P9-CRU-389

# Children and Books

Fourth Edition

# Children and Books

Fourth Edition

May Hill Arbuthnot

Zena Sutherland

Scott, Foresman and Company

Glenview, Illinois London

# Preface to Fourth Edition

*Children and Books* is meant for all adults who are interested in bringing children and books together, but it is designed particularly for classes in children's literature in English and education departments and in library schools, in colleges and universities.

As May Hill Arbuthnot said in the preface to the third edition:

> Children and Books *grew in the first place out of the tantalizing questions adults are always asking: "What kind of books do children like?" "How can we get our children to read more and better books?" It grew also out of many observations of children choosing or rejecting books in their homes, nursery schools, libraries, and classrooms. It grew from watching artist-teachers using books in such happy and meaningful ways that the children reached new heights of appreciation and taste. It grew from the eager response of college students to the beauty and fun of children's books. It grew from watching parents share their joy in books with their children, making book lovers of them by sheer contagion. And it grew primarily from liking children and books.*

Never before has there been such recognition of the importance of children's books as there is today. The body of children's literature has grown enormously, courses in the subject have multiplied, and some of the best writers today are devoting all or part of their time to writing children's books. Realization that children's literature both reflects the values of our society and instills those values in children has made increasing numbers of adults aware that children's literature is a part of the mainstream of all literature and that, like adult literature, it is worthy of our respect both for what it is and for what it does.

The title suggests the dual nature of the book's approach. The emphases are on understanding children and their needs, on perspectives and background, on criteria and types of literature, and on artists and authors. In a sense, *Children and Books* has a *major-author* approach. It is impossible to describe all of the good books that have been written for children, but it is possible to introduce readers to the works of most of the major authors of the past and present. The major-author emphasis should spare the reader, particularly the new student, from floundering in a sea of titles.

*Children and Books* is primarily about books; since the field is so broad, to include other media would mean giving them superficial treatment that would not do them justice. There are, however, some discussions of other media in Parts Six and Seven; and the bibliographies for those parts, as well as the Adult References in the appendices, refer the reader to articles and books on related media.

Library of Congress Catalog Card Number 70-188618.
Copyright © 1947, 1957, 1964, 1972 by Scott, Foresman and Company, Glenview, Illinois 60025.
Philippines Copyright 1972 by Scott, Foresman and Company, Glenview, Illinois 60025.
All Rights Reserved.
Printed in the United States of America.
Regional offices of Scott, Foresman and Company are located in Dallas, Oakland, N.J., Palo Alto, and Tucker, Ga.

028.5
A66
1972

## ORGANIZATION AND REVISION

Before her death in October 1969, May Hill Arbuthnot approved the reorganization and redevelopment carried out in this fourth edition of *Children and Books*. Much of what she had to say is preserved, but she recognized the fact that the changes in our society since her revision of the third edition in 1963, and the changes in the kinds of books children need indicated the desirability of new emphases in *Children and Books*.

In this fourth edition, newly designed, Part One is an overview of children's needs and interests, the range of books for children, types of and criteria for children's literature, and artists and their illustrations. Part Two discusses history and trends, traditional literature from *Mother Goose* to the epics, and modern fantasy. Part Three is on poets and poetry, and includes a discussion of children's poetry writing. Part Four considers animal stories, modern realistic stories about children in this country as well as in other lands, and historical fiction. It stresses the growing importance of books about minority groups and includes many books published in other countries, both translated books and those from English-speaking countries. Part Five discusses biography and informational books.

Many of the sixteen chapters in Parts One through Five have been substantially reorganized, and in all chapters the material in the text and in the bibliographies has been brought up to date, with criteria about each genre discussed at the beginnings of chapters.

Part Six, Bringing Children and Books Together, is a redevelopment and expansion of the material on methodology. It discusses the role of the adult, techniques for using books with children, and religious books in the home, and it has notes on Chapters 5–15, with suggestions for using books in each genre with children.

Part Seven, Areas and Issues Related to Children and Their Books, is wholly new. It includes discussions of research studies, the school media center, censorship, internationalism in children's literature, and book promotion. Each discussion contains suggestions for research and a bibliography.

The Appendices are Book Selection Aids, Adult References, Publishers and Their Addresses, Children's Book Awards, and Pronunciation Guide. There is a Subject Index in addition to the Author, Illustrator, Title Index.

## SPECIAL FEATURES

Throughout the discussions of books and authors in Chapters 1–16, and separated from the text, are "Viewpoints," brief statements from books and articles, not necessarily representing the point of view in *Children and Books*, but suggesting to readers some issues and interests they may wish to explore.

The bibliographies are extensive. To facilitate information for the reader, all adult references and book selection aids are listed together, with annotations and full bibliographical information, in Appendices A and B, at the end of the book. Books pertinent to chapter discussions are listed by title and author under Adult References at the end of each chapter. Books for children are listed for all chapters on types of children's literature. Books mentioned in the text are not annotated; additional entries are. Each reader undoubtedly will miss one or more favorite books; unfortunately, space limitations necessitated some omissions, even of books the authors would have liked to include. The age levels are suggestive only, since children of the same age often differ markedly in reading skills, interests, and social maturity. In the bibliographies for Chapters 13, 14, and 15, symbols are used to denote books centered on blacks, Chicanos, Indians, and religious minorities, so that such books may be more accessible to readers.

This fourth edition has been designed by John Pacyna. The drawings for the cover, the title page, and the part openings have been created by Meyer Seltzer. Included in the expanded illustration program are a sixteen-page color section and a discussion, in Chapter 3, of reproduction methods in book illustration.


## ACKNOWLEDGMENTS

For various kinds of assistance in the preparation of this fourth edition, grateful acknowledgments are due to the following people:

for suggestions for revision of the third edition, Patricia Jean Cianciolo, Bruce Clements, Jerome Cushman, Arnold Grade, James E. Higgins, J. Lynn Mortensen, Elizabeth Ann Parker, Bette Peltola, Raymond Picozzi, and Peggy Sullivan;

for her contribution to the development of Chapter 16, Ruth Gillis;

for his contribution to the development of Part Six, especially for the examples of techniques in using books with children, Raymond Lubway;

for the articles in Part Seven, Dorothy Broderick (contributor to and editor of Part Seven), Diane Chrisman, Kathleen Coleman, Caroline Feller, Sara Innis Fenwick, John Donovan, Larry N. Landrum, W. Bernard Lukenbill, Michael T. Marsden, Anne Pellowski, and Mildred Beatty Smith;

for suggesting Viewpoints to be used in Chapters 1–16, Donnarae MacCann;

for their valuable suggestions as manuscript consultants, Augusta Baker, Wayne Booth (Chapter 2), Mary Alice Burgan, Ruth K. Carlson, Peter F. Neumeyer, Bette Peltola (Part Six), Warren E. Roberts (Chapters 4–7), Sam Sebesta, Brian Sutton-Smith (Chapter 1), and Evelyn L. Wenzel;

for their aid in bibliographic research, Margaret Cory and Jean Block;

for their unflagging patience and wisdom, Frances Ekins and JoAnn Johnson, the editors;

for his sage counsel, moral support, and sustaining sense of humor, Alec Sutherland, my husband.


It would be impossible to express adequately the gratitude I feel to May Hill Arbuthnot. Everyone who works toward the goal of bringing to children the undying pleasure of a love for books knows that hers was a permanent contribution to children's literature. Her knowledge, her enthusiasm, her practical commonsense, and her boundless imagination have guided countless parents, teachers, librarians, and students. All of these qualities are evident in *Children and Books*, and it has been a joy and a challenge to adapt her work to today's needs. Her death brought an abrupt end to plans to work together, but May Hill Arbuthnot is still with us in her books, a wise and blithe spirit.

Zena Sutherland
Editor
*Bulletin of the Center for Children's Books*

# Contents

## Chapter 11
## Poets and Children's Poetry 324



# Part Four
# Realistic Fiction

## Chapter 12
## Animal Stories 392



## Chapter 13
## Modern Fiction 420

## Chapter 14 Historical Fiction 494



# Part Five
# Stranger Than Fiction

## Chapter 15 Biography 534

## Chapter 16 Informational Books 586



## Part Six Bringing Children and Books Together



## Part Seven Areas and Issues Related to Children and Their Books



### Appendices



### Indices

# Part One
# "Books, Children and Men"

# Chapter 1
# Children and Their Books

*Books are no substitute for living, but they can add immeasurably to its richness. When life is absorbing, books can enhance our sense of its significance. When life is difficult, they can give a momentary relief from trouble, afford a new insight into our problems or those of others, or provide the rest and refreshment we need. Books have always been a source of information, comfort, and pleasure for people who know how to use them. This is as true for children as for adults.*

Since that paragraph was first written—some twenty-five years ago—the world has undergone unprecedented change. The mood of the writers, editors, teachers, and librarians working in the field of children's literature a quarter of a century ago was quite different from the mood of most people today. Then there was a greater sense of security about the direction of the future. Today, change has become the predominant fact of life, accelerating at such a pace that traditional values have become confused and confusing. Still, many values of the past endure, and the assumptions in past editions of *Children and Books* about the nature and the needs of children, the value of good books, and the importance of bringing children and books together continue to have validity.

Along with television, films, filmstrips, video-tapes, and the like, there is today an amazing variety of material in print: picture books, some without text; easy-to-read books, invaluable for the beginning and the poor reader; poetry for and by children; folk literature that includes tales, myths, fables, epics, and legends; modern fanciful tales, ranging from imitations of folk tales to science fiction; historical fiction and biographies; animal stories, family stories (including the "problem stories"), realistic fiction about people of almost every land and every race; career stories and sports stories; informational books and how-to-do-it books. They are in every public and school library, in bookstores and drugstores, on supermarket racks and corner newsstands. There are reading kits, book-and-record sets, comic books and children's magazines—and a great deal of print meant for adults but read also by children.

Today there is also a new sensitivity to the variety of children in our country, children who have always been with us but who have not found their counterparts in books as they do today. For we have an infinite variety of children. They are bright, average, and dull; rural, urban, small-town, migrant, suburban. They come from happy homes and homes riven by tension, from solid houses and slum tenements. White, black, Indian, Appalachian, Chicano, Nisei; unloved and neglected, loved and cherished; bookworms and nonreaders—boys and girls whose needs to identify, to develop, to feel pride in race and acceptance in the community are being studied and served. They are infinitely different and profoundly similar.

Children's literature in recent years has taken new directions, explored new themes, and opened up possibilities for developing new attitudes. In the following chapters these changes will be discussed. Writers, artists, and editors have joined forces to make today's children's books so varied in content and so beautiful to look at that adults as well as children enjoy them. These books, like those for adults, range from the unreliable and trashy to the scrupulously accurate and permanently significant. The treasures must be sought for, but they are there, a wealth of fine books old and new.

If we are to find these treasures, the best books for children, we need standards for judging them.[1] But two facts we need to keep constantly before us: *a book is a good book for children only when they enjoy it; a book is a poor book for children, even when adults rate it a classic, if children are unable to read it or are bored by its content.* To bring children and books together, we must know hundreds of books in many fields and their virtues and limitations, and we must also know the children for whom they are intended—their interests and their needs.

## CHILDREN'S NEEDS

Despite social change, certain basic needs seem to be common to most peoples and most times. A child's needs are at first intensely and narrowly personal, but, as he matures, they should broaden and become more widely socialized. The direction they will take depends a great deal on the experiences the child encounters in his crucial early years before school. How tragically different, for example, are the experiences of the battered child living with violent, unloving, sometimes psychotic adults and the experiences of the beloved child nurtured by a warm, supportive family. Struggling to satisfy his needs, the child is forever seeking to maintain the precarious balance between personal happiness and social approval, and that is no easy task. Directly or indirectly, books may help him, particularly if they are books written by sensitive, thoughtful adults who are percipient observers of children and who remember their own childhoods vividly. Such books not only may help children better understand themselves and others but

1. See Chapter 2 for a discussion of criteria for judging stories for children.

### VIEWPOINTS

Children defend themselves, I tell you. They manifest at first a degree of inertia that resists the liveliest attacks; finally they take the offensive and expel their false friends from a domain in which they wish to remain the rulers. Nothing is done to create a common opinion among them and yet that opinion exists. They would be wholly incapable of defining the faults that displease them; but they cannot be made to believe that a book which displeases them *should* please them. Whatever their differences may be as to age, sex, or social position, they detest with common accord disguised sermons, hypocritical lessons, irreproachable little boys and girls who behave with more docility than their dolls. It is as though . . . they brought into the world with them a spontaneous hatred of the insincere and the false. The adults insist, the children pretend to yield, and do not yield. We overpower them; they rise up again. Thus does the struggle continue, in which the weaker will triumph—Paul Hazard, *Books, Children and Men*, The Horn Book, Inc., 1944, p. 49.

1. From The Guinea Pigs That Went to School by Leonard Meshover and Sally Feistel, photographs by Eve Hoffman. Copyright © 1968 by Follett Publishing Company. Used by permission.

2. From On and Off the Street by Bob Adelman and Susan Hall. Copyright © 1970 by Bob Adelman and Susan Hall. Reprinted by permission of The Viking Press, Inc.

3. From I Wish I Had an Afro, written and photographed by John Shearer. Copyright 1970. Reproduced by permission of Cowles Book Company, a subsidiary of Henry Regnery Company.

4. Photograph by Gordon Parks, Jr. From J. T. by Jane Wagner, by permission of Van Nostrand Reinhold Company.

5. Photograph by James Kilberg. From The World of Kindergarten by Clancy Goode. Copyright © 1970. Reproduced by permission of The Ward Ritchie Press.

1.

2.

3.

4.

5.

6.

6. From David, Young Chief of the Quileutes, *copyright © 1967 by Ruth Kirk. Reproduced by permission of Harcourt Brace Jovanovich, Inc.*
7. *Photographs copyright © 1970 by Arline Strong. From* A Crack in the Pavement *by Ruth Rea Howell. Used by permission of Atheneum Publishers.*
8. From Sweet Pea, *copyright © 1969 by Jill Krementz. Reproduced by permission of Harcourt Brace Jovanovich, Inc.*
9. *Copyright © 1970 by Roy Arenella. Reprinted from* City Talk, *compiled by Lee Bennett Hopkins, by permission of Alfred A. Knopf, Inc.*
10. *Photographs copyright © 1969 by John Arms. From* Today Is Saturday *by Zilpha Keatley Snyder. Used by permission of Atheneum Publishers.*

7.

8.

9.

10.

VIEWPOINTS

The young human being is intrinsically motivated to a high degree. Many elements of his environment constitute challenges for him. He is curious, eager to discover, eager to know, eager to solve problems. A sad part of most education is that by the time the child has spent a number of years in school this intrinsic motivation is pretty well dampened. Yet it is there and it is our task as facilitators of learning to tap that motivation, to discover what challenges are real for the young person, and to provide the opportunity for him to meet those challenges.—Carl R. Rogers, *Freedom to Learn*, Charles E. Merrill Publishing Company, 1969, p. 131.

also should help adults better understand and empathize with their own children and with the children in their classrooms and library centers.

## THE NEED FOR PHYSICAL WELL-BEING

A child's sense of physical security ordinarily begins in his mother's or father's arms, includes his routines of eating and sleeping, and comes gradually to embrace everything that gives him a sense of comfort and well-being. For both children and adults, material satisfactions may become the chief symbols of security. The old fairy tales were told by peoples who seldom had enough food to eat or clothing to keep them warm. So their tales are full of brightly burning fires, sumptuous feasts, rich clothes, glittering jewels, and splendid palaces. These are man's age-old symbols of security. Undoubtedly some of the appeal of the old *Elsie Dinsmore* stories and of Frances Hodgson Burnett's *Sara Crewe* and *The Secret Garden* lay in this same incredible affluence which the characters enjoyed.

Today, as in earlier times, material security is uncertain, and it continues to be one of people's most pressing needs. So in books as in life, the lack of security and the hunger for it often supply the motive for the action and the theme of the story. In Betty Erwin's *Behind the Magic Line*,[2] a black family leaves their crowded two-room city apartment to find security and a better life in a home of their own. In Louisa Shotwell's *Adam Bookout*, Adam, yearning for a better life, goes to New York on the strength of an old Christmas card from relatives who have casually written, "Come see us!" In Zilpha Snyder's *The Velvet Room*, the daughter of a migrant worker is so enchanted with the haven provided by a room in a deserted house that through her interest the family finds a permanent home as caretakers for the property. In Vera and Bill Cleaver's *Where the Lilies Bloom*, the doughty young heroine struggles

*Illustration by Jim Spanfeller for* Where the Lilies Bloom *by Vera and Bill Cleaver. Copyright © 1969. Reproduced by permission of J. B. Lippincott Company, Publishers.*

2. *Behind the Magic Line*, as well as most of the other books mentioned in this chapter, is discussed elsewhere in the text. See the Index for relevant page references.

*Illustration by Julia Iltis. From* Behind the Magic Line *by Betty K. Erwin. Copyright © 1969. Reproduced by permission of Little, Brown and Co.*

fiercely to keep her family together, lying about her father's death to prevent the authorities from separating the children, and out-maneuvering the landlord to keep the house in which they live.

In book after book, the search for security will spellbind young readers of the old fairy tales or of the modern realistic books or of the biographies of heroes, all the way from "Dick Whittington" to *Tom Sawyer* and Elizabeth Janeway's *Ivanov Seven.*

## THE NEED TO LOVE AND TO BE LOVED

Every human being wants to love and to be loved. This need is so pressing that when it is frustrated in one direction it will provide its own substitutes, centering upon almost anything from lap dogs to antiques. Children, too, set up their own substitutes. A child who feels out of favor or rejected may lavish an abnormal amount of affection upon a stray cat, perhaps identifying himself with the unwanted animal. In John Donovan's *I'll Get There. It Better Be Worth the Trip*, Davy's whole devotion is given, after his grandmother's death, to his dog, Fred. In Clyde Bulla's *White Bird*, the foundling boy, living in complete isolation with a taciturn man, becomes attached to a wounded white crow he has rescued. The small, retarded boy in Louise Dickinson Rich's *Three of a Kind* is spurred to responsiveness by the love of a kitten.

It is in his family that the child learns his first lessons in the laws of affectionate relationships. Books, too, exemplify these relationships. In Ellen Parsons' *Rainy Day*

*Illustration by Leonard Weisgard for* White Bird *by Clyde Robert Bulla. Copyright © 1966 by Clyde Robert Bulla. Reprinted with permission of Thomas Y. Crowell Company, Inc., New York, publisher.*

*Together*, the whole theme is love between parents and children. Not only does the child's sense of security develop from these family patterns, but also his whole approach to other people and later his search for and treatment of a mate. In *Queenie Peavy*, by Robert Burch, a child's personality is colored by the fact that her father, to whom she feels unswerving loyalty, is in jail. The status of the mother and the father in the family circle provides a child with his first concepts of the woman's role and the man's role in life and often determines his consequent willingness or unwillingness to accept his own sex. In older books such as *Caddie Woodlawn* and in some recent ones as well, girl heroines, despite their love of boisterous games and adventures, always learn to appreciate their "woman's role." In recent years, in response to a growing demand, there have been books in which girls can enjoy being "tomboys" without the implication that they are behaving in an unfeminine and socially unacceptable manner.

Family loyalties also provide a basis for loyal friendships as the child's social life widens. When family relationships are normal and happy, a child starts life with healthy attitudes. If he feels loved and knows his love is accepted, he in turn is predisposed toward friendly relationships with people outside the family. When the reverse is true, his approach to other people is often suspicious or belligerent. Gilly, the lonely, orphaned protagonist of Julia Cunningham's *Dorp Dead*, hides his intelligence because he mistrusts adults; and Ivan, in Paula Fox's *Portrait of Ivan*, is cautious in accepting friendly overtures from other adults because his mother is dead and his father shows him no affection.

Sometimes stories about family life may interpret to the fortunate child the significance of his own experiences which he might otherwise take for granted. A child may find traces of his own father in the father of Andy in Joseph Krumgold's *Onion John* or share

## VIEWPOINTS

The evidence in young lives of the search for something and somebody to be true to is seen in a variety of pursuits more or less sanctioned by society. It is often hidden in a bewildering combination of shifting devotion and sudden perversity, sometimes more devotedly perverse, sometimes more perversely devoted. Yet, in all youth's seeming shiftiness, a seeking after some durability in change can be detected, whether in the accuracy of scientific and technical method or in the sincerity of conviction; in the veracity of historical and fictional accounts or the fairness of the rules of the game; in the authenticity of artistic production (and the high fidelity of reproduction) or in the genuineness of personalities and the reliability of commitments.—Erik H. Erikson, "Youth: Fidelity and Diversity," in *Youth: Change and Challenge*, edited by Erik H. Erikson, Basic Books, Inc., New York and London, 1963, p. 3.

the longing of the fatherless boy in Charlotte Zolotow's *A Father Like That*, or recognize his own mother in Mrs. March of *Little Women* or in the bustling mother in Elaine Konigsburg's *About the B'nai Bagels*. He may share the brother and sister fun of Madeleine L'Engle's *Meet the Austins* or the adventures of the cousins in Elizabeth Enright's *Gone-Away Lake*, or feel the warmth of the love between Siebren and his grandfather in Meindert DeJong's *Journey from Peppermint Street*. Through reading books such as these, he may find that his own family will mean more to him. On the other hand, children who have missed these happy experiences may find in family stories vicarious substitutes which will give them some satisfaction and supply them with new insight into what families can be.

*Illustration by Peter Boston. From* A Stranger at Green Knowe. *Copyright © 1961 by Lucy Maria Boston. By permission of Harcourt Brace Jovanovich, Inc. and Faber and Faber Ltd.*

*Illustration by Emily Arnold McCully from* Journey from Peppermint Street *by Meindert DeJong. Copyright © 1968. Reproduced by permission of Harper & Row, Publishers, Inc.*

Another aspect of this need to love and to serve the beloved is the recognition of this same need in other creatures. Stories about wild animals defending their mates or their young or the herd are tremendously appealing. So, too, are stories of pets, steadfast not only in their affection for their own kind but for their human masters as well. Such stories as Sheila Burnford's *The Incredible Journey* have played upon this appeal. *A Stranger at Green Knowe* by Lucy Boston is a moving example of a boy's understanding of and sympathy for an unhappy, caged young gorilla. Fine animal stories of all kinds will undoubtedly contribute to breaking down the young child's unwitting cruelties toward animals and to building up his sensitivity to their needs.

Finally, the need to love and to be loved, which includes family affection, warm friendships, and devotion to pets, leads the child to look toward romance. In children's literature, romance begins early but remains impersonal. The fairy tales, with their long-delayed prince or their princess on a glass hill, are little more than abstract symbols of what is to come.

Then came a flood of novels of romance for teen-agers. While many of them are incredibly stereotyped and predictable, there are growing numbers of competent authors who write well and respect their young readers. They supply realistic pictures of family life, with boys and girls looking away from their families to a serious interest in someone of the opposite sex. And many of these books deal frankly with some of the heart-breaking problems of young people. Zoa Sherburne, for example, in *Too Bad About the Haines Girl*, handles with dignity the problem of the unwed mother. The establishment of a desirable romantic attachment is one of the most important tasks of growing up. A well-written story that shows all the complications of romance, its pitfalls and disappointments as well as its happiness, can provide young people with needed guidance in an approach to one of life's most vital problems.

Out of family affection and trust grows a kind of *spiritual strength* that enables human beings to surmount dangers, failures, and even stark tragedies. Such books as Louisa May Alcott's *Little Women* and the Little House books by Laura Ingalls Wilder leave children with the conviction that decent, kindly people can maintain an inner serenity even as they struggle with and master the problems that threaten them.

Particular religious groups and practices appear in children's books and reflect something of the diversities of belief in our modern world. *Thee, Hannah!* by Marguerite de Angeli gives a charming picture of Quaker customs. *Daughter of the Mountains* by Louise Rankin is a story about a little Tibetan girl's faith that she can somehow accomplish her impossible mission because she is guided and cared for by Buddha. In Mildred Jordan's *Proud to Be Amish*, the Amish people are described with sympathy. *Young Fu of the Upper Yangtze* by Elizabeth Lewis gives a rich cross section of Confucian guides to conduct. Leo Politi's *Juanita* describes and illustrates the charming Blessing of the Animals, which is one of the yearly church festivals in some Catholic countries and on Olvera Street, Los Angeles. *All-of-a-Kind Family* by Sydney Taylor is a captivating picture of Jewish family life and religious observances and Sulamith Ish-Kishor's *Our Eddie* a sober one. In Judy Blume's *Are You There God? It's Me, Margaret*, the protagonist cannot decide what church to attend (her father is Jewish, her mother is not), but this indecision does not shake her deep faith. *Waterless Mountain* by Laura Armer and *Raven's Cry* by Christie Harris present the religion of the Navaho and Haida Indians with fidelity and beauty. Joseph Krumgold's . . . *and now Miguel* has a discussion of prayer between two teen-age boys that is unique in children's literature. In Louise Fitzhugh's *The Long Secret*, Harriet gets quite different notions of God and prayer and religion from her mother, her father, and the Preacher.

Reading such books, children can find an honest picture of religious diversity as it exists today—knowledge which should help them develop respect for different groups. However firm a family may be in its adherence to a particular religious sect or in its objections to all organized religion, it will find in these books a fair picture of the world as it is today. And when children read the biographies of heroes of such divergent religious beliefs as St. Francis of Assisi, John Wesley, Father Damien, Florence Nightingale, Martin Buber, Mohandas Gandhi, and Martin Luther King, they may begin to understand that prayer and a sense of God give spiritual security and are impelling and creative forces in the lives of many men and women.

## THE NEED TO BELONG

Growing out of the need for security is the need of every human being to belong, to be an accepted member of a group. "My daddy," or "My big brother," the young child says with pride. At first these experiences are merely egocentric extensions of the child's self-love, but at least he is beginning to line himself up with his family, and this acknowledgment of others marks his growing sense of belonging to a group. In time, this same child will identify himself with his friends, his school, and later with his city and country, and perhaps with a world group.

So the child's literature should reflect this expanding sense of the group. It should begin with stories about the family, the school, and the neighborhood in warm little books such as Martha Alexander, Ezra Jack Keats, and Charlotte Zolotow write for the preschool child, Carolyn Haywood for the primer age, and Beverly Cleary for the middle grades in her amusing *Henry Huggins* books. These represent happy, normal group experiences. But there are also stories about children who must struggle anxiously to be liked by the people whose acceptance they long for. Orphaned Heidi in Johanna Spyri's book by the same name, Mary in Frances H. Burnett's *The Secret Garden*, Cissie in Mildred Lawrence's *Peachtree Island*, and the Guatemalan Indian boy in Ann Nolan Clark's *Santiago* are good examples. The story of the child who wins a respected place in groups that once rejected him is a satisfying theme from "Cinderella" to *Good-Bye to the Jungle* by John Rowe Townsend.

With the growing consciousness of a world in which all people are brought closer by the developments in communications and transportation, with children's increased awareness of such problems as war, pollution, and student unrest, there is an urgent need for books in which minority peoples gain not tolerance, but respect, books that attack the injustice and discrimination and apathy still prevalent in our society. The young today are aware of social ills. Exposed to the mass media and to the changing mores of the community, they need books that reflect the world in which they live but offer realistic and optimistic solutions. John Tunis, in his sports stories for the preadolescent and teen-ager, makes his young readers face fully the extra difficulties that beset youngsters of minority groups in winning a place on the team or in the community. This is the general theme also of Eleanor Estes' *The Hundred Dresses*. In Emily Neville's *Berries Goodman* and Hila Colman's *Mixed-Marriage*

*Illustration by Tasha Tudor. From* The Secret Garden *by Frances Hodgson Burnett. Copyright 1911 F. H. Burnett. Copyright renewal 1938 by Verity Constance Burnett. Illustrations copyright © 1962 by J. B. Lippincott Company. Reprinted by permission of the publishers, J. B. Lippincott Company. (Original in color)*

## VIEWPOINTS

If one dares to probe beneath the surface of the various forms of the present Negro protest to find the common compelling force, one will probably find that it is a rather simple and universal human desire. It is the desire to be respected for one's self—the desire to be seen and to be reacted to as an individual human being; the desire to be free of the shackles of being lumped, categorized, and stigmatized as an inchoate mass. The Negro has no more or less virtues or frailties than those found in other human beings. He is an individual who varies as much in courage and cowardice or ambivalence as do other human beings. He reacts to injustices and cruelties with the same patterns of accommodation, intimidation, rebellion, or philosophy as do others. He is here. Like others, throughout his life, he is in a relentless struggle against the void, the inner chaos. He is an individual. If life is to be tolerable for him he must be respected as an individual.—Kenneth B. Clark, *The Negro Protest*, Beacon Press, Boston, 1963, pp. 50–51.

*Daughter*, anti-Semitism is candidly portrayed; in Kristin Hunter's *The Soul Brothers and Sister Lou*, a group of black adolescents face prejudice toward and within themselves. Sometimes the problem is not one of winning acceptance but of accepting. For example, in Ann Nolan Clark's *Little Navajo Bluebird*, an Indian child passionately rejects the white man and all his ways and wants to belong only to her own tribal group. Books like these parallel the need of each individual not only to belong with pride to his own group, but to identify himself warmly and sympathetically with ever widening circles of people. When a child from suburbia weeps over Lullah's plight in Natalie Savage Carlson's *The Empty Schoolhouse* or wishes she could know Hungarian Kate in *The Good Master*, by Kate Seredy, her sense of belonging is widening. A good and honest book can strengthen the pride of the minority member and enrich all who read it.

## THE NEED TO ACHIEVE

The need for competence—the "organism's capacity to interact effectively with its environment"[3]—is a strong motivating force in human behavior. The struggle to achieve competence begins with the infant's visual exploration, with his crawling, grasping, and other primitive activities and grows into the complex physical or intellectual performances of the expert man or woman athlete, mathematician, musician, or scientist. Competence is as satisfying as inhibitions and frustrations are disruptive. To be happy or well adjusted, the child or the adult must have a satisfying sense of competence in one area or another.

Ivan Southall's *Let the Balloon Go* is devoted to the theme of achieving competence. "What you wish for, fight for," a stranger had told John. "A balloon is not a balloon until you cut the string and let it go." And John did let the balloon go. A spastic child, John had been overprotected all his life until the day he secretly climbed a tree, risking his life but succeeding for the first time in feeling that he had accomplished something that other boys could do.

In Mary J. Collier and Eugene L. Gaier's study "The Hero in the Preferred Childhood Stories of College Men,"[4] the important factor the book heroes had in common was that they performed their unique feats on their own. Whether it was Hänsel from the old fairy tale or the realistic Tom Sawyer, the hero's competence was achieved without help from adults, and his independence was the quality that made him memorable and admired. Achieving competence may become the compensation for rejection and a step toward acceptance. This is a frequent theme in stories for children—the lonely child or the shy teen-ager who develops competence in some field and so wins the admiration and

3. Robert H. White, "Motivation Reconsidered: The Concept of Competence," *Psychological Review*, Vol. 66, No. 5, 1959, p. 297.

4. *American Imago*, Vol. 16, No. 2, 1959.

*Illustration by Harold James from* Tessie *by Jesse Jackson. Copyright © 1968. Reproduced by permission of Harper & Row, Publishers, Inc.*

acceptance of the group. Taro Yashima's *Crow Boy*, Eleanor Estes' *The Hundred Dresses*, Armstrong Sperry's *Call It Courage*, Nat Hentoff's *Jazz Country*, and Jesse Jackson's *Tessie* are all built upon this theme.

The young child's first book heroes are doers, from Edward Ardizzone's Tim, who survives shipwreck and finds his lost parents, to David of the Old Testament, who slew the giant Goliath. In later childhood and adolescence young readers enjoy the competence of the heroes in adventure, mystery, and career stories and the achievements of famous men and women in biographies. *Carry On, Mr. Bowditch* by Jean Latham is a splendid, true record of competence independently achieved. More and more books are appearing that describe the accomplishments of black heroes: biographies of Matthew Henson, Benjamin Banneker, Sojourner Truth, Elizabeth Freeman, and many other Americans.

There is a stern negative aspect to this hunger for achievement. The struggle for competence may involve failures and complete frustration. Physical handicaps or mental limitations must be faced and accepted. In Jean Little's *Mine for Keeps*, a child with cerebral palsy comes home, after five years in a residential school, feeling fear and self-pity, but she adjusts to her own problems when she becomes involved in helping another child. In Esther Forbes' *Johnny Tremain*, Johnny's maimed hand prevented him from becoming the master silversmith he had expected to be. Emma Sterne's *Blood Brothers* tells the story of Charles Drew, a black ghetto child, who, despite discrimination, persisted in his pursuit of a medical career and eventually became a distinguished pioneer in

*Illustration by Lewis Parker. From* Mine for Keeps *by Jean Little. Copyright © 1962 by Jean Little. Reproduced by permission of Little, Brown and Co.*

blood research. Stories of such heroes who refuse to accept defeat help children in the task of growing up.

## THE NEED FOR CHANGE

Play is sometimes classified as a part of the desire for change, which is one of the basic needs of the human organism. If we work hard, we need rest or play. If we are serious and intent, we need relaxation and gaiety. So, in our reading, after grave and factual books or books about everyday affairs we like something light or imaginative. If we are beset with personal anxieties, we may look for a book of adventure or mystery or romance, lose ourselves completely, and come back to our own problems refreshed.

Children, too, need such liberation. They suffer more than many adults realize from the pressure of routines, adult coercion and tensions, and the necessity of conforming to a code of manners and morals whose reasonableness they do not always understand. This is especially true today, when so many aspects of our present society are being challenged by the young. Some children suffer from school failures, feelings of social or physical inferiority, difficulty in communicating with their parents, and bewilderment or resentment about the strictures of cultural patterns.

Books of many kinds may be used to meet the child's need for healthy change. The old fairy tales have about them a dreamlike quality that is a welcome change from the everyday world of here and now. Modern fantasies provide laughter and imaginative adventures that are sometimes ribtickling nonsense and sometimes humor with overtones of beauty. These range from the fun of Dr. Seuss' rambunctious *Horton Hatches the Egg* to the beauty and tragedy of Mary Norton's *The Borrowers* and the compassionate self-sacrifice of *Charlotte's Web.*

There is bland burlesque of city problems in Jean Merrill's *The Pushcart War* and of the rebellious adolescent in Hope Campbell's *Why Not Join the Giraffes?* in which a conservative teen-ager resists the influence of her beatnik parents; there is nonsense humor in John Ciardi's *The Man Who Sang the Sillies* and in Sid Fleischman's tall tale *McBroom's Ear.* Humor and suspense are combined in *Encyclopedia Brown Saves the Day*, Donald Sobol's story of a boy detective. There are adventures of the world of the future in John Christopher's *The Guardians* and suspense in Patricia Moyes' mystery story *Helter-Skelter.* All such stories afford children fun, pleasure, and respite. Fine poetry, too, that arrests the attention and stirs the emotions, light verse and nonsense jingles now and then—these may supply a child with the inspiration or laughter for which he hungers.

## THE NEED TO KNOW

Parents often complain about the bothersome curiosity of children. But this need to investigate, to know for sure, is a sign of intelligence. In fact, the keener the child is mentally, the wider and more persistent his curiosities will be. The need to know surely and accurately is a basic hunger and one which books help satisfy.

Books about Africa, desert Indians, birds, plants, stones, stars, rockets and jets, DNA, care of pets, do-it-yourself books, and, of course, dictionaries and encyclopedias properly gauged to a child's needs are all available today. Adults need only discover a child's particular interests to find books that will answer his questions reliably, stimulate new curiosities, and set him to exploring further to satisfy his need to know and give him, momentarily at least, a certain intellectual security.

Some books not only provide fascinating information but dramatically exemplify the human need to find out, to know for sure. For example, Thor Heyerdahl's *Kon-Tiki* tells the true story of five young men who set out

VIEWPOINTS

Someday civilization must be simplified and made more just and decent and honest for everyone. Air and water must be cleaned up. Cities that would appall Dante must be made habitable. We must discover how to live together in moderate amity. It will take a good deal of imagination to bring so many opposites into harmony, to create an inwardly desired cohesive order out of so many contradictory compulsions, to design a civilization permitting all decent variables to live together in at least a semblance of understanding.

Perhaps only because they are fresh to experience, children are insatiably curious, wanting to understand everything. Our adult curiosity seldom ranges beyond the small worlds in which we earn our living and relax from our labors. We are not notably addicted to a passionate desire for tolerance. If only we might add a child's fresh eagerness to be friendly to our trove of all recorded knowledge, then our social, economic, and political disorder might begin to assume reasonable clarity.—Harry Behn, *Chrysalis*, Harcourt Brace Jovanovich, 1968, p. 27.

on the flimsy raft Kon-Tiki to prove their theory of the origin and migrations of the Polynesian people. Hans Baumann's *Lion Gate and Labyrinth* tells the story of Heinrich Schliemann, who also needed to know and whose persistent curiosity and zealous investigations led to the discovery of ancient Trojan ruins. And Louis Haber's *Black Pioneers of Science and Invention* tells the stories of various men whose lives were a clear demonstration of the consuming need to know.

## THE NEED FOR BEAUTY AND ORDER

There is still another human need that seems curiously at odds with man's more utilitarian search for competence and security of various kinds. It is the need for beauty and order.

A wealth of books is available today to satisfy a child's aesthetic needs—authentic poetry, fanciful tales whose content and style are perfectly suited, books that are beautiful in themselves, books that provide various kinds of aesthetically satisfying experiences, and books that help children grow in their appreciation of beauty and order. Shirley Glubok's series about art in various cultures (*The Art of Ancient Egypt, The Art of the North American Indian, The Art of Ancient Mexico*) are simply written and related to the way people lived. *Looking at Art*, by Alice Elizabeth Chase, discusses the ways in which individual artists interpret landscapes, or people, or spatial relations. The *Time-Life* series of biographies of artists, profusely illustrated, is published for adults but is read by young people and can be enjoyed for its pictures alone even by very young children. Lamont Moore's *The Sculptured Image* describes the ways by which sculptors achieve their effects. *Ballet: A Pictorial History*, by Walter Terry, and *The Wonderful World of Music*, by Benjamin Britten and Imogen Holst, are fine examples of books about the performing arts written for children by experts in their fields.

Whether in music, dancing, drama, story, painting, or sculpture, the artist seizes upon some aspect of life and re-creates it for us in a new form. We see it whole and understandable; people, events, and places assume a new dimension beyond the mere chronicling of facts. The artist can give us a long, clear view so that we see details in relation to the complete design. It is as if a kaleidoscope were held immovable. The colors and lines fall into logical relationship and the design stands out in bold relief, not necessarily beautiful but complete and therefore satisfying.

Men are continually seeking aesthetic satisfaction in one form or another and at varying levels of taste. One man may find it in the songs of Tin Pan Alley. Another finds it in a symphony which exalts the sorrows of life to heroic proportions. Aesthetic satisfaction comes to the small child as well as to the adult, and the development of his taste depends not only upon his initial capacities but also upon the material he encounters and upon how it is presented. When a child has chuckled over Miss Muffet and the spider, he is getting ready to enjoy Stevenson's *A Child's Garden of Verses*, and to progress to Walter de la Mare's and David McCord's poetry. After he has been charmed with Beatrix Potter's *The Tale of Peter Rabbit*, he is on his way to appreciate the humor and beauty of Kenneth Grahame's *The Wind in the Willows* and the pathos of *The Borrowers* by Mary Norton.

## CHILDREN NEED GOOD BOOKS

Today's children, like today's adults, read for many reasons: to dream, to learn, to laugh, to enjoy the familiar and explore the unknown. They read for sheer pleasure and they absorb, in their reading, those facets of books that reflect the developmental values that are appropriate to the individual readers at each of the stages of their growth. The child is influenced by factors that have always affected children's reading: his sex, age, health and physical development, mental ability, emotional maturation, and home environment. But many of today's children have intellectual and social sophistication that further affects their reading habits and needs and tends to make them mature earlier than children matured in the past.

The pace of life is swifter and the media more pervasive; the problems of our society at times seem insuperable. Books may help children build a concept of the society in which they live and of their roles in that society; books may help shape and sharpen their concepts about other people and relationships; and books can contribute to an understanding of themselves.

To nurture young minds there must be books of many types. And they should be strong books, written with liveliness and honesty both in content and style, rather than little juvenile tracts designed to teach this lesson or that. There have been so many of these moralistic books that they threaten the general quality of children's books. For instance, there is the story of little Dickie or Bobbie or Jimmy who goes to kindergarten, stamps around, yells, and knocks down other people's blocks or seizes their toys. He is isolated like the bubonic plague until one day he learns to share and is, forthwith, a beloved and accepted member of the group. A juvenile "how to make friends and influence people"! Or there is the story of an obnoxious boy who says he wishes he didn't have a kid sister. But when she saves him in a social emergency his attitude changes for the better. The worst of such tracts is that children accept them and immediately assume an insufferably self-righteous attitude toward the sinner. "Isn't he awful?" they say virtuously. Such books may underscore a lesson, but they also encourage prigs. There are similar juvenile tracts, bogged down with preaching, in the field of race relationships. Such books, humorless and tame, offer nothing to lighten their dull didacticism.

There has also been a flood of small, pretty books for children four to seven years old about friendship, love, and similar abstractions. These precious trifles are purchased by nostalgic adults who hope to make the skipping, hopping child aware of the experiences he is bouncing through so heedlessly. But psychology makes it clear that for the young child such abstractions as unselfishness and kindness must be experienced objectively in this situation and that, not generalized in the large. These juvenile tracts seem thin indeed when compared with such robust tales as Wanda Gág's *Millions of Cats*, "The Three Little Pigs," Beverly Cleary's *Ramona the Pest*, or Scott O'Dell's *Island of the Blue Dolphins*. Such books are timeless because they are built around universal themes or needs—the desire for competence or love or accurate knowledge.

It may be unwise to give a child a story which deals with his particular behavior problem. In the process of growing older, a child may be confronted with pressures and problems too difficult for him to sustain or solve. As a result, he may lapse into temper tantrums or timid withdrawal or aggressiveness. To give such a child, already harassed, a story about a hero who conquers a similar fault may simply make the child more self-conscious or so resentful of the virtuous example in the book that he turns with increased fervor to the uninhibited excitement of television or the comics. A child going through one of these temporary periods of rebellion or withdrawal needs to discover books so absorbing, so alight with adventure or satisfying accomplishment that he is heartened in his own struggle to achieve and encouraged to believe that life is worth while in spite of its limitations. This is one form of indirect guidance.

*Illustration by E. Ness. From* Island of the Blue Dolphins *by Scott O'Dell. Copyright © 1960 by Scott O'Dell. Reproduced with permission of Houghton Mifflin Co. (Original in color)*

## TALKING ABOUT BOOKS WITH CHILDREN

Another method of guidance is through informal discussions of the problems these books involve, rather than of the child's own personal difficulties. For example, a teacher who was reading Beverly Cleary's *Henry Huggins* to her class stopped before she read them the solution of the ethical problem Henry faces when the original owner of his dog Ribsy turns up. "What would you do if you were in Henry's place?" she asked the children, and they played out the solution then and there, with different children taking Henry's part. Their varying interpretations told the teacher much about the children's standards and attitudes, and the activity provided a good deal of fun in the process.

A classroom group discussed Kate's outrageous behavior in the first chapter of *The Good Master*. Of course they thoroughly enjoyed her antics, but they came to the conclusion that she behaved that way because she was "mad" at her father for sending her away, and so she took it out on her uncle's family. It was further agreed that most of us are likely to behave foolishly when we think we have been unjustly treated.

A problem not unlike Kate's is to be found in that splendid family story for eleven- and twelve-year-olds, *Meet the Austins*, by Madeleine L'Engle. What triggered the wretched quarrel between the older brother and sister that almost ended in tragedy for them both? The girl was the aggressor and completely unreasonable. But why, what set her off? Can the children see how the death of their beloved uncle and the arrival in the family of a spoiled brat of a girl had all the children emotionally upset and on edge? Such accumulative disturbances sometimes result indirectly in the worst explosions, as they did in this case. But the warmth and stability of family life are restored eventually in this heart-warming story.

Righteous anger over an injustice is one of the hardest emotions to quell, for both children and adults. It is important that children learn early that almost everyone suffers at one time or another from this difficulty.

*A Dog on Barkham Street*, by Mary Stolz, turns on such a problem and so affords an impersonal situation for discussion. Edward is small and slight, perpetually bullied by the boy next door; Martin is big, burly, and insolent. Edward suspects that if he answered meekly he would not be tormented, but his indignation at an unprovoked insult goads him, at each encounter, into sarcasm. So the pattern repeats: Martin taunts, Edward retorts, Martin pounces and thumps until Edward says "Uncle."

*Illustration by Leonard Shortall from* A Dog on Barkham Street *by M. Stolz. Copyright © 1960. Reproduced by permission of Harper & Row, Publishers, Inc.*

A group of nine-year-olds to whom the book had been read aloud were in vehement agreement that Martin should bear the blame, save for one tall, domineering girl who felt that if Edward had ignored Martin there would have been no fight. The group then read *The Bully of Barkham Street*, an interesting companion volume that gives the same events, but from Martin's point of view. With parents who work, Martin is jealous of Edward, whose mother is always home. He eats for comfort yet hates being plump. When he does try to improve his behavior, Martin is irate that people still think of him as a bully.

Talking about the situation again, the children felt now that there was justification and guilt on both sides. One child commented that this was probably true about every relationship. All of the group were now much more aware of the contributing factors (friends, school life, parental conflict) and of, as one child put it, ". . . how it balances if you aren't happy." Another discussion of the ethical issues involved was held by two sixth-grade classes, each of which had read one of the two books. Interestingly enough, these older children were able to see the implications of provocation—that is, readers of the first book did not assume that Martin was wholly culpable. They commented on the roles of Martin's parents, their lack of understanding and their need for being understood themselves. This is the sort of book that lends itself very nicely to dramatization, either as an adjunct to discussion or as a purely theatrical venture that can sharpen for each viewer the issues with which the book confronts each reader.

In one class, invaluable indirect guidance grew from reading aloud *Cheaper by the Dozen*, by Frank B. Gilbreth and Ernestine Gilbreth Carey. A young teacher had a sixth-grade group of boys and girls from homes about as undesirable as one could find. Divorce, desertion, drunkenness, and quarreling were the rule rather than the exception. The children were spellbound by the hilarious goings-on of that remarkable family.

Their comments were revealing. Over and over they asked, "Is it really true? Did any family ever have fun like that?" One big overage boy commented, "A fellow wouldn't mind studying if he had a dad that helped him like that." And a girl said in surprise, "Why, those people really wanted their kids, didn't they?" Such comments gave the leader a chance not to moralize but to reassure those children. Yes, there really was such a family and these things did happen. Families have fun together when they share work, and plan and play together. He was trying to build into their concepts of family life the idea of family love and loyalty. By way of this book those children glimpsed, perhaps for the first time, the possible satisfactions and joys of family life.

Sometimes the best guidance is no guidance at all, a hands-off policy until the storm passes or the tensions are eased. Tales of laughter—for example, the books by Dr. Seuss or Keith Robertson's hilarious *Henry Reed, Inc.*—are invaluable. Invaluable too are grave books like Lucy Boston's *A Stranger at Green Knowe* or Esther Hautzig's *The Endless Steppe*, so absorbing that a young reader is carried out of himself and comes back re-created. Know your child and know books because for every child there is the right book at the right time.

## ADULT REFERENCES[5]


ALMY, MILLIE. *Ways of Studying Children.*

ALMY, MILLIE, E. CHITTENDEN, and PAULA MILLER. *Young Children's Thinking; Studies of Some Aspects of Piaget's Theory.*

AMERICAN COUNCIL ON EDUCATION, COMMISSION ON TEACHER EDUCATION. *Helping Teachers Understand Children.*

ANDERSON, VERNA. *Reading and Young Children.*

ARBUTHNOT, MAY HILL. *Children's Reading in the Home.*

BEADLE, MURIEL. *A Child's Mind; How Children Learn During the Critical Years from Birth to Age Five.* Particularly Chapters 12, 13, 14, 15, and 19.

BRUNER, JEROME S. *Toward a Theory of Instruction.*


5. Complete bibliographic data are provided in the combined Adult References in the Appendices.


CHAMBERS, AIDAN. *The Reluctant Reader.*

CHUKOVSKY, KORNEI. *From Two to Five.*

COLES, ROBERT. *Children of Crisis.*

COLES, ROBERT, and MARIA PIERS. *Wages of Neglect.*

CROSBY, MURIEL. *An Adventure in Human Relations.*

______, ed. *Reading Ladders for Human Relations.*

DUFF, ANNIS. *"Bequest of Wings"; A Family's Pleasures with Books.*

______. *"Longer Flight"; A Family Grows Up with Books.*

EGOFF, SHEILA, G. T. STUBBS, and L. F. ASHLEY, eds. *Only Connect: Readings on Children's Literature.* Article by Anthony Storr, "The Child and the Book."

ERIKSON, ERIK H. *Childhood and Society.*

FADER, DANIEL N., and ELTON B. McNEIL. *Hooked on Books: Program and Proof.*

FEATHERSTONE, JOSEPH. *Schools Where Children Learn.*

FRANK, JOSETTE. *Your Child's Reading Today.*

GESELL, ARNOLD, and FRANCES ILG. *Child Development; An Introduction to the Study of Human Growth.*

HENTOFF, NAT. *Our Children Are Dying;* and JOHN McPHEE. *The Headmaster.*

HERNDON, JAMES. *The Way It Spozed to Be; A Report on the Crisis in Our Schools.*

HOLT, JOHN. *How Children Fail.*

______. *How Children Learn.*

______. *What Do I Do Monday?*

HYMES, JAMES LEE. *Understanding Your Child.*

ILG, FRANCES L., and LOUISE BATES AMES. *Child Behavior.*

JENKINS, GLADYS GARDNER. *Helping Children Reach Their Potential.*

JENKINS, GLADYS, HELEN SHACTER, and WILLIAM BAUER. *These Are Your Children.*

KOZOL, JONATHAN. *Death at an Early Age; The Destruction of the Hearts and Minds of Negro Children in the Boston Public Schools.*

KUJOTH, JEAN SPEALMAN. *Reading Interests of Children and Young Adults.*

LARRICK, NANCY. *A Parent's Guide to Children's Reading.*

MAIER, HENRY. *Three Theories of Child Development: The Contributions of Erik H. Erikson, Jean Piaget, and Robert R. Sears, and Their Applications.*

MATHEWS, MITFORD M. *Teaching to Read; Historically Considered.*

MAYERSON, CHARLOTTE LEON, ed. *Two Blocks Apart; Juan Gonzales and Peter Quinn.*

MILLAR, SUSANNA. *The Psychology of Play.* Chapter, "Phantasy, Feeling and Make-Believe Play."

PIAGET, JEAN, and BARBEL INHELDER. *The Psychology of the Child.*

PINES, MAYA. *Revolution in Learning; The Years from Birth to Six.* Particularly Chapter 11, "Early Reading."

RICHARDSON, ELWYN. *In the Early World.*

ROBINSON, EVELYN ROSE. *Readings About Children's Literature.* Part 1, "The Child and His Reading."

SMITH, LILLIAN. *The Unreluctant Years.*

WHITE, DOROTHY MARY NEAL. *About Books for Children.*

______. *Books Before Five.*

# Chapter 2
# Selecting Books for Children

Books are written for children, but adults buy them. Editors decide on manuscripts, reviewers make judgments, teachers and librarians exhibit books, recommend them, and otherwise guide children's reading. Parents, grandparents, uncles, and aunts select a choice volume for a favorite child. But how can adults know what book a child is going to enjoy?

Actually, they can't know with any degree of certainty. Moreover, they must face the fact that youngsters are past masters at rejecting what is not for them. A book may be judged a juvenile classic by experts in children's literature, but if it is beyond the child's understanding or too subtle or sophisticated for his level of appreciation, he can turn it down with a stony indifference which leaves adults baffled and grieved. They need not mourn. Two years later the child may accept that very book with enthusiasm. It is the same with music. A simple melody may appeal to a child, while a symphony may confuse him. But if his musical experiences increase as he matures, he hears parts of the symphony, its different movements, over and over, until he understands and enjoys them. Finally, when he hears the whole symphony, he can follow it with pleasure, and its great melodies sing in his memory. So some poems must be heard repeatedly, and some stories must be talked over in parts or listened to while someone who knows and loves them reads aloud.

Through this gradual induction into better and better literature, children catch the theme and savor the beauty or the subtle humor or the meaning that eluded them at first. Sometimes an adult has the privilege of seeing this discovery take place. The children's faces come suddenly alive; their eyes shine. They may be anticipating an amusing conclusion or a heroic triumph. There is a sudden chuckle, or breath is exhaled like a sigh. The book has moved them, perhaps even to laughter or tears, but in any case there is a deep inner satisfaction, and they will turn to books again with anticipation.

## KNOWING CHILDREN

How are adults to select these books for children? It is evident from the discussion of children's needs in Chapter 1 that the first consideration in selecting books for a special child or a group of children must be the children themselves. The needs of each child are determined by his background and attitudes, his abilities and reading skill and, of course, his interests. Most small children like stories about animals and machines or vehicles, about playmates and family relationships, and about situations that reflect their own environment. They enjoy rhyme and rhythm, and they are pleased by stories that demonstrate the satisfaction of having a wish fulfilled, a problem solved, a new skill learned, or a new situation taken in stride.

The beginning independent reader wants action and variety, appreciates humor, and is beginning to be curious about his world. Some younger children enjoy word play. As their world expands, children in the primary grades become interested in children of other lands.

In the middle grades, when children have acquired a better understanding of time and a sense of history, biography begins to appeal. For a time boys tend to scorn "girls' stories" and girls tend to seek out such books. There is often an enthusiastic reaction to fantasy and nonsense humor, an interest in words, and a continuing enjoyment of action, partly seen in a devotion to series fiction, which usually leans heavily on plot. For years adults have deplored and children have relished the stereotyped *Nancy Drew* and *Tom Swift* books; today the lively adventures of *Encyclopedia Brown* and *Henry Reed* have devoted followers who eagerly await each new volume.

Many readers of nine, ten, and eleven become addicted to a topic or a genre; subject interests make informational books of growing importance, and children's desire for a clearer understanding of themselves and their relation to others is evident in their interest in fiction about interpersonal relationships, children of other lands and times, sex roles, and family patterns.

Young teen-agers today are often concerned about their roles in society and about social problems; they talk about drugs and delinquency, student revolt, the generation gap, the role of the presidency, the manipulations of the stock market, and the struggle for black equality. Many of them read adult books, while some may vary their reading patterns with an occasional book intended for younger children.

In selecting books for groups of children or individual children, adults should know as much as possible about children in general and about the particular children they are working with, and they can learn a great deal, as Chapter 1 suggests, by discussing books with children. Always the adult should keep in mind the goal: to make reading a pleasurable experience for children, so that it will always be one of their leisure-time activities.

## KNOWING BOOKS

Adults must know a great deal about books in choosing them for children. The chapters in this book will introduce many of the fine authors of the past and present, and will also suggest ways of judging books in each genre. These chapters are, of course, guides only. In the end, each adult should choose books for children on the basis of his own first-hand knowledge of the child or groups of children he is working with and of the books he recommends for their enjoyment.

The best way to know books is to read them. Book selection guides can help and lists of award books are useful, but there is no substitute for reading. Using the lists of book selection aids and prize-winning books that are included later in this volume is only a first step. Many of the best books are published in paperback, and children can be

## VIEWPOINTS

Literary criticism can be no more than a reasoned account of the feeling produced upon the critic by the book he is criticising. Criticism can never be a science: it is, in the first place, much too personal, and in the second, it is concerned with values that science ignores. The touchstone is emotion, not reason. We judge a work of art by its effect on our sincere and vital emotion, and nothing else.

. . . A critic must be able to *feel* the impact of a work of art in all its complexity and its force. To do so, he must be a man of force and complexity himself. . . . —D. H. Lawrence, *Selected Literary Criticism*, edited by Anthony Beal, Mercury Books, London, 1956, p. 118.

encouraged to start their own paperback libraries, especially if the adult can discuss books with knowledgeable enthusiasm. It really isn't enough to feel, "I like it," or "I don't like it." To make wise selections and to stimulate children's interest, one must know why. It is useful to keep records of such data as title, author, publisher, series, illustrator, availability in paperback, and of your opinion of plot, theme, style, characters, etc. You may also want to note passages that would be particularly enticing as baits to reading. Publishers usually suggest the reading level, but this you will want to judge for yourself: would a fifth-grade class enjoy this book, could a slow reader handle it, will the subject interest a particular child who can read but seldom does. While you will be careful to avoid the role of censor, you should know the book well enough to judge whether it should be given to special children or recommended to a class as a whole. If you have kept records of the books you have read, you may have the great satisfaction of being able to recommend another book when a child asks, "Is there any other book just like this one?"

In some classrooms, a teacher will have enthusiastic response to *The Wind in the Willows;* in others, he will not. In some library story hours *Mary Poppins* may produce hilarity, in others boredom—in the same library. Think how differently you would select, say, for a fourth grade of bright, enthusiastic booklovers or a fourth grade of slow, apathetic readers. Or, in working with individual children, how differently you would choose a book for a lively child with a sense of humor and a child who is quiet and thoughtful.

***Floating away over the roofs of the houses***

*Illustration by Mary Shepard. Reproduced from* Mary Poppins, *copyright, 1934, © 1962, by P. L. Travers, by permission of Harcourt Brace Jovanovich, Inc.*

You can turn to review sources for opinions of books, but in the end you must rely on your own judgment.[1] Adults should not feel restricted by children's immediate in-

1. Obviously there are various ways to approach a book. Frederick C. Crews in *The Pooh Perplex* (Dutton, 1963) has produced a devastating satire of various literary approaches to criticism. As Orville Prescott remarked in the *New York Times*, "In twelve glittering, brightly malicious essays he has poleaxed and then neatly eviscerated twelve varieties of currently fashionable literary criticism."

terests in choosing books because these are often narrower than they need to be and because they can change quite quickly. Children's reactions are often immediate and personal, and they often adhere conservatively to a known literary experience such as horse stories or science fiction. Teachers, parents, and librarians should keep children exploring both the best of the old books and the most promising of the new. Since new titles alone number over two thousand a year, the adult needs some criteria to help him select wisely. To develop judgments that are reliable and useful, you need to look closely at a book, not only to appraise its total effect on you but to examine the elements that produce that effect.

In discussion of these elements, three books will be analyzed as examples, all realistic fiction for better comparison: Rebecca Caudill's *Did You Carry the Flag Today, Charley?* for the youngest children; Laura Ingalls Wilder's *Little House in the Big Woods* for the middle group; and John Rowe Townsend's *The Intruder* for older children.[2]

## LOOKING CLOSELY AT BOOKS

### Setting

*Where and when did the story take place?*
The setting is the time and the place of the action. Its elements are the geographical location, which may be as broad as a country or city or as narrow as an isolated farm or a single classroom; and the time, which can be a historical period of several decades or more, a season, or a day. Other aspects of setting may be an occupational pattern or a general milieu or atmosphere, social or emotional.

2. Rebecca Caudill, *Did You Carry the Flag Today, Charley?* (hardback, 1966; paperback, 1971—Holt, Rinehart & Winston, Inc.). Laura Ingalls Wilder, *Little House in the Big Woods* (hardback, 1932, 1953; paperback, 1971—Harper & Row, Publishers). John Rowe Townsend, *The Intruder* (hardback, 1970—J. B. Lippincott Company).

#### VIEWPOINTS

Education must begin, as Dewey concluded his first article of belief, "with a psychological insight into the child's capacities, interests, habits," but a point of departure is not an itinerary. It is just as mistaken to sacrifice the adult to the child as to sacrifice the child to the adult. It is sentimentalism to assume that the teaching of life can be fitted always to the child's interests just as it is empty formalism to force the child to parrot the formulas of adult society. Interests can be created and stimulated. In this sphere it is not far from the truth to say that supply creates demand, that the provocation of what is available creates response. One seeks to equip the child with deeper, more gripping, and subtler ways of knowing the world and himself.—Jerome S. Bruner, *On Knowing*, Belknap Press of Harvard University Press, 1962, pp. 117–118.

For some readers, the setting of a story may be of paramount interest. For others, the action is all-absorbing, and the setting is of minor importance.

The setting of the story should be clear, believable, and, in the case of biography or historical fiction, authentic. A book like Irene Hunt's *Across Five Aprils* has strength in part because of the author's research which enabled her to reveal convincingly the tempo, the ideologies, and the language of the Civil War years—particularly in the conflict that existed in border-state families. Too often, in a mediocre book, the author substitutes for a subtly interwoven, authoritative treatment of a time or a place some laboriously detailed information awkwardly placed and often isolated from the characters and events. On the other hand, an author like Rosemary Sutcliff, who has a vast knowledge of British history, lets her characters give readers, in dialogue that is appropriate for the period in which the book is set, necessary details about costumes, for example, or information about military leaders. A less qualified writer might introduce into the dialogue an unnatural exchange of information that has the synthetic character of a travel brochure. A mediocre story with a hospital setting might have this ridiculous remark by one nurse to another: "Oh, did you know that one must go through decompression to enter a hyperbaric oxygen chamber?" Of course, the other nurse knows it, and the reader knows she knows it. The author simply hasn't been sufficiently skilled to bring in needed scientific details in a casual, natural way.

"To get to Charley Cornett's house, you turn left off the highway at Main Street, drive to the edge of town, and cross a bridge." So begins *Did You Carry the Flag Today, Charley?* and it goes on to place Charley's home in mountain country: a small house in which Charley lives with his parents, four brothers, and five sisters. Since this is a book for reading aloud to young children, it is quite fitting that there be no specific time, but the "highway" and "drive" make it clear that it is now. No confusion here. It is in the countryside, not the city; Charley is one of a large family. All of these interpretations are within the grasp of small children.

*Little House in the Big Woods* begins "Once upon a time, sixty years ago, a little girl lived in the Big Woods of Wisconsin, in a little gray house made of logs." Thus, deftly and simply, Wilder has made it clear not only that (at the time of writing) the story is set sixty years in the past, but that the little girl that was Laura Ingalls lived in pioneer fashion, in a log house. And how much more we learn about the setting because of the capitalization of "Big Woods." It immediately gives an impression of the isolation of the little gray house, and both the pinpointing of a past time and the expectation that readers will understand the locale are appropriate for the level of the readers.

In *The Intruder*, Townsend begins with "Sea, sand, stone, slate, sky." Both the staccato introduction and the paragraphs that follow, giving geographical details and historical background, lend emphasis to the importance of the place. The two-page chapter ends, "Sea, sand, stone, slate, sky. That is the landscape," a further emphasis by setting the description apart. Facing the opening lines is a map, another clue to the fact that the setting is important. Townsend assumes that his reading audience will appreciate this, and he creates, in the two pages, an atmosphere that invites an expectation of suspense that depends on the kind of reading experiences older children have had.

## Point of View

*Who tells the story?*

The author may write as an omniscient narrator, who simply describes the characters and gives their thoughts by direct exposition, perhaps at several points in the story. He may make no comment and simply let the characters' actions speak for them. If the story is told in first person, the voice may be that of an impartial bystander or of the principal character. In Emily Neville's *It's Like This, Cat*, in which the adolescent protagonist tells the story, we see his parents only through his eyes and must remember that the view of them is therefore limited, so that the author must use other ways of telling the reader what Dave's father is like—through the father's dialogue and actions and through another boy's reaction to him. In Hila Colman's *Claudia, Where Are You?* alternate chapters give the viewpoint of Claudia's mother (in third person) and of the runaway Claudia herself (in first person). If the author uses a diary form or a monologue, as Maia Wojciechowska does in *"Don't Play Dead Before You Have To,"* the point of view is restricted and the only change comes with changing attitudes of the speaker.

Rebecca Caudill's *Charley* is seen quite objectively, but the author identifies with him by making him the only character whose thoughts are given ("he remembered," "he figured out"), so that the listening audience tends to empathize with him.

In *Little House*, Mrs. Wilder does the

same thing; the story is told in third person (although it is based on her childhood) and the emphasis is put on Laura as the main character both by introducing her first and by making the first comment on Laura from her viewpoint: "So far as the little girl could see . . . ."

In *The Intruder*, even more emphasis is given to Arnold as the protagonist, the second chapter beginning, "Arnold saw the boy and girl a few minutes before he saw the stranger," and all of the subsequent actions of the stranger (who claims that *he* is the real Arnold Haithwaite) are seen from Arnold's viewpoint as those of a mysterious intruder.

## Characters

*Who are the characters? How are they revealed?*

It is clear from the discussion above that a major character is often distinguished by being the first person in the book to be introduced. In a book like *The Peterkin Papers*, however, Lucretia Hale sets the lady from Philadelphia apart by introducing her only when the Peterkin family has become so befuddled that she alone can set them straight. In *Charlotte's Web*, E. B. White presents the pig, Wilbur, through a family's discussion of him. Joseph Krumgold, in *. . . and now Miguel*, opens his story with, "I am Miguel."

We learn something more in his very next words: "For most people it does not make so much difference that I am Miguel. But for me, often, it is a very great trouble." The character may thus be revealed by what is said or done, or—as in the case of Wilbur—by what is said about him.

Characterization can be effected by physical description: if we read that a judge in Colonial Salem has pursed lips and a frowning brow, that he is dressed in somber black and walks with stiff dignity, we anticipate his stern behavior. What a character says, what he does, how he reacts to others, how others talk about him are all clues to his personality. If he is a major character, he must play a dynamic role; if he changes, the change should be logical for the sort of person the author has drawn. There should be depth of characterization, since to emphasize only one or two traits produces a one-dimensional portrait that is often more caricature than characterization.

Characters must be both believable and consistent. Children soon learn how superficial is the patterned mystery story in which no adult contributes to the solution, while an omniscient, persistent, superintelligent child adroitly sees all clues, pursues them, and solves the mystery single-handed, or the career story in which the neophyte reporter acquires an interview which none of the older writers had been able to obtain. The reader can usually prophesy that this stereotype will get a by-line and will marry the editor's daughter.

The characters should develop naturally and behave and talk in ways that are consistent with their age, sex, background, ethnic group, and education.

Whether the story is realistic or fantastic, the characters must be convincing. Although Mary Poppins is in a fanciful story, she is a very convincing character, a severe and crusty individual that no child ever forgets. When Michael asks anxiously, "Mary Poppins, you'll never leave us, will you?" the answer from his new nurse is a stern, "One more word from that direction and I'll call the Policeman." Wilbur, the "radiant pig" in *Charlotte's Web*, and Toad of Toad Hall in *The Wind in the Willows* are just as real to children as is Caddie Woodlawn, the redheaded tomboy. Long after details of plot have been forgotten, children and adults will recall with a chuckle or a warm glow of affection such characters as Jo in *Little Women*, Long John Silver, Henry Huggins, Janey the middle Moffat, Arrietty in *The Borrowers*, and dozens of other salty book characters. And it is through such well-drawn individuals that children gain new insight into their own personal problems and into their ever widening relationships with other people.

*Illustration by E. H. Shepard. From* The Wind in the Willows *by Kenneth Grahame. Published by Charles Scribner's Sons, 1954. Reproduced with permission of the publisher.*

As is appropriate for small children whose chief interest is the action in a story, *Charley* is revealed more by what he does than by what he says. Cheerfully obstreperous, Charley, who is five and having his first school experiences, *has* to climb an apple tree to see how apples are attached, and when the class is playing at "hoppity" like Christopher Robin, he hops right out the door. It is further revealing that when the teacher tells him to stay out in the rain, he happily pretends he is a rock and enjoys the rain. In all of his brothers' and sisters' daily inquiries about whether or not he has had the honor of being the flag-carrier, it is clear that they know their little brother and hardly expect it—yet they ask "anxiously" also making it clear that Charley is lovable and loved.

*Illustration by Nancy Grossman from* Did You Carry the Flag Today, Charley? *by Rebecca Caudill. Copyright © 1966 by Rebecca Caudill. Reproduced by permission of Holt, Rinehart and Winston, Inc.*

The theme of family love is strong in the *Little House* books, and the first thing we learn about Laura, as she lies in a trundle bed listening to a wolf howl, is the security she feels with Pa there to protect her. We also see in Laura's actions that she is a curious child, far less compliant than her sister Mary—and Mrs. Wilder often uses Mary's behavior as a contrast to define Laura's livelier personality.

Arnold Haithwaite is revealed as a terse, uncommunicative young man by the first passage of dialogue in the story, yet when he confronts the intruder he makes no bones about his incredulity that they have the same name. Stalwart, inflexible, and unafraid, Arnold shows his personality in the tenacious way he insists on his identity even when the intruder has usurped his place by convincing others that he is the real Arnold Haithwaite.

## Plot

*What happens in the story?*

Fiction for children usually focuses on what happens, what the action is. In some stories for adults, very little happens in a stream-of-consciousness novel or in a quiet character study. While there are some children's books of which this is true, most of them are filled with action. Children want heroes who have obstacles to overcome, conflicts to settle, difficult goals to win. It is the vigorous action in pursuit of these goals that keeps young

## VIEWPOINTS

. . . One of the prime achievements in every good fiction has nothing to do with truth or philosophy or a *Weltanschauung* at all. It is the triumphant adjustment of two different kinds of order. On the one hand, the events (the mere plot) have their chronological and causal order, that which they would have in real life. On the other, all the scenes or other divisions of the work must be related to each other according to principles of design, like the masses in a picture or the passages in a symphony. . . . Contrasts (but also premonitions and echoes) between the darker and the lighter, the swifter and the slower, the simpler and the more sophisticated, must have something like a balance, but never a too perfect symmetry, so that the shape of the whole work will be felt as inevitable and satisfying.— C. S. Lewis, *An Experiment in Criticism*, Cambridge University Press, 1961, pp. 81–82.

readers racing along from page to page to find out how the hero achieves his ends. But achieve he must, in some way or other.

A plot is basically a series of actions that move in related sequence to a logical outcome; if there is no sequence or interaction, the book may have a series of episodes (in some books, particularly books of reminiscence, this can be very effective) rather than a plot or story line. Simple as it sounds, a story needs a beginning, a middle, and an end. First the author must set the stage; then, to have development and momentum, a plot needs conflict, opposition, or a problem; last, there should be a definitive ending: a climax of action, or even a strong indication of future resolution. A dramatic example of a powerful ending is that of *Helter-Skelter*, by Patricia Moyes, in which a young girl, hunting a criminal, finds that the pleasant young man in whom she has confided is himself the culprit. Alan Garner's *The Owl Service* has an equally powerful conclusion. Here a contemporary setting is the background for a frightening reenactment of a Celtic myth. In the last scene the legend is laid to rest and young Gwyn finally discovers who his father is.

Linked to the development of the plot are the characters, who affect what happens by the sort of people they are and who are affected by what happens to them. In stories for the very young, the plot is usually simple, with no subplot, whereas older readers can both understand and enjoy the complexity of a story with many threads.

In *Charley*, the story begins with the fact that a small boy going to school for the first time is told by his brothers and sisters that one child is honored each day by being allowed to carry the flag; as the story develops it becomes evident that Charley is an unlikely candidate. Then an understanding teacher acts—and Charley proudly carries the flag.

*Little House* is an episodic story; although the book and its sequels show the children growing, the separate incidents of

*Illustration by Garth Williams. From* Little House in the Big Woods *by Laura Ingalls Wilder. Copyright 1932 Laura Ingalls Wilder; renewed copyright, © 1953, as to pictures, by Garth Williams. Reprinted by permission of Harper & Row, Publishers, Inc.*

the story might often be interchanged without affecting the outcome.

The plot of *The Intruder* has high dramatic quality. (It was, in fact, filmed for television.) Arnold Haithwaite learns almost immediately that the stranger who establishes himself in Arnold's home is a threat to him—since Arnold is not quite sure of who he really is. He calls the old man with whom he lives "Dad," not having been told that he is the old man's illegitimate grandson. In the struggle for dominance between the boy and the stranger, the plot is given momentum by the fact that the stranger wants not only to take command of the household but also to commercialize the town. The fact that Arnold does not at first know his real identity gives the author an opportunity to unravel threads of past events as well as the immediate action. The conclusion fulfills the promise of the story's opening: a desperate chase on the sands, with the drowning of the criminal in the swift tide and Arnold reaching the safety of an old church, long deserted because it has been for many years cut off from the mainland at high tide.

### Theme

*What is the main idea of the story?*
The theme of the story is its central core, its meaning. For example, the theme of *. . . and now Miguel* is the struggle to attain competence in one's chosen work and so be accepted as a responsible, mature person. The same theme appears in Bianca Bradbury's *The Loner*. In Elizabeth Coatsworth's *Bess and the Sphinx* the theme is overcoming shyness. Often in children's books the theme reflects those developmental values that are inherent in the process of growing up. The theme may be concerned with overcoming jealousy or fear, adjusting to a physical handicap, or accepting a stepparent. Books that have these or other developmental values can help not only the child who shares similar problems but also the child who does not and who needs to learn sympathy and understanding.

Not all books have such themes; some are adventure stories, some written just for fun, and some historical fiction is intended only to highlight a person, a movement, or a period. Indeed, there can be no hard and fast rule about any of the elements of fiction, since there are good books in which almost any aspect may be omitted. The elements discussed here are those which exist in most books.

The theme in *Charley* is that of achieving status and acceptance: Charley has been told that carrying the flag is the signal honor of the school day, and although he is really more excited, by the end of the story, by the fact that he owns his first book, he is well aware that the sign of approval has been carrying the flag. Although the *Little House*

*From* Bess and the Sphinx *by Elizabeth Coatsworth. Illustration by Bernice Loewenstein. Illustration © Macmillan, 1967.*

## VIEWPOINTS

. . . Participation in the continuity of narrative leads to the discovery or recognition of the theme, which *is* the narrative seen as total design. This theme is what, as we say, the story has been all about, the point of telling it. What we reach at the end of participation becomes the center of our critical attention. The elements in the narrative thereupon regroup themselves in a new way. Certain unusually vivid bits of characterization or scenes of exceptional intensity move up near the center of our memory. This reconstructing and regrouping of elements in our critical response to a narrative goes on more or less unconsciously. . . . —Northrop Frye, "The Road of Excess," in *Myth and Symbol; Critical Approaches and Applications*, Northrop Frye, L. C. Knights, and others, edited by Bernice Slote, University of Nebraska Press, Lincoln, 1963, p. 9.

books are imbued with family love and pioneer courage, there really is no underlying theme. In *The Intruder*, for all the drama of the action, the theme is the boy's quest for identity.

### Style

*How is the story written? How are the ideas expressed?*
Style is very difficult to define. Whole books have been devoted to explaining and exemplifying it. There are many brief definitions—Jonathan Swift's "Proper words in proper places make the true definition of style"; Lord Chesterton's "Style is the dress of thoughts"; Comte de Buffon's "The style is the man." Style involves the author's choice of words, the sentence patterns (simple or involved structure, long or short sentences, arrangement of the words within the sentences), the imagery used, the rhythm of the sentences. There are many styles—as many styles as authors. As Thrall, Hibbard, and Holman say in *A Handbook to Literature*, "The best style, for any given purpose, is that which most nearly approximates a perfect adaptation of one's language to one's ideas."[3] Perhaps the best way to talk about style is simply to look at some passages. Read these excerpts from "The Three Little Pigs" and *Millions of Cats* aloud:

*"Little pig, little pig, let me come in."*
*"No, not by the hair on my chinny-chin-chin."*
*"Then I'll huff and I'll puff and I'll blow your house in."*

*"Hundreds of cats, thousands of cats, millions and billions and trillions of cats."*

Sorche Nic Leodhas has the true Scottish cadence. The first tale in her *Thistle and Thyme* begins:

*From Thistle and Thyme by Sorche Nic Leodhas. Illustrated by Evaline Ness. Copyright © 1962 by Leclaire G. Alger. Reproduced by permission of Holt, Rinehart and Winston, Inc.*

3. William Thrall, Addison Hibbard, and C. Hugh Holman, *A Handbook to Literature* (Odyssey, 1960), p. 474.

*An old laird had a young daughter once and she was the pawkiest piece in all the world. Her father petted her and her mother cosseted her till the wonder of it was that she wasn't so spoiled that she couldn't be borne.*

How much more convincing that is than a peppering of *hoot-mon*'s and *dinna ken*'s.

Over and over again, Elizabeth Enright surprises her readers with her pat and amusing use of words that fit the situation or the character. In *Gone-Away Lake* five-year-old Foster is rescued from a dangerous bog of quicksand and explains that he is all right, "but I'm kind of weak from scaredness." And when Portia appears at the farm with braces on her teeth, her boy cousin comments, "When you smile it looks just like the front of a Buick!"

Sid Fleischman's tall tales appeal to children because they are nonsensical, but it is his crisp, casual style that gives such tales as *McBroom's Ear* humor and flavor:

*I guess you've heard how amazing rich our farm was. Anything would grow in it quick. Seeds would burst in the ground and crops would shoot up right before your eyes. Why, just yesterday our oldest boy dropped a five-cent piece and before he could find it that nickel had grown to a quarter.*

In *Little Calf*, a story of the first year in the life of a whale, Victor Scheffer uses words and word patterns that have a quiet, lyric quality that is admirably suited to the scene he is describing:

*On a morning in early October the sea is glass, without a ripple or sound. A feather falls from the breast of an albatross winging its lonely way northwestward to the Leeward Islands and home. The plume drifts lightly to the sea and comes to rest on a mirror image. It is a day when time itself is still.*

In style, as in the theme of a book, there should be appropriateness and integrity, the hallmarks of good writing. When they are absent, we often find pedestrian writing: flagrant repetitiveness, stiff dialogue, a gross exaggeration of humor or fantasy, conflict between realism and fantasy, didacticism, superciliousness ("Can YOU see the little duck in the tree?") or a use of language that is poorly chosen for the genre of the book or for the characters in it.

Rebecca Caudill's style in *Did You Carry the Flag Today, Charley?* is brisk and forthright, just as is Charley himself. Small children may not recognize the Appalachian setting, but they can hear the authenticity of the speech patterns and the fact that Charley's comments sound the way a five-year-old's should.

*Once inside Miss Amburgey's schoolroom, Charley looked around. Little chairs stood in a circle, with one big chair among them. Behind the big chair was a blackboard, and in a trough underneath lay pieces of chalk. Low tables stood at one side of the room. And there—there, fastened to the wall, was the white washbowl!*

Notice how much like an inquisitive child's reaction this is—and how the exclamation point prepares the way for an episode in which Charley squirts water all over himself and several others. In contrast, note the quiet simplicity and the establishment of mood in Wilder's *Little House in the Big Woods:*

*She looked at Ma, gently rocking and knitting. She thought to herself, "This is now." She was glad that the cozy house, and Pa and Ma and the firelight and the music, were now. They could not be forgotten, she thought, because now is now. It can never be a long time ago.*

And, from *The Intruder*, an example of John Rowe Townsend's writing that shows both his gift for brief characterization and the terse dialogue that is typical of Arnold:

*Ernest Haithwaite was a small man whose clothes now seemed a size too big for him. His features, always craggy, were sharpening with age.*

*His hair, once plentiful, was thinning and grizzled. He shaved every Sunday, and sometimes during the week as well.*

*The old man was putting his cup down when a tap came on the door that led to the main house. He struggled to get up. Arnold waved him down, handed him his false teeth from the mantelpiece.*

*"There's a feller staying the night," the old man said.*

*"I know," said Arnold.*

## AN ANALYSIS OF BLOWFISH LIVE IN THE SEA

As an example of analysis of the elements of a book (setting, point of view, characterization, plot, theme, and style) and the criteria used in assessing them, let's look at *Blowfish Live in the Sea* by Paula Fox.

It begins, "My brother, Ben, says that blowfish live in the sea. He says it in many ways. I've found it written on matchbook covers, on brown paper bags from the supermarket, in dust on the windows. That makes Mama mad because you can't get window cleaners to come anymore." On the next page, we learn that this "makes my father mad," and that Ben and his sister do not have the same father. Ben's father is somewhere out west "the last I heard," and the only answer Ben gives, if asked, is "I don't know, Carrie." Carrie goes on to say that she is twelve and Ben nineteen and that his uncut hair irritates his mother and stepfather.

What a lot to learn in two pages! Carrie has first of all told us that Ben is the most important character in the story, certainly the most important to her. He prefers not to talk about his father, and Carrie's laconic "the last I heard" makes it clear that he doesn't often hear from him. The viewpoint is Carrie's, but in her comments about her parents' attitude toward one thing about Ben, his hair, we suspect conflict. Then we learn Ben has dropped out of school, that after an argument with his stepfather he had stopped bringing his friends home. So the stage is set (and the setting here consists of a comfortable, conventional home and a nonconformist son).

The problem is posed when Ben gets a letter from his father, who is going to be in Boston for the weekend and wants Ben to meet him. "Can't wait," the letter ends, and the reader has been given another clue to the father who has not been heard from for so long. Ben wants Carrie to go with him, which tells us both that he is nervous about meeting his father and that the bond between brother and sister is a strong one. All of the elements of the story have now been established and will be elaborated on, but not until the close of the book is the title explained.

In Boston, Carrie and Ben learn that Ben's father is a raffish but engaging man, a liar, a drifter who has neglected his son save for an occasional boastful letter. In fact, they get to his hotel to find a letter saying that an emergency at the ranch he runs in Arizona has forced him to leave town. "Really, so disappointed for both of us! But soon. Very soon." Ben says bluntly, "He didn't want to see me," and he goes back to the hotel and finds his suspicion verified. Mr. Felix has not left town at all.

He is in his room, not quite sober, and at first puts up a bluff about his lie. Then he admits that he, like Ben, was nervous, and having confessed this, he begins to tell the truth. He owns a motel outside of Boston, not a very profitable venture, and he talks about what a wonderful life he has had. To Carrie it is a record of failure, to Ben the freedom of his father's wanderings sounds enticing. Ben decides to stay with his father and Carrie goes home alone.

Ben's decision is the climax of the plot, and it is made credible by the friction that he has felt at home; the reader has been prepared for it both by the characterization and by the tension and apprehension of Carrie as she reacts to Mr. Felix. And for Carrie, too, the outcome is credible: she misses Ben when she is back home, but she has other interests and is not desolate.

The setting, contemporary and urban, is not a major element of the story except for its underlining of the situation: the contrast between the ordered home in New York and the seedy hotel in Boston, where the young people's expectation of what Felix will be like is shaped by that atmosphere.

The theme is love and the acceptance of frailty that love implies, exemplified both by Carrie, who adores her brother despite his moodiness and rebelliousness, and by Ben, who is old enough to understand his father's ineptitude and irresponsibility and to forgive him for them. Paula Fox is a particularly adept writer in presenting the theme of a story; she lets the characters tell the reader what their concerns are. When Carrie reminisces about an incident earlier in her childhood, she reveals both Ben's sensitivity and her own appreciation of it. And Ben, facing his father with the fact that he has been lied to for years, smiles. We know that Ben is compassionate rather than vengeful. And we know, not because the author *says* people must sometimes make difficult choices but because she *shows* us, that these things happen and that people must adjust to them.

One of the criteria for the evaluation of a book is the interaction between characters and between characters and events. Are the characters firmly enough drawn so that the reader finds their reactions to events believable? And do they, in turn, behave consistently in determining what happens? In *Blowfish Live in the Sea*, Carrie very quickly establishes her own still childlike character by her comments on Ben and her tangential remarks about her friend Abby (an early bloomer), by her reaction to her mother's worries about Ben, and by her conversation with her father. Ben is clearly drawn through Carrie's expressed thoughts as well as by his own dialogue and his stepfather's irritation. We are prepared for the denouement by the mother's apprehension about the meeting, and for the touching inadequacy of Ben's father by her remarks.

Some of the components of style are comparatively easy to assess: the writing flows smoothly, the dialogue really sounds like people talking, the story has suspense and momentum. Paula Fox's ability to maintain the child's point of view while writing with adult compassion and literary grace is exemplified by Carrie's memory of a family outing years before.

> *Once when I was standing just behind him, and he was kneeling, I'd suddenly seen how much older he was than I, how much bigger. At that same picnic, a bird had flown right into our windshield just as we parked under some trees. Ben had leaped out of the back seat and run to where the bird had fallen. Then I'd walked over and found him with the bird in his hand, a little mound of smoky feathers.*
>
> *"It's dead," he said quietly.*

## VIEWPOINTS

The . . . argument, 'all taste is relative', must as a matter of simple logic lead also to the conclusion that no one book is inherently better than another. If we accept this, then one of two things is true: either all books are worthless, since if preference is impossible all books are equal and therefore without *value* (for currency depends on varying stages of value); alternatively, if preference is only possible in relative judgements, then discussion is pointless, for everybody is as right as everybody else.

. . . Either some books *can* be dismissed out of hand for reasons which can be precisely given, and which depend on moral and literary principles, or all judgement is purely personal, and there are no grounds for saying that Shakespeare is better than Noël Coward. All our experience and our most valuable traditions uphold the first view: certain books are good, others are bad, and a very large number have something of both. The books are good because they comment on experience with profundity and intelligence, and occasionally with genius; and these qualities lead us to some glimpse of the truth about human experience.

. . . The greatest works of literature challenge us so absolutely that, if we are honest, our private concerns are transcended and our experience is, in spite of ourselves, enlarged. Old ways of judging and feeling are not corroborated, but dissolved, redistributed and refined by the writing.—Fred Inglis, *An Essential Discipline*, Methuen Educational Ltd., London, 1968, pp. 3–5.

*Ben had known everything then. I thought about that bird long after winter came, and Ben standing there with it in his hand.*

In this tender story of love, Paula Fox never strikes a false note, never inserts a word for effect, never uses a polysyllabic word or a quip when they are out of place. She never comes between the child and the book; it is as though she were a channel between the reader and the characters. Only when Ben is gone does Carrie learn why he wrote "Blowfish live in the sea" everywhere. His father had once sent him a dried blowfish that he had found, he wrote, in the Amazon. It was after Ben learned that blowfish live only in salt water that he inscribed his testimony of resentment against his father's betrayal. How astute of the author not to tell us this at the first, but to let us see how Ben reacts and how his leaving home to join his father indicates the softened judgment and tolerance of maturity.

## THE ROLE OF THE CRITIC

In the evaluation of children's books there should be neither a casual, uncritical approach nor a rigid adherence to the standards for adult literature. The best in children's literature, as well as the best in adult literature, will meet those standards, but it is incumbent on critics (and this includes parents) to balance each book's strengths and weaknesses and to remember that each kind of book for children has its own requirements. As Lillian Smith points out in *The Unreluctant Years* (1953):

*A child's range of choice in his reading will always depend upon what is at hand, and this will largely depend upon his elders. Mistaken ideas among adults about what books a child likes, or should like, must prevent the very object they intend: a love for books and reading. If such misunderstanding is given widespread credence it will eventually affect what books are made generally available to children.* (p. 12)

Adults must be wary of pedestrian books, often oversize and profusely illustrated, the kind that bookstore clerks refer to as "grandmother books": slick, busy with detail, often coy, cute, or sentimental. They must try to distinguish between what appeals to some nostalgic adults and what appeals to children. They should guard against bias, preconception, or unevaluated loyalty to a favorite childhood book.

Children's literature often reflects the values that adults think are important to encourage, and those who select books for children should be aware of the author's values and assumptions as well as of their own. If an author's attitude toward parent-child relationships, sex mores, civil rights, or any other issue is in agreement with our own, we may tend to approve of his book as a whole, but if his values and assumptions are at variance with our own, we may tend to dismiss his book, regardless of its other qualities. For these reasons, it is particularly important for us to analyze books as carefully and objectively as we can. Each book must be judged on its own merits, but it is often illuminating to compare a book with the author's other books and with other authors' books on the

### VIEWPOINTS

To judge literature in terms of the racial attitudes presented in them is actually to judge whether the writer has gone beyond and behind stereotypes, myths, and ideas about blacks to develop characters whose ethnic, social, cultural, and personal experiences mesh in all the complex ways they do in real life. The literature that will truly give black children a sense of identity will not be literature-as-morality nor literature-as-propaganda, but literature as human experience. To black children, blackness is an intrinsic and desirable component of that human experience.—Judith Thompson and Gloria Woodard, "Black Perspective in Books for Children," *Wilson Library Bulletin*, December 1969, p. 422.

same topic or in the same literary genre. The professional—teacher, librarian, reviewer, or editor—should know both the books themselves and the critical literature, since criticism entails making judgments that ought to be both informed and objective.

## CRITERIA FOR SPECIFIC TYPES OF BOOKS

The special criteria for the various types of children's literature—poetry, folk tales, fables, myths, epics, fanciful tales, realistic stories, historical fiction, biography, animal stories, and informational books—are discussed in succeeding chapters, and there are also evaluations of individual books, authors, and illustrators. Many different kinds of books should be judged by the criteria for judging the elements of stories—theme, plot, setting, characters, and style. Biography, for instance, may be so evaluated, but it should also be judged by other equally important criteria (see Chapter 15). One of the essential criteria for judging informational books (see Chapter 16) is accuracy, but style, too, is important. Information can, and should, be presented in an interesting, lively fashion.

### VIEWPOINTS

. . . A good critic will indeed be aware of theme, plot, style, characterization, and many other considerations, some of them not previously spelled out but arising directly from the work; he will be sensitive; he will have a sense of balance and rightness; he will respond. Being only human he cannot possibly know all that it would be desirable for him to know; but he will have a wide knowledge of literature in general as well as of children and their literature, and probably a respectable acquaintance with cinema, theatre, television, and current affairs. That is asking a lot of him, but not too much. The critic (this is the heart of the matter) counts more than the criteria.

. . . If the book is for children, he should not let his mind be dominated by the fact, but neither, I believe, should he attempt to ignore it. Just as I feel the author must write for himself yet with awareness of an audience of children, so I feel the critic must write for himself with an awareness that the books he discusses are children's books.

. . . A book is a communication; if it doesn't communicate, does it not fail? True, it may speak to posterity, if it gets the chance; it may be ahead of its time. But if a children's book is not popular with children here and now, its lack of appeal may tell us something. It is at least a limitation, and it *may* be a sign of some vital deficiency which is very much the critic's concern.—John Rowe Townsend, "Standards of Criticism for Children's Literature," *Top of the News*, June, 1971, pp. 385–387.

## THE RANGE OF BOOKS FOR CHILDREN

Because childhood should be a time of exploring many kinds of books, adults who work with children should know the different types, both to prevent children from falling into reading ruts and to encourage them to try books of many varieties.

The books discussed in the following chapters are grouped variously—some according to subject matter (animal stories), some according to approach (realistic stories), some according to genre (biography), and so on. This kind of classification, though obviously mixed and inexact, is nonetheless useful, partly because it is based to a considerable degree on the ways that children themselves describe their books.

One means of helping a child out of a reading rut—say, all animal stories or all fairy tales—is first to discover some common elements in the books he enjoys and then to use these as a stimulus to change. For example, if a child who reads only animal stories has enjoyed Mehlli Gobhai's *Lakshmi, the Water Buffalo Who Wouldn't*, he might be led toward reading other kinds of books with some of the same elements—humor, an Indian setting, or pleasant family relationships.

### Picture Stories

For the prereaders and beginning readers, the picture stories are enchanting. Their illustrations will be considered in Chapter 3. Significantly, the older stories which have lasted over the years are, for the most part, built around one or two general themes: love or reassurance, and achievement. *Peter Rabbit*, which is over seventy years old, has both. Peter has a daring adventure but returns safely to his home where his mother tucks him into bed with a justifiably punishing dose of camomile tea. Love and reassurance make Else Minarik's *Little Bear* books, and many other stories for the youngest, completely satisfying. And then, because the young child is always in an inferior position in his relations with older children and adults, he yearns for independent achievement or competence. Hence the long life of *Mike Mulligan and His Steam Shovel*, the popularity of *Madeline* and her achievements, and the tongue-in-cheek success of *Little Tim*, who triumphs gloriously over his many mishaps, such as shipwrecks and mislaying his parents—all books with themes of satisfying achievement.

Picture books and picture-story books have not, save for the ABC books discussed in Chapter 3, been presented in a separate section because so many of them can be included as a part of a literary genre, and can perhaps be better judged as realistic stories, poems, fantasy, etc., for the very young child.

### Mother Goose and the Ballads

When evaluating the various editions of Mother Goose books, the adult is relieved of the responsibility of deciding whether or not the material will appeal to children; the rhyme and rhythm of the verses and their gay humor are established beyond controversy as appealing to the very young. The areas of decision are the format of the book, the choice of rhymes included, and the calibre of the illustrations.

The traditional ballads appeal to children primarily because of their dramatic quality, and—used with discrimination—can be a bridge between the rhythmic appeal of *Mother Goose* and narrative poetry. Children should also be made aware that ballad-writing is a living art form, the ballads of today emphasizing protest and reform.

### Folk Tales

Challenge and achievement are the heart of the folk tale themes. The heroes or heroines must perform stern tasks if they are to survive, but the fact that they deal competently with glass hills, giants, witches, wicked machinations, and come through modestly triumphant is both reassuring and encouraging. Stories such as "Cinderella," "The Three Little Pigs," "The Three Billy-Goats Gruff," and "Snow White" dramatize the stormy conflict of good and evil. And they reiterate the old verities that kindness and goodness will triumph over evil if they are backed by wisdom, wit, and courage. These are basic truths we should like built into the depths of the child's consciousness; they are the folk tales' great contribution to the child's social consciousness.

### Fables, Myths, and Epics

Older children are the primary audience for the pithy—if sometimes didactic—wisdom of the fables, although many fables have been skillfully used as single versions in picture-story format. All of these forms of literature (fables, myths, and epics) have a quality of universality, and are part of the literary heritage with which all children should become familiar. They may not fully understand the complexity or symbolism of myths and legends, but they can appreciate the drama and beauty of the stories, and the great epics can satisfy a child's reverence for courage and high deeds.

### Fantasy

No genre so satisfies the child's boundless imagination as does fantasy, from the riotous adventures of Max in Maurice Sendak's *Where the Wild Things Are* to the intricate depths of Madeleine L'Engle's *A Wrinkle in Time*. It encompasses gay little picture books about friendly ghosts and little-girl witches, low-keyed modern fairy stories like Betty Brock's *No Flying in the House*, blandly told tales like Helen Cresswell's *The Piemakers*, the romantic adventure stories by Lloyd Alexander, the picaresque books by Joan Aiken, and the polished science fiction of Ray Bradbury. All of them can extend the reader's horizons, all of them have the action that appeals to children, and almost all of them have an ingredient of durable attraction, magic.

### Humor

Children need also the therapy of laughter. Hence the value of the Seuss books from *Horton Hatches the Egg* to *The Cat in the Hat*, wild, daft nonsense matched at an older level by Astrid Lindgren's outrageously funny super-child *Pippi Longstocking*. There is also the subtler humor of *Winnie-the-Pooh* or *Charlotte's Web*, and the wry, close-to-tears humor and pathos of *The Borrowers*. For fantasy moves from nonsense to serious symbolism, as *The Wind in the Willows* or the *Narnia* stories prove.

Incidentally, there is delightful humorous realism, too, as in Keith Robertson's *Henry Reed, Inc.* From the ingenuous absurdities of Charlotte Zolotow's *When I Have a Son* and the matter-of-fact hilarity of Beverly Cleary's *Ramona the Pest* to the sophisticated humor of Campbell's *Why Not Join the Giraffes?* the young of all ages can find amusing echoes of everyday life. But whether laughter is found in a here-and-now story or in the wildest fantasy, it is so important that we should search for it and use it.

### Poetry

Poetry, too, extends children's imaginations, although in a different way. Where fantasy opens doors to things beyond belief, poetry gives new inward vision and understanding. The facile appeals of rhyme, rhythm, and repetition in simple verse and the quick humor of nonsense poetry can lead to an appreciation of the beauty of language and the crystallization in poetry of a mood, an emotion, a relationship, or the loveliness of a scene. The storytelling appeal of narrative poetry makes it a good choice for reading aloud as an introduction to the genre, and children may be led from this to lyric poetry and free verse. The increased interest of children and young people in the writing of poetry as well as in reading it is evident in the many collections and anthologies that have appeared and in the numbers of poetry magazines and workshops that have produced new young poets.

### Animal Stories

A teacher or parent confronted with a reluctant reader will find that two of the most enticing baits to reading are animal stories and what the children describe as "funny books." Stories about animal heroes, either pets or wild creatures, are exceedingly popular. Does the child identify himself with the animal, helpless in the hands of men? Or, as some people think, does this very helplessness of the beast make the child feel superior in resourcefulness and competence? Whatever the answer, the fact remains that whether it is a horse story by Marguerite Henry, the story of three intrepid pets in *The Incredible Journey*, or the story of the young gorilla in *A Stranger at Green Knowe*, children read animal tales avidly even though they are often filled with sadness or downright tragedy. Such stories call forth the young reader's desire to nurture and protect, and this is one of the values of the well-written animal tale for children. Compassion is close to love, and love is the most civilizing force in life. So let children weep over *King of the Wind* or *Gentle Ben;* they need the therapy of tears if they are to learn compassion.

### Realistic Stories

The themes of love, reassurance, and achievement continue in stories of family life. For the middle years, eight to ten, the pleasant and amusing adventures of *Little Eddie* or *Henry Huggins* take place against a permissive family background of suburbia. So does that great family story for the twelves, *Meet the Austins.* The children in these stories have their problems and difficulties, some funny, some grave, but with the reassurance of family understanding and love. This is also true of books about underprivileged migrant workers such as *Blue Willow* and *Roosevelt Grady.* These books broaden children's social understandings and deepen their

*Illustration by Peter Burchard reproduced by permission of The World Publishing Company from* Roosevelt Grady *by Louisa R. Shotwell. Copyright © 1963 by Louisa R. Shotwell.*

sympathies. It is significant that the realistic stories for today's children have gone beyond such books as the once popular *The Bobbsey Twins* and *Nancy Drew* stories and present real people confronted with real problems—from earning money for a bike to rebuilding a fairly normal life in a postwar, bombed-out European city (*The Ark*).

This realistic fiction also acquaints the child with a wider world than the city, suburbs, or regional groups of our own country. Books begin to introduce him to family life in other countries. Even in the picture-story stage, French *Madeline* or *Jeanne-Marie* are as familiar to American children as are the boys and girls of the United States in American children's books. Presently the tens will be enjoying that strange French home-in-the-making described in *Family Under the Bridge,* and the twelves will find out what happens in the aftermath of a war as described in Margot Benary-Isbert's *The Ark.* Gone are the fiesta stereotypes of foreign lands and gone are the stories about a country told by an author who has never seen it or who equates contemporary life with that of a hundred years ago. *Hans Brinker* has been supplemented by Meindert DeJong's *Wheel on the School.* Today's India is re-created by Shirley Arora in *What Then, Raman?*

### Adventure Tales

Under the broad rubric of adventure tales are those realistic stories in which the emphasis is on action. They include mystery stories, sea stories, and such classics as Robert Louis Stevenson's *Treasure Island.* Many of the elements common to other kinds of books are found in tales of adventure, notably the success of the individual over obstacles and the combining of an ordinary setting with extraordinary events, but the distinguishing element of the adventure tales is an emphasis on suspense, danger, or tension.

## Historical Fiction

Children may know Paul Revere in story or verse, but do they also know children of Revere's time—eight-year-old Sarah in *The Courage of Sarah Noble* and the twelve- or fourteen-year-old Johnny in *Johnny Tremain?* Historical fiction today is both historically authentic and well written. Indeed, in such books we find some of the best contemporary writing for children and youth. Both the 1961 and the 1962 Newbery Medals were awarded to books of historical fiction—*Island of the Blue Dolphins* and *The Bronze Bow*, two books good readers of twelve and over should not miss. In each of the books mentioned in this brief sampling, the theme—from "Keep up your courage, Sarah Noble" to the message that it is only love, not hatred, that can bend a bow of bronze—speaks strongly to children of today.

## Biography

Historical fiction and biography may and should be used to reinforce each other. *Johnny Tremain* makes a biography of Paul Revere infinitely more real; Cora Cheney's *The Incredible Deborah* is a stirring example of the valor of a colonial girl; and the homespun, frontier boys in William Steele's stories give vivid life to the scene and times of Daniel Boone. Both historical fiction and biography impress children with a sense of the reality of other days. Begin early to introduce children to these "real stories" we call biographies. Even the youngest readers can start with the d'Aulaires' picture biographies and can then move on to many excellent biographies suitable for children of each age level. Books about Paracelsus, Galileo, Penn, Columbus, Washington, Banneker, Sequoyah, Lincoln, Lee, Gandhi, and many others are authentic and as fascinating as fiction.

## Informational Books

The category of informational books is so broad and so diverse that almost any need a child has for facts about a subject can be satisfied. There is, however, a need for vigilance on the part of the adult to be familiar with the contents of such books, since many informational books give scant coverage or unbalanced treatment. This is an area in which the author's qualifications are important, and the adult working with children should know those authors—and there are many—whose books are accurate, up-to-date, and written at the right level of complexity for their intended audience. Publishers are quick to respond to expressed needs, and the past years have seen an outpouring of books about pollution and ecology, oceanology and space science, and most of the reform and protest movements that stir our society, as well as books on the arts and sciences, man's past record, and his present environment. Handbooks and experiment books, reference books, do-it-yourself books, handsome art books—books by the hundreds—exist to fulfill the child's need to know. The adult can help children choose the best of these books by being aware of the accuracy of the contents, the thoroughness of the indexing (not all informational books need an index), the placement of maps and diagrams, and the organization of the material in a logical sequence.

Children need books to widen their horizons, deepen their understandings, and give them broader social insights. They also need books that minister to their merriment and increase their appreciation of beauty. They need heroism, fantasy, and down-to-earth realism. They need information about themselves and their fast-changing world, and they need books to relieve the tensions of that world. Adults may think in terms of what the child will learn, how the book may improve an attitude, correct a misconception, or ease a fear. If books do this, fine, but the child reads primarily for pleasure. The right time for a book is fleeting, and gentle guidance may be needed to expand the interests of a child who is in a reading rut, so that he may not miss a reading experience for which there may never be another time so right.[4]

The analyses in this chapter are meant as guidelines, not as rigid specifications. There are fine books that do not measure up to every standard of good literature but that may have particular values for a particular child, or whose strengths outweigh their weaknesses. Each book should be judged on its own merits. Wide reading at all levels and careful observation of children's reactions to books and of their individual and special interests will also help adults make wise choices in guiding young readers.

## ADULT REFERENCES[5]


BECHTEL, LOUISE SEAMAN. *Books in Search of Children.*

CAMERON, ELEANOR. *The Green and Burning Tree.* Chapter, "Of Style and the Stylist."

CARLSEN, G. ROBERT. *Books and the Teen-Age Reader; A Guide for Teachers, Librarians, and Parents.*

*Chosen for Children; An Account of the Books Which Have Been Awarded the Library Association Carnegie Medal, 1936–1965.*

COLBY, JEAN POINDEXTER. *Writing, Illustrating and Editing Children's Books.*

COMMIRE, ANNE. *Something About the Author: Facts and Pictures about Contemporary Authors and Illustrators of Books for Young People.*

DE ANGELI, MARGUERITE. *Butter at the Old Price.*

DUNNING, STEPHEN. *Teaching Literature to Adolescents: Poetry.*

———. *Teaching Literature to Adolescents: Short Stories.*

EDWARDS, MARGARET A. *The Fair Garden and the Swarm of Beasts; The Library and the Young Adult*

EGOFF, SHEILA. *The Republic of Childhood; A Critical Guide to Canadian Children's Literature in English.*

EGOFF, SHEILA, G. T. STUBBS, and L. F. ASHLEY, eds. *Only Connect: Readings on Children's Literature.*

FENNER, PHYLLIS. *The Proof of the Pudding.*

———, ed. *Something Shared: Children and Books.*

FENWICK, SARA INNIS, ed. *A Critical Approach to Children's Literature.* Papers by Rosenheim and Nesbitt.

FIELD, CAROLYN W., ed., with VIRGINIA HAVILAND and ELIZABETH NESBITT, consultants. *Subject Collections in Children's Literature.*

FIELD, ELINOR WHITNEY, comp. *Horn Book Reflections: On Children's Books and Reading.*

FISHER, MARGERY. *Intent Upon Reading.*

FRYATT, NORMA R., ed. *A Horn Book Sampler.*

FULLER, MURIEL, ed. *More Junior Authors.*

GILLESPIE, JOHN, and DIANA LEMBO. *Introducing Books; A Guide for the Middle Grades.*

———. *Juniorplots; A Book Talk Manual for Teachers and Librarians.*

HAVILAND, VIRGINIA. *Children's Literature: A Guide to Reference Sources.*

HAZARD, PAUL. *Books, Children and Men.*

HILDICK, WALLACE. *Children and Fiction.* Chapter, "Adult Responsibility: Authors' and Critics'."

HUCK, CHARLOTTE S., and DORIS YOUNG KUHN. *Children's Literature in the Elementary School.*

KAMM, ANTONY, and BOSWELL TAYLOR. *Books and the Teacher.*

KARL, JEAN. *From Childhood to Childhood: Children's Books and Their Creators.*

KUNITZ, STANLEY J., and HOWARD HAYCRAFT, eds. *The Junior Book of Authors.*

LANES, SELMA G. *Down the Rabbit Hole; Adventures and Misadventures in the Realm of Children's Literature.*

LENSKI, LOIS. *Adventure in Understanding; Talks to Parents, Teachers and Librarians by Lois Lenski, 1944–1966.*

LEPMAN, JELLA. *A Bridge of Children's Books.*

LINES, KATHLEEN, ed. *Walck Monographs.* A series of biographies of authors.

MAHONY, BERTHA E., and ELINOR WHITNEY FIELD, eds. *Newbery Medal Books, 1922–1955.*

MEEKER, ALICE M. *Enjoying Literature with Children.*

PILGRIM, GENEVA HANNA, and MARIANNA McALLISTER. *Books, Young People, and Reading Guidance.*

ROBINSON, EVELYN ROSE. *Readings About Children's Literature.*

SAYERS, FRANCES CLARKE. *Summoned by Books; Essays and Speeches by Frances Clarke Sayers.*

SMITH, JAMES STEEL. *A Critical Approach to Children's Literature.*

SMITH, LILLIAN. *The Unreluctant Years.*

THOMISON, DENNIS. *Readings About Adolescent Literature.*

TOWNSEND, JOHN ROWE. *A Sense of Story.*

TREASE, GEOFFREY. *Tales Out of School: A Survey of Children's Fiction.* Chapter 1, "How Much Does It Matter?"

VIGUERS, RUTH HILL. *Margin for Surprise; About Books, Children, and Librarians.*

WALSH, FRANCES, ed. *That Eager Zest; First Discoveries in the Magic World of Books.*

WILSON, BARBARA KER. *Writing for Children; An English Editor and Author's Point of View.*

WYNDHAM, LEE. *Writing for Children and Teen-Agers.*

*Yale French Studies: The Child's Part.*


4. For additional help in choosing books for children, see Book Selection Aids in the Appendices.

5. Complete bibliographic data are provided in the combined Adult References in the Appendices.

# Chapter 3
# Artists and Children's Books

For children, books begin with pictures. A small child, given a picture book of baby animals with no text at all except the identifying labels, learns to turn pages and to look at pictures with increasing perception of pictorial details. In short, he learns to "read" pictures and with their help will soon be able to follow a narrative read to him.

Beautiful pictures can sell a trivial book, and sometimes poor illustrations can cause a first-rate story to be overlooked. With today's offset printing and remarkable color reproduction, the eye appeal of books is more important than ever before, and consequently the artist plays a very significant role in the production of books for children. The books he embellishes fall into at least three distinct categories: first, the pure *picture book* with little or no text (*Bruno Munari's ABC*, for example); second, the *picture story* in which the pictures are so integral a part of the content that the story can actually be "read" by the child from the pictures (Robert McCloskey's *Make Way for Ducklings*, for example); and third, the *illustrated book* with fewer pictures but those interpretative of both characters and situations (E. B. White's *The Trumpet of the Swan*, with Edward Frascino's illustrations, is a good example).

*Illustration by Edward Frascino from* The Trumpet of the Swan *by E. B. White. Copyright © 1970. Reproduced by permission of Harper & Row, Publishers, Inc.*

Esther Averill, in her discriminating evaluation of the art of picture books as it is found in the Caldecott Medal winners, underscores the distinction further:

> *In an illustrated book the pictures are, as the term "illustrated" implies, a mere extension—an illumination—of the text. In a picture book, as the term implies, the pictures play a livelier role, and are an integral part of the action of the book.*[1]

The "livelier role" generally means more pictures and a more complete interdependence between pictures and text than is true in an illustrated book. Obviously, then, the picture book and the picture stories are primarily for the prereader groups from two to perhaps seven. But pictures, whether they are interpretative illustrations of a text or an integral part of a story, still belong to the total stream of art, just as stories written especially for children belong to the total stream of literature and should ultimately be evaluated in that context.

Beautiful illustrations and format (the shape, size, type, paper, binding, and general arrangement) are among the most striking characteristics of modern books for children. Bright colors or soft pastels, quaint old-fashioned pictures or arresting modern designs—all clamor for attention. Black-and-white drawings or pen-and-ink sketches, too, can have a drollery or a charm that delights children. Publishers know well the effect of gay-looking books. Supermarkets and newsstands are selling literally thousands of books for children on the strength of their eye-catching colors. Some of these are worth buying, but many of them are trivial in content and pictorially worthless. Temporary pacifiers in book form!

From what they see in comics and slick magazines as well as in books from supermarket shelves, children know many kinds of pictures. Building on such knowledge, we can begin to lead them into an awareness of finer examples of graphic art, old and new. For, as Bertha Mahony says in *Illustrators of Children's Books*, ". . . art in children's books is a part of all art, not an isolated special field. In every period the greatest artists have shared in it."[2] But in the evaluation of illustrations as in the evaluation of stories, the child himself must be the starting point if we are to meet his needs and extend the range of the art he appreciates.

1. "What is a Picture Book?" in *Caldecott Medal Books: 1938–1957*, edited by Bertha Mahony Miller and Elinor Whitney Field, Horn Book Papers, 1957.

### VIEWPOINTS

. . . By illustration we mean any form of exposition or elucidation. The degree it elucidates or reveals is the degree of its goodness or badness. It can exist on its own, or it may need to be amplified by words. Or it can itself amplify a text. It can also serve decorative ends. It can be a drawing, a painting, a collage or a photograph; it can also be a thumb-print, a geometrical diagram, an ink blot or anything else that communicates. It should always be judged by the effectiveness of its statement and the media in which it appears.—Bob Gill and John Lewis, *Illustration: Aspects and Directions*, Reinhold Publishing Corp., New York, 1964, p. 34.

## CHILDREN'S PREFERENCES

Children begin as stern literalists, demanding a truthful interpretation of the text. If the hero is described as red-headed, no child is going to accept a brown topknot without protest. When the child is told by Ludwig Bemelmans that there are twelve little girls who go walking from Madeline's school, he counts to see that the artist has put them all in.

Even young children observe and enjoy all the cozy details of Caldecott's *Frog He Would A-Wooing Go* or of Eleanor Schick's

2. The Horn Book, Inc., 1947.

*Illustration by Eleanor Schick for* City in the Summer *by Eleanor Schick. Copyright 1969. Reproduced by permission of The Macmillan Company. (Original with color)*

*City in the Summer* as readily as they follow the everyday drama of weather in Roger Duvoisin's pictures for Alvin Tresselt's *Follow the Wind* or *Sun Up*. If the illustrations interpret the story, the child will take to his heart such varied techniques as the splashy colors of Nicolas Mordvinoff's *Finders Keepers*, Robert Lawson's finely detailed pen-and-ink sketches of landscapes and small animals, and Arthur Rackham's inimitable gnomes, witches, wee folk, and strangely human trees.

Being literal, the young child also wants a picture synchronized precisely with the text. When *Make Way for Ducklings* has the mother duck leading her offspring across a busy Boston thoroughfare, the child is glad that Robert McCloskey placed his unforgettable picture with the description and not a page or two later. Even older children are irked by illustrations that appear before or after the episode they are supposed to represent.

Children are as fond of action in pictures as in stories. They love Ernest Shepard's gay action drawings of the skipping Christopher Robin, the tumult of Martha Alexander's *Out! Out! Out!* and the droll, carefree abandon of Maurice Sendak's capering children.

We know that young children also like bright colors, but not to the exclusion of muted hues or blacks and whites. Some years ago, a nursery-school staff tested children on their color choices in clothes and in picture books and were surprised to find no conclusive preference for primary colors. To be sure, the brilliant reds and clear blues that the Petershams so frequently employed in their pictures are always eye-catching, but apparently children also respond happily to the gentle colors in Adrienne Adams' illustrations for Alice Goudey's *Houses from the Sea* and Marguerite de Angeli's pictures for *Mother Goose*. G. LaVerne Freeman and Ruth Sunderlin Freeman, in their evaluation of children's preferences in picture-book illustration,[3] found that children preferred bright, strong colors but that they also seemed to accept black-and-white pictures. The Freemans

3. *The Child and His Picture Book* (Century House, rev. ed. 1967).

## VIEWPOINTS

There is no point, for [the picture book illustrator], in trying to be purely representational. The meaning in his picture comes from the way he arranges colors, lines, shapes, and textures into a special synthesis—one that will please the senses and achieve an aesthetic experience for the reader. Object recognition is a criterion based on the commonplace. It is concerned with simple imitation. The arts are the very antithesis of commonplace standards of imitation, recognition, and the sense of familiarity derived from such considerations.—Olga Richard, "The Visual Language of the Picture Book," *The Wilson Library Bulletin*, December 1969, p. 435.

suggest that this acceptance may be due to familiarity with the black-and-white television screen of that period.

On the whole, there is evidence that children do prefer color to black-and-white in book illustrations. Yet young children delight also in Lynd Ward's powerful monochromes for *The Biggest Bear*, and older children are pleased with the fine, clear minutiae of William Pène du Bois' drawings for his *Twenty-One Balloons* or those of Edwin Tunis in *Shaw's Fortune*.

Adults often assume that small children do not see details in a picture, but they do. For young children of the early 1900's, half the charm of the pictures in the Palmer Cox *Brownie* books lay in their details. The illustrations seemed to have hundreds of Brownies, each doing something different, but every child always looked for his favorites, the Dude or the Policeman or the Cowboy. So children today look for the small figure of the mouse in *Anatole and the Thirty Thieves* by Eve Titus. But the same youngster who will gloat over small details in a picture may also enjoy the bold, uncluttered strength of a single figure by Rockwell Kent, or the sharp, clear outlines of Artzybasheff's illustrations for *The Fairy Shoemaker and Other Fairy Poems*.

Children, then, respond to a wide variety of book illustrations—even the crude or saccharine drawings if they help tell the story. The more they are exposed to authentic art of many styles, however, the greater the possibility that their tastes will diversify.

## REPRODUCING THE WORK OF THE ARTIST

It's a long way from the drawing board to the finished book. We enjoy today a wealth of varied and beautiful books in part because of the technological advances in printing, in part because of the growing awareness of the importance of early childhood education, and in part because good artists, designers, and editors are dedicated to giving children the best. As Jean Karl, a children's book editor, has said:

> *Picture books, of course, present the greatest problems in finding the right artist. Most authors have some kind of illustrations in mind when they write a picture book text. If they have not envisioned specific illustrations, they at least have some specific style in mind. (Many manuscripts from never-published authors suggest that Maurice Sendak, Leo Lionni, or even Andy Warhol would be the perfect illustrator for the tale they tell.) It is the publisher's responsibility to choose the illustrator for a picture book, but most try to take the author's preferences into consideration, and all try to find the illustrator who will make the manuscript into a unified book. For this, the author's vision of the finished book is important, because it is part of the author's concept of what he has done.*[4]

There are many picture books in which the artist's conception of an author's characters and mood are enchanting in their perfection (for example, Garth Williams' illustrations for Natalie Carlson's *The Happy Orpheline*

4. Jean Karl, *From Childhood to Childhood* (John Day, 1970).

and Maurice Sendak's for Else Holmelund Minarik's *Little Bear's Friend*). Some of the best picture books, however, are those written and illustrated by the same person. Leo Lionni, Martha Alexander, Edward Ardizzone, Maurice Sendak, Uri Shulevitz, Evaline Ness, and Marcia Brown are among the contemporary author-artists in whose books the text and the illustrations perfectly complement each other. This is true also of books for older children by such author-illustrators as Leonard Everett Fisher and Edwin Tunis.

The editor and the book designer must, in collaboration with the illustrator, consider all the visual aspects that contribute both to the beauty of a book and to its appropriateness for its intended audience—the size and clarity of the type, the leading (space between lines), the layout of the page, the amount of print on each page, as well as the illustrations. Of course such picture books as John Goodall's *Shrewbettina's Birthday* and Iela and Enzo Mari's *The Apple and the Moth* (the first a story, the second the record of a moth's life cycle) have no words at all, but the pictures have been so carefully planned that what happens is crystal clear. In books for older children, too, the arrangement of all visual material (Anthony Ravielli's precise drawings for *Wonders of the Human Body* are fine examples) illuminates and expands the text.

As Edward Ardizzone insists, "drawing is of paramount importance."[5] The artist must be able to draw, to interpret the story, or, in informational books, interpret accurately the given facts. Furthermore, he must understand the printing processes by which his original art work is converted into illustrations for a book.

There are three basic methods of reproduction—relief, intaglio, and surface or planographic printing. Each of these may be direct (done largely by hand) or indirect (done by mechanical procedures).

In *relief* the surface to be printed is raised. The most familiar examples of direct or manual techniques are probably the wood blocks or linoleum blocks on which a picture is drawn, the surrounding areas cut away, and the remaining portion inked to be impressed upon paper. The indirect or mechanical counterpart is the line cut (also called a

5. Edward Ardizzone, "Creation of a Picture Book," *Top of the News*, December 1959.

*From* Shrewbettina's Birthday, *copyright © 1970 by John S. Goodall. Reproduced by permission of Harcourt Brace Jovanovich, Inc. (Original in color)*

## VIEWPOINTS

The painter who stands before an empty canvas must think in terms of paint. If he is just beginning in the use of paint, the way may be extremely difficult for him because he may not yet have established a complete rapport with his medium. He does not yet know what it can do, and what it cannot do. He has not yet discovered that paint has a power by itself and in itself—or where that power lies, or how it relates to him. For with the practiced painter it is that relationship which counts; his inner images are paint images, as those of the poet are no doubt metrical word images and those of the musician tonal images.—Ben Shahn, *The Shape of Content*, Vintage Books, New York, 1960, p. 57.

line engraving or line block). In this process the illustration is photographed, being mechanically reduced to correct size, on a glass plate. When the film is hardened, it is transferred to a sensitized metal plate and is developed and washed. The lines of the drawing are brought into relief by bathing the plate in acid, which eats away the part that has no lines. The plate, nailed to a wooden block so that the drawing is type-high, will print the raised design on paper.

When a drawing has shadings, a halftone engraving is made. To obtain the shadings, tones between black and white, the drawing is photographed through a halftone screen, which has fine parallel lines at right angles. This breaks the pictorial copy into tiny dots: the darker the gray, the more dots to the inch. The acid etching for the halftone requires much more care than that for the simple line cut and must be done in stages so that the deeper parts can be re-etched. If colors are used, only one color can be printed at a time. A four-color picture with varying strengths requires four halftone blocks (black, yellow, magenta, and cyan blue can reproduce almost any color or shade of color) to reproduce the shading and intensity of the original.

The second method of reproduction is *intaglio*. In this process the part to be printed is below the surface rather than above the surface as in relief. Mezzotint, steel engraving, and etching are some of the direct or hand intaglio techniques. Photogravure is the indirect or mechanical technique. In this process the surface is broken into dots as for the halftone, but here each dot forms a pit—the variation is in depth rather than in size as in the halftone. The surface ink is scraped off with a knife and the remaining ink is picked out from the pits when paper is pressed on the cylinder. To print color photogravure, a separate plate must be made for each color.

The third method of reproduction is *surface* or *planographic* printing. Stencils and silk screens are examples of direct or hand techniques. Indirect or mechanical techniques include collotype (very expensive and seldom used) and lithography. Lithography is based on the principle that water and grease do not mix. The process was discovered accidentally in 1796, when Aloys Senefelder used a crayon to write a list on a slab of limestone, and then wet and inked the stone. The water repelled ink except for the writing, which didn't hold water because of the crayon grease. In today's printing, the stone is replaced by a sheet of emulsion-coated zinc on which the images are printed photographically, much in the way that halftones are produced, except that the dots are on the emulsion and will accept ink. The bare metal around the dots repels ink, and the dots are impressed in the printing process. Most lithographic work today is produced by offset process, using an extra roller to transfer the impression. The use of offset lithography for color work is one of today's most significant advances in the reproduction of illustrations, since it makes possible the use of type and colored illustrations on the same page without the necessity for coated paper for separate pages of illustration.

The artist must choose between two methods of preparing his colored illustrations for reproduction: either using the me-

## VIEWPOINTS

But it is not safe to identify illustration with the representational and decoration with the abstract elements of art; although this is as true as most generalizations. Both elements may be mingled in one design, and in fact must be if it is to be good. And if it were possible to divide something that is indivisible, we might say that illustration has reference to the meaning of the text and decoration to the appearance of the page. . . .

Midway between the two we have the imaginative type of illustration which rests upon the text but is itself a sort of extension of the text because it says things visually that are not possible to words.

. . . The good illustration must be a good design irrespective of the text it accompanies, and the way it fits the page is of course part of that design.—David Bland, *The Illustration of Books*, Pantheon, New York, 1952, pp. 12, 13.

chanical separation of colors already mentioned, which requires a complete understanding of the production method so that he can give specific instructions to the printer; or making his own color separations. If he does his own, he must make a separate drawing for each color, with transparent sheets perfectly aligned one over the other or with the key drawing taped on the glass top of a lighted box. If he uses only two colors that do not touch each other, he can use red and black and instruct the printer to use them as keys for any other two colors.

Evidence of the importance of children's book illustration includes the establishment of the Caldecott Medal in the United States, the Greenaway Medal in England, and the international Hans Christian Andersen Medal for illustrators as well as authors. The American Institute of Graphic Arts now includes the names of children's book illustrators and designers in their annual "Fifty Books of the Year" and holds a biennial Children's Book Show, which exhibits some 100

*Posters prepared for Children's Book Week in 1921, Jessie Willcox Smith; 1943, Elizabeth Orton Jones; 1969, Emily McCully. Published by The Children's Book Council, Inc.*

books selected for their artistic and typographic merit. The Children's Book Council's widely circulated posters by children's book illustrators call attention to Children's Book Week and also to the importance of the illustrations in children's books.

Just as the Children's Book Week posters reflect changes both in styles of illustration and in social customs, dress, mores, and the adult's conception of the child, so illustrations for the books themselves echo their own times since children first looked at pictures and print. In the following pages, some of the ABC books will be considered in a group, and then many of the artists who have contributed to children's books will be discussed in chronological order, according to their birth dates.

## ABC BOOKS

The pictorial ABC books of each generation are all variants of *Mother Goose's* "A Apple Pie." Edward Lear wrote one of the funniest, all in nonsense phonetics, and it now appears in a delightful illustrated edition. Walter Crane made a charming *Baby's Own Alphabet*, and Kate Greenaway turned *A Apple Pie* into a thing of beauty.

Modern artists have also been intrigued by the austerity of a single letter and the possibilities of making it dramatic. Wanda Gág's *ABC Bunny* has a rhyming text with continuity unusual in such miscellanies. The dark woodcuts are relieved by large scarlet capital letters which suggest the small child's ABC blocks. The pictures (1, p. 49) and story make it a favorite.

Garth Williams' *Big Golden Animal ABC*, which is also available in a small edition, makes use of amusing contrast: for each letter Williams has provided a large realistic animal in full color and, on the same page, his unrealistic comic foil. The letter *A*, for instance, has a menacing Alligator with jaws agape and, near the bottom of the page, a wee rabbit on a bicycle, scuttling madly away.

Fritz Eichenberg's *Ape in a Cape*, "an alphabet of odd animals," is both funny and phonetic. The "Goat in a boat" looks properly wild-eyed (2, p. 49) like the "Fox in a box." Young children like this book, and it inspires the older children to make rhymes of their own—e.g., "A llama in Alabama."

Roger Duvoisin's *A for the Ark*, shows Noah calling the animals alphabetically. The ducks dawdle because they like the rain. Some bears come with the B's, others with U for ursus. On they come, comical or impressive, but all decorative in the artist's most colorful style.

Also for older children is Phyllis McGinley's *All Around the Town*, an alphabet of city sights and sounds in lively verse, with Helen Stone's pictures as attractive as the text. The witty lyrics combine letter sounds with the maximum rhythm and meaning. For example, one verse begins "V is for the Vendor/ A very vocal man."

In contrast to *All Around the Town*, *Bruno Munari's ABC* depends for its charm on his masterful use of color and design to build interesting associations around each letter—"A Fly/ a Flower/ a Feather/ and a Fish" with "more Flies" at the top of the page to go buzzing on through the book (3, p. 49). So arresting are his colors and use of space that the visual impact of each page is a contribution to seeing.

*Brian Wildsmith's ABC* is a heady experience with color, an ABC book with the simplest of texts and the most glorious rainbow of subtle tints and hues. "cat CAT" says a fuchsia page with letters in three colors, and opposite, against a muted blue, is a green-eyed, black cat. One of the great pleasures of this book is to flip the pages slowly and enjoy the changing colors.

*John Burningham's ABC* has upper- and lower-case letters and illustrative words on the verso pages, facing stunning pictures in bold compositions (p. 50). The delicate details of Peter Parnall's drawings in *Apricot ABC* by Miska Miles illustrate a rhyming text that tells a story; unfortunately, on some pages the letters are partially concealed by the pictorial details. *Celestino Piatti's Animal ABC* is also in rhyme, the illustrations vigorous, richly colored, and poster simple (p. 50). This book also illustrates a weakness too often found in alphabet books, the use of an uncommon word as the key: here, for example, "U" is "Ural owl" (bright children, of course, are sometimes intrigued by these uncommon words). Thomas Matthiesen's *ABC* concentrates on familiar objects. Unusually good, simple color photographs face pages that have, in addition to the upper- and lower-case letters and the illustrative words, a few lines of text about the objects—"Shoes keep your feet safe when you walk. They have strings called laces, which often become untied."

Two books are useful for environmental awareness. Francine Grossbart's *A Big City* has words which all start with oversize capital letters: Antennas, Buildings, Cars, Doors, Elephant in a zoo, etc., on colored pages with ample blank space (p. 51). In Marguerite Walter's *City-Country ABC*, half the book has a city setting, and, turned upside down, the other half has a country setting. The emphasis is alliterative: ". . . and W was everywhere—in the woods, in the whistling wind. There was even a woodpecker."

Among the newer books, one of the most outstanding graphically is Dorothy Schmiderer's *The Alphabeast Book*, in which each letter, framed, is reshaped in two other frames to end, in a fourth frame, as an object (p. 51). This is useful for visual conceptualizing as well as for learning the alphabet. *Still Another Alphabet Book* by Seymour Chwast and Martin Stephen Moskof is an unusual book, too, the pictures varied and inventive, and the entire alphabet used as a frieze on each page. Within the frieze, the letters used in the word for the pictured object are printed in a different color; for example, on the "Q" page a queenly figure is pictured and within the frieze of the alphabet the letters in "queen" are a different color from the other letters in the alphabet, a technique that intrigues children as a game and fosters reading readiness. (See p. 51.)

There are many other ABC books and undoubtedly more to come, but these major examples illustrate some of the various types.

## JAPANESE SCROLL, TWELFTH CENTURY

In Japan in the twelfth century the artist Kakuyu (1053–1140), popularly known as Toba Sojo, produced a "Scroll of Animals" that for humor and storytelling power must have delighted both young and old. It is not in the heroic vein but is hilariously lighthearted, a sort of glorified comic strip drawn without any text by a superb artist. Velma Varner, an editor of children's books, reproduced the scroll in book form with brief

1.

2.

1. *Reprinted by permission of Coward-McCann, Inc. from* The ABC Bunny *by Wanda Gág. Copyright 1933 by Wanda Gág. Copyright renewed 1961 by Robert Janssen.*

2. *From* Ape in a Cape. *Copyright 1952 by Fritz Eichenberg. Reproduced by permission of Harcourt Brace Jovanovich, Inc. (Original in color)*

3.

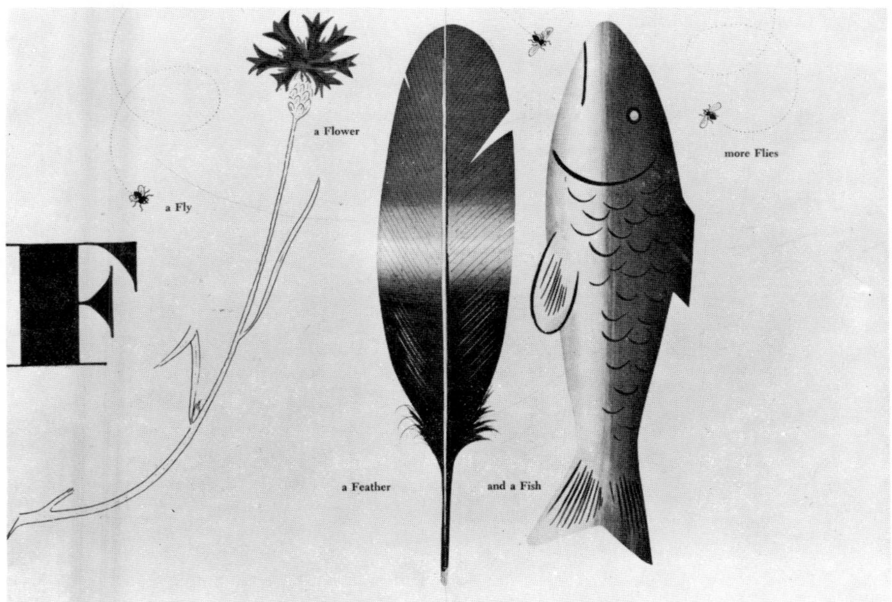


3. *From* Bruno Munari's ABC. *Copyright 1960 by Bruno Munari. Reproduced by permission of the publishers, The World Publishing Company. (Original in color)*

4.

*4. Copyright © 1965 by Artemis Verlag, Zurich, Switzerland. First U.S.A. edition 1966 by Atheneum. From* Celestino Piatti's Animal ABC. *Used by permission of Atheneum. (Original in color)*

*5. From* John Burningham's ABC, *copyright © 1964, by John Burningham, reproduced by permission of the Bobbs-Merrill Company, Inc., and Jonathan Cape Ltd., London. (Original in color)*

5.

6.

*6. Illustration by Francine Grossbart from* A Big City. *Copyright © 1966. Reproduced by permission of Harper & Row, Publishers, Inc. (Original in color)*
*7. From* The Alphabeast Book: An Abcedarium *by Dorothy Schmiderer. Copyright © 1971 by Dorothy Schmiderer. Reproduced by permission of Holt, Rinehart and Winston, Inc. (Original in color)*
*8. Illustration by Seymour Chwast and Martin Stephen Moskof for* Still Another Alphabet Book. *Copyright © 1969. Reprinted by permission of McGraw-Hill Book Company. (Original in color)*

7.

**Ii** **inchworm**

8.

*Illustration by Toba Sojo for* The Animal Frolic *by Velma Varner, G. P. Putnam's Sons. Copyright 1954 by the Temple of Kozanji, Kyoto, Japan.*

commentaries that provide minimum clues to the action. She called the book *The Animal Frolic* (1954). The pictures show the creatures convening for a picnic and enjoying swimming, feasting, athletic feats, a sword dance, and the choosing of a king-for-a-day. The characterization of each animal is droll and fascinating. Here, in spite of the original scroll form, is a true picture book with pictures that tell the story, show action, and reveal character without the necessity of words. How children who saw it some eight hundred years ago must have loved it, just as children love it today when they have the opportunity to see it and to "read" the pictures for themselves.

## WOODCUTS AND ENGRAVINGS BEFORE 1800

In 1484 William Caxton issued the first English edition of *Aesop's Fables*, illustrated with woodcuts by some unknown artist or artists. This was an adult book, but if the children saw the pictures and heard the stories, they undoubtedly appropriated the book just as they have appropriated certain adult books in every generation. Since Caxton's publication of the fables these little moralities have been continuously reprinted, usually illustrated by outstanding artists, doubtless attracted by the dramatic situations the stories embody.

Between the Caxton edition of the fables and the epoch-making *Orbis Pictus*, there were hornbooks and battledores for children but with few or no pictures. There were also the popular chapbooks, enlivened with crude woodcuts, which were beloved by the story-hungry children of the sixteenth and seventeenth centuries.

The *Orbis Pictus* of Comenius is assumed to be the first picture book prepared for children. Today, we would say that it more nearly resembles a primer. It was written in Latin, in 1657 or 1658, by a Moravian bishop and translated into most European languages, including English in 1658. The pictures and text are stilted but not without charm. The word *Flores* appears above a small woodcut showing flowers in a vase and also in a field; the picture is followed by a pleasant commentary on spring flowers. Whatever the subject, there was a conscious effort to associate words and pictures and to use the latter to lead directly into the text. Compared with the gay, action-packed Japanese "Scroll of Animals," the *Orbis Pictus* seems tame and wooden, but for English-speaking children it marked the beginning of picture books planned especially for them.

Even the Newbery publications, important as they are in the history of children's books, did little to advance the art of illustration. It is generally agreed that only for *Little Goody Two Shoes* (1765) did the artist (possibly Thomas Bewick) execute his woodcuts with unusual grace and synchronize them with the text so that they are illustrations in the true sense of the word—interpreting or illuminating the story.

For the most part these earliest producers of crude woodcuts were minor artists, usually unknown. It was not until the advent of Thomas Bewick that children's books were adorned by a major artist.

**Flowers.** **XV.** **Flores.**

| | |
|---|---|
| Amongst the Flowers the most noted, | Inter flores notissimi, |
| In the beginning of the Spring are the | Primo vere, |
| *Violet*, 1. the *Crow-toes*, 2. the *Daffodil*, 3. | *Viola*, 1. *Hyacinthus*, 2. *Narcissus*, 3. |
| Then the *Lillies*, 4. white and yellow and blew, 5. | Tum *Lilia*, 4. alba & lutea, & cœrulea, 5. |
| and the *Rose*, 6. | tandem *Rosa*, 6. |
| and the *Clove gilliflowers*, 7. &c. | & *Caryophillum*, 7. &c. |
| Of these *Garlands*, 8. and *Nosegays*, 9. are tyed round with twigs. | Ex his *Serta*, 8. & *Serviæ*, 9. vientur. |
| There are added also *sweet herbs*, 10. | Adduntur etiam *Herbæ odoratæ*, 10. |
| as *Marjoram*, *Flower gentle*, *Rue*, *Lavender*, *Rosemary*. | ut *Amaracus*, *Amaranthus*, *Ruta*, *Lavendula*, *Rosmarinus*, (Libanotis). |

From Comenius' Orbis Pictus.

### Thomas Bewick, 1753–1828

Thomas Bewick's first book designed for children was *A Pretty Book of Pictures for Little Masters and Misses or Tommy Trip's History of Beasts and Birds* (1779). This book, exceedingly rare today, is an example of the artist's skill in the use of the woodcut. He developed better tools for this work, made effective use of the white line, and carried

*FABLE XLVII.*

**The Fox and the Stork.**

*From Aesop's Fables, Thomas Bewick edition. Faithfully reprinted from rare Newcastle edition. Published by T. Saint in 1784 with the original engravings by Thomas Bewick. From the John G. White collection, Cleveland Public Library.*

the woodcut to a new level of beauty. Most of Bewick's finest drawings seem to have been for books originally planned for adults as, for instance, his various editions of Aesop's fables, particularly those of 1784 and 1818. The former was reprinted in 1878 by his publisher, T. Saint, from the original blocks. It is called *Bewick's Select Fables of Aesop and Others.* These pictures show the artist's knowledge and love of the whole outdoor world—plants, trees, birds, and beasts. Certainly Thomas Bewick, and to a somewhat lesser extent his brother John, raised the woodcut to a high level of artistic achievement.

An interesting by-product of the Bewicks' contribution is that artists of established reputations began to sign their pictures for children's books.

### William Blake, 1757–1827

William Blake's *Songs of Innocence* (1789)[6] adds special luster to the artistic achievements of the eighteenth century. The artist wrote the verses, illustrated them, engraved, hand-colored, and bound the book, with some help from his wife. It caused no great stir in its day, but it was nevertheless an epoch-making book. It is true that most of Blake's poetry and all of his finest engravings and water colors were for adults, but the artist thought of his *Songs of Innocence* as a book for children. He adorned it lovingly with garlands and scrolls. He gave it color and beautifully drawn figures of people, especially children. The pictures are not realistic but delicate fantasies, almost dreamlike in character. They in no way measure up to the greatness of his illustrations for adult books, *The Book of Job* (1825), for instance. But here are color and a tender perception of the artless grace of children. (See 2 in color section.)

6. The work of Blake, as well as that of other author-illustrators, is discussed later in the text. See Index for relevant page references.

## THE NINETEENTH CENTURY

William Blake brought delicate colors into his book for children, not by color printing but by hand. Color printing, however, was widely used from about 1803 to 1835, though at the beginning of the nineteenth century the most notable illustrators were still working in black and white.

Examine 1 and 3 in the color section. These two early colored illustrations by unknown artists are interesting proof that publishers were beginning to recognize the lure of color in books for young children. *A Continuation of the Comic Adventures of Old Mother Hubbard and Her Dog* was issued in London in 1805 by John Harris, successor to Elizabeth Newbery. Harris was deservedly famous for his children's books. As Philip James says of him, ". . . the high quality of the illustrations in all of his books during the first quarter of the nineteenth century place him above his rivals."[7] The rare little book *The History of the House That Jack Built* has "15 elegant engravings on Copper Plate," brightly colored and amusing. In 1825, Fielding Lucas, a distinguished American publisher famous for his beautifully designed and decorated maps, was also publishing well-chosen children's books. They followed the English publications of Newbery or Harris, but we are told[8] he had his own plates made, some of them drawn by John Latrobe perhaps, but unsigned. Lucas' list of children's books advertised in a newspaper in 1824 includes twenty-four familiar English titles such as *Cock Robin, The Comic Adventures of Dame Trot and Her Cat, The Cries of London,* and *The History of the House That Jack Built.* Only seventeen examples of his children's books are extant, although he is known to have published seventy between 1820 and 1845.

7. *Children's Books of Yesterday*, edited by C. Geoffrey Holme, p. 44.

8. *Proceedings of the American Antiquarian Society.* At the Annual Meeting held in Worcester, October 19, 1955. "Fielding Lucas, Jr. Early 19th Century Publisher of Fine Books and Maps," by James W. Foster, pp. 202–207.

### William Mulready, 1786–1863

So the century began propitiously with some color printing for children's books, but it is the work of William Mulready that first brought distinction to those early years of the century.

This illustrator is remembered for his gay, fanciful drawings for *The Butterfly's Ball* (1807) by William Roscoe. This rhymed description of a fairy picnic enjoyed enormous popularity for over fifty years, aided no doubt by Mulready's amusing pictures in black and white. Some of his bees, snails, butterflies, and other guests of the party have human bodies with true-to-the-species creatures atop their heads or else they are well-drawn insects or animals piloted by elfish figures perched on their backs. The mole, for instance, has a fat blind gnome for a rider. Unfortunately, the children's books this gifted artist adorned do not stand the tests of time as his drawings do. This is a fate that threatens the lasting fame of illustrators in each generation.

*Illustration by William Mulready. From* The Butterfly's Ball *by William Roscoe. Published by J. Harris, 1807.*

### George Cruikshank, 1792–1878

George Cruikshank, a great artist of this period, was a satirist and a cartoonist for England's famous *Punch*. In contrast to Mulready, Cruikshank had the good fortune to illustrate an English translation of the Grimms' *Collection of German Popular Stories* (1824 and 1826), a classic that is ageless in its appeal. In black and white, his humorous, lively, cleverly drawn pictures are the embodiment of the tales.

### Sir John Tenniel, 1820–1914

Inseparable from Lewis Carroll's *Alice's Adventures in Wonderland* (1865) and *Through the Looking Glass* (1871) are the illustrations by Sir John Tenniel, cartoonist for *Punch*. Other artists hopefully make pictures for this classic fantasy, but their illustrations usually seem inadequate when compared with the long beloved figures by Tenniel. Unforgettable are serious, pinafored, long-haired Alice, the smartly dressed, bustling White Rabbit, the Mad Hatter and his famous tea-party companions, Father William, the Cheshire Cat, and all the other mad, topsy-turvy characters of the Wonderland and the Looking Glass worlds. Strong in line and composition, drawn with beautiful clarity and poker-faced drollery, these illustrations enhance the fantasy and give it convincing reality.

### Arthur Hughes, 1832–1915

The illustrations of Arthur Hughes are as strongly associated with George Macdonald's *At the Back of the North Wind* (1871) and *The Princess and the Goblin* (1872) as are Tenniel's illustrations with *Alice's Adventures in Wonderland*. Hughes worked in black and white and was an interpreter of fantasy, but his pictures are as different from Cruikshank's or Tenniel's as the Macdonald books are different from the Grimms' fairy tales or Carroll's *Alice*. For Macdonald's two fairy tales the never-never land of the pictures is all mystery, gentleness, and lovely innocence. These qualities carry over to his more realistic pictures for Christina Rossetti's *Sing-Song* (1872), little masterpieces of tenderness and beauty.

### Walter Crane, 1845–1915

In *English Children's Books*, Percy Muir points out in the chapter "The Importance of Pictures" that it was ". . . in the sixties that publishers began first to attempt to sell books to children mainly for the interest of the illustrations." What a line of successors that movement launched! Mr. Muir then goes on to show how much modern color printing owes to Edmund Evans, a publisher and an artist in his own right. A pioneer in color printing, Evans had long inveighed against the cheap, gaudy illustrations used in books for children. He firmly believed that even an inexpensive paperback book planned for the nursery child could be beautiful in design and color. In Walter Crane, Evans found an artist to carry out his theories.

Trained as a wood engraver, Walter Crane was greatly influenced by the work of the Pre-Raphaelites and also by his study of Japanese prints. Both of these influences are evident in his pictures—in the idealized figures of women and children and in the sparse, decorative landscapes. Between 1867 and 1876 Crane produced over thirty so-called "toy books,"[9] published chiefly by Routledge and generally undated. Crane took these books so seriously that he worked over every page, including the typography, so that it came out a well-composed whole. His *Baby's Opera* and *Baby's Bouquet* were a series of English nursery songs with words, music, and pictures. Later he decorated, also in color, Hawthorne's *Wonder Book* (1892). (See 7 in color section.)

9. The term "toy book" is used today to mean books with pop-ups or cut-outs that make them more toys than books. The Crane "toy books" were simply books intended for the nursery prereading child.

### Kate Greenaway, 1846–1901

Edmund Evans was greatly taken with the delicate colors and decorative borders of Kate Greenaway's pictures for her own rhymes. He printed her book *Under the Window* (1878) by a costly process that reproduced the pictures with remarkable fidelity. To her surprise, the artist found herself famous almost overnight, and she outsold all the other artists of her day, the initial sales of *Under the Window* running to some 70,000 copies. It still sells, and Evans' firm is still printing her books.

Her style was unique—graceful figures in quaint old-fashioned clothes, at play, at tea, or otherwise decorously engaged. The pages are gay with garlands of fruits or flowers, mostly in delicate pastel colors. Her pictures often have a gentle humor, and their grace and charm still delight the eye. (See 5 in color section.)

### Randolph Caldecott, 1846–1886

Randolph Caldecott, for whom the Caldecott Medal is named, was the third of Edmund Evans' famous triumvirate and, like the others, owes much to that printer's bold experiments with color printing. Caldecott succeeded and far surpassed Walter Crane in the production of illustrated toy books.

Caldecott grew up in the Shropshire country, familiar with country fairs, the hunt, dogs, horses, and the lovely English landscape, all of which are evident in his pictures. When in 1876 Washington Irving's *Old Christmas* appeared with Caldecott's illustrations, his reputation was established. But it was not until around 1878 that he began to work on the nursery toy books with which we associate his name and fame. Probably his most famous illustrations (1878) are those for William Cowper's *The Diverting History of John Gilpin* (1785). Caldecott made Cowper's poem into a picture story, funny both to children and adults and a masterpiece of droll action. No one ever drew such humorous horses or such recklessly inept riders. His illustrated *Mother Goose* rhymes in paper-covered book form are among his loveliest and most original creations. Caldecott did a number of these toy books, selling at one shilling, and they have seldom been surpassed by our best and most expensive modern picture books. (See 10 in color section.)

### Arthur Frost, 1851–1928

For that classic collection *Nights with Uncle Remus*, Arthur Frost made pen-and-ink pictures as comic and irresistible as that gay rogue, Brer Rabbit himself. Whether he is "sashaying" down the road in his patched and droopy old pants or talking turkey to Tar Baby, he is a picture of rural shrewdness.

*Illustration by Arthur Frost. From* Uncle Remus and His Friends *by Joel Chandler Harris. Published 1892 by Houghton Mifflin.*

Frost's whole gallery of animal folk, "ourselves in fur," provides as marvelous characterizations as any Caldecott ever made.

### Howard Pyle, 1853–1911

Howard Pyle was another American artist who worked in black and white. His heroic and romantic pictures for such books as *Robin Hood* (1883), *Otto of the Silver Hand* (1888), and *Men of Iron* (1890) are meticulous in their fidelity to the historical costumes, weapons, and accouterments of the period. Yet his elaborations of robes, courtly trappings, and tournament details are always subordinated to the interpretation of character or mood. The poignancy of young Otto's tragedy moves anyone who looks at those pictures, and, in contrast, the high good humor of Robin Hood is equally evident. Here was an author-artist with a gift for telling stories in words and pictures and with the ability to inspire his students to produce great illustrations, too (see, for example, the work of Jessie Willcox Smith and N. C. Wyeth).

---

VIEWPOINTS

A good book has no need of illustration but illustration can add something that is not in the story itself—the authentic topographical or architectural background, for instance, or characteristics of dress and manners. A painterly-draughtsman-illustrator will be competent to describe, in visual terms, the psychological nuances leading to, or arising from, an incident. In this way, rather than through tidy little drawings depicting 'hair-raising episodes', will the child gain something from the illustrator.

For older children illustration of this kind must be done with all the skill of an objective painter whose work is remote from photographic image. . . .—John Ryder, *Artists of a Certain Line*, Bodley Head, London, 1960, p. 33.

---

**Leslie Brooke, 1862–1940**

Although some of the work of the English Leslie Brooke was published as late as 1935, he is so much in the Caldecott tradition that he seems to belong to the earlier century of the famous triumvirate. In delicate pastel colors he provides glimpses of the English countryside, pictures as charming as any Caldecott produced. His *Mother Goose* characters in *Ring o' Roses* (1922) are delightful, and his pigs are triumphs of whimsical characterization. The *Johnny Crow* books (1903, 1907, and 1935) are his own invention. Johnny Crow is the perfect host for two parties of birds and beasts so adroitly characterized both in verse and pictures that his books are classic examples of what picture books can be in the hands of a creative artist-writer. (See 4 in color section.)

## THE TWENTIETH CENTURY

**E. Boyd Smith, 1860–1943**

An American artist and an innovator, E. Boyd Smith produced at the turn of the century but is now almost forgotten. In 1906 he wrote and illustrated *The Story of Pocahontas and Captain John Smith*, which could be considered the forerunner of the d'Aulaires' picture-biographies. It is a moving narrative with pictures that are beautiful in composition and wonderfully interpretative. In 1910 Smith wrote and illustrated *Chicken World*, a picture book as beautiful as anything we have today. Borders portraying the changes in season frame the large pictures which show the cock strutting grandly, his feathers all a-shine, the hens sitting or proudly exhibiting their fluffy chicks. None of E. Boyd Smith's other work had the distinction of his biography of *Pocahontas* and his *Chicken World*. Both deserve to be in print today.

**Jessie Willcox Smith, 1863–1935**

Jessie Willcox Smith was a student of Howard Pyle and, like his, her figures and backgrounds are strongly drawn, but here the resemblance ends. She used soft colors, dark rather than clear and light. The heart-shaped faces are idealized and all alike, and her pictures are completely feminine. And yet her illustrations for Stevenson's *Child's Garden of Verses* (1905) still seem as right for those poems as Shepard's for Milne's.

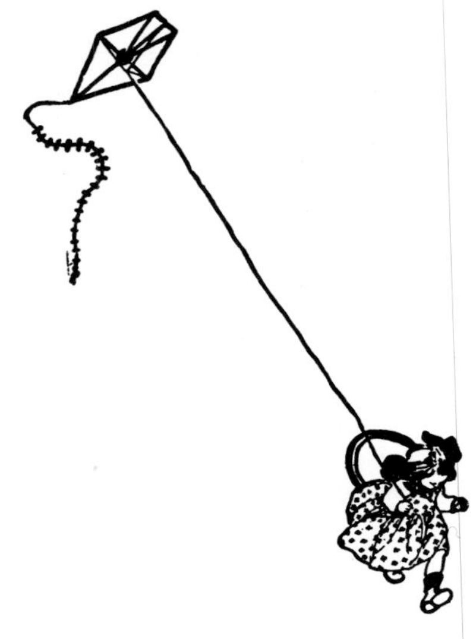

*Illustration by Jessie Willcox Smith. From A Child's Garden of Verses by Robert Louis Stevenson. Copyright, 1905, by Charles Scribner's Sons. Reproduced with permission of Charles Scribner's Sons.*

**Beatrix Potter, 1866–1943**

Beatrix Potter's *The Tale of Peter Rabbit* (1901), a milestone in children's literature, marks the beginning of the modern picture story—the book in which the pictures are so integral a part of the story that the nonreading child can soon "read" the story from the pictures. In Beatrix Potter's books, her clear watercolors show the small animals dressed up like human country folk pursuing their activities through fascinating English lanes and meadows or within cozy interiors. The pictures are as beautifully composed as the texts, and in her little books there is a perfect union of the two arts. See 8 in color section.)

### Arthur Rackham, 1867–1939

Arthur Rackham, whose distinctive work is easily recognized, illustrated well over fifty books but seemed most at home in the field of folklore. His pictures for *The Fairy Tales of Grimm* (1900) made an immediate impression, and Rackham enthusiasts and collectors began with that publication. There are no fluttering fairies to be found on his pages; instead, there are earthy old gnomes, ogres, and witches, eerie, mysterious, and sometimes menacing. In black and white or full color his pictures are alive with details that the casual observer may miss—small furry faces or elfin figures peering out from leaves or half hidden in grasses. His little girl heroines—like Snow White and Tattercoats—are fragile and lovely in a threatening world. Others, like Catskin and the heroines of the ballads, are lush, splendid creatures. We are told that Rackham drew his pictures before painting them, a technique that seems to strengthen them, because whether the colors are dark and somber or clear and light they have body and vitality. For *The Wind in the Willows* (1940), his characterizations of Mole, Ratty, Toad, and all the others are inimitable, and the details of picnics and cozy rooms enhance the warmth of that story. Here is an artist with unique gifts which he devoted almost entirely to the illustration of books for children. (See 9 in color section.)

### Ernest H. Shepard, 1879–

The deft pen of Ernest Shepard was drawing for *Punch* as early as 1907, but not until the publication of A. A. Milne's *When We Were Very Young* (1924) with the Shepard illustrations were his pen-and-ink sketches widely and affectionately known. Milne's *Winnie-the-Pooh* followed in 1926, *Now We Are Six* in 1927, and *The House at Pooh Corner* in 1928, all illustrated by Shepard. Now Ernest Shepard's pen-and-ink sketches of Christopher Robin, Pooh, and their companions seem inseparable from the poems and stories. Whether it is Christopher Robin going hoppity or meditating "half way down the stair" or Pooh trying to look like a cloud, these pictures show mood, character, and situation. Shepard's interpretative ability is shown again in his illustrations for Kenneth Grahame's *Reluctant Dragon* (1938) and *The Wind in the Willows* (1931). Even Rackham's illustrations for this latter book cannot surpass some of Shepard's sketches. Mole "Jumping off all four legs at once, in the joy of living," Toad picnicking grandly or waddling off disguised as a washerwoman, or the snug security of Badger's firelit kitchen after the cold of the Wild Wood—these pictures and many

*Illustration by E. H. Shepard. From* The House at Pooh Corner *by A. A. Milne. Copyright 1956, by A. A. Milne. Reproduced by permission of the publishers, E. P. Dutton & Co., Inc.*

others are sheer perfection. In 1957 Shepard made eight color plates for *The World of Pooh* and followed, when he was eighty years old, with eight more for the Golden Anniversary Edition of *Wind in the Willows* (1959). His color plates are beautiful but add nothing to the virtuosity of his pen-and-ink sketches. In 1962 an edition of Hans Christian Andersen's fairy tales illustrated by Shepard was published.

**N. C. Wyeth, 1882–1945**

Another pupil of Howard Pyle's, Newell Wyeth, brought to his illustrations a deep sense of drama. Whether he illustrated *Robin Hood* (1917), *Robinson Crusoe* (1920), or *Treasure Island* (1911), his pictures are powerful in composition, almost three-dimensional in effect, and rich in color. None are more appealing than his pictures for *The Yearling* (1939), but in every one of these dissimilar books his fertile imagination interprets and illumines the story. (See 6 in color section.)

**Kurt Wiese, 1887–**

Sent to China on business, taken prisoner by the Japanese, back to Germany by way of Australia and Africa—somewhere along the line, German-born Kurt Wiese determined to be an artist. This background of travel and of knowledge of many peoples has given color and authenticity to his illustrations for such books as Elizabeth Lewis' *Young Fu of the Upper Yangtze* (1932), Kipling's *Jungle Books* (1932), and that classic little story by Marjorie Flack, *The Story About Ping* (1933).

Perhaps the most outstanding characteristic of Kurt Wiese's work is his amazing versatility. He has illustrated over a hundred books, and whether it is Ping, a Chinese duck waddling up the gangplank of his particular junk, or Felix Salten's wild and beautiful *Bambi* (1929), or his own amusing stories *Rabbits' Revenge* (1940) and the Chinese *Fish in the Air* (1948), or Claire Huchet Bishop's *The Truffle Pig* (1971), and whether he is working in black and white or full color, character and situations are illustrated with humor, fidelity to the story, and fine draftsmanship. (See 12 in color section.)

To this group of artists, born in the nineteenth century but producing in the early or middle years of the twentieth century, more names could be added. Thomas Handforth (1897–1948) won the Caldecott Medal for his major contribution to children's books, *Mei Li* (1938). His black-and-white illustrations are vigorous and full of action, and they make the little Chinese heroine seem real and understandable. Another Caldecott winner is the picture book *The Big Snow* (1948) by Berta and Elmer Hader. It is typical of the Haders' work—a slight story, soft colors, and a warm feeling for birds, animals, and kindly people. Marie Hall Ets (1895–     ) did her amusing *Mister Penny* (1935) in black and white, but her sensitive and perceptive watercolors for *Play with Me* (1955), about a little girl learning to be quiet with shy woodland creatures, are quite the loveliest she has ever produced. *Nine Days to Christmas* (1959) won the Caldecott Medal but is, in spite of full, bright colors, less interesting than her earlier books. *Gilberto and the Wind* (1963) and *Talking Without Words* (1970) are among her most effective books.

*Illustration by Berta and Elmer Hader. From The Big Snow. Copyright 1948 by Berta and Elmer Hader. Reproduced with permission of The Macmillan Company. (Original in color)*

From the thirties on, there have been such numbers of picture books for the youngest children and such lavishly illustrated books for the older ones that the forties, fifties, sixties, and seventies may come to be known in the history of children's literature as the age of the illustrator. No book of this size can hope to name and appraise half the talented people who are doing fine and original illustrations for children's books. Of the sampling of these artists that follows, some were born in the nineteenth century, but most of these began their work in the thirties and have continued producing in the years following. The exception is Wanda Gág, whose epoch-making book *Millions of Cats* appeared before the thirties.

**Wanda Gág, 1893–1946**

In 1928, Wanda Gág's picture story *Millions of Cats* ushered in what came to be known as "The Golden Thirties" of picture books. It still outshines in strong story interest many of its successors. It is indeed about as close to perfection as a picture story can be. It is told with all the rhythm and cadence of the old European storytellers and is illustrated with striking black-and-white lithographs that repeat the flowing rhythm of the text. Wanda Gág was steeped in European folk tales, which she heard told as a child, and so it is not surprising that her own completely fresh and original four stories have a folk flavor. They are, in addition to *Millions of Cats*, *Funny Thing* (1929), *Snippy and Snappy* (1931), and *Nothing at All* (1941). Her illustrations for *ABC Bunny* (1933) and the four small books of *Grimms' Fairy Tales* have the same flowing lines, dramatic black-and-white areas, and homely warmth that are characteristic of everything she did.

**Conrad Buff, 1886–**

Conrad Buff, a Swiss-born Californian, is primarily a landscape painter whose pictures hang in many of the great art museums in this country and abroad and in private collections. For his wife's stories he has made striking illustrations in black and white, sepia, or full color. His pictures for Mary Buff's *Big Tree* (1946), *Dash and Dart* (1942), and its sequel *Forest Folk* (1962) show not only his keen observation and love of nature but his primary concern with problems of light. The poetry of Conrad Buff's illustrations matches the cadenced prose of Mary Buff's stories.

**Marguerite de Angeli, 1889–**

Whether Mrs. de Angeli gives us a rebellious young Quaker girl of long ago, kicking her bonnet down the stairs in *Thee Hannah!* (1940), or a too lively young pioneer schoolboy in *Skippack School* (1939), or whether she gives us some two-hundred sixty illustrations for her *Mother Goose* (1954), the people are always lovely to look at, the colors warm and soft, and the details of outdoor scenes or interiors authentic and beautifully composed. Although Mrs. de Angeli's illustrations may be somewhat reminiscent of the pretty quaintness of Jessie Willcox Smith's, they have much more vitality and action. Minority groups and historical subjects have held special interest for this artist. The Pennsylvania Dutch in *Henner's Lydia* (1936), the Amish in *Yonie Wondernose* (1944), the Polish children in *Up the Hill* (1942), and the hero of her splendid historical story *Door in the Wall* (1949 Newbery Medal) are most appealing. No matter whose story she is telling, Marguerite de Angeli's illustrations have grace, lovely colors, and eye-filling beauty. (See 13 in color section.)

**James Daugherty, 1889–**

Thomas Handforth's *Mei Li* was awarded the Caldecott Medal in 1938, but another picture story was also worthy of the award that year—

*Illustration by James Daugherty from* Andy and the Lion *by James Daugherty. Copyright 1938, copyright © renewed 1966 by James Daugherty. Reprinted by permission of The Viking Press, Inc. (Original with color)*

*Andy and the Lion* by James Daugherty. Later, this author-artist received the Newbery Medal for his *Daniel Boone* (1939). Both books are as distinguished for their illustrations as for the text. Warm earthiness and a tender appreciation of people mark his pictures. *Andy and the Lion* is entertaining, but the pictures are unforgettable. The rear view of young Andy reaching for a book on high library shelves, or Andy suddenly confronted with a lion in full roar, or Andy toppling over backward as he extracts the thorn—these have a gusto that only Daugherty can impart to awkward, beautiful, absurd human beings. On the heroic side, his illustrations for *Daniel Boone* (1939) have vigor, and those for *Poor Richard* (1941) reveal his wonderful gift for characterization. James Daugherty's portraits are as distinctive as the heroes they record.

**Maud, 1890–1971 and Miska Petersham, 1888–1960**

Maud and Miska Petersham won the Caldecott Medal for their American Mother Goose, *The Rooster Crows* (1945). They celebrated the advent of a grandchild with the charming *The Box with Red Wheels* (1949), a book with bold, bright colors, strong composition, and a slight story with a surprise ending which appeals to children four to seven. However, it is their beautiful picture story of the Nativity, *The Christ Child* (1931), that has especially endeared them to children, parents, and teachers. A year in Palestine gave them the inspiration and background for this classic, for which they wisely used the texts from St. Matthew and St. Luke. Their exquisite pictures, historically authentic in scene, costumes, and other details, have successfully caught and interpreted for young children the tender majesty of that matchless narrative.

**Feodor Rojankovsky, 1891–1970**

Russian-born Feodor Rojankovsky has unforgettable illustrations with rich, earthy colors and homely, lovable, old peasant faces for Hans Christian Andersen's *The Old Man Is Always Right* (1940). There is this same earthy quality about all of Rojankovsky's people—the sturdy, unprettified children and the stocky, dumpy grownups with their warm, woolly scarves or mittens. As for his animals there were never furrier kittens or fluffier feathered fowls. Texture, rich colors, and good draftsmanship are hallmarks of this artist. He is at his best in his illustrations for that somber story of two lone, struggling children, Mikhail Prishvin's *Treasure Trove of the Sun* (1952). Yet it was Rojankovsky's gay, amusing illustrations for *Frog Went a-Courtin'* (1955), by John Langstaff, that won him a long deserved Caldecott Medal. Some of the more recent books he illustrated are Marie Colmont's *Christmas Bear* (1966), *Over in the*

*Meadow* (1966) with John Langstaff, and Jan Wahl's *Mulberry Tree* (1970). He was one of the notable colorists among modern artists. (See 11 in color section.)

### Dorothy Lathrop, 1891–

Primarily a worker in black and white, Dorothy Lathrop has illustrated many of Walter de la Mare's books, W. L. Hudson's *Little Boy Lost* (1920), and Sara Teasdale's *Stars Tonight* (1930). These she has done with such beauty and interpretative power that story and pictures or poem and picture are a perfect whole. However, it is in the interpretation of animals that she has perhaps made her greatest contribution, and these pictures are all in pen and ink, sketched with remarkable fineness and integrity. *Animals of the Bible* (1937) was awarded the first Caldecott Medal. *Who Goes There?* (1935) is a picture book of small forest creatures who come to a winter feast spread for them in the woods. *Hide and Go Seek* (1938) is a record of those shyest of creatures, the flying squirrels. Both of these picture books are done with such exquisite details, such superb composition, that no colored illustrations could do more.

### Robert Lawson, 1891–1957

If pen-and-ink sketches can be described as witty, Robert Lawson's pictures certainly deserve the description. Who can ever forget his first glimpse of that mild young bull in *The Story of Ferdinand* (1936), peacefully inhaling the fragrance of flowers instead of snorting around the bull ring, or Mr. Popper blandly coping with his penguins in *Mr. Popper's Penguins* (1938), or the scene of the electric shock in *Ben and Me* (1939). In contrasting mood are Lawson's gravely beautiful drawings for *Pilgrim's Progress* (1939) and for *Adam of the Road* (1942), with boy and dog moving adventurously through thirteenth-century England. Robert Lawson was a master draftsman, and every detail of scenes, costumes, and characterizations is meticulously executed. But not until he wrote as well as illustrated *Ben and Me* did his admirers realize the full scope of his talents and versatility. Text and pictures are equally amusing and full of the wry wisdom that appears again in his own *Mr. Revere and I* (1953), *Rabbit Hill* (1944 Newbery Medal), and its sequel, *The Tough Winter* (1954).

### Helen Sewell, 1896–1957

No illustrator ever varied her style more radically than Helen Sewell. She belongs both to the old and to the new in art. Her pictures for *The First Bible* (1934) are grave, realistic, and monumental. The pictures for her *Book of Myths* (1941) show an entirely new technique. Sharp lines give an effect of action, so that the pictures seem to be the recorded movements of a dance. Then for the illustrations of *Grimms' Tales* (1954), she used broad brush strokes and an almost abstract representation. This she used again in her pictures for *The Three Kings of Saba* (1955) by Alf Evers. At the beginning of the story the figures of the three kings are stonelike and unbending. After the kings see the Child, the lines are curved and yielding.

### Edwin Tunis, 1897–

Each book by Edwin Tunis is a product of intensive research and a model of clean draftsmanship and scrupulous accuracy. For his first six books, the line drawings were in pen and ink; to relieve strain on his arm muscles he adopted, on medical advice, crayon-plus-wash both for his work in black and white and for the color drawings for *Chipmunks on the Doorstep* (1971). His books are handsome and vastly informative, *Indians* (1959) being used as a text in Indian schools and *Weapons* (1954) as a text for the United States Air Force. *Frontier Living* (1961) was a

Newbery Medal Honor Book; *The Young United States* (1969), *Colonial Living* (1957), and *Shaw's Fortune* (1966) are, like his other books, evidence that Edwin Tunis is a historian with a drawing board.

**Ludwig Bemelmans, 1898–1962**

Author-artist Ludwig Bemelmans produced books for adults and for children. His *Hansi* (1934) is a big book about a small boy who sent an unwilling dachshund off on a ski trip in the Alps. But it was *Madeline* (1939) that made Bemelmans famous. And with every succeeding Madeline book, Paris became more familiar to American children. Madeline falling into the Seine, Madeline grandly enjoying appendicitis, Madeline and the eleven other little girls searching for their dog, and Madeline in London—these big, handsome pictures, sketchily drawn but full of details and lovely color, have made Madeline and her creator forever beloved by children.

**Edward Ardizzone, 1900–**

Only a first-rate artist like Edward Ardizzone could bless Tim with such splendid seascapes and glimpses of port towns. Whether the books come in the handsome, outsize edition of the first *Little Tim and the Brave Sea Captain* (1936) or in the small-size edition of *Tim All Alone* (1957), the pictures are watercolors, beautifully reproduced, full of the relentless power of the sea and the jaunty courage of seafaring folk. Master of the economical line, Ardizzone has a droll quality that makes his figures memorable; his illustrations for Cecil Lewis' *The Otterbury Incident* (1969) and for Eleanor Estes' *Miranda the Great* (1967) are as beguiling as those for his own *Sarah and Simon and No Red Paint* (1966). Mr. Ardizzone's superb illustrations for *Don Quixote* (1959) have humor and pathos and, like those for *Little Tim*, show man forever confronted with something vast and beyond him, but struggling courageously nevertheless. (See 24 in color section.)

**Roger Duvoisin, 1904–**

Roger Duvoisin uses a variety of techniques and has an unfailing sense of strong composition and design. For Alvin Tresselt's books on weather and seasons, such as *White Snow, Bright Snow* (1947 Caldecott Medal), his colors are flat washes and the pictures simplified to a poster-like effect. For Louise Fatio's series of stories—*The Happy Lion* (1954), *The Happy Lion's Vacation* (1967), *The Happy Lion's Treasure* (1970)—his pictures are in soft colors with lively details. Gian-Carlo Menotti's *Amahl and the Night Visitors* (1952) is illustrated in dark, rich colors with a somber, dramatic quality that is at one with this story from the familiar opera. Duvoisin's own books about the hippopotamus Veronica and the series of tales about the goose Petunia have rare humor. Here is a major artist giving his best to children's books. (See 14 in color section.)

**Theodor Seuss Geisel (Dr. Seuss), 1904–**

What shall we say of "Dr. Seuss" as an artist? He confesses that he cannot draw anatomy as it actually is, but in his pictures the fractured legs and gangling arms have made his nizzards and wizards, his Bartholomew, Horton, Thidwick the Moose, the Cat in the Hat, and all the rest of his mad characters so beloved by children that Dr. Seuss is synonymous with laughter. This is cartoon art, but when it accompanies rhymed stories of great originality, whose words run and leap with the rhythmic lines of the pictures, the combination is irresistible. There is also a strange, wild grace about some of the pictures, with their great heights and depths, bright clear blues and reds, decorative touches to costumes or scenes. These make the grotesque arresting and even attractive.

*Illustration by Roger Duvoisin. From* The Happy Lion *by Louise Fatio. Copyright, 1954, by Louise Fatio Duvoisin and Roger Duvoisin. Reprinted by permission of Whittlesey House (McGraw-Hill). (Original in color)*

**Ingri, 1905– and Edgar Parin d'Aulaire, 1898–**

Ingri and Edgar Parin d'Aulaire are the artists who brought the picture biography into its own. It is interesting that Norwegian-born Ingri and Swiss-born and French-educated Edgar should have turned to the heroes of their adopted land for their subjects. Edgar d'Aulaire in his Caldecott Medal acceptance speech for their *Abraham Lincoln* (1939) explained this. "We counted as our biggest asset just the fact that our conceptions of our American themes had never been shaped into school clichés." After the d'Aulaires make their first sketches, they work directly on the lithograph stone, which gives their pictures unusual strength and depth. These qualities were not so effective in their *George Washington* (1936), in which the pictures have always seemed wooden. But by the time they wrote the text and made the pictures for *Abraham Lincoln*, they were using this difficult medium superbly. The colors in this book are deep and rich, and the pictures are full of authentic factual details. The lines and composition have a sort of primitive simplicity that suggests folk art. *Benjamin Franklin* (1950) is particularly rich in storytelling details, *Leif the Lucky* (1951) and *Columbus* (1955) are the most colorful, *Pocahontas* (1946) and *Buffalo Bill* (1952), the most picturesque. Their large, handsome *The Book of Greek Myths* (1962) and *Norse Gods and Giants* (1967) are other examples of their versatility. (See 23 in color section.)

**Lynd Ward, 1905–**

*The Biggest Bear* (1952) won the Caldecott Medal for Lynd Ward, who was already a well-known illustrator, and that book seems to have overshadowed the lovely pictures he made for Hildegarde Swift's *The Little Red Lighthouse and the Great Gray Bridge* (1942). In spite of its long, awkward title, this is a significant picture story that is made doubly moving by Mr. Ward's illustrations. In both books—*The Biggest Bear*, in monochrome, and *The Little Red Lighthouse*, in dark blues and grays with touches of red—it is the artist's sure sense of dramatic contrast that tells the stories and grips and holds children's attention. Ward has illustrated many books written by his wife, May McNeer, among them *America's Mark Twain* (1962) and *Stranger in the Pines* (1971); he also illustrated Esther Forbes' Newbery Medal book *Johnny Tremain* (1943).

**Leo Politi, 1905–**

Leo Politi is an artist whose pictures are deceptively simple, almost primitive. Both his figures and his landscapes are stylized, but the total composition makes a beautiful design. His children are colorful and appealing whether it is *Little Leo* (1951), capering gaily with his friends through Italian streets, the lovely procession of children and pets in *Juanita* (1948), the delightful little Chinese *Moy Moy* (1960), or the appealing dog *Emmet* (1971). (See 19 in color section.)

**Adrienne Adams, 1906–**

*Houses from the Sea* (1959) by Alice Goudey includes some of the loveliest watercolor illustrations Adrienne Adams has made. Since then, her pictures for the Grimms' *Shoemaker and the Elves* (1960) and Andersen's *Thumbelina* (1961) have been exceedingly popular. Her colors are warm and delicate, her pictures full of fascinating details. A most happy collaboration is evident in her delightful pictures for Aileen Fisher's *Going Barefoot* (1960) and *Where Does Everyone Go?* (1961), seasonal poems to which the pictures add lively charm. One of her most engaging conceptions has been the serried ranks of marching rabbits in her husband Lonzo Anderson's story *Two Hundred Rabbits* (1965). In Carl Withers' *Painting the Moon* (1970), the Grimm brothers' *Jorinda and Joringel* (1968), and Alice Goudey's *The Day We Saw the Sun Come Up* (1961), the illustrations are particularly striking for their meticulous detail and dramatic use of color. (See 20 in color section.)

**Virginia Burton, 1909–1968**

*Mike Mulligan and His Steam Shovel* (1939) and *The Little House* (1943 Caldecott Medal) are landmarks in the field of picture stories. Both have absorbing plots, perfect synchronization of text and illustrations, and both also have a social significance over and above their story appeal. Virginia Burton uses clear, bright colors and frequently a swirling line pattern that suggests the ballet, from which she turned to illustrating. Her last two contributions are *Life Story* (1962) and *The Emperor's New Clothes* (1962). Every one of her books has been a delight to children, but artistically *Song of Robin Hood* (1947) is her *tour de force*. For these old ballads she produced hundreds of pictures of great intricacy and detail, and the whole composition makes striking patterns in black and white. This book is a collector's item. (See 16 in color section.)

**Nicolas Mordvinoff, 1911–**

The team of "Will and Nicolas" made an immediate impression with their first book, *The Two Reds* (1950). It has a sequel, *Russet and the Two Reds* (1962), and in between they have produced a number of picture sto-

*Illustration by Nicolas Mordvinoff. From* Russet and the Two Reds *by Will and Nicolas. Copyright 1962 by William Lipkind and Nicholas Mordvinoff. Reproduced by permission of Harcourt Brace Jovanovich, Inc. (Original in color)*

ries, including *Finders Keepers* (1951), which won the Caldecott Medal. William Lipkind's stories are fresh, humorous, and masculine. Nicolas Mordvinoff's pictures embody the same qualities. They are a protest against the prettified art that has accompanied too many books for children, especially the mass-produced variety. His animals and children are homely creatures except for *Chaga* (1955), which has a poetic quality not found in his other illustrations. Strong lines, bold composition, color dramatically employed, and plenty of action—these are characteristic of his work.

**Evaline Ness, 1911–**

Evaline Ness uses a variety of techniques, her skills ranging from hand-worked tapestry to woodcuts printed on tissue-thin paper, with separate blocks used for each color. Her constant experimentation brings freshness to her handsomely composed illustrations. She used collage with line-and-wash for *Sam, Bangs & Moonshine,* for which she received the Caldecott Medal in 1967. For the three preceding years, the books she illustrated were Honor Books—in 1964 with illustrations for Sorche Nic Leodhas' *All in the Morning Early*; in 1965 for Rebecca Caudill's *A Pocketful of Cricket*; and in 1966 for her version of *Tom Tit Tot. Josefina February* (1963) is the first book of her own that she illustrated. Other books include *The Girl and the Goatherd* (1970); *Do You Have the Time, Lydia?* (1971); *Some of the Days of Everett*

*From the book* The Girl and the Goatherd. *Text and illustrations by Evaline Ness. Copyright © 1970 by Evaline Ness. Published by E. P. Dutton & Co., Inc., and used with their permission. (Original in color)*

*Anderson* (1970), by Lucille Clifton; *The Truthful Harp* (1967), by Lloyd Alexander; and *Joey and the Birthday Present* (1971), by Maxine Kumin and Anne Sexton.

**Garth Williams, 1912–**

Garth Williams has won a formidable number of awards and prizes, including the Prix de Rome for sculpture, a field of art in which he still works. His first venture into children's book illustration was for E. B. White's *Stuart Little* (1945). He followed this with Mr. White's famous *Charlotte's Web* (1952)—a book that might well have received both the Newbery and the Caldecott Medals. For a new edition of Laura Ingalls Wilder's *Little House* books (1953), Garth Williams spent ten years making the pictures, and as a result the pictures and stories are one. Equally successful are his illustrations for Natalie Carlson's books about the French Orphelines and Jennie Lindquist's *Little Silver House* (1959), Russell Hoban's *Bedtime for Frances* (1960), Margery Sharp's *Miss Bianca* (1962), and George Selden's *Tucker's Countryside* (1970). The artist works both in black and white and full color, and his pictures are always characterized by authenticity of details. The colors are fresh and soft, the composition vigorous. But whether the story he illustrates is realistic or pure fantasy, historical fiction or modern city life, his superb gift for characterization stands out. No pig could look more foolishly smug than Wilbur, no orphan could flee more desperately from the encircling bicyclists than Josine, no pioneers could look more cozy than the Little House dwellers, wherever they might be. (See 22 in color section.)

**Robert McCloskey, 1914–**

The first artist to be twice winner of the Caldecott Medal is Robert McCloskey, whose big, handsome picture stories are almost as popular with adults as with children. *Lentil* (1940) is a juvenile *Main Street*, complete with Soldiers' Monument, a welcoming band, and a harmonica-playing hero. *Make Way for Ducklings* (1941 Caldecott Medal) vies with *Blueberries for Sal* (1948) in popularity. He has also illustrated Keith Robertson's *Henry Reed* stories with great humor. Only in *Time of Wonder* (1958 Caldecott Medal) and *Burt Dow, Deep Water Man* (1963) has this artist used color, but in his powerful black and whites you do not miss the color, so alive they are with realistic details and storytelling power. (See 15 in color section.)

**William Pène du Bois, 1916–**

Few indeed are the children's book illustrators who can claim both a place in the New York Museum of Modern Art and a Newbery Medal. William Pène du Bois was awarded the Newbery Medal in 1948 for his *Twenty-One Balloons*, and he has written many distinguished books before and after that year, all with an illogical logic, all illustrated with paintings that are notable for their clean lines and clear colors, as evident, for example, in *Otto and the Magic Potatoes* (1970) and *Call Me Bandicoot* (1970). His boyhood love for the circus is evident in several of his books: *The Great Geppy* (1940) and *The Alligator Case* (1965). Although he has illustrated the books of other writers—George Macdonald's *The Light Princess* (1962), Rebecca Caudill's *A Certain Small Shepherd* (1965), Roald Dahl's *The Magic Finger* (1966)—the books for which he is both author and illustrator have a felicitous harmony between text and pictures seldom achieved in children's books.

**Ezra Jack Keats, 1916–**

In a tough section of Brooklyn, eight-year-old Ezra Jack Keats discovered the beneficial side effects of painting. Some neighborhood boys

1.

2.

1. *From* The History of the House That Jack Built. *Reproduced from the D'Alte Welch Collection, Cleveland.*

2. *From the facsimile of Mr. Lessing J. Rosenwald's copy of William Blake's* Songs of Innocence and of Experience, *published by the Trianon Press, London, for the William Blake Trust, 1955.*

3.

4.

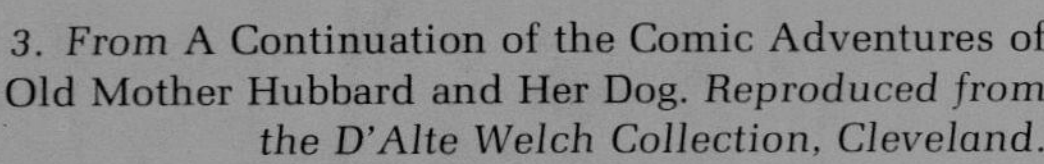

3. *From* A Continuation of the Comic Adventures of Old Mother Hubbard and Her Dog. *Reproduced from the D'Alte Welch Collection, Cleveland.*

4. *Illustration by Leonard Leslie Brooke. From* Ring o' Roses. *Reproduced with permission of Frederick Warne & Co., Inc.*

5. *From Kate Greenaway's* Under the Window. *Reproduced with permission of Frederick Warne & Co., Inc.*

YES, that's the girl that struts about,
She's very proud,—so very proud!
Her *bow-wow*'s quite as proud as she:
They both are very wrong to be
So proud—so very proud.

See, Jane and Willy laugh at her,
They say she's very proud!
Says Jane, "My stars!—they're very silly;"
"Indeed they are," cries little Willy,
"To walk so stiff and proud."

5.

6.

7.

8.

*6. Illustration by Newell Wyeth. From* Treasure Island *by Robert Louis Stevenson. Copyright 1911 by Charles Scribner's Sons, Copyright 1939 by N. C. Wyeth. Reproduced with permission of Charles Scribner's Sons.*

*7. From Walter Crane's* Baby's Bouquet. *Reproduced with permission of Frederick Warne & Co., Inc.*

*8. From Beatrix Potter's* The Tale of Peter Rabbit. *Reproduced with permission of Frederick Warne & Co., Inc.*

9.

10.

9. *Illustration by Arthur Rackham. From* English Fairy Tales. *Copyright 1918 by Macmillan & Co., London. Reproduced with permission of Macmillan & Co., London.*

10. *From Randolph Caldecott's* Hey Diddle *and* Baby Bunting. *Reproduced from the D'Alte Welch Collection, Cleveland.*

11. *Illustration by Feodor Rojankovsky. From* Frog Went A-Courtin'. *Copyright 1955 by John M. Langstaff and Feodor Rojankovsky. Reproduced by permission of Harcourt Brace Jovanovich, Inc.*

11.

12.

12. *From* Fish in the Air *by Kurt Wiese. Copyright ©
1948 by Kurt Wiese. Reprinted by permission of The
Viking Press, Inc.*

13. *From* Yonie Wondernose *by Marguerite de Angeli.
Copyright 1944 by Marguerite de Angeli. Reproduced
with permission of Doubleday and Company.*

14. *Illustration by Roger Duvoisin. From* Amahl and
the Night Visitors *by Gian-Carlo Menotti, adapted by
Frances Frost. Copyright 1952 by G. Sherimer.
Reproduced with permission of Whittlesey House,
McGraw-Hill.*

15. *From* Time of Wonder *by Robert McCloskey.
Copyright © 1957 by Robert McCloskey. Reprinted by
permission of The Viking Press, Inc.*

13.

14.

15.

He had taken
such good care of her
that she could still dig
as much in a day
as a hundred men
could dig in a week;
at least he thought she could
but he wasn't quite sure.
Everywhere they went
the new gas shovels
and the new electric shovels
and the new Diesel motor shovels
had all the jobs. No one wanted
Mike Mulligan and Mary Anne any more.
Then one day Mike read in a newspaper that the town
of Popperville was going to build a new town hall.
'We are going to dig the cellar of that town hall,'
said Mike to Mary Anne, and off they started.

16.

17.

18.

The tiger felt offended and humiliated. He forgot all the good he had received from the old man.

"No one shall tell me that I was once a mouse. I will kill him!"

19.

16. *From* Mike Mulligan and His Steam Shovel, *by Virginia Lee Burton. Houghton Mifflin. Copyright 1939 by Virginia Lee Demetrios.*

17. *From* Umbrella *by Taro Yashima. Copyright © 1958 by Taro Yashima. Reprinted by permission of The* Viking Press, Inc.

18. *From* Once a Mouse *by Marcia Brown. Copyright 1961 by Marcia Brown. Reproduced with permission of Charles Scribner's Sons.*

19. *From* Leo Politi's Moy Moy. *Copyright 1960 by Leo Politi. Reproduced with permission of Charles Scribner's Sons.*

*20. Illustration by Adrienne Adams. From* Thumbelina *by Hans Christian Andersen. Copyright 1961 by Adrienne Adams. Reproduced with permission of Charles Scribner's Sons.*

*21. Illustration by Harold Jones. From* Lavender's Blue, *Mother Goose rhymes compiled by Kathleen Lines. Copyright 1954. Reproduced with permission of Franklin Watts, Inc., and Oxford University Press, London.*

*22. Illustration by Garth Williams. From jacket for* A Brother for the Orphelines *by Natalie Savage Carlson. Copyright © 1959 by Garth Williams. Reproduced with permission of Harper & Row, Publishers, Inc.*

*23. From* Leif the Lucky *by Ingri and Edgar Parin d'Aulaire. Copyright 1951 by Doubleday, Doran & Company, Inc. Reproduced with permission of Doubleday and Co.*

21.

20.

down into the water, in the middle of which floated a large tulip petal where Thumbelina could sit and row herself from one side of the plate to the other, using a couple of white horsehairs as oars. It was a most charming sight. She could sing, too, in the sweetest little voice you ever heard.

22.

A BROTHER FOR THE ORPHELINES

by Natalie Savage Carlson
Pictures by Garth Williams

24.

25.

26.

*24. From* Little Tim and the Brave Sea Captain *by Edward Ardizzone. Reprinted by the permission of Henry Z. Walck, Inc.*

*25. Illustration by Maurice Sendak. From* Mr. Rabbit and the Lovely Present *by Charlotte Zolotow. Copyright 1962 by Maurice Sendak. Reproduced with permission of Harper & Row, Publishers, Inc.*

*26. Illustration by Charles Keeping for* Charley, Charlotte and the Golden Canary. *Copyright 1967. Reproduced by permission of Franklin Watts, Inc., and Oxford University Press, London.*

*27. From* The Snowy Day *by Ezra Jack Keats. Copyright © 1962 by Ezra Jack Keats. Reprinted by permission of The Viking Press, Inc., and The Bodley Head, Ltd. London.*

27.

28.

28. *Illustration by Nancy Ekholm Burkert from* The Nightingale, *translated by Eva Le Gallienne. Copyright © 1965. Reproduced by permission of Harper & Row, Publishers, Inc.*

29. *From* Dionysos and the Pirates, *translated by Penelope Proddow, illustrated by Barbara Cooney. Copyright © 1970 by Doubleday & Company, Inc. Reproduced by permission of the publisher.*

30. *Reprinted with the permission of Farrar, Straus & Giroux, Inc. from* The Fool of the World and the Flying Ship, *retold by Arthur Ransome, pictures by Uri Shulevitz. Pictures copyright © 1968 by Uri Shulevitz.*

31. *Illustration by Brian Wildsmith for* Puzzles. *Copyright © 1971. Reproduced by permission of Franklin Watts, Inc., and Oxford University Press, London.*

29.

30.

31.

32.

33.

And the shepherds
returned, glorifying
and praising God
for all the things
that they had
heard and seen,
as it was told
unto them.

32. *Illustration by Nonny Hogrogian for* One Fine Day, *copyright 1971. Reproduced by permission of The Macmillan Company.*

33. *From* And It Came to Pass, *arranged by Jean Slaughter. Illustration by Leonard Weisgard. Illustration © Leonard Weisgard, 1971.*

*Illustration by William Pène du Bois. From* Otto and the Magic Potatoes *by William Pène du Bois. Copyright © 1970 by William Pène du Bois. Reprinted by permission of The Viking Press, Inc. (Original in color)*

snatched a painting from him, but when they learned he was the artist, they treated him with respect. The first book he wrote and illustrated, *The Snowy Day* (1963), earned him the Caldecott Medal and later became a prize-winning film at the Venice Film Festival. Keats works as a choreographer does, hanging his illustrations in rows on the walls "to pace the text." Using oils and collage, he achieves a sunny simplicity. His books include *Whistle for Willie* (1963), *Peter's Chair* (1967), *Goggles!* (a 1970 Caldecott Honor Book), *Hi, Cat!* (1970), *Apt. 3* (1971). He also illustrated Lloyd Alexander's *The King's Fountain* (1971). (See 27 in color section.)

**Anthony Ravielli, 1916–**

A painter of murals and a designer of visual training aids during World War II, Anthony Ravielli moved into medical illustration, and after developing techniques in oil, tempera, and watercolor, arrived at the scratchboard technique which he used for the first of his five books in the area of science, *Wonders of the Human Body* (1954). For process reproduction he prefers to render full-color illustrations, but for *Wonders of the Human Body* he used colored inks on scratchboard. *An Adventure in Geometry* (1957) and *The World is Round* (1963) are good examples of his technique—he designs as well as illustrates his own books. He also illustrated the 1959 edition of Charles Darwin's *The Voyage of the Beagle*, Keith Gordon Irwin's *The Romance of Chemistry* (1959), Peter K. Weyl's *Men, Ants, and Elephants* (1959), and S. Carl Hirsch's *This is Automation* (1964), as well as his own *From Fins to Hands* (1968).

**Leonard Weisgard, 1916–**

Leonard Weisgard is a major illustrator whose pictures have sold many a second-rate text. He is a great colorist and his paintings are full of exquisite details of small flowers or frolicking animals or decorative birds. His illustrations for Margaret Wise Brown's *Little Island* (1946), painted on pressed wood in tempera and egg white, won him the Caldecott Medal. The seascapes are in deep blues and greens, with the island sometimes lost in mist. The landscapes are in lush yellow greens and flashing blues. Some of the other books illustrated by this prolific artist are Sesyle Joslin's charming stories about Baby

Elephant; Phyllis McGinley's *A Wreath of Christmas Legends* (1967); Charlotte Zolotow's *Wake Up and Goodnight* (1971); *And It Came to Pass* (1971), Bible verses and carols arranged by Jean Slaughter; and his own *The Beginnings of Cities* (1968). (See 33 in color section.)

**Barbara Cooney, 1917–**

Children were delighted by Barbara Cooney's black-and-white pictures for those two fine animal stories—Rutherford Montgomery's *Kildee House* (1949) and Barbara Reynolds' *Pepper* (1952). But in color she did not come into her own until she made the pictures for Lee Kingman's *Peter's Long Walk* (1953). They are in muted colors and interpret tenderly the child's long journey, the lovely New England countryside and village, the sad homecoming which turns out cheerfully. After this beautiful picture story it was no surprise to have her win the Caldecott Medal for her scratchboard illustrations for *Chanticleer and the Fox* (1958), adapted from Chaucer's "The Nun's Priest's Tale" in *The Canterbury Tales*. Every detail is historically accurate, but what the children love are those pages in bright clear reds, greens, and blues, alive with action, and old Chanticleer and Reynard equally gorgeous. This is one of the gayest, most exuberant picture stories children have had. Her *Little Juggler* (1961) is done with the same painstaking accuracy and gorgeous colors, but the story is a gentler one with none of the humor and gaiety of *Chanticleer*. She prefers working in full color, using acrylic paints, but has also used pen and ink for *Cock Robin* (1965), wash for the delicate pictures in Sarah Orne Jewett's *A White Heron* (1963), and charcoal for her pictures in the Grimms' *Snow White and Rose Red* (1966). Her illustrations for Natalia Belting's *Christmas Folk* (1969) and for *Dionysus and the Pirates* (1970) exemplify both her artistic diversity and the research that results in authentic detail. (See 29 in color section.)

**Marcia Brown, 1918–**

No generalizations about the work of Marcia Brown are possible, for she varies her style to suit the content of the story she is illustrating. Her illustrations for *Stone Soup* (1947) are colorful, gay, and earthy, like the rogues who taught the villagers a more generous way of life. *Puss in Boots* (1952) is a gorgeous, flamboyant feline, well adapted to the court life into which he catapults his master. Both *The Steadfast Tin Soldier* (1953) and *Cinderella* (1955 Caldecott Medal) are in misty pinks and blues grayed down to the gentle mood of the tales. The sturdy woodcuts in brown and black for *Dick Whittington and His Cat* (1950) are as substantial as the hero. And the book that won her second Caldecott Medal, *Once a Mouse* (1961), is completely different from all the others. This fable of pride laid low is in jungle colors, and the stylized woodcut pictures have subtle details of expression or posture that tell the story and repay study. Marcia Brown has written and illustrated some charming stories of her

VIEWPOINTS

Many illustrators have tried to write—with varying success—and occasionally authors have tried to draw—with less. One feels that the desire to do a book may be commendable; but without something to say to children and the means to say it, or even the desire to develop the means, one wonders at the arrogance that expects a child to be interested in halfbaked creations, texts or pictures. There is still among laymen a lack of comprehension of the discipline needed to pare a text to a basic line that looks simple. A picture book is as concise as poetry. Text and pictures combine to form an essence that expands in the child's mind.—Marcia Brown, "One Wonders . . .," in *Illustrators of Children's Books: 1957–1966*, compiled by Lee Kingman, Joanna Foster, and Ruth Giles Lontoft, The Horn Book, Inc., Boston, 1968, p. 24.

own, but her major contribution to date is her brilliant interpretations of single folk tales. She is also one of the most articulate and lucid writers on the techniques and media of the illustrator's art. (See 18 in color section.)

**Antonio Frasconi, 1919–**

Antonio Frasconi is one of the great woodcut artists of our time. His technique has softened the basic, crudely broad areas of the usual woodcut by high artistry in the use of color. He avoids the uncompromising pressure printing of the entire block by printing his woodcuts by hand, and to achieve variations of tone, rubbing a spoon over a paper laid on an inked block. Strong and vivid, his work melds the "dynamics of design and typography" with an imaginative power that pulls the young reader back to his illustrations again and again. A Uruguayan who came to the United States on a scholarship, Frasconi published his first children's book in 1955, the multilingual *See and Say*. Other Frasconi books are *The House That Jack Built*

*Illustration by Antonio Frasconi from* The House That Jack Built, *copyright © 1958 by Antonio Frasconi. Reproduced by permission of Harcourt Brace Jovanovich, Inc. (Original in color)*

(1958), *The Snow and the Sun* (1961), *See Again, Say Again* (1964) in four languages, and *Overhead the Sun* (1969), based on lines by Walt Whitman.

*Illustration © 1965 by Erik Blegvad. From* Mr. Jensen & Cat *by Lenore Blegvad. Reproduced by permission of Harcourt Brace Jovanovich, Inc. (Original in color)*

**Erik Blegvad, 1923–**

The appeal of Erik Blegvad's illustrations is in the precise detail of his tidy, humorous drawings, the delicate tints of color, and the fidelity to the author's text. For Monica Stirling's *The Cat from Nowhere* (1969), the black-and-white drawings were done in pen-and-India ink. When he works in full color, he uses a transparent watercolor wash, or a mixture of watercolor and poster colors. His tender feelings for animals are apparent in Lenore Blegvad's *The Great Hamster Hunt*

(1969) and in *Mr. Jensen and Cat* (1965), which has enchanting illustrations of Copenhagen.

**Charles Keeping, 1924–**

Born in Lambeth, English Charles Keeping won the 1967 Kate Greenaway Medal for *Charley, Charlotte and the Golden Canary.* Keeping is noted for his bold approach, his use of vivid colors, and his highly individual style. For *Joseph's Yard* (1969) he used several layers of colored acetate, with drawings in colored ink, which were then shot together as one drawing. His remarkable range shows in the bold black-and-white India ink drawings for Rosemary Sutcliff's *Heroes and History* (1966) and the unexpected perspectives in her *Knight's Fee* (1960). Only in their swirling lines is there a resemblance between his black-and-white illustrations and the vibrant color illustrations he uses in his own picture books. (See 26 in color section.)

**Nicolas Sidjakov, 1924–**

Three books illustrated by Nicolas Sidjakov are notable because the pictures are stylized and in the modern idiom. The illustrations for *The Friendly Beasts* (1957), *The Emperor and the Drummer Boy* (1962), and *Baboushka and the Three Kings* (1960 Caldecott Medal) have figures that are blocklike and stylized. There is little realism in these pictures, but they reveal character and mood. Baboushka is a flinty-looking old woman, the soldiers in the Emperor's story show a robotlike obedience in their mass marching, and the Friendly Beasts are gentle and sympathetic. Here is an artist who makes children see the world with new eyes and in new patterns.

**Beni Montresor, 1926–**

An Italian-born designer for stage and film, Beni Montresor came to the United States in 1960. As a child, he was deeply impressed by the pageantry of the church, and in his approach to illustration he sees the blank page as something to be filled with scenes, costumes, and movement. Anticipating the imaginative responses of children and without losing a focal point, he puts as many elements as he can into his pictures so that there will be many visual experiences to enjoy. In 1965 he was awarded the Caldecott Medal for his illustrations for Beatrice Schenk de Regniers' *May I Bring a Friend?* His own books include *House of Flowers, House of Stars* (1962), *The Witches of Venice* (1963), and *Cinderella* (1965). He has also illustrated Eve Merriam's *Mommies at Work* (1961), Mary Stolz' *Belling the Tiger* (1961), and Beatrice Schenk de Regniers' *Willy O'Dwyer Jumped in the Fire* (1968).

*Illustration by Beni Montresor from* Belling the Tiger *by Mary Stolz. Copyright © 1961. Reproduced by permission of Harper & Row, Publishers, Inc.*

### Maurice Sendak, 1928–

Some of Maurice Sendak's first illustrations were for humorous books like Ruth Krauss' *A Hole Is to Dig* (1952), Marcel Aymé's fantasy *The Wonderful Farm* (1951), and Beatrice de Regniers' *What Can You Do with a Shoe?* (1955). They show the tender appeal of children even when they are most absurd—roundfaced children, grinning fiendishly or preternaturally solemn, dressed up in adult clothes or kicking up their heels and cavorting like young colts. This artist with his flair for comic exaggeration is tremendously popular, but in his illustrations for Meindert DeJong's books, *Wheel on the School* (1954), for example, and for his own book *Kenny's Window* (1956), he shows a sensitive perception of the lonely, imaginative, struggling side of childhood, too. One book in full color is a superb example of his versatility. His pictures for Janice Udry's *Moon Jumpers* (1959) are in the green-blues of a moonlit summer's night. The moon-mad children are running and leaping in ecstasy or dropping with exhaustion or going quietly home. These pictures are all beauty and the very poetry of childhood. The same could be said of his glorious color pictures for Charlotte Zolotow's *Mr. Rabbit and the Lovely Present* (1962). Mr. Sendak's four original stories for his tiny *Nutshell Library* (1962) are exceedingly funny both in texts and illustrations.

Sendak moved into further prominence with *Where the Wild Things Are* (1963), which won the Caldecott Medal. Children rejoice over the ferocious, adoring creatures and over the small hero who, sated with adulation, goes home to reality to find his dinner waiting, still hot. In *Higglety Pigglety Pop!* (1967) the reader shares, in the adventures of the dog Jenny, the pathos of a loved one leaving home even though for a successful but slightly raucous career. The delicacy of the wash drawings for Else Minarik's *Little Bear* (1957), the tenderness of the pictures in Randall Jarrell's *Animal Family* (1965), and the boldness of those in Sendak's own *In the Night Kitchen* (1970) show how completely Maurice Sendak adapts his illustrations to the story and make clear why he received the Hans Christian Andersen Medal in 1970, the first time an American artist was so honored. (See 25 in color section.)

*Illustration and accompanying text from* In the Night Kitchen *by Maurice Sendak. Copyright © 1970. Reproduced by permission of Harper & Row, Publishers, Inc. (Original in color)*

### Irene Haas, 1929–

Irene Haas' pictures for Paul Kapp's *A Cat Came Fiddling* (1956) show not merely children but some indescribably funny and well-characterized animals and adults. For Beatrice de Regniers' subtle little book about a child's need for privacy, *A Little House of Your Own* (1954), she has suggested the mood of quiet withdrawal in every picture. There are also sly touches of humor—for instance, in the picture of the child and cat covered up in bed, with only the cat's tail sticking out. Her illustrations for Emma Smith's *Emily's Voyage* (1966) have the same humor, but her soft, romantic pictures for Elizabeth Enright's *Tatsinda* (1963) have an appropriate fairy-tale quality.

**Blair Lent, 1930–**

Most of Blair Lent's illustrations have been done with cardboard cuts and overlays. The 1965 Caldecott Medal Honor Book recognition was given to his illustrations for Margaret Hodges' *The Wave*, which also received a silver medal at the Sao Paulo Biennal in Brazil, and was included in the annual Fifty Books Show and the American Institute of Graphic Arts Children's Book Show. His inventive full-color paintings, which heightened the dramatic quality of William Sleator's Tlingit Indian Legend, *The Angry Moon* (1970), earned him another Caldecott Honor Book recognition. *John Tabor's Ride* (1966) and *Pistachio* (1964) are examples of Mr. Lent's work as author-illustrator. He has also illustrated Olga Economakis' *Oasis of the Stars* (1965), Franklyn M. Branley's *The Christmas Sky* (1966), Ernest Small's *Baba Yaga* (1966), and Arlene Mosel's *Tikki Tikki Tembo* (1968).

**Brian Wildsmith, 1930–**

Although he says he has "abstract tendencies," Brian Wildsmith's illustrations are strongly brilliant and representational. He sees the pictorial form as being at one with the text, yet each a thing unto itself—complementary—and each able to exist without the other. All of his work is in full color; a Wildsmith trademark is the use of bright contrasting colors in a harlequin pattern. In his technique, gouache is used, moving from impasto down to almost translucent watercolor effects. The subjects he treats lend themselves to strong impact: *Brian Wildsmith's Fishes* (1968), *Brian Wildsmith's Circus* (1970), *Brian Wildsmith's Puzzles* (1971), and *Brian Wildsmith's ABC*, which won the Kate Greenaway Award for 1962 and was published in the United States in 1963. One of the major British illustrators, Wildsmith has, in addition to his own books, created illustrations for several Jean de la Fontaine fables, for *The Oxford Book of Poetry for Children* (1964), edited by Edward Blishen, and for Kevin Crossley-Holland's *Havelock the Dane* (1965). (See 31 in color section.)

**Nonny Hogrogian, 1932–**

For the first children's books she illustrated, Nicolete Meredith's *King of the Kerry Fair* (1960), Nonny Hogrogian used woodblocks, as she did for Robert Burns' *Hand in Hand We'll Go* (1965). The illustrations for the 1966 Caldecott Medal book, *Always Room for One More* by Sorche Nic Leodhas, were done in pen and ink, with gray wash and pastels to achieve the quality of mist and heather. Her approach to illustration is that the manuscript comes first, and the pictures grow from it, the mood of the text dictating the technique as much as possible. She used pastels to illustrate the story of the gentle, lovely *Vasilisa the Beautiful* (1970), translated by Thomas Whitney; etchings for an edition of Grimms' tales; and oil paintings for her own *One Fine Day* (1971), in which the illustrations have the full and vigorous quality of the story of a sharp-nosed fox who tries to retrieve his tail. Some of the other books she has illustrated are Barbara Schiller's *The Kitchen Knight* (1965); Virginia Hamilton's *The Time-Ago Tales of Jahdu* (1971); Isaac Bashevis Singer's *The Fearsome Inn* (1967); Yulya's gentle Russian lullaby *Bears Are Sleeping* (1967); and *The Thirteen Days of Yule* (1968), edited by A. Murray. (See 32 in color section.)

### Nancy Ekholm Burkert, 1933–

As might be expected from an artist who sees "absolute perfection" in the compositions of Arthur Rackham, Nancy Burkert's work is full of exquisite detail. In her imaginative treatment of Edward Lear's *The Scroobious Pip* (1968), she is thoroughly at home with the infinite variety of nature, and both the line drawings and the full-color paintings have a firm delicacy. For Natalie Carlson's *Jean-Claude's Island* (1963) she used conté pencil and crayon, and for Eva Le Gallienne's translation of Hans Christian Andersen's *The Nightingale*, she used brush and colored ink to achieve the wonderfully rich color; the authentic detail of her illustrations for this book she provided through her study of ancient Chinese scrolls. Among the other books she has illustrated are John Updike's *A Child's Calendar* (1965), Roald Dahl's *James and the Giant Peach* (1961), and Andersen's *The Fir Tree* (1970), to which Miss Burkert gave pictures that match the grave sweetness of the story. (See 28 in color section.)

### Raymond Briggs, 1934–

Raymond Briggs is best known for his illustrations of *The Mother Goose Treasury*, which won him the Kate Greenaway Medal in 1967. To complete that collection of 400 rhymes, which he selected and illustrated, he worked for two years. Sketching with pencil and working over with pen and ink for the black-and-white pictures and with gouache for those in color, he captured the exuberance and the humor of the rhymes. A prolific worker, Briggs illustrated seven of the Coward-McCann "Champion" series in 1968 and 1969, wrote and illustrated *Jim and the Beanstalk* in 1970, and in the same year illustrated *The Elephant and the Bad Baby* by Elfrida Vipont, *The Christmas Book* compiled by James Reeves, and *The Book of Magical*

*Reprinted by permission of Coward-McCann, Inc. from* The Elephant and the Bad Baby *by Elfrida Vipont. Illustrated by Raymond Briggs. Illustrations © 1970 by Raymond Briggs. (Original in color)*

*Beasts* edited by Ruth Manning-Sanders. His pictures are deft in composition and are gay with color and movement.

### Victor G. Ambrus, 1935–

Born in Budapest, Victor Ambrus, designer, author, and illustrator, won the Kate Greenaway Medal in 1966 for *The Three Poor Tailors*. He uses a mixture of techniques: ink, watercolor, and oil pastel. His black-and-white work, as in *Flambards in Summer* (1970) by K. M. Peyton, has the bold quality of etching. Mr. Ambrus, a collector of European military relics, provides a strong sense of action in his pictures. They are vigorous and decorative, as in *The Brave Soldier Janosh* (1966), with soldiers that are authentically swashbuckling, peasants that are stolid with a skeptical humor, and horses that seem to be cynically amused at the tall tale they are participating in. Mr. Ambrus illustrated E. M. Almedingen's *Katia* (1967) and *Fanny* (1970), Hester Burton's *Time of Trial* (1964), Barbara Picard's *The Young Pretenders* (1966), and his own *The Little Cockerel* (1968) and *The Seven Skinny Goats* (1970).

### Uri Shulevitz, 1935–

Uri Shulevitz, who was born in Poland and spent some of his childhood years in Israel and in France, shares, he says, the belief of the prophet Isaiah—"And a little child shall lead them." He works chiefly in ink, sometimes using it in combination with wash; for the illustrations in *Maximilian's World* (1966), by Mary Stolz, he used a Japanese reed pen. In Dorothy Nathan's *The Month Brothers* (1967), his line drawings have a grave yet comic quality that befits the folktale style. In illustrating Arthur Ransome's *The Fool of the World and the Flying Ship*, for which he won the 1969 Caldecott Medal, his pictures in brilliant color are faithful to the art style of the Russian background of the book. He has illustrated with sensitivity the stories of many writers, but has never surpassed the evocative mood and the harmony of pictures and text in his own *One Monday Morning* (1967) and *Rain Rain Rivers* (1969). (See 30 in color section.)

## OTHER NOTABLE ARTISTS

Today there are so many creative illustrators of children's books that it is impossible to discuss them all even briefly. Obviously, this list of artists should include Henry Pitz, a prolific illustrator and an author of several books on illustration; Leonard Everett Fisher, whose stark scratchboard pictures are dramatic in black and white; Peter Parnall, whose drawings have a geometric precision; Leo Lionni, whose *Inch by Inch* (1960), done in rice paper collage, was a Caldecott Honor Book; Tasha Tudor, who works in delicate pastel colors; and Janina Domanska, whose *If All the Seas Were One Sea* (1971) and *Under the Green Willow* (1971), by Elizabeth Coatsworth, are good examples of her striking etchings.

*From* Under the Green Willow *by Elizabeth Coatsworth. Illustration by Janina Domanska. Illustration © Janina Domanska, 1971. (Original in color)*

Milton Glaser has not illustrated many books for children, but his pictures for Conrad Aiken's *Cats and Bats and Things with Wings* (1965) show amazing virtuosity, each picture in a different mood and technique. Edward Gorey's pen-and-ink illustrations are elegant and distinctive; Emily McCully's produce a free, staccato feeling. The work of Arnold Lobel, John Steptoe, and Brinton Turkle will be discussed in connection with their books. Ed Emberley won the Caldecott Award for his illustrations, with a leaded-glass effect from bright colors over woodcut lines, in *Drummer Hoff* (1967), a folk verse adapted by Barbara Emberley. Another husband-and-wife team whose books have a robust comic spirit in text and illustration are Harve Zemach, who wrote the rhyming story of *The Judge: An Untrue Tale* (1969), and Margot Zemach, who provided the imaginative illustrations. The Caldecott Award for a 1970 book went to Gail Haley for *A Story, A Story* (the retelling of an African folk tale with woodcut illustrations that are occasionally crowded but have good design and vitality). Anita Lobel, an adaptable artist, is at her best in Benjamin Elkin's *How the Tsar Drinks Tea* (1971), in which the pictures, appropriately bordered, have a quality of Russian decorative art. The soft, almost photographic drawings of Symeon Shimin, the distinctive portraiture of Ati Forberg, and the subtle shading of Tom Feelings' pictures in Muriel Feelings' *Zamani Goes to Market*, all have a gentleness that is also strength. A bold freedom is evident in the work of Josè Aruego, whose illustrations for *Leo the Late Bloomer* (1971), by Robert Kraus, have strength and vigor; and in the work of Tomi Ungerer, whose pictures are the visual equivalent of a comic tall tale. Ed Young and Bernarda Bryson are outstanding for their sense of design and their use of color. John Schoenherr, Olive Earle, and Carl Burger are all notable for their scrupulously realistic pictures of animals.

The work of several illustrators is indelibly identified with the characters they have helped bring to life: Beth and Joe Krush for the stories of the Borrowers; Louis Slobodkin for the Moffats; Paul Galdone for those mice-extraordinary, Anatole and Basil; Kurt Werth for the mendacious raconteur McBroom; and Leonard Shortall for the boy detective, Encyclopedia Brown—all of these artists of course have illustrated many other books.

*Reprinted with the permission of Farrar, Straus & Giroux, Inc. from* The Judge: An Untrue Tale *by Harve and Margot Zemach. Text copyright © 1969 by Harve Zemach, pictures copyright © 1969 by Margot Zemach. (Original in color)*

Jean de Brunhoff delighted children with the adventures of that suave French elephant Babar, and Françoise (Seignobosc) has given us a number of books in bright, decorative colors. Bettina (Ehrlich) introduces children to Italy in her big picture story *Pantaloni* (1957), and her countryman Bruno Munari provides them with so magnificent a use of color against white space that he could train the color blind to see and rejoice. The illustrations of Swiss Felix Hoffmann for *Sleeping Beauty* (1960) and *King Thrushbeard* (1970) are in the grand style, romantic and grave. The first Hans Christian Andersen Award for illustrations went to Swiss Alois Carigiet, whose *Anton and Anne* (1969) is a good example of the vibrant delicacy of his work. In contrast, another Swiss artist, Celestino Piatti, paints in bold and brilliant modern style. The English artist Harold Jones illustrates in a manner both romantic and restrained in *Lavender's Blue* (1954). (See 21 in color section.) Two other English illustrators, Margery Gill and Shirley Hughes, do work in color but are better known for their realistic, natural line drawings. C. Walter Hodges won the Kate Greenaway Medal for *Shakespeare's Theatre* (1964), and his fidelity of detail is also seen in sea scenes and the historically-based tale of a rescue operation, *The Overland Launch* (1970). John Burningham has twice won the Greenaway Medal: in 1954 for *Borka* and in 1971 for *Mr. Gumpy's Outing*, which is illustrated with quiet humor. From Japanese-born Taro Yashima have come the sensitive illustrations of children in Japan in *Plenty to Watch* (1954) and *Crow Boy* (1955), and of a Japanese child in this country in *Umbrella* (1958), and others. (See 17 in color section.) Kazue Mizumura, who also came to the United States from Japan, has created lively pictures for the stories, set in Japan, of Yoshiko Uchida.

This is indeed the day of the artist in children's books, and their pictures should afford some protection from the flood of meretricious art that is so readily available. Better one good book with distinguished illustrations than a dozen stereotypes with flashy, poorly executed pictures. For children must be trained to see truly and subtly. They must be taught to look and look again at the illustrations in their books. Pictures can help them see the comic absurdities of life or its heroic struggles and tragedies. Pictures can give children a sudden breathtaking feeling for the beauty or the wonder of life. Such pictures deepen their perceptiveness and help them to grow.

## ADULT REFERENCES[10]

*The Art of Beatrix Potter.*

*The Bewick Collector.*

BLACKBURN, HENRY. *Randolph Caldecott: A Personal Memoir of His Early Art Career.*

CIANCIOLO, PATRICIA. *Illustrations in Children's Books.*

COLBY, JEAN POINDEXTER. *Writing, Illustrating and Editing Children's Books.* Part II, "Illustrations and Production."

COMMIRE, ANNE. *Something About the Author: Facts and Pictures about Contemporary Authors and Illustrators of Books for Young People.*

DAUGHERTY, JAMES. *William Blake.*

DAVIS, MARY GOULD. *Randolph Caldecott 1846–1886: An Appreciation.*

DOYLE, BRIAN, comp. and ed. *The Who's Who of Children's Literature.*

EGOFF, SHEILA. *The Republic of Childhood; A Critical Guide to Canadian Children's Literature in English.* Chapter 7, "Illustration and Design."

EGOFF, SHEILA, G. T. STUBBS, and L. F. ASHLEY, eds. *Only Connect: Readings on Children's Literature.* Part 5, "Illustration."

ERNEST, EDWARD, comp., assisted by PATRICIA TRACY LOWE. *The Kate Greenaway Treasury.*

FREEMAN, G. LAVERNE, and RUTH SUNDERLIN FREEMAN. *The Child and His Picture Book.*

FULLER, MURIEL, ed. *More Junior Authors.*

HOPKINS, LEE BENNETT. *Books Are by People.*

HUDSON, DEREK. *Arthur Rackham: His Life and Work.*

HÜRLIMANN, BETTINA. *Picture-Book World.*

KINGMAN, LEE, JOANNA FOSTER, and RUTH GILES LONTOFT, comps. *Illustrators of Children's Books, 1957–1966.*

KLEMIN, DIANA. *The Art of Art for Children's Books.*

______. *The Illustrated Book: Its Art and Craft.*

KUNITZ, STANLEY J., and HOWARD HAYCRAFT, eds. *The Junior Book of Authors.*

LANE, MARGARET. *The Tale of Beatrix Potter; A Biography.*

MAHONY, BERTHA E., LOUISE P. LATIMER, and BEULAH FOLMSBEE, comps. *Illustrators of Children's Books, 1744–1945.*

MILLER, BERTHA MAHONY, and ELINOR WHITNEY FIELD, eds. *Caldecott Medal Books: 1938–1957.*

MOORE, ANNE CARROLL. *A Century of Kate Greenaway.*

MUIR, PERCY. *English Children's Books, 1600 to 1900.*

PITZ, HENRY C. *Illustrating Children's Books: History, Technique, Production.*

______. *The Practice of American Book Illustration.*

______, ed. *A Treasury of American Book Illustration.*

QUINNAN, BARBARA, comp. *Fables from Incunabula to Modern Picture Books.*

ROBINSON, EVELYN ROSE. *Readings About Children's Literature.* Part 5, "Illustrations and Children's Books."

VIGUERS, RUTH HILL, MARCIA DALPHIN, and BERTHA MAHONY MILLER, comps. *Illustrators of Children's Books, 1946–1956.*

WARD, MARTHA E., and DOROTHY A. MARQUARDT. *Illustrators of Books for Young People.*

WHITE, DOROTHY MARY NEAL. *About Books for Children.* Chapter 2, "Picture Books."

______. *Books Before Five.*

10. Complete bibliographic data are provided in the combined Adult References in the Appendices.

## ABC BOOKS

BROWN, MARCIA. *Peter Piper's Alphabet*, ill. by author. Scribner's 1959.

BURNINGHAM, JOHN. *John Burningham's ABC*, ill. by author. Bobbs, 1967. 4-6

CHWAST, SEYMOUR, and MARTIN STEPHEN MOSKOF. *Still Another Alphabet Book*, ill. by authors. McGraw, 1969. 3-6

CRANE, WALTER. *Baby's Own Alphabet*, ill. by author. Dodd, n.d. 5-7

DUVOISIN, ROGER. *A for the Ark*, ill. by author. Lothrop, 1952. 5-8

EICHENBERG, FRITZ. *Ape in a Cape*, ill. by author. Harcourt, 1952. 5-8

FRANÇOISE [pseud. for Françoise Seignobosc]. *The Gay ABC*, ill. by author. Scribner's, 1938. 5-7

GÁG, WANDA. *The ABC Bunny*, ill. by author. Coward, 1933. 5-7

GORDON, ISABEL. *The ABC Hunt*, ill. by author. Viking, 1961. From the A in alphabet soup to the Z in the sign at the zoo, children will enjoy the gamelike search for letters in this entertaining photographic alphabet book. 5-7

GREENAWAY, KATE. *A Apple Pie*, ill. by author. Warne, n.d. 5-7

GROSSBART, FRANCINE. *A Big City*, ill. by author. Harper, 1966. 3-6

LEAR, EDWARD. *ABC*, penned and ill. by author. McGraw, 1965. Facsimile of a manuscript, this edition has the nonsense verses set in type at the back of the book. 5-7

McGINLEY, PHYLLIS. *All Around the Town*, ill. by Helen Stone. Lippincott, 1948. 6-10

MATTHIESEN, THOMAS. *ABC; An Alphabet Book*, photos by author. Platt, 1966. 3-6

MILES, MISKA. *Apricot ABC*, ill. by Peter Parnall. Little, 1969. 5-7

MUNARI, BRUNO. *Bruno Munari's ABC*, ill. by author. World, 1960. 4-6

NEWBERRY, CLARE. *The Kittens' ABC*, ill. by author. Harper, 1946. 5-7

PIATTI, CELESTINO. *Celestino Piatti's Animal ABC*, ill. by author, English text by Jon Reid. Atheneum, 1966. 4-6

ROJANKOVSKY, FEODOR. *Animals in the Zoo*, ill. by author. Knopf, 1962. A handsome zoo alphabet book in color with an animal for every letter. 4-6

SCHMIDERER, DOROTHY. *The Alphabeast Book; An Abecedarium*, ill. by author. Holt, 1971. 3-5

SENDAK, MAURICE. *Alligators All Around*, in *Nutshell Library*, ill. by author. Harper, 1962. 4-7

TUDOR, TASHA. *A Is for Annabelle*, ill. by author. Walck, 1954.

WALTERS, MARGUERITE. *The City-Country ABC; My Alphabet Ride in the City, and My Alphabet Ride in the Country*, ill. by Ib Ohlsson. Doubleday, 1966. 5-7

WILDSMITH, BRIAN. *Brian Wildsmith's ABC*, ill. by author. Watts, 1963. 4-6

WILLIAMS, GARTH. *Big Golden Animal ABC*, ill. by author. Golden Pr., 1954. 4-7

# Part Two
# Once upon a Time . . .

# Chapter 4
# Children's Literature: History and Trends

The flood of publications in children's books is so overpowering that it is important to remind ourselves that there are old books in children's literature as fresh and serviceable today as they were a hundred years ago. There are also old books for children which have been discarded, and properly so. Age is no guarantee of a book's excellence, nor recency of its significance. Some of the discards we shall glance at briefly, only to know their kind and to be wary of their reappearance in modern dress—because that is what happens. We have not arrived at our wealth of fine modern books for children without considerable trial and error, and the errors are difficult to eradicate. We need perspective in judging children's books. We need to look at the past with modern eyes and view the present with the accumulated wisdom of the past. Where and how did children's literature begin? What has it grown out of and where is it going?

Before a child can read, his acquaintance with literature begins, as it began for the race, through listening to the songs and stories of his people. All peoples had their explanations of the beginnings of the world, the coming of their own family or tribe, and the natural phenomena that delighted or terrified them. Mothers of yesterday chanted or sang to their babies. In simpler days, old women told homely tales of the beasts and kept alive legends of strange events. Grandmothers have always been the custodians of traditional tales, both of families and of the larger group, the tribe or the village. The men told stories to the adults of daring exploits and great adventures, and we may be sure the children listened. The professional storytellers, the bards or minstrels, took these tales, embroidered and polished them, and made them into the ballads or the hero tales or the epics of the people. So unwritten folk literature grew and was passed on by word of mouth for centuries before the collectors gathered it together for printing. Much of it was bloody and terrible; some of it was romantic, some coarse and humorous, told by adults to adults. Undoubtedly the children listened and loved many of these tales never intended for their ears and begged for them again and again. We say this with confidence because that is the way they have acquired much of their literature in every generation, even our own. Today, children watch adult television programs, take over adult songs, and read the same comics that adults read. They appropriate from adult material those things they understand and enjoy.

## BOOKS BEFORE PRINT

In the several centuries before the invention of movable type, all books for children were instructional, written by monastic teachers and chiefly intended for the children of privilege. These lesson books, often in Latin, began the tradition of didacticism that was to dominate children's books for hundreds of years and to persist as an influence into contemporary times.

Aldhelm (640?–709), Abbot of Malmesbury, set the pattern used until the end of the sixteenth century of a text that was either rhymed or in question-and-answer form. In the eleventh century Anselm (1033–1109), Archbishop of Canterbury, wrote an encyclopedia that treated such topics as manners and customs, natural science, children's duties, morals, and religious precepts. Such books were meant to instruct and to instill in children edifying principles of belief and conduct; they were not meant to give delight to the young.

## FOR GROWNUPS: FABLES, ROMANCES, ADVENTURES

William Caxton (1422–1491) was England's first printer. He issued a series of books which are still appearing in various versions on our publishers' book lists for children. Caxton's books included, among other titles, Sir Thomas Malory's *Morte d'Arthur, The Recuyell of the Historyes of Troye, The Boke of Histories of Jason, The Historye of Reynart the Foxe*, and *Aesop's Fables*. Tales of King

*Illustration for the William Caxton edition of* Aesop's Fables.

Arthur still give the older child a fine introduction to romance, the story of Odysseus remains a popular adventure story, and the fables are enjoyed by young children even if they do skip the morals. Although Caxton intended his books for adults, children appropriated many of them, and versions of these same collections continue to delight each generation.

## FOR CHILDREN: HORNBOOKS AND BATTLEDORES

While textbooks will not be discussed in detail, no account of children's books seems complete without a word about the hornbooks and the battledores. The hornbooks were not books at all but little wooden paddles on which were pasted lesson sheets of vellum or parchment. These sheets were covered with transparent horn and bound along the edges by strips of brass. Most of the hornbooks were two and three-fourths by five inches. The lesson sheets began with a cross followed by the alphabet (sometimes in both large and small letters) and by syllables: *ab, eb, ib*, and other vowel and consonant combinations. There would probably be "In the Name of the Father, the Son, and the Holy Ghost" and the Lord's Prayer. The hornbooks differed in content, but in general they were designed to teach the child his letters and their combinations and to continue his religious instruction. There is still in existence a little hornbook supposedly used by Queen Elizabeth I. We know that these first hornbooks made their way to the New World for the instruction of Puritan children.

The battledore, which was conceived by one of Newbery's helpers, was in use from about 1746 to 1770. It had three folding cardboard leaves. Unlike the hornbook, it had no religious material but contained alphabets, easy reading, numerals, and woodcut illustrations. Neither the hornbook nor the battledore ever carried anything that was remotely entertaining; so children still sampled what they could from adult books.

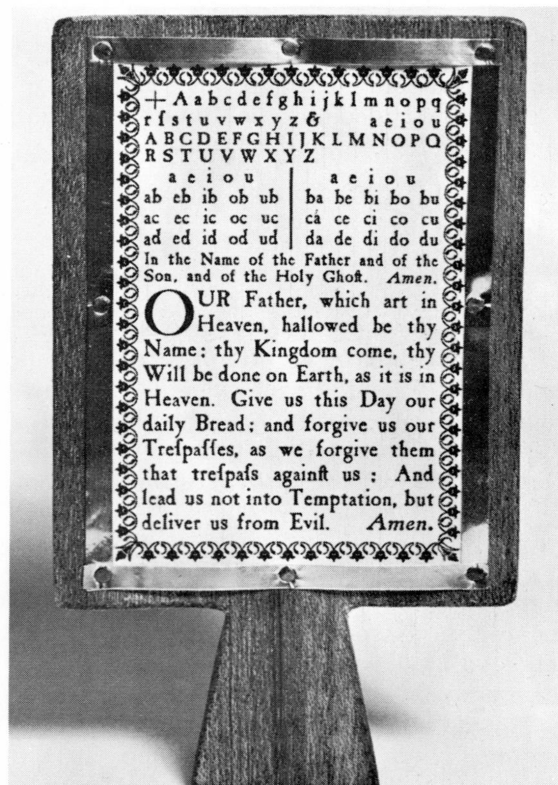

+Aabcdefghijklmnopq
rſstuvwxyz& aeiou
ABCDEFGHIJKLMNOPQ
RSTUVWXYZ

| a e i o u | a e i o u |
| --- | --- |
| ab eb ib ob ub | ba be bi bo bu |
| ac ec ic oc uc | ca ce ci co cu |
| ad ed id od ud | da de di do du |

In the Name of the Father and of the Son, and of the Holy Ghoſt. *Amen.*

OUR Father, which art in Heaven, hallowed be thy Name; thy Kingdom come, thy Will be done on Earth, as it is in Heaven. Give us this Day our daily Bread; and forgive us our Treſpaſſes, as we forgive them that treſpaſs againſt us: And lead us not into Temptation, but deliver us from Evil. *Amen.*

*From a photograph in* A Little History of the Horn-Book *by Beulah Folmsbee, The Horn Book, Inc., 1942.*

## AND A PICTURE BOOK

In 1657 a Moravian bishop and educator, John Amos Comenius (1592–1671) put into practice his belief in better education for the young by preparing what is described today as the first picture book—*Orbis Pictus* (The World Illustrated).[1] Comenius' preface indicates the author's sensitivity to children's need for interesting material: "See then here a new help for Schooles, a Picture and Nomenclature of all the chief things in the World, and of mens Actions in their way of Living!" It would serve, he hoped, "To entice Witty Children to it . . . to stir up the Attention . . . by sport, and a merry pastime." (See illustration, p. 53.)

## PEDLAR'S TREASURY: A TU'PENNY TREAT

Then came the chapmen, the pedlars of the seventeenth and eighteenth centuries, with newssheets, ballads, broadsides, and chapbooks tucked in among their trinkets. Chapbooks were cheap little books that could be bought for as little as a penny. They had from sixteen to thirty-two or sixty-four pages and were often not stitched but merely folded. F. J. H. Darton, in *Children's Books in England*, tells us that surviving copies have been found all carefully sewed with bits of silk or ribbon, perhaps by some child owner. The editors or compilers of these little books took the legends of antiquity, the old tales of the Middle Ages, elements of the fairy tales—any stories they could lay their hands on—and retold them in drastically condensed versions. All literary charm was lost; the grammar was often faulty, but what remained was a heightened sense of action with an adventure on almost every page. The educated upper classes of England may have frowned

1. An edition of *Orbis Pictus*, published in 1887 by C. W. Bardeen, has been reissued by the Singing Tree Press. See pp. 52–53 for further discussion of *Orbis Pictus*.

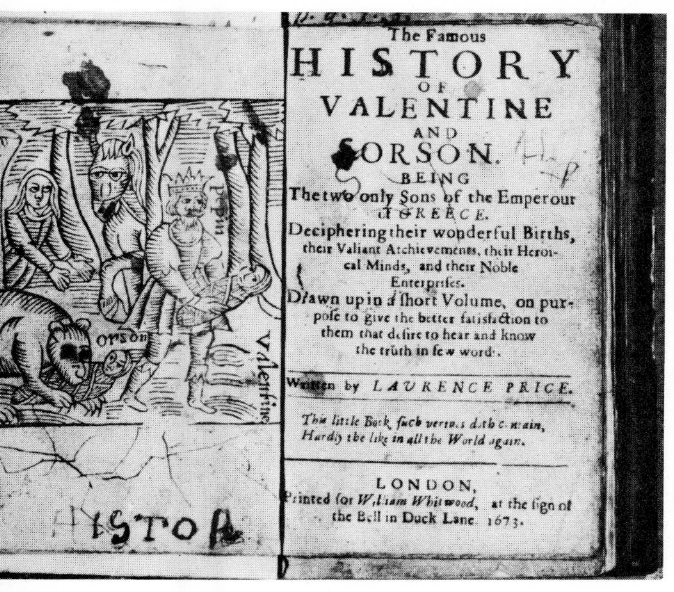

The Famous
HISTORY
OF
VALENTINE
AND
ORSON.
BEING
The two only Sons of the Emperour of GREECE.
Deciphering their wonderful Births, their Valiant Atchievements, their Heroical Minds, and their Noble Enterprises.
Drawn up in a short Volume, on purpose to give the better satisfaction to them that desire to hear and know the truth in few words.

Written by LAVRENCE PRICE.

This little Book such vertues doth contain,
Hardly the like in all the World again.

LONDON,
Printed for William Whitwood, at the sign of the Bell in Duck Lane. 1673.



*From Laurence Price's* History of Valentine and Orson. *Reproduced from an edition in the D'Alte Welch Collection, Cleveland.*

upon the chapbooks, but the common people of England loved them and bought them continually. Of course the children discovered them and became ardent patrons of the pedlar's treasures, too.

The stories were the kind that children have always liked—adventure stories with heroes who do things. The account of their doughty deeds fills a book: *Chapbooks of the Eighteenth Century*, by John Ashton. "The History of Valentine and Orson" is the story of twin brothers who were separated in infancy, Orson to be raised by a bear and Valentine to be reared by a king of France. Later, Valentine captured the wild Orson and they performed great deeds together, each winning the hand of a lovely princess. Incidentally, the bear child, Orson, is a forerunner of Mowgli in Kipling's *Jungle Books*.

One favorite, "Tom Hickathrift," is a kind of early English Paul Bunyan. "At ten years old he was six feet high and three in thickness, his hand was like a shoulder of mutton, and every other part proportionable." He pulled up trees, slew giants, and felled four highwaymen at a blow.

In contrast to the colossal Tom Hickathrift, there is Tom Thumb, whose story is told in a chapbook rhymed version of "Tom Thumb His Life and Death." The woodcuts from 1630 show this Lilliputian hero early in his career falling into a bowl of pudding but later riding valiantly into battle atop an enormous war horse.

The attitude of serious-minded adults of the day toward these crude, often vulgar little books was generally scornful. The clergy "viewed with alarm," but at least one man of letters spoke a good word for them. Richard

Tom Thumb.

How Tom Thumb fell into the Pudding-Bowl, and of his escape out of the Tinkers Budget.

He sat upon the pudding-bowl,
the Candle for to hold,

A 4 Of

*From the chapbook* Tom Thumb His Life and Death. *Reproduced from an edition (circa 1665) in the John G. White Collection, Cleveland Public Library.*

Steele, in *The Tatler* (No. 95), tells how his young godson was "much turned in his studies" to these histories and adds:

> *He would tell you the mismanagements of John Hickerthrift, find fault with the passionate temper of Bevis of Southampton and loved St. George for being the champion of England: and by this means had his thoughts insensibly moulded into the notions of discretion, virtue, and honour.*

This may be a charitable interpretation of the effects of chapbook reading, but Florence Barry, in *A Century of Children's Books*, adds a cheerful note also. She says:

> *John Bunyan was the first to reconcile the claims of religion and romance, and he could never have written* The Pilgrim's Progress *if he had not been a good customer of the pedlar in his youth. (pp. 6–7)*

Badly written, crudely illustrated, unhonored though they were, the chapbooks preserved and popularized some of the precious elements of literature that children love. But their coarseness probably paved the way for the reaction against "tales, stories, jests," the reaction which produced children's books full of somber warnings and doleful examples.

## VIEWPOINTS

. . . the evolution of juvenile literature in England has in a very real sense been an account of the gradual and often reluctant realisation that children were meant to enjoy life in their own right, and, to a great extent, on their own terms. The subject, indeed, has a wider reference than its own intrinsic importance, in reflecting a changed and broadening viewpoint towards the upbringing of children.

. . . Harking back to the Puritans and the obstinate vitality of their mental and spiritual approach to the upbringing of children, it is seen to be fundamental to their viewpoint that the only concession permissible of any important difference between children and adults implies not a smaller susceptibility to the temptations of the flesh, but a feebler capacity to withstand them.

For more than one hundred years after the time of the good, godly writers of the Commonwealth period breaks in the cloud of their sombre influence are infrequent and feeble.

. . . The significant fact is that until the eighteen-fifties and even later a carefree attitude unencumbered by moral or instructional preoccupation was strikingly exceptional in writing for children.—Percy Muir, *English Children's Books, 1600–1900*, Batsford, London, 1954, pp. 226–227.

## THE PURITANS AND PERDITION

Even while the chapmen were peddling their lurid, light-hearted "Histories," a religious movement was under way that was to affect life on both sides of the Atlantic. Beginning about the middle of Queen Elizabeth's reign, the English had become "the people of a book, and that book was the Bible." In London people went daily, in great crowds, to St. Paul's to hear the Bible read aloud, and small Bibles found their way into homes everywhere.

A group of deeply religious people whom we know as the Puritans read their Bibles with fervor. They venerated the victims of religious persecution and studied Foxe's *Book of Martyrs* (1563), with its details of death at the stake, and gave the book to their children.

As if this legacy of terror was not enough for small Puritans to endure, a clergyman, James Janeway, wrote in 1671 or 1672 a famous book that was long popular with the heaven-bent adults who ruled over Puritan nurseries. Its full title was:

> A Token For Children: *being an Exact Account of the Conversion, Holy and Exemplary Lives, and Joyful Deaths of several young Children. To which is now added, Prayers and Graces, fitted for the use of little Children.*

There were thirteen good little children in this gloomy book, and, considering their lives, it is small wonder that they died young. They spent their time trying to reform, convert, and generally improve everyone they encountered. They brooded on sin and eternal torment and the state of their souls. Morbid and unnatural as this book was with its continual dwelling on death, it grew from the earnest desire of the Puritans to make children happy—not in our modern sense of the word but in theirs. To be happy meant to be secure in the avoidance of Hell and in the assurance of Heaven. Unfortunately their method of instilling religious ideas was chiefly through the use of fear—the fear of Hell.

Out of the Puritan world there emerged one great book for children—Bunyan's *Pilgrim's Progress.* This book was intended for adults and probably reached the children piecemeal as they listened to the adults read it aloud, or discuss it, or tell the more dramatic portions. Reviewing the story, we can easily understand why the children enjoyed the book. It is told in the best tradition of the old fairy tales which John Bunyan had enjoyed in chapbook form when he was a boy.

John Bunyan (1628–1688), a humble tinker, confessed that one of the sins of his youth was his delight in the "History of the Life and Death of that Noble Knight Sir Bevis of Southampton." As he grew more and more religious, he put away all such frivolous reading and turned to the Bible and to such fear-inspiring books as John Foxe's *Book of Martyrs.* These harrowing tales of "holy deaths" obsessed Bunyan to the point where he saw visions and dreamed horrible dreams of his own sins and the torments he was to suffer because of them. He began to preach such fiery and fearsome sermons that he was locked up for nonconformity to the established Church of England. In jail for years with his Bible and his *Martyrs,* he began to write the story of a Christian soul on its troublesome pilgrimage through this world to everlasting life. Sir Bevis was not forgotten but was reborn as Christian; the giant Ascapart became the Giant Despair; and so, in good fairy-tale style, Christian fought monsters and enemies with properly symbolic names. But no chapbook tale was ever so somber and so dramatic as this progress of a Christian pilgrim. It begins as a dream:

> *As I went through the wild waste of this world, I came to a place where there was a den, and I lay down in it to sleep. While I slept, I had a dream, and lo! I saw a man whose clothes were in rags, and he stood with his face from his own house, with a book in his hand, and a great load on his back.*

In its original form, with long interludes of theological moralizing, children would have difficulty reading this book, but when the dramatic story is cleared of these obstructions, it is a moving tale. In 1939 an edition abridged and illustrated by Robert Lawson was published.

The *Mayflower* reached our shores in 1620, but the great exodus of Puritans from England to the New World did not take place until around 1630. We can well imagine that those early years of colonization were too difficult for any excursions into book-producing for either children or adults, but the Puritans' passion for education could not long be submerged. Whatever else may be said of them, the history of their activities in New England is alive with a deep and growing concern for schools and the tools of education, books. As early as 1632, there are references to hornbooks, brought from England with the crosses blotted out—crosses being for the time a religious symbol to which the Puritans objected.

The first book for children to be published in the New World appeared in 1646. It was written by John Cotton and its full title was:

> *Milk for Babes, Drawn out of the Breasts of Both Testaments, Chiefly for the Spirituall Nourishment of Boston Babes in either England, but may be of like Use for any Children.*

Beneath this title it adds *A Catechism in Verse,* and begins:

*Who is the Maker of all things?*
*The Almighty God who reigns on high.*
*He form'd the earth, He spread the sky.*

It continues with all the intricate details of Puritan theology.

Editions of the *New England Primer* published as early as 1691 have been found, although it is known to have been in print before that. Its famous rhyming alphabet begins:

*In Adam's fall*
*We sinned all.*

*Thy life to mend*
*God's Book attend.*

In addition, the book contains prayers, poems, the shorter catechism, the Ten Commandments, Bible verses, and pictures. One of these is a quaint woodcut of a Dame's school; another is the picture of a mournful figure contemplating a tombstone; and the prize is a graphic illustration of the burning of Mr. John Rogers, with his wife and ten children looking on, while a jaunty man-at-arms holds them at bay. With tombs and torture, it is difficult to justify the subtitle, "An Easy and Pleasant Guide to the Art of Reading."

As late as 1832, Boston had its own descendant of Janeway's *Token*. It was written by Perkins and Marvin and the title page reads as follows:

*Mary Lothrop*
*Who Died In*
*Boston*
*1831*

The authors add in their preface that their Memoir was prepared "for the purpose of adding another to the bright pictures set before children to allure them into the paths of piety." This was a fairly large book for those days, about three by seven inches, and fully three fourths of it is devoted to the pious Mary's interminable death. The charming little frontispiece shows Mary and her little brother kneeling beside a chair, praying. The boy has struck his sister, and Mary is praying him into a state of repentance. Shortly after that, Mary becomes ill and begins her preparations for death. Gloom descends for the remaining pages. It is to be hoped that Boston children who were given this "bright picture" had recourse to the lusty nonsense of *Mother Goose*. For, despite the Puritans, a pirated edition of this cheerful volume was printed in the New World in 1785.

24 NEW ENGLAND PRIMER.

Thou shalt not see thy brother s ass or his . s fall down by the way, and hide thyself fron. them : thou shalt surely help him to lift them up again.

THE BURNING OF MR. JOHN ROGERS.

MR. JOHN ROGERS, minister of the gospel in London, was the first martyr in Queen Mary's reign; and was burnt at Smithfield, February the fourteenth, 1554. His wife, with nine small children, and one at her breast, followed him to the stake, with which sorrowful sight he was not in the least daunted, but with wonderful patience died courageously for the gospel of JESUS CHRIST.

*From* The New England Primer; or An Easy and Pleasant Guide to the Art of Reading. *Massachusetts Sabbath School Society.*

## FAIRY TALES AND FABLES IN FRANCE

Paul Hazard in his delightful *Books, Children and Men* calls attention to the early portraits of children clad in long velvet skirts, heavily plumed hats, corsets, swords, and ornaments and he remarks, "If, for centuries, grownups did not even think of giving children appropriate clothes, how would it ever have occurred to them to provide children with suitable books?"

Yet around 1697 this miracle occurred in France with the publication of *Histoires ou contes du temps passé avec des moralités* (Histories or Tales of Long Ago with Morals), or, more familiarly, *Contes de ma Mère l'Oye* (Tales of Mother Goose). There is some question today as to whether the tales were written for adults or for children. But whatever the author's intention, they were loved by children. The stories were "La belle au bois dormant" (The Sleeping Beauty); "La petite chaperon rouge" (Little Red Riding Hood); "La Barbe Bleue" (Blue Beard); "Le Maître chat, ou le chat botté" (The Master Cat, or Puss in Boots); "Les fées" (Diamonds and Toads); "Cendrillon, ou la petite pantoufle de verre" (Cinderella, or the Little Glass Slipper); "Riquet à la houpe" (Riquet with the Tuft); and "Le petit poucet" (Little Thumb).

Did Charles Perrault (1628–1703), member of the French Academy and author of many serious but forgotten works, collect these traditional tales, or was it Pierre Perrault d'Armancour, his eldest son? No author is listed in what is probably the first edition. Opinion favored the father for years, but he never admitted authorship. On the other hand, a publication privilege was granted to young "P. Darmancour." Percy Muir gives other evidence that the son was the compiler and adds, "Today informed opinion in France also favours the son and we may very well leave it at that" (*English Children's Books, 1600–1900*, p. 49). Perrault's Fairy Tales, we call them, and their immortality is due as much to the spontaneity and charm of the style as to the traditional content.[2]

2. For a fascinating account of the "lost manuscript" of 1695, see May Hill Arbuthnot, "Puss, the Perraults and a Lost Manuscript," *Elementary English*, October 1969, pp. 715–721.

Perrault had imitators but no rivals. Using Aesop and *The Fables of Bidpai* as sources, Jean de la Fontaine (1621–1695) wrote fables to amuse court circles, but they are savored by children today just as they were when they appeared as a series of twelve books in the years 1668–1694. Mme. d'Aulnoy (1650?–1705) turned the old folk-tale themes into ornate novels for the court. "The Yellow Dwarf" and "Graciosa and Percinet" are sometimes adapted for modern collections but are rarely seen in their original form. Mme. de Beaumont (1711–1780), busy with the education of children, also took time to write some fairy tales for them. Of these, her "Beauty and the Beast" has survived deservedly. Still others took a hand at the fairy tales, but none with the freshness of Perrault.

## JOHN NEWBERY'S BOOKS IN ENGLAND

Meanwhile, in England, it was a happy day for children, steering a perilous course between the pedlar and the Puritan, when in 1729 R. Samber translated Perrault's *Tales of Mother Goose*. No chapbook was ever so thrilling as these eight tales, no "good Godly book" was ever so beloved. At the time, they must have attracted the attention of an English publisher by the name of John Newbery, because not only did his firm later use the title *Mother Goose*, but he may also have discovered through the popularity of the tales the importance of the child as a potential consumer of books.

John Newbery was what we would call today "a character." He dabbled in many things. He wrote; he published; he befriended indigent authors; he did a flourishing business manufacturing and dispensing medicines and a "Medicinal Dictionary." The caustic Samuel Johnson called him "Jack the Whirler," only to be pressed into service by busy Mr. Newbery as an occasional writer and literary adviser to a rapidly expanding publishing house. Then in 1744, along with Dr.

James' Fever Powders, Newbery offered for sale his latest publication:

A LITTLE PRETTY
POCKET-BOOK
*Intended for the*
*Instruction and Amusement*
*of*
*Little Master Tommy,*
*and*
*Pretty Miss Polly.*
*With Two Letters from*
*Jack the Giant-Killer;*
*As also*
*A Ball and a Pincushion;*
*The Use of which will infallibly make*
*Tommy*
*a good Boy and Polly a good Girl.*
*To which is added,*
*A Little Song-Book,*
*Being*
*A New Attempt to teach Children*
*the Use of the English Alphabet,*
*by way of Diversion.*[3]

For the "*amusement*" of Tommy and Polly, "by way of *diversion*"—here is a new approach to books for children and a momentous one. It marks the beginning of English books for their delight! Of course, Jack the Giant-Killer wrote two exceedingly moral letters to the readers of the *Pretty Pocket-Book*. He had evidently reformed and settled down since the chapbook days, for his lectures are as mild as milk, with no threats anywhere. The letters are followed by a series of games with rhymed directions and morals: marbles, shuttle-cock, blindman's buff, thread the needle, leap frog, and many other old favorites. There are fables, proverbs, and rules of behavior, with a rhyming alphabet and a few poems thrown in for good measure. The morals to the fables are made more romantic and palatable by the signature of Jack the Giant-Killer. The success of the *Pocket-Book* evidently encouraged the publisher because other books for children followed rapidly.

In 1765 *The Renowned History of Little Goody Two Shoes, Otherwise Called Mrs. Margery Two Shoes*, appeared. This is a small juvenile novel, the first of its kind to be written expressly for children. Oliver Goldsmith is supposed to have written *Goody Two Shoes*, which tells the story of a virtuous and clever child, Margery *Meanwell*. At the opening of the book, Margery's father suffers "the wicked persecutions of Sir Timothy *Gripe* and Farmer *Graspall*," who manage to ruin him and turn the whole family out of house and lands. The parents quickly die (evidently no Dr. James' Fever Powders available), leaving Margery and her brother Tommy destitute. Tommy goes to sea and Margery is rescued by charitable Clergyman Smith and his wife. When they buy her two shoes, the child is so overcome with pleasure that she keeps crying out, "Two shoes, Madam, see my two shoes"—hence her name.

This happiness is short-lived, for Gripe forces Smith to turn her out of the house. Back to the hedgerows once more, Margery teaches herself to read with remarkable ease by studying the schoolbooks of more fortunate children. Soon she knows more than any of them and decides to advance their learning. She makes up an alphabet of wooden blocks or "rattle traps" with both small and large letters, puts them into a basket, and goes from house to house helping children to read. The methods of the Trotting Tutoress apparently work like a charm, for all her young pupils respond immediately with never a "retarded reader" in the whole countryside.[4]

*Goody Two Shoes* is full of sociological lessons; its characters are types rather than individuals. Nevertheless, it was entertaining and it was a child's book. Many adults, nota-

3. No copies of the first English edition (1744) have survived. But in 1944, the two-hundredth anniversary of its first appearance, F. G. Melcher issued a reproduction of the first American edition, which was a reprint by Isaiah Thomas published in 1787 in Worcester, Mass. You can now examine the *Pocket-Book* gaily bedecked with a flowery gilt paper cover after Newbery's custom.

4. *The Renowned History of Little Goody Two Shoes, Otherwise Called Mrs. Margery Two Shoes.* Attributed to Oliver Goldsmith. Edited by Charles Welsh.

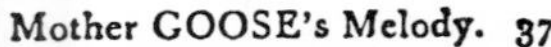

Mother GOOSE's Melody. 37

*JACK* and *Gill*
Went up the Hill,
To fetch a Pail of Water;
*Jack* fell down
And broke his Crown,
And *Gill* came tumbling after.

*Maxim.*

The more you think of dying, the better you will live.

ARISTOTLE'S

38 Mother GOOSE's Melody.

ARISTOTLE's STORY.

THERE were two Birds ſat on a Stone,
Fa, la, la, la, lal, de; [one,
One flew away, and then there was
Fa, la, la, la, lal, de;
The other flew after,
And then there was none,
Fa, la, la, la, lal, de;
And ſo the poor Stone
Was left all alone,
Fa, la, la, la, lal, de.

This may ſerve as a Chapter of Conſequence in the next new Book of Logick.

*From* The Original Mother Goose's Melody. *Reproduced in facsimile by W. H. Whitmore (Joel Munsell's Sons, 1899) from the edition reprinted by Isaiah Thomas of Worcester, Mass., about 1785.*

bly Charles Lamb, recalled the pleasure it gave them when they read it as children.

Between 1760 and 1766, John Newbery, according to many scholars, also published the first edition of *Mother Goose*,[5] but no trace of such a book remains and no contemporary reference to or advertisement of the book has ever been uncovered.[6] On the basis of their research, Jacques Barchilon and Henry Pettit[7] now assert that there was no such publication during those years. They assume that John Newbery may have planned such a book, but not until 1781 was there an advertisement announcing the first publication by his stepson, T. Carnan, of *Mother Goose's Melody*. John Newbery's firm remained in the family for many years and continued to publish books for children.

Many of the books published by Newbery were pirated by an American printer and publisher, Isaiah Thomas (1749–1831), who cheerfully and not quite legally printed his own editions of Newbery's books, possibly for mercenary motives but certainly to the benefit of young Americans.

It is fitting that John Newbery, this first English publisher of books for children, is honored annually when the Newbery Medal is presented for the year's most distinguished literature for children. Frederic G. Melcher, a publisher, in 1922 created and named this award as a tribute to the genius and foresight of the Englishman who first believed in children as discriminating patrons of books.[8]

## ROBINSON CRUSOE

One book emerged from the Puritan world to mark not only the increase of cheerfulness but the beginning of contemporary adventure tales. It was Daniel Defoe's *Robinson Crusoe*, one of the most popular books in all English literature.

Defoe (1659–1731), with a wisdom far in advance of his times, wrote on banks, insurance companies, schools for women, asylums

5. Even the scholarly Opies give 1765–1766 in their *Oxford Dictionary of Nursery Rhymes* (Oxford, 1951), p. 33.

6. See Chapter 5 for a detailed account of *Mother Goose*. Other children's classics mentioned in this chapter are discussed more fully in later chapters. See the Index for relevant page references.

7. *The Authentic Mother Goose Fairy Tales and Nursery Rhymes* (Alan Swallow, Denver, 1960), p. 11.

8. For the list of books which have been awarded the Newbery Medal see "Book Awards" in the Appendix.

for the insane, and all sorts of social problems. He turned out bitter political and religious satires which landed him in the pillory. He rose to wealth and fame and sank to penury and prison more than once. Writing was his passion, and few men have written more continuously. His most famous book, *The Life and Strange Surprising Adventures of Robinson Crusoe*, appeared in 1719, when Defoe was sixty and nearing the end of his turbulent career. We are told four editions of it were printed in four months, and for once the old fighter enjoyed fame with no unhappy repercussions of any kind.

Why has this book commended itself to children of each succeeding generation? It was addressed to adults and originally contained masses of moral ruminations that the children must have skipped with their usual agility in the avoidance of boredom. Most children's editions today omit these tiresome reflections and get on with the story.

There was a real-life Alexander Selkirk, marooned for over four years on the island of Juan Fernandez, who not only told his story to Defoe but also gave him his papers. However, it is due to Defoe's skill that Selkirk, as Robinson Crusoe, emerges a favorite world hero. The theme itself is irresistible: man pitted against nature, one man with a whole world to create and control. He must obtain food, provide himself with clothes and shelter, fight off wild animals, reckon time, keep himself civilized and sane. We are given many details of how he makes his shelter and cultivates a garden, how he domesticates his little herd of goats and acquires a parrot, and finally how he discovers an islander who becomes "my man Friday," a symbol today of faithfulness and loyalty.

Here is a book that satisfies the child's hunger to achieve competence. Identifying himself with Robinson Crusoe, he wins an ordered, controlled place in the world by his own efforts and foresight. With the coming of Friday, he has the love of a friend whom he in turn nurtures and protects. No wonder children read and reread and dramatize this book. All the details are there; every question is answered. It is reasonable and clear—a design for living, complete and satisfying.

The theme of the shipwrecked survivor is used also in *The Swiss Family Robinson*, written by Johann David Wyss (1743–1818) and published in 1812. Despite its pedantic overtones, this story of a pious, energetic family on a desert island delighted worldwide audiences with its dramatic events.

## GULLIVER'S TRAVELS

Another remarkable book emerged from this period, a political satire not intended for children but appropriated by them and known today as *Gulliver's Travels*. The author, Jonathan Swift (1667–1745), was born in Dublin and died there, Dean of the Cathedral. But between his birth and death, he spent considerable time in London and took an active part in the political life of the times. Recognized today as one of the greatest satirists in English literature, in his own day he was known as a pamphleteer and misanthrope. Despite this forbidding reputation, he had deep and lasting friendships with such famous men as Sir William Temple, Bolingbroke, and Oxford. With his two close friends, the distinguished physician John Arbuthnot and the poet Alexander Pope, he founded the Scriblerus Club. From this group came the *Memoirs* of a fictional character known as Martinus Scriblerus. Dr. Arbuthnot wrote about Martinus' childhood and Swift was supposed to carry the hero through some fantastic journeys, but he never did so. However, this book may have furnished Swift with the idea for Lemuel Gulliver.

Swift wrote his book in Ireland to lampoon the follies of the English court, its parties, its politics, and its statesmen. Worried about the reception of the book, he published it anonymously in 1726 as *Travels into Several Remote Nations of the World*, in four parts, by Lemuel Gulliver. To Swift's surprise and relief, London society, the very society he was making fun of, was highly diverted. In writing these tall tales, Swift seems to have been caught up with the richness of his own invention, and the humor sometimes overshadows the satire.

Children have always loved things in miniature, and they soon discovered the land of the Lilliputians. No one ever forgets Gulliver's waking to find six-inch people walking over him and Lilliputian ropes binding him. All the fascinating details are worked out to scale with logic and precision. Children are untroubled by any double meanings and like the fantasy for itself. The second journey, to the land of giants, Brobdingnag, is the next most popular, but man in an inferior position, treated like a toy, is not so appealing as the omnipotent Gulliver in Lilliput. The remaining books most children never read. Laputa is the land of the superminds, and a thoroughly repulsive lot they are. The country of the Houyhnhnms is strangest of all. It is ruled by beautiful and benignant horses, whereas men, the Yahoos, are horrid creatures, the beasts of the noble horses. As far as children are concerned, the first adventure makes the book, and it is Lilliput forever!

If Gulliver's travels had not fascinated artists, the book might not have survived in children's reading as long as it has. An early edition illustrated by Charles E. Brock (1894) and later editions illustrated by Arthur Rackham and by Fritz Eichenberg would lure anyone into reading the story.

*Illustration by Louis Rhead. From* Gulliver's Travels *by Jonathan Swift. Copyright 1913 by Harper & Brothers, copyright 1941 by Bertrand Rhead. Reproduced by permission of Harper & Row, Publishers.*

## POETS AND CHILDREN

About the time *Robinson Crusoe* and *Gulliver's Travels* were published, a gentle nonconformist preacher wrote a book of poetry for children. Isaac Watts (1674–1748) moralized in verse about busy bees and quarrelsome dogs, but he also wrote tender and beautiful hymns, many of which are found today in most hymnals. His *Divine and Moral Songs for Children* (1715) dwelt not on the fearful judgments of God, but on God "our refuge," and many a child must have been comforted by his tender "Cradle Hymn."

Toward the end of the century a major poet, William Blake (1757–1827), published a book of poems for and about children, *Songs of Innocence* (1789), each poem illustrated with Blake's own decorative designs. It is now considered an epoch-making book, but it caused no stir at the time of its publication. A companion volume, *Songs of Experience* (1794), followed. Although most of Blake's unique lyrics are for adults, some of his poetry appeals to children also.

Ann (1782–1866) and Jane (1783–1824) Taylor's *Original Poems for Infant Minds: By*

*Several Young Persons* (1804) teaches lessons in the manner of Watts' *Moral Songs*, but with a difference. The vigorous, fun-loving Taylors usually tell good stories in their verse and reveal something of the simple, pleasant life of rural England. The book enjoyed immediate popularity and was translated into various languages, but it is best known today for the familiar "Twinkle, twinkle, little star."

*The Butterfly's Ball*, published in book form in 1807, was written by William Roscoe (1753–1831), a lawyer and member of Parliament, for the amusement of his little son. There is no story, but there are such fascinating details as a mushroom table with a water dock leaf tablecloth, and there are William Mulready's charming pictures of the insect guests at the ball. However, the verse is tame, and the long popularity of the poem must have been due in part to lack of better verse for children.

## DIDACTICISM IN FRANCE, ENGLAND, AND THE UNITED STATES

In 1762 Jean Jacques Rousseau (1712–1778) proclaimed his theory of a new day for children through his book *Émile*. He believed in the joyous unfolding of a child's powers through a free, happy life. The child Émile was the companion of his tutor; he was free of all books except *Robinson Crusoe;* and he lived vigorously out of doors, learning from experiences and activities. Schools today reflect Rousseau's emphasis on experiences and activities.

In its day *Émile* effected a revolutionary change in people's attitudes toward both children and education. To some people, Rousseau seemed like a breeze blowing away the clouds of Puritan morbidity, and one would naturally expect the ardent Rousseau converts, if they wrote books for children, to write only the gayest ones. Instead, in France, in England, and even in the United States, they began to write painfully didactic stories, sometimes to teach religion, sometimes to inform and educate. The only thing these writers seemed to have carried over from Rousseau was the idea of following and developing the child's natural interests. In practice, they went at the business hammer and tongs. If a poor child picked strawberries, the experience was turned into an arithmetic lesson. If he rolled a snowball, he learned about levers and proceeded from those to wedges. If he took a walk, he had to observe every bird, beast, stone, and occupation of man. Day and night these ardent authors stalked their children, allowing them never a moment for play or fancy but instructing and improving on every page. No longer did they threaten the child with the fear of Hell, but the pressure of Information hung almost as heavily over his hapless head.

Here was a revival of didacticism with a vengeance—not the terrifying theological didacticism of the Puritans but the intellectual and moralistic variety. Students who wish to read more about this period should study the works of the French Mme. de Genlis (1746–1830) and Armand Berquin (1749–1791) and those of such English writers as Laetitia Barbauld (1743–1825), Sarah Trimmer (1741–1810), and Hannah More (1745–1833). For most readers, a few examples of this writing will probably suffice.

One of the classic examples of the new didacticism is *The History of Sandford and Merton* (1783–1789) in four volumes by Thomas Day (1748–1789). Tommy Merton was the spoiled, helpless, ignorant son of a rich gentleman, whereas Harry Sandford was the sturdy, industrious, competent child of an honest farmer. Harry was reared out of doors and trained to work and study; there was nothing he did not know and nothing he could not do. Father Merton, handicapped by wealth though he was, saw at once the advantage of having his young darling unspoiled and trained in the ways of the honest Harry. So poor Tommy, little knowing what was in store for him, was put in the charge of

## VIEWPOINTS

Not everyone will agree with me, but we are living in a time when literature aspires more and more to be didactic and utilitarian. It doesn't seem to matter what lesson it teaches—a sociological, psychological or humanistic one—as long as it teaches. There have never been more interpretations of texts or guides for readers who must be led by the hand by the critics. We are no longer allowed to enjoy a sunset without footnotes. . . . Thank God for the children. . . . The child is still selfish to demand an interesting story. He wants surprises and tensions. Our children, God bless them, don't read to discover their identity, as so many wiser adults pretend to do. Young as they are, fresh from the egg, they know exactly who they are, and where they belong. Neither do they read to free themselves from guilt or to quench the thirst for rebellion.—Isaac Bashevis Singer, "I See the Child as a Last Refuge," *The New York Times Book Review*, November 9, 1969, p. 66.

the same clerical tutor who had wrought such wonders with Harry. Mr. Barlow trained both boys, but Harry was always used as the perfect example to show up the ignorance, incompetence, and general orneriness of poor Tommy. All day that worthy pair, the omniscient Barlow and the admirable Harry, instructed, disciplined, and uplifted poor Tommy. Why Tommy did not have enough initiative to use one of his educational levers or wedges to haul off and clout his tormentors is beyond imagination; but no, through each of the volumes, he was plagued and polished into Rousseau-like simplicity and competence. At the end of four volumes, there he was at last—Tommy Merton remodeled, divested of all his fine apparel, his curls gone, and his life to be given over to study and philosophy forever more. Could any reform go further?

Another and perhaps the most gifted exponent of didacticism in children's books was Maria Edgeworth (1767–1849), who told her moral tales with such dramatic realism that they are still remembered. She had an excellent laboratory for developing her stories as she was the second of twenty-two children. She not only helped her father with the education of the younger ones but wrote her stories in their midst, tried them out with the children, and modified them according to their suggestions. Thomas Day himself had a hand in Maria's early education, but her own father seems to have been a greater influence in her writings than anyone else.

Maria Edgeworth wrote many short stories, some deadly dull and unnatural. But at her best, she was a born storyteller. She developed real plots—the first in children's stories since the fairy tales—with well-sustained suspense and surprise endings that took some of the sting out of the inevitable morals. The story that is most frequently quoted and that remained in the anthologies the longest is probably "The Purple Jar," which is sufficiently typical to relate here.

Rosamond, an amiable but thoughtless little girl, was out shopping with her mother. At the sight of all the delightful things displayed in the windows, Rosamond wanted something from each one, but a large purple vase in an apothecary's shop completely charmed her. She felt she could not do without it, although a large hole in her only pair of shoes made it evident that she needed shoes more than purple vases. Her mother, knowing well the fallacy of the jar, gave the guileless child her choice—shoes or jar. Rosamond chose the jar and received it in ecstasy. Once the treasure was in the house, Rosamond was sure she had made the right choice, but her mother bided her time. Wishing to put flowers in the vase, Rosamond empties the purple liquid and lo, she had only a common white glass jar! In tears she begged her mother to take it back and purchase her shoes instead, but Mother insisted that Rosamond must bide by her choice, and so she did, limping miserably for a whole month. At the end of this sad tale Rosamond remarked:

*How I wish I had chosen the shoes! They would have been of so much more use to me than the jar: however, I am sure, no, not quite sure, but I hope I shall be wiser the next time.*

This proves that Rosamond, at least, was a real human being, even if her stern mother was not.

The mother annoys us today because she is insincere and unnatural. Rosamond, on the other hand, except for her language, is all child. The picture of the little girl, standing in the shop in profound meditation over the choice of jar or shoes, is very childlike and genuine. Maria Edgeworth tells an interesting story. But her tales carry such a heavy and obvious burden of moral lessons that her characterizations and excellent plots are sacrificed to didacticism.

One writer of the period, however, not only deplored the pedantic stories written for children but tried to provide them with more entertaining fare. Charles Lamb (1775–1835) and his sister Mary's (1764–1847) best-known contribution to children's literature is their *Tales from Shakespeare* (1806), in which they retold the plays from Shakespeare and made them more easily comprehensible and presumably more enjoyable for the young.

It was inevitable that the United States should develop its own brand of didacticism. Samuel G. Goodrich (1793–1860), who wrote under the name of Peter Parley and produced five or six volumes a year, wrote laudatory biographies of famous men and poured out a continuous stream of information in the fields of science, history, and geography. Jacob Abbott (1803–1879) launched a travel series in which a youth by the name of Rollo was dragged from one city and country to another, bearing up nobly under a steady barrage of travel talks and moralizing. Both men wrote well but pedantically. We shall detect some of their literary descendants in the books of today—information attractively sugared but oppressively informative nevertheless.

Our chief moralist was Martha Farquharson, pseudonym for Martha Finley (1828–1909), whose *Elsie Dinsmore* series began in 1868 and ran to twenty-six volumes. This pious heroine had a way of bursting into tears or fainting with such effect that adult sinners were converted and even Elsie's worldly father was brought to a state of repentance. Little girls cried their way through all twenty-six volumes. Most parents developed considerable resistance to Elsie but were baffled by her powers to charm their offspring. Elsie was a spellbinder, for her author had a sense of the dramatic. To this day sensible women remember weeping over Elsie's Sabbath sit-down strike at the piano, when she refused to play the secular music for her erring father. She was made to sit on the piano stool until one of her best faints put an end to her martyrdom and Father repented. Elsie was a prig with glamour, and there is no telling how many more of her kind might have developed if certain pioneers had not appeared to clear away the artificiality and to bring laughter, fantasy, and realism to children's books.

## MODERN BOOKS BEGIN

Even while Peter Parley was dispensing information, and Maria Edgeworth was teaching little Rosamond valuable lessons, and Martha Finley's heroine, Elsie Dinsmore, was piously swooning, epoch-making books in both England and the United States were appearing that were to modify the whole approach to children's literature. These children's classics, some as popular today as when they were first published, not only brought laughter, fantasy, and realism into stories for young people, but they began the trend toward better illustrations in children's books. Each of these books will be discussed in greater detail in later chapters; they are reviewed here because they are milestones in the development of children's literature.

### Folk and Fairy Tales

*Grimms' Popular Stories* by Jacob (1785–1863) and Wilhelm (1786–1859) Grimm was translated into English by Edgar Taylor in 1823. Grimms' Fairy Tales, as they were called by the children, became as much a part of the literature of English-speaking children as their own *Mother Goose* rhymes. These stories, some of them gathered by the Grimm brothers from the lips of the old storytellers, were occasionally droll but often somber and harrowing.

*Illustration by George Cruikshank for* Grimms' Popular Stories.

The *Fairy Tales* of Hans Christian Andersen (1805–1875) appeared in England in 1846, translated by Mary Howitt. Many of these stories were Andersen's own adaptations of folk tales which he, too, had heard from the storytellers. But to these he added his own fanciful inventions and immeasurably enriched the child's world of the imagination. Andersen's stories have unusual literary and spiritual values, and they are, for the most part, in a minor key, melancholy and even tragic.

Joseph Jacobs (1854–1916) was the great compiler of English folk tales; and the folklorist Andrew Lang (1844–1912) began, in 1889, with the publication of *The Blue Fairy Book*, a series that is still deservedly popular.

### Humor

One of the first notes of gaiety was a long story poem by Clement Moore called "A Visit from St. Nicholas" (1822), but known to children as "The Night Before Christmas." This fast-moving, humorous ballad, full of fun, fancy, and excitement, with never a threat or a dire warning to spoil the children's delight, is as beloved now as it was in Moore's day.

Under Queen Victoria, England's industrial age flourished and grew prosperous and pompous. Then suddenly two eminent men produced books that sent the children off into gales of laughter. One, Edward Lear (1812–1888), was an artist who earned his living by making scientific paintings of birds and reptiles. When he grew too bored with the drawing room, he took refuge with the children. For them he would write absurd limericks which he would illustrate on the spot. His *Book of Nonsense* (1846) not only was an unprecedented collection of amusing verses and pictures but perhaps paved the way for another excursion into absurdity.

In 1865 a book appeared that is generally considered the first English masterpiece written for children. It was *Alice's Adventures in Wonderland*. The author was Charles Lutwidge Dodgson (1832–1898), an Oxford don, a lecturer in logic and mathematics, who used the pen name Lewis Carroll. *Alice* still remains a unique combination of fantasy and nonsense that is as logical as an equation. It was first told, and later written, solely for the entertainment of children, and neither it nor its sequel, *Through the Looking Glass*, has the faintest trace of a moral or a scrap of useful information or one improving lesson—only cheerful lunacy, daft and delightful. *Alice* launched the literature of nonsense and fantasy which is so gravely and reasonably related that it seems as real as rain, as natural as going to sleep.

Two more books brought laughter to children. Written in Germany in 1844 and published the next year, *Struwwelpeter* (Slovenly Peter), by Heinrich Hoffmann (1809–1894), was a collection of merry, prankish rhyming stories intended only to entertain, although the verses are regarded by some people as brutal. It is still in print, having gone into dozens of editions in English, with one translation by Mark Twain. In America, children were captivated by the antics of the Peterkin family. Lucretia Hale (1820–1900) published a series of stories about the Peterkins in magazines, collected them in a book in 1880, and gave the young an unforgettable character: the Lady from Philadelphia.

### Illustrations

Both Lear's and Carroll's laughter-provoking books have delightful illustrations—Lear's own outrageous caricatures for his *Book of Nonsense* and Sir John Tenniel's inimitable drawings for Carroll's *Alice*. Deservedly famous, too, are Walter Crane, Randolph Caldecott, and Kate Greenaway,[9] whose charming watercolors brightened the pages of children's books with decorative designs, appealing landscapes, and figures which hold their own with the best in the modern books.

When Frederic G. Melcher in 1938 sponsored a second award—this time for the most distinguished picture book for children published each year in the United States—he named it the Caldecott Medal after Randolph Caldecott. The award is a fitting memorial to the man who drew a picture of himself surrounded by children, and who left those children a legacy of gay storytelling pictures.[10]

9. See Chapter 3 for a fuller account of illustrators of children's books.

10. For a list of the books which have been awarded the Caldecott Medal see "Book Awards" in the Appendix.

### Myths: Hawthorne and Kingsley

In the United States Greek myths were introduced to children by a gifted novelist, Nathaniel Hawthorne (1804–1864). Around 1852 *A Wonder-Book for Girls and Boys* was published, followed in 1853 by *Tanglewood Tales for Girls and Boys*. These books contain stories of the Greek gods and heroes, supposedly told to a group of lively New England children by a young college student, Eustace Bright. Eustace talks down to the children; his gods lose much of their grandeur, and his heroes are often child-sized. But the stories have a delightful style, and the chatty interludes of banter between Eustace and the children provide pleasant pictures of the New England outdoor world.

In England, Charles Kingsley (1819–1875), country parson, Victorian scholar and poet, also retold the myths for children. His adaptations not only are closer to the original myths than Hawthorne's romantic versions, but convey the inner significance and grandeur of the myths in a style closer to the classic original. Here are dreams of greatness, presented with the sensitive perception of a poet. Oddly enough, in Kingsley's own day these stories were less popular than his original fantasy, *The Water-Babies* (1863), which is marred for us today by its moralizing.

### Modern Fantasy

Lewis Carroll's *Alice* was the great masterpiece of fantasy and nonsense, but the nineteenth century saw the publication of several other classics in fantasy for children. In 1841, John Ruskin (1819–1900) wrote *The King of the Golden River*, a long, serious fairy tale, and published it a decade later. In 1867, George Macdonald (1824–1905), Scottish poet and novelist, published a delightfully playful tale, *The Light Princess*, and, four years later, his most important children's fairy tale, the imaginative *At the Back of the North Wind*.

Some of the other great British writers of the period tried their hands at fantasy for children. William Makepeace Thackeray (1811–1863) contributed, in 1855, *The Rose and the Ring*, a book-length fairy tale distinguished by blithe humor; and in 1868, Charles Dickens (1812–1870) wrote, in the best fairy-tale tradition, *The Magic Fishbone*. Dickens' earlier story, *A Christmas Carol* (1843), is firmly ensconced in the list of hardy perennials of both Christmas literature and Victoriana. Rudyard Kipling (1865–1936), storyteller and poet, Nobel Prize winner and advocate of empire, wrote *The Jungle Books* (1894) and *Just So Stories* (1902) with a warmth and affection that make his animal characters part of the permanent heritage of children's lore, along with Beatrix Potter's *The Tale of Peter Rabbit* (1901) and Kenneth Grahame's *The Wind in the Willows* (1908).

From France came the stories of Jules Verne (1828–1905), who wrote for adults but whose books have fascinated children since the first, *From the Earth to the Moon*, was published in 1865. *Twenty Thousand Leagues Under the Sea* (1869) and *Around the World in Eighty Days* (1872) are still popular with adults as well as children. In Verne's work, one sees the beginning of a new genre, the science-fiction story.

*Illustration by Arthur Hughes for* At the Back of the North Wind *by George Macdonald.*

From Italy came *Pinocchio* by Collodi (pseudonym for Carlo Lorenzini, 1826–1890). Published originally in a magazine, as so many books of this period were, the story was translated in 1892 to become one of the enduring classics of the world literature for children.

Edith Nesbit (1858–1924) was one of the first and still is one of the best craftsmen in combining realism and fantasy. Her first story, *The Story of the Treasure Seekers*, was published in 1899.

### Realistic Stories

During the Victorian period there was an increasing awareness of, and response to, children's needs. In England the awareness was most evident in the work of Charlotte Yonge (1823–1901), who wrote family stories, based on her own happy childhood, and some school stories, sentimental in tone, moral in intent, and realistic in approach. Her prolific output (well over a hundred books) was read avidly by children of the period.

In the United States our epoch-making book was a modest story of family life, *Little Women*, like Charlotte Yonge's books, based on the author's own family experiences. The author, Louisa M. Alcott (1832–1888), submitted the manuscript hesitatingly, and her publisher had to tell her as gently as possible how unacceptable it was. Fortunately, he felt some qualms about his judgment and allowed the children of his family to read the manuscript. They convinced him that he was wrong. Those astute little girls loved the book, and it has remained popular with children since its publication in 1868. The story is as genuine a bit of realism as we have ever had. Family life is there—from the kitchen to the sanctuary of the attic, from reading to giving amateur dramatics in which the homemade scenery collapses. But right as all the details are, the reason the adults remember the book is the masterly characterizations of the four girls. No longer are people typed to represent Ignorance or Virtue, but here are flesh-and-blood girls, as different from each other as they could well be, full of human folly and human courage, never self-righteous, sometimes irritable but never failing in warm affection for each other. This ability to make her characters vividly alive was Louisa M. Alcott's gift to modern realism for children.

In his adventure stories for boys, England's George Henty (1832–1902) used his own experiences as a correspondent to furnish the backgrounds; in the same field in the United States, William Taylor Adams (1822–1897) wrote under the fetching pen name of Oliver Optic. That supreme purveyor of the rags to riches books, Horatio Alger (1834–1899), captivated the young with *Ragged Dick* (1867) and all the succeeding stories in the same pattern.

So far, on both sides of the Atlantic, realistic stories for children were primarily about eminently respectable characters. When Samuel Clemens (1835–1910), or Mark Twain as he signed himself, wrote *The Adventures of Tom Sawyer* in 1876, he carried realism across the tracks. In this book Huck and his disreputable father were probably the child's first literary encounters with real people who were not considered respectable but who were likable anyway. Moreover, they were not typed to show the folly of being disreputable, but Huckleberry Finn won all hearts and so nearly stole the book from Tom that he had to appear in a book of his own—*The Adventures of Huckleberry Finn* (1884). Mark Twain in these two unsurpassed books not only gave us realism with humor but also showed warm tolerance in his presentation of socially undesirable people.

## CHILDREN'S LITERATURE COMES OF AGE

The Victorian period saw the stream of cheerfulness in children's literature rise steadily. Many of the books written then are still popular and will be considered in detail later. This list is a reminder of these and others that are milestones in the development of children's literature from 1484–1908.

1484 *Aesop's Fables*, translated and printed by William Caxton.
1646 *Spiritual Milk for Boston Babes*, John Cotton.
1657 or 1658 *Orbis Pictus*, Comenius (original in Latin).
1678 *Pilgrim's Progress*, John Bunyan.
1691 *The New England Primer.*
1697 *Contes de ma Mère l'Oye*, Perrault.
1715 *Divine and Moral Songs for Children*, Isaac Watts.
1719 *Robinson Crusoe*, Daniel Defoe.
1726 *Gulliver's Travels*, Jonathan Swift.
1729 *Tales of Mother Goose*, Perrault (first English translation).
1744 *A Little Pretty Pocket-Book.*
1765 *The Renowned History of Little Goody Two Shoes.*
1781 *Mother Goose's Melody.*
1785 *Mother Goose's Melodies* (Isaiah Thomas edition).
1789 *Songs of Innocence*, William Blake.
1804 *Original Poems for Infant Minds*, Ann and Jane Taylor.
1807 *The Butterfly's Ball*, William Roscoe.
1822 *A Visit from St. Nicholas*, Clement C. Moore.
1823 *Grimms' Popular Stories* (translated into English by Edgar Taylor).
1843 *A Christmas Carol*, Charles Dickens.
1846 *Book of Nonsense*, Edward Lear.
1846 *Fairy Tales*, Hans Christian Andersen (first English translation).
1848 *Struwwelpeter*, Heinrich Hoffmann (first English translation).
1852 *A Wonder-Book for Girls and Boys*, Nathaniel Hawthorne.

1865 *Alice's Adventures in Wonderland*, Lewis Carroll (Charles Lutwidge Dodgson).
1865 *Hans Brinker, or the Silver Skates*, Mary Mapes Dodge.
1867–1876 *Sing a Song of Sixpence*, and other toy books, illustrated by Walter Crane.
1868–1869 *Little Women*, Louisa M. Alcott.
1871 *At the Back of the North Wind*, George Macdonald.
1872 *Sing-Song*, Christina Rossetti.
1876 *The Adventures of Tom Sawyer*, Mark Twain (Samuel Clemens).
1878 *Under the Window*, Kate Greenaway.
1878 *The House That Jack Built* and *The Diverting History of John Gilpin*, illustrated by Randolph Caldecott.
1880 *The Peterkin Papers*, Lucretia Hale.
1883 *Treasure Island*, Robert Louis Stevenson.
1883 *Nights with Uncle Remus*, Joel Chandler Harris.
1883 *The Merry Adventures of Robin Hood*, Howard Pyle.
1884 *Heidi*, Johanna Spyri (date of English translation).
1884 *The Adventures of Huckleberry Finn*, Mark Twain (Samuel Clemens).
1885 *A Child's Garden of Verses*, Robert Louis Stevenson.
1889 *The Blue Fairy Book*, Andrew Lang.
1891 *Pinocchio*, C. Collodi (Carlo Lorenzini). First English translation.
1894 *The Jungle Books*, Rudyard Kipling.
1899 *The Story of the Treasure Seekers*, E. Nesbit.
1901 *The Tale of Peter Rabbit*, Beatrix Potter.
1903 *Johnny Crow's Garden*, L. Leslie Brooke.
1908 *The Wind in the Willows*, Kenneth Grahame.

These are individual books that were turning points in children's literature. They not only carry us into the twentieth century with distinction, but their influence is discernible in the writing of today. Laura Richards continued the deft nonsense verses of Lear and Carroll in her *Tirra Lirra* (1932). A. A. Milne's skillful light verse, *When We Were Very Young* (1924), did as much to popularize poetry for young children in schools and homes as Robert Louis Stevenson had done earlier. The small, sweet lyrics of Christina Rossetti were followed by the exquisite poetry of Walter de la Mare and by poetry with the delicacy of Aileen Fisher, the humor of David McCord, the evocative directness of Langston Hughes.

*Illustration by Laura Bannon for* Tales from a Finnish Tupa *by James Cloyd Bowman and Margery Bianco. Copyright © 1936. Reproduced by permission of Albert Whitman & Company.*

In the field of fairy tales and fantasy, *East o' the Sun and West o' the Moon* continued the interest in folklore that began with the Grimms. American children could share in the literary heritage of other lands with books like *Tales from a Finnish Tupa* (1936), Indian fables in the several versions of the Jataka stories, and Japanese folk tales in *The Dancing Teakettle* (1949). From the Uncle Remus collections there came a new consciousness of the United States as a repository of regional and racial folklore. *The Jack Tales* (1943), southern variants of European folk tales, stemmed from this interest. If the Italian fairy tale *Pinocchio* (1891) was the gay descendant of Andersen's somber toy stories, so too was the young and equally light-hearted *Winnie-the-Pooh* (1926). Gulliver's Lilliput was not more fascinating than the miniature world of *The Borrowers* (1952). *Rabbit Hill* (1944) continued the great tradition of animal fantasy begun in *The Wind in the Willows*, to be followed by *Charlotte's Web* (1952), *The Cricket in Times Square* (1960), *Animal Family* (1965), and *Jason's Quest* (1970). And the daft world of *Alice's Adventures in Wonderland* grew perceptibly zanier in the fantastic dreams of Dr. Seuss.

True Americana began with *Little Women* and *Tom Sawyer* and continued to flourish in descendants such as *Little House in the Big Woods* (1932), *Caddie Woodlawn* (1935), the three books about *The Moffats* (1941–1943), and *Across Five Aprils* (1964). It is there, too, in the fine animal story *Smoky* (1926), written in the vernacular of a cowboy, and in an excellent story of the South in the depression era, *The Rock and the Willow* (1963). And it is certainly alive in such regional stories as *Strawberry Girl* (1945), *. . . and now Miguel* (1953), and *Island of the Blue Dolphins* (1960).

The picture story so charmingly begun by Beatrix Potter continues in the varied books of Wanda Gág, Maurice Sendak, Marie Ets, and many others. And if stories of other lands began auspiciously with *Hans Brinker* and *Heidi*, they have grown and strengthened in *The Good Master* (1935), *The Ark* (1953), *The Wheel on the School* (1954), *The Happy Orpheline* (1957), *The Silver Sword* (1959), and *Wildcat Under Glass* (1968). So the types of books that were turning points in children's literature at an earlier period are perpetuated today, although the kinship between the old and the new may sometimes seem remote.

*Illustration by Attilio Mussino for* Pinocchio *by Carlo Collodi. Copyright reissued 1969. Reproduced by permission of The Macmillan Company. (Original in color)*

Of the many good books that have been published in the twentieth century, some stand out. Probably no two people would agree on every one that merits inclusion in a list of landmark books; the older classics have proved themselves, the new ones have yet to do so. Still, some seem milestones either because they are distinguished of their kind or because they have broken new ground, or—as in the past—they are adult books that have been taken by children as their own.

1921 *The Story of Mankind*, Hendrik Willem van Loon.
1926 *Smoky, the Cow Horse*, Will James.
1926 *Winnie-the-Pooh*, A. A. Milne.
1928 *Millions of Cats*, Wanda Gág.
1928 *Abe Lincoln Grows Up*, Carl Sandburg.
1932 *Little House in the Big Woods*, Laura Ingalls Wilder.
1934 *Mary Poppins*, Pamela Travers.
1937 *The Hobbit*, J. R. R. Tolkien.

1941 *George Washington's World*, Genevieve Foster.
1941 *Paddle-to-the-Sea*, Holling C. Holling.
1943 *Homer Price*, Robert McCloskey.
1943 *Johnny Tremain*, Esther Forbes.
1944 *Rabbit Hill*, Robert Lawson.
1947 *The Twenty-One Balloons*, William Pène du Bois.
1952 *Charlotte's Web*, E. B. White.
1959 *America Is Born, a History for Peter*, Gerald W. Johnson.
1961 *The Incredible Journey*, Sheila Burnford.
1962 *The Snowy Day*, Ezra Jack Keats.
1963 *Where the Wild Things Are*, Maurice Sendak.
1964 *Harriet the Spy*, Louise Fitzhugh.
1964 *The Pushcart War*, Jean Merrill.
1964 *The Book of Three*, Lloyd Alexander.

## TRENDS IN CHILDREN'S BOOKS TODAY

What, we may ask, are the trends in writing for children today? A glance at the past makes it clear that nothing today is completely new, but certainly some types of books are better written today than ever before and are enjoying such tremendous popularity that they seem to mark a trend.

An interesting phenomenon has been the growth of the picture book. Not since that famous triumvirate, Caldecott, Crane, and Greenaway, have so many artists lavished so much effort and talent on books for young children. Lynd Ward, himself an artist, wrote ". . . the book work of the thirties that is most significant in itself, and in terms of what it contributes to the world at large, was done in picture-book form."[11] Mr. Ward's own *Biggest Bear* is an excellent example. Sharing such a book with children, adults find themselves as charmed with the pictures as are the children. Someone has said that a wonderful way to teach art appreciation would be through children's picture books which run the whole gamut of styles and techniques. Ezra Jack Keats uses collage with great effect; Marcia Brown combines quiet colors and bold designs in handsome woodcuts. Harold Jones' pictures for *Lavender's Blue (Mother Goose)* are in strong, dark colors

*Illustration by Lynd Ward for* The Biggest Bear. *Copyright © 1952. Reproduced by permission of Houghton Mifflin Company.*

### VIEWPOINTS

One thing that emerges clearly is that most . . . trends are pragmatic phenomena—they derive from market and/or need. So it goes back to the consumer, and you, dear reader, set the trends. Please make them good ones, I beg of you. The thing to keep in mind is that all trends start somewhere—with a prototype that is frequently the brainchild of an author who is lucky enough to have an editor who refuses to think in terms of trends. In my case, the refusal to believe in trends in what I publish comes from my staunch belief in the minority—if *I* really love a book, there's got to be a kid like me somewhere—and even if it develops that the audience and therefore the market for the book is a very small select minority indeed, it was still worth publishing.—Ann Durell, "Goodies and Baddies," *The Wilson Library Bulletin*, December 1969, p. 457.

11. "The Book Artist: Yesterday and Tomorrow," in *Illustrators of Children's Books, 1744–1945*, comp. by Bertha E. Mahony, Louise P. Latimer, and Beulah Folmsbee, 1947, p. 254.

and in an older style of realism with impressive composition. Marie Hall Ets' *Play with Me*, one of the most sensitive and perfect picture stories ever made for the three- to seven-year-olds, is in delicate springtime colors that illumine each episode. Nicolas Mordvinoff, in a protest against prettified art for children, uses bold, bright colors and humorous composition. Nancy Burkert, Marguerite de Angeli, and Adrienne Adams are not afraid of delicate beauty of details and figures. And for complete contrast look at the modern, stylized art in the striking picture books illustrated by Nicolas Sidjakov. Reflecting the emergence of pop art and grotesquerie, and possibly in ineffectual imitation of Maurice Sendak's illustrations, there have been increasing numbers of picture books, as well as illustrations in books for older children, with grim or bizarre illustrations. But despite some unfortunate and unsuccessful experiments, today's picture book is exciting art with endless possibilities.

There is also an increased interest in poetry both in and out of our schools. New books of poems appear often and, what is more, they sell. Many of the poets today may be "new singers of small songs," but there are authentic poets of childhood, too. Before his death, Robert Frost gave children and youth *You Come Too*, a fine selection from his poems. Harry Behn has composed some choice lyrics, and David McCord and John Ciardi enliven the scene with extraordinarily clever nonsense verse. Poetry anthologies like *Black Out Loud*, edited by Arnold Adoff, have introduced many new black American poets, and Virginia Olsen Baron's compilation of poems by young people from minority groups, *Here I Am!* reflects the interest young people have in writing poetry. A good all-around anthology is *Every Child's Book of Verse*, compiled by Sarah Chokla Gross; another excellent collection is *The Oxford Book of Poetry for Children*, edited by Edward Blishen and delightfully illustrated by Brian Wildsmith. Moreover, in the schools children are speaking poetry informally or in verse choirs with unfeigned enjoyment. Adults are reading poetry aloud and listening to poetry records and readings. Such delightful books as Aileen Fisher's *Going Barefoot* or Paul Galdone's beautifully illustrated edition of *Paul Revere's Ride* might have gone unsold twenty years ago. Today their popularity is assured.

In 1921, Hendrik Willem van Loon's *Story of Mankind* launched a fresh interest in biographies and informational books, both of which have developed into major trends. Authentic, well-written biographies are popular with adults today and equally popular with children and youth. Elizabeth Janet Gray's *Penn*, Jean Latham's *Carry On, Mr. Bowditch*, Sidney Rosen's *Doctor Paracelsus*, Elizabeth Yates' *Amos Fortune, Free Man*, Nardi Campion's *Patrick Henry*—these and many others mark biography as one of the most distinguished types of juvenile literature.

As adolescents have become more sophisticated and aware and have voiced their concern with current social problems, publishers and authors have responded with books on war, the stock market, ecology, pollution, student protest, conservation, the political scene, international relations, and the role of women.

In the sciences, books have reflected the increasing complexity of school curricula and general knowledge. Each advance in space exploration produces a throng of new books, and there is a noticeable trend toward publication of such books for younger and still younger readers. Particularly evident is the growing interest in biological frontiers and in science books with sociological implications for younger children.

Numerically, informational books threaten to outdistance all other types put together. From people and places to weather and worms, from stones to stars, from dinosaurs to missiles, from insects to astronauts, science and social studies books for children pour off the presses. The books are attractive and their content is designed for particular reading levels and understanding. Their numbers and variety are so staggering that they are more than a trend; they are practically an inundation.

A frequently used technique in informational books in the social studies has become so popular that it might be called a trend: combining photographs with a first-person text to picture a child's life in one part of another country, thus giving a detailed report rather than the usual broad, general account that covers many aspects of another land. These books are often in series; few of them have achieved the level of dependability of the Gidals' "My Village" books. The photo-documentary technique also has become popular in books about urban life, particularly life in black neighborhoods.

Certainly the books by, for, and about blacks have been one of the most significant of major trends. There were comparatively few such books earlier in the twentieth century, but the 1960s produced a spate of them, long overdue—books that have faced the problems of black people; fiction with exciting plots, interesting settings, and well-drawn, appealing black heroes and heroines for characters; picture books in which only the illustrations indicated that the characters were black (see, for example, Ezra Jack Keats' stories about Peter in *The Snowy Day* and its sequels); biographies of long-neglected black people of note (Harriet Tubman, Frederick Douglass, Mary McLeod Bethune, Benjamin Banneker, Paul Dunbar, Phillis Wheatley, etc.); and poetry about and by black people.

As adult literature has become more sophisticated and frank in its use of language, and permissive in its treatment of hitherto-taboo subjects, so books for young people have to a certain degree followed suit with such books as Emily Cheney Neville's *Fogarty* and Lee Kingman's *The Peter Pan Bag*. While many of these books seem concocted, there has been a growing number in which controversial themes are handled with dignity and honesty—books in which sexual and psychological problems are faced, in which siblings and parents may be hostile, in which teen-agers use the language that readers are well aware is used in real life. No longer are parents sacrosanct, all-wise, and benevolent; no longer do books for young people ignore drug addiction, sexual deviation, serious maladjustment, adultery, or racial violence. Like adult books, the worst are cheap shockers; and the best—fiction and nonfiction—are thoughtful avenues to clarification or solution of attitudes and problems.

Another trend is the publication in the United States, either in separate editions or translations, of books from other countries. Concurrently, many of our books are translated into other languages and are therefore familiar to the children of other nations. That this trend will continue is almost assured by the increasing intercommunication among authors, illustrators, editors, librarians, and

## VIEWPOINTS

Where American books are concerned the condition of North American society is being translated into children's books quite clearly, but with one notable difference from the past. As society in general does not seem to know what to say to its children and cannot express itself with one voice, we have both a literature of 'personal decision', which suggests that each young person has to come to terms with life on an individual basis, and a literature of conformity. Many writers move uneasily between the two, exhibiting their own cloudy view of life and of contemporary problems. The form most writers use is realistic fiction or contemporary-scene fiction and they try to 'tell it like it is' in areas such as the 'personal' problems of young people, race relationships, alcoholism, drug addiction, violence, and war. . . .—Sheila Egoff, "Precepts and Pleasures: Changing Emphases in the Writing and Criticism of Children's Literature," in *Only Connect; Readings on Children's Literature*, edited by Sheila Egoff, G. T. Stubbs, and L. F. Ashley, Oxford University Press, Toronto, New York, 1969, p. 433.

teachers who exchange journals, participate in international meetings, serve together on boards and committees, and share their concerns about children and books the world over.

What is a trend? Observe a pattern long enough and you are looking backward; to label a current change a trend is to make a judgment about the importance of a development that may prove to be ephemeral. It is within the context of the historic pattern that you must decide. It is against the background of the past—the changed concept of childhood, the establishment of universal education, the growing numbers of libraries for children, the evaluation of literary quality in the elementary school classroom—that publishers have established a broad program of special publishing for children. It is impressive by its sheer weight; it has responded with sensitivity to curricular needs and current interests; it has made reading material more accessible by mass distribution of inexpensive flats (oversized books with few pages and cheap printing) and by a rapidly expanding production of paperback editions of established books—one of the most significant trends in bookmaking. Furthermore, many publishers are broadening their programs to include book-oriented films, film strips, cassettes, and other audio-visual media; and some have established flourishing book clubs. Without any doubt, these are exciting and productive times in the field of children's literature.

## ADULT REFERENCES [12]

ASHTON, JOHN. *Chap-Books of the Eighteenth Century.*

BARCHILON, JACQUES, and HENRY PETTIT. *The Authentic Mother Goose Fairy Tales and Nursery Rhymes.*

BARRY, FLORENCE V. *A Century of Children's Books.*

BETT, HENRY. *The Games of Children; Their Origin and History.*

12. Complete bibliographic data are provided in the combined Adult References in the Appendices.

CHAMBERS, ROBERT. *Popular Rhymes of Scotland.*

COMENIUS, JOHANN AMOS. *The Orbis Pictus of John Amos Comenius.*

CROUCH, MARCUS. *Treasure Seekers and Borrowers: Children's Books in Britain, 1900–1960.*

DARLING, RICHARD L. *The Rise of Children's Book Reviewing in America, 1865–1881.*

DARTON, F. J. H. *Children's Books in England: Five Centuries of Social Life.*

DAVIS, MARY GOULD. *Randolph Caldecott 1846–1886: An Appreciation.*

DE VRIES, LEONARD. *Little Wide-Awake: An Anthology from Victorian Children's Books and Periodicals in the Collection of Anne and Fernand G. Renier.*

DOYLE, BRIAN, comp. and ed. *The Who's Who of Children's Literature.*

EDEN, HORATIA K. F. *Juliana Horatia Ewing and Her Books.*

ELLIS, ALEC. *A History of Children's Reading and Literature.*

ERNEST, EDWARD, comp., assisted by PATRICIA TRACY LOWE. *The Kate Greenaway Treasury.*

FIELD, ELINOR WHITNEY, comp. *Horn Book Reflections: On Children's Books and Reading.*

FIELD, LOUISE F. *The Child and His Book: Some Account of the History and Progress of Children's Literature in England.*

FOLMSBEE, BEULAH. *A Little History of the Horn-Book.*

FORD, PAUL LEICESTER, ed. *The New England Primer.*

FORD, ROBERT. *Children's Rhymes, Children's Games, Children's Songs, Children's Stories: A Book for Bairns and Big Folk.*

FRYE, BURTON C., ed. *A St. Nicholas Anthology; The Early Years.*

GILLESPIE, MARGARET C. *Literature for Children: History and Trends.*

GREEN, ROGER LANCELYN. *Tellers of Tales.*

HALES, JOHN W., and FREDERICK J. FURNIVALL, assisted by FRANCIS J. CHILD. *Bishop Percy's Folio Manuscript.*

HALSEY, ROSALIE V. *Forgotten Books of the American Nursery; A History of the Development of the American Story-Book.*

HAVILAND, VIRGINIA. *Children's Literature: A Guide to Reference Sources.*

HAZARD, PAUL. *Books, Children and Men.*

HEWINS, CAROLINE M. *A Mid-Century Child and Her Books.*

HÜRLIMANN, BETTINA. *Three Centuries of Children's Books in Europe.*

JORDAN, ALICE M. *From Rollo to Tom Sawyer.*

KIEFER, MONICA. *American Children Through Their Books, 1700–1835.*

LANG, ANDREW, ed. *Perrault's Popular Tales.*

McGUFFEY, WILLIAM HOLMES. *Old Favorites from the McGuffey Readers.*

MAHONY, BERTHA E., LOUISE P. LATIMER, and BEULAH FOLMSBEE, comps. *Illustrators of Children's Books, 1744–1945.*

MEIGS, CORNELIA, ANNE EATON, ELIZABETH NESBITT, and RUTH HILL VIGUERS. *A Critical History of Children's Literature.*

MOORE, ANNE CARROLL. *My Roads to Childhood.*

MUIR, PERCY. *English Children's Books, 1600 to 1900.*

OPIE, IONA and PETER. *The Lore and Language of Schoolchildren.*

———, eds. *The Oxford Dictionary of Nursery Rhymes.*

*The Original Mother Goose's Melody, As First Issued by John Newbery, of London, about A.D. 1760.*

PELLOWSKI, ANNE. *The World of Children's Literature.*

ROSELLE, DANIEL. *Samuel Griswold Goodrich, Creator of Peter Parley; A Study of His Life and Work.*

ROSENBACH, ABRAHAM S. W. *Early American Children's Books with Bibliographical Descriptions of the Books in His Private Collection.*

ST. JOHN, JUDITH. *The Osborne Collection of Early Children's Books 1566–1910; A Catalogue.*

SMITH, DORA V. *Fifty Years of Children's Books.*

SMITH, IRENE. *A History of the Newbery and Caldecott Medals.*

TARG, WILLIAM, ed. *Bibliophile in the Nursery.*

TOWNSEND, JOHN ROWE. *Written for Children: An Outline of English Children's Literature.*

TUER, ANDREW W. *Pages and Pictures from Forgotten Children's Books; Brought Together and Introduced to the Reader.*

———, *Stories from Old-Fashioned Children's Books.*

VIGUERS, RUTH HILL, MARCIA DALPHIN, and BERTHA MAHONY MILLER, comps. *Illustrators of Children's Books, 1946–1956.*

WEISS, HARRY B. *A Book About Chapbooks; The People's Literature of Bygone Times.*

WELSH, CHARLES. *A Bookseller of the Last Century, Being some Account of the Life of John Newbery, and of the Books he published with a Notice of the later Newberys.*

———, ed. *The Renowned History of Little Goody Two Shoes, Otherwise Called Mrs. Margery Two Shoes.*

# Chapter 5
# Mother Goose and the Ballads

Small children acquire a love for poetry as naturally as did people of early times, through hearing poems spoken or sung and through learning them, almost unconsciously, along with the speaker or singer. Long, long ago, mothers, grannies, and nurses diverted crying babies by playing with their toes—"This little pig went to market," or making a game—"Pat-a-cake, pat-a-cake," or chanting a nonsense rhyme with a catch tune—"Hickory, dickory, dock." In the same long ago, grownups were entertained by gifted minstrels chanting stories of heroic battles or sad romances or human absurdities. These old nursery ditties and ancient ballads were easily remembered and passed on by word of mouth for generations before they achieved the permanency of print and became known as *Mother Goose* and traditional (or popular) ballads. These folk rhymes are still important not only because children and youth continue to enjoy them and even to make up their own ballads, but because many are skillfully composed, exuberant or dramatic, and lead naturally into modern nonsense verse and narrative poems.[1]

1. Many of the poems discussed but not reprinted in this book can be found in the anthology *Time for Poetry*, gen. ed., comp. by May Hill Arbuthnot and Shelton Root, Jr. (Scott, Foresman, 1968).

## MOTHER GOOSE

One of the opening pages of an old edition of *Mother Goose* contains a picture of an ancient crone admonishing two small children. The picture is followed by the text of her lecture. Mark its words well, for this is Ma'am Goose herself, addressing her "dear little blossoms." As you read, you discover that the good dame is distinctly irritated. She is relieving her mind in no uncertain terms concerning those misguided reformers who are forever pestering mothers to discard her soothing ditties in favor of more educational and uplifting verses. After defending her jingles lustily, the good dame rends her long-faced critics with a particularly withering blast:

> *Fudge! I tell you that all their batterings can't deface my beauties, nor their wise pratings equal my wiser prattlings; and all imitators of my refreshing songs might as well write a new Billy Shakespeare as another Mother Goose—we two great poets were born together, and we shall go out of the world together.*
>
> *No, no, my Melodies will never die,*
> *While nurses sing, or babies cry.*[2]

2. *The Only True Mother Goose Melodies* (Reprinted by Lothrop, Lee and Shepard Co., Boston, 1905, from the Munro and Francis edition, Boston, 1833).

*From* Oxford Nursery Rhyme Book *by Iona and Peter Opie. Reproduced by permission of The Clarendon Press, Oxford.*

The idea of Mother Goose calmly associating herself with Shakespeare and asserting an immortality equal to his is not so farfetched as it may seem. Moreover, this spirited defense of a book that long ago proved itself a nursery classic is as timely today as it was in 1833. For some people are always arising to protest that *Mother Goose* is out of date, that her vocabulary is all wrong, that her subjects are not sufficiently "here and now."[3] Despite these protests, the children go right on crying for her ditties, and mothers know well her power to soothe "won't-be-comforted little bairns."

## WHO WAS MOTHER GOOSE?

Where did these verses come from? Who was Mother Goose? These are questions that occur to us as we turn over the pages of some beguiling modern editions. The answers are sometimes confusing; it is sometimes difficult to distinguish legends from facts, but it is illuminating to discover how these nursery songs are linked with our historical and literary past.

### Dame Goose of Boston

In the Old Granary Burying Ground in the heart of downtown Boston there is a flock of little tombstones bearing the name of Goose. One particular stone is supposed to mark the resting place of none other than the famous Dame Goose herself. Many a Boston child, gazing with awe at this small tombstone, has visualized the beak-nosed old woman, with a suggestion of wings in her sharp shoulder blades, ready to go up in glory, chanting:

*Old Mother Goose, when*
*She wanted to wander,*
*Would ride through the air*
*On a very fine gander.*

Unfortunately, the Boston Dame Goose was not the author of these verses and her son-in-law did not publish them in 1719. Both beliefs are wholly legendary. Indeed, the verses came chiefly from England and the name came from France.

### Ma Mère l'Oye

The name *Mother Goose*, as Chapter 4 explains, was first associated with the eight folk tales recorded by Perrault. Andrew Lang, in *Perrault's Popular Tales*, tells us that the frontispiece of *Histoires ou contes du temps passé, avec des moralités* (Histories or Tales of Long Ago, with Morals) showed an old woman spinning and telling stories, and that a placard on the same page bore the words "Contes de ma Mère l'Oye" (Tales of Mother Goose). But the name *Mother Goose* has now become so completely associated with the popular verses that most English

3. For example, in a July 16, 1970, *Chicago Tribune* article by Joan Beck, Mother Goose apparently was described as outdated, "bad psychology, bad philosophy, bad education and bad poetry." In "Joan Beck's Mail," *Chicago Tribune*, August 16, 1970, Mrs. Beck went on to say, "So much of Mother Goose is so far removed from the context of contemporary life that it hinders rather than helps children understand and use language for themselves. . . . In any library or bookstore, you can find excellent poems for very young children, with just as much rhyme, rhythm and fun as Mother Goose, plus meanings and imagery that are far more intriguing and relevant to youngsters."

translations of the Perrault tales omit it from the title of the collection.

The French also connect *Mother Goose* with Goose-footed Bertha, wife of Robert II of France. French legends represent the queen spinning and telling stories to children, as illustrators have sometimes pictured *Mother Goose*.

### Dame Goose in England

Lina Eckenstein, in *Comparative Studies in Nursery Rhymes* (1906), says that the name *Mother Goose* was first used in England in connection with Robert Powell's puppet shows, exhibited in London between 1709 and 1711. Powell's plays included, among others, *Robin Hood and Little John, The Children in the Wood, Whittington and His Cat*, and one called *Mother Goose*. Perhaps it was Powell who popularized the name in England, for Joseph Addison in one of the *Spectator Papers* says that Powell set up his puppet show in London opposite St. Paul's and when the sexton rang his bell, many churchgoers were deflected from piety to puppets. The sexton wrote to Addison to complain, "As things are now, Mr. Powell has a full Congregation, while we have a very thin House." What play did Mr. Powell present under the title of *Mother Goose*? It may have been one of Perrault's stories heard from a sailor. At any rate, Perrault's *Contes de ma Mère l'Oye* was translated into English in 1729, and the popularity of the eight tales undoubtedly helped establish still more firmly that delightful nonsense name, *Mother Goose*.

## EARLY EDITIONS OF MOTHER GOOSE

### Newbery Edition, 1781

The next mention of the name in England is in connection with John Newbery, who is discussed in Chapter 4. At one time, Newbery was thought to have published an edition of *Mother Goose's Melody or Sonnets for the Cradle* between 1760 and 1765, but more recent research[4] suggests that he may have planned but did not publish such a book. In 1781 Newbery's stepson, T. Carnan, who continued the Newbery publishing business, advertised in the *London Chronicle* for January 2, "The first publication of *Mother Goose's Melody*." No copy of that edition is extant, but the advertisement is considerable assurance of its one-time existence. The earliest edition we have of this famous little book is from

*LONDON*
*Printed for Francis Powers, (Grandson to the late Mr. J. Newbery,) and Co.*
*No. 65. St. Paul's Church Yard, 1791.*
*Price Three Pence*

For a complete reproduction of this rare edition we are indebted to Barchilon and Pettit in their book *The Authentic Mother Goose Fairy Tales and Nursery Rhymes*. Here the student will find the famous Preface by a "very great Writer of very little Books" (probably Oliver Goldsmith), fifty-two rhymes with their quaint and generally irrelevant "Maxims," and—a surprising inclusion—sixteen songs of Shakespeare, with a tiny woodcut for each verse or song. This pleasant juxtaposition of *Mother Goose* and Shakespeare reminds us of Dame Goose's boast, "We two great poets were born together, and we shall go out of the world together."

Whether the first Newbery edition was planned by John himself or by his stepson or grandson, we may be sure that, coming from the house of Newbery, it was "strongly bound and gilt," unlike the chapbooks which were merely "folded, not stitched" in pamphlet style. Leigh Hunt refers to these Newbery books as "certain little penny books, radiant with gold, and rich with bad pictures." So even on her first appearance in

4. Jacques Barchilon and Henry Pettit, eds. *The Authentic Mother Goose Fairy Tales and Nursery Rhymes* (Swallow, 1960).

print, *Mother Goose* seems to have been brightly adorned.

### Isaiah Thomas Edition, 1785

The first American edition of *Mother Goose* was probably a pirated reprint of an early Newbery edition. It was published by Isaiah Thomas of Worcester, Massachusetts, who was in the habit of reproducing Newbery's books. W. H. Whitmore vouched for the fact that two copies of this Isaiah Thomas edition existed in his day, and in 1889 he reproduced the book in full, calling it *The Original Mother Goose's Melody.*[5] The little book is two and one-half by three and three-fourths inches. Preface, fifty-two jingles with maxims, sixteen songs of Shakespeare and small

5. W. H. Whitmore, ed. *The Original Mother Goose's Melody* (Joel Munsell's Sons, 1889). It is reproduced in facsimile from the Isaiah Thomas edition (Worcester, Massachusetts, 1785). Mr. Whitmore's introduction gives many interesting facts about the early collections of *Mother Goose.*

Mother GOOSE's Melody. 25

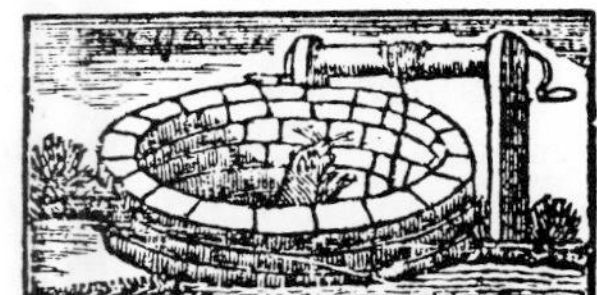

PLATO's SONG.

DING dong Bell,
The Cat is in the Well.
Who put her in?
Little *Johnny Green.*
What a naughty Boy was that,
To drown Poor Puſſy Cat,
Who never did any Harm,
And kill'd the Mice in his Father's
Barn.

Maxim. *He that injures one threatens an Hundred.*

LITTLE

26 Mother GOOSE's Melody.

LITTLE *Tom Tucker*
Sings for his Supper;
What ſhall he eat?
White Bread and Butter:
How will he cut it,
Without e're a Knife?
How will he be married,
Without e'er a Wife?

To be married without a wife is a terrible Thing, and to be married with a bad Wife is ſomething worſe; however, a good Wife that ſings well is the beſt muſical Inſtrument in the World. *Puffendorff.*

SE

Mother GOOSE's Melody. 27

SE ſaw, *Margery Daw,*
*Jacky* ſhall have a new Maſter;
*Jacky* muſt have but a Penny a Day,
Becauſe he can work no faſter.

It is a mean and ſcandalous Practice in Authors to put Notes to Things that deſerve no Notice.
*Grotius.*

GREAT

28 Mother GOOSE's Melody.

GREAT A, little a,
Bouncing B;
The Cat's in the Cupboard,
And ſhe can't ſee.

Yes ſhe can ſee that you are naughty, and don't mind your Book.

SE

*From* The Original Mother Goose's Melody. *Reproduced in facsimile by W. H. Whitmore (Joel Munsell's Sons, 1889) from the edition reprinted by Isaiah Thomas of Worcester, Mass., 1785.*

woodcuts are precisely the same as in the English edition. The maxims are surprising and often amusing, especially the one that follows "Margery Daw," which will surely be applauded by all bewildered readers of footnotes: "It is a mean and scandalous Practice in Authors to put Notes to Things that deserve no Notice."

### Munroe and Francis Editions, 1824, 1833

Two more notable American editions succeeded the Isaiah Thomas publication of 1785. Between 1824 and 1827, the Boston firm of Munroe and Francis published the *Mother Goose's Quarto, or Melodies Complete*, which contained many rhymes drawn from the Thomas reprint of Newbery's *Melody* but also many apparently old ones printed for the first time. In 1833 this firm made a reprint of the *Quarto* with the title *The Only True Mother Goose Melodies*. Fortunately, the second of these rare early editions has been made available in a modern facsimile edition with an introduction by Edward Everett Hale. It contains 169 rhymes illustrated with woodcuts. Both the *Quarto* and the 1833 edition are important sources for many of the later collections.

2

HEAR WHAT MA'AM GOOSE SAYS!

My dear little Blossoms, there are now in this world, and always will be, a great many grannies besides myself, both in petticoats and pantaloons, some a deal younger to be sure; but all monstrous wise, and of my own family name. These old women, who never had chick nor child of their own, but who always know how to bring up other people's children, will tell you with very long faces, that my enchanting, quieting, soothing volume, my all-sufficient anodyne for cross, peevish, won't-be-comforted little bairns, ought to be laid aside for more learned books, such as *they* could select and publish. Fudge! I tell you that all their batterings can't deface my beauties, nor their wise pratings equal my wiser prattlings; and all imitators of my refreshing songs might as well write a new Billy Shakespeare as another Mother Goose — we two great poets were born together, and we shall go out of the world together.

No, no, my Melodies will never die,
While nurses sing, or babies cry.

*From* The Only True Mother Goose Melodies, *an exact and full-size reproduction of the original edition published and copyrighted in Boston in the year 1833 by Munroe and Francis (Lothrop, Lee and Shepard, 1905).*

These editions include several fairly long poems such as "You owe me five shillings, say the bells of St. Helen's" and "London Bridge," each with eleven verses. They have such songs as "Johnny shall have a new bonnet" and "Lavender's blue, Rosemary green." And as many of our modern editions do, they include some poems that are not traditional, such as Walter Scott's "Pibroch of Donnel Dhu" and Shakespeare's "Jog on, jog on, the foot-path way," which are obviously out of place in a collection of folk rhymes.

## ORIGINS OF THE MOTHER GOOSE VERSES

The *Mother Goose* verses underwent many changes during the years when they were passed on by word of mouth, and later when they traveled from one printed edition to another. As with the ballads, variants of the same verses were recited or sung in different places, and which ones were the originals no one can say. Certainly they have led to considerable speculation and to some careful research. Undoubtedly many of the rhymes are mere nonsense jingles, but many others reveal interesting bits of history, old customs, manners, and beliefs.

Attempts to find historical characters to fit the people of *Mother Goose* have shown more imagination than documented research. From 1834 with John Bellenden Ker's study to 1930 with Katherine Elwes Thomas' book,

*The Real Personages of Mother Goose*, these romantic speculations caught the popular fancy and were repeated *ad infinitum*. Students were pleased to read that it was Queen Elizabeth I who rode the "cock horse to Banbury Cross" and danced to the tune of "Hey diddle diddle"; that dour old John Knox was the spider to poor Mary Queen of Scots' Miss Muffet; and that Anne Boleyn was the pretty maid hanging up her clothes and losing her head to the grim blackbird headsman. However, Iona and Peter Opie, in *The Oxford Dictionary of Nursery Rhymes*, found little evidence for these deductions. Their comment is:

> *Much ingenuity has been exercised to show that certain nursery rhymes have had greater significance than is now apparent. They have been vested with mystic symbolism, linked with social and political events, and numerous attempts have been made to identify the nursery characters with real persons. It should be stated straightway that the bulk of these speculations are worthless. Fortunately the theories are so numerous they tend to cancel each other out. The story of "Sing a song of sixpence," for instance, has been described as alluding to the choirs of Tudor monasteries, the printing of the English Bible, the malpractices of the Romish clergy, and the infinite workings of the solar system. The baby rocked on a tree top has been recognized as the Egyptian child Horus, the Old Pretender, and a New England Red Indian. Even when, by chance, the same conclusions are reached by two writers the reasons given are, as likely as not, antithetical. This game of "interpreting" the nursery rhymes has not been confined to the twentieth century, though it is curious that it has never been so overplayed as in the age which claims to believe in realism. (p. 27.)*

There is some evidence that several of the rhymes did originally refer to real people, and that some were once political lampoons. For instance, Miss Thomas gives a detailed and apparently documented account of "Little Jack Horner." The present Horner family, she says, showed her the deed to their estate, signed by Henry VIII and wrongly described as the "plum" their ancestor pulled out of the King's "pie"—a collection of deeds. According to the Opies, it is possible that this jingle did refer to a Horner ancestor, but on the whole a healthy skepticism is the safest approach to any attempts to identify nursery rhyme characters with real people.

Lina Eckenstein in *Comparative Studies in Nursery Rhymes* discusses some of the historical origins but is mainly concerned with the ancient folk origins of the verses and their counterparts in other countries. For example, she traces "Sally Waters" from its present simple game form back to its origin as part of a marriage rite in pre-Christian days. The name, she thinks, came from the Roman occupation of the city of Bath, where the temple was dedicated to Sulis-Minerva, Sul being the presiding deity at Bath. Sul of the Waters and Sally Waters do sound as if they might be related.

She devotes a whole chapter to cumulative tales—two of which have become a part of *Mother Goose*: "The house that Jack built" and "The old woman and her pig." She relates them to the Hebrew chant that begins:

*A kid, a kid, my father bought*
*For two pieces of money,*
*A kid, a kid.*
*Then came the cat and ate the kid*
*That my father bought*
*For two pieces of money,*
*A kid, a kid.*

The chant continues with the familiar sequence of dog, staff, fire, water, ox, butcher, then the angel of death, and the Holy One. This sequence, symbolizing the Hebrew people and their enemies at the time of the Crusades, is still recited as a part of the Passover liturgy and is probably older than "The old woman and her pig." Miss Eckenstein thinks that the latter is not merely what one scholar has called "a broken-down adaptation of the Hebrew poem" but that all these cumulative stories were originally incantations or rituals seriously performed.

## QUALITIES THAT APPEAL TO CHILDREN

Children enjoy the variety of subject matter and mood that continually surprises them in these verses. It ranges from the sheer nonsense of:

*Hey! diddle, diddle,*
*The cat and the fiddle,*
*The cow jumped over the moon.*

to the sad and tender ballad of "The babes in the wood":

*My dear, do you know*
*How a long time ago*
*Two poor little children,*
*Whose names I don't know . . .*

It is a rewarding task to make a list of the different kinds of verses in *Mother Goose.* Here are some obvious categories with only one or two examples of each, to which you can add dozens of others:

### VIEWPOINTS

. . . although each new generation of parents, grandfathers, and grandmothers sings and recites to children both the good and the inferior, only that which best serves the children's needs and tastes remains in their memories. And when he reaches old age, everyone who heard in his childhood these folk chants passes on to his grandchildren, in his turn, the very best, the most vivid and vital. And everything that is out of tune and incongruous with the psychology of the young child is gradually forgotten and becomes extinct; . . . In this way an exemplary children's folklore has come into existence—exemplary in its language and rhythm, as well as ideally suited to the intellectual needs of the young child. . . .

The great book that is called by the English *Mother Goose* came into being exactly the same way. The rhymes comprised in *Mother Goose*, called nursery rhymes, had been subjected to the same process of collective selection, unconsciously achieved by a long sequence of generations of children. These verses had been sifted through a thousand sieves before this book came into existence.—Kornei Chukovsky, *From Two to Five*, University of California Press, Berkeley and Los Angeles, 1963, p. 94.

*People* (a rich gallery of characters)
  Children—Little Miss Muffet
  Grownups—Old King Cole
  Imaginary—Old Mother Goose when she wanted to wander
  Grotesque—There was a crooked man
*Children's pranks*—Georgie, Porgie, pudding and pie
*Animals*—I had a little pony
*Birds and fowl*—Jenny Wren; Higgledy, piggledy, my black hen
*Finger play*—Pat-a-cake
*Games*—Ring a ring o' roses
*Riddles*—Little Nancy Etticoat
*Counting rhymes*—One, two, buckle my shoe
*Counting out*—Intery, mintery, cutery-corn
*Alphabets*—A, is an apple pie
*Proverbs*—Early to bed, early to rise
*Superstitions*—See a pin and pick it up
*Time verses*—Thirty days hath September
*Days of the week*—Solomon Grundy, born on Monday
*Verse stories*—The Queen of Hearts, she made some tarts
*Dialogue*—Who killed Cock Robin?
*Songs*—A frog he would a-wooing go
*Street cries*—Hot-cross Buns!
*Weather*—Rain, rain, go away
*Tongue twisters*—Peter Piper picked a peck of pickled peppers
*Cumulative stories*—This is the house that Jack built
*Nonsense*—Three wise men of Gotham

There is one little nature personification in *Mother Goose:*

*Daffadowndilly*
*Has come up to town,*
*In a yellow petticoat*
*And a green gown.*

And there is the charming

*The North Wind doth blow,*
*And we shall have snow,*
*And what will poor Robin do then?*

But on the whole, descriptive nature poems, in the modern sense, are conspicuously lacking. So are fairy poems; the only mention of fairies is usually:

*Oh who is so merry*
*So merry heigh-ho,*
*As a light-hearted fairy?*
*Heigh-ho, heigh-ho.*

Even this one fairy rhyme is lacking in many editions, but all the collections abound with characters absurd, grotesque, and fantastic. In what other collections of verse can you find such variety and surprise?

Lured on by the variety of these rollicking jingles, the child is also captivated by their musical quality. "Sing it again," he insists, when you finish reading or singing one of his favorites. He nods his head or rocks his body or waggles a finger, marking time to the rhythm. He himself often suits the words to his own action. A three-year-old, bouncing up and down on a spring horse chanting her version of "Ride a cock horse," mixed up the words, but she never lost her rhythm, which is perfection for galloping.

Saying these verses, the child gets a happy introduction to rhyme—perfect and imperfect—to alliteration, onomatopoeia, and other sound patterns. Happily he gets these without the burden of their labels and so enjoys them lightheartedly. He likes the exact, neat rhyming of:

*Georgie Porgie, pudding and pie,*
*Kissed the girls and made them cry.*
*When the boys came out to play*
*Georgie Porgie ran away.*

But he is not disturbed by the far from perfect rhyme of:

*Goosey, goosey, gander*
*Whither shall I wander?*
*Up stairs, down stairs,*
*And in my lady's chamber.*

Alliteration, as in "Sing a song of sixpence," tickles his sound sense to a degree that astonishes us. He is also fascinated by the staccato in "Higgledy, piggledy, my black hen" and by the explosive *tle* in "She lays eggs for gen*tle*men." Indeed, the brisk tune of this ditty turns upon its lively use of consonants, the *n* sounds making it ring delightfully. One of the many values of these melodious jingles is that they accustom the ear and the tongue to the musical aspects of our English language.

There are also in *Mother Goose* small lyrics of genuine poetic charm with a more subtle music than the examples already given: "I

## VIEWPOINTS

However fantastic, however impossible, the only obligation laid upon a work of art is that it shall establish its claim to its own existence. It must be true to its own world . . .

The relevant point is that my nursery rhymes are tiny, unconscious works of art within their own limitations; very young sisters of their grown-up brother, Poetry, but of the same parentage as he. Their quality is the same. . . .

. . . This is not to imply that . . . lines of the purest gold of poetry contain any measure of "nonsense" such as we find in the nursery rhyme, but merely that the element of suggestive evocation can be common to both. "Ninety-nine times as high as the moon" is nonsense, but it is also something more: it would not be entirely out of place as a statement in the *Ancient Mariner*. . . .

Finally, let us not forget the inherent music of the nursery jingle. . . . M. Emile Cammaerts . . . observes that the nursery rhyme is "essentially poetical because essentially musical," a comment which deserves to be pondered, for it supplies the key to our enduring affection.—V. Sackville-West, *Nursery Rhymes*, Dropmore Press, London, 1947, pp. 62–66.

saw a ship a-sailing," "Bobby Shaftoe," "Hush-a-bye, baby," "Johnny shall have a new bonnet," "Lavender's blue," "The north wind doth blow," and the charming:

*I had a little nut tree, nothing would it bear*
*But a silver apple and a golden pear;*
*The King of Spain's daughter came to see me,*
*And all for the sake of my little nut tree.*
*I skipped over water, I danced over sea,*
*And all the birds in the air couldn't catch me.*

All in all, the verses offer many opportunities for the development of a fine sense of the musical quality of language.

Still another characteristic of these verses that endears them to young children is their action. Jack and Jill fall down, Miss Muffet runs away, Mother Goose rides on her gander, the cow jumps over the moon, Polly puts the kettle on, the cat comes fiddling out of the barn, the Man in the Moon comes down too soon. Here are no meditations, no brooding introspections, no subtle descriptions to baffle the jumping, hopping, up-and-doing young child. In these verses things happen as rapidly and riotously as he would like to see them happening every day.

Some verses contain simple stories. "The Queen of Hearts," for example, is a slight but complete account of the innocent and industrious queen, her tarts stolen, the villain caught, punishment administered, and the villain left in a properly penitent frame of mind. A child lends his pony and protests:

*She whipped him, she lashed him,*
*She rode him through the mire,*
*I would not lend my pony now,*
*For all the lady's hire.*

Old Mother Hubbard and her bare cupboard involve considerable suspense before the tale is told out. Froggy has all sorts of difficulties with his wooing. The bewildered old woman who wakes to find her skirts cut short and so is not sure of her identity makes a story that is funny to the last line. "The babes in the wood" is a tragic tale but endurable because it is brief and is gently and sweetly told. The brevity of these verse stories makes them acceptable to children as young as two years old and they prepare children to enjoy longer and more involved prose and verse stories.

The sheer fun of *Mother Goose* keeps her verses alive in the hearts of every generation of children. Of course adults and children seldom see eye to eye on what is humorous. Our jaded ears, for instance, may have forgotten that the hissing s's of "s-s-sing a s-s-song of s-s-sixpence" sound funny, but the child laughs at them as he laughs at other comical sounds our dull ears miss. The child, on the other hand, may stare gravely at the story of the dish running away with the spoon, which usually strikes adults as funny. Then he turns around and giggles at the crooked man, who seems a little sad to us. So it goes, but the fact remains that on almost every page of *Mother Goose* there is a smile or a chuckle for the child. What does he laugh at? It is hard to say; we can only watch and listen. Sometimes he laughs at the sound; often he laughs at the grotesque or the incongruous. Surprise tickles him, absurd antics amuse him, and broad horseplay delights him. There are plenty of examples of all these in *Mother Goose*. A man jumps into the bramble bush to scratch his eyes "*in* again"; a pig flies up in the air; Simple Simon goes fishing in his mother's pail; Humpty Dumpty has a fall (falls always bring a laugh); Peter, Peter pumpkin-eater keeps his wife in a pumpkin shell; Tom who "was beat" runs "roaring down the street." Such humor is far from subtle, but its absurdities must be a relief to the child beset on all sides by earnest adults.

Finally, and almost above all, the child loves the pictures that illustrate his favorite book. Whether the edition is so small he can tuck it into his pocket, or so enormous that he has to spread it out on the floor, the numerous pictures enchant him. Here he shares his delight in *Mother Goose* with some of the finest illustrators of each generation, for artists also love the fun and action of these old

### VIEWPOINTS

For after all, despite the trappings, life on a block in the ghetto may not be so much unlike Tom Jones' England. Vita Sackville-West helps us remember that the eighteenth-century gentry "banged their children about physically and mentally, teaching them well in advance what to expect of life." Sometimes we forget the health and dignity that exist in the very young ghetto child. We neglect his aristocracy. The ghetto child knows by experience that he can confront and survive, which is often more than his anxious suburban counterpart knows about himself. He is a hero who needs a literature worthy of his zest and toughness, a Homer to celebrate the terror and beauty of mere existence.

I submit *Mother Goose.*—Joan Bodger, "Mother Goose: Is the Old Girl Relevant?" *Wilson Library Bulletin*, December 1969, p. 408.

rhymes and have lavished on them some of their best work. It has been said that the perfect edition of *Mother Goose* has not yet been made. Probably it never will be, because no two of us will ever see these famous characters in quite the same way. Just as there is endless variety in these stories, the mood, and the characters of these jingles, so there is a like variety in the size, the shape, the color, and the style of pictures that illustrate them. One adult prefers one edition, while a second adult greatly prefers another, but the children apparently like them all. What they ask for is *Mother Goose*—with colored pictures or black-and-white, simple or elaborate, commonplace or subtle.

## POPULAR MODERN EDITIONS

It is impractical to list all the fine editions of *Mother Goose*, but the following choices are popular with parents, teachers, librarians, and children for a variety of reasons.

*Mother Goose; or, The Old Nursery Rhymes* (1882), illustrated by Kate Greenaway, is a tiny book to fit small hands and pockets and to fill small hearts with delight. It contains forty-four of the brief rhymes, each with its own picture in the quaint Kate Greenaway style. The print is exceedingly fine, but for nonreaders this does not matter. The illustrations are gently gay, the colors are soft, and the people exquisitely decorative.

*Mother Goose; The Old Nursery Rhymes* (1913), illustrated by Arthur Rackham, one of England's great artists, is a splendid edition, now out of print, but well worth hunting up in any library that has it. The illustrations are of three types: pen-and-ink sketches, silhouettes, and full-page color. The silhouettes are amazingly effective, for example, the dripping bedraggled cat of "Ding, dong, bell." The color plates are Rackham at his best and in many moods. These are pictures by an artist with imagination and a knowledge of folklore. (See 3, p. 120.)

A good introduction to *Mother Goose* and her world is the tried and true *The Real*

### VIEWPOINTS

Let the poet Walter de la Mare speak in defense of poor Old Mother Goose. Her rhymes, he wrote [in his introduction to *Nursery Rhymes for Certain Times* (London: Faber & Faber, Ltd., 1956)] "free the fancy, charm tongue and ear, delight the inward eye, and many of them are tiny masterpieces of word craftsmanship—of the latest device in rhythm, indeed—the 'sprung'! Last, but not least, they are not only crammed with vivid little scenes and objects and living creatures, but, however fantastic and nonsensical they may be, they are a direct short cut into poetry itself."—Walter de la Mare, quoted in *The Annotated Mother Goose* by William S. Baring-Gould and Cecil Baring-Gould, Meridian Books, Cleveland and New York, 1967, p. 21.

*Mother Goose*, illustrated by Blanche Fisher Wright. The Fiftieth Anniversary Edition, 1965, has an introduction by May Hill Arbuthnot. There are colored pictures on every page, often one picture fills a whole page, or sometimes there are two or three small ones. In either case, the illustrations are simple and clear and have only a few details. The characters are dressed in period costumes and can be seen distinctly by a large group of children. The colors are clear washes, sometimes soft and pale but more often bright and lively. It is a big book with a wide selection of traditional verses which the illustrations really illustrate. This is more important than some artists have realized, because little children use pictures as clues to the meaning of the text. (See 1, p. 120.)

One edition of *Mother Goose* that no child should miss is *Ring o' Roses* (1922), illustrated by Leslie Brooke, who provides an imaginative and broadly humorous pictorial interpretation of the traditional verses. The lovely English countryside is painted in pastel colors, with yellows and tender greens giving a springtime brightness to the pages. The characters are in English period costumes and are utterly satisfying interpretations. Simple Simon *is* Simple Simon, daft and delightful. Goosey, Goosey, Gander and the outrageous old man "who would not say his prayers" will be forever your vision of that remarkable pair. But above all you will remember Leslie Brooke's pigs and after chuckling over them you will never again see pigs as plain pigs. Instead you'll see pigs with a smirk or a leer, pigs looking coy or shocked, pigs on the rampage, or pigs of complacence. This is, after all, the test of great illustrations: they do more than illustrate—they interpret the text so vividly that they become the visual embodiment of the words. There are only some twenty rhymes in *Ring o' Roses*, but every child should have the book to pore over and absorb until the pictures are his forever. (See 2, p. 120.)

*The Tall Book of Mother Goose* (1942), illustrated by Feodor Rojankovsky, is an elongated book, approximately five by twelve inches, which can be easily held. The pages lend themselves either to delightful double-page spreads like the panoramic landscape of "One misty, moisty morning," or to a sequence of small pictures like those for "The three little kittens." Mr. Rojankovsky was a master of color and realistic texture. His furry kittens, feathery chicks, or woolly mufflers have a depth that almost creates a tactual sensation. His children are husky, everyday youngsters, never beautiful and often very funny. His pop-eyed Miss Muffet, viewing the spider with alarm, always brings laughter. On the other hand, Humpty Dumpty with the face of Hitler is a mistake since Hitlers are only passing phenomena and Humpty is immortal. Fortunately, the resemblance means nothing to young children. The illustration of "Ding, dong, bell" misses the point entirely. The freckled, rosy, good boy and the wan child with a cigarette not only do not illustrate the rhyme but introduce an adult line of thought completely irrelevant to the verse. Despite these two objectionable pictures, this book, with its 150 rhymes and twice as many pictures, remains justifiably popular. (See 5, p. 121.)

Tasha Tudor's illustrations have always been notable for her delicate imagination and for her use of quaint costumes. Her *Mother Goose* (1944) is six and one-half by seven and one-half inches, an agreeable size for small hands to hold. Of the seventy-seven verses, a number are unfamiliar. The costumes of the characters include Elizabethan, colonial, American pioneer, Kate Greenaway, and Godey styles, in pastel colors or soft grays. The action is interpreted both realistically and imaginatively. For instance, the illustration for "the cow jumped over the moon" pictures the cow running downhill with the distant moon showing through the cow's four legs. The cozy domesticity of many of the pictures is very appealing, as in the illustration for "One, two, buckle my shoe," which shows a mother tenderly dressing her little girl. (See 4, p. 121.)

Marguerite de Angeli's *Book of Nursery and Mother Goose Rhymes* (1954) contains 376 jingles, 260 enchanting pictures, and innumerable decorations. It is a big book, and for the artist, it must have been a labor of love. Children and animals dance and prance across the pages. Little flowery bouquets and birds adorn the corners, and plump, pretty babies tumble here and there. The artist tells us that the faces of the family of "God bless the master of this house" were drawn from the laughing faces of her own family, and many of the other pictures seem to be sketches of real people. The book is too big for small children to handle alone, but it is fine for children and adults to look at together. The verses are not arranged in any particular order, so a nursery jingle is often followed by a ballad of sufficient substance to suit the oldest children. However, the rich offering of verses and illustrations makes this an edition to cherish and to pass on to the next generation.

*Lavender's Blue* (1954), compiled by Kathleen Lines, is distinguished by Harold Jones' illustrations. Both in color and in black and white, they suggest old engravings. The pages are neatly bordered; the figures are stiffish, not stylized yet not realistic either. Although the colors are muted and there is little humor, the composition of the pictures holds your attention. "I love little pussy" is an example. Puss sits tall, solemn, and mysterious, against an interior from which a door opens onto alluring streets. She is framed like a period portrait of a great lady. (See 21, Color Section.)

From the rich store of their scholarly study Iona and Peter Opie have compiled *The Oxford Nursery Rhyme Book* (1955), with eight hundred of the ditties that have delighted children for generations. The vast collection is skillfully organized. It begins with the simplest ditties and progresses to more mature riddles, songs, and ballads. Almost every verse has a picture—small and black only, but amazingly effective. Many of the illustrations are taken from the old chapbooks and toy books. The work of Thomas and John Bewick is well represented, and the distinguished drawings of contemporary artist Joan Hassall are in keeping with their style. Students of early children's books will find this an invaluable edition, and parents will also enjoy the book and its preface. Designed as a companion volume to *The Oxford Nursery Rhyme Book* is the Opies' *A Family Book of Nursery Rhymes*, 1964 (first published as *The Puffin Book of Nursery Rhymes*). Of its 358 rhymes, 200 are not included in the first book. Precise, delicate drawings by Pauline Baynes grace almost every page, and the notes at the back of the book are as entertaining as they are informative.

Brian Wildsmith's work is distinguished for its magnificent use of rich color, often in a patchwork of vibrant blocks. In his *Brian Wildsmith's Mother Goose* (1964) the people are gay in period clothing, and the almost theatrical quality of the pictures gives a sense of milieu as well as of the characters. (See 8, p. 122.)

Another delightful collection is *A Book of Scottish Nursery Rhymes* (1965), edited by Norah and William Montgomerie. Most of the selections are pure Scots, but anyone can recognize and enjoy such favorites as:

*"Pussy, pussy baudrons*
*Where have you been?"*
*"I've been to London,*
*To see the Queen!"*

*"Pussy, pussy baudrons,*
*What got you there?"*
*"I got a good fat mousikie,*
*Running up a stair!"*

One of the impressive collections of the 1960s is *The Mother Goose Treasury* (1966), illustrated by Raymond Briggs. Each of the over four-hundred verses, most of them from the Opie collection, has at least one illustration. The verses and pictures, many of them small, are scattered over the pages with open-handed abandon. Occasionally there is a full-page or a double-page spread in color. The

1.

2.

3.

1. *Illustration by Blanche Fisher Wright. From* The Real Mother Goose. *Copyright 1916, renewal 1944, by the publishers, Rand McNally & Co. (Original in color)*

2. *Illustration by Leonard Leslie Brooke. From* Ring o' Roses. *Reproduced with permission of Frederick Warne & Co., Inc. (Original in color)*

3. *Illustration by Arthur Rackham. From* Mother Goose. *Copyright, 1913, by Arthur Rackham, 1941, by Adyth Rackham. Reproduced by permission of D. Appleton-Century Company, Inc. (Original in color)*

4.

*4. Illustration by Tasha Tudor. From* Mother Goose. *Copyright 1944 by Henry Z. Walck, Inc., Publishers. Reprinted by permission. (Original in color)*

*5. Illustration by Feodor Rojankovsky. From* The Tall Book of Mother Goose. *Copyright, 1942, by Artists and Writers Guild, Inc. Reprinted by permission. (Original in color)*

*6. Illustration by Ed Hargis. From* The American Mother Goose *by Ray Wood. Reproduced with permission of J. B. Lippincott Company.*

5.

6.

Jay bird, Jay bird, settin' on a rail,
Pickin' his teeth with the end of his tail,
Mulberry leaves and calico sleeves
All school teachers are hard to please.

[67]

7.

7. *From* London Bridge Is Falling Down! *by* Peter Spier. *Copyright © 1967 by Peter Spier. Reproduced by permission of Doubleday & Company, Inc. and The World's Work, Ltd., Great Britain. (Original in color)*
8. *From* Mother Goose *by Brian Wildsmith. Copyright © 1964. Reproduced by permission of Franklin Watts, Inc. and Oxford University Press, London. (Original in color)*
9. *Taken from* Every Child's Book of Nursery Songs *by Donald Mitchell and Carey Blyton. Copyright © 1968 by Donald Mitchell and Carey Blyton. Used by permission of Crown Publishers, Inc.*

8.

9.

10.

*10. Copyright © 1963 by Philip Reed. From* Mother Goose and Nursery Rhymes. *Used by permission of Atheneum Publishers. (Original in color)*

*11. Reprinted by permission of Coward, McCann & Geoghegan, Inc. from* The Mother Goose Treasury *by Raymond Briggs. Copyright © 1966 by Raymond Briggs.*

*12. Illustration by Barbara Cooney for* Mother Goose in French *translated by Hugh Latham. Illustrations copyright © 1964 by Barbara Cooney. Reprinted with permission of Thomas Y. Crowell Company, Inc., New York, Publishers.*

11.

DOCTOR FELL

12.

pictures are greatly varied in mood and treatment: some are bold, some delicate, some restrained, some grotesque, some humorous, but all have charm and vitality. (See 11, p. 123.)

*Mother Goose and Nursery Rhymes* (1963) is delightfully illustrated by Philip Reed with woodcut engravings in quiet colors, which are enhanced by being set off by ample space. The characters have an ebullient and rakish humor that captures the joyful spirit of the verses. (See 10, p. 123.)

A collection of songs, many from *Mother Goose*, have been selected by Donald Mitchell and very simply arranged for piano accompaniment by Carey Blyton in *Every Child's Book of Nursery Songs* (1969). Suggestions for the use of percussion instruments or for vocal participation by children (in rounds or with spoken parts) are included. The black-and-white illustrations are gay and amusing. (See 9, p. 122.)

In recent years several very attractive editions of single verses from *Mother Goose* have been published. Both Peter Spier and Ed Emberley have illustrated *London Bridge Is Falling Down*—Emberley's fanciful version has an ornate bridge but little period detail; Spier's version has minutely and humorously detailed illustrations and notes on the history of the bridge. (See 7, p. 122.) Paul Galdone and Barbara Cooney, too, have illustrated single-verse editions. Barbara Cooney has also illustrated with delightful delicacy *Mother Goose in French*, ably translated by Hugh Latham. (See 12, p. 123.) Maurice Sendak in *Hector Protector* and *As I Went Over the Water* (1965) adds a raffish charm to two less familiar verses. And for those who enjoy a touch of the macabre, *The Chas. Addams Mother Goose* (1967) by cartoonist Charles Addams provides a sophisticated, off-beat edition.

## VARIANTS OF MOTHER GOOSE

In addition to the many editions of *Mother Goose*, there are several collections of nursery rhymes which are fairly close in style and content to the old English jingles.

*The American Mother Goose* was compiled by Ray Wood (1940) and illustrated by Ed Hargis. Children studying frontier life are interested in and amused by this collection. The verses are both rougher and funnier than the English nursery rhymes and are as indigenous to America as a "possum up a gum stump." Here are such familiar doggerels as "I asked my mother for fifteen cents," "How much wood would a woodchuck chuck," "Mother, may I go out to swim," the long "Obadiah jumped in the fire," "I went to the river," and a final section of riddles, games, and finger play. The pen-and-ink sketches are full of hilarious touches that delight adults as much as they do the children. This book is not for the youngest, but it is fun for older children. (See 6, p. 121.)

Maud and Miska Petersham's *The Rooster Crows: A Book of American Rhymes and Jingles* was awarded the Caldecott Medal in 1946. In spite of the inclusion of such American folk rhymes as "A bear went over the mountain" and "Mother, may I go out to swim," the subtitle is difficult to justify because the collection also contains such old-world rhymes as "Sally Waters" and "Oats, peas, beans and barley grows." Children enjoy the picture of colts, kittens, and bunnies which adorn the pages, of children of long ago rocking wooden cradles or going a-hunting, and children jumping off haymows and enjoying themselves generally.

*A Rocket in My Pocket* (1948), compiled by Carl Withers, carries the subtitle *The Rhymes and Chants of Young Americans*. Some four hundred ditties, tongue twisters, derisive chants, and bits of pure nonsense, together with Susanne Suba's line drawings, make this an unusually beguiling book.

*Did You Feed My Cow?* (1969), compiled by Margaret Burroughs, an authority on Afro-American culture, is a book of street games, chants, and rhymes in which traditional folk materials have been adapted by children.

Lillian Morrison has made a delightful contribution to Americana with her small collections of riddles, auguries, school and playground chants, and amusing autograph album inscriptions. The two books in the last category—*Yours Till Niagara Falls* (1950) and *Remember Me When This You See* (1961)—are never on library shelves at commencement time.

*Tongue Tanglers*, compiled by Charles Francis Potter, is popular with both children and speech teachers. There are only forty-four tongue tanglers, but they are gems, and the illustrations in full color add to the hilarity. Dr. Potter's selection, chosen from thousands of tongue twisters, includes:

*I Saw Esau kissing Kate.*
*Fact is we all three saw.*
*I saw Esau, he saw me,*
*And she saw I saw Esau.*

and ends with that perfect conclusion:

*Tongue twisters twist tongues twisted*
*Trying to untangle twisted tangles*
*My tangs tungled now.*[6]

## THE TRADITIONAL BALLADS

The ancient ballads have never been as beloved by children as *Mother Goose*, partly because their dialect and archaic language make them difficult to read and sing. Yet children are universally fond of poems that tell a story, and a more hair-raising collection of stories would be hard to find. An eleven-year-old boy, after listening to his teacher read the old ballad of "Sir Patrick Spens," remarked, "That is the best poem I ever heard."

"Why?" asked his teacher, in some surprise.

"Oh, 'cause the author gets right into the story. He doesn't waste any time describing things. It's more exciting that way."

This young critic summed up neatly the appeal that ballads and story poems have for children of all ages. They tell a story in concentrated form, with the maximum of excitement and the minimum of words.

The child makes no distinction between the types. He doesn't care whether a poem or a song is an old folk song or a folk ballad such as "The Babes in the Wood" or "Bonny Barbara Allan," or a modern song like "Robin Adair," or a modern story poem like "The Pied Piper of Hamelin." What he enjoys is the swift movement of verse or melody enhancing the dramatic appeal of a good story. The search for these story poems carries us back into folk rhymes and forward to present-day narrative poems, ranging from hilarious nonsense to romance and noble tragedy.

Like the *Mother Goose* verses and all other folk literature, the traditional ballads were passed on by word of mouth long before they were printed. In England, Scotland, Germany, and Denmark, in particular, a great many ballads were passed on from person to person, village to village, and country to country. Sailors, too, would hear ballads and take them home, much as travelers carry popular songs from country to country today. So popular were these story poems and so rapidly were they exchanged that it is difficult today to determine whether a ballad is Danish, Scottish, English, or German in origin. As Warren E. Roberts, Professor of Folklore, Indiana University, has pointed out:

*Contemporary ballad scholars hesitate to ascribe specific origins to individual ballads. They feel that the important consideration is that a given ballad has been in oral circulation long enough to have undergone changes (G. H. Gerould's phrase is "communal re-creation"). When a ballad has been in oral circulation for several generations, any given aspect of its style may be the product of the changes made in it by a series of singers, rather than a mark of the original composer. Consequently, older theories of origin have*

6. From *Tongue Tanglers* by Charles Francis Potter. Copyright 1962 by Charles Francis Potter. Published by The World Publishing Co.

*either been discarded or de-emphasized. . . . Contemporary ballad scholars freely admit that it is impossible to ever know much about the origins of individual ballads and so they simply ignore the question and concentrate on other matters. . . . Most scholars would probably agree that most of the ballads were composed by gifted, but unknown individuals who were working within a traditional framework, but further they would probably not care to go.*[7]

According to Kenneth Rexroth:

*Ballads of Scottish and English type are found from Mongolia to Spain, and they are still being made from the Appalachians to Yugoslavia. . . . The literature of balladry is enormous. Child's great collection is in paperback, five volumes. The melodies most commonly sung are in Cecil Sharp's* One Hundred English Folksongs *and* English Folk Songs from the Southern Appalachians. *Much of Grundtvig [a collection made in Denmark in the middle of the nineteenth century by S. Grundtvig and A. Olrik] is available in translation. There are many state and regional collections. . . . There are collections, in English, of ballads from Mongolia, Yugoslavia, and dozens of other countries.*[8]

## PRINTED SOURCES OF THE TRADITIONAL BALLADS

It is known that the English and Scottish ballads grew and flourished from the thirteenth to the middle of the sixteenth centuries. Eventually they must have reached the ears and captured the imaginations of the educated people. Sir Philip Sidney in his *Defence of Poesie*, published in 1595, wrote of the ballad of Chevy Chase: "Certainly, I must confess my own barbarousnesse, I never heard the olde song of *Percy* and *Duglas*, that I found not my heart mooved more then with a Trumpet. . . ."

Joseph Addison devoted two papers in *The Spectator* (Nos. 70 and 71) to an excellent analysis of the moving qualities of this same ballad, commenting that: "The old song of Chevy-Chase is the favourite ballad of the common people of England, and Ben Jonson used to say he had rather have been the author of it than all of his works."

David Garrick, the famous English actor, collected ballads and no doubt recited or sang them with telling effect. Oliver Goldsmith, noted for his good voice, enjoyed singing them. Samuel Pepys, the jovial diarist, made one of the finest collections in existence, and in the 1720's Allan Ramsay, a Scottish poet, published three volumes of ballads. However, it was not until 1765, when Bishop Percy published his famous *Reliques* that the Scottish and English ballads became widely known and appreciated.

## BISHOP PERCY, 1729–1811

*Reliques of Ancient English Poetry*

*Reliques of Ancient English Poetry*, the three-volume edition of the ancient ballads discovered by Bishop Percy, contains the Bishop's own account of how he made his famous find. While visiting his friend Humphrey Pitt, in Shiffnal, Shropshire, Bishop Percy found an old manuscript lying on the floor under a bureau. Some of it had been used by the maids to start fires, and half of its fifty-four pages were torn away. This scrubby little book contained 195 handwritten ballads. The script of the copier placed the manuscript sometime before 1650, although the ballads were undoubtedly much older. The Bishop prepared the ballads for publication under the title *Reliques of Ancient English Poetry*, and the collection soon became extremely popular in England. Unfortunately, the good Bishop did not respect this ancient manuscript. He scribbled on the margins, struck out those ballads he thought indelicate, and, in his editorial capacity, wrote and rewrote ballads that he considered

7. Letter to the editor, August 3, 1971.

8. Kenneth Rexroth, "The English and Scottish Ballad," *Saturday Review*, December 14, 1968, p. 26.

too crude for the "polished taste" of the day. It was not until 1867, over a hundred years after its discovery, that scholars reprinted the original 195 ballads, and students could compare them with the Bishop's elaborations.[9]

Certainly no ballad is more exciting than the story of the discovery of this seventeenth-century manuscript with its ballads copied laboriously by some unknown lover of these story poems. If Percy had postponed his visit to his friend for a few more weeks, perhaps the maids would have fed the whole manuscript to the flames. In that case, our present collection of traditional ballads and the romance of ballad collecting would have been much the poorer.

The Bishop's collection aroused enormous interest in ballads. Sir Walter Scott, for instance, by reading them in childhood was inspired to a lifelong search for them. Ballad "raids" he called his journeys into remote parts of Scotland to gather firsthand from a shepherd or an old woman some little-known ballad or variant of a familiar one. The publication of the ballads, though, distressed at least one of Scott's contributors, for the old woman who gave him so many of his ballads burst into tears when she first saw them in print. As she said, "They were made for singing and not for reading; but ye ha'e broken the charm now, and they'll never be sung mair."

## FRANCIS JAMES CHILD, 1825–1896

*The English and Scottish Popular Ballads*

Since Scott's day other collectors have compared, criticized, and evaluated ballad sources, but the most notable compilation is the famous *The English and Scottish Popular Ballads*, in five volumes, edited by Francis J. Child of Harvard. Child not only carried on exhaustive investigations into manuscript sources and current versions but also studied the ballads of other countries. There are 305 ballads in his collection, with copious notes and with all known and accredited variants of each ballad. "Mary Hamilton" alone has twenty-eight variants. Child's five volumes represent the most thoroughly investigated collection of ballads that exists and are the final authority on the original sources of old ballads.

It is usually agreed that these volumes are principally for scholars, and yet if a sixth-grade teacher feels moved to read "Sir Patrick Spens" to her children, she can build up a richer background by consulting the introduction in Francis Child's great edition. She may not have the time or inclination to read all the eighteen variants, but her children will be interested at least to know that "Sir Patrick Spens" was remembered in so many places and by so many people, and that there exist today some eighteen ways of telling his story.

If these five volumes are not available, then teachers should become acquainted with the one-volume edition prepared by Child's student and successor, George Lyman Kittredge—*English and Scottish Popular Ballads, Student's Cambridge Edition*. It contains not only the 305 ballads with two or three variants of each, but brief notes that are invaluable.

## CHARACTERISTICS OF THE TRADITIONAL BALLADS

The old ballad was a song story and its singing quality is still evident in the lilting verses and refrains and in the lively tunes that accompany the words. "Bonny Barbara Allan," for example, tells a tragic tale swiftly and movingly, but the opening verse suggests at once that here is a song:

*In Scarlet Town, where I was bound*
*There was a fair maid dwelling,*
*Whom I had chosen to be my own,*
*And her name it was Barbara Allan.*

9. *Bishop Percy's Folio Manuscript, Ballads and Romances.*

There are almost as many tunes to "Barbara" as there are variants to the words, and if you know any of the tunes it is difficult to read the words without singing them. This is also true of "The Gypsy Laddie," or its more familiar folk-song variant, "The Raggle, Taggle Gypsies." Its tune is a compelling one, but the ballad is also dramatic for reading. Even the most tragic ballads, like "Edward" or "Lord Randal," have wistful, tender airs that somehow soften the tragedy. The music of "Lizie Lindsay" has an attractive swing, and there are dozens of other ballads that seem to prove the old woman's contention that they were made for singing.

In many ballads this songlike quality is enhanced by refrains. The refrain of "The Cruel Brother" sounds like tripping dance steps:

*There was three ladies playd at the ba,*
*With a hey ho and a lillie gay*
*There came a knight and played oer them a'*
*As the primrose spread so sweetly.*

One version of the "The Gypsy Laddie" begins:

*There was a gip come oer the land,*
*He sung so sweet and gaily;*
*He sung with glee, neath the wildwood tree,*
*He charmed the great lord's lady.*
*Ring a ding a ding go ding go da,*
*Ring a ding a ding go da dy*
*Ring a ding a ding go ding go da,*
*She's gone with the gipsey Davy.*

"Robin Hood and Little John" starts out with a vigorous refrain:

*When Robin Hood was about twenty years old,*
*With a hey down down and a down*
*He happened to meet Little John,*
*A jolly brisk blade, right fit for the trade,*
*For he was a lusty young man.*

The second, fourth, and fifth lines suggest men banging on the table with their fists or with mugs of "nut brown ale," in jovial accompaniment to a familiar song.

Some of the ballad refrains are so lively that it is easy to imagine a still more vigorous bodily response. For instance, the refrain of "The Wife Wrapt in Wether's Skin" seems made for jig steps.

*There livd a laird down into Fife,*
*Riftly, raftly, now, now, now*
*An he has married a bonny young wife.*
*Hey Jock Simpleton, Jenny('s) white petticoat,*
*Robin a Rashes, now, now, now.*

Such a dancing, prancing refrain as this brings to mind a picture of a group of people stirring up a ballad by a kind of spontaneous combustion of high spirits, shouting and jigging while the next man thinks up another episode of the story. It reminds us also that the word *ballad* comes from *ballare*, meaning "to dance." Some of these refrains certainly seem made for dancing. It is a good idea to help children respond to the musical character of the ballads by having them sing some and suit gentle rhythmic movements to the words of others or even try lively dance steps to the lustier refrains.

Perhaps the most striking characteristic of the ballads is their dramatic and rapidly unfolding plots. In "Edward," for example,

*Illustration by Virginia Burton. From* Song of Robin Hood *edited by Anne Malcolmson. Reproduced with permission of Houghton Mifflin Company.*

you sense immediately that something is wrong; then you learn that Edward has killed his own father, but not till the last stanza do you know that the mother herself planned the crime and persuaded her son to commit it. "Lord Randal," opening peacefully with a mother questioning her son about his hunting, hints only in the melancholy last line of each verse—"For I'm wearied wi hunting, and fain wad lie down"—that all is not well. As the questioning goes on, you learn that Lord Randal's hawks and his hounds died of the food he gave them from his own plate. Then you find out that his "true love" is the poisoner and that Lord Randal will also die. The last-minute revelation of the villain is nowhere more strikingly employed than in "The Daemon Lover." In this ballad, it is only after the faithless wife has gone with her former lover on his ship that she "espies" his cloven hoof and knows she has eloped with the devil himself.

There are of course some comic plots too, but they are distinctly in the minority. "The Crafty Farmer" outwitting the thief is one of the children's favorites, and they like even better the broad slapstick farce of the stubborn old couple in "Get Up and Bar the Door." The folk-tale plot of trial by riddle with a bright person substituting for a stupid one is amusingly used in "King John and the Abbot of Canterbury" ("King John and the Bishop"). The charming "Wee Wee Man" is built on the folk-tale plot of the fairy who disappears if you take your eyes off him. "Lizie Lindsay" is mildly humorous, with the young Lord disguised as a shepherd's son and with poor Lizie tramping the soles off her shoes, but the conclusion of this ballad, where MacDonald reveals all his grandeur, turns it into a cheerful and dramatic romance.

On the whole, ballad plots are more likely to be tragic than humorous. They celebrate bloody and terrible battles, ghosts that return to haunt their true or their false loves, fairy husbands of human maids, infanticide, murder, faithless love punished, faithful love not always rewarded—sad, sad, romance and tragedies in every possible combination. Sadder still, there is not always the clear retribution characteristic of the folk tales. Ballad villains are all too likely to make a go of their fell deeds, and their victims frequently die off with hardly time to curse them properly. Since children always disapprove of this lack of poetic justice, the ballads have to be combed carefully if you are to find a fair proportion with satisfactory, or just, endings. When you wish to use a sad one like "Bonny Barbara Allan" or "Lord Randal," then you should probably sing it. The gentle music leaves the children feeling so tender toward the victim that they almost forget the villain.

The ballads often begin right in the middle of a complicated story. "The Daemon Lover" ("James Harris") opens with a brisk dialogue and not a "he said" to guide you:

## VIEWPOINTS

The ballad art is peculiarly, though unconsciously, fitted for the representation of the supernatural. The brevity of the ballad, its tendency to proceed by allusion and suggestion, its omission of essentials, its love of the unmotived and unexplained, combine to give a peculiar charm and effectiveness to ghost or fairy stories.

Most of these ballads, we have seen, are tragic, or select a situation full of emotional significance. It is easy to see, then, what part of a long story the selected incident will be: clearly, as in Greek tragedy, the last and most significant of a series, the climax and close of the story, what would be the fifth act of a romantic drama, the "moment of last suspense" and the "catastrophe." The rest of the story the ballad is inclined to omit. . . . No matter how abrupt the beginning, however, the first problem of the ballad is exposition; the hearer is to be put in possession of enough facts to enable him to follow the story intelligently.—Walter Morris Hart, *Philology and Literature (Volume XI: Ballad and Epic, A Study in the Development of the Narrative Art,* Ginn, Boston, 1907, pp. 21, 34.

*'O where have you been, my long, long love,*
*This long seven years and mair?'*
*'O I'm come to seek my former vows*
*Ye granted me before.'*

*'O hold your tongue of your former vows,*
*For they will breed sad strife;*
*O hold your tongue of your former vows,*
*For I am become a wife.'*

And there you are with a melodrama well under way. Three ragged gypsies sing at the door of a fine lady, and she comes promptly down the stairs—so the first verse of "The Raggle, Taggle Gypsies" ("The Gypsy Laddie") tells you, and you never do find out why. These are typical ballad beginnings; you have to keep reading to find out what on earth everyone is up to and why.

The conclusions are sometimes equally abrupt. In "Get Up and Bar the Door," after the old man breaks his vow and speaks first, the ballad concludes with the old woman skipping around in high glee. But what of those two roguish gentlemen? Nothing more is said about them, and you are left wondering mildly what happened next. Sometimes the ballad ends on a teasing note. What does that mean, you ask yourself, and go on wondering. In the last verse of "The Wife of Usher's Well," when the ghosts of the widow's three sons hear the cock crow and know they must be gone, one of them says:

*Fare ye weel, my mother dear!*
*Fareweel to barn and byre!*
*And fare ye weel, the bonny lass*
*That kindles my mother's fire!*

There is a suggestion of a sad romance in the last two lines—a poor ghost leaving behind not only his mother, his barn, and his byre, but his heart's delight as well! When these cryptic endings set the listener's imagination to work, they are almost as satisfactory as neat, thoroughgoing conclusions. They give the hearer a sense of making the story himself.

Intent on telling a dramatic story, ballad makers were not concerned with either the details of the landscape or the emotions of the characters. Nature is used as a highly conventionalized setting for a tale. "It fell upon a Martinmass" or "at Lammas time" or "in the merry month of May" are favorite phrases. So, depending on the season, the nights may be "lang and mirk" or green leaves "a-springing" or lovers may walk along a green road "the greenest ever was seen." Maidens are "the fairest ever seen," and men are "lords of high degree" or "proper men." These are ballad conventions that made composition easy and memorizing even easier. When "Sir Patrick Spens" receives the "braid letter," "a loud lauch lauched he" and then "a tier blinded his ee." Such conventions take care of the emotions. The characters may "rive" their hair, and of course they die for love right on schedule, so that they can be buried side by side and roses can grow from their graves—

*Until they could grow no higher,*
*And twisted and twined in a true lover's knot*
*Which made all the parish admire.*

Today such standardized phrases are called formulas. They serve a useful purpose in the ballad by easing the strain of composition and centering attention on the action.

Incremental repetition is another aid to storytelling. This is a ballad convention in which each verse repeats the form of the preceding verse but with a new turn that advances the story. Here, for instance, is a portion of "The Cruel Brother." This ballad gives a breathing space for the composer with its formal refrains and leads up to the climax with its incremental repetition. The story concerns the fate of the fair lady whose lover forgets to ask her brother John for his consent to their marriage. This oversight is punished when John stabs the bride. To her lover the bride says:

*'O, lead me gently up the hill,*
*With a hey ho and a lillie gay*

*'And I'll there sit down, and make my will.'*
*As the primrose spreads so sweetly.*

*'O what will you leave your father dear?'*
*With a hey ho and a lillie gay*
*'The silver-shode steed that brought me here.'*
*As the primrose spreads so sweetly.*

*'What will you leave to your mother dear?'*
*With a hey ho and a lillie gay*
*'My velvet pall and my silken gear.'*
*As the primrose spreads so sweetly.*

*'What will you leave to your sister Anne?'*
*With a hey ho and a lillie gay*
*'My silken scarf and my gowden fan.'*
*As the primrose spreads so sweetly.*

*'What will you leave to your sister Grace?'*
*With a hey ho and a lillie gay*
*'My bloody cloaths to wash and dress.'*
*As the primrose spreads so sweetly.*

*'What will you leave to your brother John?'*
*With a hey ho and a lillie gay*
*'The gallows-tree to hang him on.'*
*As the primrose spreads so sweetly.*

Reading these ballads that use incremental repetition, you will find it easy to imagine a leader starting the pattern by asking the question, a crowd of people singing the refrain, and the same leader, or perhaps the next man in the circle, answering the question.

Whoever the author, he always remains anonymous. Reference to the storyteller is comparatively rare, perhaps only in an opening line. The charming "Wee Wee Man" begins, "As I was walking all alone" and records the adventures of the speaker when he meets a fairy man. Nevertheless, the story concerns the fairy world and not the author of the tale. Who he was, how he felt, you never learn. He merely records the facts of the adventure as objectively as possible and remains himself completely anonymous. For the most part, the storytelling is impersonal and gives you not the slightest inkling of the author's point of view or station in life. It is "good reporting" in the modern sense.

The ballads, as we have observed, run the whole gamut of subjects and emotions. Here are some categories with a few examples:

*Farce*—The Crafty Farmer; Get Up and Bar the Door
*Comedy*—King John and the Abbot of Canterbury (King John and the Bishop); A Gest of Robyn Hode (with the exception of the account of Robin Hood's death)
*Crime*—Edward; The Bonny Earl of Murray; Lord Randal; The Twa Sisters
*Noble tragedy*—Sir Patrick Spens; The Hunting of the Cheviot; The Battle of Harlaw; The Battle of Otterburn (the ballads of the great battles are generally too involved for the elementary school)
*Romance*—Lizie Lindsay; Bonny Barbara Allan; The Raggle, Taggle Gypsies (The Gypsy Laddie)
*Fairylore*—The Wee Wee Man; Tam Lin; Hind Etin
*Ghost story*—The Wife of Usher's Well
*Melodrama*—The Daemon Lover (James Harris); Lord Randal; Bonny Barbara Allan

## FOLK BALLADS IN THE UNITED STATES

Early settlers brought the old Scottish and English ballads to this country, and children in states as remote from each other as Pennsylvania and Texas, or Wisconsin and the Carolinas, heard their parents and their grandparents singing the same ballads that *their* grandparents had sung in the mother country. "Bonny Barbara Allan," for example, was carried by the colonists and pioneer families from one end of the United States to the other.

The Child collection stimulated such an interest in these old story songs that collectors began to search for and record their American variants. They found, as you might expect, a large number of ballads being sung

### VIEWPOINTS

. . . Ballads are widely considered to be plotted narratives, rising from relatively trained minds, taken over and fostered by the folk until they become the verses and masterpieces that our collectors uncover.

The word "plotted" is of particular significance. . . . Plotting is honored by the tradition in which the Anglo-American ballad is born, but there is little evidence to support a contention that the folk, in whose oral heritage the ballad lives, care very much at all for unified action. Their myths and their tales lack unified action, except as a vestige. Generally, the folk tend to discard plotting in favor of something one might call "impact" or "emotional core." . . .

A ballad survives among our folk because it embodies a basic human reaction to a dramatic situation. This reaction is reinterpreted by each person who renders the ballad. As an emotional core it dominates the artistic act, and melody, setting, character, and plot are used only as means by which to get it across. This core is more important to the singer and the listeners than the details of the action themselves.—Tristram P. Coffin, "Mary Hamilton and the Anglo-American Ballad as an Art Form," in *The Critics and the Ballad*, readings selected and edited by MacEdward Leach and Tristram P. Coffin, Southern Illinois University Press, Carbondale, 1961, pp. 245, 246, 247.

or recited throughout the country, but especially in the Southern mountains. There the mountaineers, cut off from the main stream of immigration and changing customs, had preserved the songs their ancestors brought with them. Sometimes "Barbara Allan" was "Barbery Allen" or "Barbara Ellen," but in every version she was the same heartless girl whose cruelty caused her lover's death. "Lord Randal" might be hailed democratically as "Johnny Randall," or even "Jimmy Randolph," but he was still begging his mother to make his bed soon for he was "sick at the heart and fain wad lie down." Sometimes the verses had been so altered and patched together that they were incoherent. Most of the ballads had, however, come through with less change than you might naturally expect from several hundred years of oral transmission.

Cecil J. Sharp (1859–1924), an English musician, made early and outstanding collections of these survivals of the Scottish-English ballads in the Southern mountains of the United States. His books are valuable contributions to ballad literature in this country, and other collectors have followed his lead. Older children will enjoy the ballads in Sharp's first two volumes, while children as young as three and four are charmed with the *Nursery Songs*.[10]

These collections bear witness to the fact that the traditional ballads are still flourishing in places far removed from their source. Evidently the old woman who gave Sir Walter Scott so many of his ballads was overly pessimistic when she burst into tears at the sight of them in print. She would be surprised to hear voices of invisible singers, coming from boxes (phonographs, radios, and television), singing her ballads even as they were sung long ago. The traditional ballads of England and Scotland did not die between the covers of books but were kept gaily alive by the descendants of the early settlers who brought them to this country. Printing seems merely to have stimulated a greater pride and a more sustained interest in them.

Once the collectors set to work gathering the American variants of the old-world ballads, they began to encounter new ballads and folk songs that are as native to the United States as buckwheat cakes and hominy grits. Lumberjacks, slaves, miners, cowboys, chain gangs, railroad men, cotton pickers, and sailors had all been singing at their work, it seemed, and they had been singing less of the sufferings of Barbara Allan than of their own toil and hardships. Here was a rich

10. C. J. Sharp, compiler, *English Folk Songs from the Southern Appalachians* (Oxford, 1953); *American-English Folk Songs* (Schirmer, 1918); *Nursery Songs from the Appalachian Mountains* (Novello, 1921-1923).

treasure of ballad-making still in the process of creation. On the whole, these songs are rougher and sometimes more sordid in language and theme than their Scottish-English predecessors. They do, however, achieve a wistful melancholy or a happy-go-lucky philosophy or a sheer braggadocio that seems to distinguish certain groups of our hardy settlers or certain workers such as the Western cowboys.

The native ballads of the United States tell, on the whole, fewer coherent and dramatic stories than do the Scottish-English ballads; but they sing with or without the music. They usually have a chorus, but so completely gone are the "Hey nonny nonnies," that it is almost a shock to encounter a "Derry down, down, down, derry down" in "Red Iron Ore."[11] The refrains are more likely to repeat a phrase or to be a three- or four-line chorus. The Negro spirituals reach heights of religious fervor never attained in any old-world ballad, but for their full beauty they need their music. The cowboy ballads have sometimes a philosophic or a wistful air that is more in the mood of a song than of a story. The language is easier for us, even the dialect or vernacular, but some of it is rather rough. Among these ballads, as in the English and Scottish popular ballads, there is material composed by adults for adults with themes as well as language unsuited to children. No sensible youngster will be hurt by browsing through the collections, but ballads for use in the classroom should be selected by the teacher.

With the increasing popularity of folk singing in the middle period of the twentieth century, there has been a renaissance of the ballad form. Young people have been exposed through radio and television as well as in live performances to the songs of protest and peace, to such wistful anti-war songs as "Where Have All the Flowers Gone?" and to the social commentary of "Little Boxes." The outstanding performer-composers are the heroes of the young, the guitar the indispensable instrument, the ballad their own song. And, for the younger children, there is an echoing trend in the publication of single songs in illustrated editions.

Once children realize that ballads are still remembered and treasured, they may turn collectors and discover some ballads in their own families or communities. Once they realize that ballads are still being made not merely by professional poets imitating

11. This ballad is given in *The American Songbag* by Carl Sandburg (Harcourt, 1927).

## VIEWPOINTS

. . . [Bob] Dylan nearly abandoned established material for songs of his own composition. The transition from one to the other was nearly imperceptible since he had the good sense to keep his overall cadence within the framework of familiar traditional music. He begged and borrowed from the established ballad styles of the past (in some cases quite freely), from the prolific works of Woody Guthrie, from the contemporary production of friends like Clayton. But the stories he told in his songs had nothing to do with unrequited Appalachian love affairs or idealized whore-houses in New Orleans. They told about the cane murder of Negro servant Hattie Carroll, the death of boxer Davey Moore, the unbroken chains of injustice waiting for the hammers of a crusading era. They went right to the heart of his decade's most recurring preoccupation: that in a time of totally irreversible technological progress, moral amelioration has pathetically faltered; that no matter how much international attention is focused on macrocosmic affairs, the plight of the individual must be considered, or we are forever lost.

Such a theme has often been associated with the output of folk poets; in fact, since the time John Henry laid down his hammer and died from the competition of the industrial revolution, they have celebrated little else.—Richard Farina, "Baez and Dylan: A Generation Singing Out," in *The American Folk Scene—Dimensions of the Folksong Revival*, edited and with an Introduction by David A. De Turk and A. Poulin, Jr., Dell Publishing Co., 1967, pp. 255–256.

old forms but by isolated peoples celebrating tragic, comic, or dramatic events, the children, too, may wish to try group composition of a ballad. It is fun and less difficult than it sounds. Certainly newspapers supply stories of heroes that are the very stuff of which these story poems have always been made, Radio and television make constant use of such episodes for sketches and dramas. Why not try casting them into ballad form?

What a rich legacy children have inherited from the anonymous folk literature of the past! Young children listen to the lively verses of *Mother Goose,* say them, gallop to them, and pore over the pictures endlessly. So children begin poetry happily with *Mother Goose,* whose varied verses lead them naturally into modern lyric poetry and also into that other, more mature, form of folk verse, the traditional ballads. These exciting story poems belong chiefly to the older children, not only because of the difficult language but also because of the mature content. The ballads, too, lead into modern poetry. It may seem a far cry from "The Cruel Brother" to Robert Browning's "My Last Duchess," but after all, both poems leave much unsaid, to be read between the lines, and Browning's sad lady won't seem unfamiliar to youngsters who have encountered "The Cruel Brother." These folk verses, both *Mother Goose* and the ballads, train the ear, challenge the imagination, and familiarize children with the fun, the excitement, and the sound and melody of English verse.

## ADULT REFERENCES: MOTHER GOOSE[12]

*The Annotated Mother Goose.*

BARCHILON, JACQUES, and HENRY PETTIT. *The Authentic Mother Goose Fairy Tales and Nursery Rhymes.*

BETT, HENRY. *The Games of Children; Their Origin and History.*

12. Complete bibliographic data are provided in the combined Adult References in the Appendices.

CREIGHTON, HELEN, comp. *Songs and Ballads from Nova Scotia.*

ECKENSTEIN, LINA. *Comparative Studies in Nursery Rhymes.*

FORD, ROBERT. *Children's Rhymes, Children's Games, Children's Songs, Children's Stories: A Book for Bairns and Big Folk.*

GREEN, PERCY B. *A History of Nursery Rhymes.*

HALLIWELL-PHILLIPPS, JAMES O. *Popular Rhymes and Nursery Tales: A Sequel to The Nursery Rhymes of England.*

MAHONY, BERTHA E., LOUISE P. LATIMER, and BEULAH FOLMSBEE, comps. *Illustrators of Children's Books, 1744–1945.*

MEIGS, CORNELIA, ANNE EATON, ELIZABETH NESBITT, and RUTH HILL VIGUERS. *A Critical History of Children's Literature.*

MUIR, PERCY. *English Children's Books, 1600 to 1900.*

OPIE, IONA and PETER. *Children's Games in Street and Playground.*

______, *The Lore and Language of Schoolchildren.*

______, comps. *A Family Book of Nursery Rhymes.*

______, eds. *The Oxford Dictionary of Nursery Rhymes.*

*The Original Mother Goose's Melody, As First Issued by John Newbery, of London, about A.D. 1760.*

ST. JOHN, JUDITH. *The Osborne Collection of Early Children's Books 1566–1910; A Catalogue.*

THOMAS, KATHERINE ELWES. *The Real Personages of Mother Goose.*

## MOTHER GOOSE EDITIONS

ADDAMS, CHARLES, ill. *The Chas. Addams Mother Goose.* Harper, 1967.

ALIKI, ill. *Hush Little Baby.* Prentice, 1968. Softly colored pictures and simple format in a charming version of an old folk lullaby.

ANGLUND, JOAN WALSH, ill. *In a Pumpkin Shell.* Harcourt, 1960. Familiar nursery rhymes are imaginatively arranged to achieve an alphabet book. Colorful illustrations.

BRIGGS, RAYMOND, ill. *The Mother Goose Treasury.* Coward, 1966. Greenaway Medal.

BROOKE, L. LESLIE, ill. *Ring o' Roses: A Nursery Rhyme Picture Book.* Warne, 1922.

CALDECOTT, RANDOLPH, ill. *Hey Diddle Diddle Picture Book.* Warne, n.d. Some of Caldecott's finest pictures accompany favorite rhymes of the nursery.

DE ANGELI, MARGUERITE, ill. *Marguerite de Angeli's Book of Nursery and Mother Goose Rhymes.* Doubleday, 1954.

EMBERLEY, ED, ill. *London Bridge Is Falling Down; The Song and Game.* Little, 1967.

FRASCONI, ANTONIO, ill. *The House That Jack Built.* Harcourt, 1958. In a handsomely illustrated picture book, a favorite nursery rhyme is told in both French and English.

GALDONE, PAUL, ill. *The House That Jack Built.* Whittlesey, 1961. Colorful illustrations and picture-book format give new life to an old favorite.

GREENAWAY, KATE, ill. *Mother Goose; or, The Old Nursery Rhymes.* Warne, 1882.

GROVER, EULALIE OSGOOD, ed. *Mother Goose; The Volland Edition*, ill. by Frederick Richardson. Hubbard Pr., 1971. A revised version of the 1915 publication with original illustrations.

LINES, KATHLEEN, ed. *Lavender's Blue*, ill. by Harold Jones. Watts, 1954.

MONTGOMERIE, NORAH and WILLIAM, comps. *A Book of Scottish Nursery Rhymes*, ill. by T. Ritchie and Norah Montgomerie. Oxford, 1965.

*Mother Goose in Hieroglyphics*. Houghton, 1962. An exact reproduction of an old edition of Mother Goose using words and rebus pictures, with an explanatory key for pictures that puzzle the reader! Originally published in Boston over a century ago.

OPIE, IONA, ed. *Ditties for the Nursery*, ill. by Monica Walker. Walck, 1954.

OPIE, IONA and PETER, comps. *A Family Book of Nursery Rhymes*, ill. by Pauline Baynes. Oxford, 1964.

———, comps. *The Oxford Nursery Rhyme Book*, ill. from old chapbooks, with additional pictures by Joan Hassall. Walck, 1955.

RACKHAM, ARTHUR, ill. *Mother Goose; The Old Nursery Rhymes*. Watts, 1969.

REED, PHILIP, ill. *Mother Goose and Nursery Rhymes*. Atheneum, 1963.

ROJANKOVSKY, FEODOR, ill. *The Tall Book of Mother Goose*. Harper, 1942.

SENDAK, MAURICE, ill. *Hector Protector, and As I Went Over the Water*. Harper, 1965.

SPIER, PETER, ill. *London Bridge Is Falling Down!* Doubleday, 1967.

TENGGREN, GUSTAF, ill. *The Tenggren Mother Goose*. Little, 1956. Gay, Disney-like pictures which do not always illustrate the rhymes near which they appear.

TUCKER, NICHOLAS, comp. *Mother Goose Lost*, ill. by Trevor Stubley. T. Crowell, 1971. A collection of unfamiliar American and English rhymes.

TUDOR, TASHA, ill. *Mother Goose*. Walck, 1944.

WILDSMITH, BRIAN, ill. *Brian Wildsmith's Mother Goose*. Watts, 1965.

WRIGHT, BLANCHE FISHER, ill. *The Real Mother Goose*. Rand, 1916.

## A FEW VARIANTS OF MOTHER GOOSE

BURROUGHS, MARGARET TAYLOR, comp. *Did You Feed My Cow? Street Games, Chants, and Rhymes*, rev. ed., ill. by Joe E. DeValasco. Follett, 1969. 8-10

DEFOREST, CHARLOTTE B. *The Prancing Pony; Nursery Rhymes from Japan adapted into English verse for children*, with "Kusa-e" ill. by Keiko Hida. Walker, 1968. 3-7

DE KAY, ORMONDE, JR. *Rimes de La Mere Oie; Mother Goose Rhymes rendered into French*. Little, 1971. More colloquial than Hugh Latham's translation. Illustrations are by Barry Zaid (pedestrian), Seymour Chwast (good), and Milton Glaser (very good). 5-8

EMRICH, DUNCAN, comp. *The Nonsense Book of Riddles, Rhymes, Tongue Twisters, Puzzles and Jokes from American Folklore*, ill. by Ib Ohlsson. Four Winds, 1970. A fine collection of Americana by an eminent folklorist. A section of notes and a bibliography are appended. 7-11

FOWKE, EDITH, comp. *Sally Go Round the Sun; Three Hundred Children's Songs, Rhymes and Games*, ill. by Carlos Marchiori. Doubleday, 1970. The material, collected directly from children by an expert on Canadian folklore, is ideally suited for adult use with groups of small children. Instructions for forty of the games; musical arrangements are simple. 8-10

*How Many Strawberries Grow in the Sea? A Songbook of Mother Goose Rhymes*, music by Earl Bichel, ill. by George Suyeoka. Follett, 1969. 4-8

KAPP, PAUL, ed. and music arr. *A Cat Came Fiddling and Other Rhymes of Childhood*, ill. by Irene Haas. Harcourt, 1956. Here is enchantment for children and adults, at home or in school. The pictures are droll and perfect, and Burl Ives says of the music, "it sounds as though it had never been written but only sung." All ages

LANGSTAFF, JOHN. *Ol' Dan Tucker*, ill. by Joe Krush. Harcourt, 1963. Lively picture-book retelling of Ol' Dan Tucker's endless mishaps. Music included. 7 up

———, ed. *Over in the Meadow*, ill. by Feodor Rojankovsky. Harcourt, 1957. The old counting rhyme of little creatures who lived "in the sand in the sun" is presented in a beautiful picture book. Music included. 3-8

LATHAM, HUGH, tr. *Mother Goose in French*, ill. by Barbara Cooney. T. Crowell, 1964. 5-8

LEACH, MARIA. *Riddle Me, Riddle Me, Ree*, ill. by William Wiesner. Viking, 1970. A collection of over 200 riddles drawn from folk materials the world over. Sources are given, and a section of notes makes the book useful for adults. 8-11

LOW, JOSEPH and RUTH. *Mother Goose Riddle Rhymes*, ill. by Joseph Low. Harcourt, 1953. Mr. Low has made a modern rebus from nursery rhymes that is beautiful in design and clever in conception—a brain teaser for young and old. 6-9

MITCHELL, DONALD, comp. *Every Child's Book of Nursery Songs*, arr. by Carey Blyton, ill. by Alan Howard. Crown, 1968. 3-7

MORRISON, LILLIAN, comp. *Black Within and Red Without*, ill. by Jo Spier. T. Crowell, 1953. A scholarly collection of rhymed riddles, wise, witty, and often as charming as poetry. Here are traditional puzzlers from ancient Egypt, Greece, the British Isles, the Orient, and our own Ozarks. 8 up

———, comp. *A Dillar a Dollar*, ill. by Marjorie Bauernschmidt. T. Crowell, 1955. Here is an exceedingly funny collection of anonymous "Rhymes and Sayings for the Ten O'Clock Scholar." Over three hundred school riddles, sayings, derisive taunts, jokes, and proverbs will be sure to enliven classroom routines. 6-13

———, comp. *Remember Me When This You See*, ill. by Marjorie Bauernschmidt. T. Crowell, 1961. 9-14

———, comp. *Touch Blue*, ill. by Doris Lee. T. Crowell, 1958. "Signs and spells, Love Charms and Chants, Auguries and Old Beliefs in Rhyme." All ages

———, comp. *Yours Till Niagara Falls*, ill. by Marjorie Bauernschmidt. T. Crowell, 1950. 9-13

PETERSHAM, MAUD and MISKA. *The Rooster Crows: A Book of American Rhymes and Jingles.* Macmillan, 1945. Caldecott Medal. 5-7

POTTER, CHARLES FRANCIS, comp. *Tongue Tanglers,* ill. by William Wiesner. World, 1962. 8-11

REID, ALAISTAIR, and ANTHONY KERRIGAN, tr. *Mother Goose in Spanish,* ill. by Barbara Cooney. T. Crowell, 1968. 5-8

WINN, MARIE, comp. and ed. *What Shall We Do and Allee Galloo!* ill. by Karla Kuskin. Harper, 1970. A collection of game and activity songs, each with directions for children's participation. A preface suggests ways to introduce them and appropriate times to use them. 3-6

WITHERS, CARL, comp. *A Rocket in My Pocket,* ill. by Susanne Suba. Holt, 1948. 6-8

WOOD, RAY. *The American Mother Goose,* ill. by Ed Hargis. Lippincott, 1940. All ages

WYNDHAM, ROBERT, comp. *Chinese Mother Goose Rhymes,* ill. by Ed Young. World, 1968. 4-6

ZEMACH, HARVE. *Mommy, Buy Me a China Doll,* ill. by Margot Zemach. Follett, 1966. A charming picture-book version of the cumulative Ozark folk song. 3-7

———, ed. *The Speckled Hen: A Russian Nursery Rhyme,* ill. by Margot Zemach. Holt, 1966. One small hen starts a cascade of dire events. 4-6

## ADULT REFERENCES: THE BALLADS

ABRAHAMS, ROGER, and GEORGE FOSS. *Anglo-American Folksong Style.*

BRAND, OSCAR. *The Ballad Mongers; Rise of the Modern Folk Song.*

CHILD, FRANCIS JAMES, ed. *English and Scottish Popular Ballads.*

COFFIN, TRISTRAM P. *The British Traditional Ballad in North America.*

FRIEDMAN, ALBERT B. *The Viking Book of Folk Ballads of the English Speaking World.*

HALES, JOHN W., and FREDERICK J. FURNIVALL, assisted by FRANCIS J. CHILD. *Bishop Percy's Folio Manuscript.*

HODGART, M. J. C. *The Ballads.*

KITTREDGE, GEORGE LYMAN, ed. *English and Scottish Popular Ballads: Student's Cambridge Edition.*

KRAPPE, ALEXANDER HAGGERTY. *The Science of Folk-Lore.*

LOMAX, JOHN A., ed. *Songs of the Cattle Trail and Cow Camp.*

LOMAX, JOHN A., and ALAN LOMAX, comps. *American Ballads and Folk Songs.*

———, eds. *Cowboy Songs and Other Frontier Ballads.*

LEACH, MAC EDWARD. *Folk Ballads and Songs of the Lower Labrador Coast.*

———, ed. *The Ballad Book.*

MYRUS, DONALD. *Ballads, Blues, and the Big Beat.* Chapter, "Poems, Protests, and Put Downs."

POUND, LOUISE. *Poetic Origins and the Ballad.*

———, ed. *American Ballads and Songs.*

SCOTT, JOHN ANTHONY. *The Ballad of America: The History of the United States in Song and Story.*

SHARP, CECIL J. *Nursery Songs from the Appalachian Mountains.*

———, comp. *English Folk-Songs from the Southern Appalachians.*

*Some British Ballads.*

## BALLAD SOURCES

Many of the poetry anthologies listed on pp. 383–385 contain sections devoted to old ballads or to modern story poems. Of these anthologies, *My Poetry Book,* by Huffard, Carlisle, and Ferris, contains an unusually large and well-selected group of story poems for the elementary school.

BAKER, LAURA NELSON. *The Friendly Beasts,* ill. by Nicolas Sidjakov. Parnassus, 1957. Reverent and beautiful illustrations enhance this version of an old English carol of the first Christmas eve, when animals talked in the stable at Bethlehem. 4 up

BONI, MARGARET BRADFORD, ed. *Fireside Book of Folk Songs,* arr. for piano by Norman Lloyd, ill. by Alice and Martin Provensen. Simon, 1966. A beautiful collection of many types of folk songs to be enjoyed by the whole family. 8 up

BROWNING, ROBERT. *The Pied Piper of Hamelin,* ill. by Kate Greenaway. Warne, n.d. Kate Greenaway made some of her loveliest pictures for this poem.

———. *The Pied Piper of Hamelin,* ill. by Harold Jones. Watts, 1962. An attractive, color-illustrated, new edition. 6-12

COLE, WILLIAM, ed. *Story Poems New and Old,* ill. by Walter Buehr. World, 1957. Over 90 story poems include traditional ballads, old favorites, and choice modern verses. 9 up

DE REGNIERS, BEATRICE SCHENK. *Catch a Little Fox,* ill. by Brinton Turkle. Seabury, 1970. Variations on a folk rhyme have sprightly illustrations. 4-7

FELTON, HAROLD W., ed. *Cowboy Jamboree: Western Songs and Lore,* music arr. by Edward S. Breck, ill. by Aldren A. Watson, foreword by Carl Carmer. Knopf, 1951. This small collection of only twenty songs is especially valuable because of the little introductions to each song. 6 up

FERRIS, HELEN, comp. *Love's Enchantment,* ill. by Vera Bock. Doubleday, 1944. A collection of romantic ballads. 12 up

LANGSTAFF, JOHN. *Frog Went a-Courtin',* ill. by Feodor Rojankovsky. Harcourt, 1955. Caldecott Medal. 4-6

———, comp. *Hi! Ho! The Rattlin' Bog; And Other Folk Songs for Group Singing,* with piano settings by John Edmunds, et al., with guitar chords suggested by Happy Traum, ill. by Robin Jacques. Harcourt, 1969. 12 up

LANGSTAFF, NANCY and JOHN, eds. *Jim Along, Josie; A Collection of Folk Songs and Singing Games for Young Children,* ill. by Jan Pienkowski. Harcourt, 1970. A good collection of folk songs, action songs, and singing games with a discussion of their use with children. 5-8

LONGFELLOW, HENRY WADSWORTH. *Paul Revere's*

*Ride*, ill. by Paul Galdone. T. Crowell, 1963. Illustrations in rich color capture the somber beauty of the night and the colonial countryside. 8 up

MALCOLMSON, ANNE, ed. *Song of Robin Hood*, music arr. by Grace Castagnetta, ill. by Virginia Burton. Houghton, 1947. A collector's item, this beautiful book is invaluable as a source both for ballad text and music. 12 up

MANNING-SANDERS, RUTH, ed. *A Bundle of Ballads*, ill. by William Stobbs. Lippincott, 1961. More than sixty traditional ballads, varied in mood and theme, introduce children to an absorbing poetic form. Given England's Kate Greenaway Award in 1959. 12 up

MOORE, CLEMENT CLARK. *The Night Before Christmas*, ill. by Arthur Rackham. Lippincott, 1954. A new edition with Rackham's lovely pictures. 4-7

———. *The Night Before Christmas*, ill. by Leonard Weisgard. Grosset, 1949. Bold, bright colors and design characterize this big modern edition. 4-7

NIC LEODHAS, SORCHE. *By Loch and By Lin*. Holt, 1969. Flavorful retellings of tales from Scottish ballads. 9-12

PARKER, ELINOR, comp. *100 Story Poems*, ill. by Henry C. Pitz. T. Crowell, 1951. All the favorite old story poems are here. 8-14

———, comp. *100 More Story Poems*, ill. by Peter Spier T. Crowell, 1960. 8-14

RITCHIE, JEAN, *The Swapping Song Book*, ill. with photos by George Pickow. Walck, 1964. All ages

SCHREITER, RICK, ill. *The Derby Ram*. Doubleday, 1970. Intricate, almost Hogarthian illustrations enliven a robust nursery ballad. 7-9

SEEGER, RUTH CRAWFORD. *American Folk Songs for Christmas*, ill. by Barbara Cooney. Doubleday, 1953.

———. *Animal Folk Songs For Children: Traditional American Songs*, ill. by Barbara Cooney. Doubleday, 1950. An interesting introduction discussing our native animal folklore. Songs and illustrations are excellent. 4 up

SERRAILLIER, IAN. *Robin and His Merry Men; Ballads of Robin Hood*, ill. by Victor G. Ambrus. Walck, 1970. In both dialogue and exposition, this retelling keeps to the style and the cadence of the ballad form. 12-14

SPIER, PETER, ill. *The Fox Went Out on a Chilly Night*. Doubleday, 1961. The old folk song enjoys a handsome picture-book setting of New England at harvest time. Illustrations in color and music appended. 5 up

TAYLOR, MARK. *Old Blue: You Good Dog You*, ill. by Gene Holtan. Golden Gate, 1970. The illustrations complement the humor of a folk-based tall tale retold with zest. 8 up

TROUGHTON, JOANNA, ill. *The Little Mohee*. Dutton, 1970. Composed with poster-like simplicity, the strong colors and dramatic, heavy lines of the pictures effectively portray the sentimental story in an Appalachian ballad. 7-9

# Chapter 6
# Folk Tales

Folk tales, like the nursery rhymes and ballads, are a part of that great stream of anonymous creation known as "folklore"—the accumulated wisdom and art of simple everyday folk. In the broadest sense of the word, folklore includes superstitions, medicinal practices, games, songs, festivals, dance rituals, old tales, verses, fables, myths, legends, and epics. Folklore is sometimes called the "mirror of a people." It reveals their characteristic efforts to explain and deal with the strange phenomena of nature; to understand and interpret the ways of human beings with each other; and to give expression to deep, universal emotions—joy, grief, fear, jealousy, wonder, triumph.

Of the many varieties of folklore, the folk tale is the most familiar and perhaps the most appealing. Interest in folk tales developed in the eighteenth century, along with the interest in old ballads, but in the nineteenth century a romantic interest in the old tales grew so strong that many thousands were collected from all over the globe. Striking similarities were then noticed among the folk tales found in different parts of the world, and many theories were advanced to explain these similarities.

## THEORIES OF FOLK-TALE ORIGIN

### Monogenesis

One of the earliest explanations for the similarities among folk tales of different peoples was the *Aryan myth* theory. It involved several ideas which have now been discredited. For instance, this theory held that the language group sometimes called the "Aryans" was a pure racial strain descended from a common stock. We know today that there is no such thing as a pure racial strain. Most important for this discussion, the theory asserted that all folk tales came from the Teutonic myths of this single ancestral group. This is sometimes referred to as the theory of "monogenesis" or "single origin." Although the Aryan myth theory has been refuted, it is interesting today because it has been the springboard for some other theories of folk-tale origin.

### Polygenesis

One group of scholars believed in the theory of *polygenesis*, or "many origins." They asserted that human beings everywhere in the world are moved by much the same emotions—love and pity, fear and anguish, jealousy and hatred; that every people can observe the results of greed, selfish ambition, or quiet courage and kindliness; that they have seen the ways of cruel stepmothers (were there no loving ones in the old days, one wonders); and that they saw the neglected child come into his own. So Andrew Lang and other believers in polygenesis insisted that similar plots could develop in different parts of the world from similar situations common to all men. Lang used the widely disseminated story of Jason to prove his point. This theory would seem to account for the literally hundreds of variants of "Cinderella" found in Egypt, India, all parts of Europe, and among the North American Indians.

However, modern social anthropologists point out that people are *not* the same the world over. In some cultures, for instance, stepmothers may not be feared at all. The Andaman Islanders are apparently indifferent to whether the children they bring up are their own or other people's—no stepmother problem there! Another objection made to polygenesis is that the same story in all its peculiar details and chains of events could scarcely have grown up quite independently among entirely different groups isolated from each other. But whether or not there is any validity to the theory of polygenesis, one thing is certain: almost all peoples have produced stories and there are striking similarities among the tales of different peoples.

## Remnants of Myth and Ritual

Some students, convinced that the folk tales preserved the *remnants of nature myths*, continually interpret any traditional story as a nature allegory—whether it is about sleep or forgetfulness, about a hero battling with a dragon, or about a lassie being carried off by a polar bear. "Little Red Riding Hood," for instance, has been interpreted as an allegory of sunset and sunrise. The wolf is supposed to symbolize night, and in many versions he succeeds in devouring the little girl, who in her red cape represents the setting sun. This symbolic interpretation is extended in the Grimm version of the story, in which the hunters cut open the wolf and release "Little Red-Cap," the sun, from her imprisonment in the wolf, or night. Perrault's version of "The Sleeping Beauty," with its oddly extraneous part about the ogress, was considered another embodiment of this night and day myth. The ogress (night) first wishes to devour Beauty's two children, Dawn and Day, and then Beauty herself (the sun). The Norse "East o' the Sun" with its polar bear and its disappearing Prince was, like the Balder myth (see p. 192), supposed to explain the disappearance of the sun.

Other folklorists, while not interpreting all the old stories as nature allegories, believed that many of these tales preserved *remnants of other kinds of religious myth and ritual*. For instance, Sir George Webbe Dasent thought that the Norse folk tales contained many of the elements of the Norse myths. He explained that after Christianity came to the Scandinavian countries, the old Norse gods lost their prestige and were gradually changed into the fabulous creatures of the folk tales. Odin became the Wild Huntsman riding through the sky with his grisly crew. And perhaps the nursery tale of "The Three Billy-Goats Gruff" preserves the memory of Thor's battle with the Frost Giants, for the billy goat was the ancient symbol of Thor, and the huge, stupid trolls could easily be the inglorious descendants of the Frost Giants.

Some scholars believe that the cumulative tales like "The House That Jack Built" and "The Old Woman and Her Pig" have ritualistic origins. Other stories too, they think, preserve fragments of spells or incantations. In the Grimms' dramatic "The Goose-Girl," the heroine puts a spell on Conrad's hat:

*Blow, blow, thou gentle wind, I say,*
*Blow Conrad's little hat away. . . .*

Ancient superstitions and customs surrounding christenings and marriage ceremonies may also be found in the folk tales. So may propitiations of spirits, witches, the devil, or certain powerful animals (like the bear in the Norse tales).

## Origins in Dreams and Unconscious Emotions

Psychoanalytic writers have studied those objects and ideas which appear frequently in fairy tales from all over the world and have asserted that they are *symbols of emotional fantasy* which all people experience. Among such supposedly universal feelings are unconscious sexual love for the parent, hatred of paternal or maternal authority, love or jealousy among brothers and sisters. The ideas and objects representing these feelings are supposed to be the same in folk tales the world over and to explain the similarities among these stories. But social anthropologists object to this theory, too. They maintain that unconscious emotions vary among different peoples and so do the symbols which represent them. The unconscious emotions described, they say, may be the characteristic product of modern urban life and not universal among all peoples and times.

Some authorities think that the stories

From The Old Woman and Her Pig by *Paul Galdone. Copyright © 1960. Reproduced by permission of McGraw-Hill Book Company.*

## VIEWPOINTS

We observe that children commonly listen to fairy tales with an air of fascinated horror, or even with gusto, and demand the reading to be repeated. Yet the gruesome figures of these tales, e.g. cannibalistic giants, enter into the frightful nightmares which so many children have to endure. It would therefore seem plain sense to avoid such horror-raising stimulation. But the matter turns out to be not so simple. We find that young children *spontaneously* create in their imagination, both consciously and still more unconsciously, the same images of horror and terror, and that they suffer from nightmares without ever having listened to a fairy story. Indeed it often happens that when their own phantasies are brought into the open by a smiling mother relating a tale of horror they thereby achieve a measure of reassurance by gradually learning that the imagery they conjure up does not correspond to any outer reality.—Ernest Jones, "Preface," for *I Could a Tale Unfold* by P. M. Pickard, Tavistock Publications, London, and Humanities Press, New York, 1961, p. ix.

originated in the *wonderful dreams or nightmares* of the storytellers. Stories about a poor girl sent out to find strawberries in the middle of winter (some versions clothe her in a paper dress) might well grow from the bad dreams we have when the night turns cold and we find ourselves with too few blankets. Did the story of "Snow White" emerge from such a dream? Or consider the story of the poor lassie in "East o' the Sun," who kissed the prince and then found herself out on a lonely road—the prince gone, the castle vanished, the little bell that fulfilled her every wish lost forever, and she in rags once more. Is she the embodiment of our anxieties and our reluctance to return from our dreams to a workaday world? So the fatal questions, impossible tasks, and endless discomforts in the folk tales may suggest some of the anxieties that haunt us in our sleep now and then. Perhaps the primitive quality of some of our dreams may also explain the shocking elements in some of the tales. These always seem less horrible in the stories than they actually should seem because they are seldom attended by any realistic details but are indeed vague, dreamlike, and evanescent.

Another phase of the psychological interpretation of folk-tale origin is the idea that the people who created them found in fancy the *satisfaction of unconscious frustrations or drives*. These imaginative tales provide *wish fulfillment*. That is, the oppressed peasants who produced some of the tales were "motivated by naïve dreams of the success of the despised," and so they told stories about cinder lads and lassies going from wretched hovels to fabulous castles, or about a goose girl marrying the prince. Certain it is that fairy tales do satisfy deep human needs, particularly the needs for security and competence. In the folk tales, banquets, servants, glittering jewels, and rich clothes are concrete symbols of success. Granting that these tales are primarily for entertainment, there seems to be little doubt that they contain a deeper meaning and an inner significance which the child or adult feels without being conscious of the cause. Barchilon and Pettit in discussing Perrault's fairy tales say, "Just as the dream expresses innermost wishes in disguised form, the fairy tale masks our real wishes with the appearance of a free fantasy." And again they emphasize the symbolic character of the tales saying, ". . . the veiled symbolism of the fairy tale and its violence fulfill a need in the child's life. The fairy tale is his apprenticeship to life."[1]

Psychoanalysts also hold that "the child, through the comparison between the fantastic and the real, gradually learns to test reality. When the child realizes that the fairy tale is fictitious, he learns to enjoy it as fiction. This is one giant step not only in the process

1. Jacques Barchilon and Henry Pettit, *The Authentic Mother Goose Fairy Tales and Nursery Rhymes* (Swallow, 1960), p. 27.

of rational maturation but in aesthetic development as well."[2]

## Cement of Society

In recent times the science of folklore has merged more and more into the science of social anthropology. To understand the why and wherefore of folk tales, anthropologists have lived intimately with many peoples, visiting their homes, markets, religious ceremonies, and festal celebrations. Of course they cannot visit the early peoples who produced the folk tales we are most interested in, but their studies of modern folk societies can cast light on the origin of the old folk tales. Their conclusion may be summed up in one sentence: folk tales have been the *cement of society*. They not only expressed but codified and reinforced the way people thought, felt, believed, and behaved.

Folk tales taught children and reminded their elders of what was proper and moral. They put the stamp of approval upon certain values held by the group, and thus cemented it together with a common code of behavior. They taught kindness, modesty, truthfulness, courage in adversity—and they made virtue seem worthwhile because it was invariably rewarded and evil just as invariably punished. This idea of the folk tales as the carriers of the moral code helps explain the ethical significance and emotional satisfaction they still hold for us today.

Some of the explanations for the origins of folk tales are dubious, but many of them are reinforced by enough reasonable evidence to make them seem both plausible and probable. Folklorists now agree that the folk tale is created by most peoples at an early level of civilization. Historically, the tales may contain elements from past religions, rituals, superstitions, or past events. Psychologically, they may serve to satisfy in symbolic form some of man's basic emotional needs. Ethically, they may be "the cement of society"—reinforcing our faith in morality and the ultimate triumph of good over evil.

2. Ibid., p. 26.

### VIEWPOINTS

Children are capable, of course, of *literary belief*, when the story-maker's art is good enough to produce it.

. . . He makes a Secondary World which your mind can enter. Inside it, what he relates is 'true': it accords with the laws of that world. You therefore believe it, while you are, as it were, inside. The moment disbelief arises, the spell is broken; the magic, or rather art, has failed.

. . . at no time can I remember that the enjoyment of a story was dependent on belief that such things could happen, or had happened, in 'real life'. Fairy stories were plainly not primarily concerned with possibility, but with desirability. If they awakened *desire* satisfying it while often whetting it unbearably, they succeeded.

. . . The dragon had the trademark *Of Faërie* written plain upon him. . . . Of course, I in my timid body did not wish to have them in the neighbourhood. . . . This is, naturally, often enough what children mean when they ask: 'Is it true?' They mean: 'I like this, but is it contemporary? Am I safe in my bed?' The answer: 'There is certainly no dragon in England today,' is all that they want to hear.—J. R. R. Tolkien, *Tree and Leaf*, Houghton Mifflin, Boston, 1965, pp. 36–37, 40, 41.

## WIDE DIFFUSION OF THE FOLK TALES

Students have found recognizable variants of such tales as "Nicht Nocht Naething" ("Nix Nought Nothing"), "Jason and the Golden Fleece," and "Cinderella" in the manuscripts of ancient India, Egypt, and Greece and on the lips of storytellers in Zulu huts, Indian hogans, and Samoan villages—from the Russian steppes to African jungles and the mountains of South America. The three tasks, the flight, the pursuit, the lost slipper or sandal, and the undoing of a spell are found in innumerable racial groups. How were they carried?

First, of course, they were carried orally by the migrations of whole peoples. Later they traveled from one country to another with sailors and soldiers, women stolen from their tribes, slaves and captives of war, traders, minstrels and bards, monks and scholars, and young gentlemen on the grand tour. Some storytellers no doubt polished and improved the tales, while others debased them. If the folk tales traveled by land, they were passed on by many peoples and greatly changed in the process; but if they traveled by sea, they stayed closer to the originals. Sometimes one story theme would combine with others, producing either a variant of the original tale or a relatively new one. So ancient storytellers preserved old stories, produced variants of others, and occasionally dreamed up new ones to pass on. This process continues today as missionaries and sailors, teachers and salesmen tell their own versions of the classic tales to children and adults in distant places.

The literary (or written) sources of the popular tales did not begin to circulate in Europe until around the twelfth century. Then came the Indian and Irish manuscript collections, vivid and lively importations which were no doubt partly responsible for the flowering of folk art in the thirteenth century. Ballads and stories began to bubble up everywhere, often with the same plots or themes.

During the sixteenth century, popular literature in England made a dignified beginning in print with Caxton's fine English translations of Aesop's fables, the King Arthur stories, the Homeric epics. In England, too, the chapbooks picked up fragments of tales from everywhere and kept them alive in garbled but recognizable versions, dearly beloved by the people. In the late seventeenth century, Perrault, with the blessing of the French court, ushered the fairy tales into print. These mark the beginnings of our written sources of folk literature in Europe. Their more ancient written sources are still the debating ground for scholars. Our major concern is with the tales themselves in the collections we use today.

## PREDOMINANT KINDS OF FOLK TALES

No adult can read these tales, particularly the French, German, Norwegian, and English, without being conscious of the varied groups into which they fall: cumulative tales, talking-beast tales, drolls or humorous tales, realistic tales, religious tales, romances, and, of course, tales of magic. Many classifications have been made, but this one seems to bring in most of the kinds and to emphasize their characteristics.

### Cumulative Tales

Very young children enjoy the simplest of all stories, the cumulative or repetitional tale. Its charm lies in its minimum plot and maximum rhythm. Its episodes follow each other neatly and logically in a pattern of cadenced repetition. Sometimes, as in "The Old Woman and Her Pig," the action moves upward in a spiral and then retraces the spiral downward to the conclusion. Sometimes, as in the American-English "Johnny-Cake," the Norse "Pancake," and the American "Gingerbread Boy," the action takes the form of a race, and the story comes to an end with the capture of the runaway. Fortunately, the runaway in such stories has forfeited our sympathy by his stupidity ("Henny Penny"), or by his impudence ("The Pancake"), so that his capture becomes merely the downfall of the foolish or the proud.

"The Pancake" is one of the most delightful of these tales. The pancake—having jumped out of the frying pan and escaped from the mother, the father, and the seven hungry children—meets a series of creatures and becomes more insolent with each encounter. The following excerpt is typical of the racing-chasing style of these little tales:

> *"Good day, pancake," said the gander.*
>
> *"The same to you, Gander Pander," said the pancake.*
>
> *"Pancake, dear, don't roll so fast; bide a bit and let me eat you up."*
>
> *"When I have given the slip to Goody Poody, and the goodman, and seven squalling children, and Manny Panny, and Henny Penny, and Cocky Locky, and Ducky Lucky, and Goosey Poosey, I may well slip through your feet, Gander Pander," said the pancake, which rolled off as fast as ever.*
>
> *So when it had rolled a long, long time, it met a pig.*
>
> *"Good day, pancake," said the pig.*
>
> *"The same to you, Piggy Wiggy," said the pancake, which, without a word more, began to roll and roll like mad.* (Tales from the Fjeld.)

Here, in the last four lines, the storyteller by her ominous tone of voice warns the children that for the pancake the jig is up. Piggy Wiggy is Fate itself.

Some cumulative stories, like "The House That Jack Built," are mere chants; others, like "The Three Little Pigs" and "The Bremen Town-Musicians," are repetitional and sequential, but have well-rounded plots.

The popularity of these cumulative tales has led to a tiresome number of modern imitators which have often missed the fun, the element of surprise, and the swift movement of the old stories. Modern examples of the successful use of this pattern are Marjorie Flack's *Ask Mr. Bear*, Wanda Gág's *Millions of Cats*, and Maurice Sendak's *One Was Johnny*.

### Talking-Beast Tales

Perhaps young children love best of all among the old tales the ones in which animals talk. Sometimes the animals talk with human beings as in "Puss in Boots" and "The Three Little Pigs," but more often with other animals as in "The Cat and the Mouse in Partnership." These creatures talk every bit as wisely as humans, or as foolishly. Possibly their charm lies in the opportunity they give the reader to identify himself with the cleverest of the three pigs or the most powerful and efficient member of "The Three Billy-Goats Gruff." Perhaps the credulity of "Henny Penny" or of the two foolish pigs ministers to the listener's sense of superiority. Certainly children are amused by these old tales for the same reasons that modern children laugh at "Mickey Mouse" and "Snoopy." The animals in both the old and the modern creations are exaggerated characterizations of human beings, and in that exaggeration lie their humor and fascination.

*Illustration by Hans Fischer. Reproduced from* Grimm's Traveling Musicians, *by permission of Harcourt Brace Jovanovich, Inc. (Original in color)*

These beast tales generally teach a lesson—the folly of credulity and the rewards of courage, ingenuity, and independence—though their didacticism does not stand out so much as in the fables. The stories are so lively and diverting that they are primarily good entertainment. Perhaps the most successful of the modern descendants of the ancient beast tales are Beatrix Potter's *The Tale of Peter Rabbit, The Tale of Benjamin Bunny*, and all her other "Tales." These have joined the ranks of the immortals, along with "The Three Little Pigs."

### The Drolls or Humorous Tales

A small body of the folk tales are obviously meant as fun and nonsense. These are the stories about sillies or numskulls, such as the Grimms' "Clever Elsie."

As you may remember, Elsie had a wooer who demanded a really clever bride. On one of his visits, Elsie's family sent her down to the cellar to draw some beer, and there, just over her head, she saw a pick-axe that had been left thrust into the masonry. Immediately she began to weep, thinking to herself,

> *"If I get Hans, and we have a child, and he grows big, and we send him into the cellar here to draw beer, then the pick-axe will fall on his head and kill him."*

She cried so hard and so long that first one member of the household and then another came down cellar, listened to her tale, and began to weep, too. Finally, Hans came and, hearing how things were, decided that Elsie was indeed a thoughtful, clever girl and married her. After the marriage Hans, who had evidently taken his bride's measure at last, gave Elsie a task to do in the field and left her there alone. But Elsie, unable to decide whether to work first or sleep first, finally fell asleep in the field and slept until night. Returning home in a great fright, she asked,

> *"Hans, is Elsie within?" "Yes," answered Hans, "she is within." Hereupon she was terrified, and said: "Ah, heavens! Then it is not I."*

And so she ran out of the village and was never seen again.

Like the cumulative tales, the drolls vary in the amount of plot they develop. Some have well-rounded plots; for instance, in "The Husband Who Was to Mind the House" (he does so with disastrous results) and in "Mr. Vinegar" (who trades off his cow as the start of a series of barters which brings him less and less until he has nothing left but a good cudgeling from his wife). The Norse story "Taper Tom" has not only all the droll antics to make the princess laugh but real adventure as well. Finally, the Norse "Squire's Bride" is not only a droll story but also a capital bit of adult satire on elderly wooers of young girls.

These drolls are sometimes the only realistic stories in a folk-tale collection. Realistic stories, of course, are those in which all of the episodes, however improbable, are possible. They *could* have happened.

### Realistic Tales

For the most part, the peoples who created these old tales seem to have had no great taste for using as story material their own "here and now," the stuff of everyday living. Even when they omit all elements of magic, they still tell a fabulous tale: the monster in "Blue Beard," for example, seems to have had some historic basis, but to young readers he is a kind of cross between an ogre and a giant. His English variant, "Mr. Fox," is even less realistic, though strictly speaking there is nothing in either story that could not have happened. Perhaps the prettiest of all realistic stories in our folk-tale collections is the Norse "Gudbrand on the Hill-side." This is "Mr. Vinegar," with a loving wife instead of a shrew. Gudbrand's old wife thinks her man can do no wrong; so, sure of his wife's love

"And thanks to you for that!" said the wife.

*Illustration by Theodor Kittelsen for* Norwegian Folk Tales *collected by Peter Christian Asbjörnsen and Jörgen Moe.*

and understanding, Gudbrand makes a wager with a neighbor that his wife will not blame him no matter what he does. Just as Gudbrand expects, his wife's tender responses to his series of disastrous trades reaches a climax with her heart-felt exclamation:

> *"Heaven be thanked that I have got you safe back again; you do everything so well that I want neither cock nor goose; neither pigs nor kine."*
>
> *Then Gudbrand opened the door and said, "Well, what do you say now? Have I won the hundred dollars?" and his neighbour was forced to allow that he had.*

## Religious Tales

Folk tales using elements of religious beliefs are rarely found in children's collections but are fairly frequent in the complete editions of almost any racial group. Coming down from the morality plays of the Middle Ages, the devil and St. Peter appear usually in comic roles. The Czech tales have an especially large number of devil stories, in which the devil is always worsted. The story of the devil who begged to be taken back to hell in order to escape from a shrew of a wife is a popular plot throughout Europe.

The Virgin is usually introduced respectfully and even tenderly. Grimm has several stories in which Our Lady appears, intervening in human lives, kindly and with pity.

St. Joseph is also introduced as a figure of compassion and as the administrator of poetic justice. The religious folk tales are generally either broadly comic or didactic and are, on the whole, not well adapted to children.

## Romances

Romance in the folk tales is usually remote and impersonal, and the characters are often stereotypes. Aucassin and Nicolette are less interesting than their adventures. Enchantments and impossible tasks separate folk-tale lovers, and magic brings them together, whether they be Beauty and the Beast, the Goose Girl and the King, or the lassie who traveled east o' the sun and west o' the moon to find her love.

## Tales of Magic

Tales of magic are at the heart of folk tales. These are the stories which justify the children's name for the whole group—"fairy tales." Fairy godmothers, giants, water nixies, a noble prince turned into a polar bear, the North Wind giving a poor boy magic gifts to make good the loss of his precious meal, three impossible tasks to be performed, a lad searching for the Water of Life—these are some of the motifs and some of the magical people that give the folk tales a quality so unearthly and so beautiful that they come close to poetry. A large proportion of the folk tales is based upon magic of many kinds—so it is worth while to study these motifs and the fairy folk who flit so mysteriously through the tales.

## FAIRIES AND OTHER MAGIC MAKERS

The modern word *fairy* comes from the French word *fée*, a name for a variety of supernatural creatures who inhabited a world known in Old French as *faierie*. Into the word have been read wider meanings, borrowed from the medieval Latin word *fatare*, "to enchant," and the older Latin *fatum*, "fate" or "destiny." These ideas all enter into our concepts of fairies as supernatural creatures—sometimes little and lovely, sometimes old witch wives, or sometimes wise women like the Fates who have the power to enchant or to cast spells on human beings. To these concepts, the Celtic fairy lore has added rich details. Indeed, though the word *fairy* may come from the French, our fairy lore is predominantly Celtic.

### The Little People

The belief in fairies was once astonishingly widespread and persistent among Celtic peoples (particularly in Ireland and Scotland). Even when belief is gone, certain superstitions remain. From these countries comes the idea of trooping fairies, ruled over by a fairy queen, dwelling underground in halls of great richness and beauty. These fairy raths (or forts) are the old subterranean earthworks remaining today in Ireland and Scotland, with the gold and glitter of jewels added by the Celtic imagination. From these hiding places, according to tradition, the fairies emerge at night to carry off men, maidens, or children who have caught their fancy. They may put spells on the cattle or on the work of humans they dislike, or they may come to the assistance of those who win their gratitude. To eat fairy food or to fall asleep in a fairy ring (a ring of especially green grass) or under a thorn tree on May Eve or Halloween is to put yourself in the power of the fairies for a year and a day. May Eve (the evening before the first of May) and All Hallows Eve (the night before All Saints' Day) are the two nights when the fairies ride abroad and human beings had best beware. Leave food on the doorstep for them, by all means; keep away from their rings and their raths; and you may avoid their anger and escape their wiles.

The name by which you refer to these blithe spirits is also a matter of importance in Celtic lore. If you want to play safe, you will never use the word f-a-i-r-y, which reminds them of the unhappy fact that they have no souls. On the Day of Judgment when humans have a chance (however slight) of going up in glory, the wee folk know full well, poor soulless creatures that they are, that they will simply blow away like a puff of down in a strong wind. So address them tactfully as "the good people," "the little people," or "the wee folk," if you would be well treated in return.

Other countries have these little creatures, too. In Cornwall, they are called pixies or piskeys, and they, like their Irish relatives, ride tiny steeds over the moors. In the Arabian tales you meet the jinns, who also live in deserted ruins, often underground, and are respectfully addressed as "the blessed ones." The German dwarfs are usually subterranean in their work and sometimes in their dwelling, too. Although they seem not to insist upon any special form of address, to treat them disrespectfully is to incur sure punishment.

The Norse hill folk live underground also, as do some of the small fairy folk of England and Scotland. There are other resemblances among these three groups. The Norse countries have a house spirit, the Tomten, much like the English Lar or Lob-Lie-by-the-Fire and the Scotch Aiken-drum. Astrid Lindgren has described their kindly guardianship in a book titled *The Tomten*, so beautifully and convincingly illustrated that even our most skeptical young skeptics may secretly hope to have a Tomten on hand. All these household spirits take up their abode in a house where they are well treated and make themselves useful in many ways. They may be propitiated by bowls of milk or offerings of parsley, chives, and garlic. But woe to the misguided soul who gives them clothes! Such a gift usually offends them and always drives them away, never to return. Oddly enough, the elves in the Grimms' "Shoemaker and the Elves" were not insulted by the tiny garments, but they did depart, forever, even though they had manifested a most unorthodox delight in the offering.

### Wise Women, Witches, and Wizards

A few of the fairy folk are consistently evil, but most of them fluctuate in their attitude toward human beings and may be either helpful or ruthless. The wise women, who come to christenings or serve as fairy godmothers to bedeviled cinder lassies, are, on the whole, a grave and serious group. They are not unlike our idea of the Fates, or Norns, who mark off the life span and foretell coming events. One of these wise women aided Cinderella, while a peevish one sent Beauty off to sleep for a hundred years.

Witches and wizards are usually wicked. They lure children into their huts to eat them, or they cast spells on noble youths and turn them into beasts. Russia has a unique witch, Baba Yaga, who lives in a house that

*Illustration by Adrienne Adams (Copyright © 1960 Adrienne Adams) is reproduced by permission of Charles Scribner's Sons from* The Shoemakers and the Elves. *(Original in color)*

*Illustration by Blair Lent for* Baba Yaga *by Ernest Small. Copyright © 1966. Reproduced by permission of Houghton Mifflin Company. (Original in color)*

walks around on chicken legs. When she wishes to fly, she soars off in a pestle and sweeps her way along with a besom (two objects which may have to be explained to children in advance, by the way). She has some other unique powers that make her quite as fascinating as she is gruesome.

The magicians and sorcerers cast spells but may sometimes be prevailed upon to do a kind deed and help out a worthy youth bent on the impossible. The Celtic "Merlin" is the most romantic of all the sorcerers, but he is seldom mentioned in the folk tales. The English "Childe Rowland," however, enlists Merlin's aid in rescuing Burd Ellen from Elfland.

Occasional imps, like the German "Rumpelstiltskin" and the English "Tom Tit Tot," are hard to classify. They seem to be a kind of hybrid elf and fiend, perhaps just one of the earth dwellers turned sour, hoping to get hold of a gay, laughing child to cheer his old age.

### Giants and Ogres

Ogres and ogresses are always bloodthirsty and cruel. Giants, however, are of two kinds: the children call them "bad" and "good." The "bad giants" are a powerful clan using brute force to mow down all opponents. They swallow their antagonists whole, as tremendous power seems always to do in any age. They are ruthless and unscrupulous and must be dealt with on their own terms—deceit and trickery. But fortunately they are often thickheaded and rely too much on force, so that clever boys like Jack or the one girl giant-tamer "Molly Whuppie" can outwit them and leave them completely befuddled. The other tribe of giants is the helpful one. They aid the lad who shares his last crust of bread with them, and of course their aid is magnificent. They can drink up the sea and hold it comfortably until it is convenient to release it again. They can see a fly blinking in the sun five miles away or hear a blade of grass growing. They feel cold in the midst of fire and suffer from heat in solid ice. They can step lightly from mountain to mountain, break trees like twigs, and shatter rocks with a glance. The lad who lines up these giants on his side is guaranteed to win the princess and half the kingdom into the bargain. But no sluggard, no pompous pretender, no mean soul ever secures this aid. It is freely given only to honest lads about whom shines the grace of goodness.

### Fairy Animals

In the world of fairy, domestic animals are as kindly disposed toward human beings as they are in the world of reality. For example, there is that handsome cat of cats, "Puss in Boots"—surely a child given a magic choice of one handy assistant from all the gallery of fairy helpers would choose the witty and redoubtable Puss. The Norse "Dapplegrim" is a horse of parts and does fully as well for his master as the Russian Horse of Power in "The Firebird."

Occasionally wild animals take a hand in the magic events of the folk tales. In the Norse story, a gray wolf carries the king's son to the castle of "The Giant Who Had No Heart in His Body," and in the Czech story, old Lishka the fox gives "Budulinek" a ride on her tail, to his sorrow. Wild animals may be for or against human beings. Sometimes they serve merely as transportation, but often they are the real brains of an enterprise.

## Magic Objects

"Little Freddy with His Fiddle" makes magic music which no one has the power to resist. People cannot stop dancing even though they land in the midst of a thorn bush, even though their bones ache until they fall down exhausted. Freddy knew how to make magic with that frivolous fiddle of his, and it carried him a long way. In "Herding the King's Hares," Espen Cinderlad receives a remarkable whistle for his kindness to an old hag. With it he can bring order to every runaway bunny in the king's herd, and finally to the royal family as well:

> *Then the king and queen thought it best to give him the princess and half the kingdom; it just couldn't be helped.*
>
> *"That certainly was some whistle," said Espen Cinderlad.*

"Molly Whuppie," when pursued by the double-faced giant, runs lightly across the Bridge of One Hair, on which the giant dares take not so much as a single step. That is the kind of power every one of us needs to develop—the power to find a bridge, however slight, on which we can run lightly away from the ogres pursuing us. The folk tales are full of these "Fools of the World," who learn how to use magic tools as the pompous and pretentious never learn to do. Espen Cinderlad, with three impossible tasks to perform, hunts around until he finds the self-propelled axe, the spade, and the trickling water that could be stopped or let loose by him alone. Each of these magic objects told him it had been waiting a long, long time, just for him. Magic is always waiting for those who know how to use it.

## Enchanted People

Being put under a spell is just one of the many complications that beset the heroes and heroines of the fairy tales. Childe Rowland's sister unknowingly courted disaster by running around the church "widershins"—counterclockwise—and so put herself under the power of the fairies. "Rapunzel," of the long, long hair, was locked up in a tower by a cruel enchantress who was so clever that only a super-prince could worst her. And there are many variants of the folk tale about the royal brothers who are changed into birds, and who can be released from their enchantment only after their little sister has gone speechless for seven long years and spun each of them a shirt of thistledown. The Russians tell the marvelous story of "Sadko," who lived at the bottom of the ocean in the palace of the Czar of the Sea—this story has all the curious elusiveness of a dream. The Grimms' touching "The Frog-King" is one of the many tales in which either the husband or the wife is a fairy creature or is in the power of some witch or sorcerer. Of these, the Grimms' "The Water-Nixie" is perhaps the most exciting and the Norse "East o' the Sun and West o' the Moon," the most beautiful. In all such stories only love, loyalty, and self-sacrifice can break the enchantment and restore the beloved.

On the whole, the good and evil super-

## VIEWPOINTS

When the fairy tales are narrated pleasantly in their original version, they will not only be entertaining, but they will also exert a doubly beneficial effect upon the development of the child. In the first place, the fairy tale awakens in the child the feeling of participation with other human beings, with people not only of his immediate environment, but of all nations. He begins to sense that he is not alone with his, at times horrid and violent, fantasies, and that the latter are meaningful and valuable sources of strength for useful sublimations, as long as they never become confused with the outward reality. He also feels understood in his most tender longings, in his highest wishes. In the second place, the fairy tale communicates to the child a dim, intuitive understanding of his own nature and of his future positive potentialities. And he starts to sense that he became a human being primarily because in this world of ours he is meant to meet challenging and wondrous adventures. And so the fairy tale nourishes the child's courage to widen his horizons and to tackle all the challenges successfully. Then only, like some of the fairy tale heroes, he can hope to become a "king" within whose maturity spiritual wisdom will harmonize with his power over earthly things.—Julius E. Heuscher, M.D., F.A.P.A., *A Psychiatric Study of Fairy Tales*, Charles C. Thomas Publisher, Springfield, Illinois, 1963, pp. 185–186.

natural forces in the folk tales act according to certain laws. If magic makes wishes come true and points the way to happiness, it does so only with struggles and hardships on the part of the hero or heroine. The true princess suffers pitifully before magic opens the king's eyes and he sees her for what she is—the rightful bride for his son and a gentle, loving girl. These stories are not didactic, but one after another shows that courage and simple goodness work their own magic in this world, that evil must be conquered even if it carries us to the gates of death, and that grace and strength are bestowed upon those who strive mightily and keep honest, kindly hearts.

## DISTINCTIVE ELEMENTS OF FOLK TALES

For generation after generation, folk tales have continued to be popular with children. Modern youngsters, surrounded by the mechanical gadgets and scientific wonders of our age, are still spellbound by their magic. A brief examination of their form, style, and character portrayal may help explain the charm of the old tales for children. First of all, the form or pattern of the folk tales is curiously satisfying both to children and adults.

### The Introduction

The introduction to a folk tale does exactly what its name implies. It *introduces* the reader to the leading characters, the time and place of the story, and the problem to be solved, or the conflict which is the very breath of the story.

The stories often involve the element of *contrast*. Sometimes there is the uneven conflict, which always makes a story more exciting: "Hänsel and Gretel" and the wicked witch—two little children pitted against an evil power; Snow White and the cruel Queen. Sometimes the contrast lies within a like group; for example, in "The Three Little Pigs," there are not only pigs and wolf but also a wise pig and foolish pigs. So in "Boots and His Brothers" (or, as it is sometimes entitled, "Per, Paal, and Espen Cinderlad") the humble Cinderlad shows the wisdom his older brothers lack. "One-Eye, Two-Eyes, and Three-Eyes" has a most unusual contrast in the three sisters. Obviously, contrast heightens the conflict and rouses the reader's sympathy for the weaker or less fortunate or more kindly member of the group.

Folk tales are *objective* and *understandable*, never abstract. They have to do with winning security, earning a living or a place in the world, accomplishing impossible tasks, escaping from powerful enemies, outwitting wicked schemes and schemers, and succeeding with nonchalance. These plots are as vital today as ever and account for the vigor of these old tales.

*Time* is effectively accounted for by a conventional phrase like "Once upon a time," "Long ago and far away," "In olden times when wishing still helped one," "A thousand years ago tomorrow," or "Once on a time, and a very good time too." Such folk-tale conventions do more than convey an idea of long ago; they carry the reader at once to a dream world where anything is possible.

The *scene* is even more briefly sketched. It is a road, a bridge, a palace, a forest, or a poor man's hut—a place where something is going to happen and soon. No wonder these introductions catch the child's attention. They launch the conflict with no distracting details.

Sometimes the folk tales, like the ballads, get off to such a brisk start that the introduction is almost imperceptible. This one for "The Three Billy-Goats Gruff" is a masterpiece of brevity:

> *Once on a time there were three Billy-goats, who were to go up to the hill-side to make themselves fat, and the name of all three was "Gruff."*
>
> *On the way up was a bridge over a burn they had to cross; and under the bridge lived a great ugly Troll, with eyes as big as saucers, and a nose as long as a poker.*

There you are! The scene is a bridge with a pleasant stretch of grassy hillside just beyond. The characters are three earnest billy goats of the Gruff family who are desirous of getting fat on the hillside. Obstacle, Conflict, Problem live under the bridge in the person

*From* The Three Billy Goats Gruff *by Asbjörnsen and Moe, illustrated and copyright 1957 by Marcia Brown. Reproduced by permission of Harcourt Brace Jovanovich, Inc. (Original in color)*

*Illustrations by Enrico Arno for "Clever Manka" in* The Shepherd's Nosegay *by Parker Fillmore, copyright © 1958 by Harcourt Brace Jovanovich, Inc., and reproduced with their permission.*

of an ugly Troll. In the fewest possible words, you have all the makings of a good plot. "The Sleeping Beauty," still a fairly uncomplicated story, must introduce the king, queen, courtiers, the grand christening for the baby princess in the palace, the good fairies for whom plates of gold have been prepared, and the evil fairy who is uninvited and minus a gold plate and therefore thoroughly angry. What will happen? This is the mark of a good introduction: it whets the appetite for more; you "go on" eagerly. For children, brevity of introduction is an important part of the charm of these folk tales. The excitement gets under way with minimum description.

### The Development

The development carries forward the note of trouble sounded in the introduction. The quest begins, the tasks are initiated and performed, the flight gets under way, and the obstacles of every kind appear, with the hero or heroine reduced to despair or helplessness or plunged into more and more perilous action. This is the heart of the story—action that mounts steadily until it reaches a climax, when the problem or conflict will be resolved one way or the other.

The vigorous plots of the folk tales, full of suspense and action, appeal strongly to young readers. The heroes *do* things—they ride up glass hills, slay giants who have no hearts in their bodies, outwit wolves, get their rights from the North Wind, or pitch an old witch into an oven she intended for them. Here are no brooding introspectionists but doers of the most vigorous sort.

If these tales are to carry conviction, the development must be both logical (in the terms of the story) and plausible. When in "The Three Little Pigs" one pig is so foolish as to build a house of straw and another to build a house of sticks, you know they are doomed. But when a pig has sufficient acumen to build his house stoutly of bricks, you know perfectly well he will also be smart enough to outwit his adversaries, for such a pig will survive in any society. Another example of a logical, plausible plot development is "Clever Manka," the witty Czech story that is a favorite with older children. Manka by her cleverness wins a fine husband, a judge and burgomaster; but he warns her that she will be banished from his house if she ever uses her cleverness to interfere with his business. Knowing Manka and realizing that no one can help using what wit the Lord gave him, you feel the conflict approaching. Of course Manka learns of a case where her husband has rendered a flagrantly

unfair judgment, and in the interest of justice she interferes. She is found out and banished, but in the face of this ultimate catastrophe, she uses her wit and saves both herself and her husband from permanent unhappiness. Here is a realistic folk tale of clever mind against duller mind, with the clever one saving them both. The ending is surprising but completely logical.

Many of the tales we know preserve unity of interest. Every episode in "The Lad Who Went to the North Wind" concerns the boy's struggles to get his rights for the meal that the North Wind blew away. "The Three Little Pigs" never deflects the reader from his intense preoccupation with the third pig's attempts to win security in a wolf-haunted world. In "Cinderella," the activities of the two spiteful sisters only heighten our concern for Cinderella and our desire to have her win the place she deserves in the world. And in "The Bremen Town-Musicians," interest in the forlorn musicians is not drawn away by the new interest in the robbers. The robbers may be ever so picturesque; they may even be kind to their families—we don't know or care. Our only concern with them is that the musicians shall drive them out of the neighborhood for good and all.

To achieve unity, a story must preserve a decent *economy of incidents*. Too many episodes, too long-drawn-out suspense, or too much magic destroys the unity of the tale. The development often contains three tasks or three riddles or three trials. Perhaps there is no particular significance in the "three" except that the old storyteller, always properly audience-conscious as a good storyteller should be, could see for himself that suspense can be endured just so long before people get impatient. After the hero rides three times up a glass hill, the listeners demand results. Molly can use her bridge of one hair three times and after that she had better finish things off and get home. For it is on *suspense* that the successful development of folk-tale action depends. Suspense is built up and maintained until it reaches a peak in the climax, after which it declines and the action ends with a flourish.

## The Conclusion

The conclusion usually comes swiftly and is as brief as the introduction. In "The Three Billy-Goats Gruff," the ringing challenge of the biggest billy goat announces the climax. The fight ensues, the biggest billy goat is the winner, and the Gruff family is now free to eat grass and get fat for the rest of its days. In "The Sleeping Beauty," the kiss breaks the spell for the princess and the whole court, the royal wedding quickly takes place, and in most modern versions that is all except for the conventional blessing "and they lived happily ever after." But in some older versions of the folk tale a second story begins, a kind of sequel in which poor Beauty finds herself with an ogress for a mother-in-law and another conflict to be resolved. Children usually dislike this, and most versions now conclude with the wedding of Beauty and the prince.

The conclusion usually follows swiftly on the heels of the climax and ends everything that was started in the introduction. Not only do the heroes and heroines achieve a happy solution for their troubles and a triumphant end to their struggles, but the villains are accounted for and satisfyingly punished. Such conclusions satisfy the child's eye-for-an-eye code of ethics and apparently leave his imagination untroubled—probably because they usually have no harrowing details and are so preposterous that they move cheerfully out of reality.

The folk tale has some conventional endings that are as picturesque as the openings. "The Three Billy-Goats Gruff" concludes

*Snip, snap, snout*
*This tale's told out.*

Other endings are: "If they haven't left off their merry-making yet, why, they're still at

*Illustration by Felix Hoffmann. From Grimm's The Sleeping Beauty, copyright 1959, by H. R. Sauerlander & Co., Aarau. Reprinted by permission of Harcourt Brace Jovanovich, Inc. and Oxford University Press, London. (Original in color)*

it"; "A mouse did run, the story's done"; "And no one need ask if they were happy"; "Whosoever does not believe this must pay a taler" (or as we should say, a dollar); "And the mouth of the person who last told this is still warm"; "And now the joy began in earnest. I wish you had been there too." For little children, the chance to vary the name in the last line of the following conclusion makes it one of their favorites.

> *My tale is done,*
> *Away it has run*
> *To little Augusta's house.*

### Style

One of the charms of the folk tale is the language and manner of telling the story. For these tales were never read silently; they were told until their form and language patterns were fixed. Consider "Go I know not whither, bring back I know not what," or

> *"Little pig, little pig, let me come in."*
> *"No, no, by the hair of my chinny chin chin."*
> *"Then I'll huff and I'll puff and I'll blow your house in."*

Or in the Scotch tale "Whippety Stourie," read the conversation with the wee fairy ladies that turned the stern husband from trying to make a spinner of his wife:

> *"Would you mind telling me," he asked them, "why it is that your mouths are all as lopsided as a fir-tree leaning against the wind?"*
>
> *Then the six wee ladies burst into loud, lopsided laughter, and Whippety Stourie herself replied:*
>
> *"Och, it's with our constant spin-spin-spinning. For we're all of us great ones for the spinning, and there's no surer way to a lopsided mouth."*

Or read that matchless ending, "As for the Prince and Princess, they . . . flitted away as far as they could from the castle that lay East o' the Sun and West o' the Moon." These are brief examples of folk-tale style—frequently cadenced, sometimes humorous, sometimes romantic—with the words suited to the mood and tempo of the tale.

The beginnings and endings of the sto-

## VIEWPOINTS

. . . Among many peoples, at least, taletelling is a consciously acquired and practiced art, and it is obviously foolish to study this technique in the hands of bunglers. Only the best efforts of raconteurs most successful with their own audiences can form a basis for a study of style which will tell us anything of value.

That the narrative details of an oral story in any particular community are relatively fixed is clear to any student of the distribution of tales. Is the form of the narrative similarly stable, and is there an attempt to hand it on exactly as learned? How much liberty does the taleteller feel justified in taking with his stylistic effects? The answer would seem to be that the skillful raconteur usually handles his material very freely, but within traditional limits. There are certain commonplaces of events or background or of word order so traditional that they are an indispensable part of the manner of the story-teller. If he is gifted, he has a command of all these old, well-tried devices and he adds thereto his individual genius and often the genius of the man or men from whom he learned his art.—Stith Thompson, *The Folktale,* The Dryden Press, New York, 1951, p. 450.

ries, of course, are particularly good examples of the storyteller's skill in establishing the predominant mood of the story, or breaking off and sending the listeners back to their workaday world. But dialogue in these old stories is also a part of their style—it runs along so naturally that real people seem to be talking. Read aloud the conversation between the old man and his wife in "Gudbrand on the Hill-side." Never once does the swift interchange of news and comments falter for a descriptive phrase such as "said he *uneasily,*" or "said she *reassuringly.*" Here is just a rapid, natural give-and-take between two people:

*"Nay, but I haven't got the goat either," said Gudbrand, "for a little farther on I swopped it away, and got a fine sheep instead."*

*"You don't say so!" cried his wife; "why you do everything to please me, just as if I had been with you. What do we want with a goat! . . . Run out child, and put up the sheep."*

*"But I haven't got the sheep any more than the rest," said Gudbrand; "for when I had gone a bit farther I swopped it away for a goose."*

*"Thank you! thank you! with all my heart," cried his wife. . . .*

So they proceed from disaster to disaster without a single literary interpolation. Notice, too, that the words suffice to establish unmistakably the attitude of each speaker. Words so perfectly chosen make long descriptions unnecessary.

Another characteristic of folk-tale style is the use of rhymes. Indeed, the stories are sometimes part prose and part verse in the old sing-and-say pattern of "Aucassin and Nicolette." Cante-fables, such stories are called—that is, singing stories or verse stories. The frequency of rhymes in some of the old folk tales has caused some speculation about whether the folk tales came from the ballads or the ballads from the tales, since both often have the same subjects ("Earl Mar's Daughter," "Binnorie," "Childe Rowland," and "The Laidly Worm," to mention a few). This is a matter for the specialists to settle, but certainly the little rhymes add greatly to the interest of the tales.

"The Well of the World's End" ("The Frog-King") alternates prose and verse, with the frog singing over and over the same words except for the request in the first two lines in which he raises his demands each time:

*"Give me some supper, my hinny, my heart,*
*Give me some supper, my darling;*
*Remember the words you and I spake,*
*In the meadow, by the Well of the World's End."*

Some of the prettiest verses in the folk tales are in the Grimms' "The Goose-Girl" and in the English "The Black Bull of Norroway." The former breaks into rhyme when the faithful horse, Falada, speaks to his mistress.

## VIEWPOINTS

Beauty is the essence of the fairy-tale. Real ugliness has no place there—the grotesqueness of gnomes and gnarled but kindly woodcutters, and of crazy cottages which even the most backward rural authority would condemn, enters the fairy-tale only for the sake of contrast, so that the beauty of goose-girl and palace may be enhanced.

Many fairy-tales have made good ballets. Conversely, in judging a fairy-tale . . . something like the symmetry of the ballet should be sought. Observe the repetitive pattern which is so characteristic a feature of the folk-tale, and observe how the small child, hearing such a story read aloud, appreciates the repetitions and delights in the expected climax. . . . Variations, imposed upon a basic pattern, combining the expected and the unexpected in just the right proportions, give the child aesthetic satisfaction comparable with that which adults derive from good choreography or symphonic composition.—Geoffrey Trease, *Tales Out of School*, Heinemann Educational Books, London, 1964, pp. 48–49.

And after he has been killed and his head nailed to the dark gateway, the Goose-Girl, who is really the princess, weeps beneath the gateway saying:

> *"Alas, Falada, hanging there!"*

Then the head answered:

> *"Alas, young Queen, how ill you fare!*
> *If this your mother knew,*
> *Her heart would break in two."*

This piteous dialogue is followed by the song of the Goose-Girl, putting a spell on young Conrad, because he takes too much delight in her golden hair:

> *"Blow, blow, thou gentle wind, I say,*
> *Blow Conrad's little hat away,*
> *And make him chase it here and there,*
> *Until I have braided all my hair,*
> *And bound it up again."*

The Grimms' "Cinderella," "Hänsel and Gretel," "The Fisherman and His Wife," "The Juniper Tree," "Little Snow-White," and many others have memorable rhymes which some adults can still recite. The English tales are especially full of them. But many other folk tales are marked by the subtle art of the storyteller who has perfected a fine oral pattern in which rhymes frequently appear.

### Character Portrayal

The interest of the modern short story frequently depends far more upon characters than upon plot or action. This is not true of folk tales. Plot is of first importance, and the characters are more or less typed. The good people in these stories are altogether good, and the wicked are so completely wicked that we waste no sympathy on them when, in the end, they are liquidated. So, too, the

*Illustration by Johannes Troyer. From Grimm's Household Stories, translated by Lucy Crane. Copyright, 1954, by The Macmillan Company. Reprinted by permission of the publishers.*

animals in the folk tales stand for simple traits like loyalty, cleverness, slyness, cruelty.

But look for brief flashes of characterization here and there. Cinderella is a teen-age girl with her mind on balls and fine clothes. Red Riding Hood is good-hearted but irresponsible. The Lad who went to the North Wind to get his rights for the wasted meal is one of those dogged, stick-to-itive boys who, with right on his side, is going to get his way in the world or know the reason why. And as for the lad's mother, you can just see her, the old skeptic, shaking her head and saying, "All very true, I daresay, but seeing is believing, and I shan't believe it till I see it." There, in a flash, is a character sketch of the doubter, the cynic.

Sometimes the characters are passive, like the Sleeping Beauty, but still sufficiently individual so that each one arouses different reactions. Beauty's doom, hanging over her youth and loveliness like a black cloud, inspires only pity. But the silly, feckless girl in "Tom Tit Tot," with her big appetite and meager wit, is so absurd that you don't particularly mind the hard bargain "that" drives with her.

So while folk tale people are strongly typed as "good" or "bad" with no subtle distinctions between, they are also individualized. Sympathy or antagonism is aroused in different degrees by the brief characterizations. A whole portrait gallery of lads and lassies, goose-girls and princes, kings and queens remains in your memory, distinct and convincingly true to human nature.

## WHY USE THE FOLK TALES WITH MODERN CHILDREN?

When the poet W. H. Auden reviewed the Pantheon edition of *Grimms' Fairy Tales* for *The New York Times* (November 12, 1944), he made this rather startling statement:

> *For, among the few indispensable, common-property books upon which Western Culture can be founded—that is, excluding the national genius of specific peoples as exemplified by Shakespeare and Dante—it is hardly too much to say that these tales rank next to the Bible in importance.*

Later in the review he added:

> *It will be a mistake, therefore, if this volume is merely bought as a Christmas present for a child; it should be, first and foremost, an educational "must" for adults, married or single, for the reader who has once come to know and love these tales will never be able again to endure the insipid rubbish of contemporary entertainment.*

Yet some people raise a great hue and cry about the ethics of the fairy tales. They wonder whether children should read about Bluebeard's gory collection of ex-wives, or about a girl who tricks a giant into killing his own offspring in place of the trembling human children who had taken refuge in his castle. People so protective of children might also question whether they should read about Jacob tricking his brother Esau out of his birthright, or about the terrors of Daniel in the den of lions, or whether they should watch some of the most popular television programs.

### Ethical Truth

Of course, the folk-tale ethics are not always acceptable to the modern moral code. These stories were told by adults to adults in an age when using wits against brute force was often the only means of survival, and therefore admirable.

But folk tales are predominantly constructive, not destructive, in their moral lessons. "The humble and good shall be exalted," say the stories of "Little Snow-White," "Cinderella," "The Bremen Town-Musicians," and dozens of others. "Love suffereth long and is kind" is the lesson of "East o' the Sun" and "One-Eye, Two-Eyes, and Three-Eyes." In "The Frog-King," the royal father of

## VIEWPOINTS

The fairy tale is a basic form of literature, and of art in general. The ease and calm assurance with which it stylizes, sublimates, and abstracts makes it the quintessence of the poetic process, and art in the twentieth century has again been receptive to it. We no longer view it as mere entertainment for children and those of childlike disposition. The psychologist, the pedagogue, knows that the fairy tale is a fundamental building block and an outstanding aid in development for the child; the art theorist perceives in the fairy tale—in which reality and unreality, freedom and necessity, unite—an archetypal form of literature which helps lay the groundwork for all literature, for all art. We have attempted to show, in addition, that the fairy tale presents an image of man which follows almost automatically from its over-all style. The fairy-tale style isolates and unites: its hero is thus isolated and, for this very reason, capable of entering into universal relationships. The style of the fairy tale and its image of man are of timeless validity and at the same time, of special significance in our age.—Max Lüthi, *Once Upon a Time; On the Nature of Fairy Tales*, translated by Lee Chadeayne and Paul Gottwald with additions by the author, Frederick Ungar Publishing Co., New York, 1970, p. 146.

the princess enforces a noble code upon his thoughtless daughter. "That which you have promised must you perform," he says sternly, and again, "He who helped you when you were in trouble ought not afterwards to be despised by you." Indeed, so roundly and soundly do these old tales stand for morality that they leave an indelible impression of virtue invariably rewarded and evil unfailingly punished.

### Satisfaction of Needs

Most adults rereading these stories begin to understand Mr. Auden's feeling that they are timeless in their appeal. Plumbing, kitchen gadgets, and modes of transportation may change, but human desires and human emotions continue strong and unchanging. These old fairy tales contain in their "picture language" the symbols of some of the deepest human feelings and satisfy in fantasy human desires for security, competence, and love.

Everyone longs for security, the simple physical security of a snug house, warmth, and good food. In the fairy tales, the little hut in the forest is cozy and warm, safe from ravening wolves, and full of the peace of the fireside, with a loaf of bread baking on the hearth and a flavorsome kettle of soup on the hob. And of course there are castles, too; they may be a bit cold and drafty, but Jack or Tattercoats or Espen Cinderlad always seems to settle down very comfortably in the new grandeur. Children identify themselves with either the elegance of the castle or the snug security of the house in the woods. Both are satisfying: the castle speaks of achievement, the little hut of peace and safety.

Human beings are always in search of love. There will never be a time when people do not need loving reinforcement against the hostile world and the frightening thought of death. The old tales are full of loving compensations for fears and hardships. Hänsel reassures his little sister and protects her as long as he is able, and Gretel comes to his rescue when he is helpless and in peril. Commoners and royalty alike pursue their lost loves and endure every kind of suffering to free them from enchantments. There is cruelty in these old tales and danger, too, but the real world, like the fairy world, can be cruel and perilous. In reassuring contrast are the symbols of love, lending strength to the weak, offering sanctuary to those in peril, and in the end rewarding their faithfulness or their struggles.

People long not only for love and security but for competence. They are eager to overcome difficulties, to right wrongs, and to stand fast in the face of danger—abilities essential for heroes of any generation. The fairy tales supply unforgettable stories of wicked powers defeated and of gallant souls who in their extremity are granted supernatural strength. Whether or not children are conscious of it, these stories may become sources of moral strength—a strength which is part faith, part courage, and wholly unshakable.

### Variety

There is a folk tale for every mood. There are drolls and romances, tales of horror and of beauty. They cover every range of feeling.

Undoubtedly their first appeal to children is *exciting action*. Things happen in these stories with just the hair-raising rapidity that children yearn for in real life and rarely find. For this reason, a child who reads too many folk tales may find everyday life painfully dull and static—no beanstalks to climb, no giants to kill, no witches to outwit. The action does fill a definite need, however. Before the child is ready to understand and follow character development, these active heroes are lads after his own heart.

There is sometimes a strange quiet about these stories. The forest is so still you can hear one bird singing; a little lamb speaks softly to a fish in a brook; the enchanted castle is silent; and the prince falls asleep by the fountain from which gently flows the water of life. Reading some of these strange tales, you feel yourself relaxing. Here there is time for everything, even a little nap by magic waters. Compared with any moving-picture version of folk tales, the old words make immeasurably better pictures, create stronger moods, and refresh and relax to a degree which only music or poetry can approach. The three are closely related: children who have learned to love the folk tales will be equipped to enjoy music and poetry, too. Moreover, they will have discovered the wonders of tranquillity and quiet in the midst of a noisy, restless world.

Children are natural recipients of folk material as is shown in the ways they use rhymes in their play, from the two-year-old murmuring nursery-rhyme refrains to the older child engaging in intricate counting-out games. Most children show a predilection for the cadence and color that are a part of the oral tradition. The child's calm acceptance of magical events and talking beasts in folk tales is not far removed from his own invention of imaginary companions. And in the enjoyment of folk tales children can assimilate a sense of their own cultural identity and an appreciation of that of others.

#### VIEWPOINTS

. . . Fairy tales are survivors. Authorless, timeless, placeless, they are also flawless. . . .

And in their character how they vary! Some have morals, some laugh in the face of morals; some are savage, some merry; some are marvelously decked out, some plain. But they survive alike because they are all good stories.

Their plots have never been surpassed and are still in service. They have action—unflinching, unremitting, sometimes circular. They appeal to the senses, they charm the memory. Their formal structure pleases the sense of order and design; their conversation is suitable, intense, pragmatic, well-timed, and makes sense for its own story alone.

Children like fairy tales also because they are wonderfully severe and uncondescending. They like the kind of finality that really slams the door. "Then the Wolf pounced upon Red Riding Hood and ate her up." And fairy tales are not innocent; they have been to the end of experience and back.—Eudora Welty, "And They All Lived Happily Ever After," *The New York Times Book Review*, November 10, 1963, p. 3. Copyright © 1963 by The New York Times Company. Reprinted by permission.

## COLLECTIONS AND COLLECTORS

Four national groups of tales include most children's favorites: the French, the German, the Norwegian, and the English. These tales have so colored our thinking and entered into our language that we call them classics.

Adults should know these collections well enough to select from them the great tales no child should miss. But they should also be familiar with the collections of similar tales now available from almost every country in the world. Adults using the major national groups of tales will be interested in the collectors and their methods of gathering and handling their materials.

### French Fairy Tales

The history of Perrault's unique *Contes de ma Mère l'Oye*, published in 1697 and translated into English in 1729, has already been discussed (p. 89). This is the appreciative tribute paid to Perrault by his countryman, Paul Hazard, a distinguished member of the French Academy:

> *Perrault is as fresh as the dawn. We never reach the end of his accomplishments. He is full of mischief, humor and charming dexterity. He never seems to be achieving a* tour de force, *lifting a weight, looking for applause, but he seems to be having more fun than anyone, relating these prodigious stories entirely for his own pleasure.* (Books, Children and Men, p. 9.)

Mr. Hazard comments on the tenderness and the terror in "Hop o' My Thumb," the suspense and despair in "Blue Beard," and the sly drollery of "Puss in Boots." He reminds us that Puss "profits by every circumstance—a bath, a stroll, or a call," and, finally, wheedling the ogre into taking the form of a mouse, gobbles him up. "We shall laugh over that the rest of our lives," he concludes.

Perrault's eight stories have rather more polish and sophistication than is usual in the folk tales. It does not matter to children whether it was Perrault father or son who collected and rewrote the tales; it is their sprightly style the children have always loved. In place of dull narrative, they are lively with conversations. Cinderella's haughty sisters talk about their own finery; Cinderella has earnest discourse with "her godmother, who was a fairy," about her needs for the ball. There is hardly a child who cannot reproduce these dialogues in the very spirit of the original.

Every necessary detail is logically provided for, or its omission underscored as a pivotal point in the plot. In "The Sleeping Beauty," for instance, the fairy touches everyone with her sleep-inducing wand "and little Mopsey, too, the Princess's little spaniel, which was lying on the bed" so that the Princess will not wake "all alone in the old palace." Or, again, we see how Little Thumb finds the way home from the forest for himself and his brothers and sisters by the white pebbles he has collected and dropped. But the next time, the door is locked and he can get no pebbles; he has only one piece of bread to crumble and let fall—disaster is near. Everywhere is the perfect logic of the

*Illustration by Gustave Dore. From Charles Perrault's* French Fairy Tales *retold by Louis Untermeyer. Reproduced by permission of Didier, Publishers. (1946)*

French—no loose ends, no incredible happenings. Magic is there, but used so sparingly and with such reasonable preparation that conviction is never disturbed.

Like most adults, Perrault could not resist "improving" these traditional tales. Sometimes he dabbled with the plot, as in the moralistic conclusion of "Little Thumb." Sometimes he added contemporary touches—"hairdressers" and "patches." Often he slipped in sly bits of satire, as the offer of the king to make the Marquis of Carabas his son-in-law on the spot once he has seen the vast estate of the Marquis. The erotica of these tales is discussed by Barchilon and Pettit, who think Perrault drove it skillfully underground for children but made it slyly evident to adult readers. On the whole, these tales are related with so masterly a sense of the dramatic that they continue to be the children's favorites.

Barbara Leonie Picard's *French Legends, Tales and Fairy Stories* (1955) contains four hero tales, six courtly tales of the Middle Ages, and thirteen legends, or folk tales, with no repetition of Perrault's famous eight. There is more magic in these tales than in Perrault's; the epic tales are full of battles and various complexities, the courtly tales are highly romantic, and the folk tales, though they contain some variants of familiar themes, are more mature in style than the stories they resemble. Good readers will enjoy this collection, and the storyteller will find fresh and exciting material in such stories as "The Grey Palfrey," "The Mouse-Princess," "The Stones of Plouhinec," and "Ripopet-Barabas."

In 1968, Geneviève Massignon's annotated, scholarly collection *Folktales of France* was published by the University of Chicago Press in the "Folktales of the World" series, a varied and representative selection. A collection long out of print has been made available again with the republication of the Comtesse d'Aulnoy's *The White Cat and Other Old French Fairy Tales* (1967), edited and translated by Rachel Field.

## German Folk Tales

While Perrault altered his tales to suit the tastes of the times, the conscientious Grimm brothers (Jacob, 1785–1863; Wilhelm, 1786–1859) began with a passionate concern for sources. They were university professors—philologists—and their interest in sagas, ballads, popular tales, and all forms of traditional literature was at first secondary to their interest in the roots and development of the German language. This interest in grammar remained paramount with Jacob, but Wilhelm gradually became more interested in the tales than in any other phase of their work. When they began their collection, it

*Illustration by E. MacKinstry for* The White Cat, *arranged by Rachel Field. Reproduced by permission of The Macmillan Company.*

was not with children in mind. They undertook their research as a part of a vast and scholarly study of language origins which was to climax in the German grammar (*Deutsche Grammatik*) and the dictionary (*Deutsches Wörterbuch*).

Jacob was perhaps the greater scholar of the two, working with tremendous energy and initiative, completely immersed in his studies. Wilhelm was the artist. He loved music and was much sought after socially, for he was a gifted storyteller and a gay, animated companion. The four years after Wilhelm's death was their longest separation. "Die Brüder Grimm," they signed themselves, and so we think of them—the Grimm brothers, dedicated scholars, cheerful human beings, happily devoted to their work and to each other.

When *Kinder- und Hausmärchen*[3] appeared in 1812 (the second volume in 1815), it caused no particular stir in literary circles. Some critics considered the stories boorish; their publisher friend Brentano thought them slovenly; and yet somehow, in spite of the reviews, the stories were received with an unprecedented enthusiasm. Edition followed edition; translations began, first into Danish, Swedish, and French, then into Dutch, English, Italian, Spanish, Czech, and Polish—in all, some seventeen different languages.

The plots of these tales appeal to all ages from the seven-year-olds to adults, while the style has the peculiarly spellbinding quality of the great storytellers. The Grimms were fortunate in their sources. Besides the "storywife," Frau Viehmann, there were Wilhelm Grimm's wife, Dortchen Wild, and her five sisters, who had been raised with these old tales and could tell them with effortless fluency. Other relatives, in-laws, and neighbors contributed to the collection also, but were not equally gifted storytellers. If you check in the Pantheon edition of *Grimms' Fairy Tales* the index of the tales with Mr. Campbell's list of the people who told them, you will discover that most of your favorites—"Hänsel and Gretel," "Mother Holle," "The Goose-Girl," "Rumpelstiltskin," to mention only a few—were related either by Frau Viehmann or the members of the Wild family.

To reread these stories is to find refreshment. Here are somber tales of children who are turned out to fend for themselves but who find love and security after all their hardships. Here are morons, cheerful and irresponsible, and royal youths and maidens, dispossessed, reduced to misery and humiliation, but keeping their innate kindness and tenderness, and so finding love. Here youth responds to the call of great tasks and accomplishes the impossible. Here a girl looks upon Holiness unmoved and is stricken dumb for her hardness, and Godfather Death stalks his prey and is never outwitted. These stories have colored the attitudes of readers toward life, toward human relationships, and toward moral standards. They are both fantasy and reality, and they are supremely entertaining.

An outstanding contemporary scholar of folklore, Kurt Ranke, has compiled a collection for the "Folktales of the World" series—*Folktales of Germany*, which includes stories from all German-speaking territories except Switzerland (stories of Switzerland are in a separate volume). Like the other books in the series, this has a wealth of background information about the folklore of the country and a section of notes and indexes that are most useful.

### Norwegian Folk Tales

When people talk about the Scandinavian folk tales, they usually mean a particular book, *East o' the Sun and West o' the Moon*, the collection most people have known and loved, in one edition or another, all their lives. These stories probably rank with *Grimms' Fairy Tales* in their continuous

3. *Nursery and Household Tales* is the usual translation, but for the German *Märchen* we have no precise translation. *Märchen* is legend, fiction, a cock-and-bull story, romance—in short, a fairy tale.

*From* East of the Sun and West of the Moon *by Ingri and Edgar Parin d'Aulaire. Copyright 1938, renewed 1966, © 1969 by Ingri and Edgar Parin d'Aulaire. Reprinted by permission of The Viking Press, Inc.*

popularity, and for similar reasons. They have the ring of complete sincerity and the oral charm of the storyteller's art at its best, for they were gathered from old wives who were still telling them to their children or grandchildren. They were recorded by Peter Christian Asbjörnsen (1812–1885) and Jörgen E. Moe (1813–1882), and turned into matchless English by a British scholar, Sir George Webbe Dasent (1817–1896), who was influenced by Jacob Grimm. The names of these three men—Asbjörnsen, Moe, and Dasent—are so inextricably bound up with the tales that the book is sometimes listed under Asbjörnsen and Moe, the collectors, and sometimes under Dasent, the translator.

Peter C. Asbjörnsen and Jörgen Moe were devoted friends from early boyhood, and death separated them by only three years. Although Asbjörnsen was a zoologist and Moe a poet and a theologian, both became interested in gathering the popular tales of their native Norway from the lips of old storytellers who were still relating them as they had received them from the lips of preceding generations. When Asbjörnsen started out on a scientific expedition, he followed his folklore hobby in his spare time. Indeed the two activities could be admirably combined. Searching for specimens and studying the terrain of the countryside carried him into the isolated districts where storytelling was still the chief source of indoor entertainment. Moe spent his holidays similarly employed, traveling to remote parts of the country and gathering the legends and stories of the district from the storytellers. Dasent said of them, "For these Norse Tales one may say that nothing can equal the tenderness and skill with which MM. Asbjörnsen and Moe have collected them."

While in Stockholm in a diplomatic post, Sir George Webbe Dasent had the great good fortune to meet Jacob Grimm, who urged him to begin a thorough study of the language of the North, especially Icelandic. This Dasent did, and his first publication was an English translation of the *Prose, or Younger Edda*, followed by his *Grammar of the Icelandic or Old Norse Tongue*, and eventually an *Icelandic-English Dictionary*. In the midst of a remarkably strenuous life of study, translations, journalism, and travel, he became interested in the Norse folk tales and made his masterly translations of the Asbjörnsen-Moe collections, *Popular Tales from the Norse* (1859) and *Tales from the Fjeld* (1874), the two sources for all subsequent English editions.

Mrs. Gudrun Thorne-Thomsen, who taught and was herself one of the great exponents of the storytelling art, used to say that she enjoyed the Dasent translations of these tales as much as she did the originals. Other Norwegians have made similar comments and have remarked about the translator's

## VIEWPOINTS

Beware . . . of the defensive argument now used by "folklore" writers to justify their tampering with sources: "We have the same right as the original storytellers to tell a folktale in our own way." There is no more fundamental fallacy in the presentation of folk materials than this notion. The carrier of oral folk traditions continually alters the tale, song, or saying he has heard; such change is at the very heart of oral, unrehearsed narration. But the calculating money-writer, using the very different medium of print in a self-conscious effort to reach readers who already associate "folklore" with froth and fun, is the voice not of the folk but of the mass culture. —Richard M. Dorson, *American Folklore*, The University of Chicago Press, Chicago and London, 1959, p. 4.

ability to catch the folk flavor of the language, even to the idioms. Like the Grimm stories, the tales were told by adults to adults, and some changes are usually made in the text when they are told to children. Dasent, in his translations, made no such adaptations but gave the stories exactly as they were in the Asbjörnsen-Moe collections. The Dasent books are, therefore, English sources for adult students of folklore, but you will find that most of the children's editions have altered them as little as possible.

*Folktales of Norway*, edited by Reidar Christiansen, is another volume in the "Folktales of the World" series. In a fascinating foreword, the editor for the series, Richard Dorson, an eminent folklorist of the United States, traces the historical development of the Norwegian tale. As in the other volumes, the provision of a glossary, an index of motifs, and a bibliography make this book of inestimable value to the scholar. Other outstanding collections are *Scandinavian Legends and Folk-Tales*, by Gwyn Jones; *Norwegian Folk Tales*, translated by Pat Shaw Iversen and Carl Norman; two compilations by Mary Hatch, *Danish Tales* and *More Danish Tales;* and Sigrid Undset's adaptations from the Asbjörnsen and Moe collections, *True and Untrue, and Other Norse Tales.*

While the general mood of the Norwegian tales is serious, which is true of most folk tales, there is much more humor, or buoyancy, in the Norse collection than in the German. The people make the best of things with an amusing nonchalance. In "The Princess on the Glass Hill," Boots, or Espen Cinderlad, with the barn almost falling about his ears, reassures himself that if things get no worse he can stand it. Gudbrand's old wife, instead of clouting her husband as the German "Mrs. Vinegar" does, makes cheerful alibis for his bad management. Nothing daunts these people, and nothing quells their firm conviction that they will make out somehow.

There are no fairies in the gauzy-winged tradition, but there is a great deal of magic. Trolls, hill folk, giants, hags, and witch-wives are plentiful. There are magic objects—fiddles, axes, tablecloths, rams, and sticks. Winds talk and take a hand in the affairs of men now and then. A polar bear (another symbol of the North) and a great dun bull are both men under enchantments, and there are the colossal horse Dapplegrim, the kindly wolf Gray-legs, and talking beasts of every variety.

Rhymes are infrequent, but one of the prettiest of them is the spell "Katie Woodencloak" casts on the Prince:

*Bright before and dark behind,*
*Clouds come rolling on the wind;*
*That this Prince may never see*
*Where my good steed goes with me.*

For storytelling, "The Pancake" is probably the finest of all cumulative stories because of its humor and rollicking movement. "The Cock and Hen That Went to Dovrefell" has a witty surprise ending that is far more satisfying than its English equivalent, "Henny Penny." These tales, like the Grimms', run the whole gamut from sheer nonsense to the romantic and heroic. They are classics and matchless entertainment which all children should have a chance to hear.

### British Folk Tales

When Joseph Jacobs (1854–1916) began compiling the English folk tales, his objective was different from that of the Grimms or of the men who had preceded him in the English field. He intended his collection not for the archives of the folklore society but for the immediate enjoyment of English children. So Jacobs omitted incidents that were unduly coarse or brutal, adapted the language somewhat, especially dialect, and even deleted or changed an occasional episode. Jacobs also "prosed" some of the ballads and left one, "Childe Rowland," in the sing-and-say, or prose-and-verse, style of the original cante-fable. He admitted cheerfully that his editing was all very horrifying to his folklorist friends but observed that every one of them, even the Grimms, had made similar modifications. Jacobs was scrupulous in recording these alterations. At the back of his books, in a section for adult readers called "Notes and References," he gives the sources for each tale and its parallels, and then notes the changes he made. Studying these notes, you soon discover that his adaptations are not too heinous, and reading the stories, you realize that he has indeed attained his goal, which was "to write as a good old nurse will speak when she tells Fairy Tales."

Jacobs obtained a few of his tales from oral storytellers—some from Australia and one from a gypsy are mentioned. But most of his tales he obtained from printed sources. He acknowledged the use of stories collected by his predecessors, notably Patrick Kennedy for the Celtic group, Robert Chambers for Scotland, and James Orchard Halliwell for England. Jacobs also credited "How Jack Sought His Fortune" to the *American Folk-Lore Journal* and added, "I have eliminated a malodorous and un-English skunk." It was not until 1943 that a whole collection of the American Jack tales[4] was published, "malodorous and un-English" skunks and all! All in all, Joseph Jacobs was a sound enough folklorist. As a matter of fact, he was editor of the British journal *Folk-Lore*. But his greatest contribution is probably in selection and adaptation. Had it not been for his collections, many of these tales might still be gathering dust in antiquarian volumes.

These English tales of Jacobs' are remarkable for three things: the giant killers, the humor, and the large number suitable for the youngest children. From these collections of Jacobs come the favorites, "The Story of the Three Bears," "The Story of the Three Little Pigs," "Henny Penny," "Johnny-Cake," "The Old Woman and Her Pig," and many others. "Tom Tit Tot," one of the stories which Jacobs rescued from the dusty oblivion of the journal *Folk-Lore*, is undoubtedly the most hilarious of all the variants of "Rumpelstiltskin." This is indeed an admirable example of the cheerfulness in the British stories. The German tale is grave throughout, even somber. The English tale opens with a bit of low comedy between a mother and her greedy, witless daughter. There is a light touch throughout, and yet the story is every bit as exciting and satisfying as "Rumpelstiltskin." The superiority of this version lies in the full and consistent characterization of the silly girl, the impishness of "that," and the amusing hints as to the personality of the king.

The tales of giant killers are another striking feature of the English collections, beginning with the old national hero story "St. George and the Dragon," and continuing through "Tom Hickathrift," "Jack the Giant Killer," and their only feminine rival, the resourceful "Molly Whuppie." These stout heroes who make away with monsters were multiplied and perpetuated by the chapbooks,

4. *The Jack Tales.* Told by R. M. Ward and others. Edited by Richard Chase.

and their adventures have remained popular with British children ever since.

Jacobs remained the chief source of English folk tales until, beginning in 1954, volumes of English, Scottish, and Welsh folk tales were issued in the Oxford Myths and Legends series. Beautifully told, handsome in format and illustrations, these three books have greatly expanded the range of British folk tales.

James Reeves' *English Fables and Fairy Stories* includes many of the old favorites as well as such delightful additions as "The Pedlar's Dream," "The Two Princesses," and "The Fish and the Ring." The style is distinguished, the stories are varied in mood, and they read or tell beautifully. Another fine collection is *Fairy Tales from the British Isles*, by Amabel Williams-Ellis.

*Folktales of England*, edited by Katharine M. Briggs and Ruth L. Tongue ("Folktales of the World" series), is a collection derived almost exclusively from oral sources. Many of the tales are relics of pagan superstition, many are based on local folk history. The material is divided by types of tales: jocular tales, tall tales, modern legends, wonder tales, etc.

*Welsh Legends and Folk Tales* by Gwyn Jones includes some of the hero tales of King Arthur and his knights. There are such romances as "Pwyll and Pryderi," "How Trystan Won Esylit," and three about the fairy "Woman of Llyn-Y-Fan." The folk tales are full of magic, incantations, fairy folk, and difficult names.

In *Peter and the Piskies: Cornish Folk and Fairy Tales*, Ruth Manning-Sanders has compiled a lively selection of stories about the small supernatural creatures of Celtic lore. All of her anthologies are excellent.

The *Scottish Folk Tales and Legends* by Barbara Ker Wilson are largely unfamiliar. There are simple nursery tales for small children, broadly comic stories for older children, a few horrific scare tales, and stories of romantic beauty. Through them all runs the Gaelic fairy lore—spells, enchantments, magic, and many sorts of fairy creatures, sometimes kind, often menacing.

The delightful books by Sorche Nic Leodhas—*Claymore and Kilt*, *Gaelic Ghosts*, *Ghosts Go Haunting*, *Heather and Broom*, *Sea-Spell and Moor Magic*, and *Thistle and Thyme*—will further enrich the Scottish lore with both humor and romance. These stories have been written in such perfect storytelling form that they may be read or told without modification, and their charm is irresistible.

*From* Heather and Broom *by Sorche Nic Leodhas. Illustrated by Consuelo Joerns. Copyright © 1970 by Leclaire G. Alger. Reproduced by permission of Holt, Rinehart and Winston, Inc.*

## OTHER NATIONAL GROUPS OF FOLK TALES

In addition to the French, German, Norwegian, and British folk tales, there are stories from innumerable other national groups. Should you wish to use a collection not mentioned here, look it up in the *Children's Catalog*, that unfailing reference for librarians and all harried makers of bibliographies, or in the *Index to Fairy Tales, Myths and Legends* by Mary Huse Eastman. Or check the listing by countries or regions in the *Subject Guide to Children's Books in Print*. And of course examine in the bibliography at the end of this chapter the favorite tales of national origins. A discussion of a few of these national collections can perhaps give some idea of the richness and variety of folk tales available today from all countries.

### African Folk Tales

Although some books tapped the wealth of African folk material before the 1960's, that decade began an outpouring of such material. Among the earlier collectors—Harold Courlander, Wilfrid Hambly, Russell Davis, Brent Ashabranner—the most prolific has been Courlander, whose general and regional collections are a rich lode of cultural information as well as a source of pleasure for readers and storytellers. West African tales are retold delightfully by Verna Aardema in *Tales from the Story Hat* and its companion volume; East African tales are well represented in two fine collections: Humphrey Harman's *Tales Told Near a Crocodile* and Eleanor Heady's *When the Stones Were Soft*. In addition to the many collections of regional and tribal tales, there are distinguished single-tale editions and a steadily growing number of general collections. Some of the most notable collections are Joyce Cooper Arkhurst's *The Adventures of Spider*, Hugh Sturton's *Zomo the Rabbit*, Frances Carpenter's *African Wonder Tales*, and Edna Mason Kaula's *African Village Folktales*. An excellent source book is *African Folktales and Sculpture*, second edition, edited by Paul Radin and James Johnson Sweeney.

The stories reflect the fact that the oral tradition is still very strong in Africa, with the tales pertinent to contemporary life and the written language echoing the cadence of speech. Many of the tales are about animal heroes like Ananse, the clever spider; many explain natural phenomena as does the literature of any people who live close to nature; many have a wry and sophisticated humor.

### Arabian Nights

The origin of *The Arabian Nights* is confused and lost in antiquity, partly because they

*Reprinted by permission of Coward, McCann and Geoghegan, Inc. from* More Tales from the Story Hat *by Verna Aardema, illustrated by Elton Fax. Copyright © 1966 by Coward-McCann, Inc.*

belonged to the people and were not considered polite literature. In the Moslem world they circulated only in the coffee houses and the market place. The stories are very old, some of them seeming to stem from ancient India, others from North Africa, with an early collection from Persia. A Frenchman, Antoine Galland, made his translation of them in 1704 from a manuscript sent to him from Syria but written in Egypt. So here again are old stories which have been inveterate travelers, with sources so ancient and varied that it is impossible to determine their true origin. We do know that Galland's translation of the tales into French, under the title *Les mille et une nuits*, was so popular that it was immediately translated into other languages, including English. Indeed, some of Galland's translated stories were even translated back into Oriental languages. The stories were fortunate in falling into the hands of a translator who was also a skillful storyteller. These tales of the Orient were given a Gallic touch, so they lack nothing of drama or color. A good modern edition, handsomely illustrated, is Amabel Williams-Ellis' *Arabian Nights*.

Today, children have turned away from most of these exceedingly long stories. However, certain of these stories have entered permanently into our speech and our thinking. A child who does not know a few of them is distinctly the poorer.

*Illustration by Vera Bock. From* Arabian Nights, *edited by Andrew Lang. Copyright, 1898, 1946 by Longmans, Green and Co. Reproduced by permission of David McKay Company.*

### Czechoslovakian Folk Tales

The Czech stories are unusually amusing and have been translated into clear, vigorous English. They include many variants of the Grimm stories but often are more interesting than the German. "Clever Manka," for instance, is a far better story than Grimms' "The Peasant's Daughter." Parker Fillmore's lively English translations in *The Shepherd's Nosegay* contain the favorite tales—"Budulinek," "Smolicheck," "Katcha and the Devil," and of course, "Clever Manka."

### Finnish Folk Tales

Joseph Jacobs used to say that the Finns at Helsingfors had in manuscript form the largest group of folk tales in existence, a group that he believed exceeded twelve thousand. But John Wargelin, President of Suomi College, stated that over thirty thousand tales had been collected although only a small portion of them had been published. In spite of this wealth of stories, the Finnish tales have not been well known or much used in this country, possibly because they are both long and descriptive, and the Finnish names are undoubtedly difficult. But this strong group of tales will repay study and will be enjoyed by older children.

### Russian Folk Tales

A. N. Afanasiev collected the Russian folk tales as the Grimm brothers collected the German, and there is now an English translation of the complete Afanasiev collection in the Pantheon edition. These stories are for adult students of folklore, not for children. They are bloody and horrible but full of excitement and color. Certain of these tales are rather generally familiar to American children—"The Snow Maiden" (sometimes called "Snegourka"), "The Firebird," and "Sadko." Every one of these lends itself to dramatization as well as to storytelling. These and other popular Russian stories are found in a good storytelling form in Arthur Ransome's *Old Peter's Russian Tales.*

Miriam Morton's impressive anthology, *A Harvest of Russian Children's Literature*, has a sizable section of folk tales, and many tales have been published singly in illustrated editions.

### Spanish Folk Tales

One American storyteller, Ruth Sawyer, thinks the Irish stories are matched only by the Spanish, and her own collection seems to bear out her opinion. New and delightful stories for telling can be found in every one of the collections of Spanish tales listed in the bibliography for this chapter. The stories for the youngest children are full of fun, those for the older ones full of grace. *Padre Porko*, for instance, is one of the most enchanting series of talking beast tales to be found anywhere. The Padre, the gentlemanly pig, is both astute and benignant, and his canny solutions of neighborhood difficulties are made with great elegance.

So delightful folk tales come to us in translation from Italy, Poland, Mexico, Yugoslavia, Burma, Turkey, Korea, China, Japan, Persia, Africa, many South American countries, and from the Pacific and Caribbean islands. Indeed it is almost a case of name the country and your librarian can match it with native folk tales. Some of these have been better translated and adapted than others, but there is scarcely a collection that will not yield two or three memorable stories for reading or telling.

## FOLK TALES IN THE UNITED STATES

The United States is the fortunate recipient of folklore and folk tales from all over the world. Americans should be proud of this rich heritage, which they can discover merely by taking the pains to visit one of the intercultural libraries of the large cities, or,

*Illustration by Fritz Eichenberg. From Padre Porko by Robert Davis. Copyright 1939 by Robert Davis. Reproduced by permission of Holiday House.*

better still, by meeting and making friends with different racial groups throughout the country. American Indians have woven beautiful baskets and rugs decorated with characteristic tribal symbols, and they still tell their own old tales, some of which are reminiscent of European ones. There are embroideries from Bulgaria and Hungary, with intricate designs that for generations have been passed on from mother to daughter along with legends still more ancient. The Southern mountaineers are still weaving the Tudor rose into their textiles and still singing ballads that were already time-honored in the days of Queen Elizabeth I. Boys and girls of Swedish, Russian, Polish, and Scottish ancestry still dance the old dances, sing the old songs, and hear the old stories that have been handed down from their grandparents' grandparents. An Irish neighborhood abounds with stories straight from the Gaelic, tales that were old when Christianity was young. The Sicilian puppet shows sometimes play the popular stories of the people. A black grandmother may be heard telling a story which goes back to the folklore of West Africa. And a Bohemian child may hear her father's version of a story which the Grimm brothers found in Germany over a hundred years ago.

Folklore in the United States falls into three large categories: (1) tales from black Americans, including the collections known as the Uncle Remus stories; (2) tales from the North American Indians; and (3) variants of the European stories. In the general discussion of folk tales few references are made to these American types, for definite reasons. In the first place, the European collections came into print long before ours began, and so they rather set the standard or pattern of such tales. Moreover, our collected tales differ in so many respects from those of the European groups that they often prove the exception to the very principles discussed as typical. They are, besides, far from being a homogeneous group—no generalizations will cover all three varieties. An Uncle Remus tale differs from an Indian story quite as much as both of them differ from their European relatives. In short, each of the three types of American folk tales needs to be considered separately.

## Black Folklore

Joel Chandler Harris (1848–1908) became interested in collecting the tales he heard the plantation slaves tell. Born in Georgia and raised on such stories as a child, he knew the black man's dialect, humor, and picturesque turns of speech. Moreover, he had a deep love for the stories and for the people who told them. In the character of Uncle Remus, a plantation slave, Harris embodied the gentleness, the philosophy, the shrewd appraisal of character, and the rich imagination of all black storytellers to whom he had listened. Into the mouth of Uncle Remus, he put the stories he gathered first hand.

The stories are mostly talking-beast tales, and the hero is Brer Rabbit, the weakest and most harmless of animals, but far from helpless. Through his quick wit, his pranks, and his mischief, he triumphs over the bear, the wolf, the fox, and the lesser animals. Like the French "Reynard the Fox," he is a trickster, but unlike Reynard, he is never mean or cruel, only a practical joker now and then, a clever fellow who can outwit the big brutes and turn a misfortune into a triumph. No matter what happens to him or what he does, he remains completely lovable.

These stories are, of course, reminiscent of the talking-beast tales of other countries. Some of them may have had their roots in India, but it is generally agreed that most of them originated in Africa or were created in this country. Variants of "The Tar Baby" are found in many lands, but there is a special flavor to the Uncle Remus stories. They show a homely philosophy of life, flashes of poetic imagination, a shrewd appraisal of human nature, a childlike love of mischief, a pattern and style unsurpassed by any other beast tales.

*Reprinted from* Brer Rabbit and His Tricks, *text © 1967, by Ennis Rees and illustrations © 1967, by Edward Gorey, a Young Scott Book, by permission of Addison-Wesley Publishing Company.*

These stories do have their limitations, and the dialect is chief of them. Children in the South may be fortunate enough to hear these tales read by adults who can do justice to the flavorsome dialect. A. A. Milne's British father read these tales aloud to his children, dialect and all, and they loved them. However, it is the dialect that makes the stories almost unintelligible to most children and adults. When the stories are turned into standard English, they retain their witty folk flavor, just as tales translated from the Norwegian or East Indian or American Indian do. Perhaps translation is the answer here, too. Ennis Rees, in *Brer Rabbit and His Tricks* and *More of Brer Rabbit's Tricks*, has provided such translations with great success. The simplest version for children is Margaret Wise Brown's edition of *Brer Rabbit*.

Other objections to these stories are raised by modern American blacks. In the article entitled "Uncle Remus for Today's Children" (*Elementary English*, March 1953), Margaret Taylor Burroughs points out that the tales are full of offensive terms for blacks. She objects to the intrusion of old "Uncle's" personality and point of view. These sometimes add to the wit and wisdom of the stories, but she cites some deplorable examples also.

These objections point up the fact that the great body of seven hundred *Uncle Remus Tales* will survive chiefly as source material for gifted storytellers. Where else in any collection of folk tales can you find such droll revelations of human nature—antic, sagacious, witty? And where else can you find a colorful dialect so lovingly and perfectly recorded by a scholar with an ear for the euphony of speech?

The mighty deeds of John Henry, the black folk hero, are described in books by Harold Felton and by Ezra Jack Keats, and Keats has also provided bold, impressive illustrations. Helen Whiting, in *Negro Folk Tales for Pupils in the Primary Grades*, retells familiar stories very simply for younger children. An excellent and varied collection of black Americana is Harold Courlander's *Terrapin's Pot of Sense*.

### North American Indian Tales

The collecting of North American Indian tales began with the sporadic records of missionaries and explorers, but not until the 1830's was there any serious attempt to bring together the rich body of existing material. Henry Rowe Schoolcraft, a government agent for the Ojibwa Indians, zealously recorded their myths and legends, although not in pure form. Since his time, ethnologists and folklorists in the United States and Canada have collected a voluminous and varied storehouse of Indian folklore.

While there are recurring themes and variants of specific tales, and even variants of European folk tales, the extant material provides a body of literature that differs distinctly according to region and tribe. Because the Indian has a reverence for natural things, an affinity for the creatures of the earth and for the earth itself, much of his lore is concerned with nature as a part of religious beliefs and practices. Myths and legends that explain the origins of natural phenomena or the attributes of wild creatures are common to all the Indian cultures, since all of them invested living things with magical powers.

The major types of tales are creation myths; trickster tales, often humorous, in which the hero is either in human or in animal form, as in the stories of Coyote or Rabbit; journeys to another world, a story type that often reflects mores and taboos of a tribe; hero tales, often including tests for maturity or courage; and marriages between human beings and animals. Each region usually had its own cycle of traditional tales, and as with folklore diffusion everywhere, there are themes and patterns that occur in different regions.

### Native Variants of European Tales

The Southern "The Gingerbread Boy," printed in *St. Nicholas* in 1875, "Johnny-Cake," in Jacobs' *English Fairy Tales*, and Ruth Sawyer's "Journey Cake, Ho!" are American variants of the Scotch "The Wee Bannock" or the Norse "The Pancake." There are undoubtedly dozens of other European folk tales extant in this country in characteristically modified form, but so far the most amusing and significant collections are *The Jack Tales* and *Grandfather Tales* by Richard Chase, collected from American mountain people. Mr. Chase's account of these gay-hearted people makes you wish there were more of the stories. Old Counce "was a sight to dance. . . . Seventy years old, he could clog and buckdance as good as a boy sixteen." And he could also spellbind the mountaineer children with tales—tales that should never be *read*—"You've got to tell 'em to make 'em go right."

The stories are recorded in the vernacular of the mountain people who have modified them to local speech and customs. The god Wotan or Woden appears, ancient, mysterious, but as helpful to Jack as he was to Sigurd or Siegfried. Jack is a country boy, unassuming but resourceful, and never nonplussed by the most fantastic adventures. The language is ungrammatical and sometimes rough, but it is humorously effective when handled by as gifted a storyteller as Richard Chase. The mood is decidedly comic, the setting rural. City children may not know "The Old Sow and the Three Little Shoats," but they'll recognize it as "The Three Little Pigs." The book's appendix by Herbert Halpert predicted that many of the tales would be found elsewhere in this country, and they have been.

Try rereading these folk tales. They will move you sometimes to laughter and sometimes to tender pity. They will give you a better understanding of other people and yourself also. When you have finished, you will find that you have grown accustomed to looking at life with the eyes of a poet, searching for the spirit behind the rags or behind the fine clothes, for the selfishness or the nobility that makes the man. You will find that your ears have grown accustomed to the language of poets speaking in prose. You can never forget the measured cadence of these tales, the words dancing or stepping gravely to the mood. All the rest of your life you will unconsciously measure other prose and other stories by the fairy tales.

The multiplicity of folk-tale collections does not mean that we should use more of them. Most teachers are probably using them less than they once did because other types of fiction for children have improved in quality. But we should know that there are now available many national collections of these old tales, and we should select from them a moderate number of suitable variety and use them in balanced proportion to realistic stories and informational reading. In moments of discouragement, let's be grateful for the reassuring message these old tales carry. They say to the child, "Don't be too depressed about brute force and wickedness, because you will live to see them overthrown. Kindness and courage work their own magic in this world. Just remember the glass slipper in your pocket. It is your talisman of the triumph of virtue."

## ADULT REFERENCES[5]

AFANASIEV, ALEXANDER N. *Russian Fairy Tales.*

ASBJÖRNSEN, PETER C., and JÖRGEN MOE. *Norwegian Folk Tales.*

_____. *Popular Tales from the Norse.*

BARCHILON, JACQUES, and HENRY PETTIT. *The Authentic Mother Goose Fairy Tales and Nursery Rhymes.*

BAUGHMAN, ERNEST. *A Type and Motif Index of the Folktales of England and North America.*

BOLTON, HENRY CARRINGTON. *The Counting-Out Rhymes of Children; Their Antiquity, Origin, and Wide Distribution: A Study in Folk-Lore.*

BRIGGS, KATHARINE M. *A Dictionary of British Folk-Tales in the English Language.*

BRUNVAND, JAN H. *The Study of American Folklore, an Introduction.*

COLUM, PADRAIC, ed. *A Treasury of Irish Folklore.*

COOK, ELIZABETH. *The Ordinary and the Fabulous; An Introduction to Myths, Legends, and Fairy Tales for Teachers and Storytellers.*

DE AUGULO, JAIME. *Indian Tales.*

DORSON, RICHARD M. *American Folklore.*

_____. *Buying the Wind, Regional Folklore in the United States.*

_____, ed. Folktales of the World series.

DOUGLAS, NORMAN. *London Street Games.*

EASTMAN, MARY HUSE. *Index to Fairy Tales, Myths and Legends.*

*Funk and Wagnalls Standard Dictionary of Folklore, Mythology and Legend.*

5. Complete bibliographic data are provided in the combined Adult References in the Appendices.

GRIMM, JACOB and WILHELM. *Grimms' Fairy Tales.*

HALLIWELL-PHILLIPPS, JAMES O. *Popular Rhymes and Nursery Tales: A Sequel to The Nursery Rhymes of England.*

JACOBS, JOSEPH. See listings of his collections of English, Celtic, and Indian folk tales in the following bibliography. They contain significant introductions, and the notes in each appendix are treasures of folklore information.

KRAPPE, ALEXANDER HAGGERTY. *The Science of Folk-Lore.*

MONTGOMERIE, NORAH. *To Read and to Tell.*

PERRAULT, CHARLES. *Perrault's Complete Fairy Tales.*

SAWYER, RUTH. *My Spain; A Storyteller's Year of Collecting.*

THOMPSON, STITH. *The Folktale.*

_____. comp. *One Hundred Favorite Folktales.*

ULLOM, JUDITH C., comp. *Folklore of the American Indians; An Annotated Bibliography.*

(Note: T. Crofton Croker printed his *Fairy Legends and Traditions of the South of Ireland* in 1825, but finer collections were made by Patrick Kennedy, a Dublin bookseller whose *Legendary Fictions of the Irish Celts* was published in 1866 and followed by two more collections in 1867 and 1869. Kennedy's notes prefacing the tales are invaluable for students of Irish folklore, but unfortunately his books have been allowed to go out of print. Lady Wilde's *Ancient Legends of Ireland* (1887) is a good source for adult students of folklore.)

## GENERAL COLLECTIONS

ARBUTHNOT, MAY HILL, and MARK TAYLOR. *Time for Old Magic.* Scott, Foresman, 1970. See Adult Reference Bibliography. 8-12

ASSOCIATION FOR CHILDHOOD EDUCATION. *Told Under the Green Umbrella*, ill. by Grace Gilkison. Macmillan, 1962. Favorite tales for storytelling or reading aloud. 4-7

BAKER, AUGUSTA, comp. *The Golden Lynx and Other Tales*, ill. by Johannes Troyer. Lippincott, 1960.

_____. *The Talking Tree and Other Stories*, ill. by Johannes Troyer. Lippincott, 1955. Two fine selections by a noted storyteller. 8-11

BROOKE, L. LESLIE, ed. *The Golden Goose Book*, ill. by ed. Warne, 1906. "The Golden Goose," "Tom Thumb," "Three Little Pigs," and "Three Bears" are delightfully illustrated. 5-10

CHILD STUDY ASSOCIATION OF AMERICA. *Castles and Dragons; Read-to-Yourself Fairytales for Boys and Girls*, ill. by William Pène du Bois. T. Crowell, 1958. 9-12

DE LA MARE, WALTER. *Tales Told Again*, ill. by Alan Howard. Knopf, 1959. Gracefully told versions of familiar tales. 9-12

HUBER, MIRIAM BLANTON. *Story and Verse for Children*, ill. by Lynd Ward. Macmillan, 1955. A general anthology of children's literature with a good chapter on the values of folk tales. 10 up

HUTCHINSON, VERONICA, ed. *Chimney Corner Stories*, ill. by Lois Lenski. Putnam, 1925. 3-8

_____. *Fireside Stories*, ill. by Lois Lenski. Putnam, 1927. 8-12

Authentic, well-written, and well-illustrated adaptations, suitable for storytelling or reading aloud.

JACOBS, JOSEPH. *The Pied Piper and Other Tales*, ill. by James Hill. Macmillan, 1963. An attractively illustrated edition. 10-12

JOHNSON, EDNA, EVELYN SICKELS, and FRANCES CLARKE SAYERS. *Anthology of Children's Literature*. Houghton, 1969. The chapter on "Folk-Tales" contains a good selection. 10 up

LANG, ANDREW. *Fifty Favorite Tales*, ill. by Margery Gill. Watts, 1964. Stories selected from Lang's "color" series (*Blue Fairy Book, Crimson Fairy Book*, etc.) which contains some stories that denigrate minority groups. 9-12

LEACH, MARIA. *The Rainbow Book of American Folk Tales and Legends*, ill. by Marc Simont. World, 1958. Regional lore, proverbs, riddles, tall tales, and folk tales of North and South America. 9-12

PROVENSEN, ALICE and MARTIN, comps. *The Provensen Book of Fairy Tales*, ill. by comps. Random, 1971. A dozen modern fairy stories illustrated with gay, colorful pictures. 9-11

RACKHAM, ARTHUR, comp. *Arthur Rackham Fairy Book*, ill. by comp. Lippincott, 1950. A choice of Rackham's favorite tales. 8-10

ROSS, EULALIE, comp. *The Buried Treasure and Other Picture Tales*, ill. by Joseph Cellini. Lippincott, 1958. Tales from the "Picture Tales" series. 7-10

______. *The Lost Half-Hour*, ill. by Enrico Arno. Harcourt, 1963. Good storytelling material. 9-11

SEKOROVA, DAGMAR, comp. *European Fairy Tales*, ill. by Mirko Hanak. Lothrop, 1971. Stories from eight European countries. 9-11

SHEEHAN, ETHNA, comp. *Folk and Fairy Tales from Around the World*, ill. by Mircea Vasiliu. Dodd, 1970. Seventeen tales, each from a different country, with some appended suggestions for beginning storytellers. 9-11

UNITED NATIONS WOMEN'S GUILD. *Ride with the Sun; Anthology of Folk Tales and Stories from the United Nations*, ed. by Harold Courlander, ill. by Roger Duvoisin. McGraw, 1955. Each story has been approved by the U.N. representative of the country from which it comes. 10-12

WIGGIN, KATE DOUGLAS, and NORA A. SMITH, eds. *The Fairy Ring*, rev. by Ethna Sheehan, ill. by Warren Chappell. Doubleday, 1967. A good new edition of an old favorite. 9-11

WITHERS, CARL. *A World of Nonsense; Strange and Humorous Tales from Many Lands*, ill. by John E. Johnson. Holt, 1968. Fifty examples of the universal appeal of nonsense and exaggeration. 9-11

## SUBJECT COLLECTIONS

BELTING, NATALIA. *Calendar Moon*, ill. by Bernarda Bryson. Holt, 1964. The text, which is composed of folk lore and myth from widely varied peoples, moves through the calendar year in this distinctive, strikingly illustrated book. 10-13

______. *Cat Tales*, ill. by Leo Summers. Holt, 1959.

______. *The Earth Is on A Fish's Back: Tales of Beginnings*, ill. by Esta Nesbitt. Holt, 1965.

______. *Elves and Ellefolk: Tales of the Little People*, ill. by Gordon Laite. Holt, 1961. 8-12

CARPENTER, FRANCES. *Wonder Tales of Dogs and Cats*, ill. by Ezra Jack Keats. Doubleday, 1955. Tales from seventeen countries. 8-11

DE LA MARE, WALTER. *Animal Stories*. Scribner's, 1940. Stories, rhymes, and ballads. 10-12

GARNER, ALAN, ed. *A Cavalcade of Goblins*, ill. by Krystyna Turska. Walck, 1969. An excellent anthology of excerpts, poems, and stories from worldwide sources. A treasure for storytellers. 9-12

HARDENDORFF, JEANNE B., comp. *Tricky Peik and Other Picture Tales*, ill. by Tomie de Paola. Lippincott, 1967. A collection of trickster tales. 9-11

JABLOW, ALTA, and CARL WITHERS. *The Man in the Moon*, ill. by Peggy Wilson. Holt, 1969. Stories about the moon, sun, and stars, the diverse sources cited. 8-10

JAGENDORF, MORITZ, and C. H. TILLHAGEN. *The Gypsies' Fiddle and other Gypsy Tales*, ill. by Hans Helweg. Vanguard, 1956. 9-12

LEACH, MARIA, ed. *How the People Sang the Mountains Up: How and Why Stories*, ill. by Glen Rounds. Viking, 1967. Legends about natural phenomena from many lands. 10-12

MANNING-SANDERS, RUTH. *A Book of Devils and Demons*, ill. by Robin Jacques. Dutton, 1970.

______. *A Book of Dragons*, ill. by Robin Jacques. Dutton, 1965.

______. *A Book of Dwarfs*, ill. by Robin Jacques. Dutton, 1964.

______. *A Book of Ghosts and Goblins*, ill. by Robin Jacques. Dutton, 1969.

______. *A Book of Giants*, ill. by Robin Jacques. Dutton, 1963.

______. *A Book of Magical Beasts*, ill. by Raymond Briggs. Nelson, 1970.

______. *A Book of Mermaids*, ill. by Robin Jacques. Dutton, 1968.

______. *A Book of Princes and Princesses*, ill. by Robin Jacques. Dutton 1970.

______. *A Book of Witches*, ill. by Robin Jacques. Dutton, 1966.

______. *A Book of Wizards*, ill. by Robin Jacques. Dutton, 1967.

______. *The Red King and the Witch: Gypsy Folk and Fairy Tales*, ill. by Victor Ambrus. Roy, 1965. Each has a delightful style and well-chosen tales. 9-12

SAWYER, RUTH. *Joy to the World: Christmas Legends*, ill. by Trina Schart Hyman. Little, 1966.

______. *The Long Christmas*, ill. by Valenti Angelo. Viking, 1941. Tales by a great storyteller. 8-12

SPICER, DOROTHY. *13 Ghosts*, ill. by Sophia. Coward, 1965. Varied and sprightly. 9-11

## COLLECTIONS AND SINGLE TALES

### African and Ethiopian

AARDEMA, VERNA. *More Tales from the Story Hat*, ill. by Elton Fax. Coward, 1966. 7-10

———. *Tales for the Third Ear; From Equatorial Africa*, ill. by Ib Ohlsson. Dutton, 1969. Nine folk tales retold from original sources that give verbatim versions of African storytellers. Full of action and humor and an excellent source for storytelling. 8-10

———. *Tales from the Story Hat*, ill. by Elton Fax. Coward, 1960. 8-12

ARKHURST, JOYCE COOPER. *The Adventures of Spider*, ill. by Jerry Pinkney. Little, 1964. 8-10

ARNOTT, KATHLEEN. *African Myths and Legends*, ill. by Joan Kiddell-Monroe. Walck, 1963. Tales from south of the Sahara, thirty-four in all, tell of "animals, humans and superhumans." 11 up

BURTON, W. F. P. *The Magic Drum; Tales from Central Africa*, ill. by Ralph Thompson. Criterion, 1962. Short tales with a fablelike quality that are favorites in the Congo. Illustrated with humor and imagination. 9-12

COURLANDER, HAROLD. *The King's Drum and Other Stories*, ill. by Enrico Arno. Harcourt, 1962. Almost thirty stories from Africa identified by tribal sources. Excellent notes are appended on the origins or interpretations of these folk tales. 9-13

COURLANDER, HAROLD, and GEORGE HERZOG. *The Cow-Tail Switch, and Other West African Stories*, ill. by Madye Lee Chastain. Holt, 1947. Seventeen tales, told in lively style and revealing much about the customs of the people. 10-12

COURLANDER, HAROLD, and WOLF LESLAU. *The Fire on the Mountain and Other Ethiopian Stories*, ill. by Robert W. Kane. Holt, 1950. Outstanding in style, illustrations, and content. 10-14

COURLANDER, HAROLD, and ALBERT PREMPEH. *The Hat-Shaking Dance, and Other Tales from the Gold Coast*, ill. by Enrico Arno. Harcourt, 1957. Humorous, droll, or wise are these twenty-one tales of Anansi. 9-12

DAYRELL, ELPHINSTONE. *Why the Sun and the Moon Live in the Sky; An African Folktale*, ill. by Blair Lent. Houghton, 1968. A story about the beginnings of time from the Efik-Ibibio peoples. Beautifully detailed and stylized art work is based on African sources. 5-7

FOURNIER, CATHARINE, ad. *The Coconut Thieves*, ill. by Janina Domanska. Scribner's, 1964. An adaptation of an African folk tale. 8-9

FUJA, ABAYOMI. *Fourteen Hundred Cowries and Other African Tales*, ill. by Ademola Olugebefola. Lothrop, 1971. Unusual stories recorded many years ago by a Youruba scholar. 9-12

GILSTRAP, ROBERT, and IRENE ESTABROOK. *The Sultan's Fool and Other North African Tales*, ill. by Robert Greco. Holt, 1958. Eleven wise and witty tales, excellent for reading aloud and storytelling. 9-12

HALEY, GAIL E., ad. *A Story A Story; An African Tale*, ill. by adapter. Atheneum, 1970. The story explains the origin of that favorite African folk material, the spider tale. Bright, humorous illustrations. Caldecott Medal. 5-7

HARMAN, HUMPHREY. *Tales Told Near a Crocodile; Stories from Nyanza*, ill. by George Ford. Viking, 1967. 10-11

HEADY, ELEANOR. *When the Stones Were Soft; East African Fireside Tales*, ill. by Tom Feelings. Funk, 1968. 9-11

KAULA, EDNA MASON. *African Village Folktales*, ill. by author. World, 1968. 9-11

RADIN, PAUL, and JAMES JOHNSON SWEENEY. *African Folktales and Sculpture*, 2nd ed. Pantheon, 1964. 13 up

ROCKWELL, ANNE. *When the Drum Sang; An African Folktale*, ill. by author. Parents' Magazine, 1970. A Bantu folk tale is retold in flat, but direct and simple, style. 5-7

STURTON, HUGH. *Zomo the Rabbit*, ill. by Peter Warner. Atheneum, 1966. 9–11

## Arabian

*Arabian Nights*, retold by Amabel Williams-Ellis, ill. by Pauline Diana Baynes. Criterion, 1957. Lively retellings of the children's favorites together with several lesser known tales. 10-13

BROWN, MARCIA. *The Flying Carpet*, ill. by author. Scribner's, 1956. This story, so much a part of our language and so difficult to find, is beautifully retold and illustrated. 6-10

COLUM, PADRAIC, ed. *The Arabian Nights: Tales of Wonder and Magnificence*, ill. by Lynd Ward. Macmillan, 1964. Republished after thirty years, in a new and attractive edition, this outstanding collection will appeal to younger readers. 10-14

LANG, ANDREW, ed. *Arabian Nights*, ill. by Vera Bock. McKay, 1946. Fine black-and-white drawings and large print make this a favorite edition for children's reading. 10-14

WIGGIN, KATE DOUGLAS, and NORA SMITH, eds. *Arabian Nights, Their Best Known Tales*, ill. by Maxfield Parrish. Scribner's, 1909. Here are the favorite stories—"Aladdin," "Ali Baba," "The Voyage of Sinbad the Sailor"—gorgeously illustrated in color and well told. 10-14

## Canadian

BARBEAU, MARIUS. *The Golden Phoenix; and Other French-Canadian Fairy Tales*, retold by Michael Hornyansky, ill. by Arthur Price. Walck, 1958. Notes as to their origin give these eight tales a special interest for the student. Told with humor and zest. 10-13

CARLSON, NATALIE SAVAGE. *The Talking Cat and Other Stories of French Canada*, ill. by Roger Duvoisin. Harper, 1952. Tales told with vitality and humor and excellent for reading aloud. 8-11

HOOKE, HILDA MARY. *Thunder in the Mountains; Legends of Canada*, ill. by Clare Bice. Walck, 1947. Indian legends, stories of the coming of white men, and variants of European tales. 9-12

## Chinese

BIRCH, CYRIL. *Chinese Myths and Fantasies*, ill. by Joan Kiddell-Monroe. Walck, 1961. Ghosts and magicians and plain folk, too, are characters in this absorbing collection of tales. 11 up

BISHOP, CLAIRE. *The Five Chinese Brothers*, ill. by Kurt Wiese. Coward, 1938. This Chinese version of five brothers, each with a magical gift, has been a favorite ever since it appeared. 5-10

CARPENTER, FRANCES. *Tales of a Chinese Grandmother*, ill. by Malthé Hasselriis. Doubleday, 1937. The "Grandmother" series for different racial groups is a reliable source, with many good stories. 9-12

MERRILL, JEAN. *The Superlative Horse*, ill. by Ronni Solbert. W. R. Scott, 1961. An unassuming stable lad becomes head groom in the royal stables when he selects the perfect horse. Based on a Taoist legend and illustrated in ancient Chinese style. 9-11

MOSEL, ARLENE, ed. *Tikki Tikki Tembo*, ill. by Blair Lent. Holt, 1968. An amusing picture book to read aloud, since the crux of the story is the long, long name (for which the title is an abbreviation). The wash illustrations have an appropriately Oriental beauty. 5-7

RITCHIE, ALICE. *The Treasure of Li-Po*, ill. by T. Ritchie. Harcourt, 1949. These six original fairy tales are told with all the sincerity and dignity of the folk tales which they resemble. 10-14

YOLEN, JANE H. *The Emperor and the Kite*, ill. by Ed Young. World, 1967. A tale of ancient China about Djeow Seow, who was so tiny her father the Emperor never noticed her until she saved his life. 5-8

### Czechoslovakian

FILLMORE, PARKER. *Shepherd's Nosegay*, ed. by Katherine Love, ill. by Enrico Arno. Harcourt, 1958. Eighteen tales of Finland and Czechoslovakia compiled from Fillmore's out-of-print collections. Excellent for telling and reading aloud. 9-12

HAVILAND, VIRGINIA, ad. *Favorite Fairy Tales Told in Czechoslovakia*, ill. by Trina S. Hyman. Little, 1966. 8-10

### Danish

HATCH, MARY COTTAM. *13 Danish Tales, Retold*, ill. by Edgun (pseud.). Harcourt, 1947. These stories are excellent for reading or storytelling, and are carefully adapted from the Bay translation. 9-13

______. *More Danish Tales, Retold*, ill. by Edgun (pseud.). Harcourt, 1949. 9-13

HAVILAND, VIRGINIA, ad. *Favorite Fairy Tales Told in Denmark*, ill. by Margot Zemach. Little, 1971. Six tales are retold with directness and simplicity. Useful as a source for storytelling as well as for independent reading. 9-11

JONES, GWYN. *Scandinavian Legends and Folk Tales* (see Norwegian tales).

### English, Scottish, and Welsh

BRIGGS, KATHERINE, and RUTH TONGUE, eds. *Folktales of England*. Univ. of Chicago Pr., 1965. (Folktales of the World series) 10 up

BROWN, MARCIA. *Dick Whittington and His Cat*, ill. by author. Scribner's, 1950. A lively, readable adaptation of this classic hero tale with strong linoleum cuts in two colors. 4-8

GALDONE, PAUL, ill. *The Old Woman and Her Pig*. McGraw, 1960. The old nursery favorite is reintroduced as a lively picture book. Another nursery classic made into a picture book by the artist is *Old Mother Hubbard and Her Dog* (1960). 4-7

HAVILAND, VIRGINIA, ad. *Favorite Fairy Tales Told in Scotland*, ill. by Adrienne Adams. Little, 1963. Six of the more familiar tales retold for the reading of younger children. 8-10

JACOBS, JOSEPH, ed. *English Fairy Tales*, ill. by John D. Batten. Putnam, n.d.

______. *More English Fairy Tales*, ill. by John D. Batten. Putnam, n.d.
These not only are reliable sources for the favorite English tales but are also appealing to children in format and illustrations. 9-12

______. *Favorite Fairy Tales Told in England*, retold by Virginia Haviland, ill. by Bettina (pseud.). Little, 1959. Six tales in attractive large-print format imaginatively illustrated. 8-9

JONES, GWYN. *Welsh Legends and Folk Tales*, ill. by Joan Kiddell-Monroe. Walck, 1955. Retellings of ancient sagas as well as folk and fairy tales are included. Illustrations in color are particularly outstanding. 11-14

MANNING-SANDERS, RUTH. *Peter and the Piskies: Cornish Folk and Fairy Tales*, ill. by Raymond Briggs. Roy, 1966. 10-12

NESS, EVALINE. *Tom Tit Tot*, ill. by author. Scribner's, 1965. A very attractive picture-book variation of the Rumpelstiltskin story, good for storytelling or for reading aloud. 5-8

NIC LEODHAS, SORCHE (pseud.). *Always Room for One More*, ill. by Nonny Hogrogian. Holt, 1965. A picture-book version of an old Scottish song. Handsome illustrations. Caldecott Medal. 5-8

______. *By Loch and by Lin*, ill. by Vera Bock. Holt, 1969. 9-12

______. *Claymore and Kilt*, ill. by Leo and Diane Dillon. Holt, 1967. 12-14

______. *Gaelic Ghosts*, ill. by Nonny Hogrogian. Holt, 1964. 10-12

______. *Ghosts Go Haunting*, ill. by Nonny Hogrogian. Holt, 1965. 10-12

______. *Heather and Broom*, ill. by Consuelo Joerns. Holt, 1960. 10-12

______. *Sea-Spell and Moor-Magic; Tales of the Western Isles*, ill. by Vera Bock. Holt, 1968. 9-11

______. *Thistle and Thyme*, ill. by Evaline Ness. Holt, 1962. 10-12

REEVES, JAMES. *English Fables and Fairy Stories*, ill. by Joan Kiddell-Monroe. Walck, 1954. An attractive collection of nineteen tales illustrated in two colors. 10-14

STEEL, FLORA ANNIE. *English Fairy Tales*, ill. by Arthur Rackham, with an afterword by Clifton Fadiman. Macmillan, 1962. This book has the imaginative pictures of Rackham and the excellent adaptations of Mrs. Steel. All the favorites are here. 8-12

WILLIAMS-ELLIS, AMABEL. *Fairy Tales from the British Isles*, ill. by Pauline Diana Baynes. Warne, 1964. 10-12

WILSON, BARBARA KER. *Scottish Folk Tales and Legends*, ill. by Joan Kiddell-Monroe. Walck, 1954. In addition to the folk tales, a section of stories on the legendary exploits of the Fians is included. Attractive format and illustrations. 11-14

### Finnish

BOWMAN, JAMES CLOYD, and MARGERY BIANCO. *Tales from a Finnish Tupa*, from a tr. by Aili Kolehmainen, ill. by Laura Bannon. Whitman, 1936. Here are the everyday folk tales of the Finnish people, not the epic stories. Beautifully told, with effective illustrations. 10-14

FILLMORE, PARKER. *Shepherd's Nosegay* (see Czechoslovakian tales).

### French

COONEY, BARBARA. *The Little Juggler*, ill. by author. Hastings, 1961. In this appealing picture-story version of the old legend, an orphan boy is the little juggler who offers his only skill at the monastery altar. 8-11

D'AULNOY, MARIE C. *The White Cat and Other Old French Fairy Tales* by Mme. La Comtesse d'Aulnoy, tr. by Rachel Field, ill. by Elizabeth MacKinstry. Macmillan, 1928, 1967. 8-11

MASSIGNON, GENEVIEVE, ed. *Folktales of France*, tr. by Jacqueline Hyland. Univ. of Chicago Pr., 1968. (Folktales of the World series) 10 up

PERRAULT, CHARLES. *Cinderella; or The Little Glass Slipper*, ill. by Marcia Brown. Scribner's, 1954. Attractive pastel illustrations. Caldecott Medal. 5-9

______. *Favorite Fairy Tales Told in France*, retold by Virginia Haviland, ill. by Roger Duvoisin. Little, 1959. Five well-loved tales include "Puss in Boots," "Beauty and the Beast," and "Sleeping Beauty." Large print and attractive illustrations. 8-10

______. *Puss in Boots*, ill. by Marcia Brown. Scribner's, 1952. Wonderful pictures enliven this story of the faithful cat who helps to make a lord of his poor young master. 6-9

______. *Puss in Boots*, ill. by Hans Fischer. Harcourt, 1959. A noted Swiss artist interjects a subtle humor of his own into the pictures and his retelling of Perrault's tale. 5-8

PICARD, BARBARA LEONIE. *French Legends, Tales and Fairy Stories*, ill. by Joan Kiddell-Monroe. Walck, 1955. A rich and varied source of folklore ranging from epic literature to medieval tales; from legends to fairy tales. 10-14

### German

ANGLUND, JOAN WALSH. *Nibble Nibble Mousekin*, ill. by author. Harcourt, 1962. Mrs. Anglund's drawings of guileless children add an appealing note to this colorful picture-book tale of "Hänsel and Gretel." 5-8

GRIMM, JACOB and WILHELM. *About Wise Men and Simpletons; Twelve Tales from Grimm*, tr. by Elizabeth Shub, ill. by Nonny Hogrogian. Macmillan, 1971. Newly translated from the less familiar first edition, pithy versions of familiar tales. 9-11

______. *Favorite Fairy Tales Told in Germany*, retold by Virginia Haviland, ill. by Susanne Suba. Little, 1959. "Hänsel and Gretel," "Rapunzel," and "Frog Prince" are among the seven selections in this attractive, large-print edition. 5-8

______. *Gone Is Gone*, retold and ill. by Wanda Gág. Coward, 1935. Lively retelling of the old tale about the man and wife who exchanged household duties for a day. 6-8

______. *Grimm's Fairy Tales*, tr. by Mrs. E. V. Lucas and others, ill. by Fritz Kredel. Grosset, 1945. An edition that is thoroughly satisfactory to children. The excellent translation is supplemented by bright, appealing pictures. 9-12

______. *Jorinda and Joringel*, tr. by Elizabeth Shub, ill. by Adrienne Adams, Scribner's, 1968. A handsome edition of the story of a maiden bewitched and of her rescue by her lover. 8-10

______. *The Shoemaker and the Elves*, ill. by Adrienne Adams. Scribner's, 1960. Colorful illustrations add new beauty to one of the Grimms' best-loved tales for little children. 3-6

______. *The Sleeping Beauty*, ill. by Felix Hoffmann. Harcourt, 1960. The richly toned pictures make a rare contribution to this American edition, originally published in Switzerland. Other Grimm tales illustrated by this artist include *The Wolf and the Seven Little Kids* (1959) and *The Seven Ravens* (1963). 5-9

______. *Snow White and the Seven Dwarfs*, freely tr. and ill. by Wanda Gág. Coward. 1938.

______. *Tales from Grimm*, freely tr. and ill. by Wanda Gág. Coward, 1936.

______. *Three Gay Tales from Grimm*, tr. and ill. by Wanda Gág. Coward, 1943. Wanda Gág's narration is lively, natural, and simple. So are the illustrations. Both text and pictures preserve the folk flavor of the tales, and children feel at once that these books belong to them. 8-12

______. *The Traveling Musicians*, ill. by Hans Fischer. Harcourt, 1955. Distinctive illustrations in color make this an outstanding folk-tale picture book. 5-8

HAUFF, WILHELM. *Dwarf Long-Nose*, tr. by Doris Orgel, ill. by Maurice Sendak. Random, 1960. Poor Jacob displeases a witch and spends years as an ugly dwarf before regaining his true form and a handsome bride as well. An excellent translation, appealingly illustrated. 9-11

PICARD, BARBARA LEONIE. *German Hero-Sagas and Folk-Tales*, ill. by Joan Kiddell-Monroe. Walck, 1958. *Siegfried* and other sagas, as well as such folk tales as *Ratcatcher of Hamelin*, give children a broader background of German lore than the more familiar Grimm tales. 11-14

RANKE, KURT, ed. *Folktales of Germany*, tr. by Lotte

Baumann. Univ. of Chicago Pr., 1966. (Folktales of the World series) 10 up

### Indian and Pakistani

BABBITT, ELLEN C. *The Jataka Tales*, ill. by Ellsworth Young. Appleton, 1912.

———. *More Jataka Tales*, ill. by Ellsworth Young. Appleton, 1912.
These are valuable sources of East Indian tales. 6-10

BROWN, MARCIA. *Once a Mouse*, ill. by author. Scribner's, 1961. The timid mouse was changed by a kindly hermit into a cat, a dog, and then a tiger who became so cruel he had to be punished. Caldecott Medal. 5-8

GRAY, JOHN E. B. *India's Tales and Legends*, ill. by Joan Kiddell-Monroe. Walck, 1961. Truly distinguished retellings of India's rich lore, which will appeal to older children. 11 up

HITCHCOCK, PATRICIA. *The King Who Rides a Tiger and Other Folk Tales from Nepal*, ill. by Lillian Sader. Parnassus, 1966. A dozen colorful, varied tales, retold in a light and graceful style. 9-11

JACOBS, JOSEPH, ed. *Indian Fairy Tales*, ill. by J. D. Batten. Putnam, 1969. Like Jacobs' other collections, these stories are selected from manuscript sources. They also throw light on fable and folktale origins. 9-12

QUIGLEY, LILLIAN. *The Blind Men and the Elephant; An Old Tale from the Land of India*, ill. by Janice Holland. Scribner's, 1959. The popular and often quoted tale of the blind men who, in describing an elephant, "saw" only what they could feel. 5-9

### Irish

COLUM, PADRAIC. *The King of Ireland's Son*, ill. by Willy Pogány. Macmillan, 1921, 1967. Seven Irish folk tales about a brave young royal lad. 10-12

DANAHER, KEVIN. *Folktales of the Irish Countryside*, ill. by Harold Berson. White, 1970. Fourteen tales heard by the author from six storytellers. Delightful to read alone or aloud, and a good source for storytellers. 10-12

HAVILAND, VIRGINIA, ad. *Favorite Fairy Tales Told in Ireland*, ill. by Arthur Marokvia. Little, 1961. "Old Hag's Long Leather Bag" and "Billy Beg and the Bull" are among the popular tales included in this attractive, large-print collection. 8-11

JACOBS, JOSEPH. *Munachar and Manachar; An Irish Story*, ill. by Anne Rockwell. T. Crowell, 1970. The cumulation and the nonsense humor of this Celtic tale are appealing. Good for storytelling or reading aloud. 5-7

———, ed. *Celtic Fairy Tales*, ill. by John D. Batten. Putnam, 1892.

———, ed. *More Celtic Fairy Tales*, ill. by John D. Batten. Putnam, n.d. Jacobs includes Welsh, Scotch, Cornish, and Irish in his two Celtic collections. His copious notes are of great value. 9-12

MACMANUS, SEUMAS. *Hibernian Nights*, ill. by Paul Kennedy. Macmillan, 1963. The "last of the great Irish storytellers" compiled this rich collection of twenty-two of his favorite tales chosen from his earlier books. Padraic Colum's introduction is a gracious tribute to MacManus and his storyteller's art. 11 up

O'FAOLAIN, EILEEN. *Irish Sagas and Folk-Tales*, ill. by Joan Kiddell-Monroe. Walck, 1954. This distinguished collection contains epic tales and folk tales to delight both reader and storyteller. 10-14

### Italian

CHAFETZ, HENRY. *The Legend of Befana*, ill. by Ronni Solbert. Houghton, 1958. The old Italian Christmas legend beautifully retold and illustrated. 5-9

HAVILAND, VIRGINIA, ad. *Favorite Fairy Tales Told in Italy*, ill. by Evaline Ness. Little, 1965. 8-10

JAGENDORF, M. A. *The Priceless Cats and Other Italian Folk Stories*, ill. by Gioia Fiamenghi. Vanguard, 1956. An attractive and gay collection for the children's own reading. 10-13

### Japanese

BARUCH, DOROTHY. *Kappa's Tug-of-War with Big Brown Horse*, ill. by Sanryo Sakai. Tuttle, 1962. Retelling of an old legend of a little water-imp who steals what he wants, and is at last outwitted by Farmer Shiba. 6-8

HAVILAND, VIRGINIA, ad. *Favorite Fairy Tales Told in Japan*, ill. by George Suyeoka. Little, 1967. 8-10

HEARN, LAFCADIO. *The Wave*, ad. by Margaret Hodges from Lafcadio Hearn's *Gleanings in Buddha-Fields*, ill. by Blair Lent. Houghton, 1964. 8-10

MC ALPINE, HELEN and WILLIAM, comps. *Japanese Tales and Legends*, retold by the McAlpines, ill. by Joan Kiddell-Monroe. Walck, 1959. A choice selection from the folklore, legends, and epic tales of Japan. 10-14

STAMM, CLAUS, ed. *Three Strong Women: A Tall Tale from Japan*, ill. by Kazue Mizumura. Viking, 1962. A sturdy girl, her mother, and her grandmother train a cocky young wrestler to new heights of strength for a court performance. A humorous read-aloud, color illustrated. 8-11

———. *The Very Special Badgers; A Tale of Magic from Japan*, ill. by Kazue Mizumura. Viking, 1960. An amusing and humorous tale of how two badger clans settle a dispute. 8-10

UCHIDA, YOSHIKO. *The Dancing Kettle and Other Japanese Folk Tales*, retold, ill. by Richard C. Jones. Harcourt, 1949. Fourteen Japanese folk tales, some of them familiar, many of them new, make this a welcome addition to folklore collections.

———. *The Magic Listening Cap, More Folk Tales from Japan*, ill. by author. Harcourt, 1955. The author-artist has illustrated this second collection with the distinctive simplicity characteristic of Japanese art. 9-12

YAMAGUCHI, TOHR. *The Golden Crane*, ill. by Marianne Yamaguchi. Holt, 1963. When a sacred golden crane is injured, a small boy rescues it and risks his life to save it from the avaricious who want it as a trophy. Based on a Japanese folk tale, both story and illustrations are artistically lovely. 8-10

### Mexican and South American

FINGER, CHARLES J. *Tales from Silver Lands*. Doubleday, 1924. The author gathered these outstanding folk tales from the Indians during his South American travels. Newbery Medal. 10-14

JAGENDORF, M. A., and R. S. BOGGS. *The King of the Mountains; A Treasury of Latin American Folk Stories*, ill. by Carybé. Vanguard, 1960. More than fifty tales, listed by country of origin. 10-14

### Norwegian

ASBJÖRNSEN, PETER C., and JÖRGEN MOE. *East o' the Sun and West o' the Moon*, ill. by Hedvig Collin. Macmillan, 1953. A new and attractive edition of a title which appeared twenty-five years ago. Based on the Dasent translation. 10-14

______. *East o' the Sun and West o' the Moon*, ill. by Kay Nielsen. Doubleday, 1922. Fifteen favorite stories with highly imaginative illustrations. 10-14

______.*Norwegian Folk Tales* (see Adult References, this chapter). 10-13

______. *The Three Billy Goats Gruff*, ill. by Marcia Brown. Harcourt, 1957. A favorite folk tale appears in brightly colored picture-book format. 4-7

CHRISTIANSEN, REIDAR T., ed. *Folktales of Norway*, tr. by Pat Shaw Iversen. Univ. of Chicago Pr., 1964. (Folktales of the World series) 10 up

HAVILAND, VIRGINIA, ad. *Favorite Fairy Tales Told in Norway*, ill. by Leonard Weisgard. Little, 1961. Seven familiar tales, handsomely illustrated in three colors. Includes "Why the Sea Is Salt," "Taper Tom," and "Princess on the Glass Hill." 8-11

JONES, GWYN. *Scandinavian Legends and Folk Tales*, ill. by Joan Kiddell-Monroe. Walck, 1956. Another Oxford contribution to folk-tale collections, this contains several of the familiar stories. Others are hero tales and unusual examples of folklore told with humor and impressive art. 8-12

THORNE-THOMSEN, GUDRUN. *East o' the Sun and West o' the Moon*, rev. ed., ill. by Frederick Richardson. Row, 1946. The stories are adapted from the original by a famous storyteller. 7-12

UNDSET, SIGRID, ed. *True and Untrue and Other Norse Tales*, ill. by Frederick T. Chapman. Knopf, 1945. A good collection for storytelling and for children's own reading. The author's foreword on the subject of folklore will appeal to the student. 10-13

### Polish

BORSKI, LUCIA M., and KATE B. MILLER. *The Jolly Tailor, and Other Fairy Tales*, ill. by Kazimir Klephacki. McKay, 1957. Reissued after many years, this collection translated from the Polish offers fine material for reading and storytelling. 9-12

HAVILAND, VIRGINIA, ad. *Favorite Fairy Tales Told in Poland*, ill. by Felix Hoffmann. Little, 1963. Six tales appealingly retold and illustrated. Large-print format appeals to younger readers. 8-10

SINGER, ISAAC BASHEVIS. *When Shlemiel Went to Warsaw; And Other Stories*, tr. by author and Elizabeth Shub, ill. by Margot Zemach. Farrar, 1968. Eight stories, some based on traditional Jewish tales. The cadence of the writing is especially evident when read aloud; the length, style, and humor make them a good source for storytelling. 10 up

______. *Zlateh the Goat*, tr. by author and Elizabeth Shub, ill. by Maurice Sendak. Harper, 1966. Seven tales based on middle-European Jewish folk material, told and illustrated with distinction. 10-12

ZAJDLER, ZOE, comp. *Polish Fairy Tales*, ill. by Hazel Cook. Follett, 1968. A more extensive collection than the Borski or Haviland collections. Considerable variety. Useful as a source for storytelling or for independent reading. 9-11

### Russian

ARTZYBASHEFF, BORIS. *Seven Simeons; a Russian Tale*, retold and ill. by author. Viking, 1961. 7-10

DANIELS, GUY, tr. *Foma the Terrible; A Russian Folktale*, ill. by Imero Gobbato. Delacorte, 1970. A funnier Russian noodlehead there never was, Foma's deeds and misdeeds are told in lively style. Adapted from the Afanasiev collection. 5-8

______, tr. *The Peasant's Pea Patch; A Russian Folktale*, ill. by Robert Quackenbush. Delacorte, 1971. The tale of a stupid peasant who moves from one exaggerated predicament to another. The tall tale appeal is not buttressed by the writing style. 8-10

DOWNING, CHARLES. *Russian Tales and Legends*, ill. by Joan Kiddell-Monroe. Walck, 1957. Epic, folk, and fairy tales gathered from many areas of Russia. 11 up

HAVILAND, VIRGINIA, ad. *Favorite Fairy Tales Told in Russia*, ill. by Herbert Danska. Little, 1961. Among the five tales included in this color-illustrated, large-print book are "The Straw Ox," "Flying Ship," and "To Your Good Health." 8-11

MORTON, MIRIAM, ed. *A Harvest of Russian Children's Literature*. Univ. of Calif. Pr., 1967. All ages

PROKOFIEFF, SERGE. *Peter and the Wolf*, ill. by Warren Chappell. Knopf, 1940. Delightful picture-book story about young Peter, who outwitted the wolf to rescue the duck. Excerpts from the musical score accompany the text. 7-10

RANSOME, ARTHUR. *Old Peter's Russian Tales*, ill. by Dmitri Mitrokhim. Nelson, 1917, 1969. This is the teacher's most practical source for the Russian tales. They are in admirable style for telling or reading aloud or dramatizing. 8-12

______, ad. *The Fool of the World and the Flying Ship; A Russian Tale*, ill. by Uri Shulevitz. Farrar, 1968. A retelling of a Russian tale is brought to life again with vigorous and colorful illustrations. Caldecott Medal. 5-8

ROBBINS, RUTH. *Baboushka and the Three Kings*, ill. by Nicolas Sidjakov. Parnassus, 1960. The familiar Russian folk tale of the selfish old woman and the Wise Men is enhanced by striking modern illustrations. Caldecott Medal. 5-10

WHEELER, POST. *Russian Wonder Tales*, ill. by Bilibin. Beechhurst, 1957. Serving in diplomatic posts in various parts of the world, Post Wheeler gathered the folklore of the people. 11-14

WHITNEY, THOMAS P., tr. *The Story of Prince Ivan, the Firebird, and the Gray Wolf*, ill. by Nonny Hogrogian. Scribner's, 1968. A classic Russian fairy tale with a melodramatic plot. Striking illustrations. 8-10

———, tr. *Vasilisa the Beautiful*, ill. by Nonny Hogrogian. Macmillan, 1970. From the Afanasiev collection, a version of the Cinderella story. Handsome illustrations. 9-11

WYNDHAM, LEE, comp. *Tales the People Tell in Russia*, ill. by Andrew Antal. Messner, 1970. Ten tales told with gusto for which sources are cited in an appended note. Also contains three fables and a short list of proverbs. 8-10

ZEMACH, HARVEY, ad. *Salt; A Russian Tale*, from a literal translation by Benjamin Zemach of the Russian of Alexei Afansev, ill. by Margot Zemach. Follett, 1965. A picture-book version of a Russian story, with the familiar pattern of the youngest brother surmounting all difficulties and winning a princess. Attractively illustrated. 5-8

## Spanish

BOGGS, RALPH STEELE, and MARY GOULD DAVIS. *The Three Golden Oranges and Other Spanish Folk Tales*, ill. by Emma Brock. McKay, 1936. Stories for older children, romantic and exciting. One remarkable ghost story. 10-12

DAVIS, ROBERT. *Padre Porko*, ill. by Fritz Eichenberg. Holiday, 1958. Padre Porko, the gentlemanly pig, has all the benignance of the Buddha animals, and a certain mannerly elegance besides. Amusing tales, enhanced by good pen-and-ink sketches. 8-12

EELLS, ELSIE SPICER. *Tales of Enchantment from Spain*, ill. by Maud and Miska Petersham. Dodd, 1956. These are romantic tales, rich in magic. 10-14

HAVILAND, VIRGINIA, ad. *Favorite Fairy Tales Told in Spain*, ill. by Barbara Cooney. Little, 1963. Six delightful Spanish tales retold. 8-10

MEHDEVI, ALEXANDER, ad. *Bungling Pedro; And Other Majorcan Tales*, ill. by Isabel Bodor. Knopf, 1970. A collection with many familiar patterns and an occasional contrived moment, but on the whole, fresh and amusing. A good source for storytelling as well as for reading. 9-11

## Swiss

DUVOISIN, ROGER. *The Three Sneezes and Other Swiss Tales*, ill. by author. Knopf, 1941. Humorous tales, many of which are based on the theme of the stupid fellow who succeeds. 9-12

MÜLLER-GUGGENBÜHL, FRITZ. *Swiss-Alpine Folk-Tales*, tr. by Katharine Potts, ill. by Joan Kiddell-Monroe. Walck, 1958. These tales are a distinguished collection of national folklore in the Oxford series of Myths and Legends. 10-14

## United States and Canada: Indian and Eskimo tales

BELTING, NATALIA M. *The Long Tailed Bear and Other Indian Legends*, ill. by Louis F. Cary. Bobbs, 1961. Animal legends of twenty-two tribes make this a valuable source. The large-print format will appeal to children, and storytellers will welcome the tribal identification preceding each story. 8-10

FISHER, ANNE B. *Stories California Indians Told*, ill. by Ruth Robbins. Parnassus, 1957. A dozen Indian myths told with zest and ranging from creation myths to such humorous tales as "Why Women Talk More Than Men." 9-12

GILLHAM, CHARLES EDWARD. *Beyond the Clapping Mountains: Eskimo Stories from Alaska*, ill. by Chanimum. Macmillan, 1943. Illustrated by an Eskimo girl, these are unusual and highly imaginative tales. 10-12

HARRIS, CHRISTIE. *Once Upon a Totem*, ill. by John Frazer Mills. Atheneum, 1963. Five superb tales of the Indians of the North Pacific. 9-12

HILL, KAY. *Glooscap and His Magic: Legends of the Wabanaki Indians*, ill. by Robert Frankenberg. Dodd, 1963.

———. *More Glooscap Stories*, ill. by John Hamburger. Dodd, 1970.

Entertaining tales of the Indian hero. 8-11

MACMILLAN, CRYUS. *Glooskap's Country, and Other Indian Tales*, ill. by John A. Hall. Walck, 1956. First published in 1918 as *Canadian Wonder Tales*, this is one of the finest collections of Indian stories available. They range from simple "how" stories to complex and mystical tales of magic, superbly told and illustrated. 8-12

MARTIN, FRAN. *Nine Tales of Coyote*, ill. by Dorothy McEntee. Harper, 1950. Authentic tales of Coyote, the Indian animal god. The stories are lively and have a quality of suspense. Illustrations are in color.

———. *Nine Tales of Raven*, ill. by Dorothy McEntee. Harper, 1951. These tales of the Northwest Coast Indians appear in attractive format. 8-11

MELZACK, RONALD, ad. *Raven; Creator of the World*, ill. by Laszlo Gal. Little, 1970. Ten stories retold from the Eskimo legends about Raven, the creator of the world. The style seldom has the cadence of an oral tradition, but the book should be useful for storytelling. 9-11

REID, DOROTHY N. *Tales of Nanabozho*, ill. by Donald Grant. Walck, 1963. Stories of the mythical Ojibwa hero to whom Longfellow gave the Iroquois name of Hiawatha. 9-12

SLEATOR, WILLIAM, ad. *The Angry Moon*, ill. by Blair Lent. Little, 1970. An adaptation of a legend of the

Tlingit Indians of Alaska, the writing simple and staccato. An interesting legend useful for storytelling, with attractive illustrations. 5-7

### United States: Afro-American tales

BROWN, MARGARET WISE. *Brer Rabbit; Stories from Uncle Remus*, ill. by A. B. Frost. Harper, 1941. 8-10

COURLANDER, HAROLD. *Terrapin's Pot of Sense*, ill. by Elton Fax. Holt, 1957. Americana collected in rural regions from black storytellers. 8-11

FELTON, HAROLD. *John Henry and His Hammer*, ill. by Aldren Watson. Knopf, 1950. 10-12

HARRIS, JOEL CHANDLER. *Brer Rabbit*, ill. by A. B. Frost. Harper, 1941.

______. *Complete Tales of Uncle Remus*, ed. by Richard Chase. Houghton, 1955.

______. *The Favorite Uncle Remus*, ill. by A. B. Frost; ed. by George Van Santvoord and Archibald C. Coolidge. Houghton, 1948. 10 up

KEATS, EZRA JACK. *John Henry: An American Legend*, ill. by author. Pantheon. 1965. 5-8

REES, ENNIS. *Brer Rabbit and His Tricks*, ill. by Edward Gorey. W. R. Scott, 1967. 5-8

______. *More of Brer Rabbit's Tricks*, ill. by Edward Gorey. W. R. Scott, 1968. 5-8

WHITING, HELEN A. *Negro Folk Tales for Pupils in the Primary Grades*, ill. by Lois Mailou Jones. Associated Pub., 1939.

### United States: variants of European tales

CHASE, RICHARD, ed. *Grandfather Tales*, ill. by Berkeley Williams, Jr. Houghton, 1948. 9-12

______. *Jack and the Three Sillies*, ill. by Joshua Tolford. Houghton, 1950. 8-10

______. *The Jack Tales*, ill. by Berkeley Williams, Jr. Houghton, 1943. 9-12
The American versions of the old-world tales are as vigorous as the mountain folk of the Cumberlands and the Smokies from whom they came.

COTHRAN, JEAN, ed. *With a Wig, With a Wag, and Other American Folk Tales*, ill. by Clifford N. Geary. McKay, 1954. Many of these tales suggest variants in European and other folklores. A final chapter describes their parallels. 9-12

JAGENDORF, MORITZ. *New England Bean Pot; American Folk Stories to Read and Tell*, ill. by Donald McKay. Vanguard, 1948. Folk tales of six New England states told with zest and humor. Two other titles in this regional series are: *Sand in the Bag and Other Folk Stories of Ohio, Indiana and Illinois*, ill. by John Moment. Vanguard, 1952; and *Upstate, Downstate; Folk Stories of the Middle Atlantic States*, ill. by Howard Simon. Vanguard, 1949. 10-14

SAWYER, RUTH. *Journey Cake, Ho!* ill. by Robert McCloskey. Viking, 1953. Mountain folk-tale version of *The Pancake*. Lively illustrations make this an attractive picture book. 6-10

### United States: tales in picture-book form and general collections

EMBERLEY, BARBARA, ad. *Drummer Hoff*, ill. by Ed Emberley. Prentice, 1967. An adaptation of a folk verse, with bouncy rhythm and the twin appeals of rhyme and repetition for the very young. Delightful illustrations. Caldecott Medal. 5-7

FIELD, RACHEL, ed. *American Folk and Fairy Tales*, ill. by Margaret Freeman. Scribner's, 1929. An early collection of such diverse items as Indian legends, black folklore, and Southern mountain stories. 10-14

JAGENDORF, MORITZ, ed. *The Ghost of Peg-leg Peter and Other Stories of Old New York*, ill. by Lino S. Lipinsky, songs of old New York selected by June Lazare. Vanguard, 1966. 10-13

______, ed. *The Marvelous Adventures of Johnny Caesar Cicero Darling*, ill. by Howard Simon. Vanguard, 1949. Humorous tales of the American frontier. 10 up

SPIER, PETER. *The Erie Canal*, ill. by author. Doubleday, 1970. The words of the rollicking song are the text. The illustrations have fascinating details and are faithful to the time and locale. 9-11

### Other countries

AMBRUS, VICTOR G. *The Three Poor Tailors*, ill. by author. Harcourt, 1966. A picture-book version of a Hungarian folk tale, retold in simple, flat style with delightful illustrations. 5-8

BELPRÉ, PURA. *The Tiger and the Rabbit and Other Tales*, ill. by Tomie de Paola. Lippincott, 1965.

______. *Perez and Martina*, ill. by Carlos Sanchez. Warne, 1961.
Tales of Puerto Rico. 9-11

BROWN, MARCIA. *Backbone of the King; The Story of Paka'a and His Son Ku*, ill. by author. Scribner's, 1966. A stately retelling of a Hawaiian hero tale. Handsome illustrations. 10-12

CARPENTER, FRANCES. *The Elephant's Bathtub; Wonder Tales from the Far East*, ill. by Hans Guggenheim. Doubleday, 1962. Burma, Cambodia, Malaya, Vietnam, and other lands of the Far East are represented in the twenty-four tales of humor and enchantment. 11-14

COURLANDER, HAROLD. *The Tiger's Whisker and Other Tales and Legends from Asia and the Pacific*, ill. by Enrico Arno. Harcourt, 1959. More humorous and philosophic tales gathered by a folklorist who has made a significant contribution to the lore of faraway lands. 9-13

CURCIJA-PRODANOVIC, NADA. *Yugoslav Folk-Tales*, ill. by Joan Kiddell-Monroe. Walck, 1957. 10-14

DEUTSCH, BABETTE, and AVRAHM YARMOLINSKY. *Tales of Faraway Folk*, ill. by Irena Lorentowicz. Harper, 1952. A unique collection of tales from Baltic, Russian, and Asiatic lands. 9-12

______. *More Tales of Faraway Folk*, ill. by Janina Domanska. Harper, 1963. Fifteen more tales, many from the U.S.S.R. 7-11

GRAHAM, GAIL B., ad. *The Beggar in the Blanket; And Other Vietnamese Tales*, ill. by Brigitte Bryan. Dial, 1970. Eight folk tales translated from French language sources in Vietnam. There is less drama here than in most folk literature and more projection of cultural patterns. 9-11

HAVILAND, VIRGINIA, ad. *Favorite Fairy Tales Told in Greece*, ill. by Nonny Hogrogian. Little, 1970. 8-10

———, ad. *Favorite Fairy Tales Told in Sweden*, ill. by Ronni Solbert. Little, 1966. 8-10

JEWETT, ELEANORE MYERS. *Which Was Witch? Tales of Ghosts and Magic from Korea*, ill. by Taro Yashima (pseud. for Jun Iwamatsu). Viking, 1953. Fourteen stories with sparkle and suspense, excellent for storytelling. 9-13

KELSEY, ALICE GEER. *Once the Hodja*, ill. by Frank Dobias. McKay, 1943. Twenty-four tales from Turkey filled with humor and simple wisdom.

———. *Once the Mullah*, ill. by Kurt Werth. McKay, 1954. Stories told by Mullah give insight into Persian life and folklore. 9-12

PARKER, K. LANGLOH. *Australian Legendary Tales*, selected and ed. by H. Drake-Brockman, ill. by Elizabeth Durack. Viking, 1966. A selection of Australian aboriginal tales first published at the turn of the century. Much violence and fascinating cultural detail. 11-14

SHERLOCK, PHILIP M. *Anansi, the Spider Man; Jamaican Folk Tales*, ill. by Marcia Brown. T. Crowell, 1954. These stories are told by Jamaicans with simplicity and charm. 9-12

TASHJIAN, VIRGINIA A., ed. *Once There Was and Was Not*, based on stories by H. Toumanian, ill. by Nonny Hogrogian. Little, 1966. Seven Armenian folk tales, many with familiar elements, beautifully illustrated. A pleasure to read aloud and a good source for storytelling. 9-11

———, ed. *Three Apples Fell from Heaven; Armenian Tales Retold*, ill. by Nonny Hogrogian. Little, 1971. 9-11

# Chapter 7
# Fables, Myths, and Epics

Fables, myths, and epics, like the ballads and folk tales, are a part of the great stream of folklore. While they are not generally so popular with children as the folk tales, they have made an equally important contribution to our literary heritage. The fables have colored our attitudes toward moral and ethical problems. The myths and the epics have become a part of our everyday symbols in both writing and speech. All these three types of literature, while fundamentally different from each other, have one characteristic in common: they have a strong moral flavor.

## FABLES, PARABLES, PROVERBS

Fables are brief narratives which take abstract ideas of good or bad, wise or foolish behavior and attempt to make them concrete and striking enough to be understood and remembered. Whether the characters are men or beasts, they remain coldly impersonal and engage in a single significant act which teaches a moral lesson. These are the essential elements of the true fable. Here is an example of the simplest type:

*The Crow and the Pitcher*[1]

*A thirsty Crow found a Pitcher with some water in it, but so little was there that, try as she might, she could not reach it with her beak, and it seemed as though she would die of thirst within sight of the remedy. At last she hit upon a clever plan. She began dropping pebbles into the Pitcher, and with each pebble the water rose a little higher until at last it reached the brim, and the knowing bird was enabled to quench her thirst.*

*"Necessity is the mother of invention."*

The chief actor in most fables is an animal or inanimate object which behaves like a human being and has one dominant trait. G. K. Chesterton insists that there can be no good fables with human beings in them, and it is

1. From *Aesop's Fables*, translated by V. S. Vernon Jones, p. 17. Copyright 1912 by Doubleday & Company, Inc.

true that most fables are not concerned with people. Yet there are a substantial number of fables which tell about human beings and still retain their fable quality. Remember "The Boy Who Cried Wolf," and

*The Milkmaid and Her Pail*[2]

*A farmer's daughter had been out to milk the cows, and was returning to the dairy carrying her pail of milk upon her head. As she walked along, she fell a-musing after this fashion: "The milk in this pail will provide me with cream, which I will make into butter and take to market to sell. With the money I will buy a number of eggs, and these, when hatched, will produce chickens, and by and by I shall have quite a large poultry-yard. Then I shall sell some of my fowls, and with the money which they will bring in I will buy myself a new gown, which I shall wear when I go to the fair; and all the young fellows will admire it, and come and make love to me, but I shall toss my head and have nothing to say to them." Forgetting all about the pail, and suiting the action to the word, she tossed her head. Down went the pail, all the milk was spilled and all her fine castles in the air vanished in a moment!*

*"Do not count your chickens before they are hatched."*

Here again is a single episode pointing to a moral, as briefly and impersonally related as "The Crow and the Pitcher." It is a true fable.

Fables have a teasing likeness to proverbs and parables. All three embody universal truths in brief, striking form; and all three are highly intellectual exercises, as exact as an equation. Of the three, the *proverb* is the most highly condensed commentary on human folly or wisdom. It tells no story but presents a bit of wisdom succinctly:

*A soft answer turneth away wrath: but grievous words stir up anger.* (Proverbs 15:1)

*The wicked flee when no man pursueth: but the righteous are bold as a lion.* (Proverbs 28:1)

*He that diggeth a pit shall fall into it.* (Ecclesiastes 10:8)

*He that is slow to anger is better than the mighty; and he that ruleth his spirit than he that taketh a city.* (Proverbs 16:32)

*Boast not thyself of tomorrow; for thou knowest not what a day may bring forth.* (Proverbs 27:1)

*Better is a dry morsel and quietness therewith, than a house full of feasting with strife.* (Proverbs 17:1)

*He that diligently seeketh good procureth favour: but he that seeketh mischief, it shall come unto him.* (Proverbs 11:27)

Certainly the sixth proverb is a perfect moral for "The Town Mouse and the Country Mouse," and either the third or seventh would fit Marcia Brown's *Once a Mouse*.

It is interesting to find many examples in *Japanese Proverbs* by Rokuo Okada that are amazingly like our proverbs in their implications:

*He who wants to shoot the general must first shoot his horse.*

*A sparrow (suzume) will never forget to dance till it is a hundred years old.*

*A cornered mouse bites the cat.*[3]

Perhaps the fable grew out of the proverb, to dramatize its pithy wisdom in story form.

The *parable* is like the fable in that it tells a brief story from which a moral or spiritual truth may be inferred. But its characters, unlike the personified animals or objects of most fables, are generally human beings, like the Wise and Foolish Virgins, or the Prodigal Son, or the Good Samaritan. If the story is told in terms of animals or objects, they are never personified but remain strictly themselves. That is, the seed that falls upon rocky

2. Ibid., p. 25.

3. From *Japanese Proverbs* by Rokuo Okada. Copyright by the Japan Travel Bureau. In *Japan Times Weekly*, December 1, 1962.

ground has nothing to say for itself, and the house that was built upon sand goes down in the flood strictly a house. The parables use people or things as object lessons, and the matchless parables of Jesus point out and amplify the moral.

There are obvious differences among the stories discussed in the following pages under *Fable Collections*. Some are typical fables, some are parables, others resemble folk tales, and many contain maxims or proverbs. All of them, however, embody moral or spiritual wisdom.

## FABLE COLLECTIONS

If you say "fables" to an English-speaking child, he thinks at once of *Aesop's Fables*, the source of the two stories quoted on pages 184–185. To a French child, La Fontaine and "fables" are inseparably associated, and so in the Orient it is *The Panchatantra, The Fables of Bidpai*, or the *Jatakas*. These major collections of fables, while resembling each other, show also striking differences.

### Aesop's Fables

Planudes, a fourteenth-century monk, prefixed a story of Aesop's life to a book of fables, supposedly those of Aesop. Some modern scholars not only doubt the authenticity of this account, but doubt whether Aesop really existed. G. K. Chesterton suggests that he may be as completely a fictitious character as that other slave, Uncle Remus, who also told beast tales. But his name and fame persist through one edition of the fables after another. Aesop is said to have lived in Greece between 620 and 560 B.C. and is thought to have been a Samian slave. Because free speech under the Tyrants was risky business, Aesop is supposed to have used the fables for political purposes, protecting himself and veiling his opinions behind the innuendoes of these little stories. Legend has it that

*From Aesop's Fables by Boris Artzybasheff. Copyright 1933 by Boris Artzybasheff. All rights reserved. Reprinted by permission of The Viking Press, Inc.*

he was deformed and that he was hurled off a cliff, whether for his deformity or for his politics is not known. All we know is that the picturesque legends about Aesop have survived with his name.

Translated into Latin in the first and third centuries, the Aesop fables became the textbooks of the medieval schools. In Latin they found their way into England, France, and Germany, were translated into several languages, and were among the first books to be printed by Caxton when he started his famous press in England. Evidently there was infiltration from other sources. Joseph Jacobs said he could mention at least seven hundred fables ascribed to Aesop, although the first known collection of them, made by Demetrius of Phalerum about 320 B.C., contained only about two hundred. Since India, like Greece, had long used the beast tale for teaching purposes, undoubtedly some of the Indian fables gravitated, in the course of time, to the Aesop collection. From whatever source they came, once included in Aesop they assumed the Aesop form, which is now regarded as the pure fable type. It is a brief story with inanimate objects or animals most

## VIEWPOINTS

In every age [*Aesop's Fables*] has had the distinction of being approved of and adapted for the young reader. In style the Aesopian fable is akin to the folk-tale, but, unlike most other traditional lore, it had the good fortune in the ancient world to be moulded into an acceptable form. Often made into a schoolbook and burdened with added moralities, it never lost those pristine characteristics which endeared it to young or unsophisticated minds. Brevity in telling, clarity of style, animal characters with human attributes, pithy lessons about human conduct; these were all features to give life to the fables in every generation. There is little of high ethical purpose in the episodes: they are more like a fascinating looking-glass reflecting the follies of mankind.—M. F. Thwaite, *Primer to Pleasure*, The Library Association, London, 1963, p. 7.

frequently serving as the leading characters, and with the single action of the narrative pointing to an obvious moral lesson. James Reeves in his *Fables from Aesop* points out that the virtues which Aesop praises are not the heroic ones but rather "the peasant virtues of discretion, prudence, moderation and forethought. . . . That is why Aesop . . . has always had the affection and regard of ordinary people."

### The Panchatantra

*The Panchatantra*, meaning "five books," was composed in Kashmir about 200 B.C.,[4] and is the oldest known collection of Indian fables. *The Hitopadesa*, or Book of Good Counsel, is considered only another version of *The Panchatantra*,[5] and still another is called *The Fables of Bidpai*. These collections were translated into Persian, Arabic, Latin, and many other languages. In the Latin version the tales became popular throughout medieval Europe.

After the extreme condensation of Aesop, the stories of *The Panchatantra* seem long and involved. They are a textbook on "the wise conduct of life" and are intricate stories-within-stories, interrupted with philosophical verses so numerous that the thread of the story is almost forgotten. Some of these poems are sixteen or twenty verses long, but the quatrain is the more usual type.

*A friend in need is a friend indeed,*
*Although of different caste;*
*The whole world is your eager friend*
*So long as riches last.*

*When arrows pierce or axes wound*
*A tree, it grows together sound;*
*From cruel, ugly speech you feel*
*A wound that time will never heal.*

*Make friends, make friends, however strong*
*Or weak they be;*
*Recall the captive elephants*
*That mice set free.*[6]

These verses are summaries of the stories which seem more like folk tales than fables. On the whole, *The Panchatantra* is for adults rather than children, but some thirty-four of the best of these stories are well illustrated by E. Boyd Smith in *The Tortoise and the Geese and Other Fables of Bidpai*. This is a book children enjoy.

### The Jatakas

Another ancient collection of Indian fables is the group called the *Jatakas*. The time of their origin is not definitely known. They were in existence in the fifth century A.D., but carvings illustrating Jataka stories have

4. *The Panchatantra*, translated by Arthur W. Ryder (University of Chicago Press, 1925), p. 3.
5. Joseph Gaer, *The Fables of India* (Little, Brown, 1955) p. 53.
6. *The Panchatantra*, op. cit., pp. 5, 322, 273.

been found which were made as early as the second or third centuries B.C.

*Jatakas* is a Buddhist name for stories concerning the rebirths of Gautama Buddha, who according to tradition was reincarnated many times in the forms of different animals until he became at last Buddha, the Enlightened One. These beast tales, then, are really about a man living briefly as an animal, consorting with other animals, and deriving from these experiences certain ethical lessons.

Joseph Gaer tells us that there are two or three thousand of these stories. Generally, the introduction and body of the tale are in prose, but the conclusions are often verses. Comparatively few of them are suitable for children and then only with considerable adaptation. Ellen C. Babbitt's two books of the Jatakas were made with children in mind and so omit all reference to the Buddha.[7] Joseph Gaer's versions, in *The Fables of India*, keep closer to the original form of the Jatakas. Some Jatakas resemble parables from the Bible. Still others are like short folk tales with self-evident morals. Because the tales in Joseph Gaer's *The Fables of India* keep closer to the original form of the Jatakas, they are more suitable for children of ten or older, while Ellen C. Babbitt's *Jatakas* appeal to the younger children. All three books are delightfully illustrated in the spirit of the text.

*Illustration by Randy Monk. From* The Fables of India *by Joseph Gaer.* Copyright 1955, *by Joseph Gaer. Reproduced with the permission of Little, Brown and Company.*

### The Fables of La Fontaine

In the twelfth century, Marie de France introduced and popularized the fable in France. Others followed her lead, but Jean de La Fontaine (1621–1695), a contemporary of Charles Perrault, made the fable so completely and gracefully his own that the French coined a word for him, *le fablier*, "the fable-teller."

La Fontaine was a skilled poet and wrote his fables in graceful verses which are delightful to read and easy to memorize. Unfortunately, they lose some of their appeal when translated into English. It is a lucky child who can have them in French with the illustrations of Boutet de Monvel. There are charming bits of description in these fables which reveal the birds and little beasts and the forests and meadows of the beautiful Champagne countryside where La Fontaine grew up. The courtier and the man of the world show themselves in the shrewd appraisals of character and the worldly philosophy that permeate the *Fables*:

> *Now, as everyone knows, white paws do not grow on wolves.*

> *My dear Mr. Crow, learn from this how every flatterer lives at the expense of anybody who will listen to him. This lesson is well worth the loss of a cheese to you.*

7. Ellen C. Babbitt, *Jataka Tales* and *More Jataka Tales* (Appleton, 1912).

*But among all the fools the human kind excels. We have the eyes of a lynx for the faults of others and the eyes of moles for our own. We forgive ourselves much more easily than we do our neighbor.*[8]

Doesn't this remind you of the New Testament admonition, "And why beholdest thou the mote that is in thy brother's eye, but considerest not the beam that is in thine own eye"? (Matthew 7:3)

La Fontaine used for his sources the Latin versions of Aesop and *The Fables of Bidpai*, and the versions of his predecessor, Marie de France. In spite of the verse form and the characteristic bits of philosophy, these *Fables* of La Fontaine's are closer to the Aesop pattern than to the tales from India. They maintain the brevity, the predominant use of animal characters, and, above all, the single striking episode which points the moral.

*Used by permission. Illustration by Alice & Martin Provensen from* Aesop's Fables *selected and adapted by Louis Untermeyer. Copyright 1965 by Western Publishing Company, Inc. (Original in color)*

## FABLE EDITIONS

The fables are both didactic and universal, with their universality making their didacticism bearable if not enjoyable. A child is made uncomfortable by a story that preaches directly, but if he sees that the lessons of the fables apply to everyone, he can better appreciate their wisdom and humor.

These pithy tales have been part of the heritage of children as well as of adults from the time of the first edition of *Aesop's Fables* printed by William Caxton in the fifteenth century to the present. Two excellent collections available today are *Aesop's Fables*, edited and illustrated by Boris Artzybasheff, and a newly illustrated edition of *The Fables of Aesop*, edited by Joseph Jacobs. For children eight to ten years old, James Reeves' *Fables from Aesop* and Anne Terry White's *Aesop's Fables* are particularly good. Reeves has varied the concise narrative form by introducing conversation among the animals, and Anne Terry White has retold the stories in an easy, simple style appropriate for younger children. Louis Untermeyer, in his *Aesop's Fables*, gaily illustrated by Alice and Martin Provensen, has provided an edition of stories humorous and colorful enough to read aloud to children as young as six or seven.

The trend to present the fables in a form appropriate for younger children is most obvious in the publication of single-fable editions, such as *The Miller, His Son, and Their Donkey*, illustrated by Roger Duvoisin; Jean Showalter's *The Donkey Ride;* and Brian Wildsmith's *The Miller, the Boy, and the Donkey*. Wildsmith has retold and illustrated several other La Fontaine fables in addition to this favorite. In *John J. Plenty and Fiddler Dan*, John Ciardi has told the story of the improvident grasshopper and the industrious

8. From *The Fables of La Fontaine*, translated by Margaret W. Brown (Harper, 1940), pp. 6, 8, and 19.

ant in an amusing verse version. There are also some attractive adaptations of fables from India for young children. Notable among them are Marcia Brown's Caldecott Medal book, *Once a Mouse*, an animal fable illustrated by color woodcuts; and Paul Galdone's *The Monkey and the Crocodile*, an adaptation of a Jataka tale.

Another collection that has both fables and folk tales is Mirra Ginsburg's *Three Rolls and One Doughnut: Fables from Russia*, which has a vivacious style and is appropriate for seven- to nine-year-olds. A source of Russian fables is Ivan Krylov's *Fifteen Fables of Krylov*, in a colloquial translation by Guy Daniels. A delightful single-fable edition is Barbara Cooney's Caldecott Medal book *Chanticleer and the Fox*, which is based on Geoffrey Chaucer's "The Nun's Priest's Tale" from *The Canterbury Tales*. There are a number of fables in modern dress—a particularly good one is Jean Merrill's *The Black Sheep*, which is far longer than the usual compressed fable form but, in the true spirit of the fable, teaches a lesson about blind conformity.

*Illustration by Barbara Cooney in* Chanticleer and the Fox, *adapted by Barbara Cooney from Chaucer's* Canterbury Tales. *Copyright © 1958 by Thomas Y. Crowell Company, New York, Publishers. (Original in color)*

## MYTHS

The fables are simple, highly condensed lessons in morality. The myth is far more complicated. It attempts to explain—in complex symbolism—the vital outlines of existence:

> *(1) cosmic phenomena (e.g., how the earth and sky came to be separated); (2) peculiarities of natural history (e.g., why rain follows the cries or activities of certain birds); (3) the origins of human civilization (e.g., through the beneficent action of a culture-hero like Prometheus); or (4) the origin of social or religious custom or the nature and history of objects of worship.*[9]

It also attempts to make more acceptable the painful realities of existence—danger, disease, misfortune, and death—by explaining them as part of a sacred order in the universe.

The "explanations" may seem irrational and inconsistent to the science-minded modern. This is because they are not scientific hypotheses but were created by and appeal to the imagination. The truth of the myth was unquestioned by primitive peoples because it was so closely associated with their sacred beliefs. For them, both nature and society were areas of reverent acceptance[10]—not of objective study, as they are in this age of scientific inquiry.

9. William Reginald Halliday, "Folklore," in an earlier edition of the *Encyclopaedia Britannica*.

10. At the adult level, an excellent example of this would be the religious beliefs and practices found in Mary Renault's *The Bull from the Sea*.

## Evolution of Myths

A number of writers have called attention to the various levels of myth development, their evolution from primitive to highly complex symbolic stories. These developmental stages are important to us because they throw light upon the various types of stories (for example, the *pourquoi* tales) included in myths and help to explain their suitability, or lack of it, as story material for children.

The early part of this evolution is, of course, shrouded in the darkness of prehistoric times. Much research has been devoted to it, but the outlines are still only dimly understood. For one thing, the evolution of myth and religion differs from people to people. Suffice it to say that the Greeks, like many other peoples, passed through a primary stage in which they worshiped an impersonal force believed to pervade all aspects of the universe: sun, moon, crops, rivers. The early Greeks performed rites to propitiate these bodiless forces so that they would grant to the world fertility and life. Later these nature forces were personified in the myths.

Myths, then, did give body—both animal and human—to the mystic forces that early people felt in the universe. As these ideas developed, the tendency was to give complex human form to these impersonal forces. These bright sky-dwellers were created in man's own image but surpassed him in beauty, wisdom, and power. All the warmth and glory of the sun were embodied in the Greek ideas of Apollo, all the terror of storms in their ideas of Zeus and his fearful thunderbolts.

Imagining these supernatural beings in their own likeness, the people interpreted a flood to mean that the river god was angry with man and intended to punish him. Droughts, earthquakes, good crops, and bad crops were all dependent on how man stood in the graces of these nature gods. These primitive beginnings of myth were polytheistic; that is, they developed many gods. G. K. Chesterton, speaking of the Greek deities, commented that "the Greeks could not see trees for dryads."

Presently these beings developed relationships among each other, assumed certain powers, and suffered limitations of power. Thus in the Greek mythology the first gods were all brothers and sisters—Hestia, Demeter, Hera, Poseidon, Hades, and Zeus. Because Zeus saved them from destruction, he was chosen the supreme ruler, the sky god, while Poseidon ruled the waters and Hades, who dwelt below the earth, ruled the dominion of the dead. From their matings, their children, and the powers and limitations of each of these three powerful brothers arose endless squabbles that bear a melancholy resemblance to the earthly rows of man himself.

### VIEWPOINTS

. . . Myths are original revelations of the preconscious psyche, involuntary statements about unconscious psychic happenings, and anything but allegories of physical processes. Such allegories would be an idle amusement for an unscientific intellect. Myths, on the contrary, have a vital meaning.

. . . there is no longer any question whether a myth refers to the sun or the moon, the father or the mother, sexuality or fire or water; all it does is to circumscribe and give an approximate description of an *unconscious core of meaning*. The ultimate meaning of this nucleus was never conscious and never will be. It was, and still is, only interpreted, and every interpretation that comes anywhere near the hidden sense (or, from the point of view of scientific intellect, nonsense, which comes to the same thing) has always, right from the beginning, laid claim not only to absolute truth and validity but to instant reverence and religious devotion. Archetypes were, and still are, living psychic forces that demand to be taken seriously.—C. G. Jung, "The Psychology of the Child Archetype," *Essays on a Science of Mythology* by C. G. Jung and C. Kerényi, translated by R. F. C. Hull, Bollingen Series XXII, Princeton University Press, Second Edition, 1969, pp. 73, 75.

Each god or goddess came to assume certain powers. For instance, Hera, the wife of Zeus, was the jealous guardian of the marriage state. She kept an eagle eye on her faithless spouse, wrought bitter vengeance on his unfortunate loves, and generally waged a strenuous, if unavailing, war on anything that threatened the dignity of the lawful wife.

But every god, except Zeus, knew distinct limitations to his powers and was vulnerable to misfortunes in certain respects, even as man. Balder, the Norse sun god, whose mother, Frigga, made everything except the mistletoe promise not to harm him, was slain by the insignificant shrub which Frigga had thought too harmless to bother about. Balder the Beautiful died; he went out to sea in his fiery ship, burning like the autumn foliage; the earth wept for him, and cold and darkness followed—a picture of the coming of autumn and winter in the north country. So these man-made deities developed relationships and powers but were subject to certain limitations from other powers.

The extension of a god's powers soon turned him into a symbolic figure, standing for certain abstract virtues. So Zeus, from being at first merely a sky god, became the symbol of power and law. Apollo began as the sun god, a beautiful young man with a fiery chariot to drive across the sky daily. Then he became also the god of health and healing, the patron god of physicians. Finally this idea of healing was expanded to include the related but less physical concept of purification, and Apollo then stood for the abstract idea of purity. In some such way as this, many of the gods evolved from mere nature personifications to become symbols of abstract moral attributes.

Of course, this evolution into symbolism was not true of all gods. Pan remained ever

> *. . . the dear son of Hermes, with his goat's feet and two horns—a lover of merry noise. Through wooded glades he wanders with dancing nymphs who foot it on some sheer cliff's edge, calling upon Pan, the shepherd-god . . .*[11]

Pan never became an abstraction but remained always the joyous earthy denizen of woods and meadows, the lover of high song.

In some mythologies less sophisticated than the Greeks' the deities have never signified anything more than spirits of earth, sky, sun, moon, or even animals. The Indian "Old Man Coyote" is such a deity. On the other hand, the Navaho "Turquoise Woman" is not merely a sky goddess but seems to be also a symbol of beauty in the highest sense, meaning harmony and goodness.

Finally, when the gods had come to stand for moral attributes and powers, the next and last stage of myth-making was the development of a priesthood, temples, and a ritual of worship. Then the myth was an organized religion. Apollo had a great temple at Delphi with priests, an oracle, vestal virgins, and elaborate ceremonies and rituals. There were temples to Zeus, to Demeter, and to the splendid Pallas Athena, until by the time the Apostle Paul arrived in Athens, temples had been built to so many gods that there was even an altar to "The Unknown God" lest one be overlooked. Few gods had as elaborate ramifications to their worship as Apollo. The Apollo cult represents the last and most complex stage of myth-making, to which only the mythologies of highly civilized people attain.

## Types of Myth Stories

Among the simplest of myth stories are the little *why* stories, or *pourquoi* tales. Why the woodpecker has a red head and how the arbutus came to be are from the North American Indians. Why the sunflower turns to the sun (the story of Clytie) and how a flower was born of the blood of Apollo's accidental victim (the story of Hyacinthus) are from the Greek. Children enjoy a few such stories in connection with the study of a people and

11. Hesiod, *The Homeric Hymns and Homerica*, translated by Hugh C. Evelyn-White (Putnam, 1914), p. 443.

accept them with a comfortable sense of superiority—they know better!

In both Greek and Norse myths these *why* stories become more complex than in the American Indian woodpecker and arbutus examples. Take, for instance, the Greek explanation of summer and winter; the story goes that Demeter (the earth mother) has been deprived of her beautiful child Persephone (the grain), who has been carried off by Hades to his realm below the ground. Demeter seeks her child, weeping, but Persephone must remain in Hades' dark world for six months of each year, leaving earth to darkness and cold. Such a story is neither simple nor fully explanatory for a child. For him, it is a good fairy tale, but if he is to catch any glimpse of its seasonal significance, it has to be explained in careful detail. Similar to this tale is the story told of Balder the Beautiful, the Norse sun god, at whose death the whole earth weeps and falls into darkness. So our North American Indians of the Southwest have their desert seasonal story of little Burnt-Face, the scorched earth, who sees the invisible chief, the spring rains, and is made beautiful by him and becomes his bride. To children, these three are just good fairy tales, as interesting and objective as "Cinderella." However, if in the study of Greeks, or Romans, or Norsemen, or Desert Indians, you explain to the children the possible meaning of these stories for the people who created them, they are surprised and charmed with the secondary meaning.

Some of the myths warn against such sins as pride. Niobe, for example, boasts of her divine descent, is insolently proud of her powers and, above all, of her seven sons and seven daughters. She sets herself up as the equal of the goddess Leto, and, for this impious pride, Apollo and Artemis, Leto's twins, avenge their mother by striking down all fourteen of Niobe's children. Her pride brought low, frozen with grief, Niobe turns into a stone fountain, weeping forever for her children.

Human pride seems to be particularly offensive to the gods. Arachne was turned into a spider because she boasted of her weaving. Bellerophon, after he captured the winged horse, Pegasus, became so sure of himself that he attempted to ride into Zeus' dwelling and was promptly struck blind for his presumption. Some of these myths are almost like fables, and, like the fables, they could be summarized with a maxim or proverb. Others, like "Arachne," are little *why* stories with a moral. Still others are involved adult stories. "Cupid and Psyche," standing for Love and the Soul, is such a tale. Fortunately, we have it in folk-tale form as our favorite "East o' the Sun and West o' the Moon." Pandora is another adult tale—sin brought into the world by the "beautiful bane," woman.

Many of the myths are, on the whole, too adult in content and significance to be appropriate story material for children. But the simpler tales among them are accepted by the children exactly as they accept any folk tale. One of their favorites is "King Midas," who wished that everything he touched would turn into gold and soon found himself starving in the midst of plenty. And there is the charming tale of "Baucis and Philemon," the old couple who entertained the gods with their humble best and were granted their two wishes—to serve the gods and to be taken out of this world together. At the hour of death they were changed into an oak and a linden tree, growing side by side. Well-told versions of such stories are suitable for children and may be used with or without the background of the people and their mythology.

The *ways of the gods with men* make another group of stories which includes the two just mentioned, "King Midas" and "Baucis and Philemon." One of the most delightful of these is "Bellerophon and Pegasus." Bellerophon, a handsome youth, is sent by his host, Iobates, to kill the chimera, which is devastating Lycia. Although Iobates is sure the mission will mean the boy's death, the gods take pity upon Bellerophon and send him the winged Pegasus. That Pegasus, the winged horse of the gods, means "poetry" does not enter the children's heads, but that Bellerophon could not kill the terrible chimera until he had first captured and tamed Pegasus makes a good adventure story of unusual beauty. Such stories are really hero tales with a background of myth and they comprise a particularly good group of stories for children. Some of them, like those in the *Odyssey*, later developed into national epics.

The gods' amatory adventures among men are legion and are not often adapted for children. Zeus, Apollo, Aphrodite, and, in fact, most of the deities succumbed repeatedly to the charms of mortals. Their godly mates also wreaked ungodly vengeance on the poor humans; so these tales are both scandalous and cruel. Stories about the ways of nymphs and dryads with men are much like fairy lore. Sometimes they deserted their mortal mates; sometimes the men fled from them.

Finally, the *ways of the gods with other gods* furnish us with another body of myth stories, often complex in their significance and adult in content. Here we encounter nature myths which even the folklorists interpret differently and which leave the layman baffled and a bit weary with all the things which aren't what they seem. Frazer's *Golden Bough* is a repository for these tales. In the Greek stories we find involved accounts of creation whose interpretation is decidedly speculative. And back of the accounts of the gods and their escapades are endless double meanings which may start simply with Gaea, a personification of the Earth, who is touched by Eros (Love) and bears Uranus (Heaven). Other stories, like "Cupid and Psyche," take on more abstract significance. Moving and profound is the story of Prometheus, the Titan, who dared the wrath of the gods to bring man fire and suffered endless tortures as a result. Prometheus is so noble a symbol of sacrifice that poets and painters have repeatedly used his story as a subject. But these myths, with their symbolism and inner meanings, are both complex and abstract, and some people feel that they have no place in children's literature.

## SOURCES OF MYTHOLOGIES

### Greek Myths

Most of the Greek myths came to us by way of the poet Hesiod, who is supposed to have lived during the eighth century B.C. He was a farmer and a bachelor with an abiding love of nature and an equally firm dislike of women. While he was guarding his father's flocks, so the story goes, the Muses themselves commissioned him to be their poet. So a poet he became, winning a contest and gratefully dedicating a tripod to the Muses, who had shown him the way.

His first famous poem, *Works and Days*, is largely didactic but is also a kind of farmer's calendar, telling when to sow or plant or harvest and what seasons are most propitious for different kinds of work. There are ethical lessons on industry and honest toil, some biting criticisms of women, and the earliest known fable in Greek, "The Hawk and the Nightingale."

*Theogony*, another poem attributed to Hesiod, contains the Greek myths of the creation and the history of Zeus and Cronus, including Zeus' great battle with the Titans. Hesiod's picture of the defeated Titans, confined and guarded by giants and by Day and Night, is a convincing one.

Hesiod is credited with bringing together in organized form the major portion of Greek mythology. The English translation, although in prose, is good reading.

### Roman Myths

The Roman versions of the Greek myths are available to us in the more familiar *Metamorphoses* of the Latin poet Ovid. Born in 43 B.C., Ovid belonged to a wealthy and privileged family. He was educated under famous Roman teachers, became a poet against his father's wishes, and, in contrast to Hesiod, was married three times. Only his last marriage was happy, but he seems never to have taken love or the ladies seriously. He belonged to the pleasure-bent, dissolute set which the Emperor Augustus was trying to discourage. When the poet's *Ars amatoria* appeared, its scandalous nature, coupled with some offense whose nature is not known, furnished sufficient cause for Ovid's banishment. He was forced to live in a barbarous little town, where his writing must have been his only consolation. Since his sentence was never rescinded despite frequent petitions, Ovid died in exile.

The *Metamorphoses* consists of fifteen books recounting tales of miraculous transformations, hence the title. It begins with the metamorphosis of Chaos to order, follows the Greek development of gods and men, recounts innumerable *why* stories of flowers, rivers, rocks, and the like. It concludes, appropriately enough, with Julius Caesar turned into a star, and Ovid himself on his way to some form of immortality. These stories, even in our English prose translations, are amazingly dramatic. It is interesting to check modern versions with these stirring tales of Ovid, which are the source of most adaptations.

### Norse Myths

Whether the Norse myths began in Norway, Greenland, Ireland, Iceland, or England, it was in Iceland that they were preserved orally and first written down. Iceland, remote from the rest of the world and settled largely by Norwegians, held to the old language, once the speech of all Northern peoples, and so kept the stories alive in their original form. The two collections are the *Elder* or *Poetic Edda*, and the *Younger* or *Prose Edda*.

The *Poetic* and the *Prose Eddas* follow the sing-and-say style, with the difference that the *Poetic Edda* is mostly verse with brief prose passages, and the *Prose Edda* is mostly prose with interspersed poetic passages. Both are difficult books, but there are several adaptations to use with children.

The word *Edda* was originally the name or title for a great-grandmother. In time it came to stand for the Norwegian court-meter or the art of poetry. In both senses it seems to imply something traditional. The *Elder* or *Poetic Edda* (thirty-four poems) contains the Prophecy, which tells how the world was created, how the gods came to be, and how they fell. There is a book of proverbs, and finally there is the story of Sigurd the Volsung, the Norse epic. These heroic lays were supposedly collected from oral tradition by Saemund the Learned and committed to writing about the eleventh or twelfth century. By then they must have been exposed to Christian ideas and to other cultures, but they remain, nevertheless, primitive and vigorous.

The *Younger* or *Prose Edda* was not collected until the thirteenth century. The first book, "The Beguiling of Gylfi," contains the bulk of the Norse myths. It was the work of Snorri Sturluson, an Icelander who combined a greedy and traitorous character with a real reverence for the traditional literature he recorded so faithfully.

## WHY USE THE MYTHS WITH CHILDREN?

It is the rare child who is not enchanted with the stories of mythology. The sky-dwellers of the Greeks and Romans not only left a mark on our language, but they continue to spellbind each succeeding generation of children. Bellerophon taming the winged horse, Icarus plummeting through the sky into the sea, Hermes stepping cloudward on his winged sandals—these somehow catch the imagination with their dramatic beauty. It is not an accident that most of the examples of myth in the preceding pages have been from the Greek. If the children can sample only one

## VIEWPOINTS

There is another door that can be opened by reading legends and fairy tales, and for some children, at the present time, there may be no other key to it. *Religio*, in one Latin sense of the word, implies a sense of the strange, the numinous, the totally Other, of what lies quite beyond human personality and cannot be found in any human relationships. This kind of 'religion' is an indestructible part of the experience of many human minds, even though the temper of a secular society does not encourage it, and the whole movement of modern theology runs counter to it. In Christian 'religious instruction' there is likely to be less and less *religio:* it may very well be in reading about a vision of the flashing-eyed Athene or the rosy-fingered Aphrodite that children first find a satisfying formulation of those queer prickings of delight, excitement and terror that they feel when they first walk by moonlight, or when it snows in May, or when, like the young Wordsworth, they have to touch a wall to make sure that it is really there. Magic is not the same as mysticism, but it may lead towards it; it is mystery 'told to the children'.—Elizabeth Cook, *The Ordinary and the Fabulous*, Cambridge University Press, London, 1969, p. 5.

mythology, it should be the Greek or its Roman adaptation. Our language and our thinking are full of words and ideas derived from these sources.[12] For example, *titanic* comes from the powerful Titans; *erotic* from Eros, the god of love; *panic* from the god Pan; and *cereal* from Ceres, the grain goddess. Men "steer between Scylla and Charybdis." Travelers who cross the equator for the first time must endure a lively hazing at the court of King Neptune, while any delayed wanderer may be dubbed a Ulysses. Minerva with her owl gazes down on us from our libraries. Venus, rising from her sea shell, advertises bath salts or cosmetics. The Muses preside over our concert halls, and young ladies used to study the terpsichorean art. There is a dramatic quality about the myths which has so captured the imaginations of poets that poetry, and English poetry in particular, is filled with classical allusions. Not to know Greek-Roman mythology is to grope more or less blindly through the arts, particularly literature.

But the Norse myths too should be part of the experience of English-speaking children. The people who composed them were a vital source of our customs, laws, and speech. Yet the myths which are their finest expression and the clearest mirror of their life are not nearly so familiar to most of us as the myths of the ancient civilizations of Greece and Rome. The Norse gods do not have the beauty and grace of the classic deities, but they are cast in heroic mold, and there is a grandeur about the tales that is hard to match. Such stories as "How Odin Lost His Eye," "How Thor Found His Hammer," "The Apples of Iduna," "Thor's Visit to the Giants," and "The Death of Balder" are fascinating with or without a study of the people.

Both Greek and Norse mythologies, moreover, furnish the background for the great national epics of those countries. Children must know Greek mythology in order to understand the *Iliad* or the *Odyssey*, and they must know Norse mythology in order to understand the ideals and motives of the heroic characters in the Norse epic *Sigurd the Volsung*, or in Wagner's opera cycle *The Ring of the Nibelungs*, the Teutonic form of the Sigurd epic.

These are a few of the reasons why myths should be used with older children, but the chief reasons are, after all, the beauty and the imaginative quality of the tales themselves.

### WHAT VERSIONS OF THE MYTHS TO USE

The chief difficulty in using mythology with children is to select satisfactory versions of the stories. Nathaniel Hawthorne, artist

12. There is a book devoted to such sources: Isaac Asimov, *Words from the Myths* (Houghton, 1961).

though he was, did not scruple to turn the gods into petulant children. He told an entrancing story, but he lost almost completely the dignity of the gods, and sometimes he even lost the significance of the story. One writer protests:

> *When one reads Hawthorne's version of Pandora and Prometheus and realizes the mere babble, the flippant detail, under which he has covered up the grim Titanic story of the yearnings and strivings of the human soul for salvation here and hereafter, the very deepest problems of temptation and sin, of rebellion and expiation, he must see clearly what is most likely to happen when a complex and mature myth is converted into a child's tale.*[13]

Persephone (or Proserpina), in Hawthorne's version, is turned into a child carried off by Pluto to live underground for six months in the year and be his "little girl." While Hawthorne's versions have delighted generations of children, such writing down to children too young to hear the real stories plays havoc with any literature. The myths suffer especially from such treatment. Even many of the best modern versions are not wholly free from interpretations that are unnecessarily childish.

Good versions of the myths for children have been made and new ones are still appearing. General standards should help us in selecting the best of these.

Although some adaptation may be necessary, myths should not be written down to children. When this is done, the author is usually trying to retell myths to children who are too young for them. Six- and seven-year-old children can take only the bare bones of these stories, but children from nine or ten years old to fourteen can enjoy rich versions of some of the originals. For example, Krystyna Turska's adaptation of *Pegasus* makes the myth of the winged horse and his bold rider vividly real with its beautiful illustrations. In the home, individual children may read myths earlier, but in the mixed groups of the average classroom, the appeal of myths is distinctly to older children.

Finally, adaptations should be simple enough to be thoroughly comprehensible to children without sacrificing either the spirit or the richness of the originals. Too often, in order to simplify these stories, the adapter reduces the colorful details of the original to drab outlines devoid of charm. Simplification of some of the words is permissible enough and even essential. For example, Henry T. Riley's literal translation of Ovid's account of Phaëthon's rash entrance into the presence of his father, the Sun, describes the youth standing at a distance because "he could not bear the refulgence nearer." Sally Benson's adaptation in *Stories of the Gods and Heroes* has "for the light was more than he could bear"—a legitimate substitution. Words may be simplified, paraphrased, or explained in advance. But reject an adaptation that omits the rich, descriptive details of

*Illustration by Krystyna Turska for* Pegasus. *Copyright 1970. Reproduced by permission of Franklin Watts, Inc. and Oxford University Press, London. (Original in color)*

13. From *Literature in the Elementary School* by Porter Lander MacClintock (University of Chicago Press, 1907), p. 122.

*Illustration by William Stobbs. Reproduced from* The Gorgon's Head. *© 1961 by Ian Serraillier. By permission of Henry Z. Walck, Inc.*

Ovid's tale. It would be a pity to miss the pictures of the palace, the chariot, and the horses of the Sun, the account of Apollo's love and anxiety for the reckless youth, the portrayal of the boy's terror of the lonely heavens, and the descriptions of the rushing speed, the earth aflame, finally the Jovian bolt, and then:

> *. . . Phaethon, the flames consuming his yellow hair, is hurled headlong, and is borne in a long tract through the air; as sometimes a star from the serene sky may appear to fall, although it really has not fallen. . . . The Hesperian Naiads commit his body, smoking from the three-forked flames, to the tomb and inscribe these verses on the stone:—"Here is Phaethon buried, the driver of his father's chariot, which if he did not manage, still he miscarried in a great attempt."*[14]

Another version translates the last lines:

> *He could not rule his father's car of fire,*
> *Yet was it much so nobly to aspire.*[15]

14. *The Metamorphoses*, literal translation into English prose by Henry T. Riley (McKay, 1899), p. 59.

15. *A Book of Myths* by Helen Sewell (Macmillan, 1942), p. 39.

According to these standards, what versions of the myths are best to use with children? There has been a flood of new adaptations and some new editions of old versions. Of the latter, one of the best is *The Heroes* by Charles Kingsley, Victorian scholar and poet. His stories of Perseus, Theseus, and Jason have a nobility that should prove a wholesome antidote to the banality of much of our mass entertainment. Padraic Colum's *The Golden Fleece* and *The Children's Homer* are superb storytelling for good readers, and the d'Aulaires' big, handsome *Book of Greek Myths* represents years of preparation. The stories are brief but have continuity; the copious and colorful illustrations are uneven in quality but imaginative. This will be a splendid book for classroom use. It is also interesting to see how the myths appeal to poets, beginning with Kingsley and Colum. In 1960, the British poet Robert Graves brought out his version, called *Greek Gods and Heroes*, a lively text that makes clear what is often confusing. And Ian Serraillier, another poet, has told the stories of Perseus, *The Gorgon's Head*, and Theseus, *The Way of Danger*, with dramatic beauty. Both can be read by children or may serve as sources for storytelling. The illustrations suggest the figures on Greek vases. Other tales by Serraillier include *Heracles the Strong*, illustrated with woodcuts that echo the vigor of the story; *The Clashing Rocks*, the story of Jason; and *A Fall from the Sky*, the story of Daedalus. The eleven stories from Greek mythology adapted by Katherine Miller in *Apollo* are told in competent but not impressive brief versions. Olivia Coolidge's twenty-seven myths in *Greek Myths*, on the other hand, are mature in approach and are well told. Leon Garfield and Edward Blishen's *The God Beneath The Sea*, a flowing narrative version that clarifies the complexities of Olympian relationships, won the 1970 Carnegie Award. Two very good source books are Edith Hamilton's *Mythology*, which gives excellent background, and Roger Lancelyn Green's *A Book of Myths*, which gives variants of myths from many of the ancient lands. Examine these editions and choose the one or two that best suit your needs as sources for storytelling or references for the children to read themselves.

When you want to use the Norse myths and hero tales, turn again to Padraic Colum, to his *Children of Odin*, a stirring and understandable version of those complex tales. Less difficult for younger readers are Catharine Sellew's *Adventures with the Giants* and *Adventures with the Heroes* and Ingri and Edgar Parin d'Aulaire's *Norse Gods and Giants*, which these author-artists have illustrated with big, bold pictures and have retold in a straightforward style with occasional passages in which the oral tradition is evident. Although *Legends of the North*, by Olivia Coolidge, has a contemporary tone and lacks the lyric quality of the Colum tales, it has a special quality of vigorous spontaneity. An early adaptation that still serves well is Abbie F. Brown's *In the Days of Giants*, while Dorothy Hosford's *Sons of the Volsungs* and *Thunder of the Gods* cover the myths and the hero cycles in superb style, either for storytelling or reading by the children themselves. These are, however, the most difficult of all stories to tell.

## EPIC AND HERO TALES

In the source collections of myths, both Greek and Norse, there are (in addition to the stories of the gods) tales of human heroes, buffeted violently by gods and men but daring greatly, suffering uncomplainingly, and enduring staunchly to the end. Such tales, that have a human hero as the focus of the action and that embody the ideals of a culture, are called epics.

*From* Norse Gods and Giants *by Ingri and Edgar Parin d'Aulaire. Copyright © 1967 by Ingri and Edgar Parin d'Aulaire. Reproduced by permission of Doubleday & Company, Inc.*

## Characteristics of the Epic

Epics are sometimes written in verse, as the *Iliad* or the *Sigurd Saga*, and sometimes in prose, as Malory's *Morte d'Arthur*. The adventures of the legendary hero Robin Hood were preserved by the ballads. The term epic is often used quite flexibly to include such dissimilar materials as the great philosophical poem from the Hebrew, the Book of Job, the slight and romantic *Aucassin and Nicolette* from the medieval French, and the comparatively modern *Paradise Lost* by the English poet John Milton.

Most of us, however, think of epics as a cycle of tales, such as the *Odyssey* or the *Iliad*, gathered around one hero. These two heroic narratives have come to typify this particular field of literature. In them legendary heroes pursue legendary adventures, aided or hindered by partisan gods who apparently leave Olympus for the express purpose of meddling in human affairs. In short, myth may still be with us in the epic, but the dramatic center of interest has now shifted from the gods to a human hero. We have moved from Olympus to earth; we have transferred our sympathies from gods to men, from divine adventures to human endeavors.

The epic is strongly national in its presentation of human character. Odysseus may have never lived, but he is the embodiment of the Greek ideals of manly courage, sagacity, beauty, and endurance. Sigurd is the personification of Norse heroism; King Arthur is the code of chivalry in the flesh; and Robin Hood is the mouthpiece for England's passionate love of freedom and justice, as he is the ideal of hardy, jovial English manhood. Study the epic hero of a nation and you discover the moral code of that nation and era—all its heroic ideals embodied in one man.

Teachers sometimes say that the epics take up too much time, that there isn't space in the curriculum for such intensive living with one piece of literature. Yet it is that very time element which is important to the richness of feeling that the epic builds. Many individual stories like "Ulysses and Circe" are good stories, but it is Ulysses' struggles day after day, his resourcefulness, his vision, and his tireless endeavor that make the pathos of his homecoming and the triumph of his final bout with the wastrels a memorable experience for children. It is this living with greatness day after day that gives the epics their value for children.

## The Iliad and the Odyssey

The *Iliad* and the *Odyssey* are attributed to Homer, a legendary Greek poet. Songs about the siege of Troy are known to have been sung shortly after the events took place, although the first written forms of the epics did not appear until some six hundred years later. What Homer composed and what he compiled cannot be established, but the great epics known by his name were studied and recited by educated Greeks and there were apparently texts or arrangements of them from around 560 to 527 B.C. Authentic texts are established by 150 B.C. The date of Homer's birth has been variously estimated as from 1159 B.C. to 685 B.C., but by the time stories of Homer's life began to appear, nothing was authentically known about him. Legend has it that he was blind and poor and wandered from city to city singing his great songs. Seven cities vie with each other for the honor of being the place of his birth, but legend agrees only that his birthplace was somewhere in Ionia. George Gilbert Aimé Murray sums up this disputable evidence in the following fashion:

> *The man "Homer" cannot have lived in six different centuries nor been born in seven different cities; but Homeric poetry may well have done so. The man cannot have spoken this strange composite epic language, but the poetry could and did.*[16]

16. George Gilbert Aimé Murray, "Homer," in an earlier edition of the *Encyclopaedia Britannica*.

The *Iliad* is certainly complex and long, but the adventures in the *Odyssey*, or *Ulysses*, are exciting and understandable to children. A combined edition, *The Iliad and the Odyssey of Homer* adapted by Alfred J. Church has versions that are well suited to the nine- to eleven-year-old reader, as are the versions in the handsomely illustrated *The Iliad and the Odyssey* adapted by Jane Werner Watson. For a slightly older reader, Padraic Colum's *The Children's Homer* is a distinguished retelling. But for readers of twelve or older, Barbara Leonie Picard's *The Odyssey of Homer* gives more depth in its perceptive portrayal of character. If units on Greek life have vanished from your school, there is still no reason why the children should not have the *Odyssey*. Ask the librarian to give it to them in her story hour—a serial, one story a week, till the suitors are all wiped out and Odysseus is happily reestablished in his home with his faithful Penelope and his son Telemachus. If the librarian can't do it, why not try it yourself? No story is more rewarding to tell than this one. Superior readers can read it for themselves in the sixth or seventh grade, but it makes a strong appeal to younger children, as young as ten, and therefore seems to call for telling.

In this epic the Greek ideals of cool intelligence, patience, and resourcefulness are found in both Penelope and Odysseus. They exhibit these qualities and hold tenaciously to their goals even when men and gods are arrayed against them. Over "the misty sea," "the wine-dark sea," Odysseus sailed for twenty years and none could stay him. This is a story of fortitude which every generation of children should know.

### Sigurd the Volsung

The Norse epic *Sigurd the Volsung* is not so well known in this country as it deserves to be. There is a rugged nobility about the saga stories which boys especially appreciate. Because these tales reflect a simpler social order, many people consider them better suited to children than the Greek epics. This is a debatable point, since anyone who has ever tried to tell the saga of Sigurd knows all

*Used by permission. Illustrations by Alice & Martin Provensen. From* The Iliad and the Odyssey *adapted by Jane Werner Watson. Copyright 1956 by Western Publishing Company, Inc. (Original in color)*

## VIEWPOINTS

[The heroic ideal] had risen into the consciousness of the authors of the Sagas; it was not far from definite expression in abstract terms. In this lay the danger. An ideal, defined or described in set terms, is an ideal without any responsibility and without any privilege. It may be picked up and traded on by any fool or hypocrite. Undefined and undivulged, it belongs only to those who have some original strength of imagination or will, and with them it cannot go wrong.

All is well, however, so long as this heroic ideal is kept in its right relation, as one element in a complex work, not permitted to walk about by itself as a personage. This right subordination is observed in the Sagas, whereby both the heroic characters are kept out of extravagance . . . and the less noble or the more complex characters are rightly estimated. [The Sagas] are imaginative, dealing in actions and characters; they are not ethical or sentimental treatises, or mirrors of chivalry.—W. P. Ker, *Epic and Romance*, Macmillan, London, 1931, pp. 202–203, 206.

too well its difficulties. Obscurities in the text, difficult names much alike, and unpalatable social relationships upon which the main action of the story depends make this an epic which calls for expert handling.

Certainly the saga has some elements of violence in common with those crime stories which the modern child may be reading in the newspapers or seeing in the movies or on television. But their differences are important. In the latter, the tales of blood and murder are often sordid, ignobly motivated, and horrifying. In the Sigmund-Sigurd stories, there is the nobility of great heroism, of keeping your word even though it costs you your life, of self-sacrifice for a great cause, of death rather than dishonor, of ideals of race and family, of intrepid courage and perseverance.

### Robin Hood

Of all the hero cycles, *Robin Hood* is unquestionably the children's favorite. It may not be the loftiest epic, and Robin Hood may not be the noblest hero, but his mad escapades, his lusty fights, his unfailing good humor when beaten, his sense of fair play, and, above all, his roguish tricks and gaiety practically define "hero" for children. Children should read *Robin Hood*, see it in a moving-picture or television version, and read it again. Indeed, no other hero lends himself so readily to dramatization on screen or in classroom as does this gallant leader of the outlaws. School dramatizations of *Robin Hood* may be out-of-door affairs when the landscape includes enough trees. Otherwise the children can paint their own sets for an assembly program, or the story can be happily lived in any classroom, with a few props and plenty of spirit.

THE MERRY FRIAR CARRIETH ROBIN ACROSS THE WATER

*From* The Merry Adventures of Robin Hood *by Howard Pyle. Copyright, 1946, by Charles Scribner's Sons. Reproduced by permission of the publishers.*

If the children read for themselves the Howard Pyle version, they will discover and weep over the tragic end of Robin Hood at the hands of the false Prioress. This is omitted in most school editions, but children must learn that treachery and death exist, and that nothing lasts in this world except that little legacy of character a man leaves behind. With Robin Hood, this was so great a legacy that his name has never died, and today Robin Hood still means to us gallantry, gentleness, justice, and a warm gaiety which cannot be downed.

Children enjoy hearing some of the ballads of Robin Hood read aloud, but the prose version by Howard Pyle, with his spirited illustrations, is the text they should know. It is hard reading for most children, and if they can't read it for themselves, they should hear it. For the lucky superior readers, it remains for generation after generation of children one of the most exciting narratives in all literature. Other rewarding versions of the story are Geoffrey Trease's *Bows Against the Baron* and J. Walker McSpadden's *Robin Hood and His Merry Outlaws*, which is told in a simple but lively style and illustrated with the jaunty drawings of Louis Slobodkin.

## VIEWPOINTS

Mythological heroes typify goals to be approached, rather than readily definable human figures. While appearing in numberless guises, one of the most important is surely *the effort we make:* the effort to become what we potentially are. . . .

The hero represents the gift of love, or again, grace—the latter epitomized, for example, in Arthur's effortless raising of the sword from the rock—or, in Hindu mythology, Rama's similar lifting of the bow. Both deeds indicate how heroic feats of critical importance are enacted at moments when there no longer exists a clear dividing line between will and act, or rather when, beyond all necessity to proceed according to any attitude or "intentional" motivation whatever, performer and performance are one. This occurs when the performer himself is not even conscious that what he has done is heroic. Yet it is, perhaps, just because he is not, that he alone can have achieved his task.—Dorothy Norman, *The Hero: Myth/Image/Symbol*, World Publishing Co., Cleveland and New York, 1969, pp. 3–4, 5.

### King Arthur and the Knights of the Round Table

Opinions differ as to the appropriateness of the King Arthur stories for young children. Certainly they are more mature in content and significance than either the *Odyssey* or *Robin Hood*. The individual adventures of some of the knights are as understandable as those of the Sherwood Forest band, but the ideals of chivalry are far subtler than the moral code of Robin Hood and his men. Often brave deeds are performed for the love of a fair lady, and many feel the cycle is better for the adolescent period when romance is uppermost and codes of conduct are taken seriously.

On the other hand, there are unusually good juvenile editions of the Arthur tales for children, which, simplified though they are, satisfy the child's love of knights and knightly adventures and make an excellent introduction to the cycle which they will encounter later in Tennyson's *Idylls of the King*. Two of the older editions of the stories of King Arthur and his court remain deservedly popular: Sidney Lanier's *The Boy's King Arthur* and Howard Pyle's *The Story of King Arthur and His Knights*, which Pyle both told and romantically illustrated. Barbara Leonie Picard's *Stories of King Arthur and His Knights* uses lucid language and evokes a feeling of the period, as does Mary MacLeod's *The Book of King Arthur and His Noble Knights*, but MacLeod's book does not achieve the stylistic level of Picard's. Several books tell separate episodes from the Arthurian legend: Barbara Schiller's *The Kitchen Knight;* the collection of four Arthurian tales in T. H. White's *The Once and Future King* that begins with *The Sword in the Stone;* Ian Serraillier's poetic *The Challenge of the Green Knight*, the story of Sir Gawain's battle against the knight who had issued a challenge to the company at Camelot; and Constance Hieatt's scholarly version of the same story, *Sir Gawain and the Green Knight*. Hieatt's *The Joy of the Court* tells the romantic story of Erec and Enid, as does Barbara Schiller's *Erec and Enid*. Teachers who love the Arthur stories will have children who enjoy them. Certainly a saturation with any of these hero cycles is an enriching experience. Among the stories popular with the children are: "How Arthur Became King," "The Winning of the Sword Excalibur," "The Winning of a Queen," "The Story of Merlin," "Sir Launcelot," "Sir Gawain," "Sir Galahad's Search for the Holy Grail," and "The Passing of Arthur."

It is the gentleness and beauty of these stories and the idealistic character of King Arthur and his knights which sometimes furnish children with their first idea of strength in gentleness, of the power that comes through disciplined restraint. Not that they can put these qualities into words, but the qualities are there, embodied in the strong, gentle men who are the heroes of these tales.

### The Ramayana and the Mahabharata

There was no version of the *Ramayana* suitable for children until Joseph Gaer's *The Adventures of Rama* was published. This myth-epic of India tells how the god Vishnu came down to earth as Prince Rama, a mortal, to save mankind from the evil powers of Ravan. Once on earth, Rama behaves much like other epic heroes. He fights innumerable battles, marries the beautiful Sita, suffers banishment, gives way to suspicion and jealousy, and is put to shame by the gentle Sita's trial by fire. After that, all goes well, and throughout the ten thousand years of Rama's reign

*Unknown were want, disease and crime,*
*So calm, so happy was the time.*

The individual stories resemble Greek myths rather more than the usual epic does. The illustrations suggest the dance, in which form the adventures of Rama are often shown in India. A splendid edition of the Ramayana has been adapted by Elizabeth Seeger, who has also retold one of India's great hero tales in *The Five Sons of King Pandu*, the story of the Mahabharata. Both books are beautifully illustrated in the Indian tradition, and both have the rolling prose that is so suitable to the intricacies of the stories and to their lofty themes.

*Reprinted from* The Ramayana, *text © 1969 by Elizabeth Seeger and illustrations © 1969 by Gordon Laite, a Young Scott Book, by permission of Addison-Wesley Publishing Company. (Original in color)*

## Other Epics and Hero Tales

The length and complexity of the epic form may seem a deterrent to young readers, but it allows time for real characterization and for a continual iteration of the moral code. Although the great national epics and hero tales are of particular interest to students of literature and to folklorists, they can be enjoyed by the adolescent reader; and many of the single episodes, especially those of the hero tales, can be appreciated by the preadolescent.

An excellent introduction to the genre is *Hero Tales from Many Lands*, edited by Alice Hazeltine. Her selection of retellings is discriminating, and the book includes sources, background notes, and a glossary. Barbara Leonie Picard's *Hero Tales of the British Isles* also has notes that give historical information.

*Beowulf*, the oldest epic in English, has been retold in several editions for the young reader. Two versions that can be enjoyed by the ten- to twelve-year-olds are Dorothy Hosford's *By His Own Might, The Battles of Beowulf;* and Robert Nye's *Beowulf, A New Telling*, a quite simple prose interpretation of the epic poem. For older children, an outstanding prose version is Rosemary Sutcliff's *Beowulf*, which has a poetic grandeur of style. Ian Serraillier's *Beowulf, the Warrior* is in sonorous and stately verse.

The Babylonian story of Gilgamesh has been retold in several editions; the most notable both in style and illustration is that of Bernarda Bryson. A version that is easier to read is edited by Anita Feagles: *He Who Saw Everything, The Epic of Gilgamesh*. The ornate mythic style of Jennifer Westwood's *Gilgamesh, and Other Babylonian Tales*, has flavor but limits the book to older readers.

The deeds of Cuchulain, the Irish warrior-hero who was the descendant of a god, are combined in a continuous story in Rosemary Sutcliff's *The Hound of Ulster*. Another Irish hero, Finn MacCool, leader of the Fenians, is described by Sutcliff in *The High Deeds of Finn MacCool*, a vigorous account of the Fenian legends. These legends are also related in vivid style by Ella Young in *The Tangle-Coated Horse and Other Tales*.

From continental Europe come other tales of heroes: stories of the legendary Spanish hero, the Cid; the story of Roland from France; in romantic tales from the Kiev cycle, *The Knights of the Golden Table* by E. M. Almedingen; *The Nibelungenlied* from Germany.

Tales from other parts of the world, too, are becoming available for children. Marcia Brown, in *Backbone of the King*, retells the Hawaiian epic of the courtier Pakaa and his son Ku. Dale Carlson's *Warlord of the Gengi* recounts the valorous deeds of a Japanese folk hero. Roland Bertol's *Sundiata, The Epic*

*From the book* Beowulf: Dragon Slayer *by Rosemary Sutcliff. Illustration by Charles Keeping. Illustration copyright, ©, 1962 by The Bodley Head, Ltd. Published by E. P. Dutton & Co., Inc. and used with their permission.*

*of the Lion King*, tells of the hero-king who founded the African empire of Mali.

Fable, myth, and epic are different from each other in many ways, yet all three are a part of the great stream of folk literature and are also embodiments of moral truths in story form.

The *fable* teaches briefly and frankly and provides the child with his first excursion into the realm of abstract ideas, intellectual speculations about conduct.

The *myth* teaches through symbols which grow more and more complex. The symbolism soon ceases to have the simple, obvious moral of a fable and becomes as complicated as life, and it is then proportionately difficult for a child to understand. Fortunately, the myth stories possess a beauty that is satisfying in itself.

The *epics* have a triple value. They contribute to an appreciation of world literature, to an understanding of national ideals of behavior, and to a comprehension of the dimensions of the valor and nobility of heroism for all mankind.

By the time the child reaches fable, myth, and epic, he must be capable of deeper feeling and understanding; for fable is a theorem, myth an allegory, and epic the glorification of man.

## ADULT REFERENCES[17]


ASIMOV, ISAAC. *Words from the Myths.*

AUSLANDER, JOSEPH, and FRANK ERNEST HILL. *The Winged Horse; The Story of Poets and Their Poetry.*

BULFINCH, THOMAS. *Age of Fable; or, Stories of Gods and Heroes.*

EASTMAN, MARY HUSE. *Index to Fairy Tales, Myths and Legends.*

FRAZER, SIR JAMES GEORGE. *The Golden Bough.*

*Funk and Wagnalls Standard Dictionary of Folklore, Mythology and Legend.*

GUERBER, HELENE A. *Myths of Greece and Rome.*

HOMER. *The Odyssey.*

MONTGOMERIE, NORAH. *To Read and to Tell.*

MUNCH, PETER A. *Norse Mythology, Legends of Gods and Heroes.*

OVID. *The Metamorphoses.*

RANK, OTTO. *The Myth of the Birth of the Hero: A Psychological Interpretation of Mythology.*

SCHWAB, GUSTAV. *Gods and Heroes.*

SMITH, RUTH, ed. *The Tree of Life.*

TATLOCK, JESSIE M. *Greek and Roman Mythology.*

*Volsunga Saga: The Story of the Volsungs and Niblungs, with Certain Songs from the Elder Edda.*


17. Complete bibliographic data are provided in the combined Adult References in the Appendices.

## AESOP'S FABLES

*Aesop for Children*, ill. by Milo Winter. Rand, 1919. The fables have been expanded in this edition, making them more like stories. Children enjoy them, and the illustrations are beautiful. 10-14

*Aesop's Fables*, tr. by V. S. Vernon Jones, ill. by Arthur Rackham. Watts, 1967. This is one of the most satisfactory editions both for children and adults. Chesterton's introduction should not be missed. The illustrations appeal to older children. 10-14

*Aesop's Fables*, ill. by Fritz Kredel. Grosset, 1947. An attractive, readable edition which contains over 150 fables. Illustrated in color and black and white. 10-14

*Aesop's Fables*, ill. by Jacob Lawrence. Windmill, 1970. Stark, sophisticated illustrations for a compilation of eighteen fables, moderately well told. 9-11

ARTZYBASHEFF, BORIS, ed. *Aesop's Fables*, ill. by ed. Viking, 1933. 12-14

EVANS, KATHERINE. *A Bundle of Sticks*, ill. by author. Whitman, 1962. An amusing modern picture-book adaptation of the Aesop fable for younger readers. Other adaptations by this author include *The Boy Who Cried Wolf* (1960) and *A Camel in the Tent* (1961). 5-8

*The Hare and the Tortoise*, ill. by Paul Galdone. McGraw, 1962. Action-filled color illustrations for this Aesop fable heighten suspense for the youngest. 4-7

JACOBS, JOSEPH, ed. *The Fables of Aesop*, ill. by David Levine. Macmillan, 1964. 9-11

REES, ENNIS, ad. *Lions and Lobsters and Foxes and Frogs*, ill. by Edward Gorey. Scott/Addison, 1971. Seventeen selections taken from *Fables from Aesop* (Oxford, 1966) by Rees are here illustrated by Gorey's amiable, wild-eyed beasts. 8-10

REEVES, JAMES, ad. *Fables from Aesop*, ill. by Maurice Wilson. Walck, 1962. In his selection of fifty fables, the narrator has introduced brief dialogue and descriptive phrases to enliven them, while keeping to the spirit of the original. Illustrations, many in color, are exceptional in quality. 9-13

SHOWALTER, JEAN B., ad. *The Donkey Ride*, ill. by Tomi Ungerer. Doubleday, 1967. 5-9

*Three Aesop Fox Fables*, ill. by Paul Galdone. Seabury, 1971. Large figures, with humor and movement, make this good for group showing. 4-7

UNTERMEYER, LOUIS, ed. *Aesop's Fables*, ill. by Alice and Martin Provensen. Golden Pr., 1965. 6-9

WHITE, ANNE TERRY, ed. *Aesop's Fables*, ill. by Helen Siegl. Random, 1964. 8-10

## LA FONTAINE'S FABLES

LA FONTAINE, JEAN DE. *The Fables of La Fontaine*, tr. by Marianne Moore. Viking, 1954. These fables retain their original verse form in this translation. A scholarly edition which includes La Fontaine's twelve books of fables and his own original preface. Chiefly an adult source.

———. *The Hare and the Tortoise*, ill. by Brian Wildsmith. Watts, 1967.

———. *The Lion and the Rat*, ill. by Brian Wildsmith. Watts, 1963.

———. *The Miller, the Boy and the Donkey*, ill. by Brian Wildsmith. Watts, 1969.

———. *The North Wind and the Sun*, ill. by Brian Wildsmith. Watts, 1964.

———. *The Rich Man and the Shoe-Maker*, ill. by Brian Wildsmith. Watts, 1966.
Big pages, big print, and jewel-tone colors make these single-title editions attractive. 5-8

## OTHER FABLES

ANDERSEN, HANS CHRISTIAN. *The Ugly Duckling, The Emperor's New Clothes*, and others (see Bibliography, Chapter 8).

BRENNER, ANITA. *A Hero by Mistake*, ill. by Jean Charlot. W. R. Scott, 1953. Afraid of his own shadow, this little man accidentally captures some bandits, is hailed as a hero, and learns to behave like one. 6-8

BROWN, MARCIA. *Once a Mouse* (see Bibliography, Chapter 6).

CHAUCER, GEOFFREY. *Chanticleer and the Fox*, ad. and ill. by Barbara Cooney. T. Crowell, 1958. Pictures of colorful beauty and design add delight to the old fable of the crafty fox and the vain cock. Caldecott Medal. 6-9

CIARDI, JOHN. *John J. Plenty and Fiddler Dan*, ill. by Madeleine Gekiere. Lippincott, 1963. 4-9

DAUGHERTY, JAMES. *Andy and the Lion* (see Bibliography, Chapter 8).

GAER, JOSEPH. *The Fables of India*, ill. by Randy Monk. Little, 1955. Beast tales from three outstanding collections of Indian fables: the Panchatantra, the Hitopadesa, and the Jatakas. The stories are entertainingly presented, and there is excellent background material on the known history of fable literature for the student. 12-16

GALDONE, PAUL. *The Monkey and the Crocodile*, ill. by author. Seabury, 1969. 5-7

GINSBURG, MIRRA. *Three Rolls and One Doughnut: Fables from Russia*, ill. by Anita Lobel. Dial, 1970. 6-10

KRYLOV, IVAN. *Fifteen Fables of Krylov*, tr. by Guy Daniels, ill. by David Pascal. Macmillan, 1965. 12 up

LEAF, MUNRO. *The Story of Ferdinand* (see Bibliography, Chapter 12).

MCGINLEY, PHYLLIS. *The Plain Princess* (see Bibliography, Chapter 8).

MERRILL, JEAN. *The Black Sheep*, ill. by Ronni Solbert. Pantheon, 1969. 9-11

## GREEK AND ROMAN MYTHS AND EPICS

BENSON, SALLY. *Stories of the Gods and Heroes*, ill. by Steele Savage. Dial, 1940. 10-14

CHURCH, ALFRED JOHN, ad. *The Aeneid*. Macmillan, 1962. A simplified and dignified version. 10-14

———, ad. *The Iliad and the Odyssey of Homer* ill. by Eugene Karlin. Macmillan, 1964. 10-14

———, ad. *The Odyssey of Homer*, ill. by John Flaxman. Macmillan, 1951. First published in 1906, this attractive recent edition is an excellent source for children to read or adults to tell. Stories are arranged in chronological order. 10-14

COLUM, PADRAIC. *The Children's Homer*, ill. by Willy Pogány. Macmillan, 1925, 1962. A distinguished version in cadenced prose, simple but in the spirit of the original. Vigorous illustrations.

———. *The Golden Fleece*, ill. by Willy Pogány. Macmillan, 1921, 1962. A companion edition to *The Children's Homer*, and equally fine. 10-14

COOLIDGE, OLIVIA E. *Greek Myths*, ill. by Edouard Sandoz. Houghton, 1949. Mrs. Coolidge has retold twenty-seven of the most widely known Greek myths. Here the gods are not idealized, but the stories have authenticity. 10-16

D'AULAIRE, INGRI and EDGAR PARIN. *Ingri and Edgar Parin d'Aulaire's Book of Greek Myths*, ill. by authors. Doubleday, 1962. 8-11

DE SÉLINCOURT, AUBREY. *Odysseus the Wanderer*, ill. by Norman Meredith. Criterion, 1956. A lusty, modern retelling of the *Odyssey* that should lure many young readers into an acquaintance with this epic before high-school days. 11 up

GARFIELD, LEON, and EDWARD BLISHEN. *The God Beneath the Sea*, ill. by Zevi Blum. Pantheon, 1971. 11-14

GRAVES, ROBERT. *Greek Gods and Heroes*, ill. by Dimitris Davis. Doubleday, 1960. 12-15

———. *The Siege and Fall of Troy*, ill. by C. Walter Hodges. Doubleday, 1963. An easy-to-follow narrative history of the Trojan War. 12-16

GREEN, ROGER LANCELYN. *Heroes of Greece and Troy; Retold from the Ancient Authors*, ill. by Heather Copley and Christopher Chamberlain. Walck, 1961. The tales of the Heroic Age have been woven into a unified whole, from the coming of the Immortals to Odysseus, the last of the heroes. Beautifully written, and with an introduction that will give insight into the great variety of classic sources used in this fine version. 12 up

———, ed. *A Book of Myths*, ill. by Joan Kiddell-Monroe. Dutton, 1965. 10-12

HAMILTON, EDITH. *Mythology*, ill. by Steele Savage. Little, 1942. 12 up

HAWTHORNE, NATHANIEL. *The Golden Touch*, ill. by Paul Galdone. McGraw, 1959. The old tale of King Midas is imaginatively illustrated with gold-toned pictures. 6-9

———. *A Wonder Book, and Tanglewood Tales*, ill. by Maxfield Parrish. Dodd, 1934. Although not good interpretations of the old myths, these stories are nevertheless worth examining for their storytelling qualities. Editions illustrated by Walter Crane and Arthur Rackham are available in many libraries. 10-14

KINGSLEY, CHARLES. *The Heroes*, ill. by Vera Bock. Macmillan, 1954. Beautifully retold tales which make a fine cycle for the storyteller. 10-14

______. *The Heroes*, ill. by Joan Kiddell-Monroe. Dutton, 1963. 9-12

LANG, ANDREW. *The Adventures of Odysseus*, ill. by Joan Kiddell-Monroe. Dutton, 1962. Andrew Lang's distinguished retellings of Homer's *Iliad* and the *Odyssey* are reissued in handsome new format. Originally published in his *Tales of Greece and Troy* (1907). 12 up

MAC PHERSON, JAY. *Four Ages of Man*, ill. St. Martin's, 1962. Beautifully narrated stories from the Greek myths organized around four periods: "creation and the coming of the gods; pastoral life and the ordering of the seasons; the adventures and the labors of the heroes; war, tragic tales, and decline into history." Illustrations have been drawn from ancient vases. 13 up

MILLER, KATHERINE. *Apollo*. Houghton, 1970. 9-11

PICARD, BARBARA LEONIE. *The Iliad of Homer*, ill. by Joan Kiddell-Monroe. Walck, 1960. A truly distinguished retelling of the *Iliad*, with characters sympathetically portrayed. *The Odyssey of Homer* (1952) is an equally fine companion volume. 12-15

REEVES, JAMES. *The Trojan Horse*, ill. by Krystyna Turska. Watts, 1969. A Trojan boy describes the invasion of his city. 9-10

SELLEW, CATHARINE. *Adventures with the Gods*, ill. by George and Doris Hauman. Little, 1945. An introduction to the more familiar myths, simply written for younger children. 9-12

SERRAILLIER, IAN. *The Clashing Rocks: The Story of Jason*, ill. by William Stobbs. Walck, 1964. 10-13

______. *A Fall from the Sky: The Story of Daedalus*, ill. by William Stobbs. Walck, 1966. 10-13

______. *The Gorgon's Head; The Story of Perseus*, ill. by William Stobbs. Walck, 1962. 12-14

______. *Heracles the Strong*, ill. by Rocco Negri. Walck, 1970. 10-13

______. *The Way of Danger; The Story of Theseus*, ill. by William Stobbs. Walck, 1963. 12-14

SEWELL, HELEN. *A Book of Myths*, sel. from Bulfinch's *Age of Fable*, ill. by Helen Sewell. Macmillan, 1942, 1964. Some people dislike, others are enthusiastic about the stylized illustrations in black and white, or sharp blue, black, and white. They are undeniably authentic in spirit and detail. For a Greek ballet or dramatization, these are worth study. 10-14

TAYLOR, N. B. *The Aeneid of Virgil*, ill. by Joan Kiddell-Monroe. Walck, 1961. The epic of Aeneas and his journeys after the burning of Troy, retold in an excellent prose version. 13-15

TOMAINO, SARAH F., ad. *Persephone; Bringer of Spring*, ill. by Ati Forberg. T. Crowell, 1971. A graceful retelling of the Greek legend with delicate and dramatic illustrations. 8-10

TURSKA, KRYSTYNA. *Pegasus*, ill. by author. Watts, 1970. 9-11

WATSON, JANE WERNER. *The Iliad and the Odyssey*, ill. by Alice and Martin Provensen. Golden Pr., 1964. 11-13

## NORSE MYTHS AND EPICS

BROWN, ABBIE FARWELL. *In the Days of Giants*, ill. by E. B. Smith. Houghton, 1902. This is a sterling adaptation of the Norse myths. 10-14

COLUM, PADRAIC. *Children of Odin*, ill. by Willy Pogány. Macmillan, 1920, 1962. Norse myths and hero tales retold in a continuous narrative ending with the death of Sigurd. Our best source for children. In fine modern format. 10-14

COOLIDGE, OLIVIA. *Legends of the North*, ill. by Edouard Sandoz. Houghton, 1951. A wide variety of stories includes tales of the northern gods and heroes, the Volsungs, and other sagas. 12-14

D'AULAIRE, INGRI and EDGAR PARIN. *Norse Gods and Giants*, ill. by authors. Doubleday, 1967. 8-11

HOSFORD, DOROTHY G. *Sons of the Volsungs*, ill. by Frank Dobias. Holt, 1949. A splendid version of the Sigurd tales adapted from William Morris' *The Story of Sigurd the Volsung and the Fall of the Niblungs.* 11-14

______. *Thunder of the Gods*, ill. by George and Claire Louden. Holt, 1952. Distinguished retellings of the Norse myths: stories of Odin, Thor, Balder, Loki, and other familiar tales. Excellent for storytelling or reading aloud. 11-14

SELLEW, CATHARINE. *Adventures with the Giants*, ill. by Steele Savage. Little, 1950. 8-11

______. *Adventures with the Heroes*, ill. by Steele Savage. Little, 1954. Retold in simple language are the stories of the Volsungs and Nibelungs. 9-12

## ENGLISH EPICS AND HERO TALES

HIEATT, CONSTANCE. *The Joy of the Court*, ill. by Pauline Baynes. T. Crowell, 1970. 9-11

______. *The Knight of the Cart*, ill. by John Gretzer. T. Crowell, 1969. 10-12

______. *Sir Gawain and the Green Knight*, ill. by Walter Lorraine. T. Crowell, 1967. 10-12

HOSFORD, DOROTHY G. *By His Own Might; the Battles of Beowulf*, ill. by Laszlo Matulay. Holt, 1947. 11-16

LANIER, SIDNEY. *The Boy's King Arthur*, ill. by N. C. Wyeth, ad. from Sir Thomas Malory's *History of King Arthur and His Knights of the Round Table.* Scribner's, 1942. An authoritative and popular version of this hero cycle; the best one to use for reading or telling. 10-14

MAC LEOD, MARY. *Book of King Arthur and His Noble Knights*, ill. by Henry C. Pitz. Lippincott, 1949. 9-13

MC SPADDEN, J. WALKER. *Robin Hood and His Merry Outlaws*, ill. by Louis Slobodkin. World, 1946. 9-12

MALORY, SIR THOMAS. *Le Morte d'Arthur*, ill. by W. Russell Flint. London: Warner, publisher to the Medici Society [1921], 2 vols. Children who are superior readers are fascinated with this source of the Arthur stories. 12-16

NYE, ROBERT. *Beowulf: A New Telling*, ill. by Allan E. Cober. Hill, 1968. 10-12

PICARD, BARBARA L. *Hero Tales of the British Isles*, ill. by Eric Fraser. Criterion, 1963. 10-13

______. *Stories of King Arthur and His Knights*, ill. by Roy Morgan. Walck, 1955. 10-13

PYLE, HOWARD. *The Merry Adventures of Robin Hood of Great Renown in Nottinghamshire*, ill. by author. Scribner's, 1946. This is the great prose edition of the Robin Hood tales, the best source for reading and telling. 12-14

______. *Some Merry Adventures of Robin Hood*, rev. ed., ill. by author. Scribner's, 1954. This book contains a dozen stories adapted from the longer book, and would serve as an introduction for younger readers. 10-13

______. *The Story of King Arthur and His Knights*, ill. by author. Scribner's, 1933. Any Pyle edition is written with grace and distinction. This is no exception. 12-14

ROBBINS, RUTH. *Taliesin and King Arthur*, ill. by author. Parnassus, 1970. The young poet Taliesin entertains King Arthur's court with his storytelling. The book mingles fact and fiction and the style is poetic. 9-11

SCHILLER, BARBARA. *Erec and Enid*, ill. by Ati Forberg. Dutton, 1970. 9-11

______. *The Kitchen Knight*, ill. by Nonny Hogrogian. Holt, 1965. 9-11

______, ad. *The Wandering Knight*, ill. by Herschel Levit. Dutton, 1971. A retelling of the deeds of the young Lancelot. 9-11

SERRAILLIER, IAN. *Beowulf, the Warrior*, ill. by Severin. Walck, 1961. 12 up

______. *The Challenge of the Green Knight*, ill. by Victor Ambrus. Walck, 1967. 12-14

*Song of Robin Hood*, ed. by Anne Malcolmson, music arr. by Grace Castagnetta, ill. by Virginia Lee Burton. Houghton, 1947. Eighteen ballads illustrated with distinguished black-and-white drawings. Traditional music for many of the ballads is included. The book is the result of careful research in art and music as well as in selection of the ballads. 10-14

SUTCLIFF, ROSEMARY. *Beowulf*, ill. by Charles Keeping. Dutton, 1962. 11 up

______. *Tristan and Iseult*. Dutton, 1971. A tender retelling of a great love story. 11-14

TREASE, GEOFFREY. *Bows Against the Barons*, ill. by C. Walter Hodges. Hawthorne, 1967. 10-12

## OTHER NATIONAL EPICS

ALMEDINGEN, E. M. *The Knights of the Golden Table*, ill. by Charles Keeping. Lippincott, 1964. 12-15

______. *The Story of Gudrun*; based on the third part of the Epic of Gudrun, ill. by Enrico Arno. Norton, 1967. A German tale retold with a dignity appropriate to the romantic sweep of a medieval epic. 12-15

BERTOL, ROLAND. *Sundiata: The Epic of the Lion King*, ill. by Gregorio Prestopino. T. Crowell, 1970. 9-12

BROWN, MARCIA. *Backbone of the King*, ill. by author. Scribner's, 1966. 10-12

BRYSON, BERNARDA. *Gilgamesh*, ill. by author. Holt, 1967. 11-14

CARLSON, DALE. *Warlord of the Gengi*, ill. by John Gretzer. Atheneum, 1970. 11-14

DAVIS, RUSSELL, and BRENT K. ASHABRANNER. *Ten Thousand Desert Swords; The Epic Story of a Great Bedouin Tribe*, ill. by Leonard Everett Fisher. Little, 1960. The Bani Hilal were a great and ancient warrior tribe, and their legends are superbly retold for the discriminating reader. 12 up

DEUTSCH, BABETTE. *Heroes of the Kalevala*, ill. by Fritz Eichenberg. Messner, 1940. This version has not only literary distinction but continuity. Text and illustrations bring out the lusty humor of the tales. 10-14

FEAGLES, ANITA. *He Who Saw Everything; the Epic of Gilgamesh*. Scott/Addison, 1966. 9-11

GAER, JOSEPH. *The Adventures of Rama*, ill. by Randy Monk. Little, 1954. One of the best-loved epics of India is the story of Prince Rama and of his wife Sita, stolen from him by a demon king. The careful selection of incidents makes this an absorbing and unified tale. 12-14

GOLDSTON, ROBERT. *The Legend of the Cid*, ill. by Stephane. Bobbs, 1963. A simple version of the adventures of the Spanish hero. 10-13

HAZELTINE, ALICE, ed. *Hero Tales from Many Lands*, ill. by Gordon Laite. Abingdon, 1961. 11-15

HODGES, ELIZABETH JAMISON. *A Song for Gilgamesh*, ill. by David Omar White. Atheneum, 1971. The story of a young potter of Sumer is woven around the journey of Gilgamesh to the Land of the Living. 11-13

SEEGER, ELIZABETH. *The Five Sons of King Pandu*, ill. by Gordon Laite. Scott/Addison, 1969. 12 up

______. *The Ramayana*, ill. by Gordon Laite. Scott/Addison, 1969. 12 up

SEREDY, KATE. *The White Stag*, ill. by author. Viking, 1937. Based on the legend of the founding of Hungary, a tale of the hero Bendeguz and his son Attila. Newbery Medal. 10-14

*The Song of Roland*, tr. by Merriam Sherwood, ill. by Edith Emerson. McKay, 1938. This is one of the finest translations of the story of Roland for younger readers, and is illustrated with distinctive line drawings. 12-16

SUTCLIFF, ROSEMARY. *The High Deeds of Finn MacCool*, ill. by Michael Charlton. Dutton, 1967. 11-14

______. *The Hound of Ulster*, ill. by Victor Ambrus. Dutton, 1964. 11-14

UDEN, GRANT, ad. *Hero Tales from the Age of Chivalry; Retold from the Froissart Chronicles*, ill. by Doreen Roberts. World, 1969. Twelve tales by the great poet-historian of the fourteenth century. Historically interesting, romantic in approach. 11-13

WESTWOOD, JENNIFER. *Gilgamesh and Other Babylonian Tales*. Coward, 1970. 12 up

YOUNG, ELLA. *The Tangle-Coated Horse and Other Tales: Episodes from the Fionn Saga*, ill. by Vera Bock. McKay, 1968. 12-14

# Chapter 8
# Modern Fantasy

Although the distinction between the old folk tale and the modern fairy tale is useful to adults, it is of no importance to the child. Magic is magic to him whether he finds it in Grimm, Andersen, or Dr. Seuss. Children do not think of their stories in the conventional categories of literature or of libraries but describe their favorites broadly as animal stories or funny stories or true stories or fairy tales, by which they mean any tale of magic, old or modern. Eleanor Cameron, in *The Green and Burning Tree*, says, "If we do not quibble over fineness of categories, we then avoid the danger of becoming one of that company of scholars (some of the folklorists among them) who seem to care less about experiencing the truth and beauty of a tale than in being 'correct' in putting it into this compartment or that."[1] The characteristics of the folk tales that make them particularly appealing to children are the same ones which make the fanciful tales attractive. In fact, interesting story patterns, distinctive style, and memorable characterizations are essential to any good story for children. The special quality of fantasy is that it concerns things that cannot really happen or that it is about people or creatures who do not exist, yet within the framework of each book there is a self-contained logic, a wholeness of conception that has its own reality. If it does not, it fails. Some modern fanciful stories err because they are overwhimsical or unduly sophisticated or, worse still, because they talk down to children. As we select from the new fanciful stories being published each year, let's keep in mind (along with good story patterns, style, and characterizations) sincerity and directness as essential characteristics.

The development of modern fanciful tales has been so astonishing and varied that it merits detailed examination. Because there are so many of these tales, this chapter can consider only a few—stories which have remained favorites over the years, recent ones which have attained great popularity, and certain ones which illustrate trends.

1. Eleanor Cameron, *The Green and Burning Tree* (Atlantic-Little, Brown, 1969), p. 12.

## THE BEGINNINGS OF THE MODERN FANCIFUL TALE

Hans Christian Andersen is generally credited with launching the literary fairy tale. Actually, it began in the French court of the seventeenth century, with elaborations of traditional tales. Fairy tales moved boldly from the hut in the woods to the fashionable drawing rooms of the court and became the vogue of the sophisticates in the century of Louis XIV. Perrault's eight little *contes* were the rage, but adorned though they were with the gentle art of a skilled writer, they remained basically folk tales, perhaps a shade too simple for the intelligentsia. So the cultivated ladies of the court began their embroideries.

Mme. d'Aulnoy, with her "White Cat," "Graciosa and Percinet," "The Yellow Dwarf," and others, turned the fairy tale into an involved story full of double meanings and romance. Published around 1700, these stories in adapted or shortened form are still found in modern collections.

Mme. Leprince de Beaumont wrote chiefly in a didactic vein for children, but happily she had her lighter moments, and her "Beauty and the Beast" (1757) was the product of one of these. With this charming adaptation of a famous folk-tale theme, she forgot her need to improve children's manners and morals; sheer enchantment was the result. Her story is strongly reminiscent of the Norse "East o' the Sun and West o' the Moon" and Grimms' "Bearskin." But Beauty seems more human and convincing than the lassies in the older stories, and neither of the four-footed heroes in the folk tales has the heart-wringing pathos of Beauty's sighing Beast. Although this is not an original tale, Mme. de Beaumont has retold it so tenderly and with such inventive touches that it has long been the favorite version of that theme. Andersen, too, began with skillful adaptations of traditional tales, but his creative genius lifted the modern fairy tale to greatness and he is deservedly called its originator.

## HANS CHRISTIAN ANDERSEN 1805–1875

Hans Christian Andersen was born at Odense, Denmark. His father, a poor shoemaker, disappointed because he could never be a scholar, cherished a shelf of the classics which he shared with his son. The mother was an uneducated peasant with a protective tenderness for the strange boy whom she could only partially understand. After the father died, the mother married again but was obliged to support her son as a washerwoman. Up to her knees in the cold water of the river, suffering from the rheumatic pains which afflicted all the washerwomen of Odense, this poor soul helped her son as long as she lived.

Poor and ignorant, romantically vain and proud, young Hans avoided school and lived in a dream world of his own creation. He made a puppet theater, dressed his puppets with remarkable skill, and dramatized the stories and the plays he was reading so avidly. He was spellbound by Shakespeare's plays and soon imagined himself becoming a great dramatist. He was overtall for his age, with big hands and feet, a big nose, a shock of yellow hair over his eyes, and a gangling body which was always outgrowing the poor clothes he somehow managed to keep clean and neat. But none of these limitations disturbed him, so strong were his dreams.

At fourteen he set off for Copenhagen alone to seek the fortune which he never doubted would await him. The disillusioning years which followed would have crushed a less intrepid soul. He literally broke in upon opera singers, ballet masters, and men of literature, and sang, danced, or recited poetry for them whether they wished it or not. He was considered mildly mad, was snubbed on all sides, and was reduced to near starvation; but here and there someone always believed in the strange boy. Before starting to school again, he published his first book, *The Ghost at Palnatoke's Grave.* At the grammar school in Slagelse and at another school in Elsinore, he remained for some five or six years. These were the bitterest years of his entire life, and the schoolmaster who humiliated and tortured him used to appear in the nightmares which haunted Andersen's old age.

Returning to Copenhagen, educated to some degree, he resumed his writing of plays and poetry with only moderate success. In 1833, Andersen traveled on a modest stipend granted to him by the king, and visited all those countries whose glories he was to give back to the world in his *Fairy Tales.* The first volume of these was published in 1835. They created no special stir, but, as more of them appeared in the ensuing years, their fame grew and spread to other countries until

*Illustration by Marcia Brown (copyright © 1963) is reproduced by permission of Charles Scribner's Sons from* The Wild Swans. *(Original with color)*

Hans Andersen found himself famous as the author of the *Fairy Tales,* which became as much the vogue as the *Contes des fées* in eighteenth-century France and completely eclipsed all of the author's more pretentious works. Andersen was never wholly resigned to the allocation of his fame to his stories for children. He continued to struggle with other types of writing which never succeeded as his fairy tales did. These were translated into almost every European language and brought Andersen the friendship of notable artists all over the world. The most poignant of all his triumphs must have been his return to his native Odense. There he was carried on the shoulders of his countrymen, who filled the streets to do him honor.

The stories themselves, probably the greatest fairy tales ever written, have a freshness and range that are just as astonishing to readers today as they were to those of Andersen's generation. He may have started retelling the old folk tales and combining folk-tale motifs into new tales, but he was soon creating original patterns of his own. His stories fall into rather obvious classifications, which are worth noting because we shall find that modern tales of magic can be grouped under these same headings.

### Retelling of Old Tales

First, there are Andersen's versions of familiar folk tales such as "What the Good-Man Does Is Sure to Be Right!" which is our Norse friend "Gudbrand on the Hill-side"; "Hans Clodhopper," which is "Lazy Jack"; "Great Claus and Little Claus," which is "Hudden and Dudden"; "The Wild Swans," which is Grimms' "The Six Swans" and Asbjörnsen's "Twelve Wild Ducks." When Andersen retold these old tales, he never destroyed the essential elements of the original plots but merely added little embellishments, little characterizations so charming and so right that they are never forgotten. For instance, in "What the Good-Man Does Is Sure to Be

Right!" you get a foreshadowing of the happy end when the old wife prepares her husband for his trip to the market:

> *So she tied on his neckerchief—for that was a matter she understood better than he—she tied it with a double knot, and made him look quite spruce; she dusted his hat with the palm of her hand; and she kissed him and sent him off, riding the horse that was to be either sold or bartered. Of course, he would know what to do.*

### New Stories in Folk-Tale Style

Andersen was so steeped in folk-tale motifs and style that his own stories seem to have come out of some old folk collection. "The Elfin-Mount" sounds curiously like an Asbjörnsen tale. "Thumbelina" might be a feminine version of the Russian "Peter Pea," the English "Hop-o'-My-Thumb," or Grimms' "Thumbling." "The Little Mermaid" is remotely reminiscent both of the water nixies who desire human husbands and of the wives and sweethearts who go through untold sufferings to rescue their beloveds. Yet these and other Andersen tales are not retellings but completely new stories in the old manner, using familiar motifs in new combinations.

### Talking Beasts

The story with animals that talk is an old form which Andersen uses less frequently than others but develops into richly symbolic stories. The traditional story "The Three Little Pigs" tells a simple tale of brains against brawn and is understandable and childlike. But Andersen's story of "The Ugly Duckling" is a complex tale with symbols which are strangely moving. Writing of the ugly duckling, he says, "The poor little thing scarcely knew what to do; he was quite distressed, because he was so ugly, and because he was the jest of the poultry-yard." The duckling went out into the world to seek his fortune, but there also he was snubbed, laughed at, persecuted, and left bitterly alone. He saw the swans flying "so very high . . . he could not forget them, those noble birds!" When he could no longer see them, "he plunged to the bottom of the water, and when he rose again was almost beside himself . . . the poor, ugly animal!"

Finally, after an almost unendurable winter, the spring came again and with it the swans. He approached them expecting they would kill him, but they welcomed him as one of themselves, and when he looked in the water, he saw his own reflection—not that of an ugly duckling, but of a swan! "It matters not to have been born in a duck-yard, if one has been hatched from a swan's egg." "The Ugly Duckling" is no folk tale but a touching allegory. Do we not see ourselves as ugly ducklings, waiting for that marvelous moment of recognition when the swans shall welcome us into their noble company? This theme goes deeper than the Cinderella motif, for it shows us a human soul struggling pitiably and fiercely against its own limitations. Fortunately, it is also a convincing story of a misplaced swan baby, which pleases children eight to eleven years old, even while it gives them a sense of larger meaning, felt, if not clearly apprehended.

### Inanimate Objects Personified

Stories about inanimate objects seem to have been Andersen's invention and special delight. "The Darning Needle," "The Drop of Water," "The Flax," "The Fir Tree," "The Constant Tin Soldier," and "The Top and the Ball" are only a few of the stories in which Andersen endows objects with life and turns their exploits into stories. They are good stories, too, though many of them are sad and adult in theme and not always popular with children. Modern authors have picked up Andersen's innovation and put it to happier and more childlike uses.

### Humorous Tales

When Andersen retells a folk tale or improvises in folk-tale style, he often falls into the hearty, slapstick humor of the old stories. Good examples are his genuinely droll "Great Claus and Little Claus" and some of the fantastic episodes in "The Elfin-Mount." But the moment he begins to write original stories, his humor becomes more subtle, less childlike, often satirical. "The Real Princess," "The Swineherd," and "The Emperor's New Clothes" are all satires on adult foibles, and the humor is ironical. After presenting a picture of a princess atop twenty mattresses under which is one little pea that causes her acute suffering, Andersen concludes, with tongue in cheek, "Was not this a lady of real delicacy?" This is as sly a jibe at snobbery and the myth of blue-bloodedness as can be found anywhere.

He uses "The Swineherd" to make fun of false standards and of people who prefer the artificial and the trivial to the durable satisfactions of life. In "The Emperor's New Clothes," Andersen relieves his mind of all its pent-up bitterness against the pompous pretentiousness of the rogues and fools who sometimes inhabit high places. This is not childlike humor, but the irony of an adult lampooning some of the cruel foibles from which he has suffered. Most of the satire goes over the children's heads, and they take the stories literally. They are perfectly serious over the absurd princess on her twenty mattresses, and they accept the emperor as the broadest kind of farce.

### Fantasy

Finally, Andersen took the make-believe and the magic of the folk tales and developed tales of pure fantasy which have never been surpassed—"The Marsh King's Daughter," "The Little Mermaid," "The Girl Who Trod on the Loaf," "The Little Match Girl," and, finest of them all, "The Snow Queen." What tales these are! "The Marsh King's Daughter" is a weird tale of a changeling—a savage, cruel girl by day, a kindly, hideous frog by night. Here is man's dual nature in perpetual conflict until love and pity conquer the evil. The story is a first-rate tale and perhaps an ancestor of *Dr. Jekyll and Mr. Hyde.*

"The Little Mermaid" concerns the old folklore conflict of a fairy creature who loves

*Illustration by Erik Blegvad. Reproduced from Hans Christian Andersen's* The Swineherd, *© 1958 by Erik Blegvad, by permission of Harcourt Brace Jovanovich, Inc. (Original in color)*

a human being. The selfless love of the mermaid endures every suffering for the sake of her beloved. Finally, losing her life, she wins the hope of immortality. Love is never wasted and carries its own benediction, Andersen seems to be saying. Again, this is a story for older children and adults and so, too, is that tale of sin "The Girl Who Trod on the Loaf," despising God's gifts and suffering a terrible punishment. It recalls Grimms' "Our Lady's Child," though it is a completely new story. On the other hand, children understand and love "The Little Match Girl" and "The Snow Queen." The former may be too sad for many children, and certainly they have wept over it ever since it was written, but there is no story in all literature that speaks more movingly of God's mercy and pity for suffering.

"The Snow Queen" is almost a novelette and, aside from its rather subtle symbolism, is an exciting adventure tale in a dream world of strange beauty. Like all of the other fantasies, this begins realistically. Two real children, sitting on their rooftop under a real rose vine, share a real picture book and a loving companionship. Then a glass splinter gets into Kay's eye and the magic begins. The splinter stabs his heart, too, which becomes as cold as ice. He sees faults in everything that he used to find good, even his little friend Gerda. Finally he is whisked away to the Snow Queen's palace, where the empty iciness suits him perfectly and he can play "the ice-puzzle of reason" to his heart's content. Meanwhile Gerda, hurt by Kay's unkindness but still loving him, sets out to find him. Her adventures are like a series of dreams, each strange and incredible but linked together by Gerda's determination to rescue her little friend. She finds him at last, stonily, icily cold, but her hot tears of grief melt the mischievous splinter, and Kay is restored to joy and love.

### Characteristics of Style

"The Snow Queen" is often ranked as Andersen's masterpiece, and indeed it exhibits

## VIEWPOINTS

Inventiveness, remember, is not to be judged by how *far out* the imagination of the writer may take his readers, but rather by the degree to which he can make the readers believe in the world he has created. And after they have believed, finally returning to their own world, to what measure then will their own world seem different to them?—James E. Higgins, *Beyond Words; Mystical Fancy in Children's Literature*, Teachers College Press, Columbia University, New York, 1970, p. 28.

Andersen's characteristic style at its best. Here are conversations so lively and natural that whether a Robber-maiden, a Buttercup, or a Reindeer speaks, you feel you have known her well. Like Gerda, you are even a bit apologetic because you cannot speak Ravenish to the Raven. No one has ever handled dialogue more easily and happily than Andersen. The characterizations often suggested by a conversation are swift and masterly. For instance, Kay's sudden change of heart after the splinter strikes him is apparent in his spiteful, angry words to poor Gerda:

> *"Why do you cry?" asked he; "you look so ugly when you cry. . . . Fie!" exclaimed he again, "this rose has an insect in it, and just look at this! after all they are ugly roses! and it is an ugly box they grow in!" Then he kicked the box and tore off the roses.*[2]

The wild Robber-maiden is curiously convincing with her biting and kicking, her sudden, grave reaching out toward kindness, but with her dagger handy, just in case. The weird people in this tale all come to life, sketched briefly, sometimes with a line of description but more often only through their own words. Andersen used description most

2. Rex Whistler edition of *Andersen's Fairy Tales*, p. 122. Published by Oxford University Press.

often for the landscape, and certainly nothing he has written excels the paragraph picturing the Snow Queen's palace:

> *The walls of the palace were formed of the driven snow, its doors and windows of the cutting winds; there were above a hundred halls, the largest of them many miles in extent, all illuminated by the Northern Lights; all alike vast, empty, icily cold, and dazzlingly white. . . . Vast, empty, and cold were the Snow Queen's chambers, and the Northern Lights flashed now high, now low, in regular gradations.*[3]

Andersen's *Fairy Tales* are not only good literature but they have about them a wholesome goodness which children need to believe in. The tales are moralistic but unobtrusively so, and the morals they exhibit are the humble ones of kindness, sincerity, and faith in God. The deeply religious note in many of these tales never seems forced or dragged in but is there as naturally as sunshine on the sand, warming everything. Andersen was not afraid to show children cruelty, sorrow, even death, but they are presented so gently that the children understand and are not hurt. He shows them rogues and fools along with hosts of kind, loving people, and he seems to be saying, "Well, this is the world. Which group will you join?" Paul Hazard says:

> *It is this inner life that gives the* Tales *their deep quality. From it also comes that exaltation which spreads through the soul of the readers. From it comes, finally, a marked quality of serenity. . . .*
>
> *The children are not mistaken. In these beautiful tales they find not only pleasure, but the law of their being and the feeling of the great role they have to fill. They themselves have been subjected to sorrow. They sense evil confusedly around them, in them; but this vivid suffering is only transitory and not enough to trouble their serenity. Their mission is to bring to the world a renewal of faith and hope.*[4]

3. Ibid., p. 147.
4. *Books, Children and Men* (Horn Book, 1944), pp. 104–105.

Beautifully illustrated editions of single stories are good introductions for children who might find the whole collection of Andersen's tales too formidable. Look, for example, at Erik Blegvad's *The Swineherd*, Marcia Brown's *The Steadfast Tin Soldier*, Virginia Lee Burton's *The Emperor's New Clothes*, Blair Lent's *The Little Match Girl*, Nancy Burkert's *The Fir Tree* and *The Nightingale* (the latter translated by Eva Le Gallienne), and Bill Sokol's *The Emperor and the Nightingale*.

## MODERN ADAPTATIONS OF OLD TALES

Andersen set such an admirable standard for the retelling of old tales that it is worth keeping in mind when we are called upon to judge the modern versions which are continually appearing. Andersen's adaptations are right because they make the stories suitable and understandable for children while maintaining the integrity of the source. Of course, there must occasionally be some changes in these old tales, created by adults for adults, if they are to be read or told to children. Andersen in "Great Claus and Little Claus" endows the husband of the faithless wife with a special antipathy for "sextons"; so the infidelity motive is amusingly glossed over. Yet this change does not interfere in any way with the essential body or style of the story. This is the standard Joseph Jacobs adhered to and defended. He altered a folk tale in such ways as to make it suitable and understandable to children without changing the core of the story. In using the sources of traditional material, Jacobs and Andersen set a commendable standard. On the other hand, if the tale requires many changes, it is probably unsuitable for children either in content or style.

## MODERN TALES IN FOLK-TALE STYLE

Hans Andersen was steeped in folk-tale tradition. He could create new stories in a similar vein, and his inventions seem to have inspired a few writers in almost every generation.

## JOHN RUSKIN

*The King of the Golden River*

John Ruskin tried writing "The King of the Golden River" (1841) in the old folk-tale style. It is for children ten to fourteen, but many of them avoid it because of its length and reading difficulty. This powerful tale with something of the somber, frightening air of the medieval legends tells the story of little Gluck, a cinder lad tormented by his cruel older brothers, Hans and Schwartz. A mysterious visitor, the South-West Wind, is treated kindly by Gluck and meanly by the brothers, and the stranger vows revenge. How Gluck discovers in the melting golden mug the King of the Golden River and with the King's help wins back his inheritance makes an exciting tale. The evil brothers are disposed of in good folk-tale style and Gluck is safe forever. This story is well written and genuinely dramatic. Children should have it read aloud to them or if they wish to read it themselves, they may need a simpler version than the original.

*Illustration by Fritz Kredel. From* The King of the Golden River *by John Ruskin. Copyright 1946 by The World Publishing Company. Reprinted by permission of the publisher. (Original in color)*

## HOWARD PYLE

*Pepper and Salt*

No one, not even Andersen, has been more successful in creating new fairy tales in the old folk-tale patterns than Howard Pyle has been in his delightful *Pepper and Salt* (1885). This has long been a favorite book with teachers and parents who like to tell stories or read them aloud. There are eight stories interspersed with clever verses and equally clever drawings by the author. Humor is the prevailing tone of the whole book. Older children like to read it for themselves as well as to hear the stories read or told.

The first tale is typical of the way Pyle used old folk motifs with new and humorous invention. In "The Skillful Huntsman," Jacob, a poor and supposedly stupid lad, wishes to marry Gretchen, the Mayor's daughter. The Mayor, to get rid of him, sets Jacob a series of tasks, the first of which is to shoot the whiskers off a running hare. Jacob meets a stranger clad in red with cloven hoofs. The stranger offers to make Jacob the greatest of all hunters and to obey his commands for ten years if at the end of that time Jacob will go with him. The lad agrees on one condition: at the end of the ten years, if the stranger cannot answer Jacob's question, Jacob is free. The bargain is made; Jacob accomplishes every task and marries Gretchen. At the end of the fateful ten years, the stranger comes for Jacob. They agree to enjoy one last hunt, and the stranger is to tell Jacob what to shoot. Gretchen appears in the far distance, all covered with feathers, and he of the cloven hoof commands Jacob to shoot. "But what is it?" asks Jacob innocently. The baffled gentleman in red is obliged to admit he does not know, and so Jacob is free. The whole tale is lightly and wittily told, with old motifs in new and amusing dress.

## OSCAR WILDE

*The Happy Prince and Other Fairy Tales*

"Beauty and the Beast," "The King of the Golden River," and Pyle's stories are all written with the directness of traditional tales and legends. But Oscar Wilde's fairy tales are art forms, polished and adult. Two of Wilde's allegories, "The Happy Prince" and "The Selfish Giant," have been rather generally used for storytelling in the elementary school. Both are sentimental and melancholy, but "The Selfish Giant" has all the earmarks of a child's fairy tale. The story is about a beautiful garden enjoyed by the children until its owner, a very selfish giant, comes home and puts up a sign, "Trespassers Will Be Prosecuted." Then winter comes to the garden and remains there as long as the children are locked out. One day the giant discovers that the garden is blooming with flowers and children. He rushes out and encounters a little boy who touches the giant's hard heart. He lifts the child into a tree and bids him come daily to the garden with his little friends. After the giant has grown old, he sees his little friend again. Hastening to the child, he discovers the prints of nails on the hands and on the little feet.

> *"Who hath dared to wound thee?" cried the Giant; "tell me, that I may take my big sword and slay him."*
>
> *"Nay!" answered the child; "but these are the wounds of Love."*
>
> *"Who art thou?" said the Giant, and a strange awe fell on him, and he knelt before the little child.*
>
> *And the child smiled on the Giant, and said to him, "You let me play once in your garden; to-day you shall come with me to my garden, which is Paradise."*
>
> *And when the children ran in that afternoon, they found the Giant lying dead under the tree, all covered with white blossoms.*

If children understand that the Child is supposed to be Jesus, they are still baffled by this conclusion and uncomfortable because of the mixture of religious ideas with a fairy tale. But most children miss the point entirely and find the nail prints merely confusing and irrelevant. The significance of "the wounds of Love"—that only those we love and care for can wound us deeply—is also difficult for children.

Almost seventy years later, in 1955, Clyde Bulla told a similar story in *The Poppy Seeds*. A suspicious old man who in an arid land kept his clear spring to himself learned that to share is to be rich. The poppy seeds that the boy Pablo had dropped in fright grew and blossomed by the spring. The moral is evident, but not underscored, and children can understand every aspect of the conflict.

This renewed simplicity is characteristic of children's literature in the twentieth century. One possible explanation is that beginning in the early nineteen hundreds there was a growing awareness of the child. G. Stanley Hall had launched a new science, Child Study, and the consciousness of the child as a child rather than as a small adult was penetrating the literate world. Whatever the cause, the turn of the century brought some delightful new fanciful tales for children.

## WANDA GÁG

*Millions of Cats*

In 1928, the inimitable *Millions of Cats* appeared, a modern invention in folk-tale style.

Wanda Gág had been brought up on the traditional tales; so she had the feeling for plot and also for the fine flowing rhythms of storytelling. This same rhythm is as characteristic of her illustrations as it is of her text and makes a strong appeal to young children.

*Millions of Cats* concerns a little old man and a little old woman who wanted a little cat. The old man went out to choose one, but because he could not decide which was the prettiest he came home with "hundreds of cats, thousands of cats, millions and billions and trillions of cats." Notice the walking rhythm of that refrain which goes all through the story. How the jealous creatures destroyed each other and left only one scrawny little cat, too homely to be in the fight, and how the little old man and woman petted and fed the skinny little thing until it became a creature of beauty make the tale. Ah, but the text and the pictures! There are strength and tenderness in these illustrations, simplicity and directness in the words. Together they make a picture story so gently humorous in content, so pleasant to the eyes and the ears, so happily concluded, that adults who read it aloud and show the pictures enjoy it quite as much as the children.

*Snippy and Snappy, The Funny Thing,* and *Nothing at All* are all good stories in Miss Gág's own particular rhythms, and the pictures have the same deceptive simplicity found in the text. Children enjoy every one of them and should probably have them all.

*Illustration from Wanda Gág's* Millions of Cats. *Copyright 1928 by Coward-McCann, Inc. Copyright renewed 1956 by Wanda Gág. Reproduced with permission of the publisher.*

## JAMES THURBER

*The Great Quillow*
*Many Moons*
*The Thirteen Clocks*

The humor James Thurber showed as a cartoonist and as the author of delightfully satiric fables is evident in his fairy tales for children. *The Great Quillow* (1944) is about a toymaker who is the only person in his village clever enough to think of a way to rid the town of a voracious giant who is depleting the communal larder. Quillow's attendance at meetings of the town council enables Thurber to poke sly fun at the prim requirements of parliamentary procedure.

In *Many Moons* (1943), for which Louis Slobodkin's illustrations won the Caldecott Medal, the Little Princess Lenore lies ill, saying that only if she can have the moon will she recover. The King consults his assorted wise men, who are equally long-winded, opinionated, and useless. Only the jester has the wisdom to consult the Princess, who makes it clear that to her the moon is golden and small, since she can obscure it by holding up her thumb. She is delighted with the small golden globe the jester brings. Children can enjoy the story for its restrained whimsy even if they don't appreciate the conflicting theories of the sages about what the moon is like and about how far away it is.

In *The Thirteen Clocks,* Thurber plays with the idea of time stopping. In order to marry the Princess, her suitor must obtain the thousand jewels to start the clocks that had been stopped so that it would never be Now. *The Wonderful O* is usually most appreciated by readers who are interested in words and word play, since the elimination of the letter "o" in words and the objects to which the words refer is the theme of the story.

## J. R. R. TOLKIEN

*The Hobbit*

No other fantasy of our time has appealed to as broad an age range of readers as has *The Hobbit* (1937); children are enthralled by it, and adults probe and discuss the inner meanings of the book and of its companion tale, *The Lord of the Rings*, a complex three-volume sequel. Professor Tolkien is an eminent philologist and an authority on myth and saga, and his knowledge provides so firm a base for the mood and style of his writing that there is no need for scholarly demonstration. Middle-earth is. Tolkien writes of it as easily as one writes about one's own home, and the familiarity of approach lends credence to the world he has created.

The hero of *The Hobbit* is Bilbo Baggins, a little creature who is neat and quiet, who loves his material comforts, and who has no desire to do great deeds. When he is tricked into going along on a quest, however, the little hobbit rises to the occasion to show that common man (or hobbit) has heroism within him. The story begins with a cozy description of the sedentary Bilbo, a very respectable character with just the slightest trace of the wildness reputed to be enjoyed by his mother's family, the Tooks. And Bilbo has his Tookish moments. Bilbo is selected by the wizard Gandalf to join a group of dwarfs who are going on a mission to recover their inheritance, which is being held by the ferocious dragon, Smaug. Bilbo is to be the burglar, and this is how the long and hazardous quest begins.

There are several qualities that contribute to the stature of *The Hobbit* in addition to the fact that its author is a natural storyteller with authoritative knowledge. The adventures are exciting, the characters are differentiated and distinctive, and the book bubbles with humor. One of the amusing qualities is the aptness of the invented personal and place names. Bilbo's mother's maiden name is Belladonna Took, perfectly in accord with her reputation as a hobbit who had had a few adventures before she settled down as Mrs. Baggins. And what an admirable name for a dragon—Smaug, and what an equally appropriate name for his lair—the Desolation of Smaug. Perhaps a special appeal lies in the very fact that Bilbo Baggins is a quiet little creature, and that his achievements are due to a stout heart, tenacity, and loyalty to his friends rather than to great strength or brilliance. He puts heroism within the grasp of each reader.

The Hill: Hobbiton across the Water

*Illustration by J. R. R. Tolkien. From* The Hobbit *by J. R. R. Tolkien. Copyright © 1938. Reproduced by permission of Houghton Mifflin Company.*

## LLOYD ALEXANDER

The *Prydain* Books
*The Marvelous Misadventures of Sebastian*
*The King's Fountain*

Lloyd Alexander had planned, in writing about Prydain, only to adapt the Welsh legends he loved, but he became so engrossed in the project that, as he said in his Newbery Medal acceptance speech, "it grew into something much more than ambition."

The first of the Prydain five-book cycle is *The Book of Three* (1964), in which Taran, the hero, is introduced. Taran, Assistant Pig-Keeper, does not have great status, but of course few pig-keepers are responsible for such a pig as Hen Wen, who utters prophesies by using letter sticks. When Taran goes forth with the great warrior Gwydion to fight against the evil Horned King, they must first find the lost Hen Wen to learn from her of the king. The Horned King has sworn allegiance to Arawn, Lord of the Land of Death. On the quest, Taran and Gwydion are joined by the capricious Princess Eilonwy, the Caliban-like creature Gurgi, and the boastful harpist, Fflewddur Flam.

Each of the characters is strongly drawn. Unforgettable is the crafty, toadying, whimpering but loyal Gurgi, whose rhymed inventions delight young readers (listen, for example, to "O joyous crunchings and munchings!" and "Gurgi hears no thrummings and drummings but cooings and mooings!"). The histrionics of Fflewddur have a touch of Mr. Micawber as he pontificates and prevaricates, but his harp, given him by Taliesin, is a rein on his fancy, for whenever he lies, a string breaks.

In the second book, *The Black Cauldron*, Taran again goes on a quest, this time to the Land of Death, where Arawn creates his Cauldron-Born creatures who live on after death. In *The Castle of Llyr*, the Princess Eilonwy is kidnapped, and it is then that Taran first realizes his love for that obstreperous hoyden. In *Taran Wanderer* the hero goes forth to seek his true identity and learns that his worth, whatever it is, is dependent on his ability and his accomplishments rather than on his position. The final book in the Prydain cycle, *The High King* (1968), was awarded the Newbery Medal. It tells of the last conflict between Taran and the Death Lord.

The stories are marvelously inventive, written in an ornate and sophisticated style. The pace, the strength of the characterizations, and the humor of the dialogue are sustained throughout, and each of the books has a host of vivid minor characters. It is not until the last book, however, that the muted theme of the hero, the champion of good against the forces of evil, emerges in triumphant pianoforte.

Several of the characters from the Land of Prydain appear in two books for younger

### VIEWPOINTS

Melancholy men, they say, are the most incisive humorists; by the same token, writers of fantasy must be, within their own frame of work, hardheaded realists. What appears gossamer is, underneath, solid as prestressed concrete. . . .

Once committed to his imaginary kingdom, the writer is not a monarch but a subject. Characters must appear plausible in their own setting, and the writer must go along with their inner logic. Happenings should have logical implications. Details should be tested for consistency. Shall animals speak? If so, do *all* animals speak? If not, then which—and how? Above all, why? Is it essential to the story, or lamely cute? Are there enchantments? How powerful? If an enchanter can perform such-and-such, can he not also do so-and-so?

. . . And, as in all literature, characters are what ultimately count. . . . Fantasy . . . goes right to the core of a character, to extract the essence, the very taste of an individual personality. This may be one of the things that makes good fantasy so convincing.—Lloyd Alexander, "The Flat-heeled Muse," *The Horn Book*, April 1965, pp. 142, 143–144, 145.

readers. *The Truthful Harp* describes the beginning of Fflewddur Flam's career as a wandering bard and his first experiences with the magical harp. *Coll and His White Pig* is based on an incident in *The Book of Three*. Although these stories are much more simply written than the books in the cycle, they have the same mixture of comedy and high adventure.

Another gay and intricate fantasy, *The Marvelous Misadventures of Sebastian* (1970), received the National Book Award. This tale of a young eighteenth-century musician who goes off on a series of romantic adventures has less of the legendary quality than the Prydain books, and its humor approaches tall-tale exaggeration.

*The King's Fountain* is a picture book, with lovely illustrations by Ezra Jack Keats complementing the poetic quality of the text. A poor and simple man asks several important people to beg the king not to go ahead with his plans for a fountain to be placed on the grounds of his hilltop palace because the fountain would deprive the townspeople of water. Since no one will go, he goes himself and is granted his wish. The writing has a folk-tale cadence, and the message—that some things will never get done unless one does them oneself—is clear but does not obtrude on the story, thanks to the leaven of humor.

## Other Examples of Stories in Folk-Tale Style

On the whole, not many stories are being written in folk-tale style today, but some exceedingly good ones appear from time to time. Louis Slobodkin's *The Amiable Giant* and Margaret Friskey's *Seven Diving Ducks* have long been popular. Will and Nicolas' *Finders Keepers*, the amusing story of two dogs that found the same bone and asked for advice to decide which should keep it, belongs to this same group of picture stories for the youngest children.

Antoine de Saint-Exupéry's *The Little Prince* is a poetic fairy tale without a plot, whimsical and sophisticated in its concern with the inconsistencies of human behavior. The author writes of the small prince who left his planet to visit the earth and tells much of the story in dialogue form. The lack of action and the allusiveness of the dialogue limit the book to those readers who can appreciate the spiritual values and the writing style—readers who include not only devoted children but many adults.

*The Animal Family*, by Randall Jarrell, also has a poetic quality but is more cohesive in plot and is more smoothly written than *The Little Prince*. Alone in his home near the sea, the hunter falls in love with a mermaid, who comes to live with him. Their family is increased by a shipwrecked boy, a bear, and a lynx, and together they live in love and peace. The writing has a subtle simplicity and ingenuous humor that succeed both in making the element of fantasy believable and in avoiding any semblance of sentimentality.

In Richard Bennett's Irish fairy tale *Shawneen and the Gander*, Shawneen catches a leprechaun and gets a goose's egg. It hatches into a very demon of a gander, which is eventually the cause of Shawneen's getting the bugle he wants.

Natalie Babbitt's *Kneeknock Rise*, in which a whole village is terrified by the terrible Megrimum (that doesn't exist), and her more poetic *The Search for Delicious* are both lightened by humor. Such adventures tickle children eight to ten, the same age group that delights in Dr. Seuss' *The 500 Hats of Bartholomew Cubbins*, Elizabeth Enright's romantic fairy tale *Tatsinda*, and Carl Sandburg's *Rootabaga Stories* with their garrulous humor. A gay picture-book version of one of Sandburg's tales, "The Wedding Procession of the Rag Doll and the Broom Handle and Who Was in It" is amusingly illustrated by Harriet Pincus.

In *Alphonse, That Bearded One*, Natalie Carlson tells children ten to twelve the entertaining story of a woodsman who trains a

*Illustration copyright © 1967 by Harriet Pincus. Reproduced from her illustrated volume of* The Wedding Procession of the Rag Doll and the Broom Handle and Who Was in It *by Carl Sandburg, by permission of Harcourt Brace Jovanovich, Inc. (Original in color)*

bear to drill like a soldier and to take his place in the army. The situations are hilarious, with Alphonse the bear always triumphant.

Barbara Leonie Picard's fairy tales have the true cadence and spirit of folk material. Her *The Faun and the Woodcutter's Daughter, The Goldfinch Garden, The Lady of the Linden Tree,* and *The Mermaid and the Simpleton* have many familiar folk-tale themes, but they are freshly conceived, the stories are written with a grave simplicity that makes them particularly enjoyable when read aloud, and they are a small gold mine for storytellers.

Because of its stories within the story, another good book for reading aloud is Elizabeth Coatsworth's *Cricket and the Emperor's Son.* Cricket, a small apprentice, tells a tale each night to the little Prince who cannot sleep, the stories coming from a magic paper that never comes to an end. Miss Coatsworth's Newbery Medal book, *The Cat Who Went to Heaven,* which also has a Japanese setting, is about a struggling young artist who is commissioned to paint a picture for the temple. The temple priest refuses to accept the picture because a cat is in the procession of animals that approach Buddha. The little household cat that had been a model for the picture dies, and a miracle occurs: the painted cat is now at the head of the procession, under the hand of Buddha, which is stretched out in blessing.

These are just a few typical examples of the original modern tales in traditional style which are successful with children. There are plenty of contrived examples available also, but these come and go in short order. Unless an author has grown up with the oral tradition of folk tales, his own stories are not likely to come out in that style. If he tries consciously to reproduce it, the results are likely to be obviously labored.

## MODERN STORIES OF TALKING BEASTS

The talking beasts in the old tales were, on the whole, a cheerful lot. Silly creatures were liquidated, but the wise pig survived, and smart billy-goats gained the grassy hillside in spite of the troll. There were no brooding and no melancholy until Andersen's *Fairy Tales.* The Ugly Duckling not only was mistreated by others but suffered spiritually. In the two English talking-beast masterpieces, *The Tale of Peter Rabbit* and *The Wind in the Willows,* there are also animals with limitations, who make mistakes and commit follies but who shake them off with blithe determination. It is these lively tales rather than "The Ugly

Duckling" which have set the pattern for recent beast tales.

## BEATRIX POTTER

*The Tale of Peter Rabbit*

Beatrix Potter, English novelist of the nursery and cheerful interpreter of small animals to small children, has left her own account of how she happened to write her classic, *The Tale of Peter Rabbit*. In a letter to *The Horn Book*, May 1929, she said:

*. . . About 1893 I was interested in a little invalid child. . . . I used to write letters with pen and ink scribbles, and one of the letters was Peter Rabbit.*

*Noel has got them yet; he grew up and became a hard-working clergyman in a London poor parish. After a time there began to be a vogue for small books, and I thought "Peter" might do as well as some that were being published. But I did not find any publisher who agreed with me. The manuscript—nearly word for word the same, but with only outline illustrations—was returned with or without thanks by at least six firms. Then I drew my savings out of the post office savings bank, and got an edition of 450 copies printed. I think the engraving and printing cost me about £11. It caused a good deal of amusement amongst my relations and friends. I made about £12 or £14 by selling copies to obliging aunts. I showed this privately printed black and white book to Messers. F. Warne & Co., and the following year, 1901, they brought out the first coloured edition.*

Commenting on her method of writing, Miss Potter adds:

*My usual way of writing is to scribble, and cut out, and write it again and again. The shorter and plainer the better. And read the Bible (unrevised version and Old Testament) if I feel my style wants chastening.*

These apparently simple little stories[5] of Beatrix Potter's the children learn by heart in no time, and how they relish the names of her characters: Flopsy, Mopsy, and Cottontail, Jemima Puddle-Duck, Pigling Bland, Mrs. Tiggy-Winkle, Benjamin Bunny, Peter Rabbit. The stories are invariably built on the never-fail formula of a beginning, a middle, and an end, with plenty of suspense to bring sighs of relief when the conclusion is finally reached. Children chuckle over the funny characters, the absurd predicaments, and the narrow escapes. They pore over the clear watercolor illustrations, which are full of action. Even at four they absorb delightedly the lovely details of landscape, old houses, fine old furniture and china, and at forty, learn why they liked them.

If you were to play one of those wretched games in which you can choose only two books for a five-year-old marooned on a desert island, you would feel obliged to choose *Mother Goose* and *The Tale of Peter Rabbit*. These are the favorites of most children. Peter's adventures he can soon "read" for himself, he knows them so well; but the charms of that humorous and exciting plot never grow stale; disobedient Peter in Mr. MacGregor's cabbage patch, very complacent at first, then pursued and thoroughly frightened but still keeping his wits about him; next, Peter hiding in the watering can, and, finally, Peter at home, properly repentant, chastened by his mother, but snug in bed at last and secure. Here is a cheerful Prodigal Son, child-size.

When Beatrix Potter died in December 1943, such papers as the London *Times* and the New York *Herald Tribune* praised the reality of the little world she had brought so vividly to life and praised her excellent prose. Certainly the children for whom her little books provide an introduction to the world of animals are never going to see a rabbit skipping hurriedly out of their gardens without amusement and sympathy, for children who have known Beatrix Potter's books know this world of timid, scampering creatures as a world touchingly like their own.

5. Among the companion volumes to *Peter Rabbit* are *The Tale of Benjamin Bunny*, *The Tailor of Gloucester*, *The Tale of Squirrel Nutkin*, *The Tale of Jemima Puddle-Duck*, *The Tale of Mrs. Tiggy-Winkle*, and *The Tale of Tom Kitten*.

## RUDYARD KIPLING

*Just So Stories*

Living in India for many years and thus familiar with the Indian Jatakas and the usual pattern of a "why" story, Rudyard Kipling wrote the *Just So Stories* (1902), his own collection of explanatory tales, in amusing imitation of the old form. "How the Whale Got His Throat" and "How the Leopard Got His Spots" begin seriously and end with a logical kind of nonsense that reminds us of *Alice.*

"The Sing-song of Old Man Kangaroo" explains that the Kangaroo got his long tail because a certain Yellow-Dog Dingo chased him halfway across the world, ending in Australia, where they were both too exhausted to run another step. By that time, the Kangaroo's hind legs had lengthened, and he had grown a long and powerful tail which helped him to jump, but he complained to the god Nqong:

> *"He's chased me out of the homes of my childhood; he's chased me out of my regular meal-times; he's altered my shape so I'll never get it back; and he's played the Old Scratch with my legs."*

Yellow-Dog Dingo complains, too, and, when left together, each says, "That's *your* fault."

"The Cat that Walked by Himself, walking by his wild lone through the Wet Wild Woods and waving his wild tail" is droll and subtly true, but the children's favorite is "The Elephant's Child." This story explains how the elephant's "blackish, bulgy nose, as big as a boot" grew to the long trunk we see today. It was all because of the "'satiable curtiosity" of the Elephant's Child, who, after innumerable spankings, ran away to seek knowledge by the banks of "the great grey-green, greasy Limpopo River."

These are stories to be read aloud. They are cadenced, rhythmic, and full of handsome, high-sounding words, which are both mouth-filling and ear-delighting. It isn't nec-

*From Just So Stories by Rudyard Kipling, illustrated by Nicolas. Copyright 1952 by Artists and Writers Guild, Inc. Reproduced by permission of Doubleday & Company, Inc., New York, and A. P. Watts & Sons, London. (Original in color)*

essary to stop and explain every word. The children will learn them, even as they learn "Hey diddle diddle," and the funny meanings will follow the funny sounds, gradually. The mock-serious tone of these pseudo-folk tales adds to their humor. Once children catch on to the grandiloquent style and absurd meanings, they love them. These stories are a good cure for too tight, humorless literalness. No child should miss hearing some of them, certainly "The Elephant's Child" for one.

## KENNETH GRAHAME

*The Wind in the Willows*

Another pleasant thing about Peter Rabbit is that he paves the way for *The Wind in the Willows* (1908). Children who loved Peter are more likely to adopt Mole and Rat and Toad a few years later.

Kenneth Grahame was a lovable, literary, out-of-doorish sort of Englishman with a gift for storytelling. For his small son, nicknamed "Mouse," he used to spin continuous tales at bedtime. Once Mouse refused to go to the seaside because his trip would interrupt the adventures of Toad, to which he was listening. In order to persuade the child to go, his father promised to send him a chapter in the mail daily, and this he did. Sensing their value, the nursery governess who read the chapters to Mouse mailed them back to Mrs. Grahame for safekeeping. From these letters and bedtime stories grew *The Wind in the Willows*.

Each chapter tells a complete adventure of the four friends—Mole, kindly old Water Rat, shy Badger, and rich, conceited, troublesome Toad. The friends "mess around in boats," have picnics, dine elegantly at Toad Hall, get lost in the Wild Wood, rescue Toad from his life of folly, and even encounter once "The Piper at the Gates of Dawn." But how explain the appeal of this book? Of course, not all children like it, but those who do are likely to value it above most other books.

In the first place, the sensory experiences make the reader one with Mole or Ratty. You can just feel the sunshine hot on your fur; you, too, waggle your toes from sheer happiness or stretch out on some cool dock leaves or explore the silent silver kingdom of the moonlit river. Earth and water, a green world of woods and meadows speak to you from every page.

The humor of *The Wind in the Willows*, particularly the humor of the conversations, is a little subtle for some children but delights those who do catch it. Fortunately, Toad's antics, his bemused pursuit of his latest fad, his ridiculous conceit, the scrapes he gets into, and the efforts of his friends to reform him furnish enough broad comedy to satisfy everyone. The dialogue is so natural you might know that it grew not from written but from oral composition. It is that of the born storyteller, used to children's predilection for talk, improvising dialogue in his own fluent, individual vein. What talk it is—funniest when it is most grave, revealing more of the speaker than any explanatory paragraph.

For example, Toad, having dragged his friends Rat and Mole on an uncomfortable journey across the country in a cart, remarks fatuously:

*". . . This is the real life for a gentleman! Talk about your old river!"*

*"I don't talk about my river," replied the patient Rat. "You know I don't, Toad. But I think about it," he added pathetically, in a lower tone: "I think about it—all the time!"*

*The Mole reached out from under his blanket, felt for the Rat's paw in the darkness, and gave it a squeeze. "I'll do whatever you like, Ratty," he whispered. "Shall we run away to-morrow morning, quite early—very early—and go back to our dear old hole on the river?"*

*"No, no, we'll see it out," whispered back the Rat. "Thanks awfully, but I ought to stick by Toad till this trip is ended. It wouldn't be safe for him*

*to be left to himself. It won't take very long. His fads never do. Good night!"*[6]

No preaching about the duties of a friend, just patient, enduring friendship, loyal in service and understanding!

These conversations are as much a part of the style as the descriptions which make the book one of the masterpieces of English for readers of any age. The famous chapter in which Rat and Toad meet "The Piper at the Gates of Dawn" is shot through with poetic descriptions that are notable for their rhythm, alliteration, and assonance. After the black darkness of the river at night the friends see the moon rise:

*The line of the horizon was clear and hard against the sky, and in one particular quarter it showed black against a silvery climbing phosphorescence that grew and grew. At last, over the rim of the waiting earth the moon lifted with slow majesty till it swung clear of the horizon and rode off, free of moorings; and once more they began to see surfaces—meadows widespread, and quiet gardens, and the river itself from bank to bank, all softly disclosed, all washed clean of mystery and terror, all radiant again as by day, but with a difference that was tremendous. Their old haunts greeted them again in other raiment, as if they had slipped away and put on this pure new apparel and come quietly back, smiling as they shyly waited to see if they would be recognized again under it.*

None of these things—sensory appeal, humor, dialogue, or descriptions—accounts for the hold this book takes upon the heart and the imagination. As in Andersen's *Fairy Tales*, it is the inner significance of the story that counts. First of all, there is the warm friendliness of the animals. Each one makes mistakes, has his limitations, but no one ever rejects a friend. The three put up with Toad's escapades as long as they can; then they join together and reform him in spite of himself. Together they endure perils and pitfalls and come safely through only because they help each other. This continual kindliness, the overlooking of other people's mistakes, and the sympathetic understanding which pervade every page warm the reader's heart. No hidden meaning or didacticism here, just decent people who happen to wear tails and fur treating each other with decent kindliness.

This is a warm book, a book to read when the heart is chilled or the spirit shaken. It is one of the most reassuring and comforting books in all literature.

Why did Kenneth Grahame write only this one story for children?[7] (His delightful story "The Reluctant Dragon" was originally a chapter in *Dream Days*, an adult book. It has been published as a children's book.) Talking to an American admirer, he said:

*I am not a professional writer. I never have been, and I never will be, by reason of the accident that I don't need any money. I do not care for notoriety: in fact, it is distasteful to me. . . .*

*What, then, is the use of writing for a person like myself? . . . A large amount of what Thoreau called life went into the making of many of these playful pages. To toil at making sentences means to sit indoors for many hours, cramped above a desk. Yet, out of doors, the wind may be singing through the willows, and my favourite sow may be preparing to deliver a large litter in the fullness of the moon.*[8]

So he left children only one book, a masterpiece, and an American admirer and critic said of him when he died:

*And yet it is a truth that, on that day, the translators of the King James version of the Bible, seated at an eternal council-table, admitted to their fellowship the last great master of English prose. . . .*[9]

6. This passage and the following one are from *The Wind in the Willows* by Kenneth Grahame; copyright 1908, 1935 by the publishers, Charles Scribner's Sons.

7. He also wrote *Dream Days* and *The Golden Age*, which were about children.

8. Quoted by Elspeth Grahame, in *First Whisper of "The Wind in the Willows,"* pp. 31–32, from an article by Clayton Hamilton in *The Bookman*, January 1933.

9. Ibid., p. 33.

Most children like this book if it is read aloud to them as it was told to Mouse, a chapter at a time. For this is decidedly a book to be shared. Its richness grows when it is mulled over, discussed, and savored to the full. If a child likes it, then it is one book he ought to own—in his favorite edition, illustrated by Arthur Rackham, or Ernest Shepard, or Paul Bransom, or whichever artist he prefers. Certainly if *The Wind in the Willows* is enjoyed in childhood, it will be reread when the child is grown up, and it will be passed on to his children as a precious inheritance.

## WALTER DE LA MARE

*The Three Royal Monkeys*

It is difficult to classify Walter de la Mare's *The Three Royal Monkeys*—originally entitled *The Three Mulla Mulgars* (1919)—but since it seems a not-too-distant relative of "The Ugly Duckling," it is grouped here with the other talking beasts. It has the same curious blend of realism and fantasy that characterizes the poet's novel *Memoirs of a Midget*. Grave and completely convincing fantasy is characteristic of Walter de la Mare's verse and prose, and is bewildering to some readers.

*The Three Royal Monkeys* is a long story dealing with the adventures of three little monkeys, or Mulgars, of the Blood Royal, who go in search of their father, a prince from the Valley of Tishnar. Tishnar stands for hope and beauty and peace beyond our world. Little Nod, the youngest of the royal monkeys, is a Nizza-neela; that is, he has magic about him, and he carries the Wonderstone, which marks him as a true prince. The brothers suffer endless hardships, but always their bravery and Nod's magic bring them through. They know that they have reached their father's land of Tishnar when they suddenly meet "a Mulgar of a presence and a strangeness, who was without doubt of the Kingdom of Assasimmon."

The book is full of wise sayings. The unhappy panther, dressed in man's clothes, is asked if she is comfortable and replies:

> *"O my friend, my scarce-wise Mulgar-royal, when did you ever hear that grand clothes were comfortable?"*

Later, Nod remarks philosophically,

> *"Who is there wise that was not once foolish?"*

But it is the descriptions that give it a strange eerie beauty unlike any other:

> *Over the swamp stood a shaving of moon, clear as a bow of silver. And all about, on every*

*Illustration by Dorothy Lathrop. From* The Three Mulla-Mulgars *by Walter de la Mare. Copyright, 1919, by Alfred A. Knopf, Inc. Reproduced by permission of the publisher. (Original in color)*

*twig, on every thorn, and leaf, and pebble; all along the nine-foot grasses, on every cushion and touch of bark, even on the walls of their hut, lay this spangling fiery meal of Tishnar—frost.*

Comparatively few youngsters—probably none under twelve—will read this long story for themselves. But those who have the capacity to enjoy such a book will discover that when a poet tells a fairy tale, the result is often a strange and heady enchantment.

## MARIE HALL ETS

*Mister Penny*

The hero of *Mister Penny* (1935) has to work hard in the factory of Friend-in-Need Safety-Pins in order to support his family of lazy, good-for-nothing animals. He loves them all—Limpy the horse, Mooloo the cow with beautiful eyes, Splop the goat, Pugwug the pig, Mimkin the lamb, Chukluk and Doody the hen and rooster. Yet the varmints do nothing to assist Mr. Penny. Instead, they get into the most expensive kind of mischief. Finally, when they destroy the rich neighbor's garden, old Thunderstorm delivers his frightful ultimatum. He'll take the worthless animals unless his garden is completely restored. The animals decide that even work is preferable to falling into the hands of old Thunderstorm. So they firmly resolve to work! A completely black page bears the caption "Here they are working in the neighbor's garden"—at night. Before the time limit elapses they have not only completely restored old Thunderstorm's garden, but they have become so enthusiastic over their labors and their successes that they go right on and make a splendid garden for Mr. Penny, too.

The story ends on a note of triumph. Mister Penny is out of the Friend-in-Need factory forever. He is installed in a fine new house, too, which everyone comes to look at because, besides climbing roses and a superb garden, the pink house boasts a separate door for each one of the animals and one for Mr. Penny—seven doors in all. The villagers think it a little queer, but they have to admit "They're the happiest family in Wuddle." This little fable about the satisfaction that comes from working and helping is a kindly tale and is delightfully humorous.

In similar vein is Marie Hall Ets' story of the animals who saved the hero of *Mr. T. W. Anthony Woo* from the interference of a meddlesome sister. *In the Forest* and *Another Day* are slight but charming stories for the nursery child, for whom Mrs. Ets is writing and illustrating some beautiful books. Her talking beasts have been admirable, and in *Play with Me* they have ceased to talk but are equally effective.

## ROBERT LAWSON

*Ben and Me*
*Rabbit Hill*

Robert Lawson, with his easy storytelling style and beautiful illustrations, added much to the glory of the talking-beast tale. The children consider *Ben and Me* (1939) one of the genuinely "funny books." These biographical memoirs of Benjamin Franklin are supposedly written by Amos, a cheeky mouse who modestly admits that he supplied Ben with most of his ideas. Take that little matter of the stove, for instance. They were almost frozen and Ben had a bad case of sniffles when Amos thought out the idea of a stove. Ben was a little slow at catching on but finally worked out a very satisfactory contraption. Amos admits that he thoroughly disapproved of Ben's experiments with electricity, but he stuck by his friend in spite of many a shock and some novel results caused by Amos' interference. The mouse, tucked snugly away in the famous fur cap, appeared at the French court with Ben. What Amos did there is too fearful to relate.

A series of these fantastic biographies followed, of which the best one by far is *Mr.*

*Revere and I* (1953). Unlike *Ben and Me*, Paul Revere's story is told by a cultured English horse who loathed the "American peasants" when he first landed in Boston. But after he falls into Revere's hands, he becomes an ardent patriot. He even carries Revere on his fateful ride in spite of the silversmith's atrocious horsemanship. It is quite possible that children will get as much from this picture of the American Revolution as from some of their histories.

Good as these humorous biographies are, Mr. Lawson really came into his own as a creative writer with *Rabbit Hill* (1944), a Newbery Medal winner. This is the story of Father and Mother Rabbit, their high-leaping son, Little Georgie, and an aged Uncle Analdas, who are the leading characters, with Willie Fieldmouse and Porkey the Woodchuck playing important parts. The story begins with the pleasant rumor that new folks are moving into the big house. The question is, what kind of folks will they turn out to be—mean and pinching, or planting folks with a thought for the small creatures who have always lived on the hill? The new folks begin well with a sign "Please Drive Carefully on Account of Small Animals." They plant gardens without fences, sow fields without traps, provide generous "garbidge," and permit no poison. They rescue little Willie from drowning and Little Georgie from an automobile accident. Their crowning beneficence is a beautiful pool and feeding station for their furry and feathered friends, presided over by the good St. Francis—a little sanctuary which bears the kindly legend "There is enough for all."

*The Tough Winter* (1954) is the sequel to *Rabbit Hill*. It tells a moving story of what happens to small beasts when snow and ice last too long and there are no kind-hearted human beings to help. If ever there was a plea for aid to winterbound beasts, it is this story.

These books may not have the superlative literary qualities of *The Wind in the Willows*, but they are exceedingly well written and marvelously illustrated. All of the animals, from suspicious Uncle Analdas to worrying Mother Rabbit, are delightfully individualized. Their precarious lives, their small needs, and their many hardships are sympathetically related, and the happy conclusions are not too idealistic, as anyone can testify who has harbored wild creatures. These stories and their illustrations should do more than any lectures to develop in young children a feeling of tenderness and regard for small animals.

To fully appreciate the range and power in Mr. Lawson's pictures of animals, you will need to examine all of his illustrated books. *Rabbit Hill*, which was also the name of his own country home, is a pleasant assembling of all the small creatures he watched and recorded with humorous understanding in his own books as well as in those by other authors which he illustrated. Even in *Pilgrim's Progress* they bob up gaily. Mr. Lawson evidently enjoyed mice, because not only is little Willie engagingly recorded in *Rabbit Hill*, but the redoubtable Amos in *Ben and Me* is a very prince of mice and as chummily convincing as Ferdinand, the languishing bull. Mr. Lawson's illustrations show his creatures not as types but as individuals in varying

*From* Rabbit Hill *by Robert Lawson. Copyright 1944 by Robert Lawson. Reprinted by permission of The Viking Press, Inc.*

moods. In *Rabbit Hill*, Porkey's out-thrust, drooping lower lip is stubbornness personified; Georgie, leaping with a powerful push from those hind legs of his, is very different from the relaxed Georgie, hands folded over his fat paunch, making up his happy chant about "New Folks coming, Oh my!" In any group of the animals you can pick out Father, the bluegrass gentleman of the old school, and Uncle Analdas, the agitator.

Because Mr. Lawson drew with exquisite detail and complete clarity, he is sometimes characterized as old-fashioned. But Helen Dean Fish tells of another appraisal of Robert Lawson by a small boy who was looking at an exhibit of contemporary illustrations. He said, "I like *his* best. He draws them up neat, and you can see what they mean."[10] So you can, and there is meaning in every line and a humor that will set you to chuckling.

## E. B. WHITE

*Charlotte's Web*

E. B. White, essayist and editorial writer for *The New Yorker*, noted for his lucid, effortless prose, wrote *Stuart Little*, the story of a baby who resembled a mouse, "in fact he was a mouse." Some children liked Stuart's adventures, but many adults were disturbed by the biology of this mouse child of a human family. *The Trumpet of the Swan*, the story of a mute swan who learned to play an instrument so that he could woo his beloved, is a fascinating blend of fantasy and realistic details. But White's masterpiece is *Charlotte's Web* (1952), which had the distinction of being enthusiastically reviewed in both the adult and children's sections of our most important literary magazines. It is a delight to read aloud, and adults as well as children enjoy it.

Fern, a farmer's child, persuades her father to give her a runt of a pig he is about to liquidate. "Wilbur," Fern names her pet, and she raises him in a doll buggy with a doll's nursing bottle for a feeder. But when Wilbur gains girth, Father firmly banishes him to the barnyard, and here the fantasy begins. Fern spends long periods of time with her pet daily and discovers that she understands what the animals are saying to each other. Wilbur has learned about the fall butchering and he doesn't want to die. Charlotte, the aloof, intelligent spider, feels sorry for the silly little pig and promises to save him. Her devices for doing this are unique and exceedingly funny. The progress of Wilbur, the "radiant pig," involves all the people on two farms and most of the barnyard creatures, including Templeton, the selfish rat. In the end, Wilbur is saved but Charlotte dies, true to her kind, leaving hundreds of eggs. Birth and death and life go on in their strange and moving cycles.

*Illustration by Garth Williams. From* Charlotte's Web *by E. B. White. Copyright 1952 by E. B. White. Reprinted by permission of Harper & Row, Publishers, and Hamish Hamilton, Ltd., London.*

10. "Robert Lawson," *The Horn Book*, January-February 1940, p. 20.

Children laugh hilariously over this story, but they weep at its conclusion—even the ten-year-olds. Said one seven-year-old whose grandmother had read him the book, "Mother, Charlotte died."

And his mother, not knowing about Charlotte, replied casually, "Oh, did she?"

Shocked, the boy cried, "Mother, don't you care?" and burst into tears.

A book that can so delight and so move children carries with it the therapy of laughter and a growing compassion as well.

## GEORGE SELDEN

*The Cricket in Times Square*
*Tucker's Countryside*

The Garth Williams illustrations add immeasurably to the charm of *The Cricket in Times Square* (1960) and *Tucker's Countryside* (1969). The New York setting provides a solid base of realism, for the animal characters live in the Times Square subway station. Tucker is a tough, slangy city mouse, a pure Damon Runyon character, and his friend Harry the Cat is a sage creature who joins him in welcoming the cricket Chester, who has been brought into town in somebody's picnic basket. Chester is also befriended and given publicity by Mario, the boy whose parents run the station newspaper stand. The cricket makes a name for himself when it is discovered that he has perfect pitch and is a concert-grade chirper. The style is breezy, the dialogue entertaining, the whole situation fresh and imaginative.

Just as charming and cheerful is the sequel, *Tucker's Countryside*, which also has a painless message about conservation. Chester, who has gone back to Connecticut, appeals to his old friends to help save the meadow in which he and his country friends live. Like E. B. White, Selden brings his animal characters so vividly to life that they have unforgettable personalities, and both books pay tribute to the tenderness and loyalty of friendship. *Sparrow Socks* is a brief story for younger children, not so distinguished in writing style, but amusing. A Scottish family's business is saved when the wee red socks that the youngest McFee makes to warm a sparrow's cold feet become the rage of the town, and everybody demands red and white sparrow socks.

## LOUISE FATIO

*The Happy Lion*
*The Three Happy Lions*
*The Happy Lion's Treasure*

In the series of *Happy Lion* books, who can say which is better—the stories by Louise Fatio or the illustrations by Roger Duvoisin? This husband-and-wife team has produced inimitable picture stories, witty and beautiful. The first book, *The Happy Lion* (1954), introduces the Lion at home in a small French park, greeted daily and politely by his friends, in particular the zoo keeper's little boy. One day, when someone inadvertently leaves the gate unlocked, the Lion saunters out to find his friends, and people flee, women faint, and the band panics. Only the little boy greets the Lion as usual and leads him gently home to his place in the park. Through the succeeding three books the Lion travels, roars, and, after kidnaping a beautiful lioness, has himself a family (*The Three Happy Lions*). In *The Happy Lion's Treasure*, the lion learns that a visitor to the zoo had commented on his "rich life." Should he make a will? What is his treasure? Much discussion among the animals gives the answer: It is the happy lion's loving heart. Not only are these stories well told with good plots, sly humor, and surprise endings, but the pictures are rich in details that children pore over. A *Happy Lion* devotee could find his way to every shop in that particular French village and would know at precisely which street corner the panic began.

**Other Examples of Talking Beasts**

Four other series, like the *Happy Lion* books popular with the nursery-kindergarten children, are the *Curious George* books by Hans A. Rey, the *Anatole* books by Eve Titus, the *Paddington* books by Michael Bond, and the old favorites the *Babar* books by Jean de Brunhoff. *Curious George* (1941), illustrated by the author, is a monkey who gets in and out of scrapes with a successful agility children envy. *Anatole and the Cat* (1957), gloriously illustrated by Paul Galdone, is the story of a French cheese-tasting mouse, complete with beret and brief case. His enemy the cat is a source of considerable danger and must be put in his place by Anatole. Paddington, who appears first in *A Bear Called Paddington* (1960), is a lovable Peruvian bear who lives with a London family, a family that is remarkably patient with his many escapades. *The Story of Babar* (1937), illustrated by the author, was the first of innumerable books about Babar, now being continued by Jean de Brunhoff's son Laurent. Babar is a sophisticated elephant who comes to Paris, obtains a wealthy patroness, is outfitted with an elegant wardrobe, and returns to Africa to set up such a dynasty as never was before or since. *Babar and Father Christmas* is one of the favorites.

Most of the fantasy tales about animals are humorous, some as gently funny as Margery Sharp's *Miss Bianca* stories, and some as pointed as *Belling the Tiger* and its companion volumes by Mary Stolz. Miss Bianca is the most genteel of mice, but her courage is unbounded. With her faithful (but *quite* ordinary) admirer, Bernard, she embarks on adventures as lurid and melodramatic as those of any detective story, but she is always calm, always complete mistress of the situation. The mice who bell the tiger (a cat, of course) are innocent young males, and their conversations take many a subtle dig at the foibles of our social structure; in fact, the books can almost be read on two levels. It is evidence of the author's skill that a child may read for the plot alone and find her books entertaining—but it's icing on the cake for the readers who see the satire. In Jacqueline Jackson's *The Orchestra Mice*, a family of musical mice are hailed for their virtuoso performance.

There have been an enormous number of talking-beast stories for two- to six-year-old children in the last several decades. All sorts of creatures, from pandas to goldfish, are talking and adventuring. Many of these tales are thin in content and undistinguished in style, but some are delightful. One of the best of these stories is Margaret Wise Brown's *The Runaway Bunny*. In this brightly colored picture story, a young bunny warns his mother that he is going to run away:

> *"If you run away," said his mother, "I will run after you. For you are my little bunny."*
>
> *"If you run after me," said the little bunny, "I will become a fish in a trout stream and I will swim away from you."*
>
> *"If you become a fish in a trout stream," said his mother, "I will become a fisherman and I will fish for you."*

So they play the game of make-believe, and Clement Hurd's pictures show the bunny as a little fish with his mother as a fisherman, or the bunny as a bird with his mother as a big rabbit-shaped tree. The word pattern goes on like a song until it ends reassuringly:

> *"Shucks," said the bunny, "I might just as well stay where I am and be your little bunny."*
>
> *And so he did.*

Marjorie Flack's *Ask Mr. Bear* is a nursery-school and kindergarten favorite. A small boy, not knowing what to give his mother for a birthday present, asks a series of animals for advice. Finally Mr. Bear whispers just the right thing in his ear. He hurries home and gives his mother—a great big Bear Hug. The surprise ending never fails to bring pleasure no matter how many times the children have heard it.

*The Country Bunny and the Little Gold Shoes* is a choice Easter rabbit story by Du Bose Heyward. More recently, Roger Duvoisin has written and illustrated a droll series about Petunia, a genius of a goose, whose predicaments delight her young followers. The amiable crocodile Lyle is the hero of several books by Bernard Waber, and in the Caldecott Medal book *Sylvester and the Magic Pebble* by William Steig, it is a young donkey who is the central figure. In Doris Orgel's *Phoebe & the Prince*, the hero is a flea with a distinguished past, and in Betty Brock's *No Flying in the House*, a cat and a dog are articulate rivals.

Other popular talking animals are the quarrelsome dogs of *Finders Keepers*, by Will and Nicolas, and the enterprising young mouse, Ralph, who makes friends with a boy in Beverly Cleary's *The Mouse and the Motorcycle* and continues his adventures in *Runaway Ralph*. There is a gentle poignancy in the story of *The Mousewife*, by Rumer Godden, and in Agnes Smith's *An Edge of the Forest*, a beautifully written book in which the innocence of a small black lamb inspires such love that other animals who are natural enemies become friends. In *Jason's Quest*, by Margaret Laurence, a staunch young mole travels to London with an owl and two cats, searching for a remedy for the wasting sickness that has afflicted his community. Jason finds that London is a swinging town, a situation that enables the author to draw some entertaining parallels with human society.

*Illustration by William Steig from* Sylvester and the Magic Pebble *© by William Steig 1969. Reprinted by permission of Windmill Books/Simon and Schuster. (Original in color)*

Modern talking-beast tales should be chosen with discrimination. If Beatrix Potter went back to her Bible-reading when she felt her style needed chastening, we had better reread Beatrix Potter and *The Wind in the Willows* when we are in doubt about choosing from the multitude of these new beast tales.

## PERSONIFIED TOYS

Although the fanciful story about the secret life of toys and other inanimate objects was Andersen's invention, it took the writers of the twentieth century to use this form at the child's level, with an inventiveness and charm that already have made some of these stories children's classics. Andersen's tales of the little china shepherdess and the chimney sweep or the rusty tin soldier are faintly sad and decidedly adult. Later writers have avoided both these pitfalls. Their dolls, trains, and airplanes are usually cheerful and lively.

### RICHARD HENRY HORNE

*Memoirs of a London Doll*

In the nineteenth century there was one popular example of this type of story, the English

*Memoirs of a London Doll* (1846) by Richard Henry Horne (pseudonym Mrs. Fairstar). In this book, Maria Poppett, the doll, tells her own story.

Tom Plummy traded an elegant Twelfth-cake for Maria as a present for his little sister, Ellen Plummy. The doll tells all the things she and her mistress did and saw together in the London of over a hundred years ago. The Christmas pantomime, the Lord Mayor's show, a typical Punch and Judy entertainment, the food, and the clothes of long ago are described. Although some little girls enjoy this early doll story, it is not an important book today, but it is interesting to adults as the ancestor of the American *Hitty*, the Newbery Medal winner written by Rachel Field.

## CARLO LORENZINI

*The Adventures of Pinocchio*

The strongest impetus to the modern personification type of story may well stem not from Hans Andersen's tales but from that popular Italian classic *Pinocchio*. Written in 1880 by a witty Tuscan, Carlo Lorenzini (pseudonym Collodi), it was apparently first translated into English and published in this country in 1892. From then on, it has held a high place in the affections of American children and has undoubtedly influenced American writers.

The story concerns a rogue of a puppet which old Geppetto painstakingly carves out of wood. Hardly has the poor wood carver finished his manikin when the saucy creature kicks him, leaps down from the bench, and makes off through the door in pursuit of life, liberty, and his own sweet way. Pinocchio is full of good resolutions: to buy new clothes for his dear papa Geppetto, to go to school, to learn his lessons, and to be a good boy generally. Instead, he wastes his money, lies about it, plays hooky from school, and chooses for his companions the villains and the boobies. Every time he lies to his friend the Blue Fairy, his nose grows longer, until soon he can't turn around in a room without colliding with the walls. Neither the Talking Cricket nor the Blue Fairy can check his follies. The climax is his journey to the Land of Toys, where there is never any school and where he finds presently that he has grown a fine pair of donkey ears and a body to match. Saved again and again by the good Blue Fairy, he learns that she is ill and starving. He is roused at last, earns money to feed and care for both Geppetto and the Fairy, and wakes in the morning to find himself no longer a puppet but a real boy, living with Geppetto in a well-kept home. Geppetto explains,

> *". . . when bad boys become good and kind, they have the power of making their homes gay and new with happiness."*

And the irrepressible Pinocchio, looking at the remains of the puppet dangling on the wall, remarks to himself with great complacency:

> *"How ridiculous I was as a marionette! And how happy I am, now that I have become a real boy!"*

Despite all the sinning and repenting, here he is—still cocky, still vain and boastful! This is the children's own epic, themselves in wood, full of good resolutions, given to folly, sliding through somehow, but with one difference—Pinocchio always comes out on top and never quite loses face.

No child's book of the nineteenth century in any country is more completely on the child's level. Pinocchio's wickedness is bloodcurdling from the child's angle—kicking his good papa, running away, lying like a trooper—but then the swift punishments which follow every misdeed are equally bloodcurdling and objective. Suppose our noses started growing every time we told a lie? The children giggle a little uneasily and can hardly wait to read what happens next.

Even the jokes are understandable, which is not always true in the great English classics, and there are laughs on almost every page.

## MARGERY WILLIAMS BIANCO

*The Velveteen Rabbit*

Margery Williams Bianco's books have the same sensitive, imaginative quality that Andersen's tales have, and they are often similarly moving.

*The Velveteen Rabbit* (1926) develops the idea that toys come to life if they are loved enough. The Velveteen Rabbit suffers more than the ordinary vicissitudes of toys and is finally, during the illness of his little owner, thrown out on the ash pile. But the child misses his companion. It does not matter to him that his toy is dilapidated and dirty; he loves his Velveteen Rabbit and wants him more than anything else. Then, out-of-doors once more, he sees a tame rabbit. The two gaze at each other. There is no doubt in the child's heart—here at last is his dear Velveteen Rabbit come to life.

## A. A. MILNE

*Winnie-the-Pooh*
*The House at Pooh Corner*

A. A. Milne's *Winnie-the-Pooh* (1926) and *The House at Pooh Corner* (1928) are different from anything that preceded them. They seem to have grown as a natural sequence to the poems about Christopher Robin and Pooh, and they also developed, as the author says, from his small son's demands to hear a story for Pooh:

> *"What sort of stories does he like?"*
> *"About himself. Because he's that sort of Bear."*
> *"Oh, I see.". . .*
> *So I tried.*

The accommodating Mr. Milne forthwith begins to spin a series of tales about Pooh, when he lived in the forest "under the name of Sanders." He calls on Rabbit and eats so much that he sticks in the door and can't get out. He flies up in a balloon to get some honey out of a tree, tries to imitate a cloud in order to distract the suspicious bees, and finally has to have the balloon shot in order to get down. There are adventures with Piglet, Eeyore the old donkey, Kanga, and Little Roo. *The House at Pooh Corner* introduces Tigger, a new and amusing character, but the tales go on in much the same vein.

Ernest Shepard's illustrations make it clear that most of the animals are really toys like Winnie-the-Pooh. Christopher appears in their midst rallying them for an "expotition" to the North Pole, or rescuing them from various mishaps, but he, too, lives in a tree in the forest in quite a cozy bearlike den. The pictures are full of the fascinating details Mr. Shepard knows how to put in. For instance, Mr. Owl's house has two signs at the door. One, under the knocker, says

> *PLES RING*
> *IF AN RNSER*
> *IS REQIRD*

The other, under the bell rope, reads

> *PLEZ CNOKE*
> *IF AN RNSR*
> *IS NOT REQID*

The stories are unusual in that Christopher goes in and out of them on a familiar forest-dwelling level with the animals, but in the end he brings everything back to reality when he sets off up the stairs of his own house, headed for a bath, dragging Pooh by one leg. The stories are finished, Christopher is himself, and Pooh is Pooh. This is not only a tale about toys come to life, but also a clever fantasy for the youngest—not too complicated, no fairies, just a little boy sharing make-believe adventures with his toys and the little creatures of the woods, but knowing all the time that they *are* make-believe. It's a game of "let's pretend" put into story form, and many children anywhere from five to ten enjoy both of these books.

## RACHEL FIELD

*Hitty, Her First Hundred Years*

Rachel Field and the artist Dorothy Lathrop were fascinated by an old doll in a New York antique shop. She was carved from mountain ash and dated back to whaling days in Maine. Rachel Field bought the doll, started a book about her to be illustrated by Dorothy Lathrop, and prophesied, as a justification for her extravagance, that this story was going to win the Newbery Medal. Indeed, *Hitty* (1929) was so honored and was present in person when Rachel Field made her acceptance speech and received the medal.

The book, which is enjoyed by girls ten to twelve years old, records Hitty's numerous adventures which range all the way from being shipwrecked and serving as a heathen idol on a remote island to hearing Jenny Lind sing and to being on exhibition in New Orleans.

## CAROLYN SHERWIN BAILEY

*Miss Hickory*

*Miss Hickory* (Newbery Medal, 1947), a mere twig with a hickory nut head and personality plus, begins as a doll left behind by the children. Waspish, but sound as a nut, she faces adversity bravely and with Crow's help makes a home for herself in a robin's nest. Her adventures come to a strange end when a squirrel bites off her head and is then frightened out of his wits when the twig that was Miss Hickory walks serenely away. That this twig becomes the graft on an old tree and gives it new life is a conclusion that leaves most children baffled. Perhaps a few of them get the suggestion of the continuity of life, but whether they do or don't, the characters are amusing, and the story of tart, competent Miss Hickory is beautifully told.

## RUMER GODDEN

*The Dolls' House*
*Impunity Jane*
*Miss Happiness and Miss Flower*

The novelist Rumer Godden has written a series of doll stories that are unsurpassed in variety and charm, for her dolls have distinct personalities and in her books they talk and act in character. Only in one respect are they alike. In the hands of their owners they are often misunderstood and badly treated, and always helpless, except for the sheer force of their unique personalities. The first of the series, *The Dolls' House* (1947, 1962), is one of the most dramatic. An exquisite old Victorian doll house is inhabited by proper, genteel dolls. When a strange, haughty doll is added to the group, a doll-sized tragedy takes place, but this ending is as gentle as the spirit of the old house.

Perhaps the most popular of the books is *Impunity Jane* (1954), so called because the clerk tells the buyers that this finger-sized doll can be dropped "with impunity." But her owner does not think much of Jane; so she relegates her to a stuffy old doll house where she sits for years, bored and pining for adventure. When a small boy named Gideon carries her off in his pocket, life begins for Jane. What that boy thinks up for Jane to do is a caution. She sails his boats, flies his airplanes, rides on his bicycle, dwells in igloos and wigwams, and generally enjoys life. When Gideon's conscience forces him to own up to his kidnapping, the solution is a joyous one, and he and Jane return happily to a life of exploration and adventure.

In contrast to the intrepid Jane, *Miss Happiness and Miss Flower* (1961) are two exquisite Japanese dolls, too gentle it would

*Illustration by Adrienne Adams. From* Impunity Jane *by Rumer Godden. Copyright 1954 by Rumer Godden. By permission of The Viking Press, Inc. (Original with color)*

seem to enjoy any adventures. Yet they are the promoters of a long series of activities which help a homesick, timid little girl and quell a jealous one. They are the inspiration for a carefully constructed, authentic, and exquisite Japanese doll house. What is more, these dolls give rise to another series of adventures in a book called *Little Plum*. In this story the interest centers less on the dolls and more on their owner Belinda's naughty curiosity and behavior in relation to a new child next door. However, the culmination of the amusing action is a most felicitous Feast of the Dolls in Japanese style. Other doll stories by Miss Godden are *Candy Floss, The Fairy Doll, Home Is the Sailor*, and *The Story of Holly and Ivy*. Doll-loving little girls should indeed be grateful to Rumer Godden for these varied and absorbing books.

### Other Stories About Toys

One of the most touching stories about a toy is Russell Hoban's *The Mouse and His Child*. They are a single unit, a wind-up tin toy that has been discarded. Repaired by a tramp, they go on a quest for love and security. The story has humor and tenderness, and an adventurous plot with general appeal, but the sophistication of its latent meaning and of its social comment and the difficulty of the vocabulary put special demands on young readers.

*Ellen's Lion*, by Crockett Johnson, is a collection of twelve short stories about the wildly imaginative Ellen and her sedate, practical stuffed lion. The author captures to perfection the intent fantasy of a small child playing alone, and the dry, sensible comments of the lion are a dramatic foil for Ellen's volatile personality.

*The Return of the Twelves*, by Pauline Clarke, is an ingenious story about the wooden soldiers that had been the playthings of the Brontë children. Years after the Brontë times, eight-year-old Max Morley finds the Twelves and learns that they "freeze" when they are observed. He wins their confidence and they talk of the past. Max and his sister decide that the soldiers belong in their old home, Haworth, and let them march off rather than offend their dignity by carrying them. Winner of the Carnegie Medal, the book has a polished style, delightful individual characterizations of the soldiers, and enough literary references to intrigue adults as well as young readers.

In Ursula Moray Williams' *The Toymaker's Daughter*, a doll wants desperately to become a real child, but realizes that her friends will grow up while she would remain the same age. The fantasy is made convincing by the children's matter-of-fact acceptance of the doll's behaving like a human being.

## OTHER PERSONIFIED INANIMATE OBJECTS

Tales in which inanimate objects are personified furnish the child with something he desires and seems likely to enjoy permanently. There were a few forerunners of the recent stories about machinery. Every kindergarten teacher told "The Little Engine That Could" to delighted groups of five-year-olds. This story with its refrain, "I think I can, I think I can, I think I can," is still popular and still fun to tell. Lucy Sprague Mitchell followed with another repetitional engine story, "How the Engine Learned the Knowing Song," which, if not as spontaneous as its predecessor, is still enjoyed by the youngest children. Then in 1939 *Mike Mulligan and His Steam Shovel* took the five-year-olds by storm and was almost equally popular with older children. Virginia Burton, the author-artist of *Mike Mulligan*, repeated her success with other books.

## VIRGINIA BURTON

*Mike Mulligan and His Steam Shovel*
*The Little House*

If artists have any facility with words, they should make good storytellers, because graphic representation requires the ability to see clearly and to bring to life for others what is taking place. Virginia Burton used her brush and words in the happiest possible combination. In her picture stories, the pictures are an integral part of the text, interpreting and even adding to the text. Some of her subjects are machines, very likely a natural response to the interests of her sons when they were small.

*Mike Mulligan and His Steam Shovel* (1939) tells the story of Mike, who owns a fine steam shovel with which he does important jobs of excavation until his machine, Mary Anne, is outmoded by new and more powerful models. Jobs no longer come his way, and Mike and his faithful shovel are in a bad state. Then Mike reads about a town which wishes to have its Town Hall excavation dug in a great hurry. Mike and Mary Anne hasten to the scene of action and offer to dig it in one day or no pay. The city fathers agree, seeing a chance to get their excavation done for nothing, since such a feat seems obviously impossible. The next morning Mary Anne and Mike go to work. Dirt flies in all directions, and the watching crowds grow to a mob and hang breathlessly over the heaving, bouncing Mary Anne, driven by Mike. At last, exactly on the hour, the excavation is finished, deep and well squared off at the corners. The crowd bursts into loud cheers. The only trouble is that Mike, in his excitement, has dug himself in, and there is no way of getting Mary Anne out. So Mary Anne just becomes the furnace of the new Town Hall and Mike her attendant. Both live a warm, prosperous, and respected life ever after.

*Katy and the Big Snow*, the story of a snow shovel, has a similar format and manner but is not so popular as *Mike*. *Choo Choo*, the story of a runaway engine, preceded *Mike* by two years and is a favorite also.

These machine stories have certain marked characteristics which help to explain their popularity. The plot always involves a staggering task or action and has considerable suspense. The illustrations heighten the feeling of action by swirling, circular lines that rush across the page and stem from or center on the cause of it all. You can almost see movement in the pictures of Mary Anne tearing around that hole with dirt flying in all directions and of the crowd of tiny figures with their gaze focused on the snorting steam shovel. In the pictures of *Choo Choo*, trees, bridges, and telegraph poles yield to the onrushing momentum of the reckless runaway. The eye follows Choo Choo past or into or out of the next set of obstacles. The action in the text and pictures keeps young readers (or read-tos) fairly breathless.

*The Little House*, the winner of the Caldecott Medal for 1943, is Virginia Burton's finest and most distinguished book. It tells the story of a house in the country which presently finds itself in the center of a village, and then in the midst of a great city where it is an insignificant obstruction between skyscrapers, with elevated trains overhead, subways beneath, and swarms of peo-

*From* The Little House *by Virginia Lee Burton. Houghton Mifflin Company, 1942. Caldecott Medal. Reproduced with the permission of the publisher. (Original in color)*

ple everywhere. Rescued by the descendants of its builder, the little house is taken back to the country where it can once more watch the cycle of the four seasons revolving in comely and ordered beauty.

There is a significance to this book that should make it permanently valuable as literature and art. The evolution of cities in all their complexity and the resultant loss of some of the sweetness of earth and sky are implied in text and picture. The house has only a delicately suggested face, and the personification is subordinate to the pattern of these illustrations, something for children and adults to study with growing astonishment and delight. The pattern of every picture is the same—rhythmical curving lines which in the country are gracious and gentle but in the city become more and more violent and confused. The children's activities on the farm in each of the four seasons, the new event in each picture of urban growth, and the hundreds of dashing, darting people in the city are a part of the rich panorama and minute details which make this a book to be looked at again and again.

## HARDIE GRAMATKY

*Little Toot*

The same year that *Mike Mulligan* appeared, another artist launched the first of a popular series of fanciful personifications of machinery. Hardie Gramatky is a watercolorist of distinction. His story of *Little Toot*, an irresponsible tugboat, appeared in 1939. Toot is hilariously personified, as are all his tugboat relatives. Toot is a lazy youngster, a disgrace to his hard-working family. How he finally reforms and makes a heroic rescue is amusingly told and pictured. Toot was followed by *Hercules*, the story of a horse-drawn fire engine forced to retire. Hercules comes into his own for one last grand run, and the pictures, in the loudest, fieriest colors, are as exciting as the text. *Loopy* is the story of an airplane used by student pilots for practice, but Loopy yearns to be a skywriter. Mr. Gramatky's personifications are extremely funny, and his tales have a breezy touch that all children enjoy.

### Other Stories of Inanimate Objects

Two stories that might be classified either as science fiction or as tales of inanimate objects are Lester Del Rey's *The Runaway Robot* and Carol Ryrie Brink's *Andy Buckram's Tin Men. The Runaway Robot* comes closer to science fiction, since it is set in the future when robots are common, but it is an uncommon robot that becomes so close a friend of his human companion that the two run away together. Andy in *Andy Buckram's Tin Men* is a twelve-year-old who builds four robots out of tin cans, but not until they are struck by lightning during a storm do the four come alive and save Andy's life during the flood caused by the storm.

Quite unlike any other heroine is *Miss Osborne-the-Mop*, by Wilson Gage. Jody, who has discovered that she has the magical power of making objects materialize, soon wishes she had never used her power, since Miss Osborne, a mop brought to life, is a tart character who insists on Jody's participation in a vigorous clean-up campaign.

## HUMOROUS TALES

Adults may speak of "drolls" or "tales of laughter" or "humorous stories," but the children say to librarians, "I want a *funny* book," and so do all of us now and then. Chapter 10 discusses the therapeutic value of nonsense and the need to break our tensions with laughter. One of the best ways to get a double dose of this curative property is to read aloud to a child one of his favorite "funny books." He laughs so hard you have to stop reading, and presently you find yourself beginning to give way to the rib-tickling humor that captivates the child. Just to discuss a funny book with a child or to hear him tell about it is to regain instantly your sense of the wholesome gaiety of life.

These humorous books are not a class by themselves but cut across all other groups. Some are talking beasts, some are fantasies, some are told in folk-tale style, some are personifications, and some, like the folk-tale drolls, are improbable but almost realistic. Many adults would head the humorous list with *Alice's Adventures in Wonderland*, but, on the whole, its humor is a little subtle for children; they smile rather than laugh at *Alice*. The following discussion of humorous tales includes only a few types—stories written primarily for sheer fun.

### LUCRETIA HALE

*The Peterkin Papers*

In the latter part of the nineteenth century, Lucretia Hale began to create for her friends' children a series of tales about a certain Peterkin family. These stories continue to seem as funny as the day they were published. Miss Eliza Orne White tells us that the episode which furnished Mrs. Hale with the idea for her stories was as absurd as any in the book. While visiting the White family, Mrs. Hale was about to start for a drive with her friends when the horse refused to go. They discovered, after all efforts to move him had failed, that he was still tied to the hitching post. Hence the story "Mrs. Peterkin Wishes to Go to Drive."

The Peterkin family consists of Mr. and Mrs. Peterkin, Solomon John, Agamemnon, Elizabeth Eliza, and the little boys in india-rubber boots. They learn wisdom by consulting "the lady from Philadelphia." For instance, Mrs. Peterkin puts salt instead of sugar in her morning coffee. They call the chemist, who makes it worse. The herb woman puts in a little of everything, and the coffee is frightful. The lady from Philadelphia suggests that they throw it out and make a fresh cup of coffee. A happy solution! A new piano is moved into the house, but the movers leave it with the keyboard against a window. Elizabeth Eliza, seated on the porch, plays the piano through the window, a satisfactory arrangement as long as the weather is warm. When winter comes, it takes the lady from Philadelphia to suggest that they turn the piano around. The stories continue in this vein.

Here is "Clever Elsie" multiplied into a whole family. The humor is so obvious and robust that an upper-grade class can even make up its own *Peterkin Papers*.

### P. L. TRAVERS

*Mary Poppins*
*Mary Poppins Comes Back*

P. L. Travers grew up in Australia, where high, wild winds blow everyone into a dither and make almost anything possible. So an east wind blows *Mary Poppins* (1934) straight into the nursery of the Banks family, and a west wind carries her off. The children first see her coming up the walk, bag in hand, and the next thing she strikes the house with a bang. Once their mother has engaged her as a nurse, Mary slides lightly *up* the banisters as neatly as the children slide down. When she opens her bag, they see it is quite empty, but out of it she takes everything from a folding cot to a bottle of medicine from which she doses the children with incredibly delicious liquid, tasting of strawberry ice or lime-juice cordial or whatever you prefer. "You won't leave us, will you?" Michael asks her anxiously, and she replies, "I'll stay till the wind changes," and she does.

Strange things happen during her stay. Having inhaled a little laughing gas, the children enjoy an elaborate tea party sitting comfortably on nothing at all around a table suspended in mid-air. They find a compass and journey north, south, east, and west without an effort. But a day comes when there is a wild west wind, and Mary is all gentleness. Her manner troubles the children and they beg her to be cross again. "Trouble trouble and it will trouble you!" she replies tartly and leaves them. Then they see her in the yard, the wind tugging at her skirts, her umbrella lifted. Suddenly she smiles at the wind, and if lifts her steadily and swiftly up and away from the children—Mary Poppins is gone. But, of course, she comes back in another book.

The Poppins books are extremely British, with cooks, gardeners, maids, nannies, nurseries, and teas. The humor is sometimes adult and sometimes whimsical, but children who like these books like them enormously and wear them to shreds with rereadings; others dislike them with scornful heartiness. These violent differences seem to occur more often about fanciful books than about any others. At any rate, the Poppins books have enjoyed a continuous popularity and are now being paid the compliment of rather frequent imitations. The character of Mary Poppins herself has a flavor all its own. Vain, stern, crotchety, continually overtaken by magic but never admitting it, adored by the children she disciplines and enchants, Mary is what the Irish would call "a char-ácter."

## THEODOR SEUSS GEISEL

*And to Think That I Saw It on Mulberry Street*
*The 500 Hats of Bartholomew Cubbins*

Theodor Seuss Geisel chose his middle name for a pen name and then added the "Dr." as a purely honorary touch. But Dartmouth, his own college, decided to make it official. The college said he had long possessed a D.D.C.—doctor of delighted children—so it would merely add a doctor of humane letters!

Dr. Seuss' first book for children, *And to Think That I Saw It on Mulberry Street* (1937), is still a favorite. A small boy sees only a horse and a wagon on Mulberry Street but begins working up a bigger and bigger yarn to tell his father. Each succeeding page pictures the next addition to his tale until finally two pages across are necessary to get everything in. Then his father fixes him with a cold stare and his tale diminishes suddenly, leaving only the horse and wagon on Mulberry Street.

This rhymed narrative was only a sample of more and better nonsense to come. Of all the Seuss books *The 500 Hats of Bartholomew Cubbins* (1938) is certainly one of the best. Bartholomew Cubbins takes off his hat to the King only to find the royal coach stopping, and the King commanding him to take off his hat. Puzzled, he puts his hand to his head and finds a hat there. He jerks it off hastily only to find another in its place, and another, and another, and another. He is seized and threatened with death, but still the hats continue to crown his bewildered head. The horrid little Grand Duke Wilfred assures the King that it will be a pleasure to push Bartholomew off the highest parapet.

Up the stairs they go, hats falling at every step. Finally the King sees upon the boy's head the most gloriously regal hat he has ever beheld. In exchange for this hat of elegance, he spares Bartholomew's life, and, as the befeathered hat goes on the King's head, Bartholomew finds his own head bare at last. The outline of this story gives no idea of the humor of both pictures and text—Bartholomew bewildered, helpless, wild-eyed; the King outraged and frustrated; the headsman unable to behead because his clients must take their hats off. All of these are hilariously pictured and solemnly described. This story has a lively sequel, *Bartholomew and the Oobleck.*

Many children and adults think *Horton Hatches the Egg* is the funniest. *Dr. Seuss's Sleep Book* is also good fun. But these stories are all funny and most of them are delightful.

## RICHARD AND FLORENCE ATWATER

*Mr. Popper's Penguins*

Another humorous book is *Mr. Popper's Penguins* (1938), written by Richard and Florence Atwater. This wild yarn is a nonsense tale narrated with gravity and giving every indication of being a simple, realistic story. Strictly speaking, nothing in the book is impossible, but because the narrative carries improbability to its uttermost limits it ends where Mr. Popper himself began—in the realm of the fanciful.

It tells the story of Mr. Popper, an untidy paperhanger with a passion for the Antarctic. An explorer rewards his admiration with a penguin. That one becomes twelve, and then the penguins revolutionize the lives of the entire Popper family. Eventually, the children return to school, Mrs. Popper gets to the meeting of the Ladies' Aid and Missionary Society, but Mr. Popper ——? Well, when last seen, Mr. Popper and his penguins were headed due north.

## ASTRID LINDGREN

*Pippi Longstocking*

A Swedish writer of excellent detective stories for children (the *Bill Bergson* series) is also responsible for creating a superchild, the heroine of *Pippi Longstocking* (1950). Pippi is an outrageous and delightful child who lives competently with her monkey and horse and takes control of any situation in which she finds herself. She cows some bullying boys, disrupts a school session, and manhandles two policemen when they try to take her to an orphanage. (Indeed, after carrying one in each hand, she sets them down so hard that it is some time before they can get up.) Then they report she is not a fit child for the orphanage!

Pippi's antics are exceedingly funny to children though some adults find a little of Pippi goes a long way.

## JEAN MERRILL

*The Pushcart War*

Certainly one of the most original fanciful stories of our time, *The Pushcart War* (1964), has all the ingredients of good fiction. The characters are unusual and distinctively drawn, the setting is colorful, the plot has a tight structure, the style is light and polished, and the theme is significant. Add humor, pace, and the element of fantasy made wholly believable, and the result is sheer delight. The time is 1976, the place New York City, and the problem the fact that there are so many huge trucks that traffic on Manhattan Island is in a constant snarl. The three big men in trucking decide that the first step in their campaign to eliminate other vehicles is to attack the pushcart owners. But the little people won't be put down; they fight with pins, and the ensuing number of flat tires puts such a strain on repair facilities that trucks are left stranded all over the island.

Led by General Anna, the brave little army of pushcart owners outwits the big business sharks, to say nothing of the mayor whose attitude has been swayed by making him a stockholder. In the most ingenuous fashion, Jean Merrill attacks both corruption in office and monopoly in business, and she does it with a bland humor that avoids any note of bitterness. The characters and the situation are given validity by an introduction that cites invented sources and by a foreword that is written by an invented historian. The concept is original and the development of the story line amusing, but it is the dialogue that gives the book flavor. In the pushcart owners' strategy session, Old Anna says, "Of course, we have got to fight." "Fight the trucks?" a colleague asks. "How can the pushcarts fight the trucks?" Anna's reply is a clincher: "Maybe you'd rather be dead?" What nicer compliment can one pay a book than to smile whenever it comes to mind?

*Reprinted from* The Pushcart War, *text © MCMLXIV, by Jean Merrill and illustrations © MCMLXIV, by Ronni Solbert, a Young Scott Book, by permission of Addison-Wesley Publishing Company.*

## Other Humorous Books

Different kinds of humor appeal to different readers or may be favorites at different times. Tove Jansson, whose work received the Hans Christian Andersen Award, is popular internationally. Her books about those engaging imaginary creatures the *Finn Family Moomintroll* have a daft logic all their own.

Most of the contemporary humorous tales, however, combine realism and fantasy, the solid practicality of the background affording contrast for the impossible or improbable events. Oliver Butterworth's *The Enormous Egg* blandly injects the hatching of a dinosaur into the modern scene, and Scott Corbett's *Ever Ride A Dinosaur?* tells of a brontosaurus (who can make himself invisible) sneaking in to have a look at the dinosaur exhibit at the New York Museum of Natural History. Butterworth's *The Trouble with Jenny's Ear* is the hilarious tale of a small girl whose extrasensory perception is used to advantage in television appearances. Corbett's *The Limerick Trick* and others in the series are rollicking adventure tales that have an element of magic and a large portion of breezy slapstick. This is true, too, of Betty Erwin's stories about *Aggie, Maggie, and Tish.*

Another type of humor that is quiet and pervasive is the sort inherent in the situation. In Helen Cresswell's *The Piemakers,* for example, a family of bakers competes for the prize given for the biggest and best pie in the world. To make a pie for two thousand eaters requires heroic measures, a tight security system, and intricate logistics in handling. In

*Illustration by W. T. Mars for* The Piemakers *by Helen Cresswell. Illustrations copyright 1968. Reproduced by permission of J. B. Lippincott Company.*

another amusing tale, Roger Drury's *The Finches' Fabulous Furnace*, the fact that a small-size volcano is industriously heating the Finch home is accepted with equanimity.

In *Island Mackenzie* and *The Cruise of the Happy-Go-Gay*, Ursula Moray Williams combines realism and fantasy with sparkling wit, although the latter book is marred by a stereotyped depiction of a native chief. Two parodies of fairy tales are Phyllis McGinley's *The Plain Princess*, with a heroine whose appearance improves as she becomes less selfish, and Joseph Schrank's *The Plain Princess and the Lazy Prince*, a sophisticated spoof in which the royal parents are forced to advertise for a dragon and the princess rescues the hapless prince.

## TALL TALES

The characteristic of the tall tale that distinguishes it from other humorous stories is its blatant exaggeration. Our older tall tales—with their swaggering heroes who do the impossible with nonchalance—embody delusions of power: dreams of riding a cyclone or mowing down forests, or, in short, blithely surmounting any and every obstacle. They are such flagrant lies that the lyingest yarn of all is the best one, provided it is told with a straight face and every similitude of truth. Babe, Paul Bunyan's blue ox, measures "forty-two axhandles between the eyes—and a tobacco box—you could easily fit in a Star tobacco box after the last axhandle." Pecos Bill, after riding the cyclone successfully, must figure a convenient way of getting down. In short, one characteristic of tall-tale humor is that there must be a great show of reasonableness and accuracy in the midst of the most hilarious lunacy.

There are no complete or satisfying answers to the questions about where all these tales came from or who started them. Some of the older stories are classified as folk tales, but many are probably best described as "fake lore."[11] But regardless of their origins, they are almost invariably humorous. The New England coast produced Captain Stormalong. Paul Bunyan and his blue ox came from the lumber camps. The Western plains started Pecos Bill and his horse the Widow Maker on their careers. Mike Fink was a keelboatman on the Mississippi, while Davy Crockett, Tony Beaver, and John Henry all belong to the South. One artist has covered a map of the United States with these heroes,[12] and it is the most astonishing array of rip-roaring, snarling, snorting he-men that any country ever produced. Walter Blair has contributed to the tall tale in *Tall Tale America*

11. See particularly Richard M. Dorson, "Twentieth-Century Comic Demigods," *American Folklore* (University of Chicago Press, 1959), pp. 214–226.

12. See Glen Rounds' end pages for Walter Blair's *Tall Tale America*, an amusing group of fabulous stories.

as has Adrien Stoutenburg in *American Tall Tales* and *American Tall-Tale Animals*. Moritz Jagendorf has compiled several volumes of regional material: *The Ghost of Peg-Leg Peter and Other Stories of Old New York*, *New England Bean Pot* a book of tales from the middle Atlantic region, and another from some of the midwestern states. Of the several collections by Maria Leach, an outstanding one is *The Rainbow Book of American Folk Tales and Legends*, which includes tall tales.

Most of the recent books in this genre are for older readers, but several have been designed for the read-aloud audience. In Shan Ellentuck's *A Sunflower as Big as the Sun* and in Victor Ambrus' *The Brave Soldier Janosh*, the fun lies in the boastfulness of the farmer and of the Hungarian soldier who is a self-acclaimed superhero. Another tale about a soldier is Tom McGowen's *The Apple Strudel Soldier*, whose conquest by apple strudel bombardment has a comic-opera quality.

Some ghost stories are close to tall tales; Robert Bright's books about Georgie, the lovable ghost, are on the tongue-in-cheek borderline. Edna Mitchell Preston's *Horrible Hepzibah* has just a trace of Pippi, although she is deliciously consistent in her dreadfulness, and her parents are delighted to have her go off and live with the equally horrible aunt for whom she is named.

Natalie Babbitt's *Dick Foote and the Shark* is a story in verse, the internal rhyme and the rhythm giving it a gay sweep just right for the antics of the poetic youth whose declamation so astounds a hungry shark that both the boy and his father escape from the gaping jaws. While this book is for children from nine to eleven, it can be enjoyed by younger children if it is read aloud to them. For the same age group, Sid Fleischman's McBroom stories have a braggadocio appeal, as does Ennis Rees' *Windwagon Smith*.

The incredible acumen of a boy detective is made clear (by the boy detective, no shrinking violet) in William Pène du Bois' *The Alligator Case* and *The Horse in the Camel Suit*. *The Three Policemen; or, Young Bottsford of Farbe Island* is one of Du Bois' most successful fantasies and one of the first really good books with a black boy as the hero. Spontaneous, inventive, and full of action, the books are illustrated with flair by the author-artist. Lorrie McLaughlin's *Shogomoc Sam* is a Canadian tall tale in the folk-hero pattern, with Sam helping the giant lumberjack, the Main John. In William Steele's *Andy Jackson's Water Well*, Andy and his pal Chief Ticklepitcher bring a well from eastern Tennessee to end the drought in Nashville.

The quality that is exaggerated in *Contrary Jenkins*, by Rebecca Caudill and James Ayars, is obstinacy. Contrary, the taciturn hero, was once known to stay on for three years as an unwelcome visitor just because somebody had carelessly said, "Too bad you're in such a big hurry." In all of the stories by Henderson LeGrand, the humor is of a broadly ridiculous kind. In *How Baseball Began in Brooklyn*, for example, it is blandly explained that ten boys in a Dutch Colonial family named Denboom were bowling one day when the ball hit a war club held by a watching Indian, and that the youngest child marked the spot with a plate he had brought from home. Home plate, what else? The Indians couldn't pronounce the boys' name, unfortunately. Dembums, they said.

Three authors who have been outstanding in their stories of tall-tale adventures are Joan Aiken, Sid Fleischman, and Ben Stahl. Aiken's *The Wolves of Willoughby Chase* tells a Gothic tale that drips with Victorian sentimentality and drama. In *Nightbirds on Nantucket* and *Black Hearts in Battersea* she displays a Dickensian relish for names that indicate character, and a sense of the ludicrous that results in such situations as a pink whale obligingly towing a trans-Atlantic cannon. *Smoke from Cromwell's Time and Other Stories* is a good collection of short stories on fanciful themes, and *The Whispering Mountain* is a broad burlesque of the fanciful adventure story. It has a rollicking plot that incorporates a spurned grandchild, a

*From* Nightbirds on Nantucket *by Joan Aiken, illustrated by Robin Jacques. Copyright © 1966 by Joan Aiken. Reprinted by permission of Doubleday & Company, Inc.*

magic harp, a foreign potentate, and a breed of little men who live in a mountain; and it has a spectrum of dialects overdone to the point of absurdity.

Ben Stahl's *Blackbeard's Ghost* and its sequel, *The Secret of Red Skull*, are swashbuckling tall tales about the ghostly crew of Captain Teach, the famous pirate Blackbeard. The style and the plots are equally extravagant, and the dialogue drips with gore and brine.

Sid Fleischman's stories are also large-canvas affairs. In *The Ghost in the Noonday Sun*, a pirate kidnaps a boy who can, he thinks, lead him to the treasure of the man he murdered. A tropic isle, plank-walking, buried treasure, and mutinous pirates are just a few of the standard ploys at which the author pokes fun. In *Chancy and the Grand Rascal* the young hero (so skinny he has to stand twice to cast a shadow) goes off to find his little sister Indiana, meets a rogue and shyster, Colonel Plugg, and then finds his uncle, whose ability to lie magnificently routs even the lying Plugg. *By the Great Horn Spoon* is a picaresque tale about the California Gold Rush, in which Young Jack and the family butler, Mr. Praiseworthy, go off to recoup their losses, with Praiseworthy the Compleat Gentleman: polite, suave, honest, brave, and able to cope with any and every situation.

*Illustration by Warren Chappell for* The Ghost in the Noonday Sun *by Sid Fleischman. Copyright © 1965 by Albert S. Fleischman. Reproduced by permission of Little, Brown and Co.*

## STORIES OF FANTASY

One of Hans Christian Andersen's most successful story types is the fantasy, a tale of magic, often beginning realistically but merging quickly into adventures strange, astonishing, and dreamlike. Andersen's stories of this type are invariably melancholy or tragic—for example, "The Marsh King's Daughter," "The Snow Queen," and "The Little Mermaid." In England, the best examples of this type of tale are exactly the reverse. Just as the humorous "Tom Tit Tot" contrasts with the somber "Rumpelstiltskin," so Alice, the English equivalent of Gerda, starts on her dreamlike adventures, not in pursuit of an icy-hearted boy but of an utterly frivolous rabbit wearing a fancy waistcoat and carrying a gold watch. Before following Alice down her famous rabbit hole, let's look briefly at one of her predecessors.

### CHARLES KINGSLEY

*The Water-Babies*

Charles Kingsley, a clergyman and a scientist, wrote a book for his own little boy which enjoyed great popularity for many years. It told the story of Tom, a poor little chimney sweep who was carried off by the fairies to the world under the waters, where he became a Water-Baby. For the most part this story makes little appeal to modern children. It is interesting historically not only because it embodies magic, but because the water creatures are true to their species. Here, perhaps, is the ancestor of the modern animal tale which permits the creatures to speak but keeps them otherwise true to their kind. *The Water-Babies* (1863) also teaches moral lessons, and the unwieldy combination of magic, morals, and lessons in science is enough to account for its waning popularity.

### LEWIS CARROLL

*Alice's Adventures in Wonderland*
*Through the Looking Glass*

The "Alice" books cannot be accounted for on the basis of anything that had preceded them. The comfortable, solid life of Charles Lutwidge Dodgson, author of *Alice's Adventures in Wonderland*, was as different from the tragic irregularities of Hans Andersen's as it could well be. Yet in the end both men achieved somewhat similar fame. Both loved children and were loved by them; both were bachelors; and both were disconcerted when their fame was attached not to their professional work but to their books for children.

As a child, young Charles complicated the family garden with an elaborate miniature railroad, which he built and ran. He also launched a newspaper, wrote poems for it, and drew the illustrations. He made a puppet theater, and he kept all sorts of curious animals for pets. Indeed, it is hard to believe that this active, enterprising boy could grow up to be a sober, sedate cleric with ambitions toward mathematical research. But his childhood may account in part for *Alice*.

Fortunately, Dr. Liddell of Christ Church, where Dodgson lectured, had three little girls called by their mathematical friend Prima, Secunda, and Tertia. Secunda was Alice, evidently Dodgson's favorite:

*Child of the pure unclouded brow*
*And dreaming eyes of wonder!*

So he described her, in the introductory poem to *Through the Looking Glass*. The charming photographs he has left of her bear out his description. To these little girls, Dodgson used to tell stories, teasing them by breaking off in the middle with "And that's all till next time." Whereupon "the cruel Three" would cry, "But it *is* the next time!"

Then came that famous summer afternoon (the fourth of July, by the way) when

Dodgson rowed his little friends up the Cherwell River to Goodstow, where they had tea on the riverbank. There the young man told them the fairy tale of "Alice's Adventures Under Ground." Secunda hoped there'd be nonsense in it, and no hopes ever materialized more gloriously. The next Christmas, Dodgson wrote his story as a gift for "a dear child in memory of a Summer day." The story was exquisitely written in clear script, as legible as print, and charmingly illustrated by the author. Years later that little green volume of ninety-two pages was sold to a private collector in the United States for £15,400 or about $77,000, "the highest price which any book has ever brought in an English auction room."

Three years after the famous picnic, the story appeared in book form, somewhat enlarged, with the new title *Alice's Adventures in Wonderland* and with Sir John Tenniel's matchless illustrations. That was 1865, and six years later the companion volume appeared, both books under the pseudonym Lewis Carroll. Then a strange thing happened. Charles Lutwidge Dodgson, still an obscure mathematician, found Lewis Carroll a famous person—sought after, praised, discussed, even advertised. Gentle, sensitive soul that he was, Dodgson was horrified. He announced firmly that "Mr. Dodgson neither claimed nor acknowledged any connection with the books not published under his name." Autograph hunters hunted in vain. He wrote several more books under his pseudonym, but when Queen Victoria asked for the rest of his works, he sent her all his learned treatises on mathematics and nothing else. If the name "Lewis Carroll" was supposed to provide Charles Dodgson with a shield against publicity, it was a dismal failure. Instead it practically obliterated the mathematician. Like Andersen's, Dodgson's declining years were serene and uneventful. Nothing else he ever wrote enjoyed the success of his two companion volumes about Alice.

Does anyone who has read the *Adventures in Wonderland* ever forget those opening paragraphs, with the child's comment on books?

> *Alice was beginning to get very tired of sitting by her sister on the bank, and of having nothing to do: once or twice she had peeped into the book her sister was reading, but it had no pictures or conversations in it, "and what is the use of a book," thought Alice, "without pictures or conversations?"*

Then plop! Right into the third short paragraph comes the White Rabbit, with waistcoat and watch. Down he goes into the rabbit hole, murmuring "Oh dear! Oh dear! I shall be too late!" And down the rabbit hole after him goes Alice, "never once considering how in the world she was to get out again." From then on madness takes over.

Alice finds a little glass table on which is a tiny golden key that unlocks the door to more bewilderment. She drinks from a little bottle and shrinks to ten inches, swallows a piece of cake and finds she is "opening out like the largest telescope that ever was!" This goes on, but never is Alice the proper size for the place she is in. She nearly drowns in a lake of her own tears; she is forever catching glimpses of the hurrying White Rabbit, but hurrying where? She encounters strange creatures. There is the smiling Cheshire Cat who can vanish leaving only his grin behind. There is the Queen of Hearts who disposes of all who disagree with her with a simple "Off with her head!" and the Red Queen who has to run for dear life in order "to keep in the same place." All these characters talk nonsense in the gravest way. The best example is "A Mad Tea-Party," where the conversation reminds you uncomfortably of some of the disjointed small talk which you have not only heard but perhaps, horrid thought, even contributed to. The characters appear and disappear, behave with a kind of wild logic, and burst into verses which sing in your head in place of the serious poetry you might prefer to recall. There are eighteen verses of the mock tragedy relating how "The Walrus and the Carpenter" lured some young oysters to a "dismal" end. Equally delightful nonsense are "The Lobster-Quadrille," "Jabberwocky," and "Father William."

These ditties, which occur every few chapters, are memorized with ease and are popular with children. They represent a kind of humor which some people enjoy and others find hard to understand. Paul Hazard in *Books, Children and Men* says of the English people and *Alice:*

> *The English are a calm and cold people. But let them relax, for a single day, that compulsion for self-control which governs them and they will show a capacity for boisterous unrestraint that is surprising. . . . It is the same with laughter. When they enjoy looking at the universe on its fantastic side, distorting it with deforming mirrors, there is no stopping them. . . . A foreigner can try to understand* Alice in Wonderland; *but to appreciate fully this marvelous story one must be English. (p. 140)*

This last statement should be qualified, for many Americans revel in the book and it has been translated into many languages. The puzzling question is when do children enjoy *Alice?* Needless to say, it should never be required reading. Some children heartily dislike fantasy and to make them read *Alice* would be to turn reading into a penalty instead of a delight. If for certain children it rouses no laughter, it is worse than useless for them. When college students are asked what books they remember enjoying as children there is more disagreement over *Alice* than over any other book. Some disliked it heartily or were bored by it; some say *Alice* was one of their favorite books, not as children but at the high-school age. This is perhaps where it really belongs. Most of those who liked *Alice* as children, ten or under, had heard it read aloud by adults who enjoyed it. Those who had to read the book for themselves rarely found it funny until they were older. Here are some clues. Try reading *Alice* aloud to the children if you yourself like it. If the story captures their interest, keep on; if it rouses no enthusiasm, put it away until later. But somewhere, sometime, children should be exposed to this fantasy and allowed to accept it joyously or reject it without apologies. And as adults they may reread it as political satire and find to their astonishment famous contemporary figures neatly caricatured.

Sir John Tenniel in his illustrations for *Alice* has fixed forever the face, figure, and dress of this beloved little girl. Long, straight hair, a grave, prim face, a neat, perky dress covered with a pinafore, and the straight, slim legs clad in horizontally striped stockings make an appealing little figure which no one ever forgets. This is Alice, the Alice who remains impeccably Alice even when her neck has grown as long as a giraffe's. The Tenniel rabbit is an equally unforgettable figure with his sporty tweed coat, his massive gold watch and chain, his swagger walking stick, just the kind of fellow who *would* keep the Duchess waiting. For Tenniel does not merely illustrate. He interprets, giving the mood and the manner of the creature as well as his outer appearance.

You also have to admire the remarkable technique of these pictures. Tenniel draws Alice stepping through the looking glass,

*Illustration by Sir John Tenniel. From* Alice's Adventures in Wonderland, *by Lewis Carroll.*

with curious and plausible ease, half of her on one side, half on the other. The Cheshire Cat disappearing, leaving only his grin behind, and the playing-card and chess people are only a few of his pen-and-ink wonders. These sketches are so alive, so profoundly interpretative that no one has ever wished for colored illustrations of Alice, at least not until Leonard Weisgard created them color-drenched and beautiful. But certainly no artist has illustrated Alice with greater magic than Tenniel. If possible, let children's first experience with Alice include the drawings of her first illustrator, Sir John Tenniel, most excellent interpreter of Wonderland.

## GEORGE MACDONALD

*At the Back of the North Wind*
*The Light Princess*

George Macdonald was a personal friend of Charles Dodgson, and *Alice* was read to the Macdonald children when it was still in manuscript form. However, when Macdonald began to write fairy tales himself, he wrote more in the vein of Hans Christian Andersen. Indeed his first book, *At the Back of the North Wind* (1871), is reminiscent of "The Snow Queen." This story of Diamond's adventures is a long one, carrying the little boy through thirty-eight adventures (chapters), some with the North Wind herself, some with his flesh-and-blood friends or foes. The North Wind first comes to Diamond in his hayloft bed. She carries him out into the night, teaches him to follow her through the air and to go from his dream life with her to play a brave part in his difficult everyday life. This continual change from fantasy to reality and back again to fantasy confuses some children. Some like the North Wind parts but others prefer the earthly adventures of the boy.

Diamond is an appealing little figure when he is not being too angelic. His flesh-and-blood adventures are often as incredible as those with the North Wind: he reforms a drunkard, rescues a street sweeper from slavery to an infamous old woman, drives his father's cab through the London streets, and generally guides and improves all the adults with whom he comes in contact. Despite the moralistic side of the book, many of the chapters tell an imaginative and thrilling story. The chapter that tells how the real Diamond was seriously ill and the other Diamond miraculously passed through the North Wind herself and came to the country which lies at her back is a beautifully related bit of mysticism implying, perhaps, death. It is one of the most moving episodes in the book. Probably few children ever catch this inner meaning, but whether they do or don't, the chapter is reassuring.

The other Macdonald books, like this one, seem overlong. *The Princess and the Goblin* and *The Princess and Curdie* present interminable adventures above and below ground with cobs and humans and with considerable general moralizing into the bargain. The books are well written and have a strong imaginative appeal, but because of their length and complexity they are enjoyed today only by the exceptional child.

A short story, *The Light Princess* (1893), has neither of these drawbacks, and is as engaging today as it was when it was first published in a collection called *Dealings with the Fairies*. In an unedited edition illustrated by Maurice Sendak, the sweetness and humor of the tale about the princess who had no gravity and couldn't keep her feet on the ground are echoed in the delicacy and beauty of the pictures. In another edited edition, William Pène du Bois takes advantage of the changes in the text to stress the humor of the story: where the original speaks of "a stamp with her feet would have sent her aloft again but for the hold she had on his arm. . . ." this edited edition gives ". . . aloft again had he not caught her toe . . ." and the accompanying illustration shows the fuming princess floating in the air above the lake with her one toe held daintily between the amused prince's thumb and forefinger.

*From* The Light Princess *by George Macdonald with pictures by Maurice Sendak, pictures copyright © 1969 by Maurice Sendak. Reprinted with the permission of Farrar, Straus & Giroux, Inc.*

## JAMES BARRIE

*Peter Pan*

Of all Sir James Barrie's delightful plays and books, none has been so beloved as *Peter Pan* (1904). Exquisitely performed by Maude Adams at the beginning of the century and by Mary Martin in a musical version in the middle of the century, it has been as popular with adults as with children. The book *Peter and Wendy* was made from the play but was never so successful, probably because the writing was too subtle for the average child. The play makes dramatically clear the story of Peter Pan, the boy who will not grow up; Tinker Bell, the fairy who loses her shadow; and the three children—Wendy, John, and Michael—who go off with Peter Pan to Never Never Land. Their adventures with pirates, redskins, and a ticking crocodile are exciting, but in the end they return to their parents to begin the serious business of growing up. Peter Pan is left alone with Tink, whose life is in danger. Only one thing will save her, and so Peter calls through the dusk to all children, "Do you believe in fairies?" Always, at this point in the play, a great cry goes up from the audience, "*I* do!" "*I* do!"—the children's testimony of faith!

## C. S. LEWIS

The *Narnia* stories

Well known as a theologian, poet, and author, C. S. Lewis created for children a strange new world—Narnia—which they first enter through an old wardrobe. *The Lion, the Witch, and the Wardrobe* (1950) is the first of a series of books about the adventures of four children. Narnia is no Utopia. In fact, once the children have become kings and queens of Narnia, they find themselves engaged in the endless conflict between good and evil symbolized by the benignant Lion Aslan and the malicious Witch. After reigning for many years, the children return to their own world, only to find that they have not even been missed.

*Prince Caspian* carries the children back to Narnia for further adventures. *The Magician's Nephew* goes back to the creation of Narnia by the Lion. When the Lion sings into existence the world, the stars, the land, and then the creatures, the sheer goodness of creation is too much for the Witch. She flees, but the reader knows she will return. *The Last Battle* concludes the series. As the title implies, the loyal followers of the king of Narnia are making their last stand against the forces of evil which seek to destroy the noble Lion Aslan and the world he has created. Another theologian, Chad Walsh, considers this the best of the series, a book full of Christian symbolism, and a "deeply moving and hauntingly lovely story apart from its doctrinal content." Children never suspect the doctrine, but a world of good and evil seems strangely plausible.

## MARY NORTON

*The Borrowers*

In 1943 a book called *The Magic Bed-knob* appeared. It caused no great stir but was well liked by children who encountered it. Then in 1953 came *The Borrowers* by the same author, Mary Norton. Most reviewers agreed that here was a treasure of lasting value. As British as tea for breakfast, but with action, suspense, and characters of universal appeal, it was immediately popular in the United States as well as in Great Britain.

Borrowers are not fairies but small creatures who live in old houses and take their names from the places they inhabit—the Overmantels, for instance, the Harpsichords, and the Clocks, who live under a huge old grandfather's clock in the hall. Homily, Pod, and their daughter Arrietty Clock are the only surviving family of Borrowers in the old house. When a Borrower is *seen*, there is nothing for him to do but emigrate. Only Pod, climbing curtains with the aid of his trusty hatpin, borrowing a useful spoon now and then or a bit of tea or a portrait stamp of the Queen, only Pod has escaped detection. Arrietty is the problem now. Arrietty wants to see the world and she goes exploring, happily and trustingly even after the boy sees her. They become fast friends, but even the boy cannot prevent the tragic ending. It was so catastrophic that children could not accept it as final. There had to be a sequel, and so we follow the fortunes of these fascinating characters in *The Borrowers Afield*, *The Borrowers Afloat*, and *The Borrowers Aloft*, with which the series ends, although Homily reminisces about a past event in *Poor Stainless*.

No briefing of these stories can give any conception of their quality. Every character is unforgettably portrayed. There is poor Homily with her hair forever awry, loving but a chronic worrier, "taking on" first and then going capably to work. Pod is the sober realist, a philosopher and a brave one. Arrietty is youth and adventure, springtime and hope, too much in love with life to be afraid even of those mammoth "human beans." To read these books aloud is to taste the full richness

*Illustration by Beth and Joe Krush. Reproduced from* The Borrowers, *copyright, 1952, 1953, by Mary Norton, by permission of Harcourt Brace Jovanovich, Inc.*

of their humor and good writing. Children read and reread them and presently, in classrooms, homes, and camps, they create their own versions of a Borrower's house. None is ever as clever as Pod's under-clock domain, but each one, done with loving inventiveness, is a tribute to Pod, Homily, Arrietty, and Mary Norton.

## LUCY M. BOSTON

The *Green Knowe* books

Another distinguished English fantasy, beautifully written and completely absorbing, is *The Children of Green Knowe* (1955), by Lucy M. Boston. It is a juvenile *Berkeley Square*, going back in time from the present and a boy named Tolly to the seventeenth century and three children of his family who died in the great plague.

A lonely child, Tolly is sent to live with his great-grandmother, Mrs. Oldknow, at the family's ancient manor house The Green Knowe. He is soon aware of the presence of other children who come and go. He hears them but cannot see them although he knows his grandmother sees them. She shows him the portrait of the three and tells him the story of each child and their great horse Feste, and presently Tolly sees them also, but he can never touch them. Play with these children from the past involves Tolly in a terrifying situation. He is saved by St. Christopher, and the story ends serenely. It is safe to say that no reader young or old will ever forget Mrs. Oldknow or Tolly or the mysterious and beautiful old manor house.

There are more books in this setting—*Treasure of Green Knowe*, in which Tolly and his great-grandmother again appear; *An Enemy at Green Knowe*, in which Tolly meets a practitioner of black magic; and *The River at Green Knowe*, in which a new set of characters appears—in all of these stories real life and fantasy are successfully mingled. *A Stranger at Green Knowe*, one of the most moving boy and animal tales ever written, is discussed in Chapter 12, page 414.

*The Castle of Yew* is an imaginative adventure story which takes place in a topiary garden where the yews have the shape of chessmen. *The Sea Egg*, a deft blend of realism and fantasy, tells of two small boys who find a stone that hatches into a water creature through whom they learn the magical secrets of the sea. In *Nothing Said*, another blend of realism and fantasy, a child, visiting a friend of her mother's, becomes intrigued by the idea of a tree spirit and does indeed meet a dryad.

### VIEWPOINTS

. . . deeper meaning is essential in fantasy. For the characters involved, there is no need for very deep thought. They can enjoy the pleasure of realizing their dearest wishes, only occasionally speculating about their origin. Sometimes (as in E. Nesbit's stories) they can be changed a little, can learn a little from their adventures, as they miraculously travel the world, change their shape, or exploit the power of a button, a lamp-post or a pencil. But the reader who vicariously enjoys these delights should expect something more. The fantasy should exercise his imagination. For the characters in the story there is little time for Why and How. Questions are blown away as they rush from one adventure to another. But the reader can and should ask How and Why. He should be left with a sense of expansion, as if he himself had been flying on a magic carpet and breathing an air more rarefied than his accustomed oxygen, . . .—Margery Fisher, *Intent Upon Reading*, Watts, 1961, pp. 149–150.

## A. PHILIPPA PEARCE

*Tom's Midnight Garden*

Known to American children as the author of a fascinating English mystery story *The Minnow Leads to Treasure*, Philippa Pearce won

*Illustration by Susan Einzig for* Tom's Midnight Garden *by A. Philippa Pearce. Copyright 1958 Oxford University Press. Reproduced by permission of J. B. Lippincott Company.*

the Carnegie Medal for *Tom's Midnight Garden* (1959), an equally engrossing fantasy, with time as a theme. Young Tom, much bored by life in his aunt and uncle's apartment, hears an ancient clock strike thirteen. Immediately he slips into an enchanting garden where he plays with Hatty, a child from the past. Their play is imaginative but made credible because of the logic of "Time no longer," the motto on the clock. These strange midnight adventures of Tom's are later half explained by what adults might call thought-transference. However, they seem quite clear and uncomplicated to young readers once they accept Tom's timeless midnight garden.

### MAURICE DRUON

*Tistou of the Green Thumbs*

From France comes a subtle allegory called *Tistou of the Green Thumbs* (1958). As a little boy, Tistou is different from other children, but it is the gardener who discovers that the child has green thumbs which cause flowers to bloom immediately. The old man says, "Hidden talent often leads to trouble. . . . Well, keep it to yourself." And the two of them do, only Tistou can not help using his talent. When he sees the misery of prisoners, he makes the prison courtyards blaze with roses, and likewise the slums, the zoo, and, finally, even the guns in his father's munition factory. Only on the last page does the reader discover Tistou's identity, and the little parable ends gently. Some children will miss the social satire of the story, but the joyous changes Tistou brings about are memorable pictures.

### JULIA SAUER

*Fog Magic*

Before Tolly played with his ancestors at Green Knowe, a Nova Scotian child, Greta Addington, abroad in a fog, walks straight into Blue Cove, a village of long ago. There she finds a friend her own age to play with and is accepted by the family as one "from over the mountain." Greta can find the village only on days of heavy fog, so she hopes her twelfth birthday will be foggy. But it isn't, until nightfall. Then she hurries to Blue Cove, where her friends give her a kitten for a birthday gift with a wish for "Safe passage for all the years ahead." Somehow Greta knows this is goodbye to fog magic and she is not surprised to discover that her father on his twelfth birthday had received a small knife and had never seen the village again.

Notice how Tolly, Tom, and Greta, in these stories that go back and forth in time, are temporarily lonely children in search of companionship. Psychologists say such stories vicariously fill a need, but *Fog Magic* (1943) does one thing better than the others. It terminates the play with finality. Maturity lies ahead and reality must be accepted. *Fog Magic* has rare beauty and significance.

## PENELOPE FARMER

*Charlotte Sometimes*
*Emma in Winter*
*The Summer Birds*

*Charlotte Sometimes* (1969) is a fantasy adventure that borders on science fiction. Its time-shift theme is a familiar one in that genre, but it has seldom been used more dramatically, perhaps because Charlotte alternates between two worlds. Somehow, while in boarding school, Charlotte finds that she is back in the days of World War I and that her name is Clare. Slowly she begins to realize that Clare is her double and that whenever she is in Clare's world, her place is taken by her doppelgänger. The mystery and suspense are maintained to the end.

In *Emma in Winter* (1966), Charlotte's sister finds that she shares the same dreams as a boy she dislikes, a boy she and Charlotte met in *The Summer Birds*, the most moving of these books. In *The Summer Birds* (1962), a strange boy teaches the sisters to fly, and then all the children in their school enjoy the soaring bliss and freedom of flight. When the summer ends, they learn the boy's identity and the magic is lost. They are again earthbound. In these three books and in *The Magic Stone* as well, the style is smooth, the mood subdued, and the characterization perceptive, but *The Summer Birds* has an almost palpable aura of magic and an ending that has the inevitability of Greek drama.

## WILLIAM PÈNE DU BOIS

*The Twenty-One Balloons*

The fantasies of William Pène du Bois are as orderly and logical as mathematics, and his illustrations have the same graceful balance. He himself credits his passion for order to his regimented school life at Lycée Hoche, for which he is as grateful as he is for glorious weekly excursions to the French circus. These and other lifelong interests are reflected in his books—his love of France, the circus, all forms of mechanized transportation, islands, Utopias, and explosions! Look at some of his most notable books: *Bear Party* is a reasonable fable of some quarrelsome bears who grow genuinely fond of each other when they have a fancy dress party. A bear Utopia results. *The Giant* is a logical story of an eight-year-old giant, already seven stories tall but wistfully amiable. He can disrupt a whole city and send the people into a panic by picking up streetcars or automobiles or people for a better look. It is all drawn to scale as precisely as an architect's plan. In *Lazy Tommy Pumpkinhead* the author takes a healthy poke at the electronic age and what can happen when machines fail.

And best of all there is his Newbery Medal book, *The Twenty-One Balloons* (1947). When its hero, Professor William Waterman Sherman, tires of teaching little boys arithmetic, he sets off in a balloon to see the world and be alone. He tells his story of landing on the island of Krakatoa (a real island, by the way) and finding its inhabitants inventors of the most amazing super-gadgets. These are described in detail and drawn meticulously. Since the island is volcanic, the people have planned a machine for escape should the volcano erupt, and of course it does. And off they go in their airy-go-round. Related with the utmost simplicity, the story piles up suspense until the explosion is a relief.

## MAURICE SENDAK

*Where the Wild Things Are*
*Higglety Pigglety Pop!*
*In the Night Kitchen*
*Nutshell Library*

Maurice Sendak's versatility and craftsmanship as an artist have been discussed in Chapter 3, and they are qualities that contribute both to the books he has illustrated for other authors and to those he has written himself. He has become equally distinguished as a writer of fantasy. The integrity of his conception and the respect he has for children are nowhere more evident than in his fanciful stories. Best known of his books is the 1964 Caldecott winner, *Where the Wild Things Are*, a picture book that was greeted with delight by many and apprehension by some. Max is a small boy whose noisy ebullience causes his mother to call him a Wild Thing. "I'll eat you up!" he retorts, and is sent to his room, where he solaces himself by imagining a kingdom of wild things, fanged and clawed, all bowing respectfully to their beloved ruler, Max, king of all the wild things. "Let the wild rumpus start," he proclaims, and a mammoth frolic takes place. When Max leaves, his creatures plead with him to stay because they love him so. But he goes back to his room, to real life, and to his supper waiting for him, "and it was still hot." The psychological implications are sound, and the reassuring note in closing has a touching quality. Those adults who were apprehensive about the possibility of the wild things (they are deliciously hideous) frightening children seem to have been mistaken: the pictures amuse and delight small children, and many Sendak fans have sent him their own pictures of wild things which, he says, outdo his own beasts in ferocity. And children see the reassurance in Max's return home from his fantasy land when he "wanted to be where someone loved him best of all."

The subtitle of *Higglety Pigglety Pop!* (1967) is *There Must Be More to Life*. Its heroine is Jenny, who has everything a dog could want and leaves home because she is not content. She wants something she does not have, and feels "there must be more to life" than having everything. Jenny is drawn from life, a dearly loved pet who has been immortalized in the soft, tender, and amusing black-and-white pictures so different from the bold exaggeration and flamboyance of the wild things. Jenny eventually becomes the leading lady of the World Mother Goose Theater, starring as The Dog (typical Sendak humor) in a production of "Higglety Pigglety Pop!" Written with bland directness that belies the nonsensical situation, the story ends with a poignant note from Jenny to her old master in which she says that she cannot tell him how to get to Castle Yonder, because she doesn't know where it is. "But if you ever come this way, look for me."

Maurice Sendak's childhood memories are the basis for much of the setting for *In the Night Kitchen* (1970). The smell of baking, the warmth and light in the room below, the buildings seen against a night sky, and the "Mickey Oven" label (Sendak has an impressive collection of Mickey Mouse objects) all contribute to the story of a small boy who, in his dream, falls down into the night kitchen where three identical bakers (all Oliver Hardy) try to stir him into the batter. Mickey soars off into the night in an airplane of dough and brings the bakers the milk they need to complete their cake. Dawn comes, and a sleepy child tumbles back into bed. The illustrations, drawn to accentuate the solidity and simplicity of the figures, make imaginative use of kitchen objects and food package labels, and there are small personal touches like a tiny sign that says, "Jennie Street." Sendak's draftsmanship is particularly impressive in these illustrations, and both the pictures and the story are remarkable in their identification with a child's vision.

The four irresistible books that make up Maurice Sendak's *Nutshell Library* (1962) are approximately two and one-half by three and three-fourths inches; they are tidily contained in a small box, and the box, the book jackets, and the books are illustrated with Mr. Sendak's impish, round-faced boys. The text of the four little books is as original as the pictures. *One Was Johnny* is a counting book, which winds up and unwinds in fine, cumulative style. *Pierre*, subtitled "a cautionary tale," describes the horrible fate of a boy who keeps saying "I don't care." But the ending is droll. *Alligators All Around* is one of the funniest alphabet books yet, and *Chicken Soup with Rice* is hilarious nonsense about the months of the year. These are "funny books," original and beguiling in miniature form.

## ROALD DAHL

*James and the Giant Peach*
*Charlie and the Chocolate Factory*
*The Magic Finger*

The fantasies of Roald Dahl have improved in style and simplicity with each of his books. *James and the Giant Peach* (1961), which tells of a boy's flight in a peach made gigantic by magic, is an inventive and elaborate story. In *Charlie and the Chocolate Factory* (1964), five children are given a chance to prove their strength of character by the eccentric factory owner whose wonderfully ingenious plant is operated by pygmies—a device that has been criticized as anti-black. The author uses the faults of the children as an opportunity to discourse on social behavior, but the fantastic setting, lively dialogue, and exaggeration in plot have appealed to many readers. *The Magic Finger* (1966) is simpler in structure and stronger in its message: shooting animals for sport is deplorable. An indignant eight-year-old girl points her magic finger at her neighbors who are hunters. The father and sons shrink to tiny winged creatures and the ducks grow enormous, sprout arms that can hold guns, and move into the family's house. Able to understand the animal point of view, the hunters make a pact with the ducks. Less humorous than *Charlie*, this has better construction and a light, easy style.

*Illustration by William Pène du Bois for* The Magic Finger *by Roald Dahl. Copyright © 1966. Reproduced by permission of Harper & Row, Publishers, Inc.*

### Other Stories of Fantasy

The most convincing modern fantasies have come chiefly from England, but American writers are working in this field with increasing success.

Alan Garner's fanciful stories have a mystical, fairy-tale quality that is particularly appealing to some readers. In *The Owl Service*, which won the Carnegie Award, there is a fine balance between the realistic problems of the young people in the story and their involvement in a mysterious reenactment of a Welsh legend. In William Mayne's *Earthfasts*, there is a double movement in time

## VIEWPOINTS

I feel that if you are going to use fantasy, that is if you are going to write in this peculiar way, then you must relate this to the known facts, that is to the material world. It goes back to my original point that mythology is not an escape, it is not an entertainment. It is an attempt to come to terms with reality. . . . it is a clarification.

. . . anybody could write a story about a moonlit hillside near Tintagel with some nice romantic ruins and have a unicorn careering across the landscape and that would be lovely. It would also be a pastiche of everything that has ever been written about unicorns since about 1400 and would not add anything to anybody's experience and therefore, to my mind, would not be worth writing.—Alan Garner, "Coming to Terms," *Children's Literature in Education*, July 1970 (#2), p. 17.

that brings fantasy to the edge of science fiction. Both books have a literary distinction that is found in few fantasies by American authors, although Lloyd Alexander's books with their intricate and humorous style and John Lawson's *You Better Come Home with Me* and *Spring Rider* with their elegant prose are outstanding. In the United States, writers have been markedly successful in books of humorous fantasy, both in books like *Magic to Burn* by Jean Fritz, which combines fantasy and realism, and in the tongue-in-cheek fairy tales of Joseph Schrank and Phyllis McGinley.

Most of the modern fantasies combine realism and fantasy. May Massee spoke soundly when she said: "The right story of fantasy has its feet on the ground."[13] That is, the more real and everyday the setting and the people, the more reasonable and convincing the story.

13. Bertha Mahony Miller and Elinor Whitney Field, eds., *Newbery Medal Books: 1922–1955* (Horn Book, 1957), p. 297.

## SCIENCE FICTION

Mankind has always been fascinated by the possibility of movement in space and time and by the extension into the unknown of facts known about the structure of society or the physical laws of the universe. Science fiction is a combination of the known and the unknown, the unknown usually based on current scientific theories; and children of today have seen the fulfillment of many prophecies of science fiction of the past. In this type of literature, there are endless combinations of science-based fantasy and hard fact, but most of the best writing is concerned with space travel, travel in time, or the world of the future.

### ROBERT HEINLEIN

*Rocket Ship Galileo*
*Podkayne of Mars*

The fun and danger of *Rocket Ship Galileo* (1947) and Robert Heinlein's many other books about interspace travel is that they seem completely reasonable and factual. No "airy-go-rounds" in these tales. Instead the reader has to pinch himself to remember that we are not pioneering on Mars, sending colonies to Ganymede, or commuting to Hespera. Although many science-fiction stories include girls, few of them have a girl as the central character. In *Podkayne of Mars* (1963), a sixteen-year-old girl goes on her first trip to Venus. Most space fiction falls into predictable patterns but not Robert Heinlein's. His characters are well-drawn human beings, with human faults, unique problems, and moments sometimes of despair and sometimes of triumph. The stories are so well told they swing the reader along in a state of almost unbearable suspense. Nevertheless, even with the best space stories, a few too many and the reader may tire of the genre. The fad passes and the fact remains that no classic has yet emerged from this field of imaginative writing unless time and young readers bestow that honor on the 1963 Newbery Medal winner, *A Wrinkle in Time.*

## MADELEINE L'ENGLE

*A Wrinkle in Time*

Madeleine L'Engle's notable book *Meet the Austins* is a fine realistic family story. The opening of *A Wrinkle in Time* (1963 Newbery Medal) suggests that it will be a similar kind of story. A storm is raging outside, but within the cozy kitchen Meg Murry and her brother, precocious five-year-old Charles Wallace Murry, are having hot cocoa with their mother. Into this family group comes a strange old woman, Mrs. Whatsit. She explains that she was "caught in a down draft and blown off course." But having finished her cocoa, she departs with one final word to the mother, ". . . there *is* such a thing as a tesseract." That is what the children's scientist father had been working on for the government when he disappeared. The next day, Meg, Charles Wallace, and Calvin O'Keefe, a friend, meet Mrs. Whatsit and two other strange old women, who warn the children that their father is in grave danger and that only they can save him and only if they are willing to tesseract. This involves the "fact" that the shortest distance between two points is not a straight line, but a fold or wrinkle. The children agree to try it. There follows in the complex course of the rest of the book a battle between good and evil, love and hate, that in spite of being complicated with science, philosophy, religion, satire, and allegory, carries the story on at a horrifying pace. In the end Meg's love triumphs and her father is saved. All of them tesseract back to earth where their lives pick up as they were except for their new-found knowledge of good and evil.

This space story is written in terms of the modern world in which children know about brainwashing and the insidious, creeping corruption of evil. The last third of the book is confused, but the fact that many children and young people read it avidly suggests that they get more of its underlying significance than might be expected. It is a tribute to their growing maturity and to Madeleine L'Engle's style of writing.

### VIEWPOINTS

In almost any fantasy of time travel, or of the mingling of different times, there inevitably arises the intriguing question of who, rightfully, is a ghost to whom, it being usually a matter of whose time the scene is being played in, though this is not invariably easy to decide—the mood or feeling being often ambiguous or even wittily paradoxical. . . .

. . . traveling back and forth in Time, or on different levels of Time, meeting one's self or others coming and going or existing in various dimensions at once, can all become enormously complicated so that the writer, not to speak of the reader, is continually required to keep his wits about him.

But happenings and devices in themselves, no matter how outré and mind-bending, are not what give lasting nourishment. They do not deeply satisfy and some of us they do not satisfy at all. For what one remembers from the great piece of writing is the voice speaking in a way that is indefinably different from any other voice, the unforgettable personalities, the sense of a profound life that can go on after the story is ended. . . .—Eleanor Cameron, *The Green and Burning Tree,* Little, Brown, Boston, Toronto, 1969, pp. 90, 76–77.

## JOHN CHRISTOPHER

*The White Mountains* trilogy

When stories of the future are written as science fantasies rather than science fiction, they need both a breadth of conception and a fidelity of detail to lend conviction. John Christopher succeeds admirably in *The White*

*Mountains* (1967) in establishing the believability of his twenty-first-century world. In this world, machine creatures called the Tripods control the earth and perpetuate their mastery over human beings by inserting steel caps in the skulls of all children when they reach the age of fourteen, an operation that renders them forever subservient. Three boys —Will, Henry, and Beanpole—have heard that in a land the ancients called "Switzerland," there is a haven, and having learned from a Vagrant that free men live in the White Mountains, they decide to escape before they are capped. They cross the channel to a land where the language is different, discover that the French have a medieval society unlike their own rustic culture, and have a hazardous but successful journey to the small colony of free men who live secluded in a mountain. In the second volume, *The City of Gold and Lead*, Will takes part in an athletic contest, the winners of which are to have the privilege of serving the Masters, the Tripods. The other boys go in a spirit of sacrifice; Will goes as a spy. In *The Pool of Fire*, Will (who tells the story in the previous books as well) describes the intricate operation of sabotage by which the Tripods are defeated, and the new freedom of mankind to set up its own government. As has happened before, there is quarreling and competition, so Will gives up his own plans to work with a small group of men whose goals are world unity and peace. The ending is sober and realistic, a reminder that vigilance against tyranny must be constant. The whole concept of the trilogy is developed with pace and skill, the pitting of good against evil, in a world where few can see the evil, adding suspense to the well-structured action.

*The Guardians* is straight science fiction with no fantasy element. It is set in the year 2052, when England is divided into two societies: the megalopolis, huge and sprawling, sharply divided by a frontier from the rest of England occupied by the landed gentry and their servants.

*The Lotus Caves* is a fantasy in which two boys living on a research station on the moon find a cavern where there is a rich environment ruled by a Plant, an entity that offers everything to its visitors but freedom.

In *The Prince in Waiting*, man has destroyed his own civilization and there is fear and hatred (as in Peter Dickinson's books) of machines and technology, but the young heir to a city-state finds a secret group, the Seers, who have in their underground sanctuary every taboo mechanical and electronic device. All of Christopher's books are concerned with serious problems of mankind and man's environment; his gift as a science-fiction writer is his ability to treat these problems seriously without making a tract out of an absorbing adventure story.

### PETER DICKINSON

*The Weathermonger*
*Heartsease*
*The Devil's Children*

An editor of the English humor magazine *Punch* and the author of adult mystery stories, Peter Dickinson was immediately successful as a writer for children. His first book, *The Weathermonger* (1969), is a vigorous and well-written fantasy about an England of the near future, a time in which the British Isles have become mysteriously subject to a state of feudalism in which any mechanical object is taboo, and in which the weather is controlled by magic. Geoffrey, a young weathermonger, escapes to France and comes back secretly with his younger sister on a mission, the cause of the enchantment. The plot is inventive, the characterization vivid, and the thoroughly contemporary dialogue, often lightly humorous, a good contrast to the mystic elements of the story.

The second book in this trilogy about England in the time of the Changes is *Heartsease*. Only a few people are unmarked by the hatred of machines, the fear of strangers, the belief in witches. Margaret and her cousin Jonathan find a "witch," buried beneath a

*Illustration by Nathan Goldstein for* Heartsease *by Peter Dickinson. Copyright © 1969 by Peter Dickinson. Reproduced by permission of Little, Brown and Co.*

pile of stones, who is still alive. He is an American, and he can hardly believe the hysteria and bigotry of the villagers who attacked him. The children plan to help him escape, and they eventually get the man on board the tugboat *Heartsease* and take off, pursued by angry villagers. The book is, as are its companion volumes, an indictment of prejudice. It is also the most dramatic of the three, with a taut suspense in the escape and chase sequences.

In *The Devil's Children*, a small girl who has been left alone in London joins a group of Sikhs, who are unaffected by the prevailing thrall that grips the native population. She is used by them to prevent their making innocent blunders, and she clings to them at first for security despite the fact that they are reviled as the Devil's Children by the villagers in the area where they settled. But she comes to respect them for their intelligence and good will, as the village people eventually do also. Logical plot development, strong characterization, and a sprightly writing style add to the appeal of a cracking good tale. These are superb examples of one facet that is common to many science-fiction stories, the expressed belief in brotherhood and love as necessary ingredients in a shrunken world.

### Other Examples of Science Fiction

There are several writers whose science-fiction stories for older readers are good if not distinguished and whose audience greets each new volume avidly. Most of Alice M. Lightner's books have a medical theme, like that of *Doctor to the Galaxy*, in which a problem of medical research is pursued on a mythical planet. In her *The Galactic Troubadours*, however, the theme is the revival of musical performance in a society that frowns on young people who aren't satisfied with perfectly good taped music. Also realistic rather than fantastic is Sylvia Engdahl's *Journey Between Worlds*, which explores the theme of prejudice of Terrans against Martian colonists. Ben Bova, who has written some good scientific material about space investigation, turns to fiction in *The Weathermakers*. Other dependably good writers are Alan Nourse, Andre Norton, and Suzanne Martel, whose *The City Under Ground* is on a theme that has often been used by writers of adult science fiction: the emergence of a new civilization, conscious of ethical values, from the ruins of the old.

For much younger children, anywhere from eight to ten or eleven, there are no science-fiction masterpieces but numerous thoroughly amusing and plausible space fantasies. Ruthven Todd's *Space Cat*, Edward Ormondroyd's *Time at the Top*, Patricia Wrightson's *Down to Earth*, Jerome Beatty's

*Matthew Looney* stories, Jay Williams' and Raymond Abrashkin's *Danny Dunn* books, Louis Slobodkin's *Space Ship Under the Apple Tree*, Ellen MacGregor's *Miss Pickerell Goes to Mars*, and Eleanor Cameron's *Wonderful Flight to the Mushroom Planet*, together with their sequels, make absorbing reading and good introductions to this popular type of literature. Indicative of the way in which very young children have become interested in subjects that were formerly considered outside their sphere of interest has been their response to such picture books as Robert Kraus' *The Unidentified Flying Elephant* and Jerome Coopersmith's *A Chanukah Fable for Christmas*, an amusing story that has both an identified flying vehicle and a message of brotherhood.

## BOOKS THAT STIR CONTROVERSY

It is hardly necessary to say that a book is not likely to excite discussion if it does not have some excellent qualities. Books that are patterned in plot and pedestrian in style fall by the wayside; books that have a few minor flaws outweighed by their strengths can be approved by adults and enjoyed by successive waves of young readers; and books that are the best of their kind live on to become classics.

Some of the controversial books of the past can be seen, in retrospect, to have been breakers of barriers, and small classics of their time. Sometimes it is the content, sometimes the treatment, sometimes only a small facet of the story that causes disagreement about a book. The discussion here of fanciful books that have aroused controversy is meant not to disparage them but to point to some of the areas of fantasy writing that trouble many adults.

Certainly one perennial bone of contention has been the Oz books of L. Frank Baum. *The Wizard of Oz* and, to a lesser degree, its sequels have remained favorites of many children despite the fact that many authorities in the field of children's literature feel that the style is flat and dull, and that the inventiveness of the first book was followed by mediocrity and repetition in subsequent volumes. Another book that has been condemned by some adults is Helen Bannerman's *The Story of Little Black Sambo*, which is set in India. It is offensive to many adults because of the illustrations and because the name "Sambo" has derogatory connotations. Some adults defend the book on the grounds that the nonsense humor and the exaggeration make it a fine tale for telling or for reading aloud, and that the character was not intended to demean black people.

Also attacked, with considerable justification it would seem, as casting aspersion on black people are the *Dr. Dolittle* books by Hugh Lofting, one of which (*The Voyages of Dr. Dolittle*) won the Newbery Medal in 1923. Children have enjoyed the humorous reversal of roles in the series, with animals guiding and taking care of helpless human beings, and the gravity with which preposterous events are treated. Although the stories have action and humor, many adults are disturbed by the racial epithets, illustrations, and incidents, and some have suggested that the offending sections be deleted in new editions of the books. Similar questions have been raised in discussing Anne Parrish's *Floating Island*, in which the cook is a black doll. No one seems to dispute the fact that this shipwreck fantasy told from the doll's viewpoint is both highly original and wryly comic.

Quite another sort of difference of opinion has been generated by the books of Julia Cunningham, some of which are fantasy (*Viollet*, in which a bird, a fox, and a man unite to save the life of a gentle old man) and others (like *Dorp Dead*) which can be taken as fantasy or as realism. Indeed, some of the controversy has been on this very point. Some adults dislike the books because they are sophisticated, complex, and heavy with symbolism and psychological import; others defend the books on the ground that the symbolism and the author's concern with the struggle between good and evil in our society entitle the stories to be classed among the significant books of our time. Most agree that the writing style is polished and distinctive.

In another book that has caused criticism, Mary Chase's *Loretta Mason Potts*, the heroine is the oldest of five children, but her brothers and sisters are unaware of her existence. Bewitched by the people of a small, enchanted world, Loretta appears to be living with the uncouth Mr. and Mrs. Potts and is visited there secretly and periodically by her mother, Mrs. Mason. When the next oldest of the Mason children learns by chance about Loretta, a train of events begins that leads to her return to her family. The writing is light but pithy, the characterization sharp, and the idea fresh, but the book has been criticized both because the mother had given up her child and because she kept her existence a secret.

Ian Fleming's *Chitty-Chitty-Bang-Bang* is a burlesque of detective stories by a popular writer of adult detective fiction. The marvelous car Chitty-Chitty can rise to an occasion both literally and figuratively, since she takes to air and can (and does) take charge of events when the going gets rough in her family's encounter with a gang of French smugglers. The sophisticated style and zany story line have amused children, and the book has been used as the script for a film, but the sophistication of the parody and the style are felt by many adults to be inappropriate for the audience most interested in stories of animated machines.

Edward Eager's stories (*Magic or Not? The Well Wishers, Half Magic, Seven-Day Magic* and others) have intriguing plots and a good style, save for those books in which segments are purportedly but unconvincingly told by the child characters. The author has been criticized by those who feel his material is derivative and his children precocious.

The writing of Norton Juster in *The Phantom Tollbooth* delights many readers, young and old, who are intrigued by words and word play (a light meal consists of lights; a bee is a Spelling Bee) and by the Bunyan-like place names (for example, the Mountain of Ignorance and the Foothills of Confusion). To others the dependence on latent content and on comprehension of allusions makes the book seem heavily burdened with references that will daunt many readers.

Under each category of modern fanciful tales many more stories could be listed. Most of the examples discussed in this chapter are outstanding because they pointed the way or were exceptions or became classics or seem likely to attain that distinction. Even with innumerable omissions, the list is a long one, and the numbers of these books are increasing yearly.

Generally, children enjoy fantasy as a change from the here and now, as a breathing space in the serious process of growing up. It is a rare child who does not like some of them, and most children enjoy many of them. Adults sometimes wonder why. The probable reason is that they provide children with another kind of flight, a flight into other worlds, incredible, exciting, satisfying. A little boy is driving an airplane when his mother calls him to come in for his bath. She can't see the pilot affronted by this indignity. Or someone says to a little girl, "No, you can't take that battered old doll downtown," and the child has to comfort the mutely hurt and unhappy doll. Children walk about their own yards as pirates, princesses, and fire engines, and we who have eyes do not see them thus transformed and free. Most children are "wind-runners" by nature and if they aren't, what a pity! These tales will help the swift wind-runners soar higher and will teach those who have never learned to run on the wind at least how to walk a little more boldly, with more faith in the unseen. Hans Christian Andersen, Kenneth Grahame, Beatrix Potter, Mary Norton, E. B. White, C. S. Lewis, Lucy Boston, and the others can reach a hand to the child and teach him to turn somersaults in the clouds or climb skyward on the rainbow.

## ADULT REFERENCES[14]

CAMERON, ELEANOR. *The Green and Burning Tree; On the Writing and Enjoyment of Children's Books.* Part 1, "Fantasy."

CARROLL, LEWIS [pseud.]. *The Annotated Alice; Alice's Adventures in Wonderland & Through the Looking Glass.*

COLLINGWOOD, STUART DODGSON. *The Life and Letters of Lewis Carroll (Rev. C. L. Dodgson).*

CREWS, FREDERICK C. *The Pooh Perplex; A Freshman Casebook.*

EGOFF, SHEILA, G. T. STUBBS, and L. F. ASHLEY, eds. *Only Connect; Readings on Children's Literature.* Part 2, "Fairy Tales, Fantasy, Animals."

FIELD, ELINOR WHITNEY, comp. *Horn Book Reflections.* Part 5, "Fantasy, Yesterday and Today."

GODDEN, RUMER. *Hans Christian Andersen: A Great Life in Brief.*

GREEN, PETER. *Kenneth Grahame.*

HAZARD, PAUL. *Books, Children and Men.*

HIGGINS, JAMES E. *Beyond Words; Mystical Fancy in Children's Literature.*

LANE, MARGARET. *The Tale of Beatrix Potter; A Biography.*

LENNON, FLORENCE BECKER. *Victoria Through the Looking Glass.*

LEWIS, C. S. *Of Other Worlds: Essays and Stories.*

STIRLING, MONICA. *The Wild Swan; The Life and Times of Hans Christian Andersen.*

TOWNSEND, JOHN ROWE. *Written for Children.* Chapter 13, "The New Fantasy."

WILLIAMS, SIDNEY H., and FALCONER MADAN. *The Lewis Carroll Handbook.*

## CHILDREN'S BOOKS

AIKEN, JOAN. *Black Hearts of Battersea*, ill. by Robin Jacques. Doubleday, 1964. 9-12

______. *Nightbirds on Nantucket*, ill. by Robin Jacques. Doubleday, 1966. 10-12

______. *Smoke from Cromwell's Time; and Other Stories.* Doubleday, 1970. 10-12

______. *The Whispering Mountain*, ill. by Frank Bozzo. Doubleday, 1969. 10-14

______. *The Wolves of Willoughby Chase*, ill. by Pat Marriott. Doubleday, 1963. 11-13

ALEXANDER, LLOYD. *The Black Cauldron.* Holt, 1965. 11-13

______. *The Book of Three.* Holt, 1964. 11-13

______. *The Castle of Llyr.* Holt, 1966. 10-13

______. *Coll and His White Pig*, ill. by Evaline Ness. Holt, 1965. 8-10

______. *The High King.* Holt, 1968. Newbery Medal. 11-13

______. *The King's Fountain*, ill. by Ezra Jack Keats. Dutton, 1971. 5-8

______. *The Marvelous Misadventures of Sebastian.* Dutton, 1970. National Book Award. 9-11

______. *Taran Wanderer.* Holt, 1967. 11-13

______. *The Truthful Harp*, ill. by Evaline Ness. Holt, 1967. 8-9

AMBRUS, VICTOR. *The Brave Soldier Janosh*, ill. by author. Harcourt, 1967. 5-8

ANDERSEN, HANS CHRISTIAN. *The Complete Andersen*, tr. by Jean Hersholt, ill. by Fritz Kredel. Heritage, 1952. Jean Hersholt captures both the spirit and fine literary style of Andersen in this translation of 168 tales. 12 up

______. *Fairy Tales*, ill. by Jean O'Neill. World, 1946. 10-12

______. *Fairy Tales*, ill. by Tasha Tudor. Walck, 1945. 10-12

______. *Fairy Tales*, ed. by Svend Larsen, tr. by R. P. Keigwin, ill. by Vilhelm Pedersen. Scribner's, 1951. The Danish literary folk consider this translation, together with those of the late Paul Leyssac and Jean Hersholt, the closest to the original manuscript. The book contains nineteen favorite tales. The small print would discourage younger readers, but the Andersen enthusiast will delight in its content. 12 up

______. *It's Perfectly True, and Other Stories*, tr. by Paul Leyssac, ill. by Richard Bennett. Harcourt, 1938. This translation of twenty-eight stories by a famous Danish storyteller has been a favorite collection for younger readers. 11-14

______. *Seven Tales*, tr. by Eva Le Gallienne, ill. by Maurice Sendak. Harper, 1959. Favorite stories chosen for their appeal to younger readers. 7-12

______. Single-story editions:

*The Emperor and the Nightingale*, ill. by Bill Sokol. Pantheon, 1959. 9-10

*The Emperor's New Clothes*, ill. by Virginia Burton. Houghton, 1962. 7-10

*The Fir Tree*, ill. by Nancy Burkert. Harper, 1970. 9-11

*The Little Match Girl*, ill. by Blair Lent. Houghton, 1968. 9-11

*The Nightingale*, tr. by Eva Le Gallienne, ill. by Nancy Burkert. Harper, 1965. 9-11

*The Steadfast Tin Soldier*, tr. by M. R. James, ill. by Marcia Brown. Scribner's, 1953. 6-10

*The Swineherd*, tr. and ill. by Erik Blegvad. Harcourt, 1958. 5-9

*Thumbelina*, tr. by R. P. Keigwin, ill. by Adrienne Adams. Scribner's, 1961. 6-9

*The Ugly Duckling*, tr. by R. P. Keigwin, ill. by Johannes Larsen. Macmillan, 1967. 6-9

*The Wild Swans*, ill. by Marcia Brown. Scribner's, 1963. 6-10

ANDERSON, LONZO. *Two Hundred Rabbits*, ill. by Adrienne Adams. Viking, 1968. Based on a French folk tale, this is a humorous picture book in which the author proves, at the end of the story, to be a rabbit himself. 5-7

ARTHUR, RUTH M. *Requiem for a Princess*, ill. by Margery Gill. Atheneum, 1967. Having worried herself sick over the discovery that she is adopted, fifteen-year-old Willow spends her nights in dreams in which she lives the life of a sixteenth-century Spanish girl whose portrait she has seen. 11-14

ASSOCIATION FOR CHILDHOOD EDUCATION. *Told*

14. Complete bibliographic data are provided in the combined Adult References in the Appendices.

*Under the Magic Umbrella.* Macmillan, 1939. This collection of fanciful tales includes such favorites as "Ask Mr. Bear" and "Peter the Goldfish." 8-12

ATWATER, RICHARD and FLORENCE. *Mr. Popper's Penguins*, ill. by Robert Lawson. Little, 1938. 8-12

AYER, JACQUELINE. *Little Silk*, ill. by author. Harcourt, 1970. The doll Little Silk had lain unloved for years until she was taken for a walk, lost, and found by an old man who takes her to a child who gives her the love and attention she had missed. Gentle and poetic, but not sentimental. Set in Hong Kong. 5-7

AYME, MARCEL. *The Wonderful Farm*, tr. by Norman Denny, ill. by Maurice Sendak. Harper, 1951. The wonderful farm is quite an ordinary French farm except that the animals happen to talk. This is a book both children and adults will enjoy. 7-10

BABBITT, NATALIE. *Dick Foote and the Shark*, ill. by author. Farrar, 1967. 9-11

______. *Kneeknock Rise*, ill. by author. Farrar, 1970. 9-11

______. *The Search for Delicious.* Farrar, 1969. 9-11

______. *The Something*, ill. by author. Farrar, 1970. A pithy and funny story about Milo, a hairy little cave dweller, who is afraid of Something in the night. It turns out to be a modern girl. When they meet in dreams, each stoutly declares he is not afraid of the other. 4-6

BAILEY, CAROLYN. *Miss Hickory*, ill. by Ruth Gannett. Viking, 1968. Newbery Medal. 10-13

BANNERMAN, HELEN. *The Story of Little Black Sambo*, ill. by author. Lippincott, 1923 (first pub. in 1900). Historically interesting but unacceptable to many. 4-7

BARRIE, SIR JAMES. *Peter Pan*, ill. by Nora Unwin. Scribner's, 1950. Peter Pan and all his delightful companions are visualized for the children by Nora Unwin's illustrations for this new edition. 9-12

BATE, NORMAN. *Who Built the Bridge? A Picture Story*, ill. by author. Scribner's, 1954. A slight but serious personification of machinery gives this story great appeal. 5-7

______. *Who Built the Dam?* ill. by author. Scribner's, 1958. Dramatically told picture tale of the building of a hydroelectric dam. 5-7

BAUM, L. FRANK. *The Wizard of Oz*, ill. by W. W. Denslow. Reilly, 1956 (first pub. in 1900). This edition has many of the original illustrations. 8-11

BEATTY, JEROME, JR. *Matthew Looney in the Outback*, ill. by Gahan Wilson. Scott/Addison, 1969.

______. *Matthew Looney's Invasion of the Earth*, ill. by Gahan Wilson. Scott/Addison, 1965.

______. *Matthew Looney's Voyage to the Earth*, ill. by Gahan Wilson. Scott/Addison, 1961. 9-12

BENNETT, RICHARD. *Shawneen and the Gander*, ill. by author. Doubleday, 1937, 1961. 6-9

BIANCO, MARGERY. *The Velveteen Rabbit*, ill. by William Nicholson. Doubleday, 1926. 6-9

BIEGEL, PAUL. *The King of the Copper Mountains*, English version by Gillian Hume and Paul Biegel, ill. by Babs Van Wely. Watts, 1969. A highly original modern fairy tale that has within it a variety of tales told by a series of animals to sustain an old and fragile king. 9-11

BLAIR, WALTER. *Tall Tale America: A Legendary History of Our Humorous Heroes*, ill. by Glen Rounds. Coward, 1944. 10-14

BOMANS, GODFRIED. *The Wily Wizard and the Wicked Witch; And Other Weird Stories*, tr. by Patricia Crampton, ill. by Robert Bartelt. Watts, 1969. A collection of original fairy tales with unusual treatment and a refreshing blend of orthodox magic and brisk touches of humor. 9-11

BOND, MICHAEL. *A Bear Called Paddington*, ill. by Peggy Fortnum. Houghton, 1960. A small brown bear from Peru arrives complete with hat and suitcase, and upsets a conservative English household with his unusual activities. Further humorous incidents follow in other stories about Paddington. 9-11

BONTEMPS, ARNA, and JACK CONROY. *The Fast Sooner Hound*, ill. by Virginia Lee Burton. Houghton, 1942. How this tall-tale hound could outrun any train, even the Cannon Ball, is gravely related and hilariously pictured. 8-12

BOSTON, LUCY M. *The Castle of Yew*, ill. by Margery Gill. Harcourt, 1965.

______. *The Children of Green Knowe*, ill. by Peter Boston. Harcourt, 1955.

______. *An Enemy at Green Knowe*, ill. by Peter Boston. Harcourt, 1964.

______. *Nothing Said*, ill. by Peter Boston. Harcourt, 1971.

______. *The Sea Egg*, ill. by Peter Boston. Harcourt, 1967.

______. *Treasure of Green Knowe*, ill. by Peter Boston. Harcourt, 1958.

______. *The River at Green Knowe*, ill. by Peter Boston. Harcourt, 1959. 9-11

BOVA, BENJAMIN. *The Weathermakers.* Holt, 1967. 12-15

BOWMAN, JAMES CLOYD. *Mike Fink*, ill. by Leonard Everett Fisher. Little, 1957. Mike Fink was one of the greatest legendary riverboatmen, and his adventures are related in tall-tale tradition. 11 up

______. *Pecos Bill*, ill. by Laura Bannon. Whitman, 1937. Pecos Bill is the gayest of our heroes and the closest to the child's sense of humor. The illustrations add to the book's appeal. 9-12

BRIGGS, RAYMOND. *Jim and the Beanstalk*, ill. by author. Coward, 1970. A silly and engaging sequel to the original tale. Jim climbs a tall plant and meets a sad and aging giant who complains that some boy once came up and robbed his father. 4-7

BRIGHT, ROBERT. *Georgie*, ill. by author. Doubleday, 1959.

______. *Georgie and the Magician*, ill. by author. Doubleday, 1966. 5-7

BRINK, CAROL RYRIE. *Andy Buckram's Tin Men*, ill. by W. T. Mars. Viking, 1966. 10-11

BROCK, BETTY. *No Flying in the House*, ill. by Wallace Tripp. Harper, 1970. 7-9

BROOKS, WALTER. *Freddy and the Men from Mars.* Knopf, 1954.

______. *Freddy Goes to Florida.* Knopf, 1949. Between these two books lies a long series of Freddy stories that enjoy enormous popularity. Whether Freddy the pig is leading the animals of Mr. Bean's farm to Florida or playing detective, he can be counted on for fun and excitement. 9-12

BROWN, MARCIA. *Stone Soup*, ill. by author. Scribner's, 1947. Three soldiers reform a selfish village by persuading the people to make a remarkably inexpensive soup—with a few additions! 7-10

BROWN, MARGARET WISE. *The Runaway Bunny*, ill. by Clement Hurd. Harper, 1942. 4-6

BULLA, CLYDE. *The Poppy Seeds*, ill. by Jean Charlot. T. Crowell, 1955. 7-10

BURTON, VIRGINIA. *Choo Choo*, ill. by author. Houghton, 1937. 5-7

———. *Katy and the Big Snow*, ill. by author. Houghton, 1943. 4-9

———. *The Little House*, ill. by author. Houghton, 1942. Caldecott Medal. 5-8

———. *Mike Mulligan and his Steam Shovel*, ill. by author. Houghton, 1939. 6-8

BUTTERWORTH, OLIVER. *The Enormous Egg*, ill. by Louis Darling. Little, 1956. 9-13

———. *The Trouble with Jenny's Ear*, ill. by Julian de Miskey. Little, 1960. 9-11

BYFIELD, BARBARA NINDE. *The Haunted Spy*, ill. by author. Doubleday, 1969. A spy who has wearied of his life of intrigue retires to a remote castle where he is forced to solve another mystery. An amusing concept. 8-10

CALHOUN, MARY (HUISKAMP). *The Pixy and the Lazy Housewife*, ill. by Janet McCaffery. Morrow, 1969. The humorous tale, told in folk style, of Old Bess, the laziest woman there was, who trapped some pixies to help with her work. But they outwit her and she changes her lazy ways. 5-8

CAMERON, ELEANOR. *Stowaway to the Mushroom Planet*, ill. by Robert Henneberger. Little, 1956.

———. *The Wonderful Flight to the Mushroom Planet*, ill. by Robert Henneberger. Little, 1954. 9-11

CARLSON, NATALIE. *Alphonse, That Bearded One*, ill. by Nicolas [pseud. for Nicolas Mordvinoff]. Harcourt, 1954. 8-11

CARROLL, LEWIS [pseud. for Charles Lutwidge Dodgson]. *Alice's Adventures in Wonderland* and *Through the Looking Glass*, ill. by John Tenniel. Heritage, 1944 (first pub. in 1865 and 1871). One of the best-loved and most quoted fantasies for children.

Ill. by John Tenniel. Grosset, 1963.
Ill. by John Tenniel. Macmillan, 1963.
Ill. by John Tenniel. World, 1946.
Ill. by Arthur Rackham. Watts, 1966. 10 up

CAUDILL, REBECCA, and JAMES AYARS. *Contrary Jenkins*, ill. by Glenn Rounds. Holt, 1969. 5-8

CHASE, MARY. *Loretta Mason Potts*, ill. by Harold Berson. Lippincott, 1958. 9-11

CHRISMAN, ARTHUR BOWIE. *Shen of the Sea: Chinese Stories for Children*, ill. by Else Hasselriis. Dutton, 1925; redesigned, 1968. Brisk and humorous fairy tales that were awarded the 1926 Newbery Medal. 10-12

CHRISTOPHER, JOHN. *Beyond the Burning Lands*. Macmillan, 1971. A sequel to *The Prince in Waiting*.

———. *The City of Gold and Lead*. Macmillan, 1967.

———. *The Guardians*. Macmillan, 1970.

———. *The Lotus Caves*. Macmillan, 1969.

———. *The Pool of Fire*. Macmillan, 1968.

———. *The Prince in Waiting*. Macmillan, 1970.

———. *The White Mountains*. Macmillan, 1967. 11-14

CLARKE, ARTHUR C. *Dolphin Island*. Holt, 1963. A fine science-fiction tale of teen-age Johnny Clinton, who becomes interested in dolphins when they rescue him from drowning. 12-15

CLARKE, PAULINE. *The Return of the Twelves*, ill. by Bernarda Bryson. Coward, 1964. 10-12

CLEARY, BEVERLY. *The Mouse and the Motorcycle*, ill. by Louis Darling. Morrow, 1965. 9-11

———. *Runaway Ralph*, ill. by Louis Darling. Morrow, 1970. 8-10

COATSWORTH, ELIZABETH. *The Cat Who Went to Heaven*, ill. by Lynd Ward. Macmillan, 1930 and 1959. Newbery Medal. 10-14

———. *Cricket and the Emperor's Son*, ill. by Juliette Palmer. Norton, 1965. 10-11

COLLODI, CARLO [pseud. for Carlo Lorenzini]. *The Adventures of Pinocchio*, tr. by Carol Della Chiesa, ill. by Attilio Mussino. Macmillan, 1963.

Ill. by Charles Mozley, large type ed. Watts, 1967. 9-12

COOMBS, PATRICIA. *Lisa and the Grompet*, ill. by author. Lothrop, 1970. The story has a fresh fancy; Lisa, unhappy because every member of her family orders her around and scolds her, meets a grompet, homeless and unhappy because he had never been told by anybody to do anything. 4-7

COOPERSMITH, JEROME. *A Chanukah Fable for Christmas*, ill. by Syd Hoff. Putnam, 1969. 5-8

CORBETT, SCOTT. *Ever Ride a Dinosaur?* ill. by Mircea Vasiliu. Holt, 1969. 9-11

———. *The Limerick Trick*, ill. by Paul Galdone. Little, 1964. 8-11

CREDLE, ELLIS. *Tall Tales from the High Hills*, ill. by author. Nelson, 1957. Lively folk tales from the North Carolina Blue Ridge country, fine for reading and telling. 9-12

CRESSWELL, HELEN. *The Piemakers*, ill. by W. T. Mars. Lippincott, 1968. 9-11

CUNNINGHAM, JULIA. *Dorp Dead*, ill. by James Spanfeller. Pantheon, 1965. 12 up

———. *Viollet*, ill. by Alan E. Cober. Pantheon, 1966. 10-11

CURRY, JANE LOUISE. *Mindy's Mysterious Miniature*, ill. by Charles Robinson. Harcourt, 1970. Mindy and her neighbor, Mrs. Bright, are captured by a Mr. Putt, who has inherited a magic contraption that miniaturizes houses and the people in them. The concept is entertaining and the writing has suspense and pace. 9-11

DAHL, ROALD. *Charlie and the Chocolate Factory*, ill. by Joseph Schindelman. Knopf, 1964. 10-11

———. *James and the Giant Peach*, ill. by Nancy E. Burkert. Knopf, 1961. 10-11

———. *The Magic Finger*, ill. by William Pène du Bois. Harper, 1966. 10-11

DAUGHERTY, JAMES. *Andy and the Lion*, ill. by author. Viking, 1938. Young Andy has read about lions but never expected to meet one. The encounter ends in high adventure for both of them, and for enthusiastic young readers. 6-8

DE BRUNHOFF, JEAN. *The Story of Babar, the Little Elephant*, ill. by author. Random, 1937. A series of these books follows and has been continued since the author's death by his son Laurent. 5-8

DE LA MARE, WALTER. *A Penny a Day*, ill. by Paul Kennedy. Knopf, 1960. Walter de la Mare brings poetic beauty to his prose style in six tales of fantasy which offer choice reading aloud. Followed by a companion volume, *The Magic Jacket* (1962). 10-13

______. *The Three Royal Monkeys*, ill. by Mildred Eldridge. Knopf, 1948. Originally published as *The Three Mulla-Mulgars*. 12-15

DEL REY, LESTER. *The Runaway Robot*. Westminster, 1965. 11-14

DICKINSON, PETER. *The Devil's Children*. Little, 1970. 10-14

______. *Heartsease*. Little, 1969. 10-14

______. *The Weathermonger*. Little, 1969. 10-14

DOLBIER, MAURICE. *Torten's Christmas Secret*, ill. by Robert Henneberger. Little, 1951. A fresh, gay Christmas story involves Santa's toy factory, hard-working gnomes, lists of good and bad children, and lovely glimpses of Santa's frosty, sparkling arctic world. 4-8

DOMANSKA, JANINA. *Marilka*, ill. by author. Macmillan, 1970. An engagingly silly story that subtly incorporates both tall-tale elements and a dash of noodlehead humor. Illustrated with charming, stylized peasant figures. 5-7

DRUON, MAURICE. *Tistou of the Green Thumbs*, ill. by Jacqueline Duhème. Scribner's, 1958. 9-11

DRURY, ROGER. *The Finches' Fabulous Furnace*, ill. by Erik Blegvad. Little, 1971. 9-11

DU BOIS, WILLIAM PÈNE. *The Alligator Case*, ill. by author. Harper, 1965. 9-11

______. *Bear Party*, ill. by author. Viking, 1951 and 1963. 5-8

______. *Call Me Bandicoot*, ill. by author. Harper, 1970. Fourth in the author's series on the seven deadly sins, this has stinginess as the leit-motif, but the imaginative embroidery of the central character's storytelling almost eclipses the theme. Witty and sophisticated with elegant illustrations. 10-14

______. *The Giant*, ill. by author. Viking, 1954. 9-12

______. *Great Geppy*, ill. by author. Viking, 1940. 10-14

______. *The Horse in the Camel Suit*, ill. by author. Harper, 1967. 9-11

______. *Lazy Tommy Pumpkinhead*, ill. by author. Harper, 1966. 7-9

______. *Otto and the Magic Potatoes*, ill. by author. Viking, 1970. The broadly nonsensical story of Otto the giant dog and his master who are kidnapped. 9-11

______. *Peter Graves*, ill. by author. Viking, 1950. 10-14

______. *Three Policemen; or, Young Bottsford of Farbe Island*, ill. by author. Viking, 1938 and 1960. 10-12

______. *The Twenty-One Balloons*, ill. by author. Viking, 1947. Newbery Medal. 10-12

DUVOISIN, ROGER. *Petunia*, ill. by author. Knopf, 1950. The first of a number of books about the adventures of that silly goose Petunia. 5-8

EAGER, EDWARD M. *Half Magic*, ill. by N. W. Bodecker. Harcourt, 1954.

______. *Magic or Not?* ill. by N. M. Bodecker. Harcourt, 1959.

______. *Seven-Day Magic*, ill. by N. M. Bodecker. Harcourt, 1962.

______. *The Well-Wishers*, ill. by N. M. Bodecker. Harcourt, 1960. 9-11

ELKIN, BENJAMIN. *Six Foolish Fishermen*, ill. by Katherine Evans. Childrens Pr., 1957. At the end of their day on the river each of the six fishermen forgot to count himself and was sure one had drowned. A small boy points out their foolish mistake. A perfect read-aloud. 4-7

ELLENTUCK, SHAN. *A Sunflower as Big as the Sun*, ill. by author. Doubleday, 1968. 5-8

ENGDAHL, SYLVIA. *Journey Between Worlds*, ill. by James and Ruth McCrea. Atheneum, 1970. 11-14

ENRIGHT, ELIZABETH. *Tatsinda*, ill. by Irene Haas. Harcourt, 1963. 9-12

______. *Zeee*, ill. by Irene Haas. Harcourt, 1965. A small, grumpy fairy is befriended by a Person. 9-11

ERWIN, BETTY. *Aggie, Maggie, and Tish*, ill. by Paul E. Kennedy. Little, 1965. 9-11

ERWIN, JOHN. *Mrs. Fox*, ill. by Wallace Tripp. Simon, 1969. Mrs. Fox had a glib and boastful tongue that might have got most animals in trouble, but she would go to any length to maintain her aura. A brittle, pointed, funny book that demands a certain level of reader sophistication. 10-11

ESTES, ELEANOR. *The Witch Family*, ill. by Edward Ardizzone. Harcourt, 1960. Their pleasant game of drawing witches leads two small girls into incredible adventures when their witches come alive! 10-12

ETS, MARIE HALL. *In the Forest*, ill. by author. Viking, 1944. Walking through the forest, a small boy has a highly satisfying time meeting imaginary wild animals in friendly mood. 4-7

______. *Mister Penny*, ill. by author. Viking, 1935. 6-8

______. *Mister Penny's Race Horse*, ill. by author. Viking, 1956. All the animals get into mischief going to the Fair, and Limpy finds that he can be a race horse. 6-8

______. *Mr. T. W. Anthony Woo*, ill. by author. Viking, 1951. 6-8

FAIRSTAR, MRS. [pseud. for Richard Horne]. *Memoirs of a London Doll*, ill. by Emma L. Brock. Macmillan, 1968 (first pub. in 1846). 9-12

FARMER, PENELOPE. *The Summer Birds*, ill. by James J. Spanfeller. Harcourt, 1962.

______. *Charlotte Sometimes*, ill. by Chris Connor. Harcourt, 1969.

______. *Emma in Winter*, ill. by James J. Spanfeller. Harcourt, 1966. 10-12

______. *The Magic Stone*, ill. by John Kaufmann. Harcourt, 1964. 11-12

FATIO, LOUISE. *The Happy Lion*, ill. by Roger Duvoisin. Whittlesey, 1954. Other titles in this consistently popular series include: *The Happy Lion in Africa* (1955), *The Happy Lion Roars* (1957), *The Three Happy Lions* (1959), *The Happy Lion's Quest* (1961), *The Happy Lion's Treasure* (1970). 5-7

FELTON, HAROLD W. *Bowleg Bill, Seagoing Cowpuncher*, ill. by William Moyers. Prentice, 1957. Tall-tale nonsense about a cowboy who solves his problems in his own cowboy way. 10 up

———. *John Henry and His Hammer*, ill. by Aldren A. Watson. Knopf, 1950. The author has compiled a dramatic and effective account of the black superman's life, a part of our railroad epic. 10-13

FERMAN, EDWARD L., and ROBERT P. MILLS, eds. *Twenty Years of the Magazine of Fantasy and Science Fiction*. Putnam, 1970. Some of the best science fiction writers who published in the magazine are represented here, though not all at their best. 11 up

FIELD, RACHEL. *Hitty: Her First Hundred Years*, ill. by Dorothy P. Lathrop. Macmillan, 1929. Newbery Medal. 11-14

FISCHER, HANS E. *The Birthday*, ill. by author. Harcourt, 1954. The animals in *Pitschi* fete their old mistress, Lisette, with a wonderful surprise party on her seventy-sixth birthday. 5-8

———. *Pitschi, the Kitten Who Always Wanted to Be Something Else*, ill. by author. Harcourt, 1953. A dissatisfied little kitten tries to emulate every creature on the farm, with discouraging results. The color illustrations are beautiful and appealing. 5-8

FLACK, MARJORIE. *Ask Mr. Bear*, ill. by author. Macmillan, 1932, 1958. 3-7

———. *Walter the Lazy Mouse*, ill. by Cindy Szekeres. Doubleday, 1963. The reform of a naughty little mouse who was always tardy. A welcome reissue. 4-7

FLEISCHMAN, SID. *By the Great Horn Spoon!* ill. by Eric von Schmidt. Little, 1963. 10-12

———. *Chancy and the Grand Rascal*, ill. by Eric von Schmidt. Little, 1966. 10-12

———. *The Ghost in the Noonday Sun*, ill. by Warren Chappell. Little, 1965. 10-12

———. *McBroom's Ear*, ill. by Kurt Werth. Norton, 1969. Another blithe tall tale about the marvelous McBroom farm which produces magnificent crops of food and stories. Enjoyable for reading aloud or storytelling. 8-11

FLEMING, IAN. *Chitty-Chitty-Bang-Bang; The Magical Car*, ill. by John Burningham. Random, 1964. 10-11

FRANÇOISE [pseud. for Françoise Seignobosc]. *Jeanne-Marie at the Fair*, ill. by author. Scribner's, 1959. Jeanne-Marie enjoyed every minute at the village fair, but her runaway pet lamb Patapon was most unhappy until he was rescued. Illustrated with appealing pastel drawings. One of several books about the quiet adventures of Jeanne-Marie. 4-6

FRISKEY, MARGARET. *Seven Diving Ducks*, ill. by Lucia Patton. McKay, 1940, 1965. 5-7

FRITZ, JEAN. *Magic to Burn*, ill. by Beth and Joe Krush. Coward, 1964. 10-11

GÁG, WANDA. *The Funny Thing*, ill. by author. Coward, 1920. 4-9

———. *Millions of Cats*, ill. by author. Coward, 1928. 5-8

———. *Nothing at All*, ill. by author. Coward, 1941. Through the use of a magic phrase, a lonesome little invisible puppy becomes "see-able," and finds a happy home. 5-7

GAGE, WILSON. *Miss Osborne-the-Mop*, ill. by Paul Galdone. World, 1963. 9-11

GARD, JOYCE. *Talargain*. Holt, 1965. Talargain, the hero, was a foundling in seventh-century England. He had learned to swim with the seals who saved his life when he came home to save his king. 11-14

GARFIELD, LEON. *The Restless Ghost; Three Stories*, ill. by Saul Lambert. Pantheon, 1969. Three splendid ghost stories, all set in the past and all with an authentic ring. 12-15

GARNER, ALAN. *The Owl Service*. Walck, 1968. 10-12

GODDEN, RUMER. *Candy Floss*, ill. by Adrienne Adams. Viking, 1960. 8-10

———. *The Dolls' House*, ill. by Tasha Tudor. Viking, 1962. 8-10

———. *Home Is the Sailor*, ill. by Jean Primrose. Viking, 1964. 10-11

———. *Impunity Jane*, ill. by Adrienne Adams. Viking, 1954. 8-10

———. *Little Plum*, ill. by Jean Primrose. Viking, 1963. 8-11

———. *Miss Happiness and Miss Flower*, ill. by Jean Primrose. Viking, 1961. 8-11

———. *The Mousewife*, ill. by William Pène du Bois. Viking, 1951. Expanded into a story from a note in Dorothy Wordsworth's journal, this is an exquisitely written little fable of the friendship of a mouse and a dove. 7-10

———. *The Story of Holly and Ivy*, ill. by Adrienne Adams. Viking, 1958. 7-9

GOODALL, JOHN S. *The Adventures of Paddy Pork*, ill. by author. Harcourt, 1968. The appealing adventures of Paddy are told without text. The illustrator uses a half-page insert between pages as an effective device in advancing his story. 3-5

GRAHAME, KENNETH. *The Reluctant Dragon*, ill. by Ernest H. Shepard. Holiday, 1953. 9-11

———. *The Wind in the Willows*, ill. by Ernest H. Shepard. Scribner's, 1953 (first pub. in 1908). 10-12

GRAMATKY, HARDIE. *Hercules*, ill. by author. Putnam, 1940.

———. *Homer and the Circus Train*, ill. by author. Putnam, 1957.

———. *Little Toot*, ill. by author. Putnam, 1939. 5-7

———. *Loopy*, ill. by author. Putnam, 1941. 5-7

GRIPARI, PIERRE. *Tales of the Rue Broca*, tr. by Doriane Grutman, ill. by Emily McCully. Bobbs, 1969. The author says he called on the neighborhood children in Paris to collaborate on these six stories. The tales have a fresh, imaginative quality that is childlike, but they are mature in style and interpretation. 10-12

HALE, LUCRETIA P. *Peterkin Papers*, ill. by Harold Brett. Houghton, 1960 (first pub. in 1880). 10-12

HARRIS, ROSEMARY. *The Moon in the Cloud*. Macmillan, 1970. Reuben and Thamar are a young couple who live in a tent near Noah and his family, and Reuben goes to Egypt to hunt for the animals needed to make up Noah's quota. A fanciful story with sophisticated humor. 10-13

———. *The Seal-Singing*. Macmillan, 1971. Not until Miranda comes to the Scottish isle of her ancestors does she discover that she is a reincarnation of a sixteenth-century ancestress who had the power of calling the seals. 11-14

______. *The Shadow on the Sun*. Macmillan, 1970. A sequel to *The Moon in the Cloud*. Reuben plays a secondary role in this book which is primarily a love story in which the young king wins the love of the Court Chamberlain's daughter. The vigorous characterization and dialogue make this as diverting as its predecessor. 10-13

HEINLEIN, ROBERT A. *Have Space Suit—Will Travel*. Scribner's, 1958. An improbable but convincing tale of two youngsters who journey through space and save humanity from immediate destruction. 12-16

______. *Podkayne of Mars; Her Life and Times*. Putnam, 1963. 12-15

______. *Rocket Ship Galileo*, ill. by Thomas Voter. Scribner's, 1947. Working together with an inventor, a trio of teen-age boys complete a rocket ship and make a trip to the moon. Entertaining science fiction based on a background of scientific knowledge. 12 up

______. *Space Cadet*, ill. by Clifford N. Geary. Scribner's, 1948. It is the year 2075, and at the rocketship training school at Terra Base, Colorado, boys from different planets come to train as cadets for Solar Patrol's interplanetary communication system. 12 up

HERRMANN, FRANK. *The Giant Alexander in America*, ill. by George Him. McGraw, 1968. The giant Alexander sails for the United States when the President wires asking his help. There he helps in the program to land a man on the moon and also does some sightseeing. 5-7

HEYWARD, DU BOSE. *The Country Bunny and the Little Gold Shoes*, ill. by Marjorie Flack. Houghton, 1939, 1969. 5-9

HOBAN, RUSSELL C. *The Mole Family's Christmas*, ill. by Lillian Hoban. Parents' Magazine, 1969. The brisk and often funny dialogue saves the story from sentimentality. The book is not too Christmas oriented for year-round use. 5-7

______. *The Mouse and His Child*, ill. by Lillian Hoban. Harper, 1967. 9-11

HOFF, SYD. *The Horse in Harry's Room*, ill. by author. Harper, 1970. Harry's horse is imaginary, and when he decides at the end of the book to stay with Harry, the reader and Harry are relieved. Light and amusing, but not superficial, for beginning independent readers. 6-7

______. *Oliver*, ill. by author. Harper, 1960. Poor Oliver was the surplus elephant in a circus shipment. How his unexpected talents won him a place on the program offers delightful reading. 6-7

HUNTER, MOLLIE. *The Kelpie's Pearls*, ill. by Joseph Cellini. Funk, 1966. Set in the Scottish Highlands, the story of old Morag and the kelpie who became her friend has a vitality of construction and a fragility of mood that are echoed in the lovely illustrations. 10-13

______. *The Walking Stones*, ill. by Trina Schart Hyman. Harper, 1970. A suspenseful story set in Scotland and reflecting Celtic folklore. A successful blend of realism and fantasy. 10-12

HURD, EDITH THACHER. *Johnny Lion's Bad Day*, ill. by Clement Hurd. Harper, 1970. Intended for independent readers, this book seems better for reading aloud, both because of the subject and the occasional difficult word. The charming story describes Johnny's day in bed with a cold. 5-7

HUTCHINS, PAT. *Rosie's Walk*, ill. by author. Macmillan, 1968. A very funny picture book, its big, bold illustrations just right for showing to a group of children. 3-6

______, ill. *Changes, Changes*. Macmillan, 1971. A book without text for the very young child who delights in "reading" by himself. 2-5

JACKSON, JACQUELINE. *The Orchestra Mice*, ill. by Robert Morrow. Reilly, 1970. 5-8

JAGENDORF, MORITZ ADOLF. *The Ghost of Peg-Leg Peter and Other Stories of Old New York*, ill. by Lino S. Lipinsky. Vanguard, 1965.

______. *New England Bean-Pot; American Folk Stories to Read and to Tell*, ill. by Donald McKay. Vanguard, 1948. 10-13

JANEWAY, ELIZABETH. *Ivanov Seven*, ill. by Eros Keith. Harper, 1967. An uproarious spoof about the Russian army discipline upset by an ingenuous peasant. 11-14

JANSSON, TOVE. *Finn Family Moomintroll*, ill. by author. Walck, 1965. And its sequels. 9-12

JARRELL, RANDALL. *The Animal Family*, ill. by Maurice Sendak. Pantheon, 1965. 10-12

JOHNSON, CROCKETT. *Ellen's Lion; Twelve Stories*. Harper, 1959. 6-8

______. *Harold's Trip to the Sky*, ill. by author. Harper, 1957. Little children enjoy this Martian tale and other stories of Harold, who crayons himself and his equipment into one lively adventure after another. 5-7

JONES, ELIZABETH ORTON. *Twig*, ill. by author. Macmillan, 1943. When Twig found the red tomato can in the yard, she thought it would make a beautiful home for a fairy. And a fairy did come to delight a city child. 8-10

JOSLIN, SESYLE. *What Do You Do, Dear?* ill. by Maurice Sendak. Scott/Addison, 1961. Delightful nonsense situations inspire the correct thing to do in this gay sequel to the 1958 book. 5-7

______. *What Do You Say, Dear?* ill. by Maurice Sendak. Scott/Addison, 1958. Manners for the youngest in a delightful read-aloud in which simple phrases of courtesy become memorable through the nonsense situations which inspire them. Children will invent others. 4-7

JUSTER, NORTON. *The Phantom Tollbooth*, ill. by Jules Feiffer. Random, 1961. 11-13

KAHL, VIRGINIA. *Away Went Wolfgang!* ill by author. Scribner's, 1954. Wolfgang was the least useful dog in the tiny Austrian village, until the housewives discovered that when Wolfgang ran, he could churn a whole cartful of milk into butter! 5-8

______. *The Baron's Booty*, ill. by author. Scribner's, 1963. Amusing rhyming tale of a wicked robber baron who steals for ransom the thirteen little daughters of the Duke and Duchess. His frantic efforts to return his troublesome booty provide good read-aloud entertainment. 6-9

______. *The Duchess Bakes a Cake*, ill. by author. Scribner's, 1955. There was consternation in the kingdom when the duchess was carried skyward atop the light fluffy cake she had baked. The story is told in lively rhyme and bright pictures and is satisfyingly funny. 6-10

______. *The Perfect Pancake*, ill. by author. Scribner's, 1960. A clever beggarman wins an unlimited supply of pancakes from the town's best cook by always belittling the last batch! Told in lively rhyme and bright pictures. 5-8

KÄSTNER, ERICH. *The Little Man*, ill. by Rick Schreiter; tr. by James Kirkup, Knopf, 1966. The diverting adventures of little Maxie, two inches high, who becomes a circus performer. Written in lively style by a distinguished German author. 10-11

KEMPADOO, MANGHANITA. *Letters of Thanks*, ill. by Helen Oxenbury. Simon, 1969. A sophisticated little spoof with delightful period-piece illustrations. The receipt of a partridge and a pear tree is welcomed with joy but as milking maids, etc., arrive the pleasure turns to coolness and then hostility. 10 up

KENDALL, CAROL. *The Gammage Cup*, ill. by Erik Blegvad. Harcourt, 1959. Children who enjoy Tolkien's *The Hobbit* will appreciate this tale of mild revolt among the Minnipins, or little people, and its surprising outcome. A protest against conformity. 10-13

KINGSLEY, CHARLES. *The Water-Babies*, ill. by Harold Jones. Watts, 1961. 8-12

KIPLING, RUDYARD. *The Elephant's Child*, ill. by Leonard Weisgard. From the *Just So Stories*, 1902. Walker, 1970. 9-11

______. *Just So Stories*, ill. by author. Doubleday, 1902. Ill. by J. M. Gleeson. Doubleday, 1912, 1946. Ill. by Nicolas [pseud. for Nicolas Mordvinoff]. Doubleday, 1952. 8-12

KRAUS, ROBERT. *Leo the Late Bloomer*, ill. by Jose Aruego. Windmill, 1971. Parental worry doesn't help. A small lion blooms in his good time. 3-5

______. *The Unidentified Flying Elephant*, ill. by Whitney Darrow. Windmill, 1968. 5-8

LANGTON, JANE. *The Diamond in the Window*, ill. by Erik Blegvad. Harper, 1962. This is a beautifully written tale of fantasy and suspense for the exceptional reader. The background is Concord, Massachusetts, with numerous allusions to Emerson and Thoreau. Good sequels, too. 11-14

LARSON, JEAN RUSSELL. *The Silkspinners*, ill. by Uri Shulevitz. Scribner's, 1967. The gently humorous fanciful story of the wanderings of a young hero Li Po who seeks an isolated colony of silk spinners since the art had been lost in China. 8-11

LAURENCE, MARGARET. *Jason's Quest*, ill. by Steffan Torell. Knopf, 1970. 9-11

LAWSON, JOHN. *The Spring Rider*. T. Crowell, 1968. 11-13

______. *You Better Come Home With Me*, ill. by Arnold Spilka. T. Crowell, 1966. 11-12

LAWSON, ROBERT. *Ben and Me*, ill. by author. Little, 1939. 9-12

______. *Mr. Revere and I*, ill. by author. Little, 1953. 11-14

______. *Rabbit Hill*, ill. by author. Viking, 1944, 1968. Newbery Medal. 9-12

______. *The Tough Winter*, ill. by author. Viking, 1970. 9-12

LEACH, MARIA. *The Rainbow Book of American Folk Tales and Legends*, ill. by Marc Simont. World, 1958. Includes tall tales. 12-14

LE GRAND, HENDERSON. *How Baseball Began in Brooklyn*, ill. by author. Abingdon, 1958. 7-9

LE GUIN, URSULA K. *A Wizard of Earthsea*, ill. by Ruth Robbins. Parnassus, 1968. An intricate and brooding fantasy, set in an imaginary world of a hundred small islands, Earthsea, in which the art of wizardry is taught and revered. The conception is original and imaginative but at times the pace is slow. 11-13

L'ENGLE, MADELEINE. *A Wrinkle in Time*. Farrar, 1962. Newbery Medal. 11-14

LENT, BLAIR. *John Tabor's Ride*, ill. by author. Atlantic, 1966. A tall tale based on a New England legend about a shipwrecked sailor. The appeal of the telling is in the exaggeration, the fantastic situations, and the abundance of salty marine terms. 5-8

LEWIS, CLIVE STAPLES. *Horse and His Boy*, ill. by Pauline Baynes. Macmillan, 1954.

______. *The Last Battle*, ill. by Pauline Baynes. Macmillan, 1956.

______. *The Lion, the Witch, and the Wardrobe*, ill. by Pauline Baynes. Macmillan, 1950. 8-12

LIFTON, BETTY JEAN. *Joji and the Dragon*, ill. by Eiichi Mitsui. Morrow, 1957. Poor Joji, the discarded Japanese scarecrow, was restored as guardian of the rice fields through a scheme of his loyal friends, the crows. 5-8

LIGHTNER, ALICE. *Doctor to the Galaxy*. Norton, 1965. 11-14

______. *The Galactic Troubadours*. Norton, 1965. 12-14

LINDGREN, ASTRID. *Pippi Longstocking*, tr. by Florence Lamborn, ill. by Louis S. Glanzman. Viking, 1950. 9-12

______. *The Tomten*, adapted from a poem by Viktor Rydberg, ill. by Harald Wiberg. Coward, 1961. Unforgettably lovely pictures of the wintry Swedish countryside illustrate the story of the kindly little troll who secretly goes about helping the people and animals. 5-7

______. *The Tomten and the Fox*, adapted from a poem by Karl-Erik Forsslund, ill. by Harald Wiberg. Coward, 1966. The resident Tomten saves the hens from a hungry fox. 5-7

LIONNI, LEO. *Alexander and the Wind-up Mouse*, ill. by author. Pantheon, 1969. Friendship triumphs over self-interest in a slight but engaging fanciful story about a real mouse, Alexander, and a toy mouse, Willy. Handsome illustrations. 4-6

______. *Frederick*, ill. by author. Pantheon, 1967. Handsome collage illustrations and direct, simple text tell the story of Frederick, a mouse that gathered words and colors against the winter. 5-7

______. *Inch by Inch*, ill. by author. Obolensky, 1960. A wise little inch worm escapes becoming a robin's dinner by proving his talents. A nature theme ingenuously framed in fantasy and illustrated with humor and imagination. 4-6

LOFTING, HUGH. *The Story of Dr. Dolittle*, ill. by author. Lippincott, 1920. 9-12

______. *The Story of Mrs. Tubbs*, ill. by author. Lippincott, 1923. 6-8

______. *The Voyages of Dr. Dolittle*, ill. by author. Lippincott, 1922. Newbery Medal. 9-12

MC CLOSKEY, ROBERT. *Burt Dow, Deep-Water Man; A Tale of the Sea in the Classic Tradition*, ill. by author. Viking, 1963. Jonah's story pales by comparison with this exuberant tall tale. 5-8

MACDONALD, GEORGE. *At the Back of the North Wind*, ill. by George and Doris Hauman. Macmillan, 1950.

______. *The Light Princess*, ill. by William Pène du Bois. T. Crowell, 1962.

______. *The Light Princess*, ill. by Maurice Sendak. Farrar, 1969.

______. *The Princess and Curdie*, ill. by Nora S. Unwin. Macmillan, 1954.

______. *The Princess and the Goblin*, ill. by Nora S. Unwin. Macmillan, 1964.

Attractive editions of old favorites. 9-12

MC GINLEY, PHYLLIS. *The Plain Princess*, ill. by Helen Stone. Lippincott, 1945. 7-10

MC GOWEN, TOM. *The Apple Strudel Soldier*, ill. by John E. Johnson. Follett, 1968. 5-8

MAC GREGOR, ELLEN. *Miss Pickerell Goes to Mars*, ill. by Paul Galdone. McGraw, 1951. Hilarious tale, one of many Miss Pickerell stories, of a determined old lady's adventures when she unwillingly goes to Mars. 8-11

MC LAUGHLIN, LORRIE. *Shogomoc Sam*, ill. by Randy Jones. St. Martin's, 1970. 9-11

MAHY, MARGARET. *A Lion in the Meadow*, ill. by Jenny Williams. Watts, 1969. The theme of a parent coping with a little boy's imaginative play ("Mother, there is a lion in the meadow") is nicely handled in this brightly illustrated picture book. 5-7

MALCOLMSON, ANNE. *Yankee Doodle's Cousins*, ill. by Robert McCloskey. Houghton, 1941. This is one of the finest collections of real and mythical heroes of the United States. 10-14

MARTEL, SUZANNE. *The City Under Ground*, tr. by Norah Smaridge, ill. by Don Sibley. Viking, 1964. 11-14

MAYNE, WILLIAM. *Earthfasts*. Dutton, 1967. 11-14

MERRILL, JEAN. *The Pushcart War*, ill. by Ronni Solbert. Scott/Addison, 1964. 10-12

MILNE, A. A. *The House at Pooh Corner*, ill. by Ernest Shepard. Dutton, 1928.

______. *Winnie-the-Pooh*, ill. by Ernest Shepard. Dutton, 1926.

These stories were reprinted in 1961, with larger type and more attractive format.

______. *The World of Pooh*, ill. by E. H. Shepard. Dutton, 1957. Distinctive color illustrations give a festive air to this new large-print volume, containing *Winnie-the-Pooh* and *House at Pooh Corner*. 8-10

MINARIK, ELSE. *Little Bear*, ill. by Maurice Sendak. Harper, 1957. And many sequels. 6-7

MORGAN, HELEN. *Satchkin Patchkin*, ill. by Shirley Hughes. Macrae, 1970. Eight short tales that are particularly suited for reading aloud or for storytelling. Good style, satisfying action. 8-10

NORTON, MARY. *Bed-Knob and Broomstick*, ill. by Erik Blegvad. Harcourt. 1957. Prim Miss Price was studying how to be a witch when the Wilson children discovered her. The bit of magic she gave them to ensure silence leads to some enchanting adventures. 9-13

______. *The Borrowers*, ill. by Beth and Joe Krush. Harcourt, 1953. This book was followed by *The Borrowers Afield* (1955), *The Borrowers Afloat* (1959), *The Borrowers Aloft* (1961). 9-12

______. *Poor Stainless*, ill. by Beth and Joe Krush. Harcourt, 1971. 8-10

O'BRIEN, ROBERT C. *Mrs. Frisby and the Rats of NIMH*, ill. by Zena Bernstein. Atheneum, 1971. The impossible is made believable in a deft and imaginative story about a group of laboratory rats who become super-intelligent. 9-11

ORGEL, DORIS. *Phoebe and the Prince*, ill. by Erik Blegvad. Putnam, 1969. 5-9

ORMONDROYD, EDWARD. *Broderick*, ill. by John Larrecq. Parnassus, 1969. An industrious mouse finds fame and fortune as a surfer. A delightful story, told with a straight face in polished style. 5-7

______. *Theodore*, ill. by John M. Larrecq. Parnassus, 1966. When he is caught in a laundromat load, Theodore, an aging toy bear, must arrange a few small capers to return him to his ordinary dirty state. A good read-aloud story. 3-6

______. *Time at the Top*, ill. by Peggie Bach. Parnassus, 1963. 11-13

PARRISH, ANNE. *Floating Island*, ill. by author. Harper, 1930. 9-11

PEARCE, A. PHILIPPA. *Tom's Midnight Garden*, ill. by Susan Einzig. Lippincott, 1959. 10-13

PECK, LEIGH. *Pecos Bill and Lightning*, ill. by Kurt Wiese. Houghton, 1940. A brief edition with copious illustrations to aid the slow reader. 8-12

PICARD, BARBARA LEONIE. *The Faun and the Woodcutter's Daughter*, ill. by Charles Stewart. Criterion, 1964. 10-12

______. *The Goldfinch Garden*, ill. by Anne Linton. Criterion, 1965. 9-12

______. *The Lady of the Linden Tree*, ill. by Charles Stuart. Criterion, 1962. 10-12

______. *The Mermaid and the Simpleton*, ill. by Phillip Gough. Criterion, 1969. 9-11

POTTER, BEATRIX. *The Tale of Peter Rabbit*, ill. by author. Warne, 1903. Between 1903 and 1930, nineteen books were published in this series. 3-8

PRESTON, EDNA MITCHELL. *Horrible Hepzibah*, ill. by Ray Cruz. Viking, 1971. 7-9

______. *Pop Corn and Ma Goodness*, ill. by Robert Andrew Parker. Viking, 1969. Vigorous illustrations and rhyming text in folk style describe the love and married life of Pop Corn and Ma Goodness. 4-6

PYLE, HOWARD. *Pepper and Salt*, ill. by author. Harper, 1923 (first pub. in 1885).

______. *Wonder Clock*, ill. by author. Harper, 1943 (first pub. in 1887). 10-12

RASKIN, ELLEN. *And It Rained*, ill. by author. Atheneum, 1969. A slight but amusing story about three silly animals who every afternoon have their tea and biscuits ruined by the rain. 5-7

______. *Nothing Ever Happens on My Block*, ill. by author. Atheneum, 1966. Chester is a small and dour curb-sitter who complains nothing ever happens on his block. Meanwhile, back of Chester, action on every page. A small and entirely diverting book. 5-8

REES, ENNIS. *Windwagon Smith*, ill. by Peter P. Plasencia. Prentice, 1966. 9-10

RESSNER, PHIL. *August Explains*, ill. by Crosby Bonsall. Harper, 1963. A very small bear loses all desire to be changed to a human when he hears about all the complexities of a boy's life. 5-7

REY, HANS A. *Curious George*, ill. by author. Houghton, 1941. The first of a well-liked series. 4-8

ROUNDS, GLEN. *Ol' Paul, the Mighty Logger*, ill. by author. Holiday, 1949. These Paul Bunyan stories are retold with an earthy, exuberant zest. 10 up

RUSKIN, JOHN. *The King of the Golden River*, ill. by Fritz Kredel. World, 1946. 10-14

SAINT-EXUPÉRY, ANTOINE DE. *The Little Prince*, tr. by Katherine Woods, ill. by author. Harcourt, 1943. 12 up

SANDBURG, CARL. *Rootabaga Stories*, ill. by Maud and Miska Petersham. Harcourt, 1922. 8-12

______. *The Wedding Procession of the Rag Doll and the Broom Handle and Who Was in It*, ill. by Harriet Pincus. Harcourt, 1967. 4-8

SAUER, JULIA. *Fog Magic*. Viking, 1943. 10-12

SAWYER, RUTH. *The Enchanted Schoolhouse*, ill. by Hugh Troy. Viking, 1956. When Brian Boru Gallagher came to America he brought a fairyman with him to show the glories of Ireland. They turned Lobster Cove topsy-turvy. 9-12

SCHLEIN, MIRIAM. *The Big Cheese*, ill. by Joseph Low. W. R. Scott, 1958. Proudly bearing his prize cheese to the king, the farmer shares it too generously and arrives with but a taste for His Majesty. A humorous read-aloud. 5-8

SCHRANK, JOSEPH. *The Plain Princess and the Lazy Prince*, ill. by Vasiliu. Day, 1958. 11 up

SELDEN, GEORGE. *The Cricket in Times Square*, ill. by Garth Williams. Farrar, 1960. 9-12

______. *Sparrow Socks*, ill. by Peter Lippman. Harper, 1965. 5-8

______. *Tucker's Countryside*, ill. by Garth Williams. Farrar, 1969. 9-11

SENDAK, MAURICE. *Higglety Pigglety Pop! or There Must Be More to Life*, ill. by author. Harper, 1967. 8-10

______. *In the Night Kitchen*, ill. by author. Harper, 1970. 5-7

______. *Nutshell Library*, ill. by author. Harper, 1962. 4-7

______. *Where the Wild Things Are*, ill. by author. Harper, 1963. Caldecott Medal. 5-7

SEUSS, DR. [pseud. for Theodor Seuss Geisel]. *And to Think That I Saw It on Mulberry Street*, ill. by author. Vanguard, 1937. 5-8

______. *The Cat in the Hat*, ill. by author. Random, 1957. The Cat provides novel entertainment for two house-bound children.

______. *The Cat in the Hat Comes Back!* ill. by author. Random, 1958. More fun with the Cat and his helpers. Easy-to-read stories. 5-8

______. *The 500 Hats of Bartholomew Cubbins*, ill. by author. Vanguard, 1938. 6-10

______. *Horton Hatches the Egg*, ill. by author. Random, 1940. 5-8

______. *Horton Hears a Who!* ill. by author. Random, 1954. 5-8

______. *McElligot's Pool*, ill. by author. Random, 1947. 7-10

SHAPIRO, IRWIN. *Heroes in American Folklore*, ill. by Donald McKay and James Daugherty. Messner, 1962. Five tall-tale heroes include Casey Jones, Joe Magarac, John Henry, Steamboat Bill, and Old Stormalong.

______. *Yankee Thunder, the Legendary Life of Davy Crockett*, ill. by James Daugherty. Messner, 1944. The author is torn between writing about the real Davy and the mythical Davy, but chooses the latter—"Yaller blossom of the forest, half horse, half snapping turtle, the ring-tailed roarer. . . ." The pictures are as vigorous as the hero. 10-14

SHARP, MARGERY. *The Rescuers*, ill. by Garth Williams. Little, 1959. Witty fantasy of three brave mice who rescue a Norwegian poet from imprisonment in a deep, dark dungeon. *Miss Bianca* (1962) relates another brave rescue. 10-13

SHEPHARD, ESTHER. *Paul Bunyan*, ill. by Rockwell Kent. Harcourt, 1941. The most complete edition of these tales, this book also has Rockwell Kent's superb pictures. 10-14

SINGER, ISAAC BASHEVIS. *The Fearsome Inn*, tr. by author and Elizabeth Shub, ill. by Nonny Hogrogian. Scribner's, 1967. A fanciful tale mingling the Polish-Jewish humor and gusto with the fairy tale genre most deftly. The illustrations have a graceful vitality and a restrained use of color. 10-12

______. *Mazel and Shlimazel; or the Milk of a Lioness*, tr. by author and Elizabeth Shub, ill. by Margot Zemach. Farrar, 1967. A tale in the folk tradition, illustrated with lively, lovely illustrations and told with eloquent simplicity by a master storyteller. 8-10

SLEIGH, BARBARA. *Carbonel: The King of the Cats*, ill. by V. H. Drummond. Bobbs, 1957. Humorous magical tale of two children who rescue the king of cats from the spell of an old witch. 9-12

______. *The Kingdom of Carbonel*, ill. by D. M. Leonard. Bobbs, 1960. Carbonel battles for the rights of his royal kittens. 9-12

SLOBODKIN, LOUIS. *The Amiable Giant*. Vanguard, 1966. 6-8

______. *Space Ship Under the Apple Tree*, ill. by author. Macmillan, 1967. Eddie's farm vacation at grandmother's proves anything but quiet when he is joined by Marty, the little man from Martinea, complete with his space ship. 8-10

SMITH, AGNES. *An Edge of the Forest*, ill. by Roberta Moynihan. Viking, 1959. 11-14

SOUTHEY, ROBERT. *Goldilocks and the Three Bears*, ed. by Edith Lowe, ill. by Marion Smith. Follett, 1966. The old favorite usually attributed to Southey. 5-8

STAHL, BEN. *Blackbeard's Ghost*, ill. by author. Houghton, 1965. 9-11

______. *The Secret of Red Skull*, ill. by author. Houghton, 1971. 10-11

STEELE, MARY Q. *Journey Outside*, ill. by Rocco Negri. Viking, 1969. The Raft People float down the dark underground river, looking for a Better Place, but the boy Dilar leaves and makes his way to the strange world of grass and sunshine where he encounters several cultures, each convincingly portrayed. 10-12

STEELE, WILLIAM O. *Andy Jackson's Water Well*, ill. by Michael Ramus. Harcourt, 1959. Andy Jackson achieves the incredible by bringing back water to drought-ridden Nashville. A hilarious tall tale that is ideal for storytelling. 9-13

STEIG, WILLIAM. *Sylvester and the Magic Pebble*, ill. by author. Simon, 1969. Caldecott Medal. 5-7

STOCKTON, FRANK RICHARD. *The Bee-Man of Orn*, ill. by Maurice Sendak. Holt, 1964. The Bee-Man is completely content until he is informed that he has been transformed from some other sort of thing. A charming story, now republished with Sendak's delightful illustrations. 10-12

______. *The Griffin and the Minor Canon*, ill. by Maurice Sendak. Holt, 1963. The lonesome last griffin, curious as to how he looks, flies far from his native haunts to see his statue image on an old church. His reception by the people, and especially by the Minor Canon, make this an intriguing tale. 6-10

STOLZ, MARY S. *Belling the Tiger*, ill. by Beni Montresor. Harper, 1967. 7-10

______. *Pigeon Flight*, ill. by Murray Tinkelman. Harper, 1962. Sulky Mr. Pigeon, indignant over a fancied slight, departs to the country from his established roost in Central Park. His brief bout with country living is engagingly funny. 7-10

STOUTENBURG, ADRIEN. *American Tall-Tale Animals*, ill. by Glen Rounds. Viking, 1968. 7-10

______. *American Tall Tales*, ill. by Richard M. Powers. Viking, 1966. 9-11

TAMCHINA, JURGEN. *Dominique and the Dragon*, ill. by Heidrun Petrides. Harcourt, 1969. Bold, imaginative pictures show the dreaded dragon who proves to be the epitome of kindness after a child is friendly to him. 5-8

THURBER, JAMES. *The Great Quillow*, ill. by Doris Lee. Harcourt, 1944. 8-11

______. *Many Moons*, ill. by Louis Slobodkin. Harcourt, 1943. Caldecott Medal. 7-10

______. *The Thirteen Clocks*, ill. by Marc Simont. Simon, 1950. 11-12

______. *The Wonderful O*, ill. by Marc Simont. Simon, 1957. 10 up

TITUS, EVE. *Anatole and the Cat*, ill. by Paul Galdone. McGraw, 1957. The first of a series of books about the adventures of that dauntless French mouse Anatole. 5-7

TODD, RUTHVEN. *Space Cat*, ill. by Paul Galdone. Scribner's, 1952. Flyball was a daring cat, and when he accompanied his favorite pilot on a trip to the moon, he not only saved his life but made an important scientific discovery. 8-10

TOLKIEN, JOHN R. R. *Farmer Giles of Ham*, ill. by Pauline Diana Baynes. Nelson, 1962. Humorous tale of a simple farmer who finds himself rescuing his village from dragons! 9-12

______. *The Hobbit*, ill. by author. Houghton, 1938. 5-8

TRAVERS, P. L. *Mary Poppins*, ill. by Mary Shepard. Harcourt, 1934.

______. *Mary Poppins Comes Back*, ill. by Mary Shepard. Harcourt, 1935.

______. *Mary Poppins in the Park*, ill. by Mary Shepard. Harcourt, 1952.

______. *Mary Poppins Opens the Door*, ill. by Mary Shepard and Agnes Sims. Harcourt, 1943. 8-12

TRESSELT, ALVIN. *The Frog in the Well*, ill. by Roger Duvoisin. Lothrop, 1958. Forced to leave his home in the well, the little frog discovers what a very small part of the world it was. 4-7

UDRY, JANICE MAY. *Glenda*, ill. by Marc Simont. Harper, 1969. Perky illustrations reflect the nonsensical humor of an easy-to-read book about a witch who finds that life as a human is not as easy as she's expected. 7-9

UNGERER, TOMI. *Émile*, ill. by author. Harper, 1960. Émile was an octopus with as many talents as appendages. 5-8

VIPONT, ELFRIDA. *The Elephant and the Bad Baby*, ill. by Raymond Briggs. Coward, 1970. The meeting of the elephant and the Bad Baby results in a series of petty thieveries, with a cumulating group of shopkeepers irately chasing the two. Charming illustrations. 4-7

WABER, BERNARD. *Lyle and the Birthday Party*, ill. by author. Houghton, 1966.

______. *Lyle, Lyle, Crocodile*, ill. by author. Houghton, 1965.

______. *Lovable Lyle*, ill. by author. Houghton, 1969. 5-7

WHITE, E. B. *Charlotte's Web*, ill. by Garth Williams. Harper, 1952. 10 up

______. *Stuart Little*, ill. by Garth Williams. Harper, 1945. 9-11

______. *The Trumpet of the Swan*, ill. by Edward Frascino. Harper, 1970. 9-11

WILDE, OSCAR. *The Happy Prince and Other Stories*, ill. by Peggy Fortnum. Dutton, 1968. 9-11

______. *The Selfish Giant*, ill. by Gertrude and Walter Reiner. Harvey, 1968. 9-11

WILL and NICOLAS [pseuds. for William Lipkind and Nicolas Mordvinoff]. *Finders Keepers*. Harcourt, 1951. Caldecott Medal. 4-7

WILLIAMS, JAY, and RAYMOND ABRASHKIN. *Danny Dunn and the Antigravity Paint*, ill. by Ezra Jack Keats. McGraw, 1956.

______. *Danny Dunn and the Smallifying Machine*, ill. by Paul Sagsoorian. McGraw, 1969.

______. *Danny Dunn and the Voice from Space*, ill. by Leo. R. Summers. McGraw, 1967. 10-12

WILLIAMS, URSULA MORAY. *The Cruise of the Happy-Go-Gay*, ill. by Gunvor Edwards. Meredith, 1968. 9-11

______. *Island Mackenzie*, ill. by Edward Ardizzone. Morrow, 1960. 10-12

______. *The Moonball*, ill. by Jane Paton. Meredith, 1967. A group of resourceful English children appoint themselves protectors of the moonball—a weird, silky-haired, grapefruit-size, living object—which a professor wishes to subject to scientific investigation. 7-9

———. *The Toymaker's Daughter*, ill. by Shirley Hughes. Meredith, 1968. 9-10

WRIGHTSON, PATRICIA. *Down to Earth*, ill. by Margaret Horder. Harcourt, 1965. 10-12

YOLEN, JANE H. *The Seventh Mandarin*, ill. by Ed Young. Seabury, 1970. Beautifully illustrated tale, in legend style, of seven mandarins who guarded their king, long ago in an eastern land. Good style and good storytelling, despite a rather pallid ending. 7-9

ZEMACH, HARVE. *The Judge; An Untrue Tale*, ill. by Margot Zemach. Farrar, 1969. An engaging and humorous nonsense story, told in rhyme and illustrated with raffish deftness. 5-7

ZOLOTOW, CHARLOTTE. *The Bunny Who Found Easter*, ill. by Betty Peterson. Parnassus, 1959. The bunny's quest for Easter did not end until he discovered that spring and Easter meant the beginning of all things beautiful. 5-7

———. *Mr. Rabbit and the Lovely Present*, ill. by Maurice Sendak. Harper, 1962. Aided by Mr. Rabbit, who makes the most impractical suggestions, a little girl finally decides on a gift for her mother's birthday. 4-6

# Part Three
# Sing It Again

# Chapter 9
# Children and Poetry

*Keep a poem in your pocket*
*and a picture in your head*
*and you'll never feel lonely*
*at night when you're in bed.*

*The little poem will sing to you*
*the little picture will bring to you*
*a dozen dreams to dance to you*
*at night when you're in bed.*

*So—*
*Keep a picture in your pocket*
*and a poem in your head*
*and you'll never feel lonely*
*at night when you're in bed.*[1]

*Illustration © 1958 by Irene Haas. Reproduced from* Something Special *by Beatrice Schenk de Regniers, by permission of Harcourt Brace Jovanovich, Inc., and William Collins Sons & Company Ltd., London.*

Here in the lightest of light verses, Beatrice Schenk de Regniers gives us one reason for using poetry with children. Like music, it carries its own therapy. To cold or timid hearts it can bring warmth, reassurance, even laughter. It can stir and arouse or quiet and comfort. Above all it gives significance to

1. "Keep a Poem in Your Pocket." From *Something Special* by Beatrice Schenk de Regniers and Irene Haas. Copyright © 1958 by Beatrice Schenk de Regniers. Reprinted by permission of Harcourt Brace Jovanovich, Inc., and William Collins Sons & Company Ltd., London.

everyday experience. To miss poetry would be as much of a deprivation as to miss music. For these reasons it is essential that we know poetry and that we know how to introduce it to children. The experience of poetry should come with so much pure pleasure that the taste for it will grow and become a permanent part of a child's emotional and intellectual resources.

For some years, there has been a groundswell of interest in poetry, both in producing it for young people and in encouraging them to write it. Not all of the qualities that distinguish poetry from prose are common to all its forms, but basic to the genre are the concentration or crystallization of mood, emotion, or experience; the use of words or sounds that are evocative; and the use of imagery, oblique or vividly clear. The verse can be free, but most poetry provides the satisfaction and challenge of pattern and uses words in a way that is more musical or fluid than all but the most lyric prose. The alliteration and refrain that can be obtrusive or redundant in prose become, in a good poem, part of its appeal; in a mediocre poem, an abuse of these devices or a rigid adherence to rhyme, especially when it is forced, can result in doggerel. Rhyme and rhythm, particularly attractive to younger children, reinforce aural enjoyment, for poetry must be heard to be fully savored. The essence of poetry is revelation: by the way words are put together, by the richly imaginative use of those words, by the condensation of the poet's conviction, we see with sharpened understanding our own experiences or share with quickened empathy the experiences or dreams of others.

Definitions of poetry are, of course, valueless to children, but they are valuable to adults since they throw light on the manner in which to present poetry. For instance, Eleanor Farjeon asks

*What is Poetry? Who knows?*
*Not the rose, but the scent of the rose;*
*Not the sky, but the light in the sky;*
*Not the fly, but the gleam of the fly;*
*Not the sea, but the sound of the sea;*
*Not myself, but what makes me*
*See, hear, and feel something that prose*
*Cannot; and what it is, who knows?*[2]

This is a poet's way of saying that a poem is a distillation of an experience: not the rose but the essence of the rose, not the sea but its light and sound.

Robert Frost develops the same idea when he says that "A poem is a momentary stay against confusion. Each poem clarifies something. . . . A poem is an arrest of disorder."[3] Frost implies that our experiences come pellmell, but a poem sorts them out, gives them order and meaning—not merely the essence of an experience but its significance.

Here are a few more definitions of poetry:

*Absolute poetry is the concrete and artistic expression of the human mind in emotional and rhythmical language.*—Encyclopaedia Britannica

*The essence of poetry is invention; such invention as, by producing something unexpected, surprises and delights.*—Samuel Johnson

*If I read a book and it makes my whole body so cold no fire can ever warm me, I know that is poetry. If I feel physically as if the top of my head were taken off, I know that is poetry. These are the only ways I know it. Is there any other way?* —Emily Dickinson

*I always know it is a good poem when the small hairs rise on the back of my neck.*—William Rose Benét

*A living poem begins with a lump in the throat; a homesickness or a lovesickness. It is a reaching out toward expression to find fulfillment.*

2. "Poetry." Copyright, 1938, by Eleanor Farjeon. Renewal, ©, 1961 by Gervase Farjeon. From the book *Poems for Children* by Eleanor Farjeon. Copyright, 1951, by Eleanor Farjeon. Reprinted by permission of J. B. Lippincott Company and David Higham Associates, Ltd. for Michael Joseph Ltd.

3. John Ciardi, "Robert Frost: Master Conversationalist at Work," *Saturday Review*, March 21, 1959.

*A complete poem is one where an emotion has found its thought and the thought has found words.* —Robert Frost

If you examine these definitions and others, you will discover certain ideas recurring: poetry surprises and delights; it sings like music; it makes you feel intensely; poetry gives you an arresting thought often in rhythmic words, plus a shiver up your backbone. When poetry means these things to you, you have genuinely enjoyed it; it is poetry to you. When it leaves you just where you were, neither aroused nor amused, neither enchanted nor solaced, then poetry has not happened to you; it has passed you by. So it is with children.

## ELEMENTS OF GOOD POETRY

But how about adults who enjoy doggerel, and children who accept anything that rhymes? Does their enjoyment make the jingles they read poetry? Perhaps for them it does temporarily, but doggerel need not remain their top level of appreciation. Good taste in any field—music, interior decoration, clothes, poetry—is largely a matter of experience. As a person becomes familiar with the best in one field, he gains discrimination there, while in another field in which his experience is limited he may show very poor taste. Harry Behn says, "I believe that children's judgment of what books are best for them to expand into is better than *our* judgment if we make the best as easily available as television."[4] So we should be patient with children's enjoyment of poor poetry. Their taste will improve if they have repeated experiences with good poetry.

### Singing Quality: Melody and Movement

One of the most important characteristics of good poetry is its singing quality, its melody and movement. In the nonsense jingles and humorous verse, for example, words and lines trip along with the lightness of children jumping rope. Clumsy doggerel—in contrast to the verses of Lear, Richards, and Milne—is heavy footed, and its words and lines have no sparkle. If, as Lillian Smith says in *The Unreluctant Years*, the verses of Milne and Lear are not true poetry, they are certainly as debonair and as skillfully written as light verse can be. If a poem is in a mysterious or meditative or wistful mood, the lines move slowly and the words fall subtly on the ear. These are clues to reading poetry aloud—emphasize the musical pattern. The poems of Blake, Rossetti, and De la Mare contain many examples of the perfect accompaniment of melody and movement to mood. On the whole the poetry small children like is more lively and dancing than poetry for adults—no blank verse for most young children and very little free verse. The fact that children enjoy marked rhythms and crisp rhymes accounts for their ready acceptance of second-rate verse if it has these characteristics. But if their ears become attuned to the subtleties

4. Harry Behn, *Chrysalis* (Harcourt Brace Jovanovich, 1968), p. 16.

### VIEWPOINTS

Poetry is essentially a game, with artificial rules, and it takes two—a writer and a reader—to play it. If the reader is reluctant, the game will not work.

. . . Poetry, . . . is a kind of musical word game which we value because of its expressive qualities. Not all poems are equally musical, or equally playful, or equally expressive. Nor are they necessarily musical, playful, or expressive in the same way. But we can consider these three qualities as the basic constituents of poetry. . . . If a piece of writing is neither especially rhythmical nor especially ironic or metaphorical in its language, it is not poetry, regardless of its dramatic situations or the ideas it presents.—Robert Scholes, *Elements of Poetry*, Oxford University Press, New York, Toronto, London, 1969, pp. 1, 7, 60.

and varieties of rhythmic patterns found in poems like those by Stevenson, De la Mare, and Behn, they may detect the labored rhythms and forced rhymes which characterize masses of mediocre verse.

### Words of Poetry

Poetry uses strong, vigorous words or warm, rich words or delicate, precise words that define with accurate perfection. Of course, prose may employ the same words, but poetry ordinarily uses them with greater condensation and in more melodious combinations so that their effect is more striking. Think of the amusing "sneezles and freezles" of Christopher Robin, of John Updike's "stripped and shapely Maple" grieving in November for "the ghosts of her departed leaves," or of Blake's "echoing green," which suggests the calls and shouts of children at their play. Read through these poems and notice both the exact, descriptive words and the sensory, connotative words and phrases which distinguish good poetry from the ordinary: "the still dark night," "skipping along alone," "rain in the city" falling "slant-wise where the buildings crowd," "soaked, sweet-smelling lane," "Apple trees are snowing." How hushed and how piercingly vivid are the words of De la Mare's "Silver":

*Slowly, silently, now the moon*
*Walks the night in her silver shoon;*
*This way, and that, she peers, and sees*
*Silver fruit upon silver trees;*
*One by one the casements catch*
*Her beam beneath the silvery thatch;*
*Couched in his kennel, like a log,*
*With paws of silver sleeps the dog;*
*From their shadowy cote the white breasts peep*
*Of doves in a silver-feathered sleep;*
*A harvest mouse goes scampering by,*
*With silver claws, and silver eye;*
*And moveless fish in the water gleam,*
*By silver reeds in a silver stream.*[5]

Words that stir the imagination, that speak to the senses, that provoke laughter, that move us deeply and strongly—such words are part of the secret of good poetry.

### Content of Poetry

While poetry is primarily emotional in its appeal, it is built around subjects or ideas, and appeals to the intellect as well as the emotions. Even a slight verse like "Little Miss Muffet" has a well-defined idea—security, fright, escape. The child's emotional response to this unit depends upon his grasp of the content. Of course poetry may have almost as varied subject matter as prose, but like any of the other arts, it must invest that content with arresting significance. A slippery baby in a bathtub is Carl Sandburg's "fish child," and Marianne Moore's jelly fish is "an amber-tinctured amethyst." Rachel Field sees city "Taxis"[6]—"Scudding through the snow," "flashing back the sun," and rolling along "like spools of colored thread." A vivid picture to city children! When mother cooks fish, the child chuckles over the memory of De la Mare's "a fish that *talks* in the frying pan." John Ciardi's "thin grin-cat" stalking a bird is ominous in its suggestion of hunger and anticipated satisfaction. So poetry takes the strange or everyday facts of life and gives them fresh meaning. We see new colors in the world because poetry has revealed them.

## SELECTING POETRY FOR CHILDREN

When we choose a poem for children, we may well test it with these questions: First, *does it sing*—with good rhythm, true, unforced rhymes, and a happy compatibility of

5. "Silver" by Walter de la Mare from *Peacock Pie*. Reprinted by permission of The Literary Trustees of Walter de la Mare, and the Society of Authors as their representative.

6. Many of the poems cited in Chapters 9–11 appear in *Time for Poetry*, Third Edition (Scott, Foresman, 1968) and *The Arbuthnot Anthology of Children's Literature* (Scott, Foresman, 1971).

## VIEWPOINTS

In choosing poems for young children . . . we would do well to remember that wit has its beginnings in simply being funny, or in the Comic Spirit, if I may borrow an almost-classic designation. . . . I have had the experience of reading Carl Sandburg's "Arithmetic" to several groups of nine- and ten-year-olds. The laughter is a little tentative at first, then grows to a shout as they begin to recognize their own struggles and puzzlements. What astonishes them most, however, is the realization that this set of lines, with its combination of truthfulness and absurdity, its juxtaposition of arithmetic problems and fried eggs, is a poem. One can almost hear the wheels go round as the children begin to consider the question of what poetry is. Now, "Arithmetic" is not "Paradise Lost," but doesn't it achieve for the nine-year-old that crystallization of experience, that new way of looking at something we knew all along, that we call poetry? Another way of putting it is to say that poetry is partly about something you know and partly about something you don't know quite yet. Children are quick to grasp this idea. . . .—Helen Plotz, "All Who Hide Too Well Away," *The Horn Book*, April 1959, pp. 113, 114.

sound and subject—whether it is nonsense verse or narrative or lyric poetry? Second, *is the diction distinguished*—with words that are rich in sensory and connotative meanings, words that are unhackneyed, precise, and memorable? Third, *does the subject matter of the poem invest the strange or the everyday experiences of life with new importance and richer meaning?* When a poem does these three things, it is indeed good poetry—it may add to the child's day one brief moment of laughter or give him a new dream to dream over in solitude or bring him a sharpened awareness of life.

People who do not like poetry usually have had unpleasant introductions to poems when they were children: they had too much analyzing of poems, or they had to memorize poems they didn't enjoy, or they were given many selections that were boring. "Lots of poems are too long," they complain, or "Poetry is hard to understand and it's hard to read." Sometimes, when poetry is read aloud to children, it is badly read—in a dull singsong or with unnatural affectations or with a "holy tone." Sometimes adults choose poems that appeal to them because they are *about* children but not really *for* children. Any one of these afflictions is enough to induce a permanent distaste for poetry.

Many children have learned to distrust the *subject matter* of poetry largely because of our blundering choice of selections for them. We have given them pedantic verse designed to teach manners or morals or safety or health. In some adaptations of nursery rhymes, Jack and Jill fall down because they didn't look both ways before they started up the hill. Then we have given children poems that voice the philosophy of old age rather than that of exuberant childhood:

> *Tell me not, in mournful numbers,*
> *Life is but an empty dream!*

So speaks middle age, or perhaps dreams wistfully of Innisfree:

> *I shall have some peace there, for peace comes*
> *dropping slow.*

But the last thing most children want is peace. What they yearn for is action, and if we are going to foster children's natural liking for poetry we had better avoid these elderly daydreams and find selections that speak to youth.

We have also given children poetry whose meaning is obscure. If these obscurities cannot be cleared up in a brief discussion, then we should drop such poems for the time being. A selection may be great literature, but if it leaves the children baffled and suspicious, it is not good literature for them at that point.

In choosing poetry for children, select poems whose subject matter is sufficiently common to their experiences and emotions so that they can understand what the poem is about and share the feeling underlying the words. We need not be too literal about this. The child need not have shared every experience he encounters in poetry, but there should be some common ground between the child and the poem.

The city child, for example, may not know meadows and cowslips, but he knows all about trying to decide where to go and what to do; so he understands this little conversation piece by Kate Greenaway:

*Susan Blue*[7]

*Oh! Susan Blue,*
*How do you do?*
*Please may I go for a walk with you?*
*Where shall we go?*
*Oh! I know—*
*Down in the meadow where the cowslips grow!*

The city child might make his own ending and say "Over in the park where the tulips grow," or "Over on the hill to slide in the snow."

The simplicity of the conversation in David Ignatow's poem about "Two Friends" makes it as comprehensible and poignant as the tender duet between the crippled child and his mother in Gian-Carlo Menotti's *Amahl and the Night Visitors.*

*Two Friends*[8]

*I have something to tell you.*
*I'm listening.*
*I'm dying.*
*I'm sorry to hear.*
*I'm growing old.*
*It's terrible.*
*It is, I thought you should know.*
*Of course and I'm sorry. Keep in touch.*
*I will and you too.*
*And let me know what's new.*
*Certainly, though it can't be much.*
*And stay well.*
*And you too.*
*And go slow.*
*And you too.*

7. "Susan Blue." From *Marigold Garden* by Kate Greenaway. Published by Frederick Warne & Company.

8. "Two Friends." Copyright © 1963 by David Ignatow. Reprinted from *Figures of the Human* (British title: *Earth Hard*), by David Ignatow, by permission of Wesleyan University Press and Rapp and Whiting.

*Illustration by Kate Greenaway for "Susan Blue." From* Marigold Garden, *published by Frederick Warne & Company. (Original in color)*

*Figures of speech* have proved particularly baffling to young children. Blanche Weekes, in a study called *Influence of Meaning on Children's Choices of Poetry,* found that the literal-minded child does not understand most figures of speech and tends to misinterpret them rather consistently. Sixth-grade children, for instance, interpreted "the lion of thunder roared" to mean that the lion roared at the thunder. So if the young child hears a poem about the stars looking like daisies that "dot the meadows of the night," he may visualize a topsy-turvy world with daisies sticking headfirst down from heaven instead of popping up from the ground as self-respecting daisies should. In short, involved figures of speech or even a plethora of adjectives are more likely to muddle than to inspire the young. One reason Stevenson and A. A. Milne are successful with young children is that they rarely use figurative language, but maintain an understandable directness most of the time.

Not that we are herewith going to abandon every poem for children that uses figurative language—not at all. But it is safe to say that the younger the child the fewer and simpler the figures of speech should be, particularly since many of them are decidedly platitudinous. Magazines abound with endless ditties about mewing pussy willows, sprightly Jacky Frost, and willful autumn leaves—outworn expressions which probably never appealed to children and which can well be discarded.

*Long descriptions* are another stumbling block to an easy enjoyment of poetry. Children usually skip descriptions in prose, and they have often spoken out fully and frankly about how much they dislike them. Yet adults have never hesitated to give them poetry that is little else. They may enjoy a few descriptive poems if they are brief, but too many and too long descriptions send them away from poetry bored and discouraged.

The *form* of poetry presents even more reading problems than the content. The mere look of a page of poetry is strange with its short lines and stanza patterns, so different in appearance from a page of prose. Attacking it gingerly, the child encounters both rhythm and rhyme, which do odd things to his reading. For instance, they heighten the child's tendency to pause at the end of each line, a pause usually marked by dropping the voice. This, in turn, results in singsong that frequently destroys the meaning.

Inverted sentences also cause singsong reading and a consequent loss of understanding. Read these lines of Stevenson's:

*When to go out, my nurse doth wrap*
*Me in my comforter and cap . . .*

Drop your voice conclusively after "wrap," and you have a strange second line. Or if the poet delays the completion of his sentence for several lines, the young reader is immediately befuddled. Take, for example, the familiar opening lines of William Cullen Bryant's "To a Waterfowl":

*Whither, 'midst falling dew,*
*While glow the heavens with the last steps of day,*
*Far, through their rosy depths, dost thou pursue*
*Thy solitary way?*

The exclamatory question that begins with "Whither," is not completed until "dost thou pursue thy solitary way?"—a conclusion that is distributed over two lines. Here the archaic expressions *Whither, 'midst, dost, thou*, and *thy* can be distracting, too. Such examples emphasize the pitfalls that await the unskilled reader of verse. The child, lost in such entanglements, knows he isn't making sense and becomes suspicious of this thing called poetry.

*Dialogue* can be another source of trouble in verse, because the poets have a way of blithely omitting the helpful "said he" or "said she." Look at the little conversation piece by Kate Greenaway (page 283). Does Susan Blue's unknown friend speak all the lines, or does Susan herself break in with the question and then the joyous solution of the last two lines? This latter interpretation turns the poem into a charming little dialogue which seems sufficiently appealing to justify such a reading. In Blake's imaginary dialogue between an adult and a tiny baby, the words are simple, but who says what? Read the poem aloud with the proper interpretation of the dialogue, and it is immediately understandable.

*Infant Joy*

| | |
|---|---|
| **Baby** | *"I have no name;* |
| | *I am but two days old."* |
| **Narrator** | *What shall I call thee?* |
| **Baby** | *"I happy am,* |
| | *Joy is my name."* |
| **Narrator** | *Sweet joy befall thee!* |
| | |
| **Narrator** | *Pretty joy!* |
| | *Sweet joy, but two days old.* |
| | *Sweet joy I call thee;* |
| | *Thou dost smile,* |
| | *I sing the while;* |
| | *Sweet joy befall thee!* |

The moral of all this is that children still in the process of learning to read should get most of their poetry through their ears before they are asked to cope with it on the printed page. It also means perhaps that poems of the older poets such as Blake, Stevenson, De la Mare, Milne, etc., should be liberally mixed with more recent poetry in which the language and content are more familiar to today's children.

## TO MAKE POETRY-LOVERS OF CHILDREN

### Know What Children Like About Poetry

This brings us to the delight of using poetry with children. We must know what they like about poetry and how to expose them to it so the liking grows. Fortunately, its first and strongest appeal is its *singing quality*, the *melody* and *movement* of the word patterns and the lines. Walter de la Mare calls these qualities "tune and runningness," and they make poetry an aural art like music, to be heard and spoken just as music is to be heard and played. Our business as adults is to savor this singing quality of verse and to learn how to maintain it in our reading.

Next, children like the *story element* in poetry, from "Little Miss Muffet" to "The Highwayman." This is so strong an interest that we should search for fine narrative poetry for every age level. Children will accept the feeblest doggerel if it tells a story. Often the surprising and provocative little story suggestions in the poetry of Walter de la Mare account for the children's enjoying subtler and lovelier verse than they would otherwise appreciate.

*Nonsense* and *humor* in poetry have great appeal to children. They delight in the daft lunacy of cows jumping over the moon and they move happily from the gaiety and nonsense of *Mother Goose* and Edward Lear to the modern hilarity of Ogden Nash and John Ciardi. They enjoy the sound of nonsense words, alliteration, and the repetition of phrases in a refrain. But on the way, nonsense merges naturally into light verse. Children chuckle over the gay drama of "The King's Breakfast" and a few years later are grinning over the more intellectual humor of "Macavity the Mystery Cat." For humor can be subtle, and well-written humorous verse is an exercise not only in ear-training but also in quick associations, double meanings, satire, or witty implications.

The *sensory content* of poetry (the words and images that evoke seeing, hearing, tasting, smelling responses) constitutes one of its strongest appeals, or, in some cases, accounts for its failure with certain children. If the sensory content is familiar or understandable, then they respond to it with zest. Unfortunately, over half the children in the United States are from urban areas while a large proportion of our poetry is distinctly rural in its sensuous imagery. (Of course, this situation is changing as more and more of the recent poetry has an urban setting.) The city child and the country child have certain experiences in common—wind, rain, snow, sun, moon, stars, heat, cold, fog—but how differently these experiences impinge on the consciousness of each of them. Take snow, for instance, which in the crowded areas of the city is soon a blackish, soggy slush. How, then, can the city child, who knows neither down, nor lambs, nor even clean, soft snow (at least for very long), respond to the feeling of stepping upon "white down," of walking upon "silver fleece," as described in Elinor Wylie's "Velvet Shoes"? By the time these are laboriously explained to him, there is not much left of the dreamlike quality of that walk

*At a tranquil pace,*
*Under veils of white lace.*[9]

In the last several years, fortunately, more and more city poems have appeared. In two poems from *I Thought I Heard the City*, Lilian Moore captures the beauty and quiet of snow in an urban setting.

*Night Snow*[10]

*A ghostly snow*
*floats*
*out of the sky*
*tonight,*
*and snow moths*
*dance*
*in the pale street light.*

*Snowy Morning*[10]

*Wake*
*gently this morning*
*to a different day.*
*Listen.*
*There is no bray*
*of buses,*
*no brake growls,*
*no siren howls and*
*no horns*
*blow.*

*There is only*
*the silence*
*of a city*
*hushed*
*by snow.*

There are now a good many anthologies intended particularly for city children: for example, Robert Froman's *Street Poems*, Nancy Larrick's *On City Streets*, Arnold Adoff's *City in All Directions*, and Lee Bennett Hopkins' *City Talk*.

Still, it does seem as if much more time should be spent providing city children with some of the lovely sensory experiences that crowded city streets deny them. Somewhere they should see frisky lambs and colts at play, smell the good smells of earth after a spring rain, bury their noses in lilies of the valley, or hear a wood thrush calling at twilight. They should have the fun of plopping through mud, wading creeks, getting lost in a cornfield, or whooping down a hillside on a windy autumn day. But lacking these experiences, which are the very stuff of dreams, of poetry, and of a lifetime of sensory joys, children in the big cities find their own beauty—skyscrapers against scudding clouds, rainy streets at night reflecting the lights of the cars, the whine of wind around tall buildings, airplanes heard when still unseen, and over the roar of city noises the eerie sound of fog horns or boat whistles. These are good experiences, too, and well worth savoring and expressing in words or colors. These, too, are the stuff of dreams.

A child does not need to be a small black boy like Everett Anderson, indeed does not even need to be a boy, to appreciate the zestfulness and coziness of the poems in Lucille Clifton's *Some of the Days of Everett Anderson.*

*Being six*
*is full of tricks*
*And Everett Anderson knows it.*
*Being a boy*
*is full of joy*
*And Everett Anderson shows it.*

9. From "Velvet Shoes" from *Collected Poems of Elinor Wylie*. Copyright 1921, 1932 by Alfred A. Knopf, Inc. Reprinted by permission.

10. "Night Snow" and "Snowy Morning." Text copyright © 1969 by Lilian Moore. From *I Thought I Heard the City*. Used by permission of Atheneum Publishers.

*Swishing one finger*
*in the foam*
*of Mama's glass*
*when she gets home*
*is a very*
*favorite thing to do.*
*Mama says*
*foam is a comfort.*
*Everett Anderson*
*says so too.*[11]

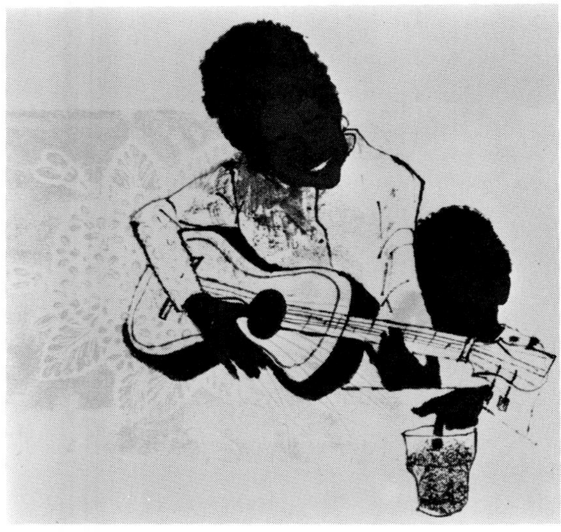

*From* Some of the Days of Everett Anderson *by* Lucille Clifton. *Illustrated by Evaline Ness. Copyright © 1970 by Evaline Ness. Reproduced by permission of Holt, Rinehart and Winston, Inc. (Original with color)*

Poetry should be comprehensible to children, but that does not mean they must have experienced everything they read about. Few children have had an opportunity to observe an ostrich closely, yet how enticingly Aileen Fisher leads them to an easy understanding of ostriches by contrasting ostriches with birds that *are* familiar.

*Most birds surely*
*Walk quite poorly*
*Most birds merely*
*hop around.*

*They're securest,*
*swiftest, surest*
*on their wings*
*above the ground,*
*but OSTRICHES . . . .*[12]

So, with humor, suspense, rhyme, and rhythm, the child is led through enjoyment to comprehension.

*Illustration by Peter Parnall for* But Ostriches . . . *by Aileen Fisher. Text copyright © 1970 by Aileen Fisher, illustrations copyright © 1970 by Peter Parnall. Reprinted with permission of Thomas Y. Crowell Company, Inc., New York, Publishers.*

### Provide Children with Rich Poetry Experiences

Children's encounters with poetry should include three types of response—*enjoyment, exploration*, and *deepening understandings*. These do not occur as separate steps but simultaneously. Certainly, the child must

11. From *Some of the Days of Everett Anderson*. Copyright © 1970 by Lucille Clifton. Reprinted by permission of Holt, Rinehart and Winston, Inc.

12. From *But Ostriches . . .* by Aileen Fisher. Copyright © 1970 by Aileen Fisher. Illustrations copyright © 1970 by Peter Parnall. With permission of Thomas Y. Crowell Company, Inc., Publishers.

## VIEWPOINTS

While in all other Arts it is agreed that a student should be trained only on the best models, wherein technique and aesthetic are both exemplary, there has been with respect to Poetry a pestilent notion that the young should be gradually led up to excellence through lower degrees of it; so that teachers have invited their pupils to learn and admire what they expected them to outgrow: and this was carried so far that writers, who else made no poetic pretence, have good-naturedly composed poems for the young, and in a technique often as inept as their sentiment. — Robert Bridges, *The Chilswell Book of English Poetry*, compiled by Robert Bridges, Longmans and Green and Co., London, 1924, p. ix.

start with enjoyment or his interest in poetry dies. But if from the beginning, he finds delight in the poems he hears, he is ready and eager to explore further — more books and more poems of different sorts. Even the youngest children can learn to read between the lines. For example, they can be helped to decide what is back of the conversation between "Pussy cat, pussy cat" and his owner: Is Cat telling a tall tale as an excuse, or did he really see the queen? Does Cat's owner believe the runaway? To read between the lines is to identify oneself with the poet, to ask the poet's questions. This is reading for deeper understanding, taking a thoughtful look at what lies beneath the surface. Enjoyment, exploration, and deeper understanding must all be part of children's experience with poetry if we are to build poetry-minded children.

### Read Poetry to Children

Poetry began as a spoken art; people listened to it and remembered it because rhyme and meter make it easier to recall than prose. So it should begin for children. Adults should read or speak it aloud and encourage the children to join in until, without even realizing it, they have memorized effortlessly dozens of poems which they can speak naturally and gaily. Saying or reading poetry to children should continue all through their first twelve years. By that time they will have mastered the mechanics of reading for themselves; they will also be steeped in poetry; and they will have the habit of saying it so well established that they will go right on reading it and enjoying it on their own.

Poetry should never be used as a reading exercise. When children have to struggle with a poem as a reading lesson, they are baffled and discouraged. John Erskine, writing for older students, says in *The Kinds of Poetry*: "The office of the teacher of poetry is easily defined; it is to afford a mediation between great poets and their audience." With children, effective oral reading is the surest mediation.

The poets themselves agree. At the turn of the century, the Irish poet William Butler Yeats wrote:

> *I have just heard a poem spoken with so delicate a sense of rhythm, with so perfect a respect for its meaning, that if I were a wise man and could persuade a few people to learn the art I would never again open a book of verse.*[13]

Yeats implies that to read a poem silently is to miss the potent appeal of its music and perhaps even its meaning. He himself read poetry with spellbinding charm, and John Masefield in his autobiography, *So Long to Learn*, testifies to Yeats' powerful influence on the young poets of the day. He convinced them of the importance of the aural effect of poetry on the reader or listener. Later, Robert Frost, in a series of cryptic comments on poetry, said:

13. William Butler Yeats, *Ideas of Good and Evil* (Macmillan, 1907), p. 16.

*The eye reader is a barbarian. So also is the writer for the eye reader, who needn't care how badly he writes since he doesn't care how badly he is read.*

*Mother Goose* is a natural starting point with children from two to six or seven years old. Her pages are alive with "tune and runningness" and the children respond with vigor. They soon discover that "Ride a cock horse" is a gallop and "To market, to market" is an everyday walk, quite unlike the military tread of "The grand Old Duke of York." The same bounce and gaiety are in Clyde Watson's *Father Fox's Pennyrhymes.* Children may try marching, skipping, galloping, hopping, running, rocking their babies, with most of the group speaking the poem while two or three respond to its rhythm. They don't know that it is meter and rhyme, line and word patterns that produce these contagious rhythms, but they feel the "goingness" of the verses. They discover that the words hop like the rabbit in Christina Rossetti's

*And timid, funny, brisk little bunny,*
*Winks his nose and sits all sunny.*

The introduction to poetry for older children should begin as painlessly as it begins for the nonreaders. That is, they should hear many poems read aloud vigorously for sheer pleasure, with no analysis during this exploratory stage. As this casual exposure to a variety of verses continues, lovely bits of authentic poetry should be slipped in and introduced with a comment like this: "A new poem is like new music. Sometimes you have to hear it several times before you know whether or not you like it." Children of eight or older should not be asked to respond to poems with bodily rhythms, but they may well identify the gallop of Stevenson's "Windy Nights" or the clacking rhythm of the trains in Mary Austin's "Texas Trains and Trails." So, too, they will show you by their response that they feel the tranquillity of Elizabeth Madox Roberts' "Evening Hymn," even though they cannot analyze the mood in words.

It may be asked, "How long must children have their poetry read to them? Aren't they ever going to explore books of poetry on their own?" Of course they are! That is what this program is for. If, during the years when they are still trying to master their reading skills, children hear poetry well read by someone who thoroughly enjoys it, they too enjoy it unabashedly and begin to accept it as naturally as they accept stories. If they hear enough authentic poetry over these formative years, they will never suffer from what the poet W. H. Auden calls a "tin ear"[14] for merely tin pan alley verses. Instead many will develop a sensitivity to the beauty and power of the spoken word, and by the time they are eleven and twelve years old and competent readers they will explore poetry for themselves. This is the goal of the aural and oral approach to poetry for sheer enjoyment. When it succeeds, children will enter high school with trained ears, good diction, and the ability to interpret and enjoy the major poets to whom they will be exposed.

### Explore Poetry Books with Children

In the process of enjoying poetry, children will encounter many books and different types of verse. Their explorations will include books by a single author and anthologies of poetry by many poets.

Anthologies are invaluable, and there is no reading experience more satisfying, either in a classroom or at home, than to settle down with your children to explore a new anthology. Needless to say, you will have explored it first to know its range and contents and to have chosen in advance a group of poems that you feel sure the children will understand and enjoy. Modern anthologies

14. W. H. Auden, "An Appreciation of the Lyric Verse of Walter de la Mare." *New York Times Book Review.* Feb. 26, 1956, p. 3.

usually provide a high quality of poetry selections and convenient subject matter arrangements, and they rescue from oblivion such out-of-print treasures as "The Pirate Don Durk of Dowdee," "Overheard on a Saltmarsh," and the best of Winifred Welles and Mary Austin. Camps, classrooms, and homes should own not less than two anthologies. Here are a few criteria for selecting an anthology from among the many excellent ones available:

1. Examine the author index to discover the range and quality of writers represented. Does it lean heavily on poets of the past, Eugene Field, Riley, Stevenson, Longfellow, or are the best of these balanced by many good modern poets?

2. How many poems does the book contain? Oddly enough one anthology will contain over seven hundred poems while another at approximately the same price will include two to three hundred. If the quality of the two books is equally good, the first is obviously a better choice.

3. Look for indexes and classifications. The indexes should include authors, titles, and, preferably, first lines. Teachers will find classifications by subjects equally important—such groupings as people, animals, nonsense, magic, our country, seasons, and the like. Organization by subjects is far more important than organization by grades. Indeed, grade levels for poems are impossible and undesirable, no matter how teachers yearn for them, because children's tastes and capacities vary as much as the poems themselves and depend on their varied experiences.

4. Format is important. A heavy volume may be useful in the school library as a reference book, but it will not be good for a child to use or an adult to handle with the child. Good paper, clear type, well-spaced pages, all add to the attractiveness of a book.

Some anthologies not only meet these basic criteria, but provide extra dividends in the form of attractive illustrations, brief introductions to or explanations of poems, and suggestions for reading aloud and choral speaking.

Teach children how to explore and use an anthology. A forthcoming festival, for example, means a search for the best Halloween or Christmas poems. Undoubtedly the greatest value of a fine anthology is the feeling it gives the child for the range and variety of poetry. He will look, browse further, and make discoveries.

In the same way, children should become acquainted with the books of single poets, not merely Stevenson's *A Child's Garden of Verses*, but David McCord's *For Me to Say*, Harry Behn's *Little Hill*, June Jordan's *Who Look at Me*, and others. This exploration of the works of individual poets guarantees that the child will encounter a range of

*Illustration by Henry Kane from* For Me to Say *by David McCord. Copyright © 1970 by David McCord. By permission of Little, Brown and Co.*

poetry from the imaginative and subtle lyrics of Walter de la Mare to the robust nonsense of John Ciardi. Such exploration will also help children to grow emotionally and intellectually with poetry.

### Deepen Children's Understanding of Poems

A third phase of poetry experience involves a more intellectual response than either enjoyment or exploration. It is what John Ciardi has called "reading in depth" or reading for a more complete understanding of the poet's meaning. With the youngest children this begins with talking about word meanings and background experiences and with older children it progresses to a fuller consciousness of implications, double meanings, and possible symbols, and even to some analysis of form.

To help younger children understand the meaning of a poem, we often need to *evoke or supplement their background of experience*. For instance, suppose a child has never been on an escalator or even seen one, real or pictured. Explain to him, "It looks like a stairway, but when you step on the first step, *you* stand still and the whole stairway moves upward, carrying you along until you hop off at the next floor." Then, Phyllis McGinley's "E is the escalator" becomes amusingly real. Or suppose a city child has never seen a snail. Show him a picture of a snail or bring one to school. Then Hilda Conkling's "Little Snail" with "his house on his back" will be visually clear. Walter de la Mare never says in his poem "The Huntsmen" that it is about three boys riding their hobbyhorses upstairs, and so unless children understand this, the "clitter clatter" of those wooden sticks on the stair and the whole meaning of the poem will be obscure. Older children who have never seen a great bird swoop downward, stop himself in full flight, and then slowly ascend may not understand the averted crash in Robert Frost's

*Questioning Faces*[15]

*The winter owl banked just in time to pass*
*And save herself from breaking window glass.*
*And her wings straining suddenly aspread*
*Caught color from the last of evening red*
*In a display of underdown and quill*
*To glassed-in children at the window sill.*

But almost every child knows about braking a car suddenly and swerving sharply to avoid a crash or may have watched airplanes bank

---

#### VIEWPOINTS

We have a cliché we use too often when we discuss the reading of poems. We talk about "levels." We say, at this level it means this; at a second level something quite different; at a third . . . at a fourth. . . . It is a word which saves time perhaps and may even mean something as a shorthand sign but as a metaphor it is deceptive. It implies that a poem is like an apartment house: you climb from one story to the next and each floor is separate and distinct: the rooms—the arrangement of the rooms—are identical but everything else is different . . . the furniture . . . the view. One does not read a poem in this way. . . .

. . . And one does not read one's self *up* or *down*. One stands there and reads *through:* through the sounds, but never leaving the sounds, into their references, through the references to the images they make, through the images to their relation to each other, through their relation to each other to the feel of meaning. It is perspective one reads for in a poem, and perspective includes the near things as well as the far and includes them all at the same time and in the same scene.—Archibald MacLeish, *Poetry and Experience*, Houghton Mifflin, Boston, 1961, pp. 85–86.

---

15. "Questioning Faces." From *The Poetry of Robert Frost* edited by Edward Connery Lathem. Copyright 1916, 1923, 1928, 1934, © 1969 by Holt, Rinehart and Winston, Inc. Copyright 1936, 1942, 1944, 1951, ©1956, 1962 by Robert Frost. Copyright © 1964, 1970 by Lesley Frost Ballantine. Reprinted by permission of Holt, Rinehart and Winston, Inc. and Jonathan Cape Ltd. for the Estate of Robert Frost.

for a landing. If he understands that word *bank* in the sense of descending and then making a corrective ascent, he can visualize what those watching children saw through the window pane when the great owl saved herself from a crash. Most children can illustrate this with a swift movement of arm and hand. These are just a few examples of evoking or amplifying background experiences to clarify meaning.

Sometimes the musical pattern of a poem affects its meaning in ways even very young children can sense. For instance, the fives know that the words in Stevenson's "The Swing" really swing and that the words of Milne's "Hoppity" do hop with Christopher Robin to the very last line which hops to a standstill. Their young ears can also be trained to hear the quietness of Winifred Welles' "Green Moth," the hushed quality of the words in De la Mare's "Some One" or "The Horseman," the quick movement in Mary O'Neill's "Wind Colors the World," and the very place in Edna St. Vincent Millay's "The Ballad of the Harp-Weaver," where the spinning music begins—as truly a spinning song as Schubert's. Hearing poetry read with an emphasis on its musical patterns, young children can be trained to the point where they are aware, consciously or unconsciously, of what the patterns are making them feel or understand. For instance, an upper-grade boy who especially liked "The Snare" by James Stephens said to his teacher, "Everytime you read that poem or I say it to myself it makes me feel as if I were running and had to hurry faster." His teacher replied, "Well, that is what the poem is about; that is the idea the poet wanted you to understand." If the boy had asked "But what makes me feel that way?" the teacher could have shown him how the repetition of the last line of each verse as the first line of the next verse compels an emphasis that hurries one on. If you read the poem without that first line repetition, you will discover that the push has gone out of the poem completely. Should the teacher have raised the question herself? This depends on the boy. In some instances, it would be enough that he had felt the poem's meaning and the teacher had praised his thoughtful response. But a boy that intelligent and inquiring could probably be carried one step further to understand the effect of pattern on feeling response.

Or take Elizabeth Coatsworth's beautiful study in contrasts—"Swift things are beautiful," p. 362. Help the children to hear how the words and lines of the first stanza hurry along, with no long, sonorous vowels or words to delay the crisp, brisk movement. But in the second verse, the long vowels in such mouth-filling phrases as "The pause of the wave/That curves downward to spray" and the heavy last lines, "And the ox that moves on/In the quiet of power," compel a slow, deliberate reading. You simply cannot dash off those last lines briskly.

Having helped the children discover Elizabeth Coatsworth's effective use of words to enhance contrast, let them explore some of her other poems for contrasts. They will find "The sea gull curves his wings," in which the first couplet is smooth as silk and as gentle as the sailing flight of the gull; the second, a sharp, harsh staccato like the cry of warning, which it is. The second verse repeats this contrast. See also "Cold winter now is in the wood" and again note the contrasts.[16] Eleanor Farjeon uses similar contrasts in "For Christmas Day," and many other examples can be found.

These brief, simple examples of the way poets use the words and patterns of their verse to suggest action, mood, or meaning are obvious enough for children and are the beginnings of a deeper look at the poetry they enjoy. This deeper look will carry them into the below-the-surface meaning or implications or symbols the poet uses.

In the discussion of the traditional ballads in Chapter 5, there was some suggestion

16. See pages 361–363 for a discussion of Elizabeth Coatsworth's poetry. Chapter 11, *Poets and Children's Poetry*, discusses the work of a number of older and more recent poets. See the Index for individual poets.

of the importance of reading between the lines. Why did the Lady leave her fine house and go off with the Raggle Taggle Gypsies? Why in the last lines of "The Wife of Usher's Well" that sad reference to the maid? For children from sixth grade on, these old ballads with their cryptic condensations are good exercises in reading for meanings that are implied but never fully stated, and therefore not to be settled neatly and without questions and differing speculations.

From a gifted teacher of English in the Montreal schools comes this interesting experience with Robert Frost's

*Stopping by Woods on a Snowy Evening*[17]

*Whose woods these are I think I know.*
*His house is in the village though;*
*He will not see me stopping here*
*To watch his woods fill up with snow.*

*My little horse must think it queer*
*To stop without a farmhouse near*
*Between the woods and frozen lake*
*The darkest evening of the year.*

*He gives his harness bells a shake*
*To ask if there is some mistake.*
*The only other sound's the sweep*
*Of easy wind and downy flake.*

*The woods are lovely, dark and deep.*
*But I have promises to keep,*
*And miles to go before I sleep,*
*And miles to go before I sleep.*

The teacher read it to the children of his seventh grade, and they discussed it first as a scene so vividly sketched that you could draw or paint it. The teacher said, "Do you think it is only a description of a scene, an incident?" And he read the poem again. They thought it was more than a scene. It referred to the feeling of lateness with still many things to do. Perhaps they were thinking of homework, but at least they caught the idea that "miles to go" might well mean many things to do, night coming, and the day's work still unfinished. The teacher agreed. Then he said, "Listen again and see if it says anything more to you," and he read it once more. A child spoke slowly, "Could the poet be thinking of death, do you suppose?" The discussion was lively. Some thought "before I sleep" might well mean death. Others disagreed and still preferred the idea of unfinished work. John Ciardi, in his provocative analysis of this poem, "one of the master lyrics of the English language," in *The Saturday Review*, referred to the dark and the snowfall as fairly obvious symbols of the death-wish.[18] This may be true, but to many older people, "and miles to go before I sleep" refers to all the wonderful things still to do, to see, to learn, to express—all the richness of life—and so little time left. By the way, it is more than likely that those children, in their own silent reading of the poem, would never have looked below the surface of this scenic description. But hearing the poem repeatedly—"lovely, dark and deep . . . And miles to go before I sleep," the children discovered meanings that they would never have found in a cursory silent reading. They were able to find at least three kinds of meaning: (1) a simple episode, a scene vividly described, (2) the day nearly over and much work still to do, (3) the nearness of the long sleep of death, with still so many things to see and do and time running out.

It is interesting to go through Frost's poems and see how he has repeatedly used trees as symbols. One verse in "Come In" suggests "Stopping by Woods," for again the poet is at the edge of a woods, listening—

*Far in the pillared dark*
*Thrush music went—*

17. "Stopping by Woods on a Snowy Evening." From *The Poetry of Robert Frost* edited by Edward Connery Lathem. Copyright 1916, 1923, 1928, 1934, © 1969 by Holt, Rinehart and Winston, Inc. Copyright 1936, 1942, 1944, 1951, © 1956, 1962 by Robert Frost. Copyright © 1964, 1970 by Lesley Frost Ballantine. Reprinted by permission of Holt, Rinehart and Winston, Inc. and Jonathan Cape Ltd. for the Estate of Robert Frost.

18. John Ciardi, "Robert Frost: The Way to the Poem," *The Saturday Review*, April 12, 1958.

*Almost like a call to come in*
*To the dark and lament.*[19]

The same idea recurs in the first verse of

*Into My Own*[19]

*One of my wishes is that those dark trees,*
*So old and firm they scarcely show the breeze,*
*Were not, as 'twere, the merest mask of gloom,*
*But stretched away unto the edge of doom.*

And the poet goes on to imagine that "into their vastness I should steal away"—probably another image of death.

There is a remarkable sense of companionship with "Tree at My Window" ending—

*That day she put our heads together,*
*Fate had her imagination about her,*
*Your head so much concerned with outer,*
*Mine with inner, weather.*[19]

Undoubtedly, some teacher has already helped her students discover the remarkable likeness of themes in Gerald Johnson's *America Is Born* and Robert Frost's poem "The Gift Outright." In his book Mr. Johnson says:

*At the start nobody intended to become an American, but everybody did if he stayed in this country. They were changed simply by living [here]. . . . George Washington still thought of himself as a trueborn Englishman, although it was impossible for him to be anything of the sort.*

*What made us Americans was not long and careful thinking about it, but simply seeing what had to be done and doing it. What had to be done here was not exactly what had to be done in England; and in doing it we became something different from Englishmen. (p. 140)*

Read the children this and then read "The Gift Outright" several times until they see the connection.

19. "Come In," "Into My Own," "Tree at My Window," and "The Gift Outright." From *The Poetry of Robert Frost* edited by Edward Connery Lathem. Copyright 1916, 1923, 1928, 1934, © 1969 by Holt, Rinehart and Winston, Inc. Copyright 1936, 1942, 1944, 1951, © 1956, 1962 by Robert Frost. Copyright ©1964, 1970 by Lesley Frost Ballantine. Reprinted by permission of Holt, Rinehart and Winston, Inc. and Jonathan Cape Ltd. for the Estate of Robert Frost.

*The Gift Outright*[19]

*The land was ours before we were the land's.*
*She was our land more than a hundred years*
*Before we were her people. She was ours*
*In Massachusetts, in Virginia,*
*But we were England's, still colonials,*
*Possessing what we still were unpossessed by,*
*Possessed by what we now no more possessed.*
*Something we were withholding made us weak*
*Until we found out that it was ourselves*
*We were withholding from our land of living,*
*And forthwith found salvation in surrender.*
*Such as we were we gave ourselves outright*
*(The deed of gift was many deeds of war)*
*To the land vaguely realizing westward,*
*But still unstoried, artless, unenhanced,*
*Such as she was, such as she would become.*

The relation between this poem and the Johnson passage lies, of course, in the lines, "She was our land more than a hundred years/Before we were her people." Why? Because we were "Possessed by what we now no more possessed"—in other words, England. Which is just another way of saying what Gerald Johnson said. The children can readily fill in the wars involved in "(The deed of gift was many deeds of war)," but it is more important to challenge the children with those enigmatic last lines—"Such as she was, such as she would become." What would they like our country to become, our United States? This is important because the answer may well lie with them, the children of today, the adults of tomorrow. What would they have our country become that she is not today? The children's answers may not be profound, neither would the answers of average adults, but at least the poem will have made them look beneath the surface of evolving life in their own country and sense the fact that they, too, are going to play a part in its future. This poem is a perfect example of Frost's own pronouncement that "Each poem clarifies something."

The poems of Frost have a deceiving simplicity, which is good for children. They catch meanings with the first reading or listening. But as children grow chronologically, they also grow intellectually. In their reading of poetry this growth includes a more perceptive grasp of undertones of meaning. No poet offers them richer food for growth than Robert Frost. (See also pp. 349–351.)

Robert Penn Warren, when he received the 1970 National Medal for Literature, said in his acceptance speech:

> *If we take poetry at its broadest meaning of emotive language, there has never been so much poetry as in our age of mass communication. . . . Poetry not only utters itself in such a language as reminds us of our deepest being, but embodies ideas and values; and so its images are, in one dimension, a sophisticated dialectic.*

The children who are reading and writing poetry today are young, but they are searching and probing issues and problems of our time. They want, in addition to poetry that is beautiful in its grace and melody, poetry that is beautiful in strength and candor. They need to explore the new forms, to hear the angry voices, for they are, many of them, angry about what is happening in their world. They should read Coatsworth, De la Mare, and Frost, but they should also read Rod McKuen, Nikki Giovanni, Leonard Cohen, Mari Evans, Karl Shapiro, and the many other poets who are concerned, as the children are, with the way things are now.

## HOW TO READ POETRY ALOUD

Throughout this chapter there has been an emphasis on reading poetry aloud to children as long as their own reading fluency is limited. This puts a heavy responsibility on adults, and the question is often asked, "How can a person with little knowledge of poetry and less knowledge of oral interpretation learn to read poetry acceptably?" The answer is, only by reading a poem aloud repeatedly until its tune and its meaning grow. Fortunately, the nonsense ditties of *Mother Goose*, Lear, and Laura Richards, with their crisp or explosive consonants and brisk rhythms, practically force the reader into vigorous, precise speech and give him a sense of tempo and variety. Milne, too, writes his lines so that they compel a correct interpretation. The subtle lyrics of Blake, Rossetti, and De la Mare, and the thought-provoking poetry of Robert Frost, however, require something more than vigor and swing. The works of these poets demand delicate, precise interpretation, and such interpretation must be grown into. So read a poem aloud to yourself first to get the general mood or feeling. Obviously, Blake's "Laughing Song" carries a gentle gaiety with it; listen to your own reading and see if you hear the suggestion (and only a suggestion) of laughter growing and finally coming to a climax in the last line. "Some One" by Walter de la Mare is mysterious and hushed—you can almost hear the speaker listening and whispering his speculations about the unseen knocker-at-his-door.

You make many such discoveries when you read poetry aloud, because skilled poets write for the ear, and they employ melody and movement consciously for specific ends: (1) Sometimes melody and movement are used to suggest the action described in the poem. (2) Sometimes they help to establish the mood of the poem, or (3) they may even furnish clues to its meaning. When you read a poem aloud, therefore, you catch elements you miss when you read it silently, and the second time you try it orally you will interpret it better because you understand it better.

*Melody and movement are used to suggest action.* Read aloud Dorothy Baruch's "Merry-Go-Round" and you discover that the carousel winds up, gains momentum, and obviously runs down to a full stop as her line patterns suggest. Or read aloud the running of the rats in Browning's "Pied Piper of Hamelin":

*And the muttering grew to a grumbling;*
*And the grumbling grew to a mighty rumbling;*
*And out of the house the rats came tumbling.*

*Great rats, small rats, lean rats, brawny rats,*
*Brown rats, black rats, gray rats, tawny rats,*
*Grave old plodders, gay young friskers,*
*Fathers, mothers, uncles, cousins,*
*Cocking tails and pricking whiskers,*
*Families by tens and dozens,*
*Brothers, sisters, husbands, wives—*
*Followed the Piper for their lives.*

As you read, you find yourself biting off the words in fine staccato style and gaining momentum as the thunderous race goes on. This is quite different from the broken, tripping, skipping, helter-skelter of the children's procession later in the poem. In still sharper contrast is this Greek lament, written over two thousand years ago, for a little dog. It moves slowly, gravely.

*A Maltese Dog*[20]

*He came from Malta; and Eumêlus says*
*He had no better dog in all his days.*
*We called him Bull; he went into the dark.*
*Along those roads we cannot hear him bark.*

This suggests the broken, halting movement of Ravel's music "Pavane for a Dead Princess," and the melody is in the same minor key. These auditory qualities force you to a reading very different from the one you would use for the spinning music of Edna St. Vincent Millay's "The Ballad of the Harp-Weaver" or the nonsense of Milne's "The King's Breakfast."

*Melody and movement help to establish mood.* A galloping rhythm suggests excitement, and in Stevenson's "Windy Nights" it heightens the mystery of the unseen rider. In Browning's "How They Brought the Good News from Ghent to Aix" it makes the ride almost unbearably exciting and full of suspense. And in Alfred Noyes' "The Highwayman" it adds enormously to the romantic thrill and tragedy of that perennial favorite. But there are subtler rhythms and tunes that are just as potent. Read Langston Hughes' "April Rain Song" slowly, thoughtfully, and feel the tranquillity it induces:

*Let the rain kiss you.*
*Let the rain beat upon your head with silver*
*liquid drops.*
*Let the rain sing you a lullaby.*

*The rain makes still pools on the sidewalk.*
*The rain makes running pools in the gutter.*
*The rain plays a little sleep-song on our roof*
*at night—*

*And I love the rain.*[21]

So, in contrast, Ivy Eastwick's "Where's Mary?" is a comic study of irritability, a nagging woman getting more and more shrewish with every line. You find yourself growing sharper with every word. Heaven help poor Mary!

For an example of two entirely different poems about the same general subject, look at "Something Told the Wild Geese" by Rachel Field, and "The Last Word of a Bluebird" by Robert Frost. Both poems are about the migration of birds in the autumn, but their tunes and rhythms are as unlike as possible, and each one induces a completely different mood. "Something Told the Wild Geese" has caught the wild poignancy of the autumn flight of geese southward. The last two lines almost give you the shiver up the backbone that you feel when you hear wild geese honking overhead. Now look at "The Last Word of a Bluebird." It sounds as colloquial as two old men meeting on a street corner to discuss the late lamented cold snap. Only it happens to be a crow talking. It is laconic, earnest, and comic. Two different tunes compel two different moods and do something to your reading if you explore them orally a time or two.

20. "A Maltese Dog" by Tymes, translated by Edmund Blunden, from *The Oxford Book of Greek Verse in Translation* edited by T. F. Higham and C. Bowra. Used by permission of the Clarendon Press.

21. "April Rain Song" from *The Dream Keeper* by Langston Hughes. Copyright 1932 and renewed 1960 by author. Reprinted by permission of Alfred A. Knopf, Inc.

*Illustration by Clare Leighton in* Imagination's Other Place, *compiled by Helen Plotz. Copyright 1955 by Thomas Y. Crowell Company, New York, Publishers.*

*Melody and movement furnish clues to meaning.* Although these clues are not always apparent, we often use them unconsciously. For example, the minor note in that last verse of Robert Frost's "Stopping by Woods on a Snowy Evening" is the clue to its meaning. Look also at the small, quiet words of Elizabeth Madox Roberts' "Firefly." Words and lines suggest the idea of a small, evanescent creature, the "little bug all lit."

Notice, for contrast, the hammer stroke of the words in T. S. Eliot's

*The world turns and the world changes,*
*But one thing does not change.*
*In all of my years, one thing does not change.*
*However you disguise it, this thing does not change:*
*The perpetual struggle of Good and Evil.*[22]

This is the sound of the preacher, pounding home a moral truth. Even if you understood no English, you would know that you were being preached at, and that is the idea back of the words. So the beat of words and lines helps to convey the meaning and clarifies obscurities.

Reading poems aloud will, then, help to train your ear, improve your diction, and develop your taste for poetry. But, for your own sake, do not confine yourself to poetry for children; explore adult poetry as well. Treat yourself to a book by a modern poet—William Butler Yeats, Theodore Roethke, Archibald MacLeish, T. S. Eliot, or Robert Frost—or to books by some of the younger poets. Treat yourself to at least one fine anthology of poetry. Walter de la Mare's *Come Hither;* Helen Plotz's *Imagination's Other Place;* Stephen Dunning, Edward Lueders, and Hugh Smith's *Reflections on a Gift of Watermelon Pickle . . . and other modern verse;* David Mackay's *A Flock of Words;* Robert Hayden's *Kaleidoscope;* and Myra Cohn Livingston's *A Tune Beyond Us* are treasures to be used by the whole family

*Illustration by James J. Spanfeller, copyright © 1968 by Harcourt Brace Jovanovich, Inc. Reproduced from* A Tune Beyond Us, *edited by Myra Cohn Livingston, by permission of the publishers.*

22. From *The Rock* by T. S. Eliot, copyright, 1934, by Harcourt Brace Jovanovich, Inc.; renewed © 1962 by T. S. Eliot and reprinted by permission of the publishers, and Faber and Faber Ltd.

through the years. Between the covers of an anthology you will find excitement when you feel dull, peace when you are harassed, refreshment when you are weary.

Poetry has the same power of healing that music has. Prove it for yourself. Some night when you find yourself exhausted or disturbed or "all tied in knots," read aloud, slowly and quietly, these first lines of John Keats' "Endymion":

*A thing of beauty is a joy forever:*
*Its loveliness increases; it will never*
*Pass into nothingness; but still will keep*
*A bower quiet for us, and a sleep*
*Full of sweet dreams, and health, and quiet breathing.*
*Therefore, on every morrow, are we wreathing*
*A flowery band to bind us to the earth,*
*Spite of despondence, of the inhuman dearth*
*Of noble natures, of the gloomy days,*
*Of all the unhealthy and o'er-darkened ways*
*Made for our seaching: yes, in spite of all,*
*Some shape of beauty moves away the pall*
*From our dark spirits. Such the sun, the moon,*
*Trees old and young, sprouting a shady boon*
*For simple sheep; and such are daffodils*
*With the green world they live in; and clear rills*
*That for themselves a cooling covert make*
*'Gainst the hot season; the mid-forest brake,*
*Rich with a sprinkling of fair musk-rose blooms:*
*And such too is the grandeur of the dooms*
*We have imagined for the mighty dead;*
*All lovely tales that we have heard or read:*
*An endless fountain of immortal drink,*
*Pouring unto us from the heaven's brink.*

Visualize these lines as you read; then, start memorizing the selection as a whole, that is, going through all the lines each time. You won't learn it perfectly the first night, perhaps, but by the time you have mulled over it four or five times, savoring the words, catching new meanings that escaped you at first, you will discover that your tenseness is gone, that you are relaxed, renewed, healed. For those who have cultivated a listening ear, poetry has the same therapeutic quality as music. When you have made this discovery, you will be ready to use poetry with children as it should be used.

With children the success of a poem depends in part upon the way you read or say it, and in part upon the mood and the setting in which the poem is introduced. One father used to settle down in the evening with his small boy in his lap. Sometimes there was an open fire, and always the child was undressed, ready for bed, comfortably snug in bathrobe and slippers. Then, in a leisurely, rumbling voice, the father would read or say the poems they both enjoyed. Occasionally the boy's thin treble would chime in, making a piccolo-bassoon duet. Invariably, along with requests for Stevenson and Milne, the child would demand, "Now say that about 'cloud-capp'd towers.'" Father would roll out those sonorous lines in his rich, deep voice, and the boy would listen intently but without comment. Occasionally he would murmur, "Say it again."

*The cloud-capp'd towers, the gorgeous palaces,*
*The solemn temples, the great globe itself,*
*Yea, all which it inherit, shall dissolve*
*And, like this insubstantial pageant faded,*
*Leave not a rack behind. We are such stuff*
*As dreams are made on; and our little life*
*Is rounded with a sleep.*—The Tempest.

Do you suppose that small boy would have listened to or been absorbed by those lines of Shakespeare had his father tried saying them to him on an automobile trip or at the breakfast table? Probably not. Mothers have always known the value of words spoken quietly at the going-to-sleep period, and the stories they tell are remembered always. So that small boy will probably carry with him as long as he lives "cloud-capp'd towers" happily associated with the warmth and security of his father's arms.

Schools usually have no such period of peace and affection, but perhaps they should create one. Of necessity a schoolroom must be functional; it must be a workshop, a study, a playroom, and a laboratory, all combined. But it is still possible to create a small area that suggests relaxation and enjoyment. In one classroom there was a little spot of ordered beauty—a table placed against a wall on which hung a bright-colored textile. On the table there was sometimes a bowl of flowers, or a vase with bare twigs, or some shining brasses borrowed from home, or a copy of a fine bit of sculpture. The children took turns arranging this table, which was a continual source of interest and pride. In another room, a teacher had one narrow window to the north. This she had turned into a glowing feast for the eyes, with glass shelves on which she and the children arranged colored glass vases. Some of them were from the ten-cent store, some the children brought from home as temporary loans, but the result was eyefilling sparkle and color. In still another classroom, there was space for a rug and some easy chairs over in a corner with the piano nearby. Such areas in the midst of our busy classrooms invite the imagination and are ideal settings for both music and literature.

For poetry, teachers and children should make themselves as comfortable as possible. Let there be no sitting up straight with hands folded. If there are any rockers or easy chairs, sit in them. If not, be as relaxed as classroom chairs permit. If the children sit on their feet, loll around, or curl up in strange postures, let them. Get the children close to you for poetry; relax, and let it be known that this is the time for enjoyment.[23]

23. For the combined poetry bibliography, see pages 382–389.

# Chapter 10
# The Range of Poetry for Children

Although some children cling to one genre or subject in their reading, most like variety, and their preferences change with mood and age. Fortunately, there is such variety in poetry as to satisfy any taste: narrative, dramatic, or lyric; bound verse or free; poems about animals, people, nature, fairies, emotions, causes; poems that are thoughtful or stirring, tender or hilarious. In this chapter we shall cross the lines of form and content in discussing both the wide variety of poetry for children and the poetry children are writing today. We shall consider poetry ranging from nonsense verse and the more serious poems about children's everyday experiences to the quiet probings of Langston Hughes' poetry and the patterned intricacies of poems by May Swenson.[1]

A poem may be written in free verse, which has no requirements of rhyme and meter, or in bound verse, which does. It can be narrative, dramatic, or lyric. Dramatic poetry, a form seldom used in children's poems, reveals the personality of a character primarily through his speech or through the speech of other characters. Narrative poetry tells a story and is enjoyed by children for that reason, whether the poems are long and serious or brief and humorous. Lyric poetry, which is usually short, expresses an emotion of some kind, often highly personal, and it may range in content from the expression of a child's delight in "wiggly mud" to a sad farewell to departing summer.

## NONSENSE VERSE

There is no better way to introduce children to poetry than with nonsense verse. For young children the gay tradition of nonsense verse was given a rousing start by *Mother Goose*'s rhymes (see Chapter 5). Children enjoy these amusing jingles, and most adults find a lifelong source of fun in humorous limericks and verse.

It is good for us to laugh. Someone has said that a teacher should count the day lost when her children have not, at one time or

1. See Chapter 11, Poets and Children's Poetry, for the discussion of the work of a wide range of poets. See the Index to locate individual poets.

another, thrown back their heads and laughed spontaneously and heartily. This unknown philosopher should have added that teachers and parents need this release also; for a hearty laugh provides just that—a release from all the miserable little tensions that have gradually crept up on us and tied us in hard knots. We say that we are "weak with laughter," which means that our knots are untied, we are relaxed once more. If nonsense verse can provide such a release, blessed be nonsense!

Not all people and not all ages are amused by the same jokes. Two-year-olds may chuckle over the hissing s's of "sing a song of six-pence." The hilarity of older children is roused by other forms of humor. Just listen to seven-year-olds enjoying Laura Richards' "Eletelephony" (see p. 340). And try reading this traditional poem to the twelve-year-olds:

*Whistle, Whistle*[2]

*"Whistle, whistle, old wife, and you'll get a hen."*
*"I wouldn't whistle," said the wife, "if you could give me ten!"*

*"Whistle, whistle, old wife, and you'll get a cock."*
*"I wouldn't whistle," said the wife, "if you gave me a flock!"*

*"Whistle, whistle, old wife, and you'll get a coo."*
*"I wouldn't whistle," said the wife, "if you could give me two!"*

*"Whistle, whistle, old wife, and you'll get a gown."*
*"I wouldn't whistle," said the wife, "for the best one in the town!"*

*"Whistle, whistle, old wife, and you'll get a man."*
*"Wheeple, whauple," said the wife, "I'll whistle if I can!"*

2. "Whistle, Whistle" from *Choral Verse Speaking* by Elizabeth H. Keppie. Published by Expression Company.

## VIEWPOINTS

. . . the technique of good nonsense verse is just as skilful and difficult as that of any other kind of verse. The grotesque impression is produced, not by ignoring the general laws of good poetry, but by upsetting them purposely, and by making them, so to speak, stand on their heads. . . . There is no more severe criticism of a poet than to question the spontaneity of his rhyming power. All of his words must obey his inspiration, without being subservient to it.

Practically every nursery rhyme shows a deliberate contempt of this rule. The rhyme, not the thought, becomes the source of inspiration, and the singer builds his story around it. Once the poet has sung 'Barber, barber, shave a pig,' there is no escaping the image of the 'wig,' . . .

. . . The more liberties he takes, the better his nonsense. He uses a perfect orgy of refrains, repetitions, new words apparently meaningless, new beings never heard of before.—Émile Cammaerts, *The Poetry of Nonsense*, George Routledge and Sons, London, 1925, pp. 40–41, 44.

The grotesque and the incongruous, which make up the content of nonsense verse, provide needed escape from the weight of the realistic and the reasonable. "The Jumblies" go to sea in a sieve and have a successful voyage instead of being properly drowned for their folly. The cow jumps over the moon and apparently her milk doesn't even curdle. The world of nonsense is a gay, exuberant world of irresponsible behavior and impossible results. It affords an innocent escape from gravity.

Nonsense verse, if it is skillfully composed, introduces the child to rhyme, rhythm, and meter and to various types of verse patterns. The neatly turned limerick and the patter of humorous couplets or quatrains in exact meter train the ear to enjoy the sound of words and rhythms, a training that should carry over to catching similar sound patterns in poetry of a higher order.

After *Mother Goose*, Edward Lear (see p. 330) is chronologically the first poet to conjure up laughter. From the time *The Book of Nonsense* appeared in 1846, children and adults have been chuckling over Lear's limericks and verse stories.

Eleven years later came the astonishingly mad nonsense poetry of Lewis Carroll in *Alice's Adventures in Wonderland* (see p. 338), to make "galumphing," "frabjous," and "burbled" an imperishable part of children's language, even if they have never read "Jabberwocky." Laura Richards, called the American Poet Laureate of Nonsense for Children, was born only eighteen years after Lewis Carroll and as a child began writing poetry and stories, but it wasn't until 1932 that her best-known book was published—*Tirra-Lirra; Rhymes Old and New* (see p. 339). Like Carroll, she invented words; in one of her poems, for example, a giraffe burns his mouth on a just-baked apple pie "so terribly he yelped and yammered yerribly." Another versifier for children, English Leslie Brooke (see p. 345), born in 1862, wrote the *Johnny Crow* verse stories that are delightful first nonsense rhymes for preschool children.

Time has not withered the horrendous appeal of Hilaire Belloc's *The Bad Child's Book of Beasts* (1896) or his *Cautionary Verses* (1941), one of which has been illustrated with gusto by Steven Kellogg: *Matilda, Who Told Lies and Was Burned to Death*, a nonsensical spoof of a Victorian morality tale. Ogden Nash was one of the most successful practitioners of the art of nonsense verse and a master of the outrageous surprise rhyme. Most of his verses are somewhat sophisticated humor, but it is a poor anthology that cannot find among Mr. Nash's riches a rib-tickling selection for all ages. "The Octopus"[3] is a good example.

*Tell me, O Octopus, I begs,*
*Is those things arms, or is they legs?*
*I marvel at thee, Octopus;*
*If I were thou, I'd call me Us.*

Nash was also the compiler of anthologies of humorous poetry—*I Couldn't Help Laughing* and *The Moon Is Shining Bright as Day.*

They ran their ladders through a score
Of windows on the ballroom floor;

*Illustration by Steven Kellogg from* Matilda, Who Told Lies and Was Burned to Death *by Hilaire Belloc. Pictures copyright © 1970 by Steven Kellogg. Reprinted by permission of the publisher, The Dial Press.*

Poet John Ciardi (p. 374) starts his children with nonsense verse. The Bugle-Billed Bazoo in *The Reason for the Pelican* and the Glurk in *Someone Could Win a Polar Bear* are examples of his silly invented names. Ciardi also turns a deft limerick.

3. "The Octopus" from *Good Intentions* by Ogden Nash. Copyright 1942, by Ogden Nash. Reprinted by permission of Little, Brown and Co. and J. M. Dent & Sons Ltd.

*The Music Master*[4]

*"My sons," said a Glurk slurping soup,*
*"We would make a fine musical group.*
*Put your spoon to your lip*
*And slurp when you sip,*
*But don't spill. Like this, children—oop!"*

Other writers who have contributed nonsense verses include William Jay Smith (p. 378), whose *Laughing Time*. a collection of often sophisticated verses and rhymes, makes amusing use of invented words; William Cole, who not only writes humorous verse but collects it (for example, in *Oh, What Nonsense!*), and Polly Cameron, whose jingling verses in *"I Can't," Said the Ant* and *The Green Machine* are simple enough for many beginning readers.

## FROM NONSENSE TO HUMOR

Although no hard and fast line divides humor from sheer nonsense, there is, nevertheless, a difference. Nonsense is more daft, more impossible, with Pobbles, Jumblies, potatoes that dance, chickens that go out to tea, gargoyles, and griffins—a wild crew close kin to the "cow that jumped over the moon." Humorous verse, on the other hand, deals with the amusing things that befall real people, or might conceivably befall them. Edward Lear and Laura E. Richards sometimes wrote humorous verse, but for the most part their verse is hilarious nonsense. In contrast, A. A. Milne (see p. 355) wrote occasional nonsense, but on the whole his poems involve people and situations that are amusingly possible, however improbable they may be.

Again we find a juggling with funny words: "sneezles and freezles," foxes who didn't wear "sockses," "biffalo-buffalo-bisons," "badgers and bidgers and bodgers," and a mouse with a "woffelly nose." The children seize upon them as their very own, for these words are exactly what they might have said. If you study Milne's funny words, you discover that they fall within the range of the child's own vocabulary. Here we find no "fatally fair flamingo" of the older child's level, but the measles and "sneezles" that "teasles" the funnybone of the little child because they are all close to words he recognizes.

Usually "The King's Breakfast" is the favorite with most Milne addicts. This starts reasonably with the king asking for a little butter on the "Royal slice of bread," and it moves along smoothly until the sleepy Alderney upsets all royal regularity by suggesting "a little marmalade instead." From then on the dialogue becomes entirely daft, reaching a joyous climax when the king bounces out of bed and slides down the banisters. This is, of course, the essence of the fun—the incongruity of a king who is so deeply concerned with marmalade that he whimpers, sulks, bounces, and slides down banisters. The verse pattern of each episode reinforces the mood.

Most of Rose Fyleman's poems are dedicated to fairies, but she also wrote amusing poems like "The Dentist" and "Mary Middling." In addition to these humorous verses she is responsible for an international *Mother Goose* called *Picture Rhymes from Foreign Lands*, with translations of nursery rhymes from many countries. Young children learn and like her galloping "Husky Hi" as much as they like "Ride a cock horse." "My Donkey," with its delicate refrain, and the clumping, thumping "Goblin" make a pleasant contrast. Both poems are fine material for verse choirs. Rose Fyleman's musical gifts were never employed to better advantage than in these rollicking nursery rhymes which she translated so effectively.

Other writers of humorous verse before the 1950s include the once popular James

4. "The Music Master." From the book *Someone Could Win a Polar Bear* by John Ciardi. Copyright, ©, 1964, 1965, 1967, 1970 by John Ciardi. Reprinted by permission of J. B. Lippincott Company.

Whitcomb Riley and Eugene Field. Riley's verses have a mild humor, but they rarely bubble or sparkle. They are newspaper verse with a rural flavor that appealed strongly to many people when they first appeared. His two best-known poems are "The Raggedy Man" and "Little Orphant Annie." Field, a newspaper poet like Riley, wrote many sentimental verses, but "The Duel" is still enjoyed by children of five or six. This mock tragedy about the gingham dog and the calico cat who "ate each other up" has a pleasant swing and a delightful refrain. Another tragicomic verse is Vachel Lindsay's "The Potatoes' Dance," which tells of the blighted romance of a "tiny Irish lady" and a hapless sweet potato (see p. 352).

There are, of course, many other writers of humorous verse for children and many humorous poems to be found here and there in the books of serious writers. Shakespeare resorts to pure nonsense now and then, usually by way of a song. Christina Rossetti (see p. 334) includes in her charming lyrics one or two which might have come from *Mother Goose*. Walter de la Mare (see p. 345) in his subtle and highly imaginative poetry pauses to describe poor Henry taking a dose of physic, or to give us a startling account of the woebegone fish in a frying pan in "Alas, Alack!"

## HUMOROUS VERSE SINCE THE FIFTIES

One of the most outstanding and prolific writers of humorous verse for children since the 1950s is David McCord (p. 365), who wrote for adults before he began writing for children. McCord's poems are not all humorous, but the best of them have a captivating playfulness and ebullience which infectiously communicate an enjoyment of words and word play.

*You Mustn't Call It Hopsichord*[5]

*You mustn't call it* hopsichord,
*It's not played by a toad.*
*You mustn't say a* chevaleer—
*It wasn't he who rode.*
*It's* sacred *to the memory of,*
*Not* scared, *as you prefer.*
*You put apostrophes in* we're
*And keep them out of* were.
Undurfed? *No, no, it's* underfed;
*Bed-raggled isn't right, I said.*
*You shirr an egg—how could you shear it?*
*Music's not hominy or grits;*
*The thing is* ferret, *though you fear it;*
*Twist twist, and twist is twits.*
*Please never say again you're* mizzled;
*Mis-led you are, or led astray.*
*The word is wizened and not* wizzled;
*Hens don't lie down—they lay.*

In a section called "Write Me a Verse," in *Take Sky*, McCord uses a mythical Professor Swigly Brown to explain the couplet, the quatrain, the triolet, and the limerick in rhymes that exemplify each of these poetic forms. In "Write Me Another Verse" from *For Me to Say*, he continues with the tercet, the villanelle, the clerihew, the cinquain, and haiku. In these two sections of both books all the directions are given in the verse form itself.

Despite the title of William Cole's large anthology *Humorous Poetry for Children*, many of the selections are for teen-agers or adults rather than for children, but there are enough poems for the nines to twelves to make the book decidedly worth adding to the library of laughter in elementary school libraries, children's collections in public libraries, and in homes. His *Oh, What Nonsense!* and *Oh, How Silly!* are also anthologies of humorous poems, the first containing many counting rhymes and jump-rope chants, the second song lyrics and folk rhymes. In both books, the illustrator, Tomi Ungerer, wittily echoes the gay and deft silliness. His *What's Good for a Four-Year-Old?* and similar separate volumes for five- and

5. "You Mustn't Call It Hopsichord" by David McCord from *Take Sky*. Copyright 1961, 1962 by David McCord. Reprinted by permission of Little, Brown and Co. and Curtis Brown, Ltd..

*From* Oh, What Nonsense! *by William Cole and Tomi Ungerer. Illustrations copyright © 1966 by Tomi Ungerer. Reprinted by permission of The Viking Press, Inc.*

six-year-olds have bouncy, lighthearted verse in which children express their preferences.

Kaye Starbird (p. 375), in *Speaking of Cows*, her first book of poetry for children, immediately established herself as a capable writer of amusing verse with an informal, ruminative quality. Her later books carried out the promise of the first: *Don't Ever Cross a Crocodile, A Snail's a Failure Socially*, and *The Pheasant on Route Seven*. Her casual, easy style is evident in the title poem of *The Pheasant on Route Seven*. In it the pheasant comments, when he unwisely lands on a busy highway, "Well, *that* was darned surprising. Not to mention darned unpleasant."

Theodore Roethke (p. 373), whose adult poetry is enjoyed by many adolescent readers as well as by adults, has written some humorous verse that amuses children, such as "Dirty Dinky" and "The Sloth."

*The Love Letters of Phyllis McGinley* is a treasury of light verse for adults and clever teen-age youngsters but not for children. But Phyllis McGinley has also written some delightful verses for children in her ABC book, *All Around the Town*, and two Christmas books, *Mince Pie and Mistletoe* and *A Wreath of Christmas Legends*.

In each of her collections of poetry, Eve Merriam (see p. 377) provides some amusing gems. Like David McCord, she sometimes uses poetic forms to explain the forms themselves, giving six examples of the couplet in "Couplet Countdown" and demonstrating in "Leaning on a Limerick" both the form and the playful use of words at which she excels.

Sara and John Brewton have specialized in limericks in their anthology *Laughable Limericks*. And in *Yours Till Niagara Falls, A Dillar, A Dollar*, and *Touch Blue*, Lillian Morrison has gathered verses of the kind found in autograph albums, popular sayings related to school life, and rhymes about spells. For older readers, Myra Cohn Livingston's (see p. 380) *Speak Roughly to Your Little Boy* is both diverting and instructive. It is a collection of parodies and burlesques, each paired with the original material on which it was based—Swinburne parodies himself; Carroll makes fun of several poets, including Longfellow in a poem called "Hiawatha's Photographing." It begins:

*From his shoulder Hiawatha*
*Took the camera of rosewood,*
*Made of sliding, folding rosewood;*
*Neatly put it all together.*
*In its case it lay compactly,*
*Folded into nearly nothing . . . .*[6]

Some of the selections will also be enjoyed by younger children who can recognize little nuggets of burlesque like J. B. Morton's "Now We Are Sick."

Other poets who have a light and knowing hand with verse for children are Felice Holman, whose *At the Top of My Voice* contains many poems that have a wry humor, and Maxine Kumin, whose *No One Writes a Letter to the Snail* has a fresh and entertaining bounce. Richard Armour's blithe rhymes in *Odd Old Mammals, A Dozen Dinosaurs*, and *All Sizes and Shapes of Monkeys and*

6. Reprinted in Myra Cohn Livingston's *Speak Roughly to Your Little Boy* (Harcourt Brace Jovanovich, 1971), p. 55.

*Apes* add zest to well-researched information. Jack Prelutsky, known for his translations of German children's poetry, has himself written entertaining light verse in *A Gopher in the Garden and Other Animal Poems* and *Toucans Two and Other Poems*. Older children savor Conrad Aiken's delightfully illustrated *Cats and Bats and Things with Wings*, but it is also a good book to read aloud to young children. Doris Orgel, in *The Good-Byes of Magnus Marmalade*, lets Magnus speak for her as he bids farewell to various people. To the dentist, for instance, he says:

> *"You filled my tooth with gentle care*
> *And yet I leave your dental chair*
> *With such great joy it must be true*
> *It's not your drill I hate, it's you!"*[7]

Since anthologists have not found all the humorous verse that has been written, it is a rewarding activity for teachers to make a collection of favorites, or to encourage children to make such a collection. Clever, well-written verses which provoke a chuckle are worth having not only because they bring laughter into this grave old world, but because their rollicking jingles cultivate the ear and lead naturally and painlessly to the enjoyment of lyric poetry.

*Reprinted by permission of G. P. Putnam's Sons from* The Good-Byes of Magnus Marmalade *by Doris Orgel, illustrated by Erik Blegvad. Copyright © 1966 Text by Doris Orgel, illustrations by Erik Blegvad.*

*Illustration copyright © 1965 by Milton Glaser. From* Cats and Bats and Things with Wings *by Conrad Aiken. Used by permission of Atheneum Publishers.*

## POETRY OF THE CHILD'S EVERYDAY WORLD

The world of fantastic nonsense and the child's everyday world of people, pets, and the outdoors may seem far apart. Yet many poets move easily from one to the other and, like the child, are at home in both worlds.

Actually, in the years before Edward Lear introduced children to his madcap world of nonsense, they had been given to understand that life was not only real but decidedly earnest. Poems were written and read to children for the purpose of improving their manners and uplifting their morals. Yet didactic as some of these early efforts seem today, they marked a dawning recognition of the child's everyday world of people and play, both real and imaginative. Slowly the

7. Reprinted by permission of G. P. Putnam's Sons from *The Good-Byes of Magnus Marmalade* by Doris Orgel. Text Copyright © 1966 by Doris Orgel.

idea took form and grew, the idea of a child, not as a small adult, but as an intensely active person, functioning in a world of his own.

The poems of Kate Greenaway (see p. 338) marked the transition from verse written for children's instruction to verse written for their entertainment, verse which records the child's play world from his point of view. "What is Tommy running for?" she asks, and sagely concludes that Tommy is running so that Jimmy can run after him. Reason enough for any child! Even though her verses are often wooden and occasionally unchildlike, most of them have a gentle gaiety, as for example, this one from *Under the Window:*

*In go-cart so tiny*
*My sister I drew;*
*And I've promised to draw her*
*The wide world through.*

*We have not yet started—*
*I own it with sorrow—*
*Because our trip's always*
*Put off till to-morrow.*[8]

This poem as well as many other verses of Kate Greenaway reflect a new consciousness of the real child and his everyday play.

Other poets caught this new point of view and began to write a new kind of verse for and about children. Their poems reflect both the child's everyday world of active play and his inner world of imaginative play.

Robert Louis Stevenson (see p. 341) wrote only one book of poetry for children, *A Child's Garden of Verses*, but with that one book he became one of the greatest of children's poets. There was nothing comparable to these verses when they were written, no literary precedents, even though Stevenson himself said that the idea for his book came to him while he was glancing over one of Kate Greenaway's little books. Fortunately, he goes far beyond Greenaway at her best, both in the reflection of the child's point of view and in the quality of his poetry.

The poems are truly childlike in their approach to play and in the manner in which they mirror the small adventures of a child's day. They are rhythmic and musical, and they see both the imagined and the real with a child's clear eye.

The poetry of Eleanor Farjeon (see p. 353) cuts across any classification which could be devised. She wrote skillful nonsense verse, her lyrics are tender and beautiful, and her poetry reflects a sure knowledge of the child's world and wonderment. Her first book, for which she wrote her own music, was *Nursery Rhymes of London Town*. Many of her books of poems for children have been collected in *Poems for Children* and *Then There Were Three*, and both poetry and prose are included in *The Children's Bells*. Her writing has zest and playfulness, and enjoyment of words, and a variety of subjects and patterns with a seeming spontaneity and an unquestionable charm.

James S. Tippett's small books, just pocket size, make an immediate appeal to the young child. For him the author is interpreting the skyscraper environment of a large city—elevators, endless stairways, switchboard girls, the subway—all the complexities of New York City experienced through the eyes of an inquiring child. Some of this subject matter in *I Live in a City* might be foreign to a suburban child of another large city, but some of the verses make a general appeal. Mr. Tippett's virtue is that he is never arch. His directness and sincerity are admirable. His books are records of modern children's curiosities, their response to their environment, both in the city and in the country. As language records, these books have their place. Most of the favorites are in the anthologies.

Elizabeth Madox Roberts (see p. 359) had the ability to see, feel, and think as a child, an ability that strikes the adult as unerringly right and true. Her single book of poetry for children, *Under the Tree*, uses words and

8. From *Under the Window* by Kate Greenaway. Published by Frederick Warne & Company.

phrases that sound like a child speaking, but only an artist could have chosen words so brilliantly descriptive. Her narrative is as direct as prose, with no "proud words," no fanciness, no ethereal theme, but the imagery, the sensitivity, and the identification with the concerns of children bring her poems directly into the child's world of poetry.

Of Rachel Field's (see p. 363) books of poetry, *Taxis and Toadstools* is the one children usually like best. Here are poems that are direct and forthright, that share the child's vision of the sights of ordinary things in city and country, things that are to him quite extraordinary in their importance.

Dorothy Aldis' verses are popular with children six to eight years old, although her verse patterns are neither varied nor interesting, and she rarely achieves anything unusual either in form or content. Yet she makes a sure appeal to young children. Her strength lies in her knowledge of the small child's everyday interests, his play, and his observations. Mrs. Aldis' verse-children keep pets, have brothers and sisters, wonder about their hands and feet, celebrate Fourth of July, and enjoy a happy relationship with their parents. "Hiding," which is the most popular verse she ever wrote, can be found in most anthologies. A prime favorite with six- and seven-year-olds, it is beloved in part because it reflects a parent-child relationship that every child longs for. Here are a mother and father playing with their child, entering into his make-believe with proper gravity and no condescension.

In Frances Frost's (see p. 370) two books, *The Little Whistler* and *The Little Naturalist*, the simply written poems reflect the author's familiarity with, and affection for, the wild animals she observed with accuracy.

Gwendolyn Brooks' (see p. 377) *Bronzeville Boys and Girls* is probably the best-known single volume of children's poetry by a black author, each discerning poem named for a child.

Beatrice Schenk de Regniers' poems have a gay, lilting quality that appeals to young children. Her *Something Special* fairly bubbles with humor.

Karla Kuskin's *In the Middle of the Trees* is also for younger children, and her *Alexander Soames: His Poems* is imaginative and humorous. Alexander refuses to speak in prose, and his mother's challenging suggestions for verse subjects give the collection both variety and a unifying theme.

Mary Ann Hoberman's *Hello and Good-By* has forty-one brief verses. The title poem voices an intriguing idea and "Brother" will undoubtedly find many sympathizers. It is an amusing patter verse to say.

The simplicity and the rhythmic quality of Myra Cohn Livingston's (see p. 380) poetry are appealing to children, and in *Whispers and Other Poems, Happy Birthday*, and *Wide Awake and Other Poems*, there are such small gems as "Lamplighter Barn":[9]

*I can play*
*in the prickly hay*
*and I can find*
*where the chickens lay*
*and take off my shoes*
*and stay*
*and stay*
*in the tickly hay*
*on a rainy day.*

John Updike, distinguished as a writer for adults and as the 1964 winner of the National Book Award for Fiction, has, in *A Child's Calendar*, written with fresh imagery about the familiar phenomena of the child's changing year.

*June*[10]

*The sun is rich,*
*And gladly pays*
*In golden hours,*
*Silver days,*

9. From *Wide Awake and Other Poems*, copyright © 1959 by Myra Cohn Livingston. Reprinted by permission of Harcourt Brace Jovanovich, Inc.

*And long green weeks*
*That never end.*
*School's out. The time*
*Is ours to spend.*

*The playground calls,*
*The ice-cream man,*
*And, after supper,*
*Kick-the-Can.*

*The live-long light*
*Is like a dream,*
*And freckles come*
*Like flies to cream.*

Here is just a sampling of the many poets who have brought their lyric gifts to interpret the everyday world the child sees and wonders about. Of all the poems available for children, however, those that tell a story have a special appeal, for poetry lovers as well as self-proclaimed detesters of poems.

## NARRATIVE POEMS

The story poems and the old ballad form have proved as attractive to poets as they have to readers. The list of poets who have enjoyed writing narrative poems is a long one and includes such distinguished names as Scott, Allingham, Southey, Browning, Tennyson, Longfellow, Whittier, Swinburne, Rossetti, Kipling, and Masefield. The majority of these poems, however, belong to high school or even to college level. They are too long or the plots are too mature or the language too difficult for elementary-school children to struggle with, even when the poems are read aloud. Still there are some narrative poems that not only are suitable for children but provide them with the fun, the thrills, and the satisfaction which only a dramatic verse story can give. The rapid course of events, the refrains and repetition, and the rhythm all contribute to the interest and impetus of the story poems.

*Illustration by Nancy Burkert from A Child's Calendar, by John Updike. Copyright © 1965 by John Updike and Nancy Burkert. Reprinted by permission of Alfred A. Knopf, Inc. (Original with color)*

For the youngest children, from five to eight or nine, there are two masterpieces—"A Visit from St. Nicholas" by Clement Clarke Moore and "The Pied Piper of Hamelin" by Robert Browning.

In 1822, Christmas Eve found a certain Mr. Clement Moore obliged to make a last-minute visit to the market. Darkness had come, sleigh bells jingled, snow crunched underfoot and, where the street lights fell upon it, sparkled and twinkled. Mr. Moore

10. "June" from *A Child's Calendar*, by John Updike and Nancy Burkert. Copyright © 1965 by authors. Reprinted by permission of Alfred A. Knopf, Inc.

did his errand at the market, hurried home with his package, delivered it to his wife, and then hastened to his study where he shut the door and remained alone for several hours. When he rejoined his family, he brought with him "A Visit from St. Nicholas."

This Saint Nicholas with his reindeer has become the American Santa Claus. Clement Moore gave him a personality, a great dramatic role, a dreamlike existence all his own. The poem was not published until a year after it was written, but from 1823, no American Christmas which includes young children has been complete without it.

It is interesting to recall that Robert Browning wrote his "The Pied Piper of Hamelin" for the amusement of a sick child, with the special intention of supplying him with subject matter he could illustrate. Perhaps this accounts, in part, for the visual quality of the poem, which endears it to illustrators young and old. The story of "The Pied Piper" is too familiar to need reviewing, but particular qualities of the poem are worth noting. In the first place, the story moves rapidly. Words hurry and all but trip the reader's tongue; episodes follow each other swiftly; and lines have the racing tempo first of the scurrying rats and later of the skipping children. They slow down only for the pompous Mayor and his devious cogitations, and for the little lame boy's wistful account of being left behind. Some readers like to conclude with this episode, omitting the last two parts entirely. The dramatic conflict between greed and honor is sufficiently objective for children to understand, and they approve of the Piper's retributive revenge. Children usually dislike descriptions, but Part II, describing the destructiveness of rats, they roll over their tongues. Above all they like the mystery of the Piper himself. "Who was he? Was there ever such a person? Where did he take the children?" they wonder.

For broad comedy Eugene Field's "The Duel" (the tale of "the gingham dog and the calico cat") and Laura Richards' "The Monkeys and the Crocodile" are perennial favorites. William Allingham's "The Fairy Shoemaker" and Laura Richards' "Little John Bottlejohn" are unusual fairy and mermaid poems, the latter simple enough for the five-year-olds. Willis Barnstone's *A Day in the Country* is a narrative in free and fluid verse, a sunny story of a child's happy summer day. An amusing venture into history is Arnold Lobel's *On the Day Peter Stuyvesant Sailed into Town*. The eights will enjoy "The Pirate Don Durk of Dowdee" by Mildred Plew Meigs. The funny words and phrases tickle them: "squizzamaroo," "a floppety plume on his hat," and the dramatic "Oh jing! went the gold of Dowdee."

Vachel Lindsay's "The Potatoes' Dance" and Walter de la Mare's "The Lost Shoe" are unique tales children also enjoy.

Kaye Starbird's "The Palace" is the story of a benighted pair of modern star-crossed lovers, somehow brisk despite the pathos of their fate. In Natalie Babbitt's *Dick Foote and the Shark*, the poetic hero saves his own life and that of his terrified father by so doggedly spouting poetry from the bow that the befuddled shark swims away. *Phoebe's Revolt* describes the rebellion of a Victorian child against the ruffles and bows of that period's clothing. In John Ciardi's *The King Who Saved Himself from Being Saved*, the peaceful monarch who enjoys the status quo outwits a stranger who is determined to be a hero no matter how much it disrupts palace life.

Christina Rossetti's story poem, "Goblin Market" (p. 334), is a dramatic story of two sisters, one of whom rescues the other from the goblins' thrall. The story of Noah's Ark, more than slightly adapted, has two verse versions: *The Cruise of the Aardvark*, in which Ogden Nash's pompous hero discovers belatedly that he is not on an ordinary pleasure cruise; and Countee Cullen's *The Lost Zoo*, which is a good choice for reading aloud to younger children. A perennial favorite is "Custard the Dragon" by Ogden Nash. Search your anthologies and books by single poets for more story poems, because even the fives and sevens enjoy the swiftness and suspense which the rhythmic flow of verse gives to a story.

Older children will like many of the poems allotted to the younger ones. If, for instance, the twelves or fourteens have missed "The Pied Piper," give it to them, by all means. Another story poem with a wide appeal is Ruth Crawford Seeger's *Let's Build a Railroad*. Six railroad work songs are connected by a cadenced narrative, with lively pictures by Tom Funk. The format suggests that the book is for children five to seven, but the text will have more meaning for ten- or twelve-year-olds. It would make a stirring class performance for an assembly, with solo voices and groups speaking or singing the narrative and the songs.

Children in the middle grades often like Longfellow's moving "The Wreck of the Hesperus." Also tragic, and of high poetic beauty, is Edna St. Vincent Millay's "The Ballad of the Harp-Weaver." This the twelves and fourteens should not miss. It is a fantasy, eerie and wistful, built around a mother's love and sacrifice for her child. A poem as full of pity and tenderness as this lovely ballad will help to balance the stark and often brutal tragedies to which children are exposed through our newspapers and magazines.

Scott's "Young Lochinvar," a gay, swashbuckling romance with a galloping tempo, is particularly enjoyed by older children; "The Highwayman" by Alfred Noyes is their favorite romance. Robert Southey's "The Inchcape Rock" tells a good pirate story, but unlike "Dowdee," it is a grim one. "Johnny Appleseed" by Stephen Vincent Benét and Rosemary Carr Benét is a simple and charming narrative. William Cowper's "John Gilpin" is only one of many humorous ballads they enjoy. May Sarton has written with sensitivity and grace "The Ballad of Ruby," based on an episode described in Robert Coles' *Children of Crisis*. It tells of a small black child's experience of discrimination when she goes to school. In a lighter vein, "The Ballad of Johnny" is the story of a child whose name tag was eaten by a goat while he was visiting the zoo. And let's not forget that gem of Americana, Ernest L. Thayer's "Casey at the Bat."

For the eleven- to fourteen-year-olds there are many story poems about great events in American history. Certainly they should know "The Landing of the Pilgrim Fathers" by Felicia Dorothea Hemans, with its unforgettable picture of that desolate arrival and its significance in our history. Children should also thrill to the galloping hoofbeats of Longfellow's "Paul Revere's Ride" before they meet the more complex and workaday Revere of the biographies. The gallantry of old "Barbara Frietchie" defying Stonewall Jackson is good, too, provided the children have a biography of Jackson and learn to appreciate him for the rare human being he was. Texas children should not be the only ones to tingle with pride over "The Defense of the Alamo" as Joaquin Miller relates it. Arthur Guiterman has written a number of fine historical ballads, but especially recommended are his "Daniel Boone" and "The Oregon Trail." These are significant, both as poems and as history. In *Independent Voices*, Eve Merriam has written poems that tell, in a variety of rhyming verse patterns and with a vivid sense of the dramatic, the stories of Benjamin Franklin, Elizabeth Blackwell, Frederick Douglass, Henry Thoreau, Lucretia Mott, Ida B. Wells, and Fiorello La Guardia. In Rosemary and Stephen Benét's (see p. 368) *A Book of Americans*, there are many poems you will wish to use with history, but the pair, "Nancy Hanks" and "Abraham Lincoln," are the great favorites. The plaintive, wistful ghost of Nancy asking if anyone knows her son, "did he have fun, did he get on," is poignantly moving, while the concluding lines of the Lincoln poem remain in your mind to be thought about over and over:

*Lincoln was the green pine.*
*Lincoln kept on growing.*[11]

11. "Abraham Lincoln." From *A Book of Americans* by Rosemary Carr and Stephen Vincent Benét. Copyright 1933 by the authors. Used by permission.

These poems are typical of the fine narrative verse about people and events in United States history. Such poems can be introduced casually as the history chronology unfolds, or the children may become interested in the theme of heroism and start searching for hero poems of their own. Such a search will include other countries, of course. They will discover Browning's "Incident of the French Camp," brief, sharp tragedy, full of youthful gallantry, or they may find Henry Newbolt's "Drake's Drum" with its eerie, haunting verse:

*"Take my drum to England, hand et by the shore,*
*Strike et when your powder's runnin' low;*
*If the Dons sight Devon, I'll quit the port o' Heaven,*
*An' drum them up the Channel as we drummed them long ago."*

They should also discover Robert Nathan's "Dunkirk," a story poem about two children who steered their little boat, along with sailors of other small craft, to bring the trapped soldiers home from that tragic beach. The return voyage with fourteen men finds the boy recalling the great English heroes of the sea.

Why do people fear that we will overromanticize history? The vision, the fortitude, and the selflessness of human beings can never be sufficiently celebrated. These put heart in youngsters, build their ideals, and help mold the temper of their minds and spirits. There cannot be too many such poems.

## LYRIC POETRY

Ask any teacher or parent who reads aloud to children what kind of poems they like and the answer will be, "Funny ones." The made-up words in so many of the nonsense poems and the amusing characters and situations in the humorous narratives always delight children. A mouse running up a clock or somebody going to sea in a sieve and coming safely home are surprises that tickle the funny bone. The rhythm and melody of verse are also primary sources of satisfaction to children just as are the rhythm and melody of music. But it is a long way from the tumpity-tump skips and gallops of early childhood to Bach and Beethoven and it is just as far from *Mother Goose* and Edward Lear to Walter de la Mare and Robert Frost. How can we help children grow up in poetry as successfully as music teachers help them grow up in music? Like the music teachers, we should start where the children are.

For instance, children begin as young as two years old to play with words and respond to their sounds. "Pickle-lillie, pickle-lillie," chants one child, savoring the ear-tickling *l*'s with evident enjoyment. "Upsey-daisy," sings another with broad smiles. Such responses to the humor of sounds are fairly common. But when a four-year-old repeated over and over in a soft, sad little voice, "Far, far away, far, far away!" everyone was surprised because none of the nursery-school stories or poems had included such a phrase or such a mood. Although he was ordinarily a rambunctious little boy, he spoke the words wistfully. He never added to the phrase, but throughout the day he would murmur, always in the same sad tone, "Far, far away!"[12] So other children are caught by the charm of other words and phrases, and without knowing why, they respond to the mood evoked by the words. In some such accidental way, children's taste for lyric poetry may begin. It is the responsibility of parents and teachers to provide poetry experiences for children that will help them grow up happily with poetry.

A group of seven-year-olds who had enjoyed Milne's poetry and other humorous verse heard for the first time some poems by Walter de la Mare, among them "The Horseman." It was read to them twice with no comment.

12. Marie L. Allen, *A Pocketful of Rhymes*.

*I heard a horseman*
*Ride over the hill;*
*The moon shone clear,*
*The night was still;*
*His helm was silver,*
*And pale was he;*
*And the horse he rode*
*Was of ivory.*[13]

After the second reading a boy spoke slowly, "That makes me think of knights . . . it has a sort of nice sound." When these children had an opportunity to receive a copy of the poems they had enjoyed the most and wished to hear again, "The Horseman" was one of their most frequent choices. Why? Its meaning is open to debate, but its mood of quiet and mystery somehow reaches young children, partly because of the associative qualities of such words as *horseman, still, helm,* and *ivory* but mostly because of the poem's gently melodic sound.

These examples are not intended to suggest that lyric poetry is characteristically obscure or that its sound is more important than its meaning. But they do imply that authentic poetry not only conveys meaning but generally evokes an emotional response. Children who have the good fortune to hear a poem that gives them a shiver up their backbones or a swift upsurging flood of elation or a sense of quiet and peace are discovering some of the joys of poetry.

Meaning is also important. After the early years of exploring poetry, children can and should profit from a close study of some poems for their ideas, secondary meanings, and possible implications. The study of poetic form can probably wait for high school and college. Just when this more intellectual approach to poetry should begin depends upon the child or group of children, their poetry experiences, and general background. But certainly, even within the elementary school years, they should grow in poetry appreciation both aesthetically and intellectually.

13. "The Horseman" by Walter de la Mare from *Peacock Pie*. Reprinted by permission of The Literary Trustees of Walter de la Mare, and The Society of Authors as their representative.

## VIEWPOINTS

The lyric has to be condensed and intense and its technical achievement must be sophisticated and impeccable. As a result the level of workmanship is very high. This is a fine ideal, yet the final test of lyric poetry is that it should get off the ground, and should not be so cumbered with craft that it can't use its wings. We miss the rhythms of pure song in most contemporary verse. Yeats and Walter de la Mare were perhaps the last in that tradition. . . . —Elizabeth Drew, *Poetry*, W. W. Norton, and Co., New York, 1959, pp. 48–49.

Meanwhile, the adult's responsibility is to find for the child at each age level those rich treasures of authentic poetry that suit his emotional range, cultivate his ear for the more subtle music of verse, and give him fresh ideas that are the essence of an experience.

Fortunately, the stream of English lyric poetry flows brighter than that of almost any other country. From this great body of verse, the child will appropriate certain poems that suit him, and when he has spoken them repeatedly until he knows them, they become truly his. He will ask about them, too, and through discussions meaning will be enriched. If most children still prefer the lightest of light verse, just remember that most adults do, too. But a child's acceptance of one lovely lyric poem means he is on his way to greater appreciation of authentic poetry.

William Shakespeare is one of those poets who, although writing for adults, have songs that children enjoy. Children hearing the songs of Shakespeare without being forced to analyze or memorize them soon know the poems by heart, and the words sing in their heads like a popular tune. "Under the greenwood tree," from *As You Like It*, seems to belong with Robin Hood:

*Under the greenwood tree*
*Who loves to lie with me,*
*And tune his merry note*
*Unto the sweet bird's throat,*
*Come hither, come hither, come hither:*
*Here shall he see*
*No enemy*
*But winter and rough weather.*

*Who doth ambition shun,*
*And loves to live i' the sun,*
*Seeking the food he eats*
*And pleased with what he gets,*
*Come hither, come hither, come hither:*
*Here shall he see*
*No enemy*
*But winter and rough weather.*

"Jog on, jog on," from *The Winter's Tale*, is a good march for any excursion of children, and Ariel's song, "Where the bee sucks," from *The Tempest*, is a pleasant fairy poem. "Who is Sylvia?" from *The Two Gentlemen of Verona;* "When icicles hang by the wall," *Love's Labour's Lost;* and "Hark, hark! the lark," *Cymbeline*—these poems have a singing quality and a simplicity of content that bring them within the enjoyment range of our older children, especially if they hear the poems before they read them.

William Blake's (see p. 325) *Songs of Innocence* is a landmark in English literature as well as in children's literature. The average child may not particularly enjoy some of the more difficult poems, but he will enjoy many of them if he hears them read aloud by someone who likes their melodies. For Blake's poems are songs, full of cadences and lovely sounds.

Christina Rossetti provides the young child with an ideal introduction to lyric poetry in the verses of *Sing Song*, published in 1872. Many of the verses have homely, familiar subjects, but they are written with lyric grace and with a subtle simplicity in the choice of words. What gentleness there is in "The Caterpillar":

*Brown and furry*
*Caterpillar in a hurry*
*Take your walk*
*To the shady leaf or stalk*
*Or what not,*
*Which may be the chosen spot.*
*No toad spy you,*
*Hovering birds of prey pass by you;*
*Spin and die,*
*To live again a butterfly.*

*Illustration by Arthur Hughes for Sing Song by Christina Rossetti (1872 edition).*

## POETRY OF NATURE

Most of the poets mentioned in the following pages are dissimilar in most respects, but they have one characteristic in common: they observe nature with precision and record its beauty with sensitive interpretation and an imaginative turn that kindles a responsive spark in the reader.

The poems of Sara Teasdale (see p. 358) are largely descriptive and often too subtle for the child under ten, but their lyric beauty and poignance captivate some children. Elizabeth Coatsworth's (see p. 361) poems are less musical but rich with imagery, less complex but lucid and gay with a quick appeal, as in "May Morning":[14]

*A joy of apple blossoms,*
*A flowering of cows,*
*The fern uncurling in the green,*
*The shine where water sings—*
*Something has found a burrow,*
*Each song bird has her nest,*

*Now! Now! The crow in the bright sun*
*Has white and glassy wings!*

Hilda Conkling's (see p. 373) largely unrhymed, sensitively perceptive verses were written when she was a child, and they are an enduring demonstration of the extent to which a ten-year-old can appreciate beauty, although few children her age have the command of language that produces a poem like "Water."[15]

*The world turns softly*
*Not to spill its lakes and rivers.*
*The water is held in its arms*
*And the sky is held in the water.*
*What is water,*
*That pours silver,*
*And can hold the sky?*

Aileen Fisher (see p. 371), many of whose longer poems have been published singly in picture-book form, has been a prolific writer of verses for children. Her writing is pleasant and patterned, and all of her nature poetry reflects both her awareness of the child's interests, and her own deep love of the outdoors and of small, wild creatures.

The Danish explorer Knud Rasmussen brought back from his fifth expedition to the Arctic a large collection of Eskimo poetry. A selection from these has been made into a rarely beautiful book for children, *Beyond the High Hills*, illustrated with breath-taking color photographs by a missionary priest, Father Guy Mary-Rousselière. The result is sheer beauty pictorially and verbally, with a dramatic re-creation of Eskimo thoughts, feelings, and way of life.

Like Hilda Conkling's verses these are in free form but they have greater strength and maturity. The bitter contrast between the two seasons is evident in this—

*There is joy in*
*Feeling the warmth*
*Come to the great world*
*And seeing the sun*
*Follow its old footprints*
*In the summer night.*

*There is fear in*
*Feeling the cold*
*Come to the great world*
*And seeing the moon*
*—Now new moon, now full moon—*
*Follow its old footprints*
*In the winter night.*[16]

Some of the poems sing the joys of the hunt and of food after famine, some are warmly personal—a first kill, the mood of approaching womanhood. This is a rune of hospitality:

*The lands around my dwelling*
*Are more beautiful*
*From the day*
*When it is given me to see*
*Faces I have never seen before.*
*All is more beautiful,*
*All is more beautiful,*
*And life is Thankfulness.*
*These guests of mine*
*Make my house grand.*

To quote briefly from this book gives no conception of its sweep. Here are the joys, terror, and casual everyday heroism of a people who have maintained life under almost unendurable hardships. To read these poems with the loneliness and beauty of the photographs is a moving experience. They will give children more of Eskimo life and thought than many factual books. *The Wind Has Wings*, a varied and handsomely illustrated collection of Canadian poetry compiled by Mary Downie and Barbara Robertson, includes Eskimo and French songs.

14. "May Morning." Reprinted from *The Sparrow Bush* by Elizabeth Coatsworth. Copyright © 1966 by W. W. Norton & Company, Inc. A Norton Book published by Grosset & Dunlap, Inc. Reprinted by permission of Grosset & Dunlap, Inc. and Mark Paterson for Elizabeth Coatsworth.

15. "Water" from *Summer-Day Song*, by Hilda Conkling. Copyright 1920 and renewed 1948 by author. Reprinted by permission of Random House, Inc.

16. "There is joy" and The lands around my dwelling." Reprinted by permission of The World Publishing Company from *Beyond the High Hills: A Book of Eskimo Poems* edited by Knud Rasmussen. Copyright © 1961 by The World Publishing Company.

Mary Austin's *The Children Sing in the Far West*, published in 1928, is an older collection of children's poems about our great Southwest. Yet the Indian lore, flora, fauna, desert, and mountains are as important to the children of that region as the landscape and creatures of New England are to the children there. "Grizzly Bear" is a joke children of any age enjoy. "Texas Trains and Trails," "A Song of Western Men," and "A Feller I Know" are satisfying Westerns. "Seven Rhyming Riddles" are delightful, but Mary Austin's finest poems are her interpretations of Indian feeling and philosophy. Perhaps the children will prefer her at her second best, in the rollicking "Texas Trains and Trails" style, but teachers should slip in some of her best and most characteristic poems now and then—"Charms," "Prayers," and "A Song of Greatness," for example—and at least a few of the children will respond.

*A Song of Greatness*[17]

*When I hear the old men*
*Telling of heroes,*
*Telling of great deeds*
*Of ancient days,*
*When I hear that telling*
*Then I think within me*
*I too am one of these.*

*When I hear the people*
*Praising great ones,*
*Then I know that I too*
*Shall be esteemed,*
*I too when my time comes*
*Shall do mightily.*

Mary Austin's own mysticism and her sympathetic understanding of the Indian's religion make "Morning Prayer" and "Evening Prayer" particularly fine.

The old Indian wisdom of killing only for food, never for the mere sport of killing, is expressed in

*For Going A-Hunting*[18]

*O my brothers of the wilderness,*
*My little brothers,*
*For my necessities*
*I am about to kill you!*
*May the Master of Life who made you*
*In the form of the quarry*
*That the children may be fed,*
*Speedily provide you*
*Another house;*
*So there may be peace*
*Between me and thy spirit.*

These poems give young readers a new understanding of and respect for our American Indians. At her best, Mary Austin transcends local color and writes with universal significance.

*The Trees Stand Shining*, a selection of poetry of the North American Indians, has been compiled by Hettie Jones. The poems are, in fact, untitled songs, fragmentary and brief, often with the terse quality of haiku, that show the affinity the Indian feels for the beauty and strength of nature. Man's close relationship to nature is also depicted in John Bierhorst's anthology *In the Trail of the Wind: American Indian Poems and Ritual Orations*. This volume includes poems of the Maya, the Aztec, and the Eskimo as well as those of North American Indian tribes. William Brandon's collection, *The Magic World: American Indian Songs and Poems* is unusual for its inclusion of a large number of Nahuatl ceremonial songs.

In *A Few Flies and I*, some of the poems of the great Japanese poet Issa have been brought together by Jean Merrill and Ronni Solbert. Richard Lewis, in *Of This World*, also chose some of the Issa poems that show an infinite tenderness toward the small creatures of the world. Rebecca Caudill's *Come Along!* has simple haiku poems that celebrate the cycle of the year.

17. "A Song of Greatness" from *The Children Sing in the Far West*. Copyright renewed 1956 by Kenneth M. Chapman and Mary C. Wheelwright. Reprinted by permission of the publisher, Houghton Mifflin Company.

18. "For Going A-Hunting." From *The Children Sing in the Far West* by Mary Austin. Used by permission of the publishers, Houghton Mifflin Company.

Of all the books that share this affection for animals, French Carmen Bernos de Gasztold's *Prayers from the Ark* and *The Creatures' Choir*, translated by Rumer Godden, are the most beguiling, each poem a percipient picture of the animal that speaks.

*The Hedgehog*[19]

*Yes, Lord, I prick!*
*Life is not easy—*
*but You know that—*
*and I have too much on my shoulders!*
*I speak of my prickles*
*but thank You for them.*
*You at least*
*have understood me,*
*that is why You made me*
*such a pinball.*
*How else can I defend myself?*
*When people see me,*
*my anxious nose*
*searching for the fat slugs*
*that devastate the garden,*
*why can't they leave me alone?*
*Ah! But when I think proper,*
*I can roll myself up*
*into my hermit life.*

*Amen*

*Illustration by Jean Primrose. From* The Creatures' *Choir by Carmen Bernos de Gasztold, translated by Rumer Godden, decorations by Jean Primrose. Copyright © 1965 by Rumer Godden. Illustrations reprinted by permission of The Viking Press, Inc.*

Two other books about wild creatures are *Cats and Bats and Things with Wings* by Conrad Aiken and *Brownjohn's Beasts* by the British poet Alan Brownjohn, whose animals, like those of Carmen Bernos de Gasztold, speak for themselves—and with great wit. Some of these poets are included in William Cole's excellent anthology, *A Book of Nature Poems*, but both this book and *The Wind Is Round*, a similar anthology edited by Sara Hannum and John Terry Chase, concentrate on poetry written for adults.

19. From *The Creatures' Choir* (British Title: *The Beasts' Choir*), by Carmen Bernos de Gasztold, translated by Rumer Godden. Copyright © 1965 by Rumer Godden. Reprinted by permission of The Viking Press, Inc., and Macmillan London and Basingstoke.

20. "The Fairies." From *Robin Redbreast* by William Allingham. Published by The Macmillan Company.

## POETRY OF FAIRYLAND

The name of William Allingham immediately brings to mind one poem, "The Fairies." *Robin Redbreast*, the collection of Allingham's poems, is out of print, but many anthologies contain "The Fairies," a fine lyric poem that children enjoy. They like it because it has a singing quality and because it contains vital statistics about the little people. The first verse is most familiar:

*The Fairies*[20]

*Up the airy mountain,*
*Down the rushy glen,*
*We daren't go a-hunting*
*For fear of little men;*
*Wee folk, good folk,*

*Trooping all together;*
*Green jacket, red cap,*
*And white owl's feather!*

Many poets have written an occasional poem about fairies, but unlike Rose Fyleman and Walter de la Mare, very few have written a number of poems about these creatures. Rose Fyleman has a trick of combining fairies with the child's everyday, modern world in a way that is very convincing. Of her poems about fairyland in *Fairies and Chimneys*, a favorite is "Oxford Street," in which a fairy hops on a bus and seems to enjoy peering at shop windows. In Walter de la Mare's *Rhymes and Verses*, there are many fairy poems with a great range of mood and style. Too many of them make a too highly spiced diet for children, but the simpler ones are among the best poems of fairy lore that we have for children.

## WORLD POETRY

*There Are Two Lives*, edited by Richard Lewis, is one of the many new books that are bringing poetry of other lands to English-speaking children. Producing such books is a phenomenon not wholly new but noticeably burgeoning. Lewis chose Japanese and Chinese poetry for *Moment of Wonder* and selected haiku for younger readers in *In a Spring Garden*. He selected poems of the haiku poet Issa in *Of This World* and edited the work of another great haiku poet in *The Way of Silence: The Prose and Poetry of Basho*.

Also Japanese are Charlotte De Forest's adaptation of Japanese nursery rhymes in *The Prancing Pony;* Virginia Baron's *The Seasons of Time*, a selection of ancient tanka poetry; and Harry Behn's two collections of haiku poetry, *Cricket Songs* and *More Cricket Songs*. In a discussion of children and poetry, Behn explains haiku thus:

*A haiku is a poem in three lines of five, then seven, then five syllables. It is made by speaking of something natural and simple suggesting spring, summer, autumn, or winter. There is no rhyme. Everything mentioned is just what it is, wonderful, here, but still beyond.*

*What a thing to see!*
*miles and miles of mountains, white*
*with cherries in bloom . . .*

*Sometimes we all make such poems and hardly think about it. The best are as natural as breathing.*[21]

*Illustration by Keiko Hida from* The Prancing Pony; Nursery Rhymes from Japan, *adapted by Charlotte De Forest. Copyright © 1968 by Walker Publishing Company, Inc. Reprinted by permission of the Publisher. (Original in color)*

Another book of nursery rhymes in translation is Robert Hyndman's *Chinese Mother Goose Rhymes*, with some verses that will remind children of the ones with which they are familiar, such as a counting rhyme very much like our "This little pig went to market." Barbara Cooney has created charming illustrations for *Mother Goose in French* and *Mother Goose in Spanish* that can be enjoyed by children learning those languages.

In William Jay Smith's *Poems from*

21. From *Cricket Songs: Japanese Haiku*, translated and © 1964 by Harry Behn. Reprinted by permission of Harcourt Brace Jovanovich, Inc. and Curtis Brown, Ltd.

*France* and Kenneth Canfield's *Selections from French Poetry*, each poem in French has the English translation on the facing page. Undoubtedly the French poetry best known to English-speaking children is that of Carmen Bernos de Gasztold, whose *Prayers from the Ark* and *The Creatures' Choir* were mentioned on page 317.

In Jean Longland's *Selections from Contemporary Portuguese Poetry*, Seymour Resnick's *Spanish-American Poetry* and *Selections from Spanish Poetry*, and Richard Lewis' *Still Waters of the Air: Poems by Three Modern Spanish Poets*, again the English translation is printed on the page facing the original. These are all intended for older readers.

Also bilingual are the poems in Mario Benedetti's *Unstill Life*, an introduction to the Spanish-American poetry of Latin America; and the poems in Angelo de Luca and William Giuliano's *Selections from Italian Poetry*.

Vladimir Rus' *Selections from German Poetry* and Helen Plotz' *Poems from the German*, both of which provide the poems in the original and in English translation, are for older children. For younger readers there are several editions of Heinrich Hoffmann's *Slovenly Peter*, now a children's classic, one version of which was translated by Mark Twain. Max Knight's translation of Christian Morgenstern's *The Three Sparrows* makes available the fanciful nursery rhymes popular with German children.

The first section of Miriam Morton's anthology *A Harvest of Russian Children's Literature* has verses for young children, and there are a few other poems in the book, notably a long narrative poem, "The Little Humpbacked Horse," a fairy tale in verse that is also popular in Russia in dramatized form. Ivan Krylov's *The Fifteen Fables of Krylov* has a dry wit.

From India there is the poetry in Gwendolyn Reed's *The Talkative Beasts: Myths, Fables and Poems of India*, and in Rabindranath Tagore's slim volume *Moon, For What Do You Wait?* In *We, the Vietnamese: Voices from Vietnam*, edited by François Sully, there is a representative section of poetry from a portion of "Kim Van Kieu," Vietnam's best-known epic poem, to folk songs of protest and the poetry of today's underground.

The indefatigable Richard Lewis has selected some of the poetry of ancient Greece for *Muse of the Round Sky* and has chosen poems and songs of primitive peoples of the world for *Out of the Earth I Sing*, most of the selections being from African and North American Indian tribes. *A Crocodile Has Me by the Leg*, compiled by Leonard Doob, has African poems that clearly stem from the oral tradition and have folk wisdom and humor.

For *The Singing and the Gold*, an excellent anthology of world literature compiled by Elinor Parker, many poets contributed to the translations of poetry from thirty-four different languages. It is probable that this trend toward international diffusion of an art that is, of all types of literature, the one most elemental, perceptive, and universal will increase as our children grow toward a world less partitioned by boundaries than the world of the past.

## CHILDREN AS POETS

There have always been children who wrote poetry, and there have been some—like Hilda Conkling and Aliki Barnstone—whose writing has been published and extolled. Never before today, however, has there been such a poetic ferment, so much encouragement by adults working with children in small groups and in classrooms, so many young people forming their own groups to read, write, and discuss poetry.

One of the most sympathetic and informed explorations of this activity is in *Somebody Turned on a Tap in These Kids*, edited by Nancy Larrick and containing articles by such poets as June Jordan, Myra Cohn Livingston, and Eve Merriam, and by others who work with children. In *Poetry Is*, Ted Hughes, a British poet, addresses his remarks about technique, acuity of observation and expression, and imagery, to young people. In *Let Them Be Themselves*, author Lee Bennett Hopkins discusses poetry as one of the ways in which the language arts program may be enriched for disadvantaged children. The spontaneity of even very young children is evident in the dictated poem of a child of five.

*Joe's Story*[22]

*My brother doesn't like me in the morning.*
*But he likes me in the afternoon.*
*He likes me today.*
*After school I nap.*
*Then I fight with my little sister.*
*She's only 4. I'm only 5.*
*When she kicks me she runs away.*
*I catch her. I jump on her.*
*Then my mother comes. I go to Stephen's house.*
*I'm kind of scared when fire engines come at night.*
*I dream about them.*
*It's really scared.*
*The fire and the fire engine.*
*At morning I'm not scared . . .*

Not every child is capable of writing poetry, and it is true that some of the work being done with children is directed as much toward therapeutic as esthetic goals, but the amount of fine poetry that has been published is a testament to the emotional and imaginative capacity of the young. The work of one outstanding young black writer, Vanessa Howard, has been included in several anthologies of poetry by children. The two following poems are examples of the inward vision and of the poetry of protest.

*Truly My Own*[23]

*I think if I searched a thousand lands*
*and twice the number in rainbows,*
*I'd never find one human being*
*who chose the things I chose*
*a person who wanted the things I wanted*
*or sought what I sought to be*

*I'd never find one human being*
*like or comparison to me*
*and if I traveled seven seas*
*I would still be alone*
*for there is no one who thinks like me*
*for my dreams are truly my own.*

And, untitled:

*I am frightened that*
*the flame of hate*
*will burn me*
*will scorch my pride*
*scar my heart*
*it will burn and i*
*cannot put it out.*
*i cannot call the fire department*
*and they cannot put out the flame within my soul*
*i am frightened that the flame*
*of hate will burn me*
*if it does*
*I will die*

*The Voice of the Children*, compiled by June Jordan and Terri Bush, comprises some of the best of the poetry written in a creative writing workshop; Virginia Baron's anthology *Here I Am!* contains poems written by young people from diverse minority groups. "Inevitable poets," Arnold Adoff calls the young people whose poems poured in from all parts of the country to be selected for *it is the poem singing into your eyes.* Kenneth Koch's *Wishes, Lies, and Dreams* contains both the author's description of his work with children in a New York City school and their poetry.

*I Heard a Scream in the Streets*, edited by Nancy Larrick, is a collection of poems written by young people in the city. Her

22. "Joe's Story" from *Teaching the Unteachable* by Herbert R. Kohl. Reprinted with permission from *The New York Review of Books*. Copyright © 1967 Herbert Kohl.

23. "Truly My Own" and "I am frightened that" by Vanessa Howard from *The Voice of the Children* collected by June Jordan and Terri Bush. Copyright © 1968 by The Voice of the Children, Inc. Reprinted by permission of Holt, Rinehart and Winston, Inc. and Julian Bach Literary Agency, Inc.

*Illustration by Emily Arnold McCully from the book* Here I Am! *edited by Virginia Olsen Baron. Illustrations copyright © 1969 by Emily Arnold McCully. Published by E. P. Dutton & Co., Inc. and used with their permission.*

other anthology of children's poetry, *Green Is Like a Meadow of Grass*, shows the results of children's observation of nature, encouraged by teachers who had participated in a poetry workshop.

Richard Lewis has gathered children's poetry in several fine anthologies: *Miracles*, a collection of poetry by children of the English-speaking world; *The Wind and the Rain*, nature poems; and *There Are Two Lives*, poems by Japanese children, a collection in which restraint in the use of language is the most marked difference between these poems and those of American children.

## POETRY FOR NOW

In the explosive increase of children's interest in reading and writing poetry, there are several striking trends. One is the subject matter with which the young are concerned: they are writing poems about anything and everything they see around them, and although they are still aware of natural beauty and intrigued by the intricacies and mystery of themselves and other people, some of their poetry seethes with anger, sees beauty as well as despair in the urban scene, and faces with candor the afflictions of the world they inherit. In form, too, there is a new freedom: most of the poetry they write and much of the poetry they read is free verse, some of it in shaped patterns, like that of May Swenson's "Redundant Journey," in which the

### VIEWPOINTS

The search for what is real has led many a poet and his readers to topics once thought of as unpoetic: traffic lights, for example, and escalators, subways and littered sidewalks. On crowded streets and in cluttered hallways man's inhumanity to man shows up dramatically. Adults who have equated poetry with "a host of golden daffodils" may find it difficult to accept this harsh reality for children. Yet this is the children's world, too. . . .

It should not surprise us, then, to find that today's children seek the realistic poetry of bolder voices, speaking in a blunt conversational style. They like poems which debunk the phony and unveil hypocrisy. I think this is one of the reasons why they are held by Eve Merriam's *The Inner City Mother Goose*, which is a biting commentary on the injustices of the American ghetto.

"This is real," explained one fourteen-year-old. "The trouble with poetry at school is it's all covered over with the beautiful."—Nancy Larrick, "Poetry That's Real," *Somebody Turned on a Tap in These Kids*, edited by Nancy Larrick, Delacorte Press, New York, 1971, pp. 4–5.

print forms a sinuous pattern on the page, or it is the concrete poetry that moves from the oral tradition to appeal to the eye. Free verse, of course, is not new, but it has never been so enthusiastically employed. Some years ago, Carl Sandburg, in "A Short Talk on Poetry," said, "We have heard much in our time about free verse being modern. . . . Now, if free verse is a form of writing poetry without rhyme, without regular meters, without established and formal rules governing it, we can easily go back to the earliest style of poetry known to the human family—and the style is strictly free verse."[24]

Young people are reading avidly the contemporary voices of protest, white and black. There is a marked increase in the numbers of black poets being heard and being represented in anthologies of modern poetry chosen especially for young readers. And—no surprise in a world in which communication has brought peoples closer to each other—there is a growing amount of poetry from other cultures now available in English.

There is no age limit for poetry that is distinguishably, and often distinctively, contemporary. Some of the urban poetry written for very young children is concerned with subjects and problems that were never mentioned in children's literature before, an acknowledgment of the sophistication of the young. "The City Question" in Robert Froman's *Street Poems* poses the problem of the man lying on the sidewalk. Wino? Junkie? Or ill? Is he dangerous, or should one try to help? Another poem is called "Hail, Polluters." Froman plays with shapes in this intriguing book that manipulates print to accentuate the message of the words; the names of objects in a garbage heap are, for example, actually piled helter-skelter; and in a poem about a dandelion, the print forms a stem and a flower head. Ian Hamilton Finlay's *Poems to Hear and See* are experiments in form by a poet who is a participant in the Concrete Poetry movement, which intends the word to stand for itself as does an ideogram.

In *Mazes*, by Muriel Rukeyser, a picture-book format and color photographs are the setting for a poem about a child who explores his surroundings, a lovely lyric but complex enough to make demands on the reader.

May Swenson, in *Poems to Solve* and *More Poems to Solve* makes demands on the reader quite deliberately. She says in the preface of *More Poems to Solve:*

*A Poem Is a Thing*[25]

*A poem is a thing that can intensify the current of consciousness, make you see, hear, feel keenly—like an electrode to the brain. This power is not generated by the ideas so much as by the language in the poem. The poet works (and plays) with the elements of language, forming and transforming his material, to the point where a new perception emerges: something simple or ordinary may be seen as wonderful, something complex or opaque becomes suddenly clear.*

*A poet hopes that the output of the poem for the reader will equal the dynamic input—the initial "brain-touch"—that made him start the poem. But all expectations for its future, or any assessment of aims, occur only after the poem is done. It is a thing in itself, and it lets the writer know when it's done—*what *it has done—sometimes* why *it was done. Making it, the poet doesn't know, any more than you do until you read the last line, what it intends to show him. The making is a groping, a solving, a process something like trying to trap a flash of light into form.*

May Swenson's poetry has enormous vitality and impact, and is filled with striking images, with patterns in print that she calls Shape Poems, and with the Riddle Poems that require the reader to make his own contribution toward interpretation. (See p. 380.)

June Jordan's *Who Look at Me* is a long poem that moves, as in a gallery, from one portrait to another of black people. The

24. Carl Sandburg, *The Sandburg Treasury* (Harcourt Brace Jovanovich, 1970), p. 169.

25. Reprinted by permission of Charles Scribner's Sons from *More Poems to Solve* by May Swenson. Copyright © 1971 May Swenson.

paintings are by distinguished artists, the poem a passionate statement of the dignity, the pain, the anger, and the pride of the black people.

*Who see the block we face*
*the thousand miles of alabaster space*
*inscribed keep off keep out don't touch*
*and Wait Some More for Half as Much?*[26]

Robert Hayden, himself a poet, has compiled the work of American black poets in *Kaleidoscope*, an anthology that begins with the poetry of the "Sable Muse" of Colonial times, Phillis Wheatley, and proceeds chronologically, with biographical notes, to contemporary writers. Arnold Adoff, in *I Am the Darker Brother* and *Black Out Loud* confines his selections to the work of modern black poets; such established writers as Langston Hughes, LeRoi Jones, Mari Evans, and Arna Bontemps are included, but there are many poems by writers less well known.

There are a dozen or so very good anthologies of modern poetry for young people, and many of them include poems by older poets who have struck a note consonant with today's themes, or poems that are the lyrics of contemporary ballads and protest songs. David Morse's selections in *Grandfather Rock* have been made to show the kinship between such lyrics and poems from Homer's time on; indeed, Morse, in his preface, refers to such poetry as "the rock and roll of the past."

Among the best of the anthologies of modern poetry are *Lean Out of the Window*, by Sara Hannum and Gwendolyn Reed; *Sounds and Silences: Poetry for Now*, by Richard Peck; and *Reflections on a Gift of Watermelon Pickle*, by Stephen Dunning, Edward Lueders, and Hugh L. Smith. Additional anthologies including other collections by these same compilers will be found in the bibliography on pages 383–385.

26. From *Who Look at Me* by June Jordan. Copyright © 1969 by June Jordan. With permission of Thomas Y. Crowell Company, Inc., Publishers.

Young poetry lovers do read the poetry of the past, but for most of them the modern poets have a greater appeal, speaking as they do to the issues, and in the language of the present. There has been no lessening of admiration for the poems of Emily Dickinson, Robert Frost, Edna St. Vincent Millay, and W. H. Auden, but there are other poets whose names (in addition to those already mentioned in this chapter) crop up in almost every anthology index: Babette Deutsch, James Dickey, Galway Kinnell, Denise Levertov, Edward Lueders, Rod McKuen, Howard Nemerov, Pauli Murray. Indeed, almost every contemporary poet is represented and has his or her faction of admirers.

One fact that emerges from a survey of poetry for children is that poets can no more be pigeonholed than light can be captured and boxed. Another fact is that a poem, more than any other kind of literature, has no boundaries and that a suggestion for a reading level is only that—an indication that for many children the poem will probably be most appreciated at a certain age. For children often have a far greater comprehension in listening to a poem than in reading it for themselves, and the poem that awakens a response will produce a greater investment of attention and understanding on the part of the reader or listener than the poem that he can accept placidly.

Not every poem is for every child, and some of the poetry he likes needs his intellectual as well as his emotional participation.[27] As Agnes Repplier says, in her introduction to a poetry anthology:

*In the matter of poetry, a child's imagination outstrips his understanding; his emotions carry him far beyond the narrow reach of his intelligence. He has but one lesson to learn,—the lesson of enjoyment.*[28]

27. For the combined poetry bibliography see pp. 382–389.

28. From *An Anthology of Modern Verse*, ed. by A. Methuen (Methuen, 1921), p. xiii.

# Chapter 11
# Poets and Children's Poetry

In contemplating the poetry that children enjoy, it is clear that the range is as varied as the children themselves. In tracing the development of a body of poetry, it is even more clear that there are no boundaries. Some of the poets who are favorites did not write for children at all; some—like Theodore Roethke and Randall Jarrell—wrote occasionally for them; and others wrote only for them. Those contemporary poets who write in protest or who experiment with form are read as avidly as are the more conventional poets, old and new. "The poet writes for his own sake," said Randall Jarrell, "for the sake of that order in which the poem takes the place that has awaited it."[1]

In briefly examining the work of some of the major contributors to children's poetry, it is possible to see both the diversity and the pattern not only of what children read but of what their society's changing ideas of a child's capabilities and preferences have been.

1. Randall Jarrell, "The Obscurity of the Poet," from *Poetry and the Age*. Faber & Faber, 1955.

## ISAAC WATTS, 1674–1748

*Divine and Moral Songs for Children*

As a young man Isaac Watts was a tutor in the home of a private family, and he was later famous for his textbooks on *Logick* and *Principles of Geography and Astronomy*. Today this nonconformist preacher is best known for his hymns and for certain little moralistic verses for children. Old school readers and anthologies always included such selections as this:

*Against Idleness and Mischief*

*How doth the little busy bee*
*Improve each shining hour*
*And gather honey all the day*
*From every op'ning flow'r.*

*How skilfully she builds her cell;*
*How neat she spreads her wax,*
*And labors hard to store it well*
*With the sweet food she makes.*

*In works of labor or of skill,*
*I would be busy too;*

*For Satan finds some mischief still*
*For idle hands to do.*

*In books, or work, or healthful play,*
*Let my first days be past;*
*That I may give for ev'ry day*
*Some good account at last.*

In his "Introduction to Parents and all who are concerned in the Education of Children," Watts wrote:

> *What is learnt in verse, is longer retained in memory, and sooner recollected.*
>
> *This will be a constant furniture for the minds of children that they may have something to think of when alone; and may repeat to themselves.*

He concluded, then, that since a child learns and recalls rhymes so easily, he might as well learn moral lessons in that form. So he composed his *Divine and Moral Songs for Children*. It was first published in 1715, and so many succeeding editions were published that there is a whole book devoted to its history and the listings of the numerous editions.[2] Read over the Watts hymns to be found in any modern hymnal and see how meaningful most of them still are: "Joy to the world," "Come, Holy Spirit," and "O God, our help in ages past." Little children also like the first verse of his "Cradle Hymn":

*Hush! my dear, lie still and slumber,*
*Holy Angels guard thy bed!*
*Heavenly blessings without number,*
*Gently falling on thy head.*

Such hymns make a center of peace and encouragement for children.

2. Wilbur Macy Stone, *The Divine and Moral Songs of Isaac Watts: An Essay thereon and a tentative List of Editions.* Privately printed for *The Triptych*, 1918.

## WILLIAM BLAKE, 1757–1827

### *Songs of Innocence*

It has always seemed easier to understand William Blake's poems, their beauty and their limitations, if we know something not only of the man himself but of his art, for Blake was primarily an artist. Some of the stories about Blake's life, particularly his childhood, might well be told to the older children as an introduction both to his poems and to his illustrations. For younger children, we omit biographical data and expose them only to those poems they are capable of enjoying.

William Blake was the second of five children. He was ordinarily an amiable, gentle child, but when roused sometimes showed a violent temper. From the time he was four years old he saw visions, and he continued to see them throughout his seventy years. At four, he saw the face of God looking at him through the window. He told his mother he had met and talked with Ezekiel, and she punished him for telling a lie. As a man, he insisted that he talked with his dead brother, with the poet Milton, the Apostle Paul, and other great ones, who, though dead, gave him continual guidance. All his life he told people about his visions as a matter of course, and so he was called "mad Blake" by the skeptical.

Blake was apprenticed at fourteen to a famous engraver, James Basire, who appreciated and understood his strange pupil, but Blake's descriptions of his conversations with the prophets made him the butt of ridicule among the other students, and his temper led to frequent fights. Basire, wishing to rescue this odd and talented boy, sent him off to the cathedrals to make drawings in solitude. After seven years of apprenticeship, Blake studied for a short time at the newly formed Royal Academy, and this completed his art education.

At twenty-five, Blake married Catherine Boucher, the daughter of a market-gardener, an uneducated but lovely young woman both in physical appearance and in character. She had a gentle, affectionate disposition along with great fortitude and unswerving loyalty. Blake taught his wife to read and write, shared with her his visions, and loved her throughout his life.

In the early days of their marriage the young couple seems to have enjoyed a prosperous and happy time. Blake was showing pictures yearly at the exhibitions of the Royal Academy. The rising young artists of the day were his friends. Besides painting his pictures, Blake was writing poems and composing the music to accompany them. Then suddenly Blake turned against the people who were making much of him and withdrew completely from society. The companionship of "the mighty dead" was more important to him than the society of his lighthearted contemporaries. He felt that his friends interfered with his visions; so he turned away from people despite their kindness.

In 1789, *Songs of Innocence* was published. This book was a labor of love on the part of both William and Catherine Blake and was literally a handmade book. Blake wrote the poems and made the decorative designs that accompanied each one, engraving them upon copper plates. He published his own book, with his wife helping him print, add the hand-coloring, and even bind it. Notable as this book seems to us now, imaginative and lovely as were its poems and decorations, it was not appreciated at the time. *Songs of Experience* was published five years later, and between the two collections of *Songs* came many of those poems Blake called his works of prophecy. Their mysticism and their incoherence led people to judge Blake insane. This judgment was reversed even during Blake's lifetime, and today—however people regard his visions and his more confused writings—the best of Blake's poems are ranked among England's finest lyric poetry and a large proportion of his illustrations among the world's greatest engravings.

If Blake's pictures for the Book of Job are available to you, examine them by all means; or study the illustrations reproduced by Darrell Figgis in *The Paintings of William Blake*, and those found in that useful little book by Philippe Soupault, *William Blake*. For purposes of comparison, consider "Oberon and Titania" and "The Procession from Calvary." These are typical engravings but do not, of course, represent his great range of subject matter.

Look first at "Oberon and Titania." The fairy figures have the dancing lightness of those in Botticelli's "Spring" but seem more unearthly because of the way both faces and bodies melt into the landscape. Only the impish Puck is sharply drawn. His smiling face attracts the eye immediately and not only is a center of interest but suggests the mood of the whole picture—light-hearted merrymaking. The four fairies dancing in a ring at the right are dimly drawn—one is only half visible—but their movement and speed are unmistakable. The whirling effect of their dance is heightened by contrast with the static figures of Oberon and Titania at the extreme left. So Blake, using no photographic details, suggests the rushing movement of an elfin dance and a mood of heedless gaiety.

*"Oberon and Titania" by William Blake.*

"The Procession from Calvary" by William Blake.

Look now at "The Procession from Calvary," which makes use of lines and masses to produce an opposite effect—not light gaiety but majestic power. The men in the procession are carrying the body of the dead Christ and they are followed by three sorrowing women. They are moving against a gloomy background: faintly suggested tree trunks and tree tops, buildings, and distant hills, one of which is surmounted by three black crosses. Dark masses and severe vertical lines are repeated over and over with increasing emphasis and growing clarity, from the dim background to the foreground of marching figures. The robes on the figures sweep downward with columnlike strength and solidity except at the head and feet, where they break into curving lines that produce an astonishing illusion of movement. Here, again, Blake has given us not a realistic representation but a powerful interpretation of an idea and a feeling.

Blake uses in his poetry the same interpretative rather than realistic method. In verse his mediums are no longer lines and masses but the sounds and the associative meanings of words and the rhythmic flow of lines. These he uses to create a mood or to convey an idea or feeling—not through a logical reporting of facts, but through words and rhythms that speak to the emotions and the imagination. For example, read aloud the first verse of

*Spring*

*Sound the flute!*
*Now 't is mute;*
*Birds delight,*
*Day and night,*
*Nightingale*
*In the dale,*
*Lark in sky,—*
*Merrily,*
*Merrily, merrily to welcome in the year.*

This opening verse suffices to set the mood of joy for the whole poem. The short, tripping lines and the brief words are like quick dance steps. The clear vowel sounds and the refrain, with its thrice-repeated "merrily," make a melody of every verse. Titania's fairies might dance to this song—the lines move with the same lightness and speed. But should children get every picture in every line, each in turn? Should they be told that larks and nightingales are not American but British birds? Heaven forbid! Four-year-old children like the sound of this poem with its rushing movement. Older children will like it, too, if it is read to them for just what it is: a song that suggests the exuberance of spring.

For contrast in mood, turn to those two companion poems, "The Little Boy Lost" and "The Little Boy Found." Read the former aloud. Doesn't it remind you, in both mood and tempo, of Schubert's famous song "The Erl King"?

*The Little Boy Lost*

*"Father, father, where are you going?*
*Oh, do not walk so fast!*
*Speak, father, speak to your little boy,*
*Or else I shall be lost."*

*The night was dark, no father was there,*
*The child was wet with dew;*
*The mire was deep, and the child did weep,*
*And away the vapour flew.*

Do you feel the terror of a lost child crying out to his father? The poem does not say where the father is or how the child lost him; its rapidly moving eight lines convey only the feelings of anguish and mystery. Notice how the metrical lines suggest the running of the child, just as Blake's graphic lines suggest movement in his pictures. Now turn to the tender reassurance of

*The Little Boy Found*

*The little boy lost in the lonely fen,*
*Led by the wandering light,*
*Began to cry, but God, ever nigh,*
*Appeared like his father, in white.*

*He kissed the child, and by the hand led,*
*And to his mother brought,*
*Who in sorrow pale, through the lonely dale,*
*The little boy weeping sought.*

This poem begins on a minor note, but the hurry and the terror are gone. The words and lines move quietly and gently, telling how God, appearing to the child in the guise of his father, leads him safely into the arms of his mother. Was the father dead? Blake never says, because in these two poems he seems to be concerned not with reporting facts but with conveying powerfully and briefly (with no distracting details) the terror of being lost, the sense of guidance and comfort outside ourselves, and the blessed relief of coming home to love and security. Not circumstance but emotion is important in these poems—one a poem of terror, one a poem of reassurance.

These examples perhaps are sufficient to emphasize that Blake is not striving for realistic effects in his poems any more than he was in his illustrations. So when you read the *Songs* with children, do not bear down heavily on the factual details. Read the poems aloud for their melody and for the feeling-response they invariably arouse. If the children hear them read well enough, they experience a momentary feeling of gaiety or wonder, terror, or peace. Then Blake speaks to them as he wished to speak—in terms of universal feeling. Of course, if the children ask questions or comment on a poem, encourage them to discuss it.

The effortless melody of many of these songs makes them sing in your head with a few readings. That is true of "Piping down the valleys wild," in which Blake describes the feeling that brought him to write these poems. Blake called this poem "Introduction," and so it may serve to introduce children to his *Songs*.

"The Shepherd" and "The Lamb" are in a quiet mood—the latter, with "The Little Boy Lost" and "The Little Boy Found," belongs to the religious literature of early childhood. Pictures of children at play are found in "Nurse's Song" and "The Echoing Green." Isn't that title—"Echoing Green"—a melody in itself? Young children like "Infant Joy,"

*Illustration by Harold Jones for William Blake's "The Echoing Green" from* Songs of Innocence. *Copyright 1961 by A. S. Barnes & Company, Inc. By permission of A. S. Barnes & Company, Inc., and Faber & Faber, Ltd., of London.*

*From William Blake's* Songs of Innocence *(facsimile from British Museum copy, published by Minton, Balch, 1926. Original in color).*

(p. 285), an imaginary dialogue between a two-day-old baby and a grownup who is wondering what to name it. This poem is typical of Blake's unrealistic style, as you can readily discover if you try to imagine how Dorothy Aldis or A. A. Milne would present the same situation. It is not with the question of naming a baby John or Peter that Blake is concerned but with the feeling of joy that a baby arouses. This little dialogue is not easy to read but is worth your best efforts to bring it to a child's understanding.

There are perhaps only nine or ten of Blake's *Songs* that belong in the literature of the elementary school, and not more than four or five of these can be used in the primary grades. But if, through hearing them read aloud, the children like one or two of these songs well enough to ask for them at poetry time, or if they discover that they can say some of them aloud with you, or if they find that one of the songs is running through their heads, then you have accomplished all you could hope for. Their liking for authentic poetry is beginning and may become a permanent source of refreshment.

## ANN TAYLOR, 1782–1866
## JANE TAYLOR, 1783–1824

*Original Poems for Infant Minds*

Ann and Jane Taylor are credited with being the first English authors to write wholly for children. Although in time they were far closer to Blake than to Isaac Watts, they were literary descendants of Watts at his most moralistic. They did not, however, achieve the serene beauty of Watts' best religious poetry. To their credit, they ventured further into the child's world, and they wrote some nature lyrics without moral lessons.

Ann and Jane were the daughters of intellectual parents and enjoyed a happy family life in the lovely English countryside. The sisters wrote so much alike that only the initial which sometimes follows a verse identifies the author.

The titles of the verses indicate their didactic intentions: "The Vulgar Little Lady," "Dirty Jim," "Meddlesome Matty," "Contented John." But the sisters had a gift for storytelling, and many of their narrative poems profit by cleverly sustained suspense. "Ball" is a good example:

*Ball*

*"My good little fellow, don't throw your ball there,*
*You'll break neighbor's windows, I know;*
*On the end of the house there is room, and to spare,*
*Go round, you can have a delightful game there,*
*Without fearing for where you may throw."*

*Harry thought he might safely continue his play*
*With a little more care than before;*
*So, heedless of all that his father could say,*
*As soon as he saw he was out of the way*
*Resolved to have fifty throws more.*

*Already as far as to forty he rose,*
*And no mischief had happened at all;*
*One more, and one more, he successfully throws,*
*But when, as he thought, just arrived at the close,*
*In popped his unfortunate ball.*

*"I'm sure that I thought, and I did not intend,"*
*Poor Harry was going to say;*
*But soon came the glazier the window to mend,*
*And both the bright shillings he wanted to spend*
*He had for his folly to pay.*

*When little folks think they know better than great,*
*And what is forbidden them, do,*
*We must always expect to see, sooner or late,*
*That such wise little fools have a similar fate,*
*And that one in the fifty goes through.*

*A. T.*

Children will listen to these little sermons because of their story interest, but the poems are commonplace. The nature lyrics are sometimes genuinely pleasing when they are not too lengthy or marred by extraneous "lessons." "The Snowdrop" is one of the prettiest; and "Twinkle, twinkle, little star" is the enduring favorite.

## EDWARD LEAR, 1812–1888

*The Book of Nonsense*
*Nonsense Songs and Stories*

In England, about 1820, several small books of limericks appeared, the first of which, *Anecdotes and Adventures of Fifteen Gentlemen*, Edward Lear probably read, because in his introduction to *More Nonsense* he writes:

> *Long years ago, in days when much of my time was passed in a country house where children and mirth abounded, the lines beginning "There was an old man of Tobago" were suggested to me by a valued friend as a form of verse lending itself to limitless variety for rhymes and pictures; and thenceforth the greater part of the original drawings and verses for the first Book of Nonsense were struck off with a pen, no assistance ever having been given me in any way but that of uproarious delight and welcome at the appearance of every new absurdity.*

*There was an Old Man of Tobago,*
*Lived long on rice gruel and sago;*
*But at last, to his bliss,*
*The physician said this—*
*To a roast leg of mutton you may go.*

These were the lines that set Lear to writing some of the most famous nonsense in the English language and illustrating it with sketches so amusing that a Lear limerick without the Lear drawing is only half as funny as the two together. Lear's own life and personality also gave impetus to his writing and drawing sheer nonsense. Older children, to whom most of Lear's verse belongs, may enjoy knowing something about him.

Edward Lear was one of twenty-one children, most of whom died in childhood or early youth. He was a pale, sickly child beset by an illness that he referred to all his life as the "Terrible Demon," a mild form of epilepsy. While he never allowed his illness to prevent him from doing anything he wished to do, we can readily imagine that it served as a stimulus to all sorts of activities that would help him forget it.

As a little boy, Lear knew the security of wealth. Then at thirteen he suffered the shock of seeing all the luxuries disappear as if by magic. His father was imprisoned for debt and his mother plunged into poverty and anxiety. Eventually all the debts were paid, but by that time the family had scattered: the boys had left England, several of the girls had died, and the others had married except Lear's beloved Ann. This sister, twenty-one years older than Edward, raised the delicate little boy from the time he was a baby. By fifteen Lear was beginning to earn

## VIEWPOINTS

Where is the charm of Lear? It lies (as it always does with poets) in his love of words: their cadences, their very look on the page, their mystery, their endless, exciting power of evocation. Lear played delightedly with language; and if, at times, he deliberately misused it (where else have we heard 'a promiscuous oration'?), even his misuse seems to have a meaning. . . .

Lear coined a vocabulary, and he did so with gusto. I think it is in his gusto that he differs most from Carroll. One never feels with Lear that his nonsense is an intellectual recreation; one never has the sense of contrivance. We can almost hear him pottering round his garden at San Remo, spontaneously christening his plants Sophtsluggia Glutinosa, or Minspysia Deliciosa. —Joanna Richardson, *Edward Lear*, published for The British Council and the National Book League by Longmans, Green and Co., London, 1965, pp. 34–35.

money with sketching. When he was in London he made scientific drawings for doctors, and when he was in the country he perfected his technique of drawing birds, butterflies, and flowers in the most minute detail. It was this latter skill that brought him an appointment to make drawings of the parrots at the zoo in Regent's Park. From the time of the publication of the book on parrots, with Lear's large colored drawings, his reputation as an artist was established, and he later prepared the drawings for another large volume, *Tortoises, Terrapins and Turtles*. It was while Lear was at work on the parrots that the Earl of Derby discovered him and invited the young artist to come down to his country estate and make drawings of his collection of birds and animals.

During his stay with this family (he was eventually employed by four Earls of Derby) he began the nonsense verses, and Lear the artist became also Lear the humorist.

Lear himself gives us a clue to this change. He sometimes grew a little tired of the formal gatherings to which he was subjected in the Earl's household and, as he wrote to a friend:

> *The uniform apathetic tone assumed by lofty society irks me dreadfully; nothing I long for half so much as to giggle heartily and to hop on one leg down the great gallery — but I dare not.*

So instead of giggling and hopping on one leg, Lear evidently took refuge with the innumerable grandchildren of the Earl. They adored him, and the Earl presently discovered that all the children on the place followed this serious-looking but irrepressibly gay young artist as if he were the Pied Piper. It was to these children that Lear must have shown his limericks as he produced them—limericks and sketches that were published in 1846 as the first *Book of Nonsense*. For Lear himself, writing them must have been great fun. They were a rest from those painstakingly detailed scientific drawings; they were a safe release for the high spirits and childlike mischief of the man who wanted to hop on one leg through the halls of the great; and, above all, they must have been a blessed escape from the illness which pursued but never conquered him.

The first book contained only limericks, and these became so famous it is sometimes

*From Edward Lear's* The Complete Nonsense Book.

erroneously assumed that Lear invented the form. Although he did not invent the limerick, he certainly became a master of its neat form and surprising content.

The second book, *Nonsense Songs and Stories*, published in 1871, includes a variety of humorous verses, among them the pseudo-serious narrative poems that seem all the funnier because they are gravely told. Every generation of five- and six-year-olds delights in "The Owl and the Pussy-Cat," that begins:

*The Owl and the Pussy-Cat went to sea*
*In a beautiful pea-green boat;*
*They took some honey, and plenty of money,*
*Wrapped up in a five-pound note.*
*The Owl looked up to the stars above,*
*And sang to a small guitar,*
*"O lovely Pussy! O Pussy, my love,*
*What a beautiful Pussy you are,*
*You are,*
*You are!*
*What a beautiful Pussy you are!"*

*Illustration by William Pène du Bois.* From The Owl and the Pussy-Cat *by Edward Lear. Illustration copyright © 1962 by William Pène du Bois. Reproduced with permission of Doubleday and Company.*

*Illustration by Leslie Brooke.* From Nonsense Songs *by Edward Lear. Published and copyrighted by Frederick Warne & Co., Inc. Reproduced with the permission of the publishers.*

Two sparkling editions of this single poem appeared in 1961 and 1962—*Le Hibou et la Poussiquette*, translated into French by Francis Steegmuller and illustrated by Barbara Cooney; and *The Owl and the Pussy-Cat*, illustrated by William Pène du Bois. The French poussiquette is a languishing siren. Mr. du Bois' feline is a bit flinty. Both are hilarious.

Dale Maxey illustrated still another version of *The Owl and the Pussy-Cat* and also provided gay, antic pictures for *Incidents in the Life of My Uncle Arly*. Two of the loveliest editions of Lear's verses have been illustrated by Helen Oxenbury, whose pictures for *The Quangle Wangle's Hat* have fascinating and colorful details; and Nancy Ekholm Burkert, whose delicate and intricate pictures for *The Scroobious Pip* have a wealth of animal forms. And all of Lear's humor is available in *The Complete Nonsense Book*, edited by Lady Strachey.

*Illustration by Barbara Cooney. From* Le Hibou et la Poussiquette *by Edward Lear, trans. by Francis Steegmuller. Illustration copyright © 1961 by Barbara Cooney. Reprinted by permission of Little, Brown and Company.*

A favorite with older children is "The Jumblies." The poem "The Duck and the Kangaroo," together with Lear's drawings, is popular with children from six years old to sixteen. It is characteristic Lear nonsense, merrily imagined and deftly written, and should be read with mock gravity. It begins:

*Said the Duck to the Kangaroo,*
*"Good gracious! how you hop!*
*Over the fields, and the water too,*
*As if you never would stop!*
*My life is a bore in this nasty pond,*
*And I long to go out in the world beyond!*
*I wish I could hop like you!"*
*Said the Duck to the Kangaroo.*

Lear's made-up words are one of the most obvious sources of amusement in these jingles. You find the Pobble who has no toes, the Quangle Wangle with the beaver hat, and the amorous Yonghy-Bonghy Bò. There's a Crumpetty Tree and a Dong with a Luminous Nose, and in the Torrible Zone you can get bottles of ring-bo-ree. The words in Lear's five different sets of alphabet rhymes are mostly of this tongue-twister variety. Of these five alphabet rhymes, none is better than the one that begins

*A was once an apple-pie,*
*Pidy,*
*Widy,*
*Tidy,*
*Pidy,*
*Nice insidy,*
*Apple-pie!*

B *was once a little bear,*
*Beary,*
*Wary,*
*Hairy,*
*Beary,*
*Taky cary,*
*Little bear!*

C *was once a little cake,*
*Caky,*
*Baky,*
*Maky,*
*Caky,*
*Taky caky,*
*Little cake!*

Lear is an excellent craftsman. His meters are exact, his rhymes neat and musical, and his verse has a pleasant sound even at its wildest. Much of it is decidedly melodious. Undoubtedly part of the appeal of "The Owl and the Pussy-Cat" for young children is its melody. They chant it happily and linger over the refrains.

Children also like the ridiculous and eccentric characters in these verses and are especially entertained by the mad troop that populates the limericks.

*There was an Old Man with a beard,*
*Who said, "It is just as I feared!—*
*Two Owls and a Hen,*
*Four Larks and a Wren,*
*Have all built their nests in my beard!"*

*There was a Young Lady of Norway,*
*Who casually sat in a doorway;*
*When the door squeezed her flat,*
*She exclaimed, "What of that?"*
*This courageous Young Lady of Norway.*

Over and over Edward Lear caricatured himself with words and with sketches which must have convulsed his friends, both juvenile and adult. In a note protesting his inability to keep an engagement because, "Disgustical to say," he had a cold in his head, he added these words with an accompanying picture:

*I have sent for 2 large tablecloths to blow my nose on, having already used up all my handkerchiefs. And altogether I am so unfit for company that I propose getting into a bag and being hung up to a bough of a tree till this tyranny is overpast.*[3]

Another portrait of himself dancing, together with the poem beginning "How pleasant to know Mr. Lear!" might be a good way of introducing Lear to children.

## CHRISTINA ROSSETTI, 1830–1894

### *Sing Song*

Christina Rossetti gave to children a small treasury of verses called *Sing Song*. Only a few incidents in her life will appeal to children, but to students of English literature and art she is interesting not only because she was the sister of the poet and painter Dante Gabriel Rossetti, and the model for several Pre-Raphaelite paintings, but also because she was an artist in her own right. Christina Rossetti contributed a fresh, if melancholy, note to English lyric poetry.

The Rossetti family was unusual in several ways. Apparently every member was beautiful to look at, highly intelligent, and uniquely gifted. The father, a distinguished Italian scholar, came to London as a political exile and found there not only the opportunity of continuing his writing on Dante, but also a charming wife, Frances Polidori. Even when Mrs. Rossetti was an old woman, visitors commented on her beauty and her intelligence. Her husband and her four children adored her, and quoted her word as final authority, painted her portrait, and wrote poems to and about her. Christina wrote a series of valentine poems all dedicated to her mother. It is amusing to discover that the recipient of this adoration found her artistic family a bit trying now and then. Mrs. Rossetti wrote:

*I had always a passion for intellect, and my wish was that my husband should be distinguished for intellect, and my children too. I have had my wish; and now I wish that there were a little less intellect in the family, so as to allow for a little more common sense.*[4]

Christina was always delicate, but the gay child grew gradually into a melancholy, deeply religious young woman, something of a recluse, unnaturally indifferent to clothes, wrapped up in her adored family, her books, and her writings. There were good reasons for this change, chief of them the unhappy conclusion of two love affairs. During her years of emotional vicissitudes, Christina must have found release and satisfaction in the recognition and praise given to her poetry. *Goblin Market and Other Poems* appeared in 1862 and immediately attracted wide attention, particularly the title poem, which was praised by the leading critics of the day, and is undoubtedly her masterpiece. When

3. *The Complete Nonsense Book*, pp. 13–14.

4. Dante Gabriel Rossetti, *His Family Letters*, p. 22.

*From the book* Goblin Market *by Christina Rossetti. Illustrated and adapted by Ellen Raskin. Illustrations and Adaptation copyright © 1970 by Ellen Raskin. Published by E. P. Dutton & Co., Inc. and used with their permission. (Original in color)*

Laura tastes the magical fruit hawked by the cunning goblins, she is bewitched and only the love and courage of her sister Lizzie save her. The plight of the two little girls is touching, their adventure with the goblins fraught with suspense, and the whole poem is woven through with vivid and colorful descriptions of the luscious wares of the bodeful little creatures. Arthur Rackham and Ellen Raskin have provided illustrations for two fine editions.

Christina Rossetti became more and more of an invalid until her death in her sixty-fourth year. Oddly enough, it was during these years of sadness and pain that she wrote her gayest poems and dedicated to a baby, "without permission," that nursery classic *Sing Song*, which appeared in 1872. The light-hearted verses of this little book she herself translated into Italian under the title *Ninna Nanna*—a charming gift for the children of her father's country!

*Sing Song* verses lead the child imperceptibly from the patter of nonsense verse to the subtle and lovely cadences of authentic poetry. "If a pig wore a wig" might have come out of *Mother Goose* and so might the popular

*Mix a pancake,*
*Stir a pancake,*
*Pop it in the pan;*
*Fry the pancake,*
*Toss the pancake,—*
*Catch it if you can.*

But Christina Rossetti's little songs have a music which is obviously more subtle than that of *Mother Goose*, and they express more complex ideas. For instance, the personification of the daffodil as a lady in yellow and green is found in both *Mother Goose* and *Sing Song*, but notice the difference. *Mother Goose* gives us the briefest personification with no embellishments:

*Daffadowndilly*
*Has come up to town,*
*In a yellow petticoat*
*And a green gown.*

But Christina Rossetti gives us hills and vales, a chilly springtime, and the suggestion of the daffodil's fragility in those clear, clipped words "straight and frail" and the delicate sounds of "chilly," "hilly," "dilly"—all slight as the flower.

*Growing in the vale*
*By the uplands hilly,*
*Growing straight and frail,*
*Lady Daffadowndilly.*

*In a golden crown,*
*And a scant green gown*
*While the spring blows chilly,*
*Lady Daffadown,*
*Sweet Daffadowndilly.*

Christina Rossetti makes subtle and repeated use of vowel and consonant sounds to suggest the feeling or idea described by the words. Take her wind poems, for instance.

Each one describes a different kind of wind, which you can almost hear in the sounds of the words. There is a stormy, ominous wind from the sea:

*The wind has such a rainy sound*
*Moaning through the town,*
*The sea has such a windy sound,—*
*Will the ships go down?*

*The apples in the orchard*
*Tumble from their tree.—*
*Oh will the ships go down, go down,*
*In the windy sea?*

Notice the use of the *n* and *d* sounds, which heighten the minor note of the poem. Then there is the poem about a tender little breeze:

*O wind, where have you been,*
*That you blow so sweet?*
*Among the violets*
*Which blossom at your feet.*

*The honeysuckle waits*
*For summer and for heat;*
*But violets in the chilly spring*
*Make the turf so sweet.*

And, finally, there is that gentle wind you can hear whispering in the soft, slight words of "Who has seen the wind?"

Every reader of *Sing Song* will have favorite examples of the skillful use of tone color. This is worth noting because the way in which word sounds fit the mood or sensory impression of the poems largely determines how they should be read. For instance, with just the slightest exaggeration in emphasis you will discover that the words actually hop in that amusing couplet describing a rabbit:

*And timid, funny, brisk little bunny*
*Winks his nose and sits all sunny.*

Or read aloud the couplets of that remarkable color poem "What is pink? A rose is pink," noticing particularly these last four verses:

*What is yellow? pears are yellow,*
*Rich and ripe and mellow.*

*What is green? the grass is green,*
*With small flowers between.*

*What is violet? clouds are violet*
*In the summer twilight.*

*What is orange? why, an orange,*
*Just an orange!*

Young children respond with delight to the music of Christina Rossetti's slight, exquisite little lyrics, and, fortunately, most of the subject matter is understandable and appealing to them. There are, to be sure, a number of elegies about dead babies which should be omitted, but her live babies are delightful from the first poem:

*Angels at the foot,*
*And angels at the head,*
*And like a curly little lamb*
*My pretty babe in bed.*

to "I know a baby, such a baby" and the lullaby that begins

*Lullaby, oh lullaby!*
*Flowers are closed and lambs are sleeping;*

She also brings in other members of the family circle: there is Father "hot and tired, knocking at the door," Mother shaking the cherry tree, "Minnie and Mattie and fat little May," and an eight o'clock visit from the postman. Then there are all the small creatures the child delights in: a cock crowing "Kookoorookoo," "a frisky lamb and a frisky child," "hopping frogs," "plodding toads," the "brown and furry caterpillar," and robins and wrens. There is a whole garden full of flowers, the sun, moon, and stars, and the rainbow seen in the poem "Boats sail on the rivers." Moralizing is rare but amusingly handled. If the verse is gaily read, children will invariably smile at

*Seldom "can't,"*
*Seldom "don't";*
*Never "shan't,"*
*Never "won't."*

For the most part, Christina Rossetti keeps to the small creatures and objects of the young child's world and to the family and playmates he knows the best.

For older children, there are some choice bits of wit and wisdom that the young child cannot grasp. In these poems the same idea or play on words is repeated several times. For example, "A pin has a head, but has no hair" is a pattern that occurs again in "The peacock has a score of eyes." The weighing of values in "A diamond or a coal?" is repeated in this still finer comparison:

*An emerald is as green as grass;*
*A ruby red as blood;*
*A sapphire shines as blue as heaven;*
*A flint lies in the mud.*

*A diamond is a brilliant stone,*
*To catch the world's desire;*
*An opal holds a fiery spark;*
*But a flint holds fire.*

It takes an older child to interpret such fables as these, but what vivid, colorful bits of wisdom they are!

## EMILY DICKINSON, 1830–1886

*Poems*

Only a half-dozen of the hundreds of poems Emily Dickinson wrote were published during her lifetime. One of the greatest of American poets, and certainly one whose life has aroused more conjecture, disputed theories, and interpretation than most, she was a poet whose style was revolutionary in its time, and whose work has become increasingly beloved by the young.

Whether an unrequited love drew Emily Dickinson into retirement or not, she did go into seclusion in her home. The few poems she offered for publication were so changed by editing that they lost the quality that made them uniquely hers. After her death, over 1700 poems were discovered, and the first volume of her poems was printed in 1890. They had a mixed reception. The broken meter, the incomplete rhymes, the unusual idioms, and perhaps most of all the absence of "lofty thought, elegantly expressed," were not in keeping with the standards of poetic writing in that period.

The poems are short, usually in four-line stanzas, flashing with brightness or taut with emotion, and her most important poems concern the relationship between the inner self and the outer world. Sharply perceptive, Dickinson could be playful or witty, but more often her outlook is somber, aware of the inflexibility of nature and expressing a yearning for immortality and for communication with a Deity seemingly remote.

There are several editions of her poems chosen for children: *Letter to the World* (1969), edited by Rumer Godden; *Poems* (1964), edited by Helen Plotz; and *Poems for Youth* (1934), edited by Alfred Hampson. Most children who are poetry lovers read Dickinson and can appreciate her at the age of eleven, and some younger children will enjoy hearing her work read aloud. Her poems are now included in many anthologies for children and in the several biographies of which she is the subject. Here is one lovely, lyric selection:

*New feet within my garden go—*
*New fingers stir the sod—*
*A Troubadour upon the Elm*
*Betrays the solitude.*

*New children play upon the green—*
*New Weary sleep below—*
*And still the pensive Spring returns—*
*And still the punctual snow!*

## LEWIS CARROLL, 1832–1898

*Alice's Adventures in Wonderland*
*Through the Looking-Glass*

In 1865 appeared the delightful and astonishing book *Alice's Adventures in Wonderland* by "Lewis Carroll," the pseudonym for Charles Lutwidge Dodgson, an Oxford don and a mathematician (see p. 248). The book was several degrees wilder than Lear's books at their wildest. There was the Duchess with her amazing advice:

*"Speak roughly to your little boy,*
*And beat him when he sneezes:*
*He only does it to annoy,*
*Because he knows it teases."*

CHORUS

*"Wow! wow! wow!"*[5]

There was the gibberish poem, "Jabberwocky," which Alice found in the looking-glass book. Even Alice found it "*rather* hard to understand."

*'Twas brillig, and the slithy toves*
*Did gyre and gimble in the wabe:*
*All mimsy were the borogoves,*
*And the mome raths outgrabe.*

*"Beware the Jabberwock, my son!*
*The jaws that bite, the claws that catch!*
*Beware the Jubjub bird, and shun*
*The frumious Bandersnatch!"*

There were "You are old, Father William," "How doth the little crocodile," and many other nonsense verses interspersed throughout the prose of *Alice's Adventures in Wonderland* and later *Through the Looking-Glass*. To quote them is a temptation, but the fact is that these rhymes are much funnier in their context than they are apart from it. The full flavor of his humor is in most cases best appreciated by boys and girls in their early teens rather than by younger children.

Certainly Carroll gave the "gay nineties" a good start on their gaiety. And the gaiety was further increased by the operas of Gilbert and Sullivan, operas whose lyrics were chanted by adults in England and America, and were also taken over by the children. The satiric conversation in *H.M.S. Pinafore* between the boastful Captain, the "Ruler of the Queen's Navee," and the skeptical chorus has become a byword for all boasters.

Captain *For I'm never, never sick at sea!*
Chorus *What, never?*
Captain *No, never.*
Chorus *What, never?*
Captain *Well,—hardly ever!*

## KATE GREENAWAY, 1846–1901

*Under the Window*
*Marigold Garden*

Like Jane and Ann Taylor, Kate Greenaway wrote undistinguished verse for children, but she did write with artless gaiety, and her illustrations have all the lyric grace the verses lack. Her balanced pages—decorated with flowers, fruits, merry children, and pleasant landscapes—possess a freshness and charm, and a kind of rhythmic grace that seem to lift the accompanying quatrains into the realm of genuine poetry. Without the pictures, the rhymes probably would not have survived, but the two in combination constitute a unique contribution to children's books.

This modest and charming woman was born in London and worked there most of her life. The daughter of an artist, she began her own study of art as a matter of course. When she was still only twenty-two years old, her exhibitions of watercolors were exciting favorable comment, but it was her Christmas cards which started her vogue. From the Christmas cards she turned to the illustration

5. This poem is a parody of David Bates' "Speak Gently." Both poems are reprinted in Myra Cohn Livingston's collection of parodies and burlesques, *Speak Roughly to Your Little Boy*.

of children's books and soon enjoyed a tremendous popularity.

The tiny *Mother Goose* with the Greenaway pictures and decorations still remains an exquisite edition of the old favorite. The artist's popularity reached new heights with the publication of her own book of verses and drawings, *Under the Window* (1879), which is said to have sold 150,000 copies. This, together with her *Birthday Book*, *Marigold Garden*, and her *Almanacs*, brought her a large income and made her famous in every great city of Europe and of the United States.

When she moralizes, as she does frequently, it is not with the heavy hand of the Taylors but with sly humor. Here is a good example, from *Under the Window:*

*Yes, that's the girl that struts about,*
*She's very proud,—so very proud!*
*Her bow-wow's quite as proud as she:*
*They both are very wrong to be*
*So proud—so very proud.*

*See, Jane and Willy laugh at her,*
*They say she's very proud!*
*Says Jane, "My stars!—they're very silly";*
*"Indeed they are," cries little Willy,*
*"To walk so stiff and proud."*

The verses, together with the gentle caricature that illustrates them, are an excellent satire on pride as children see it.

The following poem might have come out of *Mother Goose*. Children like it for the contagious excitement of its lines.

*Higgledy, piggledy! see how they run!*
*Hopperty, popperty! what is the fun?*
*Has the sun or the moon tumbled into the sea?*
*What is the matter, now? Pray tell it me!*

*Higgledy, piggledy! how can I tell?*
*Hopperty, popperty! hark to the bell!*
*The rats and the mice even scamper away;*
*Who can say what may not happen to-day?*

"Susan Blue" is a little conversation piece—two small girls talking over a garden gate and wondering where to play. "Tommy was a silly boy" relates the amusing mishap of a small boy who thought he could fly. "Blue Shoes," "Shall I Sing!" "Under the Window," and "My House Is Red" are all pleasant, if uninspired, little verses. In the Greenaway books, we see and read about children racing and skipping, dancing to the piper's tune, flying kites, rolling hoops, chasing each other, going primly to tea, or quietly enjoying their own little red house—in short, real children. For this is Kate Greenaway's contribution to children's poetry: verses that are simple in language and idea, but with a spark of humor that brings a smile, because her children are truly childlike.

## LAURA E. RICHARDS, 1850–1943

*Tirra Lirra; Rhymes Old and New*

Laura E. Richards came from an American home of unusual distinction and in turn added her unique contribution to its distinction. Her father was Samuel Gridley Howe, who devoted himself to such diverse social causes as the Greek War for Independence, the education of the blind, and the founding of the first school for feeble-minded children. Her mother, the beautiful and gifted Julia Ward Howe, author of "The Battle Hymn of the Republic," was not only a poet but an excellent musician who "knew all the songs in the world," or so her children thought. Mrs Howe sang to them in three languages, and she made a special song for each child.

Laura grew up with her brother and three sisters in a house called Green Peace. The children shared the family heritage of music, poetry, and wide interests, together with the companionship of happy, intelligent adults. It is not surprising that the children in turn scribbled stories and poetry. It was not, however, until after she was married and had her own children that Laura thought much about writing. Then, remembering her own delight in her mother's songs, she, too, began to sing to her children. First she sang the old ballads that she knew so well. Then she found herself making up her own ditties, just as her mother had done, probably because she could adapt them to the special demands of the child in her lap or at her knee. In her book, *Stepping Westward*, she tells about these songs. In the four years that saw the birth of her first three children (there were seven in all), she writes that she enjoyed

> *. . . contemporary with these births, the acquisition of my hurdy-gurdy . . . I had always rhymed easily; now . . . came a prodigious welling up of rhymes, mostly bringing their tunes (or what passed for tunes; the baby, bless it, knew no better!) with them. I wrote, and sang, and wrote, and could not stop. The first baby was plump and placid, with a broad smooth back which made an excellent writing desk. She lay on her front, across my lap; I wrote on her back, the writing pad quite as steady as the writing of jingles required.*

No wonder these "jingles" of Laura Richards have a spontaneity and a freshness that are only equaled by their lyric quality. Nor are we surprised to find that at eighty-one her "hurdy-gurdy" was still turning furiously, reeling out as delightful ditties for the third generation of babies as for the first.

It was her husband who suggested that she send some of her verses to the new magazine for children, *St. Nicholas*, and this she did. From then on, stories and poems came from her flying pen at an amazing rate. There was the long series known as the *Hildegarde* books, which were tremendously popular with the children of her generation. *Captain January* told the story of a baby rescued from the sea and raised by a good old lighthouse keeper. Between stories and biographies, the verses continued to "bubble up" with undiminished charm. But it wasn't until 1932 that a book of her verses, called *Tirra Lirra; Rhymes Old and New*, was published—a book which she dedicated to her youngest grandchild and her eldest great-grandchild.

Laura Richards' verses abound in humorous, made-up words. Lear gave us "meloobious" and "torrible," and Carroll presented us with "galumphing," "beamish," and "whiffling," but Mrs. Richards matches them with "Muffin Bird," "Rummyjums," "bogothybogs," "Lolloping Lizard," "a Glimmering Glog," and those remarkable museum specimens, "Wiggledywasticums" and "Ptoodlecumtumsdyl." Moreover, no one can play with words with more joyous confusion than she. Children from five to any age chuckle over

*Eletelephony*[6]

*Once there was an elephant,*
*Who tried to use the telephant—*
*No! no! I mean an elephone*
*Who tried to use the telephone—*
*(Dear me! I am not certain quite*
*That even now I've got it right.)*

*Howe'er it was, he got his trunk*
*Entangled in the telephunk;*
*The more he tried to get it free,*
*The louder buzzed the telephee—*
*(I fear I'd better drop the song*
*Of elephop and telephong!)*

Like "Eletelephony," "Some Fishy Nonsense," "Doggerel," "Sir Ringleby Rose," and many other jingles depend for their fun upon this juggling with words.

But Mrs. Richards carries her fun beyond mere play with words. She has, in addition to the verse-maker's skill, the dramatic art of a first-rate storyteller. The gentle tale of "Little John Bottlejohn," lured away by a cajoling mermaid; the gory record of "The Seven Little Tigers and the Aged Cook," the exciting "The Monkeys and the Crocodile"—these and a dozen others depend for their interest upon the skillful storytelling of the author as well as upon her irrepressible sense of the absurd.

6. "Eletelephony" and "The Umbrella Brigade." From *Tirra Lirra: Rhymes Old and New* by Laura E. Richards. Published by Little, Brown and Company.

Her characters and situations are also a source of amusement for the children. And even four- and five-year-olds feel superior when they giggle understandingly over the blunders of the two dogs "Jippy and Jimmy." The older children who know Kipling's "yellow dog Dingo" will also appreciate the ridiculous plight of "Bingo the Dingo," who fell in love with the "fatally fair flamingo." The funny situations in *Tirra Lirra* are laugh provoking, even without the funny words.

Laura Richards has caught in her verses some of the singing quality of words that children enjoy. For example, "A Song for Hal," "Little John Bottlejohn," "The Song of the Corn-Popper," "Talents Differ," "Will-o'-the-Wisp," and "Prince Tatters" are lyrics that almost sing themselves. To test this quality, read aloud the chorus of "The Umbrella Brigade":

*But let it rain,*
*Tree-toads and frogs,*
*Muskets and pitchforks,*
*Kittens and dogs!*
*Dash away! plash away!*
*Who is afraid?*
*Here we go,*
*The Umbrella Brigade!*[6]

This lyric quality not only gives distinction to her most extravagant nonsense but makes children more sensitive to the musical qualities of words.

*Illustration by Marguerite Davis. From Tirra Lirra by Laura Richards. Copyright, 1930, 1932, 1934, by Laura E. Richards. Copyright, 1955, by Little, Brown and Company. Reprinted by permission of the publishers.*

## ROBERT LOUIS STEVENSON, 1850–1894

*A Child's Garden of Verses*

The title "poet laureate of childhood" has often been bestowed upon Robert Louis Stevenson, who first captivated adult readers with his essays and fiction, then caught and held the affectionate regard of children with *A Child's Garden of Verses*.

The facts of Stevenson's life are too well known to need much reviewing. There has been, however, far too much emphasis on the pathology of his life, and on his recurrent illnesses, and not enough emphasis on the indomitable spirit that kept him working and playing with tremendous energy and enjoyment to the very end of his short life.

He was always a frail child, to be sure, and the sullen, severe climate of Edinburgh could not have helped his health. Fortunately, Louis sometimes got away for visits to his grandfather Balfour's house at Colinton on the Water Leith. There he played outdoors with his cousins, and made friends with all the small creatures and with the garden blossoms he names so lovingly in his poem "The Flowers." There he discovered the "thrushes on the lawn," the lilacs, and the lawn itself which he later said was "a perfect goblet of sunshine." There, too, at the foot of the garden, flowed the dark brown river over its golden sand "with trees on either hand," just as he recalls it in "Where Go the Boats?"

Fortunately, too, the young Louis went on journeys with his father to visit the great lighthouses of the Scottish coast, many of them built by the grandfather, Robert Stevenson, for whom he was named. These lighthouses and the daring feats of engineering which they represented captured the imagination of the child and helped his spirit grow robust.

Of his adult life more tales can be told than he himself ever wrote. He studied law but soon turned to writing, and no author ever took his profession more earnestly nor worked at it more zealously. We know of his continual travels all over the world for health and for pleasure, and we know how his notebooks went with him everywhere and how there was never a journey that did not yield fat notes to be used later in essays, poems, plays, novels, short stories, and letters.

In France he fell in love with an American, a Mrs. Osbourne, and followed her to California, where they were married in 1880. Their life together was remarkably happy, and Stevenson found himself in a kind of family partnership for writing. He dictated to his stepdaughter Isobel; he read everything he wrote to his wife, who was one of his best critics; and on Lloyd Osbourne, his stepson, he tried out his boys' stories, chapter by chapter. *Treasure Island* grew and flourished by way of Lloyd's enjoyment, Lloyd's criticism, Lloyd's robust approval. "No women in the story, Lloyd's orders," wrote Stevenson. Again—"the trouble is to work it off without oaths. Buccaneers without oaths—bricks without straw. But youth and the fond parent have to be consulted. . . . It's awful fun boys' stories; you just indulge the pleasures of your heart; that's all; no trouble, no strain."

Stevenson's last four years were spent in Samoa, and no part of his brief life is more picturesque. He built himself a great house in the midst of a tropical estate, which he cultivated with astonishing success. He gathered round him a kind of feudal clan of natives who adored him and whom he protected like a kindly patriarch. He aided their deposed king, wrote a book in behalf of his native friends, hoping to help their cause in England, and was himself a sort of island king and judge.

When Stevenson died suddenly, his native friends came from all over the island to look upon the face of the dear friend they called "Tusitala," teller of tales. They brought their finest mats to honor the dead, they filled his room with their brightest flowers, and they carved a road up the great mountain to a peak where Stevenson had said he wished to lie. Sixty Samoans carried their friend up that precipitous road and left him forever in the land he loved.

*A Child's Garden of Verses* appeared in 1885 as *Penny Whistles*, with sixty-three poems and this fond dedication to Stevenson's childhood nurse: "To Alison Cunningham (From Her Boy)." Not all these poems are for children; a few of them are merely about children or are adult reminiscences of childhood. Such poems creep into almost every collection of juvenile poetry but are nevertheless to be avoided; for example, Stevenson's "Keepsake Mill," "Whole Duty of Children," and the rarely included "To Any Reader" and "To Willie and Henrietta."

With these exceptions, no careful reading of the poems can fail to leave you impressed with the author's genuine understanding of children. The opening poem, "Bed in Summer," is every child's complaint:

*And does it not seem hard to you,*
*When all the sky is clear and blue,*
*And I should like so much to play,*
*To have to go to bed by day?*

His children get up shivering with cold on winter mornings; they yearn to travel; they discover the sea miraculously filling up their holes on the beach; they struggle with table manners; they have a deep respect for "System," an orderly world; they enjoy good days and bad ones, mostly good; they can't understand why the gardener doesn't want "to play at Indian wars" with them; they watch for the lamplighter; they wonder why they can't see the wind; and they enjoy a world of play and a world of the imagination as well. Children's interest in tiny things is found not only in "The Little Land" but over and over again in other verses. Here are real children, many-sided and with many interests.

Especially true to child life are the poems involving dramatic play. Imagination transforms a clothes basket into a boat. Climbing up in the cherry tree, the child glimpses not merely the next-door garden but foreign lands and even fairyland. In "A Good Play," the children explain:

*We built a ship upon the stairs*
*All made of the back-bedroom chairs.*

The sick child's fleets go "all up and down among the sheets" in "The Land of Counterpane"; and in "The Land of Story Books," he has a forest adventure, "Away Behind the Sofa Back." The poems bristle with the properties and imaginative transformations of that arch magician, the child of about four to seven years old.

People have complained that this child of the *Verses* is a solitary child, and they have read into the poems some of the pathos of the sick Louis. But if you study these verses, you will find several children playing pirates in the "Pirate Story"; building ships together in "A Good Play"; being "mountaineers" in "The Hayloft"; crawling "through the breach in the wall of the garden" to "Keepsake Mill"; tramping round the village in the "Marching Song" with Johnnie, Willie, Peter, and "great commander Jane"; and in "Northwest Passage," facing together the "long black passage up to bed." These give us a fair proportion of other children and of social play. They emphasize also the normal play activities of healthy children. Nothing of the invalid here!

Perhaps the largest group of poems under a single general classification is made up of those concerned with night. What an imaginative group it is, and sometimes scary, too: "Young Night Thought," "My Bed Is a Boat," "The Land of Story-Books," "Night and Day," "The Moon," "Windy Nights," "Shadow March," "The Land of Nod," "Escape at Bedtime," "Good-Night," and "In Port." Of these, "Escape at Bedtime" is one of the most interesting.

There are two poems in this night group which are also notable for their rhythm. "Shadow March" is in perfect marching time, but it is an eerie, frightening march of bogies

*Used by permission. Illustration by Alice & Martin Provensen from* A Child's Garden of Verses *by Robert Louis Stevenson. Copyright 1951 by Western Publishing Company, Inc. (Original in color)*

and shadows, not to be used before the children are seven or eight years old and stout enough to stand it. Less scary and still finer is that pounding gallop called

*Windy Nights*

*Whenever the moon and stars are set,*
*Whenever the wind is high,*
*All night long in the dark and wet,*
*A man goes riding by.*
*Late in the night when the fires are out,*
*Why does he gallop and gallop about?*

*Whenever the trees are crying aloud,*
*And ships are tossed at sea,*
*By, on the highway, low and loud,*
*By at the gallop goes he,*
*By at the gallop he goes, and then*
*By he comes back at the gallop again.*

Another fine example of the use of rhythm to suggest the subject is "From a Railway Carriage." Notice that the verse has the tempo and the driving speed of the train.

*Faster than fairies, faster than witches,*
*Bridges and houses, hedges and ditches;*
*And charging along like troops in a battle,*
*All through the meadows the horses and cattle:*
*All of the sights of the hill and the plain*
*Fly as thick as driving rain;*
*And ever again in the wink of an eye,*
*Painted stations whistle by.*

These examples of rhythm illustrate another of the outstanding qualities in Stevenson's *Child's Garden of Verses:* the poems are markedly lyrical. Of course, numbers of them have been set to music, but they sing anyway, without benefit of notes. Take the concluding line of "A Good Boy": "And hear the thrushes singing in the lilacs round the lawn." Or listen to the refrain in "The Wind":

*O wind, a-blowing all day long,*
*O wind, that sings so loud a song!*

Go through page after page of these poems and you'll find them singing in your memory with their own melody. One of the most lyrical of them all is

*Where Go the Boats?*

*Dark brown is the river,*
*Golden is the sand.*
*It flows along forever,*
*With trees on either hand.*

*Green leaves a-floating,*
*Castles of the foam,*
*Boats of mine a-boating—*
*Where will all come home?*

*On goes the river*
*And out past the mill,*
*Away down the valley,*
*Away down the hill.*

*Away down the river,*
*A hundred miles or more,*
*Other little children*
*Shall bring my boats ashore.*

Notice the slow, smooth-flowing melody of the first two verses, like the flow of the river. In the third verse, the repetition of "Away" gives an impetus to the lines as if the current were really flowing faster and carrying the boats farther until, abruptly, as if in a little eddy, the boats come to anchor in the last two lines. Except that the poem has no gaiety, the smooth glide of the lines suggests the flowing melody of "The Moldau," by Smetana.

Stevenson was evidently fond of the poem pattern which seems to begin close at hand and go farther and farther away. He uses it again effectively in "Foreign Lands," and, for the youngest, in the brief

*Rain*

*The rain is raining all around,*
*It falls on field and tree,*
*It rains on the umbrellas here,*
*And on the ships at sea.*

Although teachers and mothers who were raised on *A Child's Garden of Verses* may feel that the verses are overfamiliar, they must not forget that these poems are new to each generation of children. "The Cow," "My Shadow," "The Swing," "Winter-time," and "Time to Rise," in addition to the verses already quoted, are perennial favorites, and children should not miss them. New poets of childhood may make their contributions, but Robert Louis Stevenson has left to young children a legacy of small lyrics, just their size.

## LESLIE BROOKE, 1862–1940

*Johnny Crow's Garden*
*Johnny Crow's Party*

Young children, four to six, are fortunate if they are introduced to their first nonsense after *Mother Goose* through the Johnny Crow books. Leslie Brooke always loved the stories about Johnny Crow, which his father, a novelist, used to tell him, and so when he grew up and had two sons of his own, he also made up stories about Johnny Crow. At his wife's suggestion he translated this genial bird into pictures and verse, and in 1903 published *Johnny Crow's Garden*, which he dedicated to his sons. A few years later came *Johnny Crow's Party*, but some thirty years passed before *Johnny Crow's New Garden* appeared, dedicated to young Peter Brooke, a grandson. These three books would amuse small children of any generation. The mannerly Johnny Crow himself, the "preposserous rhinoserous," the cow and the sow who sing "Squeal and Low"—these and other friendly beasts come and go with grave absurdity through the pages of the three picture books.

Mothers and fathers should know these books and should take time to talk over and savor the jokes with the small children for whom they were intended. Good manners are exemplified by Johnny Crow, the perfect host, and by the appreciative guests. In these famous picture books Leslie Brooke has created a choice array of illustrations and nonsense rhymes for children.

## WALTER DE LA MARE, 1873–1956

*Rhymes and Verses: Collected Poems for Children*
*Peacock Pie*

Adults and children of the English-speaking world lost a great lyric poet when Walter de la Mare died in Twickenham, England, on June 22, 1956. He was born in the little village of Charlton in Kent. When he was only seventeen, he finished his schooling and went into the London office of the Anglo-American (Standard) Oil Company. For eighteen years he worked in the statistical department of that company, during which time he wrote stories and poems and published them under the pseudonym of Walter Ramal. The treasured *Songs of Childhood* was published in 1902, when he was still engaged in this statistical work.

When he was thirty-five, he received a small civil pension and had sufficient income from book reviewing to enable him to retire from business. Later, a legacy enabled him to drop all work except his own creative writing.

All of his poems for young people are now collected in *Rhymes and Verses*. (There is also *Come Hither*, De la Mare's own selection of poems for children.) *Peacock Pie* has been reissued and is a choice book for the special child to own. Many of his poems are beyond the comprehension of children. Nevertheless, this work yields a precious residue of pure poetry that no child should miss. Choose your favorite poems; try them with the children; then try certain others that are beautiful but that are not so sure to be enjoyed at first hearing. Who knows what words will catch the imagination of children and set their spirits winging? When you are using the poetry of a great lyric poet, be adventurous and try a wide selection for the sake of that occasional child who may suddenly be carried out of himself by the magic of poetry.

One characteristic of Walter de la Mare's poems is the use of the unanswered question which leaves the reader wondering. Reading the gravely beautiful "The Horseman," you discover that the content is slight, the melody is utterly satisfying, but the picture it produces is an enigma. "Is it a knight?" "Maybe

*Illustration copyright © 1961 by Barbara Cooney. Reprinted from* Peacock Pie, *by Walter de la Mare, by permission of Alfred A. Knopf, Inc.*

it's the moon." "Or maybe it's white clouds," the children say. When you read them the last lines of "Some One"—

> *So I know not who came knocking,*
> *At all, at all, at all.*[7]

the children ask, "But who *was* knocking?" and immediately start answering their own question. Many of Walter de la Mare's poems have this enigmatic quality. Whether he is writing for children or adults, his poems frequently leave you possessed and wondering. You keep on saying them, trying to find the answer from the poet himself, or, failing in this, supplying first one answer of your own and then another. Children speculate over "The Mocking Fairy," "Jim Jay," and "The Little Green Orchard," to mention only a few.

Of course, too much ambiguity may be discouraging to those children who are literal creatures and like things straight and plain. A little, however, stimulates children's imagination and provokes not only a healthy speculation but the ability to transcend the factual and go over into the world of dreams. Some people make this transition with music. Why not with poetry as well?

Walter de la Mare could be straight and plain when he wished to, and his children are real flesh-and-blood children. The account of "Poor Henry" swallowing physic is as homely a bit of family life as you can find anywhere. Little Ann waking up and tumbling out of her bed in the morning is any child waking happily. Small children enjoy the matter-of-fact subject matter and the straightforward treatment of such poems as "Chicken," "Bread and Cherries," "Tired Tim," "The Barber's," and the Elizabeth Ann parts of "A Child's Day." Even these poems for the youngest children, however, are illumined with little touches that invariably lift them above the commonplace. Contrast the

7. "Some One," "Tired Tim," and "The Barber's" by Walter de la Mare from *Peacock Pie*. Reprinted by permission of The Literary Trustees of Walter de la Mare, and The Society of Authors as their representative.

dragging words of "Tired Tim" with the gay, skipping words of "The Barber's":

*Tired Tim*[7]

*Poor tired Tim! It's sad for him.*
*He lags the long bright morning through,*
*Ever so tired of nothing to do;*
*He moons and mopes the livelong day,*
*Nothing to think about, nothing to say;*
*Up to bed with his candle to creep,*
*Too tired to yawn, too tired to sleep:*
*Poor tired Tim! It's sad for him.*

*The Barber's*[7]

*Gold locks, and black locks,*
*Red locks and brown,*
*Topknot to love-curl,*
*The hair wisps down;*
*Straight above the clear eyes,*
*Rounded round the ears,*
*Snip-snap and snick-a-snick,*
*Clash the Barber's shears;*
*Us, in the looking-glass,*
*Footsteps in the street,*
*Over, under, to and fro,*
*The lean blades meet;*
*Bay Rum or Bear's Grease,*
*A silver groat to pay—*
*Then out a-shin-shan-shining*
*In the bright, blue day.*

Walter de la Mare wrote many of these poems for his own children. He knew what caught their fancy and what jokes they liked. So he sometimes gave them rare nonsense in the preposterous vein they appreciated, for example, "Alas, Alack!"

The poet also knew children's curious penchant for names. In nursery schools they can be heard sometimes chanting each other's names, not for the sake of calling or addressing each other but just for fun. Walter de la Mare must have observed this delight in saying names, for he wrote several poems using them including the introduction to "A Child's Day," "O Dear Me!" and "Bunches of Grapes." Walter de la Mare's children are indeed real, from pert little Mima and her taunting sister, to the hammering and sawing small boy who speaks from "The Little Green Orchard," and to the three children in "Bunches of Grapes."

There are many nature poems in *Rhymes and Verses*. There are "The Hare," "The Warbler," "A Goldfinch," "Mrs. Earth," "The Pool in the Rock," "The Snowflake," "Silver," "Full Moon," "Wanderers" (the planets), "Snow," the simple and beautiful "The Rainbow," and many others. Throughout the poems you find intimate glimpses of flowers, birds, beasts, the sea, and the countryside—all caught and colored with the poet's own peculiar insight. No poetry is more intensely visual than Walter de la Mare's. A "sun-washed drift of seabirds," "horned snails," "four-clawed moles," "moths like ghosties," a "martin's sun-baked nest," "rain-sweet lilac on the spray," and, for another sensory experience, those "chuffling" pigs making their "grizzling, gruzzling and greedy" sounds. Sometimes you feel as if Walter de la Mare shared his famous midget's ability to stand grass-high and look intimately at bluebells and beetles, cobwebs and dewdrops, so vividly did he record them.

Forrest Reid characterizes Walter de la Mare's poetry by saying that it is chiefly "poetry of imagination and *vision* with its hints of loveliness belonging to a world perhaps remembered, perhaps only dreamed, but which at least is not *this* world."[8] The fairy poems, with a great range of mood and style, begin at nonsense level with such delightful absurdities as "Tillie," the old woman who swallowed some magic fern seeds when she yawned and has ever since been floating around on the wind.

For the older children, there is that hilarious "The Dwarf," which is almost a study in laughter. One of the children's favorite fairy poems is "Sleepyhead," with its interesting contrast between the child's matter-of-fact narrative and the wild, sweet singing of

8. *Walter de la Mare: A Critical Study*. Faber and Faber Ltd., 1929.

the "gnomies." By the way, this is one of those poems of which there are at least three variants in the different editions. The version given below was the first one, in the 1902 printing. It was called "The Gnomies" in that edition but is "Sleepyhead" in most of the books.

*Sleepyhead*[9]

*As I lay awake in the white moonlight,*
*I heard a faint singing in the wood—*
*'Out of bed,*
*Sleepyhead,*
*Put your white foot now,*
*Here are we,*
*'Neath the tree*
*Singing round the root now!'*

*I looked out of the window in the white moonlight,*
*The leaves were like snow in the wood—*
*'Come away*
*Child and play,*
*Light wi' the gnomies;*
*In a mound,*
*Green and round,*
*That's where their home is!*
*Honey sweet,*
*Curds to eat,*
*Cream and frumènty,*
*Shells and beads,*
*Poppy seeds,*
*You shall have plenty.'*

*But soon as I stooped in the dim moonlight*
*To put on my stocking and my shoe,*
*The sweet, sweet singing died sadly away,*
*And the grey of the morning peep'd through:*
*Then instead of the gnomies there came a red robin*
*To sing of the buttercups and dew.*

If you read all of the poems mentioned in this group and add "Melmillo," "Bewitched," "The Pedlar," "As Lucy Went A-Walking," and half a dozen others, you soon discover that here are no fairies with gauzy wings and jeweled wands, but rather the witches, the dwarfs, the occasionally droll, homely wee women or wee men of ancient folklore.

*Illustration by Boris Artzybasheff for Walter de la Mare's "Sleepyhead" from* The Fairy Shoemaker and Other Fairy Poems. *Copyright, 1928, by The Macmillan Company.*

Walter de la Mare has left behind him a rich legacy of both poetry and prose for children and adults. If *Memoirs of a Midget* is brilliant fiction for mature readers, *The Three Royal Monkeys* is equally distinguished fantasy for children. If his adult poetry is frequently compared to William Blake's, many of his poems for children merit the same comparison and have, besides, a range and variety not found in Blake. That his work for children has the same beauty found in his books for adults is not surprising when he himself said in his Introduction to *Bells and Grass*, "I know well that only the rarest kind of best in anything can be good enough for the young." If anyone has given children "the rarest kind of best" in poetry, it is Walter de la Mare.

9. "Sleepyhead" by Walter de la Mare from *Collected Poems*. Reprinted by permission of The Literary Trustees of Walter de la Mare, and The Society of Authors as their representative.

## ROBERT FROST, 1874–1963

*You Come Too*

Everyone thinks of Robert Frost as a New Englander, but he was born in San Francisco and did not arrive in New England until he was eleven years old. However, his forebears had been there for generations and his spirit was so completely akin to the region that he spoke with the laconic wit, plain words, and arresting understatements of a native.

Frost seems to have taken college lightly, with less than one term at Dartmouth and two years at Harvard. In later years many universities honored him with positions on their faculties and with honorary degrees. Some forty academic hoods might have been gathering dust in his closets except that he had them made into a splendid patchwork quilt, commenting, "It's knowing what to do with things that counts"[10]—a line that sounds as if it came from one of his poems! Besides holding professorship in many universities and colleges, Robert Frost traveled the lecture circuit throughout the United States to literally hundreds of institutions, clubs, and groups of every sort. He read his own poems inimitably and talked wisely and simply about poetry.

Robert Frost was four times the recipient of the Pulitzer Prize for poetry. In 1950 the United States Senate adopted a "resolution of felicitation" on his seventy-fifth birthday, and in 1961, President-elect John F. Kennedy invited Frost to read one of his poems at the inaugural ceremony, the first time a poet had been so honored.

In 1962, the poet's eighty-eighth year, a new book of his poems was published, *In the Clearing*, an arresting title for a last book. Robert Frost died early in 1963. John F. Kennedy said of the poet, ". . . he will live as a poet of the life of man, of the darkness and despair, as well as the hope. . . ."[11] And the poet John Ciardi wrote of Frost, "If he is half radiance he is also half brimstone, and praise be. His best poems will endure precisely because they are terrible—and holy."[12] But the poet himself had the last word. In a poem called "Into My Own," he wrote of death as walking deeper and deeper into "those dark trees" that "stretched away unto the edge of doom" and he prophesied that for those who missed and followed him—

*They would not find me changed from him they*
*knew—*
*Only more sure of all that I thought was true.*[13]

Which of Robert Frost's poems are simple enough for young children? The poet answered this question with the title of his own selections—*You Come Too, Favorite Poems for Young Readers*. In this book young children will enjoy the riddle about the grasshopper, "One Guess," and the amusing "Fireflies in the Garden." Children can understand "Blue-Butterfly Day" with that wonderful line, "But these are flowers that fly and all but sing"; and of course they chuckle over "Last Word of a Bluebird." If the nines are given help with the unusual word "rue," they like "Dust of Snow," just as an episode. But they, too, can think of days that have gone wrong and suddenly are right when something pleasant unexpectedly happens. Here is a poem that will be as perfect at eighty-nine as at nine, which is one test of a good poem.

For the nines and tens and older, almost any poem in this selection will carry meaning, more meaning perhaps for the rural than for the urban child. The latter probably has never "out-walked the furthest city light," nor watched "A Hillside Thaw," nor tried

10. Lawrence Thompson, "A Native to the Grain of the American Idiom," *Saturday Review*, March 21, 1959, p. 55.

11. Quoted from President Kennedy's "Comments" on "Accent," February 24, 1961, in *Saturday Review*, Feburary 23, 1963, p. 18.

12. "Robert Frost: American Bard," *Saturday Review*, March 24, 1962, p. 15.

13. "Into My Own." From *The Poetry of Robert Frost* edited by Edward Connery Lathem. Copyright 1916, 1923, 1928, 1934, © 1969 by Holt, Rinehart and Winston, Inc. Copyright 1936, 1942, 1944, 1951, © 1956, 1962 by Robert Frost. Copyright © 1964, 1970 by Lesley Frost Ballantine. Reprinted by permission of Holt, Rinehart and Winston, Inc. and Jonathan Cape Ltd. for the Estate of Robert Frost.

## VIEWPOINTS

If I maintain that no poet in America has ever so effectively combined play and profundity [as Robert Frost], it is only because it has usually been the critic's habit to appraise the latter and neglect the former. Frost has been praised for the unity of his thought, for the intellectual steadfastness which is not deceived by the schools and slogans of the moment. He has been applauded for the symmetry of his form and the shapeliness of his technique. He has been acclaimed as one who unearthed a new kind of poetry from old and stony soil, finding his material in what was "common in experience, uncommon in writing."

. . . His style, so characteristic, so seemingly simple and yet so elusive, so colloquial and yet so elevated, has a way of uniting opposites. It combines fantasy with matter-of-fact; or, rather, it is not so much a combination as an alternation, an intellectual legerdemain in which fact becomes fancy and the fancy is more compelling than the fact.—Louis Untermeyer, *Play in Poetry*, Harcourt, Brace and Co., New York, 1938, pp. 100–101, 102.

---

"Mending Wall." But fortunately, we can all learn by vicarious experiences, and in every poem, the pictures or episodes or ideas are sharply and clearly told with words that have a tonal beauty as captivating as music.

Robert Frost once said, "Every poem is a new metaphor inside or it is nothing"[14]—which implies that the surface meaning of a poem is only the beginning. Frost's poems grow in richness with thoughtful rereading. We may not wish to discuss the various levels of meaning in every poem, but it would be a pity to leave children with nothing more than the obvious scenes the verses report. "A Drumlin Woodchuck" is, for instance, the amusing soliloquy of a canny old denizen of a hilltop (drumlin) telling how he has managed to evade the hunters. Here is the last verse—

> *It will be because, though small*
> *As measured against the All,*
> *I have been so instinctively thorough*
> *About my crevice and burrow.*[15]

Here is obviously more than meets the eye. The poet himself referred to it as "my most Vermonty poem." And it is obviously rich, good-humored satire. It might be the poet speaking for himself or any other human being who is trying to maintain a little privacy, to protect his own right to be himself, to live his own life, to keep his own secrets, to protect his spirit from unwanted intrusions. Older boys and girls fighting for a place of their own can appreciate this. In a different vein, "The Death of a Hired Man" is a dramatic, poignant story none too tragic to confront the insensitivity that sometimes marks youth. Discuss with them how the husband must have felt at the close of that dialogue, after his harsh, unpitying words. "The Road Not Taken" has a different meaning for every human being. Even twelve-year-olds can sense the choices that lie ahead. "The Tuft of Flowers" is the delightful discovery of a kindred spirit, a heart-warming experience at any age, and fairly easy for children to parallel. "Two Tramps in Mud Time" is more difficult—must we *not* work at work we love, if someone else needs such work? That is a difficult social problem. What should the poet have done?

Poems such as these from this one small collection of Frost's poetry will help the children move gradually from the purely objective to deeper meanings. Slipped in among the lighter fare, these poems should be read and discussed, paralleled with personal experiences or the experiences of people we know or of people from history, and then they should be read still again for pure enjoyment and enriched meaning. Children should

14. Charles R. Anderson, "Robert Frost," *Saturday Review*, February 23, 1963, p. 20.

15. "A Drumlin Woodchuck." From *The Poetry of Robert Frost* edited by Edward Connery Lathem. Copyright 1916, 1923, 1928, 1934, © 1969 by Holt, Rinehart and Winston, Inc. Copyright 1936, 1942, 1944, 1951, © 1956, 1962 by Robert Frost. Copyright © 1964, 1970 by Lesley Frost Ballantine. Reprinted by permission of Holt, Rinehart and Winston, Inc. and Jonathan Cape Ltd. for the Estate of Robert Frost.

*Illustration by Thomas W. Nason from* You Come Too *by Robert Frost. Copyright, © 1959, by Holt, Rinehart and Winston, Inc. Reproduced by permission of Holt, Rinehart and Winston, Inc.*

encounter some of Robert Frost's poems so that they can live with the poetry over the years. The poems will grow in significance as the children grow in years and experience. (See also p. 293.)

## CARL SANDBURG, 1878–1967

*Early Moon*
*Wind Song*

Carl Sandburg was almost forty years old before he began to be recognized as a writer. He became the author of what is certainly one of the greatest biographies of Abraham Lincoln, *The Prairie Years* and *The War Years*, and he occupies a secure position in American letters.

When Sandburg was thirteen, his schooling was apparently over and he went to work. His occupations were numerous and carried him all through the Midwest and eventually to Puerto Rico. As porter, dishwasher, trucker, driver, scene-shifter, harvest hand, and soldier in the Spanish-American War, he learned to know working men and people of all kinds. He saw poverty and brutality, along with the nobility and vision that make life in the United States the curious composite that it is. After the Spanish-American War was over, he worked his way through college and went into newspaper work. He was with the Chicago *Daily News* for many years, and some of his poems first appeared in that paper. The publication of his *Chicago Poems* in 1915 created a sensation and brought down upon his head both hostility and enthusiasm. Critics seemed to feel either that poetry was going rapidly downhill or that there was another Walt Whitman, a prophet of a new day. His two books of poetry for children are *Early Moon* (1930) and *Wind Song* (1960), both included in *The Sandburg Treasury* along with *Rootabaga Stories*, *Prairie-Town Boy*, and *Abe Lincoln Grows Up*.

Sandburg's verse is free, the language sturdy and direct, the subjects often indicating his interest in all things American and his sympathy for its little people. Here is an example of his robust simplicity:

*Bubbles*[16]

*Two bubbles found they had rainbows on their curves.*
*They flickered out saying:*
*"It was worth being a bubble just to have held that rainbow thirty seconds."*

Older children can also appreciate the ironical "Southern Pacific." Its biting brevity is exceedingly effective. Easier for them to understand are "Summer Grass" (waiting for rain), "Again?" (about the Woolworth building), the poignant "Buffalo Dusk" (good for Western units), "People Who Must" (about a steeplejack), "Manual System" (about a switchboard operator), and the fine "To Beachey, 1912" (which might be about any aviator of any year).

Sandburg has given some good advice to the children themselves in "Primer Lesson."

16. "Bubbles" © 1960 by Carl Sandburg. Reprinted from his volume, *Wind Song*, by permission of Harcourt Brace Jovanovich, Inc.

## VIEWPOINTS

The Seeing eye—Mr. Sandburg has it to a superlative degree, and, wedded to it, an imaginative utterance which owes nothing whatever to literature or tradition. It is a fascinating and baffling study, this of examining how Mr. Sandburg does it. The technique of this magic is so unusual that no old knowledge applies. It is, more than anything else, the sharp, surprising rightness of his descriptions. . . .

Some people have had difficulty in understanding Mr. Sandburg's rhythms, these long, slow cadences, like the breath of air over an open moor. Indeed, they are the very gift of the prairies, for where else do we find them? Not in Whitman, . . . not among his contemporaries.—Amy Lowell, *Poetry and Poets*, Houghton Mifflin, Boston, 1930, pp. 157–158.

If you read this to children, let them talk it over. It is good advice for anyone.

*Primer Lesson*[17]

*Look out how you use proud words.*
*When you let proud words go, it is not easy to call them back.*
*They wear long boots, hard boots; they walk off proud; they can't hear you calling—*
*Look out how you use proud words.*

## VACHEL LINDSAY, 1879–1931

Vachel Lindsay was born in Springfield, Illinois, and spent his childhood there. One of Lindsay's heroes was Abraham Lincoln, and his "Abraham Lincoln Walks at Midnight" is one of his most famous poems. "The Congo," perhaps his best-known poem, is typical of the chanting style that distinguishes some of his work.

Lindsay's poetry is markedly rhythmic, and many of the poems he wrote for children are amusing nonsense. However, in *Springfield Town Is Butterfly Town*, published many years after his death, there are, in addition to humor and fantasy, some serious poems that he wrote for his own children.

He enchants small children with his nonsensical "The Potatoes' Dance." If they hear it twice, they begin to chant it with you, memorizing it in a jiffy. Lindsay himself called it a "poem game." Here are the first twenty-eight lines:

*The Potatoes' Dance*[18]

*"Down Cellar," said the cricket,*
*"Down cellar," said the cricket,*
*"Down cellar," said the cricket,*
*"I saw a ball last night,*
*In honor of a lady,*
*In honor of a lady,*
*In honor of a lady,*
*Whose wings were pearly white.*
*The breath of bitter weather,*
*The breath of bitter weather,*
*The breath of bitter weather,*
*Had smashed the cellar pane.*
*We entertained a drift of leaves,*
*We entertained a drift of leaves,*
*We entertained a drift of leaves,*
*And then of snow and rain.*
*But we were dressed for winter,*
*But we were dressed for winter,*
*But we were dressed for winter,*
*And loved to hear it blow*
*In honor of the lady,*
*In honor of the lady,*
*In honor of the lady,*
*Who makes potatoes grow,*
*Our guest the Irish lady,*
*The tiny Irish lady,*
*The airy Irish lady,*
*Who makes potatoes grow."*

Most of Vachel Lindsay's contribution belongs to youth and adults rather than to

17. From *Slabs of the Sunburnt West* by Carl Sandburg, copyright, 1922 by Harcourt Brace Jovanovich, Inc.; renewed, 1950, by Carl Sandburg. Reprinted by permission of the publishers.

18. "The Potatoes' Dance." Reprinted with permission of the Macmillan Company from *Collected Poems* by Vachel Lindsay. Copyright 1917 by The Macmillan Company, renewed 1945 by Elizabeth C. Lindsay.

children. "Daniel," "The Santa Fe Trail," "General William Booth Enters into Heaven," and "The Congo" should not be missed by older boys and girls. These poems use repetition to develop a great swinging rhythm that is almost hypnotic in its effect. The two poems enjoyed by young children, "The Potatoes' Dance" and "The Mysterious Cat," develop this same hypnotic rhythm. One little group of six-year-olds who loved "The Potatoes' Dance" used to step it, from one foot to the other, as they said it. This brought a group swing that added greatly to the effect of the lines. Step, step, step, step, they went until they reached the line,

*There was just one sweet potato.*

Then their stepping ceased and that sudden cessation of all movement marked with dramatic intensity the coming of the mock tragedy. This was an entirely spontaneous, almost reflex response of young children to Vachel Lindsay's swinging rhythm that seems to demand a bodily response.

## ELEANOR FARJEON, 1881–1965

*Eleanor Farjeon's Poems for Children*
*The Children's Bells*
*Kings and Queens*

Surely no child ever grew up in a more amusing household than little "Nellie" Farjeon enjoyed. For a picture of childhood in a family which was as brilliant as it was unusual, you should read her delightful *Portrait of a Family*.

Although the four Farjeon children grew up on friendly terms with many of London's distinguished people, none seemed as wonderful to them as their gentle mother and their gay, irrepressible father. The mother was the daughter of America's beloved actor, Joseph Jefferson of Rip Van Winkle fame. From the Jeffersons, Eleanor thinks, the four children inherited their love of music. Certainly pretty "Maggie" Jefferson gave them a good start, singing for them all the American songs with which she had grown up and which they soon learned to know and love as well as she did.

When Nellie was about ten years old, her father began the pleasant custom of presenting each child with a book after Sunday dinner. Nellie's first one was *In Memoriam*, and she remembers her father telling her about Tennyson and reading her parts of the poem. He read aloud much poetry, and of all the poets Shakespeare was their favorite.

When Eleanor Farjeon began to write, she always took her manuscripts to her father's study, pushed them under the door, and then ran away. "I had a stomach-ache till he came and told me if he liked it," she wrote. "He never kept me waiting. Even if he was writing his own stories, he stopped at once to look at my last poem, and came straight to the Nursery to talk it over with me. He taught me how to correct proofs and to be particular in the clearness of my 'copy' for the printers, long before I had any printers to consider." Once, when she was ill, Nellie wrote a twenty-thousand-word story, sent it down to her father, and then waited in bed fearful and anxious to learn his opinion. When he came, he exclaimed, "I have hopes of you, Nell! I have hopes of you!" and she knew complete satisfaction. The story might not win a prize but she was on her way. Her father thought she might be a writer!

After the death of her father, she spent one year in the United States with her grandfather, Joseph Jefferson. Her first book was published shortly after she returned to London. It was the amusing *Nursery Rhymes of London Town*, for which she wrote her own music. This was followed by the lively historical nonsense, *Kings and Queens*, by her brother and herself, and from then on she wrote prolifically, both prose and poetry.

*Kings and Queens*, written with her brother Herbert, was republished in 1953 and will delight children wrestling with the solemnity of English history. For instance,

"Henry VIII"[19] opens with:

*Bluff King Hal was full of beans;*
*He married half a dozen queens;*
*For three called Kate they cried the banns,*
*And one called Jane, and a couple of Annes.*

And it continues with blithe irreverence to account for the six ladies and their much-marrying spouse.

At their best, Eleanor Farjeon's poems for children, whether nonsense or serious lyrics, are skillfully written. Her rhythms are often as lively as a dance; her meters and rhyme schemes are varied and interesting; and her subject matter has exceptional range.

Unfortunately, the quality of her poems is uneven. She is not, for instance, so adroit at describing the modern child's everyday activities as A. A. Milne, although such poems as "Bedtime," "Breakfast," and "What I've Been Doing" are well liked by the children.

But the moment she turns imaginative, something wonderful happens. Take, for example, that curious and lovely night poem, whose very title arrests attention:

*The Night Will Never Stay*[20]

*The night will never stay,*
*The night will still go by,*
*Though with a million stars*
*You pin it to the sky.*
*Though you bind it with the blowing wind*
*And buckle it with the moon,*
*The night will slip away*
*Like sorrow or a tune.*

This poem might well give a child his first sense of time, rushing irresistibly along in a pattern of starry nights that will not stand still. Not that the child can so translate the poem, but he will say it and say it again, because both the ideas and the words are as haunting as a melody. In *The Children's Bells*, her "What Is Time?" supplements this poem in a gayer mood. Children like the sound of her companion poems, "Boys' Names" and "Girls' Names," and the surprise endings amuse them.

Of her fairy poems, "City Under Water" is perhaps the loveliest and the most usable for children. There are not many of these, but they are invariably good fairy lore and are well written.

Nature poems occur throughout the books. Of these, children like especially "The Kingfisher," "A Dragon-Fly," "Heigh-Ho, April," "Farewell to Summer," and the favorite, "Mrs. Peck-Pigeon."

One of Eleanor Farjeon's most valuable contributions is her Christmas poetry, which is unique in its variety and spirit. Sometimes the poems have the hushed reverential mood of a Christmas hymn; sometimes they are gay and rollicking. Often she uses contrast to point ever so gently the lesson of Christmas, as in "For Christmas Day." "The Shepherd and the King" is filled with tender joy, and young children will like the spirited "In the Week When Christmas Comes." There are no poems more true to the Christmas spirit, thoughtful, tender, imaginative. Her "Prayer for Little Things" is often used at Christmas but is actually timeless in its appeal. Even though Eleanor Farjeon had written nothing else, her Christmas poems would still give her a high place among the poets who have written poetry that children love.

Eleanor Farjeon was the first writer for children to receive the Hans Christian Andersen Award when it was established in 1956, and each year in her memory the Children's Book Circle in England presents the Eleanor Farjeon Award for "distinguished services to children's books."

19. "Henry VIII" by Herbert and Eleanor Farjeon from *Kings and Queens*. Reprinted by permission of Harold Ober Associates Incorporated. Copyright 1933, 1961 by Eleanor Farjeon.

20. "The Night Will Never Stay." From the section "Meeting Mary" in *Poems for Children* by Eleanor Farjeon. Copyright, 1951, by Eleanor Farjeon. Reprinted by permission of J. B. Lippincott Company and David Higham Associates, Ltd. for Michael Joseph Ltd.

## A. A. MILNE, 1882–1956

*When We Were Very Young*
*Now We Are Six*

A pleasant way to meet A. A. Milne is to read his *Autobiography*. This book contains more than the life of an author. It is a series of significant reminiscences of a man who not only enjoyed his own childhood but had a rare understanding of children. Milne tells us that his mother, usually so competent and practical in most matters, *would* dress the three brothers like Little Lord Fauntleroys and keep their blond curls long. He testifies that old ladies instinctively adored them, and boys yearned to kick them.

Milne's father, the head of the first school the boys attended, was evidently a born teacher. A walk with him meant learning about caterpillars or the law of gravity, or doing fascinating problems. Here, evidently, was no dull pedant, because grown-up Alan testifies that he learned what his father taught and failed to learn what others taught. He recalls his brothers' and his great delight in the books their father read aloud to them. They loved *Uncle Remus* when their father read it and could not abide the sound of it when the nurse took it over. They found *Pilgrim's Progress* a thriller even though they suspected it was meant to be uplifting. Anything they did with their father they enjoyed.

After Cambridge, where Milne disappointed his father by coming out only third in mathematics instead of first, the two of them faced the fact that writing was the one thing Alan wished to do. With £320 he went to London and began writing a thousand words a day, sending his finished pieces to various magazines. By the end of the second year he was supporting himself, and the third year he was appointed assistant editor of *Punch* with an assured income and the chance to increase it. He was just twenty-four years old.

Financially secure, he married and had just started writing plays when the First World War came. He wrote of the needless brutality of war with understandable bitterness, but he managed to keep on writing and actually produced three plays during his years in service.

After the war, a son was born to the Milnes—Christopher Robin. As soon as he could talk he gave himself the name of "Billy Moon," and "Moon" he was called by everyone. For this reason, Milne explains, the name "Christopher Robin" always seemed to belong entirely to the public's little boy, not to his own.

At the time Milne was writing plays and other adult literature, he gave his wife a verse about Christopher Robin—"Vespers"—which she sent off to a magazine and which was accepted for publication. Then Rose Fyleman, who was publishing a magazine for children, asked Milne to contribute some children's verses. At first he refused but changed his mind and sent them after all. When both the editor and the illustrator advised him to write a whole book of verses, he felt it was a foolish thing to do, but again he complied. He had, he said, as preparation for the task, three years of living with his son and "unforgettable memories of my own childhood." The result was *When We Were Very Young*, a major sensation in children's books both in England and America. It shares with the second book, *Now We Are Six*, an undiminishing popularity year after year. Milne's plays are amusing, but it is probable that Milne's reputation as a writer will rest more securely upon his two books of verse for children and his two books of stories about Pooh than upon any of his adult stories and dramas.

Milne had a remarkable ability of presenting small children as they are. He gives us their bemused absorption in their private inner world of make-believe, their blithe egotism, their liking for small animals, their toys and games, and the peculiar angle from which they view the odd behavior of those adults who move vaguely on the fringe of their private world.

Christopher Robin speaks for the make-believe of children around four to six years old. His imaginative world is not peopled with the fairies of the eight-year-old but is just the everyday sort of play of the nursery age. One chair is South America and another is a lion's cage. When walking with his nurse becomes just too dull to be endured, Christopher scares himself into a pleasant spinal chill by imagining that bears are skulking around the corner and are watching his approach with a sinister smacking of the lips. This is characteristic play for a solitary child. So, too, are his imaginary companions. There is Binker, visible only to Christopher Robin, and there is the omnipresent Pooh, who appears both in the poems and in the prose adventures.

Much has been written about the egocentricity of the young child's thought and language, but it has never been recorded more accurately than by A. A. Milne. Christopher Robin goes to the market looking for a rabbit and is naïvely astonished that the market men should be selling mackerel and fresh lavender when *he*, Christopher Robin, wants rabbits. He catalogues his articles of clothing, fascinating because they are his. You can hear the smug emphasis on the personal pronoun. Changing the guard at Buckingham may be very impressive, but the child's only concern is, "Do you think the King knows all about Me?" This is a typical four-year-old, thinking and speaking of everything in terms of himself—an amusing and endearing little egotist!

Knowing children's interests, Milne reflects them in his writing. There we find the child's love of small animals whose antics and vicissitudes enliven the verses. Toys are there, too—balls, tops, hoops, and the beloved teddy bear. The verses are full of the small child's activities, also. He walks, rolls, and plays. He stalks down the sidewalk missing all the lines. He sits on the stairs and meditates, or he goes hoppitty, hoppitty, hop. He sometimes refuses rice pudding (or rather Mary Jane does), and he often resents foolish adult questions. On the whole, he is a busy, active child, immersed in his own affairs and oblivious of any world beyond his own horizon.

Read Milne's two little books, *When We Were Very Young* and *Now We Are Six*, and you will discover an author who knew how to write verse that dances, skips, meditates, and changes to reflect changing moods. We can analyze his tripping trochees, his iambics and dactyls, but those academic labels do not seem to convey any idea of the fluid and flashing use Mr. Milne made of words, rhyme, and rhythm to convey character, mood, and action. For example, read "Buckingham Palace" aloud and hear the marching of soldiers in the background throughout those brief descriptions and the whispered conversations of Alice and Christopher. The feet thud, thud, thud through every line. So, too, when Christopher Robin hops through the jingle called "Hoppity," the lines go in exactly the pattern of a child's hop, ending with a big one and a rest, just as hopping always does. But best of all is that juvenile meditation "Halfway Down." Ernest Shepard's sketch, too, has caught the mood of suspended action that is always overtaking small children on stairs. Why they like to clutter up stairs with their belongings and their persons Milne knew, and he has told us with arresting monosyllables that block the way as effectually as Christopher Robin's small person blocks the stairs. In this first stanza from "Halfway Down"[21] notice "It" and "Stop," which sit as firmly in the middle of the verse as Christopher on the stair.

*Halfway down the stairs*
*Is a stair*
*Where I sit.*

21. "Halfway Down." From the book *When We Were Very Young* by A. A. Milne. Decorations by E. H. Shepard. Copyright 1924 by E. P. Dutton & Co., Inc. Renewal, 1952, by A. A. Milne. Published by E. P. Dutton & Co., Inc. Reprinted by permission of The Canadian Publishers, McClelland and Stewart Limited, Tononto, E. P. Dutton & Co., Inc., and Methuen & Co. Ltd.

*There isn't any*
*Other stair*
*Quite like*
*It.*
*I'm not at the bottom,*
*I'm not at the top;*
*So this is the stair*
*Where*
*I always*
*Stop.*

Over and over again, Mr. Milne makes a monosyllable or a single word equal by sheer intensity three or four words in a preceding line. It is a device that compels correct reading of the lines, regardless of scansion.

With all of these virtues, it is not surprising that some moderns have come to feel that Milne is the child's greatest poet, certainly his favorite poet. However, delightful as Milne's verses are, they do not cover the full range either of the child's interests or of his capacity for enjoying poetry. Many poets achieve greater lyric beauty, more delicate imagery, and deeper feeling for the child's inner world, but certainly we shall never encounter a writer who understood more completely the curious composite of gravity and gaiety, of supreme egotism and occasional whimsy that is the young child.

We cannot leave Milne's books without considering the illustrations. Never was an author more happily paired with an artist than A. A. Milne with Ernest Shepard. The tiny pen-and-ink sketches capture the mood of every poem. You have only to glance at one of these tiny figures to know exactly what is happening inwardly as well as outwardly. In "Halfway Down," the small figure is planted in a dreamy, meditative but solid pose that makes you feel just how hard it's going to be to dislodge him. Pooh is there,

## VIEWPOINTS

. . . I know that a great many children did, and do, like *When We Were Very Young*. I think that such merit as attaches to the verses for this (as distinct from the illustrations to which the book is so obviously indebted) was won by taking pains: more pains, perhaps, than is usual. Whatever else they lack, the verses are technically good. The practice of no form of writing demands such a height of technical perfection as the writing of light verse in the Calverley and *Punch* tradition. *When We Were Very Young* is not the work of a poet becoming playful, nor of a lover of children expressing his love, nor of a prose-writer knocking together a few jingles for the little ones; it is the work of a light-verse writer taking his job seriously even though he is taking it into the nursery. It seems that the nursery, more than any other room in the house, likes to be approached seriously.—A. A. Milne, *Autobiography*, E. P. Dutton and Co., New York, 1939, p. 282.

*Illustration by E. H. Shepard. From the book* When We Were Very Young *by A. A. Milne. Copyright, 1924, by E. P. Dutton & Co., Inc. Renewal, 1952, by A. A. Milne. Reproduced by permission of the publishers.*

too, the same solid, jaunty teddy bear we shall meet later on in the Pooh stories. The interpretative quality of these pictures makes them illustrations in the best sense of the word.

## SARA TEASDALE, 1884–1933

*Stars To-night*

If children can suddenly catch the charm of even one or two of Sara Teasdale's lyrics, they will have a surer sense of poetry and the stirring of the spirit that it can bring.

Sara Teasdale was born in St. Louis of wealthy parents. She was a delicate child who went to school irregularly, read and traveled widely, and after her marriage lived in New York. The summer before she died she was in London in search of material for a biography of Christina Rossetti. She wrote much about love, the stars, the night, and the sea. In her last book with its enigmatic title, *Strange Victory*, the concluding poem, "There Will Be Rest,"[22] ends with these lines:

*I shall find the crystal of peace, — above me*
*Stars I shall find.*

Those stars shine all through her poetry, and to the selection from her poems made for boys and girls she gave the title *Stars To-night.* When Macmillan added to this unusual collection the illustrations of Dorothy Lathrop, the result was a book of rare beauty. These pen-and-ink drawings have a frosty, sparkling quality that is as delicate and sensitive as the poems themselves.

The first poem in the book is one of the favorites and is characteristic of Teasdale's highly individual style and mood:

*Night*[23]

*Stars over snow,*
*And in the west a planet*
*Swinging below a star—*
*Look for a lovely thing and you will find it,*
*It is not far—*
*It never will be far.*

For the second poem, "Stars," Lathrop has captured the enchantment of the experience with a picture of a child alone, looking up at the night sky and awed by the great procession of stars marching up the dome of heaven, "stately and still." You can almost imagine the child whispering to herself the concluding lines of "Stars":

*Up the dome of heaven*
*Like a great hill,*
*I watch them marching*
*Stately and still,*
*And I know that I*
*Am honored to be*
*Witness*
*Of so much majesty.*[24]

In the winter when the zenith is ablaze with stars, older children should have these poems. But even a five-year-old child can enjoy

*The Falling Star*[25]

*I saw a star slide down the sky,*
*Blinding the north as it went by,*
*Too burning and too quick to hold,*
*Too lovely to be bought or sold,*
*Good only to make wishes on*
*And then forever to be gone.*

22. "There Will Be Rest" from *Collected Poems* by Sara Teasdale. Reprinted by permission of the Macmillan Company.

23. "Night." Reprinted with permission of The Macmillan Company from *Collected Poems* by Sara Teasdale. Copyright 1930 by Sara Teasdale Filsinger, renewed 1958 by Guaranty Trust Company of New York, Executor.

24. "Stars." Reprinted with permission of The Macmillan Company from *Collected Poems* by Sara Teasdale. Copyright 1920 by The Macmillan Company, renewed 1948 by Mamie T. Wheless.

25. "The Falling Star." Reprinted with permission of The Macmillan Company from *Collected Poems* by Sara Teasdale. Copyright 1930 by Sara Teasdale Filsinger, renewed 1958 by Guaranty Trust Company of New York, Executor.

No child should miss this book. Don't force the poems. Read the easier ones first—those already mentioned, along with "Winter Noon," "February Twilight," and "Redbirds." You will probably not use all these at once but will read just one poem several times and then leave the book around where the children can look at it. Poring over the pictures helps establish the mood of the poems, and presently some child may bring you the book and say, "Read this one." So the range of appreciation will grow. If the children appropriate only one of these poems but really enjoy it and make it their own, then you have given them a treasure.

*Illustration by Dorothy P. Lathrop for* Stars To-night *by Sara Teasdale. Copyright 1930 by Sara Teasdale Filsinger. Reprinted by permission of the publishers, The Macmillan Company.*

## ELIZABETH MADOX ROBERTS, 1886–1941

### *Under the Tree*

Elizabeth Madox Roberts was born and grew up in Perryville, Kentucky, where her forebears had settled in Daniel Boone's time. From her novels we know that she must have been steeped from childhood in the balladry, the folklore, and the history of her state. From her poems we guess she must have had an unusually happy childhood with the other children in her family—enjoying the normal village experiences of picnics, church, lessons, and the glorious treat of the circus.

From 1917 to 1921, she attended the University of Chicago and graduated not only Phi Beta Kappa but with the McLaughlin prize for essay and the Fisk prize for poetry. The poetry was later published in the book called *Under the Tree*, about which Louis Untermeyer has remarked, "few American lyricists have made so successful a debut." After her graduation from the university, she lived in New York for a while and began writing her novels. Later she retired to her own Kentucky and continued her work there. She won several poetry prizes while writing her novels, but she is best known as the author of *The Time of Man, Jingling in the Wind, The Great Meadow*, and other stories of Kentucky. A year before her death, a second volume of poems, *Song in the Meadow*, appeared.

One reviewer, J. Donald Adams, has said of Elizabeth Madox Roberts: "Everything she writes bears the unmistakable mark of her highly individual gifts; nothing she has ever done could possibly be mistaken for the work of another writer."

This is particularly true of her one book of poems for children, which is unlike any other juvenile poetry. It has a deceptive air of simplicity that gives the unwary reader no immediate clues to the artistry which makes these poems emotionally satisfying and full of everyday enchantment. "The Worm" will serve as an example:

*Dickie found a broken spade*
*And said he'd dig himself a well;*
*And then Charles took a piece of tin,*
*And I was digging with a shell.*

*Then Will said he would dig one too.*
*We shaped them out and made them wide,*
*And I dug up a piece of clod*
*That had a little worm inside.*

*We watched him pucker up himself*
*And stretch himself to walk away.*
*He tried to go inside the dirt,*
*But Dickie made him wait and stay.*

*His shining skin was soft and wet.*
*I poked him once to see him squirm.*
*And then Will said, "I wonder if*
*He knows that he's a worm."*

*And then we sat back on our feet*
*And wondered for a little bit.*
*And we forgot to dig our wells*
*A while, and tried to answer it.*

*And while we tried to find it out,*
*He puckered in a little wad,*
*And then he stretched himself again*
*And went back home inside the clod.*[26]

The children are digging; but, notice that they are digging with a broken spade a piece of tin, and a shell—tools accepted as a matter of course by the child. Then the worm distracts them from their original plan of digging a well, and they experiment with it for a while until a strange idea makes them forget their experiments. They sit back and wonder if "he knows that he's a worm"—an idea that only a child could think of.

The Roberts child ruminates about things, wonders, and has several scares, but she is never fairy-conscious or full of those delicate whimsies so frequently found in British juveniles. This child has a wholesome earthiness and a healthy identification with and delight in nature. She enjoys milking time; she makes herself a little house under "The Butterbean Tent." She has all the fun of wading in "The Branch." She listens to the "Water Noises" that seem to say, "And do you think? And do you think?" She grows suddenly joyous over the "Crescent Moon," and the verse skips as ecstatically as the children:

Crescent Moon[26]

*And Dick said, "Look what I have found!"*
*And when we saw we danced around,*
*And made our feet just tip the ground.*

*We skipped our toes and sang, "Oh-lo.*
*Oh-who, oh-who, oh what do you know!*
*Oh-who, oh-hi, oh-loo, kee-lo!"*

*We clapped our hands and sang, "Oh-ee!"*
*It made us jump and laugh to see*
*The little new moon above the tree.*

She shares her shelter from a "Little Rain" with a shivery chicken and a ladybug. She is haunted by stars, amazed at the miracle of a "Firefly." And she is struck by the odd three-layer cake arrangement of the universe:

The People[26]

*The ants are walking under the ground,*
*And the pigeons are flying over the steeple,*
*And in between are the people.*

A very tidy arrangement when you come to think of it!

Then there is talk, back and forth, between the child and her world. She listens to the hens going to roost and speaking their "little asking words." Twice a bush speaks to her, quite naturally, just a passing word. Around sleep time there is a gay little brown jug that talks, and in broad daylight an old horse, in the poem called "Horse," gives her a piece of his mind and sends her on her way:

*He didn't talk out with his mouth;*
*He didn't talk with words or noise.*
*The talk was there along his nose;*
*It seemed and then it was.*

*He said the day was hot and slow,*
*And he said he didn't like the flies;*

26. "The Worm," "Crescent Moon," "The People," "Horse," and "Mr. Wells." From *Under the Tree* by Elizabeth Madox Roberts. Copyright 1922 by B. W. Huebsch, Inc., renewed 1950 by Ivor S. Roberts. Reprinted by permission of The Viking Press, Inc.

*They made him have to shake his skin,*
*And they got drowned in his eyes. . . .*

*And then he shut his eyes again.*
*As still as they had been before.*
*He said for me to run along*
*And not to bother him any more.*[26]

So children interpret dog or cat talk in their earnest and commendable efforts to reach the animal's point of view. This poem is horse-talk indeed, and you can fairly hear the snort with which horse asserts "'I'm horse,' he said, 'that's what!'"

The poems are full of pleasant people and reflect the child's interest not only in other children, but in the grownups at home and abroad. Father fills the little girl's mug at milking time and sings or tells stories to all the children. Mother sends them on picnics and corrects their manners. There are brothers: Clarence, Charles, and the twins, Will and Dick. In "Christmas Morning" the child recalls the details of the Nativity in terms of her own mother and baby John—as naïve and lovely an interpretation as you can find! The townspeople vary from pretty "Miss Kate-Marie," the Sunday school teacher, to Mr. Pennybaker, who makes faces when he sings bass, and the notable Mr. Wells:

Mr. Wells[26]

*On Sunday morning, then he comes*
*To church, and everybody smells*
*The blacking and the toilet soap*
*And camphor balls from Mr. Wells.*

*He wears his whiskers in a bunch,*
*And wears his glasses on his head.*
*I mustn't call him Old Man Wells—*
*No matter—that's what Father said.*

*And when the little blacking smells*
*And camphor balls and soap begin,*
*I do not have to look to know*
*That Mr. Wells is coming in.*

The intense curious interest that children feel toward the strange antics of grownups is reflected in poem after poem and is summarized in the amusing "People Going By."

Reading these poems, you realize their integrity. No word, no line is dressed up or prettified to sound "cute." Cuteness afflicts some modern verse for children and is indeed the curse of juvenile poetry. Here in these poems by Elizabeth Madox Roberts is complete fidelity to child nature. They are grave, simple, and full of the unconscious beauty of a child's narrative when he is moved to tell you earnestly of something he enjoys. You can live with these poems, use them year after year, and never exhaust their richness. No adult can read them without knowing much more about children when he finishes, and no child can hear them without feeling a kinship with that child who likes to play with wiggletails, smell the aromatic herbs of fennel, and eat cherry pie, but who occasionally suffers from fears no less intense from being imaginary.

## ELIZABETH COATSWORTH, 1893–

*Summer Green*
*Poems*
*The Sparrow Bush*
*Down Half the World*

Elizabeth Coatsworth went to a private school as a child and comments that its "English system" resulted in severe, scholarly discipline. After graduation from Vassar, she took her M.A. at Columbia University. Meanwhile she had traveled in this country, in Mexico, Europe, and Egypt, and, after her graduate degree, spent a year in the Orient.

Coatsworth's *The Cat Who Went to Heaven* won the Newbery Medal for 1930 but is not as popular with children as her historical tales such as *Away Goes Sally, Five Bushel Farm*, and *The Fair American*. Within the pages of these books are some of her best poems, and her poetry is collected in

*Summer Green, Poems, The Sparrow Bush,* and *Down Half the World.*

A certain style in her poetry is well illustrated by the frequently quoted "Swift things are beautiful," from *Away Goes Sally:*

*Swift things are beautiful:*
*Swallows and deer,*
*And lightning that falls*
*Bright-veined and clear,*
*River and meteors,*
*Wind in the wheat,*
*The strong-withered horse,*
*The runner's sure feet.*

*And slow things are beautiful:*
*The closing of day,*
*The pause of the wave*
*That curves downward to spray,*
*The ember that crumbles,*
*The opening flower,*
*And the ox that moves on*
*In the quiet of power.*[27]

Here are the comparisons that the author uses, not incidentally but as the theme of the entire poem. You can find other examples of contrasts in all three books. From *Five Bushel Farm* there is another one on swiftness, but treated differently—"Swift comes the summer." In *The Fair American* there is a comparison of sorrow, danger, and courage, long ago and today, in the poem beginning "So long ago," and in a still more striking poem there is a comparison of a clipper ship with flame, bird, deer, and horse. Building a poem around a series of comparisons seems then to be a favorite pattern for Elizabeth Coatsworth. It is an exceedingly provocative one for children to study and to try for themselves.

Another aspect of her style is the smooth, flowing lines that fall so gently on the ear. Poem after poem has this quietness. The lyric text of *Under the Green Willow*, a picture book, has a subdued, rhythmic quality. From *Away Goes Sally* read "Hard from the southeast blows the wind," with its description of a gathering storm without and the cozy comfort of an open fire within. Note these lines, for example:

*And the cat comes to bask herself*
*In the soft heat,*
*And Madame Peace draws up her chair*
*To warm her feet.*[27]

With those concluding lines, you can fairly feel yourself relaxing and stretching a bit. "No leaf is left," "How gray the rain," and "In the forest it is cool" are only a few examples of that quietness with which the poems abound. Although the lines can frolic now and then, slow-moving calmness predominates. For this reason, reading many of the poems at a time is monotonous.

Both in her prose and in her poetry, Elizabeth Coatsworth makes an effective use of words, often rich with associative meaning, such as "Madame Peace" drawing up her chair to the fire to "warm her feet"—not extraordinary words but laden with associations of peace, warmth, and comfort. On the whole these poems are not markedly musical, but they are rich in sensory words; for instance: fallen apples that "smell cidery on the air," sleigh bells that ring "icily sweet," children with their "mouths stained with berry juice," "bright-veined lightning," and little buds "no larger than a mouse's ear." You can find examples of her use of words which make you see, smell, taste, touch, and hear.

The single lines and phrases already quoted reveal her sensitive response to nature. Her nature poems seem to fall into two classes. Some are straight nature descriptions, and others are brief, lovely descriptions which lead toward, or climax in, a human mood or situation. One of the finest examples of the second type, "How gray the rain," from *Five Bushel Farm*, ends with

27. "Swift things are beautiful" and "Hard from the southeast blows the wind." Reprinted with permission of The Macmillan Company and Blackie & Son Limited from *Away Goes Sally* by Elizabeth Coatsworth. Copyright 1934 by The Macmillan Company, renewed 1962 by Elizabeth Coatsworth Beston.

*Serene and bright*
*The rainbow stands*
*That was not anywhere before,*
*And so may joy*
*Fill empty hands*
*When someone enters through a door.*[28]

These poems linking together nature and human concerns are notable but they may prove a bit subtle for children and may require discussion before the literal minded children catch their implications. But the nature descriptions are understandable to all children. For those who know salt marshes, the first poem in *Away Goes Sally*, "This is the hay that no man planted," is particularly good.

The following verse from *The Fair American* is typical of a small group of the poems that present an occasional bit of homely wisdom:

*He who has never known hunger*
*Has never known how good*
*The taste of bread may be,*
*The kindliness of food.*[29]

Such verses lack the epigrammatic and sparkling quality of similar poems by Christina Rossetti but have instead a straightforward simplicity. In this same book there is the philosophic

*To have nothing at all*
*Is to have much still.*[29]

and the interesting application to human life of the plant:

*The plant cut down to the root*
*Does not hate.*
*It uses all its strength*
*To grow once more.*

*Turn, boy, to the unknown field*
*Beyond the gate.*
*Never look back again*
*To the bolted door.*[29]

There are examples of everyday wisdom in her other books, but these suffice to illustrate this type of poem and the style in which it is written.

Small animals appear throughout the poems, but cats are favorites. There are a number of poems about them, usually in a humorous mood. The liveliest of these from *Away Goes Sally* begins, " 'Who are you?' asked the cat of the bear," and contains a dialogue that is thoroughly amusing. Certainly one of the loveliest poems about animals, also from *Away Goes Sally*, is "The Rabbit's Song Outside the Tavern." All the gay wildness of small beasts on a moonlit night is in these lines.

The poetry of Elizabeth Coatsworth is more ideational than most juvenile verse. It belongs chiefly to older children and will stretch their minds and imaginations.

## RACHEL FIELD, 1894–1942

*Taxis and Toadstools*
*Poems*

Rachel Field must have been a delightful human being, judging from the amusing account of her early years she wrote for *The Junior Book of Authors*, and from the varied tributes paid her in the Memorial edition of the *Horn Book* (July-August 1942). These give you the impression of a warm, vivid personality, full of exuberance, loving people and the outdoor world. She worked at top speed, as if from some inner compulsion, and gave to her books the vigor and integrity that were hers.

She was born in the lovely old town of

28. "How gray the rain." Reprinted with permission of The Macmillan Company and Blackie & Son Limited from *Five Bushel Farm* by Elizabeth Coatsworth. Copyright 1939 by The Macmillan Company, renewed 1967 by Elizabeth Coatsworth Beston.

29. "He who has never known hunger," "To have nothing at all," and "The plant cut down to the root." Reprinted with permission of The Macmillan Company and Blackie & Son Limited from *The Fair American* by Elizabeth Coatsworth. Copyright 1940 by The Macmillan Company, renewed 1968 by Elizabeth Coatsworth Beston.

Stockbridge, Massachusetts. There she started school and, she confides, did so poorly that she dreaded the days when report cards were due. She began to write poetry at an early age, but mathematics was forever a mystery and a terror. In high school in Springfield, Massachusetts, she won an essay prize and determined to go to college if she could avoid mathematics. Radcliffe accepted her as a special student, and throughout four happy years she took all the English she could get, both literature and composition.

After Radcliffe, she settled in New York to begin the serious business of writing. Her *Six Plays* were published in 1924, and that same year the Yale University Press published her poems for children, *The Pointed People*. These attracted favorable attention even though they appeared at the same time that A. A. Milne's *When We Were Very Young* was creating a sensation. She illustrated her book with her own cutout silhouettes, and in 1926 did the decorations for her second book of poems, *Taxis and Toadstools*. This clever title signified her own way of life: eight months in New York City, with taxis, street-vendors, and skyscrapers; four months on an island off the coast of Maine with fogs, wood-strawberries, and toadstools.

From 1924 to 1942, in a period of only eighteen years, she published some thirty-six books, many of which she herself illustrated. Among her best-known books for children are *Calico Bush*, a historical novel; and the 1930 Newbery Medal book, *Hitty*, the story of a hundred-year-old doll.

The last six years of her sunny life must have been among the happiest. After her marriage she went to California with her husband and there she wrote the adult novel *All This, and Heaven Too*, which was made into a successful motion picture. In California, when their daughter Hannah was only two-and-a-half years old, Rachel Field died. In the closing paragraph of her last novel, *And Now Tomorrow*, she writes, "Once I might have faltered before such a transplanting. But that was yesterday. Now I am ready for tomorrow."

An inland child once said with awe that she was going to spend the summer on an island. "A real island with the sea all around; just think, with the sea on every side of us!" she breathed, recalling:

> *If once you have slept on an island*
> *You'll never be quite the same.*

How could Rachel Field know so unerringly the child's sense of the miracle of islands? Over and over, she catches the curious wonderment of children. She shows a child turning back to look at the china dog with the "sad unblinking eye" and wishing for magic words to bring him to life; or feeling "strange and shivery" when a parrot looks at him with his "beadbright eyes"; or wondering if skyscrapers ever want to lie down and never get up! These are authentic child-thoughts, and the children respond to their integrity with spontaneous pleasure.

Out-of-doors, the children of her poems voice that curious kinship with birds, beasts, and growing things that is part of the magic of childhood. Some people, like Rachel Field herself, keep this all their lives. In "Barefoot Days" the child is "glad in every toe," and the first verse is alive with the feeling of cool grass and curly fern under small, naked feet. Children go to the woods for wild strawberries and forget that there is anything else in the world to do but "fill my hands and eat." They understand the wild creatures, and when they see "The Dancing Bear," they know at once something is wrong, for his eyes look bewildered "like a child's lost in the woods at night."

Field's unique contribution to children's verse is perhaps the three groups of city poems in *Taxis and Toadstools*, called "People," "Taxis and Thoroughfares," and "Stores and Storekeepers." A ten-year-old boy of the city streets used to recite Rachel Field's "Taxis" with a shine in his eyes and a gusto that seemed to say, "Now listen to this. Here's something!"

*Taxis*[30]

*Ho, for taxis green or blue,*
*Hi, for taxis red,*
*They roll along the Avenue*
*Like spools of colored thread!*

*Jack-o'-Lantern yellow,*
*Orange as the moon,*
*Greener than the greenest grass*
*Ever grew in June.*
*Gayly striped or checked in squares,*
*Wheels that twinkle bright,*
*Don't you think that taxis make*
*A very pleasant sight?*
*Taxis shiny in the rain,*
*Scudding through the snow,*
*Taxis flashing back the sun*
*Waiting in a row.*

*Ho, for taxis red and green,*
*Hi, for taxis blue,*
*I wouldn't be a private car*
*In sober black, would you?*

In the collection of her verses called *Poems*, "Song for a Blue Roadster" is equally popular. Children like "Good Green Bus," "At the Theater," "The Florist Shop," "The Animal Store," and the favorite "Skyscrapers."

One of the pleasantest poems in this group is "City Rain." The first verse is so clear a picture that children often want to illustrate it. The cozy feeling in the second verse is heightened by the rainy sound of that next-to-the-last line, with its humming *n*'s or *ing*'s:

*City Rain*[30]

*Rain in the city!*
*I love to see it fall*
*Slantwise where the buildings crowd*
*Red brick and all.*
*Streets of shiny wetness*
*Where the taxis go,*
*With people and umbrellas all*
*Bobbing to and fro.*

*Rain in the city!*
*I love to hear it drip*
*When I am cosy in my room*
*Snug as any ship,*
*With toys spread on the table,*
*With a picture book or two,*
*And the rain like a rumbling tune that sings*
*Through everything I do.*

The child who speaks in the first person throughout these poems likes people and watches them with friendly keenness. Interest in people is characteristic of children, and it is recorded in these poems with sensitive perception. When the child sees "Sandwich Men," there is a recognition of something wrong. The men are "dreary round the eye" with something about them that makes her "want to cry." And this is not an unchildlike observation. Children study lame people or anyone who deviates from the normal with a passionate intentness that seems bent upon finding out why, at all costs.

Rachel Field's poetry never attains the power and sureness of her best prose, but the complete absence of artificiality or juvenile cuteness in these poems commends them to both children and adults.

## DAVID McCORD, 1897–

*Far and Few*
*Take Sky*
*All Day Long*
*Every Time I Climb a Tree*
*For Me to Say*

Speaking at a conference on children's literature, David McCord gave as one of his rules for writing for children:

*First, just be a child before you grow up and let nothing interfere with the process. Write it all out of yourself and for yourself. . . . Next, never take the phrase "writing verse for children" seriously. If you write for them you are lost. Ask your*

30. "Taxis" and "City Rain" copyright 1926 by Doubleday & Company, Inc. from the book *Taxis and Toadstools* by Rachel Field. Reprinted by permission of Doubleday & Company, Inc. and World's Work Ltd.

*brain's computer what you know about a child's mind. The answer is zero.*[31]

McCord first began writing verse at fifteen, encouraged, he believes, by two solitary years on an Oregon ranch. After his college years at Harvard, his verses appeared frequently in newspaper columns and magazines. One of his books won the William Rose Benét Award of the Poetry Society of America. *Far and Few*, his first book for children, is his fifteenth book of verse, a choice collection of poems. They range from pure nonsense to quiet little meditations that reflect, perhaps, those solitary years out of doors.

*Far and Few* opens with a poem about "Joe," the greedy squirrel who keeps the birds waiting. It closes with "Fred," an intrepid flying squirrel, the original glider. Children and adults who provide feeding tables will recognize both these characters. Here is

*Joe*[32]

*We feed the birds in winter,*
*And outside in the snow*
*We have a tray of many seeds*
*For many birds of many breeds*
*And one gray squirrel named Joe.*
*But Joe comes early,*
*Joe comes late,*
*And all the birds*
*Must stand and wait.*
*And waiting there for Joe to go*
*Is pretty cold work in the snow.*

Other small beasts are presented—bats, grasshoppers, a snail, starfish, and an especially convincing crowd of crows "spilling from a tree." For sheer nonsense "Five Chants," "In the Middle," "Who Wants a Birthday?" and "Isabel Jones & Curabel Lee" are fun. Children under six like to roll the onomatopoetic refrains of "Song of the Train" and "The Pickety Fence" on their tongues. But it takes a perceptive older child to appreciate "The White Ships," "The Shell," "The Starfish," "Tiggady Rue," and "The Star in the Pail."

*Take Sky*, McCord's second book of verse for children, is on the whole more completely humorous than *Far and Few*, although it begins seriously with

*Take Sky*[33]

*Now think of words. Take sky*
*And ask yourself just why—*
*Like sun, moon, star, and cloud—*
*It sounds so well out loud,*
*And pleases so the sight*
*When printed black on white.*

For fifty-six lines the poet plays with the sounds and meanings—denotations and connotations—of words. His "Write Me a Verse" should appeal to youngsters wrestling with verse forms. In these poems couplets, quatrains, limericks, and triolets are amusingly defined and illustrated. However, there is also much entertainment in this book for the youngest children. In "Sing Song," "Three Signs of Spring," "Sally Lun Lundy," and many other verses, Mr. McCord has a wonderful time playing with the sounds of words. He also makes many clever uses of dialogue. The series on "Food and Drink" opens with

*Cup*[33]

*"Cup, what's up?*
*Why, it's cocoa scum!*
*And who likes that?"*
*"Some."*

31. From David McCord's "Poetry for Children," in *A Critical Approach to Children's Literature*, ed. by Sara Innis Fenwick. University of Chicago Press, 1967, p. 53.

32. "Joe" by David McCord from *Far and Few*. Copyright 1952 by David McCord. Reprinted by permission of Little, Brown and Co. and Curtis Brown, Ltd.

33. "Take Sky" and "Cup." From *Take Sky* by David McCord. Copyright 1961, 1962 by David McCord. Reprinted by permission of Little, Brown and Co. and Curtis Brown, Ltd.

The funniest of this series is the tongue twister, "Jug and Mug."

*Illustration by Henry B. Kane. From* Take Sky *by David McCord. Copyright © 1961, 1962, by David McCord. Reprinted by permission of Little, Brown and Company.*

## HARRY BEHN, 1898–

*The Golden Hive*
*The Little Hill*
*Windy Morning*
*The Wizard in the Well*

Harry Behn was born in Arizona, then still a territory, and was educated at Harvard and abroad. He has written both prose and poetry for children, and has translated Japanese haiku with precise and delicate sensitivity in *Cricket Songs* and *More Cricket Songs*, both of which are illustrated by reproductions of the paintings of Japanese artists.

In his book on poetry, *Chrysalis*, Behn points out that children see a world in every least little thing, and his poems explore with an ever-fresh awareness the child's delight in little things about them. *The Golden Hive* is for older readers and includes some fine lyric poems, of which "The Painted Desert" and "Summer" are particularly evocative. His other small books of verse, decorated by the author, speak to young children, five to nine, with lyric charm and unusual variety. There are a few nonsense jingles like "Mr. Pyme," "Dr. Windikin," "Shopping Spree," and the lively "Tea Party."

Of the comparatively few fairy poems, particularly pleasing are the imaginative "The Merry-Go-On," "The Fairy and the Bird," the philosophical "The Wizard in the Well," and the gentle, wistful "Undine's Garden." In quite a different mood of conscious make-believe is the amusing

*The Gnome*[34]

*I saw a gnome*
*As plain as plain*
*Sitting on top*
*Of a weathervane.*

*He was dressed like a crow*
*In silky black feathers,*
*And there he sat watching*
*All kinds of weathers.*

*He talked like a crow too,*
*Caw caw caw,*
*When he told me exactly*
*What he saw,*

*Snow to the north of him*
*Sun to the south,*

34. "The Gnome." From *Windy Morning*, copyright 1953 by Harry Behn. Reprinted by permission of Harcourt Brace Jovanovich, Inc.

*And he spoke with a beaky*
*Kind of a mouth.*

*But he wasn't a crow,*
*That was plain as plain*
*'Cause crows never sit*
*On a weathervane.*

*What I saw was simply*
*A usual gnome*
*Looking things over*
*On his way home.*

There are many verses about the child's play world, both real and imaginative. "The New Little Boy" is refreshingly antisocial. "Picnic by the Sea" is a child's view of the queer grownups who sit sunning themselves when there are so many wonders to be explored. "Hallowe'en" is a particularly shivery celebration of that favorite festival and is delightful for verse choirs to speak.

Mr. Behn's unique contribution is found in those poems where he is helping the child to look at his everyday experiences with the eyes of the spirit. Notice the philosophy in

Others[35]

*Even though it's raining*
*I don't wish it wouldn't.*
*That would be like saying*
*I think it shouldn't.*
*I'd rather be out playing*
*Than sitting hours and hours*
*Watching rain falling*
*In drips and drops and showers,*
*But what about the robins?*
*What about the flowers?*

Read aloud "Early Awake," "Trees," "Spring," "Spring Rain," "The Little Hill," "Lesson," and you will feel the reassurance, the acceptance, and the happy peace that emanate from these and many other poems. "This Happy Day" begins with a child's cheerful greeting to the sun on a bright new day and concludes with a note of thanksgiving. Without any religious pronouncements, these are religious poems in which the poet helps children to appreciate their everyday experiences, the sheer magic of being alive. One of the finest of these is "Gardens." The young child may not understand its full meaning without a little explanation, but it is a reverent expression of the mystery of creation.

Gardens[36]

*Clouds are flowers*
*Around the sun.*

*The summer breeze*
*Hums with bees.*

*One drop of dew*
*Holds only me,*

*But there is one*
*That holds the sun*

*And clouds and flowers*
*And everyone.*

This quiet note of reassurance is characteristic of Mr. Behn's poetry for children.

## STEPHEN VINCENT BENÉT, 1898–1943
## ROSEMARY CARR BENÉT, 1898–1962

*A Book of Americans*

Stephen Vincent Benét, a member of a famous family of writers, was born in Bethlehem, Pennsylvania, and published his first book of verse while he was a student at Yale University. Twice winner of the Pulitzer

35. "Others." From *The Wizard in the Well*, © copyright 1956 by Harry Behn. Reprinted by permission of Harcourt Brace Jovanovich, Inc.

36. "Gardens." From *The Little Hill*, copyright 1949 by Harry Behn. Reprinted by permission of Harcourt Brace Jovanovich, Inc.

Prize for poetry, Benét's best-known work is probably his epic poem about the Civil War, *John Brown's Body*. With his wife, Rosemary, he wrote *A Book of Americans*, in which popular figures in American history are described in moods ranging from the nonsensical to the deeply serious.

"Pilgrims and Puritans" is a humorous presentation of the two sides of these colonists. It begins:

*Pilgrims and Puritans*[37]

*The Pilgrims and the Puritans*
*Were English to the bone*
*But didn't like the English Church*
*And wished to have their own*
*And so, at last, they sailed away*
*To settle Massachusetts Bay.*

*And there they found New England rocks*
*And Indians with bows on*
*But didn't mind them half as much*
*(Though they were nearly frozen)*
*As being harried, mocked and spurned in*
*Old England for the faith they burned in.*

*The stony fields, the cruel sea*
*They met with resolution*
*And so developed, finally,*
*An iron constitution*
*And, as a punishment for sinners,*
*Invented boiled New England dinners.*

Children like "Captain Kidd," "Peregrine White and Virginia Dare," and the larruping "Theodore Roosevelt." These are genuinely funny. The poem about the Wright brothers is particularly appreciated today by nine- and ten-year-olds for its humorous account of a momentous event in human history.

This is not great poetry, but it gives the reader a series of vivid portraits of some great Americans, written with vigor and simplicity. It can be a delightful addition to the study of the lives of these Americans or of periods in American history.

## LANGSTON HUGHES, 1902–1967

*Don't You Turn Back*

Langston Hughes was born in Joplin, Missouri, and began writing verse while he was in high school in Cleveland. Encouraged by Vachel Lindsay to continue his writing, Hughes joined the New York group of black writers of the Harlem Renaissance movement, and much of his poetry is in a spirit of racial pride and protest. The poem, "I, Too," is in many anthologies, including Lee Bennett Hopkins' selection of Hughes' poems for children, *Don't You Turn Back:*

*I, Too, Sing America*[38]

*I am the darker brother.*
*They send me to eat in the kitchen*
*When company comes,*
*But I laugh,*
*And eat well,*
*And grow strong.*

*Tomorrow,*
*I'll be at the table*
*When company comes.*
*Nobody'll dare*
*Say to me,*
*"Eat in the kitchen,"*
*Then.*

*Besides,*
*They'll see how beautiful I am*
*And be ashamed—*

*I, too, am America.*

37. From *A Book of Americans*. Copyright 1933 by Rosemary and Stephen Vincent Benét. Copyright renewed © 1961 by Rosemary Carr Benét. Used by permission.

38. "I, Too" Copyright 1926 and renewed 1954 by Langston Hughes. Reprinted from *Selected Poems of Langston Hughes*, by permission of Alfred A. Knopf, Inc.

*Illustration copyright © 1969 by Ann Grifalconi. Reprinted from* Don't You Turn Back, *by Langston Hughes, by permission of Alfred A. Knopf, Inc.*

Although many of his poems spoke for and about black people, Hughes also wrote poetry that speaks for all mankind.

*Silence*[39]

*I catch the pattern*
*Of your silence*
*Before you speak.*

*I do not need*
*To hear a word.*

*In your silence*
*Every tone I seek*
*Is heard.*

These are both serious poems, but there is an ironic humor in much of Hughes' writing, both poetry and prose. Although he wrote several books for children (on jazz, on Africa, on black heroes), his poetry was not designed for them. They have, however, overruled him and claimed his poetry for their own. His last book, published after his death, is *Black Misery*, a series of pithy sentences that are a bitter comment on what a black child faces in our society.

David Littlejohn says of Langston Hughes:

> *By moulding his verse always on the sounds of Negro talk, the rhythms of Negro music, by retaining his own keen honesty and directness, his poetic sense and ironic intelligence, he has maintained through four decades a readable newness distinctly his own.*[40]

## FRANCES FROST, 1905–1959

*The Little Whistler*
*The Little Naturalist*

Frances Frost's two small books of verses are not so well known as they deserve to be. The title poem of *The Little Whistler* is an account of a child's vain attempts to produce a whistle. The poems of the four seasons in this book reveal the author's delight in seasonal changes and her enjoyment of the outdoor world. But her best observations of nature are to be found in the posthumous book, *The Little Naturalist*. Both books are written from a child's point of view. Typical is her

*Green Hill Neighbors*[41]

*When I look at our green hill,*
*I think of all the wild*

39. "Silence," from *Fields of Wonder* by Langston Hughes. Copyright 1947 by Langston Hughes. Reprinted by permission of Alfred A. Knopf, Inc.

40. David Littlejohn, *Black on White: A Critical Survey of Writing by American Negroes.* Viking, 1969 (originally published in 1966 by Grossman).

41. "Green Hill Neighbors" by Frances Frost from *The Little Naturalist.* Copyright 1959 by the Estate of Frances Frost, and Kurt Werth. Copyright © renewed 1970. Reprinted by permission.

*Small hearts that live inside it:*
*The woodchuck's chubby child,*

*Rabbits with busy whiskered faces*
*Peering out of rocks,*
*The big-eared meadow mouse, the dainty*
*Gold-eyed baby fox.*

*When I look at our green hill*
*Beneath the sunny sky,*
*I'm pleased to have such friends inside—*
*And glad I live nearby!*

"Green Afternoon" is an account of two nervous mothers, a cow and a doe, anxiously watching their youngsters frolicking together. "Fox Cub Goes Home" is the dramatic account of a fox baby following a child. Otters at play seem almost neighbors in "Otter Creek." "The Foxes" playing ball is a beguiling picture. Every poem reflects Frances Frost's love for and close observation of the small creatures of field, forest, and meadow. These poems will enrich science courses and should make a young naturalist of any child who reads them.

## AILEEN FISHER, 1906–

*Runny Days, Sunny Days*
*Going Barefoot*
*But Ostriches . . .*
*Feathered Ones and Furry*

Aileen Fisher was born in Iron River, Michigan, and studied at the University of Chicago and the University of Missouri. She sold her first verses to *Child Life Magazine* while working in Chicago. Yearning to return to the outdoors, she decided to buy a one-way ticket to Colorado, and there she has stayed, writing poetry about the wild creatures she loves. She has also written some excellent biographies and several collections of plays, and has published many books of poetry in addition to the titles listed above. Her topics cover the seasons, children's pets, nature as the child encounters it. Typical of her early work is

*My Cat*[42]

*My cat rubs my leg*
*and starts to purr*
*with a soft little rumble,*
*a soft little whir*
*as if she had motors*
*inside of her.*

*I say, "Nice Kitty,"*
*and stroke her fur,*
*and though she can't talk*
*and I can't purr,*
*she understands me,*
*and I do her.*

With *Going Barefoot* Miss Fisher has attained a new freedom of verse patterns, a lighter, gayer touch, and a melodic line that makes this book a delight to read aloud either at one sitting or in parts day by day. It begins with the boy's question—

*How soon*
*how soon*
*is a morning in June,*
*a sunny morning or afternoon*
*in the wonderful month*
*of the Barefoot Moon?*[43]

Then the young philosopher observes that rabbits go barefoot all year round, so do raccoons, bees, cats, deer, and other creatures, while he must suffer the handicap of socks, shoes, and even galoshes. At last comes the day when he and his mother consult the calendar and the narrative reaches a triumphant conclusion—

42. "My Cat." From *Runny Days, Sunny Days* by Aileen Fisher. Copyright 1933, 1938, 1946, 1958. Reprinted by permission of Abelard-Schuman, Ltd. All Rights Reserved.
43. "How soon" and "June." From *Going Barefoot* by Aileen Fisher. Text copyright © 1960 by Aileen Fisher. Illustrations copyright © 1960 by Adrienne Adams. With permission of Thomas Y. Crowell Company, Inc., Publishers.

*June!*[43]

*The day is warm*
*and a breeze is blowing,*
*the sky is blue*
*and its eye is glowing,*
*and everything's new*
*and green and growing . . .*

*My shoes are off*
*and my socks are showing . . .*

*My socks are off . . .*

*Do you know how I'm going?*
BAREFOOT!

This is free and melodic and as full of movement as the restless child waiting for the big day of emancipation from shoes. The poetry about the rabbits, the kangaroos, and other creatures may be read and enjoyed separately or enjoyed as part of the whole. Adrienne Adams' illustrations in full color, with authentic paw prints adorning the end pages, add enchantment to this delightful book. The autumnal *Where Does Everyone Go?* is not quite so exhilarating but exceedingly pleasant to hear and look at. *Up, Up the Mountain* and *In the Middle of the Night* are lyric comments on the beauties of nature; *Feathered Ones and Furry* and *But Ostriches . . .* communicate with humor an affection for animals.

*The Furry Ones*[44]

*I like*
*the furry ones—*
*the waggy ones*
*the purry ones*
*the hoppy ones*
*that hurry,*

*The glossy ones*
*the saucy ones*
*the sleepy ones*
*the leapy ones*
*the mousy ones*
*that scurry,*

*The snuggly ones*
*the hug-ly ones*
*the never, never*
*ugly ones . . .*
*all soft*
*and warm*
*and furry.*

*I Like Them Feathery, Too*[44]

*I like them feathery, too—*
*I certainly, certainly do:*
*canary yellow*
*and lovebird green*
*and magpie black*

*Illustration by Eric Carle for* Feathered Ones and Furry *by Aileen Fisher. Illustration Copyright © 1971 by Eric Carle. Reprinted with permission of Thomas Y. Crowell Company, Inc., New York, Publishers.*

44. "The Furry Ones" and "I Like Them Feathery, Too." From *Feathered Ones and Furry* by Aileen Fisher. Copyright © 1971 by Aileen Fisher. Illustrations copyright © 1971 by Eric Carle. With permission of Thomas Y. Crowell Company, Inc., Publishers.

*with a shimmery sheen,*
*and fluttery bluebird blue.*

*I like them patterned*
*or feathery plain*
*from a tilt-tailed wren*
*to a long-legged crane.*

*But I like them best*
*for the news they bring*
*when you see the flash*
*of a feathery wing*
*at the end of winter,*
*and hear one sing,*
*so all of a sudden*
*you know it's SPRING.*

## THEODORE ROETHKE, 1908–1963

*I Am! Says the Lamb*

Theodore Roethke, a distinguished American poet, was born in Michigan and took his B.A. and M.A. degrees at the University of Michigan. At the time of his death he was teaching at the University of Washington. He received many awards and honors for his poetry, including Guggenheim and Ford Foundation Fellowships, the Pulitzer Prize in 1954 and the National Book Award posthumously in 1965.

Some of his poems are included in anthologies for young people, but *I Am! Says the Lamb* is the only collection that can be enjoyed as a whole by children. Roethke wrote with an ebullience and humor that are especially appealing in such nonsense poems as "The Kitty-Cat Bird." That some of his other poems can be enjoyed by children is obvious on reading

*The Bat*[45]

*By day the bat is cousin to the mouse.*
*He likes the attic of an aging house.*

*His fingers make a hat about his head.*
*His pulse beat is so slow we think him dead.*

*He loops in crazy figures half the night*
*Among the trees that face the corner light.*

*But when he brushes up against a screen*
*We are afraid of what our eyes have seen:*

*For something is amiss or out of place*
*When mice with wings can wear a human face.*

It is interesting to compare this poem with "Man and Bat" by D. H. Lawrence and with the poem that begins, "A bat is born . . ." in Randall Jarrell's *The Bat-Poet.*

## HILDA CONKLING, 1910–

*Poems by a Little Girl*
*Shoes of the Wind*

That a little girl living much in the company of her poet-mother should begin "talking" her own poems is not surprising, but the quality of Hilda Conkling's poems *is.* They are beautiful both in ideas and in expression.

Hilda's mother, Grace Hazard Conkling, was a professor of English at Smith College, a gifted musician, and a writer of poems in free verse. Her two little girls, Elsa and Hilda, grew up in the lovely New England country of Northampton, Massachusetts, with daily enjoyment of garden and countryside, books and music. Not only must the companionship of the three have been unusually close, but the whole environment was favorable to creative expression. At first, both little girls "dictated" their poems to their mother.

When Hilda was ten years old, *Poems by a Little Girl* was published with a laudatory introduction by the poet Amy Lowell. Since it created something of a sensation, Mrs. Conkling gave occasional lectures on how the poems happened. She said the poems often came when they were walking or just conversing. Hilda never hesitated for a word,

45. "The Bat," copyright 1938 by Theodore Roethke, from the book *Collected Poems of Theodore Roethke.* Reprinted by permission of Doubleday & Company, Inc. and Faber and Faber Limited.

and the mother made notes as best she could. Later she read her copy to Hilda, who would correct any word that had been inadvertently changed. The poems stand exactly as the child spoke them. When Hilda was twelve, her second book, *Shoes of the Wind*, was published (selections from the two books have been published under the title *Silverhorn*). After her second book, there were no more poems from Hilda so far as we can discover. Speculations as to why she ceased writing are beside the point. Our concern is with these poems that have important qualities for children.

First of all, their lack of rhyme is sometimes an asset. The time always comes when children are obsessed with rhyming everything and calling it poetry; then it is a good thing to read them some of young Hilda's verses and say, "Here is poetry written by a little girl. It has no rhyme. Why do you suppose it is called poetry?" That question is a poser for some children, but eventually they arrive at certain unmistakably poetic qualities in these unrhymed stanzas. "She *sees* things good," one child said after hearing "Moon Song." Another child, hearing "Chickadee" and "Red Rooster," thought the poet remembered how things *sounded*. Eventually, they discover that it is the fresh or different way in which she tells something with just a few words that makes these little verses different from prose. For instance:

*Tree-toad is a leaf-gray shadow*
*That sings.*
*Tree-toad is never seen*
*Unless a star squeezes through the leaves,*
*Or a moth looks sharply at a gray branch.*[46]

Hilda Conkling's free style is, then, a salutary antidote for the rhyming passion when it produces only doggerel and seems to handicap the development of original observation and expression. Her limitation for children is that she is predominantly descriptive. She is chiefly concerned with finding the precise words that tell how something looked or felt or appealed to her imagination. That the short feathers along the rooster's back

*Are the dark color of wet rocks*
*Or the rippled green of ships*
*When I look at their sides through water.*[47]

is a remarkably fine and discriminating observation, but too much of this kind of detailed description swamps children. They cannot see rooster for words, or, rather, after a number of these short, highly descriptive verses, children cannot follow the idea. Their attention is gone.

## JOHN CIARDI, 1916–

*I Met a Man*
*John J. Plenty and Fiddler Dan*
*The Man Who Sang the Sillies*
*You Read to Me, I'll Read to You*

Boston-born John Ciardi has for a number of years been active as a teacher, lecturer, critic, and writer, and as poetry editor of *Saturday Review*. Much of his poetry for both adults and children has a brisk candor. In his poetry for children, though, the humor and nonsense soften a forthrightness that is sometimes tart. Many of his poems are satirical comments on the reprehensible behavior of children, a vein most appreciated by the sophisticated reader. However, the topics he develops are usually fresh and original, as, for example, "How to Tell the Top of a Hill," "The River Is a Piece of the Sky," "The Reason for the Pelican." And when he chooses a familiar subject like "Halloween," he treats it freshly, so that it is unlike any other Halloween poem ever written—dramatic and weird,

46. From "Tree-Toad" from *Summer-Day Song* by Hilda Conkling. Copyright 1920, renewed 1948 by Hilda Conkling. Reprinted by permission of Random House, Inc.

47. From "Red Rooster" by Hilda Conkling from *Poems by a Little Girl*. Copyright 1920 by J. B. Lippincott. Reprinted by permission of Random House, Inc..

and a brain-tickler for the oldest and best readers.

*Scrappy the Pup*, in rollicking couplets, tells the story of a sleepy pup who was supposed to be a watch dog. One night a fox got into the hen house, which was responsible for the first of a series of noises that kept the farmer on the move all night while Scrappy drifted around in an "ocean of sleep." The surprise ending will tickle children and adults who have owned such a pet.

The omission of words in "Summer Song" makes a good language game.

*Summer Song*[48]

*By the sand between my toes,*
*By the waves behind my ears,*
*By the sunburn on my nose,*
*By the little salty tears*
*That make rainbows in the sun*
*When I squeeze my eyes and run,*
*By the way the seagulls screech,*
*Guess where I am? At the. . . . . !*
*By the way the children shout*
*Guess what happened? School is. . . !*
*By the way I sing this song*
*Guess if summer lasts too long?*
*You must answer* Right or. . . . . !

One of Mr. Ciardi's interesting experiments in verse for children is *I Met a Man*, written with a controlled vocabulary of some four hundred words. It was planned as a first book for his daughter to read on her own, and it moves from easy to more difficult in both words and content. "Poetry," the author says, "is especially well designed to lead the child to such recognition [of new words] for rhyme and pattern are always important clues."

Mr. Ciardi continued his experiment with a limited vocabulary in *You Read to Me, I'll Read to You*, in which he alternates a poem the child is supposed to read with one for the adult to read, unrestricted by word lists. These, too, are clever verses. In *The King Who Saved Himself from Being Saved*, Ciardi tells an amusing and pointed story that spoofs the stereotypical hero who insists on improving a situation with which everyone else concerned is perfectly content. This narrative poem is illustrated by Edward Gorey, whose elegant grotesquerie is admirably suited to Ciardi's wit. Many young people read Ciardi's poetry for adults, and nobody who writes poetry should fail to read this critic of contemporary poetry.

## KAYE STARBIRD, 1916–

*Speaking of Cows*
*A Snail's a Failure Socially*
*Don't Ever Cross a Crocodile*
*The Pheasant on Route Seven*

Kaye Starbird was born in Fort Sill, Oklahoma, and studied at the University of Vermont. She wrote verses as a child and she had poems published in magazines while she was still in college. She has written both satirical verse and serious poetry for adults. In her writing for children she uses a conversational tone and sees everyday experiences from the child's point of view, as, for example, in the title poem of *Speaking of Cows:*

*Speaking of Cows*[49]

*Speaking of cows*
*(Which no one was doing)*
*Why are they always*
*Staring and chewing?*
*Staring at people,*
*Chewing at clover,*
*Doing the same things*
*Over and over.*

48. "Summer Song." From the book *The Man Who Sang the Sillies* by John Ciardi. Copyright, ©, 1961, by John Ciardi. Reprinted by permission of J. B. Lippincott Company.

49. "Speaking of Cows." From the book *Speaking of Cows* by Kaye Starbird. Copyright, ©, 1960, by Kaye Starbird. Reprinted by permission of J. B. Lippincott Company.

*Once in awhile,*
*You see a cow mooing,*
*Swishing her tail*
*At a fly that needs shooing.*
*Most of the time, though,*
*What's a cow doing?*
*Munching and looking,*
*Staring and chewing.*
*Eyes never blinking,*
*Jaws always moving.*
*What are cows thinking?*
*What are cows* proving?

*Cows mustn't care for*
*New ways of doing.*
*That's what they stare for;*
*That's why they're chewing.*

These poems present a child voicing his honest opinions or questions about the bugs, beasts, people, and ideas he encounters. There is the unloved lizard "O'Toole," "Living his life in a quiet way," but still unloved. There is "My Cousin Kitty," who no matter what wonders you show her continues to cry "I want a balloon." The poems about the kitten in the mailbox, the toad that needed a baby sitter, Patsy Doolin, the naughty, imaginary sprite who takes over the body of a child who is misbehaving—these and many others are inventive and skillfully composed.

With each book, Kaye Starbird has grown as a poet. Her verse patterns are more deft, her moods more varied. Compare, for example, the humor of the first of the following poems with the nostalgic thoughtfulness of the second—"One Leaf."

*Illustration by Rita Fava. From* Speaking of Cows *by Kaye Starbird. Copyright © 1960 by Kaye Starbird. Reproduced by permission of the publishers, J. B. Lippincott Company.*

*A Snail's a Failure Socially*[50]

*A snail's a failure socially,*
*Which means you very seldom see*
*A crowd of happy, laughing snails*
*Collected all at once.*
*The reason's this: when asked to dine*
*A snail could answer "Yes" or "Fine,"*
*But if he lived a field away*
*The trip would take him months.*

*In short, the most excited snail,*
*Though pleased to hit the party trail,*
*Could promptly tidy up and take*
*A shortcut through the clover;*
*But asked to Easter luncheon—say—*
*And getting there Columbus Day,*
*There'd be at least an even chance*
*He'd find the party over.*

*One Leaf*[51]

*At least a month away from the autumn season*
*I saw a leaf from the maple break and fall,*
*Fluttering down for no apparent reason*
*One windless day when nothing else moved at all.*

*A sea gull cried in notes that tended to linger.*
*A sailboat lay becalmed on the summer ocean.*
*I reached to touch the falling leaf with my finger*
*And asked myself what fate had put it in motion.*

*Now in the scarlet glory of late September*
*As leaves drift down, too many to notice well,*
*It's odd how often and clearly I remember*
*The summer day when the single green leaf fell.*

50. "A Snail's a Failure Socially." From the book *A Snail's a Failure Socially* by Kaye Starbird. Copyright, ©, 1966, by Kaye Starbird. Reprinted by permission of J. B. Lippincott Company.
51. "One Leaf." From the book *The Pheasant on Route Seven* by Kaye Starbird. Copyright, ©, 1968, by Kaye Starbird. Reprinted by permission of J. B. Lippincott Company.

## EVE MERRIAM, 1916–

*Catch a Little Rhyme*
*Finding a Poem*
*It Doesn't Always Have to Rhyme*
*There Is No Rhyme for Silver*

Eve Merriam was born in Philadelphia, studied at the University of Pennsylvania and at Columbia, and is a teacher of creative writing as well as a writer of prose and poetry for adults and for children. Her first book of poetry for adults, *Family Circle*, won the Yale Series of Younger Poets prize.

Eve Merriam's verse is varied in form, inventive, and often humorous. It usually speaks directly to the child's experience and is especially appealing to the reader who enjoys word-play. Her essay on "Writing a Poem," in *Finding a Poem*, describes the poet's search for the exact word or phrase to express and illuminate her meaning. Both this essay and the chapter entitled "'I,' Says the Poem" in Nancy Larrick's *Somebody Turned on a Tap in These Kids* are good reading for anyone working with children.

Some notion of the range of Eve Merriam's poetry can be seen in two contrasting poems:

Landscape[52]

*What will you find at the edge of the world?*
*A footprint,*
*a feather,*
*desert sand swirled?*
*A tree of ice,*
*a rain of stars,*
*or a junkyard of cars?*

*What will there be at the rim of the world?*
*A mollusc,*
*a mammal,*
*a new creature's birth?*
*Eternal sunrise,*
*immortal sleep,*
*or cars piled up in a rusty heap?*

52. "Landscape" and "Ping-Pong" by Eve Merriam from *Finding a Poem*. Copyright © 1970 by Eve Merriam. Reprinted by permission of Atheneum Publishers, and Eve Merriam c/o International Famous Agency.

Ping-Pong[52]

*Chitchat*
*wigwag*
*rickrack*
*zigzag*

*knickknack*
*gewgaw*
*riffraff*
*seesaw*

*crisscross*
*flip-flop*
*ding-dong*
*tiptop*

*singsong*
*mishmash*
*King Kong*
*bong.*

"Landscape" has the provocative imagery and the concern with today's problems that are typical of Eve Merriam's poetry and are qualities that she encourages in the writing of her students. The intensity of her protest against social ills is most clearly seen in *The Inner City Mother Goose*, a collection of angry poems written for adults but relished by many young people.

"Ping-Pong" is a good example of the way she uses words for aural effect; bouncy and rhythmic, the poem evokes the patterned clicking of the game's sound. In *There Is No Rhyme for Silver, It Doesn't Always Have to Rhyme*, and *Catch a Little Rhyme*, Merriam—like David McCord—uses poems to illustrate such terms as cliché, homonym, limerick, onomatopoeia, simile, and metaphor.

## GWENDOLYN BROOKS, 1917–

*Bronzeville Boys and Girls*

Gwendolyn Brooks was born in Topeka, Kansas, but her family moved to Chicago soon

## VIEWPOINTS

Gwendolyn Brooks has always been committed and lyrical and relevant. Before it was fashionable, she was tone deep in blackness. In the fifties, she was writing poems about Emmett Till and Little Rock and the black boys and girls who came North looking for the Promised Land and found concrete deserts. In fact, she has always written about the sounds and sights and flavors of the black community. Her poems are distinguished by a bittersweet lyricism and an overwhelming concreteness. . . . Her poems celebrate the truth of her life. They celebrate the truth of blackness, which is also the truth of man.—From *To Gwen With Love* edited by Patricia L. Brown, Don L. Lee, and Francis Ward. Johnson Publishing Co., Chicago, 1971, pp. 3, 1.

after her birth. Her first poem was published when she was thirteen; in 1949 she won the annual prize given by *Poetry* magazine, and in 1950 she received the Pulitzer Prize for Poetry, never before awarded to a black writer.

In all her poetry there is a concern for racial and personal identity. Dan Jaffe says, "The label 'Black poetry' ignores Gwen Brooks' ability to speak as a hunchbacked girl, a male preacher, a white spokesman, in varying voices all clearly her own . . . it forgets that though Gwen Brooks learns from Langston Hughes, she also learns from T. S. Eliot; and that she must be more than a replica of either or both."[53]

Her poems for and about children, *Bronzeville Boys and Girls,* speak for any child of any race. The poems are each named for a boy or girl. They show a rare sensitivity to the child's inner life—his wonderments, hurts, and gay sense of make-believe and play. Here are two in contrasting mood.

*Cynthia in the Snow*[54]

*It SUSHES.*
*It hushes*
*The loudness in the road.*
*It flitter-twitters,*
*And laughs away from me.*
*It laughs a lovely whiteness,*
*And whitely whirs away,*
*To be*
*Some otherwhere,*
*Still white as milk or shirts.*
*So beautiful it hurts.*

*Vern*[54]

*When walking in a tiny rain*
*Across the vacant lot,*
*A pup's a good companion—*
*If a pup you've got.*

*And when you've had a scold,*
*And no one loves you very,*
*And you cannot be merry,*
*A pup will let you look at him,*
*And even let you hold*
*His little wiggly warmness—*

*And let you snuggle down beside.*
*Nor mock the tears you have to hide.*

### WILLIAM JAY SMITH, 1918–

*Laughing Time*
*Boy Blue's Book of Beasts*
*Mr. Smith and Other Nonsense*

William Jay Smith was born in Winnfield, Louisiana, and studied at several universities in the United States and abroad. He was a Rhodes Scholar and won, among other honors, the Young Poets' Prize of *Poetry* magazine in 1945. He has served as Consultant in Poetry to the Library of Congress, and has written poetry for children as well as poetry and criticism for adults.

53. "Gwendolyn Brooks: An Appreciation from the White Suburbs," by Dan Jaffe. From *The Black American Writer,* v. 2, ed. by Christopher Bigsby (Everett/Edwards, 1969).

54. "Cynthia in the Snow" and "Vern" from *Bronzeville Boys and Girls* by Gwendolyn Brooks. Copyright © 1956 by Gwendolyn Brooks Blakely. Reprinted by permission of Harper & Row, Publishers.

*Illustration by Ronni Solbert. From* Bronzeville Boys and Girls *by Gwendolyn Brooks. Copyright © 1956 by Gwendolyn Brooks Blakely. Reproduced with permission of Harper & Row, Publishers.*

*"I like this book," said the King of Hearts.*
*"It makes me laugh the way it starts!"*

*"I like it also," said his Mother.*
*So they sat down and read it to each other.*[55]

This is an ideal approach to verse, and, in the case of the verses in *Laughing Time*, repeat performances are inevitable. They are not too subtle for very young children and not too simple for the sevens and for the adults who must, perforce, read them aloud. "Laughing Time" is such infectious nonsense that you begin to smile as you look at the pictures and read the verses.

*Laughing Time*[55]

*It was laughing time, and the tall Giraffe*
*Lifted his head and began to laugh:*

*Ha! Ha! Ha! Ha!*

*And the Chimpanzee on the ginkgo tree*
*Swung merrily down with a Tee Hee Hee:*

*Hee! Hee! Hee! Hee!*

*"It's certainly not against the law!"*
*Croaked Justice Crow with a loud guffaw:*

*Haw! Haw! Haw! Haw!*

*The dancing Bear who could never say "No"*
*Waltzed up and down on the tip of his toe:*

*Ho! Ho! Ho! Ho!*

*The Donkey daintily took his paw,*
*And around they went: Hee-Haw! Hee-Haw!*

*Hee-Haw! Hee-Haw!*

*The Moon had to smile as it started to climb;*
*All over the world it was laughing time!*

*Ho! Ho! Ho! Ho! Hee-Haw! Hee-Haw!*
*Hee! Hee! Hee! Hee! Ha! Ha! Ha! Ha!*

After the children have heard this once, the obvious next step is for the adult to read the narrative, with the child or children coming in on the laughing choruses.

Children enjoy the idea behind "The Toaster."

*A silver-scaled Dragon with jaws flaming red*
*Sits at my elbow and toasts my bread.*
*I hand him fat slices, and then, one by one,*
*He hands them back when he sees they are done.*[55]

"Moon" belongs to cat lovers of any age, from children to T. S. Eliot. This "proud, mysterious" feline is in the best tradition.

*Boy Blue's Book of Beasts* is equally good nonsense about animals wild and tame—considerably wilder in verse form! There is "a tough Kangaroo named Hopalong Brown/ Boxed all the badmen out of town" and "Trim my whiskers! Bless my soul!/ Here comes a big brown one-eyed Mole." "A long-haired

55. "The King of Hearts," "Laughing Time," and "The Toaster" from *Laughing Time* by William Jay Smith. Copyright, 1953, 1955, by William Jay Smith. Reprinted by permission of Atlantic-Little, Brown and Co., and the author.

*Illustration by Juliet Kepes. From* Laughing Time *by William Jay Smith. Copyright 1953 by The Curtis Publishing Company. Copyright, 1953, 1955, by William Jay Smith. Reproduced by permission of Atlantic-Little, Brown and Co.*

Yak" in a barber's chair presents a problem and so does a little Raccoon who wants to be something else. All the verses are cleverly written. Mr. Smith's *Typewriter Town* is less successful, but it is good to discover a writer of poetry for adults who starts his own children with the musical inventions of nonsense verse.

William Jay Smith is also co-editor with Louise Bogan of an excellent anthology, *Golden Journey: Poems for Young People;* and with Virginia Haviland of an annotated bibliography, *Children and Poetry,* which includes a selective listing of poetry anthologies.

## MAY SWENSON, 1919–

*Poems to Solve*
*More Poems to Solve*

May Swenson was born in Logan, Utah, and took a degree at Utah State University, and she has gone on to win innumerable awards and fellowships. She writes with sharp imagery, her free and flowing verse filled with an awareness of sensory stimuli and imaginative vision.

Her poems are studded with evocative phrases that spring to life; in "At Truro," for example

> *The sea is unfolding scrolls*
> *and rolling them up again.*
> *It is an ancient diary*
>
> *the waves are murmuring.*
> *The words are white curls,*
> *great capitals are seen.*[56]

In the preface to *More Poems to Solve,* she discusses the patterns of words in her poems, and explains that "Riddles, Shapes, Riddle-Shapes, Word-Things, Shape-Word-Things (not to mention the poems whose modes, by contrast, are more conventional) all present some unexpected facet or internal feature to be discovered *as part* of the recognition to be reached for in each." Her poems to solve, then, at least invite and at most demand the participation of the reader.

## MYRA COHN LIVINGSTON, 1926–

*Whispers and Other Poems*
*Wide Awake and Other Poems*
*A Crazy Flight and Other Poems*

Omaha-born Myra Cohn Livingston was interested in writing and music throughout all

56. "At Truro." Reprinted by permission of Charles Scribner's Sons from *More Poems to Solve* by May Swenson. Copyright © 1971 May Swenson.

her school years, finally abandoning her music study to become a writer and teacher. As a teacher of creative writing, she feels very strongly about the paramount importance of free expression. As she has said in "What the Heart Knows Today":[57]

*Happily, we are no longer concerned with those who copy patterns or fill in blanks; the beginning acceptance of blank verse, free verse, haiku has helped somewhat to break the rhyme barrier, but we have a long way to go before we can succeed in recognizing that the tools of poetry are not poetry.*

Nevertheless, her own mastery of rhyme and meter makes it clear that she herself is in command of the tools of poetry. Her books of verse (some of which are listed above) deal with the sensory experiences, activities, and imaginings of young children.

*Whispers*[58]

*Whispers*
*tickle through your ear*
*telling things you like to hear.*
*Whispers*
*are as soft as skin*
*letting little words curl in.*
*Whispers*
*come so they can blow*
*secrets others never know.*

*Wide Awake*[59]

*I have to jump up*
*out of bed*
*and stretch my hands*
*and rub my head,*
*and curl my toes*
*and yawn*

*Illustration by Jacqueline Chwast. Reproduced from* Wide Awake and Other Poems, *© 1959, by Myra Cohn Livingston, by permission of Harcourt Brace Jovanovich, Inc.*

*and shake*
*myself*
*all wideawake!*

Although *A Crazy Flight and Other Poems* is for children eight to eleven, there are no age barriers to the enjoyment of poetry, and many of the selections may please both the read-aloud audience and adults. A recognition of changing speech patterns can be observed in "The Sun Is Stuck":[60]

*The sun is stuck.*
*I mean, it won't move.*
*I mean it's hot, man, and we need a red-hot*
*poker to pry it loose,*
*Give it a good shove and roll it across the sky*
*And make it go down*
*So we can be cool,*
*Man.*

Mrs. Livingston had also edited an excellent anthology for adolescent poetry lovers—*A Tune Beyond Us*—which includes many poems from other languages. As she says in "Editor's Note": "This collection has been

57. "What the Heart Knows Today" by Myra Cohn Livingston. From *Somebody Turned on a Tap in These Kids*, ed. by Nancy Larrick. Delacorte, 1971, p. 11.

58. "Whispers" from *Whispers and Other Poems*, © 1958 by Myra Cohn Livingston. Reprinted by permission of Harcourt Brace Jovanovich, Inc.

59. "Wide Awake" from *Wide Awake and Other Poems*, © 1959 by Myra Cohn Livingston. Reprinted by permission of Harcourt Brace Jovanovich, Inc.

60. "The Sun Is Stuck" from *A Crazy Flight and Other Poems*, copyright © 1969 by Myra Cohn Livingston. Reprinted by permission of Harcourt Brace Jovanovich, Inc. and McIntosh and Otis, Inc.

chosen, largely, from the lesser known works of great poets or from the work of little-known poets: A German who tells of a railroad man in Ohio, an Irishman who sees the Devil, a Latin poet of the ninth century writing of Easter Sunday . . . an American speaking of flying saucers. . . . In an age of science and definition, it sometimes seems important to reflect that art escapes definition by its appeal to man's senses, sensitivities, and emotions."

Here, then, are some of the poets who have written joyously and seriously for children. There are of course many other poets whose work is cherished by children. Beatrice Schenk de Regniers' books are gay and imaginative—a good example is *Something Special*, with its beguiling verses embellished by Irene Haas' interpretative drawings. Zhenya Gay has written some really giddy nonsense verses for young children, and Karla Kuskin and Mary Ann Hoberman have also contributed some appealing books of poetry for them. Mary O'Neill's *Hailstones and Halibut Bones* is a happy experiment with words and colors, associating colors with objects, moods, and feelings. Most anthologies include one or more of the poems of James Tippett, E. V. Rieu, James Reeves, William Allingham, and Rose Fyleman. With the flourishing of new black poets, older boys and girls read with interest some of the earlier writers like Paul Laurence Dunbar and Countee Cullen. The bibliography at the end of this chapter reflects children's interest in modern poetry. It cannot possibly cite all of the anthologies that have now been published for children and young people, but it includes some excellent general anthologies and a selection of subject anthologies.

Not all of the poets discussed in this chapter and listed in the bibliography have been gifted with lyric genius, but each one has made a contribution which serves to underscore the fact that *children like poetry*. If the lesser of our poets are at first more popular with children than our major poets, it is probably because they are direct and clear; they choose subjects children can understand easily, and they treat the subject briefly and cheerfully. These are standards we must respect in our choice of verse for children. We must remember, too, that they may turn away from obscurity in a poem—just as many adults do; that they will endure length usually only in narrative verse that is swift-moving and exciting; and that in general they shun long descriptions. So lyric poets who catch their favor generally do so with poetry that is brief and gay, or markedly melodious. And of course many young people prefer the poetry that speaks to the problems and issues of today.

The poetry in Randall Jarrell's *The Bat-Poet* is graceful and perceptive, but no more so than the creative musing of the little brown bat who, disappointed at the criticism of his poetry, says, "The trouble isn't making poems, the trouble's finding somebody that will listen to them."[61] Children are listening. They are listening to older poets and younger ones, to poetry of all peoples the world over, to poems that make them laugh and cry and question and see or feel things they have never seen or felt before.

## ADULT REFERENCES[62]

ARNSTEIN, FLORA. *Children Write Poetry: A Creative Approach.*

AUSLANDER, JOSEPH, and FRANK ERNEST HILL. *The Winged Horse; The Story of Poets and Their Poetry.*

BARROWS, HERBERT, HUBERT HEFFNER, JOHN CIARDI, and WALLACE DOUGLAS. *How Does a Poem Mean?*

BEHN, HARRY. *Chrysalis; Concerning Children and Poetry.*

BREWTON, JOHN E. and SARA W., comps. *Index to Children's Poetry.*

DEUTSCH, BABETTE. *Poetry in Our Time.*

DREW, ELIZABETH, and GEORGE CONNOR. *Discovering Modern Poetry.*

DUNNING, STEPHEN. *Teaching Literature to Adolescents: Poetry.*

61. Randall Jarrell, *The Bat-Poet.* Macmillan, 1967, p. 15.

62. Complete bibliographic data are provided in the combined Adult References in the Appendices.

EASTMAN, MAX. *The Enjoyment of Poetry.*
FRANKENBERG, LLOYD. *Pleasure Dome: On Reading Modern Poetry.*
HAVILAND, VIRGINIA, and WILLIAM JAY SMITH, comps. *Children and Poetry; A Selective Annotated Bibliography.*
HILLYER, ROBERT. *In Pursuit of Poetry.*
HOPKINS, LEE BENNETT. *Let Them Be Themselves.*
HUBER, MIRIAM BLANTON. *Story and Verse for Children.*
HUGHES, TED. *Poetry Is.*
ISAACS, J. *The Background of Modern Poetry.*
KOCH, KENNETH. *Wishes, Lies, and Dreams; Teaching Children to Write Poetry.*
LARRICK, NANCY, ed. *Somebody Turned on a Tap in These Kids.*
READ, HERBERT. *This Way, Delight.*
RIBNER, IRVING, and HARRY MORRIS. *Poetry: A Critical and Historical Introduction.*
SANDBURG, CARL, ed. *The American Songbag.*
SANDERS, THOMAS E. *The Discovery of Poetry.*
SHAW, JOHN MACKAY. *Childhood in Poetry: A Catalogue.*
WITUCKE, VIRGINIA. *Poetry in the Elementary School.*

## CHILDREN'S BOOKS: ANTHOLOGIES

There are so many good anthologies of poetry for children that it is not possible to list them all here. The following are especially useful for reasons the text or the notes make clear.

ADOFF, ARNOLD, ed. *Black Out Loud*, ill. by Alvin Hollingsworth. Macmillan, 1970. 11-14
———. *City in All Directions*, ill. by Donald Carrick. Macmillan, 1969. 12 up
———. *I Am the Darker Brother*, ill. by Benny Andrews. Macmillan, 1968. 11 up
———. *it is the poem singing into your eyes; anthology of new young poets.* Harper, 1971. 10 up
ADSHEAD, GLADYS L., and ANNIS DUFF, eds. *An Inheritance of Poetry*, ill. by Nora S. Unwin. Houghton, 1948. A large collection of unusual poems, chiefly for adolescents, but with some exquisite bits for children. 10-16
ALDAN, DAISY, comp. *Poems from India*, ill. by Joseph Low. T. Crowell, 1969. A collection of poems ranging from ancient times to the present, conservative and idealistic, on the whole. 14 up
ARBUTHNOT, MAY HILL, and SHELTON L. ROOT, JR., eds. *Time for Poetry*, 3rd gen. ed., ill. by Arthur Paul. Scott, Foresman, 1968. There are more than seven hundred poems in this newest edition of a favorite collection, ranging from *Mother Goose* to T. S. Eliot. The discussion of reading poetry to children and using poetry in verse choirs and the notes throughout the text are invaluable for adults. Also included in *The Arbuthnot Anthology.* 4-14
Association for Childhood Education, Literature Committee. *Sung Under the Silver Umbrella*, ill. by Dorothy Lathrop. Macmillan, 1935, 1962. A small collection of choice poetry, including selections from the Bible, modern poems, nonsense verse, and Japanese haiku. 4-9
BARON, VIRGINIA, ed. *The Seasons of Time; Tanka Poetry of Ancient Japan*, ill. by Yasuhide Kobashi. Dial, 1968. 11 up
———. *Here I Am! An Anthology of Poems Written by Young People in Some of America's Minority Groups*, ill. by Emily Arnold McCully. Dutton, 1969. 8-11
BEHN, HARRY, tr. *Cricket Songs; Japanese Haiku*, with pictures selected from Sesshu and other Japanese masters. Harcourt, 1964. 10 up
———, tr. *More Cricket Songs*, ill. with pictures by Japanese masters. Harcourt, 1971. 10 up
BENEDETTI, MARIO, ed. *Unstill Life*, tr. by Darwin Flakoll and Claribel Alegria, ill. by Antonio Frasconi. Harcourt, 1969. 11 up
BIERHORST, JOHN, ed. *In the Trail of the Wind*, ill. Farrar, 1971. 12 up
BLISHEN, EDWARD, comp. *Oxford Book of Poetry for Children*, ill. by Brian Wildsmith. Watts, 1963. An excellent anthology covering a wide variety of subjects, moods, and styles with superb illustrations. 9-12
BOGAN, LOUISE, and WILLIAM JAY SMITH, eds. *The Golden Journey; Poems for Young People*, ill. by Fritz Kredel. Reilly, 1965. 10-14
BRANDON, WILLIAM, ed. *The Magic World: American Indian Songs and Poems.* Morrow, 1971. 11 up
BREWTON, SARA and JOHN, comps. *Birthday Candles Burning Bright; A Treasury of Birthday Poetry*, ill. by Vera Bock. Macmillan, 1960. A delightful anthology of poems arranged by age groups, illustrating the general fun of birthdays and including a choice selection of Christmas poems. 5 up
———, comps. *Laughable Limericks*, ill. by Ingrid Fetz. T. Crowell, 1965. 9 up
———, comps. *Sing a Song of Seasons*, ill. by Vera Bock. Macmillan, 1955. Poems of school days and vacation time. 6-12
CANFIELD, KENNETH, ed. *Selections from French Poetry*, ill. by Tomi Ungerer. Harvey, 1965. 12 up
COLE, WILLIAM, ed. *Beastly Boys and Ghastly Girls*, ill. by Tomi Ungerer. World, 1964. Varied and humorous. 10-12
———, ed. *The Birds and the Beasts Were There*, ill. by Helen Siegl. World, 1963. A choice and lovely collection of verses about animals, birds, and insects, both real and fantastic. 6 up
———, ed. *A Book of Nature Poems*, ill. by Robert Andrew Parker. Viking, 1969. 10-14
———, ed. *Humorous Poetry for Children*, ill. by Ervine Metzl. World, 1955. 8 up
———, ed. *Oh, How Silly!* ill. by Tomi Ungerer. Viking, 1970. 8-10
———, ed. *Oh, What Nonsense!* ill. by Tomi Ungerer. Viking, 1966. 9-11
———, ed. *Poems for Seasons and Celebrations*, ill. by Johannes Troyer. World, 1961. From the year's beginning to its end, poems follow the cycle of seasons and holidays in a refreshing collection of

modern and traditional verses. 8-15

______, ed. *Poems of Magic and Spells*, ill. by Peggy Bacon. World, 1960. Goblins and ghosts, witches and other magical creatures are highlighted in a novel and attractive anthology. 9-13

______, ed. *The Poet's Tales: A New Book of Story Poems*, ill. by Charles Keeping. World, 1971. From folk ballads to sophisticated modern poems. 10-14

COLUM, PADRAIC, ed. *Roofs of Gold; Poems to Read Aloud*. Macmillan, 1964. The editor's favorites from Shakespeare to Dylan Thomas. 11-15

DE FOREST, CHARLOTTE B., ad. *The Prancing Pony; Nursery Rhymes from Japan*, adapted into English verse for children, ill. by Keiko Hida. Walker, 1968. 3-7

DE LA MARE, WALTER, ed. *Come Hither*, 3rd ed., ill. by Warren Chappell. Knopf, 1957. 12 up

______, ed. *Tom Tiddler's Ground*, ill. by Margery Gill. Knopf, 1962. First American edition of a choice compilation of verses for younger children. As in *Come Hither*, De la Mare's perceptive notes distinguish his anthologies. 9 up

DE LUCA, MICHAEL, and WILLIAM GUILIANOS, eds. *Selections from Italian Poetry*. Harvey, 1966. 13 up

DOOB, LEONARD, ed. *A Crocodile Has Me by the Leg; African Poems*, ill. by Solomon Irein Wangboje. Walker, 1967. 9-14

DOWNIE, MARY, and BARBARA ROBERTSON, comps. *The Wind Has Wings; Poems from Canada*, ill. by Elizabeth Cleaver. Walck, 1968. 9-12

DUNNING, STEPHEN, EDWARD LUEDERS, and HUGH SMITH, comps. *Reflections on a Gift of Watermelon Pickle*. Scott, Foresman, 1967. 11 up

______, comps. *Some Haystacks Don't Even Have Any Needle*, ill. Scott, Foresman, 1969. A splendid collection of poems complemented by reproductions of modern art in full color. 11 up

EATON, ANNE THAXTER, comp. *Welcome Christmas!* ill. by Valenti Angelo. Viking, 1955. A garland of some fifty Christmas poems, chosen with exquisite taste and given format and decorations of fitting beauty. all ages

FERRIS, HELEN, comp. *Favorite Poems Old and New*, ill. by Leonard Weisgard. Doubleday, 1957. Here is a splendidly varied collection of over 700 poems to appeal to the tastes and interests of children and grownups, too. 5 up

FUJIKAWA, GUY, comp. *A Child's Book of Poems*, ill. by comp. Grosset, 1969. A profusely and attractively illustrated collection of poems, standard fare. Selections are not grouped or arranged. 3-7

FYLEMAN, ROSE, ed. *Picture Rhymes from Foreign Lands*. Lippincott, 1935. 5-8

GREGORY, HORACE, and MARYA ZATURENSKA, eds. *The Crystal Cabinet*, ill. by Diana Bloomfield. Holt, 1962. A refreshingly original anthology of lyric poetry, wide in range, from Chinese translations to poems by Edith Sitwell, chosen for special appeal to children and young people. 12 up

HANNUM, SARA, and JOHN TERRY CHASE, comps. *The Wind Is Round*, ill. by Ron Bowen. Atheneum, 1970. 10 up

HANNUM, SARA, and GWENDOLYN REED, comps. *Lean Out of the Window; An Anthology of Modern Poetry*, ill. by Ragna Tischler. Atheneum, 1965. 10-14

HAYDEN, ROBERT, ed. *Kaleidoscope; Poems by American Negro Poets*. Harcourt, 1967. 13 up

HOPKINS, LEE BENNETT, comp. *City Talk*, ill. with photos by Roy Aranella. Knopf, 1970. 7-9

______, comp. *I Think I Saw a Snail; Young Poems for City Seasons*, ill. by Harold James. Crown, 1969. A selection of poems (four or five for each season) by accepted authors. A few are not particularly city poems. 5-8

JONES, HETTIE, ed. *The Trees Stand Shining; Poetry of the North American Indians*, ill. by Robert Andrew Parker. Dial, 1971. 8-11

JORDAN, JUNE, and TERRI BUSH, comps. *The Voice of the Children*. Holt, 1970. 10 up

LARRICK, NANCY, ed. *Green Is Like a Meadow of Grass*, ill. by Kelly Oechsli. Garrard, 1968. 5-9

______, ed. *I Heard a Scream in the Streets; Poems by Young People in the City*, ill. with photos by students. Evans, 1970. 10 up

______, ed. *On City Streets*, ill. with photos by David Sagarin. Evans, 1968. 10-14

LEWIS, RICHARD, ed. *I Breathe a New Song: Poems of the Eskimo*, ill. by Oonark. Simon, 1971. Poems that reflect the Eskimo's life and closeness to nature. 9 up

______, ed. *In a Spring Garden*, ill. by Ezra Jack Keats. Dial, 1965. 5-9

______, ed. *Miracles*. Simon, 1966. all ages

______, ed. *The Moment of Wonder; A Collection of Chinese and Japanese Poetry*, ill. with paintings by Chinese and Japanese masters. Dial, 1964. all ages

______, ed. *Muse of the Round Sky; Lyric Poetry of Ancient Greece*, tr. by Willis Barnstone and others. Simon, 1969. 8 up

______, ed. *Out of the Earth I Sing; Poetry and Songs of Primitive Peoples of the World*. Norton, 1968. 8 up

______, ed. *Still Waters of the Air; Poems by Three Modern Spanish Poets*, ill. by Arvis Stewart. Dial, 1970. 11 up

______, ed. *There Are Two Lives; Poems by Children of Japan*, tr. by Haruna Kimura. Simon, 1970. 8-10

______, ed. *The Wind and the Rain*, ill. with photos by Helen Buttfield. Simon, 1968. 8-10

LIVINGSTON, MYRA COHN, ed. *Speak Roughly to Your Little Boy; A Collection of Parodies and Burlesques, Together with the Original Poems, Chosen and Annotated for Young People*, ill. by Joseph Low. Harcourt, 1971. 11 up

______, ed. *A Tune Beyond Us*, ill. by James J. Spanfeller. Harcourt, 1968. 12 up

LONGLAND, JEAN, ed. *Selections from Contemporary Portuguese Poetry*. Harvey, 1966. 11 up

MC DONALD, GERALD D., comp. *A Way of Knowing; A Collection of Poems for Boys*, ill. by Clare and John Ross. T. Crowell, 1959. A varied and popular collection, representative of modern and traditional poets. Appeals to girls as well as to boys. 10 up

MAC KAY, DAVID, comp. *A Flock of Words*, ill. by Margery Gill. Harcourt, 1970. 11 up

MORRISON, LILLIAN, comp. *A Dillar, A Dollar; Rhymes and Sayings for the Ten O'Clock Scholar*, ill. by Marjorie Bauernschmidt. T. Crowell, 1955. 6-13

______, comp. *Touch Blue; Signs and Spells, Love Charms and Chants, Auguries and Old Beliefs, in Rhyme*, ill. by Doris Lee. T. Crowell, 1958. 6-13

______, comp. *Yours till Niagara Falls*, ill. by Marjorie Bauernschmidt. T. Crowell, 1950. 9-13

MORSE, DAVID, ed. *Grandfather Rock*. Delacorte, 1972. 11 up

MORTON, MIRIAM, ed. *A Harvest of Russian Children's Literature*. Univ. of Calif. Pr., 1967. all ages

*Mother Goose in French*, tr. by Hugh Latham, ill. by Barbara Cooney. T. Crowell, 1964. 10-11

*Mother Goose in Spanish*, tr. by Alastair Reid and Anthony Kerrigan, ill. by Barbara Cooney. T. Crowell, 1968. 10-11

NASH, OGDEN, comp. *I Couldn't Help Laughing*. Lippincott, 1957. 12-14

______, comp. *The Moon Is Shining Bright as Day*, ill. by Rose Shirvanian. Lippincott, 1953. 12-14

PARKER, ELINOR, comp. *The Singing and the Gold*, ill. by Clare Leighton. T. Crowell, 1962. 12 up

PECK, RICHARD, ed. *Sounds and Silences: Poetry for Now*. Delacorte, 1970. 12 up

PLOTZ, HELEN, comp. *The Earth Is the Lord's; Poems of the Spirit*. T. Crowell, 1965. Emphasizes work of contemporary poets. 11 up

______, comp. *Imagination's Other Place; Poems of Science and Mathematics*, ill. by Clare Leighton. T. Crowell, 1955. 12 up

______, comp. *The Marvelous Light; Poets and Poetry*. T. Crowell, 1970. The poets and their work reflect a variety in style and mood. 11 up

______, comp. *Poems from the German*, ill. by Ismar David. T. Crowell, 1967. 11 up

______, comp. *Untune the Sky: Poems of Music and the Dance*. T. Crowell, 1957. Ranges from reverence to gaiety. 10 up

READ, HERBERT. *This Way, Delight*, ill. by Juliet Kepes. Pantheon, 1956. A poet's choice of over 100 poems within the understanding of younger readers. Selected to delight children, they are followed by a distinguished essay on *What Is Poetry?* 8 up

REED, GWENDOLYN, comp. *Out of the Ark; An Anthology of Animal Verse*, ill. by Gabriele Margules. Atheneum, 1968. The selections include old favorites and some lesser-known poems representing many centuries. Useful for independent reading or for reading aloud. 10-14

______, comp. *The Talkative Beasts: Myths, Fables and Poems of India*, ill. by Stella Snead. Lothrop, 1969. 8-12

RESNICK, SEYMOUR, ed. *Selections from Spanish Poetry*, ill. by Anne Marie Jauss. Harvey, 1962. 11 up

______, ed. *Spanish-American Poetry; A Bilingual Selection*, ill. by Anne Marie Jauss. Harvey, 1964. 11 up

RUS, VLADIMIR, ed. *Selections from German Poetry*, ill. by Elizabeth Korolkoff. Harvey, 1966. 13 up

SECHRIST, ELIZABETH, comp. *One Thousand Poems for Children*, based on the selections of Roger Ingpen, ill. by Henry C. Pitz. Macrae, 1946. A tremendous collection, excellent for a reference source in school or home. all ages

SEEGER, RUTH CRAWFORD, ed. *Let's Build a Railroad*, ill. by Tom Funk. Dutton, 1954. 4-9

SMITH, JANET ADAM, comp. *The Faber Book of Children's Verse*. Faber, 1953. Eight- to fourteen-year-old English children may rise to this collection, but in this country it will fit chiefly the high-school levels. An unusual selection of fine poetry makes it well worth knowing. 12 up

SMITH, WILLIAM JAY, ed. *Poems from France*, ill. by Roger Duvoisin. T. Crowell, 1967. 9 up

SULLY, FRANÇOIS, ed. *We, the Vietnamese: Voices from Vietnam*. Praeger, 1971. Includes poetry. 13 up

UNTERMEYER, LOUIS, ed. *Rainbow in the Sky*, ill. by Reginald Birch. Harcourt, 1935. Mr. Untermeyer was one of the first and most indefatigable anthologists for children. This is only one of his many books. They lean heavily on old and familiar poems. 7-12

VAN DOREN, MARK, ed. *Anthology of World Poetry*, rev. and enl. ed. Harcourt, 1936. A collection of choice poems on an international scale, including ancient literatures and modern poetry as well. 12 up

WYNDHAM, ROBERT, comp. *Chinese Mother Goose Rhymes*, ill. by Ed Young. World, 1968. 4-6

## CHILDREN'S BOOKS: BY INDIVIDUAL POETS

AIKEN, CONRAD. *Cats and Bats and Things with Wings*, ill. by Milton Glaser. Atheneum, 1965. 5-8

ALDIS, DOROTHY. *All Together: A Child's Treasury of Verse*, ill. by Helen D. Jameson. Putnam, 1952. Poems about everyday happenings. 5-9

______. *Quick as a Wink*, ill. by Peggy Westphal. Putnam, 1960. Insect poems. 4-7

ALLINGHAM, WILLIAM. *The Fairy Shoemaker and Other Fairy Poems*, ill. by Boris Artzybasheff. Macmillan, 1928. Poems by Allingham, Walter de la Mare, and Matthew Arnold. 9-12

______. *Robin Redbreast and Other Verses*, ill. by Kate Greenaway, Helen Allingham, Caroline Paterson, and Harry Furness. Macmillan, Little Library, 1930. 7-12

ARMOUR, RICHARD. *All Sizes and Shapes of Monkeys and Apes*, ill. by Paul Galdone. McGraw, 1970. 5-8

______. *A Dozen Dinosaurs*, ill. by Paul Galdone. McGraw, 1967. 6-9

______. *Odd Old Mammals; Animals After the Dinosaurs*, ill. by Paul Galdone. McGraw, 1968. 9-11

AUSTIN, MARY. *The Children Sing in the Far West*, ill. by Gerald Cassidy. Houghton, 1928. 8-12

BABBITT, NATALIE. *Dick Foote and the Shark*, ill. by author. Farrar, 1967. 9-11

______. *Phoebe's Revolt*, ill. by author. Farrar, 1968. 8-9

BARNSTONE, WILLIS. *A Day in the Country*, ill. by Howard Knotts. Harper, 1971. 5-8

BEHN, HARRY. *The Golden Hive*, ill. by author. Harcourt, 1966. 9-12

______. *The Little Hill*, ill. by author. Harcourt, 1949.

______. *Windy Morning*, ill. by author. Harcourt, 1953.

______. *The Wizard in the Well*, ill. by author. Harcourt, 1956. 5-9

BELLOC, HILAIRE. *The Bad Child's Book of Beasts*, ill. by B.T.B. Knopf, 1965. 6-9

______. *Cautionary Verses*, ill. by B.T.B. and Nicolas Bentley. Knopf, 1959. 9-12

______. *Matilda, Who Told Lies and Was Burned to Death*, ill. by Steven Kellogg. Dial, 1970. 9-12

BENÉT, ROSEMARY and STEPHEN VINCENT. *A Book of Americans*, rev. ed., ill. by Charles Child. Holt, 1952. 8-14

BLAKE, WILLIAM. *Songs of Innocence*, ill. by Harold Jones. Barnes, 1961. A welcome edition which contains nineteen of Blake's more childlike poems. 6 up

BROOKE, L. LESLIE. *Johnny Crow's Garden*. Warne, 1903.

______. *Johnny Crow's New Garden*. Warne, 1935.

______. *Johnny Crow's Party*. Warne, 1907. 3-7

______. *Leslie Brooke's Children's Books*, 4 vols. Warne, n.d. 5-12

______. *Ring o' Roses* (see Bibliography, Chapter 5).

BROOKS, GWENDOLYN. *Bronzeville Boys and Girls*, ill. by Ronni Solbert. Harper, 1956. 7-11

BROWNJOHN, ALAN. *Brownjohn's Beasts*, ill. by Carol Lawson. Scribner's, 1970. 9-11

CAMERON, POLLY. *The Green Machine*, ill. by Consuelo Joerns. Coward, 1969. 4-7

______. *"I Can't," Said the Ant*, ill. by author. Coward, 1961. 4-6

CARROLL, LEWIS. *Alice's Adventures in Wonderland* (see Bibliography, Chapter 8).

______. *The Annotated Snark*, with an introduction and notes by Martin Gardner. Simon, 1962. The full text of Lewis Carroll's great nonsense epic *The Hunting of the Snark* and the original illustrations by Henry Holiday.

CAUDILL, REBECCA. *Come Along!* ill. by Ellen Raskin. Holt, 1969. 7-9

CHAUCER, GEOFFREY. *A Taste of Chaucer*, selections from *The Canterbury Tales*, chosen and ed. by Anne Malcolmson, ill. by Enrico Arno. Harcourt, 1964. A careful and discriminating adaptation of—and introduction to—Chaucer for young people. The introduction describes Chaucer and the period in which he lived. 12 up

CIARDI, JOHN. *The Reason for the Pelican*, ill. by Madeleine Gekiere. Lippincott, 1959. 5-9
Nonsense verses and imaginative poems in this collection launched John Ciardi's books for children. Others are:

______. *I Met a Man*, ill. by Robert Osborn. Houghton, 1961. 4-8

______. *John J. Plenty and Fiddler Dan* (see Bibliography, Chapter 7—Modern Fables).

______. *The King Who Saved Himself from Being Saved*, ill. by Edward Gorey. Lippincott, 1965. 9-11

______. *The Man Who Sang the Sillies*, ill. by Edward Gorey. Lippincott, 1961. 4-8

______. *Scrappy the Pup*, ill. by Jane Miller. Lippincott, 1960. 4-8

______. *Someone Could Win a Polar Bear*, ill. by Edward Gorey. Lippincott, 1970. 5-8

______. *You Read to Me, I'll Read to You*, ill. by Edward Gorey. Lippincott, 1962. 5-8

CLIFTON, LUCILLE. *Some of the Days of Everett Anderson*, ill. by Evaline Ness. Holt, 1970. 5-7

COATSWORTH, ELIZABETH. *Away Goes Sally* (see Bibliography, Chapter 14).

______. *Down Half the World*, ill. by Zena Bernstein. Macmillan, 1968. 12 up

______. *The Fair American* (see Bibliography, Chapter 14).

______. *Five Bushel Farm* (see Bibliography, Chapter 14).

______. *The Sparrow Bush*, ill. by Stefan Martin. Norton, 1966. 9-12

______. *Summer Green*, ill. by Nora S. Unwin. Macmillan, 1948. 7 up

______. *Under the Green Willow*, ill. by Janina Domanska. Macmillan, 1971. 5-7

COLE, WILLIAM. *What's Good for a Four-Year-Old?* ill. by Tomi Ungerer. Holt, 1967. One of a series. 3-4

CONKLING, HILDA. *Poems by a Little Girl*. Lippincott, 1920. 6-10

______. *Shoes of the Wind*. Lippincott, 1922. 6-10

______. *Silverhorn; The Hilda Conkling Book for Other Children*, ill. by Dorothy P. Lathrop. Stokes, 1924.

CULLEN, COUNTEE. *The Lost Zoo*, ill. by Joseph Low. Follett, 1969. 10 up

DE GASZTOLD, CARMEN BERNOS. *The Creatures' Choir*, tr. by Rumer Godden, ill. by Jean Primrose. Viking, 1965. 11 up

______. *Prayers from the Ark*, tr. by Rumer Godden. Viking, 1962. 12 up

DE LA MARE, WALTER. *Peacock Pie*, ill. by Barbara Cooney. Knopf, 1961. 6 up

______. *Rhymes and Verses: Collected Poems for Children*, ill. by Elinore Blaisdell. Holt, 1947. 5 up

DE REGNIERS, BEATRICE SCHENK. *May I Bring a Friend?* ill. by Beni Montresor. Atheneum, 1964. A young child brings his (animal) friends with him when invited to visit the king and queen. Caldecott Medal. 5-7

______. *Something Special*, ill. by Irene Haas. Harcourt, 1958. 3-6

DICKINSON, EMILY. *Letter to the World*, ed. by Rumer Godden, ill. by Prudence Seward. Macmillan, 1969.

______. *Poems*, ed. by Helen Plotz, ill. by Robert Kipness. T. Crowell, 1964.

______. *Poems for Youth*, ed. by Alfred Hampson. Little, 1934. 11 up

ELIOT, T. S. *Collected Poems 1909–1935*. Harcourt, 1936. 13 up

FARJEON, ELEANOR. *The Children's Bells*, ill. by Peggy Fortnum. Walck, 1960.

______. *Eleanor Farjeon's Poems for Children*. Lippincott, 1951. 5-12

______. *Then There Were Three*, ill. by Isobel and John Morton-Sale. Lippincott, 1965. 4-7

FIELD, EUGENE. *Poems of Childhood*, ill. by Maxfield

Parrish. Scribner's, 1904. First published in 1896. 8-12

FIELD, RACHEL. *Poems*, ill. by author. Macmillan, 1957. Favorite selections from this versatile author's earlier books with a few new poems. 6-12

______. *Taxis and Toadstools*, ill. by author. Doubleday, 1926. 7-12

FINLAY, IAN HAMILTON. *Poems to Hear and See*. Macmillan, 1971. 8-10

FISHER, AILEEN. *But Ostriches. . .*, ill. by Peter Parnall. T. Crowell, 1970. 8-10

______. *Feathered Ones and Furry*, ill. by Eric Carle. T. Crowell, 1971. 5-8

______. *Going Barefoot*, ill. by Adrienne Adams. T. Crowell, 1960. 4-8

______. *In the Middle of the Night*, ill. by Adrienne Adams. T. Crowell, 1965. 5-7

______. *Listen, Rabbit*, ill. by Symeon Shimin. T. Crowell, 1964. A small boy sees a rabbit from time to time and comes to love it and then he finds a nest of young. A lovely picture book in which the gentle text and the beautiful illustrations are completely in harmony. 5-7

______. *Runny Days, Sunny Days; Merry Verses*, ill. by author. Abelard, 1958. 6-8

______. *Up, Up the Mountain*, ill. by Gilbert Riswold. T. Crowell, 1968. 8-10

______. *Where Does Everyone Go?* ill. by Adrienne Adams. T. Crowell, 1961. 4-8

FROMAN, ROBERT. *Street Poems*. McCall, 1971. 8-10

FROST, FRANCES. *The Little Naturalist*, ill. by Kurt Werth. Whittlesey, 1959. 8-12

______. *The Little Whistler*, ill. by Roger Duvoisin. Whittlesey, 1949. 8-12

FROST, ROBERT. *Complete Poems of Robert Frost*. Holt, 1949.

______. *In the Clearing*. Holt, 1962.

______. *You Come Too*, ill. by Thomas W. Nason. Holt, 1959. 11 up

FYLEMAN, ROSE. *Fairies and Chimneys*. Doubleday, 1944. 8-10

GREENAWAY, KATE. *Marigold Garden*, ill. by author. Warne, 1910.

______. *Under the Window*, ill. by author. Warne, 1910. 4-7

HOBERMAN, MARY ANN. *Hello and Good-By*, ill. by Norman Hoberman. Little, 1959. 4-9

HOFFMANN, HEINRICH. *Slovenly Peter, or Pretty Stories and Funny Pictures for Little Children*. Tuttle, 1969. 5-8

HOLMAN, FELICE. *At the Top of My Voice; and Other Poems*, ill. by Edward Gorey. Norton, 1970. 8-10

HUGHES, LANGSTON. *Black Misery*, ill. by Arouni. Eriksson, 1969. 10-14

______. *Don't You Turn Back*, selected by Lee Bennett Hopkins, ill. by Ann Grifalconi. Knopf, 1969. 10 up

______. *Fields of Wonder*. Knopf, 1947. 11 up

______. *Selected Poems of Langston Hughes*. Knopf, 1959. 11 up

ISSA. *A Few Flies and I; Haiku by Issa*, ed. by Jean Merrill and Ronni Solbert, from tr. by R. H. Blyth and Nobuyaki Yuasa, ill. by Ronni Solbert. Pantheon, 1969. 8-11

JARRELL, RANDALL. *The Bat-Poet*. Macmillan, 1967. 9-11

JOHNSON, JAMES WELDON. *God's Trombones*, ill. by Aaron Douglas. Viking, 1927. Seven verse sermons. Introduction discusses dialect and vernacular. 11 up

JORDAN, JUNE. *Who Look at Me*. T. Crowell, 1969. 10 up

KRYLOV, IVAN. *The Fifteen Fables of Krylov*, tr. by Guy Daniels, ill. by David Pascal. Macmillan, 1965. 10-12

KUMIN, MAXINE. *No One Writes a Letter to the Snail*, ill. by Bean Allen. Putnam, 1962. 8-10

KUSKIN, KARLA. *Alexander Soames: His Poems*, ill. by author. Harper, 1962. 5-8

______. *The Bear Who Saw the Spring*, ill. by author. Harper, 1961. A most amiable bear inducts a small dog into the beauties of each of the four seasons. Rhyming text makes this a delightful read-aloud picture book. 5-6

______. *In the Middle of the Trees*, ill. by author. Harper, 1958. 5-8

LEAR, EDWARD. *The Complete Nonsense Book*, ed. by Lady Strachey. Dodd, 1942. This volume includes both books referred to in the text: *The Book of Nonsense* and *Nonsense Songs and Stories*. These are available in the original attractive separate volumes from Warne. 8-14

______. *Le Hibou et la Poussiquette*, tr. by Francis Steegmuller, ill. by Barbara Cooney. Little, 1961.

______. *Incidents in the Life of My Uncle Arly*, ill. by Dale Maxey. Follett, 1969.

______. *The Jumblies*, ill. by Edward Gorey. W. R. Scott, 1968.

______. *The Owl and the Pussy Cat*, ill. by William Pène du Bois. Doubleday, 1962.

______. *The Owl and the Pussy-Cat*, ill. by Dale Maxey. Follett, 1970. 5-8

______. *The Quangle-Wangle's Hat*, ill. by Helen Oxenbury. Watts, 1969. 4-8

______. *The Scroobious Pip*, completed by Ogden Nash, ill. by Nancy Ekholm Burkert. Harper, 1968. 9 up

LENSKI, LOIS. *City Poems*, ill. by author. Walck, 1971. Most of the poems are new and their chief attraction is, for the urban child, the familiarity of the sights and activities they describe. 5-7

LEWIS, RICHARD, comp. *Of This World; A Poet's Life in Poetry*, ill. with photos by Helen Buttfield. Dial, 1968. 10 up

______. *The Way of Silence: The Prose and Poetry of Basho*. Dial, 1970. 10 up

LINDSAY, VACHEL. *Johnny Appleseed, and Other Poems*, ill. by George Richards. Macmillan, 1928. 10 up

______. *Springfield Town Is Butterfly Town*, ed. by Pierre Dussert, ill. by Vachel Lindsay. Kent State Univ. Pr., 1969. 7-11

LIVINGSTON, MYRA COHN. *A Crazy Flight; And Other Poems*, ill. by James Spanfeller. Harcourt, 1969. 8-11

______. *Happy Birthday!* ill. by Erik Blegvad. Harcourt, 1964. 5-7

______. *The Moon and a Star and Other Poems*, ill. by Judith Shahn. Harcourt, 1965. Poems about familiar phenomena or activities. 5-7

______. *Whispers and Other Poems*, ill. by Jacqueline Chwast. Harcourt, 1958. 5-7

______. *Wide Awake and Other Poems*, ill. by Jacqueline Chwast. Harcourt, 1959. 5-7

LOBEL, ARNOLD. *On the Day Peter Stuyvesant Sailed into Town*, ill. by author. Harper, 1971. 5-8

LOW, JOSEPH. *There Was a Wise Crow*, ill. by author. Follett, 1969. 5-8

MC CORD, DAVID. *All Day Long: Fifty Rhymes of the Never Was and Always Is*, ill. by Henry B. Kane. Little, 1966. 9-11

______. *Every Time I Climb a Tree*, ill. by Marc Simont. Little, 1967. 7-9

______. *Far and Few: Rhymes of the Never Was and Always Is*, ill. by Henry B. Kane. Little, 1952. 5-10

______. *For Me to Say: Rhymes of the Never Was and Always Is*, ill. by Henry B. Kane. Little, 1970. 9-11

______. *Take Sky: More Rhymes of the Never Was and Always Is*, ill. by Henry B. Kane. Little, 1962. 8 up

MC GINLEY, PHYLLIS. *All Around the Town* (see Bibliography, Chapter 3).

______. *Mince Pie and Mistletoe*, ill. by Harold Berson. Lippincott, 1961. 6-12

______. *A Wreath of Christmas Legends*, ill. by Leonard Weisgard. Macmillan, 1967. 10-13

MERRIAM, EVE. *Catch a Little Rhyme*, ill. by Imero Gobbato. Atheneum, 1966. 5-9

______. *Finding a Poem*, ill. by Seymour Chwast. Atheneum, 1970. 11 up

______. *Independent Voices*, ill. by Arvis Stewart. Atheneum, 1968. 10-12

______. *It Doesn't Always Have to Rhyme*, ill. by Malcolm Spooner. Atheneum, 1964. 10-14

______. *There Is No Rhyme for Silver*, ill. by Joseph Schindelman. Atheneum, 1962. Jaunty little verses full of rhythm, nonsense, and child appeal, for the youngest. 5-7

MILNE, A. A. *Now We Are Six*, ill. by Ernest Shepard. Dutton, 1927.

______. *When We Were Very Young*, ill. by Ernest Shepard. Dutton, 1924. These verses were reprinted in 1961, in larger type and more attractive format.

______. *The World of Christopher Robin*, ill. by Ernest Shepard. Dutton, 1958. The complete verses from *Now We Are Six* and *When We Were Very Young* appear in attractive single-volume format with eight new color illustrations. 5-10

MIZUMURA, KAZUE. *I See the Winds*, ill. T. Crowell, 1966. A small book with a brief poem on each page, and on the facing page an illustration. The illustrations vary from attractive to lovely; the poetry ranges from adequate to good. 8-10

MOORE, LILIAN. *I Thought I Heard the City*, ill. by Mary J. Dunton. Atheneum, 1969. 8-10

MORGENSTERN, CHRISTIAN. *The Three Sparrows, and Other Nursery Poems*, tr. by Max Knight, ill. by Nonny Hogrogian. Scribner's, 1968. 5-7

NASH, OGDEN. *The Cruise of the Aardvark*, ill. by Wendy Watson. Evans, 1967. 7-9

______. *Good Intentions*. Little, 1942. 10 up

O'NEILL, MARY. *Hailstones and Halibut Bones*, ill. by Leonard Weisgard. Doubleday, 1961. 6 up

ORGEL, DORIS. *The Good-Byes of Magnus Marmalade*, ill. by Erik Blegvad. Putnam, 1966. 8-9

PRELUTSKY, JACK. *A Gopher in the Garden; And Other Animal Poems*, ill. by Robert Leydenfrost. Macmillan, 1967. 9-10

______. *Toucans Two*, ill. by José Aruego. Macmillan, 1970. 5-7

RASMUSSEN, KNUD, comp. *Beyond the High Hills: A Book of Eskimo Poems*, ill. by Guy Mary-Rousselière. World, 1961. 7 up

REEVES, JAMES. *Prefabulous Animiles*, ill. by Edward Ardizzone. Dutton, 1960. Extraordinary, fantastic animals of a poet's creation make this a fun-filled collection of nonsense verse. In more varied vein is the poet's *Blackbird in the Lilac* (1959), an excellent selection of some fifty poems. 4-8

RICHARDS, LAURA E. *Tirra Lirra; Rhymes Old and New*, ill. by Marguerite Davis, foreword by May Hill Arbuthnot. Little, 1955. 5-12

RIEU, E. V. *The Flattered Flying Fish*, ill. by E. H. Shepard. Dutton, 1962. Lovely light verses that savor of Milne and Lewis Carroll and yet have a special quality of their own. There is a tenderness when touching on a child's woes and a happy imaginativeness in the nonsense rhymes. 7-12

ROBERTS, ELIZABETH MADOX. *Under the Tree*, ill. by F. D. Bedford. Viking, 1922. 6-10

ROETHKE, THEODORE. *Collected Poems*. Doubleday, 1966. 12 up

______. *I Am! Says the Lamb*, ill. by Robert Leydenfrost. Doubleday, 1961. 10 up

ROSSETTI, CHRISTINA. *Goblin Market*, ill. by Arthur Rackham. Watts, 1970. 9 up

______. *Goblin Market*, ill. by Ellen Raskin. Dutton, 1970. 9 up

______. *Sing Song*, ill. by Marguerite Davis. Macmillan, 1952. 4-10

RUKEYSER, MURIEL. *Mazes*, ill. with photos by Milton Charles. Simon, 1970. 8-10

SANDBURG, CARL. *Early Moon*, ill. by James Daugherty. Harcourt, 1930. 10-14

______. *Wind Song*, ill. by William A. Smith. Harcourt, 1960. Poems chosen for child appeal cover a wide range of subjects from prayers and people to nature and nonsense. 11-14

______. *The Sandburg Treasury; Prose and Poetry for Young People*, ill. by Paul Bacon. Harcourt, 1970. 10-14

SMITH, WILLIAM JAY. *Boy Blue's Book of Beasts*, ill. by Juliet Kepes. Little, 1957. 5-9

______. *Laughing Time*, ill. by Juliet Kepes. Little, 1955. 4 up

______. *Mr. Smith and Other Nonsense*, ill. by Don Bolognese. Delacorte, 1968. 8-12

______. *Typewriter Town*. Dutton, 1960.

STARBIRD, KAYE. *Don't Ever Cross a Crocodile*, ill. by Kit Dalton. Lippincott, 1963. 5-10

______. *The Pheasant on Route Seven*, ill. by Victoria de Larrea. Lippincott, 1968. 10-13

______. *A Snail's a Failure Socially; And Other Poems, Mostly About People*, ill. by Kit Dalton. Lippincott, 1966. 9-11

______. *Speaking of Cows*, ill. by Rita Fava. Lippincott,

1960. 5-10

STEARNS, MONROE. *Ring-A-Ling*, ill. by Adolf Zábransky. Lippincott, 1959. The verses, adapted from folk songs, are uneven in quality, but the illustrations are unforgettably beautiful. 4-8

STEVENSON, ROBERT LOUIS. *A Child's Garden of Verses*. There are many editions of this classic. These are representative.

Ill. by Jessie Willcox Smith. Scribner's, 1905, 1969. A large book with appealing pictures in soft colors.

Ill. by Tasha Tudor. Walck, 1947. A full edition with pictures in soft pastels using the young Robert Louis himself as the child.

Ill. by Brian Wildsmith. Watts, 1966. The loved and familiar poems are illustrated with the usual Wildsmith riot of color. 5-9

SWENSON, MAY. *More Poems to Solve*. Scribner's, 1971. 10 up

______. *Poems to Solve*. Scribner's, 1969. 12 up

TAGORE, RABINDRANATH. *Moon, For What Do You Wait?* ed. by Richard Lewis, ill. by Ashley Bryan. Atheneum, 1967. 9 up

TEASDALE, SARA. *Stars To-night*, ill. by Dorothy Lathrop. Macmillan, 1930. 8-12

TIPPETT, JAMES S. *I Live in a City*. Harper, 1924. 5-7

UPDIKE, JOHN. *A Child's Calendar*, ill. by Nancy Ekholm Burkert. Knopf, 1965. 8-10

WATSON, CLYDE. *Father Fox's Pennyrhymes*, ill. by Wendy Watson. T. Crowell, 1971. 3-6

WELLES, WINIFRED. *Skipping Along Alone*. Macmillan, 1931. Imaginative poems with a lyric quality. 7-9

# Part Four
# Realistic Fiction

# Chapter 12
# Animal Stories

Almost all children are interested in animals. Rhymes about "The Three Little Kittens" or the mouse that ran up the clock are early favorites. *Mother Goose* is supplemented by the more realistic animal picture books, first in linen or heavy paper and later in well-bound editions. With these picture books, children learn to name all the beasts under the sun from hippopotamuses to anteaters. The folk tales with animal heroes come next and seem never to wear out their welcome. "The Three Little Pigs," "The Little Red Hen," and all the other favorites are heard over and over with endless satisfaction.

From these, children progress to the more complex, realistic stories about animals, and for many people the interest lasts a lifetime. Consider the tremendous popularity—in book form, in films, and in television—of such animal stories as Eric Knight's *Lassie Come-Home* and Mary O'Hara's *My Friend Flicka*, and of television programs such as Disney's nature films, *Wild Kingdom*, and *Flipper*. Ernest Thompson Seton probably launched this favorite type of story with his *Lives of the Hunted* and other animal sagas.

## CRITERIA FOR JUDGING ANIMAL STORIES

Three groups of animal stories are discussed here under Ourselves in fur (animals that behave like human beings), Animals as animals but talking, and Animals as animals. The categories could be subdivided, but there is no point in spinning the distinctions too fine. These categories are important only because they call attention to diverse purposes and points of view in these stories and because they suggest somewhat our approach to and judgment of such stories.

Unquestionably, the books in the first category are the gayest, the stories in which the animals strut about with the same virtues and foibles as human beings. In the stories about Babar by Jean and Laurent de Brunhoff and *Ferdinand* by Munro Leaf, in Dr. Seuss' *Horton Hatches the Egg* and Michael Bond's *Paddington*, these absurd animals are doubly funny because they parody the people we know. The stories in this group are mostly animal comics, with Robert Lawson's *Rabbit Hill* and Kenneth Grahame's *The Wind in the Willows* striking more serious and mature notes. These beast tales are chiefly for children three to seven years old, with a few for the tens and even twelves. Of the folk-tale type we ask only good entertainment and good style. Such stories to be sound must be true to human, not animal, nature, and they must be told with lighthearted wisdom.

Books in the second category, the stories of animals scientifically represented with the exception of their power to think and speak, are a more serious group. In the *Tail* series by Gall and Crew for children from seven to ten, disasters and death are gently suggested but unmistakably present. *Charlotte's Web* by E. B. White remains lighthearted until death impinges at the end. In the stories for older children, nine to twelve, there are the real hardships and suffering, the cruelty and tragedy of books like Felix Salten's *Bambi*. Such stories make children aware of the hard lives of animals, constantly threatened by other animals, natural forces, and man.

This hybrid literary form is likely to become sentimental or to present an overly humanized animal. But Rudyard Kipling's *Jungle Books* are scrupulously true to the nature and the ways of each species, in spite of endowing the animals with speech. In short, when animals are described as animals but talking, their behavior and their problems must be only those of their animal world.

In the third category of books, the animals are objectively portrayed. The author may never interpret the animal's motives or behavior through giving the animal speech or thought. He may guess at the motives of his animal hero, but those guesses must accord with the interpretation of animal behavior as reliable observers have recorded it.

The books in which animals are objectively recorded as animals are popular with children from seven or eight to maturity; these stories range from mere thrillers to substantial literature. They may be as gay and humorous as Phil Stong's *Honk: the Moose*, but they are likely to be harrowing or tragic. The authors do not necessarily wish to play on the reader's emotions merely to rouse or hold interest, but the lives of most animals, whether wild or domestic, run into tragedy sooner or later. It has been said that wild creatures rarely die a natural death. The books show this to be true. Even pets are subject to the changing fortunes and whims of the human beings to whom they belong. They may be sold or given away or misunderstood to a tragic degree. Such dramatic situations make up the plots of many of these tales, and such stories are almost unavoidably melancholy.

If the animal hero is sufficiently appealing or the human and animal relationship sufficiently strong, such tragedies will attract

## VIEWPOINTS

. . . insofar as man, either primitive or modern, has had any tinge of philosophy he has also asked questions. Why did God bother to create [animals] or, in terms of a different vocabulary, what is their "place in nature"? Were they put on earth merely to serve man's need or pleasure and, as one medieval writer is said to have maintained, were they endowed with life only in order that their flesh should not decay before some human being got around to eating them? Are they, on the other hand, to some degree fellow creatures with some rights and privileges of their own? How much do they resemble and how greatly do they differ from man himself? What conclusions are to be drawn from the likeness and the difference?

For all these reasons a collection of writings about animals is also about the men who have been moved, for one reason or another, to write on that subject. Sometimes consciously and sometimes unconsciously (but always inevitably) the writer implies an answer to one or more of the questions which any concern with an animal must raise, and this is quite as true in the case of one who describes merely how he collected a trophy as in that of the biologist or the mystic.—From *The World of Animals*, compiled with commentary by Joseph Wood Krutch. Simon and Schuster, New York, 1961, p. 19.

readers even to a poor story. In these strongly emotional plots we need to be more than ordinarily alert to what is a true and consistent story, and to what is pure animal melodrama. A little melodrama or a few trashy books are not going to hurt children, but they should not miss the great animal tales in a welter of second-rate ones.

## TALKING BEASTS—OURSELVES IN FUR

The oldest type of animal story is the folk tale (talking beast) in which the animals are given the characteristics of human beings—they are ourselves in fur. These stories are completely unscientific. The third little pig belongs to no Poland China nor any other swine species. He is called Pig, but he is really our industrious and capable selves, triumphing over every difficulty. So in the modern talking-beast stories, Hans Rey's *Curious George*, the irresponsible, mischievous monkey is a four-footed Andrewshek or a Little Pear or a Johnny Jenks next door, always in hot water. The animals in *The Wind in the Willows* are more like our neighbors than they are like moles and toads and river rats. Toad is the perfect picture of some vacuous and reckless young playboy, and Ratty is the Good Samaritan, the guardian angel which such young scamps seem always to acquire.

There is a great variety in these animal takeoffs on human behavior. Some of them are close to fables. Marjorie Flack's *Ping* shows children that home is best even with a spank—a moral for four-year-olds, without any moralizing. In Robert Lawson's *Rabbit Hill* pompous Father Rabbit, worrying Mother, and suspicious, complaining Uncle Analdas are thoroughly entertaining—and they are also satires on types of people we have known. The same characters in *The Tough Winter* reveal the helplessness of creatures in the grip of natural forces more effectively than a factual account could do.

In hilarious contrast to *The Tough Winter* is Anne H. White's *Junket*, a story about a canine who teaches a city family the proper ways of farm living from a dog's-eye view. Junket is all dog, but he has the determination of a wise, patient great-uncle who gets things done, one way or another. This is a lastingly popular story.

From the talking tortoise and Balaam's ass to Mickey Mouse, these unscientific talking-beast tales have had a long life. Why have they lasted, and why does the stream of new ones continue? Apparently it is the fun of their exaggerated pictures of human foibles. Donald Duck, with his hoarse roarings, is so ridiculously like someone we know that he makes us chuckle. Or the timid seventh duck in Margaret Friskey's *Seven Diving Ducks* makes the timid child feel brave by comparison, and he is consoled. Or Mary Chalmers' *Be Good, Harry* can reassure the child who worries about being left with a baby-sitter. Or the Babar stories offer children amusing pictures of the adult world and social relationships.

In the chapters on the old folk tales, the fables, and the modern fanciful tales, many of the talking-beast stories have already been reviewed. A few more examples of the type, then, will suffice—two unusual talking-beast stories: Toba Sojo's *The Animal Frolic* and Munro Leaf's *The Story of Ferdinand*, Else Minarik's *Little Bear* books, Russell Hoban's stories about Frances, and Arnold Lobel's *Frog and Toad Are Friends*.

### TOBA SOJO

*The Animal Frolic*

If you have a chance to share with children that collector's item *The Animal Frolic* (1954),[1] you will doubly enjoy some of the most subtle and beautiful satires on human behavior you have ever seen. The book is a reproduction of a twelfth-century scroll by a famous Japanese artist. Here is the officious

1. See page 48 for an additional discussion of this book.

rabbit as chairman of the hospitality committee and master of ceremonies. The text does not say he is, but he must be, because throughout this animal picnic he welcomes, bosses, organizes, interferes, and decides. Contests are set up to choose the king of the picnic. (Evidently beauty contests had not yet troubled twelfth-century Japan.) Some of the contests are fair and square, but the frog wins on an undetected foul. He bites the rabbit's ear and hangs on. However, he does make a very decent king, after all. The text is slight, but children can provide their own interpretations of what is happening. And the droll antics of the animals in these matchless pictures will delight both children and adults.

### MUNRO LEAF

*The Story of Ferdinand*

No adult ever forgets his first surprised examination of the small book bearing the picture of a mild-looking bull and the title *The Story of Ferdinand* (1936). Munro Leaf's brief, succinct text, together with some of Robert Lawson's finest drawings, achieves a droll perfection that is hard to account for.

Ferdinand, the peaceful bull, accidentally sits down on a bee, is stung into wild action, and is mistaken for the "fightingest" bull of the whole countryside. He is carted off to the city for a bullfight, but once in the arena he merely returns to his favorite occupation, smelling flowers, and so is ignominiously sent back to his meadow.

Why does this small tale induce such prolonged chuckles? First, it has a genuinely funny situation: peaceful Ferdinand cast in the role of a frightful monster! Ferdinand's plight suggests amusing human parallels. Probably every adult has at one time or another found himself in the thick of some battle for which he was never intended; some awful committee he should never have been put on; some exalted public task he is supposed to work at brilliantly when all he really wants is a little spare time to go his own way and sniff peacefully at such fine flowers of leisure as life affords. So adults, identifying themselves with the absurdly miscast Ferdinand, are much amused with his tribulations. But children like this story, too. The youngest take it literally. They say gravely, "Did the bee hurt Ferdinand?" Older children are entranced by the drawings and catch the fine humor of the text.

*From* The Story of Ferdinand the Bull *by Munro Leaf and Robert Lawson. Copyright 1936 by Robert Lawson (illustrations), renewed © 1964 by James W. Boyd. Reprinted by permission of The Viking Press, Inc.*

### ELSE H. MINARIK

*The Little Bear stories*

Else Minarik's series of books about *Little Bear* (1957), his mother, father, friends, and activities have enjoyed a well-deserved popularity. Little Bear is any small child. He pretends he is going to take off for the moon, but after falling kerplop, he approaches his mother, who enters into his make-believe by asking him who he is. When this pretending goes a little too far for his comfort,

*Illustration by Maurice Sendak from* Little Bear *by Else Holmelund Minarik. Copyright 1957. Reproduced by permission of Harper & Row, Publishers, Inc. (Original with color)*

*Little Bear put his arms around Mother.*
*He said, "Mother Bear, stop fooling.*
*You are my Mother Bear*
*And I am your Little Bear,*
*And we are on earth, and you know it.*
*Now may I have my lunch."*

These books are of the easy-to-read variety, but they are completely satisfying stories, with Maurice Sendak's irresistible pictures.

## RUSSELL HOBAN

*Bedtime for Frances*

In all of Russell Hoban's stories about Frances, the small badger, there is affection for and understanding of children. In *Bedtime for Frances* (1960) the bright-eyed heroine goes through all the techniques of stalling with which every child save the most sanctimonious is familiar. She wants a glass of milk. She asks to be carried to her room. May she sleep with her doll? Mother gives her the doll. "Did you kiss me?" Yes, but Mother and Father kiss her again. She wants the door open, she sees a tiger in the corner and goes to report on this, and then she sees a giant, and thinks it would be nice to stay with her parents and watch television. She remembers that she forgot to brush her teeth. By then her parents are in bed, and Father cocks a leery eye when she comes in to tell him that something is moving the curtains. Finally Father asserts himself and tells Frances the train of consequences that may possibly, just possibly, result in a spanking. These characters are indeed ourselves in fur: the fact that Frances is a badger makes the story applicable without being didactic, but

*Illustration by Lillian Hoban from* Best Friends for Frances *by Russell Hoban. Copyright 1969. Reproduced by permission of Harper & Row, Publishers, Inc. (Original in color)*

in each of the stories about Frances (*A Baby Sister for Frances* [1964], *Best Friends for Frances* [1969], *A Bargain for Frances* [1970], and others) there is some very familiar childhood situation used as a basis for an amusing story—with beguiling illustrations—that can contribute to a small child's understanding of himself, his relationships with other people, and the fulfillment of his emotional needs.

### ARNOLD LOBEL

*Frog and Toad Are Friends*

Two more amiable and ingenuous creatures than Frog and Toad do not exist, and their fond, patient give-and-take is an admirable example for the beginning reader for whom they were created. The book comprises five very short stories, and the illustrations as well as the text have charm and simplicity. One story: the friends go for a long walk, Toad returning in a state of irritation because he has lost a button from his jacket. Several friends offer buttons, but they don't match, and the irate Toad then finds the button at home and realizes how much trouble he has caused Frog. He sews the buttons on securely, and next day gives his jacket to Frog as a gift. This little gem of 1970 was a Caldecott Honor Book and one of the finalists for the National Book Award.

*Illustration by Arnold Lobel from* Frog and Toad Are Friends *by Arnold Lobel. Copyright 1970. Reproduced by permission of Harper & Row, Publishers, Inc. (Original in color)*

## ANIMALS AS ANIMALS BUT TALKING

The second type of animal story is a paradox. In these tales the animals are scientifically true to their species, but they are given the human abilities of thought and speech. The boy Mowgli, in the *Jungle Books*, first learns the language of each kind of animal; then he converses with his four-footed friends much as he might talk with his parents. But Bear always advises from the standpoint of bear experience, and Panther from panther experience. In Felix Salten's *Bambi*, the deer thinks and speaks only of deer matters, never of human. Except that we are told the thoughts of the animals, the story is scientifically true to deer life and to the lives of the other creatures.

This is a difficult type of story to tell convincingly, for it is easy to sentimentalize or humanize the animals falsely. But if these stories are honestly written, they are good for children to have. Told from the standpoint of the animal, they dramatize the creature and point up his hardships, his fears, and his tragedies. The children gain from such stories a closer kinship with animals, more tenderness for them, and a greater desire to help them.

## VIEWPOINTS

The creative writer, in depicting an animal's behaviour, is under no greater obligation to keep within the bounds of exact truth than is the painter or the sculptor in shaping an animal's likeness. But all three artists must regard it as their most sacred duty to be properly instructed regarding those particulars in which they deviate from the actual facts. They must indeed be even better informed on these details than on others which they render in a manner true to nature. There is no greater sin against the spirit of true art, no more contemptible dilettantism than to use artistic licence as a specious cover for ignorance of fact.—Konrad Z. Lorenz, *King Solomon's Ring; New Light on Animal Ways*, Thomas Y. Crowell Co., New York, 1952, pp. xviii–xix.

Hans Christian Andersen's "Ugly Duckling" is an admirable example of this type of animal tale. The young swan, in a barnyard full of cackling hens, chickens, ducks, and turkeys, is confronted with the problems of being a swan. He is rejected because he is different; he suffers the perils of being outcast and alone; he yearns to belong to his own kind without knowing why; and when his maturity is accomplished, he is welcomed by the swans to whom he belongs. This is an allegory, but it is also the story of a swan, scientifically true to its species except that we are told what this swan thinks and says.

Of course, children have always thought of their pets' noises as talk. "Soot says he is hungry," they interpret helpfully when the dog barks. And this is good, because it means they are developing a sensitivity to the needs of animals and to their discomfort or suffering when they are neglected or mistreated. These talking-beast tales which are also authentic animal lore speak for the vulnerability of all animals—the fear of the hunted creature as well as the joy of the pet in the companionship of his beloved master.

### ANNA SEWELL
*Black Beauty*

In contrast to "The Ugly Duckling," there is that old animal classic *Black Beauty*, by Anna Sewell, first published in 1877. It enjoyed tremendous popularity for many years. Some children wept over Beauty's sufferings and were never thereafter able to ride or drive a horse without being haunted by its probable agonies of mind or body. Only parents with a sense of humor could laugh and talk them out of Black Beauty vapors.

*Black Beauty* was written as a protest against the tight checkrein and other more serious cruelties to horses. It relates, in the first person, a good story of the ups and downs of a carriage horse. Black Beauty tells us about his happy childhood. Then things go wrong. Black Beauty is sold farther and farther down the horse social scale. People inexperienced with horses handle him; he is whipped, abused, underfed, and neglected. Through a series of happy accidents he falls into the hands of Joe, the now prosperous man who as an unskilled groom almost killed him. He makes amends to the old horse, and Beauty lives in clover ever after.

This story sounds all right, yet *Black Beauty* is rarely listed in careful bibliographies in spite of new and beautiful editions of it. One reason is that Black Beauty, while presumably a real horse, thinks and talks out of horse character. He is humanly sensitive to the social and moral tone of the people with whom he lives. His social judgments are those of a genteel lady, not a horse. He is ultraconservative about such habits as smoking, of which he heartily disapproves. Bad language, dirty clothes, and the smell of liquor offend his refined sensibilities—not as a horse, which might associate these things with cruel treatment, but as a perfect Victorian lady. Black Beauty is so full of human proprieties that he ceases to be convincing as a horse. The story is also morbidly sad, but it is the sentimentality and the overhumanizing of the species that make *Black Beauty* unconvincing as a horse story, and that violate one of the criteria for this type of fiction.

### RUDYARD KIPLING

*The Jungle Books*

The greatness of Rudyard Kipling's *Jungle Books* (1894) lies in part in his scrupulous avoidance of this temptation to overly humanize the animals. Mowgli, the human baby, is raised by the wolves and vouched for by them at the council rock. Later he is repudiated by his foster brothers because he is not wolf. They remain true to their wolfishness, knowing that Mowgli can never be one with them. Thereafter Mowgli hunts alone. Another example from these stories of the way Kipling scrupulously reveals the nature of the animal and never permits sentimentality to mar the picture is "Kaa's Hunting." Usually the animals avoid the great snake, Kaa. They know his wiles and have a healthy respect for his powers, but when Mowgli is stolen by the irresponsible monkeys, his protectors, the Bear and the Panther, have to summon Kaa to help them. He graciously consents, only because of the prospect of a delectable feast on the silly monkeys. All goes well. Mowgli is released, but before he and his protectors can depart, Kaa has begun his dance before the monkeys. Spellbound, they watch him, and spellbound, the Bear and the Panther watch also. Mowgli has to bring them out of their trance and get them away, or they, too, like the helpless monkeys, would soon find themselves a part of Kaa's feast.

It would have been easy for a less skillful writer to have made Kaa altruistic, or at least temporarily loyal to his friends of the hunt, but Kipling knew his jungle animals too well and was too scrupulous a writer to make any such mistakes. It is for these reasons, as well as for the exciting episodes in the stories and for their powerful imaginative appeal, that no recent books ever displace the *Jungle Books*.

### VIEWPOINTS

It is obvious that the naturalist would not indulge in anthropomorphism—the endowment of animals with human traits. It is not so clear that the writers of even the best animal stories should not or do not do so. Some transfer of human intelligence and emotion to the animal character can, in good hands, heighten the emotional impact of a story and strengthen the rapport between writer and reader. . . . But it takes a sure sense of the limits of credibility to keep the realistic animal story from being maudlin or, worse, so confused as to be neither animal story nor outright fantasy.—Sheila Egoff, *The Republic of Childhood*, Oxford University Press, Toronto, 1967, p. 107.

Children get from these stories an insight into wild-animal nature, into the curious likeness of animals and humans, and into the still more curious lines of demarcation.

### FELIX SALTEN

*Bambi*
*Bambi's Children*

*Bambi* (1931) and *Bambi's Children* (1938) by Felix Salten are also fine animal stories. Bambi is a deer, and we follow him from his first day of life in a little forest glade to the absentee parenthood of the mature male deer. The books are exquisitely written and the animals well characterized. They are all there, from little field mice and rabbits to foxes and great elk. There is also "He," the enemy of all the forest creatures. His scent carries terror; his pale, hairless face chills them with horror because just beneath it are "legs" which reach out with a stick, and the stick shoots fire and death far beyond its reach. *Bambi* tells a story of man's hunting from the standpoint of the hunted and is therefore desperately tragic in places. The account of the hunters encircling the animals and then frightening them from their hiding places with terrible noises and constant shooting is so horrible it should make readers hate this barbarous practice. The larger proportion of the two Bambi books has to do with the training of the young deer, with the relationship of the males and females in the organization of the herd, and with some of the idyllic qualities of forest life as well as with the hard struggle for existence in the winter months. Children nine to eleven can read these books, but younger children enjoy hearing them, too.

## ALICE CREW GALL
## FLEMING CREW

*The Tail books*

The *Tail* books by Alice Crew Gall and Fleming Crew are animal stories that are scientifically accurate except for the animals' power of speech. The first of the series, *Wagtail* (1932), is the story of pond life, told from the viewpoint of a polliwog. Wagtail's universe is the Blue Pool and the bordering banks, where he must learn to distinguish between friends and foes. Once Wagtail has achieved legs, the old Patriarch frog teaches him the basic law of his kind, which is to jump first at the sight of a strange creature and find out about him afterward. Wagtail remembers this advice when he is idly wondering about an approaching heron. He jumps just as the heron opens his mouth to catch the frog—"another second would have been too late." Decidedly, action is the thing. From the friendly woodchuck, he learns a strange fact: the Blue Pool is not there in the cold months. It is gone completely; only white snow is everywhere. This is baffling, particularly since the Patriarch has told Wagtail about their long winter sleep, buried in mud at the bottom of the pond, and has also hinted very gently of a still longer sleep, a sleep from which some warm spring the old frog will not return, and Wagtail will take his place on the old log and be the new Patriarch. This, too, is baffling, but something to be accepted without anxiety. Meanwhile, the sun shines hot and comforting on Wagtail's back, and the pond is clear and blue. Frog life is good, despite these mysteries. Whether it is *Ringtail* the raccoon or *Flat Tail* the beaver, these stories are true to the species, and each book gives the reader a clear understanding of a particular species and its ways of life.

Following *Bambi* and the *Tail* books there were no outstanding contributions to this type of animal story until E. B. White wrote his *Charlotte's Web*, which has been discussed in Chapter 8 under fantasy. To be sure, each animal in the book remains true to his species. Wilbur, the silly pig, fights death in every way he knows. Templeton, the rat, fattens happily on the rich garbage of the county fair. And Charlotte, the spider, dies according to the biological laws of her species. But the animals are also embodiments of human folly, greed, and selflessness, and this distinguished contribution to children's literature remains more fantasy than animal lore.

## RANDALL JARRELL

*The Bat-Poet*

In *The Bat-Poet* (1963), poet and critic Randall Jarrell wrote a story of grave sweetness, a quality echoed in the Maurice Sendak illustrations. It is at the same time a small homily on the writing of poetry. His creatures speak and think, but their behavior is true to their animal natures, and the poetry written by the bat gives marvelously vivid pictures of the owl, the mockingbird, the chipmunk, and the bat. The little brown bat discovers all of the activity going on during the day and tries to convince his companions that they should stay awake, but they share neither his curiosity nor his poetic vision. Listening to the virtuoso performance of the mockingbird, the bat feels stirred to write, and he reads his poetry to the subjects of his portraits in verse. When winter comes, the small brown bat gets more and more sleepy, and he cuddles in among the other bats, upside down, and drowses off. For all of the discussion of poetry, the actions and reactions of the bat and his friends are in general animallike.

### GUIDO ROCCA

*Gaetano the Pheasant*

Although there are occasional episodes in *Gaetano the Pheasant* (1966) where the birds are not birdlike (books often refuse to be classified), it is primarily a tale in which the animals are in the main true to their species. Indeed, the plot centers on their plight as creatures helpless against the sportsmen who decimate their numbers. Gaetano, more observant and thoughtful than the other pheasants, has noticed that there are ways of escaping the guns of the hunters in the game preserve: one can slow down and fool the man with a gun, or one can give up flying and walk. The other birds deride him, but Gaetano determines to escape and with his mate goes off on a long flight to the safety of an uninhabited island. The conversation among the birds is witty and pointed, and more perceptive children will understand the parallels between birds and men. For any reader there is a double value in the book: it is a story with pace and humor, and it helps readers understand the cruelty of killing for sport. As in other books in this category, it is written from the animal's point of view.

### JACQUELINE JACKSON

*Chicken Ten Thousand*

*Chicken Ten Thousand* (1968) is one of the few picture books that depict animals that speak but act like animals. Chicken Ten Thousand is a victim of progress, a mere number in a hatchery, a hen not quite understanding the frustration she feels. Crated for market, she escapes when her crate is jolted off the truck. "What was this green sawdust that felt so cool and smelled so sweet? What was this brown floor so rough and scratchy under claw with tasty tidbits scurrying around?" She meets a rooster, a boastful creature who deigns to add her to his harem, and when she subsequently lays eggs, expecting again the disappointment of the hatchery, Chicken Ten Thousand learns the satisfaction of motherhood. The book deftly combines information about the egg business and a pleasant story that should arouse children's sympathetic understanding. In describing the hen's reactions to earth and grass, sun and pond (to her, "what must be the largest water pan in all the world"), the book also subtly suggests the way in which our interpretation can be determined by our experience.

## ANIMALS AS ANIMALS OBJECTIVELY REPORTED

The third type of animal story is the one told from observation, with fidelity to all the

*From the book* Anna and the Baby Buzzard *by Helga Sandburg. Illustrations by Brinton Turkle. Illustrations copyright © 1970 by Brinton Turkle. Published by E. P. Dutton & Co., Inc. and used with their permission. (Original with color)*

modern knowledge of a species. It may deal with animals by themselves in their own world, as reliable observers have seen them, holding their own against their particular enemies and solving their own problems. Or it may deal with human beings and animals together. In this case the animals are most frequently pets—dogs, kittens, or horses—recorded objectively as human beings see them. For example, in Helga Sandburg's *Anna and the Baby Buzzard* (1970), based on an incident in the author's childhood, it is Anna and her father who realize that the buzzard, now large and quite tame, will soon be flying off to seek her kind. The story may be factual and told in the first person, as is Sterling North's *Rascal* (1963). This story of an engaging pet raccoon is handsomely illustrated by John Schoenherr, and was so popular that the author wrote a simplified version, *Little Rascal* (1965). The animals are permitted no thoughts, except as people guess at them, and no language other than the barks or whines or purrs or cringing or hissing or exuberant cavortings appropriate to their kind.

Such stories are in the majority and are on the whole the most popular of all types of animal books with children over seven or eight. In these stories, the child finds himself a spectator in a humorous or tragic or dramatic series of events whose import he cannot always fathom. He finds himself looking in on an unfamiliar world, enough like his own so that it rouses his curiosity and sympathy but so strange that he cannot predict what will happen. He knows the mother creature will defend her young at the risk of her life, even as the human mother will, but the animal mother's means of defense will be strange to him and her defeat or triumph uncertain. He tries to guess at what his dog is pleading with him to do, but he may not guess right and so may blunder on a happy or a tragic solution of the dog's difficulty. It is the element of uncertainty in these objective modern animal tales that makes them more convincing and more exciting than other types. If such stories are genuinely true to animal nature and abilities, they constitute an excellent source of enlightenment and engrossing entertainment for the modern child.

*From the book Rascal by Sterling North. Illustration by John Schoenherr. Illustration copyright © 1963 by E. P. Dutton & Co., Inc., publishers, and used with their permission.*

## DOROTHY LATHROP

*Who Goes There?*
*Hide and Go Seek*

There are some outstanding picture books designed for the youngest child which give equal delight to adults and to all ages in between. Dorothy Lathrop's *Who Goes There?*

(1935) pictures in exquisite drawings the small creatures who come to eat the food left for them in the snowy forest. Chipmunks, red squirrels, gray squirrels, rabbits, field mice, a crow, a porcupine, and even flying squirrels come to the feast. By way of an index, their tracks are recorded behind each animal. Here is a book to take out and look at again every winter. Children who study these pictures will know these animals intimately. In *Hide and Go Seek* (1938), Miss Lathrop has drawn the flying squirrels from birth to maturity, in every type of activity, until this tiny nocturnal animal is as familiar as a pet dog. One teacher, never having seen flying squirrels in the flesh, knew them instantly from these pictures when they began to come and go on her window sill after dusk, for all the world like small flashes of furry lightning. In time, the food and quiet allayed their fears, and she could observe how truly the artist had recorded her own living models. Miss Lathrop's art has already been discussed (p. 63), but nowhere is it finer than in these two books.

## MARY AND CONRAD BUFF

*Dash and Dart*
*Forest Folk*

Mary and Conrad Buff have made a number of beautiful picture stories for young readers and prereaders. *Dash and Dart* (1942) tells about the first year in the lives of twin fawns. *Forest Folk* (1962) continues the story of Dash to the time when he fights his way to become king of the herd. *Hurry, Skurry, and Flurry* (1954) are three forest squirrels, frolicsome but aware of the lurking danger which always threatens them and finally catches up with one. The tiny *Elf Owl* (1958) looks out of his home in a spiny saguaro cactus and views the drama of desert creatures from a safe distance. The pictures in these books have a poetic beauty that matches the cadenced text. The stories read aloud beautifully and provide a background of understanding for the more complex animal stories to come.

*Illustration by Dorothy Lathrop from* Who Goes There? *by Dorothy Lathrop. Copyright, 1935 by The Macmillan Company.*

## MARJORIE FLACK

*The Angus books*
*The Story about Ping*

Realistic animal stories for the youngest children are on the whole a cheerful group containing some excellent pictures and some of

*From* Hurry, Skurry, and Flurry *by Mary and Conrad Buff. Copyright 1954 by Mary Marsh Buff and Conrad Buff. Reprinted by permission of The Viking Press, Inc.*

the children's favorite tales. Early favorites were the dog stories of Marjorie Flack.

The *Angus* books are worn to shreds by athletic young devotees of four or five. *Angus and the Ducks* (1930), the first of the series, is typical. Angus is a small, curious Scotch terrier. Even as he dozes on or under his favorite sofa he wishes to get out and discover things for himself. One day his chance comes. He runs out the open door, through the hedge, into the next garden. There he encounters some strange creatures who go "Quack, quack, quack." He barks at them and they run away. This is very satisfactory to Angus, and he feels well pleased with himself. He explores the ducks' territory, but suddenly they turn on him, both of them, and, with a terrible "sssing" and flapping of wings, they chase him through the garden and through the hedge back to his own house. There the terrified Scottie takes refuge under the sofa and forgets to be curious for all of three minutes. A simple enough narrative, you may think, but just try to do something like it. Here at the simplest level are all the elements of a good plot—a problem, action, and a surprising, humorous climax and conclusion.

*The Story about Ping* (1933), with pictures by Kurt Wiese, carries the children to China, and so it is generally allocated to the sixes and sevens, although the fours enjoy it thoroughly. Ping is a duck, a youthful member of a large duck family living on a boat in the Yangtze River. In the morning all the ducks walk down a gangplank and go swimming in the river. Toward evening they return to their boat, and the last duck to waddle up the gangplank always gets a little spank from a small switch. Ping, returning late one evening, decides that he won't submit to this spank, and so he hides in the rushes all night. The next day all sorts of things happen to him. Finally, he is captured by a strange family which intends to cook him, but a kindhearted boy sets him free. Ping hastily returns to his own family. Home and security, even with a spank, look good to the adventurous young duck after the dangers he has endured.

The story is told with a directness that makes ducks on the Yangtze River as understandable and homey as ducks on the local duck pond, and the prodigal Ping receiving his spank gratefully is an amusing final touch. No need to moralize. "Home's best after all" is written all over Ping's contented acceptance of the family pattern. Kurt Wiese's pictures add to the fun of the story.

## LYND WARD

*The Biggest Bear*

A delectable comedy is Lynd Ward's *The Biggest Bear* (1952), which won the Caldecott Medal almost by public acclamation. Young Johnny is so mortified because his family has no bearskin nailed up on their barn door that he sets off to capture a bear all by himself. He does it, too, and brings it home alive. That bear grows and grows and grows, and Johnny's problems grow right along with the bear. The solution, like most things in life, is a compromise, but not half bad for either Johnny or the bear. Adults are as captivated by this story and its pictures as the children are. (For an additional comment on Ward's illustrations, see p. 66.)

## CLARE TURLAY NEWBERRY

*Percy, Polly, and Pete*

Clare Turlay Newberry's little books have no importance as literature, but as exquisite picture books for the youngest they are unexcelled. Her cats have a fluffy, furry look that tempts you to touch them, and so have the woolly snowsuits and the hair of the children. There is a softness, a rotundity, and a depth of textures in her pictures to which children and adults respond with equal delight.

*Mittens*, *Babette*, *Barkis*, and *Marshmallow* are cat stories, but they also include one puppy, one rabbit, and the children. *Percy, Polly, and Pete* (1952) is the amusing story of an old mother cat who tries to hide her three kittens, in order to protect them from the strenuous affection of two-year-old Shasha. This is Mrs. Newberry's nearest approach to a plot, but the tender appeal of her pictures and the kindliness that pervades the stories make them worthwhile.

## TOM ROBINSON

*Buttons*

A picture story which has never enjoyed the popularity it deserves is *Buttons* (1938) by Tom Robinson, superbly illustrated by Peggy Bacon. There have been innumerable stories about fluffy kittens, Siamese exotics, and felines of various ages and colors, but *Buttons* is the first tale about an alley cat, the son of an alley cat, a hero to the last scratch. Born in an ash can, orphaned at six weeks, fighting his way to the kingship of the alley mousers – how he managed to leave all this behind and attain cleanly security makes a grand tale. These are not pretty cats, and starvation looks out of their gaunt faces, but they have desperate courage and the will to live. Perhaps for these reasons *Buttons* shouldn't be given to all four-year-olds, but from five on children can well afford to pore over these pictures and sympathize with the forlorn but unquenchable hero, Buttons.

## MISKA MILES

*Nobody's Cat*

In *Nobody's Cat* (1969), another alley cat, tough and self-sufficient, fights, hunts for food, and sleeps wherever he can find shelter. One day he stalks into a school when he smells the lunchroom food, and allows himself to be petted by the children. He narrowly escapes being run over by a car and eventually finds his way back to the safety of his own alley. With no sentimentality, no happy ending, the book awakens sympathy by showing the alley cat just as he is: lean, homely, and lonely. The animal stories of Miska Miles include *Fox and the Fire* (1966), *Mississippi Possum* (1965), and *Eddie's Bear* (1970). They have in common a quiet tone and absence of anthropomorphism. Illustrated by John Schoenherr, they differ from Schoenherr's *The Barn* in having more plot, more interaction with other animals and with human beings, but are the same in their identification with the animal's point of view.

## JOHN SCHOENHERR

*The Barn*

John Schoenherr's beautiful, realistic drawings of animals that grace the stories of Miska Miles and other writers have a quiet fidelity to nature also evident in Schoenherr's pictures for his own book, *The Barn* (1968). There is no hint of anthropomorphism – the animals are true to their species, and their existence is a struggle for survival, a struggle in which there are no heroes and no villains. In *The Barn*, a skunk, hungry in a time of drought, leaves the safety of the barn to venture forth into daylight and finds that another predator is about, an owl who snatches the mouse the skunk is stalking. The skunk retreats, the owl flies after it and catches it, then loses it and goes her way. A small event, this is the perennial drama of wild creatures, and Schoenherr makes it all the more effective by his subdued writing and by the acuity with which he has observed and recorded it.

## AILEEN FISHER

*Valley of the Smallest*

Written in a smooth narrative style, Aileen Fisher's story of the life cycle of a shrew, *Valley of the Smallest* (1966), is meticulous in detail, giving not only a vivid picture of the shrew but also of the ecological pattern of which she is a part. Tiny, nervous, always hungry, the mountain shrew's whole life is a search for food, the pattern of her days governed by the behavior of other animals and the climate as much as by the drive to fulfill her own needs.

## C. W. ANDERSON

*The Blaze stories*
*Salute*

C. W. Anderson's books range in their appeal from the five-year-old level to high school. They are simply written, substantial stories with splendid drawings of horses by a man who knows every muscle, every stance, and every cavorting of these big, amiable creatures. The books begin for the five-year-olds with *Billy and Blaze* (1936), the simple story of a little boy who gets his first pony and names it Blaze for the star on its forehead. Children of five like the *Blaze* stories, but slow readers of eight and nine will read them with pleasure also, because of the horse pictures and the direct style of the narratives.

In addition to the *Blaze* books, Mr. Anderson has written stories of the race horses he knows so well. He has child characters in these books, too—horsy children who read everything there is to read about the great racers and study horse training humbly and devotedly. One value of these books is the picture they give of the patience needed to make a racer. *Salute* and *High Courage* are great favorites. Fine human relationships are to be found in all the Anderson stories.

## ERIC KNIGHT

*Lassie Come-Home*

Appearing first as a magazine short story, Eric Knight's *Lassie Come-Home* was published in book form in 1940. When Joe's father had to go on dole, their valuable collie is sold to a duke. But faithful Lassie escapes and makes a 400-mile journey from Scotland to Yorkshire to rejoin her young master. In 1971 the story of the come-home dog was revised by Knight's widow and his editors to contain changes made by the author before his death, including the minimization of some of the Yorkshire and Cockney dialects.

## GLEN ROUNDS

*The Blind Colt*

*The Blind Colt* (1941) by Glen Rounds is a mildly sad horse story for children eight to eleven. It is quite moving, but it does have humor, too, and is, besides, a completely satisfying "Western."

Whitey watches a blind colt until he wants it more than any other colt on the range. His uncle tells him it must be shot, and the boy is inconsolable. Finally he wins a reprieve for the blind but spirited animal. When it survives all the dangers of a hard winter and marauding wolves, Whitey begins the colt's training. His success convinces Uncle Torval that this is really a smart colt and will make a good "Sunday horse" at least. So Whitey keeps his colt and the colt finds security.

Written in the cowboy vernacular, this book makes an instant appeal to boys. The pictures by the author convey some of the excitement of the colt's adventures. *Blind Colt* is followed by several good Westerns with young Whitey as the resourceful hero in all of them.

## MARGUERITE HENRY

*King of the Wind*
*Brighty of the Grand Canyon*

Marguerite Henry is probably the most successful writer of horse stories we have ever had. Her success rests on a sound basis. Every book represents careful research, the stories are well told, the animal heroes are true to their species, and the people in her books are as memorable as the animals.

*Justin Morgan Had a Horse* (1954) is an example of the careful research Mrs. Henry puts into a book. For this book she conducted an intensive search for information about the ancestor of the Morgan breed and the people responsible for establishing it. It is the story of a poor teacher and singing master who accepted two horses in payment for a debt. One of them was a big, handsome creature and the other was a runt of a colt. It was Justin Morgan's young pupil, Joel, who saw in the colt a rare combination of intelligence, strength, and willingness. When Little Bub, as Joel called him, showed that he had both strength and speed, men began to exploit him. Joel, because he was too poor to buy his beloved horse, had to stand by and see Little Bub overtaxed but a winner in a pulling bee. After that the horse was matched against thoroughbreds in a race, and later he was sold out of the state. The story of the reunion, years later, of Joel and Bub is as moving as the Clint and Smoky reunion. Bub lived to achieve new honors, sire innumerable colts, and establish the Morgan line.

*Misty of Chincoteague* (1947) followed the history of the little wild horses on the island of Chincoteague, Virginia. Mrs. Henry wrote *Sea Star, Orphan of Chincoteague* (1949) a few years later, but in between was the Newbery winner, *King of the Wind* (1948). For this story, the author pursued the history of the great Godolphin Arabian, which changed the physical conformation of race horses and sired a line of thoroughbreds from which Man o' War was descended. It is one of the most exciting and moving horse stories ever written, and it is enormously popular with both children and teachers.

*Brighty of the Grand Canyon* (1953) is the story of the legendary burro, wild and solitary, whose hoofs galloping up and down the walls of the Grand Canyon are said to have made that terrifying path known as Bright Angel Trail. Brighty is the most winning of all Mrs. Henry's four-footed heroes. He is a comic, like all burros, but lonely too. His search for companionship, his loyalty to those who are kind to him, and his gay flights back to freedom make a thrilling story of animal and human adventure.

In *Gaudenzia* (1960) Mrs. Henry writes with vitality and color of the mare that broke all records for the Palio, the annual horse race held in Siena, Italy, with costumes and rites used since their medieval beginnings. *White Stallion of Lipizza* (1964) is also based on one of the romantic realities of the horse world, the precision-drilled Lippizaners, the performing horses of the Spanish Riding School of Vienna.

What gives these books by Marguerite Henry their unique quality? First of all, she can make the true pattern of animal life so vivid that readers identify themselves with the animals. Yet the animals are never humanized. With complete integrity to their species, these creatures exhibit traits that children admire in human beings—fortitude, loyalty, and a blithe zest for life.

## JOSEPH WHARTON LIPPINCOTT

*Wilderness Champion*
*Wahoo Bobcat*

*Wilderness Champion* (1944) is the story of a red setter pup which is lost in the mountains, raised by a black wolf, and finally found, caught in an illegal trap. The dog is nursed back to health and develops a fondness for his master, but despite this and his subsequent training, he is dispirited, and so he is turned loose to rejoin his wild friend. After the wolf's death, the setter returns to live with his master, and becomes a man's dog again.

*Wahoo Bobcat* (1959) is the more unusual story of the friendship that developed between a huge bobcat and a small, solitary boy. The story centers on the bobcat's struggle to survive in a changing environment where he is ceaselessly pursued by the hunters and their dogs.

## PHILIP DUFFIELD STONG

*Honk: the Moose*

There is so much inevitable sadness about animal stories that it is a satisfaction to remind readers young and old that *Honk: the Moose* is a tale of sheer hilarity. Written in 1935 and joyously illustrated in color by Kurt Wiese, it is the story of a huge moose which insists upon being housed and cared for during the Minnesota winter. There is no attempt to present scientific animal lore in this perennial favorite—just a problem moose on the loose!

## WILL JAMES

*Smoky*

One of the greatest animal stories for children is the Newbery winner for 1927, *Smoky*, told and illustrated by the cowboy Will James. Adults are sometimes shocked when they read the author's preface:

> *I've never yet went wrong in sizing up a man by the kind of a horse he rode. A good horse always packs a good man, and I've always dodged the hombre what had no thought nor liking for his horse or other animals, for I figger that kind of gazabo is best to be left unacquainted with.* (p. v)[2]

Then the story begins:

> *It seemed like Mother Nature was sure agreeable that day when the little black colt came to the range world, and tried to get a footing with his long wobblety legs on the brown prairie sod.*

*Smoky* is written in the vernacular of the Western cowboy, his everyday speech, with something of the easy, loping style of his riding too. There are such verbs as *knowed*, *figgered*, *throwed*, *sashayed*—not academic English, but the cowboy's lingo. And there are horsy words like *stud*, *mare*, *stallion*, and *gelding*. If children are troubled by the large number of strange words or such highly descriptive phrases as *crowhopped*, *hightailed*, and the like, a little help in the beginning will tide them over these minor difficulties, and they will get from this easy narrative a portrait of a horse they will never forget.

The story is simple, but the details are rich and absorbing. Smoky is a little range colt "fetched up" by his mammy and by his own high spirits and intelligence. When it comes his turn to be broken, he puts up a terrific fight, but he has the luck to fall into the skillful hands of the cowboy Clint, who loses his heart to this spunky, handsome pony. Smoky is broken and trained but will allow no one to handle him except Clint. The little horse gains a reputation for being the finest cow pony on the range and is Clint's special pride. Then Smoky is stolen by a vicious man who treats the horse so cruelly that he turns into a killer. Under the name of The Cougar, he fights all rodeo riders until he is worn out. After cruel treatment by a succession of owners, he is found and reclaimed by Clint. Smoky does not even know him. Back at the range where he was born, old Smoky is

2. Selections from *Smoky, the Cowhorse* by Will James, copyright 1926 by Charles Scribner's Sons. Used by permission of the publishers, Charles Scribner's Sons.

fed, rubbed, doctored, and presently turned out in the spring sunshine with the colts.

No briefing of this book and no excerpts give any idea of its power. Never once does the author sentimentalize or humanize his horses. If children are going to weep over animal stories, here is one that is worth their tears.

## MARY O'HARA

*My Friend Flicka*
*Thunderhead*
*Green Grass of Wyoming*

*My Friend Flicka* (1941), *Thunderhead* (1943), and *Green Grass of Wyoming* (1946), a trilogy by Mary O'Hara (Mary Sture-Vasa), were written for adults but have been appropriated by the children who can read them. They deal with the biology of horse breeding on the McLaughlins' ranch, where the problems are complicated by a bad wild-horse strain from a white stallion they call the Albino. Ken, the juvenile hero of *My Friend Flicka*, falls in love with a colt from this strain. When he is finally allowed to choose a young horse for his very own he chooses—to his father's distress—this half-wild filly, which he later calls Flicka. His father warns him that he will never be able to break her, that the whole breed is "loco"—crazy.

Ken lives to see his horse gentled at last, as tractable and intelligent as any. Ken apparently is right about Flicka, but the father is not convinced. Through both of these books runs the conflict of the strong-willed father and son, much alike, loving each other dearly, but critical of each other, too, because they are so much alike. Family relationships are strained from time to time but on the whole are understanding and affectionate. The horses are the center of interest for the whole family.

*Thunderhead* is the name given to Flicka's first colt, which, to everyone's horror, turns out to be pure white. This means that Flicka has mated with the Albino, and the loco strain will be intensified in the colt. Indeed, Thunderhead has intelligence, tremendous speed, but complete instability, and, in the end, goes back to the wild strain from which he came. *Green Grass of Wyoming* shows Ken growing up, and includes a teen-age romance.

## THEODORE J. WALDECK

*The White Panther*

Theodore J. Waldeck has written some fine stories of jungle animals in their native haunts. *The White Panther* (1941) is a favorite. It follows this rare, beautiful, and hunted creature from cub days to maturity. Life is mostly eating, sleeping, stalking prey, killing, and eating again, broken only by fights with enemies and accompanied by a continual alert against man. Ku-Ma, with his coat like faintly dappled white velvet, is an appealing creature only because of his uncanny beauty. He is a sleek bundle of appetite and ferocity, though, unlike man, he kills only to eat or to preserve his life. His perils are many, especially from man, who hunts his rare pelt. How Ku-Ma escapes even the clever man-made trap is the triumphant conclusion of the book. The Waldeck stories leave the reader with no delusions about the possible sweetness and light of these wild creatures. Rather they build up in his mind a respect for their skill, resourcefulness, and courage.

## MARJORIE KINNAN RAWLINGS

*The Yearling*

Although *The Yearling* (1938) by Marjorie Rawlings was written for adults, many children have appropriated it even as they have appropriated adult books in every generation. It is a beautifully written story of Jody, a lonely boy, living in the primitive wilds of inland Florida with his family and his pet deer, Flag. Together the boy and the deer frolic and grow, make mistakes and are punished, only to forget and play again. Finally Flag, the year-old deer, begins to eat the family's scanty crops as fast as they grow. There is not enough food for the maturing deer and the family. Penny, the father, knows the dreaded time has come to make Jody face facts: Flag must be shot. The boy is frantic and will not listen to his father. Penny is bedridden and so cannot do what needs to be done. The tragedy of those last hours of the boy with his deer are too much for Jody, and he runs away. When he returns, father and boy talk together for a long time. Penny says, "You've takened a punishment. You ain't a yearlin' no longer."

This poignant story of growing up is more boy than deer, but it turns upon a child's devotion to a pet. A child forced to betray the creature which loves him may suffer just as passionately as Jody did over Flag. And that suffering, as adults may fail to realize, is compounded of bitter, if temporary, hatred for those who demand such a sacrifice, as well as of lacerating sorrow over the loss of the loving and beloved creature. Not all children have the wise tenderness of a father like Penny, who could help his son grow up. Penny could not spare his son pain, but he could help him understand the reason for the pain and give him the courage to stand it. Children who have suffered these heartbreaking separations from a loved and loving pet may read *The Yearling* over and over. A better catharsis for such pent-up emotions could hardly be found.

No comment on *The Yearling* is complete without a word about its illustrator, Newell Convers Wyeth. Wyeth journeyed down to the hammock country of Florida to study both the land and the people. The results were pictures so true and yet so imaginative that they represent a high point in the remarkable achievement of this dean of illustrators of children's books.

## JAMES ARTHUR KJELGAARD

*Big Red*

Jim Kjelgaard writes dog stories as good as Marguerite Henry's horse stories. His books are equally absorbing, with the very breath of the wilderness blowing through the pages. His dogs are lovable and courageous, true to their breeds and devoted to the men who love them.

Beginning with *Big Red* (1945), Kjelgaard has written three books about the champion Irish setters in Mr. Haggin's kennels. Ross Pickett and his son Danny care for, train, and completely devote themselves to the "Irishmen" above all other breeds of dogs. In the first story, Danny and Big Red both prove their mettle in a series of exciting adventures culminating in the tracking down of a great bear.

*Illustration by N. C. Wyeth. From The Yearling by Marjorie Kinnan Rawlings. Charles Scribner's Sons, 1939. Reprinted by permission of the publisher. (Original in color)*

## VIEWPOINTS

. . . In the fragments of old Greek poetry is an epitaph which begins, "Laugh not, I pray thee; though this is a dog's grave, tears fell for me."

I am sure that is one reason the dog story is such an enduring part of our literature. Even when it is banal or downright lachrymose, there is a recognizable grain of truth somewhere in it; and when it is properly told it is classic, as fundamental as the love story or the story of man's valiant struggle with fate. At its best, it is a tale of fidelity; often it is a tale of heroism; and the hero is at the heart of the legends by which man preserves his own dreams of greatness and nobility.—Hal Borland, "It's the Dog That Wags the Tale," *The New York Times Book Review*, November 11, 1962. Copyright © 1962 by The New York Times Company. Reprinted by permission.

In *Irish Red, Son of Big Red* (1951), Mr. Haggin imports some English setters and a new trainer. When the Picketts leave, Mike, the "mutton-headed" son of Big Red, trails them. Their winter in the woods is rugged for all of them, but when they return to the kennels, Mike is a disciplined and worthy son of Big Red. *Outlaw Red* (1953), the third book, is almost all dog. Pampered Sean, another son of Big Red, is lost in the wilderness and is almost shot as a suspected sheep killer. Bewildered and lonely, the dog makes a painful adjustment to his new life. The story of how he manages to survive, secure a mate of his own breed, and raise his pups may stretch the long arm of coincidence a bit, but it is convincingly told.

*Illustration by Bob Kuhn from* Big Red *by Jim Kjelgaard. Copyright 1945. Reproduced by permission of Holiday House, Inc., Publishers.*

Jim Kjelgaard has written other dog stories and stories about other animals. In all his books, he interprets the world of nature truthfully and shows the nobility and courage of animals.

## MICHEL-AIMÉ BAUDOUY

### *Old One-Toe*

*Old One-Toe* (1959) is a variant of the master fox versus the master hunter, but it is enlivened by four delightful children, two unique adults, an earnest hunting dog, and a clown of a city dog intoxicated with country life. The four children, who have come from Paris to live on their aunt's chicken farm, are horrified when a fox destroys her whole brood of young chickens. They vow they will get the fox, old One-Toe. Under the master hunter, the boy Piet begins to track the fox without a gun. Observing the creatures of the forest, including the fox, Piet comes to love their wildness and resourcefulness. By the time the big hunt is organized, Piet and the other children are secretly on the side of old One-Toe. The hunt is a comedy of errors for the hunters, complicated by the children and their wildly excited, unsportsmanlike dog. It is near tragedy for One-Toe and his vixen, but the children save them. This well-written book is full of the outdoor magic of fields and forests, the gallantry of hunted creatures, and lively characterizations of both the children and the adults.

## JOHN GEORGE AND JEAN GEORGE

*Vulpes, the Red Fox*

Zoologist John George and artist Jean George turned their combination of talents to the production of books about wild animals. In most of the books the story follows the animal's life cycle: his discoveries, mistakes, and escapes; his mating and raising of young; and his continual search for food and struggle against enemies—always with death just around the corner.

The hero of *Vulpes, the Red Fox* (1948), for instance, is known to every hunter for his superb pelt, his raids on barnyards, and his skillful escapes from both dogs and men with guns. Actually, Vulpes is so swift and so powerful that he sometimes courts the hunt to enjoy the befuddlement of the hounds, or at least so the hunters think. Meanwhile, readers follow his search for a mate. Rejecting a nervous weakling, he courts a strong, handsome vixen, a worthy mate. Cubs are born, and the relentless battle for food continues. Finally, one unwary moment, death comes to Vulpes at the hands of the hunters. Yet somehow this inevitable ending is not sad. Vulpes has lived a zestful life. He has loved the sun on his fur, the excitement of the chase, and the sweetness of mate and cubs. And death comes swiftly, a good end.

*Masked Prowler* (1950) follows a similar pattern except that at the finish old Procyon, the aged raccoon, after an epic battle with the dogs, retires in triumph to lick his wounds and become a forest myth. *Bubo, the Great Horned Owl* (1954) is one of the most dramatic of these stories. Most of us know little about great horned owls, the "tigers" of the forest. Their size and the ferocity of their hunting would seem to make them invulnerable. Instead, they are hunted by every creature in the forest in one way or another.

Although *Meph, the Pet Skunk* (1952) follows the amusing development of the skunk, it is chiefly the story of the reclamation of an eroded farm, and of an unhappy

*From the book* Masked Prowler: The Story of a Raccoon *by John and Jean George. Illustrated by Jean George. Copyright, 1950, by John and Jean George. Reproduced by permission of E. P. Dutton & Co., Inc.*

farmer and his disturbed teen-age boy. It is a fine story for young people. This book foreshadows Jean George's immensely popular *My Side of the Mountain* (see Chapter 13).

In all of these books, both the writing and the wonderful illustrations show acute observation and a scientific knowledge of these woodland creatures and their habitat.

Of the many books that Jean George has written alone, two of the most unusual are *Gull Number 737* (1964) and *Coyote in Manhattan* (1968). The first is the story of a boy who in helping his father with research on herring gulls becomes so interested that he develops his own research project. The book is admirable for its story (especially in its depiction of the boy's need to gain independence from his father) and for the scientific accuracy with which the author describes the habits and habitat of the gulls, and it is also an excellent example of the lure of scientific research and of its methodology. In *Coyote in Manhattan*, a wild animal is loose in Central Park and is eventually captured. Although the substructure of the story is frail, the descriptions of the coyote's behavior are carefully realistic, and the animal—without being endowed with human traits or abilities—has a strong personality.

## VICTOR B. SCHEFFER

*Little Calf*
*The Year of the Seal*

Victor Scheffer is a marine biologist who in *Little Calf* (1970) and *The Year of the Seal* (1970) follows marine mammals through the cycle of their first years. The framework for these books is lightly fictionalized, but the descriptions adhere scrupulously to whale and seal behavior. *Little Calf*, the story of a sperm whale, was adapted from the adult title *The Year of the Whale*. Tales of sea creatures are comparatively rare, and so it is most gratifying to have these books written by a scientist who is an authority in his field and a fine literary stylist.

## EMIL E. LIERS

*An Otter's Story*

A more lovable creature than the playful, affectionate, freshwater otter doesn't exist. That it should be so ruthlessly hunted by farmers is hard to understand. Mr. Liers tells a delightful story of one otter family and makes clear their harmlessness as well as their usefulness to the balance of nature both for farmers and fishermen. *An Otter's Story* (1953) is based upon long observation, and every incident is vouched for. Tony Palazzo's handsome illustrations are as spirited as the text.

## MEINDERT DeJONG

*Along Came a Dog*

*Along Came a Dog* (1958), illustrated by Maurice Sendak, is only one example of Meindert DeJong's many excellent stories about animals (other DeJong books are discussed in Chapter 13). Gentle but never sentimental, his books often emphasize the animal characters, here achieved in part because the human being in the story is referred to only as "the man." Crippled, the little red hen is befriended by a dog which the man shoos off, but the dog persists as guardian of the hen and when he sees the hen attacked by a hawk, he saves her and her chicks. Finally the man understands and gives the dog a home. The story has a quiet, poignant appeal, and the animals have definite personalities.

## SHEILA BURNFORD

*The Incredible Journey*

The year 1961 saw the publication of a remarkable animal story, *The Incredible Journey*, a detailed account of three heroic animals who travel through two hundred and fifty miles of Canadian wilderness to the place and people that mean home and love to them. A young red-gold Labrador retriever instigates the journey and leads the way. A Siamese cat and an old English bull terrier complete the triumvirate. The old bull dog gives out first, and the cat feeds him till he regains his strength. The cat is the most competent of the trio, and even after he is half drowned he manages to rejoin his companions and keep them going. The retriever gets a face full of porcupine quills which fester. Then cat and terrier bring him the kill, so he can lap the blood when he cannot chew anything. Mauled by bears, nearly starved, attacked by a bobcat, delayed by the blandishments of occasional human beings they encounter, the trio, led by the retriever who

*Illustration by Carl Burger. From* The Incredible Journey *by Sheila Burnford. Copyright © 1960, 1961 by Sheila Burnford. Reprinted by permission of Little, Brown and Co.—Atlantic Monthly Press and Hodder and Stoughton Limited.*

never loses his sense of direction or purpose, traverse a final fifty miles of such hazardous forest terrain the rangers say they cannot possibly survive. The reunion with the human beings they love is an unforgettable scene, written with restraint and integrity. The animals are never humanized or sentimentalized, and this beautifully written saga of three gallant animals is a superb story to read aloud either in the home or classroom.

## WALT MOREY

*Gentle Ben*
*Gloomy Gus*
*Kävik the Wolf Dog*

All of Walt Morey's stories are set in the far North and all are imbued with his love for that region and his affection for animals. In *Gentle Ben* (1965), a lonely boy makes a pet of an Alaskan brown bear which, goaded by some teasing men, retaliates and as a result is isolated on an island. When the family moves to the island to tend a salmon trap, the huge, docile Ben and the boy are happily reunited. In this book and in *Gloomy Gus* (1970), the story of a tame Kodiak bear which is put into a circus, Morey creates animal personalities that vie with his perceptively characterized human beings. *Kävik the Wolf Dog* (1968) is the story of a sled dog, found by a boy who is the first person to treat him kindly. Sent to Seattle, Kävik escapes and makes his way north to Alaska and the boy. Kävik is vividly portrayed but is consistently an animal. That portion of the story in which he is traveling alone is particularly dramatic.

## PETER HALLARD

*Puppy Lost in Lapland*

In Peter Hallard's *Puppy Lost in Lapland* (1971) Vedge, an injured puppy, falls off a sledge in a blinding snowstorm and is on his own in the desolate wilderness. The culmination of his struggle for survival brings him leadership of a wolf pack, but when he finds the old grandfather of the boy to whom he had belonged, Vedge chooses to protect the man rather than join the wolves in their attack. The long sequence in which the dog is alone is, as in *Kävik*, the most absorbing part of the story, and the book, like those by Morey, is excellent in its sharp evocation of the still solitude of the land.

## LUCY M. BOSTON

*A Stranger at Green Knowe*

Green Knowe, an old English manor house, is associated with three remarkable fantasies, the most notable of which is *The Children of*

*From the book* Kävik the Wolf Dog *by Walt Morey. Illustrated by Peter Parnall. Copyright © 1968 by Walt Morey. Published by E. P. Dutton & Co., Inc. and used with their permission.*

*Green Knowe* (p. 254), so it comes as a surprise to find that *A Stranger at Green Knowe* (1961) is completely realistic. It is the story of Ping, a small Chinese refugee, and Hanno, a thirteen-year-old gorilla, two displaced creatures who have known years of dreary gray cement. They meet in a dismal zoo, the gorilla inside a cage, the boy outside. The boy gives the gorilla his peach, and they eye each other with what seems to the boy complete understanding. Later, by a series of coincidences, they meet in the small, dense forest of Green Knowe. Both have escaped their prisons, both are happy in the freedom of this green wildness, and they adopt each other. But they are too close to civilization to be safe, and the story moves inevitably toward a tragic conclusion. It is nobly met by both Ping and Hanno. The peace of Green Knowe is temporarily shattered, but there is new hope for Ping, thanks to the remarkable Mrs. Oldknow. The introductory picture of the gorilla tribe in its native jungle and the horrible hunt that leads to the capture of Hanno are memorable scenes. Mrs. Boston is one of the most distinguished writers in the juvenile field, and while this book may not enjoy the popularity of *The Incredible Journey*, *A Stranger at Green Knowe* is a powerful and original book no child should miss. It too reads aloud magnificently.

There is rarely any need to urge children to read stories about animals. Pet stories bring out the child's desire to nurture and protect, and, as he matures, he learns about the piteous vulnerability of animals at the hands of cruel masters or hunters and trappers. Such stories encourage a compassionate sense of kinship with animals. Many of these books teach sex casually in the course of an absorbing story. For children who have little or no knowledge of breeding and the raising of young, these stories are especially valuable. From the stories that center on the proper training of dogs and horses, young readers gain a background for the training of their own pets. There is, of course, a great deal of overlap between such stories and informational books. Much of the fiction gives accurate information, and many informational books about animals have a narrative framework; indeed, it is at times difficult to decide in which class a book belongs.

Best of all, these four-footed heroes display some of the very qualities that children admire in human beings—courage in the face of danger, fortitude in suffering, loyalty to cubs, mate, or master, and finally, a gay, frolicsome zest for life that is much like the child's own frisky, coltish enjoyment of each day. These are all good reasons why the child enjoys fine books about animals.

Since the mere nature of the wild animal's life means chiefly pursuit or being pursued, escape or death; and since the drama of a pet's life turns upon the upsetting of its happy security with a tragic or triumphant outcome, there is bound to be a certain similarity in these tales. Too many of them in a row are monotonous or overly harrowing.

Such stories should be read along with other books. But any child is the richer for having had his sympathies expanded and his tenderness stirred by such great animal books as *Along Came a Dog, Smoky, Big Red, Gentle Ben*, and *The Yearling*. Any child is the poorer for having missed the drama of the *Jungle Books, King of the Wind, The Incredible Journey*, and *A Stranger at Green Knowe*.

## ADULT REFERENCES

ARBUTHNOT, MAY HILL, and DOROTHY M. BRODERICK. *Time for Stories of the Past and Present*. Part 1, "Animal Stories."

EGOFF, SHEILA. *The Republic of Childhood; A Critical Guide to Canadian Children's Literature in English*. Part 4, "The Realistic Animal Story."

EGOFF, SHEILA, G. T. STUBBS, and L. F. ASHLEY, eds. *Only Connect: Readings on Children's Literature*. Part 2, "Fairy Tales, Fantasy, Animals."

TOWNSEND, JOHN ROWE. *Written for Children*. Chapter 9, "Articulate Animals."

WHITE, DOROTHY, and MARY NEAL. *Books Before Five*.

## BOOKS FOR THE YOUNGEST READERS

ANDERSON, CLARENCE. *Billy and Blaze*, ill. by author. Macmillan, 1936, 1962. And its sequels. 5-8

BROWN, MARCIA. *How, Hippo!* ill. by author. Scribner's, 1969. Mother teaches Little Hippo different kinds of roars and has to rescue him the first time he strays from her side. Attractive woodcuts. 3-5

BUFF, MARY and CONRAD. *Dash and Dart*, ill. by Conrad Buff. Viking, 1942.

______. *Elf Owl*, ill. by Conrad Buff. Viking, 1958.

______. *Forest Folk*, ill. by Conrad Buff. Viking, 1962.

______. *Hurry, Skurry, and Flurry*, ill. by Conrad Buff. Viking, 1954. 5-8

BULLA, CLYDE. *Star of Wild Horse Canyon*, ill. by Grace Paull. T. Crowell, 1953. The disappearance of the wild white horse which Danny has so carefully trained creates a mystery in this easy-to-read Western story. 7-9

CHALMERS, MARY. *Be Good, Harry*, ill. by author. Harper, 1967. 3-6

DE BRUNHOFF, JEAN. *The Story of Babar, the Little Elephant*, ill. by author. Random, 1937. And its sequels. 5-8

DENNIS, MORGAN. *Burlap*, ill. by author. Viking, 1945. A worthless farm dog suddenly proves himself by helping to capture an escaped circus bear. 6-8

FLACK, MARJORIE. *Angus and the Cat*, ill. by author. Doubleday, 1931.

______. *Angus and the Ducks*, ill. by author. Doubleday, 1930, 1939.

______. *Angus Lost*, ill. by author. Doubleday, 1932, 1941. 4-7

______. *Restless Robin*, ill. by author. Houghton, 1937. Mr. Robin starts north in February and finally arrives in New Hampshire with the spring. 6-8

______. *The Story about Ping*, ill. by Kurt Wiese. Viking, 1933. 5-8

FREEMAN, DON. *Fly High, Fly Low*, ill. by author. Viking, 1957. Scenic San Francisco offers a colorful background for this picture tale of a pigeon which temporarily loses its mate when their electric-sign home is moved. 6-8

FRISKEY, MARGARET. *Seven Diving Ducks*, ill. by Jean Morey. Childrens Pr., 1969. 5-7

GEORGE, JEAN. *Snow Tracks*, ill. by author. Dutton, 1958. Distinctively illustrated nature picture story of animal tracks and of a boy who followed them to acquire a whitefoot mouse for a pet. 6-8

HADER, BERTA and ELMER. *The Big Snow*, ill. by authors. Macmillan, 1948. Beautiful pictures of small animals preparing for a winter that was worse than they dreamed. With the aid of human friends they survive. Caldecott Medal. 6-9

HOBAN, RUSSELL. *A Baby Sister for Frances*, ill. by Lillian Hoban. Harper, 1964. 3-6

______. *A Bargain for Frances*, ill. by Lillian Hoban. Harper, 1970. 6-8

______. *Bedtime for Frances*, ill. by Garth Williams. Harper, 1960. 3-6

______. *Best Friends for Frances*, ill. by Lillian Hoban. Harper, 1969. 5-7

JACKSON, JACQUELINE. *Chicken Ten Thousand*, ill. by Barbara Morrow. Little, 1968. 5-7

JOHNSTON, JOHANNA. *Penguin's Way*, ill. by Leonard Weisgard. Doubleday, 1962. In the cold bleakness of the Antarctic, Emperor Penguins care for their young. A life-cycle picture book of unusual charm and distinction. 5-8

KRASILOVSKY, PHYLLIS. *The Cow Who Fell in the Canal*, ill. by Peter Spier. Doubleday, 1957. After a tumble into the canal, Hendrika, the cow, climbs on a raft and is soon drifting down to the city. Beautiful Dutch scenes in crisp clear colors. 6-8

LATHROP, DOROTHY. *Hide and Go Seek*, ill. by author. Macmillan, 1938. 7-10

______. *Who Goes There?* ill. by author. Macmillan, 1935, 1963. 6-10

LEAF, MUNRO. *The Story of Ferdinand*, ill. by Robert Lawson. Viking, 1936. 5 up

LOBEL, ARNOLD. *Frog and Toad Are Friends*, ill. by author. Harper, 1970. 6-7

MCNEER, MAY. *My Friend Mac*, ill. by Lynd Ward. Houghton, 1960. An orphaned and fast-growing moose provides plenty of diversion for lonely little Baptiste of the Canadian woods. 7-9

MILES, MISKA. *Eddie's Bear*, ill. by John Schoenherr. Little, 1970. 5-8

______. *Fox and the Fire*, ill. by John Schoenherr. Little, 1966. 7-8

______. *Mississippi Possum*, ill. by John Schoenherr. Little, 1965. 7-9

MINARIK, ELSE. *Little Bear*, ill. by Maurice Sendak. Harper, 1957. Other books in the series include *Father Bear Comes Home* (1959), *Little Bear's*

Friend (1960), *Little Bear's Visit* (1961), and *A Kiss for Little Bear* (1968). 4-8

NEWBERRY, CLARE. *April's Kittens*, ill. by author. Harper, 1940. When April's cat Sheba has kittens, April's father agrees to move from a one-cat to a two-cat apartment.

———. *Babette*, ill. by author. Harper, 1937.

———. *Barkis*, ill. by author. Harper, 1938.

———. *Marshmallow*, ill. by author. Harper, 1942.

———. *Mittens*, ill. by author. Harper, 1936.

———. *Percy, Polly, and Pete*, ill. by author. Harper, 1952. 5-8

REY, HANS A. *Curious George*, ill. by author. Houghton, 1941. And its sequels. 4-8

ROBINSON, TOM. *Buttons*, ill. by Peggy Bacon. Viking, 1938, 1968. 6-9

SANDBURG, HELGA. *Anna and the Baby Buzzard*, ill. by Brinton Turkle. Dutton, 1970. 5-7

SCHOENHERR, JOHN. *The Barn*, ill. by author. Little, 1968. 7-9

SEUSS, DR. (pseud. for Theodor Seuss Geisel). *Horton Hatches the Egg*, ill. by author. Random, 1940. 5-8

SOJO, TOBA. *The Animal Frolic*, ill. with reproductions from the drawings of Kakuyu. Text by Velma Varner. Putnam, 1954. 6-8

STOLZ, MARY S. *The Story of a Singular Hen and Her Peculiar Children*, ill. by Edward Frascino. Harper, 1969. With no animal mothers in sight, a hen adopts all the barnyard young as her own. On the surface, a lighthearted animal story, deftly told; below the surface, sagacious perception. 5-8

TRESSELT, ALVIN. *The Rabbit Story*, ill. by Leonard Weisgard. Lothrop, 1957. The little wild rabbit lost her freedom to become a pet and then escaped to raise her own family. An appealing nature story beautifully illustrated in brown tones. 4-7

WABER, BERNARD. *A Firefly Named Torchy*, ill. by author. Houghton, 1970. Torchy's maladjustment is solved by a fact of urban environment. Blithely told, the story has humor in style and concept. 5-7

WARD, LYND. *The Biggest Bear*, ill. by author. Houghton, 1952. Caldecott Medal. 5-8

## BOOKS FOR THE MIDDLE READERS

AGLE, NAN HAYDEN. *My Animals and Me*, ill. with photos by Emily Hayden. Seabury, 1970. Reminiscences of an animal lover in a book that combines warmth, humor, family anecdotes, and memories of beloved pets in a rural pre-World War I background. 8-10

ANDERSEN, HANS CHRISTIAN. *The Ugly Duckling*, tr. by R. P. Keigwin, ill. by Adrienne Adams. Scribner's, 1965. 9-11

ANDERSON, CLARENCE. *High Courage*, ill. by author. Macmillan, 1941. 10-13

———. *Salute*, ill. by author. Macmillan, 1940. 9-12

ARUNDEL, JOCELYN. *Simba of the White Mane*, ill. by Wesley Dennis. McGraw, 1958. In an exciting tale of Africa young Toki saves a lion from the ruthless safari leader. Handsomely illustrated, and with an underlying theme of animal conservation. 9-12

BOND, MICHAEL. *A Bear Called Paddington*, ill. by Peggy Fortnum. Houghton, 1960. 9-11

BOSTON, LUCY M. *A Stranger at Green Knowe*, ill. by Peter Boston. Harcourt, 1961. 11-14

CLARK, BILLY C. *The Mooneyed Hound*, ill. by Nedda Walker. Putnam, 1958. Jeb's handicapped dog proves his mettle as a hunter in the field trials.

———. *The Trail of the Hunter's Horn*, ill. by Veronica Reed. Putnam, 1957. Jeb's happiness in his new hunting dog was crushed when the puppy proved to be half blind. Two distinctive stories of Kentucky mountain life, rich in human values. 9-11

DEJONG, MEINDERT. *Along Came a Dog*, ill. by Maurice Sendak. Harper, 1958. 10-12

———. *The Last Little Cat*, ill. by Jim McMullan. Harper, 1961. The timid seventh kitten strays away from his friend, the old blind dog, and encounters many cat enemies before he reaches home and safety. 8-10

ENGELHARD, GEORGIA. *Peterli and the Mountain*, ill. by Madeleine Gekiere. Lippincott, 1954. No one really knows what made Peterli, the cat, climb the Matterhorn, but climb it he did, with the aid of a friendly guide. An amusing tale based on a true incident. 8-12

GALL, ALICE CREW, and FLEMING CREW. *Flat Tail*, ill. by W. Langdon Kihn. Walck, 1935.

———. *Ringtail*, ill. by James Reid. Walck, 1933.

———. *Splasher*, ill. by Else Bostelmann. Walck, 1945. A flood is a great adventure for a young muskrat and his friends.

———. *Wagtail*, ill. by Kurt Wiese. Oxford, 1932. 8-10

GATES, DORIS. *Little Vic*, ill. by Kate Seredy. Viking, 1951. When Pony River, a black boy, sees Little Vic, he believes the colt will be as great as his sire, Man o' War. The boy endures every hardship willingly in his devotion to the colt. 9-12

GRAHAME, KENNETH. *Wind in the Willows*, ill. by Ernest H. Shepard. Scribner's, 1953. 10 up

HALLARD, PETER. *Puppy Lost in Lapland*, ill. by Wallace Tripp. Watts, 1971. 10-12

HENRY, MARGUERITE. *Born to Trot*, ill. by Wesley Dennis. Rand, 1950. The true story of Ben and Gib White, trainer and owner of a famous trotting mare, with a good deal of history of trotting races.

———. *Brighty of the Grand Canyon*, ill. by Wesley Dennis. Rand, 1953.

———. *Justin Morgan Had a Horse*, ill. by Wesley Dennis. Rand, 1954.

———. *King of the Wind*, ill. by Wesley Dennis. Rand, 1948. Newbery Medal.

———. *Misty of Chincoteague*, ill. by Wesley Dennis. Rand, 1947.

———. *Sea Star*, ill. by Wesley Dennis. Rand, 1949. 9-14

HOLLING, HOLLING C. *Pagoo*, ill. by author and Lucille W. Holling. Houghton, 1957. A quietly paced, beautifully illustrated life story of a hermit crab. 9-12

JARRELL, RANDALL. *The Bat-Poet*, ill. by Maurice Sendak. Macmillan, 1967. 10 up

LAWSON, ROBERT. *Rabbit Hill*, ill. by author. Viking, 1944. Newbery Medal. 9-12

———. *The Tough Winter*, ill. by author. Viking, 1954. 9-12

LIERS, EMIL. *An Otter's Story*, ill. by Tony Palazzo. Viking, 1953. 10-13

LINDQUIST, WILLIS. *Burma Boy*, ill. by Nicolas Mordvinoff. Whittlesey, 1953. A thrilling tale of an elephant of the teakwood forests which goes wild, and of young Haji, the elephant boy, who wins his confidence and saves the villagers from disaster. 10-13

LIPPINCOTT, JOSEPH WHARTON. *Gray Squirrel*, ill. by George F. Mason. Lippincott, 1954.

______. *Little Red, the Fox*, ill. by George F. Mason. Lippincott, 1953.
Authentic life stories of native animals. 9-11

MILES, MISKA. *Nobody's Cat*, ill. by John Schoenherr. Little, 1969. 8-9

MONTGOMERY, RUTHERFORD. *Kildee House*, ill. by Barbara Cooney. Doubleday, 1949. Story of an elderly would-be hermit who, building a house in the redwood forest, soon finds it filled with small animals and visited by warring children. The tragicomic episodes make this a nature story of unusual sensitivity and beauty. 10-13

MOREY, WALT. *Gloomy Gus*. Dutton, 1970. 10-12

MOWAT, FARLEY. *Owls in the Family*, ill. by Robert Frankenberg. Little, 1962. A funny and heartwarming story of two owls of Northern Canada, told by their youthful rescuer. 9-12

NORTH, STERLING. *Little Rascal*, ill. by Carl Burger. Dutton, 1965. 9-11

ROCCA, GUIDO. *Gaetano the Pheasant; A Hunting Fable*, ill. by Giulio Cingoli and Giancarlo Carloni. Harper, 1966. 9-10

ROUNDS, GLEN. *The Blind Colt*, ill. by author. Holiday, 1941, 1960.

______. *Stolen Pony*, ill. by author. Holiday, 1948, 1969. Two stories with a background of the Dakota Badlands. With the care and training given by a ten-year-old boy, the blind colt earns his right to live. The sequel tells how the pony was stolen by horse thieves and then abandoned, to make his way home with the aid of a faithful dog. 9-12

______. *Whitey's First Roundup*, ill. by author. Holiday, 1960. Maybe it was an accident that small Whitey roped his first cow, but he had all the fun of feeling like a first-class cowhand. 8-10

SALTEN, FELIX. *Bambi*, ill. by Kurt Wiese. Grosset, 1931.

______. *Bambi's Children*, ill. by Robert Kuhn. Grosset, 1948. 10-14

SETON, ERNEST T. *Lives of the Hunted*, ill. by author. Schocken, 1967. 10 up

STOLZ, MARY S. *Fredou*, ill. by Tomi Ungerer. Harper, 1962. Fredou, a Parisian cat of great wisdom, takes a homesick young American boy in hand and provides him with a memorable summer. The French background is a joy in this most delightful tale. 8-10

STONG, PHIL. *Honk: the Moose*, ill. by Kurt Wiese. Dodd, 1935. 9-10

WALKER, DAVID E. *Big Ben*, ill. by Victor Ambrus. Houghton, 1969. Fine writing style and characterization in this story about a St. Bernard who is unjustly suspected of being a sheep-killer. 9-11

WHITE, ANNE H. *Junket*, ill. by Robert McCloskey. Viking, 1955. 9-11

## BOOKS FOR THE OLDEST READERS

BALL, ZACHARY. *Bristle Face*. Holiday, 1962. Orphaned Jase tells his own tale of the unexpected talents of his homely dog, Bristle Face, and of the kindly storekeeper, Lute Swank, who found a home for them. Background is rural Mississippi in the early 1900's. 12-16

BAUDOUY, MICHEL-AIMÉ. *Old One-Toe*, tr. by Marie Ponsot, ill. by Johannes Troyer. Harcourt, 1959. 11-13

BURNFORD, SHEILA. *The Incredible Journey*, ill. by Carl Burger. Little, 1961. 11 up

CHIPPERFIELD, JOSEPH E. *Wolf of Badenoch*, ill. by C. Gifford Ambler. McKay, 1959. An outstanding tale of the Scottish Highlands and of the vindication of a great sheep dog which was suspected of being a killer. 12-16

CLARK, DENIS. *Black Lightning*, ill. by C. Gifford Ambler. Viking, 1954. Black Lightning, a rare black leopard of Ceylon, regains his jungle freedom after harsh captivity in a shabby little circus. An exciting and well-written wild animal story.

______. *Boomer*, ill. by C. Gifford Ambler. Viking, 1955. An absorbing tale of an Australian kangaroo, orphaned and adopted as a household pet, who later returns to the wild and becomes a leader of his kind. 12-16

FISHER, AILEEN. *Valley of the Smallest; The Life Story of a Shrew*, ill. by Jean Zallinger. T. Crowell, 1966. 11-14

GEORGE, JEAN. *Coyote in Manhattan*, ill. by John Kaufman. T. Crowell, 1968. 11-13

______. *Gull Number 737*. T. Crowell, 1964. 12-15

______. *The Summer of the Falcon*, ill. by author. T. Crowell, 1962. A unique story of growing up, in which a sixteen-year-old loses interest in the falcon training that has absorbed her earlier years. The descriptions of the sparrow hawk and its training are the highlights of the book. 12-15

GEORGE, JOHN, and JEAN GEORGE. *Bubo, the Great Horned Owl*, ill. by Jean George. Dutton, 1954.

______. *Masked Prowler; the Story of a Raccoon*, ill. by Jean George. Dutton, 1950.

______. *Meph, the Pet Skunk*, ill. by Jean George. Dutton, 1952.

______. *Vison, the Mink*, ill. by Jean George. Dutton, 1949. 11-14

GIPSON, FRED. *Old Yeller*, ill. by Carl Burger. Harper, 1956. Travis' mongrel dog is bitten by a rabid wolf while loyally defending his family. He becomes infected and has to be destroyed. This is a moving tale of a boy and his dog, set in pioneer Texas of the 1870's. In a sequel, *Savage Sam* (1962), Travis, now fifteen, is aided by Old Yeller's equally gallant son in rescuing two small children from Apache captivity. 11-14

HENRY, MARGUERITE. *Gaudenzia; Pride of the Palio*, ill. by Lynd Ward. Rand, 1960. 11-14

______. *White Stallion of Lipizza*, ill. by Wesley Dennis. Rand, 1964. 11-13

JAMES, WILL. *Smoky, the Cowhorse*, ill. by author. Scribner's, 1926. Newbery Medal. 11-16

JOHNSON, JAMES RALPH. *Utah Lion*, ill. by author.

Follett, 1962. The wild rugged country near the Grand Canyon is the background for this powerful story of an orphaned mountain lion and his struggle for survival. 11-15

KIPLING, RUDYARD. *The Jungle Book*, ill. by Kurt Wiese. Doubleday, 1932. Ill. by Fritz Eichenberg. Grosset, 1950. First published in 1894. 12-14

KJELGAARD, JIM. *Big Red*, ill. by Bob Kuhn. Holiday, 1956.

______. *Irish Red, Son of Big Red*. Holiday, 1951.

______. *Outlaw Red, Son of Big Red*. Holiday, 1953. 12-16

KNIGHT, ERIC. *Lassie Come-Home*, ill. by Marguerite Kirmse. Holt, 1940; rev. ed., ill. by Don Bolognese. 1971. 11-14

LEIGHTON, MARGARET. *Comanche of the Seventh*, ill. by Elliot Means. Farrar, 1957. In the life story of Comanche, the horse that survived Custer's Last Stand, the author achieves fine historical fiction and an absorbing animal tale. 11-15

LIPPINCOTT, JOSEPH WHARTON. *The Wahoo Bobcat*, ill. by Paul Bransom. Lippincott, 1950.

______. *Wilderness Champion*, ill. by Paul Bransom. Lippincott, 1944. 12-15

LOKEN, ANNA BELLE. *The Colt from the Dark Forest*, ill. by Donald Bolognese. Lothrop, 1959. Sensitively written story of a young Norwegian farm boy who overcomes every obstacle to feed and train the newborn red colt he found in the forest. 11-13

MAXWELL, GAVIN. *The Otters' Tale*, ill. with photos. Dutton, 1962. A juvenile edition of the author's memorable nature tale of his otter pets, *Ring of Bright Water*. 12-15

MOREY, WALT. *Gentle Ben*, ill. by John Schoenherr. Dutton, 1965. 11-14

______. *Kävik the Wolf Dog*, ill. by Peter Parnall. Dutton, 1968. 11-14

MUKERJI, DHAN GOPAL. *Gay-Neck*, ill. by Boris Artzybasheff. Dutton, 1927, 1968. Gay-Neck's training as a carrier pigeon in India made him valuable as a messenger in France during the war. Newbery Medal, 1928. 11-14

______. *Hari, the Jungle Lad*, ill. by Morgan Stinemetz. Dutton, 1924.

______. *Kari, the Elephant*, ill. by J. E. Allen. Dutton, 1922.

These two stories of East India are rich in atmosphere. The first book is the story of a boy of the jungle and how his meeting with Kari brings good fortune to his family. The second book tells of elephant life and adventure. 11-14

NORTH, STERLING. *Rascal: A Memoir of a Better Era*, ill. by John Schoenherr. Dutton, 1963. 12 up

O'HARA, MARY [pseud. for Mary Sture-Vasa]. *My Friend Flicka*. Lippincott, 1941. 12 up

______. *Thunderhead*. Lippincott, 1943. 14 up

______. *Green Grass of Wyoming*. Lippincott, 1946. 12 up

RAWLINGS, MARJORIE KINNAN. *The Yearling*, ill. by N. C. Wyeth. Scribner's, 1939, 1962. 12 up

SCHEFFER, VICTOR B. *Little Calf*, ill. by Leonard Everett Fisher. Scribner's, 1970. 12 up

______. *The Year of the Seal*, ill. by Leonard Everett Fisher. Scribner's, 1970. 12 up

WALDECK, THEODORE J. *Lions on the Hunt*, ill. by Kurt Wiese. Viking, 1942. A young lion becomes the leader of his pack, hunted by the people of a Zulu village on the South African veldt.

______. *On Safari*, ill. by Kurt Wiese. Viking, 1940. An account of the author's days as a cub explorer.

______. *White Panther*, ill. by Kurt Wiese, Viking, 1941. 11-15

# Chapter 13
# Modern Fiction

Modern realistic fiction for children was off to a spirited start with such books as *Hans Brinker, or the Silver Skates* (1865), *Little Women* (1868), *The Adventures of Tom Sawyer* (1876), and *Heidi* (1884, first English translation). While there are signs that moralistic and sentimental didacticism is not dead, present-day realistic fiction, like these fine books, is predominantly honest. Most authors assume, as did Samuel Clemens, that children are sensible, normal human beings, interested in how other children and adults get along in the world. On the whole, modern realistic fiction for children includes, along with a great number of mediocre stories, some of the finest children's books ever written.

Realistic stories may be just as exciting or humorous or romantic or imaginative as fanciful tales, but they are always plausible or possible. In a realistic story everything that happens *could* happen. Sometimes the adventures of the hero or heroine may seem rather improbable but still merit the classification of realistic because they are possible. Sometimes the hero's exploits may be possible but are so extravagant that they are classified as fanciful. On the whole, a realistic story may be defined as a tale that is convincingly true to life.

Realistic fiction for children is divided into many categories including some animal stories (Chapter 12), historical novels for children (Chapter 14), stories about peoples of other lands, and stories about contemporary life in the United States, the last two categories the major concern of this chapter. These stories are particularly valuable to children because they give everyday life something of the excitement and charm of fiction. They also help children better understand the problems and issues of their own lives, empathize with other people, and see more clearly the complexities of human relationships.

The books discussed in this chapter have been divided into three major groups: books for the youngest children, books for the middle group, and books for older children. These divisions are not hard and fast, since many children read above their usual reading level when they are interested or may go back to a childhood favorite of their past reading experience. And many adults have found that they can read aloud books intended for children older than those in their audience. The reading levels suggested in the bibliography are of course equally flexible. In addition to these three major categories, there are two minor categories: sports stories and myster-

## VIEWPOINTS

The only obligation to which in advance we may hold a novel, without incurring the accusation of being arbitrary, is that it be interesting. . . . The ways in which it is at liberty to accomplish this result (of interesting us) strike me as innumerable, and such as can only suffer from being marked out or fenced in by prescription. They are as various as the temperament of man, and they are successful in proportion as they reveal a particular mind, different from others. A novel is in its broadest definition a personal, a direct impression of life: that, to begin with, constitutes its value, which is greater or less according to the intensity of the impression. But there will be no intensity at all, and therefore no value, unless there is freedom to feel and say. The tracing of a line to be followed, of a tone to be taken, of a form to be filled out, is a limitation of that freedom and a suppression of the very thing that we are most curious about.—Henry James, "The Art of Fiction," in *Makers of Literary Criticism* (vol. II), compiled and edited by A. G. George, Asia Publishing House, London, 1967, p. 352.

ies, two of the favorite subject-matter interests of children.

The stories in this chapter are not divided by ethnic or regional groups or by countries. The chapter bibliography, however, is marked so that those who are interested, say, in finding books about black children can do so; and the Subject Matter Index, too, will help readers find such stories.

In the past ten years or so, realistic fiction has shown more change than any other kind of books for children. Chapter 1 touched briefly on those changes and Chapter 4, pages 105–106, discussed some of the present-day trends: the increased number of books by and about blacks; the growing publication in the United States, either in separate editions or translations, of books from other countries; and, particularly notable, the greater frankness in language and the treatment of hitherto taboo subjects.

## CRITERIA FOR REALISTIC STORIES

How can we evaluate this wealth of realistic fiction for children, when it ranges from picture stories for the youngest to mystery stories and romance for young people? First of all, it may be helpful to review the section in Chapter 2, entitled "Looking Closely at Books," pp. 23–32, and to consider in these books just how effectively setting, point of view, characters, plot, theme, and style are handled. The primary consideration is Does the story captivate the reader and keep him racing along from page to page, and does it have sufficient literary distinction to develop the child's taste as it enchants him?

Most of this fiction, in addition to telling good stories, satisfies some of children's basic needs. From *One Morning in Maine* to *Where the Lilies Bloom* there is continual emphasis on winning or holding security. The satisfaction of belonging is very important in *Plain Girl, Little Navajo Bluebird*, and the picture story *Wait for William*. Loving and being loved is a powerful motive in *Wild in the World, Zeely*, and *Cotton in My Sack*. Children's love of change and fun is a motivating force in *Henry Huggins*, the Ransome books, and *Little Eddie*. The need to know is important in *Tom Sawyer, Portrait of Ivan, . . . and now Miguel, Roosevelt Grady*, and in the mystery tales.

*Illustration by Lois Lenski from* Cotton in My Sack. *Copyright, 1949, by Lois Lenski. Published by J. B. Lippincott Company. Reprinted by permission of author.*

The need for competence is a strong motivating force in *Yonie Wondernose, Olaf Reads, My Side of the Mountain*, and many other realistic stories of the past and present.

If these books center on the child's basic needs; if they give him increased insight into his own personal problems and social relationships; if they show that people are more alike than different, more akin to each other than alien; if they convince young readers that they can do something about their lives—have fun and adventures and get things done without any magic other than their own earnest efforts—then they are good and worthwhile books for children to read.

### Stories About Minority Groups

No other country in the world has the variety of peoples to be found in the United States. We have such regional groups as the mountaineers, the Cajuns, and the migrant groups that follow the crops—picking cotton or beans or strawberries or oranges. Then there are the close-knit communities of immigrants and their descendants making a little Italy or Hungary or Sweden within a larger community. There are groups representing all the major and innumerable minor religious sects, and Americans of every racial background. Since all of these diverse peoples have contributed richly to our national life, it is important that children should meet them vicariously in books in order that they may meet them in person sympathetically and with respect. Children see in books their own images, and if these are distorted or if there is stigma by omission, such self-images are damaged. And it is especially important that the minority group is pictured not as "them" but as "one of us," that the books about children of minority groups show the diversity within the group rather than a stereotype. When there is a need and a response, as there has been for books about black children, there are always the twin specters of the bandwagon book, tailored to fit the need, and of the tract, written with good intent but too burdened by its message to be a good story. Some of these books may be useful temporarily despite their mediocrity, but it is to be hoped that the day will come when there are so many good books for and about every kind of child that we can dismiss those that do not meet all the standards of good literature.

#### VIEWPOINTS

Fiction at its best, then, is the fruit of perfect self-identification of the writer with his materials—with beings, with situations, with objects, with time and place. It is the application to life of a heightened perception which experiences people and all things as if the writer *were* those people, those things. For the fiction writer "There, but for the grace of God, go I" is heightened to "There go I," is heightened to "While there is a poorer class, I belong to it, while there is a criminal class, I am of it, while there is a soul in jail, I am not free." It is the literal self-identification "with every fault, frailty and futility," and also with every magnification and enhancement of the human being. It is to see within, it is to see through, it is to see all material, as it were, as intimate and as *warm* as one's self. These walls, this separation of being which we set up and imagine, are specious. The appearance—and this is what the realist deals with—is separative; but the consciousness, which the creative writer deals with, is one.—Zona Gale, "Writing as Design," in *The Writer and His Craft*, edited by Roy W. Cowden, The University of Michigan Press, Ann Arbor, 1954, p. 35.

### Stories About Children from Other Lands

In early stories about other lands there was a tendency to present the picturesque at the expense of the usual. They gave us the China of bound feet, the Holland of wooden shoes and lace caps, South America by way of a primitive type of Indian tribe. Some of these faults are still to be found in recently published books (both those written in the United States and those selected for importation from other countries), but such misconceptions are far less common. We must be careful to check the information given in such stories against what we believe to be true of the present everyday life of people we know. And we must question any implication that a way of life of people we don't know is queer or quaint rather than simply different. In many of these books the themes are universal, and the stories point up the fact that differences between children of one country and those of another are superficial, based on cultural rather than on inherent factors.

## REALISM FOR YOUNG CHILDREN

Our youngest children, anywhere from two years old to seven, seem to have special need for stories that are as factual and personal as their fingers and toes and the yards and neighborhoods they are beginning to explore. At the beginning of the nineteen twenties, Lucy Sprague Mitchell in her *Here and Now Story Book* (1921) called attention to the fact that there were few if any stories for children under five concerned with their modern world. The four- and five-year-olds were given "The Three Little Pigs," "The Gingerbread Boy," and "The Three Billy-Goats Gruff" over and over again. Of course they liked these stories and still do, regardless of lunar modules and Telstar. But they should also have been supplied with stories about children like themselves and about the everyday things of their everyday world.

Mrs. Mitchell set out to supply these tales. She did her best with earnestness and sincerity, but she turned away from plot, centered on the child's own activities, and wrote from the child's own talk—using many sensory-motor words and repetitional phrases. She launched the purr, purr, pat, pat school of writing, which offers the young child pitterpatter in place of plot. Nevertheless, her idea of a modern realism for the youngest was sound, and she soon had a devoted group of followers. Mrs. Mitchell's work fulfilled a need which few adults had noticed before.

One book of realistic tales which appeared a few years after Mrs. Mitchell's stories was nothing short of epoch-making. *The Poppy Seed Cakes* (1924) broke every one of the canons of realism which had been developed by Mrs. Mitchell. The stories have a Russian atmosphere with beautifully unfamiliar and mouth-filling names like Andrewshek, Erminka, and Auntie Katushka. Every story in the series has a lively plot—something happens. Mostly the stories turn upon Andrewshek's irresponsibility. He starts bouncing on the feather bed, and the goose walks in and gobbles up Auntie Katushka's poppy seed cakes. Andrewshek repents, but the next time he forgets to watch the picnic basket. Off it goes down the lake,

BOUNCING UP IN THE AIR FOR THE NINTH TIME

*Illustration by Maud and Miska Petersham. From* The Poppy Seed Cakes *by Margery Clark. Copyright, 1924, by Doubleday and Company, Inc. Reprinted by permission of publisher. (Original in color)*

Then he dyed his wool himself until it was all, all blue.

*Illustration by Elsa Beskow from* Pelle's New Suit. *Harper & Row, Publishers, 1929. Reprinted by permission of Stig Beskow, Stockholm. (Original in color)*

propelled by a predatory swan. Every story involves plenty of action and laughter.

Here are no stories by a formula but a book full of tales as gay and funny as any fanciful tale could possibly be. Boys recognize themselves in Andrewshek and so delight in his mishaps. Girls see themselves in Erminka with her passion for red boots. The stories have a warm, human atmosphere, which is enhanced by Maud and Miska Petersham's gay illustrations.

Another example of realism for the youngest came from the Swedish. It was a translation of *Pelle's New Suit* (1929), told and illustrated by Elsa Beskow.

Text and pictures in color tell how the little boy Pelle needs a new suit. He raises his own lamb and then, for each person who helps him with his suit, he performs some useful service. He follows the tailoring even as he assists the tailor. Finally, for his Sunday best he triumphantly wears his beautiful blue suit. A similar story, save for the child's participation, is K. Ushinsky's *How a Shirt Grew in the Field*, translated from the Russian by Marguerita Rudolph (1967). These processes of making cloth and clothes may be dated, but pictures and text make them understandable and give children a sense of the sequential activities involved in producing a suit of clothes. This is what Mrs. Mitchell was moving toward. A plot for small children need not have elaborate complications if it has enough significance.

## MARGARET WISE BROWN

*The City Noisy Book*
*The Dead Bird*

The most notable of the early followers of Lucy Sprague Mitchell's pattern was Margaret Wise Brown, who wrote also under the name of Golden MacDonald. It was said that at the peak of her remarkable productivity she turned out some fifty-four books in two years. One of them, *The Little Island*, was so beautifully illustrated by Leonard Weisgard that it won the Caldecott Medal in 1947. The style of her books was cadenced, in order to stimulate the sensory perceptions and awareness of young children.

*The City Noisy Book* (1939) was a pioneer

in this awareness school of writing. It was followed by several more *Noisy* books. Then there was a series contrasting bigness and littleness. The hero of *The Little Fisherman* caught little fish and the big fisherman caught big fish, and so on.

Many books have appeared since her death, the most outstanding being *The Dead Bird* (1958), which is a direct and simple story of some children's burial of a bird they have found. Her contribution lies chiefly in her sensitive perception of the child's sensory responses to the big booming confusion of the world.

The books by Margaret Wise Brown launched a torrent of awareness compositions for the young. There were books about night sounds, day smells, wetness, coldness, colors, and "plink plink goes the water in the sink." By the nineteen fifties it began to look as if we were in for a kind of pernicious anemia of theme and plot, with language experiences in place of stories and pitter-patter in place of events. These books give the child back himself with little more—no rich entertainment, no additional insight, and no laughter.

## RUTH KRAUSS

*A Hole Is to Dig*
*A Very Special House*

In 1947 Ruth Krauss' *Growing Story* caused no great stir. It is about a small boy who sees various things growing but does not realize that he too is lengthening until he tries on his last year's clothes. *A Hole Is to Dig* (1952) is a series of definitions by children: "a hole is to dig," "a face is so you can make faces." Boys and girls in the upper grades enjoyed experimenting with their own definitions: "ice is to suck and to fall down on," "trees are what you tear your pants on." This is conscious language play for children old enough to know what they are doing and to enjoy giving vent to their pent-up silliness.

*A Very Special House* (1953) is an imaginative spree by a small child who for once in his life does everything he shouldn't, such as drawing on the walls, jumping up and down on a bed, and shouting "ooie ooie ooie." And nobody ever says "stop stop stop." Herein lies Ruth Krauss' particular skill: she uses cadence so cleverly that it is as orderly and lyrical as verse. *I Write It* (1970) celebrates the joy of being able to write one's own name. Maurice Sendak's action pictures would predispose anyone to the texts. Like Margaret Wise Brown, Ruth Krauss has been fortunate in her illustrators.

## MARJORIE FLACK

*Wait for William*

*Wait for William* (1935) is a "here and now" story whose whole plot turns on a small boy's struggle to get his shoelaces tied. Any four-year-old can understand and sympathize with William's predicament, and so can adults.

On his way to watch a circus parade, being hurried of course by the older children, who never pay any attention when he pleads with them to wait, William just *has* to stop to tie his shoelaces. When he finishes, the children have vanished. Things look dark for William, until suddenly the parade he was waiting for overtakes him. Moreover, he is lifted high on the top of the elephant by a sympathetic circus man and allowed to ride with the parade. A more joyous story of the humble being exalted and the meek inheriting the earth was never told.

Marjorie Flack, it is said, not satisfied with privately working over her little story patterns, always submitted them to the critical responses of two different school groups, whose reactions helped her to determine the final form of these tales. This perhaps accounts for their unfailing popularity with children everywhere.

### ALVIN TRESSELT

*Hide and Seek Fog*
*White Snow, Bright Snow*

Midway between the awareness and the theme-plot schools of writing for young children lie the picture stories of Alvin Tresselt and Leo Politi. Mr. Tresselt constructs his stories about weather in simple, rhythmic prose, and with Roger Duvoisin's pictures, they develop a real sense of drama. *Hide and Seek Fog* (1965), for example, describes how the fog affects sea and seaside activities. These little everyday miracles of the weather are made exciting, something to be watched and enjoyed, never feared. Texts and pictures are full of reassurance and beauty. *White Snow, Bright Snow* won the 1948 Caldecott Medal for Mr. Duvoisin.

### LEO POLITI

*Pedro* and other stories

Leo Politi's picture stories are simple in theme and plot and are frequently centered on the activities of small children living in a homogeneous racial group in the midst of one of our big cities. *Pedro, the Angel of Olvera Street* (1946) and *Juanita* (1948) are both about the Mexican-Americans of Los Angeles—*Pedro* tells of Olvera Street at Christmas time and *Juanita* of the Olvera pre-Easter ceremony, the Blessing of the Animals. *Song of the Swallows*, the 1950 Caldecott Medal book, tells of the coming of spring to the old mission of Capistrano. *Moy Moy* (1960) is about a little Chinese-American girl observing the Chinese New Year (see 19 in color section). *Little Leo* (1951) journeys to Italy and converts a whole village of children to the charms of playing Indian. An affectionate understanding of children is reflected in every book and every picture Politi has made.

### EDWARD ARDIZZONE

The *Little Tim* stories

Even young children need a touch of wildness now and then, which is precisely what the English Mr. Ardizzone gives them in *Little Tim and the Brave Sea Captain* (1936), his spirited account of Tim's adventures at sea. It all starts with Tim, who plays in and out of boats on the beach. How he becomes a stowaway, learns to be an efficient if reluctant deck hand, and experiences shipwreck makes a thrilling story for the five- to eight-year-olds. Mr. Ardizzone's watercolors are as vigorous as his tale. Here is realism for the youngest at its most adventurous level. Tim is a do-it-yourself hero if ever there was one, and his competence and achievements through a series of stories rouse the admiration of his young devotees. Mr. Ardizzone's books introduce other heroes, but Tim is still the favorite young hero.

### ROBERT McCLOSKEY

*Make Way for Ducklings*
*Time of Wonder*

Robert McCloskey was the first artist to win the Caldecott Medal twice, 1942 and 1958. If you look over his picture stories—*Make Way for Ducklings* (1941), *One Morning in Maine* (1952), and *Time of Wonder* (1957)—you discover that they are all built on a theme of reassurance. Children know the ducklings will come safely through their first perilous trip in city traffic because their mother has them in charge. And in that superb book in full color *Time of Wonder*, the safe, secure world of woods and beach is threatened by the oncoming darkness of a hurricane. How the family prepares for and survives this menace is so convincingly told and pictured that children feel they too can meet and endure danger. The pictures in the first two

*Illustration by Robert McCloskey from* Make Way for Ducklings *by Robert McCloskey. Copyright, 1941, by Robert McCloskey; copyright © renewed 1969 by Robert McCloskey. By permission of The Viking Press, Inc.*

books have humor and strength, and some of the paintings in *Time of Wonder* have a breathtaking beauty. *Lentil* (1940) is the story of a boy who plays a harmonica and saves the day in a small town's welcome to a returning citizen. McCloskey's books for older children, *Homer Price* (1943) and *Centerburg Tales* (1951), are both written with a humor that has given them enduring popularity.

## WILL AND NICOLAS

*The Two Reds*
*Russet and the Two Reds*

William Lipkind's and Nicolas Mordvinoff's books are lively picture stories for the youngest. Their first collaboration was the amusing *The Two Reds* (1950), in which Red, a city boy, and Red, an alley cat, are pursued by a militant gang known as the Signal Senders. In the second book (1962), Russet, a girl redhead, has moved upstairs over the two Reds. They ignore her, but when the Signal Senders pursue again, Russet proves her worth. Once secure, the three go home, a united trio. These are slight stories but they have the realism of city streets.

## CAROLYN HAYWOOD

*"B" Is for Betsy*
*Little Eddie*

With the *Betsy* and the *Little Eddie* books of Carolyn Haywood, children progress from the picture story to the illustrated story, with the pictures of secondary importance to the tale. Another mark of increasing maturity is that against a familiar background of family life, the young heroes and heroines are moving into an ever widening circle of neighborhood and school adventures, camps, and even travel.

*"B" Is for Betsy* (1939) launched the series of books about the everyday activities of a little girl in suburbia. Children took Betsy to their hearts immediately. As she grew with each succeeding book, her experiences widened. Other books about Betsy's circle of friends appeared each year, but the characters remained very close to stereotypes. It was the interpretation of their activities or the problems connected with school or camp or typical mistakes and accidents that held the attention of young readers. These gave the child greater self-knowledge, more understanding of other people and experiences, and a greater confidence in approaching the next level of life.

With *Little Eddie* (1947) Carolyn Haywood developed a real boy, and laughter began. Eddie is as earnest as Betsy, but much more alive. He is an avid collector of "valuables," which his long-suffering family calls "junk." Still the family endures patiently even an old but full-sized fire engine. However, Gardenia the goat is too much for Father, and Eddie and his pet are banished to an uncle's ranch, far, far away. The picture of ranch life is a bit vague, but not Eddie. He saves Gardenia's life but remains definitely Eddie, traveling home with the largest miscellany of "valuables" ever collected. In the next book, *Eddie's Pay Dirt* (1953), our hero is confronted with a grave ethical problem. His father helps him see it, but wisely leaves the decision to Eddie. *Eddie and His Big Deals* (1955) and the more recent *Eddie's Happenings* (1971) show many signs of maturity.

These simply written stories have a warmth and a directness that win and hold young readers.

## TARO YASHIMA

*Crow Boy*

Taro Yashima's striking picture stories are set in his native Japan. *Plenty to Watch* (1954) by Taro and Mitsu Yashima tells of the shops and workers that Japanese children stop to watch as they walk home from school. The stores and the workers may differ from ours, but the children's insatiable curiosity about both is universal.

*Crow Boy* (1955), Taro Yashima's third book, was a Caldecott Honor Book and also won the Child Study Award. It has unusual social values as well as pictorial beauty. Crow Boy is a small, silent child who walks to school alone, sits alone, and does not talk. The children call him derisively "Chibi"—tiny boy. But a new schoolmaster discovers that the small outcast walks in from a great

*Illustration by Taro Yashima from* Crow Boy *by Taro Yashima. Copyright 1955 by Mitsu and Taro Yashima. By permission of The Viking Press, Inc. (Original in color)*

distance. He knows where wild potatoes and wild grapes grow, and he knows every call the crows make and can imitate them perfectly. When he does this for the children they call him "Crow Boy" with respect, and he is one of them at last. Not since Eleanor Estes' *The Hundred Dresses* has this theme of the outsider been so sensitively handled.

### MYRA BERRY BROWN

*First Night Away from Home*
*Benjy's Blanket*
*Sandy Signs His Name*

Myra Brown's picture books for very young children have a natural, easy style and each presents a situation with which a child can identify. *First Night Away from Home* (1960) describes the mingled qualms and joys of such an experience, and *Benjy's Blanket* (1962) is the story of a security blanket that is given up when Benjy decides the kitten next door needs it more than he does. In *Sandy Signs His Name* (1967), a child, delighted with his new skill, prints his name everywhere he can—and a few places he shouldn't. Other books deal with such universal experiences as adjustment, in *Amy and the New Baby* (1965), and the satisfaction of achievement, in *Ice Cream for Breakfast* (1963), in which two children make breakfast for their mother on Mother's Day.

### JOAN LEXAU

*Olaf Reads*
*Benjie*

Joan Lexau's stories have diversity of style, mood, and subject, but all of them have an understanding of the child's viewpoint, whether they are written for older readers or for kindergarten children. Her books for the youngest children are permeated with love and humor.

*Olaf Reads* (1961) is an amusing tale of a child so enthralled by his new prowess that he takes literally a sign that says "Pull," and finds the whole school responding with a fire drill. In *Benjie* (1964), a very shy black child discovers, when he hunts for his grandmother's lost earring, that it isn't really so hard to talk to people; in *Benjie on His Own* (1970)

*Illustration by Don Bolognese from* Benjie on His Own *by Joan Lexau. Illustrations copyright © 1970 by Don Bolognese. Reprinted by permission of the publisher, The Dial Press. (Original in color)*

he learns that he can call on his neighbors for help when grandmother is ill. *Finders Keepers, Losers Weepers* (1967) is for beginning readers, a story of a small boy's trials in taking care of his still smaller sister. *Striped Ice Cream* (1968) tells of a child in a working-class family who, tired of hand-me-down dresses from her sisters, is thrilled by a new dress *and* striped ice cream for her birthday. *Me Day* (1971) describes a small boy's joy in seeing his father, who has left home, on his birthday. Two excellent realistic books for older children, *The Trouble with Terry* (1962) and *A Kite Over Tenth Avenue* (1967), are cited in the bibliography at the end of this chapter.

## CHARLOTTE ZOLOTOW

*Big Sister and Little Sister*
*The Hating Book*
*A Father Like That*

Few writers for small children so empathize with them as does Charlotte Zolotow, whose books—with some exceptions—are really explorations of relationships cast in story form and given vitality by perfected simplicity of style and by the humor and tenderness of the stories. *Big Sister and Little Sister* (1966) is typical of Zolotow's later books, exploring the balances in a one-to-one relationship, as are *When I Have a Son* (1967) and its companion volume, *When I Have a Little Girl* (1965). Each of these is a bravado statement of independence: the boy, for example, can have triple malts just before dinner, never have to go to sleep until he finishes a chapter, and so on—exaggerations that can make the small child see the humor of his own demands. *The Hating Book* (1969) describes the ups and downs of friendship, a theme also used in Miriam Cohen's *Best Friends* (1971). The mother of a fatherless child listens, in *A Father Like That* (1971), to her son's catalog of virtues in his dream-father, who would *never* show off at parent-teacher meetings. Zolotow's understanding of children's emotional needs and problems, and her ability to express them with candor have made her one of the major contemporary writers of realistic books for small children.

## MARTHA ALEXANDER

*Out! Out! Out!*
*The Story Grandmother Told*
*Sabrina*

Tidy, charming little drawings in soft colors add to the appeal of Martha Alexander's realistic stories. In *Out! Out! Out!* (1968) she tells a story without words, the pictures showing the delightful commotion that ensues when a

*Illustration by Martha Alexander from* Bobo's Dream *by Martha Alexander. Copyright © 1970 by Martha Alexander. Reprinted by permission of the publisher, The Dial Press. (Original with color)*

bird flies into the house. In *The Story Grandmother Told* (1969) a bright-faced black child prompts Gramma to tell a favorite tale by telling it herself. *Sabrina* (1971) finds, when she starts nursery school, that other girls like her unusual name. Each story touches on some familiar situation, and the behavior of the children is convincingly natural. *Blackboard Bear* (1969) and *Bobo's Dream* (1970) use a daydream sequence to gain self-confidence for their protagonists.

## OTHER NOTABLE BOOKS FOR THE YOUNGEST

The profusion of picture-story books and books for the beginning reader makes it impossible to include every one of the many worthy books that have been published. Some authors whose best-known books are in another category have written stories that are admirable examples of realism for young children; Russell Hoban, for example, whose *Frances* books are described in the chapter on animal stories, has also written books like *The Sorely Trying Day* (1964), in which the chain effect of hostile, then friendly, behavior is seen in a family, a plot also used in Charlotte Zolotow's *The Quarreling Book* (1963). Lois Lenski, whose regional stories are discussed later in this chapter, pioneered in realism in books for the youngest children. The series that began with *The Little Auto* (1934) and the later series about Debby and Davy are direct and simple, with no wasted words. In Heidrun Petrides' *Hans and Peter* (1963) the children have the satisfaction of seeing a project fulfilled by their own efforts. The engagingly homely children and deft humor of Harriet Pincus' illustrations add immeasurably to the bland text of Lore Segal's *Tell Me a Mitzi*, which has three stories of family life—as it really is. One tale is totally and amusingly improbable, but Mitzi and her little brother Jacob remain sturdily childlike.

*Illustration by Harriet Pincus. Reprinted with permission of Farrar, Straus & Giroux, Inc. from* Tell Me a Mitzi, *text copyright © 1970 by Lore Segal, pictures copyright 1970 by Harriet Pincus. (Original in color)*

In the blithe *Emmet's Pig* (1969), Mary Stolz, who writes for all ages, faces the problem of a child who wants a pet inappropriate for apartment living. Beatrice Schenk de Regniers, in *A Little House of Your Own* (1955), gives a childlike introduction to the idea that it is good to be alone at times. Many author-illustrators have contributed to the store of realistic picture books: Virginia Lee Burton, Tasha Tudor, Ezra Jack Keats. Keats' Caldecott book, *The Snowy Day* (1962), started a trend of showing black children in illustrations with no reference to racial identity in the text. One of the most outstanding earlier books about black children is Ellen Tarry's and Marie Hall Ets' *My Dog Rinty* (1946), in which a child faces giving up a pet. *Two Is a Team* (1945), by Lorraine and Jerrold Beim, is a simple story of cooperation. Such books were, however, rare. Of the trends observable in contemporary publishing, the increased numbers of books about black children is a major one. Some of the books are simply affirmations of pride, like Jean Bond's *Brown Is a Beautiful Color* (1969) or Ann McGovern's *Black Is Beautiful* (1969), and some are stories of black children showing competence, as in Janice Udry's *Mary Jo's Grandmother* (1970); overcoming jealousy and learning to love, as Robert does in John Steptoe's beautifully illustrated *Stevie* (1969); seeking quiet in a crowded home, in Elizabeth Hill's *Evan's Corner* (1967). In some, the theme is the problems raised by prejudice against color, such as Billy meets in *A New Home for Billy* (1966), by May Justus. In this story, a black family, anxious to move from a tenement to a house in the country, encounters barriers before they find a community that welcomes them. And Lennie, in Justus' *New Boy in School* (1963), must adjust to being the only black child in his class.

*Illustration by Emily A. McCully from* Friday Night Is Papa Night *by Ruth A. Sonneborn and Emily A. McCully. Illustrations copyright © 1970 by Emily A. McCully. Reprinted by permission of The Viking Press, Inc. (Original with color)*

*Illustration by John Steptoe from* Stevie *by John Steptoe. Copyright 1969. Reproduced by permission of Harper & Row, Publishers, Inc. (Original in color)*

Ruth Sonneborn's stories are about Puerto Rican children in the United States; they are stories of universal problems and joys, like the happiness of having the family all together in *Friday Night Is Papa Night* (1970), rather than difficulties faced because the children are Puerto Rican. *Magdalena* (1971), by Louisa Shotwell, is the story of a lively Puerto Rican child and her beloved grandmother. There is still a paucity of books about other minority groups for the youngest readers, but this will surely change.

Almost every trend in realistic fiction for older children seems to be followed by a similar trend in books for younger children. Topics that have been hitherto abjured are emerging, as does divorce in Beth Goff's *Where Is Daddy?* (1969).

Although children in the United States are enjoying more books from other countries than ever before, there are fewer picture stories being written about children of other lands. However, such books as Eleanor Lattimore's *Little Pear* (1931) and—in 1971!—its sequel, *More About Little Pear*, the sprightly stories of Françoise, and Ludwig Bemelmans' *Hansi* (1934) and *Madeline* (1939) are still read and loved. Marie Hall Ets is one of the few authors who writes about Mexican children; her *Bad Boy, Good Boy* (1967) describes the problems of learning a new language and the effect of marital conflict on a child, while *Gilberto and the Wind* (1963) is a simpler story of a child's play.

*Illustration by Edward Ardizzone from* The Wrong Side of the Bed *by Edward Ardizzone. Copyright © 1970 by Edward Ardizzone. Reproduced by permission of Doubleday & Company, Inc. and The Bodley Head, London. (Published in Britain under the title* Johnny's Bad Day.*)*

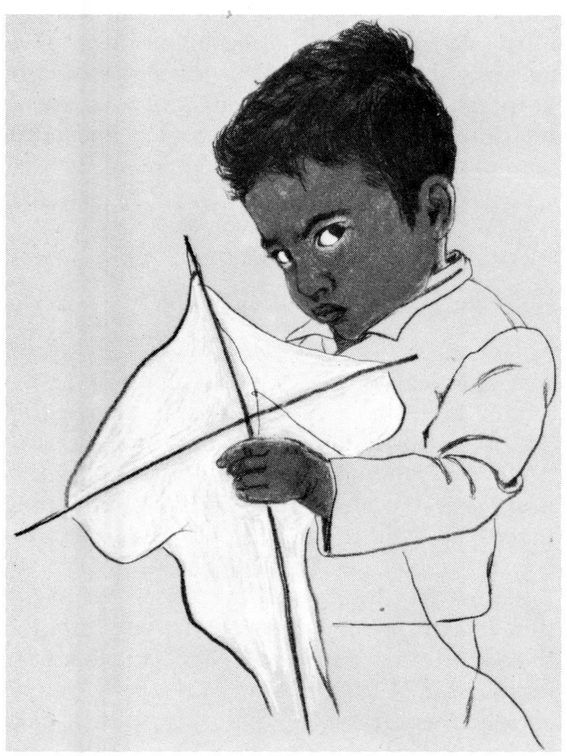

*Illustration by Marie Hall Ets from* Gilberto and the Wind *by Marie Hall Ets. Copyright © 1963 by Marie Hall Ets. Reprinted by permission of The Viking Press, Inc. (Original with color)*

Two other significant developments in books for the youngest children are the numbers of lively and entertaining books for beginning readers and the smaller, but growing, numbers of books with no text. Several of Martha Alexander's books are of this type, and some of the best are Edward Ardizzone's *The Wrong Side of the Bed* (1970), Eleanor Schick's *Making Friends* (1969), and Mercer Mayer's *Frog, Where Are You?* (1969). Among the best books for independent reading are those in the Harper "I Can Read" series.

## FORERUNNERS OF REALISM

Before examining present-day realistic stories for the middle and older children, it may be helpful to review some of the classic realistic stories: *The Adventures of Tom Sawyer* (1876), *Little Women* (1868), *Hans Brinker, or the Silver Skates* (1865), and *Heidi* (1884).

## SAMUEL L. CLEMENS (MARK TWAIN)

### *The Adventures of Tom Sawyer*

Almost a century ago, Tom Sawyer introduced children to the seamy side of village life. At that time, automobiles, superhighways, airplanes, and television had not tied the small towns so intimately to the large cities that there was little difference between the two. There in *Tom Sawyer* was the isolated country town Samuel Clemens himself had grown up in, with respectable churchgoers on one side and the village ne'er-do-wells on the other. Tom was the link between the two groups. By way of his friendship with Huck, the son of the town drunkard, he knew all the shady characters as well as his Aunt Polly's churchgoing friends. He saw a grave robbery and a murder and had other hair-raising adventures. The book's special appeal is to children around ten, eleven, and twelve. At those ages, it gives them chills up and down their spines, but it is not lurid or sensational. Along with the excitement and the humor, there is a steady emergence of the boy's code: he keeps his word to a friend; he may be scared to death, but he sees things through; in real peril, he protects a weaker person; he uses his head, keeps cool, and keeps trying. This is as good a code today as it ever was.

## LOUISA MAY ALCOTT

### *Little Women*

*Little Women* deals with a family of four girls of teen age, but it is the preadolescent girls to whom this book makes the greatest appeal, because of their interest in what lies just ahead, their first sense of romance, their dream of being grown up. Many girls still enjoy *Little Women* as much as their great-great-grandmothers did. Here is the first great juvenile novel of family life—a warm, loving family group, struggling with poverty and with individual problems but sustained by an abiding affection for each other and an innocent kind of gaiety that could make its own fun. Not until the Laura Ingalls Wilder series or perhaps Hilda Van Stockum's *The Cottage at Bantry Bay* do we again encounter such a picture of a family, and in no one of them is each member of the group more distinctly drawn than are the unforgettable Beth, Jo, Meg, and Amy. Here is characterization that makes each girl a real human being—exasperating, lovable, heroic, absurd, delightful.

*Little Women* also provides a wholesome introduction to romance and to the inevitability of death even among loved ones, who, because they are loved, seem somehow invulnerable. There is a continuity in social relationships, with the home as the necessary core of all happy living.

## MARY MAPES DODGE

### *Hans Brinker, or the Silver Skates*

Mary Mapes Dodge is notable not only as the author of *Hans Brinker* but also as the first editor of the famous old magazine for children, *St. Nicholas* (1873). This magazine, numbering among its contributors such names as Louisa May Alcott, Henry Wadsworth Longfellow, Frances Hodgson Burnett, Rudyard Kipling, and John Greenleaf Whittier, is said to have marked the beginning of the Children's Age,[1] but Mrs. Dodge's own famous novel for children and young people certainly contributed to its propitious start. *Hans Brinker, or the Silver Skates* (1865) was

1. Bertha Mahony and Elinor Whitney, comps., *Realms of Gold in Children's Books*. Garden, 1929, p. 611.

immediately successful. It was translated into many languages, and the Dutch people accepted it as the best picture of childhood in Holland that had ever been written up until that time.[2]

In this country *Hans Brinker* has remained on most book lists, as a good story and a picture of Dutch life of the time, though its popularity is beginning to wane. Dodge had become deeply interested in the history of the Dutch republic and had saturated herself with the best references she could find on the subject. When she began to write her book she had a twofold purpose: to tell a story about the children of Holland and to weave into that story as much of the history and customs of the people as she could. It is this burden of information that bogs it down here and there, or even interrupts the story entirely. Some of the digressions are interesting in themselves; others are less so; but all of them disrupt the unity of the exciting plot which Mrs. Dodge develops so successfully. If these digressions were deleted, the story might go right on being as popular as ever because it is exciting, with a competition for the wonderful silver skates and two fascinating mysteries to be solved. Some of the episodes seem melodramatic but not too incredible considering the date of the narrative. It is, on the whole, still a lively and satisfying tale, with mysteries and suspense aplenty.

## JOHANNA SPYRI

### *Heidi*

*Heidi* was written in German by Johanna Spyri, a Swiss, and translated into English (1884) soon after its publication. This book continued the fine tradition of *Hans Brinker* by introducing American children to children of other lands through a delightful story.

2. Ibid., p. 610.

*Heidi* uses the most popular of all themes—a variation of Cinderella, the unwanted, neglected child who comes into her own—but there is a convincing quality about *Heidi* which many of the modern Cinderellas lack. The child is full of the joy of living. She skips and leaps and she falls in love with an apparently grouchy old grandfather, the goats, and the mountains, all with equal vehemence and loyalty.

No child who has read and loved *Heidi* will ever enter Switzerland without a feeling of coming home. This is what books about other lands should do for children—leave them feeling forever a part of that country, forever well disposed toward the people. In such stories of other people, they have no sense of oddity, no feeling of irreconcilable differences, but a desire to know these people so like themselves.

To accomplish this, a book about other lands must be completely authentic and sincere. *Heidi* has both these virtues because of the experiences and character of the author, Johanna Spyri. She was a doctor's daughter, greatly moved by the ill health of her father's patients. She, too, knew the bounding health of this free life under sunny skies, amid the great mountain peaks, and she breathed the crystal-clear air. Nothing in the book is labored or superficial. Heidi is as wholesome and real as her mountains.

## REALISM FOR THE MIDDLE GROUP

For a long period after *Tom Sawyer*, *Little Women*, *Hans Brinker*, and *Heidi* appeared, there was as little substantial realism for older children as there was for the youngest. Of course the books by Frances Hodgson Burnett, which began in 1877 with *That Lass o' Lowrie's* and continued until the last book came out in 1922, span the gap between these older books and those realistic stories which are comparatively recent.

## FRANCES HODGSON BURNETT

*The Secret Garden* and other stories

When Frances Hodgson Burnett's *Little Lord Fauntleroy* was published in 1886, it is said to have "caused a delirium of joy," and *Sara Crewe* (1888) equaled *Fauntleroy.* Then about a quarter of a century after *Fauntleroy*, Burnett wrote *The Secret Garden* (1909), which has maintained a following of devoted readers to this very day. Like her earlier stories, it tells a fairy tale of unimaginable riches, of children misunderstood and suffering but conquering all. Burnett enjoys describing great wealth and then showing how it often brings neither a normal nor a happy life—very consoling to those without such wealth. The heroine of *The Secret Garden*, Mary, is plain and bad tempered as well as orphaned and neglected. In the huge estate where she is sent to live, Mary discovers a secret garden, a master with a crooked back, and his ailing son, Colin. Martha, the hearty Yorkshire maid, provides a healthy contrast, and Martha's little brother, Dickon, is the very spirit of the earth as is his wise, kind mother, who has love enough for her own brood of twelve and for the poor little rich children besides. Among them, they get the wretched Colin into the secret garden with Mary. Under Dickon's guidance, the children make the garden grow and bloom once more, without realizing that in the process they, too, will grow and bloom.

Dickon is as unreal as Fauntleroy, but Mary, sour and homely, and Colin, with his temper tantrums, are convincing. In spite of the heavy metaphysical suggestion at the close of the story about the "magic" of the earth and right thinking, this book is probably Burnett's most lasting contribution.

## ARTHUR RANSOME

*Swallows and Amazons* and other tales

After the publication of *Old Peter's Russian Tales*, Arthur Ransome started a series of stories about English children living in the Lake district of England. These were so popular for a while that children read every book in the series. Now, although their popularity has declined, they still have special values.

*Swallows and Amazons* (1931) is the first of the series. "The Swallows" are the four Walker children, who wish to camp out completely on their own. When Mother cables their seafaring father for permission, he cables back, "Better drowned than duffers if not duffers won't drown." Decidedly the children are not duffers. They set up shipshape living quarters on their island, establish a regular schedule, and have as little to do with the "natives" (adults) as possible.

The outstanding characteristic of these Ransome children is their competence. They meet every emergency with resourcefulness and intelligence. No one talks about courage. It is taken for granted like cleanliness and a decent sense of responsibility.

## KATE SEREDY

*The Good Master*

*The Good Master* (1935), written and beautifully illustrated by Kate Seredy, was an instantaneous favorite with children. If they were to be consulted, they might give this book the Newbery Medal rather than Seredy's *White Stag. The Good Master* is the story of a Hungarian tomboy, Kate—a regular brat of a child. She is sent by her father to stay on her uncle's ranch. Her young cousin Jancsi imagines she will be a frail, dainty girl, and so he is horrified by the wild, impish Kate. She causes a runaway of horses; she climbs the rafters and there eats sausage until she is sick; she knows how to do nothing useful and is a general pest. The gentling of Kate makes a charming story. "The Good Master" is the understanding uncle. The aunt is just as patient with Kate, and Jancsi takes a hand, too, in the girl's reformation. But it is Kate's growing love of the horses and riding, as well as her affection for her newly found relatives, that helps her learn gentler ways. Hungarian festivals and legends, the household crafts, the work of the ranch, the good food, and the warm family life add color and charm to a delightful story. The sequel to *The Good Master* is *The Singing Tree*, which sees Kate and Jancsi into their teens and the father gone to World War I. Anti-Semitism arises, but, in this story, it is happily banished. It comes perhaps too close to the didactic to be a popular story, but it is well worth reading.

## ARMSTRONG SPERRY

*Call It Courage*

*Call It Courage* (1940), a Newbery Medal book, is an exciting story about Mafatu, the son of a Polynesian chief, rejected by his people for his cowardice and marooned on a desert island. This island proves to be the sinister shrine of man-eaters. Mafatu maintains life, develops all the necessary arts and skills, makes his own weapons and his own canoe, finally escapes the man-eaters, and returns home a hero. This book about the conquest of fear will give young readers many a spinal chill and subsequent shiver of relief. The illustrations are beautiful.

*Illustration by Armstrong Sperry from* Call It Courage *by Armstrong Sperry. Copyright 1940, The Macmillan Company. Reprinted by permission of the publishers and The Bodley Head Ltd., London.*

## MONICA SHANNON

*Dobry*

One of the great children's books about people of other countries is Monica Shannon's *Dobry*, Newbery Medal winner for 1935. Because this book is not immediately popular with children, it needs some help from adults in promoting it. Read it aloud, discuss and savor the colorful episodes. The Bulgarian Christmas celebration, climaxing in Dobry's fine snow carving of the Nativity, makes a beautiful excerpt to read aloud for Christmas.

Dobry is a Bulgarian peasant boy whose family has been at work on the land for generations and who finds himself longing both to stay at home and to go away to become a sculptor. His mother is frightened and disappointed that he should think of anything but the land. The old grandfather, a remarkable character, believes that there lives in every human being "a spark of God" and only when that burns clear does life have any value. Even the mother comes to see, at last, that Dobry's "spark of God" belongs not to the land but to the creation of another kind of beauty.

The coming of the gypsies with their massaging bear, the snow-melting contest which lusty old Grandfather wins, the diving into the icy river for the crucifix on a cold St. John the Baptist Day, and the everyday work make this story of a boy's choice of his life's work a picture of rich living. We who guide children should remember Grandfather's philosophy:

> *. . . Everything is different, each leaf if you really look. There is no leaf exactly like that one in the whole world. Every stone is different. No other stone exactly like it. That is it, Dobry. God loves variety. . . . He makes a beautiful thing and nothing else in the whole world is exactly like it. . . . In odd days like these . . . people study how to be all alike instead of how to be as different as they really are.*

## MARY and CONRAD BUFF

*Dancing Cloud*
*Magic Maize*
*Hah-Nee*

Mary and Conrad Buff lived among the Indians, and in *Dancing Cloud* (1937) they tell about the Navahos in story and in wonderful pictures. The story is not so memorable as the pictures. Each chapter is a separate episode dealing with the activities of these people and their children—weaving, herding and shearing sheep, making jewelry, preparing food.

*Magic Maize* (1953) is about Guatemalan Indians, but their problems are much like those faced by some of the remote tribes in this country. The characters in this story are more fully realized than those in *Dancing Cloud*. And again Mr. Buff has captured the calm strength of the Indians and the glowing colors of their country.

*Hah-Nee* (1956) goes back in time to explain why the great Pueblo cities of the Southwest were abandoned. Hah-Nee does not quite emerge as a flesh-and-blood boy but is chiefly a name to carry the story. The effect of long-continued drouth will be understood by modern desert dwellers. To other children the book will supply an exciting background for the enigma of those vast, empty Pueblo cities.

## NOEL STREATFEILD

The *Shoes* stories

Noel Streatfeild's *Shoes* books are all vocational in their themes, but they manage to avoid the heavy earnestness that generally pervades such books. The two best are *Ballet Shoes* and *Circus Shoes*.

In the first story, *Ballet Shoes* (1937), the three Fossil children determine to become famous, so famous that their names will be in every history book. This book follows particularly the training of the would-be ballerina in the Academy of Dancing and Stage Training. The work is hard; there are bitter disappointments and also moments of triumph as brief as they are rare, but always the child's own unwavering determination to succeed keeps her working. How such a story manages to be as gay as it is rests entirely with Streatfeild's ability to make everyday events somehow amusing.

In *Circus Shoes* (1939) we meet poor Peter and Santa, who have been raised to be excessively genteel and never to appear outdoors without their gloves! Suddenly they find themselves running away to the only relative they have left in the world, an unknown Uncle Gus, of Cob's Circus. Uncle Gus is as horrified by his genteel relatives as the poor children are by the rough and ready life of the circus. Presently it begins to dawn upon Peter and Santa that they are surrounded by experts and perfectionists: these circus people are artists.

For the child with a special interest in ballet or any sort of theatrical life, these books are valuable. They take a serious attitude toward professions and amplify the difficulties without minimizing the satisfactions.

Of Streatfeild's later books, one that also has a background of the entertainment world is *The Children on the Top Floor* (1965), who live with a television celebrity. In *The Family at Caldicott Place* (1968) the most interesting character is the father of the family, who is having a slow recovery from deep neurosis. *Thursday's Child* (1971) is the story of an indomitable foundling girl.

## HILDA VAN STOCKUM

*The Cottage at Bantry Bay* and other stories

Having spent a childhood divided between Holland and Ireland, and later raising her own family in the United States, Hilda Van Stockum writes delightful stories of family life in all three countries. Children seldom think of the Irish twins, Francie and Liam, or the tomboy Pegeen as children of a foreign land.

*The Cottage at Bantry Bay* (1938) is the first of the series dealing with the O'Sullivan family. The mother and father are poor in this world's goods but rich in understanding and love. Francie has a clubfoot and there is no money to have it cared for, but this misfortune bothers only his mother and father, not Francie. There are mishaps and sadness, gaiety and triumph in this charming story, but the center of it all is the love of the family for each member of the group. Every episode is satisfying, and the fine human relationships of these obscure people make the book memorable.

*Francie on the Run* (1939) is a surprising sequel. Money is obtained to have Francie's foot taken care of. A successful operation is performed, but before Francie can be officially discharged from the large city hospital, he walks out.

In the story of *Pegeen* (1941), Francie is safely home, and a new child, Pegeen, an orphan, shares the love of the O'Sullivan family. Always there hangs over their heads the dread day when Pegeen will have to leave them and go to her only relative in America. The happy solution of this problem makes a heartwarming conclusion to this pleasant trilogy.

## ELEANOR ESTES

The *Moffat* stories

Within the United States one of the most captivating book families is unquestionably "the Moffats," created by Eleanor Estes. There are three of these books—*The Moffats* (1941), *The Middle Moffat* (1942), and *Rufus M.* (1943). Some adults consider either *Rufus M.* or *The Middle Moffat* the best of the series, but the children like them all.

There is no general theme, no long suspense, and no exciting climax to these books. Each chapter is a complete episode in the life of one of the Moffats. The funniest episode is Janey's performance in a dramatization of "The Three Bears." She carries on mostly without her middle-bear's head, which she mislaid, and she finishes with it on backward, after it has been hastily retrieved and chucked over her head.

*Illustration by Louis Slobodkin. Reproduced from* The Middle Moffat, *copyright, 1942, by Eleanor Estes, by permission of Harcourt Brace Jovanovich, Inc.*

The ultimate humor in these Moffat situations is touched off by the artist—Louis Slobodkin. The Moffat tales and Mr. Slobodkin's illustrations represent the perfect union of story and pictures—Rufus M. leaping for a deadly catch in a baseball game; Janey viewing the world amiably from an upside-down angle, looking between her own stout legs, head almost on the ground.

Also illustrated by Slobodkin, Estes' *The Hundred Dresses* (1944) is one of the most effective indictments of prejudice in children's literature, and a poignant story told in an easy, natural style. Wanda Petronski is an outsider, poor and ill-clad, who wears the same dress every day. Taunted, she says she has a hundred dresses at home. She does, and she's drawn them all. Her pictures, exhibited at school, win a medal, but Wanda isn't there. A note from her father says they have moved to a place where "No more holler Polack. No more ask why funny name. . . ." Eleanor Estes was awarded the Newbery Medal for *Ginger Pye* (1951). It is not up to the standard of the Moffat books but is a delightful story about a family that loses its dog and finds him through the kind offices of three-year-old Uncle Benny. The plot in *The Alley* (1964) revolves around burglary, but the book's appeal is in its picture of a small faculty community.

## ELIZABETH ENRIGHT

*The Saturdays*
*Gone-Away Lake*

Elizabeth Enright had a gift for realism, and her Melendy children in *The Saturdays*, *The Four Story Mistake*, and *Then There Were Five* are as popular with the nine-, ten-, and eleven-year-olds as *The Moffats* are with children just a little younger. *The Saturdays* (1941) introduces the four Melendys, ranging in age from six to thirteen, and deals with their $1.60 Saturdays. These are achieved by pooling all their allowances and by permitting one child to use the whole amount for a Saturday on his own. The results are often startling and always amusing. *The Four Story Mistake* (1942) and *Then There Were Five* (1944) continue the family activities in the country and lead to the adoption of a country boy.

The Melendy family has been almost superseded by the popular cousins in *Gone-Away Lake* (1957) and its sequel. In the first book, Portia and her cousin Julian discover an abandoned colony of summer cottages near a swamp that was once a lovely, sparkling lake. In the second book, *Return to Gone-Away* (1961), the family makes the joyous decision to restore one of the old houses and live there the year round. Mrs. Enright's style is so forthright and lively that this unusual setting becomes completely real and the reader shares the family's joy in that final decision.

The Newbery Medal was given to Mrs. Enright's *Thimble Summer* (1938). Here is the germ of a family story which developed more successfully in her Melendy family. The setting of *Thimble Summer* is a Midwestern farm in the midst of a burning drouth. Just as the drouth is broken by a drenching rain, Garnet finds a silver thimble, which she is convinced will bring her a lucky summer.

## MARGUERITE DE ANGELI

*Bright April*
*Yonie Wondernose*
*Thee, Hannah!*

*Bright April* (1946) was one of the earliest books to focus on a black child's problems. The youngest in a prosperous, middle-class family, April finds a happy solution to her difficulties with a prejudiced member of her Brownie troop. There are many books for and about black children now, but this was a rarity when it was published. Marguerite de

Angeli was also a pioneer in relating stories about the minority groups around her home in Philadelphia. Her stories are slight, but the warm pictures she paints, both with colors and words, of Amish, Quaker, and Pennsylvania-Dutch children are important. *Henner's Lydia* (1936), *Skippack School* (1939), *Yonie Wondernose* (1944), and *Thee, Hannah!* (1940) are all pleasant stories about interesting people.

*Yonie Wondernose* with his wondering is the favorite, especially when, like the hero of the folk tale, his wondering pays off and he proves his courage as well. Particularly appealing, too, is the little Quaker girl in *Thee, Hannah!* who despises her Quaker garb until she finds herself chosen, because of it, to serve a great cause. This book goes back in time to the Civil War.

Of first importance are Mrs. de Angeli's illustrations. These are beautiful in color with springtime freshness and innocence. To be sure, her children—whatever their sex, nationality, or disposition—have always the same little heartshaped faces and wistful beauty, but they have also a skipping gaiety which is the very essence of all childhood.

## VIRGINIA SORENSON

*Plain Girl*
*Miracles on Maple Hill*

*Plain Girl* (1955) is another delightful story about a Pennsylvania minority group. Ten-year-old Amish Esther is both worried and pleased when she knows she must attend a public school. But she makes friends and is surprised to find that her very best friend, she of the glorious pink dress, actually admires Esther's plain clothes. In *Miracles on Maple Hill*, awarded the 1957 Newbery Medal, ten-year-old Marly and her family move to the country in hopes that her father will regain his health after being in a war prison. The "miracle" happens, and the family decides to stay at Maple Hill. *Lotte's Locket* (1964) is the brisk and appealing story of a Danish child's adjustment to the fact that she is going to move to the United States. The story has good background material about Copenhagen and Danish holiday customs. In *Around the Corner* (1971) a black family welcomes white newcomers to their neighborhood.

## SYDNEY TAYLOR

*All-of-a-Kind Family*

Sydney Taylor's *All-of-a-Kind Family* (1951), *More All-of-a-Kind Family* (1954), and *All-of-a-Kind Family Uptown* (1958) are stories of a Jewish family in New York in the early 1900's. The fact that the children are all girls accounts for the titles, although to Papa's great delight a boy arrives eventually.

The family lives on New York's lower East Side in a Jewish neighborhood, but the adventures of the girls are such as might happen to any city children anywhere. Their warm home life is deeply rooted in Jewish religious customs. Hard-working Papa and pretty, capable Mama keep all the fasts and feasts of the Jewish year with deep reverence and thanksgiving. Pleasanter emissaries for religious piety and family love than these entertaining and heartwarming books could hardly be found. *A Papa Like Everyone Else* (1966), another story of Jewish family life, is set in a Czechoslovakian village just after World War I. There are some episodes about Czech and Hungarian customs, but most of the story concerns the culture of the Jewish community.

## ELLIS CREDLE

*Down Down the Mountain*

Ellis Credle's *Down Down the Mountain* (1934) is a story about two Southern mountaineer children, Hetty and Hank, who yearn to possess a pair of squeaky shoes. They must earn them, but how? Their mountain is so steep that pumpkins might roll right off the side; so they plant turnips, which flourish. Then the fair with prizes for the finest specimens unexpectedly provides shoes for Hetty and Hank. Their turnip of turnips wins a prize! They get the most elegantly squeaky shoes in town and enjoy a triumphant return home, with shoes and presents. These children have energy, good humor, and a nice generosity, which make them likable but never priggish.

## LOIS LENSKI

*Strawberry Girl*
*Cotton in My Sack*
*Boom Town Boy*

In 1940 *Blue Willow*, a tender and beautifully written book by Doris Gates, was a Newbery Medal Honor Book. A story of migratory farm workers and their camps, it centers on ten-year-old Janey's longing for a permanent home where her family will be a part of a settled community. Then in 1946, when the Newbery Medal was given to Lois Lenski's *Strawberry Girl*, attention was called to a unique series of books about regional groups of many kinds, all over this country.

Lois Lenski began her series with *Bayou Suzette* (1943), a story about the French-speaking people in the bayou section of Louisiana. After *Strawberry Girl* of Florida came *Blue Ridge Billy* (1946), about the North Carolina mountaineer group, and *Judy's Journey* (1947), which followed the crop-pickers from California to Florida and back to New Jersey, and there are many more, including *Project Boy* (1954), which is set in a veterans' housing project and *High-Rise Secret* (1966), in a high-rise housing project.

*Strawberry Girl* (1945) is typical of these books at their best. It is the story of Birdie Boyer's family, newly moved to Florida's backwoods for the purpose of raising small crops of "sweet 'taters," strawberries, oranges, and the like.

In *Cotton in My Sack* (1949) the mother can't cook or keep her house and children clean. Everyone in the family, except the baby, toils endlessly picking cotton, only to indulge in a weekly orgy of aimless spending. So in *Boom Town Boy* (1948), Orvie's family when it strikes oil goes on a spending spree that is silly and purposeless. Yet these books have a wry humor about them, and children like the stories.

The values of this series are to be found in its objective realism and compassion. Young members of disadvantaged families meet their own kind in these regional stories of Lois Lenski's. And they take heart, because always the ups and downs of these hard-pressed, courageous people yield a ray of hope. Things are, or give promise of becoming, better. As for the well-cared-for children of suburbia, these books give them a picture of family love and loyalty.

## BEVERLY CLEARY

*Henry Huggins*
*Ramona the Pest*
*Mitch and Amy*

Probably no reviewer of children's books has forgotten the excitement and fun of reading the first of Beverly Cleary's *Henry Huggins* books in 1950. Pure Americana, from supermarkets to backyard barbecues, the stories are delightfully humorous.

The Huggins family is an average group. The parents are sympathetic to Henry's enterprises but not overly indulgent. All the children in the stories are pursuing their own goals with the frustrations usual to children. The first book begins with Henry's determination to keep and support a stray dog he has acquired and named Ribsy. After Ribsy has been accepted, the next problem concerns the speedy multiplication of a pair of guppies Henry buys at a sale. By midsummer the neighborhood is glutted with guppies and they are occupying his mother's entire supply of mason jars. This is a dilemma in the canning season! Then when the original owner of Ribsy turns up and claims his dog, Henry is in a still more serious spot. He earnestly wants to do the right thing, but he also wants Ribsy. The solution is a masterly piece of diplomacy.

There are several other books about Henry and even one about *Ribsy* (1964). Each book is built around a real struggle on Henry's part and involves some very funny situations before a hard-won success.

One of the most delightful books about Henry's nemesis is *Ramona the Pest* (1968), in which Ramona is probably the first kindergarten dropout on record, having become convinced that the teacher, whom she adores, doesn't love her any more. A serious problem for many children is presented in a realistic and encouraging way in *Mitch and Amy* (1967). Mitch and Amy are fourth-grade twins, he a slow reader and she a proficient one. They are, except when under attack, very competitive, yet it is Amy that finds the book that starts Mitch on the path to self-motivated reading.

These books may not all be gems of literary style, but the characters are real boys and girls, convincingly alive.

## MEINDERT DeJONG

*The Wheel on the School*
*Journey from Peppermint Street*

*The Wheel on the School* (1954), a tenderly told story which won the Newbery Medal, gives a remarkably detailed picture of life in a Dutch fishing village and also has unusual social values. The story begins in the tiny village school, when Lina, the only girl, asks, "Do you know about storks?" This leads to more questions, "Why are there no storks in Shora?" and "How can we bring them back?" These two questions launch a series of activities that begin with the six children and the schoolmaster but presently draw into the circle every person in the village. Everything is ready for the storks when a terrible storm kills or drives off course hundreds of the birds. But at last the storks do settle in Shora again.

*Illustration by Maurice Sendak. From* The Wheel on the School *by Meindert DeJong. Copyright, 1954, by Meindert DeJong. Reprinted by permission of Harper & Row, Publishers.*

Although the book is too long for its story, it reads aloud wonderfully and can promote many discussions about the people, the lonely land of sea and sky that is Holland, and the wonder of those great birds that fly home all the way from Africa.

One of DeJong's stories has been discussed in the preceding chapter, since books about animals, or children and animals, are prevalent among his works. *Shadrach* (1953) is a sensitive study of a boy and his pet rabbit. *The Easter Cat* (1971) is the story of a child who hides a kitten, knowing that her mother is allergic to cats; she is satisfied when an understanding sister-in-law offers to keep the kitten for her.

*Journey from Peppermint Street* (1968), which won the National Book Award for Children's Literature, is set in Holland in the early 1900's. Beautifully written, it is the story of a small boy who goes with his grandfather on a long night walk to visit an "inland aunt." The relationship between the old man and the child, the satisfaction at conquering his nervousness in a strange place, and the confidence gained by little Siebren as he meets new people, have a universality that transcends the setting.

Another story set in Holland is *Far Out the Long Canal* (1964). Because the ice has been bad for several years, and he has had a long illness, nine-year-old Moonta is the only child in town who cannot skate. Any reader can sympathize with his embarrassment, his secret struggles, and the alternate teasing and comfort he gets from friends and family. *The House of Sixty Fathers* (1956) is for readers eleven to thirteen, but younger children have enjoyed this vividly realistic story, set in China, of a boy who searches for his lost family.

Meindert DeJong has the gift of wonder and delight. Whatever the outward action of his tales, it is the inner grace of his children and animals that moves readers, young or old. It is not surprising that in 1962 he won the Hans Christian Andersen International Award for his contribution to the world of children's literature.

*Illustration by Garth Williams. From* The Family Under the Bridge, *copyright © 1958 by Natalie Savage Carlson. Pictures copyright © 1958 by Garth Williams. Reprinted by permission of Harper & Row, Publishers, Inc.*

## NATALIE SAVAGE CARLSON

*The Family Under the Bridge*
*The Happy Orpheline*
*The Empty Schoolhouse*

Some of the gayest stories about Paris are Natalie Carlson's *The Family Under the Bridge* (1958) and her series about the Orphelines. *The Family Under the Bridge* has to do with that post-World War II period in Paris when housing was at a premium. The hero is an elderly, jaunty hobo named Armand, completely averse to work, family life, and especially "starlings," as he calls children. Armand has found himself a snug corner under an old bridge. So imagine his horror to return there one night and find it occupied by three children. This is the beginning of the end for carefree, soft-hearted Armand. His series of adventures with the starlings are sometimes very funny and sometimes sad, but in the end he finds himself the adopted grandfather of a family. No pathos here, just a determined struggle for a stable, decent way of life.

The books about the Orphelines reverse the usual pattern of sad, sad orphans hoping to be adopted. These French orphans love their home to the point where their one fear is adoption. When in *The Happy Orpheline* (1957) poor Brigitte is about to be adopted, she knows she must perform a very wicked deed of some kind to prove she isn't fit for adoption. What she does is hilarious and makes a fitting if confused climax to the adventures of the twenty Orphelines who are still twenty strong at the end. *A Brother for the Orphelines* (1959) and *A Pet for the Orphelines* (1962) are fun, too, and follow the pattern of the others. Each chapter is a complete adventure in the course of which young readers see French life from a child's-eye view.

Emma, who tells the story of *The Empty Schoolhouse* (1965), has dropped out of school but is proud of her bright little sister Lullah. Lullah is black, her friend Oralee white, and they are delighted that there is going to be an integrated school in their Louisiana parish. There is trouble, though, and parents keep their children away. When Lullah is hurt in a racial incident, the rift between her and Oralee grows—but it is healed, and the episode shocks some parents into a reversal of their decision. The first-person narrative gives consistency and immediacy to an honest and thoughtful story.

*Ann Aurelia and Dorothy* (1968) is another book about an interracial friendship, and *Marchers for the Dream* (1969) tells about an eleven-year-old girl who goes with her grandmother to Washington to join the Poor People's March. *The Half Sisters* (1970) and its sequel, *Luvvy and the Girls* (1970), are amusing stories about Luvvy, one of six sisters, who longs to be old enough to go away to a Catholic boarding school but finds when she does that there are adjustments to be made. Set early in the century, the stories have good period details and lively characters.

### JACQUELINE JACKSON

*The Paleface Redskins*
*A Taste of Spruce Gum*

One of the things that the Richards children had always loved about their vacation home was the continuing game of playing at being Indians. When a Scout camp is built one summer on land they have used as their own, war is declared by *The Paleface Redskins* (1958). The skirmishes and ploys of the children are enjoyable, and the author handles with true sensitivity the musings of Marcy, the central character, on her budding breasts and on her acceptance of the inevitable changes that are a part of growing out of childhood.

In *The Taste of Spruce Gum* (1966), set in Vermont lumber country at the turn of the century, an eleven-year-old girl adjusts to the rough life and to her new stepfather, and gains new confidence when she copes with the problems engendered by her stepfather's accident. *Julie's Secret Sloth* (1953) takes full advantages of the humorous possibilities of having a giant two-toed sloth as a pet.

### KEITH ROBERTSON

The *Henry Reed* stories

Children need books also which demonstrate that life is not always earnest, that it can in fact be highly entertaining. *Henry Reed, Inc.* (1958) is such a book. It is Henry's private journal. On a visit to his uncle and aunt who live in the country near Princeton, Henry hears all about the research at that University; so he decides to go into research. He takes over an old barn and paints an enormous sign: HENRY REED, RESEARCH. To the sign a girl who finds her way into this intellectual domain adds: PURE AND APPLIED. She wants her name added too, but Henry is adamant—she must prove her worth first. Their research activities make this book hilarious reading.

Other Henry Reed stories are direct narrative, equally amusing and often mirroring some new social trend. In *Henry Reed's Big Show* (1970), for example, Henry and Midge put on a rock music festival. These books are highly exaggerated in the pace of their plots, but in every separate episode the activities of the ploymasters Henry and Midge are within the realm of possibility.

### SHIRLEY ARORA

*"What Then, Raman?"*

A young Indian woman studying in the United States protested that children's books about India are generally more exotic than authentic. However, she cited *"What Then, Raman?"* (1960) as a happy exception. It is the story of a shy, earnest Indian boy who has learned to read, the only person in his village with this accomplishment. His ambition is to become a scholar and possess a beautiful black and gold copy of the *Ramayana*, the great Indian classic. But his learning sets him apart. The village boys avoid or taunt him, and Raman feels no special responsibility for them or for the needs of his family. To earn money for the book, he works for an American teacher. Slowly she brings him to the realization that the privilege of learning carries with it responsibility for teaching and helping others. Raman begins with his little sister, teaching her to read, then the boys in the village, and presently he finds himself not only accepted but deeply involved in their longings and needs. When he finally has the money for his precious book, somehow he can't buy it; his family comes first. Still Raman keeps his dreams. Someday he will be a scholar and own the book. This is not so moralistic as it sounds but is sensitively written with a deep perception of the boy's conflict and a thorough knowledge of India today.

*The Left-Handed Chank* (1966), a story for older readers, is also set in India.

## MARY STOLZ

*By the Highway Home*
*The Noonday Friends*
*A Wonderful, Terrible Time*
*The Dragons of the Queen*

Mary Stolz is a prolific author and one of the few authors who write with admirable acuity for all ages. Some of her fanciful and humorous animal tales have already been discussed; *A Dog on Barkham Street* (1960) and *The Bully of Barkham Street* (1963) were considered in Chapter 1 as companion volumes that narrate the same events from different viewpoints.

In *By the Highway Home* (1971), the death of an older brother, the loss of the father's job, and a subsequent move to a new home create problems of adjustment for a girl of thirteen. A lost job also adds to the tensions in *The Noonday Friends* (1965), in which Franny sees her friend only at lunch time because Franny must take care of her little brother after school. The story is perceptive in reflecting the way emotions are affected by circumstances and in drawing the relationship between Franny and the small brother, who knows her as the most dependable person in his world.

The two friends in *A Wonderful, Terrible*

*Illustration by Louis S. Glanzman for* A Wonderful, Terrible Time *by Mary Stolz. Copyright 1967. Reproduced by permission of Harper & Row, Publishers, Inc.*

*Time* (1967) are black girls who go to an interracial summer camp. Sue Ellen is apprehensive; Mady is thrilled and enjoys every moment. Sue Ellen never wants to talk about serious things; Mady—whose father had been killed in a voter registration drive—does. Integration is not the issue of the book but is one of several problems considered to show the differences in the reactions of the two girls.

*The Dragons of the Queen* (1969) tells about a middle-aged American couple who are enchanted by the dignity and grace of an old Mexican woman. Appropriate for children because it is so simply written, the story can give a young reader an appreciation of the values of a different way of life and a sympathy for the old. Also set in Mexico, *Juan* (1970) is the story of an orphaned boy. The characterization is very fine, the writing style distinctive.

### WILLIAM MAYNE

*A Grass Rope*
*Whistling Rufus*
*The Old Zion*

One of William Mayne's many talents is his evocative description of settings, as, for example, his depiction of the Yorkshire landscape in *A Grass Rope* (1962), which won the Carnegie Medal. In this story, four children become intrigued by an old legend and set about investigating it, the older ones gravely tolerating little Mary's firm belief that there is indeed a unicorn and that she will lead it home by the grass rope she has prepared.

*Whistling Rufus* (1965) is the story of two children who find an old ship on dry land and decide to work on it together as their school project. Mayne's dialogue and characterization are always outstanding; here the most interesting facet of the story is the ambivalence of one child: wildly imaginative while working on the ship, quite matter-of-fact and practical at other times.

*The Old Zion* (1967) takes place on an island in the South Seas, where a church, the Old Zion, is being shifted to a new location. The story of the planning and execution of the project is permeated with humor and local color. Other books by the versatile William Mayne are discussed later in this chapter under books of mystery and suspense.

### JEAN LITTLE

*Mine for Keeps*
*Home from Far*
*Look Through My Window*

Born blind, Canadian Jean Little understands the child who is different, and has the ability to spin a good story which makes such differences natural and comprehensible. In *Mine for Keeps* (1962), Sally, who has cerebral palsy, comes home after five years at a school for handicapped children, her apprehension about getting along mixed with self-pity. Through the help of her family and through her own interest in others, Sally gradually overcomes her fears and becomes more independent. The story treats the difficulties of a handicapped child matter-of-factly and emphasizes the point that the family has to adjust to the situation and that each of them makes mistakes. In the sequel, *Spring Begins in March* (1966), Sally smooths the way of her little sister.

In *Home from Far* (1965) Jenny's twin brother Michael is killed, and soon after the accident, Jenny's parents bring two foster children into the home, one named Mike and the same age as Jenny. This is a sensitive study of the attitudes and emotions of children, particularly of Jenny, who at first bitterly resents Mike, and of Mike, who misses his real father.

In *Look Through My Window* (1970) Emily's family takes in four little cousins whose mother is hospitalized. From resentment, Emily moves to love and acceptance, and her horizons are further broadened by a new friend who has one Jewish parent. The discussions between Emily and Kate are candid, those between Emily and her mother tender and sensible, and those between Kate and her father perceptive and honest, as they talk about what it is to be Jewish. In the sequel, *Kate* (1971), the girl moves further to explore her ambivalence and to discover why her father had severed connections with his family. Jean Little has a rare ability to see problems and their ramifications from the viewpoint of the child.

## MARILYN SACHS

The *Laura and Amy* stories
The *Peter and Veronica* stories
*Marv*

In *Amy Moves In* (1964), Amy's family moves in the 1930s to another section of the Bronx; the pleasant family story about the Sterns ends with mother going into a hospital. In *Laura's Luck* (1956) Laura and Amy go off to camp, Laura jealous of her younger sister because she adjusts so much more easily. Laura gains confidence and decides she likes camp in a story that is, like the first book, realistic in dealing with small problems and lightly humorous. Not until the third book, *Amy and Laura* (1966), is there a real problem in interpersonal relationships. Laura finds it difficult to accept her invalid mother, so long away, and is relieved at the close of the story when Mama rebels and declares she is going to run her home and be a mother, not a liability.

In *Veronica Ganz* (1968) and *Peter and Veronica* (1969), Marilyn Sachs introduces a perennial bully who becomes friends with the smallest boy in the class. Peter, in the second book, is first angry with his mother because she doesn't want his non-Jewish friend to come to his bar mitzvah, then—after he has persuaded his mother—angry at Veronica because she doesn't show up. Both in the candor with which Peter and Veronica discuss their mothers' prejudices and in the new maturity with which they mend their quarrel the story is honest and percipient.

*Marv* (1970) tells of a boy who admires his sister Frances more than anyone else in the world, and repeatedly tries to impress her with his accomplishments, always seeking her approval. There are poignant moments and funny ones, but the book's import is the resilience with which youth strives for competence and approval.

## LOUISE FITZHUGH

*Harriet the Spy*
*The Long Secret*

The very funny and very touching story of *Harriet the Spy* (1964) aroused vigorous controversy for the portraits it drew of prying, fractious Harriet and of her parents, too busy with their social life to pay much attention to their child until she was in real trouble. Eleven-year-old Harriet aspires to be a writer, and, encouraged by her nurse Ole Golly, keeps notes about everything that happens to her and her friends and to the people she studies on her after-school spy route. She keeps notes on her thoughts and observations, too, as when, on the way to see Ole Golly's "family," she writes:

> *This is incredible. Could Ole Golly have a family? I never thought about it. How could Ole Golly have a mother and father? She's too old for one thing and she's never said one word about them and I've known her since I was born. Also she doesn't get any letters. Think about this. This might be important.*

The sequel, *The Long Secret* (1965), is less intense, more sophisticated, and equally funny at times. Harriet, curious as ever but now on very close terms with her parents, is at the beach for the summer. So is the shy Beth of *Harriet the Spy*, now terrified because her mother, a jet set butterfly, has come

*Illustration by Louise Fitzhugh from* Harriet the Spy *by Louise Fitzhugh. Copyright © 1964. Reproduced by permission of Harper & Row, Publishers, Inc.*

to disrupt the quiet life Beth and her grandmother lead. The inclusion of an evangelist family, several jaded characters of the jet set, and a wise old man make the book more cluttered and not as effective as *Harriet*, but it has two episodes that are particularly perceptive. In one, Harriet and her mother have a serious discussion of faith and religion, and in the other Harriet and her friends talk about menstruation, a long-standing taboo subject in children's books.

## ROBERT BURCH

*Queenie Peavy*
*Simon and the Game of Chance*

*Queenie Peavy* (1966) is a story of the depression era, set in Georgia, where Queenie, thirteen, has a deserved reputation as a troublemaker and a hoyden. Fiercely loyal to her father who is in jail, she faces a painful readjustment when he comes home, shows neither affection nor responsibility, breaks his parole, and is returned to jail. Queenie, a staunch little character, realizes that any change in her status must now come from her own changed attitude and behavior. Candid in treatment of the father, this is one of the books that lucidly exemplifies the end of the perfect-parent image in children's literature.

The father in *Simon and the Game of Chance* (1970) is also the harsh character of the story, stern and tyrannical, a man whose rigidity affects the whole life of the family. Simon's immediate problem is his fear that he is in some way culpable for the death of his sister's fiancé, since he had resented the planned marriage. Like Queenie, Simon adjusts in a way consistent with his character and his need to be loved and accepted. *Joey's Cat* (1969), a pleasant story for younger children, is about a small black boy who is delighted when his mother changes her mind and lets him bring his cat and her kittens into the house.

## PAULA FOX

*Maurice's Room*
*A Likely Place*
*The Stone-Faced Boy*
*Portrait of Ivan*

With the publication of *Maurice's Room* (1966) it became immediately clear that Paula Fox is one of the finest new writers in the field of children's literature. Her style is quiet, her vision penetrating, her understanding of children deep and sympathetic. Maurice is an only child whose room is a haven for anything and everything he finds. His parents attempt subtle distractions, but there is no stopping a born collector: when the family moves to the country, Maurice is bored until he sees the barn, full of Old Things.

*A Likely Place* (1967) is a testament to the joy of competence. Lewis, tired of the adults who want to help or to improve him, takes great delight in his friendship with an elderly gentleman who treats him as an equal and asks his help.

In *The Stone-Faced Boy* (1968) a child who is shy and withdrawn in the midst of a boisterous family takes refuge in looking impassive. Only one elderly great-aunt sees what lies behind the stoic facade. This empathetic relationship between a child and someone outside his immediate family is used again in *Portrait of Ivan* (1969), in which lonely Ivan's friendship with the artist who is painting his portrait helps Ivan gain confidence to approach his busy, remote father. The writing is skilled, and the characters are superbly drawn. *Blowfish Live in the Sea* (1970) is discussed at some length in Chapter 2. *How Many Miles to Babylon?* (1967) is the story of a black child persecuted by a gang of older boys.

## ELEANOR CLYMER

*My Brother Stevie*
*The Spider, the Cave and the Pottery Bowl*
*The House on the Mountain*

"She was always going away, even before Pa died, and leaving us with Grandma," twelve-year-old Annie says of her mother in *My Brother Stevie* (1967). This is a sober and convincing story about what can happen to children who feel rejected. Annie worries about the gang her younger brother is in, but her concern is not as effective as the affection of a wise, warm teacher. Another book with an urban setting, *The Big Pile of Dirt* (1968), tells a story of children with no play space who enjoy the pile of dirt left by demolition. It is all the more poignant for being told in matter-of-fact style.

In *The Spider, the Cave and the Pottery Bowl* (1971) young Kate goes back to her mother's home on the mesa, the Indian village where grandmother teaches her to make pottery. The story is a simple one, but it is imbued with the dignity of tradition and has a positive approach: Kate is irked when a white tourist is patronizing but she is no less proud of her heritage.

*The House on the Mountain* (1971) has a slight plot, but in the story of a group of black children, enthralled by a little house they see on a country outing, there is a touching yearning for space and beauty, and a moving pride in their dignified withdrawal when the angry owners find them inside the house.

*Drawings copyright © 1971 by Ingrid Fetz. From* The Spider, the Cave, and the Pottery Bowl *by Eleanor Clymer. Used by permission of Atheneum Publishers.*

## ZILPHA KEATLEY SNYDER

*The Egypt Game*
*The Changeling*

One of the notable books of 1967 and a Newbery Honor Book, *The Egypt Game* is an absorbing story of sustained, imaginative group play and of interracial friendship. Surprisingly for a child's book, the characters include a murderer who almost captures one of the girls. The children are vividly real, their Egypt Game absorbing, their conversation and personalities distinctive.

In *The Changeling* (1970) a quiet child from a conservative family becomes friends with an unusual girl and only years later realizes how much the disreputable and wildly imaginative Ivy contributed to her own growth and flexibility.

The interest of the young in astrology and the supernatural is reflected in *The Headless Cupid* (1971), in which an unhappy adolescent persuades her newly-acquired stepbrothers and stepsisters to become her disciples in the occult. Only when there seems to be evidence of a poltergeist does Amanda lose her pose of superiority. *The Velvet Room* (1965) is the story of Robin, one of the children in a family of migrant workers, who finds a haven in the Velvet Room, the library of a deserted house. While there is a mystery, the book is less a mystery than a story of the need for security and belonging.

## VIRGINIA HAMILTON

*Zeely*
*The Time-Ago Tales of Jahdu*

A gifted black writer, Virginia Hamilton has shown versatility with each of her books. In *Zeely* (1967) a child visiting in the country is smitten by the beauty of a neighbor who looks like a Watusi queen. The book is impressive both as a picture of a girl's crush on an adult and as a record of a child's growing understanding of racial identity.

*Illustration from Zeely by Virginia Hamilton. Illustrations by Symeon Shimin. Illustration © Macmillan, 1967.*

In *The Time-Ago Tales of Jahdu* (1969) Lee Edward stays each day with Mama Luka until his mother is home from work, and each day he hears another story of the legendary Jahdu, crafty and powerful. The tales are beautifully told in the folk tradition, and the small boy learns the joy of being black and proud.

*The House of Dies Drear* (1968) is a dramatic story set in an old house that had been a station on the Underground Railroad; and *The Planet of Junior Brown* (1971), a memorable book for older readers, is an imaginative and touching story of a friendship between two boys who are loners, each in a different way.

## VERA and BILL CLEAVER

*Ellen Grae*
*Where the Lilies Bloom*
*I Would Rather Be a Turnip*

Although there had been other books about children of divorce before *Ellen Grae* (1967) was published, none had so firmly stated by implication the fact that a parent's love and responsibility are not changed by divorce. Ellen Grae tells her own story, and it becomes instantly apparent that she is an accomplished and artistic teller of tall tales and that she is a child with great sensitivity and loyalty. Despite the seriousness of the problem that faces Ellen Grae and despite its less than satisfactory resolution, the story is permeated with humor. Its sequel, *Lady Ellen Grae*, has less impact but is written with vivacity and sharp characterization. The hero of *Grover* (1970) is Ellen Grae's friend, and his adjustment to his mother's suicide (she has cancer) and to his father's grief is described in a story that shows the sensitivity of the young.

The heroine of *Where the Lilies Bloom* (1969) is one of the strongest characters in children's fiction. Fourteen-year-old Mary Call Luther buries her father herself, and valiantly tries to hold together the family—which includes a retarded older sister—so that the four children will not be sent to a county charity home. This is an excellent example of the need for security as well as of the need to achieve.

In *I Would Rather Be a Turnip* (1971) twelve-year-old Annie Jelks faces a problem that is seldom presented in children's books, the acceptance of an illegitimate child. Annie is aware that everyone in her small town knows that her sister's child was born out of wedlock, and when eight-year-old Calvin comes to live with Annie and her father, she is jealous of her father's love for the boy and apprehensive about the feelings of her friends. Again, the Cleavers deal perceptively with the intricacies of a serious problem yet lighten the story with humor both in the dialogue and in the affectionate depiction of a child who is understandably belligerent. These books are prime examples of the changes that have occurred in what has been considered appropriate in children's books.

## ELAINE KONIGSBURG

*From the Mixed-Up Files of Mrs. Basil E. Frankweiler*
*Jennifer, Hecate, Macbeth, William McKinley, and Me, Elizabeth*
*(George)*
*About the B'nai Bagels*

In 1968 Elaine Konigsburg made history in children's books when her *From the Mixed-Up Files of Mrs. Basil E. Frankweiler* was awarded the Newbery Medal and her *Jennifer, Hecate, Macbeth, William McKinley, and Me, Elizabeth* was voted a Newbery Honor Book. They were her first two books. *From the Mixed-Up Files* is an engaging story of two children who leave home and take up residence in the Metropolitan Museum of Art, the details of the expedition capably planned by the older child, Claudia. The unlikely setting is made believable by the bland perfection of details.

*Jennifer, Hecate* is a story of interracial friendship and sustained imaginative play in which Jennifer, a self-declared witch, permits Elizabeth (who tells the story) to become her apprentice. Both in the relationship between the two protagonists and in their relationships to others there is delightful warmth and humor.

*(George)* (1970) deals with a serious problem, the schizoid personality, yet the book has high humor, tenderness, and a lively plot. The distinctive achievement of *(George)* is that it enables the reader to see that the child with psychological problems is not beyond the pale: Ben is human, intelligent, loving.

*Illustration by E. L. Konigsburg. Copyright © 1967 by E. L. Konigsburg. From* From the Mixed-Up Files of Mrs. Basil E. Frankweiler. *Used by permission of Atheneum Publishers.*

*About the B'nai Bagels* (1969) is a cheerful story, less dramatic than the other Konigsburg books, but enjoyable for the felicity with which Mark describes the awfulness of having his mother manage his Little League team, the nervous pleasure of his first look at a girly magazine, and the indignation aroused by his first encounter with anti-Semitism. *Altogether, One at a Time* (1971) is a collection of four deftly written short stories, different in plot and mood, alike in their theme of compromise with circumstance.

## OTHER NOTABLE BOOKS FOR THE MIDDLE GROUP

In books for children, realism in the 1970s tends to mirror the contemporary scene, but there have been fine realistic stories written in the past and so vividly true to life that they are enjoyed by today's children. One of these is Ruth Sawyer's Newbery Medal book, *Roller Skates* (1936), in which ten-year-old Lucinda makes friends as she skates about New York. Another is Eve Garnett's *The Family from One End Street* (1939), the story of the big, cheerful Ruggles family who live in a poor neighborhood in an English city.

Another British writer enjoyed by children everywhere is Janet McNeill, whose *The Battle of St. George Without* (1968) and other stories are set in a heterogeneous urban

### VIEWPOINTS

The short story, like any form of literature that pretends to the status of art, must become an organic whole. While it is composed of various identifiable elements, each must be seen as having its existence only in relation to the others and each must contribute a proper share toward the achieving of a final, integrated form. Incident must not exist for its own sake, as it does in anecdote and sometimes does in certain forms of popular fiction. Action must grow out of the conflicting motives of its characters. Similarly, atmosphere should not display a merely sentimental grouping of oddities, as it sometimes did in what we call "local color" stories. Creation of atmosphere must become one of the techniques whereby the total scene achieves its appropriate tone as the result of an underlying consistency of attitude towards the subject. Theme, or "meaning," represents not the mere drawing of a moral or the delivering of a message. The idea must be embodied in the total form, must become as much an integrated segment of the total work as are the characters and the place where they act. – Ray B. West, Jr., *The Art of Writing Fiction*, Thomas Y. Crowell Co., New York, 1968, p. 121.

neighborhood. Rumer Godden's *The Kitchen Madonna* (1967) is a tender story about an aloof, sensitive boy who reaches out to help the homesick Ukrainian maid in his London home. In Ursula Moray Williams' *A Crown for a Queen* (1969) a small, shy child enjoys a wish come true when she becomes "Beauty Queen of Baggott Street." The meticulously realistic pen drawings by Shirley Hughes add to the appealing image of grave, wistful little Jenny.

The Australian stories of Reginald Ottley, Mary Patchett, and Joan Phipson demonstrate that children are the same everywhere despite the fascinating differences of setting and idiomatic language, but the most moving story from an Australian author is probably Patricia Wrightson's *A Racecourse for Andy* (1968), its main character a gentle, retarded child whose mistaken belief that he owns a race track is treated with great sympathy and understanding by all his friends.

*Illustration by Kazue Mizumura (copyright © 1963 by Kazue Mizumura) is reproduced by permission of Charles Scribner's Sons from* The Forever Christmas Tree *by Yoshiko Uchida. (Original with color)*

*Illustration by Shirley Hughes for* A Crown for a Queen *by Ursula M. Williams. Copyright 1969. Reprinted with permission of Hamish Hamilton, Ltd., London.*

Astrid Lindgren's stories of Swedish children today (*The Children on Troublemaker Street* [1964], for example) are no more appealing than Edith Unnerstad's tales of the past (*The Spettecake Holiday* [1958], for example) and Karin Anckarsvärd's *Doctor's Boy* (1965), a lively tale set early in the twentieth century. Jennie Lindquist's *The Golden Name Day* (1955) is a warm story of a Swedish-American family.

Yoshiko Uchida brings a Japanese girl to the United States in *The Promised Year*

(1959) but sets most of her stories in Japan, one of the most charming being *The Forever Christmas Tree* (1963).

Of the many books about changing cultural patterns in Africa, Reba Paeff Mirsky's *Thirty-one Brothers and Sisters* (1952) was one of the first and is still one of the best. Others that show life in Africa today are Lorenz Graham's *I, Momolu* (1966), Duane Bradley's *Meeting with a Stranger* (1964), Naomi Mitchison's *The Family at Ditlabeng* (1970), Edna Walker Chandler's *With Books on Her Head* (1967), and Muriel Feelings' *Zamani Goes to Market* (1970).

Among the books about black children in the United States, Louisa Shotwell's *Roosevelt Grady* (1963) is one that has as its theme the migrant family's desire for a settled life and educational opportunity. Shotwell's *Adam Bookout* (1967) is an interracial story set in Brooklyn. John Durham's *Me and Arch and the Pest* (1970), the story of two boys who acquire a large dog, is especially appealing because of the warm relationships, the natural dialogue, and the candid, casual way in which Arch and Bit discuss their parents' unreasonable attitudes toward large dogs, the difference in their color (Bit is white, Arch black) and the difference between natural speech and schoolroom language. Nan Hayden Agle's *Maple Street* (1970) shows the kindness of a black Baltimore neighborhood community to a hostile white family they

*Illustration by Tom Feelings for* Zamani Goes to Market *by Muriel Feelings. Copyright © 1970. Reproduced by permission of The Seabury Press. (Original with color)*

*Illustration from* Me and Arch and the Pest *by John Durham, illustrations by Ingrid Fetz. Copyright © 1970 by Ingrid Fetz. Reprinted by permission of Four Winds Press, a division of Scholastic Magazines, Inc.*

help in a time of trouble. Betty Erwin's *Behind the Magic Line* (1969) is the story of an imaginative black child and the serious problems of a ghetto family, a book particularly warm in its family relationships. In Alfred Slote's *Jake* (1971) a small boy's uncle gives up his free time to coach a baseball team.

In Mildred Jordan's *Proud to be Amish* (1968) little Katie feels guilty because she envies the red dress of a child in a family that is "Lutheran and Gay." In Judy Blume's *Are You There God? It's Me, Margaret* (1970), the heroine is troubled about whether she should follow her father's religion (Jewish) or her mother's, and decides, her faith as strong as ever, that God is not as real to her during a formal service as when she is talking to Him alone. In *Then Again, Maybe I Won't* (1971) Blume writes with great insight about the problems of an adolescent boy who is disturbed by his family's changed attitude when they become well-to-do and by his first sexual stirrings.

A charming boarding-school story is Ursula Nordstrom's *The Secret Language* (1960), in which a homesick child adjusts to the pattern of school life. Michele Murray's *Nellie Cameron* (1971) is the story of a black child who feels left out in a large family, and whose feelings of rejection are complicated by her problems as a slow reader, a situation that improves when she attends the school's reading clinic.

There is a poignant sympathy for the girl in Constance Greene's *A Girl Called Al* (1969). Plump and caustic, Al is a nonconformist who is won by the understanding friendship of the building superintendent and who is catapulted into maturity by his death. Plot and subplots are skillfully woven together in Eleanor Cameron's *A Room Made of Windows* (1971), in which a self-centered adolescent becomes more mature and responds to the needs of others with increasing perception. In Molly Cone's *The Other Side of the Fence* (1967) a white child is torn between his better instincts and his desire to stay with the majority when a black family moves into the neighborhood and meets with hostility. He makes his decision when a spiteful man paints one side of his fence white and his black neighbor's side black, but the child's efforts to welcome the newcomers are received with realistic moderation. Another reflection of life as it is today is given in Gudrun Alcock's *Run, Westy, Run* (1966), in which Westy runs away from home to escape the truant officer, gains enough confidence to talk to a social worker, but when he gets home finds that there is no magic ending—he must prove himself.

## REALISM FOR OLDER CHILDREN

Although there have been many changes in realistic fiction for younger children and for children in the middle group, the most striking changes have been in realistic fiction for older children. In the most recent books, subjects which were once taboo or elided, such as premarital pregnancy or illegitimate children, are fairly common, and the image of the perfect parent appears in fewer and fewer stories. Problems that confront today's youth are treated with understanding: the generation gap, the drug scene, the dissatisfaction with a materialistic society. And the language used reflects the speech of today, both in the admission of words that were once considered shocking and in the use of black English. Some of the stories are didactic, but the best fiction can win young people because it shows their world and its relationships as they know them to be. The older stories, though, are still popular.

## LAURA ARMER

*Waterless Mountain*

Laura Armer's books about the Navaho Indians were written for children twelve to fifteen years old. The hero of her Newbery winner, *Waterless Mountain* (1931), is

Younger Brother, whose secret name is Dawn Boy. Younger Brother knows that he is going to be a medicine man when he grows up, and the story tells much about his training in the mysticism of the Navaho religion. It is a beautifully written story but decidedly difficult for many children to understand and share. To be sure, teachers who love this book can have a whole roomful of young Navaho mystics completely in sympathy with Younger Brother, but most children must be helped to an enjoyment of this unusual story. The everyday life of the tribe emerges clearly, and there is one exciting adventure when the boys catch horse thieves and reclaim a beloved pony.

## JESSE JACKSON

*Call Me Charley*
*Tessie*

Jesse Jackson has given a full and moving account of the kind of discriminations a black child may encounter. In *Call Me Charley* (1945), the young black, the only one in the neighborhood, is not welcome in the school but is tolerated. He has some bitter disappointments but gradually wins the respect and friendship of some of the boys. It is a touching story made more poignant by Charley's quiet, patient acceptance of his lot. When his friends finally sense his heartbroken disappointment over his exclusion from the school play, they do something about it. Charley is in the play and happy for the present. The author has too realistic an approach to suggest a complete solution, but he tells a good story of a brave, likable boy in a difficult world.

*Charley Starts from Scratch* (1958), a sequel, finds Charley graduated from high school and trying to find a job in a strange city. Many doors are closed to him, but coming in first in Olympic trials gives Charley fresh courage and convinces several employers of the boy's worth and perseverance. Like the first book, this story is sensitively told.

*Tessie* (1968) is the story of a fourteen-year-old girl in Harlem who wins a scholarship to an all-white private school. Her parents are apprehensive, but Tessie is determined to use her educational opportunity even if it means social rebuffs—as it does, both from her new schoolmates and from her old friends. The development is believable, with actions that proceed logically from attitudes and motivations, so that Tessie's firm insistence on making the best of both her worlds is natural.

## EVELYN SIBLEY LAMPMAN

*Treasure Mountain*
*Navaho Sister*
*Half-Breed*

Evelyn Lampman has concentrated on writing stories about the Indian child who is faced with conflicting ways of life. In *Treasure Mountain* (1949) an Indian brother and sister from a government school spend a summer with their great-aunt who is a full-blooded "blanket Indian." Accustomed to white men's ways, the children at first are shocked by their aunt's customs and beliefs, but as the summer passes their respect and love for her grow. The title comes from the children's hunt for treasure to raise the money for taxes, but the primary interest in this story lies in their deepened appreciation of values in the old ways of Indian life as well as in the new.

In *Navaho Sister* (1956) orphaned Sad Girl goes to a government school where she feels isolated and is thoroughly unhappy. The episodes in the book bring out the difficult adjustment an Indian child must make to a modern school. Sad Girl's need to be more outgoing and tolerant is a problem in social adjustment most children can understand.

The story of a twelve-year-old *Half-Breed* (1967) is set in Oregon Territory, where Hardy has come to find his white father and finds instead an aunt who had not known Hardy existed. Hardy is homesick and his father too much of a wanderer to make a home for his son, but the boy becomes so fond of Aunt Rhody that he is content. The plot is thin, but the style, the setting, and the boy's need to belong and to establish his identity are strong. In *The Year of Small Shadow* (1971) an eleven-year-old Indian boy comes to stay with a white lawyer for a year while his father is in jail.

## ELIZABETH YATES

*A Place for Peter*

*A Place for Peter* (1952) deals with another kind of growing-up problem, a conflict between a father and son. Peter, who has appeared in an earlier book, is now a sturdy thirteen-year-old fighting for recognition as a mature human being. But his father keeps him at small-boy chores which he does sloppily or neglects. When the understanding mother is called away from home for a long period of time, Peter faces with dread the prospect of life with his father alone. Added responsibilities challenge all of Peter's energies and good sense. He swings the sugar bush alone, plants a garden, deals with rattlesnakes, and manages to enjoy himself in the process. By spring, Peter discovers to his surprise that he and his father are friends as they never were before, partners in the demanding tasks of running the farm.

*Illustration by Nora S. Unwin. From* A Place for Peter *by Elizabeth Yates. Copyright, 1952, by Coward-McCann, Inc. Reprinted by permission of the publisher.*

## JOSEPH KRUMGOLD

*. . . and now Miguel*
*Onion John*

Joseph Krumgold has given the preadolescent two fine stories of growing up, both winners of the Newbery Medal.

The members of Miguel's family in *. . . and now Miguel* (1953) have been sheepherders for generations, first in Spain, now in the Southwest country around Santa Fe, New Mexico. Twelve-year-old Miguel is struggling to prove to his father that he is as mature and competent a sheep man as his adored brother Gabriel, who is eighteen. This is a universal problem, differing only in its symbols for the city boy, the coastal boy, or Miguel, the sheepherder. His attempts to prove his maturity and responsibility supply the action of the story. After many disheartening blunders, success comes, but it is tempered with regret. This book, written in the first person, may have to be introduced to children, but it is well worth the time and effort. Here are strong family love and loyalty with a profound respect for the family tradition of work, and here is pride in the expert performance of that work. Here too is the hero worship of a younger for an older brother. There is a feeling for the cycle of the seasons, each one bringing its special work and special satisfactions. And finally there is a closeness to God that makes prayer a natural part of life. This remarkable book began as a documentary film and is still available in that form.

*Onion John* (1959) was not so universally approved as *Miguel*, but it too is concerned with problems in family relationships that are part of growing up. Andy is temporarily fascinated by a picturesque old hobo who lives in a shanty at the edge of town. This hero worship causes the first rift between Andy and his father. The story of the whole town trying to uplift and "do good" to the old tramp is an exceedingly funny and characteristic bit of Americana. But not until Onion John has fled from his do-gooders does Andy realize that he would rather be exactly like his father than anyone else—the respected owner of the town hardware store.

Here is an important theme—hero worship centered in the home. It was "Pa" for Jody in *The Yearling* and for the girls in the *Little House* books. It was his brother Gabriel for Miguel and the father again for Andy. Such family love and respect can ease the pangs of growing up as nothing else can and in addition can give the child a picture of his own life stretching ahead of him, rich with promise.

In *Henry 3* (1967) the boy and his family have moved to suburban affluence and the artificiality of conformist behavior, and the boy is disturbed by the values of adults and the superficial standards by which many people live.

## ANN NOLAN CLARK

*Secret of the Andes*
*Santiago*
*Medicine Man's Daughter*

*In My Mother's House* (1941) and *Secret of the Andes* (1952) represent something of Mrs. Clark's range of experience with primitive peoples. Furthermore, she is able to interpret their ways of life so that modern children respect them. Her writing reflects her love for these peoples. *Secret of the Andes*, a Newbery Medal winner, is the story of a dedicated Peruvian Indian boy, the last of a royal line, who has been brought up in the mountains and grows to understand his heritage and his responsibilities. *Santiago* (1955) is about a Guatemalan youth, raised in a Spanish home but determined to find his place in the world as an Indian. Both of these perceptive stories are beautifully written. *Medicine Man's Daughter* (1963) is the story of a girl who, at fifteen, has been chosen by her father as his successor. Stunned when a white man heals a child she cannot help, Tall-Girl rides off to a mission school and in time learns to appreciate the values of both cultures. The story moves slowly, but the information about Navaho life is interesting and the book sustains the mood of Tall-Girl's dedication.

For younger children Mrs. Clark has written books that give authentic pictures of the life and ideals of the desert Indians. For the oldest or the youngest children, she writes with a sense of the inner life and ideals of a people. Her cadenced prose is beautiful and unique.

## MARGOT BENARY-ISBERT

*The Ark*
*Rowan Farm*

*The Ark* and *Rowan Farm* give children an impressive account of the aftereffects of war on the people, cities, and countryside of Germany, where these stories were exceedingly popular.

In *The Ark* (1953) the Lechow family, a mother and four children, are trying to reestablish something approaching a normal life in a bombed-out city. The story centers on Margret, a kennel maid to Mrs. Almut, who has brought her farm and famous breed of Great Danes through the war with the minimum care and the maximum grit. Margret loves and nurses the dogs back into condition, serves as midwife to the stock on the farm, and even helps to restore an old railroad car, which becomes "The Ark" to shelter the whole Lechow family.

In *Rowan Farm* (1954) the father has returned, new characters are introduced, and Margret suffers the pangs of first love and jealousy. These stories are chiefly focused on the gallant struggles of one family to reestablish normal life, not only for themselves but for others more lost than they. Both are superlative stories, and through the eyes of these vividly drawn characters young readers see the rubble of bombed-out cities and the wastelands of what were once beautiful farms.

## ARCHIE BINNS

*Sea Pup*

For most children there comes a time when they are called upon to put away childish things. *The Yearling* (p. 409) and . . . *and now Miguel* (p. 458) both turn upon this necessity. Growing up means taking on responsibility, making decisions with a long-range view of life, and turning away from pleasant immediacy. Because this is hard to do, it is important that children gain some insight into this problem of coming into man's estate before they have to meet it. Fortunately, there are a number of fine books to help them.

In Archie Binns' *Sea Pup* (1954) Clint is a budding oceanographer. He lives on a remote shore of Puget Sound. When Clint finds a day-old seal pup, the family accepts the orphan with many dire warnings. But from the first, Buster is so friendly and so funny that he wins the affection of the whole family, in spite of such misdemeanors as milking the neighbor's cows. Clint is sure he can control his pet by one method or another. The climax comes when a Seattle professor urges Clint to come to the city where he can get the proper pre-college course in science. But what about Buster? Clint's father talks it over with his son but leaves the decision to him, and Clint grows up by facing his problem. This book has rare values as a family story, as a record of a beguiling pet, and as a presentation of the deep love that can develop between a lonely boy and an animal.

## JAMES STREET

*Good-bye, My Lady*

*Good-bye, My Lady* (1954) by James Street presents a boy entirely different from Clint in *Sea Pup*. Skeeter lives on the edge of a great swamp. He has never possessed anything of his own in his whole life. Yet he is rich and secure, secure because he shares Uncle Jesse's one-room cabin and his love, rich because now he has a dog, and what a dog! She is a small, trembling creature that laughs instead of barks, licks herself clean like a cat, and sheds tears when she is scolded. Even Uncle Jesse has never seen her like.

Skeeter trains his dog painstakingly, and people come from miles around to watch her phenomenal performance in the field. But her spreading fame brings tragedy to Skeeter. She turns out to be an African Basenji, lost from a famous kennel that has been advertising for her. No one will tell on Skeeter if he decides to keep the dog, but loving his "Lady" has made Skeeter mature. He gives up the dog, and then he and Uncle Jesse head for home.

The lonely beauty of river and swamp is in this book, and the kindliness of humble people to each other.

## JAMES RAMSEY ULLMAN

*Banner in the Sky*

*Banner in the Sky* (1954) is a book about Switzerland by the author of the adult novel *The White Tower*. It gives children a dramatic story of self-discipline and the stern code of ethics that governs the famous guides of the Alps. Rudi is the son of the greatest of these guides. His father, Josef Matt, gave his life for the men in his care in their unsuccessful attempt to scale the Citadel. Since then, the guides of Kurtal have decided the mountain cannot be climbed. But brash young Rudi is determined that someday he is going to conquer the great peak and put his father's red shirt at the top of it. The story tells of Rudi's training, his mistakes, discouragement, and stubborn determination. When a party finally sets off, young Rudi is along, a sternly disciplined climber, well aware of his obligations. The suspense grows with the inclusion in the party of a treacherous guide from another village. In the end, Rudi is called upon to make the greatest sacrifice to duty that a guide can. He yields his chance of success to save a life. But in spite of this, his father's red shirt flies from the peak of the Citadel at last.

For young outdoor enthusiasts, this combination of meticulous discipline and thrilling action provides a wonderful story.

### E. C. SPYKMAN

*A Lemon and a Star*

*A Lemon and a Star* (1955) is a unique and genuinely funny book. More completely individualized, flesh-and-blood children than the four motherless Cares youngsters are not to be found in literature.

Thirteen-year-old Theodore is the pompous elder of the tribe, against whom the three younger children are united in a book-long feud. It all starts with Jane's tenth birthday, when Ted gives her a magnificent-looking package which turns out to be only a lemon! War is on. These children live in the country, and their adventures abroad and in the nearby village are often hair-raising. When the final revolt against Ted gets under way, complete with battle axes, that young man knows it is time to move. He heads for the marsh, and the result is more mud than gore. But Janey, returning from her near-triumph dirty and disheveled, barges right in on a brand-new stepmother. In the end it is "Madam," as Janey calls her, who unites the tribe in affectionate amity. *The Wild Angel* (1957), *Terrible, Horrible Edie* (1960), and *Edie on the Warpath* (1966) continue the adventures of the Cares children.

### FLORENCE CRANNELL MEANS

*Knock at the Door, Emmy*
*Us Maltbys*
*Our Cup Is Broken*

*Knock at the Door, Emmy* (1956) is the story of the child of a migrant family who is bent on receiving an education, using public libraries avidly, going to school whenever she can. Emmy's single-minded tenacity finally brings her a college scholarship and a chance to reach her goal of doing social work with migrant people.

*Us Maltbys* (1966) is an excellent book about the acceptance of foster children. The two Maltby girls are stunned when their parents announce that they are going to take in five teen-age girls with problems, and both the Maltby girls and their foster-sisters have a slow and often painful period of adjustment. Mrs. Maltby then decides to test the town rule that no black may stay overnight and brings home a baby boy after the family has discussed her proposal and agreed to it. Hoping that little Jamie will charm people into accepting him, the Maltbys give a party—and their hopes are realized. This is an interesting contrast to John Neufeld's *Edgar Allan* (see bibliography), in which the outcome is quite different.

*Our Cup Is Broken* (1969) is heavily laden with tragedy, but it is, like other books by Means, a searching exploration of a social problem. Sarah had lived with a white family since she was twelve, and went back to her Hopi village in deep despair because the parents of the white boy who was in love with her had ruthlessly broken up the attachment. She found herself no more at home in the Indian community than she had been in the white, and the bitter story of intercultural conflict ends with marriage and a move to a new community only after Sarah has been raped and borne a blind child.

*Shuttered Windows* (1968), which was one of the earliest books to portray blacks realistically, describes the problems faced by a young girl from the north who comes to a South Carolina island.

## JEAN GEORGE

*My Side of the Mountain*

*My Side of the Mountain* (1959) is the record of a New York City boy who breaks away from his family to prove that he can maintain life completely on his own in a mountain wilderness for a year. This competent young nonconformist writes, "I am on my mountain in a tree home that people have passed without ever knowing I am here. The house is a hemlock tree six feet in diameter, and must be as old as the mountain itself." How fourteen-year-old Sam perfects his house and how he makes a lamp from deer fat in a turtle's shell, clothes from deer skins, flour from acorns, and a balanced diet from roots, wild onions, leaves, and livers of animals make absorbing reading. Only the concluding reunion with his family seems mildly contrived. Jean George, an artist and a naturalist, not only writes well but knows what she is writing about.

## DOROTHY STERLING

*Mary Jane*

Dorothy Sterling's *Mary Jane* (1959) faces fully the violence that met the first black children to try out school integration in a segregated community. Mary Jane's grandfather is a scientist and former college professor, living in quiet retirement on his farm. When Mary Jane tells him that in the autumn she is going to enter the white high school in order to get certain subjects not taught in their segregated school, her grandfather tries gently to prepare her for trouble. When she returns home, her lawyer father tries to do so also, but Mary Jane is adamant. Nothing, not even her father and the police escort, has prepared her for the jeering, howling mob shouting, "Go back to Africa," or the white mothers' faces distorted with hate, yelling, "Pull her black curls out," or the boys inside the school chanting, "We don't want her. . . . She's too black for me." Mary Jane is frightened right down to the pit of her stomach, but, along with one black boy, she keeps her chin up and stays in school.

The indignities they suffer in and out of school are many, but Mary Jane wins the friendship of one white girl. With Sally's encouragement and the understanding kindness and backing of two teachers, Mary Jane hangs on. By the year's end, things are better and the future a shade more hopeful. Is this too easy and too quick a conclusion? Who can say? Both black and white children must have courage and hope. Books can help to build both.

## MADELEINE L'ENGLE

*Meet the Austins*

*Meet the Austins* (1960), another family-centered book, is one of the first since *Little Women* to handle the death of a loved one so well.

The story begins in a modern kitchen where mother is preparing a gala dinner for a visiting relative. The small children are underfoot with dog and toys, the twelve-year-old daughter is doing her homework, and the record player is midway through Brahms' Second Piano Concerto when the telephone rings. It announces the death in an airplane crash of a beloved uncle. The next night, realizing that the two oldest children are not sleeping, the mother gets them up and dressed and they drive up the mountain to talk. The children demand bitterly why God had to take a good man like Uncle Hal, and the mother replies, "Sometimes it's very hard to see the hand of God instead of the blind finger of Chance. That's why I wanted to come out where we could see the stars." They talk it out quietly in between long healing silences, and then they go home. The children's ups and downs, a serious brother-sister conflict, some funny and some grave situations—all develop against a background of family love. This is a fine family story, as unusual and provocative throughout the whole book as is its first chapter.

*The Moon by Night* (1963) is a sequel in which the family goes on a camping trip and Vicky, now fourteen, is concerned with some of the problems of a maturing adolescent: boys, faith, prejudice, and society's conflicting values.

## ZOA SHERBURNE

*Jennifer*
*Too Bad About the Haines Girl*

While Zoa Sherburne's writing style is not distinctive, her books are notable for the balance and objectivity with which serious problems are treated. In *Jennifer* (1959) the problems of alcoholism and its effect on the lives of others are handled with dignity and compassion. Jennifer's sister had been hit by a car, and her mother turned to drink in her grief. Helped by Alcoholics Anonymous, she had quite recovered by the time the family moved to a new town, but Jennifer lived in dread that the truth would come out. The book may help young people understand others who face such dread, and the fact that Jennifer feels both sympathy and shame may help others in the same position feel less guilty about their own resentment. In *Stranger in the House* (1963) the problem is adjustment to a mother returned from a mental hospital. *Evening Star* (1960), though a placid story, is valuable for the sturdy pride Nancy feels in the fact that she is part Indian.

*Too Bad About the Haines Girl* (1967) is one of the best of the growing number of books about teen-age pregnancy. Melinda Haines is a nice girl from a loving family, and she suffers from the shame of telling her parents, from the knowledge that her future mother-in-law will always feel disdain, and especially from the terrible realization that she has damaged her younger sister. There is no cant in the story, and its pathetic candor delivers a potent message.

## AIMEE SOMMERFELT

*The Road to Agra*
*Miriam*
*My Name Is Pablo*

Aimée Sommerfelt is a distinguished Norwegian writer whose familiarity with India gives *The Road to Agra* (1961) a convincing background. It won the Norwegian State Prize for Children's Literature, as did its sequel, *The White Bungalow* (1964). In the

*Illustration by Ulf Aas. Reprinted from* The White Bungalow *by Aimée Sommerfelt. All rights reserved. Copyright year 1963. By permission of Criterion Books.*

first book, a boy of thirteen takes his small sister on the long trek to Agra, where he hopes her rapidly deteriorating eyesight can be saved. Turned away from the hospital, the children are picked up and cared for by a UNICEF unit. Impressed by this, Lalu decides, in the second book, to become a doctor—but he is needed at home, and is himself surprised that he is content to stay there. The books give a vivid picture of Indian village life, but their power lies in the universality of the theme of the choice that many young people must make.

*Miriam* (1963) is the story of a Jewish family in occupied Norway during World War II, a candid picture of the range of attitudes toward Jews among the Norwegians, and, again, a book with far wider implications than the immediate setting.

*My Name Is Pablo* (1966) is set in Mexico City, where young Pablo has been sent to a reformatory for shining shoes without a license. Released, he fears reprisal from two tough boys who have tried to get him to help them sell marijuana. Colorful and candid, the book gives a stirring picture of the pressures that operate on the poor in an urban environment.

## EMILY NEVILLE

*It's Like This, Cat*
*Berries Goodman*

There is no startling drama in *It's Like This, Cat* (1963), a Newbery Medal book, but it is impressive both for its lightly humorous, easy style and the fidelity with which it portrays a fourteen-year-old boy, Dave, who tells the story. Dave has found the first girl with whom he really feels comfortable (her mother is delightfully sketched as an urban intellectual), and he learns, by seeing the relationship between his father and his friend, that his father really is a pretty good guy. The experience of seeing one's parents through a friend's eyes is a common one, usually revelatory and seldom touched on in books for young people.

*Berries Goodman* (1965) looks back on the two years in which his family lived in a suburb, years in which he had a friend who was Jewish and learned the subtle signs of adult prejudice: the nuances of tone and the light dismissal of subjects with painful implications. He also learns that Sidney's mother is just as biased. The book is an invitation to better understanding, and its serious import is not lessened by a light humor.

## ESTER WIER

*The Loner*

The year 1963 brought children a new book and a new author of unusual promise. This story of the reeducation of a "loner" is a notable one.

Boy—with no name, no family, and no home—has picked crops as long as he can remember. He learns early that the only way to get along in this world is to look out for oneself and no one else. Starving and at the end of his strength, he curls up in a little hole in the earth, somewhere in the lonely grazing lands of Montana. There Boss, a big, competent sheep woman, finds him and cares for him until he is on his feet once more. He yearns to please Boss and stay with her, but over and over he fails her. From his dismal failures to measure up and from Boss herself, he learns what it means to give oneself completely to a job, to do it perfectly and completely.

The characterizations of people, dogs, and sheep are so vivid that even an ornery old ewe called Cluny becomes memorable. The hardships of sheepherding demand deep devotion. The details of this life are made clear in a story with a noble theme.

While none of Wier's other books has quite the depth and impact of *The Loner*, *The Barrel* (1966) is a story with a tight plot construction, a basis of action that rings true psychologically, richly idiomatic dialogue, and a setting that adds atmosphere. Orphaned Chance Reedy is twelve when he learns for the first time that he has a grandmother and a brother living in the Florida swampland. He is sent there by Child Welfare authorities only to find his older brother boastful and hostile. For timid Chance the turning point in his adjustment is the moment he proves himself more courageous than his braggart brother.

## IVAN SOUTHALL

*Hills End*
*Ash Road*
*Let the Balloon Go*

One of Australia's most notable writers of children's books, Ivan Southall is particularly adept at placing his child characters in a situation of stress or danger, and showing in realistic and exciting fashion how the common sense and courage of the young can prevail over obstacles. In *Hills End* (1963) a group of children who have been exploring a cave with their teacher come back to find their home town flooded and deserted, and so they organize for survival and rehabilitation. In *Ash Road* (1966), which won the Australian Children's Book of the Year Award, three boys who have been careless while camping start a bush fire. The suspense is built by Southall's use of fragmented incidents fitted together in jigsaw pattern.

Most of Southall's books concern a group, but in *Let the Balloon Go* (1968) the supreme effort of a spastic child, the great achievement of climbing a tree, is as tense and exciting as the flood or the fire of the earlier books. The theme of the story is that all young people want a chance to make their own decisions and take their own risks. All of Southall's books combine a faith in the abilities of the young and a dramatic setting in which they demonstrate their capability. *To the Wild Sky* (1967) also won the Book of the Year Award in Australia.

## HILA COLMAN

*Classmates by Request*
*The Girl from Puerto Rico*
*Claudia, Where Are You?*

Carla is one of a group of white high-school students who have asked to transfer to an all-black school in *Classmates by Request* (1964). Her overtures of friendship are rejected by Ellen, who has remained aloof from her family's participation in the campaign for civil rights and who is angry because neither her father nor any other black man was asked to serve on a commission appointed by Carla's father. It is Ellen's father who emerges as the pacifier, stating bluntly that he is not qualified and should not have been asked, and that his friendship with Carla's father is not impaired. The two girls end by marching together in a demonstration. The ending is a bit pat, but the subjects of school integration and race relations are made an integral part of the story rather than a springboard, and the changing attitudes of Ellen and Carla develop naturally out of events.

*The Girl from Puerto Rico* (1961) has a slight plot but a warm understanding of the situation of the newly-arrived Puerto Rican who comes to the United States in happy anticipation and is unprepared for cultural differences, dismayed by housing conditions, and shocked by the discrimination against her people.

A story about the generation gap, *Claudia, Where Are You?* (1969), is Colman's most effectively written book. The chapters alternate, either being written by Claudia or written from the viewpoint of her mother. A successful woman who deludes herself into thinking always that everything about her is just what she wants it to be, Claudia's mother cannot understand her daughter's rebellion against her own values. Claudia runs away to the East Village, calling on her parents only when she needs money. Her distraught mother cannot understand Claudia's need for freedom; Claudia cannot live in suburban affluence. The characterization is excellent, the theme universal, the unsweetened ending faithful to the theme.

### MAIA WOJCIECHOWSKA

*Shadow of a Bull*
*Tuned Out*
*"Don't Play Dead Before You Have To"*

*Shadow of a Bull* (1964) richly deserved the Newbery Award, for in the conflict of a Spanish boy torn between his inclination and obligation, there are the themes of youth's similar conflict in any time and place, and of the courage of a boy who dares to admit he is afraid. Manolo, whose father had been the greatest bullfighter in Spain, is being trained in his footsteps by the hopeful elders of his Andalusian village. He knows himself a coward, yet he practices and prays—and when he is eleven and has had his first experience in the ring, he decides he is through.

In *Tuned Out* (1968) an adolescent boy's journal describes, in a stark and honest story, the painful experiences of a loved and respected older brother who has become a drug addict, the sober message particularly effective because it is seen through Jim's eyes.

*"Don't Play Dead Before You Have To"* (1970) explores the sense of commitment and the values of young people in a time of protest. The literary form is unusual, the book being a long monologue by teen-ager Byron, babysitting a five-year-old genius who immediately accepts all Byron's shallow values. But Byron changes through the course of the book, and—although the form becomes monotonous—there is great impact in his growing concern for others and in his intense yearning for a better world. It is this belief that our only hope is in young people which distinguishes Maia Wojciechowska's writing.

### FRANK BONHAM

*Durango Street*
*The Nitty Gritty*
*The Vagabundos*

Although *Durango Street* (1965) has a black youth as its protagonist, it is less about black delinquents than it is about the slum neighborhood that breeds delinquency. Rufus is a paroled adolescent more suspicious of the social worker assigned to his case than he would be if Alex Robbins were white. While the patient, firm Robbins does have a realistically small effect on Rufus and his gang, the book is more interesting as a fictional study of gang behavior and protocol than as a story.

In *The Nitty Gritty* (1968), another black adolescent is torn between the indolent life of his favorite uncle and the benefits of continuing his education. Again, the story lacks impetus but is perceptive in interpretation of character and motivation, its candor lightened by moments of humor.

In *The Vagabundos* (1969) a white adolescent follows the trail of his father, who has disappeared from home. By the time he catches up with his father, Eric understands why the simple life of the local fishermen, the vagabundos, holds more satisfaction than do the indolence and boredom of retirement. The book has vivid characterization of the Americans and Mexicans Eric meets, the suspense of the chase, and a perceptive delineation of the relationship between father and son.

### SUSAN HINTON

*The Outsiders*
*That Was Then, This Is Now*

*The Outsiders* (1967) are the members of a tough, lower-class gang who have a running feud with a middle-class gang. Ponyboy is the outsider who tells the story, stark and vivid, of running off to a hideout with a pal who has committed murder. The two give themselves up, and Ponyboy's pal dies in the hospital. Ponyboy faces the fact that the advantage is with those on the inside of society's line, yet knows that if he cannot have help, he must and will help himself and end the vicious circle of hostility and reprisal. Honest and forthright, the story shows the desperation of the need to belong; it has also a bittersweet quality, especially in young Ponyboy's relationship with his older brothers.

The seventeen-year-old author's candor and insight that made the book so popular are evident also in her *That Was Then, This Is Now* (1971), which is basically a story of friendship and the choice that teen-aged Byron must make when he finds that his best friend is pushing dope. Especially bitter because he has seen drugs ruin a younger boy of whom he is fond, Byron turns Mark in—and hates himself. The characters are vividly real, and no didactic tract on drug abuse could be more convincing than is the story seen from the viewpoint of an adolescent who has himself been a fringe delinquent.

### NAT HENTOFF

*Jazz Country*
*I'm Really Dragged But Nothing Gets Me Down*

In *Jazz Country* (1965) Tom Curtis is a trumpet player who describes the people whose influence has helped him decide to go to college rather than join a band. Most of the jazzmen he meets are black, and Tom is white; he finds that his new friends will accept no phonies and that he has to prove himself before he is accepted by them. A fine book about jazz and about New York City, this is distinguished for its candor about racial attitudes and relationships.

In *I'm Really Dragged But Nothing Gets Me Down* (1968) not a great deal happens, but a great deal is there: it is the scope of understanding and the depth of perception that give vitality and impact to a story of the unsure adolescent and the generation gap. Jeremy and his father don't understand each other, but then Jeremy hardly understands himself. He is in conflict about the draft, unsure of his goals, worried about his responsibilities. The same theme is explored in Barbara Wersba's *Run Softly, Go Fast* (1970), also a perceptive study of a father and son who are at odds, but it lacks the sense of dramatic conflict of the Hentoff book, largely because *I'm Really Dragged* makes both viewpoints understandable. *In the Country of Ourselves* (1971) is a tough, honest account of the protest and rebellion in a high school, an upheaval in which faculty, students, and community forces are split and struggling for power.

### CONSTANCE BARTUSIS

*Shades of Difference*

In *Shades of Difference* (1968), Greg is a high-school boy who runs with the crowd but loses his prejudiced white friends after he has learned, working at a recreation center, to see the black people there as people and to make a real friend of Jake, one of the black members. When a white staff member introduces him to her black fiancé, Greg is shocked by his own resentment and realizes for the first time that there are "shades of difference" in prejudice. The book closes on a hopeful note, as Greg's father assures him that changing attitudes takes time and that he has made a start. The book is weakened by a crowded story line, but is unusual in its perception and candor.

### KRISTIN HUNTER

*The Soul Brothers and Sister Lou*

Which side was she on? Lou, at fourteen, wasn't militant, but she didn't trust white policemen, and she warned the gang with whom she sang that a policeman was near and was acting provocative. She knew the gang carried weapons, but she also saw an unarmed boy shot by the police, and found it hard to believe that any white people had good motives. Yet the more she learned of her black heritage, the more proud and confident Lou became, until she made her decision: moderation, not militancy. *The Soul Brothers and Sister Lou* (1968) has too many episodes and a weak ending (sudden success as a vocal group), yet the book is valuable because it gives a vivid and honest picture of one segment of black society and of the dilemma of its young people.

## JOHN ROWE TOWNSEND

*Trouble in the Jungle*
*Hell's Edge*
*Good Night, Prof, Dear*

John Rowe Townsend, children's book editor of the Manchester *Guardian*, is one of the major writers of realistic fiction for young people in England. His *Trouble in the Jungle* (1969) tells of some slum children who show their mettle when they are temporarily abandoned by adults. To avoid being forced into an institution, the two older children take the younger ones to a refuge in a deserted warehouse and have a dangerous skirmish with criminals who also seek a hideout. The story, which has good characterization and pace, ends on a realistic note: the shiftless father and his mistress return, and the children go back to their home. Although published earlier in the United States (1967), *Good-Bye to the Jungle* is a sequel in which the family moves to a better home and a better life.

*Hell's Edge* (1969) was a runner-up for the Carnegie Medal when it was first published in England. It is the story of a grimy Yorkshire town, Hallersage, in which several young people are interested in an urban renewal project. There is an element of mystery, but this is not a mystery story.

In *Good Night, Prof, Dear* (1971) a shy and overprotected sixteen-year-old falls in love with a waitress he meets when his parents are away on a trip. Although the girl verges on a fallen-woman-with-heart-of-gold type, it is the contrast between her knowledgeable resilience and Graham's diffidence and insecurity that gives the story its real drama. *The Intruder*, another story about a sixteen-year-old, is discussed in Chapter 2.

*Illustrations copyright 1969 by W. T. Mars for* Trouble in the Jungle *by John Rowe Townsend. Copyright 1961. Reproduced by permission of J. B. Lippincott Company.*

## THEODORE TAYLOR

*The Cay*

Although the fact that German submarines are attacking islands along the Venezuelan coast during World War II serves as a catalyst for Phillip's departure, this is in no sense a historical novel, since all of the action takes place on a small Caribbean island, *The Cay* (1969), with only two characters. The ship Phillip and his mother are on is torpedoed and the boy finds himself, some hours later, alone on a raft with Timothy, an old black man. Infected by his mother's prejudice, Phillip feels only aversion for his companion at first, but he becomes totally dependent on Timothy when he goes blind as a delayed result of the shipwreck injury. Slowly, patiently, stubbornly, Timothy teaches the boy to fend for himself, refusing to coddle him—and when old Timothy dies, Phillip knows how much he has come to love and respect the wise and charitable man. The bleakness of the setting is a dramatic foil for the action, and there is taut suspense within the economical framework of the plot.

## JOHN DONOVAN

*I'll Get There. It Better Be Worth the Trip*
*Wild in the World*

In a compassionate story of childhood's end, John Donovan draws a picture of thirteen-year-old Davy, caught and shaped by his environment in *I'll Get There. It Better Be Worth the Trip* (1969). His beloved grandmother has just died, and Davy comes to New York to live with his mother, a divorced, bitter alcoholic. All he clings to is his beloved dog, and the dog irritates his mother. Sent to a boys' school, Davy meets another pupil adjusting to bereavement, and the two have a brief homosexual relationship. It is handled with great dignity and compassion, not the core of the book but one of the scarring episodes that make Davy know his strength must be in himself.

*Wild in the World* (1971) is a quite different and an even stronger book, memorable for its stark setting and the dramatic impact of a solitary boy's deep need for love and companionship. John lives alone on a remote mountainside farm until a stray dog—or it may be a wolf, John is not sure—learns to trust him. For the first time, John plays and laughs with the creature he has named "Son." When John dies, still alone, and neighbors find him, his "Son" is chased off but steals back later to sleep and keep his vigil in John's house.

## OTHER NOTABLE BOOKS FOR OLDER CHILDREN

In Mildred Lee's *The Skating Rink* (1969) a shy fifteen-year-old boy's life is changed by the skating rink, because the owner teaches Tuck to skate so expertly that he is able to partner an exhibition skater on opening night. Tuck works doggedly to achieve competence and realizes he has won respect, not for his performance but for his application. Lee's *The Rock and the Willow* (1963) was chosen a Notable Book, and deservedly. It is

### VIEWPOINTS

Every writer re-creates in words what *he* sees, and there are different ways of seeing. The honest writer can give only his own view of the world, and if it is truly his, there is likely to be something new and different about it. . . . he has to work out his own forms, and every good novel or short story is a successful experiment in technique.—Leon Surmelian, *Techniques of Fiction Writing*, Doubleday and Co., New York, 1968, pp. 3, 4.

a powerful and incisive story set in rural Alabama during the depression years, bleak in its honest portrayal of a hard life, with young Enie bearing the brunt of caring for the family after her mother's death and grudgingly accepting a stepmother. The characters are cameo-clear, and Enie's dream of getting away from home and going to college is realistically achieved.

An unusual setting for another depression era story is the Montana ranch on which Adrienne Richard's *Pistol* (1969) works as a wrangler, grows from boy to man, and goes home to see with a new perspective that his father is a weakling and that he must leave home permanently to find freedom. The story has a serious theme but is lightened by delightful scenes of cowboy humor.

William Armstrong's *Sounder* (1969), a Newbery Medal book, is the grim and moving story of a black sharecropper's family whose father is jailed for stealing food for his wife and children.

Not distinguished in style but noteworthy for the importance of the subject and the candor of treatment is the trilogy by Lorenz Graham: *South Town* (1958), *North Town* (1965), and *Whose Town?* (1969). The Williams family leaves South Town because of discrimination against them, and David Williams, wary about trusting white people, finds that there is a range of attitudes in the black community. Himself torn by indecision, David wavers between moderation and black militancy, influenced by his middle class, middle-of-the-road parents on the one hand and by his resentment against discriminatory treatment on the other. The books are based in part on Graham's experiences with his own family.

In Gretchen Sprague's *A Question of Harmony* (1965) three young people are refused service in a snack bar because one of them is black, and the subsequent publicity clarifies for Jeanne, the protagonist, her own values. The unusual aspect of the book is that the bond among the three is classical music which they perform as a trio.

The democratic process is the theme of William Huntsberry's *The Big Wheels* (1967), in which one boy in a group of six describes the way in which his gang organized to take over the positions of power in their senior class. He suspects that there has been dishonesty in elections as well as collusion and drops out, having learned that there is no such thing as partial involvement in deceit.

*Our Eddie* (1969), by Sulamith Ish-Kishor, is the trenchant story of a tyrannical father so dedicated to helping others that he neglects his own family. The Raphels are English Jews who have moved to New York, where Papa refuses to see that Eddie is truly ill, and only after the boy's death softens his behavior somewhat to his other children.

In Hope Campbell's *Why Not Join the Giraffes?* (1968) there is an amusing reversal. While other adolescents rebel against conservative parents, Suzie grieves because hers are free spirits—very embarrassing when you have a stuffy boy friend. Yet she learns to prefer her parents' honesty to his conformist materialism.

*The Pigman* (1968) was what John and Lorraine called Mr. Pignati, whom they had met when pretending to collect for a charity. The lonely, elderly man is delighted to have the young people as friends, but when he comes back from a hospital stay to find them having a wild party, Mr. Pignati is stunned. Remorseful, they try to make amends, but the old man has had too much excitement and dies of a stroke. Only then do John and Lorraine know that each person's cage is of his own making: "there was no one else to blame any more . . . And there was no place to hide." Told alternately by John and Lorraine, this story, by Paul Zindel, shows more clearly than a reporter could the restless, pliant amorality that so often marks adolescent behavior and the deep sensitivity beneath it.

Other popular books about young people today include Lee Kingman's *The Peter Pan Bag* (1970), in which a girl participates in communal living in Boston and finds her new acquaintances serious about establishing their independence but often pathetic or irritatingly irresponsible; and Barbara Rinkoff's *Member of the Gang* (1968), in which a probation officer convinces one boy that delinquent behavior has only one outcome—trouble (a particularly effective story because it shows the potency of the need to belong and because the probation officer realistically has only moderate success with the gang). Anita Feagles' *Me, Cassie* (1968) is the amusing and sophisticated story of a suburban girl whose mother is a frustrated liberal in a community where there isn't enough for her to reform. Cassie is almost crowded out of her home by her mother's causes: two African exchange students and some orphaned cousins.

The girl in Barbara Corcoran's *Sam* (1967) has been taught by her father, who keeps her on their island home until she is in high school because he so mistrusts people, but Sam discovers for herself that there are all kinds of people, and that even those like Uncle Everett, a weakling and a gambler, have some good things about them. In Corcoran's and Bradford Angier's *A Star to the North* (1970) a brother and sister learn to accept each other's inadequacies on a trek through the Canadian wilderness.

It is interesting that two prize books from Holland are about children in other countries. Siny van Iterson's *Pulga* (1971) is the story of a Colombian waif who gets a job as a trucker's helper and gains self-confidence from his experience; and Jaap Ter Haar's *Boris* (1970) is a story of brotherhood set in Russia. One of the best of the translations from Russia is Vadim Frolov's *What It's All About* (1968), in which a teen-age boy copes with the bitter fact that his mother has left his father to be with another man. Sasha's self-doubt, his budding love affair, and his relationships with classmates give the story balance and depth.

Hesba Fay Brinsmead's *Pastures of the Blue Crane* (1966) is set in Australia, its theme the intrinsic worth of all men. A girl of sixteen who has been living in boarding schools inherits property and finds, in her new home, that her most trustworthy friend is Perry, a quartercaste. Indignant at the slurs cast on him, Amaryllis is not dismayed when she discovers that she herself is not, as she had always assumed, all white.

Of William Mayne's books for older children, *A Swarm in May* (1957) is the most distinctive. Set in a choir school in England, it has a colorful atmosphere, delightful characterization and dialogue, a polished and witty style, and a considerable amount of information about church music. The story line is solid, and the ingenious ploys of the boys make this one of the most entertaining of all school stories.

Although the story takes place during the blitz of London, *Fireweed* (1970), by Jill Paton Walsh, is not historical fiction, but a tender story of two adolescents who find each other and set up housekeeping in an abandoned building, their relationship innocent and touching. When Julie is hurt in a bombing, Bill realizes that he loves her, but when he visits her in hospital and meets her family, he is snubbed by them and thinks she too is rejecting him. A convincing and dramatic story is given poignancy by the wholly unsentimental writing.

## SPORTS STORIES

If there is one fault common to most sports stories, it is the formula plot: the beginner, from school playground to professional team, who can't get along with another member of the team or the whole team or the coach because he is cocky or because he wants things his own way, eventually rises to heights of glory and acceptance by all because he saves the final game in the final minute of play. Another fault common to such stories is the thin plot wrapped around long and often tedious game sequences. Perhaps more than any other kind of realistic fiction, the sports story needs good characterization and good style to give it depth, especially since there is usually little variation in setting and often little opportunity for a meaningful theme.

There are few realistic sports stories for the beginning reader, but Leonard Kessler's *Here Comes the Strikeout* (1965) has simplicity, humor, and an emphasis on perseverance and achievement. Bobby (white) cannot get a hit until he has been coached by his friend Willie (black) and has worked hard to correct his faults. Leonard Shortall, in a good story for seven- to nine-year-olds, describes a boy's first attempts at skiing in *Ben on the Ski Trail* (1965). Beman Lord has written several books for this age group, one of which, *Shrimp's Soccer Goal* (1970), reflects the increasing interest in that sport and is unusual in presenting a woman teacher as the founder and coach of the team. Another good soccer story from Sweden is Kerstin Thorvall's *Gunnar Scores a Goal* (1968).

*Illustration by Harold Berson for* Shrimp's Soccer Goal *by Beman Lord. Copyright © 1970. Reproduced by permission of Henry Z. Walck, Inc., publishers.*

The popularity of each individual sport is echoed proportionately in children's books, with baseball and football stories far outnumbering all others. One of the most dependable writers for the nine-to-eleven group is Matt Christopher, whose productivity is impressive. *Johnny Long Legs* (1970) and *Tough to Tackle* (1971) are examples of his style: simple, undistinguished plots; good game descriptions; and an emphasis on sportsmanship and team effort. *The Baseball Bargain* (1970) by Scott Corbett has more depth, since the protagonist is tempted to steal a mitt and strikes a bargain with the storekeeper whereby he earns it by working in the store—*if* he can first do three good deeds in a day. Corbett's light, easy style and humor make this a pleasant tale with serious overtones— and good baseball. Alfred Slote's *Stranger on the Ball Club* (1970) also is concerned with ethical values and has good sports writing and deeper characterization than is found in most books at this level. William Pène du Bois, in *Porko von Popbutton* (1969), writes a merry tale of ice hockey at a boys' school.

Margaret Potter's *The Touch-and-Go Year* (1969) is flawed by several uses of coincidence in the plot, but is otherwise a fine story about a boy who works to become a professional tennis player—a sport that receives rather scant attention.

The response by publishers to the demand for more books about blacks and other minority groups has included sports fiction, but many of these stories seem obtrusive in their inclusion of such minorities. Indeed, one of the formulas has seemed to be the team in which each player represents a different ethnic background. Stories that approach the particular problems of the black player in sports with honesty and concern are rare, and therefore John Tunis' *All American* (1942) was all the more exciting when it appeared. It tells the story of a boy who plays high-school football and learns to appreciate each player for his own worth and to fight discrimination. In Jesse Jackson's *Anchor*

*Man* (1947) an influx of black students into a small town school leads to misunderstanding on both sides, and the author, who is black, gives a good study of a range of attitudes. Two of the more recent books that deal incisively with the special problems of the black player are Robert Lipsyte's *The Contender* (1967), in which a Harlem youth decides, after a successful start in a boxing career, to get an education instead; and Donald Honig's *Johnny Lee* (1971), a story of a black baseball rookie who finds discrimination as well as friendship on the team and in the Virginia town where he plays in a minor league.

Another story with rare depth and characterization is *Stubborn Sam* by William Gault. Sam Bogosian goes to college as his father asks—but he still wants to play baseball, and does. In Robert Weaver's *Nice Guy, Go Home* (1968), an Amish boy is drawn into a civil rights conflict in the town where his pro team plays; although he respects the Amish ideals, Johnny cannot remain neutral when he sees injustice.

As in other kinds of fiction, sports stories follow trends and issues. The few books about girls' sports have been undistinguished, but more are beginning to appear and there will be better books among them. The interest in the problem of drugs is reflected in William Heumann's *Fastbreak Rebel* (1971), in which the white protagonist on a pro basketball team encourages his coach to sign on a black player who has given up drugs and is especially anxious to show the young people of his deprived neighborhood that there is a better way than the marijuana-to-heroin path.

Although few American readers understand the fine points of cricket, nobody can miss the high-spirited humor of P. G. Wodehouse's *Mike and Psmith* (1969), first published in 1909, but a timeless piece of school humor. Shinty is enough like hockey to be comprehensible to fans, and Margaret McPherson's *The Shinty Boys* (1963) has a cohesive plot, plenty of action, lively characters, and the flavorful dialogue and atmosphere of the Isle of Skye. Last, for really mature readers, *Today's Game* (1965), by Martin Quigley, is valuable both because of the author's expert knowledge of baseball behind the scene and because of the brisk, professional approach to the problems of a manager, his moves and counter-moves in a crucial game. This is a side of baseball seldom described, and it paves the way for some of the baseball classics.

## MYSTERY AND ADVENTURE

A classification of children's books which cuts across all groups of realistic fiction in all countries and times is the mystery story. The mystery tale is certainly a striking example of the way in which children's books parallel predominant trends in adult reading interests. With mothers, fathers, and even grandparents all devoted to the "whodunit" school of writing, it is not surprising to find a seven-year-old marching into the children's room of a library and demanding a good mystery story. In libraries today, children can find racks upon racks of juvenile mysteries which include, along with mediocre ones, some fine books by authors whose names are a guarantee of wholesome, well-written fiction.

Not only do adventure and mystery stories cut across realistic fiction, but also infringe with impunity on historical fiction, as do many of Mollie Hunter's books: are they historically-based tales of adventure or are they historical tales filled with dramatic incidents? Townsend's *The Intruder* and Virginia Hamilton's *The House of Dies Drear*, both mentioned earlier in this chapter, seem primarily realistic stories, yet they may well be considered mystery tales.

The extreme popularity of the mystery tale at present may be a fad as far as children are concerned, artificially stimulated by adult emphasis. An element of mystery has always been a source of interest in a story and always will be. But when innumerable books are written merely for the sake of the mystery, the pattern and mood of such tales are liable to become tiresomely repetitious and the stories are likely to be mere trash. At their worst, such books are marked by preposterous plots, details left unaccounted for, too many episodes, violence piled upon violence, typed characters, and, finally, poor style.

The virtues of good mystery tales for children are numerous, but first among these is the atmosphere of excitement and suspense which serves as the most tempting of all baits for nonreaders. Comic-strip-addicted and television-fed children demand a highly spiced book fare if they are going to read at all, and these mystery tales are usually adventure stories with plenty of breathtaking action to keep young thrill-seekers absorbed. Another useful feature of such stories is that they help establish a much needed reading skill—rapid silent reading. Children unconsciously speed up their usual reading rate under the stimulus of an agreeable suspense. They will cover pages of a mystery tale at breakneck speed in their desire to find the answers and solve the mystery. This rapid rate of silent reading, together with a little skipping or skimming on the way, is a useful habit for fiction readers to establish—the younger the better.

Finally, if children can be supplied with adventure and mystery stories which are also well written and not too difficult for them to read, unbookish children can be persuaded to read a better type of literature than they might otherwise attempt.

The appeal of suspense often leads children to read above their usual level. Older children will plunge happily into adult mystery stories, and children in the middle grades may have favorite authors whose books are intended for older children. Even the youngest now have mystery tales: short, easy to read, and wisely laced with humor. Some of these are Joan Lexau's *The Rooftop Mystery* (1968) and *The Homework Caper* (1966); Ben Shecter's *Inspector Rose* (1969), which has a circus setting; and the lively interracial group in Crosby Bonsall's stories—*The Case of the Cat's Meow* (1965) and others.

Popular with the eight to ten age group are the tales by Donald Sobol about a boy detective; in *Encyclopedia Brown Saves the Day* (1970) the astute ten-year-old solves a series of short mysteries, with answers at the back of the book. Catherine Storr's *Lucy* (1968) is determined to be a detective, and, much to her surprise, she effects the capture of a gang of thieves.

For the nine- to eleven-year-olds, there's an enticing locked room in Elizabeth Ladd's *A Mystery for Meg* (1962). Erich Kästner's *Emil and the Detectives* was published in 1930, but the charm of this German author's style is such that the book is still enjoyed. This is true as well for William Mayne's *The Battlefield* (1967), in which the Yorkshire setting adds to the appeal of a mystery about some odd, carved, apparently very old stones.

It is for the ten- to twelve-year-olds that mystery stories begin to appear in large numbers, although any true fan will read any good mystery—and even some not so good. In Eleanor Cameron's *A Spell Is Cast* (1964) there are logical explanations for all the things that puzzle Cory, and the book has fine characterization. Although the plot of Frank Bonham's *Mystery in Little Tokyo* (1966) is somewhat contrived, Bonham draws a fine picture of the Japanese section of Los Angeles as a solid neighborhood community with rich tradition. Two good stories with a country setting are Eda and Richard Crist's *The Secret of Turkeyfoot Mountain* (1957), in which the unusual treasure hunted is ginseng root, and Wilson Gage's *The Ghost of Five Owl Farm* (1966), with a haunted house and Something in the barn.

Two books for this age group that are notable both for their distinctive style and their well-paced plots are William Mayne's *The Changeling* (1963) and Phillipa Pearce's

*The Minnow Leads to Treasure* (1958). In Mayne's book, three children zealously unravel the mystery of events in the life of an elderly woman who cannot remember anything that happened before she was twenty. In *The Minnow*, two boys recover a family treasure that had been lost since the time of the Armada. To the lure of the subject and the suspense of the story are added superbly natural characters, humor, and an evocative atmosphere of long, golden summer days. Florence Hightower's *The Fayerweather Forecast* (1967) is a good example of a piquant family atmosphere and is one of the few stories in which there has been a (past) murder. The style is lively and there are some highly entertaining episodes, such as the one in which mother is working for a new school and little Bitsy obligingly quavers out a pitiful tale about the horrors of the decrepit old school. Two writers whose tales of adventure and suspense are dependably exciting are Karin Anckarsvärd of Sweden and Nina Bawden of England.

*Catch as Catch Can* (1970), by Josephine Poole, is an English mystery story in which two children witness an incident on a train and are pursued by criminals, a basic plot often used in adult tales and here executed with finesse. In Keith Robertson's *The Money Machine* (1969) two boys pursue the trail of a counterfeiter, and in Eva-Lis Wuorio's *Save Alice!* (1968) three children have a romping journey through Spain, trying to discover why Alice (a bird) had been shoved into their car and what the dastardly villains who did it are up to. In addition to the fun, the story has delightful dialogue between the British and American contingents of the party.

When we come to the mystery and adventure tales for children of eleven and up, we face an avalanche. One of the great classic tales of adventure is Robert Louis Stevenson's *Treasure Island* (1883), which has been published in many fine editions. The story of Long John Silver and his pirate crew has suspense, masterly characterization, a rousing plot, and an adroit contrast in moral codes. *Crystal Mountain* (1955), by Belle Dorman Rugh, was a Newbery Honor book. Set in Lebanon, the story has good intercultural relations as well as an interesting setting and the satisfying solution to a minor mystery. Among Keith Robertson's mysteries for this age group are *Three Stuffed Owls* (1954) and *Ice to India* (1955), a sea story with a wonderfully villainous villain. Another good sea story is *Secret Cargo* (1946), by Howard Pease, in which the timid young hero gains self-confidence and eventually solves the mystery of a shipboard death that was in reality a murder.

One of the master storytellers of our time in the realm of high adventure is Leon Garfield. His stories are set in the eighteenth century, abound in picturesque language, period details, complicated plots, exaggerated characters (usually of very high or very low estate), and are written so deftly that the wildly implausible is made wholly convincing. In *Black Jack* (1968), for example, a hanged man revives, captures an orphaned boy and holds up a coach from which an insane girl escapes. The boy and girl join a caravan, she regains her sanity, her father is murdered, she goes to an asylum, the repentant highwayman rescues her, and the boy and girl sail off as stowaways in his uncle's ship, presumably to a quieter life.

Another fine, complicated tale is Joan Aiken's *Nightbirds on Nantucket* (1966), which is a parody of nineteenth-century melodrama, very tongue-in-cheek and very blandly told, a combination that is used in most of Aiken's books with great success. It begins with an absentminded sea captain and his fragile little daughter, Dutiful Penitence Gasket, and really gets into action with the sea rescue of eleven-year-old Dido, who is so exhausted that she sleeps for ten months. The further adventures of Dido are described in *The Cuckoo Tree* (1971), a sequel so involved and so laden with dialect that it almost loses its footing.

In Henry Winterfeld's *Mystery of the Roman Ransom* (1971) the exuberant boys of

*Illustration by Fritz Biermann from* Mystery of the Roman Ransom, *copyright © 1969, 1971 by Henry Winterfeld. Reproduced by permission of Harcourt Brace Jovanovich, Inc.*

ancient Rome, who solved a puzzler in *Detectives in Togas* (1956), again become involved in a dramatic detective venture when a slave from Gaul tells them he bears a secret message that a senator is doomed to die. The boys are all sons of senators, and they immediately spring into action, lots of it. The story has the pace and suspense that a good mystery story should have, and although it has no historical significance, it gives a modicum of information about ancient Rome; it also has a minor anti-slavery message, vigorous style, and good characterization.

Leon Garfield and Joan Aiken are British, and Henry Winterfeld is German. From France come the mystery stories of Paul Berna, whose *A Truckload of Rice* (1970) is a good example of the solid plots, lively chase sequences, and Parisian settings characteristic of most of his books.

The books of Philip Turner are more boys-and-ploys than they are mysteries, though in *Colonel Sheperton's Clock* (1966) the boys, busily investigating an old mystery, find themselves involved with criminals. The first sequel, *The Grange at High Force* (1967), was awarded the Carnegie Medal, and all of the books are distinguished by a vivid picture of an English town and by the sparkling dialogue, which is tossed back and forth from boy to boy like a ping pong ball. Roderic Jeffries, who writes adult mysteries as Jeffrey Ashford, excels at logical plot construction and authoritative details in police procedure in *Patrol Car* (1967) and *River Patrol* (1969).

Felicity Bell tells her own story in Patricia Moyes' *Helter-Skelter* (1968), an artfully plotted tale of a security leak at a British naval research base, during which the heroine confides in the culprit himself and endangers her life thereby. In Madeleine L'Engle's complex adventure story, *The Arm of the Starfish* (1965), a precocious girl of twelve is kidnaped. Her father is a marine biologist working on regeneration of parts, and there are spies and agents prying about the Portuguese island that is the setting. Despite the complications of plot, the story is strong in appeal because of its theme of the triumph of good over evil, or at least of the humane over the inhumane.

Two authors who have written many suspense stories are Phyllis Whitney and Eilis Dillon. Whitney's *Secret of the Spotted Shell* (1967) is set in the Virgin Islands, and is casual in its acceptance of the mixed racial background of many residents. Eilis Dillon's stories are set in her native Ireland, and each has distinctive characterization and dialogue flavored, rather than burdened, with the musical cadence of Irish speech. In a skillfully constructed, well-paced story, *A Herd of Deer* (1970), Peter Regan is hired as a spy by a man who suspects his hostile neighbors of depleting his herd.

A fledgling spy almost muffs his first assignment in Christopher Nicole's *Operation Destruct* (1969), a story that has the mad pace of the adult spy stories it mocks, light humor, and refreshing variation in detail, such as the pretty girl reporter who is far more adept than the hero and who falls for a pop singer. William Mayne's *Ravensgill* (1970) unfolds and clarifies an old family feud in a tale taut with suspense and delightfully imbued, as are so many Mayne stories, with Yorkshire atmosphere.

Frank Bonham's *Mystery of the Fat Cat* (1968) is set in a poor neighborhood, Dogtown, where the fate of the Boys' Club is contingent upon a cat. The boys suspect that the cat's caretaker has substituted another animal so that he will not lose his job (he is paid out of an estate which goes to the Boys' Club after the cat's death). The efforts of the boys to prove a fraud has been perpetrated are exciting and believable, and the inclusion of a retarded child as a sympathetic character who contributes to the solution is a bonus.

Of the many mystery anthologies, one that approaches the quality of the best compilations for adults is Joan Kahn's *Some Things Fierce and Fatal* (1971). Other anthologies and single mysteries are given in the bibliography for this chapter.

The books discussed here should suffice to show how mystery cuts across most forms of fiction. Unlike adult "whodunits," the juvenile stories seldom involve murder. Rather, the element of mystery is introduced to heighten interest and suspense. Few of these books have literary distinction, though many are competently written, and mystery tales for children are particularly valuable when, in the course of exciting action, they also emphasize desirable attitudes and social relationships.

The books mentioned in this chapter do not by any means exhaust the list of good realistic fiction for children and young people. To give only the best to children, the adult should be aware of the pedestrian books that are written as "bandwagon" books to satisfy a demand, and should evaluate new books with a critical appraisal of how well they meet the standards discussed in Chapter 2 and fulfill the needs discussed in Chapter 1. The best in this genre will always be those books that depict life honestly and accurately, that are interesting in themselves, that present characters who evoke understanding or even self-identification, and that give children new insights into the familiar and the unknown.

## ADULT REFERENCES[3]


ARBUTHNOT, MAY HILL, and DOROTHY M. BRODERICK. *Time for Stories of the Past and Present.*
CLARK, ANN NOLAN. *Journey to the People.*
CROSBY, MURIEL, ed. *Reading Ladders for Human Relations.*
DUNNING, STEPHEN. *Teaching Literature to Adolescents: Short Stories.*
EGOFF, SHEILA, G.T. STUBBS, and L.F. ASHLEY, eds. *Only Connect: Readings on Children's Literature.* Part 6, "The Modern Scene."
ELLIS, ANNE W. *The Family Story in the 1960's.*
FENWICK, SARA INNIS, ed. *A Critical Approach to Children's Literature.* "Literature for Children Without" by Marion Edman.
HILDICK, WALLACE. *Children and Fiction.*
HOPKINS, LEE BENNETT. *Books Are by People.*
LEPMAN, JELLA. *A Bridge of Children's Books.*


*For help in locating books with special purposes or about minorities, see the section "Book Selection Aids" in the Adult References in the Appendices. In the following bibliography these symbols have been used to identify books about a particular religious or ethnic group:*

§ Black
★ Chicano or Puerto Rican
☆ Indian
● Religious minority

3. Complete bibliographic data are provided in the combined Adult References in the Appendices.

## SOME FORERUNNERS OF REALISTIC FICTION

ALCOTT, LOUISA M. *Little Women*, ill. by Barbara Cooney. T. Crowell, 1955 (first pub. in 1868–69).

———. *Little Women*, ill. by Jessie W. Smith. Little, 1968. 10-13

BURNETT, FRANCES HODGSON. *Little Lord Fauntleroy*, ill. by R. Birch. Scribner's, 1955 (first pub. in 1886). 9-11

———. *Sara Crewe*. Scholastic Book Services, paper (first pub. in 1888). 9-11

———. *The Secret Garden*, ill. by Tasha Tudor. Lippincott, 1962 (first pub. in 1909). 9-11

DODGE, MARY MAPES. *Hans Brinker, or the Silver Skates*, ill. by Hilda Van Stockum. World, 1948 (first pub. in 1865). 10-12

SPYRI, JOHANNA. *Heidi*, ill. by Greta Elgaard. Macmillan, 1962 (first pub. in 1884). 9-11

TWAIN, MARK (pseud. for Samuel Clemens). *The Adventures of Huckleberry Finn*, ill. by John Falter. Macmillan, 1962 (first pub. in 1885). 10 up

———. *The Adventures of Tom Sawyer*, ill. by John Falter. Macmillan, 1962 (first pub. in 1876). 10-14

———. *The Adventures of Tom Sawyer* and *The Adventures of Huckleberry Finn*, ill. by Norman Rockwell, 2 vols. in 1. Heritage, 1952. 10-14

## REALISTIC FICTION: THE UNITED STATES

§ ADOFF, ARNOLD, ed. *Brothers and Sisters; Modern Stories by Black Americans*. Macmillan. 1970. A discriminating selection of twenty short stories about black youth, varied in period, setting, style, and mood, chosen from a 40-year span. 12 up

§ AGLE, NAN HAYDEN. *Maple Street*, ill. by Leonora E. Prince. Seabury, 1970. 8-10

ALCOCK, GUDRUN. *Run, Westy, Run*, ill. by W. T. Mars. Lothrop, 1966. 10-11

ALDRIDGE, JOSEPHINE H. *A Penny and a Periwinkle*, ill. by Ruth Robbins. Parnassus, 1961. Old Sy's day spent fishing near his Maine coast home proves more satisfying than any city adventure. 7-9

ALEXANDER, MARTHA. *Blackboard Bear*, ill. by author. Dial, 1969. 3-6

§ ———. *Bobo's Dream*, ill. by author. Dial, 1970. 3-6

———. *Out! Out! Out!* ill. by author. Dial, 1968. 3-5

§ ———. *Sabrina*, ill. by author. Dial, 1971. 3-5

§ ———. *The Story Grandmother Told*, ill. by author. Dial, 1969. 3-6

ALLEN, ELIZABETH. *You Can't Say What You Think; And Other Stories*. Dutton, 1968. Eight short stories that share a suburban high school as a setting, but do not overlap. Candid, varied, the stories are concerned with the familiar problems of young people. 12-15

ANGELO, VALENTI. *The Bells of Bleecker Street*, ill. by author. Viking, 1949. An Italian neighborhood comes vividly to life in this amusing story of twelve-year-old Joey's struggles to return the toe from a statue of St. John. 10-13

☆ ARMER, LAURA. *Waterless Mountain*, ill. by author and Sidney Armer. McKay, 1931. Newbery Medal. 10-13

§ ARMSTRONG, WILLIAM. *Sounder*, ill. by James Barkley. Harper, 1969. Newbery Medal. 12-15

ASSOCIATION FOR CHILDHOOD EDUCATION. *Told Under the Blue Umbrella*, ill. by Marguerite Davis. Macmillan, 1933 and 1962. A collection of realistic stories. Mary G. Phillips' "Paddy's Three Pets" is a gem for storytelling. 4-10

§★●☆ ———. *Told Under the Stars and Stripes*, ill. by Nedda Walker. Macmillan, 1945. An interracial collection. 8-12

☆ BAKER, BETTY. *Little Runner of the Longhouse*, ill. by Arnold Lobel. Harper, 1962. Little Runner finally gains his reward of maple sugar in the Iroquois New Year rites. An amusing repetitive Indian tale for beginning readers. 6-7

☆ ———. *The Shaman's Last Raid*, ill. by Leonard Shortall. Harper, 1963. Two Apache children of today learn something of their tribal culture when great-grandfather visits them. 9-11

★ BARTH, EDNA. *The Day Luis Was Lost*, ill. by Lilian Obligado. Little, 1971. Newly arrived in the city, a Puerto Rican child has trouble finding his way to school. 8-10

§ BARTUSIS, CONSTANCE. *Shades of Difference*. St. Martin's, 1968. 13-15

§ BEIM, LORRAINE and JERROLD. *Two Is a Team*, ill. by Ernest Crichlow. Harcourt, 1945. 5-8

★ BELPRÉ, PURA. *Santiago*, ill. by Symeon Shimin. Warne, 1969. Missing his pet, left behind in Puerto Rico, a child finds that his picture of her brings him a new friend. 8-9

BINNS, ARCHIE. *Sea Pup*, ill. by Robert Candy. Little, 1954. 10-14

BLEGVAD, LENORE. *The Great Hamster Hunt*, ill. by Erik Blegvad. Harcourt, 1969. When the hamster Nicholas is taking care of for his friend Tony disappears, his family buys Tony another one. When the first hamster reappears, what can his reluctant family say except that Nicholas might keep hamster number two. 7-9

● BLUME, JUDY. *Are You There God? It's Me, Margaret.* Bradbury, 1970. 10-12

———. *Then Again, Maybe I Won't*. Bradbury, 1971. 10-12

§ BOND, JEAN. *Brown Is a Beautiful Color*, ill. by Barbara Zuber. Watts, 1969. 5-7

§ BONHAM, FRANK. *Durango Street*. Dutton, 1965. 14 up

§ ———. *The Nitty Gritty*, ill. by Alvin Smith. Dutton, 1968. 11-14

★ ———. *Viva Chicano*. Dutton, 1970. A Chicano youth on parole fights to escape from the burdens that have trapped him into delinquency. 13-16

BORACK, BARBARA. *Someone Small*, ill. by Anita Lobel. Harper, 1969. A tender, realistic, low-keyed story about a little girl who gets a pet bird. The bird eventually dies, is buried, and life goes on. The lesson quietly insinuates itself. 5-7

BRADBURY, BIANCA. *Andy's Mountain*, ill. by Robert MacLean. Houghton, 1969. A warm and lively picture of a cantankerous and determined old man who refuses to give up his farm to the state for a highway and of the love and loyalty between him and his grandson. 10-12

———. *The Loner*, ill. by John Gretzer. Houghton, 1970. Twelve-year-old Jay's resentment of his older brother Mal works itself out in the course of a summer job. Easy writing style, realistic incidents, and economic structure give the book vitality and verisimilitude. 10-12

———. *Two on an Island*, ill. by Robert MacLean. Houghton, 1965. Twelve-year-old Jeff and his nine-year-old sister Trudy are accidentally marooned for three days on an off-shore island. They have not been friends, but in a believable way, they learn to appreciate each other. 10-12

BROWN, MARCIA. *The Little Carousel*, ill. by author. Scribner's, 1946. Into the crowded tenement neighborhood comes the little traveling merry-go-round. Its kindly owner lets Anthony earn the rides he cannot pay for. 5-8

BROWN, MARGARET WISE. *The Dead Bird*, ill. by Remy Charlip. W. R. Scott, 1958. 5-7

———. *The Little Fisherman*, ill. by Dahlov Ipcar. W. R. Scott, 1945. 4-6

———. (Golden MacDonald, pseud.). *The Little Island*, ill. by Leonard Weisgard. Doubleday, 1946. Caldecott Medal. 4-8

———. *The City Noisy Book*, ill. by Leonard Weisgard. Harper, 1939. 4-6

BROWN, MYRA BERRY. *Amy and the New Baby*, ill. by Harriet Hurwitz. Watts, 1965. 3-6

———. *Benjy's Blanket*, ill. by Dorothy Marino. Watts, 1962. 3-5

———. *First Night Away from Home*, ill. by Dorothy Marino. Watts, 1960. 4-6

———. *Ice Cream for Breakfast*, ill. by Lawrence Beall Smith. Watts, 1963. 3-6

———. *Sandy Signs His Name*, ill. by Betty Fraser. Watts, 1967. 7-8

☆ BUFF, MARY. *Dancing Cloud*, rev. ed., ill. by Conrad Buff. Viking, 1957. 8-10

☆ BUFF, MARY and CONRAD. *Hah-Nee of the Cliff Dwellers*, ill. by Conrad Buff. Houghton, 1956. 10-12

● ———. *Peter's Pinto*, ill. by Conrad Buff. Viking, 1949. A Utah ranch summer is highlighted for Peter when he acquires a wild pinto pony of his own. Mormon background. 9-11

☆ BULLA, CLYDE. *Eagle Feather*, ill. by Tom Two Arrows. T. Crowell, 1953. Eagle Feather, a young Navaho, loved the outdoor life of a shepherd and had no wish to go to school until changed circumstances made school a longed-for goal. 7-10

☆ ———. *Indian Hill*, ill. by James Spanfeller. T. Crowell, 1963. Adjustment of a Navaho Indian family moved from a reservation to a city apartment. 8-10

———. *A Ranch for Danny*, ill. by Grace Paull. T. Crowell, 1951.

———. *Surprise for a Cowboy*, ill. by Grace Paull. T. Crowell, 1950. A story and its sequel about a little city boy who wanted to be a cowboy, and how his desired ranch became a reality. 7-9

———. *White Bird*, ill. by Leonard Weisgard. T. Crowell, 1966. Brought up in a remote valley, a foundling child makes a pet of a white bird and learns that his harsh foster parent loves him even as he loves his pet. 9-12

§ BURCH, ROBERT. *Joey's Cat*, ill. by Don Freeman. Viking, 1969. 3-6

§ ———. *Queenie Peavy*, ill. by Jerry Lazare. Viking, 1966. 11-14

———. *Simon and the Game of Chance*, ill. by Fermin Rocker. Viking, 1970. 10-12

BUTLER, BEVERLY. *Light a Single Candle*. Dodd, 1962. The stirring story of Cathy Wheeler, blinded at fourteen, and her courageous struggle to regain her place in the school crowd. 12-15

BYARS, BETSY C. *Go and Hush the Baby*, ill. by Emily A. McCully. Viking, 1971. An appealing story about Will, who is asked by his mother to pacify the baby just as he is about to leave the house, bat in hand. 2-5

———. *The Midnight Fox*, ill. by Ann Grifalconi. Viking, 1968. Sent to stay two months on a farm with his aunt and uncle, Tom never expected to have an animal—a fox—become the focus of his life. Written with quick, quiet humor. 9-11

———. *The Summer of the Swans*, ill. by Ted CoConis. Viking, 1970. The summer that has been the worst in her life for fourteen-year-old Sara climaxes when Charlie, her younger retarded brother, is lost. Sharp characterization, good dialogue, and fine balance in relationships. Newbery Medal. 10-12

CAMERON, ELEANOR. *A Room Made of Windows*, ill. by Trina Schart Hyman. Little, 1971. 10-13

CAMPBELL, HOPE. *Why Not Join the Giraffes?* Norton, 1968. 11-14

§ CARLSON, NATALIE SAVAGE. *Ann Aurelia and Dorothy*, ill. by Dale Payson. Harper, 1968. 8-10

§ ———. *The Empty Schoolhouse*, ill. by John Kaufmann. Harper, 1965. 9-11

———. *The Half Sisters*, ill. by Thomas di Grazia. Harper, 1970. 9-11

———. *Luvvy and the Girls*, ill. by Thomas di Grazia. Harper, 1971. 8-11

§ ———. *Marchers for the Dream*, ill. by Alvin Smith. Harper, 1969. 9-11

CARROLL, RUTH and LATROBE. *Beanie*, ill. by authors. Walck, 1953. A warm family story set in the Smoky Mountains. Followed by *Tough Enough* (1954) and its sequels. 8-11

§ CAUDILL, REBECCA. *A Certain Small Shepherd*, ill. by William Pène du Bois. Holt, 1965. An Appalachian Christmas story. When a young Negro couple's baby is born in a church across the road, young Jaime, who has trouble talking, offers the child the orange from his own Christmas stocking and says clearly, "Here's a Christmas gift for the Child." Movingly told. 9-11

———. *Did You Carry the Flag Today, Charley?* ill. by Nancy Grossman. Holt, 1966. 5-7

———. *A Pocketful of Cricket*, ill. by Evaline Ness. Holt, 1964. On his first day of school Jay takes a pet cricket with him in his pocket. A charming picture book that captures a universal quality of childhood. 5-7

CAVANNA, BETTY. *Fancy Free*. Morrow, 1961. Her father's archaeological expedition to Peru reveals to teen-age Fancy Jones a new world of sights and sounds, and of human values too. 12-15

CHURCH, RICHARD. *Five Boys in a Cave*. Day, 1951. Five boys carefully plan their expedition into an old tunnel. When an accident occurs, it is the quiet unassuming lad who takes over leadership of the group and brings them to safety. 11-14

☆ CLARK, ANN NOLAN. *Along Sandy Trails*, photos by Alfred A. Cohn. Viking, 1969. Not really a story, this book with its beautiful color photos, follows an Indian child in the Arizona desert and gives a feeling of the peaceful life and of the color and beauty of the dry land's flowering. 8-10

☆ ______. *In My Mother's House*, ill. by Velino Herrera. Viking, 1941. 8-12

☆ ______. *Little Navajo Bluebird*, ill. by Paul Lantz. Viking, 1943. 8-12

☆ ______. *Medicine Man's Daughter*, ill. by Donald Bolognese. Farrar, 1963. 11-13

CLARK, MARGERY (pseud. for Mary E. Clark and Margery C. Quigley). *The Poppy Seed Cakes*, ill. by Maud and Miska Petersham. Doubleday, 1924. 7-9

CLEARY, BEVERLY. *Ellen Tebbits*, ill. by Louis Darling. Morrow, 1951. 8-12

______. *Emily's Runaway Imagination*, ill. by Beth and Joe Krush. Morrow, 1961. In between her zealous efforts to start a town library, imaginative Emily frequently finds herself the victim or the heroine of some very funny situations. A lively story of Oregon in the 1920s. 9-11

______. *Fifteen*, ill. by Beth and Joe Krush. Morrow, 1956. Jane at fifteen wants above all a handsome boy friend. Her progress, along with the essential family life of fifteen-year-olds, is told with a light and satisfying reality. 12-15

______. *Henry Huggins*, ill. by Louis Darling. Morrow, 1950. And other books in the series. 8-10

______. *Jean and Johnny*, ill. by Beth and Joe Krush. Morrow, 1959. The author creates a sympathetic family life around fifteen-year-old bespectacled Jean and the cocky senior who temporarily captures her heart. 12-15

______. *Mitch and Amy*, ill. by George Porter. Morrow, 1967. 9-11

______. *Ramona the Pest*, ill. by Louis Darling. Morrow, 1968. 8-10

______. *Ribsy*, ill. by Louis Darling. Morrow, 1964. 9-11

CLEAVER, VERA and BILL. *Ellen Grae*, ill. by Ellen Raskin. Lippincott, 1967. 9-11

______. *Grover*, ill. by Frederic Marvin. Lippincott, 1970. 9-11

______. *I Would Rather Be a Turnip*. Lippincott, 1971. 10-12

______. *Lady Ellen Grae*, ill. by Ellen Raskin. Lippincott, 1968. 9-11

______. *Where the Lilies Bloom*, ill. by Jim Spanfeller. Lippincott, 1969. 11-14

CLYMER, ELEANOR. *The Big Pile of Dirt*, ill. by Robert Shore. Holt, 1968. 8-10

§ ______. *The House on the Mountain*, ill. by Leo Carty. Dutton, 1971. 8-9

______. *My Brother Stevie*. Holt, 1971. 9-11

☆ ______. *The Spider, The Cave and the Pottery Bowl*, ill. by Ingrid Fetz. Atheneum, 1971. 8-10

______. *We Lived in the Almont*, ill. by David K. Stone. Dutton, 1970. The first-person account of Linda and her family who move into the once elegant Almont Apartment. A perceptive picture of the concerns of a young adolescent and the small group of varied tenants. 9-11

COHEN, MIRIAM. *Best Friends*, ill. by Lillian Hoban. Macmillan, 1971. 3-5

§ COLMAN, HILA. *Classmates by Request*. Morrow, 1964. 12-15

______. *Claudia, Where Are You?* Morrow, 1969. 12-15

★ ______. *The Girl from Puerto Rico*. Morrow, 1961. 12-15

§ CONE, MOLLY. *The Other Side of the Fence*, ill. by John Gretzer. Houghton, 1967. 8-10

CORCORAN, BARBARA. *The Long Journey*, ill. by Charles Robinson. Atheneum, 1970. Laurie, thirteen, is sent on horseback by her grandfather across the state of Montana to find her uncle. The story has pace and suspense, memorable characters, an appealing heroine, and a satisfying ending. 10-12

______. *Sam*, ill. by Barbara McGee. Atheneum, 1967. 11-14

CRAIG, MARGARET MAZE. *Now That I'm Sixteen*. T. Crowell, 1959. A teen-age story of real substance, in which Chip, a boy classmate, steers timid, insecure Beth on the road to genuine popularity and success. 12-15

CREDLE, ELLIS. *Down Down the Mountain*, ill. by author. Nelson, 1934. 7-8

CRETAN, GLADYS YESSAYAN. *All Except Sammy*, ill. by Symeon Shimin. Little, 1966. The misfit in a musical Armenian-American family, Sammy finds status and satisfaction in art. 8-10

§ DE ANGELI, MARGUERITE. *Bright April*, ill. by author. Doubleday, 1946. 8-11

● ______. *Henner's Lydia*, ill. by author. Doubleday, 1936. 8-10

● ______. *Skippack School*, ill. by author. Doubleday, 1939 and 1961. 9-11

● ______. *Thee, Hannah!* ill. by author. Doubleday, 1940. 9-11

● ______. *Yonie Wondernose*, ill. by author. Doubleday, 1944. 6-9

DEJONG, MEINDERT. *The Easter Cat*, ill. by Lillian Hoban. Macmillan, 1971. 8-10

DE REGNIERS, BEATRICE. *A Little House of Your Own*, ill. by Irene Haas. Harcourt, 1955. 5-7

______. *The Snow Party*, ill. by Reiner Zimnik. Pantheon, 1959. On a lonely Dakota farm, a blinding snowstorm brings a houseful of company to a little old woman who pined for a party. 5-9

DONOVAN, JOHN. *I'll Get There. It Better Be Worth the Trip*. Harper, 1969. 11-14

______. *Wild in the World*. Harper, 1971. 11-14

§ DURHAM, JOHN. *Me and Arch and the Pest*, ill. by Ingrid Fetz. Four Winds, 1970. 8-10

☆ EMBRY, MARGARET. *Shadi*. Holiday, 1971. A story of cultural conflict for an adolescent Navajo girl. 11-14

ENRIGHT, ELIZABETH. *The Four-Story Mistake*, ill. by author. Holt, 1942. 9-11

______. *Gone-Away Lake*, ill. by Beth and Joe Krush. Harcourt, 1957. 8-10

______. *Return to Gone-Away*, ill. by Beth and Joe Krush. Harcourt, 1961. 8-10

______. *The Saturdays*, ill. by author. Holt, 1941. 9-12

———. *Then There Were Five*, ill. by author. Holt, 1944. 10-13

———. *Thimble Summer*, ill. by author. Holt, 1938. Newbery Medal. 10-12

§ ERWIN, BETTY. *Behind the Magic Line*, ill. by Julia Iltis. Little, 1969. 9-11

ESTES, ELEANOR. *The Alley*, ill. by Edward Ardizzone. Harcourt, 1964. 9-11

———. *Ginger Pye*, ill. by author. Harcourt, 1951. Newbery Medal. 9-11

———. *The Hundred Dresses*, ill. by Louis Slobodkin. Harcourt, 1944. 9-11

———. *The Middle Moffat*, ill. by Louis Slobodkin. Harcourt, 1942. 9-11

———. *The Moffats*, ill. by Louis Slobodkin. Harcourt, 1941 and 1968. 9-11

———. *Rufus M.*, ill. by Louis Slobodkin. Harcourt, 1943. 9-11

★ ETS, MARIE HALL. *Bad Boy, Good Boy*, ill. by author. T. Crowell, 1967. 5-8

★ ———. *Gilberto and the Wind*, ill. by author. Viking, 1963. No indication is given as to whether the Mexican child is in Mexico or the U.S. 3-5

———. *Just Me*, ill. by author. Viking, 1965. A very small boy describes his imaginative imitating of farmyard animals as he plays alone. 3-6

———. *Play with Me*, ill. by author. Viking, 1955. An exquisite picture story showing how a little girl makes many animal friends when she learns to be still in the woods. 3-6

§ FAULKNER, GEORGENE, and JOHN BECKER. *Melindy's Medal*, ill. by Elton C. Fax. Messner, 1945. A humorous and tender story of a black girl, Melindy, who is boundlessly happy when the family moves to a new housing project. When a fire breaks out at her school, Melindy proves her bravery. 8-10

● FEAGLES, ANITA. *Me, Cassie*. Dial, 1968. 12-15

FITZHUGH, LOUISE. *Harriet the Spy*, ill. by author. Harper, 1964. 10-12

———. *The Long Secret*, ill. by author. Harper, 1965. 11-13

FLACK, MARJORIE. *Wait for William*, ill. by author and R. A. Holberg. Houghton, 1935. 4-8

FOX, PAULA. *Blowfish Live in the Sea*. Bradbury, 1970. 11-14

§ ———. *How Many Miles to Babylon?* ill. by Paul Giovanopoulos. White, 1967. 9-10

———. *A Likely Place*, ill. by Edward Ardizzone. Macmillan, 1967. 9-11

———. *Maurice's Room*, ill. by Ingrid Fetz. Macmillan, 1966. 8-10

———. *Portrait of Ivan*, ill. by Saul Lambert. Bradbury, 1969. 10-12

———. *The Stone-Faced Boy*, ill. by Donald A. MacKay. Bradbury, 1968. 9-11

☆ FREDERICKSEN, HAZEL. *He-Who-Runs-Far*, ill. by John Houser. W. R. Scott, 1970. The book is chiefly devoted to years spent by Pablo, a Papago Indian, in the government school where he learns English and the white man's ways. He becomes convinced he must bring understanding and change to his people but realizes as the book closes that they are not yet ready to accept his ideas. 10-13

GAGE, WILSON. *Big Blue Island*, ill. by Glen Rounds. World, 1964. When Darrell is sent to live with a great-uncle on an island in Tennessee, he is bored and resentful. The depiction of the boy is powerful: a child who has no parents, no education, and no future begins to feel that he has a place and a role. 10-12

———. *Dan and the Miranda*, ill. by Glen Rounds. World, 1962. Dan chose spiders for his school science project, and the family, especially his sister, regarded the choice with mixed feelings! A delightful family tale developed around a nature theme. 9-10

GATES, DORIS. *Blue Willow*, ill. by Paul Lantz. Viking, 1940. 10-12

GEORGE, JEAN. *My Side of the Mountain*, ill. by author. Dutton, 1959. 11-14

GOFF, BETH. *Where Is Daddy? The Story of a Divorce*, ill. by Susan Perl. Beacon, 1969. 3-5

GOFFSTEIN, M. B. *Goldie the Dollmaker*, ill. by author. Farrar, 1969. A gentle story, simply written and illustrated with clean-lined, almost naive drawings. 8-10

———. *Two Piano Tuners*, ill. by author. Farrar, 1970. Orphaned Debbie lives with her grandfather, an expert piano tuner. He wants Debbie to be a concert pianist; she wants to be a piano tuner as good as Grandpa. The story has humor, affection, and charm. 8-9

§ GRAHAM, LORENZ. *North Town*. T. Crowell, 1965.

§ ———. *South Town*. Follett, 1958.

§ ———. *Whose Town?* T. Crowell, 1969. 11-14

GREENE, CONSTANCE. *A Girl Called Al*, ill. by Byron Barton. Viking, 1969. 9-11

———. *Leo the Lioness*. Viking, 1970. The theme of the adolescent who grows into a more mature person is handled unusually well here. The writing is convincingly that of a teen-ager, the dialogue is excellent, and the relationships are drawn sympathetically. 10-12

GUILFOILE, ELIZABETH. *Nobody Listens to Andrew*, ill. by Mary Stevens. Follett, 1957. Humorous cumulative tale of Andrew's attempts to tell everyone there was a bear in his bed! An easy-to-read book for the primary grades. 6-7

§ HAMILTON, VIRGINIA. *The House of Dies Drear*, ill. by Eros Keith. Macmillan, 1968. 11-14

§ ———. *The Planet of Junior Brown*. Macmillan, 1971. 12-14

§ ———. *The Time-Ago Tales of Jahdu*, ill. by Nonny Hogrogian. Macmillan, 1969. 8-10

§ ———. *Zeely*, ill. by Symeon Shimin. Macmillan, 1967. 9-11

HAYWOOD, CAROLYN. *"B" Is for Betsy*, ill. by author. Harcourt, 1939, 1968. And other books in the series. 6-8

———. *Eddie and His Big Deals*, ill. by author. Morrow, 1955. 8-10

———. *Eddie's Happenings*, ill. by author. Morrow, 1971. 8-10

———. *Eddie's Pay Dirt*, ill. by author. Morrow, 1953. 8-10

———. *Little Eddie*, ill. by author. Morrow, 1947. And other books in the series. 7-9

HEILBRONER, JOAN. *The Happy Birthday Present*, ill. by Mary Chalmers. Harper, 1962. Peter and Davy, with little money and endless time, shop thoroughly for mother's birthday gift. One of the most delightful of the books for beginning readers. 6-7

●§ HENTOFF, NAT. *I'm Really Dragged But Nothing Gets Me Down*. Simon, 1968. 14-17

●§ ______. *In the Country of Ourselves*. Simon, 1971. 12-17

§ ______. *Jazz Country*. Harper, 1965. 13 up

HILDICK, E. W. *Top Boy at Twisters Creek*, ill. by Oscar Liebman. White, 1969. The book concerns a popularity contest (tied to grocery purchases) in a small academic community in Ohio. A deft jibe at college politics and an amusing story about some lively boys. 11-14

§ HILL, ELIZABETH. *Evan's Corner*, ill. by Nancy Grossman. Holt, 1967. 5-7

HINTON, S. E. *The Outsiders*. Viking, 1967.

______. *That Was Then, This Is Now*. Viking, 1971. 13-15

HOBAN, RUSSELL C. *Herman the Loser*, ill. by Lillian Hoban. Harper, 1961. A most refreshing picture story of a little boy with a talent for losing who one day becomes a victorious finder. 5-6

______. *The Sorely Trying Day*, ill. by Lillian Hoban. Harper, 1964. 5-7

HOLLAND, ISABELLE. *Amanda's Choice*. Lippincott, 1970. Twelve-year-old Amanda is an *enfant terrible*. When Manuel, a nineteen-year-old musical prodigy from a New York slum, comes to occupy the guest cottage at her family's summer home, Amanda feels he is the first person who understands her. Memorable characterization and good style. 12-14

HORVATH, BETTY. *Be Nice to Josephine*, ill. by Pat Grant Porter. Watts, 1970. Charley's mother insists he spend Saturday with a visiting cousin—a girl. The day turns out exceptionally well in this pleasant and believable story. 7-9

HUNT, IRENE. *Up a Road Slowly*. Follett, 1967. Julie Trelling, left motherless at age seven, is sent to live with an aunt and uncle who provide her with insight into the qualities necessary to become a mature, happy individual. Newbery Medal. 11-14

§ HUNTER, KRISTIN. *The Soul Brothers and Sister Lou*. Scribner's, 1968. 12-15

HUNTSBERRY, WILLIAM. *The Big Wheels*. Lothrop, 1967. 13-15

● ISH-KISHOR, SULAMITH. *Our Eddie*. Pantheon, 1969. 11-14

JACKSON, JACQUELINE. *Julie's Secret Sloth*, ill. by Robert Henneberger. Little, 1953. 10-12

______. *The Paleface Redskins*, ill. by author. Little, 1958. 9-11

______. *The Taste of Spruce Gum*, ill. by Lilian Obligado. Little, 1966. 10-12

§ JACKSON, JESSE. *Call Me Charley*, ill. by Doris Spiegel. Harper, 1945. 10-13

§ ______. *Charley Starts from Scratch*. Harper, 1958. 12 up

§ ______. *Tessie*, ill. by Harold James. Harper, 1968. 11-14

JOHNSON, ANNABEL and EDGAR. *The Grizzly*, ill. by Gilbert Riswold. Harper, 1964. David accompanies his father to the woods for a weekend of fishing. The dangers they encounter, the relationship between father and son who hardly know each other since the parents have been separated for some years—all this is perceptively and convincingly described. 11-14

● JORDAN, MILDRED. *Proud to Be Amish*, ill. by W. T. Mars. Crown, 1968. 10-11

JUDSON, CLARA INGRAM. *The Green Ginger Jar; They Came from China*, ill. by Paul Brown. Houghton, 1949. A young Chinese-American brother and sister thought their grandmother and parents adhered too closely to old country ways, and so they set out to change them. 9-12

§ JUSTUS, MAY. *New Boy in School*, ill. by Joan Balfour Payne. Hastings, 1963. 7-8

§ ______. *A New Home for Billy*, ill. by Joan Balfour Payne. Hastings, 1966. 5-8

KANTROWITZ, MILDRED. *I Wonder If Herbie's Home Yet*, ill. by Tony De Luna. Parents' Magazine, 1971. Good drawings illustrate the woeful thoughts of a small boy whose friend has gone off to play with somebody else. 5-7

§ KEATS, EZRA JACK. *Goggles!* ill. by author. Macmillan, 1969. Peter is knocked down by a group of bullies who want the motocycle goggles he has found but he outmaneuvers them. A slight story with lovely illustrations. 5-7

§ ______. *The Snowy Day*, ill. by author. Viking, 1962. Caldecott Medal. 5-7

§ ______. *Whistle for Willie*, ill. by author. Viking, 1964. A delightful picture book in which a small boy Peter tries and tries to learn to whistle for his dog Willie. 3-6

KINGMAN, LEE. *The Peter Pan Bag*. Houghton, 1970. 13-16

______. *The Year of the Raccoon*. Houghton, 1966. Joey is an ordinary middle child who is helped to overcome feelings of inferiority and inadequacy through his attachment to a pet raccoon. 11-14

§ KONIGSBURG, E. L. *Altogether, One at a Time*, ill. by Gail E. Haley and others. Atheneum, 1971. 9-11

______. *From the Mixed-Up Files of Mrs. Basil E. Frankweiler*, ill. by author. Atheneum, 1967. Newbery Medal. 10-12

______. *(George)*, ill. by author. Atheneum, 1970. 11-14

§ ______. *Jennifer, Hecate, Macbeth, William McKinley, and Me, Elizabeth*, ill. by author. Atheneum, 1967. 9-11

KRAUSS, RUTH. *The Growing Story*, ill. by Phyllis Rowland. Harper, 1947. 4-6

______. *A Hole Is to Dig*, ill. by Maurice Sendak. Harper, 1952. 5-7

______. *I Write It*, ill. by Mary Chalmers. Harper, 1970. 4-6

______. *A Very Special House*, ill. by Maurice Sendak. Harper, 1953. 4-7

§ KREMENTZ, JILL. *Sweet Pea; A Black Girl Growing Up in the Rural South*, ill. with photos by author. Harcourt, 1969. Ten-year-old Sweet Pea tells her own story: living with a working mother and four little brothers in a rented house in rural Alabama, a hard but not intolerable life with family love and religion looming large. Good photos. 8-10

★ KRUMGOLD, JOSEPH. *. . . and now Miguel*, ill. by Jean Charlot. T. Crowell, 1953. Newbery Medal. 13-17

______. *Henry 3*, ill. by Alvin Smith. Atheneum, 1967. 11-14

______. *Onion John*, ill. by Symeon Shimin. T. Crowell, 1959. Newbery Medal. 11-14

☆ LAMPMAN, EVELYN SIBLEY. *Half-Breed*, ill. by Ann

Grifalconi. Doubleday, 1967. 15-17

☆ ———. *Navaho Sister*, ill. by Paul Lantz. Doubleday, 1956. 10-13

☆ ———. *Treasure Mountain*, ill. by Richard Bennett. Doubleday, 1949. 12-14

☆ ———. *The Year of Small Shadow*. Harcourt, 1971. 10-12

LANGTON, JANE. *The Majesty of Grace*, ill. by author. Harper, 1961. Even her family's straitened finances did not discourage young Grace Jones, for she was convinced she was heir to the British throne! 10-12

☆ LAURITZEN, JONREED. *The Ordeal of the Young Hunter*, ill. by Hoke Denetsosie. Little, 1954. A distinguished story of a twelve-year-old Navaho boy who grows to appreciate what is good in the cultures of the white man and the Indian. Background of the story is Flagstaff, Arizona. 11-14

LAWRENCE, MILDRED. *Peachtree Island*, ill. by Mary Stevens. Harcourt, 1948. After having been passed about among numerous relatives, nine-year-old Cissie finds a real home with Uncle Eben in the Great Lakes peach-growing area. Cissie loves the work, Uncle Eben, and the happy winter when the harvest is in. 8-10

LEE, MILDRED. *The Rock and the Willow*. Lothrop, 1963. 14-16

———. *The Skating Rink*. Seabury, 1969. 11-13

L'ENGLE, MADELEINE. *Meet the Austins*. Vanguard, 1960. 10-13

———. *The Moon by Night*. Ariel, 1963. 11-14

LENSKI, LOIS. *Blue Ridge Billy*, ill. by author. Lippincott, 1946. 8-10

———. *Boom Town Boy*, ill. by author. Lippincott, 1948. 8-12

———. *Cotton in My Sack*, ill. by author. Lippincott, 1949. 8-12

———. *High-Rise Secret*, ill. by author. Lippincott, 1966. 8-9

———. *Judy's Journey*, ill. by author. Lippincott, 1947. 8-10

———. *The Little Auto*, ill. by author. Walck, 1934. The first in a popular series about Mr. Small. 5-7

———. *Project Boy*, ill. by author. Lippincott, 1954. 7-9

———. *Strawberry Girl*, ill. by author. Lippincott, 1945. Newbery Medal. 9-12

LEWIS, RICHARD S., comp. *Journeys; Prose by Children of the English-Speaking World*. Simon, 1969. Selections by children from four to fourteen, ranging from a single line to a page or two. Delightful for browsing and for discussion. 8-12

★ LEWITON, MINA. *Candita's Choice*, ill. by Howard Simon. Harper, 1959. A warm and understanding story of an eleven-year-old who adjusts slowly to the move from Puerto Rico to New York. When she has a chance to return, Candita decides to stay in New York where she no longer feels an alien. 9-11

§ LEXAU, JOAN. *Benjie*, ill. by Don Bolognese. Dial, 1964. 5-7

§ ———. *Benjie on His Own*, ill. by Don Bolognese. Dial, 1970. 5-8

———. *Finders Keepers, Losers Weepers*, ill. by Tomi de Paola. Lippincott, 1967. 6-8

——— *A Kite over Tenth Avenue*, ill. by Symeon Shimin. Doubleday, 1967. A five-foot Chinese kite is an exciting birthday present for a child in New York's tenement area. 8-10

§ ———. *Me Day*, ill. by Robert Weaver. Dial. 1971. 5-8

———. *Olaf Reads*, ill. by Harvey Weiss. Dial, 1961. 6-7

§ ———. *Striped Ice Cream*, ill. by John Wilson. Lippincott, 1968. 7-9

———. *The Trouble with Terry*, ill. by Irene Murray. Dial, 1962. A realistic and perceptive picture of a summer of change for a tomboy. 9-11

LINDQUIST, JENNIE. *The Golden Name Day*, ill. by Garth Williams. Harper, 1955. 8-10

LOBE, MIRA. *The Grandma in the Apple Tree*, tr. by Doris Orgel, ill. by Judith Gwyn Brown. McGraw, 1970. A young boy who longs for a grandmother and has even invented an imaginary one and an old woman who yearns for her faraway grandchildren discover each other. 8-9

MC CLOSKEY, ROBERT. *Centerburg Tales*, ill. by author. Viking, 1951. 10-12

———. *Homer Price*, ill. by author. Viking, 1943. Lively, funny stories about an irrepressible boy; one of the first books to spoof comic books. 9-12

———. *Lentil*, ill. by author. Viking, 1940. 7-9

———. *Make Way for Ducklings*, ill. by author. Viking, 1941. Caldecott Medal. 6-8

———. *One Morning in Maine*, ill. by author. Viking, 1952. 5-7

———. *Time of Wonder*, ill. by author. Viking, 1957. Caldecott Medal. 8-10

MC GOVERN, ANN. *Black Is Beautiful*, ill. by Hope Wurmfeld. Four Winds, 1969. 5-8

MC KAY, ROBERT. *Dave's Song*. Meredith, 1969. Well written, this book is both realistic and romantic. Kate (who considers Dave a loner, an odd-ball) and Dave (who considers Kate, but secretly) are drawn together in their reaction to the unjust treatment of a rehabilitated ex-convict. 12-15

MAYER, MERCER. *Frog, Where Are You?* ill. by author. Dial, 1969. 3-5

MEANS, FLORENCE CRANNELL. *Knock at the Door, Emmy*, ill. by Paul Lantz. Houghton, 1956. 12-14

☆ ———. *Our Cup Is Broken*. Houghton, 1969. 12-15

§ ———. *Shuttered Windows*, ill. by Armstrong Sperry. Houghton, 1938. 11-14

★§ ———. *Us Maltbys*. Houghton, 1966. 11-14

MITCHELL, LUCY SPRAGUE. *Here and Now Story Book*, rev. and enl. ed., ill. by H. Willem Van Loon and Christine Price. Dutton, 1948 (first pub. in 1921). 2-7

§ MURRAY, MICHELE. *Nellie Cameron*, ill. by Leonora E. Prince. Seabury, 1971. 9-11

NASH, MARY. *While Mrs. Coverlet Was Away*, ill. by Garrett Price. Little, 1958. Light-hearted nonsense tale of the three Persever children, whose cat-food formula opens the road to modest riches. 9-11

NESS, EVALINE. *Sam, Bangs & Moonshine*, ill. by author. Holt, 1966. Sam is a small, mendacious girl and Bangs is her cat and moonshine is the word for all the lies she tells. Attractive illustrations. Caldecott Medal. 5-7

§ NEUFELD, JOHN. *Edgar Allan*. Phillips, 1968. A poignant story of a white family's adoption of a black child, and the pressure that forces them to give him up. 11-14

§ NEUMEYER, PETER. *The Faithful Fish*, ill. by Arvis L. Stewart. W. R. Scott, 1971. The children of a white family are followed by those of a black family in a vacation cottage where fishing is the great attraction. 5-8

● NEVILLE, EMILY. *Berries Goodman*. Harper, 1965. 11-14

______. *Fogarty*. Harper, 1969. A thoughtful, timely book about a young college dropout whose plans to be a playwright come to naught but who realizes there is another place in the world for him. 13-15

______. *It's Like This, Cat*, ill. by Emily Weiss. Harper, 1963. Newbery Medal. 11-14

§ NEWELL, HOPE. *A Cap for Mary Ellis*. Harper, 1953. Two young nursing students enter as the first black trainees in a New York State hospital. There they make a happy adjustment to the new life, their fellow workers, and the patients. The story is told with warmth and humor. Followed by *Mary Ellis, Student Nurse* (1958). 12-16

NORDSTROM, URSULA. *The Secret Language*, ill. by Mary Chalmers. Harper, 1960. 7-9

ORGEL, DORIS. *Next Door to Xanadu*, ill. by Dale Payson. Harper, 1969. Patricia, called "fatsy Patsy" by the boys, has no close friends. When she becomes bosom pals with a girl only to learn she's going to move away, she's at first stricken but then pulls herself together. Realistic events and relationships. 8-10

§ PANETTA, GEORGE. *The Shoeshine Boys*, ill. by Joe Servello. Grosset, 1971. Tony, an Italian-American, becomes a shoeshine boy to help out with the finances when his father loses his job. He joins forces with MacDougal Thompson, a black boy, and the Black and White Shoeshine Company is a great success. The style is gently and humorously affectionate. 8-10

★ POLITI, LEO. *Juanita*, ill. by author. Scribner's, 1948. 5-7

______. *Little Leo*, ill. by author. Scribner's, 1951. 5-8

______. *Moy Moy*, ill. by author. Scribner's, 1960. 5-7

★ ______. *Pedro, the Angel of Olvera Street*, ill. by author. Scribner's, 1946. 6-9

★ ______. *Song of the Swallows*, ill. by author. Scribner's, 1949. Caldecott Medal. 5-7

PRESTON, EDNA MITCHELL. *The Boy Who Could Make Things*, ill. by Leonard Kessler. Viking, 1970. A quiet book about role-projection in a small boy's imaginative play (he makes a paper family which he manipulates). Effective despite the burden of message because of the restraint and simplicity of the writing. 4-7

RASKIN, ELLEN. *Spectacles*, ill. by author. Atheneum, 1968. An amusing picture book about the trials and errors of a small girl who myopically sees strange creatures and finally is won over to wearing glasses. 5-7

RICH, LOUISE DICKINSON. *Three of a Kind*, ill. by William M. Hutchinson. Watts, 1970. A foster child forgets her own problems in helping the four-year-old autistic grandson of the couple she lives with. Realistic characters and a warmly portrayed Maine setting. 9-11

RICHARD, ADRIENNE. *Pistol*. Little, 1969. 12-15

§ RINKOFF, BARBARA. *Member of the Gang*, ill. by Harold James. Crown, 1968. 10-12

______. *Name: Johnny Pierce*. Seabury, 1969. A lonely teen-age boy drifts toward a gang and delinquency, then decides only he can stop himself. 10-14

ROBERTSON, KEITH. *Henry Reed, Inc.*, ill. by Robert McCloskey. Viking, 1958. 11-13

______. *Henry Reed's Big Show*, ill. by Robert McCloskey. Viking, 1970. 10-12

ROBINSON, JOAN G. *Charley*, ill. by Prudence Seward. Coward, 1970. The story of Charley who, through a misunderstanding, believes she is unwanted by the aunt with whom she is living and runs away. Good characters, plenty of action, and the perennial appeal of making-it-on-your-own. 9-11

§ RODMAN, BELLA. *Lions in the Way*. Follett, 1966. A story of school integration in a Tennessee town. 11-14

§ ROSE, KAREN. *A Single Trail*. Follett, 1969. Ricky is white and entering a new sixth grade after nine moves. Earl is black and antagonistic in school. Their friendship comes very slowly with help from an understanding teacher. The story has a sturdy honesty. 10-11

● SACHS, MARILYN. *Amy and Laura*, ill. by Tracy Sugarman. Doubleday, 1966. 9-11

● ______. *Amy Moves In*, ill. by Judith G. Brown. Doubleday, 1964. 9-11

● ______. *Laura's Luck*, ill. by Ib Ohlsson. Doubleday, 1965. 9-11

● ______. *Marv*, ill. by Louis Glanzman. Doubleday, 1970. 9-12

● ______. *Peter and Veronica*, ill. by Louis Glanzman. Doubleday, 1969. 9-12

● ______. *Veronica Ganz*, ill. by Louis Glanzman. Doubleday, 1968. 10-12

SAUER, JULIA. *Mike's House*, ill. by Don Freeman. Viking, 1954. The library is "Mike's House" to young Robert because it houses his favorite book, *Mike Mulligan and His Steam Shovel*. 5-7

SAWYER, RUTH. *Roller Skates*, ill. by Valenti Angelo. Viking, 1936. Newbery Medal. 12-13

SCHICK, ELEANOR. *Making Friends*, ill. by author. Macmillan, 1969. 3-6

§ SCOTT, ANN HERBERT. *Sam*, ill. by Symeon Shimin. McGraw, 1967. Although the story is more an expanded situation than a plot, it is a pleasant and realistic picture of Sam and his black, middle-class family. 3-6

SEGAL, LORE. *Tell Me a Mitzi*, ill. by Harriet Pincus. Farrar, 1970. 5-7

SHARMAT, MARJORIE WEINMAN. *Gladys Told Me to Meet Her Here*, ill. by Edward Frascino. Harper, 1970. When Gladys is late meeting Irving at the zoo, he indulges himself alternately in daydreams of his best friend suffering and memories of her staunch loyalty. As enjoyable for the adult reader-aloud as for the young listener. 5-7

______. *Goodnight Andrew Goodnight Craig*, ill. by Mary Chalmers. Harper, 1969. Two small boys, who have gone to bed, get noisier and and noisier until their father comes in with an ultimatum. The illustrations echo the engaging tone of the story, which is all in dialogue. 4-6

§ SHEARER, JOHN. *I Wish I Had an Afro*, ill. with photos by author. Cowles, 1970. The candor and pathos of the text are uncommon and the quality of the photos is exceptional. 9-11

☆ SHERBURNE, ZOA. *Evening Star*. Morrow, 1960. 12-15

———. *Jennifer*. Morrow, 1959. 13-15

———. *Stranger in the House*. Morrow, 1963. 13-15

———. *Too Bad About the Haines Girl*. Morrow, 1967. 13-17

§★ SHOTWELL, LOUISA R. *Adam Bookout*, ill. by W. T. Mars. Viking, 1967. 9-11

★ ———. *Magdalena*, ill. by Lilian Obligado. Viking, 1971. 10-12

§ ———. *Roosevelt Grady*, ill. by Peter Burchard. World, 1963. 9-11

SHULEVITZ, URI. *One Monday Morning*, ill. by author. Scribner's, 1967. A fine read-aloud book about the imaginative play of a small, solitary child. The setting is urban, inner city, lower class. 5-7

———. *Rain Rain Rivers*, ill. by author. Farrar, 1969. There is so much action and so sustained a mood in the illustrations that the absence of a story line seems of little importance. 5-8

SKORPEN, LIESEL MOAK. *Elizabeth*, ill. by Martha Alexander. Harper, 1970. Kate was disappointed when she got a rag doll for Christmas instead of the one she wanted. How she came to love the rag doll is told without sentimentality. 5-7

SLOBODKIN, FLORENCE and LOUIS. *Too Many Mittens*. Vanguard, 1958. Small mitten-losers will delight in this humorously repetitive picture tale of Ned and Donny, the twins, who were also mitten-losers. 5-7

☆ SMUCKER, BARBARA. *Wigwam in the City*, ill. by Gil Miret. Dutton, 1966. One of the few stories about discrimination against Indians in an urban setting. A Chippewa family in Chicago turns to the American Indian Center for help. 10-12

SNYDER, ZILPHA KEATLEY. *The Changeling*, ill. by Alton Raible. Atheneum, 1970. 10-12

§ ———. *The Egypt Game*, ill. by Alton Raible. Atheneum, 1967. 9-12

———. *The Headless Cupid*, ill. by Alton Raible. Atheneum, 1971. 9-11

———. *The Velvet Room*, ill. by Alton Raible. Atheneum, 1965. 10-12

★ SONNEBORN, RUTH. *Friday Night Is Papa Night*, ill. by Emily A. McCully. Viking, 1970. 6-7

§ SORENSON, VIRGINIA. *Around the Corner*, ill. by Robert Weaver. Harcourt, 1971. 10-12

———. *Miracles on Maple Hill*, ill. by Beth and Joe Krush. Harcourt, 1956. Newbery Medal. 10-12

● ———. *Plain Girl*, ill. by Charles Geer. Harcourt, 1955. 9-11

§ SPRAGUE, GRETCHEN. *A Question of Harmony*. Dodd, 1965. 12-15

SPYKMAN, E. C. *Edie on the Warpath*. Harcourt, 1966. 10-13

———. *A Lemon and a Star*. Harcourt, 1955. 10-12

———. *Terrible, Horrible Edie*. Harcourt, 1960. 10-13

———. *The Wild Angel*. Harcourt, 1957. 10-12

§ STEPTOE, JOHN. *Stevie*, ill. by author. Harper, 1969. 5-7

§ STERLING, DOROTHY. *Mary Jane*, ill. by Ernest Crichlow. Doubleday, 1959. 10-13

STOLZ, MARY. *The Bully of Barkham Street*, ill. by Leonard Shortall. Harper, 1963. 10-12

———. *By the Highway Home*. Harper, 1971. 11-13

———. *A Dog on Barkham Street*, ill. by Leonard Shortall. Harper, 1960. 10-12

———. *Emmett's Pig*, ill. by Garth Williams. Harper, 1959. 6-8

★ ———. *The Noonday Friends*, ill. by Louis S. Glanzman. Harper, 1965. 9-11

———. *Who Wants Music on Monday?* Harper, 1963. A sharply perceptive story of a sensitive adolescent who sees clearly the shallowness of her popular older sister, the amiable stupidity of her mother. Also candid are the discussions between her brother and his black college roommate. 13-15

§ ———. *A Wonderful, Terrible Time*, ill. by Louis S. Glanzman. Harper, 1967. 9-11

STORR, CATHERINE. *Lucy Runs Away*, ill. by Victoria de Larrea. Prentice, 1969. Lucy, bored by her sedentary summer, decides that she will run away as soon as she turns ten. And she does and has some satisfying adventures. Light style and a satisfying plot. 8-10

STREET, JAMES. *Good-bye, My Lady*. Lippincott, 1954. 11-17

★ TALBOT, CHARLENE JOY. *Tomas Takes Charge*, ill. by Reisie Lonette. Lothrop, 1966. Two motherless Puerto Rican children, fearing the dreaded Welfare, hide in an abandoned New York building when their father fails to come home. The boy's tender protection of his older, timid sister is beautifully drawn. 9-12

§ TANNER, LOUISE. *Reggie and Nilma*. Farrar, 1971. Nilma, a black woman, and her son, Reggie, enjoy a close relationship with the white family she works for. When Reggie is wrongly suspected of robbing the white family's apartment, the breach is irreparable. Despite the serious problems, the story is not somber. 11-15

§ TARRY, ELLEN, and MARIE HALL ETS. *My Dog Rinty*, ill. by Alexander and Alexandra Alland. Viking, 1946. 8-10

● TAYLOR, SYDNEY. *All-of-a-Kind Family*, ill. by Helen John. Follett, 1951. 9-11

● ——— *All-of-a-Kind Family Uptown*, ill. by Mary Stevens. Follet, 1958. 9-11

● ———. *More All-of-a-Kind Family*, ill. by Mary Stevens. Follett, 1954. 9-11

§ TAYLOR, THEODORE. *The Cay*. Doubleday, 1969. 12-15

★ THOMAS, DAWN C. *Mira! Mira!* ill. by Harold L. James. Lippincott, 1970. A Puerto Rican child adjusts to a move to New York not through the usual pattern of recognition in some situation but rather when he sees his first snowfall which he feels "fell from the sky to say 'Welcome.'" 5-7

TRESSELT, ALVIN. *Hide and Seek Fog*, ill. by Roger Duvoisin. Lothrop, 1965. 5-8

———. *White Snow, Bright Snow*, ill. by Roger Duvoisin. Lothrop, 1947. Caldecott Medal. 5-7

TUDOR, TASHA. *Pumpkin Moonshine*, ill. by author. Walck, 1938 and 1962. This Halloween story makes a good introduction to the other books of Tasha Tudor. Reissued in larger format. 4-7

TURKLE, BRINTON. *The Sky Dog*, ill. by author. Viking, 1969. A satisfying story for the read-aloud audience about a boy who finds and keeps a stray dog. Simply and touchingly told and engagingly illustrated. 4-6

UCHIDA, YOSHIKO. *The Promised Year*, ill. by William M. Hutchinson. Harcourt, 1959. 9-11

UDRY, JANICE MAY. *The Moon Jumpers*, ill. by Maurice Sendak. Harper, 1959. Beautiful color illustrations enhance this mood picture book which describes children frolicking in the moonlight until bedtime interrupts their imaginative play. 5-8

§ UDRY, JANICE. *Mary Jo's Grandmother*, ill. by Eleanor Mill. Whitman, 1970. 5-7

WEBER, ALFONS. *Elizabeth Gets Well*, ill. by Jacqueline Blass. T. Crowell, 1970. One of the best of the books intended to prepare a child for hospital procedures. 4-7

§ WEIK, MARY HAYS. *The Jazz Man*, ill. by Ann Grifalconi. Atheneum, 1966. A story that combines harsh realism and brooding lyricism gives a poignant picture of a crippled child in Harlem. This has had high praise for its tender treatment of the child and stringent criticism for the depiction of parental neglect. 9-11

WERSBA, BARBARA. *The Dream Watcher*. Atheneum, 1968. Albert is an adolescent loner until he meets an old woman who tells him about her glamorous career on the stage and becomes his friend. When she dies, he is shocked to find she had lied to him about almost everything, but he realizes keenly that she gave him something precious and durable. Excellent characterization. 11-14

● ______. *Run Softly, Go Fast*. Atheneum, 1970. 13-15

WIER, ESTER. *The Barrel*, ill. by Carl Kidwell. McKay, 1966. 10-12

______. *The Loner*, ill. by Christine Price. McKay, 1963. 11-14

WILL and NICOLAS. *Russet and the Two Reds*, ill. Harcourt, 1962. 5-8

______. *The Two Reds*, ill. Harcourt, 1950. 5-8

WOJCIECHOWSKA, MAIA. *Don't Play Dead Before You Have To*. Harper, 1970. 13-15

______. *Tuned Out*. Harper, 1968. 14-16

YASHIMA, TARO. *Umbrella*, ill. by author. Viking, 1958. To small Momo it seemed that rain would never come so that she might use her new blue umbrella and bright red boots. New York background. 4-6

YATES, ELIZABETH. *Mountain Born*, ill. by Nora Unwin. Coward, 1943. Young Peter cares for Biddy, the little black lamb, proudly wears a coat woven from her wool, and endures the grief of losing her after she dies in a mountain storm. 8-11

______. *A Place for Peter*, ill, by Nora Unwin. Coward, 1952. 12-14

YORK, CAROL BEACH. *Nothing Ever Happens Here*. Hawthorn, 1970. Young Elizabeth lives a quiet life in a dull town, but the author has written a truly touching book about the ordinary lives around her. Perceptive characterization. 11-14

ZINDEL, PAUL. *The Pigman*. Harper, 1968. 12-14

ZION, GENE. *Dear Garbage Man*, ill. by Margaret Bloy Graham. Harper, 1957. Popular for community units as well as highly entertaining is this picture story of Stan, the brand-new rubbish collector. 5-8

______. *The Plant Sitter*, ill. by Margaret Bloy Graham. Harper, 1959. Tommy crowded the house with the plants of vacationing neighbors, and his zeal in their care precipitates a family crisis! A novel and humorous picture book. 5-7

ZOLOTOW, CHARLOTTE. *Big Sister and Little Sister*, ill. by Martha Alexander. Harper, 1966. 5-7

______. *A Father Like That*, ill. by Ben Shecter. Harper, 1971. 5-7

______. *The Hating Book*, ill. by Ben Shecter. Harper, 1969. 5-7

______. *The Quarreling Book*, ill. by Arnold Lobel. Harper, 1963. 5-7

______. *The Storm Book*, ill. by Margaret B. Graham. Harper, 1952. Little boy and his mother share the beauty and excitement of a summer storm. Brief text and charming illustrations. 5-7

______. *When I Have a Little Girl*, ill. by Hilary Knight. Harper, 1965. 5-8

______. *When I Have a Son*, ill. by Hilary Knight. Harper, 1967. 5-7

## REALISTIC FICTION: FOREIGN LANDS

### Africa

BRADLEY, DUANE. *Meeting with a Stranger*, ill. by E. Harper Johnson. Lippincott, 1964. 10-12

CHANDLER, EDNA WALKER. *With Books on Her Head*, ill. by Charles Keeping. Meredith, 1967. 11-14

FEELINGS, MURIEL. *Zamani Goes to Market*, ill. by Tom Feelings. Seabury, 1970. 5-8

GRAHAM, LORENZ. *I, Momolu*, ill. by John Biggers. T. Crowell, 1966. 12-15

MIRSKY, REBA. *Seven Grandmothers*, ill. by W. T. Mars. Follett, 1955. A sequel to the title below.

______. *Thirty-one Brothers and Sisters*, ill. by W. T. Mars. Follett, 1952. 9-11

MITCHISON, NAOMI. *The Family at Ditlabeng*, ill. by Joanna Stubbs. Farrar, 1970. 9-11

STEVENSON, WILLIAM. *The Bushbabies*, ill. by Victor Ambrus. Houghton, 1965. A most unusual story, both in the setting and in the beautifully built-up relationship between two people different in age, sex, race, and station. The story moves from one dangerous episode to another across wild African country. 11-14

### Australia

BRINSMEAD, HESBA FAY. *Pastures of the Blue Crane*. Coward, 1966. 13-15

OTTLEY, REGINALD. *Boy Alone*, ill. by Clyde Pearson. Harcourt, 1966. The story of a young adolescent in the Australian outback. The atmosphere is wonderfully created; the writing is perceptive. 10-12

PHIPSON, JOAN. *Birkin*, ill. by Margaret Horder. Harcourt, 1966. An engaging story about several children in a small Australian town who care for a calf. Plenty of action and humor. 10-12

———. *The Boundary Riders*, ill. by Margaret Horder. Harcourt, 1963. The suspense-filled journey to safety of three Australian children and their dog. 10-13

———. *The Family Conspiracy*, ill. by Margaret Horder. Harcourt, 1964. The large Barker family lives on an isolated Australian sheep station. A warm and convincing family story with good characterization and an unsentimental ending. 10-11

SOUTHALL, IVAN. *Ash Road*, ill. by Clem Seale. St. Martin's, 1966. 11-14

———. *Hills End*. St. Martin's, 1963. 11-14

———. *Let the Balloon Go*, ill. by Ian Ribbons. St. Martin's, 1968. 11-13

———. *To the Wild Sky*, ill. by Jennifer Tuckwell. St. Martin's, 1967. 12-14

SPENCE, ELEANOR. *Jamberoo Road*, ill. by Doreen Roberts. Roy, 1969. Two orphans, Cassie and Luke, go to the prosperous Marlow homestead as governess and stable boy. The book has a bit of everything: drama and love interest, excellent characterization, good plot, and an interesting Australian setting. 11-14

WRIGHTSON, PATRICIA. *A Racecourse for Andy*, ill. by Margaret Horder. Harcourt, 1968. 10-12

## Canada

CORCORAN, BARBARA, and BRADFORD ANGIER. *A Star to the North*. Nelson, 1970. 11-14

LITTLE, JEAN. *Home from Far*, ill. by Jerry Lazare. Little, 1965. 10-13

● ———. *Kate*. Harper, 1971. 10-13

● ———. *Look Through My Window*, ill. by Joan Sandin. Harper, 1970. 9-11

———. *Mine for Keeps*, ill. by Lewis Parker. Little, 1962. 10-12

———. *Spring Begins in March*, ill. by Lewis Parker. Little, 1966. 10-12

VAN STOCKUM, HILDA. *Canadian Summer*, ill. by author. Viking, 1948. Adventures of the Mitchell family in a summer cottage near Montreal. 10-14

## Central and South America

BEHN, HARRY. *The Two Uncles of Pablo*, ill. by Mel Silverman. Harcourt, 1959. Small Pablo copes with two antagonistic uncles as well as his own problem of trying to gain an education. An appealing story of Mexico written by a poet very popular with children. 9-11

BONHAM, FRANK. *The Vagabundos*. Dutton, 1969. 12-15

BUFF, MARY, and CONRAD BUFF. *Magic Maize*, ill. by authors. Houghton, 1953. 9-12

BULLA, CLYDE. *Benito*, ill. by Valenti Angelo. T. Crowell, 1961. The encouragement of a successful artist helps orphaned Benito assert his need for time from the endless farm drudgery at Uncle Pedro's to develop his talent. 8-10

CLARK, ANN NOLAN. *Santiago*, ill. by Lynd Ward. Viking, 1955. 12-14

———. *Secret of the Andes*, ill. by Jean Charlot. Viking, 1952. Newbery Medal. 12-14

ETS, MARIE HALL, and AURORA LABASTIDA. *Nine Days to Christmas*, ill. by Marie Hall Ets. Viking, 1959. Ceci, a little girl of Mexico, discovers the fun of Christmas with her first piñata. Caldecott Medal. 5-8

GARRETT, HELEN. *Angelo the Naughty One*, ill. by Leo Politi. Viking, 1944. The amusing reform of a small Mexican boy who did not like to take baths. 6-9

NESS, EVALINE. *Josefina February*, ill. by author. Scribner's, 1963. A warm, quiet read-aloud story set in Haiti. 5-7

O'DELL, SCOTT. *The Black Pearl*, ill. by Milton Johnson. Houghton, 1967. The stark simplicity of the story and the deeper significance it holds in the triumph of good over evil add importance to the book, but even without that it would be enjoyable as a rousing adventure tale with beautifully maintained tempo and suspense as Ramon searches for a giant black pearl in the waters of Baja California. 12-17

RHOADS, DOROTHY M. *The Corn Grows Ripe*, ill. by Jean Charlot. Viking, 1956. Twelve-year-old Tigre, spoiled and lazy, grows up suddenly when his father is injured. Background of the story is Yucatan, among the Mayan Indians. 9-12

SOMMERFELT, AIMÉE. *My Name Is Pablo*, tr. by Patricia Crampton, ill. by Hans Norman Dah. Criterion, 1966. 11-14

STOLZ, MARY. *The Dragons of the Queen*, ill. by Edward Frascino. Harper, 1969. 10-12

———. *Juan*, ill. by Louis S. Glanzman. Harper, 1970. 9-11

SURANY, ANICO. *Ride the Cold Wind*, ill. by Leonard Everett Fisher. Putnam, 1964. The story of a small Peruvian boy who wishes to go fishing with his father on Lake Titicaca. He and his sister go boating alone, and when a storm comes up, must be rescued. An appealing theme and setting. 8-10

VAN ITERSON, S. R. *Pulga*, tr. from the Dutch by Alexander and Alison Gode. Morrow, 1971. 11-14

## China and Japan

BRO, MARGUERITE. *Su-Mei's Golden Year*, ill. by Kurt Wiese. Doubleday, 1950. It is Su-Mei and her friends of the younger generation who save their Chinese village from famine when the wheat crop is endangered. 11-14

BUCK, PEARL. *The Big Wave*, ill. by Hiroshige and Hokusai. Day, 1948. Jiya leaves the coast after a tidal wave destroys his home and the entire fishing village. When he is grown, he courageously returns to his traditional occupation. There is a heroic quality in the telling which makes this Japanese story a memorable one. 9-13

DEJONG, MEINDERT. *The House of Sixty Fathers*, ill. by Maurice Sendak. Harper, 1956. 11-13

HANDFORTH, THOMAS. *Mei Li*, ill. by author. Doubleday, 1938. The pleasant adventures of a little Chinese girl at the Fair. Caldecott Medal. 5-8

LATTIMORE, ELEANOR. *Little Pear*, ill. by author. Harcourt, 1931. 8-10

______. *More About Little Pear*, ill. by author. Morrow, 1971. 8-10

MATSUNO, MASAKO. *A Pair of Red Clogs*, ill. by Kazue Mizumura. World, 1960. A little Japanese girl chooses beautiful but impractical new red clogs and soon rues her choice. Beautifully illustrated in color, with a universal theme. 5-8

MUHLENWEG, FRITZ. *Big Tiger and Christian*, ill. by Rafaello Busoni. Pantheon, 1952. An English and a Chinese boy cross the Gobi Desert on a dangerous mission for a Chinese general. Here are nearly six hundred pages packed with adventure, people, and strange places. A rare treat for the superior reader. 12 up

UCHIDA, YOSHIKO. *The Forever Christmas Tree*, ill. by Kazue Mizumura. Scribner's, 1963. 5-7

______. *Hisako's Mysteries*, ill. by Susan Bennett. Scribner's, 1969. Although there is some awkwardness in the appearance of Hisako's father, who was presumed dead, the book is otherwise well written and interesting both for the picture of life in Japan today and of a typical thirteen-year-old. 10-12

______. *Sumi and the Goat and the Tokyo Express*, ill. by Kazue Mizumura. Scribner's, 1969. Sumi has a brief but delicious moment in the limelight when she is the only one who can get old Mr. Oda's goat to move from the path of the new Tokyo express. A charming book. 7-9

YASHIMA, MITSU and TARO. *Plenty to Watch*, ill. by Taro Yashima. Viking, 1954. 8-10

YASHIMA, TARO. *Crow Boy*, ill. by author. Viking, 1955. 8-10

### England, Ireland, Scotland

ARDIZZONE, EDWARD. *Little Tim and the Brave Sea Captain*, ill. by author. Walck, 1955 (first pub. in 1936). First of several books about Tim's adventures at sea. 4-6

______. *Nicholas and the Fast Moving Diesel*, ill. by author. Walck, 1959. Two small boys avert a train wreck when fireman and engineer become ill. High adventure for the youngest. 5-7

______. *The Wrong Side of the Bed*, ill. by author. Doubleday, 1970. 3-6

CRESSWELL, HELEN. *The Night Watchmen*, ill. by Gareth Floyd. Macmillan, 1970. Josh and Caleb, the most distinctive pair of tramps in contemporary fiction, fascinate young Henry with their enthralling talk and their do-as-you-please life. Not deep characterization, but marvelously vivid characters. 9-11

DIVINE, DAVID. *The Stolen Seasons*. T. Crowell, 1970. Two British children and their American friend organize an expedition to get over Hadrian's Wall without being spotted. The first part of the book is entertaining, the second tense with suspense when they flee some men, who have stolen a valuable artifact and know the children have seen them. 11-14

GARNETT, EVE. *The Family from One End Street*, ill. by author. Vanguard, 1960. 11-13

GODDEN, RUMER. *The Kitchen Madonna*, ill. by Carol Barker. Viking, 1967. 8 up

MACKELLAR, WILLIAM. *Wee Joseph*, ill. by Ezra Jack Keats. McGraw, 1957. Young Davie prayed hard, and a small miracle and a great scientific event combine to save Wee Joseph, his runt puppy, from being drowned. A heartwarming story of Scotland. 8-10

MC LEAN, ALLAN CAMPBELL. *Storm over Skye*, ill. by Shirley Hughes. Harcourt, 1957. A story rich in Scottish atmosphere tells of two brothers' efforts to solve the sheep stealing that has thrown their community into an uproar. A bit of romance, too. 13-16

MC NEILL, JANET. *The Battle of St. George Without*, ill. by Mary Russon. Little, 1968. 10-12

______. *Goodbye, Dove Square*, ill. by Mary Russon. Little, 1969. In this sequel to the above title, all the Dove Square residents have left the area, cleared for renewal. A realistic picture of urban life. 10-13

______. *The Other People*. Little, 1970. Kate visits her aunt's guest house, which she had envisioned as a glamorous resort, and finds it shabby and filled with unexciting people. Her initiative and sympathy are the fulcrum for events that change, to some extent, the lives of most of the others and her own as well. Well-drawn characters. 11-13

MAYNE, WILLIAM. *A Grass Rope*, ill. by Lynton Lamb. Dutton, 1962. 10-12

______. *A Swarm in May*, ill. by C. Walter Hodges. Bobbs, 1957. 11-13

______. *Whistling Rufus*, ill. by Raymond Briggs. Dutton, 1965. 10-11

NESBIT, EDITH. *The Conscience Pudding*, ill. by Erik Blegvad. Coward, 1970. A Christmas story taken from *The New Treasure Seekers*, one of the books about the Bastable children that have become classics. When money is short, the children plan and produce an elaborate Christmas pudding. The period details are charmingly picked up in the illustrations. 9-11

PEARCE, PHILLIPA. *A Dog So Small*, ill. by Antony Maitland. Lippincott, 1963. An unusual story of a gentle, withdrawn young boy's obsessive desire to own a dog. 10-12

RANSOME, ARTHUR. *Swallows and Amazons*, ill. by Helene Carter. Lippincott, 1931. 12-13

ROBINSON, VERONICA. *David in Silence*, ill. by Victor Ambrus. Lippincott, 1966. The story, set in a small English town, concerns a new boy David, who has always been deaf. A poignant and interesting story about the isolation and hostility that often are the lot of the deaf. 10-12

STREATFEILD, NOEL. *Ballet Shoes*, ill. by Richard Floethe. Random, 1950. 11-13

______. *The Children on the Top Floor*, ill. by Jillian Willett. Random, 1965. 10-12

______. *Circus Shoes*, ill. by Richard Floethe. Random, 1939. 11-13

______. *The Family at Caldicott Place*, ill. by Betty Maxey. Random, 1968. 9-11

______. *Thursday's Child*, ill. by Peggy Fortnum. Random, 1971. 9-11

TOWNSEND, JOHN ROWE. *Good-bye to the Jungle*. Lippincott, 1967. 12-14

______. *Good Night, Prof, Dear*. Lippincott, 1970. 12-14

———. *Hell's Edge*. Lothrop, 1969. 11-14
———. *The Intruder*. Lippincott, 1970. 11-14
———. *Trouble in the Jungle*, ill. by W. T. Mars. Lippincott, 1969. 10-12

TURNER, PHILIP. *War on the Darnel*, ill. by W. T. Mars. World, 1969. Three lively English boys engage in a mighty battle with another set of boys who have set up a river barricade. Good characterization and even better dialogue. 10-14

VAN STOCKUM, HILDA. *The Cottage at Bantry Bay*, ill. by author. Viking, 1938.
———. *Francie on the Run*, ill. by author. Viking, 1939.
———. *Pegeen*, ill. by author. Viking, 1941. 10-12

WALSH, JILL PATON. *Fireweed*. Farrar, 1970. 11-14

WILLIAMS, URSULA MORAY. *A Crown for a Queen*, ill. by Shirley Hughes. Meredith, 1969. 8-10

### France

BEMELMANS, LUDWIG. *Madeline*, ill. by author. Viking, 1939. Other titles in the series include *Madeline's Rescue* (1953), *Madeline and the Bad Hat* (1957), *Madeline and the Gypsies* (1959). 5-7

BISHOP, CLAIRE HUCHET. *All Alone*, ill. by Feodor Rojankovsky. Viking, 1953. Villagers in the French Alps learn to work together when two children, herding in the mountains, are isolated by an avalanche. 9-11

———. *Pancakes-Paris*, ill. by Georges Schreiber. Viking, 1947. A half-starved postwar French child receives a miraculous package of American pancake mix. How he meets two American soldiers and gets the recipe makes a heart-warming tale. 8-12

CARLSON, NATALIE SAVAGE. *A Brother for the Orphelines*, ill. by Garth Williams. Harper, 1959.
———. *The Family Under the Bridge*, ill. by Garth Williams. Harper, 1958.
———. *The Happy Orpheline*, ill. by Garth Williams. Harper, 1957.
———. *The Orphelines in the Enchanted Castle*, ill. by Adriana Saviozzi. Harper, 1964. The fourth book about the lively French orphans who live—this time in a small castle—with Madame Flattot. A light and charming story with important (but not obtrusive) overtones about social behavior. 9-11
———. *A Pet for the Orphelines*, ill. by Fermin Rocker. Harper, 1962. 8-10

### Germany

BENARY-ISBERT, MARGOT. *The Ark*, tr. by Clara and Richard Winston. Harcourt, 1953. 12-14
———. *Rowan Farm*, tr. by Richard and Clara Winston. Harcourt, 1954. 13-17

PETRIDES, HEIDRUN. *Hans and Peter*, ill. by author. Harcourt, 1963. 7-9

VON GEBHARDT, HERTHA. *The Girl from Nowhere*, tr. by James Kirkup, ill. by Helen Brun. Criterion, 1959. No one believes her father will return, but a little German girl's faith surmounts mockery and pity and is happily rewarded. 10-13

### Holland

DEJONG, MEINDERT. *Far Out the Long Canal*, ill. by Nancy Grossman. Harper, 1964. 10-13
———. *Journey from Peppermint Street*, ill. by Emily Arnold McCully. Harper, 1968. National Book Award. 9-11
———. *Shadrach*, ill. by Maurice Sendak. Harper, 1953. 9-12
———. *The Wheel on the School*, ill. by Maurice Sendak. Harper, 1954. Newbery Medal. 9-12

DODGE, MARY MAPES. *Hans Brinker; or the Silver Skates* (see Forerunners).

VAN STOCKUM, HILDA. *The Winged Watchman*, ill. by author. Farrar, 1962. The Verhagen family, in constant danger from an informer, conceal a British pilot during the occupation. 10-12

### India

ARORA, SHIRLEY. *The Left-Handed Chank*. Follett, 1966. A village in India accepts modern ideas. 11-14
———. *"What Then, Raman?"* ill. by Hans Guggenheim. Follett, 1960. 10-12

BOTHWELL, JEAN. *The Little Flute Player*, ill. by Margaret Ayer. Morrow, 1949. Minor disasters stalk Teka, the little village flute player, and grow into tragedy when famine comes. The ten-year-old boy takes his father's place and saves his family from starvation. 9-12

GOBHAI, MEHLLI. *Lakshmi; The Water Buffalo Who Wouldn't*, ill. by author. Hawthorn, 1969. A simply written story about a family in India today. The tale has humor as well as an interesting setting, and the theme (mother and son amused at the come-down of father) a broad applicability. 7-9

MEHTA, RAMA. *The Life of Keshav; A Family Story from India*. McGraw, 1969. A very good story of contemporary India, the young protagonist caught between traditional patterns of living and the desire for an education that will inevitably change those patterns. 11-14

RANKIN, LOUISE. *Daughter of the Mountains*, ill. by Kurt Wiese. Viking, 1948. Tells of the journey of a little Tibetan village girl to far-off Calcutta in search of her stolen puppy. 10-13

SINGH, REGINALD LAL, and ELOISE LOWNSBERY. *Gift of the Forest*, ill. by Anne Vaughan. McKay, 1942 and 1958. In this distinguished story of rural India, Young Bim, a Hindu boy, finds a tiger cub and cares for it until he is forced to return it to the jungle. 11-14

SOMMERFELT, AIMÉE. *The Road to Agra*, ill. by Ulf Aas. Criterion, 1961. 10-11
———. *The White Bungalow*, ill. by Ulf Aas. Hale, 1963. 10-12

### Italy

BETTINA (pseud. for Bettina Ehrlich). *Pantaloni*, ill. by author. Harper, 1957. Colorfully illustrated, this is a warm story of Italian village life and of a little boy's search for his lost dog. 5-8

FLETCHER, DAVID. *Confetti for Cortorelli*, ill. by George Thompson. Pantheon, 1957. To be in the Children's Fancy Dress Parade, Angelo, an orphan of Sicily, needed a costume. How he earned it and gained a home as well makes an original and distinctive story. 6-8

REGGIANI, RENEE. *The Sun Train*, tr. from the Italian by Patrick Creagh. Coward, 1966. A mature story about a family that moves from an almost-feudal society in Sicily to find other problems just as serious in a contemporary Italian urban setting. 11-14

### Russia

FROLOV, VADIM. *What It's All About*, tr. by Joseph Barnes. Doubleday, 1968. 13-15

KASSIL, LEV. *Once in a Lifetime*, tr. by Anne Terry White. Doubleday, 1970. The first-person story of a thirteen-year-old Russian girl's experience as a movie find. The story has a Moscow setting, with good balance of school and family life and excellent characterization. 11-14

MAYAKOVSKY, VLADIMIR. *Timothy's Horse*, ad. by Guy Daniels, ill. by Flavio Costantini. Pantheon, 1970. A rhyming text that tells of a small boy whose wish comes true when he and his father buy a hobby horse. Marvelous illustrations. 5-7

TER HAAR, JAAP. *Boris*, tr. from the Dutch by Martha Mearns, ill. by Rien Poortvliet. Delacorte, 1970. 10-12

USHINSKY, K. *How a Shirt Grew in the Field*, ad. from the Russian by Marguerita Rudolph, ill. by Yaroslava. McGraw, 1967. 5-7

### Sweden

ANCKARSVÄRD, KARIN. *Aunt Vinnie's Invasion*, tr. by Annabelle MacMillan, ill. by William M. Hutchinson. Harcourt, 1962. The six Hallsenius children live with Aunt Vinnie for a year. This is an amusing story of modern Sweden. 10-13

———. *Doctor's Boy*, tr. from the Swedish by Annabelle MacMillan, ill. by Fermin Rocker. Harcourt, 1965. 10-12

BESKOW, ELSA. *Pelle's New Suit*, ill. by author. Harper, 1929. 12-15

LINDE, GUNNEL. *The White Stone*, tr. by Richard and Clara Winston, ill. by Imero Gobbato. Harcourt, 1966. Set in Sweden, the story of two children whose friendship ended a rather lonely life for each of them. The writing style is light and amusing and the relationship between the two is charming. 10-11

LINDGREN, ASTRID. *The Children on Troublemaker Street*, tr. by Gerry Bothmer, ill. by Ilon Wiklund. Macmillan, 1964. 7-9

———. *Rasmus and the Vagabond*, tr. by Gerry Bothmer, ill. by Eric Palmquist. Viking, 1960. Written in a more serious vein than the author's *Pippi Longstocking* series, this is an appealing story of a runaway orphan and the part-time tramp who befriended him. 9-12

LINDMAN, MAJ. *Snipp, Snapp, Snurr and the Red Shoes*, ill. by author. Whitman, 1932. The humorous adventures of three small boys earning money to buy their mother a pair of red shoes. 4-8

UNNERSTAD, EDITH. *The Saucepan Journey*, ill. by Louis Slobodkin. Macmillan, 1951. The Larrson children, all seven of them, spend a wonderful summer in the traveling caravan, helping father sell his saucepans through Sweden. 9-12

———. *The Spettecake Holiday*, tr. by Inger Boye, ill. by Iben Clante. Macmillan, 1958. 8-10

### Switzerland

BEMELMANS, LUDWIG. *Hansi*, ill. by author. Viking, 1934. 6-8

CHONZ, SELINA. *A Bell for Ursli*, ill. by Alois Carigiet. Walck, 1953. One of the most beautiful picture stories to come out of Europe, this is also the exciting story of a small Swiss boy determined to have the largest bell to ring in the spring procession. 6-9

RUTGERS VAN DER LOEFF-BASENAU, ANNA. *Avalanche!* tr. by Dora Round, ill. by Gustav Schrotter. Morrow, 1958. Holland's prize-winning children's book for 1955 tells the dramatic story of an avalanche that struck the tiny Swiss village of Urteli and how it affected three young boys. 11-13

SPYRI, JOHANNA. *Heidi* (see Forerunners).

ULLMAN, JAMES RAMSEY. *Banner in the Sky*. Lippincott, 1954. 12-14

### Other countries

AYER, JACQUELINE. *Nu Dang and His Kite*, ill. by author. Harcourt, 1959. A colorful introduction to Siamese life is provided by this story of a small boy's search along the river banks for his lost kite. *The Paper Flower Tree* (1962) is the story of a little girl of Thailand who at last finds her longed for ornamental tree. 6-8

BALET, JAN B. *Joanjo; A Portuguese Tale*, ill. by author. Delacorte, 1967. The story of Joanjo, a small Portuguese boy's acceptance of the independent life of the fisherman after dreams of glory. 5-7

BONZON, PAUL-JACQUES. *The Orphans of Simitra*, tr. from the French by Thelma Niklaus, ill. by Simon Jeruchim. Criterion, 1962. Orphaned by an earthquake in Greece, Porphyras and his little sister find a new home in Holland. The homesick Marina disappears and Porphyras works his way to Paris in search of her. Sensitively written and rich in background of people and places. 11-14

FREUCHEN, PETER. *Whaling Boy*, ill. by Leonard Everett Fisher. Putnam, 1958. Per List, not quite twelve, finds life aboard a Danish whaling ship a rugged and adventurous experience. A powerfully written and moving story. 10-13

FRIIS-BAASTAD, BABBIS. *Don't Take Teddy*, tr. from the Norwegian by Lise Sømme McKinnon. Scribner's, 1967. A moving story about a small boy who protects his older retarded brother. 10-13

HOUSTON, JAMES. *Akavak; An Eskimo Journey*, ill. by author. Harcourt, 1968. Young Akavak sets out on a dangerous journey alone with his grandfather. They reach their goal after seeming to be hopelessly lost, because of the acumen of the old man and the determination of the young one, and the courage of both. The stark illustrations reflect the elemental isolation of the setting. 9-11

KRUMGOLD, JOSEPH. *The Most Terrible Turk; A Story of Turkey*, ill. by Michael Hampshire. T. Crowell, 1969. Uncle Mustafa and Ali are all that are left of a once-large family. Their relationship is warm and appealing, and the setting, Turkey today, is interesting. 8-10

LINDQUIST, WILLIS. *Burma Boy*, ill. by Nicolas Mordvinoff. McGraw, 1953. Suspense and atmosphere combine to make this an absorbing story of a boy's search for a lost elephant. 9-11

MAYNE, WILLIAM. *The Old Zion*, ill. by Margery Gill. Dutton, 1967. 10-12

MERRILL, JEAN. *Shan's Lucky Knife*, ill. by Ronni Solbert. W. R. Scott, 1960. Young Shan outwits the tricky boatman who has taken all his possessions. An excellent read-aloud with a Burmese background and folk-tale flavor. 7-10

SEREDY, KATE. *The Good Master*, ill. by author. Viking, 1935. 10-12

———. *The Singing Tree*, ill. by author. Viking, 1939. 10-14

SHANNON, MONICA. *Dobry*, ill. by Atanas Katchamakoff. Viking, 1934. Newbery Medal. 10-13

● SOMMERFELT, AIMÉE. *Miriam*, tr. by Pat Shaw Iversen. Criterion, 1963. 12-15

SORENSON, VIRGINIA. *Lotte's Locket*, ill. by Fermin Rocker. Harcourt, 1964. 9-11

SPERRY, ARMSTRONG. *Call It Courage*, ill. by author. Macmillan, 1940. Newbery Medal. 10-13

● TAYLOR, SYDNEY. *A Papa Like Everyone Else*, ill. by George Porter. Follett, 1966. 9-11

● WATSON, SALLY. *To Build a Land*, ill. by Lili Cassel. Holt, 1957. War-orphaned Leo and his small sister, rescued from the streets of Naples, find a new life in a children's camp in Israel. 11-14

WOJCIECHOWSKA, MAIA. *Shadow of a Bull*, ill. by Alvin Smith. Atheneum, 1964. Newbery Medal. 12-15

WUORIO, EVA-LIS. *The Island of Fish in the Trees*, ill. by Edward Ardizzone. World, 1962. The day-long adventure of two little sisters who trail the doctor around the island to get him to mend their broken doll. The setting is the Balearic Islands, and both story and pictures are exceptionally appealing. 7-9

## SPORTS BOOKS

BISHOP, CURTIS. *Little League Victory*. Lippincott, 1967. Ed's temper tantrums make it difficult for him to be accepted as a member of the team, but he succeeds in getting over this obstacle. 9-11

CARSON, JOHN F. *The Coach Nobody Liked*. Farrar, 1960. A basketball coach who puts sportsmanship ahead of winning finds himself the central issue of a divided community. 12-15

CHRISTOPHER, MATT. *Johnny Long Legs*, ill. by Harvey Kidder. Little, 1970. 9-11

———. *Tough to Tackle*, ill. by Harvey Kidder. Little, 1971. 8-10

CORBETT, SCOTT. *The Baseball Bargain*, ill. by Wallace Tripp. Little, 1970. 9-11

DU BOIS, WILLIAM PÈNE. *Porko von Popbutton*, ill. by author. Harper, 1969. 9-11

GAULT, WILLIAM. *Stubborn Sam*. Dutton, 1969. 11-14

§ HEUMANN, WILLIAM. *Fastbreak Rebel*. Dodd, 1971. 11-14

§ HONIG, DONALD. *Johnny Lee*. McCall, 1971. 10-14

§ JACKSON, JESSE. *Anchor Man*, ill. by Doris Spiegel. Harper, 1947. 12 up

§ KESSLER, LEONARD. *Here Comes the Strikeout*, ill. by author. Harper, 1965. 7-8

● KONIGSBURG, E. L. *About the B'nai Bagels*, ill. by author. Atheneum, 1969. 10-12

§ LIPSYTE, ROBERT. *The Contender*. Harper, 1967. 12-15

LORD, BEMAN. *Shrimp's Soccer Goal*, ill. by Harold Berson. Walck, 1970. 7-9
All of Lord's stories about several sports are sound and enjoyable for readers in the middle group. 8-10

MAC PHERSON, MARGARET. *The Shinty Boys*, ill. by Shirley Hughes. Harcourt, 1963. 11-13

POTTER, MARGARET. *The Touch-and-Go Year*. Meredith, 1969. 10-12

§ QUIGLEY, MARTIN. *Today's Game*. Viking, 1965. 13 up

RENICK, MARIAN. *Boy at Bat*, ill. by Paul Galdone. Scribner's, 1961. An amusing story of a boy who gets into one baseball game and demands that his family now call him "Lefty." 7-9

———. *Take a Long Jump*, ill. by Charles Robinson. Scribner's, 1971. A track story that also has good family relationships. 9-11

SHORTALL, LEONARD. *Ben on the Ski Trail*, ill. by author. Morrow, 1965. 7-9

SLOTE, ALFRED. *Stranger on the Ball Club*. Lippincott, 1970.

§ ———. *Jake*. Lippincott, 1971. 9-11

THORVALL, KERSTIN. *Gunnar Scores a Goal*, tr. from the Swedish by Anne Parker, ill. by Serge Hollerbach. Harcourt, 1968. 8-10

§ TUNIS, JOHN. *All-American*, ill. by Hans Walleen. Harcourt, 1942. 10-14

———. *The Duke Decides*, ill. by James MacDonald. Harcourt, 1939.

———. *The Iron Duke*, ill. by Johan Bull. Harcourt, 1938. Among the best college stories we have for the precollege boy. *The Iron Duke* is about an Iowa boy's adjustments to Harvard. *The Duke Decides* finds him a member of the Olympic track team. 12-16

● ———. *Keystone Kids*. Harcourt, 1943. A fine sports story for the teen age—the happy resolution of anti-Semitic feeling is achieved by the students. 12-16

———. *The Kid from Tomkinsville*, ill. by J. H. Barnum. Harcourt, 1940. Roy Tucker, a small-town boy, makes a big-league baseball team. Fine story of his training, mistakes, and triumphs. The Tunis books are popular sports stories with a strong emphasis on community ideals. 11-15

● WEAVER, ROBERT. *Nice Guy, Go Home.* Harper, 1968. 12-15

WODEHOUSE, P. G. *Mike and Psmith.* Meredith, 1969. 11 up

## MYSTERY AND ADVENTURE BOOKS

AIKEN, JOAN. *The Cuckoo Tree,* ill. by Susan Obrant. Doubleday, 1971. Further adventures of Dido Twite. 10-12

______. *Nightbirds on Nantucket,* ill. by Robin Jacques. Doubleday, 1966. 10-12

ANCKARSVÄRD, KARIN. *The Robber Ghost,* tr. from the Swedish by Annabelle Macmillan, ill. by Paul Galdone. Harcourt, 1961. The disappearance of money from the post office housed in a wing of an old and supposedly haunted Swedish castle arouses the detective instincts of young schoolmates Michael and Cecilia. Good atmosphere and suspense for both boys and girls. 10-12

BERNA, PAUL. *A Truckload of Rice,* tr. from the French by John Buchanan Brown, ill. by Prudence Seward. Pantheon, 1970. 10-12

BONHAM, FRANK. *Mystery in Little Tokyo,* ill. by Kazue Mizumura. Dutton, 1966. 10-12

§★ ______. *Mystery of the Fat Cat,* ill. by Alvin Smith. Dutton, 1968 10-14

§ BONSALL, CROSBY. *The Case of the Cat's Meow,* ill. by author. Harper, 1965. All of the Bonsall books are charming and useful. 7-8

CAMERON, ELEANOR. *A Spell Is Cast,* ill. by Beth and Joe Krush. Little, 1964. 10-12

______. *The Terrible Churnadryne,* ill. by Beth and Joe Krush. Little, 1959. Did a strange prehistoric creature really stalk San Lorenzo peak? Tom and Jennifer and the whole town of Redwood Cove are caught up in the strange controversy. A unique, well-written tale of suspense. 9-12

CRIST, EDA and RICHARD. *The Secret of Turkeyfoot Mountain,* ill. by Richard Crist. Abelard, 1957. 10-12

DILLON, EILIS. *A Herd of Deer,* ill. by Richard Kennedy. Funk, 1970. 12-15

______. *The Singing Cave,* ill. by Stan Campbell. Funk, 1960. Suspense and mystery abound in this outstandingly written tale of the discovery and disappearance of Viking remains from a cave on an Irish isle. 12-15

GAGE, WILSON. *The Ghost of Five Owl Farm,* ill. by Paul Galdone. World, 1966. 10-12

GARFIELD, LEON. *Black Jack,* ill. by Antony Maitland. Pantheon, 1968. Other Garfield books, too. 11-14

GIBSON, WALTER B., ed. *Rogues' Gallery; A Variety of Mystery Stories,* ill. by Paul Spina. Doubleday, 1969. A better than usual anthology of mystery and detective stories, each one prefaced with a page of information about the author or the background for the particular story. 13 up

HIGHTOWER, FLORENCE. *Dark Horse of Woodfield,* ill. by Joshua Tolford. Houghton, 1962. The Woodfield home was a shabby relic, but it housed Buggsie and Maggie Armistead, who trained a horse, solved a mystery, and even bred cocoons to restore the family fortunes. A highly humorous and substantial family story with a background of New England. 11-13

______. *The Fayerweather Forecast,* ill. by Joshua Tolford. Houghton, 1967. 10-13

______. *The Ghost of Follonsbee's Folly,* ill. by Ati Forberg. Houghton, 1958. The newly bought dilapidated house in the country soon had the young Stockpoles trying to solve the mystery of its strange sounds and another puzzle as well. 11-14

______. *Mrs. Wappinger's Secret,* ill. by Beth and Joe Krush. Houghton, 1956. Eccentric Mrs. Wappinger of a Maine resort island is quite sure she has ancestral buried treasure somewhere on her property. Young Charlie Porter, summer visitor, is more than delighted to aid her in a secret treasure-hunting alliance. 11-14

JEFFRIES, RODERIC. *Patrol Car.* Harper, 1967.

______. *River Patrol.* Harper, 1969. 11-14

KAHN, JOAN, ed. *Some Things Fierce and Fatal.* Harper, 1971. 11-14

KÄSTNER, ERICH. *Emil and the Detectives,* ill. by Walter Trier. Doubleday, 1930. 9-11

LADD, ELIZABETH. *A Mystery for Meg,* ill. by Mary Stevens. Morrow, 1962. 9-11

L'ENGLE, MADELEINE. *The Arm of the Starfish.* Farrar, 1965. 12-15

§ LEXAU, JOAN. *The Homework Caper,* ill. by Syd Hoff. Harper, 1966. 6-7

§ ______. *The Rooftop Mystery,* ill. by Syd Hoff. Harper, 1968. 6-8

LINDGREN, ASTRID. *Bill Bergson Lives Dangerously,* tr. by Herbert Antoine, ill. by Don Freeman. Viking, 1954.

______ *Bill Bergson Master Detective,* tr. by Herbert Antoine, ill. by Louis Glanzman. Viking, 1952. These two mystery stories from the Swedish are told with considerable humor in spite of their dramatic plots. In *Bill Bergson, Master Detective* Bill and his friends Anders and Eva Lotta track down stolen jewels and restore them to the police. In the other book they identify a murderer. 10-13

MCLEAN, ALLAN CAMPBELL. *Master of Morgana.* Harcourt, 1959. Sixteen-year-old Niall solves the mystery of his older brother's injuries in this suspense-filled tale of fishermen and poachers on the Isle of Skye. 13-15

MAYNE, WILLIAM. *The Battlefield,* ill. by Mary Russon. Dutton, 1967. 9-11

______. *The Changeling,* ill. by Victor G. Ambrus. Dutton, 1963. 10-12

______. *Ravensgill.* Dutton, 1970. 12-15

MEADER, STEPHEN. *The Fish Hawk's Nest,* ill. by Edward Shenton. Harcourt, 1952. Exciting tale of smuggling on the New Jersey coast in the 1820's. Good characterizations and background. 11-14

MOYES, PATRICIA. *Helter-Skelter.* Holt, 1968. 12-15

NICOLE, CHRISTOPHER. *Operation Destruct.* Holt, 1969. 12-15

PEARCE, PHILLIPA. *The Minnow Leads to Treasure,* ill. by Edward Ardizzone. World, 1958. 10-12

PEASE, HOWARD. *Secret Cargo.* Doubleday, 1946. 12-14

POOLE, JOSEPHINE. *Catch as Catch Can,* ill. by Kiyo Komoda. Harper, 1970. 10-12

ROBERTSON, KEITH. *The Crow and the Castle*, ill. by Robert Greiner. Viking, 1957. A superior mystery tale involving two youthful amateur detectives. 11-14

———. *Ice to India*, ill. by Jack Weaver. Viking, 1955. 12-14

———. *The Money Machine*, ill. by George Porter. Viking, 1969. 10-12

———. *Three Stuffed Owls*, ill. by Jack Weaver. Viking, 1954. 12-14

RUGH, BELLE DORMAN. *Crystal Mountain*, ill. by Ernest H. Shepard. Houghton, 1955. 11-13

SHECTER, BEN. *Inspector Rose*, ill. by author. Harper, 1969. 6-8

SOBOL, DONALD. *Encyclopedia Brown Saves the Day*, ill. by Leonard Shortall. Nelson, 1970. 8-10

STEVENSON, ROBERT LOUIS. *Treasure Island*, ill. by C. B. Falls. World, 1946 (first pub. in 1883).

———. *Treasure Island*, ill. by N. C. Wyeth. Scribner's, 1945. 11-16

STORR, CATHERINE. *Lucy*, ill. by Victoria de Larrea. Prentice, 1968. 8-10

TURNER, PHILIP. *Colonel Sheperton's Clock*, ill. by Phillip Gough. World, 1966.

———. *The Grange at High Force*, ill. by W. T. Mars. World, 1967. 11-14

WHITNEY, PHYLLIS. *Mystery of the Green Cat*. Westminster, 1957. The discovery of a message long hidden in a ceramic cat brings peace to an old neighbor. 11-14

§ ———. *Secret of the Spotted Shell*, ill. by John Mecray. Westminster, 1967. 11-14

WINTERFELD, HENRY. *Detectives in Togas*, tr. from the German by Richard and Clara Winston, ill. by Charlotte Kleinert. Harcourt, 1956. 10-12

———. *Mystery of the Roman Ransom*, tr. from the German by Edith McCormick, ill. by Fritz Biermann. Harcourt, 1971. 10-13

WUORIO, EVA-LIS. *Save Alice!* Holt, 1968. 10-12

# Chapter 14
# Historical Fiction

The authors of historical fiction are usually aware that their young audience wants more than warmed-over history. To attract and hold children, these stories must not only be accurate but they must fulfill all the criteria of good fiction. The way the characters speak and dress must be right for the historical period in which they live; background information about social customs, prevalent ideas, and concurrent events should be accurate both for the sake of informing the child correctly and for the verisimilitude they give the story. It is in the small details of everyday living that the past is made understandable. When she first comes to the new land, the heroine of Patricia Clapp's *Constance* longs to look out the familiar diamond-paned window of her London bedroom, to feel "civilized cobbles" under her feet, to debark from the "stench-filled, rolling *Mayflower*." The best stories are so re-created that the people, places, and problems of the past seem almost as real to us as those we know today. They tell a good story regardless of the period—a story so absorbing that the historical background and details fall into a properly secondary place and do not seem an end in themselves. In Rachel Field's *Calico Bush* the details of pioneer life are vivid, but what we remember is the discrimination suffered by the French "bound-out" girl. And in the best of this genre, the problems and difficul-

## VIEWPOINTS

The historical novelist with a proper respect for history has a very stiff task before him; . . . the atmosphere of belief, the attitudes and assumptions of society that he conveys, must be in accordance with what is known of the mental and emotional climate of the place and period. It is by the striking of a false note here that one distinguishes the writer who has "got up" his subject, however painstakingly, from the one who has really soaked himself in it.—Helen Cam, *Historical Novels*, The Historical Society, London, 1961, pp. 4, 8.

ties of the past throw a helpful and sometimes reassuring light upon our problems today.

Hester Burton, in discussing her approach to the writing of historical fiction, mentions three rules: "First, I must acquaint myself as thoroughly as I possibly can with the historical period and the event I am describing. . . . My second rule is never to use a famous historical person as the pivot of my story and never to put into his mouth words or sentiments for which there is no documentary evidence. . . . When I come to describe the historical situation which I have chosen, I try to view it through the limited vision of a single character or group of characters."[1]

Like every rule that was ever made, Hester Burton's rules can be disregarded, but most writers of historical fiction are equally careful to back up their stories with research, to treat their historical characters with cautious respect, to confine their inventiveness to fictional ones, and to maintain with consistency the viewpoint of the main character or group of characters.

When does history stop being history and become "now"? Certainly the nine-year-old does not think of the 1950s as part of the recent past as his father may—and certainly his grandfather does! Children's time sense grows with experience and with the perspective that time itself brings. Therefore, what to include as "historical" fiction has required an arbitrary decision: this chapter discusses only those books whose backgrounds are no later than World War II. The books are divided into those for the youngest readers, the middle group, and the older readers, and are arranged within each group by the period or year of the setting for the title discussed, or the first title if there are several titles. All of the books, in varying degrees, comply with a major requirement of good historical fiction for young readers. The research and the authoritative historical milieu are there, but they do not overpower the story.

1. Hester Burton, "The Writing of Historical Novels," *Horn Book*, June 1969, pp. 271–272. Adapted from a paper given at the Loughborough School of Librarianship, August 1968.

## BOOKS FOR THE YOUNGEST

For young children who have little understanding of the past, historical fiction should be presented very simply, focusing on a person or just a few people, or on one problem or event. The story needs action and drama, and should avoid any references to events that demand knowledge not provided in the book. There is more historical fiction for young children being written now than in the past, and this trend will probably continue in order to meet the needs of the changing curriculum.

### BYRD BAYLOR SCHWEITZER

*One Small Blue Bead*

*One Small Blue Bead* (1965) lies lost and forgotten now, in the desert sand of Arizona, but once it was held in the hand of Boy. Very simply, a rhyming text tells a story about primitive men. Sitting around a cave fire, they talk of the possibility of there being other men somewhere, and the old man of the clan says he wants to see for himself, to wander to far-off lands. No, say his people, every man is needed to do his work. But Boy offers to do the old man's share, and he is happy when the old man comes back, and with him is—another boy! The stranger talks of drawings scratched in rock, of the roaring sea, and of roaming, restless bands of other men, and he gives Boy the brilliant blue bead he has brought. Beautifully illustrated, this book can evoke for the youngest children the prehistory of America and the beginnings of cultural diffusion, and it also suggests that people of a remote time were very like us.

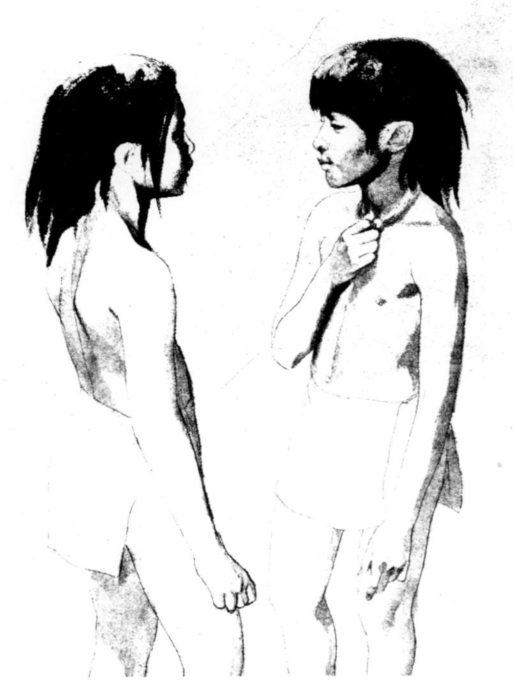

*Illustration by Symeon Shimin for* One Small Blue Bead *by Byrd Baylor Schweitzer. Copyright 1965. Reproduced by permission of The Macmillan Company, and World's Work Ltd., England. (Original with color)*

## CLYDE ROBERT BULLA

*John Billington, Friend of Squanto*

Clyde Bulla's books for children, both fiction and nonfiction, are distinguished for their simplicity of style combined with a dignified tone that makes them an excellent choice for the older child who finds reading difficult. *John Billington, Friend of Squanto* (1956) is a sequel to *Squanto* (1954) but is a more vigorous story and more detailed. Set in the Plymouth Colony, it concerns the lively boy captured by an unfriendly tribe and released through the intercession of Squanto.

In several periods in which there is little historical fiction for the middle group of readers, stories by Bulla can be found. *The Sword in the Tree* (1956), set in the reign of King Arthur, is the story of an eleven-year-old boy who goes to Camelot to ask for help when his wicked uncle takes possession of his father's castle. In *Viking Adventure* (1963) young Sigurd sails to Wineland with his father.

## NATHANIEL BENCHLEY

*Sam the Minuteman*

*Sam the Minuteman* (1969) is perhaps the most historically oriented of the books for young children, giving such background as "At that time, America was not a country of its own. It belonged to England," while avoiding such words as "colony," which might need explanation. Historically accurate, the book tells a lively tale that brings home, through the involvement of one boy, the impact of war on a child, and it adheres to a child's viewpoint. Sam had been told that if Paul Revere was right, and the British did show up, he might go along. "They want to keep us from being too strong," Father explained (another example of wise simplification). The first encounter with the British teaches the Minutemen to snipe at them rather than meet them. After this initiation, Sam goes to bed tired, worried about a wounded friend, and unaware that a war has started, but he has lost his fear and is ready to fight again.

## BRINTON TURKLE

*Obadiah the Bold*

*Obadiah the Bold* (1965), set in the early nineteenth century, is an engaging tale of the dreams of glory of a small Quaker boy who wants to become a pirate. He decides he will be a sailor like Grandfather after Father very cleverly talks about how brave a man Captain Obadiah Starbuck had been. The story has minimal historical significance, but the illus-

*Illustration by Brinton Turkle from* Obadiah the Bold *by Brinton Turkle. Copyright © 1965 by Brinton Turkle. Reprinted by permission of The Viking Press, Inc. (Original in color)*

trations show details of early Nantucket, and both this book and its sequel, *Thy Friend, Obadiah* (1969), can give children a sense of the period, the Quaker community, and the loving kindness of family life. The soft details of the illustrations are charming in themselves and they are accurately informative in showing costume, architecture, and artifacts of the period.

## FERDINAND MONJO

### *The Drinking Gourd*

A fine story about the Underground Railroad is told in *The Drinking Gourd* (1970), in which young Tommy Fuller, sent home from church because of a prank, wanders into the barn and finds a runaway slave family. The explanation given Tommy of the Railroad clarifies it for the reader as well as for Tommy, and he understands for the first time the degradation of slavery and the danger runaways face. When a search party comes along, Tommy quickly pretends that he himself is running away from home; the Marshal laughs and decides not to search the hay wagon, and so Tommy helps the cause. That night Father explains that he is, he knows, breaking a law but that he must. These are *people*. The story has suspense and action, and in Tommy's participation there is both the joy of achievement and an appreciation of ethical issues. In this, and in other books by Monjo set in other historical periods, there is always a sense of history and an emphasis on such qualities as courage, loyalty, and family love.

Monjo's *Pirates in Panama* (1970) describes the way in which Brother John defeated the pirate Henry Morgan and saved the gold for the church altar.

## CATHERINE COBLENTZ

*Martin and Abraham Lincoln*

Based on a true incident, *Martin and Abraham Lincoln* was first published in 1947 and reissued twenty years later. Martin's father is a prisoner of war, and his family is often dependent on the kindness of Snowden, a black neighbor, for their food. Martin, dressed in a soldier's garb, is waiting for Snowden one day when a tall man sees the small boy in Union blue and stops to talk. Martin knows it is Abraham Lincoln, but as he talks about his father in Andersonville, he cannot hold back his tears, and soon the man's long arms are holding him close. Lincoln solemnly complains about a nail in his shoe, knowing that Martin wants to be a cobbler like his father; Martin happily pounds out the nail in the President's shoe and when Snowden appears, the two new friends gravely salute each other and separate. The dialogue gives information about the war, and the story not only characterizes Lincoln but shows, poignantly, how the duress of war affects a child.

## OTHER BOOKS FOR THE YOUNGEST CHILDREN

One of the gayest books of historical fiction for young children is Arnold Lobel's *On the Day Peter Stuyvesant Sailed into Town* (1971), delightfully illustrated by the author, a story in rhythmic verse that describes the irascible Governor's successful efforts to clean up New Amsterdam.

Another story of colonial times is Alice Dalgliesh's *The Thanksgiving Story* (1954), a fictional account of the voyage of the *Mayflower* and the first year at Plymouth, culminating in the thanksgiving feast with the Indians. Centered in the experiences of the Hopkins family, especially the children, it is a remarkably moving little story told with dignity and avoiding stereotyped episodes. The colorful, somewhat stylized drawings complement the text.

Peggy Parish's *Granny and the Indians* (1969) is a humorous tale of pioneer times. Doughty Granny never realizes what a nuisance she is to the braves. The book is a pleasant antidote for stories of Indian savagery.

Betty Baker's *The Pig War* (1969) is based on a minor event in American-British relations, a dispute in 1859 over possession of a coastal island. In *Hill of Fire* (1971) by Thomas Lewis, the eruption of Paricutin in Mexico in 1943 is seen from the viewpoint of the farmer on whose land the volcano stood.

## BOOKS FOR THE MIDDLE GRADES

By the time they reach the middle grades, children have acquired a sense of the past and some perspective on its relation to the present. Their lively curiosity leads to conjecture about people of other times, and historical fiction that tells a good story about such people satisfies both their need to know and their appreciation of action. In the books for this group, most of the stories stress courage and problem-solving, and the preponderance of historical fiction is set in the comparatively familiar bounds of our own country's past.

## MARGUERITE DE ANGELI

*The Door in the Wall*

Marguerite de Angeli's Newbery Medal book, *The Door in the Wall* (1949), is set in thirteenth-century England. Robin's noble father is off to the wars and his mother is with the Queen when the plague strikes. Robin falls ill, unable to move his legs, and is deserted by the servants. Brother Luke finds the boy, takes him to the hospice, and cares for him. To the despairing Robin he says, "Always remember . . . thou hast only to follow the wall far enough and there will be a door in it." The monks teach the boy to use his hands and his head, "For reading is another door in the wall. . . ."

Robin learns to swim and to get around swiftly on his crutches, but his bent back never straightens. However, his spirit is strong, and he plays so heroic a part in saving a beleaguered city that the king honors him, and his parents are moved with joy and pride. This heartwarming story is beautifully illustrated in the author's most colorful style. The characters are less convincing than the situations, but the book is of great interest to all children, and brings special comfort to the handicapped.

### WILMA PITCHFORD HAYS

*May Day for Samoset*

Many of the books by Wilma Pitchford Hays are, like *May Day for Samoset* (1968), set in colonial times: *Pilgrim Thanksgiving* (1955) has good Indian-white relations, and *Christmas on the Mayflower* (1956) conveys something of the courage and faith of the first settlers. The setting for *May Day* is unusual—the island of Monhegan, Maine, where the colonists prepare to celebrate in the traditional English style with a Maypole. Susan Lull's decision to give her most precious possession, a kitten, to her good friend Samoset rather than fill his May Day basket with flowers is the focus of action in the story, but its historical interest is in the details of the May Day traditions and in the disapproval of the celebration expressed by the dour guests from the Plymouth colony.

### JEAN FRITZ

*The Cabin Faced West*
*Brady*

In *The Cabin Faced West* (1958) there isn't much to console little Ann. She misses her cousin in Gettysburg and there isn't another child in the pioneer country of Western Pennsylvania for her to play with until she finds a boy her own age. The high point of the story is a surprise visit from George Washington, an episode based on historical fact, but the most engaging incident is the one in which Ann's mother stops her work to play tea party with her lonely child.

*Brady* (1960) is a more mature story, set in the years just before the Civil War. Living in an area where people's feelings are divided, Brady is embarrassed by his father's strong anti-slavery feelings until events move him to take a position of responsibility. Both books are smoothly written and are convincing in their setting and in period details, but *Brady* also has a depth that stems from strong characterization and a vivid portrayal of the moral issues involved in the Abolitionist position.

*From Brady by Jean Fritz, illustrated by Lynd Ward. Copyright © 1960 by Jean Fritz. Reprinted by permission of Coward, McCann & Geohegan, Inc.*

## ALICE DALGLIESH

*The Bears on Hemlock Mountain*
*The Courage of Sarah Noble*

Alice Dalgliesh's *The Bears on Hemlock Mountain* (1952) can be read to five-year-olds and read by the eights. At first the story seems almost contemporary—a little boy is sent to his aunt's to borrow a kettle. But the kettle is a huge iron one, and Jonathan must go up and over a mountain—and there could be bears up there. His mother says that's all nonsense, that there are no bears on Hemlock Mountain. But there *are*, and Jonathan meets two big ones. What he does to save himself is surprising. For young children this story is a thriller, and they love quick-thinking Jonathan of long ago.

*The Courage of Sarah Noble* (1954) is more richly historical and, according to Miss Dalgliesh, a real episode of 1707. Little eight-year-old Sarah is sent into the wilderness to cook and care for her father because her mother cannot leave or move a sick baby. But before Sarah and her father set off, her mother wraps the little girl in a cloak as warm as her love and says, "Keep up your courage, Sarah Noble." Little Sarah travels to her mother's marching words, and when wolves threaten them in the forest, or they sleep in strange cabins with unfriendly folk, or Sarah is left alone with an Indian family, she wraps her mother's cloak and her words warmly about her and keeps up her courage. When this story was read to a particularly timid urban youngster just Sarah's age, her teacher asked, "Pat, do you think you could do what Sarah did?" Pat, big-eyed and grave, said slowly, "Well, I'd be awful scared but I'd try. Yes, I could do it, I know I could." That is one of the wonderful results of historical stories—they give youngsters new vistas and stretch their young spirits.

*The Fourth of July Story* (1956) must have been more difficult to write, with its large gallery of leading characters and the complex theme of independence and restoration of good relationships with England. But again Miss Dalgliesh has selected her people and episodes so carefully that the story is dramatic and not too complicated for the understanding and enjoyment of children.

*Adam and the Golden Cock* (1959) is a Revolutionary War story in which a boy is caught in the conflict between friendship and loyalty, for Adam's friend Paul is from a Tory family. Children of today, aware of conflicting opinions about controversial issues, may see the timeless application of such conflict.

## WALTER D. EDMONDS

*The Matchlock Gun*

Walter D. Edmonds is the author of the popular adult book *Drums Along the Mohawk*. His first book for children, *The Matchlock Gun*, was given the Newbery Medal in 1942. A mother, alone with her baby and young son, suddenly discovers that Indians are near. Her little boy, who has been trained to fire an old matchlock gun at her signal, stays on guard in the house while she watches outside until the Indians discover her. As the Indians start for her, she gives the signal, the gun goes off on schedule, but she falls unconscious with a tomahawk through her shoulder. The suspense in this story is almost unbearable, and the terrifying climax is heightened by lurid pictures.

Unfortunately, whatever the book offers in showing the child's courage and his achievement, however dramatic the suspense, *The Matchlock Gun* gives only one side of red-white relations and perpetuates the false image of the Indian as a cruel savage. The book is well written, and the preliminary glimpse of happy family relationships balances somewhat the harrowing quality of the story, one that reminds us that historical fiction for children must be more than authentic. It must seem as probable and possible as life today. The extraordinary may enter in, as it does in modern life, but it should not constitute the whole story. Life for most people has only its occasional moments of terror or rapture or triumph. Focusing a whole story upon such moments not only leans toward sensationalism but puts an undue strain on the reader's credulity. Mr. Edmonds barely skirts these pitfalls.

## ELIZABETH COATSWORTH

*Away Goes Sally*
*The Fair American*

The Newbery Medal was given to Elizabeth Coatsworth's *The Cat Who Went to Heaven*, a fanciful tale, exquisite and sad, involving a poor artist, a humble cat, and a Buddhist miracle. But the children like her historical fiction much better, particularly *Away Goes Sally* (1934), *Five Bushel Farm* (1939), and *The Fair American* (1940). Her writing has an easy flow and establishes unerringly the mood and temper of the tale. Take the opening page of *The Fair American:*

> *The first thing that Pierre saw as he wakened was the moonlight that lay across the darkness of his room like the blade of some great sword. Jean, the old valet, was beside him, or at least the boy thought so; but since the man, whoever he was, carried no light, he could not be certain until he heard Jean's voice low and urgent:*
>
> *"Get up, Master Pierre, quickly. They are coming back, I think."*[2]

Here is suspense, something hushed and fearful in every line, and that one phrase, "like the blade of some great sword," strikes the note of terror that is to recur throughout the book. The story has to do with a boy of the French aristocracy, escaping from the terrorists after the French Revolution. This beginning establishes the atmosphere and the suspense. Contrast it with the first page of *Away Goes Sally*. There the chatter of the aunts sounds the prevailing feminine note.

2. From *The Fair American*. The Macmillan Company, 1940. Reprinted by permission.

*Away Goes Sally* has to do with the migration of Sally's whole family of uncles and aunts from Massachusetts to Maine not long after the American Revolution. The family travels in a little house on sledges pulled by six yoke of oxen, and the story moves along as leisurely as the little house. *Five Bushel Farm* sees the family established on their new farm. Andy joins Sally's circle of friends and introduces a desirable masculine note into their activities. In *The Fair American*, the French boy, Pierre, ships on an American sailing vessel. Sally's resourcefulness saves Pierre's life when a French officer boards the ship to look for refugees. Again, as in the books of Cornelia Meigs, the past throws fresh light on some of the poignant problems of the present, and the *Fair American*, bearing to our shores the stricken refugee child, is a moving symbol. These three books about the early nineteenth century appeal to children of ten or eleven. The exquisite poems dividing the chapters (see p. 362) add to their unusual value and charm.

## CAROL RYRIE BRINK

*Caddie Woodlawn*

In addition to the great historical stories about our country, there is another kind of book which, although its scenes may be laid in the colonial or Revolutionary period, is not primarily historical fiction because interest is centered in the *story*, and not in a historical period. *Little Women* is such a book; its setting is the Civil War period, but it is predominantly a story of family life.

Like *Little Women, Caddie Woodlawn* (1935) belongs to the Civil War period, but the war plays no part in the story. Caddie and her family lived in Wisconsin when Indians were considered a menace, but life on the whole was fairly comfortable. Red-headed Caddie, the tomboy, and her two brothers extracted every possible bit of fun and adventure the frontier settlement could yield.

Caddie's long friendship with the Indians and her courageous personal appeal to them helped prevent a threatened uprising.

The fun Caddie gets out of life suggests the usefulness of this book in the historical group in counteracting the overseriousness of most historical fiction. One little girl said, "I just hate pioneer stories. All the people do is struggle and struggle and struggle!" To such a child we may well give *Caddie Woodlawn*, if only to prove that the children of the frontier had their fun, too.

## LAURA INGALLS WILDER

*Little House in the Big Woods*
and other stories

As has been noted, children's sense of the past is a confused one at best. Gas burners are more incredible to them than candlelight, and horse-and-buggy travel quite as odd as a trip by canal boat. Indeed, it may be easier for them to understand and enter into the colonial period of American history than into the more immediate past. The pioneering and settling of the Midwest have fewer picturesque details than has the dramatic first colonization. Frontier life has more of the humdrum "struggle" the little girl complained of, less romantic adventure. Until Laura Ingalls Wilder undertook the writing of her family's experiences in settling the Midwest, there were no books of this period which really held children's interest.

In 1953 Mrs. Wilder's publisher reissued the books with new illustrations by Garth Williams, and the Children's Services Division of the American Library Association presented a special and long overdue award to Mrs. Wilder for her "substantial and lasting contribution to children's literature." Children love all the books and grow up with the Ingalls girls and the Wilder boys, from *Little House in the Big Woods* (1932) to the romantic *These Happy Golden Years* (1943) when Laura Ingalls and Almanzo Wilder are married. The first book appeals to children of eight or nine; the last is written for the almost-grown-up girl, who by this time may feel that Laura is an old and dear friend. Few other books give children this sense of continuity and progress.

The saga begins with the Ingalls family in their log cabin in the Wisconsin forests, *Little House in the Big Woods*. (See also the discussion of this book in Chapter 2.) The children are all girls. The oldest is Mary (who later goes blind), then the active Laura, and baby Carrie. Grace eventually displaces Carrie as the baby. In this first book we become acquainted with Ma's skill in cooking wonderful, triumphant meals out of limited resources, and especially we know her good bread, baked every Saturday. It fills the small cabin with its delicious fragrance and nourishes the girls' growing bodies even as Pa's gay songs and fiddle music nourish their spirits. Here, too, we first see the little china woman which Ma is to carry with her through all their journeys. She puts it over the fireplace only when the dwelling is worthy, a real house and home. All these things give the children a sense of comfort and security.

Next, the family moves out to the wild Kansas country and begins the adventures described in the *Little House on the Prairie* (1935). *On the Banks of Plum Creek* (1937) finds the Ingalls family in Minnesota; *By the Shores of Silver Lake* (1939) carries them to the Dakota Territory, where they remain either on their lake or in town.

*Farmer Boy* (1933) begins the account of the Wilder family of boys on their prosperous New York farm. We follow Almanzo Wilder from his first day at school to the proud moment when he is given his own colt to break and train. In this book the modern child is given incidentally a sense of money values in terms of human labor. Almanzo knows fifty cents as so many hours of backbreaking toil over the family potato crop.

*The Long Winter* (1940) finds the Ingalls family living in town. Of the whole series,

## VIEWPOINTS

. . . the historical novelist does not merely acquire information about the past, but absorbs it into his mind. Atmosphere comes out in his books as the overflow of a personality that has made a peculiar appropriation of history. It comes as part of the man himself.

. . . The virtue and power of the novelist's depiction of men, is not that he observes perpetually and arranges data, but that he enters into the experiences of others, he runs his life into the mould of their lives, he puts himself under the conditioning circumstances of their thinking. He can feel with people unlike himself and look at the world with their eyes and grapple with the issues of life that meet them, because he can put himself in their place, that is to say, because his experience is not entirely and merely his own. It is precisely because personality is not cut off from personality, and a man is not entirely locked up within himself, . . . that the novelist can so to speak transpose himself and catch life into a person other than himself.—H. Butterfield, *The Historical Novel*, Cambridge University Press, London, 1924, pp. 107, 111.

this book is one no modern child should miss. One blizzard follows another until the railroads cease to run and the little town is cut off from supplies for months. Fuel gives out, and the family has to twist straw into sticks to burn. Ma devises a button lamp to save oil. All day the sound of their little hand mill is heard as different members of the family take turns grinding wheat, their last stand against hunger. Finally the wheat begins to give out, and the whole community faces starvation. Then it is Almanzo Wilder, not Pa Ingalls, who rides out into the trackless, snow-driven prairie to buy wheat from a farmer who has it. He succeeds, and the conclusion of the book is happy and humorous. *Little Town on the Prairie* (1941) and *These Happy Golden Years* (1943) carry Laura into teaching and then into marriage with Almanzo. *The First Four Years* (1971), a posthumous book, tells of Laura and Almanzo's first year as struggling farmers. In *These Happy Golden Years*, a title which speaks for the whole series, Laura Ingalls Wilder wrote in her daughter's copy:

> *And so farewell to childhood days,*
> *Their joys, and hopes and fears.*
> *But Father's voice and his fiddle's song*
> *Go echoing down the years.*[3]

### OTHER BOOKS FOR THE MIDDLE GROUP

Although *The Apple and the Arrow* (1951), by Mary and Conrad Buff, is set in 1292, the story of Switzerland's revolt against Austria has pertinence for young readers today. The tale of the legendary William Tell's leadership is seen from the point of view of the young son from whose head, according to the story, the apple was shot. Roderick Haig-Brown's *The Whale People* (1963) describes the training of a young chief of the Hotsath people of the Nootka Indians in pre-Columbian times, a book that gives a dignified picture of the great whale hunters. Set in the sixteenth century, Sulamith Ish-Kishor's *A Boy of Old Prague* (1963) explores the theory that acquaintance can eradicate prejudice. In this story a Bohemian peasant boy learns, when he comes to work for a Jewish family, how many misconceptions he had had. The martial figures of Nicolas Sidjakov's handsome four-color illustrations add to the appeal of a story based on an incident in Napoleon's life—*The Emperor and the Drummer Boy* (1962), by Ruth Robbins.

Two good Civil War stories for the middle group are Ferdinand Monjo's *The Vicksburg Veteran* (1971) and Rhoda Bacmeister's *Voices in the Night* (1965). In the Monjo

3. Irene Smith, "Laura Ingalls Wilder and the Little House Books," *The Horn Book*, September-October 1943, p. 306. Delightful account of Mrs. Wilder, with family photographs of Ma, Pa, the four girls, and Almanzo.

*Illustration by Nicolas Sidjakov. From* The Emperor and the Drummer Boy *by Ruth Robbins. Copyright 1962 by Nicolas Sidjakov and Ruth Robbins. Reproduced with permission of Parnassus Press. (Original in color)*

story, General Grant's son participates in the victory that gains the Union forces control of the Mississippi; in the Bacmeister story, a small girl visiting a family that operates a station on the Underground Railroad uses her wits to help one runaway escape.

The story of Little Big Horn is told by fifteen-year-old Red Hawk in *Red Hawk's Account of Custer's Last Battle* (1970), by Paul and Dorothy Goble. Red Hawk, the only fictional character, says, sadly, "Once all the earth was ours; now there is only a small piece left which the White Men did not want." He knows that the cause is lost despite the victory won by the Indians. The list of sources indicates the research that gives the book its authenticity of historical detail.

Another story of the 1870s is *Molly's Hannibal* (1957), by Robert J. Willis. The setting is an Erie Canal houseboat, and added to the interest of the locale and the period is the perception Molly gains. When she makes a sacrifice to help pay for a veterinarian for her mule Hannibal, she learns what it means to love and why her mother has given up a settled life to be with her husband on his journeys.

For children who have never experienced the horror of war, books that tell of the plight of children in wartime can evoke a deeper understanding. Alki Zei's *Wildcat Under Glass* (1968, first published in 1963 in Greece), translated from the Greek by Edward Fenton, is a story of life under the oppression of dictatorship as it is seen through the eyes of a child, Melia, who lived on a Greek island during the time of prewar German occupation. The story, which begins in August 1936, has drama and momentum, and is particularly effective in showing the reactions of the very young to a rigid regime.

In Susan Cooper's *Dawn of Fear* (1970) a small group of boys, busy with their games and school, is shocked into awareness and fear when one of their number is killed in an air raid. Arnold Elliott's *A Kind of Secret Weapon* (1969) is a book for the more mature readers in this group, the story of a Danish boy who risks his life to help his parents run an underground newspaper.

## BOOKS FOR OLDER CHILDREN

For older readers, there are no time barriers, and in their historical fiction there is no need to avoid the complexities of social movements and relationships that existed in the past as they do today. Erik Haugaard's Hakon can move from one cultural pattern to another, Rosemary Sutcliff's Aquila can have a divided allegiance that young people understand. They can enjoy the rich tapestry of a story that has intricate patterns of action in an unfamiliar setting and the implications that past events have for the present.

## LUCILE MORRISON

*The Lost Queen of Egypt*

For the superior reader, the child who at twelve or thirteen can read anything he wishes to, Lucile Morrison's *The Lost Queen of Egypt* (1937) is a thrilling story. The heroine is Ankhsenpaaten, the Pharaoh's third daughter, a lively, mischievous five-year-old at the beginning of the story. Through her eyes, the reader sees the court ceremonies, the dress, the foods, and the customs of an ancient Egyptian kingdom.

The story begins about 1580 B.C. in the royal nurseries of Akhenaten, Pharaoh of Egypt, and Nefertiti, his queen. Their six little daughters are being arrayed for the arrival of the Great Royal Mother, who decides that three of the little girls must be betrothed at once to guarantee the succession. Ankhsenpaaten is relieved when the soldierly Tutankhaten is chosen for her, since he alone of the royal blood has shown a reckless courage and vitality equal to her own.

Later, a series of deaths calls this popular young pair to the throne; they become Tutankhamon and Ankhsenamon and seem destined to happiness and a long reign. Instead, the young king dies by poisoning, and the queen is trapped in the palace to be forced either to marry the traitorous Ay or to die herself. How Kenofer the artist rescues her; how, in disguise, they turn to the river and live on their boat like hundreds of humble river people; and how the tragic young queen learns at last that she can find happiness only by ceasing to be a queen make a satisfying end to a fine story.

*The King and Queen Hunting*

*Illustration by Winifred Brunton. From* The Lost Queen of Egypt *by Lucile Morrison. Copyrighted 1937 by J. B. Lippincott Company. Reprinted by permission of the publishers.*

## ELOISE JARVIS McGRAW

*Mara, Daughter of the Nile*

Another novel of ancient Egypt is *Mara* (1953), which parents may possibly read along with their twelve-year-olds. It is a hair-raising tale of royal intrigue, spies, and true love, in the days when a feminine Pharaoh, Hatshepsut, has usurped the throne from the rightful king. Mara is a slave who vaguely remembers better days and is determined to escape. She is bought by a mysterious man who offers her luxury if she will serve at court as a spy for the queen. She accepts, and also sells her services as a spy for the king to a young nobleman, Lord Sheftu. Eventually, her love for Sheftu and a deep pity for the wronged king change her from a liar and a cheat to a selfless heroine who endures torture rather than betray her new loyalties. The action is terrifying. Detailed pictures emerge of the daily life of different classes—shopkeepers, rivermen, soldiers, slaves, and royalty.

A second book about ancient Egypt by this writer is *The Golden Goblet* (1961). While it is not quite so powerful a tale as *Mara*, it, too, affords a detailed picture of the times, with a vigorous plot and convincing characters.

## HANS BAUMANN

*I Marched with Hannibal*

Hans Baumann, a German schoolteacher, chooses dramatic material, so that his stories are always exciting, even though sometimes slowed down by details. In *I Marched with Hannibal* (1962), an old man tells two children about his boyhood experiences, a narrative device that gives the book a sense of immediacy and scope for vivid personal accounts of the marches and battle scenes. Baumann's historical fiction usually concerns an important figure and a worthwhile theme. In *The Barque of the Brothers* (1958) the theme is the affectionate bond between two Portuguese sailors of the fifteenth century, a bond echoed in the relationship between Prince Henry, who inspired the naval expeditions, and his brother Fernando. In *Sons of the Steppe*, two of Genghis Khan's grandsons, who were young warriors together, meet as enemies later in life after their paths have diverged. Baumann's historical personages are never stock characters but are vividly depicted to add depth to splendid stories with authentic background.

## OLIVIA E. COOLIDGE

*Egyptian Adventures*

Although the stories in *Egyptian Adventures* (1954) are at junior-high-school reading level, many of them may be read aloud to elementary-school children who are having their first look at the ancient world. Olivia E. Coolidge is a scholar, and in the course of these entertaining tales she gives children lively pictures of the Egyptians' superstitions and magic, harvests and hunts, festivals and funerals. The characters emerge fully drawn and colorfully alive. These twelve well-written stories will do much to develop children's feeling for the people and adventures of a far-distant past.

*Men of Athens* (1962), *Roman People* (1959), and *People in Palestine* (1965) are in the same format, each tale complete in itself and the whole giving a remarkably vivid picture of the diversity of the culture in a historical period. *The King of Men* (1966) is a complex and absorbing novel based on the Agamemnon legend, and *Marathon Looks on the Sea* (1967) provides a sharp immediacy to the Battle of Marathon. The central character is a boy whose allegiance is torn between his own Greek people and the Persian king who has become his friend. In all these books, the combination of scholarly research and a fine writing style creates the period so convincingly that the reader has no sense of a disparate culture; each detail of rites and customs, of mores and superstitions is an integral part of the story.

## ISABELLE LAWRENCE

*The Gift of the Golden Cup*

Isabelle Lawrence's stories pile action upon action and intrigue upon intrigue, but her characters are exuberantly alive and entertaining. In *The Gift of the Golden Cup* (1946) twelve-year-old Atia and her seven-year-old brother, Gaius, are children of the famous Roman family of Julians, with Julius Caesar for an uncle. While their parents are away from home, there is a well-organized revolt of the slaves, a terrifying experience for the children. They find themselves, after a series of misadventures, on a pirate ship, slaves of the captain. Their captor is kind to them, but both children learn the bitterness their own slaves, some of them of noble birth, must feel. The adventures of the young Julians include sea battles, the sinking of a ship, rescue, and a long journey home with a young Roman and two slaves. Once home, the children persuade their father to free the two Greek slaves who helped them. Later the mother of the former slaves invites Atia and Gaius to visit the family in Athens. This visit provides an interesting chance to contrast Roman and Greek life. It also supplies more action and a mystery which continues in the second book, *The Theft of the Golden Ring* (1948), an equally complex and exciting story.

Were it not for Isabelle Lawrence's ability to bring her characters vividly to life, from the irrepressible Gaius to Caesar himself, these books might be merely action-packed thrillers of small value. But besides an impressive gallery of well-drawn characters, the stories provide unforgettable pictures of Greek and Roman houses, cities, ships, clothes, food, slave conditions, patrician luxuries and obligations, schools for the boys, and the duties of girls and women. These may remain in memory when some of the action is forgotten.

### HENRY TREECE

*Viking's Dawn*

An English poet, critic, and teacher, Henry Treece is distinguished both for the sonorous quality of his prose and for his ability to create convincingly the mood and language of the distant past. *Viking's Dawn* (1956) is the first of a trilogy about Harald Sigurdson who, in the eighth century, was the only man on his crew to return from a voyage filled with disasters. In *The Road to Miklagard* (1957) Sigurdson becomes a Moorish slave and travels to Constantinople and then to Russia; and in *Viking's Sunset* (1961) the Vikings come to a new land and live with Eskimos and Indians.

Treece uses ancient Britain as a setting for such lively tales as *The Centurion* (1967), a story of a Roman legionnaire. Like Rosemary Sutcliff, he is so steeped in history that his stories have a remarkable unity: details of dress and architecture, language, and references to other events have a consistency that makes his books convincing and alive.

### ERIK CHRISTIAN HAUGAARD

*Hakon of Rogen's Saga*

*Hakon of Rogen's Saga* (1963) is not a traditional saga but a realistic story taking place in the last days of the Vikings. The rocky, mountainous island of Rogen, where Hakon was born, has been handed down in his family from father to son for generations. To Hakon, Rogen Island and his powerful father seem indestructible and their home the best of all places to live, especially after Thora, his gentle stepmother, comes bringing love both to the boy and his father. But Thora was a kidnapped bride, and so when spring comes, her father sends three ships and many men to bring her back. When the bloody battles are over, Hakon is an orphan at the mercy of his treacherous uncle, who wants Rogen for his own. How Hakon suffers enslavement and brutal treatment, bides his time, finds a hideout in the mountain caves, mobilizes his few loyal men, and eventually takes Rogen again reads much like an old Norse saga. The author, a Dane steeped in Icelandic sagas, says at the beginning:

> *"Your dog, your horse, your friend, and you yourself: all shall die. Eternally live only your deeds and man's judgment over them," this was the credo of the Vikings.*

Throughout the book their philosophy of living and dying is stated or chanted and at the end of the book when Hakon has won Rogen and rescued Helga, with whom he had been raised, he says to her:

> *That is everyone's birthright, his freedom, and the gods have only one message for us, that we must live.*

In this book the Vikings are of heroic stature and the author clothes their story with nobility.

Its sequel, *A Slave's Tale* (1965), is told by the small slave girl Helga, to whom Hakon is like a beloved brother. Their affection ripens into love, but this is a minor facet of the story, which is primarily a tale of a voyage to Frankland in a longboat. The writing, in explication and dialogue as well as in the period details, vividly creates the historical milieu and has the sweep and cadence of a Norse epic.

*The Rider and His Horse* (1968) is set in ancient Israel, and *Orphans of the Wind* (1966) takes place during the time of the American Civil War.

## ROSEMARY SUTCLIFF

*The Lantern Bearers*
*Dawn Wind*

Most critics would say that at the present time the greatest writer of historical fiction for children and youth is unquestionably Rosemary Sutcliff. Her books are superior not only because they are authentic records of England's earliest history with its bloody raids and its continuous wars for occupation by Norsemen, Romans, Normans, and Saxons, but also because every one of her memorable books is built around a great theme. Her characters live and die for principles they value and that men today still value.

The theme of all her stories, as Margaret Meek[4] points out, is "the light and the dark. The light is what is valued, what is to be saved beyond one's own lifetime. The dark is the threatening destruction that works against it." In *The Lantern Bearers* (1959)[5] the blackness of despair is concentrated in the heart of Aquila, a Roman officer who, when a Saxon raid sweeps down on his father's farm, sees his father slain, and his sister Flavia carried off by the raiders. He himself is left tied to a tree for the wolves and later made a slave by another band. Years later, after he has escaped his thralldom, an old friend says to him:

> *It may be that the night will close over us in the end, but I believe that morning will come again. . . . We are the Lantern Bearers, my friend; for us to keep something burning, to carry what light we can forward into the darkness and the wind.*

No briefing of these stories can give any conception of their scope and power, and when young people read them they live with nobility. The sooner our children can begin to read these Sutcliff books the better, as they will help to build intellectual maturity. Nevertheless, these are difficult books, not because of vocabulary problems, but because of the complexities of the plots in which many peoples are fighting for dominance. In England, where the children have some background of their own history, these books are recommended for the elevens to sixteens. Most of our eleven-year-olds would find them hard going.

Fortunately, *Dawn Wind* (1962), one of the finest of the books, is also the least complex. Chronologically it follows *The Lantern Bearers*, but it is complete in itself and will undoubtedly send some readers to the trilogy. For the fourteen-year-old hero Owain, the light of the world seems to have been extinguished. He finds himself the sole survivor of a bloody battle between the Saxons and the Britains in which his people, the Britains, were completely destroyed. In the gutted remains of the city from which he had come, the only life the boy finds is a pitiable waif of a girl, lost and half-starved. At first Owain and Regina are bound together in mutual misery, but eventually they are united in respect and affection. So when Regina is sick and dying, Owain carries her to a Saxon settlement, even though he knows what will happen to him. The Saxons care for the girl but sell Owain into slavery. Like Aquila, Owain can do nothing less than serve his master with all his skill and strength. This proud, competent youth is loved and trusted by his master and his family. If sometimes despair almost overcomes Owain, his work, in which there is both conflict and triumph, absorbs him. After eleven years, he is freed and sets out at once

4. *Rosemary Sutcliff.* A Walck Monograph, Walck, 1962.
5. *The Lantern Bearers* is the third book in a trilogy which also includes *The Eagle of the Ninth* and *The Silver Branch.*

to find his people and Regina, who has never doubted he would come for her.

So life is not snuffed out by the night. A dawn wind blows and two people start all over again with those basic qualities that have always made for survival. Whether it is her great trilogy or *The Shield Ring* (1957) or *The Outcast* (1955) or *Warrior Scarlet* (1958), Rosemary Sutcliff gives children and youth historical fiction that builds courage and faith that life will go on and is well worth the struggle.

## HOWARD PYLE

*Otto of the Silver Hand*
*Men of Iron*

Howard Pyle was steeped in the traditions and customs of the Middle Ages. He not only wrote fascinating stories about them, but provided powerful illustrations for his own books from a storehouse of detailed and seemingly inexhaustible information. The convincing dialogue in his tales, while not of course reproducing exactly the speech of the period, suggests it. Old speech forms and difficult words make hard reading in places but add to the flavor of the tale. His running narrative is always clear, direct, and vigorous, and how he loves fights! These range from terrible to farcical, but each story has a liberal sprinkling of them. His books are excellent to read aloud and are exciting materials on which the good readers may try their mettle.

*Otto of the Silver Hand* (1888) is a horrifying tale of the robber barons of Germany. One of these had plundered ruthlessly. For revenge, his enemies struck off the hand of his only son, the delicate Otto. Later, because of the silver substitute, the boy was known as Otto of the Silver Hand. The story presents two phases of the life of the period: the turbulent life within the castle strongholds of the robber barons and the peaceful, scholarly pursuits of the monks within their great monasteries. The mutilation of the boy is gently handled. There are no details, only the infinite pathos of a child in the power of cruel men.

Pyle's *Men of Iron* (1892) is popular with boys from twelve to fourteen. The sixteen-year-old Myles Falworth is sent to be a squire to a powerful earl. There he learns that his own father is practically an outlaw, suspected of being one of the plotters against the king's life. In the earl's great castle, Myles is trained in all the intricate feats of knighthood and in the code of chivalry and is eventually knighted. He frees his father from suspicion and wins the earl's daughter for his wife. Myles has to battle with his own impulsiveness and his too-quick temper as well as with his enemies. This is one of the outstanding books about medieval England.

*Illustration by Howard Pyle from* Otto of the Silver Hand *by Howard Pyle. Copyright, 1916, by Anne Poole Pyle. Reprinted by permission of the publisher, Charles Scribner's Sons.*

## CYNTHIA HARNETT

*Nicholas and the Wool-Pack*
*Caxton's Challenge*

Cynthia Harnett's sketches add to the wealth of informative detail about fifteenth-century England in *Nicholas and the Wool-Pack*, winner of the Carnegie Award in 1951 under its British title, *The Wool-Pack*. It is not only an exciting story with an element of mystery, but also a colorful picture of the weaving industry and of everyday life of the period. Nicholas, an apprentice to his father, a wool merchant, foils the two Lombardians who are secretly attempting to ruin his father.

Another smoothly written story of the same period is *Caxton's Challenge* (*The Load of Unicorn* [1968] in the British edition), which gives a vivid picture of London at that time, both the text and the maps indicating the careful research that lends authenticity to historical fiction. Again an apprentice is a leading character; Bendy is entranced by the printing machines of his master, William Caxton, and becomes involved in the struggles Caxton has against the resentful scriveners.

## MARCHETTE CHUTE

*The Wonderful Winter*
*The Innocent Wayfaring*

Marchette Chute, the author of *Shakespeare of London* and similar studies of Chaucer and Ben Jonson for adult readers, has also written some delightful stories for young people. *The Wonderful Winter* (1954) carries young readers straight into Shakespeare's theater with young Robin, Sir Robert Wakefield, who has escaped from an intolerable home situation. London seems to spell starvation for him until he is befriended by some actors and is taken into the home of the famous John Heminges. Through the warmth and affection of this crowded household, young Robin learns to give and accept love and gaiety. Meanwhile he works and plays small parts in the Burbage Theater, knows the great Shakespeare, and falls in love with *Romeo and Juliet*. When Robin returns to his castle and his duties, he is happy and confident as a result of his wonderful winter.

*The Innocent Wayfaring* (first published in 1943 and reissued in 1955) is fourteenth-century England brought vividly and authentically to life. Anne is so averse to learning the arts of housewifery that she runs away from her convent school with the prioress' pet monkey for company. The monkey is responsible for her meeting Nick, a poet and a most resourceful young man. He tries to get away from her, but Anne sticks like a bur. Their adventures provide a view of fourteenth-century life, from seamy inns to manor houses. After three days Nick takes Anne back to her family with the agreement that when she has learned housewifery and he his father's business, Nick will come for her. Meanwhile, they have the memory of three enchanting days which led them back to home and responsibility.

Both books are beautifully written by a scholar who can paint a glowing background for her charming stories.

## ELIZABETH JANET GRAY

*Adam of the Road*
*I Will Adventure*

Another book about the medieval period which children should not miss is the Newbery Medal winner for 1943, Elizabeth Janet Gray's *Adam of the Road*. Elizabeth Gray has also written a distinguished series of American historical fiction and some excellent biographies (see Bibliography, Chapter 15).

Elizabeth Gray is a born storyteller, although paradoxically she is weak in plot construction. Her books develop little excitement; the conflicts are mild; no breathtaking suspense leads to a smashing climax. Yet she is a careful historian, and her tales have all the authentic minutiae of everyday life long ago which make history convincing. But chiefly she is concerned with people.

Children from twelve to fourteen years old will find that Adam is a boy much like themselves. It just happened that he lived in the thirteenth century instead of today. Adam's two loves are his golden cocker spaniel and his minstrel father, but he loses them both for a time. How he seeks the two of them up and down the roads of old England gives children a glimpse into every variety of medieval life—that of jugglers, minstrels, plowmen, and nobles, as real as the people today.

The hero of *I Will Adventure* (1962) is Andrew Talbot, a most beguiling young imp, who takes to himself a line from Shakespeare's *Romeo and Juliet*, "I will adventure." Andrew is journeying to London to be a page to his uncle Sir John Talbot when he has the good luck to hear this play and by way of a fight with one of the boy players, meets Master Burbage and Shakespeare himself. Andrew is all for signing up with the players, but they won't take him, though Shakespeare, grieving for his own boy Hamnet, lets Andrew ride with him for a day's journey. Through Andrew's eyes the reader comes to know intimately many facets of London life in 1596, especially the theater, the plays, and the audiences. Andrew's problems are happily solved, thanks to Shakespeare and a sympathetic uncle.

*Illustration by Corydon Bell. From* I Will Adventure *by Elizabeth Janet Gray. Copyright © 1962 by Elizabeth Janet Gray. Reprinted by permission of The Viking Press, Inc.*

## MOLLIE HUNTER

*The Ghosts of Glencoe*

Mollie Hunter's research for the historic events of the Massacre of Glencoe was done at the West Highland Museum. Ensign Robert Stewart, the protagonist of *The Ghosts of Glencoe* (1969), is an officer of the king's army, dedicated to keeping peace in the Highlands, where the clans who had supported the deposed James II were in rebellion, and were refusing to take the oath of allegiance to William III. Like many other Scottish officers, Ensign Stewart is torn between loyalty to his king and sympathy for his countrymen. Shaken by the vengefulness of those who do not share that sympathy, Stewart finally warns the rebels when an attack is planned. The dialogue rings true, and the period details are as meticulously correct as is the historical material.

This careful treatment of fact is a firm base in all of Mollie Hunter's books, although most of them are more highly fictionalized than is *The Ghosts of Glencoe*. *The Spanish Letters* (1967) is a cloak-and-dagger adventure story, set in Edinburgh in the late sixteenth century, in which two Spanish agents are allied with Scottish traitors planning to abduct King James. *The Lothian Run* (1970) is a tale of spies and smugglers which, like

*The Spanish Letters*, is full of plot and counterplot, romantic and sinister. Less dramatic but just as suspenseful is the more somber *A Pistol in Greenyards* (1968), a tale of the Highland evictions of the tenant farmers in the 1850s.

## PATRICIA CLAPP

*Constance*

With the exception of one character, all of the people described by *Constance* (1968) in her journal existed, and the events are based on the real life of an ancestress of Patricia Clapp Cone's husband. The historical details are smoothly woven into the story, and the description of the early days of the Plymouth Colony is unusually vivid. As she tells of her growing understanding of the Indians, her relationship with her stepmother, her doubts about herself, and her satisfaction when young men find her attractive, Constance sounds always like a young girl. The book, which concludes with her marriage in 1626, is particularly valuable because of the graphic depiction of the hardships of the first grim winter and the struggles of the colonists with their English backers. *Constance* was one of the five finalists in the children's books category for the 1969 National Book Award.

## HESTER BURTON

*Beyond the Weir Bridge*
*Time of Trial*

*Beyond the Weir Bridge* (1970) is a vivid piece of historical writing, consistent in language and viewpoint, informative about the period in which it is set, and a truly dramatic story. Richard and Richenda, whose fathers had been killed in 1644 in Cromwell's service, are both fond of shy, bookish Thomas although he is a Royalist. Richenda, indeed, comes to love him when they are grown and with him joins the Quakers, a denomination then reviled. It is only when Richard, who has become a doctor, sees Thomas' faith bring him to plague-ridden London to help as best he can, that he understands the true humility of the Quaker credo.

*Time of Trial*, winner of the 1963 Carnegie Award, also is concerned with the courage of the nonconformist. Seventeen-year-old Margaret Pargeter is the daughter of a London bookseller who is sent to prison for advocating social reform and for printing a book judged inflammatory. Burton's characters always reflect the mores and customs in a time of change yet are developed as distinctive individuals, and the story is all the more convincing because their efforts have a realistically modest effect.

### VIEWPOINTS

If writing historical novels has its own special pleasures, it also has its own special difficulties—especially if one knows that one's books are going to be read primarily by children. Children are not less intelligent than grownups. The problem is that they *know* less. In particular, they know less history. The first difficulty, then, is to give the historical setting of one's story and to impart the necessary historical facts without appearing to teach or to preach and—what is more important—without slowing up the pace of the narrative. Both the child and the writer want to hurry on to the action of the story. Yet, if the historical background is not firmly painted in, both child and author come to grief. The characters in the story move in a kind of featureless limbo, and both reader and writer lose interest in them. For this reason, I find the writing of the first chapter of every novel extremely difficult. There is so much to do all at the same moment: there are the characters to describe, the geographical setting to depict, the plot to be introduced, and, on top of all, the problem of history. I know from children themselves that I have not entirely mastered this difficulty, for I sometimes receive letters which begin: "I liked your story except for the beginning which I found boaring [sic]."—Hester Burton, "The Writing of Historical Novels," *The Horn Book*, June, 1969, p. 276.

## ELIZABETH GEORGE SPEARE

*The Witch of Blackbird Pond*
*The Bronze Bow*

*The Witch of Blackbird Pond,* winner of the 1959 Newbery Medal, is well worthwhile for mature readers of the sixth and seventh grades. Orphaned Kit, luxuriously raised in tropical Barbados, comes to live with her Puritan relatives in Connecticut. These cousins try to be kind but they disagree with Kit about almost everything. Her silk dresses and befeathered bonnets scandalize the whole community, and Kit willfully flouts local customs in many ways, most seriously by making friends with an old Quaker woman, Hannah Tupper, the suspected witch of Blackbird Pond. Kit's recklessness climaxes in her arrest, imprisonment, and trial for witchcraft. This terrifying experience brings Kit to realize that no one of us can live to himself alone. Her stern old uncle defends her even at considerable danger to himself and his family. A forlorn waif Kit had befriended stands by her, and her disapproving, seafaring beau Nat finally manages to extricate Kit. The strength of this book lies in its theme and its well-drawn characters. They are neither wholly good nor wholly bad but a very human mixture of heroism and bigotry, frailty and courage, rebellious recklessness and generous loyalty.

The title of the 1962 Newbery Medal winner, *The Bronze Bow,* comes from II Samuel 22:35—"He trains my hands for war, so that my arms can bend a bow of bronze." This verse fascinates young Daniel, who, along with many Israelites, is looking for the Deliverer to drive the cruel Romans out of their land. Daniel had seen his mother and father wantonly slain by these conquerors. So, thinking Rosh is perhaps such a deliverer, Daniel deserts his grandmother and sister to join Rosh's band. Daniel's loyal friends try to tell him that Rosh is no more than a greedy bandit. They tell Daniel also about another Deliverer called Jesus, a gentle teacher who preaches love and says that he who wields the sword will perish by the sword. But Daniel, consumed with bitterness, believes violence is the only way. Blinded by his hatred, Daniel kills his sister's hope of love, thereby driving her into mental darkness. Not until he has seen his mute but devoted follower killed and has almost lost his love Thacia, does Daniel come face to face with the healing love of Jesus. Then at last he understands that it is not hatred and violence, but only love that is strong enough to bend the bow of bronze.

## RACHEL FIELD

*Calico Bush*

One of the finest books Rachel Field ever wrote is *Calico Bush* (1931), the story of Marguerite Ledoux, a French bound-out girl of thirteen, who travels to the state of Maine with a Massachusetts family in 1743. On the long sail from Marblehead to Mount Desert, Marguerite comes to know the Sargent family and proves to them her grit and resourcefulness. She remains, nevertheless, a servant and an alien in their midst. When the Sargents finally reach Maine, they locate their land, but the house has been burned down by the Indians. What is more, they are told that the Indians want no settlers on that particular property. (One criticism of the book is that it ignores the Indians' point of view—the land taken is sacred land—and it draws Indians, for the most part, as savages.) Joel Sargent builds his house there anyway.

In this new country Marguerite makes a fast friend of a remarkable old woman, Aunt Hepsa. There are brief days of joy in the new settlement, but there are tragic and frightening days, too—the Sargent baby is burned to death, and an Indian raid is diverted only by Marguerite's courage and ingenuity. At the end of the story, the Sargents gratefully offer Marguerite her freedom, but she will not leave them.

The picture of the times and the people is authentic and well balanced. The hardships, the monotony, and the perils of pioneer life are there, unvarnished and frightening. The compensatory rewards may seem slight to modern readers, but there can be no doubt in their minds about the sturdy, undismayed character of these early settlers.

## JOHN and PATRICIA BEATTY

*At the Seven Stars*

John and Patricia Beatty's historical novels are based on sound research, and their aim is to entertain rather than to instruct their readers. As Patricia Beatty says, "We hope that our books are more than escape fiction, but we are aware that all fiction offers escape."[6] In *At the Seven Stars* (1967) a fifteen-year-old boy from Philadelphia comes to London in 1752 and meets some of the very real people of that turbulent period. Richard becomes involved in the struggle between the Hanoverian and Stuart supporters, takes refuge in William Hogarth's home, is imprisoned, escapes, enlists the aid of the actor David Garrick, and gets back to America with the help of the Duke of Newcastle. There is never a dearth of action in books by the Beattys or in the books that Patricia Beatty writes alone. In *Hail Columbia* (1970), for example, a suffragette in Oregon in 1893 stirs up the town of Astoria by her vigorous dedication to causes.

## ESTHER FORBES

*Johnny Tremain*

Esther Forbes received the 1942 Pulitzer Prize for her adult biography *Paul Revere and the World He Lived In*. Her *Johnny Tremain*, which was an outgrowth of the research expended on *Paul Revere*, received the 1944 Newbery Medal. In her Newbery acceptance speech, she explained that while she was working on the adult biography she had to stifle any tendency toward fiction. But she was continually teased by the story possibilities of Boston's apprentices, who were always getting into scrapes of one kind or another. To illustrate her point, she related the hilarious doings of one of these apprentices who precipitated the Boston Massacre, and she concluded:

> *In this way an apprentice of whom we know nothing except that he was "greasy and diminutive" played his minute part in our history and disappears forever. I'd like to know more of him.*[7]

So she promised herself that as soon as possible she would write some fiction about the apprentices. The resulting book, *Johnny Tremain*, represents a high point in American historical fiction for children and young people. It is a great book for children to read at twelve or fourteen and to reread with added appreciation in college. In fact, like all of the greatest juveniles, it is a book as much for adults as for children.

*Johnny Tremain* tells the story of a silversmith's apprentice who lived in the exciting days that marked the beginning of the American Revolution. Johnny's master is second only to the famous Paul Revere as a silversmith, but Johnny knows that he himself is unrivaled among all apprentices. Competent and cocky, a humble artist but an unbearably conceited boy, Johnny is harsh and overbearing with his fellow apprentices and ambitious for himself. Just as he achieves a notable design, the apprentices decide to play a joke on him. The results are far worse than they intended. Not only is Johnny's design lost but he is left with a burned hand, maimed for life. His career as a silversmith is

6. Patricia Beatty, "The Two-headed Monster," *The Horn Book*, February 1967, p. 100.

7. Esther Forbes, "The Newbery Medal Acceptance," *The Horn Book*, July-August 1944, p. 264.

*Illustration by Lynd Ward. From Johnny Tremain by Esther Forbes. Copyright, 1943, by Esther Forbes Hoskins. Reprinted by permission of the publishers, Houghton Mifflin Company. (Original with color)*

over even before it is well begun. Out of work and embittered, he still must stand on his own feet or go under. He stands.

This is the beginning of a story that carries Johnny and his friend Rab into the thick of Boston's pre-Revolutionary activities. In the first little skirmish of the Revolution, men and boys lined up in the square—some to die. But they knew what they were dying for, Miss Forbes assures us, and they believed it "was worth more than their own lives."

*Johnny Tremain* has so many values they are difficult to summarize. To children carrying any physical handicaps, Johnny's bitterness over his maimed hand is understandable. The book gives no one-sided account of pre-Revolutionary days but makes the colonists and Red Coats alive as the histories never seem to. The British, especially, are amazingly human in their forbearance, while the confusion and uncertainty of the colonists are frighteningly real. All the details of the everyday life of the period are expertly woven into the story, never dragged in for themselves.

## REBECCA CAUDILL

### *Tree of Freedom*

*Tree of Freedom* (1954), a story about the Revolutionary War period, is sound historical fiction because of its vivid characterizations and homely details of everyday living, which make the past understandable and natural. Each child of a family moving to Kentucky may take one prized possession. Stephanie carries an apple seed, because that is what her grandmother brought from France. When Noel, the eldest son, wants to take his dulcimer, it starts anew the feud between father and son. But the mother intervenes, "'Twon't hurt him any. An' a little music won't hurt Kentucky, either. . . . He's got his rifle, ain't he, as well as his dulcimore? He'll use it like a man. See if he don't." And he does, but the quarrel is not resolved until the end of the war.

In the stockade, where the family takes refuge from the Indians, the mother is horrified by the smells, the flies, the bad water, and the crowding. After they are on their own land, the father, Jonathan, and Noel go to war, and the backbreaking care of the crops falls to the mother, Rob, and Stephanie. There are anxieties, too, big and little ones. But always Stephanie tends her little sprout of an apple tree, "tree of freedom," she calls it. This is the theme of the story, and it speaks to us today, because in every generation the tree of freedom must be nurtured if it is to survive.

Another fine story is Caudill's *The Far-Off Land* (1964), in which a young girl is taken by flatboat in 1780 from the Moravian settlement in Salem to French Lick. Although she becomes accustomed to the rough ways of the settlers, Ketty cannot accept their hostile behavior toward Indians, since she has been brought up to practice brotherly love. The characterization is strong, the period details convincing and smoothly incorporated into the story.

## LEONARD WIBBERLEY

The *Treegate* series

Leonard Wibberley paints his stories of Peter Treegate's adventures during the Revolutionary War on a broad canvas. In the first book, *John Treegate's Musket* (1959), John Treegate is a solid, respectable Boston citizen who is loyal to his king, but his son Peter becomes increasingly convinced of the rectitude of the Patriot cause and fights against the British at Bunker Hill. In *Peter Treegate's War* (1960), Peter becomes a war prisoner, escapes, crosses the Delaware with Washington, and goes to the southern mountains. *Sea Captain from Salem* (1961) tells the story of Peace of God Manly, who saved Peter's life in the first book, and who is sent on a mission by Benjamin Franklin, in an effort to win French support for the cause. The move to France gives the series variety, and the plot provides some rousing sea battles. In *Treegate's Raiders* (1962), Peter is on a recruiting trip through the mountains, trying to persuade Scottish settlers to forget their clan loyalties and feuds and unite as Americans. The story has vivid martial scenes and ends with the defeat of Cornwallis. All the books give marvelously vivid pictures not only of the Revolutionary War but of the significance of that war to the ordinary citizen of the time and to history. In *Leopard's Prey* (1971), Wibberley moves almost to the War of 1812, his young protagonist the nephew of Peter, Manly Treegate.

## CORNELIA MEIGS

*Clearing Weather*
*Master Simon's Garden*

Cornelia Meigs is interested not only in our historical past but also in the beginnings of ideas and their development. Her stories, however, are always something more than historical fiction. Indeed, she manages frequently, in these stories of the past, to illuminate certain problems of the present.

For example, *Clearing Weather* (1928) deals with Nicholas Drury's struggles to keep alive his uncle's shipbuilding business in the discouraging days following the American Revolution. Only through the cooperation of the whole community is the little town able to reestablish itself. The theme of community cooperation is a good one today.

*Master Simon's Garden* (1929) carries a still more striking theme. In the little Puritan New England settlement called Hopewell, where everything is done for utility and thrift, Master Simon develops his beautiful garden—a riot of colorful flowers and sweet herbs. It is an expression of his philosophy of tolerance and love in complete contrast to the intolerance and suspicion of some of his neighbors.

But these are not propaganda stories, and Cornelia Meigs is not writing with a message always in mind. Every one of her books has plots that are absorbing and often exciting. However, the plots are stronger because of their genesis in a strong theme. It is the theme which gives unity to the action and significance to the conclusion.

Meigs' inability to create memorable characters may help explain why her books are not so popular as they might be. The dominance of ideas rather than vivid, individual characters means that these stories are more intellectual than those most children are used to. Certainly the books should be discussed if children are to grasp their implications and enjoy fully the exciting action with which most of the stories culminate.

## VIEWPOINTS

Readers and critics who wish to laud historical literature frequently say that the author has succeeded in lending life to the period he has portrayed. . . . Academicians who have authored historical novels may well have had that in mind as their principal purpose. But the creative writers desire only to treat contemporary matters even in those of their creations which have history as their subject. . . . [Homer and the poets about him] did not write the *Iliad* for the purpose of re-creating the period of Achaean penetration into Asia. They described instead the knighthood and adventures of their own ninth or eighth century rather than the barbaric events of the thirteenth century in which their story took place. . . . The portrayal of times past was never the point and purpose but always only a means or vehicle for expressing their own experience of their own time. — Leon Feuchtwanger, *The House of Desdemona or The Laurels and Limitations of Historical Fiction*, Wayne State University Press, Detroit, 1963, pp. 129, 130.

## SALLY WATSON

*Jade*

One of the things that appeals to the readers of Sally Watson's historical fiction is that the characters in her stories, which span generations, are part of the same family. Another is her light, lively style, and a third is the careful research that nevers appears obtrusively as edifying information but is smoothly incorporated into the story. *Jade* (1968) is, for example, a descendant of *Mistress Malapert* (1955), and her adventures are vouched for in an appended historical note in which Sally Watson says, ". . . I should never have dared invent any fiction so improbable — and I didn't. I got it from the records of the time — directly or indirectly." The story *is* improbable: Melanie Lennox (Jade's real name), a sixteen-year-old girl of an eighteenth-century Virginia family, attempts to free the passengers on a slave ship, is publicly flogged, becomes a pirate, is jailed along with the very real pirate queen, Anne Bonney, and released, with the proviso that she never again come to the West Indies. Other books by Sally Watson, set in various historical periods, are noted in the bibliography.

## WILLIAM O. STEELE

*Wayah of the Real People*
*The Perilous Road*
*The Far Frontier*

Few writers today can re-create wilderness life more vividly and movingly than William Steele. His stories are well written in the vernacular of the times, with good dialogue, plenty of suspense and action, and flesh-and-blood characters — grownups who struggle and survive in a tough pioneer world and expect their children to do the same; frontier boys, ignorant, prejudiced, or wrong-headed, but resourceful and enduring. The significant thing about William Steele's boys is that life changes and develops them, so that the reader sees them grow.

*Wayah of the Real People* (1964) is an unusual story about a Cherokee boy's year of schooling at Brafferton Hall in mid-eighteenth-century Williamsburg. Wayah suffers all the problems of any child placed in an environment culturally different from his own. Afraid that he has changed, Wayah finds when he has returned to the Real People, that his year away has helped him mature.

In *The Perilous Road* (1958), young Chris Brabson, who hates the Yankees, cannot understand how his parents can accept the fact that his older brother has joined the Union Army. After Union soldiers have raided the Brabson livestock, Chris tries a bit of revenge and is surprised, when he gets to know some of the soldiers, that they are people like himself. The story has action and suspense, and,

*Illustration by Paul Galdone. Reproduced from* The Far Frontier, *© 1959, by William O. Steele, by permission of Harcourt Brace Jovanovich, Inc.*

to his chest, and the blows rained down over him. His spectacles fell off, and the Indian left off hitting him and picked up the eyeglasses. He looked at them carefully, felt the glass between his thumb and finger, squinted through them, and then stuck them on his nose. The others ran up to see.

Mr. Twistletree stayed with head bowed, right where he'd been left and never made a murmur.

134

Even when he was lying beside Tobe later, tied up tight and with the red men all about him, he didn't seem to see or hear them or notice where he was. He was still mourning his book, Tobe knew. It was gone for sure now, most of it used to get the wood burning.

The braves moved around their campfire, talk-

135

like many of Steele's other books, is set in the Tennessee mountain region.

*The Far Frontier* (1959) shows another strong-willed boy who is outraged when he finds himself bound out to an absent-minded scientist from Philadelphia. But before their long, danger-beset journey through the Tennessee wilderness is over, Tobe has acquired a deep respect for his brave, eccentric companion. Best of all, the boy survives with a lasting hunger for learning and is well on his way with both reading and figuring. Tobe and the naturalist, Mr. Twistletree, are a memorable pair.

## EVELYN LAMPMAN

*The Tilted Sombrero*
*Cayuse Courage*

Evelyn Lampman's *The Tilted Sombrero* (1966) takes place at the start of the Mexican War of Independence in 1810, and it includes some real people prominent in that struggle, primarily Father Hidalgo y Costilla, the priest who led the first Indian revolt against Spain. In addition to historical interest, however, the story gives a vivid picture of the stratification of Mexican society. Its protagonist, Nando, is a proud Creole whose family has always been loyal to Spain, and at first he is greatly displeased to learn that his family is not pure Creole, that they have an Indian grandmother. Won over to the patriot cause, Nando changes his attitude. The book has a colorful setting and an action-filled plot, but it is the theme of rebellion against oppression that is its most memorable quality. Another historical period (1847) is the setting for a fine pioneer story, *Tree Wagon* (1953), and Lampman's sympathetic identification with the Indians of America is evident in both *Cayuse Courage* (1970), a story of the Whitman Massacre told from the viewpoint of a young Indian boy, and *Once Upon the Little Big Horn* (1971), a detailed account of the four-day struggle popularly known as "Custer's Last Stand," also described in *Red Hawk's Account of Custer's Last Battle*, by Paul and Dorothy Goble (see p. 504).

## SCOTT O'DELL

*Island of the Blue Dolphins*
*The King's Fifth*

There seem to be more good realistic stories about the American Indian set in the past than in the present. Of these stories of the past, the most powerful is *Island of the Blue Dolphins* (1961 Newbery Medal).

In the early 1800s off the coast of California, a twelve-year-old Indian girl boarded a ship that was to carry the tribe away from their island home where they were being harried and destroyed by Aleutian seal hunters. But when Karana saw that her little brother had accidentally been left behind, she jumped off the moving ship and swam back to him and their island home. A pack of wild dogs killed her brother and began to stalk the solitary girl. This is the beautifully told story of her survival on the island for eighteen years. She had to prepare her own weapons, build a shelter with a strong fence, maintain a continual search for food, replace her worn out clothes, all with an eye on the savage pack of dogs. The need to love and nurture was strong. So when she wounded the leader dog, she nursed him back to health and he became her inseparable companion and defender. Shining through her struggles and hardships are her quiet resignation, her endurance, her genuine love for her island home, and the great fortitude and serenity she developed. The story of Karana is historically true. Her incredible battles with a bull sea elephant, a devilfish, and the ferocious dogs, and, above all, her years of solitude command the reader's humble admiration for human courage.

Also based on history is the story told by Esteban in *The King's Fifth* (1966), his reminiscences of the journey made as a fifteen-year-old cartographer to Coronado. Put ashore to find Coronado's camp, his small group has a dangerous journey searching for the fabled gold of Cibola, and Esteban is later imprisoned on the charge that he has withheld the king's share of the treasure. The transitions between past and present are smoothly bridged, and the historical details are used to enhance rather than obscure an adventurous tale.

## WEYMAN JONES

*The Talking Leaf*
*The Edge of Two Worlds*

In two stories about Sequoyah, Weyman Jones brings vividly to life the half-white Cherokee who conceived the idea of giving to his people a written alphabet. In *The Talking Leaf* (1965) a young Cherokee, Atsee, had hoped to become a great scout like his father but found that times had changed, that the Cherokee nation would have to change as well. Knowing that his people must become literate, Atsee sought Sequoyah. Sympathetic, dignified, and beautifully written, the story is moving, its theme apparent in Sequoyah's comment when Atsee asks bitterly if the bolt he is making for a bridge is so that the whites can come into Cherokee country more easily. "Part of growing up," Sequoyah says, "is learning that a bridge goes two ways." In *The Edge of Two Worlds* (1968) a white boy who is the only survivor of an Indian attack on a wagon train travels with Sequoyah, now an old man, for mutual protection, but when the time comes that they part, the boy has learned to respect and trust the gentle and dignified old man. There is no stereotype, no sentimentality in these stories, but a deep understanding and reverence for the man who learned to interpret the written word so that he might help his people.

## CHRISTIE HARRIS

*Raven's Cry*
*West with the White Chiefs*

*Raven's Cry* (1966) was given the Canadian Library Association's award as the best children's book of the year in English, the research having been done through a Canada Council Grant. The dramatic and impressive story describes the dreadful consequences for the Haida people when white men came in 1775 to hunt sea otter, cheating the people and destroying their way of life until only a handful remained. The story is told from the Indian viewpoint, in a vigorous narrative that is complemented by the strong illustrations of Bill Reid, a descendant of the last Haida chief, who duplicates the form of Haida art.

*West with the White Chiefs* (1965) is based on the journal written by two Englishmen, a story of high adventure in which a small party crosses the Rockies in 1863. The characterization of the whites and Indians, who become friends on the journey, is excellent, and there is some comedy in the pedantic, quarrelsome schoolmaster who foists himself on the party of explorers.

*Illustration by Bill Reid. Copyright © 1966 by Christie Harris from* Raven's Cry. *Used by permission of Atheneum Publishers.*

## BETTY BAKER

*The Dunderhead War*
*Walk the World's Rim*

*The Dunderhead War* (1967) is one of the few good stories for young people about the Mexican War, which serves as a background for Betty Baker's story of seventeen-year-old Quincy, who is too young to enlist, but travels with his Uncle Fritz and shares some of the adventures of the volunteers. Uncle Fritz has just come to the United States, and his complacent superiority and criticism of that "army of dunderheads" give an outsider's viewpoint and add humor to a lively story.

Many of Baker's books, from stories for beginning readers to serious fiction for adolescents, are about Indians. Two of the best are *Walk the World's Rim* (1965), the story of the black slave Esteban, who wandered across the country with Cabeza de Vaca and became the hero of the Indian boy Chakoh; and *And One Was a Wooden Indian* (1970), a sensitive novel about a young Apache of the nineteenth century and his first encounter with white men. It is interesting to compare Baker's Cabeza de Vaca with Maia Wojciechowska's in *Odyssey of Courage*, in which de Vaca's affection for the Indians, and theirs for him, are stressed.

## HAROLD KEITH

*Rifles for Watie*

*Rifles for Watie*, winner of the 1958 Newbery Medal, is the most substantial historical fiction for children we have had in this country since *Johnny Tremain*. The hero of the book is young Jefferson Davis Bussey, who despite his name is a Kansas farm boy and a rabid Unionist. Once in the army, Jeff's name and his stubborn forthrightness get him into trouble with a brutal officer, who persecutes him endlessly. Finally, Jeff is sent as a spy behind the Rebel lines to try to discover where Confederate Stand Watie, full-blooded Cherokee Indian, is getting the new rifles issued for the Union armies. Jeff is captured by the Rebels, but his name, together with a plausible story, allays suspicions. Jeff lives, works, and fights with this Indian regiment for fourteen months. When he finally gets his information and escapes to the Northern side, he leaves his Confederate friends with real regret. He leaves them also with the disturbing realization that heroic, well-intentioned men are fighting and dying on both sides in this horrifying struggle.

Among the unforgettable characters is Jimmy Lear, the fourteen-year-old drummer boy, too young to carry a gun but old enough to die gallantly. There is big-eared, ugly Heifer, the cook, who is like a father to Jeff, and Lucy, the beautiful Confederate half-breed, and finally, Watie himself, much like a gentle old farmer but in action a ruthless raider and fighter. All the hunger, dirt, and weariness of war are in this book to balance the heroism of men and boys on both sides. This is a magnificent story to use along with the biographies of Lincoln and Lee.

*Illustration by Peter Burchard. Reprinted by permission of Coward, McCann & Geoghegan, Inc., from* Jed *by Peter Burchard. Copyright © 1960 by Coward, McCann, Inc.*

## PETER BURCHARD

*Bimby*
*Jed*

Peter Burchard's approach to the writing of historical fiction is to pinpoint his theme by using a compressed, concise account of an incident or a single day and creating thereby a dramatic impact. In *Bimby* (1968) he follows a young slave through one crucial day in which the boy sees an old friend killed and also learns that his father had died of the punishment he received when he tried to escape. Knowing that she will never see her son again, Bimby's mother gives him information that will enable him to escape, both of them aware that life without freedom is empty. The writing is subdued, so that the poignancy and tension of the story emerge from the events themselves.

In *Jed* (1960), Burchard again avoids didacticism and lets the ethical implications of a boy's conduct make its own impact on the reader. Although he is only sixteen, Jed has already fought at Shiloh, and he is disturbed by the behavior of some of the Yankee soldiers who are his companions at arms. Foraging is stealing, and war is no excuse; war, in fact, is not glamorous. When he finds a small boy who has been hurt, Jed takes the child back to his Confederate family and befriends them. It is interesting to compare Burchard's approach with the broader view taken by Anna Gertrude Hall in *Cyrus Holt and the Civil War* (1964), in which a boy of nine finds the war exciting when it starts but becomes increasingly aware as time goes by of the men wounded and dead, and of the growing burden of deprivation and unwonted responsibilities.

## K. M. PEYTON

The *Flambards* trilogy

Some of Kathleen Peyton's earlier books were written with her husband Michael, hence the "K. M.," which she now uses for all her writing. Before the *Flambards* trilogy, she produced a series of excellent adventure stories, many of which are set in the past but have little sense of history. With the publication of *Flambards* (1968), Peyton made the Edwardian period an integral part of the book. Flambards is the Russell estate to which Christina Parsons, a young orphan, comes to live with her uncle and his two sons, Mark and Will. World War I is looming, and quiet Will is enthralled by flying. The emphasis on the first frail, experimental planes is a major part of the story, although the plot focuses on Christina's rejection of the powerful bully Mark and her love for Will. One of the ways in which Peyton reflects the changing mores of the period is in Christina's ambivalence about servants: she resents her uncle's treatment of them, yet cannot quite feel that the groom, Dick, is a person.

The book was a runner-up for the Carnegie Award, which was won by Peyton for the second book of the three, *The Edge of the Cloud* (published here in 1970). In this book Will and Christina take refuge with an aunt in Battersea, since Mark and his father were irate because of Christina's choice. For two years they are engaged, Christina always apprehensive because of Will's dangerous vocation. The story ends with their marriage, but it is less a love story than an account of the early days of flying, with its stunt men, and the camaraderie of the still-small group of flyers.

In *Flambards in Summer* (1970) the time is 1916, and Christina is a widow. She finds that Mark has an illegitimate son and brings the boy to Flambards, the neglected estate that she manages. Eventually she falls in love again. It is significant of the changes in Christina and of the changes in the times that Dick, the former groom, is the man she plans to wed. The characterization is strong and the heroine's development into maturity is a convincing characterization and also a microcosmic picture of the new social structure that came out of World War I.

## ELIZABETH FOREMAN LEWIS

*Young Fu of the Upper Yangtze*
*To Beat a Tiger*

Elizabeth Lewis, who lived long in China, wrote *Young Fu of the Upper Yangtze*, winner of the 1933 Newbery Medal. It is the exciting story of a thirteen-year-old Chinese country boy who is brought to the rich city of Chungking in the 1930s and apprenticed to a skillful coppersmith. In time, Young Fu becomes a fine craftsman, but neither easily nor quickly. Meanwhile, he explores the great modern city and finds everywhere the conflict of old and new ideas. Fu is no idealized hero but exhibits the usual contradictory human traits. He is brave and honest, yet he wastes his master's time and gets into trouble. He works hard, grows skillful, and then gets unbearably cocky. He is frugal one moment and wasteful the next.

Mrs. Lewis has a later book, *To Beat a Tiger* (1956), for teen-agers and young adults. It is the grim story of sixteen Chinese boys living by their wits on the outskirts of Shanghai. They all know the proverb, "To beat a tiger, one needs a brother's help." Their tiger is starvation and death, and so they lie, steal, and cheat, but share their wretched scraps of food, their hut, filthy rags, and scanty heat. Death strikes one of the gang, and the chance to rise by sheer villainy claims another. Nationalists and Communists are not named, but the two factions are there and the boys are involved. It is a complex story, but once the large gallery of characters is identified, the plot gains momentum and suspense is high.

## OTHER BOOKS FOR OLDER CHILDREN

When a poet tells a story, poetry often results. In *The Faraway Lurs* (1963), Harry Behn has written a story that has the poignancy of *Romeo and Juliet*. It is set in Denmark during the Bronze Age, where a girl of the peaceful Forest People falls in love with a young man from a hostile tribe, the Sun People, whose great bronze lurs, or trumpets, she has heard. The lovers come to a tragic end, a fate that is realistic within the framework of cultural conflict.

*Illustration by C. Walter Hodges. Reprinted by permission of Coward, McCann & Geoghegan, Inc., and G. Bell & Sons, Ltd., London, from* The Marsh King *by C. Walter Hodges. Copyright © 1967 by C. Walter Hodges.*

Another story of ancient times is Madeleine Polland's *To Tell My People* (1968). A British girl, taken by Roman invaders, is sent to Rome as a slave. When she escapes and returns to her colony, she hopes to share with her people the knowledge she has gained, but they are ignorant and only sneer. She has hoped to bring them peace; they will do nothing but fight.

*The Namesake* (1964) and *The Marsh King* (1967), by Cyril Walter Hodges, are sequential tales of King Alfred's struggle against the Danish invaders, stories full of action and fascinating historical details. Another English writer, Geoffrey Trease, moves his hero in *The Red Towers of Granada* (1967) from England in the time of Edward I to Spain. Cast out of his village as a leper, young Robin is told by a Jewish doctor that he has a minor skin disease. Since it was illegal for Jews to practice medicine at that time, Robin stays secretly in the doctor's home and goes with him to Spain.

Fifteenth-century Poland is the setting for Eric Kelly's 1929 Newbery Medal book, *The Trumpeter of Krakow*, a story based on the oath of the Krakow trumpeters to sound their defiant song every hour. The setting is colorful, the story intriguing both because it has dramatic adventure and because it gives an absorbing picture of the problems of the Polish people.

*I, Juan de Pareja* (1965), for which Elizabeth Borton de Trevino was awarded the Newbery Medal, is the story of the black slave of the painter Velazquez. Written in autobiographical form, it comes close to biography, but is told as a story. An aspiring artist himself, de Pareja painted secretly until his master realized that here was another artist—and freed him. In de Pareja's descriptions of court affairs and of Velazquez as a person, there is appeal for the reader interested in history and in art, and the story itself moves with pace and dignity.

Another story with a black protagonist is Ann Petry's *Tituba of Salem Village* (1964), a dramatic fictionalization of the inexorable hysteria of the Salem witch-hunt and trials. In Alice Marriott's *Indian Annie: Kiowa Captive* (1965), Annie comes to love her foster parents and marries into the tribe. The story is set in the antebellum years, and Annie is struck by the fact that a freed slave cannot identify, as she does, with another minority group.

E. M. Almedingen has written many charming historical novels set in Russia, most of them based on family records. *Katia*

*Illustration by Victor Ambrus. Reprinted with the permission of Farrar, Straus & Giroux, Inc. and Oxford University Press, London, from* Katia *by E. M. Almedingen, illustrated by Victor Ambrus, copyright © 1966 by E. M. Almedingen.*

(1967) is an adaptation of a great-aunt's memoirs, published in Russia in 1874. *Young Mark* (1968) is the true and romantic story of Almedingen's great-great-grandfather, who became a court favorite because of his beautiful singing, grew wealthy, and established the family fortune. The writing is intricate and mature, but for those children who are able to enjoy it the style and the fidelity of the historical background are very appealing.

No group of stories within the genre of historical fiction demonstrates so clearly that literature is an international heritage as do the books about World War II. From Denmark comes Anne Holm's *North to Freedom* (1965), the story of a boy of twelve who escapes from a prison camp in eastern Europe and makes his way to his mother in Copenhagen. Josef Carl Grund's *Never to Be Free* (1970) and Hans Peter Richter's *Friedrich* (1970), both translated from the German, are alike in being told by boys who are at first loyal to Hitler but who change; in Grund's book Gustav is disillusioned by his army experience; in Richter's, the boy who tells the story is disillusioned by what happens to his Jewish friend Friedrich. Both stories are all the more effective for their portrayal of ordinary people. This is also true of a book from France, Colette Vivier's *House of the Four Winds* (1969), for the people who live in the house (an apartment building) are a cross-section of middle-class Parisians, and their valor (or cowardice) during the German occupation has a homeliness that makes the historical period come alive. Margaret Balderson's *When Jays Fly to Barbmo* (1969) moves slowly, but the style fits the bleak setting of a Norwegian island where the German invaders burn the farmhouses.

In Hester Burton's *In Spite of All Terror* (1969), a girl who has been sent out of London for her safety comes back to do her bit on the eve of Dunkirk. One of the most powerful books in this group is Erik Haugaard's *The Little Fishes* (1967), told by a twelve-year-old waif in wartime Italy. Guido lives by stealing because he must to exist. Children compete with adults for survival, yet Guido has faith in mankind. Terrible and true, the story is a testament of hope as much as it is an indictment of war.

The ravages of war are a recurrent theme in James Forman's books. *Horses of Anger* (1967), like Grund's *Never to Be Free*, concerns a Nazi soldier who begins to doubt the propaganda he has heard and to understand his own prejudice. In Forman's *The Traitors* (1968), a Bavarian pastor suffers because his congregation and his only child espouse the Nazi cause, and he joins the underground rebellion. Forman's books are mature and sophisticated, often profound and provocative, demanding the most of a young reader.

Because books of historical fiction may so obviously enrich social studies in the schools, there may be a tendency to use them with too heavy an emphasis on their social implications. *The Gift of the Golden Cup* contrasts Greek and Roman life and demonstrates the evils of slavery, but it is primarily a rousing story of adventure and revolt. *The Tilted Sombrero* is concerned with the struggle for independence and the inanity of prejudice, but it focuses on the exciting events in a boy's life. Historical fiction may supplement the school curriculum, but children read it for enjoyment. It includes some of the finest literature for children, and there are fortunately so many good books in the genre that this chapter can only call atttention to some of the best and list a slightly wider selection in the bibliography.

## ADULT REFERENCES[8]

ARBUTHNOT, MAY HILL, and DOROTHY M. BRODERICK. *Time for Stories of the Past and Present.*

EGOFF, SHEILA. *The Republic of Childhood: A Critical Guide to Canadian Children's Literature in English.* Part 3, "Historical Fiction."

EGOFF, SHEILA, G. T. STUBBS, and L. F. ASHLEY, eds. *Only Connect: Readings on Children's Literature.* Part 3, "Historical Fiction."

FIELD, ELINOR WHITNEY, comp. *Horn Book Reflections.* Part III, "Recreating Other Times."

*Historical Fiction.*

*World Culture.*

8. Complete bibliographic data are provided in the combined Adult References in the Appendices.

*Some historical fiction titles may be found in the bibliography for Chapter 13. In the following bibliography these symbols have been used to identify books about a religious or a particular ethnic group:*

§ Black
★ Chicano or Puerto Rican
☆ Indian
● Religious minority

## HISTORICAL FICTION: THE ANCIENT WORLD

BAUMANN, HANS. *I Marched with Hannibal,* tr. by Katherine Potts, ill. by Ulrik Schramm. Walck, 1962. 12-15

BEHN, HARRY. *The Faraway Lurs.* World, 1963. 12-15

COOLIDGE, OLIVIA. *Egyptian Adventures,* ill. by Joseph Low. Houghton, 1954. 12-16

______. *King of Men,* ill. by Ellen Raskin. Houghton, 1966. 12 up

______. *Marathon Looks on the Sea,* ill. by Erwin Schachner. Houghton, 1967. 12-15

● ______. *People in Palestine.* Houghton, 1965. 12 up

______. *Roman People,* ill. by Lino Lipinsky. Houghton, 1959. The Rome of Augustus comes alive in ten stories, each of which portrays a different social or economic level. *Men of Athens* (1962) portrays Athens' Golden Age. 12-15

GARD, JOYCE. *The Mermaid's Daughter.* Holt, 1969. An intricate novel set in Britain at the time of the Roman occupation, based on the mermaid-goddess cult. 11-14

HAUGAARD, ERIK CHRISTIAN. *The Rider and His Horse,* ill. by Leo and Diane Dillon. Houghton, 1968. 12-17

HAYS, WILMA PITCHFORD. *The Story of Valentine,* ill. by Leonard Weisgard. Coward, 1956. A vivid story of a Christian priest who, when imprisoned, achieved a miracle of faith. 9-12

LAWRENCE, ISABELLE. *The Gift of the Golden Cup,* ill. by Charles V. John. Bobbs, 1946. 11-14

______. *The Theft of the Golden Ring,* ill. by Charles V. John. Bobbs, 1948. 11-14

MCGRAW, ELOISE JARVIS. *The Golden Goblet.* Coward, 1961. 11-15

______. *Mara, Daughter of the Nile.* Coward, 1953. 11-15

MADDOCK, REGINALD. *The Great Bow,* ill. by Victor

Ambrus. Rand, 1968. A tightly constructed and convincing story about prehistoric man. Atta is a thoughtful fourteen-year-old who fails his test of manhood because he does not want to kill. 10-12

MORRISON, LUCILE. *The Lost Queen of Egypt*, ill. by Franz Geritz and Winifred Brunton. Lippincott, 1937. 12-14

POLLAND, MADELEINE. *To Tell My People*, ill. by Richard M. Powers. Holt, 1968. 11-13

☆ SCHWEITZER, BYRD BAYLOR. *One Small Blue Bead*, ill. by Symeon Shimin. Macmillan, 1965. 7-9

SNEDEKER, CAROLINE DALE. *The Forgotten Daughter*, ill. by Dorothy Lathrop. Doubleday, 1933. A good tale and a thorough study of Roman life. 10-14

______. *Theras and His Town*, ill. by Dimitris Davis. Doubleday, 1961. Life in Sparta and Athens is sharply contrasted as young Theras is forced to live under the Spartan regime. First published almost 40 years ago. 9-11

SPEARE, ELIZABETH G. *The Bronze Bow*. Houghton, 1961. Newbery Medal. 12 up

TREECE, HENRY. *The Centurion*, ill. by Mary Russon. Meredith, 1967. 11-15

## EUROPEAN HISTORICAL FICTION

ALMEDINGEN, E. M. *Katia*, ill. by Victor G. Ambrus. Farrar, 1967. This has often been classified as a biography. 11-14

______. *Young Mark: The Story of a Venture*, ill. by Victor G. Ambrus. Farrar, 1968. 12-15

BALDERSON, MARGARET. *When Jays Fly to Barbmo*, ill. by Victor G. Ambrus. World, 1969. 11-14

BAUMANN, HANS. *The Barque of the Brothers*, tr. by Isabel and Florence McHugh, ill. by Ulrik Schramm. Walck, 1958. 13-17

BEATTY, JOHN and PATRICIA. *At the Seven Stars*, with Hogarth prints and line drawings of Douglas Gorsline. Macmillan, 1963. 12-14

BENNETT, JOHN. *Master Skylark*, ill. by Reginald Birch. Grosset, 1924 (first pub. in 1897). One of the outstanding tales of Shakespeare's day. 12-14

BUFF, MARY. *The Apple and the Arrow*, ill. by Conrad Buff. Houghton, 1951. 9-12

BULLA, CLYDE. *The Sword in the Tree*, ill. by Paul Galdone. T. Crowell, 1956. 8-10

● BURTON, HESTER. *Beyond the Weir Bridge*, ill. by Victor G. Ambrus. T. Crowell, 1970. 12-15

______. *In Spite of All Terror*, ill. by Victor G. Ambrus. World, 1969. 11-14

______. *Time of Trial*, ill. by Victor G. Ambrus. World, 1964. 12-15

CHUTE, MARCHETTE. *The Innocent Wayfaring*, ill. by author. Dutton, 1955.

______. *The Wonderful Winter*, ill. by Grace Golden. Dutton, 1954. 11-14

COOLIDGE, OLIVIA. *Tales of the Crusades*, ill. adapted from prints by Gustave Doré. Houghton, 1970. Each of the stories that chronicle some facet of the long years of the Crusades is a splendid entity, wonderfully evocative and vividly written. The book does not give a cohesive picture of all those centuries but is impressive both as a literary and a historical work. 13 up

COOPER, SUSAN. *Dawn of Fear*, ill. by Margery Gill. Harcourt, 1970. 10-11

DE ANGELI, MARGUERITE. *The Door in the Wall*, ill. by author. Doubleday, 1949. Newbery Medal. 8-11

ELLIOTT, ARNOLD. *A Kind of Secret Weapon*. Scribner's, 1969. 10-13

FORMAN, JAMES. *Horses of Anger*. Farrar, 1967. 13 up

______. *Ring the Judas Bell*. Farrar, 1965. A story of Greece just after the time of the Nazi occupation when the Andarte were kidnapping children from the villages. A dramatic and sophisticated story; honest, grim, and moving. 13 up

● ______. *The Traitors*. Farrar, 1968. 13 up

GRAY, ELIZABETH JANET. *Adam of the Road*, ill. by Robert Lawson. Viking, 1942. Newbery Medal. 12-14

______. *I Will Adventure*, ill. by Corydon Bell. Viking, 1962. 11-14

GRUND, JOSEF CARL. *Never to Be Free*, tr. by Lucile Harrington. Little, 1970. 12-15

HARNETT, CYNTHIA. *Caxton's Challenge*, ill. by author. World, 1960. 12-16

______. *Nicholas and the Wool-Pack*, ill. by author. Putnam, 1953. 11-15

HAUGAARD, ERIK CHRISTIAN. *Hakon of Rogen's Saga*, ill. by Leo and Diane Dillon. Houghton, 1963. 11-14

______. *The Little Fishes*, ill. by Milton Johnson. Houghton, 1967. 12 up

______. *A Slave's Tale*, ill. by Leo and Diane Dillon. Houghton, 1965. 11-14

HAWES, CHARLES B. *Dark Frigate*. Little, 1924. An exciting sea tale in the days of the Stuarts. Newbery Medal. 12-14

HODGES, C. WALTER. *Columbus Sails*, ill. by author. Coward, 1950. This well-liked story of Columbus and his voyages is fiction based on facts and is tremendously moving. 11-14

______. *The Marsh King*, ill. by author. Coward, 1967. 12-15

______. *The Namesake*, ill. by author. Coward, 1964. 12-14

HOLM, ANNE. *North to Freedom*, tr. from the Danish by L. W. Kingsland. Harcourt, 1965. 11-13

HUNTER, MOLLIE. *The Ghosts of Glencoe*. Funk, 1969. 11-14

______. *The Lothian Run*. Funk, 1970. 12-15

______. *A Pistol in Greenyards*. Funk, 1968. 11-14

______. *The Spanish Letters*. Funk, 1967. 12-15

● ISH-KISHOR, SULAMITH. *A Boy of Old Prague*, ill. by Ben Shahn. Pantheon, 1963. 10-12

KELLY, ERIC. *The Trumpeter of Krakow*, rev. ed. Macmillan, 1966. Newbery Medal. 12-14

KENT, LOUISE ANDREWS. *He Went with Magellan*, ill. by Paul Quinn. Houghton, 1943. Fun and adventures, with enough background to make the book good historical fiction. 10-14

● LEVITIN, SONIA. *Journey to America*, ill. by Charles Robinson. Atheneum, 1970. The first-person story of a young Jewish girl and her family from Germany in the late 30s. Dramatic and well written. 10-12

LEWIS, HILDA. *The Gentle Falcon*. Criterion, 1957. A poignant and moving story of little Princess Isabella of France, who was married to Richard II of England when she was seven. Romantic in vein and rich in historical detail. 12 up

MAC PHERSON, MARGARET L. *The Rough Road*, ill. by Douglas Hall. Harcourt, 1966. Jim finds life difficult indeed living with unkind foster parents on the Isle of Skye during the depression of the 30's. Vivid atmosphere, characterization, and dialogue. 12-15

OLIVER, JANE [pseud.]. *Faraway Princess*, ill. by Jane Paton. St. Martin's, 1962. Princess Margaret, in flight from England after the Norman Conquest, finds sanctuary in Scotland and later a throne. Excellent historical fiction. 10-13

PEROVSKAYA, OLGA. *The Wolf in Olga's Kitchen*, tr. from the Russian by Fainna Glagoleva, ill. by Angie Culfogienis. Bobbs, 1969. The childhood reminiscences of a writer of Russian children's books, much of which concerns the family's endless parade of pets. The anecdotes have an appealing warmth and universality. 9-11

PEYTON, K. M. *The Edge of the Cloud*, ill. by Victor G. Ambrus. World, 1970.

______. *Flambards*, ill. by Victor G. Ambrus. World, 1968.

______. *Flambards in Summer*, ill. by Victor G. Ambrus. World, 1970. 12-15

PLOWMAN, STEPHANIE. *Three Lives for the Czar*. Houghton, 1970. The fascinating first-person story of Andrei Hamilton, whose family had for many generations lived in Russia and whose childhood playmate had been the Grand Duchess Olga. Successfully combines romantic appeal and sociological value. 13 up

POLLAND, MADELEINE. *Children of the Red King*, ill. by Annette Macarthur-Onslow. Holt, 1961. Grania and Fergus, children of Ireland's embattled king, are sent as captives to their father's enemy. The events leading to reunion with their father offer a vivid story of the Norman Conquest. 11-13

PYLE, HOWARD. *Men of Iron*, ill. by author. Harper, 1891.

______. *Otto of the Silver Hand*, ill. by author. Scribner's, 1888. 10-14

● RICHTER, HANS PETER. *Friedrich*, tr. from the German by Edite Kroll. Holt, 1970. 11-14

ROBBINS, RUTH. *The Emperor and the Drummer Boy*, ill. by Nicolas Sidjakov. Parnassus, 1962. 9-12

SERRAILLIER, IAN. *The Silver Sword*, ill. by C. Walter Hodges. Criterion, 1959. The unforgettable journey of four children who make their way from Warsaw to Switzerland and safety during World War II. 11-14

SEUBERLICH, HERTHA. *Annuzza: A Girl of Romania*, tr. by Stella Humphries, ill. by Gerhard Pallasch. Rand, 1962. A poignant story of rural pre-war Rumania tells of a gifted peasant girl who wins a scholarship and for a time loses her perspective on home and family. 12-15

● SLOBODKIN, FLORENCE. *Sarah Somebody*, ill. by Louis Slobodkin. Vanguard, 1970. The warm and sympathetic story of a nine-year-old girl in a Polish village in 1893 who gets a chance to learn to read and write—and to become somebody. 8-10

SUTCLIFF, ROSEMARY. *Dawn Wind*, ill. by Charles Keeping. Walck, 1962.

______. *The Eagle of the Ninth*, ill. by C. Walter Hodges. Walck, 1954. The story of a lost legion in Roman Britain of the second century.

______. *The Lantern Bearers*, ill. by Charles Keeping. Walck, 1959.

______. *The Mark of the Horse Lord*. Walck, 1965. Set in Scotland during the second century, this exciting adventure novel is fast paced with no slackening of suspense up to the last stunning episode.

______. *The Outcast*, ill. by Richard Kennedy. Walck, 1955. Unwanted by either Briton tribesmen or the Romans, orphaned Beric is forced to build a new life. Service as a galley slave is an unforgettable part of the story.

______. *The Shield Ring*, ill. by C. Walter Hodges. Walck, 1957. Eleventh-century England is the background for this tale of Norsemen against Norman invaders, and of the advance of two young people in the war-torn land.

______. *The Silver Branch*. Walck, 1958. Two young Romans, involved in the bitter intrigue between the ruler of Roman Britain and his rival, play a heroic part in bringing an assassin to justice.

______. *Warrior Scarlet*, ill. by Charles Keeping. Walck, 1958. In a unique tale of Bronze Age England, Drem kills his wolf and regains his tribal status despite a crippled arm. 12-16

______. *The Witch's Brat*, ill. by Richard Lebenson. Walck, 1970. An evocative story of Norman England, based on the actual founding of St. Bartholomew's Hospital. The story has strong, taut structure and good characterization, but is most distinguished by the colorful picture of a historical period. 11-14

● TREASE, GEOFFREY. *The Red Towers of Granada*, ill. by Charles Keeping. Vanguard, 1967. 11-14

TREECE, HENRY. *The Road to Miklagard*, ill. by Christine Price. Criterion, 1957. 11-14

______. *Viking's Dawn*, ill. by Christine Price. Criterion, 1956. First in an absorbing trilogy of eighth-century Viking life, in which youthful Harald Sigurdson accompanies his father on his first dangerous sea journey. In *The Road to Miklagard* (1957) his voyages are interrupted when he becomes a Moorish slave. In *Viking's Sunset* (1961) Harald, now a chieftain, sails his longboat to the shores of Lake Superior, and death intervenes on this last voyage. Harald's life saga conveys the vast scope of early Viking travels. 11-14

______. *Viking's Sunset*, ill. by Christine Price. Criterion, 1961. 11-14

§ TREVIÑO, ELIZABETH B. DE. *I, Juan de Pareja*. Parrar, 1965. Newbery Medal. 12-15

TUNIS, JOHN R. *Silence over Dunkerque*. Morrow, 1962. The evacuation of Dunkirk is the dramatic background for the story of British Sergeant Williams stranded in enemy-occupied France. A powerful story. 12-15

● VIVIER, COLETTE. *The House of the Four Winds*, tr. and ed. by Miriam Morton. Doubleday. 1969. 11-14

WATSON, SALLY. *Highland Rebel*, ill. by Scott Maclain. Holt, 1954. Scotland at the time of Bonnie Prince Charlie.

______. *Linnet*. Holt, 1971. Linnet is trapped by a criminal into involvement in a plot to overthrow Elizabeth I.

______. *Mistress Malapert*. Holt, 1955. 11-14

WILLIAMS, URSULA MORAY. *The Earl's Falconer*, ill. by Charles Geer. Morrow, 1961. Training falcons was not the privilege of peasant boys, but young Dickson's rare talent earned him the Earl's favor. A colorful tale of medieval England. 11-14

ZEI, ALKI. *Wildcat Under Glass*, tr. from the Greek by Edward Fenton. Holt, 1968. 10-12

## UNITED STATES HISTORICAL FICTION

§ BACON, MARTHA. *Sophia Scrooby Preserved*, ill. by David Omar White. Atlantic, 1968. A romantic tale of a cultured black girl whose lively adventures are described in the mannered style of early English novelists. 11-13

§ BACMEISTER, RHODA. *Voices in the Night*, ill. by Ann Grifalconi. Bobbs, 1965. 9-11

☆ BAKER, BETTY. *And One Was a Wooden Indian*. Macmillan, 1970. 11-15

______. *The Dunderhead War*. Harper, 1967. 11-14

______. *The Pig War*, ill. by Robert Lopshire. Harper, 1969. 7-8

☆§ ______. *Walk the World's Rim*. Harper, 1965. 11-14

BALL, ZACHARY [pseud.]. *North to Abilene*. Holiday, 1960. The thousand-mile cattle drive from Texas to Abilene challenges the resourcefulness of orphaned Seth in this fine tale of the early cattle industry. 12-15

BEATTY, PATRICIA. *Hail Columbia*, ill. by Liz Dauber. Morrow, 1970. 10-12

______. *A Long Way to Whiskey Creek*. Morrow, 1971. Set in Texas in 1879, a story in which two boys overcome the lingering hostility between Northern and Southern supporters. 10-12

☆ BELL, MARGARET. *Daughter of Wolf House*. Morrow, 1957. The coming of the white trader and his sons to the Alaskan salmon country changes the lives of the Indian villagers and brings romance to Nakatla, granddaughter of the chief. 12-15

BENCHLEY, NATHANIEL. *Sam the Minuteman*, ill. by Arnold Lobel. Harper, 1969. 7-9

BERRY, ERICK [pseud. for Allena Best]. *Hay-Foot, Straw-Foot*, ill. by author. Viking, 1954. Tale of a little drummer boy in the French and Indian War who inspired the tune of "Yankee Doodle." 9-12

BOLTON, CAROLE. *Never Jam Today*. Atheneum, 1971. Young Maddy becomes involved, through her Aunt Augusta, in the cause of women's suffrage. A realistic story with a commendable conclusion: Maddy passes up two love interests for the time being in favor of college and a career. 11-14

☆ BRINK, CAROL RYRIE. *Caddie Woodlawn*, ill. by Kate Seredy. Macmillan, 1935. Newbery Medal. 9-12

BULLA, CLYDE ROBERT. *Down the Mississippi*, ill. by Peter Burchard. T. Crowell, 1954. Erik leaves his Minnesota farm to go down the great river on a log raft as a cook's helper. Storms and an Indian raid add plenty of excitement. 8-10

☆ ______. *John Billington, Friend of Squanto*, ill. by Peter Burchard. T. Crowell, 1956. 7-9

______. *Riding the Pony Express*, ill. by Grace Paull. T. Crowell, 1948. An easy-to-read but never commonplace story of a boy who carried the mail in an emergency. 8-10

§ BURCHARD, PETER. *Bimby*, ill. by author. Coward, 1968. 9-11

______. *Jed*, ill. by author. Coward, 1960. 10-13

______. *North by Night*, ill. by author. Coward, 1962. Swift moving escape tale of two Yankee soldiers from a South Carolina Confederate prison. 12 up

CATTON, BRUCE. *Banners at Shenandoah*. Doubleday, 1955. Bruce Catton, Pulitzer Prize winner, writes absorbingly of Civil War days in this story of young Bob Hayden, flag bearer for General Sheridan. 12-16

● CAUDILL, REBECCA. *The Far-Off Land*, ill. by Brinton Turkle. Viking, 1964. 12-14

______. *Tree of Freedom*, ill. by Dorothy Bayley Morse. Viking, 1949. 12-14

☆ CLAPP, PATRICIA. *Constance; A Story of Early Plymouth*. Lothrop, 1968. 12-15

COATSWORTH, ELIZABETH. *Away Goes Sally*, ill. by Helen Sewell. Macmillan, 1934.

______. *The Fair American*, ill. by Helen Sewell. Macmillan, 1940.

______. *Five Bushel Farm*, ill. by Helen Sewell. Macmillan, 1939. 10-12

§ COBLENTZ, CATHERINE. *Martin and Abraham Lincoln*, ill. by Trientja. Childrens Pr., 1967. 7-10

CONSTANT, ALBERTA WILSON. *Those Miller Girls!* ill. by Joe and Beth Krush. T. Crowell, 1965. A period story set in Kansas early in the century. The motherless Miller girls come with their father to his new job at Eastern Kansas Classical College. 10-12

DALGLIESH, ALICE. *Adam and the Golden Cock*, ill. by Leonard Weisgard. Scribner's, 1959. 8-9

______. *America Travels*, rev. ed., ill. by Hildegard Woodward. Macmillan, 1961. Short stories about each phase of transportation from the stagecoach to the space age. 9-11

______. *The Bears on Hemlock Mountain*, ill. by Helen Sewell. Scribner's, 1952.

☆ ______. *The Courage of Sarah Noble*, ill. by Leonard Weisgard. Scribner's, 1954.

______. *The 4th of July Story*, ill. by Marie Nonnast. Scribner's, 1956.

☆ ______. *The Thanksgiving Story*, ill. by Helen Sewell. Scribner's, 1954. 7-10

☆ EDMONDS, WALTER D. *The Matchlock Gun*, ill. by Paul Lantz. Dodd, 1941. Newbery Medal. 10-12

ERSKINE, DOROTHY WARD. *Big Ride*, ill. by Hubert Buel. T. Crowell, 1958. The story of Captain De Anza's colonizing expedition from Mexico to California and the dangers encountered on the long and perilous journey. 10-14

§ FALL, THOMAS. *Canalboat to Freedom*, ill. by Joseph Cellini. Dial, 1966. Orphaned Benja is indentured as a canalboat worker. There he meets Lundius, a freed slave who becomes his friend and teacher. When Lundius is killed working for the Underground Railroad, Ben grieves. The emphasis in the story is on their developing friendship and on Ben's gradual realization of the horrors of slavery. 11-14

☆ FIELD, RACHEL. *Calico Bush*, ill. by Allen Lewis. Macmillan, 1931. 10-14

FLEISCHMAN, SID. *Mr. Mysterious & Company*, ill. by Eric von Schmidt. Little, 1962. Traveling under their intriguing stage name, the delightful Hackett family give magic shows in small pioneer towns as they work their way west from Texas to a San Diego ranch. A very different and appealing story of the early West. 10-12

FORBES, ESTHER. *Johnny Tremain*, ill. by Lynd Ward. Houghton, 1943. Newbery Medal. 12-14

§ FRITZ, JEAN. *Brady*, ill. by Lynd Ward. Coward, 1960. 10-13

______. *The Cabin Faced West*, ill. by Feodor Rojankovsky. Coward, 1958. 8-10

______. *Early Thunder*, ill. by Lynd Ward. Coward, 1967. Set in Salem in 1775, the story of a boy whose loyalty moves from King to Patriot cause. 11-14

______. *I, Adam*, ill. by Peter Burchard. Coward, 1963. A good period story, set in New England in the mid-19th century, about a young man who decides that his real goal is an education. 11-14

☆ GOBLE, PAUL and DOROTHY. *Red Hawk's Account of Custer's Last Battle*, ill. by authors. Pantheon, 1970. 10-12

☆ HAIG-BROWN, RODERICK. *The Whale People*, ill. by Mary Weiler. Morrow, 1963. 10-12

HALL, ANNA GERTRUDE. *Cyrus Holt and the Civil War*, ill. by Dorothy Bayley Morse. Viking, 1964. 9-11

HAUGAARD, ERIK CHRISTIAN. *Orphans of the Wind*, ill. by Milton Johnson. Houghton, 1966. 10-12

HAYS, WILMA PITCHFORD. *Christmas on the Mayflower*, ill. by Roger Duvoisin. Coward, 1956. 7-9

☆ ______. *May Day for Samoset*, ill. by Marilyn Miller. Coward, 1968. 8-10

☆ ______. *Pilgrim Thanksgiving*, ill. by Leonard Weisgard. Coward, 1955. 8-10

HUNT, IRENE. *Across Five Aprils*. Follett, 1964. An impressive book both as a historically authenticated Civil War novel and as a beautifully written family story. The realistic treatment of the involved emotional conflicts within a border-state family is superb. 12 up

JOHNSON, ANNABEL and EDGAR. *Torrie*. Harper, 1960. It took the grim realities of a covered-wagon journey to California to jolt rebellious fourteen-year-old Torrie from her self-centered ways. Family relationships are well depicted in this pioneer story of the 1840s. 13-15

☆ JONES, WEYMAN. *The Edge of Two Worlds*, ill. by J. C. Kocsis. Dial, 1968. 10-13

☆ ______. *The Talking Leaf*, ill. by Harper Johnson. Dial, 1965. 10-12

☆ KEITH, HAROLD. *Rifles for Watie*. T. Crowell, 1957. Newbery Medal. 12-16

☆ LAMPMAN, EVELYN. *Cayuse Courage*. Harcourt, 1970. 11-14

☆ ______. *Once Upon the Little Big Horn*, ill. by John Gretzer. T. Crowell, 1971. 10-12

☆ ______. *Tree Wagon*, ill. by Robert Frankenberg. Doubleday, 1953. 10-13

☆ LATHAM, JEAN. *This Dear-Bought Land*, ill. by Jacob Landau. Harper, 1957. An outstanding story of Captain John Smith and the settlement of Jamestown. 11-14

LENSKI, LOIS. *Puritan Adventure*, ill. by author. Lippincott, 1944. Massachusetts is the background of this vivid tale of colonial times. A light-hearted young aunt from England visits a strict Puritan family, bringing gaiety and laughter with her. 11-14

§ LEVY, MIMI COOPER. *Corrie and the Yankee*, ill. by Ernest Crichlow. Viking, 1959. Corrie, a little black girl on a South Carolina plantation, rescues a wounded Yankee soldier and helps him to safety. 10-13

LOBEL, ARNOLD. *On the Day Peter Stuyvesant Sailed into Town*, ill. by author. Harper, 1971. 5-8

LOWREY, JANETTE. *Six Silver Spoons*, ill. by Robert Quackenbush. Harper, 1971. A British soldier helps two children carry safely the silver spoons made by Paul Revere during the Revolutionary War. 6-8

☆ MARRIOTT, ALICE. *Indian Annie: Kiowa Captive*. McKay, 1965. 11-14

MASON, MIRIAM. *Caroline and Her Kettle Named Maud*, ill. by Kathleen Voute. Macmillan, 1951.

______ *Little Jonathan*, ill. by George and Doris Hauman. Macmillan, 1944.

Easy-to-read pioneer stories full of humor and action. 8-10

MEADER, STEPHEN W. *Boy with a Pack*, ill. by Edward Shenton. Harcourt, 1939. An exciting story of a young Yankee peddler. 11-14

§ MEADOWCROFT, ENID. *By Secret Railway*, ill. by Henry C. Pitz. T. Crowell, 1948. The story of a white boy's rescue of a freed black who had been carried to the South again illegally. 11-14

MEIGS, CORNELIA. *Clearing Weather*, ill. by Frank Dobias. Little, 1928. 11-14

______. *Master Simon's Garden*, ill. by John Rae. Macmillan, 1929. 11-14

______. *The Willow Whistle*, ill. by E. B. Smith. Macmillan, 1931. 8-10

Well-written historical tales little used today.

§ MONJO, FERDINAND. *The Drinking Gourd*, ill. by Fred Brenner. Harper, 1970. 7-8

☆ ______. *Indian Summer*, ill. by Anita Lobel. Harper, 1968. A Kentucky family defends itself against Indian attack while their father is away fighting with George Washington. 7-8

______. *The Vicksburg Veteran*, ill. by Douglas Gorsline. Simon, 1971. 7-10

☆ O'DELL, SCOTT. *Island of the Blue Dolphins*. Houghton, 1960. Newbery Medal. 11-14

☆ ______. *The King's Fifth*, ill. by Samuel Bryant. Houghton, 1966. 12-15

☆ ______. *Sing Down the Moon*. Houghton, 1970. Bright

Morning is a young Navaho girl whose tribe is forced out of their homes by white men and driven to Fort Sumner. She persuades her husband to escape and they start their peaceful life anew. The simple, almost terse, style makes more vivid the tragedy and danger. 11-14

☆ PARISH, PEGGY. *Granny and the Indians*, ill. by Brinton Turkle. Macmillan, 1969. 7-8

§ PETRY, ANN. *Tituba of Salem Village*. T. Crowell, 1964. 12-15

POPE, ELIZABETH MARIE. *The Sherwood Ring*, ill. by Evaline Ness. Houghton, 1958. Beautifully told romances of Revolutionary times and of today are skillfully interwoven in a story rich in suspense and mystery. 12-16

☆ SANDOZ, MARI. *The Story Catcher*, ill. by Elsie J. McCorkell. Westminster, 1963. The dramatic and moving story of Lance, a young Sioux brave who longs to achieve status with his people. The blending of style and subject is impressive. 11-14

SCHAEFER, JACK. *Mavericks*, ill. by Lorence Bjorklund. Houghton, 1967. This is a deeply romantic picture of the old West, written in a strong and flavorful prose, moving back and forth from old Jake Hanlon's past to the present. 12-15

☆ SHARP, EDITH LAMBERT. *Nkwala*, ill. by William Winter. Little, 1958. Stirringly written historical tale of a young Spokane Indian who at last wins his adult name. 11-13

☆ SPEARE, ELIZABETH GEORGE. *Calico Captive*, ill. by W. T. Mars. Houghton, 1957. Stirring junior novel of Miriam Willard, a young Indian captive taken to Canada during the French and Indian Wars. 11-15

● ______. *The Witch of Blackbird Pond*. Houghton, 1958. Newbery Medal. 12-16

STEELE, WILLIAM O. *The Buffalo Knife*, ill. by Paul Galdone. Harcourt, 1952. A thousand-mile flatboat trip is an exciting adventure for a boy of nine. 9-12

______. *The Perilous Road*, ill. by Paul Galdone. Harcourt, 1958. 11-13

☆ ______. *Wayah of the Real People*, ill. by Isa Barnett. Holt, 1964. 11-13

______. *Wilderness Journey*, ill. by Paul Galdone. Harcourt, 1953. A sickly boy becomes a resourceful pioneer. 9-12

§ SWIFT, HILDEGARDE H. *Railroad to Freedom*, ill. by James Daugherty. Harcourt, 1932. A true story of a black slave who helped her people to freedom during the Civil War. 10-14

● TURKLE, BRINTON. *Obadiah the Bold*, ill. by author. Viking, 1965. 8-9

● ______. *Thy Friend, Obadiah*, ill. by author. Viking, 1969. 7-9

UCHIDA, YOSHIKO. *Journey to Topaz*, ill. by Donald Carrick. Scribner's, 1971. A Japanese-American family is sent to a World War II relocation center in Utah. 10-12

WIBBERLEY, LEONARD. *John Treegate's Musket*. Farrar, 1959. First in an outstanding series. Other titles are: *Peter Treegate's War* (1960), *Sea Captain from Salem* (1961), *Treegate's Raiders* (1962). 12-15

§ ______. *Leopard's Prey*. Farrar, 1971. 11-14

WILDER, LAURA INGALLS. *The First Four Years*, ill. by Garth Williams. Harper, 1971. Found among Mrs. Wilder's papers after her death, and published without revision, this is the story of her first years as a farmer's wife on a South Dakota homestead. The same charm and virtues as the Little House books. 10-14

______. *Little House in the Big Woods*, ill. by Garth Williams. Harper, 1953. Other titles in the series are: *Little House on the Prairie, On the Banks of Plum Creek, By the Shores of Silver Lake, Farmer Boy, The Long Winter, Little Town on the Prairie, These Happy Golden Years*. 9-14

WILLIAMSON, JOANNE S. *The Glorious Conspiracy*. Knopf, 1961. Ben Brown was a half-starved child laborer in the Manchester cotton mills when he escaped to America. In New York City he found a richer future and a chance to work for the Federal Party's democratic ideals. 12-16

WILLIS, ROBERT J. *Molly's Hannibal*, ill. by Ursula Koering. Follett, 1957. 8-10

☆ WILSON, HAZEL. *His Indian Brother*, ill. by Robert Henneberger. Abingdon, 1955. Based on a true incident of the 1800s is this story of Brad Porter, left alone in a Maine pioneer cabin and rescued from starvation by an Indian chief and his son. 10-14

☆§ WOJCIECHOWSKA, MAIA. *Odyssey of Courage: The Story of Álvar Núñez Cabeza de Vaca*, ill. by Alvin Smith. Atheneum, 1965. 12-14

☆§ WORMSER, RICHARD. *The Black Mustanger*, ill. by Don Bolognese. Morrow, 1971. Set in Texas in the period after the Civil War, the story of a white boy whose mentor is a cowboy, half black and half Apache. 10-14

§ WRISTON, HILDRETH. *Susan's Secret*, ill. by W. T. Mars. Farrar, 1957. Suspense-filled story of a little Vermont girl who undertook her absent family's task of guiding fugitive slaves to the next Underground station. 9-12

YATES, ELIZABETH. *Carolina's Courage*, ill. by Nora S. Unwin. Dutton, 1964. A pioneer story for girls, written in sedate style, realistic and slow-moving. 8-10

## HISTORICAL FICTION: OTHER COUNTRIES

BARTOS-HÖPPNER, B. *Hunters of Siberia*, tr. by Anthea Bell. Walck, 1969. A novel set in the early part of the century that is both a plea for conservation of wild life and a remarkable picture of a way of life now ended. 12-15

BAUMANN, HANS. *Sons of the Steppe*. Walck, 1958. 12-16

BULLA, CLYDE ROBERT. *Viking Adventure*, ill. by Douglas Gorsline. T. Crowell, 1963. 8-10

☆ HARRIS, CHRISTIE. *Raven's Cry*, ill. by Bill Reid. Atheneum, 1966. 10-15

☆ ______. *West with the White Chiefs*, ill. by Walter Ferro. Atheneum, 1965. 11-15

☆ HOUSTON, JAMES. *The White Archer; An Eskimo Legend*, ill. by author. Harcourt, 1967. Kungo is a young Eskimo who vows revenge when his parents are killed and his sister is taken captive by a band of Indians. The description of his years of cold, patient planning is in low key. 10-12

☆ LAMPMAN, EVELYN. *The Tilted Sombrero*, ill. by Ray Cruz. Doubleday, 1966. 11-14

LEWIS, ELIZABETH FOREMAN. *To Beat a Tiger; One Needs a Brother's Help*, ill. by John Heuhnergarth. Holt, 1956. 14-17

______. *Young Fu of the Upper Yangtze*, ill. by Kurt Wiese. Holt, 1932. Newbery Medal. 13-15

LEWIS, THOMAS. *Hill of Fire*, ill. by Joan Sandin. Harper, 1971. 6-8

MONJO, FERDINAND. *Pirates in Panama*, ill. by Wallace Tripp. Simon, 1970. 7-9

RITCHIE, RITA. *The Golden Hawks of Genghis Khan*, ill. by Lorence F. Bjorklund. Dutton, 1958.

______. *Secret Beyond the Mountains*. Dutton, 1960.

______. *The Year of the Horse*, ill. by Lorence F. Bjorklund. Dutton, 1957.

These are outstanding tales of the years of Mongol supremacy. 12-15

● VINEBERG, ETHEL. *Grandmother Came from Dworitz; A Jewish Story*, ill. by Rita Briansky. Tundra, 1969. The first of a series of books on the origins of Canadians (a French edition of each will be published), the story based on the life of the author or illustrator of the book. The text here is sedate but the material is fascinating, giving a vivid picture of the restrictions upon nineteenth-century Russian Jews, their communal life, and their emigration. 9-12

§ WATSON, SALLY. *Jade*. Holt, 1968. 11-14

# Part Five
# Stranger Than Fiction

# Chapter 15
# Biography

The *Oxford English Dictionary* defines biography as "the history of the lives of individual men as a branch of literature." Here, as Harold Nicolson indicated, are the three points of emphasis: *history*, that is, facts authentic and verifiable; an *individual*, not a paragon or a type; *literature*, that is, a conscious work of art. This description with some amplifications not only defines biography, but suggests the standards by which we should judge it.

## BIOGRAPHY AS HISTORY

### Authenticity

If a biography is the history of a person's life, it should be as accurate and authentic as research can make it. The biographer must read the complete literary works of his hero if he is a writer, and study everything he has created or accomplished. He must examine any letters or diaries or journals left by the man. He must in turn compare the man's personal papers with the comments of his contemporaries as recorded in their books or letters or diaries. If these seem contradictory, the biographer must discover what the attitude of the contemporary was—friendly, worshipful, or definitely antagonistic. This may involve consulting the available writings of still other contemporaries who knew both men and who in turn left records of their relationships. The mass of personal papers and documents which a conscientious modern biographer goes through in order to be even reasonably certain of the authenticity of his material is staggering. Esther Forbes in her meticulous research for her *Paul Revere and the World He Lived In* gathered enough information about the lively antics of Boston's apprentices to give body to a second book, *Johnny Tremain* (p. 514). The limitations of biography had prevented her from using her imagination or guessing at some of the things that happened in the life of Paul Revere; so *Johnny* was the fictional outlet for all her wonderings about those busy apprentices.

### Objectivity

Esther Forbes' experience in writing the life of Paul Revere suggests another test for biography as history. A biographer is not free to give his own opinions as fact or to present an

## VIEWPOINTS

Certainty of knowledge not only excludes mistake, but fortifies veracity. What we collect by conjecture, and by conjecture only can one man judge of another's motives or sentiments, is easily modified by fancy or by desire; as objects imperfectly discerned take forms from the hope or fear of the beholder. But that which is fully known cannot be falsified but with reluctance of understanding, and alarm of conscience: of understanding, the lover of truth; of conscience, the sentinel of virtue.

He that writes the life of another is either his friend or his enemy, and wishes either to exalt his praise or aggravate his infamy: many temptations to falsehood will occur in the disguise of passions, too specious to fear much resistance. Love of virtue will animate panegyric, and hatred of wickedness embitter censure. The zeal of gratitude, the ardour of patriotism, fondness for an opinion, or fidelity to a party, may easily overpower the vigilance of a mind habitually well disposed, and prevail over unassisted and unfriended veracity.—Samuel Johnson, *The Rambler*, No. 60, Sat. Oct. 13, 1750.

---

interpretation for which he has no evidence. His hero's deeds should speak for themselves. If they seem ambiguous, the author may speculate about the contradictory evidence, but he may not take sides or tell the reader what to think. Was Sam Houston completely honest and disinterested in his dealings with the Indians and with his Cherokee foster father? Marquis James in *The Raven*, a biography of Sam Houston, never tells us how he regards Houston's actions. He presents the evidence and lets the reader draw his own conclusions. And readers of *The Raven* differ in their judgment of Sam, just as Sam's contemporaries themselves differed.

It also follows that the biographer may report only those words and thoughts which the hero has recorded or is known to have spoken. Some biographers have got around this strict limitation by saying, "Perhaps he thought . . ." or "Perhaps he meant what he said, who knows?" Lytton Strachey uses this device repeatedly in his *Queen Victoria*. When the gouty old king whom she was to succeed asked the young Victoria for her favorite tune, she replied without a moment's hesitation, "God Save the King." This, Strachey tells us, "has been praised as an early example of a tact which was afterwards famous." Then he adds cryptically, "But she was a very truthful child, and perhaps it was her genuine opinion." He closes his book with a dramatic use of this device. Describing the dying queen, old, blind, and silent, he suggests that she *may perhaps* have recalled her past. Then, as if Victoria were thinking aloud, he briefly and tenderly reviews her life, going back to the little girl in "sprigged muslin, and the trees and the grass at Kensington." André Maurois uses this same device differently but just as dramatically in relating the possible "dreams" of the old and ailing Disraeli. So Jeanette Eaton also uses it in her account of the dying Washington in *Leader by Destiny*. It is a legitimate device, but when it is overused it may become a not too subtle method of influencing the opinions of the reader.

### Documentation

For many people, one of the most important tests of a good biography is the accuracy and thoroughness of its documentation. Nicolson in *The Development of English Biography* insists that a biography should be as scrupulously documented as history. Strachey's *Queen Victoria* is a model in this respect, for every incident and every description is conscientiously documented in the footnotes.

Juvenile biographies are usually not documented by footnotes, although the author may supply sources in a separate section, a bibliography, or an afterword. Although children may never read the author's comments on sources, careful documentation and acknowledgment of sources is an indication to adults of the authenticity of the material, and it could serve a similar purpose for older children and young people. A respect for objective, verifiable reporting can be started with any child old enough to read substantial biographies.

## BIOGRAPHY AS THE INDIVIDUAL

All of us are familiar with the older biographies which presented a man as a type—Washington the ever truthful, Lincoln the sad, and Benjamin Franklin the thrifty. Franklin seems to have been cast in the role of the *thrifty* merely because he wrote a number of wise saws on the desirability of this virtue. As a matter of fact, he sent home from England a continual stream of handsome and extravagant presents, such as silver-handled knives, fine china, a whole box of table glass, carpets, even a harpsichord for Sally.[1] Later, in France, his bills for his wine cellar were lavish, and he finally remarked plaintively that frugality was "a virtue I never could acquire in myself."[2] So "perhaps," as the biographers say, his adages on thrift were reminders for his unthrifty self, as well as for the rest of the world.

Franklin is indeed a good example of a figure almost spoiled for young people in the past because he had been typed as a paragon. Today in the new biographies young people and even children may catch a glimpse of the real Franklin—witty, worldly, urbane, adored by the ladies and adoring them in turn, equally at home in the wilderness and in the court, a scientist, a man of letters, a diplomat, an amateur musician, lazy and prodigiously industrious, in short, a composite of strength and weakness on a grand scale, with a tremendous brain directing the whole. To have made Franklin, of all men, into the image of a stuffy prig was a crime. To rediscover the whole man and reveal him to this generation, as Carl Van Doren has done, is a crowning achievement of modern biography.

1. Carl Van Doren, *Benjamin Franklin*, pp. 276–277.
2. Ibid., p. 637.

### VIEWPOINTS

A biography is not an encyclopedia, it is the story of a life. George Macaulay Trevelyan has said it is in narrative that modern historical writing is weakest. I think this happens when the writer tries to crowd too much information on his page at one time, or, sinning in the opposite direction, assumes the reader is familiar with names and events simply because he, the writer, knows them so well. All this information, gathered in the library, has its place, a canny page or paragraph where it will fit painlessly—which means clearly and entertainingly, so that the reader will feel he has made a discovery.—Catherine Drinker Bowen, *Biography: The Craft and the Calling*, Little, Brown and Co., 1968, pp. 50–51.

### The Whole Man

Carl Van Doren's *Benjamin Franklin* is an example of the way in which modern historical research, in the hands of skillful writers, is destroying the typed hero of the past and portraying the whole man. The book that is generally considered the greatest biography in the English language, James Boswell's *Life of Samuel Johnson* (1791), is as modern in this respect as Strachey's *Queen Victoria* (1924). But despite Boswell's early demonstration of what a good biography should be, the typed life somehow or other became firmly established in the years before Strachey and as such was thoroughly disliked by youngsters.

But, it is objected, while it may be all right to give adults the whole truth about a man—his vices, the tragedies in his life, his failures—still children cannot and should not have the complete account. This may be true. The younger children are, the less they are able to understand or to accept the ultimate tragedy of a life. A child's life of Mozart[3] terminates with his first adult triumphs, and a biography of Shelley[4] for the teen age concludes before the tragedies and the scandals begin. Neither record is falsified; it just does not continue long enough to catch up with sorrow. *The Raven*, Marquis James' adult biography of Sam Houston, tells about Sam's taking an Indian mate and abandoning her when it was convenient. *Six Feet Six*, the Bessie and Marquis James version of this biography for children, omits such episodes. This certainly is not presenting the whole man. But while adults are entitled to a complete picture, children are not always ready for it. Juvenile biographies should be true as far as they go, with no falsifications, but the whole adult truth may not be within younger children's range of comprehension and judgment.

## VIEWPOINTS

. . . we cannot thank [the biographer] sufficiently for what he does for us. For we are incapable of living wholly in the intense world of the imagination. The imagination is a faculty that soon tires and needs rest and refreshment. But for a tired imagination the proper food is not inferior poetry or minor fiction—indeed they blunt and debauch it—but sober fact, that 'authentic information' from which, as Lytton Strachey has shown us, good biography is made. When and where did the real man live; how did he look; did he wear laced boots or elastic-sided; who were his aunts, and his friends; how did he blow his nose; whom did he love, and how; and when he came to die did he die in his bed like a Christian, or . . . .—Virginia Woolf, "The New Biography," *The New York Herald Tribune*, October 30, 1927. Reprinted in *Granite and Rainbow* by Leonard Woolf, Harcourt, Brace, New York, 1958, p. 155.

### Vivid Details

Boswell remains the greatest of all biographers, partly because of his tremendous gusto for details. We know how Samuel Johnson dressed, how he went through a door—it had to be with one particular foot or he backed up and tried it again. We know what prayers he said; how desperately he feared death and how he loved the company of men; how he sneaked out at night so that the servants would not know about his buying oysters for Hodge, his cat; what he thought about taverns and second marriages; how he regarded David Garrick. In fact, we scarcely know anyone else so well as we know Samuel Johnson when we have finished reading Boswell. In the same way, Catherine Drinker Bowen brings *John Adams and the American Revolution* to life, and Van Doren portrays the real *Benjamin Franklin*—not through large generalizations but through a multitude of rich and arresting details.

In the past, biographies written for young people failed at precisely this point. They told children about the large affairs in which their heroes played a part but neglected to give any account of the individual man with his amusing idiosyncrasies, peculiar bents, and special talents which made him unique among other men. Children delight in Franklin's account of himself as a boy floating in a pond on his back propelled by a kite;[5] or in the story of Davy Crockett crossing an icy river in December, sometimes in and sometimes out of the water, but managing to keep dry his keg of gunpowder, a bundle, and his gun, "Betsy";[6] or of Haydn cutting off the pigtail of a fellow chorister;[7] or of Lewis and Clark, the intrepid explorers, feeling uncomfortable when the Indians at a ceremonial feast served a stewed dog, reminding them of their own Spot;[8] or of Lincoln holding a child upside down to make tracks on

3. Opal Wheeler and Sybil Deucher, *Mozart, the Wonder Boy*.
4. Laura Benét, *The Boy Shelley*.

5. Carl Van Doren, *Benjamin Franklin*, p. 17.
6. Constance Rourke, *Davy Crockett*, pp. 94–97.
7. Opal Wheeler and Sybil Deucher. *Joseph Haydn: The Merry Little Peasant*, p. 45.
8. Julia Davis, *No Other White Men*, p. 71.

the ceiling as a joke on the stepmother he dearly loved, a joke he righted with a fresh coat of whitewash.[9]

To be told that Penn dressed in sober clothes is dull enough. To learn that even after he turned Quaker he still loved good apparel and went to meet the velvet-clad Lord Baltimore in sober brown but cut by the best London tailor from the finest materials—ah, that is more human.[10] To read that Penn was tried for holding a meeting with other Quakers is dreary, but young people warm immediately to the picture of Penn on trial, shut up in a cage at the back of the courtroom, shouting out his own defense so effectively that he won the jury to his side and later won the right of the jury to have its decisions upheld in the English courts.[11] Little incidents and big ones which reveal the spirited human being who will not be downed and who travels his own unique way bring the individual to life for the reader. Revealing details are the very essence of good biography.

## BIOGRAPHY AS LITERATURE

If biography is a branch of literature, then it, like any other work of art, should be a consciously planned composition. It has a subject, a theme, unity attained through that theme, style, a pattern of the whole, and a pattern of the parts. These may not be evident to the casual reader, but if the life is written with any skill, they are there.

### Theme and Unity

Biography like history is based on documented facts. No liberties may be taken with these facts; no flights of fancy are permissible. The biographer begins by assembling all the documents and examining all the evidence. But the modern biographer feels that he should not give his accumulated research to the reader in its endless and often trivial details. He must choose those which he thinks will most truly reveal the man as the author has come to know him. It is in this matter of selection and organization that the biography ceases to be purely history and becomes a work of art. For the author, through his reading of all the sources and his weighing of all the evidence, gradually develops a theme. Around this theme he organizes the facts so that they not only reveal the man as he has come to see him but give unity to that life and to the book. If he selects his theme before he examines the evidence, he will write a biased, subjective biography. If he sees no theme emerging out of the chaos of events, he will write a chronological record which may lack wholeness and charm. This is the modern point of view, influenced especially by the French. André Maurois, for example, in *Aspects of Biography*, compares the writing of a biography to painting:

> *The biographer, like the portrait painter and the landscape painter, must pick out the essential qualities in the whole subject which he is contemplating. By such a choice, if he can make the choice without weakening the whole, he is very precisely performing the artist's function.*

Maurois speaks too of the symmetry of certain lives and remarks that even Byron's life, with all its incidents, "must also have its hidden unity; the problem is to find it." So the author of a biography must first saturate himself with facts; then he must synthesize these facts until the hero begins to emerge as an integrated human being in spite of contradictions, with purposes and a direction of energies that give wholeness and significance to the life. In this unity of a life the author finds his theme, and around the theme composes his book.

Carl Van Doren, in his *Benjamin Frank-*

9. Ingri and Edgar d'Aulaire, *Abraham Lincoln* (unpaged).
10. Elizabeth Janet Gray, *Penn*, p. 206.
11. Ibid., Chapter 15.

*lin*, states his theme clearly in his last paragraph. Franklin, says the author, "seems to have been more than any single man: a harmonious human multitude." There it is, the core of the man's life—his remarkable diversity, all the interests and powers of the man in balance, "a harmonious human multitude."

Turning to children's or young people's biographies, we often find the theme in the title—*Carry On, Mr. Bowditch* (Nathaniel Bowditch), *He Heard America Sing* (Stephen Foster), *Invincible Louisa* (Louisa M. Alcott).

In *Leader by Destiny*, the life of George Washington, Jeanette Eaton shows how over and over again circumstances and the times interfered with Washington's life and called him to other ways of living. He might have been a homespun frontiersman, playing a gallant part no doubt, but his brother's death gave him Mount Vernon and turned him into a country gentleman. This role was forwarded by his neighbor's wife, the lovely Sally Fairfax (destiny again), who taught him the manners and ways of gentlemen. Then the country squire was called upon for soldiery and more soldiery, and finally he was made the head of the Continental Army. Seven long years of campaigning followed, with his whole heart yearning for the gracious life of Mount Vernon. Then came peace and a chance to realize his desires, but destiny called him once more, this time to the Presidency, the gravest responsibility an American had ever faced. Washington played a great part in every role he undertook, but it would seem that these roles were not of his own choosing. He would have been a leader in any situation, but destiny called him to national greatness.

Not all biographies adhere so closely and obviously to theme and unity as those just cited, certainly not the early examples of biography. But modern biographies, including those for young people, seem to follow this pattern and are organized around a central theme which gives a dramatic unity to the book.

### Style and Pattern

If biography is to be judged as literature, it must also have a pleasing style. As one authority has said, style is "the auditory effect of prose." The prose must be good to read and it must be appropriate to the subject matter and to the mood of the story. Read aloud this excerpt from James Daugherty's *Daniel Boone:*

> *When Daniel came back to the Boones' farm in the Yadkin valley, he up and married his Irish sweetheart, Rebecca Bryan, whose family had settled in the valley near them. There was a hilarious shindig with the Carolina fiddles shaking down the moon. When the logs were all cut for the house-raising, the neighbors for miles around took a hand. By sundown they stuck a pine tree on the ridgepole of a brand new cabin in the clearing and ate and danced till morning. (p. 21)*

Notice the strong swing and rhythm of this prose. Notice, too, the homespun quality of the words—pioneer talk, not recorded in tiresome detail but richly suggested.

This book, deservedly a Newbery Award, is one of the finest modern biographies written for young people and serves as an example of the way in which style may reflect the subject matter and mood of the narrative. James Daugherty's illustrations for this book have the same sweep and swing of his verbal style. Fat babies "wrassling" with wildcats and coasting "down the Cumberlands in three cornered pants," North Carolinian youth dancing the moon down, big husky women cradling their babies tenderly—these pictures have an epic flow and a stirring sense of movement which rightly illustrate the tale.

A fine example of style and pattern in biography is Carl Sandburg's *Abe Lincoln Grows Up*, adapted from the first twenty-seven chapters of his book for adults, *The Prairie Years*. Picking the book up anywhere, you discover that it reads aloud so easily and naturally you just keep reading. Of Tom Lincoln, the father, Sandburg writes:

## VIEWPOINTS

Biography *is* a craft—like all the other arts—in that it employs techniques which can be learned by anybody, which are outside personal commitment. It can be loosely called a science in that, for part of his labors, the biographer proceeds inductively: he collects facts in order to arrive at conclusions from them. It is an art, however lowly, because the biographer is himself interfused into what he has made, and, like the novelist and the painter, shapes his material in order to create effects.

. . . The novelist's pen is a delicate instrument. If the biographer holds something like that pen in one hand, he has to wield a shovel with the other. His ore is not inner experience, the quicksilver stuff of gland and nerve. It is brute matter, wrested from the earth. . . . To exist at all, it must feed upon the truth of facts, and yet to exist on its highest level, it must pursue the truth of interpretation.—Paul Murray Kendall, *The Art of Biography*. W.W. Norton and Co., New York, 1965, p. xii.

---

*He wasn't exactly lazy, he was sort of independent, and liked to be where he wasn't interfered with. . . . He was a wild buck at fighting, when men didn't let him alone. A man talked about a woman once in a way Tom Lincoln didn't like. And in the fight that came, Tom bit a piece of the man's nose off. . . . Though he was short spoken, he knew yarns, could crack jokes, and had a reputation as a story-teller when he got started.* (pp. 12–13)

Of Nancy Hanks, Sandburg writes differently:

*The Lincolns had a cabin of their own to live in. It stood among wild crab-apple trees.*

*And the smell of wild crab-apple blossoms . . . came keen that summer to the nostrils of Nancy Hanks.*

*The summer stars that year shook out pain and warning, strange laughters, for Nancy Hanks.* (p. 30)

A different use of pattern is well illustrated by the opening chapter of Elizabeth Janet Gray's *Penn*. She describes Penn's father, young Captain Penn, already rising in the English navy, in which eventually he becomes admiral; his wife with her Irish estates; the king with his two sons, James and Charles; a shoemaker named George Fox; an eight-month-old heiress, Gulielma Springett; and the lusty baby, William Penn.

*And all these scattered lives were to play their part in the life of the baby who slept and cried and ate and slept again in sight of the steep walls of the old, grim Tower, into which had gone, down the centuries, many prisoners, young and old, frightened and defiant; and from which fewer had come out. The Tower too had its part.* (p. 7)

Here, we are told, are all the threads of the story, all the important elements in the life of the baby, who grew to be the man of whom it was said later, "the world has not yet caught up with William Penn." There in that first chapter are the small patterns which will make up the large pattern.

These examples show how biography, although as scrupulously documented as history, may become in the act of composition a branch of literature. Yet good adult biographies are as sound sources for facts as histories. This may also be true of biographies for children and young people but with certain differences.

## BIOGRAPHICAL TYPES FOR CHILDREN

As we have already seen, juvenile biographies differ from adult biographies in several important respects. First, biographies for children are often not documented. Second, these biographies may not be complete accounts of the men—particularly if the men's lives include objectionable incidents or many unrelieved tragedies.

In the third place, biographers for the young usually feel that it is legitimate to cast known facts about an episode into actual dialogue and to interpret the thoughts of their characters. In other words, they put sentences into their heroes' mouths and thoughts into their heads for which there is no actual documentary evidence. Their excuse, and it is a legitimate one, is that this makes the narrative more dramatic. They contend that anyone who starts to relate a hero tale to a child invariably begins to tell what the people thought or said. It is true that the moment we start some episodes about George Washington or Abraham Lincoln we find ourselves saying, "So George thought to himself . . . ." or "When Sarah Bush saw her new stepson, Abe, she liked the boy at once, and said to him . . . ." Of course such methods bring the scene more vividly to life for a child. Furthermore, the author of such fictionalized conversations would justify them by saying that while they are not to be found in so many words in any record, they have a basis in known facts. Certainly whether fictionalized dialogue is justified or not, we find a great deal of this sort of thing in most biographies written for the young, and if the authors give no sources the casual reader cannot tell whether or not there is a sound reason for such free interpretation.

If these biographies for children carried footnotes and source references, we could tell which authors had done a scholarly piece of work in a partially fictionalized vein, and which ones had simply used the hero as a basis for a creative story. There are two hybrids in this field: First, there is *fictionalized biography*, in which the facts are documented and only a few liberties are taken, such as occasional dialogue for which there is no actual record. Second, there is *biographical fiction*, which takes a historical character as a basis for a story semihistorical in nature.

## Fictionalized Biography

Most of the biographies for children are fictionalized. That is, they are based on careful research, but known facts are often presented in dramatic episodes complete with conversation. For instance, Elizabeth Janet Gray in relating the moving quarrel between Admiral Penn and his young son lately turned Quaker begins the account with the old Admiral exploding wrathfully, ". . . three people you may *not* thee and thou—the King, the Duke of York, and myself." This speech is much more exciting than the plain statement, "The Admiral objected to his son's Quaker use of thee and thou." The quarrel continues the next day, climaxing in the Admiral's terrible threat:

> *"I am going to kneel down and pray to God that you may not be a Quaker, nor go ever again to any more of their meetings."*

and in William's frenzied reply:

> *"Before I will hear thee pray after any such manner," he cried, "I'll leap out of the window."*

It was a high window, too, and, according to Elizabeth Gray, William was saved only by the interruption of one of his father's most elegant friends come to call. Since Elizabeth Gray is a scrupulous research scholar, she probably had some sort of documentary evidence for this quarrel. She does, for instance, give the Admiral's actual letters to William summoning him home for this grim conference. Assuming then that there is a historical basis for the scene, we accept the dialogue, which certainly heightens the drama, the words fairly crackling with suppressed emotion.

Perhaps fictionalized biography is the best pattern of biography for young people and children. There is no doubt that dialogue based on facts, written by a scholar and an artist, brings history to life and re-creates living, breathing heroes, who make a deep impression on children.

## Biographical Fiction

Jean Lee Latham's Newbery Medal book, *Carry On, Mr. Bowditch*, is sometimes catalogued as fiction, but the reason is not clear. In her acceptance speech the author describes her book as fictionalized biography. She probably makes no more use of imaginary dialogue than does Elizabeth Janet Gray in *Penn*, which is listed as biography. *Mr. Bowditch* does include around a dozen imaginary characters, such as members of ships' crews, but the author adds that "there are about four dozen historical characters . . . handled with accuracy as to time, place, and personality."[12] Certainly this book, based on all the historical documents available, is a magnificent record of a little-known genius. In purpose and in effect on the reader it is biography.

These distinctions among different types of historical literature are not greatly important to the children's use of the books. When young people read biographical fiction, they might be warned, "This is the way it may have happened, but history does not tell us for sure." And when they read biography or even fictionalized biography, they might be told, "In so far as the author can find historical records, this is the way it *did* happen."

Briefly, the chief distinctions between good biographies for adults and those for children are that, in the latter, sources are less often stated, unsavory episodes are usually omitted, and recorded events are more likely to be enlivened with imaginary dialogue. On the whole, however, modern biographies for children represent scholarly research and conscientious retelling of events in a dramatic style. Such characteristics make these books one of the finest modern contributions to children's literature.

## WORK METHODS OF BIOGRAPHERS

From book-jackets, authors' notes, lists of suggested readings, prefatory remarks, articles by authors on their research methods, and even from those pages in which a writer expresses his thanks to those who have helped him, it is clear that the research for biographies for children is taken very seriously indeed. Evidence of careful documentation is found in more and more books for younger and younger children.

Dorothy Sterling, for example, when working on *Captain of the Planter*, a biography of Robert Smalls, went to Beaufort and Charleston, where she talked to people who had known Mr. Smalls, and had two visits with his son. She pored over old newspapers and photographs, ransacked library collections and archives, and picked up every lead by correspondence.

Aileen Fisher and Olive Rabe, in "Writing About the Alcotts,"[13] explain how they used the source material collected and published by others and the biographies of men and women who had played a part in the Alcotts' lives, reading whatever could be found about the family and the period. Each worked on the same chapter separately; one welded the two versions and the other edited and revised the resulting chapter. The authors decided to write the story from the viewpoint of a family member so that the book would have an intimate feeling, although they knew it restricted the action to what could be observed.

Fruma Gottschalk notes in a statement on the jacket of *The Youngest General*, a biography of Lafayette, that she had participated in the research done by her husband, a specialist in eighteenth-century European history, who had been working on Lafayette for twenty years. No wonder the historical background is so marvelously detailed and accurate!

There are small variations in the ways in which authors patiently dig, sift, compare, record, and revise, but one thing is paramount: a respect for the truth. Marchette Chute says it beautifully:

12. *Horn Book*, August 1956.

13. Aileen Fisher and Olive Rabe, "Writing About the Alcotts," *Horn Book*, October 1968.

*A biographer is not a court record or a legal document. He is a human being, writing about another human being, and his own temperament, his own point of view . . . are unconsciously imposed upon the man he is writing about. . . .*

*It is easy enough to make good resolutions in advance, but a biographer cannot altogether control his sense of excitement when the climax of his years of research draws near and he begins to see the pieces fall into place. Almost without his volition, A, B, and D fit together and start to form a pattern, and it is almost impossible for the biographer not to start searching for C. Something turns up that looks remarkably like C, and with a little trimming of the edges and the ignoring of one very slight discrepancy it will fill the place allotted for C magnificently.*

*It is at this point that the biographer ought to take a deep breath and sit on his hands until he has had time to calm down. He has no real, fundamental reason to believe that his discovery is C, except for the fact that he wants it to be. He is like a man looking for a missing piece in a difficult jigsaw puzzle, who has found one so nearly the right shape that he cannot resist the desire to jam it into place.*

*If the biographer had refused to be tempted by his supposed discovery of C and had gone on with his research, he might have found not only the connecting, illuminating fact that he needed but much more besides. He is not going to look for it now. Desire has blocked the way. And by so much his biography will fall short of what might have been the truth.*

*It would not be accurate to say that a biographer should be wholly lacking in desire. Curiosity is a form of desire. So is the final wish to get the material down on paper in a form that will be fair to the reader's interest and worthy of the subject. But a subconscious desire to push the facts around is one of the most dangerous things a biographer can encounter, and all the more dangerous because it is so difficult to know when he is encountering it.*

Marchette Chute concludes:

*To put the whole thing into a single sentence: you will never succeed in getting at the truth if you think you know, ahead of time, what the truth ought to be.*[14]

## VIEWPOINTS

Biography, like fiction, should have its characters so completely realized, its background so true, that everything that happens will seem inevitable. But the characters in the series books are all of a pattern. There is a convention that great men and women invariably started out as normal and likeable youngsters, good mixers, and good sports. There is no inkling of the fact that loneliness and oddity often bear a dark fruit of their own. . . .

In two popular biographies in the Childhood of Famous Americans Series, *Nancy Hanks, Kentucky Girl*, and *Mary Todd Lincoln*, the heroines are so conventional as to be startling to anyone who has read Carl Sandburg's *Abraham Lincoln*. Mary Todd's disastrous disposition, which was to harry the great president so sorely, is passed off as "that terrible Todd temper." She is represented as spunky and lovable, gay, generous, and impulsive, flying off the handle, shaking her curls, and stamping her little foot.

. . . What is gained by telling children that the great of the world have always been well adjusted and genteel?—Fran Martin, "Stop Watering Down Biographies." Reprinted from *Junior Libraries*, December 1959, published by R. R. Bowker Co. Copyright © 1959, R. R. Bowker Co.

### THE SERIES

The Bobbs-Merrill Childhood books seem to have launched, in 1932, the biography fever with both children and publishers. As a result, not only is the numerical impact of these books staggering, but the duplication of biographies has reached the point where it is a major feat of memory to recall which George Washington is whose and whose Abraham Lincoln is which.

It would be convenient to be able to make a judgment of each series as a whole, but this is impossible, because within one set

14. Marchette Chute, "Getting at the Truth," *Saturday Review*, September 19, 1953.

of books some are thin or pedestrian and others are of major importance. Although it is difficult to select from a list, it is wasteful for schools or homes or libraries to order every one of any series. It is best to watch for authoritative reviews of individual books. Many of the books discussed in this chapter are from one or another of the series. However, since each series is designed to perform a definite function in the child's reading program, several should be familiar to adults working with children.

Two outstanding series for the beginning reader are the Harper and Row "I Can Read" history books and the Young Crowell Biographies. The former includes several life stories told from the child's viewpoint; the latter emphasizes minority group members, although it does not focus on them exclusively. The Bobbs-Merrill Childhood of Famous Americans series has high-interest low-vocabulary books, rigidly patterned and often determinedly merry and gay. The Random House Step-Up Books, the Putnam See-and-Read Books, and the Watts Picture Life series are all simply written and variable in quality. The Garrard Discovery Books follow a set format, and although there are exceptions, many of the titles in this extensive series for young children are bland or stilted. Most of these series are useful as supplementary curricular material, yet they are enjoyed by children for their narrative quality.

Scribner's Initial Biographies by Genevieve Foster are well-written, brief, and useful—but staid in tone. Like the Foster books, the Grosset and Dunlap Signature Books, which the publishers call "life stories," are for the middle grades, but are highly fictionalized and sometimes of dubious accuracy. There are exceptions: the books of Hazel Wilson, Margaret Leighton, Iris Vinton, Enid Meadowcroft, and Nina Brown Baker are above average.

In 1950, Random House launched the Landmark Books, and later added the World Landmark Books, presenting men, movements, and moments in history that have been landmarks in our national life. Reading levels and interest levels are indicated by the publisher. Some of the contributors are notable, and some of the books are of superior literary quality, but in a series as extensive as this one, it is not surprising that high standards are not always maintained.

The Crowell biographies of women and of poets are outstanding series for older readers, as are the Harper and Row Breakthrough Books, which emphasize, as the title indicates, a breakthrough in achievements or in human relations. Putnam publishes both a Sports Hero series and an American Hero series, which, like the Houghton Mifflin North Star series, contains lives of heroes in American history. The Horizon Caravel Books and the American Heritage Junior Library are both distinguished for their profuse and beautiful illustrations as well as for the accuracy of the material.

## COLLECTIVE BIOGRAPHIES

Because of the brevity of treatment of each subject in collective biographies, they will not be discussed singly in this chapter. However, many are included in the bibliography, since this form of the genre serves two purposes admirably. The collective biography is an excellent choice for the child whose span of attention is limited, and for the reader who is particularly interested in the career, race, sex, period, or country that is the common denominator for the collection. This is an especially popular form for sports biographies—or biographical sketches—but it is also used widely to catch the interest of those children who are infatuated, say, with ballet or medicine (*anything* about ballet or medicine) or with women who broke into new professional fields or with black scientists. This is not to suggest that collective biographies are catch-alls: such books as Isaac Asimov's *Breakthroughs in Science* (1960), Victor Seroff's *Men Who Made Musical History* (1969), or *Leaders of New Nations* (1968) by Leonard Kenworthy and Erma Ferrari are exciting books and an irreplaceable contribution to children's literature.

The following discussions of biographies are grouped under three main divisions: Biographies for the Youngest, Biographies for the Middle Group, and Biographies for Older Readers. Within each of these main groups, the discussions are arranged according to the birth date of the subjects of the biographies, so that there is a chronological progression within each section.

The main emphasis throughout is on the authors who are outstanding biographers. However, most of the author-title subsections not only highlight one biography of the author and give some indication of the range of his work, but also mention parallel biographies of the principal subject by other authors.

## BIOGRAPHIES FOR THE YOUNGEST

It was often assumed in the past that young children had little interest in biography, but, as a matter of fact, when the small child says, "Mom, tell me about when you were a little girl," he is asking for biography. It is true that small children are not interested in certain kinds of biographies, and when they ask for a story about mother's childhood they want to hear what she *did*, not how she conquered her bad temper or became interested in science and decided to make it her life's work.

There have been some good biographies for young children in the past; they are still valuable, especially for reading aloud. What is flourishing now is the simply written life story or partial biography for the beginning independent reader. The best of this kind are just as accurate as books for older readers, but the person's life is often seen from a child's viewpoint—as in Ferdinand Monjo's *The One Bad Thing About Father*, which gives a son's-eye-view of Theodore Roosevelt. For the young child whose time sense cannot fully encompass the past, this is one of the best—but not the only—ways to give a biography immediacy and reality.

*Illustration by Rocco Negri for* The One Bad Thing About Father *by F. N. Monjo. Copyright 1970. Reproduced by permission of Harper & Row, Publishers, Inc. (Original with color)*

## ALICE DALGLIESH

### *The Columbus Story*

The text of the picture biography *The Columbus Story* (1955) is less than thirty pages long. It is vividly alive and re-creates with simple dignity, in a direct writing style, the boyhood of Columbus and the struggles he had in getting support for his first successful voyage. The book carries Columbus through that journey, with none of the tragedy of the later years, and can be read aloud to children as young as five or six. Some second-graders and most third-graders can read it for themselves. Leo Politi's brilliantly colored illustrations complement the dignified tone of the story.

With Dalgliesh's gift for making the past alive for young children (see Chapter 14), it is logical that she should also succeed in writing enjoyable biographies for young children. In her picture biography for readers in the middle grades *Ride on the Wind* (1956) she describes the dramatic solo flight of Charles Lindbergh across the ocean in "The Spirit of St. Louis."

Of the other biographies or partial biographies of Columbus written for young children, two gauged for the beginning reader are Gertrude Norman's *A Man Named Columbus* (1960), slight but useful because of its simplicity; and Clara Ingram Judson's *Christopher Columbus* (1960), a straightforward account in which style is sacrificed to the demands of a controlled vocabulary. An appendix in Ann McGovern's *The Story of Christopher Columbus* (1963) gives information about the way facts were obtained from source materials.

## PATRICIA MILES MARTIN

*Pocahontas*

Patricia Miles Martin begins her story of *Pocahontas* (1964) when the Indian girl is eleven years old and sees an English ship arrive. She learns English, becomes friendly with the Jamestown colonists, marries John Rolfe when she is grown, and dies in England, homesick and ready to return to America. Written for beginning independent readers, the book is hampered stylistically by the demands of a limited vocabulary, but it is not dull and not unduly fictionalized. The story of Pocahontas has all the requisites of romantic drama, although there is some question about whether the familiar scene in which she saves the life of John Smith did occur, since Smith did not include it in the first edition of his own book.

Jan Wahl's *Pocahontas in London* (1967) focuses on the Indian girl's experiences in London. However, the writing is stiff and the book notable only for the brilliant color and striking composition of John Alcorn's illustrations. A good choice for reading aloud to young children is *Pocahontas* (1949) by Ingri and Edgar Parin d'Aulaire, with its direct approach, large and colorful pictures, and emphasis on action. (See also Bulla's *Pocahontas and the Strangers.*)

*Daniel Boone* (1965) is a good example of the many other biographies that Patricia Martin has written for young readers, most of them about famous persons in America's history. *Daniel Boone* tends to be somewhat oversimplified in style, with short sentences and large print, but it gives the major facts about Boone's life at a level comprehensible to the beginning reader. These books are useful but not outstanding, giving young children information rather than an understanding of the biographee's role in history.

## CLYDE ROBERT BULLA

*Squanto, Friend of the Pilgrims*

Children are usually enthralled by the amazing story of Squanto's life. He was taken to England in 1605 and lived there for eight years. Then he returned to this country with John Smith only to be captured and sold to Spain by slave hunters. In Spain he was rescued by the friars and returned once more to his native land. The story is beautifully told by Clyde Bulla, who has a gift for writing easy-to-read books that are never commonplace. His historical tales have a pleasant lilt and swing and substantial content. *Squanto* was published in 1954 with the subtitle

*Friend of the White Men*, and in 1969 the title was changed to *Squanto, Friend of the Pilgrims*. The book has the same virtues as Bulla's historical fiction, the genre used in *John Billington, Friend of Squanto* (1956). The other biographies of Squanto for this age group are dull and stilted when compared to Bulla's story.

Bulla's *Pocahontas and the Strangers* (1971) is written for eight- to ten-year-olds, but the suspense of the story and the simplicity of style make it appropriate for reading aloud to younger children, especially if read in installments. Other good biographies by Bulla for the beginning independent reader are *Song of St. Francis* (1952), *Lincoln's Birthday* (1966), and *Washington's Birthday* (1967).

## INGRI and EDGAR PARIN d'AULAIRE

*Abraham Lincoln*

*From* Abraham Lincoln *by Ingri and Edgar Parin d'Aulaire. Copyright 1939 by Doubleday & Company, Inc. Reprinted by permission of the publisher. (Original in color)*

The picture-book biographies of Ingri and Edgar Parin d'Aulaire are a real contribution to the youngest. They are large books, copiously illustrated with full-page lithographs in deep, glowing colors on alternate pages, and with black and whites and innumerable small pictures in between. These small pictures fulfill a definite purpose in each book, sometimes adding droll touches to the interpretation of the hero's character, sometimes showing something of his work or progress. In *Benjamin Franklin* (1950), for instance, the decorative borders throughout the book carry a series of Franklin's wise sayings. These are fun for children to discover and read, and they make *Poor Richard's Almanac* more real. Throughout the series, the illustrations are somewhat stylized and occasionally stiff. But this is a minor criticism of pictures that are alive with action and full of humor.

Study the details of the pictures in *Abraham Lincoln* (1939). No need to talk about the doorless dwellings—in one picture a horse has stuck his head into the single room of the cabin and seems to be taking a neighborly interest in the new baby. Notice the little boys' single galluses upon which hang all the responsibility for holding up their scanty pants. No need to say that Mary Todd was something of a termagant, nor that she had a few problems to contend with in Abe. That picture of the wildly disordered parlor, with Abe on the floor in stocking feet, and with Mary, arms akimbo, reflected in the elegant mirror, is a demonstration of their fundamental unlikeness. The book is full of just the sort of sly humor that characterized Abe.

It is something of a shock to discover in the d'Aulaires' fine picture-book life of *George Washington* (1936) for the youngest children this repellent phrase, "He learned to be good and honest and never tell a lie." Fortunately, the d'Aulaires give other and more winning pictures of Washington. The children will probably forgive the authors this absurdity and remember George racing his horse to school with his hard-riding playmates.

In the early books of this series, the texts were simple and the life stories were incomplete. But with *Benjamin Franklin*, *Pocahontas* (1949), *Buffalo Bill* (1952), and *Columbus* (1955), the content has grown richer, with more details. In the case of *Columbus*, the man's whole life is related, even those tragic last voyages.

Of the many other biographies of Abraham Lincoln, one of the best is Clyde Bulla's *Lincoln's Birthday* (1966). Wilma Hays' *Abe Lincoln's Birthday* (1961), despite the similarity of title, is fiction, based on the events of Lincoln's twelfth birthday. Clara Ingram Judson's *Abraham Lincoln* (1961) has a rather flat style, but is useful because it is easy to read, factually accurate, and balanced in coverage. See also Aileen Fisher's *My Cousin Abe*.

*Illustration by Aliki from the book* A Weed Is a Flower: The Life of George Washington Carver *by Aliki. © 1965 by Aliki Brandenburg. Published by Prentice-Hall, Inc., Englewood Cliffs, New Jersey. (Original in color)*

## ALIKI BRANDENBURG

*A Weed Is a Flower*

Aliki Brandenburg, who writes as "Aliki," illustrates her own books. In *A Weed Is a Flower* (1965), a biography of George Washington Carver, her pictures have a realistic range of skin tones. The story of the great black naturalist is told in a dry, quiet style with a simple vocabulary. The title is based on a comment attributed to Dr. Carver: "A weed is a flower growing in the wrong place." Born of slave parents, Carver worked his way through school, leaving the college where he had been a student and then a faculty member to join the staff of Tuskegee Institute at the invitation of Booker T. Washington. His distinguished career in agricultural research brought him many honors, and he is probably, along with Martin Luther King, the most popular black person of note as a subject of biographies for children. Another biography for this group is *George Washington Carver* (1960) by Samuel and Beryl Epstein, a stolid but factual account.

Aliki also has written and illustrated attractive picture biographies: *The Story of Johnny Appleseed* (1963) and *The Story of William Penn* (1964). The latter, like *A Weed Is a Flower*, invests its subject with dignity and stature.

## MARGARET B. YOUNG

*The Picture Life of Martin Luther King, Jr.*

Margaret Young's biography of Martin Luther King was written before his assassination (although published in the same year, 1968) and it concludes with his being awarded the Nobel Prize. The book fulfills every requisite for the very young reader: it has large print on pages with plenty of space, and the photographs on facing pages are clear and are either self-explanatory or have a succinct caption. The style is simple and dignified, and the important facets of Dr. King's life are picked up in a list of notes at the end of the book. The treatment is balanced in giving attention to periods in Dr. King's life and in giving facts about his personal life and his career.

Young has also written *The Picture Life of Ralph Bunche* (1968) and *The Picture Life of Thurgood Marshall* (1971) in the same format, and collections of biographies: *Black American Leaders* (1969) and *The First Book of American Negroes* (1966), a record of the struggles of contemporary black people who have become prominent. The two collections are for children of ten to twelve.

*Meet Martin Luther King, Jr.* (1969), by James T. De Kay, also has photographic illustrations and large print and is simple enough to be read by the second-grade child. The book is weakened by two flaws common to many biographies written for young readers: it is "written down" with a note of coyness in the passages describing King's early childhood, and it has an adulatory tone that lessens, rather than enhances, the stature of King. However, this book is more detailed than the biography by Margaret Young. Both are suitable for slow older readers.

Of the several biographies of Martin Luther King written for the middle grades, Ed Clayton's *Martin Luther King: The Peaceful Warrior* (1964) and Lillie Patterson's *Martin Luther King, Jr.: Man of Peace* (1969) give balanced coverage and a strong impression of personality as well as of King's role in the civil rights struggle. Both can be used by adults to augment information for younger readers.

For readers in the upper grades, Don McKee's *Martin Luther King, Jr.* (1969) is quite factual, giving more information about the civil rights struggle and King's leadership than about his personal life, and including the attempted assassination of King by a black woman, an episode missing from most of the biographies about him.

## OTHER BIOGRAPHIES FOR THE YOUNGEST READERS

There have been increasing numbers of very simply written biographies to satisfy the curiosity of children in the primary grades. In part because young children's sense of history is not fully developed, most of the books are about important men and women in American history. Maggi Scarf's *Meet Benjamin Franklin* (1968) touches on the most familiar events and achievements in Franklin's life. In *The Story of Ben Franklin* (1965), Eve Merriam gives a brief but balanced treatment of Franklin as a family man, a statesman, and an inventor-scientist.

Ormonde De Kay's *Meet Andrew Jackson* (1967) is one of the better books in the Random House Step-Up Series. Bernice Kohn's *Talking Leaves: The Story of Sequoyah* (1969) tells of the Cherokee who devised a way to record the language of his people.

Like the biographies for older readers, biographies for this age group give evidence of the response of authors and publishers to the need for materials about minority groups. The Crowell Biographies series is outstanding in this area (many of the books in the series are listed in the chapter bibliography). Some examples are Midge Turk's *Gordon Parks* (1971), the story of a versatile and creative black writer and photographer; Tobi Tobias' *Maria Tallchief* (1970), the biography of one of our great American dancers; and Ruth Franchere's *Cesar Chavez* (1970), a good picture both of the plight of the migrant worker and of the Chicano labor leader. Not all of the books in this series are about people of minority groups; for example, Molly Cone's *The Ringling Brothers* (1971) tells of a circus-smitten family who achieved the dream so many children have.

## BIOGRAPHIES FOR THE MIDDLE GROUP

Children in the middle grades want to know everything there is to know about their special heroes, the doers—from explorers and scouts of the Old West to today's astronauts and baseball stars. The child is not usually ready for career stories unless they are stories of action, nor is he concerned with character development. Least of all are most children able to appreciate an account of the pursuit of an abstract idea. Penn, with his deep concern for Quakerism and social ideals, is a hero for older children, as is Jefferson, who was so predominantly a man of ideas.

However, through their reading of fairy tales and realistic fiction, children arrive gradually at some broad standards of right and wrong. They may not understand altruism or self-abnegation, but they know all about fair play, kindness, bravery, and justice. These actions they respect, and they admire the heroes and heroines who embody these virtues.

The increasing awareness on the part of authors and editors that young readers like their biographies to be tales of action and achievement rather than stories of the childhood pranks of a great man or woman, straightforward and accurate rather than adulatory, has brought a decided improvement in most of the books for this age group.

### AILEEN FISHER

*Jeanne d'Arc*

Aileen Fisher's *Jeanne d'Arc* (1970) is beautifully illustrated with Ati Forberg's quiet, reverent pictures. The story begins with Jeanne at the age of eleven, listening to her father's angry plaints about the English invaders and to his expressed hope that the Dauphin somehow could ascend the throne left vacant by his father's death. When first Jeanne sees a dazzling light and hears a voice tell her that she will be guided by the saints, she is happy and trustful but not, in her piety, surprised. The faith she has in her power to defeat the English and to see the Dauphin crowned, and the tragedy of her imprisonment and death are described with grave simplicity. Aileen Fisher writes in a direct and unembellished prose appropriate to Jeanne's modesty and conviction and she successfully portrays her as a heroine by describing her acts rather than by commenting on them.

In *Joan of Arc: Her Life as Told by Winston Churchill* (1969), reprinted from Churchill's *A History of the English-Speaking Peoples*, comments by the author such as these are frequent: "Unconquerable courage, infinite compassion, the virtue of the simple, the wisdom of the just, shone forth in her." For older readers, Albert Paine's *The Girl in White Armor* (1967; abridged from an earlier version) is well written, historically accurate and detailed, and broad in scope.

Fisher's other biographies are for older readers. In both *We Dickinsons* (1965) and *We Alcotts* (1968), written with Olive Rabe, the story is told supposedly by a member of the family: Emily Dickinson's brother Austin describes Emily's life within the family, and Mrs. Alcott tells—in language delightfully stately and appropriate for the period—about the family's participation in the intellectual ferment of their circle, the abolitionist movement, and new educational theories. A similar, and equally successful device, is used in *My Cousin Abe* (1962), in which Dennis Hanks gives a warm and intimate picture of his cousin Abraham Lincoln.

### RONALD SYME

*Columbus, Finder of the New World*

Ronald Syme's series of biographies of explorers began as easy-to-read books for the

*Illustration by William Stobbs. From* Columbus, Finder of the New World *by Ronald Syme. Copyright 1952 by William Morrow and Company, Inc. Reprinted by permission of the publishers.*

middle and upper grades—Columbus, Cortes, Champlain, Balboa, Magellan, and others—and broadened to include more detailed biographies of La Salle, John Smith, and Henry Hudson. *Columbus, Finder of the New World* (1952) is typical of the style and approach of all the books. Christopher Columbus is a difficult character to present in a full biography, since the drama of his life rises grandly to the successful conclusion of his first voyage. After that, failure and tragedy stalk his path. It is greatly to Syme's credit that he presents the gloom as well as the glory. In this brief, well-written biography, the Admiral of the Ocean Sea goes down to his death apparently defeated, but his name and his achievements live after him.

Other biographies of Columbus that readers of nine to twelve may enjoy are Armstrong Sperry's *Voyages of Christopher Columbus* (1950); Clara Ingram Judson's *Admiral Christopher Columbus* (1965), not to be confused with her biography of Columbus for younger children; and August Derleth's *Columbus and the New World* (1957). For another slant on the Admiral, children can read Nina Brown Baker's *Amerigo Vespucci* (1956), which, in discussing why America was named for Amerigo rather than for Columbus and in discussing the relationship between the two explorers, gives a picture of Columbus that helps explain his downfall.

In addition to his books about explorers, Syme has written several biographies of heroes of Latin-American countries. For older children, *Bolivar the Liberator* (1968) is a good example of the dramatic pattern of events, set off by a restrained style, that makes Ronald Syme's books as exciting as they are informative. Bolivar became president of the Republic of Great Colombia, which included Venezuela, Colombia, Peru, Ecuador, and Bolivia. Although his fortune and his power were lost, and he died in poverty and isolation, Bolivar's reputation as the most important political figure in South American history has grown with the passing of time. "Few liberators," comments Syme, "have lived long enough to enjoy the benefits derived from their achievement of victory for others." As always, Syme is candid in appraisal and lucid in explaining the complexities of political upheaval. These are characteristics also of *Garibaldi: The Man Who Made a Nation* (1967), of *Toussaint: The Black Liberator* (1971), and of *Zapata, Mexican Rebel* (1971), the latter for readers of nine to twelve, simply written, not as smooth in style as the books for older readers but just as objective.

## HAROLD W. FELTON

*Mumbet: The Story of Elizabeth Freeman*

In our era of consciousness of the exclusion, for many years, of the black contributors to American history, such heroes as Benjamin

Banneker and Matthew Henson and such heroines as Sojourner Truth and Mary McLeod Bethune have been described many times. Elizabeth Freeman, though, is one heroine whose true story, dramatic and courageous, is seldom heard. Harold Felton's *Mumbet* (1970) tells how "Elizabeth" had become "Mumbet" to the Ashleys, the Massachusetts family whose slave she was. When Elizabeth heard of the new Massachusetts constitution which stated that all men were created equal, she called on a lawyer who had visited the Ashley home. He argued her case and in 1781 the black slave won her freedom in the courts of Massachusetts. Uneducated but intelligent, firm in her resolve, Elizabeth Freeman is a fascinating heroine, her triumph given suspense by the obstacles put in her way by the Ashleys, and her later years graced by the indomitable way in which she drove Shays' raiders from the lawyer's home.

Adroitly fictionalized, *Mumbet* is written in a vigorous style, the lengthy introduction making evident the research (with many sources quoted) that provided a firm base for the biography.

Harold Felton's other books are primarily about the heroes of America's tall tales or about such black heroes of the West as *Jim Beckwourth* (1966), *Edward Rose* (1967), and *Nat Love* (1969), all action-filled stories.

*Illustration by Donn Albright. Reprinted by permission of Dodd, Mead & Company, Inc. from* Mumbet, The Story of Elizabeth Freeman *by Harold W. Felton, illustrations by Donn Albright. Copyright © 1970 by the University of Nebraska Foundation.*

## GENEVIEVE FOSTER

### The Initial Biographies

The Initial Biographies by Genevieve Foster are brief and add little to our knowledge of the American heroes they describe, but they are written in restrained literary style and provide children with a summary of each man's childhood, youthful struggles, and mature contributions. *George Washington* (1949) has the same accuracy that distinguishes Foster's *George Washington's World*, but is more simplified, yet not written down. Many of the legendary exploits are omitted. In *Abraham Lincoln* (1950) the legends are included and explained—especially the Ann Rutledge affair. The biographies of Theodore Roosevelt and Andrew Jackson provide the liveliest reading, and all of the books are an excellent introduction to the lives of their subjects. Most of the children's books about Andrew Jackson have played down the scandal which dogged his life, and yet the cruel injustice of that scandal points up the man's deep feelings and loyalty. For that reason the biography by Margaret Vance, discussed in the next section, is particularly important.

## OPAL WHEELER and SYBIL DEUCHER

Biographies of musicians

The happy collaboration and later the individual work of Opal Wheeler and Sybil Deucher have resulted in a series of biographies of musicians for younger children, about seven to ten, which have proved unusually popular. The books follow a similar pattern—family, birth, amusing or extraordinary episodes of childhood, hardships (but never tragedies), artistic achievements and triumphs. With Mozart the story terminates before the tragedies begin. The title indicates the theme—*Mozart, the Wonder Boy* (1934).

Knowing the tragedies in the lives of many of these musicians, the biting poverty and the humiliations, you may wonder if the tone of these books is not a shade too merry and lighthearted. Perhaps this treatment is legitimate, since the books are directed to an audience under eleven. Some teachers and parents, on the other hand, feel that young children should not be protected from all harsh realities, that they should know of the ultimate tragedy in Mozart's life, of Beethoven's deafness, and Schubert's poverty.

The fact remains, however, that for young children the Wheeler-Deucher formula has been extremely popular. The books are easy and popular introductions to musicians and to biography. In addition to Haydn, Mozart, Schubert, Bach, Beethoven, and Grieg, the books include two American composers—Edward MacDowell and Stephen Foster. In every case, the authors have chosen musicians whose music is enjoyed by young children.

Reba Paeff Mirsky's biography *Mozart* (1960) does include information about the poverty and tribulations of Mozart's later life, although it emphasizes his childhood, and it is given added authenticity by the inclusion of letters from Mozart to his family. Mirsky's *Haydn* (1963) covers Haydn's childhood and his thirty years as a court musician, culminating in the composition of "The Creation."

## HAZEL WILSON

*The Story of Lafayette*

In spite of the fact that *The Story of Lafayette* and *The Story of Mad Anthony Wayne* (both Signature biographies) read as conversationally as fiction, Hazel Wilson is too conscientious a research student not to base her episodes on documented facts. *The Story of Lafayette* (1952) gives children a convincing portrait of a man whose life is more romantic than any novel.

Lafayette's coming to the aid of our struggling colonies was inevitable, but the wonder lies in his immediate recognition of Washington's greatness. This helped him to forget the Congress which received him so miserably, half starved and half paid his men, and gave Washington himself inadequate and delayed support. The author holds children's interest not only through this familiar story but also through her account of the French Revolution and Lafayette's long imprisonment. Mrs. Wilson finishes her full-length portrait of the man with Lafayette, full of years and honors, making a triumphal tour of this country and receiving a tardy but generous recognition of his services from another Congress. A coincidence which will delight children is the fact that the first man on our shores to receive Lafayette cordially into his home had a little boy who, when he had grown up, attempted a gallant rescue of Lafayette from the French prison. The attempt failed, but Lafayette's heart must have warmed when he knew his would-be rescuer's identity.

Mrs. Wilson's *The Little Marquise: Madame Lafayette* (1957) is a biography for older readers that also provides much information about Lafayette, as does Fruma Gottschalk's *The Youngest General: A Story of Lafayette* (1949), which ends with Lafayette's being given the command of a division by Washington. Another good biography of Lafayette is Alberta Graham's *Lafayette: Friend of America* (1952), which tells of his life from his youth to his visit to America in 1824. This book may be useful for slow older readers.

Other biographies by Mrs. Wilson include *The Last Queen of Hawaii: Liliuokalani* (1963), which is rather heavily fictionalized but depicts its subject well and also provides some background of Hawaiian history. In her *The Years Between: Washington at Home at Mount Vernon 1783-1789* (1969), Mrs. Wilson gives a detailed and fascinating picture, based on contemporary reports and on Washington's letters and diaries, of the period between the end of the Revolutionary War and the election of Washington as the first President.

### DORIS FABER

*I Will Be Heard: The Life of William Lloyd Garrison*

The subject of Doris Faber's *I Will Be Heard: The Life of William Lloyd Garrison* (1970) is no idealized figure: opinionated, irascible, with no small estimate of his own ability, he was a man whose greatest virtues were a belief in the equality of man and an unwillingness to compromise in any way in the pursuit of that belief. It was a meeting with Benjamin Lundy, whose experiences in the South had caused him to devote his life to speaking against slavery, that started Garrison on the long fight for abolition of that evil. Reviled for many years for the stridency of his views, Garrison did not catch up with the times—the times caught up with him. By the time the Civil War was over, he—who had been threatened, mobbed, and jailed—was lauded and cheered, welcomed by the President, and carried through the streets of Charleston by freed slaves. Through Garrison's biography, the whole pattern of the fight against slavery can be seen. Describing her sources in an afterword, Faber warns that much of the material about abolition is not readily available but was gathered from the files of contemporary journals and from the four-volume biography published by Garrison's sons. Older readers may prefer Jules Archer's *Angry Abolitionist: William Lloyd Garrison* (1969).

Other Faber biographies for the middle grades include *Enrico Fermi: Atomic Pioneer* (1966), *Horace Greeley: The People's Editor* (1964), and *Clarence Darrow: Defender of the People* (1965). One of her best-written books, *Printer's Devil to Publisher: Adolph S. Ochs of the New York Times* (1963), is for readers of eleven to thirteen.

### CLARA INGRAM JUDSON

*Abraham Lincoln, Friend of the People*

Clara Ingram Judson began writing biography in 1939 with a modest little book about Frances Willard called *Pioneer Girl*. That was followed by *Boat Builder: The Story of Robert Fulton* (1940) and others. In 1950, when her *Abraham Lincoln, Friend of the People* appeared, it was evident that this writer, competent in so many fields, had attained new stature as a biographer. It was also evident that Mrs. Judson's research into source materials was to yield a fresh slant on the man. Her careful studies convinced her, for example, that Abe's childhood was no more "poverty stricken" than that of most of the neighbors. She also brought out the warm family love and loyalty of the Lincoln tribe, and Abe himself emerges as a real person.

Many think *Abraham Lincoln, Friend of the People* is the finest book in Mrs. Judson's biography series. Certainly it can take its place with the Sandburg and Daugherty Lincolns. The illustrations are unique also. In addition to the pen-and-ink drawings, there are colored photographs of the Lincoln dioramas from the Chicago Historical Society. These pictures are eye-catching and vivid.

Mrs. Judson believed that the only justification for new biographies of such well-known national figures as George Washington, Thomas Jefferson, Andrew Jackson, and Theodore Roosevelt is that they throw fresh light on, and give children new facts or a new point of view about, the man. Before she wrote a biography, she read the letters, journals, or papers of her hero, searched contemporary magazines and newspapers, and studied the life of the times. As a result, she rescued Washington from the stereotypes that had nearly obliterated him. She even made Jefferson, the man of ideas, intelligible to children. Mrs. Judson's writing is sometimes stilted, but somehow her deep love of family, her respect for all kinds of people, and her sense of the struggles through which these men came to greatness communicate themselves to children.

## OTHER BIOGRAPHIES FOR THE MIDDLE GROUP

Many biographies for the middle grades seem to have been published with more thought for their usefulness as supplementary curricular material than for their literary merit, but they should be used for that purpose and for giving information only if better books are not available. Fortunately, there are now so many good biographies that a reader who enjoys the genre and is not just seeking information about a particular individual has a wide choice.

For Alcott fans, Helen Papashvily's *Louisa May Alcott* (1965) gives a brisk and capable summary of the writer's work and family life. *Nothing Is Impossible: The Story of Beatrix Potter* (1969) by Dorothy Aldis is simply written and uses extracts from Potter's letters and journal to give added color and establish atmosphere. Margaret Davidson's *The Story of Eleanor Roosevelt* (1969) and Jeanette Eaton's 1956 book with the same title are two of the better biographies of that indomitable woman for this age group. Another hardy heroine is delightfully described in Evelyn Lampman's *Wheels West: The Story of Tabitha Brown* (1965). Grandma Brown went to Oregon by wagon train at the age of sixty-six and became one of its educational pioneers.

*The Story of George Washington Carver* (1954) by Arna Bontemps is one of the best of the Carver biographies. Another good biography of a scientist is Dan D'Amelio's *Taller Than Bandai Mountain: The Story of Hideyo Noguchi* (1968), which tells of the Japanese doctor who achieved success in bacteriological research despite severe obstacles. An excellent biography of an explorer is Jean Latham's *Far Voyager: The Story of James Cook* (1970).

Arnold Adoff's *Malcolm X*, a 1970 Notable Book, is very simply written; *The Life of Malcolm X* (1971) by Richard Curtis, for the more mature reader, is candid and comprehensive.

*Martin de Porres, Hero* (1954), by Claire Huchet Bishop, is a moving story of the Peruvian child, half-black, half-Spanish, who devoted his life in the sixteenth century to helping the poor and who was beatified in 1837. Another good biography of a man devoted to his people is Reginald Reynolds' *The True Story of Gandhi, Man of Peace* (1964), which gives full background information about conditions in India as well as a sympathetic treatment of Gandhi's life and his beliefs.

Although the writing in Mary Malone's *Actor in Exile: The Life of Ira Aldridge* (1969) is not outstanding, the dramatic story of the black actor makes fascinating reading. With no chance of gaining a place in American theater, Aldridge went to England in 1824. There was prejudice enough there to make his career difficult, but in time he was acclaimed a great tragedian.

With as many biographies as are published today, it is impossible to mention them all. Additional titles are listed in the chapter bibliography, and more are available through sources cited in Appendix A, Book Selection Aids.

## BIOGRAPHIES FOR OLDER READERS

Children in the middle grades usually demand action, but adolescent readers are also interested in men and women of ideas and ideals. While they enjoy a biography that is dramatic and well told, they may also read biographies for their historical background, their association with causes and movements, or their association with a field in which the reader has a special interest. One reader may consume avidly any biography with a Civil War background; another, any book about a musician; others, books about people whose lives as dancers, chemists, doctors, or teachers satisfy an orientation toward the profession.

Throughout this chapter, parallel biographies have been mentioned, and they exist in profusion for older readers. Adults working with children will want to know such books so that they may help children explore various presentations. Comparing Catherine Owens Peare's *Mahatma Gandhi: Father of Nonviolence* (1969, rev. ed.) and Olivia Coolidge's *Gandhi* (1971), the reader can see that Peare's book with its fictionalized, rather informal narrative style is easier to read and more dramatic, but that Coolidge's is more detailed, dignified, and analytical. Jeanette Eaton's *Gandhi: Fighter Without a Sword* (1950) is notable for the perceptive picture it gives of Gandhi as a man and a spiritual leader. Comparing biographies gives children an opportunity to understand how emphasis, style, and author's viewpoint, the amount of fictionalization or of documentation, and the amount of historical background or period details can shape a book.

### SIDNEY ROSEN

*Doctor Paracelsus*

In *Doctor Paracelsus* (1959), Sidney Rosen tells the story of Theophrastus Bombastus von Hohenheim, the son of an honest and dedicated Swiss doctor in a day of quacks. Thoroughly grounded in Latin and Greek and such science as his father could teach him, Theophrastus set off for a university to study medicine. But when he discovered that the professors only read notes copied from ancient Greek and Roman doctors, he was disgusted and moved on from university to university. In the course of his career he took the name of Paracelsus to indicate his own superiority to Celsus, an ancient authority on remedies. This was so typical of the man's cocksureness that the name Bombastus became, even in his lifetime, a synonym for brash, blustering conceit. Yet here was a bold, original mind unafraid to challenge the superstitions of the day or to try new methods. Reading this fascinating account of a contradictory personality, young people will catch a glimpse of early medical research and gain some understanding of the stubborn heroism it takes to stand out against the beliefs and practices of the times.

*Illustration by Rafaello Busoni. From* Doctor Paracelsus *by Sidney Rosen. Copyright, ©, 1959, by Sidney Rosen. By permission of Little, Brown and Company.*

This sort of heroism is even more evident in Rosen's *Galileo and the Magic Numbers* (1958). Like Paracelsus, Galileo began with the study of medicine, but he was so fascinated with mathematics and physics that he transferred his studies to those fields. In nontechnical language, this biography manages to give young readers absorbing accounts of Galileo's discovery of many important mathematical, physical, and astronomical truths and his invention of the thermometer and the telescope. His theories were contrary to the theological beliefs of the time, and so Galileo became a victim of the Inquisition.

*Wizard of the Dome* (1969) is an appealing biography for the general reader, since Buckminster Fuller is drawn as a lively, tenacious inventor whose patterns of success and failure as a designer-inventor have a cliffhanger appeal; to the scientifically-oriented girl or boy, it has the added attraction of presenting with unusual clarity the theories for which Fuller is now famous. Out of his concepts about the tetrahedron in nature and the application of geodesic structure have come his now-famous geodesic dome construction. The book has a good balance of personal life and of information about Fuller's professional career; it is written in a dignified but informal style, and it makes clear the importance and the innovatory nature of his work.

## ELIZABETH YATES

*Amos Fortune, Free Man*

Born an African prince, sold in Boston, well treated by a series of masters, Amos Fortune learned the tanner's trade and eventually bought his freedom. After that, this humble, mighty soul devoted everything he earned to buying freedom for other slaves. Freedom and education were the greatest things in his life. He died a respected member of the little New Hampshire town of Jaffrey, where he had lived so long. When Elizabeth Yates saw the tombstone of Amos, she tells us, she knew she must write his biography. *Amos Fortune, Free Man* (1951 Newbery Medal winner) is written with the same warmth and human compassion that mark her stories *Mountain Born* and *A Place for Peter.* Since most books about slavery deal with the South, it is important to have this picture of slave running and sales in the North. The details are grim, but Amos Fortune carried suffering lightly because his eyes were on the freedom of the future.

*Pebble in a Pool: The Widening Circle of Dorothy Canfield Fisher's Life* (1958) and *Prudence Crandall: Woman of Courage* (1955) are other biographies by Yates. The latter is a competent treatment of the Quaker schoolmistress who engendered bitter hostility in 1833 when she opened a school for black girls in a Connecticut town; a parallel biography for more mature readers is Edmund Fuller's *Prudence Crandall* (1971), which incorporates source material into the text but is not as readable.

## JAMES DAUGHERTY

*Poor Richard*

James Daugherty's superb *Daniel Boone* (1939) (p. 539) is one of the finest bits of Americana we have for children. The old woodsman was a contemporary of Andrew Jackson; Audubon knew him, and so perhaps did Davy Crockett; and it was over his "Wilderness Road" through the Cumberland Gap that Lucy Hanks carried her baby Nancy. So Daniel Boone seems to be a link which pulls together different men and periods.

For a fuller biography of the man at a more mature level, some children should read John Mason Brown's *Daniel Boone.*

For superior readers with mature interests, Daugherty's *Poor Richard* (1941) has unusual distinction. This book covers Franklin's whole life, his manifold activities, and his amazing talent for friendship among people of all varieties and ages. The chapter called "An American in Paris" opens in this way.

*One man alone captured a city. An American had taken Paris single-handed.*

*All the king's horses and all the king's men could not do what the friendly seventy-year-old journeyman printer was doing in spite of himself. He was surprised and pleased to find himself a hero. He was ready to act the part, knowing all that it might mean for America.*

The chapter includes a visit with John Paul Jones, "a one-man navy," and a little later we are treated to the scandalized Abigail Adams' report of a dinner where Mme. Helvétius sat with one arm around Franklin's shoulder and the other on the chair of Abigail's own John. "After dinner," wrote the outraged Mrs. Adams, "she threw herself on a settee where she showed more than her feet." Here, obviously, is a somewhat mature interpretation of the times, written and illustrated with Daugherty's usual gusto and swing.

Daugherty's *Abraham Lincoln* (1943) covers Lincoln's whole life. This book avoids the usual anecdotes found in most of the other juveniles, and with remarkable clarity and power tells the story of Lincoln in relation to the stormy war years. A reviewer summarizing Mr. Daugherty's contribution in his three biographies writes:

*. . . "Daniel Boone," "Poor Richard" and now "Abraham Lincoln"—are linked together in unity of spirit, an appreciation, in the true sense, of the restless, surging, visionary America which, with all its faults, has borne Titans.*[15]

There is something in the spirit which animates Mr. Daugherty's pen and brush that seems particularly adapted to the interpretation of titans. His *Abraham Lincoln* illustrations show all the rowdy vigor of his earlier drawings, but predominant in the book is the brooding melancholy of the strangest and perhaps loneliest of our great men. *Abraham Lincoln* is the most serious of Mr. Daugherty's three biographies, as we should expect, and is a magnificently clear if tragic picture of this great man.

15. Ellen Lewis Buell, "The Story of Honest Abe," a review of Mr. Daugherty's *Abraham Lincoln* in *The New York Times Book Review*, December 19, 1943.

## NARDI REEDER CAMPION

*Patrick Henry, Firebrand of the Revolution*

Patrick Henry was one of the leaders of the American Revolution, and yet his character and achievements have always been open to question. In her book *Patrick Henry* (1961), Mrs. Campion shows why. She never glosses over the weaknesses of her hero. As a boy, growing up in a cultured home where education was highly valued, he was lazy and irresponsible and soon discovered that he could talk himself out of most scrapes. He developed a fine speaking voice and a feeling for words and the cadence of language that were to be his greatest assets as long as he lived. Amiable and talented, he married when he was still penniless, failed twice at storekeeping, but, with three children to support, decided to become a lawyer. For once he studied intensively, if briefly, and became a close friend of the scholarly Jefferson. Once admitted to the bar, he won an unpopular case against the clergy and the king that rocked the State and made him famous.

This was the beginning. Caught up in the rising tide of pre-Revolutionary activity, Patrick Henry in the Virginia House of Burgesses became the spellbinding voice of the Revolutionists. It was said that without the fiery oratory of Patrick Henry there would have been no successful break with England. And somehow, that dream of freedom from tyranny and a union of the colonists so possessed the man that it forged him into a finer person than he had been. Yet after years of devoted friendship, Jefferson broke with him completely and denounced him venomously.

Mrs. Campion records his words and accusations but concludes that there were no valid stains on Henry's honor.

On July 5, 1776, he was overwhelmingly elected first governor of Virginia, an office which he administered wisely and well in five different terms. Jefferson was wrong, the author concludes, and this strange, passionate "Son of Thunder" died gently and courageously, much loved by his family and his State. This is a fascinating and carefully-documented biography, well adapted to elementary school children but enjoyed at high school level also.

## LEONARD WIBBERLEY

The Thomas Jefferson Cycle

The four volumes of Leonard Wibberley's biography of Thomas Jefferson constitute an impressive addition to Jeffersonia. The first volume, *Young Man from the Piedmont: The Youth of Thomas Jefferson* (1963), describes the years before 1776; the second, *A Dawn in the Trees* (1964), the years 1776-1789, giving the important historical background and a sympathetic portrayal of Jefferson as a husband and father. The third volume, *The Gales of Spring* (1965), covers the period 1789-1801; and the fourth, *The Time of the Harvest* (1966), describes Jefferson's years in office and his busy years of retirement until his death. The four volumes were condensed and slightly revised in 1968 – chiefly by minor deletions – in *Man of Liberty: A Life of Thomas Jefferson*.

In his prefatory note for the single-volume edition, Wibberley says that he felt his task as a biographer was to round out the picture usually given of Jefferson the statesman by including more information about his personal life. However, the comments he makes about his sources are much more specific and detailed than such notes usually are, and it is clear that Wibberley's choice of material is based on exhaustive as well as discriminating research. He concludes, "I do not think that, however much I had read about Jefferson, I could have written this book about him without having lived in America. It is something that is in the air, and if you press me to say what that something is, I have to answer: Jefferson."[16]

This admiration is not explicit in the text itself. Wisely, Wibberley draws Thomas Jefferson (and the historical figures with whom

### VIEWPOINTS

For how can a book be educational which discourages children from reading? What is educational about a book which is so thin in its characterization, so stilted in its prose, and so contrived in its plotting that the young reader goes to it as to a penance, eyeing his baseball mitt for succor. Unfortunately, there are quite a number of such "educational" books published today. . . . In a large part they consist of the lives of famous men who, judging by the books, could hardly be said to have lived at all. They seem merely to have passed through the Ten Commandments, nodding dutifully to each one of them, never guilty of an error of judgment, let alone a sin, and then died honored by their countrymen, who secretly must have been very glad to get rid of them. . . . But it is a paradox of writing that books which are written for the purpose of being educational (I exclude school books from this discussion) are not. The very emphasis on being educational kills the spirit of the book. While those which are written with a love of a story or of a character or of a time or a place are educational, for something comes to life from between the pages and we stand on Tower Hill in the sixteenth century and hear the executioner cry in anguish, "God pardon me," as he brings down his ax and severs the head of Sir Thomas More from his body. . . . – Leonard Wibberley, "The Land of the Ever Young," *The California Librarian*, January, 1962, pp. 19 – 20.

16. Leonard Wibberley, *Man of Liberty* (Farrar, 1968), pp. v, vii.

he lived and worked) so astutely that the man's intellect, ability, and versatility speak for him. The biography is mature in approach, an excellent source of information about the period as well as a fascinating study of Jefferson.

Another good biography of Jefferson for older readers is Henry Moscow's *Thomas Jefferson and His World* (1960) in the American Heritage series. It gives a clear picture of the accomplishments and wide interests of Jefferson, and because of the profuse illustrative material can be used by younger readers. Thomas J. Fleming's *Thomas Jefferson* (1971) is a partial biography; it begins with Jefferson's marriage in 1772 and recounts the remainder of his life in a competent, vigorous style. Other good Jefferson biographies for this age are Clara Ingram Judson's *Thomas Jefferson, Champion of the People* (1952) and Johanna Johnston's *Thomas Jefferson, His Many Talents* (1961), which is organized about such areas as "Architect and Builder" and "Scientist and Naturalist."

*That Jefferson Boy*, written for the middle grades by Earl Schenck Miers, is a lively fictionalized account of Jefferson's life up to the signing of the Declaration of Independence. Simply written for still younger children is Marvin Barrett's *Meet Thomas Jefferson* (1967).

Other Wibberley biographies are *The Complete Life of Winston Churchill* (1968) and *Zebulon Pike: Soldier and Explorer* (1961). There is seldom a suggestion in Wibberley's biographical writing of the humor that has made his adult fiction popular with young readers, but both have a graceful, easy style.

## JEANETTE EATON

*Leader by Destiny*

Washington is undoubtedly one of the most difficult figures to bring alive for children, both because he has been belittled by the trivial anecdotes told about him and because he has the subtle, intangible qualities of a highly civilized human being. Self-discipline and restraint are not easy for children to understand or to appreciate, and for this reason in particular Washington is a better character for adolescents than for children.

The best juvenile biography of Washington, Jeanette Eaton's *Leader by Destiny* (1938), is for the teen age, but it is such an extraordinary book that adults could also profit by reading it. You catch in it, for instance, Washington's lifelong regret for his inadequate education. You also find in this book Washington's single indiscretion, in his relations to his friend's wife, the beautiful Sally Fairfax. He wrote her one letter declaring his love. This letter Sally kept secret until the day of her death, and it remained secret for a hundred years after. In this book you see Washington's affectionate relations with his wife's children, and you see Martha herself as a charming and devoted helpmate to Washington, who came to appreciate her more and more. This book will help young people and adults know Washington as a very human, often bewildered man with a remarkable gift for inspiring confidence in other men.

For less able or less mature readers, Jeanette Eaton has written *Washington, the Nation's First Hero*. Her two biographies of Washington may be supplemented with those by Clara Judson and Genevieve Foster. And from these biographies some children will turn to biographies of Lafayette. Jeanette Eaton has written one of the finest, *Young Lafayette*, in the mature style of *Leader by Destiny*.

*Young Lafayette* (1932) gives a picture of the young French idealist, and again throws an interesting light on Washington. In Lafayette's almost awed reverence for his hero, we see the strange power of Washington over the men who surrounded him. He never lost his stature as a hero to them in spite of his very human weaknesses. This biography of Lafayette, which carries him through the French

Revolution, is both authentic and finely written.

## ELIZABETH RIPLEY

*Hokusai*

To supplement her background of art education, Elizabeth Ripley studied numerous sources to gain information for her biographies of artists. For *Hokusai* (1968), her story of the Japanese artist (1760–1849), she spent a month in Japan to get background. One of the best in a series of good books, *Hokusai* is particularly charming because of the vivacity and humor of the artist himself. Dismissed by his master from a print design shop because of his unorthodox approach to art, Hokusai lived in poverty until he at long last became famous for the beauty of his prints. A nonconformist, a showman, a cheerful spendthrift, he died at eighty-nine after having changed his name fifty times and having squandered his money. He chose his own tombstone inscription: "Old Man Mad About Painting."

In *Michelangelo* (1953) Ripley shows the artist as almost the victim of his two gifts for painting and for sculpture. Painting with its vision of endless details seemed to enslave him, while sculpture freed his energies and let his creative spirit soar. Each of the books in Elizabeth Ripley's series follows a similar pattern, with a brief coverage of the artist's childhood and youth, and with the beginning of his productivity, a discussion of his life as it related to his major works.

Another excellent biography of Michelangelo is Robert Coughlan's *The World of Michelangelo 1475–1564* (1966) in the Time-Life Library of Art, written for the mature reader. The text gives full historical background and a discussion of the artist's work, as well as a perceptive picture of the man. The book is profusely illustrated with reproductions of Michelangelo's paintings and photographs of his sculpture.

## ESTHER M. DOUTY

*Forten the Sailmaker: Pioneer Champion of Negro Rights*

James Forten, born ten years before the American Revolution in the Colony of Pennsylvania, was the grandson of a slave and the son of a father both free and proud. When he was eight, he began his schooling with the gentle Quaker Anthony Benezet. At fourteen he signed on a privateer as powder boy, was captured by the British, and gave up his chance to go home as an exchange prisoner to a white friend who was ill. Released later, he shipped to England and worked as a stevedore, returning to Philadelphia to become an apprentice in the sail loft, where his industry and ability so impressed the white owner that he offered to sell the business to James. Thus he became an independent man, *Forten the Sailmaker* (1968), who in time became wealthy and influential in the community.

In 1800, Forten and other free blacks of the city petitioned Congress for a revision of the Fugitive Slave Act, and throughout the rest of his life he gave generously of his time and his fortune helping others, buying the freedom of many slaves, working with the Underground Railroad. Over three thousand people, white and black, attended the funeral of this quiet and respected citizen of Philadelphia.

Carefully written, the book is based on extensive research, both the bibliography and the author's acknowledgments showing Esther Douty's meticulous probing. The book is a good example of how biography shows the valor of a lifetime dedicated to a worthy cause.

The information garnered for this book has also been used in part as background for Douty's *Charlotte Forten: Free Black Teacher* (1971), which is mentioned in the discussion of Longworth's biography of Charlotte Forten. Other biographies by Douty include *America's First Woman Chemist, Ellen Richards* (1961), which emphasizes her work rather than the fact that she was a pioneer in a field hitherto restricted to men; and *The Story of Stephen Foster* (1954), which is for nine- to eleven-year-olds.

## MARGUERITE VANCE

*The Jacksons of Tennessee*

Despite the title, *The Jacksons of Tennessee* (1953) is somewhat more the story of Rachel Jackson than it is of her husband, Andrew Jackson. Beautiful and kindly Rachel Donelson had made an unfortunate first marriage. In the days when news traveled slowly, she had every reason to believe her divorce was complete when she married Jackson. Mrs. Vance presents the details of this tragic misunderstanding (for such it was) which almost wrecked Jackson's career. The gentle beauty of Rachel, their all too brief moments of fun and triumph, their love of the children they gathered around them—nothing could ameliorate the shadow of that bitter story. In the end it killed Rachel. This is a mature and complex social problem, compassionately handled. It brings out what youth should know—the often disastrous effect of malicious gossip—and it tells a moving story of two high-spirited and devoted people.

An excellent biography of Jackson is the American Heritage book, *Andrew Jackson, Soldier and Statesman* (1963), written by Ralph K. Andrist and profusely illustrated with material from the period. The style of the narrative is simple and entertaining, and the historical background well detailed.

Among the many other biographies by Marguerite Vance, those she has written about women rulers are outstanding. *Elizabeth Tudor, Sovereign Lady* (1954) gives an objective picture of the imperious queen, although most of the book is devoted to her childhood. Helene Hanff's *Queen of England: The Story of Elizabeth I* (1969) gives a broader picture of Elizabethan England and of Elizabeth's maturity. Other biographies by Vance include *Scotland's Queen: The Story of Mary Stuart* (1962) and *The Empress Josephine: From Martinique to Malmaison* (1956).

## JEAN LEE LATHAM

*Carry On, Mr. Bowditch*

Between the great leaders in the American Revolution and the sturdy frontiersmen of the push westward is the unique figure of Nathaniel Bowditch. Born in Salem, Massachusetts, in 1773, he never had a day's schooling after he was ten years old. Yet he became an outstanding astronomer, mathematician, and author of *The New American Practical Navigator*, published in 1802 and still a basic text of modern navigation.

When Nathaniel was twelve, his father bound him out for nine years to a ship's chandlery. The boy was near despair, when an old fellow told him, "Only a weakling gives up when he is becalmed! A strong man sails by ash breeze!" That is, he "sails" his boat with ash oars. So Nat sailed. His story is one of continuous toil in the chandlery by day and with books at night. Then came the end of his indenture, and a knowledgeable young man set off on the first of his five adventurous voyages. There is romance in Nat's story, and some tragic as well as some extremely humorous episodes. The climax came when Harvard, to which he had yearned to go, bestowed upon this unschooled but brilliant scientist an honorary degree. It is a thrilling story of New England fortitude and love of learning. Jean Latham has told it splendidly, and strong illustrations add to the distinction of this 1956 Newbery Medal book.

Another Latham biography of a great American navigator is *Trail Blazer of the Seas* (1956), the story of Matthew Maury, who worked to establish a naval academy. *Young Man in a Hurry: The Story of Cyrus W. Field* (1958) is as exciting as an adventure story.

*Illustration by John O'Hara Cosgrave II. From* Carry On, Mr. Bowditch *by Jean Lee Latham. Copyright, 1955, by Jean Lee Latham and John O'Hara Cosgrave II. Reproduced by permission of the Houghton Mifflin Company.*

## EDWIN P. HOYT

*James Knox Polk*

Edwin Hoyt is a dependably good biographer, his style rather heavy and serious but his books valuable because of their historical accuracy and their objective approach. In his Presidential series, Hoyt's outstanding contribution is his presentation of the lives of some of our lesser-known Presidents and his stress on memorable facets of their lives. In *James Knox Polk* (1965), he emphasizes Polk's years of development in state and national politics rather than his term as President, though the latter is given adequate coverage. In *William McKinley* (1967), he stresses McKinley's role as an internationalist before his time.

In Hoyt's biography of James Polk, comparatively little is said about his personal life, and the discussion of his rise to the office of the Presidency includes not only an account of Polk's legislative accomplishments and personal growth but also a description of the intricacies of party politics and intraparty struggles for power. Polk's early political career was undistinguished: he showed little interest in social problems, he was a rather cold and silent man, and he was regarded as a tool of the slave owners. But he was a careful man, and he believed in the "manifest destiny" of the United States in a time when the country was in a mood for expansion. During his term of office, James Polk achieved almost every goal he had set himself: an equitable tariff law, an independent treasury, a settlement of the Oregon boundary dispute, and the annexation of Texas and California.

Hoyt's Presidential biographies do more than simply give the historical events of the periods they cover. To read the life of Polk, or *Martin Van Buren* (1964), or *John Tyler* (1970) is to gain a clearer understanding of how a man can affect his times and how the times can influence a man.

Other biographies of Polk for older children are Milton Lomask's *This Slender Reed, a Life of James K. Polk* (1966) and William Severn's *Frontier President: James K. Polk* (1965), which is better written than the Lomask book and a little lighter in tone than that of Hoyt. Severn devotes more attention to Polk's childhood and personal life than does Hoyt, but is no less adroit in giving a vivid and accurate historical background, particularly in details of the development of the major political parties.

## ELIZABETH KYLE

*Girl with a Pen: Charlotte Brontë*

Elizabeth Kyle's *Girl with a Pen* (1964) is a story of Charlotte Brontë's life from her seventeenth year to her thirty-first. Competently fictionalized, the biography evokes vividly the bleak parsonage and the beloved moorland country, the affection among the Brontë children, and the growing development of their literary interests.

Particularly engaging is the section that describes the reception at the London publishing house of Smith and Elder of a book titled *Jane Eyre* by a writer who called herself Currer Bell. The subsequent acclaim of the book is followed by Charlotte's timid report to her father that she had had a book published and his announcement to her sisters: "Girls, do you know that Charlotte has been writing a book, and it is much better than likely?"

The portraits of Charlotte and her sisters are candid, and the establishment of their restricted horizons is so strong that the reader is always conscious of the courage it must have taken the three Brontë sisters as women—and particularly as women from a modest parsonage—to submit their manuscripts.

In her afterword, Kyle refers to this book as a story rather than a biography, but it succeeds in the task of a good biography: it reveals the character of its subject and her achievements, and in stimulating interest in its subject, this captivating biography—or story, as Kyle describes it—is exceptionally successful.

Hilda White's *Wild Decembers* (1957) is a semi-fictionalized, biographical portrait of the Brontë family presumably told from Charlotte's retrospective viewpoint as she looks over her life after her sisters and brother have died. *Wild Decembers* is not as entertaining as Kyle's book, but is more psychologically analytical. In Phyllis Bentley's *The Brontës and Their World* (1969), the sisters are considered not only as literary figures, but as mirrors, in their lives and their books, of socially significant changes taking place during their lifetimes.

Another one of Elizabeth Kyle's lively biographies of writers is *Great Ambitions: A Story of the Early Years of Charles Dickens* (1968), covering in great detail Dickens' life between the ages of twelve and twenty-seven. Kyle has also written two biographies of musicians: *Song of the Waterfall* (1970), which is almost as much a discussion of cultural life in nineteenth-century Norway as it is the story of Edvard and Nina Grieg; and *Duet: The Story of Clara and Robert Schumann* (1968). Of all Kyle's books, *Princess of Orange* (1966) has the greatest historical interest, because it is the story of the daughter of James II, Mary, whose unhappiness at an arranged marriage changed to love and respect for William of Orange, eventually joint sovereign with her when she became Mary II of England.

## JAMES PLAYSTED WOOD

*Spunkwater, Spunkwater! A Life of Mark Twain*

"The United States has always paid its entertainers extravagantly," says James Wood in *Spunkwater, Spunkwater!* (1968). "Whatever his other excellences, and he had many—and whatever deep, dark mystique ingenious critics have read into his life and work—Mark Twain was first and last an entertainer. It was his celebrity as an entertainer that led to his being enthroned as the American sage. He was the articulate and even voluble symbol of the kind of practical wisdom Americans most admired. He was about as tragic as anyone else, applauded and honored everywhere he went, who was having a wonderful time. . . ." Such candid comment is typical of the fresh and thoughtful approach of James Wood, whose sophisticated style pays the reader the compliment of assuming that he will appreciate the nuance of humor and oblique reference.

Mark Twain's life as river pilot, newspaperman, author, lecturer, caustic world traveler, and deeply devoted husband is familiar material, included in most of the biographies of Twain. Wood gives an added dimension by his perceptively analytical discussion of Twain's volatile and ebullient personality and by his criticism of Twain's writing. A list of important dates and a bibliography add to the book's usefulness, and some delightful photographs add to its appeal.

Few books about the wives of famous men are really centered on the wife; *Dear, Dear Livy* (1963) by Adrien Stoutenburg and Laura Nelson Baker is one that is. An interesting book in itself, it is particularly so when read as a companion volume to Wood's book on Twain, and it gives an almost stereoscopic view of the surprisingly happy marriage of a frail, shy woman and an obstreperous man.

The mature wit and percipience of Wood's analysis of Twain are also evident in his other biographies of writers. In *The Lantern Bearer: A Life of Robert Louis Stevenson* (1965), he is candid in appraisal of Stevenson as a romantic, often illogical man and a superb craftsman. In *I Told You So* (1969), he is equally frank in picturing H. G. Wells as aggressive and irritable but brilliant and energetic. Wood's *The Admirable Cotton Mather* (1971) is particularly interesting because he disputes Mather's reputation as vindictive and bigoted.

## POLLY LONGSWORTH

*I, Charlotte Forten, Black and Free*

Polly Longsworth's *I, Charlotte Forten* (1970) is based on Ray Allen Billington's edition of Charlotte's diary, and, according to the author in her acknowledgments, is "as close a re-creation of Miss Forten's life and experiences as I am capable of achieving." This explains why the biography begins with Charlotte's sixteenth year, when she came to Salem, Massachusetts, so that she might attend an unsegregated school.

As the granddaughter of the wealthy and respected James Forten, she had been brought up in a home in which good breeding and cultural interests were taken for granted, and in which the leaders of the antislavery movement were accustomed guests. Charlotte continued to meet in Salem such dignitaries as Whittier, Garrison, Douglass, and Phillips, and she decided to devote her life to helping her own people.

Having become a teacher, she volunteered to join the Port Royal Commission that was going to the South Carolina Sea Islands to teach the neglected blacks of Saint Helena. In 1864, she came North to attend her father's funeral, and there the biography ends, although a final chapter describes the Grimké family and her marriage to Francis Grimké, and speaks briefly of their joint years of dedication to helping the black cause through the hard days of antebellum disillusionment.

The book is written in first person, in a heavy and rather ornate style appropriate for a nineteenth-century woman of good family. It is nevertheless an exciting book, in part because the pages read like a roll call of all the early crusaders against slavery, in part because the events are intrinsically dramatic, and in part because the picture of a frail and gentle girl so unselfishly devoted to a cause is romantic in the best sense.

Esther Douty's *Charlotte Forten: Free Black Teacher* (1971), a biography for the middle grades, is based on the diary also, but written in third person; it, too, ends with Charlotte Forten's return to the North after her father's death. An afterword briefly describes her subsequent life. More fictionalized than the Longsworth book, this has a few childhood episodes that contribute little to the book and includes some quotations from the diary. Otherwise the books cover most of the same incidents and major events, though there is much more detail and more background in Longsworth's account.

Another outstanding biography by Longsworth is *Emily Dickinson: Her Letter to the World* (1965), written in a quiet style that is a good foil for the romantic subject, and with a balanced attention to the poet's writing and to her personal life.

## DOROTHY STERLING

*Captain of the Planter:*
*The Story of Robert Smalls*

Robert Smalls' owner was Henry McKee. Because he could earn more money for McKee by being hired out, Smalls was sent to Charleston, where he worked in a sailing loft and watched the pilots carefully until he became adept at handling boats himself. In 1861, Smalls shipped on the *Planter* as a deckhand. The ship was in the service of the Confederate Navy, and it was the resemblance between its captain and himself that gave Smalls his great idea: an idea that would bring him freedom and put the ship into Union hands. At three A.M. on the morning of May 13, 1862, the black crew quietly maneuvered the ship out of the harbor, stopping to take on some of their wives and children; they were given freedom to pass by the sentinel at Fort Sumter, and the crew proudly hailed a Union ship and turned the *Planter* over to the Union.

Disappointed by the fact that the Union Army included no black troops, Smalls visited President Lincoln and persuaded him to change his policy. Dedicated to the causes of freedom and equality, he became a public speaker and a member of Congress.

Dorothy Sterling's story of Robert Smalls, well documented by a list of sources and an extensive bibliography, is dramatic because of its subject matter: Smalls' personal achievement and the events of the years of the Civil War and the Reconstruction. What Sterling has added to the inherent drama of the *Captain of the Planter* (1958) is a powerful picture of the tragedy of the postwar years and a personal portrait of a man whose true greatness lay not in one single courageous act but in the fact that he never compromised his principles for the sake of expediency.

Other biographies by Sterling are *Freedom Train: The Story of Harriet Tubman* (1954), *Lucretia Mott, Gentle Warrior* (1964), and *The Making of an Afro-American: Martin Robison Delaney 1812–1885* (1971), an extensively documented account of an early exponent of black nationalism. While Dorothy Sterling has written stories, informational books on such diverse topics as caves and caterpillars, and series books, her strongest commitment is clearly to the cause of black equality. Young readers who enjoy her biographies may also want to read her study of events related to the Emancipation Proclamation in *Forever Free* (1963) and her history of the American civil rights movement in *Tear Down the Walls!* (1968).

## SHANNON GARST

*Crazy Horse*

Toward the end of the period of westward expansion came the terrible struggles between the advancing hordes of white men and the defending Indians. Several fine biographies of Indian leaders of this period give children the story of these events from the Indians' point of view. *Crazy Horse* (1950) is one of the best of these. It begins with his training as a boy, shows his bitter experiences with the bad faith and cruelties of the white men and his growing determination to stop their invasion at all costs. The end is sheer tragedy. Crazy Horse is defeated, his people scattered or herded into a reservation, and Crazy Horse, rather than submit, fights to his death. No child who reads this moving record will ever believe the cruelties were all on one side.

Shannon Garst also writes sympathetically of the Sioux way of life in *Sitting Bull, Champion of His People* (1946) and of Sitting Bull's tenacious and courageous fight in a losing battle against the encroachment of the white men. Garst's *Kit Carson, Trailblazer and Scout* (1942) is a lively book of frontier life, full of action and the romance of the Old West.

## SHIRLEY GRAHAM

*Booker T. Washington*

Shirley Graham's memoirs of her late husband, William E. B. Du Bois, *His Day Is Marching On* (1971), make clear the difference in viewpoint between the militant Du Bois and the conservative Booker Taliaferro Washington. But in her biography *Booker T. Washington* (1955) she has given an objective and sympathetic picture of Washington.

Born a slave, Booker was nine when the Emancipation Proclamation brought him freedom and an opportunity to go to West Virginia, where he worked in a salt mine and a coal mine. He took the name "Washington," in fact, from the name of the salt mine and the "Taliaferro" from the name of his father. According to Graham, he didn't learn this until he went off to attend Hampton Institute in 1872. Bent on getting an education, young Washington worked doggedly to pay his way through school, his academic prowess earning him an appointment as principal of Tuskegee, the new normal school that became Tuskegee Institute.

Although Booker T. Washington became famous for his development of Tuskegee, for bringing George Washington Carver to the faculty, for dining with presidents, and for being the first black man to get an honorary degree from Harvard University, he has always stirred some controversy because of the stand he took on race relations in the famous speech often referred to as the "Atlanta Compromise." In her biography, Shirley Graham has submerged any difference in viewpoint she might have with Washington. Her story is told with an understanding of how Washington's life and experience shaped his ideas. The biography is adroitly fictionalized, many of the incidents based on Washington's autobiography *Up from Slavery*, with anecdotes and dialogue woven smoothly into the narrative. A bibliography gives sources, and a lengthy index makes textual material accessible.

*The Story of Phillis Wheatley* (1949) is well researched but even more fictionalized. Graham has also written biographies of Frederick Douglass (*There Was Once a Slave* [1947]), Benjamin Banneker (*Your Most Humble Servant* [1949]), and other figures in black history, and, for children in the middle grades, *The Story of Pocahontas* (1953).

For very young children, William Wise's *Booker T. Washington* (1968) is simply written and gives adequate information; other biographies for the early and middle grades are pedestrian, although the brief treatment in *Lift Every Voice* (1965), a collective biography written for older children by Dorothy Sterling and Benjamin Quarles, can be used by many nine- and ten-year-old readers. For older readers, the best book is Booker T. Washington's autobiography, *Up from Slavery*, available in both hardbound and paperback editions.

## CATHERINE OWENS PEARE

*The Louis D. Brandeis Story*

Catherine Owens Peare is never adulatory in her attitude toward the men and women whose biographies she writes, but her affection and respect for her subjects are usually clear, as they are in *The Louis D. Brandeis Story* (1970). Coming of a close-knit Austrian-Jewish family that had migrated to Louisville, Brandeis grew up in a circle in which it was taken for granted that cultural, academic, and political interests would be shared and discussed. An ardent student, Louis Brandeis made a distinguished record at Harvard Law School.

With a passion for justice and a concern for the underprivileged, Brandeis became a respected figure in the legal hierarchy of Boston, and grew wealthy enough to espouse reform measures and to take cases without a fee to protect the public interest against the depredations of big business monoliths. In his years as an Associate Justice of the Supreme Court, he won distinction for his idealism, his concern for humanity, and his farseeing understanding of ethical and social implications of the issues involved in cases heard. An ample bibliography of sources is included.

Many of Peare's biographies are concerned with public figures: *The Herbert Hoover Story* (1965) stresses Hoover's role in humanitarian projects, and *The Woodrow Wilson Story* (1963), Wilson's idealism and his influence on world events. In *Mary McLeod Bethune* (1951), she draws an exciting picture of the remarkably energetic black educator.

## IRIS NOBLE

*Emmeline and Her Daughters: The Pankhurst Suffragettes*

*Emmeline and Her Daughters* (1971), like many of Iris Noble's other biographies, describes with enthusiastic sympathy a pioneer in a reform movement, a champion of a cause. The book's bibliography includes works by Mrs. Pankhurst and by each of her three daughters, clearly the source of many of the intimate details that give the account vitality and authenticity. The tumultuous record of the Pankhursts is seen both as a personal narrative and as the opening salvo in the long battle for equality for women.

Emmeline Pankhurst had been a demure, cultured Victorian wife and mother until the day her husband, who had long fought for feminine liberation, challenged her to take an active part in the struggle. He began her education as a militant participant by taking her to hear debates in Parliament, helping her organize the Women's Franchise League, and encouraging her to run for a minor political office. She was forty when he died, and without his backing her role was even more difficult. It was her daughter Christabel who conceived the idea of a new organization, "*of* women *for* women, one that will lead all the women of Britain into militant action." So the Women's Social and Political Union was born, the group that was a vigorous spearhead for feminine equality. Reviled by Herbert Asquith and rejected by Winston Churchill, oppressed by the police and the courts, jeered at by the public and the press, the W.S.P.U. grew in strength and determination through all of the years in which its members were jailed, force-fed, ostracized, and beaten. The actions taken against this dedicated army of women led them to mass demonstrations and acts of violence, but their courage in the face of brutal reprisals eventually won them public admiration, the support of much of the press, and, in 1928, at long last, full suffrage.

Iris Noble deals objectively with dramatic and important events and shows the long struggle as not only a dominating motive in the lives of the four Pankhurst women but the cause of a bitter rupture between Christabel and Sylvia Pankhurst.

Objectivity in reporting and sympathetic understanding of a crusader's ardor are also evident in Noble's *Labor's Advocate: Eugene V. Debs* (1966), in which, as in *Emmeline*, there is a vivid portrayal of the protagonist as well as a broad picture of the movements in which he was a pioneer. In Noble's biographies of rulers (*Empress of All Russia* [1966], *Spain's Golden Queen Isabella* [1969]), there is also a combination of broad historical coverage and a vigorous, perceptive characterization of the individual.

## MIRIAM GURKO

### *Restless Spirit: The Life of Edna St. Vincent Millay*

Miriam Gurko's *Restless Spirit* (1962) is a mature and thoughtful biography for adolescent readers, the sources for which include published and unpublished material, letters, and interviews. "Curiously, as the mass of notes grew, the more elusive the subject seemed to become," Gurko states in her foreword. And she goes on, "From this assortment of fact and characterization I have had to select those elements which appeared the most credible, and which seemed to have undergone the least alteration as a result of the passage of time or the presence of certain personal factors."

Brought up by her mother after her parents had separated, Vincent and her sisters had a childhood in which they early became self-reliant. Vincent wrote poetry at the age of five, and many of her childhood poems were published in *The St. Nicholas Magazine*. She had already published "Renascence" and become modestly famous when she entered Vassar at the age of twenty-one. After her graduation, Edna, who no longer used "Vincent" as her name, went to New York to join in the intellectual ferment of Greenwich Village life and in the activities of the newly formed Provincetown Players. After several abortive love affairs, she married Eugen Boissevin, a marriage that was ideal for a poet, since Eugen felt it his role to protect Edna and encourage her work.

The biography includes quotations from Edna St. Vincent Millay's poetry only when they are relevant to the text, and Gurko has integrated smoothly the personal material, the background of the artistic and literary circles in which Edna moved, and the discerning discussion of the poet's work and its place in modern poetry.

Toby Shafter's biography *Edna St. Vincent Millay: America's Best-Loved Poet* (1957) is lighter in style, with much more fictionalization and with approximately half the book devoted to Millay's childhood. However, it is factually reliable and a good introduction for less mature readers.

Other biographies by Miriam Gurko include *Clarence Darrow* (1965), interesting both as an account of the famous Scopes trial and as a study of the nonconformist lawyer who was a defender of unpopular causes. Much of the story also reflects the history of the labor movement. *The Lives and Times of Peter Cooper* (1959), as the title indicates, is concerned with other figures as well as with that of the protagonist, for the inventor and industrialist Cooper was constantly involved in industrial, political, and educational movements.

## LEO GURKO

*Ernest Hemingway and the Pursuit of Heroism*

Leo Gurko, in *Ernest Hemingway* (1968), writes for the adolescent reader who is seriously interested in Hemingway as a writer rather than as a person. Only the first fourth of this biography is devoted to Hemingway's life. Colorful to the point of flamboyance, Ernest Hemingway was a nonconformist adolescent in a conventional suburban home. When he refused to go to college and was rejected by the Army during the First World War, he joined the staff of the Kansas City *Star* as a cub reporter until he discovered that he could serve with the Red Cross. Much of his experience in Italy appears again in *A Farewell to Arms*. His years in Paris, his service in Spain during the Civil War, his string of marriages, and his winning of the Nobel Prize for Literature are described in a concise and objective account. The remainder of the book is devoted to an astute critical analysis of Hemingway's writing, learned but never dry, in which Gurko explores the persistence of the theme of heroism, not the heroism of great deeds but the heroism of the individual who struggles for humanity and his own salvation.

In *The Two Lives of Joseph Conrad* (1965) Gurko again relates, in polished prose style, the man and his experiences to the content of his books (in which there are often thinly disguised counterparts of the people and the incidents in the subject's own life). *Tom Paine: Freedom's Apostle* (1957) is more simply written than Gurko's other books and equally objective and perceptive.

## THEODORA KROEBER

*Ishi: Last of His Tribe*

At the end of the nineteenth century a small band of Yahi Indians lived in solitude and secrecy at the foot of Mount Lassen, their way of life threatened by the white settlers and seekers of gold. *Ishi* (1964) and his people knew that they could survive only if they remained hidden, their ancient villages having been destroyed by the ruthless invaders. As long as they could, the people clung to the sacred ways, the quiet and peaceful pattern of Yahi life. One by one, the others died, and Ishi was alone. "There is nothing to wait for in this empty land, nothing—I am free to go." And so he left, and took the trail to the west, lost his way, and met the saldu, the whites.

To his surprise, they did not kill him; a Stranger was brought, a museum-saldu, who spoke in the tongue of the People, and took Ishi on a train. And so Ishi came to live with the white men in peace, an adviser to the museum people on the ways and the crafts of the Yahi. One of the most striking aspects of *Ishi* is the consistency with which Theodora Kroeber maintains Ishi's viewpoint; even after he comes to live and work with the museum staff, the relationships are seen through Ishi's eyes, and the writing continues to have the beautiful cadence and dignity of Yahi. At the end, "Death came to him as he wished—

*Illustration by Ruth Robbins for* Ishi, Last of His Tribe *by T. Kroeber. Copyright 1965. Reproduced by permission of Parnassus Press.*

with his friends in the museum-watgurwa. Majapa and the museum men released his spirit in the old Yahi way. And they saw to it that Ishi had with him those things that a Yahi hunter must take from the World of the Living, for the journey to the west. . . ." The names used are always the Yahi names that Ishi had given.

Alfred Kroeber was Curator of the Museum of Anthropology and Ethnology at the University of California when Ishi was brought there, and his wife had the benefit of his professional knowledge as well as first-hand information from Ishi. Such familiarity permits a biographer to incorporate cultural details so that they are as intrinsic a part of a life story as they are in *Ishi*, and in Theodora Kroeber's anthropological study for adult readers, *Ishi in Two Worlds*.

## MILTON MELTZER

*Langston Hughes*

Perhaps because *Langston Hughes: A Biography* (1968) is about a colleague and friend, it has an immediacy and warmth that Meltzer's other biographies do not have. Perhaps it is that the poet himself sheds light and grace. "Within a few years of his first book," Meltzer says, "he was the poet laureate of his people." Hughes' life and work were a testament to his belief that it was a proud thing to be black, his poetry more bittersweet than bitter.

In Topeka, Kansas, he was the only black child in school; he spent some time on his father's Mexican ranch; he washed dishes in a Paris cafe and worked on a Staten Island truck farm. While working as a waiter in a Washington hotel, he put three of his poems on Vachel Lindsay's table, and that night Lindsay read the poems aloud in public. He went to Spain as a reporter during the Civil War there, and he traveled in Asia and in Russia – in short, he had an exciting and colorful life.

But his travels, his involvement in causes, and his amazingly varied and prolific outpouring of magnificent prose and poetry are almost overshadowed by his passion for truth and justice. That is what Milton Meltzer has succeeded in conveying to the readers of *Langston Hughes*.

Another biography of Hughes for the older reader is *Black Troubadour: Langston Hughes* (1970) by Charlemae Rollins. It covers most of the incidents that are in Meltzer's book, although it refers to Hughes' patron, Mrs. Mason, only as "an elderly woman." While this is not as discerning as the Meltzer biography, it has the intimacy borne of personal friendship, a full list of Hughes' works, and many photographs of him and of other black authors.

The reader will want to explore Hughes' poems, some of which are discussed in the poetry chapters; his short stories, the amusing stories about "Simple," with *The Best of Simple* (1961) comprising selections from earlier books; and his two autobiographical books, *I Wonder as I Wander* (1956, reprinted 1964) and *The Big Sea* (1963).

In an article on the distortions in children's history books, Milton Meltzer says, "Biography is another way to re-create the past. The life of a Tom Paine, a Benjamin Banneker, a Sojourner Truth . . . lets the reader see history from inside, from the mind and heart of an individual struggling to reshape his own time. In history books, Wendell Phillips and William Lloyd Garrison are only a paragraph or a line, too often dismissed as irresponsible fanatics. Or there is a glancing reference to that other 'fanatic,' Thaddeus Stevens, painted darkly in the sky of Washington like some vulture hovering over the capital to pick the bones of Southern heroes ennobled in defeat."[17]

Meltzer's *Thaddeus Stevens* (1967) destroys this picture and presents a mature and thoughtful biography of the Pennsylvania

17. Milton Meltzer, "The Fractured Image," *Library Journal*, Oct. 15, 1968, p. 3923.

lawyer whose tenure in the national Congress was marked by bitter opposition from the South, particularly because of his battle against the fugitive slave laws. Thaddeus Stevens was a champion of public education and racial equality, his efforts on behalf of black people's civil rights continuing after the Civil War and through the years of Reconstruction. Meltzer's description of those years and of Stevens' leadership in the move to impeach President Andrew Johnson is direct and vigorous, one of the most valuable aspects of a fine biography that does, indeed, see history from the viewpoint of "an individual struggling to reshape his own time."

*Tongue of Flame: The Life of Lydia Maria Child* (1965) and *A Light in the Dark: The Life of Samuel Gridley Howe* (1964) are, like the Stevens biography, imbued with enthusiasm for the causes to which the subjects were dedicated, yet they are not eulogistic in tone. Howe was a pioneer in work for the blind and for prison reform, in programs to aid the retarded, and provide help to fugitive slaves. Mrs. Child founded the first children's magazine in this country, ran a newspaper, and was a pioneer in the fight against slavery. Meltzer has let their amazing records speak for them, serving their reputations simply by recording their lives.

## OTHER BIOGRAPHIES FOR OLDER READERS

By far the greatest number of biographies are written for readers in the upper grades and high school. Many are, of course, read by younger children. It is not possible to include discussion of all the fine books that are available; fortunately reference books in the field of biography make the material easily accessible to readers seeking information about individuals' lives. Here will be added just a few more outstanding biographies to indicate further the scope of the genre.

Margaret Leighton's *Cleopatra: Sister of the Moon* (1969) gives a good picture of the complicated pattern of Mediterranean countries and depicts Cleopatra, not as a siren but as an intelligent woman aware of the transitory nature of her power. In Alice Curtis Desmond's *Cleopatra's Children* (1971) the picture of shifting alliances, feuds, and intrigue is even stronger.

Cornelia Spencer writes objectively and authoritatively of the brothers-in-law whose lives are so important in Chinese history—*Sun Yat-sen, Founder of the Chinese Republic* (1967) and *Chiang Kai-shek, Generalissimo of Nationalist China* (1968), both books having slight fictionalization in conversation but not in the events described.

Among the notable biographies of American figures are Esther Forbes' *America's Paul Revere* (1946), which used the material from *Paul Revere and the World He Lived In*, an adult title by the same author.

Ann Petry has told a well-documented story of another famous American in *Harriet Tubman: Conductor on the Underground Railroad* (1955). The dramatic story of this courageous woman is also told in Hildegarde Swift's *Railroad to Freedom* (1932).

*Invincible Louisa: The Story of the Author of Little Women* (1968) by Cornelia Meigs was first published in 1933 and won the Newbery Medal. It gives a remarkably broad view of the period and of the people in Louisa May Alcott's life as well as a perceptive study of Alcott herself.

The National Book Award went to Isaac Bashevis Singer for *A Day of Pleasure: Stories of a Boy Growing Up in Warsaw* (1969). Illustrated with photographs of the Singer family and of scenes of Warsaw, the nineteen autobiographical stories, told in delightful style, provide a lively picture of the ghetto community and of the author as a child.

Biography, like many other literary forms, reflects contemporary interests, and so there have been increasing numbers of books about minority group representatives in the United States, about leaders of other countries, and about women. One such is James

Terzian and Kathryn Cramer's *Mighty Hard Road: The Story of Cesar Chavez* (1970), which is liberally fictionalized but a good study both of Chavez and of the migrant workers' struggle against exploitation. Another is Addison Gayle's *Oak and Ivy: A Biography of Paul Laurence Dunbar* (1971), the black writer who, Gayle feels, was forced by the prejudice of his times to compromise unhappily in his writing of negritude. *Hidalgo, Mexican Revolutionary* (1971) by Mark Lieberman is the engrossing story of Miguel Hidalgo y Costilla, the priest who became Generalissimo of a rebel army—a book that also gives a vivid picture of eighteenth-century Mexico and its struggle for independence from the Spanish hierarchy.

Nardi Campion's *Look to This Day! The Lively Education of a Great Woman Doctor: Connie Guion, M.D.* (1965) gives a long, detailed story of the woman who entered medical school when she was thirty-one, and provides interesting glimpses of the beginnings of higher education for women. Cora Cheney's *The Incredible Deborah: A Story Based on the Life of Deborah Sampson* (1967) describes a heroine whose adventures are indeed stranger than fiction. Deborah would not be denied a chance to prove her patriotism; and so, dressed as a man, she served in the Revolutionary War, her sex being discovered only when she fell ill. She left her husband and children years later to lecture on her experiences, and she was awarded a pension as an invalid soldier!

There is a growing trend toward presenting the subject of a biography without omitting important facts about unpleasant or unsavory incidents or traits, a trend that recognizes the right of young readers to know the whole truth and thus to understand more clearly the men and women about whom they are reading. As Paul Murray Kendall says:

> *Biography attempts the simulation, in words, of a man's life, from what is known about that life, from the paper trail, the enigmatic footprint. Thus it differs from the other literary arts. They seek to evoke reality from illusion; biography hopes to fasten illusion upon reality, to elicit, from the coldness of paper, the warmth of a life being lived.*[18]

## ADULT REFERENCES[19]

ALTICK, RICHARD D. *Lives and Letters: A History of Literary Biography in England and America.*

ARBUTHNOT, MAY HILL, and DOROTHY M. BRODERICK. *Time for Biography.*

BERRY, THOMAS ELLIOTT, ed. *The Biographer's Craft.*

BOWEN, CATHERINE DRINKER. *Biography: The Craft and the Calling.*

CLIFFORD, JAMES L. *From Puzzles to Portraits: Problems of a Literary Biographer.*

———, ed. *Biography as an Art.*

CRAVEN, PAUL R. *Biography.*

NICHOLSEN, MARGARET. *People in Books: A Selective Guide to Biographical Literature Arranged by Vocations and Other Fields of Reader Interest.*

SILVERMAN, JUDITH. *An Index to Young Readers' Collective Biographies.*

STANIUS, ELLEN, comp. *Index to Short Biographies: For Elementary and Junior High Grades.*

*In the following bibliography these symbols have been used to identify books about a religious or a particular ethnic group:*

§ Black
★ Chicano or Puerto Rican
☆ Indian
● Religious minority

## COLLECTIVE BIOGRAPHIES

§ ALEXANDER, RAE PACE, comp. *Young and Black in America.* Random, 1970. Well-known black men and women describe the problems they encountered in their youth. 11 up

§● ASIMOV, ISAAC. *Breakthroughs in Science,* ill. by Karoly and Szanto. Houghton, 1960. 11 up

BAKELESS, KATHERINE. *Story-Lives of American Composers.* Lippincott, 1953.

———. *Story-Lives of Great Composers.* Lippincott, 1953.
For each collection, nineteen composers have been selected. 12-15

● BEARD, ANNIE E. S. *Our Foreign-born Citizens,* 6th ed. T. Crowell, 1968. Short biographies of Americans of foreign birth or parentage. 10-14

BEARD, CHARLES AUSTIN. *The Presidents in American History.* Messner, 1961. Offers good historical background for each Presidential career. 12-16

18. Paul Murray Kendall, *The Art of Biography* (Norton, 1965), p. 28.

19. Complete bibliographic data are provided in the combined Adult References in the Appendices.

BENÉT, LAURA. *Famous American Poets*, ill. with photos. Dodd, 1950. Over twenty poets both recent and past are introduced in brief biographies. 11-14

BENTLEY, PHYLLIS. *The Brontës and Their World.* Viking, 1969. 14 up

§ BONTEMPS, ARNA. *Famous Negro Athletes.* Dodd, 1964. Short sketches include personal and career information. 10-12

§ BUCKMASTER, HENRIETTA. *Women Who Shaped History.* Macmillan, 1966. A fine collective biography of Dorothea Dix, Prudence Crandall, Elizabeth Stanton, Harriet Tubman, and Mary Baker Eddy. 12-15

CHASE, ALICE. *Famous Artists of the Past.* Platt, 1964. Twenty-six brief biographies include discussions of the artists' styles. Many of the reproductions are in color. 10-13

§● COHEN, TOM. *Three Who Dared.* Doubleday, 1969. Three young men who risked their safety to help bring civil rights to the southern black people. 11-14

COMMIRE, ANNE. *Something About the Author: Pictures about Contemporary Authors and Illustrators of Books for Young People.* Vol. 1. Gale, 1971. Each biographical sketch is followed by a list of the author's works and his or her comments on those works. Not comprehensive, but the book has reference use. 10 up

COY, HAROLD. *The First Book of Presidents*, rev. ed., ill. by Manning Lee. Watts, 1964. A useful ready reference source. 8-10

CRAWFORD, DEBORAH. *Four Women in a Violent Time.* Crown, 1970. Mary Dyer, Anne Hutchinson, Penelope Van Princes, and Deborah Moody fought for personal liberty in colonial times. 11-14

DAUGHERTY, SONIA. *Ten Brave Men*, ill. by James Daugherty. Lippincott, 1951. Good accounts of such national heroes as Roger Williams, Patrick Henry, Thomas Jefferson, and Andrew Jackson.

______. *Ten Brave Women*, ill. by James Daugherty. Lippincott, 1953. 11-15

§ DOBLER, LAVINIA, and WILLIAM A. BROWN. *Great Rulers of the African Past*, ill. by Yvonne Johnson. Doubleday, 1965. Five brief biographies of rulers of African kingdoms during the years 1312–1617. 10-13

§ DOUTY, ESTHER. *Under the New Roof: Five Patriots of the Young Republic.* Rand, 1965. Smoothly-written and well-researched sketches of five less familiar figures of Revolutionary War days. 10-13

DUNSHEATH, PERCY. *Giants of Electricity.* T. Crowell, 1967. Useful both for its biographical and scientific information. 12 up

FANNING, LEONARD M. *Fathers of Industries.* Lippincott, 1962. Emphasis is on men who from industrial revolution days to the present have contributed significantly to inventions having social and economic significance. 12 up

FISHER, AILEEN, and OLIVE RABE. *We Alcotts*, ill. by Ellen Raskin. Atheneum, 1968. 11-14

FLEMING, ALICE. *Doctors in Petticoats.* Lippincott, 1964.

§ ______. *Great Women Teachers.* Lippincott, 1965.
Succinct and lively, both books give information about the profession as well as its practitioners. 11-14

FORSEE, AYLESA. *Men of Modern Architecture: Giants in Glass, Steel and Stone.* Macrae, 1966. Emphasis is on professional rather than personal material. 13 up

FREEDMAN, RUSSELL. *Teen-Agers Who Made History.* Holiday, 1961. Stories of eight famous people of the past and present who became eminent in their careers before the age of twenty. 12-14

FULLER, MURIEL. *More Junior Authors.* Wilson, 1963. A companion volume to the Kunitz and Haycraft book cited below. 9 up

§ HABER, LOUIS. *Black Pioneers of Science and Invention.* Harcourt, 1970. A few of the fourteen biographees are famous, but most have not been written about for young people. 10-13

HIRSHBERG, AL. *The Greatest American Leaguers.* Putnam, 1970. Typical of many such sports biographies, this is breezy and anecdotal. 10-14

§ KAULA, EDNA MASON. *Leaders of the New Africa*, ill. by author. World, 1966. Competent and thoughtful. 12 up

KENNEDY, JOHN. *Profiles in Courage*, Young Readers Memorial ed. abr. Harper, 1964. The Pulitzer Prize was awarded this compilation of stories of men who took courageous stands in some decisive moments in our history. 10-12

§ KENWORTHY, LEONARD, and ERMA FERRARI. *Leaders of New Nations*, ill. by Michael Lowenbein. Doubleday, 1968. Revised edition of 1959 title, with four new leaders added and older material brought up to date. 12 up

KUNITZ, STANLEY, and HOWARD HAYCRAFT. *The Junior Book of Authors.* Wilson, 1951. Informal in style, and liberally illustrated, an excellent source of information. 9 up

LAWSON, ROBERT. *They Were Strong and Good*, ill. by author. Viking, 1940. Simply written stories of the author's parents and grandparents. Caldecott Medal. 8-10

§ MC NEER, MAY, and LYND WARD. *Armed with Courage*, ill. by Lynd Ward. Abingdon, 1957. Brief, entertaining biographies of seven dedicated men and women: Florence Nightingale, Father Damien, George W. Carver, Jane Addams, Wilfred Grenfell, Gandhi, and Albert Schweitzer. 9-12

§ MEYER, EDITH PATTERSON. *Champions of Peace*, ill. by Eric von Schmidt. Little, 1959. Timely sketches of fourteen Nobel Peace Prize winners, followed by a complete listing of all the award winners up to 1959, Nobel's will, and the rules for the award. 11 up

§ MITCHISON, NAOMI. *African Heroes*, ill. by William Stobbs. Farrar, 1969. Eleven tales of great Africans from the sub-Sahara, told in the fluent prose of a storyteller. Much history is included, but the book's impact lies in the richness and dignity of the people and their complex traditions. 12 up

MONTGOMERY, ELIZABETH RIDER. *The Story Behind Great Books*, ill. by Friedebald Dzubas. Dodd, 1946.

______. *The Story Behind Great Stories*, ill. by Elinore Blaisdell. Dodd, 1947.

______. *The Story Behind Modern Books.* Dodd, 1949.
Short sketches about authors and illustrators of children's books, both classic and recent. 11 up

ORR, FRANK. *Hockey's Greatest Stars.* Putnam, 1970. A Canadian sports writer gives a lively and informative account of twenty-odd outstanding players. 10-13

POOLE, LYNN, and GRAY POOLE. *Men Who Dig Up History.* Dodd, 1968. A good survey of the work of ten contemporary archeologists. 12 up

§ RICHARDSON, BEN. *Great American Negroes*, rev. by William A. Fahey, ill. by Robert Hallock. T. Crowell, 1956. Vivid accounts of twenty black people who have overcome obstacles and who have contributed to American culture in many fields. 12-16

§ ROLLINS, CHARLEMAE HILL. *They Showed the Way: American Negro Leaders.* T. Crowell, 1964. Each life story is very brief, but the book is valuable for information about black leaders not available elsewhere. Other Rollins' biographies are about black poets and black entertainers. 11-14

ROSENBLUM, MORRIS. *Heroes of Mexico.* Fleet, 1970. A survey of emperors, revolutionaries, artists, statesmen, and others who influenced the country's development. 12 up

SEROFF, VICTOR. *Men Who Made Musical History.* Funk, 1969. 10 up

SIMON, CHARLIE MAY. *Art in the New Land.* Dutton, 1945. Stories of famous American artists from Benjamin West to Grant Wood, with illustrations and descriptions of their work. 12-14

§ STERLING, DOROTHY, and BENJAMIN QUARLES. *Lift Every Voice*, ill. by Ernest Crichlow. Doubleday, 1965. 11-14

§ STEVENSON, JANET. *Pioneers in Freedom: Adventures in Courage.* Reilly, 1969. Life histories of men and women, slave and free, who had the courage to fight for the truths stated in the Declaration of Independence. 9-11

STODDARD, HOPE. *Famous American Women.* T. Crowell, 1970. An unusually good collective biography, distinguished by a sprightly style, a variety of fields of endeavor, and the evidence of careful research that makes the book a reference source as well as entertaining reading. 11-15

● SULLIVAN, NAVIN. *Pioneer Germ Fighters.* Atheneum, 1962. The discoveries of a dozen scientists, ranging from Leeuwenhoek to Salk. 10-12

SUTCLIFF, ROSEMARY. *Heroes and History*, ill. by Charles Keeping. Putnam, 1966. Detailed accounts of the years and deeds of glory of ten British figures. 13 up

●§ WEBB, ROBERT. *Heroes of Our Time.* Series 1. Watts, 1964. Followed by companion volumes; Series 4, for example (Watts, 1969), describes influential leaders of their countries and includes Brandt, Dayan, Gandhi, Ho Chi Minh, Nixon, and others. 11-13

WEINBERT, ARTHUR and LILA. *Six Dissenting Voices: The Story of Six American Dissenters.* World, 1970. Life stories of Steffens, Debs, Darrow, Altgeld, Addams, and Ingersoll, with emphasis on their ideas. 11-15

WHITE, HILDA. *Truth Is My Country: Portraits of Eight New England Authors.* Doubleday, 1971. Well-researched and perceptive in analysis, sketches of Emerson, Dickinson, Frost, Hawthorne, Millay, Stowe, Robinson, and Thoreau. 11 up

———. *Wild Decembers: A Biographical Portrait of the Brontës.* Dutton, 1957. 13-15

YOUNG, BOB and JAN. *Liberators of Latin America.* Lothrop, 1970. Eleven biographical sketches are preceded by a chapter giving historical background and a concluding section on the rise of the new republics. 11-14

§ YOUNG, MARGARET B. *Black American Leaders.* Watts, 1969. 10-14

§ ———. *The First Book of American Negroes*, ill. with photos. Watts, 1966. 10-14

## BIOGRAPHIES

ADAMS, SAMUEL (1722–1803)

Alderman, Clifford Lindsey. *Samuel Adams, Son of Liberty.* Holt, 1961. Distinguished writing and an outstanding evaluation of one of the American Revolution's most controversial figures. 12-16

ADDAMS, JANE (1860–1935)

Meigs, Cornelia Lynde. *Jane Addams; Pioneer for Social Justice.* Little, 1970. The writing has warmth and cohesion and gives a vivid picture of an era in this excellent biography of an important social reformer. 11-15

ALCOTT, LOUISA MAY (1832–1888)

Meigs, Cornelia. *Invincible Louisa.* Little, 1968 (first pub. in 1933). Newbery Medal. 12-14

Papashvily, Helen. *Louisa May Alcott*, ill. by Bea Holmes. Houghton, 1965. 11-14

§ ALDRIDGE, IRA (1807–1867)

Malone, Mary. *Actor in Exile: The Life of Ira Aldridge*, ill. by Eros Keith. Crowell-Collier, 1969. 9-11

ALEXANDER THE GREAT (356–323 B.C.)

Mercer, Charles. *Alexander the Great*, ill. American Heritage, 1963. The stirring account of Alexander's conquests, colorfully illustrated. 13 up

ALLEN, ETHAN (1738–1789)

Holbrook, Stewart. *America's Ethan Allen*, ill. by Lynd Ward. Houghton, 1949. Spirited illustrations in color add to the dramatic story of the "Green Mountain Boys" and their fighting leader. 11-15

ANDERSEN, HANS CHRISTIAN (1805–1875)

Collin, Hedvig. *Young Hans Christian Andersen*, ill. by author. Viking, 1955. Sensitively told story of the Danish writer from his childhood years to his first literary recognition. 11-14

ASOKA, EMPEROR OF INDIA (3rd century B.C.)

Lengyel, Emil. *Asoka the Great: India's Royal Missionary.* Watts, 1969. The life of the man who spread Buddhism to India, China, and Japan. This is one of a series, "Immortals of Philosophy and Religion," that includes St. Augustine, Confucius, Martin Luther, Moses Maimonides, and St. Francis. 12 up

AUDUBON, JOHN JAMES (1785–1851)

Fisher, Clyde. *The Life of Audubon*, ill. by John James Audubon. Harper, 1949. Written by a former staff member of the American Museum of Natural History, this biography is enhanced with reproductions of Audubon's own paintings in black and white and full color. 10-14

AUSTEN, JANE (1775–1817)

Becker, May L. *Presenting Miss Jane Austen*, ill. by Edward Price. Dodd, 1952. This picture of the life and times of Jane Austen, written by an Austen enthusiast, is a good introduction to the novels. 14-16

§ ARMSTRONG, LOUIS (1900–1971)

Eaton, Jeanette. *Trumpeter's Tale: The Story of Young Louis Armstrong*, ill. by Elton Fax. Morrow, 1955. Good biographical writing, and a good history of the development of jazz. 12-14

BACH, JOHANN SEBASTIAN (1685–1750)

Goss, Madeleine. *Deep Flowing Brook: The Story of Johann Sebastian Bach*, ill. by Elinore Blaisdell. Holt, 1938. Mrs. Goss writes unusually perceptive and comprehensive studies of musicians and their works. Her books are highly recommended. 12-16

Wheeler, Opal, and Sybil Deucher. *Sebastian Bach: the Boy from Thuringia*, ill. by Mary Greenwalt. Dutton, 1937. 9-10

BALBOA, VASCO NUNEZ DE (1475–1517)

Syme, Ronald. *Balboa, Finder of the Pacific*, ill. by William Stobbs. Morrow, 1956. Other explorer biographies include *Champlain of the St. Lawrence* (1952), *Henry Hudson* (1955), *Magellan, First Around the World* (1953). 10-12

§ BANNEKER, BENJAMIN (1731–1806)

Graham, Shirley. *Your Most Humble Servant: Story of Benjamin Banneker*. Messner, 1949. 14 up

BARTON, CLARA (1821–1912)

Boylston, Helen Dore. *Clara Barton, Founder of the American Red Cross*, ill. by Paula Hutchison. Random, 1955. Emphasizes Barton's work as a Civil War nurse rather than as the founder of the American Red Cross. 9-12

BEETHOVEN, LUDWIG VAN (1770–1827)

Goss, Madeleine. *Beethoven: Master Musician*, ill. by Carl Schultheiss. Holt, 1946. 12-16

Wheeler, Opal. *Ludwig Beethoven, and the Chiming Tower Bells*, ill. by Mary Greenwalt. Dutton, 1942. 9-10

§ BECKWOURTH, JAMES PIERSON (1798–1867)

Felton, Harold. *Jim Beckwourth: Negro Mountain Man*, ill. with photos and prints of the period and maps. Dodd, 1966. 11-14

● BERNSTEIN, LEONARD (1918– )

Ewen, David. *Leonard Bernstein: A Biography for Young People*. Chilton, 1960. Story of the notable American composer and conductor. 13 up

§ BETHUNE, MARY MCLEOD (1875–1955)

Peare, Catherine Owens. *Mary McLeod Bethune*. Vanguard, 1951. 13-15

Sterne, Emma Gelders. *Mary McLeod Bethune*, ill. by Raymond Lufkin. Knopf, 1957. A substantial biography about the child of a slave-born mother who did so much to advance the education of her people. 12-16

BOLIVAR, SIMON (1783–1830)

Syme, Ronald. *Bolivar the Liberator*, ill. by William Stobbs. Morrow, 1968. 9-12

BOONE, DANIEL (1734–1820)

Brown, John Mason. *Daniel Boone: The Opening of the Wilderness*, ill. by Lee J. Ames. Random, 1952. Fine characterization adds distinction to this biography of the Kentucky pioneer. 12-15

Daugherty, James. *Daniel Boone*, ill. by author. Viking, 1939. Newbery Medal. 12-15

Martin, Patricia Miles. *Daniel Boone*, ill. by Glen Dines. Putnam, 1965. 7-9

BOWDITCH, NATHANIEL (1773–1838)

Latham, Jean Lee. *Carry On, Mr. Bowditch*, ill. by John O'Hara Cosgrave II. Houghton, 1955. Newbery Medal. 11-15

BRAILLE, LOUIS (1809–1852)

De Gering, Etta. *Seeing Fingers*, ill. by Emil Weiss. McKay, 1962. Beautifully told story of Louis Braille, who was blinded at three, and of his development of the raised alphabet. 11-13

● BRANDEIS, LOUIS (1856–1941)

Peare, Catherine Owens. *The Louis Brandeis Story*. T. Crowell, 1970. 11-13

BRONTË, CHARLOTTE (1816–1855)

Jarden, Mary Louise. *The Young Brontës: Charlotte and Emily, Branwell and Anne*, ill. by Helen Sewell. Viking, 1938. An exceedingly well-written biography for girls who are interested in the Brontës. 14-16

Kyle, Elizabeth. *Girl with a Pen: Charlotte Brontë*. Holt, 1964. 12 up

Vipont, Elfrida. *Weaver of Dreams; The Girlhood of Charlotte Brontë*. Walck, 1966. A good biography of Charlotte Brontë, giving a quite absorbing and dramatic picture of the isolated family. Some instances of fairly florid writing and imaginary conversation. 11-14

BROWN, TABITHA (1780–1858)

Lampman, Evelyn. *Wheels West: The Story of Tabitha Brown*, ill. by Gil Walker. Doubleday, 1965. 10-12

§ BUNCHE, RALPH JOHNSON (1904–1971)

Young, Margaret B. *The Picture Life of Ralph J. Bunche*, ill. with photos. Watts, 1968. 7-8

BUONARROTI, MICHELANGELO (1475–1564)

Coughlan, Robert. *The World of Michelangelo*. Time-Life, 1966. Like other volumes in the magnificent Time-Life Library of Art, this is profusely illustrated with reproductions of the artist's work. 12 up

Ripley, Elizabeth. *Michelangelo*. Walck, 1953. 12-15

CABOT, JOHN (1450–1498)

Hill, Kay. *And Tomorrow the Stars; The Story of John Cabot*, ill. by Laszlo Kubinyi. Dodd, 1968. An excellent biography, convincingly fictionalized and carefully researched, giving vivid pictures of the dream-driven mariner Cabot and of Venice at the zenith of her power. 12 up

§ CAMPANELLA, ROY (1921– )

Schoor, Gene. *Roy Campanella: Man of Courage*. Putnam, 1959. A warm life story of the Dodger catcher who fought against crippling injuries. 9-11

CARSON, CHRISTOPHER (1809–1868)

Bell, Margaret E. *Kit Carson, Mountain Man*, ill. by Harry Daugherty. Morrow, 1952. A short dramatic biography with large print and many illustrations. 8-11

Garst, Shannon. *Kit Carson, Trail Blazer and Scout*, ill. by Harry Daugherty. Messner, 1942. 11 up

CARSON, RACHEL (1907–1964)

Sterling, Philip. *Sea and Earth; The Life of Rachel Carson*. T. Crowell, 1970. A beautifully balanced biography, written with skill and restraint. 12 up

CATHER, WILLA SIBERT (1873–1947)

Franchere, Ruth. *Willa*, ill. by Leonard Weisgard. T. Crowell, 1958. Willa Cather's pioneer childhood in Nebraska is vividly portrayed, and younger readers unfamiliar with her novels will enjoy the biography as a good story. 11-14

§ CARVER, GEORGE WASHINGTON (1864?–1943)

Aliki. *A Weed Is a Flower; The Life of George Washington Carver*, ill. by author. Prentice, 1965. 5-8

Bontemps, Arna. *The Story of George Washington Carver*, ill. by Harper Johnson. Grossett, 1954. 11-15

Epstein, Samuel and Beryl. *George Washington Carver*, ill. by William Moyers. Grosset, 1963. 7-10

CASSATT, MARY (1845–1926)

Wilson, Ellen. *American Painter in Paris: A Life of Mary Cassatt*. Farrar, 1971. Photographs and reproductions of paintings enliven the story of a distinguished artist. 11 up

CATHERINE II, EMPRESS OF RUSSIA (1729–1796)

Noble, Iris. *Empress of All Russia; Catherine the Great*. Messner, 1966. 12-15

§ CHAMBERLAIN, WILT (1936– )

Rudeen, Kenneth. *Wilt Chamberlain*, ill. by Frank Mullins. T. Crowell, 1970. The basketball star is described in a simply written and balanced book. 7-9

CHAPMAN, JOHN (1774–1845)

Aliki. *The Story of Johnny Appleseed*, ill. by author. Prentice, 1963. 7-8

Hunt, Mabel Leigh. *Better Known as Johnny Appleseed*, ill. by James Daugherty. Lippincott, 1950. The life of John Chapman, "American pioneer, missionary, and apple lover," based on old legends and reminiscences gathered by the author. 12-16

★ CHAVEZ, CESAR (1928– )

Franchere, Ruth. *Cesar Chavez*, ill. by Earl Thollander. T. Crowell, 1970. 7-9

Terzian, James, and Kathryn Cramer. *Mighty Hard Road: The Story of Cesar Chavez*. Doubleday, 1970. 11-14

CHIANG KAI-SHEK (1896– )

Spencer, Cornelia. *Chiang Kai-shek, Generalissimo of Nationalist China*. Day, 1968. 12 up

CHILD, LYDIA MARIA (1802–1880)

Meltzer, Milton. *Tongue of Flame: The Life of Lydia Maria Child*. T. Crowell, 1965. 13-15

§ CHISHOLM, SHIRLEY (1924– )

Brownmiller, Susan. *Shirley Chisholm*, ill. Doubleday, 1970. Courageous, outspoken, articulate, Mrs. Chisholm is an exciting subject, and her story is completely told. The book focuses primarily on her political career. 10-14

CHURCHILL, SIR WINSTON LEONARD SPENCER (1874–1965)

Coolidge, Olivia. *Winston Churchill and the Story of Two World Wars*, ill. with photos. Houghton, 1960. The twentieth century becomes vividly alive and significant in this story of the great British statesman. 13-16

Wibberley, Leonard. *The Complete Life of Winston Churchill*, rev. ed. Farrar, 1968. 12-16

CLEMENS, OLIVIA (1845–1904)

Stoutenburg, Adrien, and Laura Nelson Baker. *Dear, Dear Livy*. Scribner's, 1963. 12-16

CLEMENS, SAMUEL LANGHORNE (1835–1910)

Eaton, Jeanette. *America's Own Mark Twain*, ill. by Leonard Everett Fisher. Morrow, 1958. Mississippi riverboat days and life in the West are absorbing highlights of this well-rounded story of one of America's most colorful authors. 12-16

Mc Neer, May. *America's Mark Twain*, ill. by Lynd Ward. Houghton, 1962. Colorful illustrations and a lively text make this biography attractive to a wide range of readers. 10-14

Proudfit, Isabel. *River Boy: The Story of Mark Twain*, ill. by W. C. Nims. Messner, 1940. An excellent life of the author of *Tom Sawyer* for older boys and girls. 12-14

Wood, James Playsted. *Spunkwater, Spunkwater! A Life of Mark Twain*, ill. with photos. Pantheon, 1968. 11-15

CLEOPATRA, QUEEN OF EGYPT (69–30 B.C.)

Desmond, Alice Curtis. *Cleopatra's Children*, ill. with maps, charts, and photos. Dodd, 1971. 11-14

Leighton, Margaret. *Cleopatra: Sister of the Moon*. Farrar, 1969. 12-15

☆ COCHISE, APACHE CHIEF (d. 1874)

Johnson, Enid. *Cochise: Great Apache Chief*, ill. by Lorence F. Bjorklund. Messner, 1953. A tragic story of a great leader's trust and disillusionment. 11-15

CODY, WILLIAM (BUFFALO BILL) (1846–1917)

d'Aulaire, Ingri and Edgar Parin. *Buffalo Bill*, ill. by authors. Doubleday, 1952. 7-9

COLUMBUS, CHRISTOPHER (1451–1506)

Dalgliesh, Alice. *The Columbus Story*, ill. by Leo Politi. Scribner's, 1955. 8-10

d'Aulaire, Ingri and Edgar Parin. *Columbus*, ill. by authors. Doubleday, 1955. 7-9

Derleth, August. *Columbus and the New World*, ill. by Dirk Gringhuis. Farrar, 1957. 9-12

Judson, Clara Ingram. *Admiral Christopher Columbus*, ill. by W. T. Mars. Follett, 1965. 10 up

______. *Christopher Columbus*, ill. by Polly Jackson. Follett, 1960. 7-9

McGovern, Ann. *The Story of Christopher Columbus*. Random, 1963. 7-10

Norman, Gertrude. *A Man Named Columbus*, ill. by James Caraway. Putnam, 1960. 7-8

Sperry, Armstrong. *Voyages of Christopher Columbus*, ill. by author. Random, 1950. 8-10

Syme, Ronald. *Columbus, Finder of the New World*, ill. by William Stobbs. Morrow, 1952. 10-13

CONRAD, JOSEPH (1857–1924)

Gurko, Leo. *The Two Lives of Joseph Conrad*. T. Crowell, 1965. 13 up

COOK, JAMES (1728–1779)

Latham, Jean. *Far Voyager: The Story of James Cook*, maps by Karl W. Stuecklen. Harper, 1970. 10-13

Syme, Ronald. *Captain Cook: Pacific Explorer*, ill. by William Stobbs. Morrow, 1960. The English navigator's eighteenth-century explorations of the South Pacific climax a fast-paced, fully illustrated biography. 10-13

COOPER, PETER (1791–1883)
Gurko, Miriam. *The Lives and Times of Peter Cooper*, ill. by Jerome Snyder, diagrams by Ava Morgan. T. Crowell, 1959. 12 up

CRANDALL, PRUDENCE (1803–1889)
Fuller, Edmund. *Prudence Crandall.* Wesleyan Univ. Pr., 1971. 12 up
Yates, Elizabeth. *Prudence Crandall: Woman of Courage*, ill. by Nora S. Unwin. Aladdin, 1955. 12-15

☆ CRAZY HORSE, OGLALA CHIEF (1842?–1877)
Garst, Doris Shannon. *Crazy Horse, Great Warrior of the Sioux*, ill. by William Moyers. Houghton, 1950. This biography gives good perspective on why the Indians so bitterly opposed the white men. 12-15
Meadowcroft, Enid. *The Story of Crazy Horse*, ill. by William Reusswig. Grosset, 1954. Biography of the Oglala chief who opposed Custer and who died escaping imprisonment. 9-12

DAMIEN, FATHER (1840–1889)
Roos, Ann. *Man of Molokai: The Life of Father Damien*, ill. by Raymond Lufkin. Lippincott, 1943. Moving story of a great modern saint who spent his life in the service of lepers. 11-14

DARROW, CLARENCE (1857–1938)
Faber, Doris. *Clarence Darrow: Defender of the People*, ill. by Paul Frame. Prentice, 1965. 10-12
Gurko, Miriam. *Clarence Darrow.* T. Crowell, 1965. 13 up

● DAVID, KING OF ISRAEL
Bolliger, Max. *David*, ill. by Edith Schindler. Delacorte, 1967. The life of David up to the point of his becoming King of Israel. 9-12

DA VINCI, LEONARDO (1452–1519)
Noble, Iris. *Leonardo da Vinci; The Universal Genius*, ill. Norton, 1965. Despite a considerable amount of fictionalization, the painter comes alive as a distinctive personality. 11-14

DEBS, EUGENE VICTOR (1855–1926)
Noble, Iris. *Labor's Advocate: Eugene V. Debs.* Messner, 1966. 11-14

§ DELANY, MARTIN ROBISON (1812–1885)
Sterling, Dorothy. *The Making of an Afro-American: Martin Robison Delany 1812–1885.* Doubleday, 1971. 11 up

DICKENS, CHARLES (1812–1870)
Kyle, Elizabeth. *Great Ambitions: A Story of the Early Years of Charles Dickens.* Holt, 1968. 12-15

DICKINSON, EMILY (1830–1886)
Fisher, Aileen, and Olive Rabe. *We Dickinsons; The Life of Emily Dickinson as Seen Through the Eyes of Her Brother Austin*, ill. by Ellen Raskin. Atheneum, 1965. 12-15
Longsworth, Polly. *Emily Dickinson: Her Letter to the World.* T. Crowell, 1965. 13 up

§ DOUGLASS, FREDERICK (1817?–1895)
Douglass, Frederick. *Life and Times of Frederick Douglass*, ad. by Barbara Ritchie. T. Crowell, 1966. First published in 1842 and last revised by the author in 1892, this is a very good adaptation with no deletion of important material. 11-15
Graham, Shirley. *There Was Once a Slave: The Heroic Story of Frederick Douglass.* Messner, 1947. 12 up

§ DREW, CHARLES RICHARD (1904–1950)
Bertol, Roland. *Charles Drew*, ill. by Jo Polseno. T. Crowell, 1970. First director of the Red Cross Blood Bank, the distinguished black doctor fought prejudice throughout his life. 7-9
Hardwick, Richard. *Charles Richard Drew, Pioneer in Blood Research.* Scribner's, 1967. Story of the great authority on blood storage. 10-12

§ DU BOIS, W. E. B. (1868–1963)
Lacy, Leslie Alexander. *Cheer the Lonesome Traveler; The Life of W. E. B. DuBois*, ill. by James Barkley and with photos. Dial, 1970. An excellent biography for young people of one of the most eminent black American leaders. The writing style is brisk, competent, and dispassionate. 12-15

§ DUNBAR, PAUL LAURENCE (1872–1906)
Gayle, Addison. *Oak and Ivy: A Biography of Paul Laurence Dunbar.* Doubleday, 1971. 12-15

DVORAK, ANTON (1841–1904)
Purdy, Claire. *Antonin Dvorák: Composer from Bohemia.* Messner, 1950. A warm and sympathetic story of a great musician. 13 up

EDISON, THOMAS ALVA (1847–1931)
North, Sterling. *Young Thomas Edison*, ill. by William Barss. Houghton, 1958. Outstanding biography of Edison both as a man and as an inventive genius. 11-15

ELIZABETH I, QUEEN OF ENGLAND (1533–1603)
Hanff, Helene. *Queen of England: The Story of Elizabeth I*, ill. by Ronald Dorgman. Doubleday, 1969. 10-13
Vance, Marguerite. *Elizabeth Tudor, Sovereign Lady*, ill. by Nedda Walker. Dutton, 1954. This story is sympathetically and dramatically told and should be a stimulus to further historical reading. 12-15

ERICSSON, JOHN (1803–1889)
Burnett, Constance Buel. *Captain John Ericsson: Father of the "Monitor."* Vanguard, 1961. Failure as well as success marked the life of the Swedish-born genius. 12-16

ERIKSSON, LEIF (b. tenth century)
Shippen, Katherine. *Leif Eriksson; First Voyager to America.* Harper, 1951. Well-written, exciting biography of the explorer of Vinland. 11-13

FERMI, ENRICO (1901–1954)
Faber, Doris. *Enrico Fermi: Atomic Pioneer*, ill. by David Hodges. Prentice, 1966. 9-12

FIELD, CYRUS (1819–1892)
Latham, Jean Lee. *Young Man in a Hurry: The Story of Cyrus Field*, ill. by Victor Mays. Harper, 1958. An account of the laying of the Atlantic cable and of the unconquerable Cyrus Field. 12 up

§ FORTEN, CHARLOTTE (1838–1914)
Douty, Esther M. *Charlotte Forten: Free Black Teacher.* Garrard, 1971. 9-11
Longsworth, Polly. *I, Charlotte Forten, Black and Free.* T. Crowell, 1970. 11-14

§ FORTEN, JAMES (1766–1842)
Douty, Esther M. *Forten the Sailmaker: Pioneer Champion of Negro Rights*, ill. with photos. Rand, 1968. 12-15

§ FORTUNE, AMOS (1709?–1801)
Yates, Elizabeth. *Amos Fortune, Free Man*, ill. by Nora S. Unwin. Dutton, 1950. Newbery Medal. 10-13

FOSTER, STEPHEN COLLINS (1826–1864)
Douty, Esther. *The Story of Stephen Foster*, ill. by Jo Polseno. Grosset, 1954. 9-11
Purdy, Claire. *He Heard America Sing: The Story of Stephen Foster*, ill. by Dorothea Cooke. Messner, 1940. A well-balanced picture of an undisciplined, likable man. 12-14

FRANCIS OF ASSISI, SAINT (1182–1226)
Bulla, Clyde. *Song of St. Francis*, ill. by Valenti Angelo. T. Crowell, 1952. The appealing story of St. Francis of Assisi presented in simple fashion for younger readers. 8-10

FRANKLIN, BENJAMIN (1706–1790)
Daugherty, Charles Michael. *Benjamin Franklin; Scientist-Diplomat*, ill. by John Falter. Macmillan, 1965. This very simple biography gives a quite adequate biographical outline. Barely fictionalized and not written down. 8-10
Daugherty, James. *Poor Richard*, ill. by author. Viking, 1941. 12-15
d'Aulaire, Ingri and Edgar Parin. *Benjamin Franklin*, ill. by authors. Doubleday, 1950. 7-9
Eaton, Jeanette. *That Lively Man, Ben Franklin*, ill. by Henry C. Pitz. Morrow, 1948. Franklin's many-sided career, from printer to ambassador. 11-14
Merriam, Eve. *The Story of Ben Franklin*, ill. by Brinton Turkle. Four Winds, 1965. 7-9
Scarf, Maggi. *Meet Benjamin Franklin*, ill. by Harry Beckhoff. Random, 1968. 7-11

§ FREEMAN, ELIZABETH (1744?–1829)
Felton, Harold W. *Mumbet: The Story of Elizabeth Freeman*, ill. by Donn Albright. Dodd, 1970. 9-11

FULLER, RICHARD BUCKMINSTER (1895– )
Rosen, Sidney. *Wizard of the Dome: R. Buckminster Fuller, Designer for the Future*. Little, 1969. 12 up

FULTON, ROBERT (1765–1815)
Judson, Clara Ingram. *Boat Builder; The Story of Robert Fulton*, ill. by Armstrong Sperry. Scribner's, 1940. 9-11

GALILEI, GALILEO (1564–1642)
Bixby, William, and the editors of *Horizon* Magazine, in consultation with Georgio De Santillana. *The Universe of Galileo and Newton*, ill. American Heritage, 1964. A most impressive dual biography, beautifully illustrated and written in a lively style. The scientific material is authoritative. 13 up
Rosen, Sidney. *Galileo and the Magic Numbers*, ill. by Harve Stein. Little, 1958. 12 up

GANDHI, MOHANDAS K. (1869–1948)
Coolidge, Olivia. *Gandhi*. Houghton, 1971. 11-14
Eaton, Jeanette. *Gandhi: Fighter Without a Sword*, ill. by Ralph Ray. Morrow, 1950. 13-15
Peare, Catherine Owens. *Mahatma Gandhi: Father of Non-Violence*. Hawthorne, 1969. 12 up
Reynolds, Reginald. *The True Story of Gandhi, Man of Peace*. Childrens Pr., 1964. 9-11

GANNETT, DEBORAH (SAMPSON) (1760–1827)
Cheney, Cora. *The Incredible Deborah: A Story Based on the Life of Deborah Sampson*. Scribner's, 1967. 11-14

GARIBALDI, GIUSEPPE (1807–1882)
Syme, Ronald. *Garibaldi: The Man Who Made a Nation*, ill. by William Stobbs. Morrow, 1967. 11-14

GARRISON, WILLIAM LLOYD (1805–1879)
Archer, Jules. *Angry Abolitionist: William Lloyd Garrison*. Messner, 1969. 12 up
Faber, Doris. *I Will Be Heard: The Life of William Lloyd Garrison*. Lothrop, 1970. 9-12

☆ GERONIMO, APACHE CHIEF (1829–1909)
Wyatt, Edgar. *Geronimo, the Last Apache War Chief*, ill. by Allan Houser. Whittlesey, 1952. The story of a great Indian hero. 11-14

● GERSHWIN, GEORGE (1898–1937)
Ewen, David. *The Story of George Gershwin*, ill. by Graham Bernbach. Holt, 1943. Memories of an American composer of popular music by a personal friend. 12-16

GREELEY, HORACE (1811–1872)
Faber, Doris. *Horace Greeley: The People's Editor*, ill. by Paul Frame. Prentice, 1964. 9-12

GREENAWAY, KATE (1846–1901)
Newcomb, Covelle. *The Secret Door: The Story of Kate Greenaway*, ill. by Addison Burbank. Dodd, 1946. Entertaining fictional biography about one of the popular early illustrators for children. 12-15

GRIEG, EDVARD (1843–1907)
Deucher, Sybil. *Edvard Grieg, Boy of the Northland*, ill. by Mary Greenwalt. Dutton, 1946. 9-10
Kyle, Elizabeth. *Song of the Waterfall, The Story of Edvard and Nina Grieg*. Holt, 1970. 10-12

GUION, DR. CONNIE M. (1882–1971)
Campion, Nardi Reeder, with Rosamond Wilfley Stanton. *Look to This Day!* ill. with photos. Little, 1965. A long, lively biography of Dr. Connie Guion, a famous physician and delightful character. Her story gives interesting glimpses of the beginnings of higher education for women. 12-15

HAMILTON, ALICE (1869–1970)
Grant, Madeleine P. *Alice Hamilton: Pioneer Doctor in Industrial Medicine*. Abelard, 1968. The inspiring story of a woman whose career encompassed both science and social reform. 12-14

HANCOCK, CORNELIA (1840–1926)
McConnell, Jane. *Cornelia*. T. Crowell, 1959. Youthful Cornelia Hancock literally had to fight her way into serving as a Civil War nurse in a period when only mature women were considered adequate. 12-15

● HAUTZIG, ESTHER
Hautzig, Esther. *The Endless Steppe; Growing Up in Siberia*. T. Crowell, 1968. The true and harrowing story of five arduous years spent by Esther and her family in forced labor in Siberia, all the more effective because it is told with direct simplicity and no bitterness. 11-15

HAYDN, FRANZ JOSEPH (1732–1809)
Mirsky, Reba Paeff. *Haydn*, ill. by W. T. Mars. Follett, 1963. 9-11

HEMINGWAY, ERNEST (1899–1961)
Gurko, Leo. *Ernest Hemingway and the Pursuit of Heroism*. T. Crowell, 1968. 14 up

HENRY, PATRICK (1736–1799)
Campion, Nardi Reeder. *Patrick Henry: Firebrand*

*of the Revolution*, ill. by Victor Mays. Little, 1961. 12 up

HERSCHEL, SIR WILLIAM (1738–1822)

Crawford, Deborah. *The King's Astronomer: William Herschel*. Messner, 1968. Although highly fictionalized, the dialogue uses language that seems so right for the period that it is an asset to the book. A good balance of personal and scientific material. 11-14

HIDALGO Y COSTILLA, MIGUEL (1753–1811)

Lieberman, Mark. *Hidalgo, Mexican Revolutionary*. Praeger, 1971. 11-14

HITLER, ADOLF (1889–1945)

Shirer, William L. *The Rise and Fall of Adolf Hitler*, ill. with photos. Random, 1961. In this biography of the Nazi dictator, emphasis is on political events, stirringly recorded for younger readers. 11-14

HOKUSAI (1760–1849)

Ripley, Elizabeth. *Hokusai*. Lippincott, 1968. 11-14

● HOOVER, HERBERT CLARK (1874–1964)

Peare, Catherine Owens. *The Herbert Hoover Story*. T. Crowell, 1965. 11-14

HOUSTON, SAM (1793–1863)

James, Bessie and Marquis. *Six Feet Six*. Bobbs, 1931. 10-12

HOWE, SAMUEL GRIDLEY (1801–1876)

Meltzer, Milton. *A Light in the Dark: The Life of Samuel Gridley Howe*. T. Crowell, 1964. 12-15

§ HUGHES, JAMES LANGSTON (1902–1967)

Meltzer, Milton. *Langston Hughes: A Biography*. T. Crowell, 1968. 12 up

Rollins, Charlemae. *Black Troubador: Langston Hughes*. Rand, 1970. 12-15

HUMBOLDT, ALEXANDER, FREIHERR VON (1769–1859)

Thomas, M. Z. (pseud.). *Alexander von Humboldt*, tr. by Elizabeth Brommer, ill. by Ulrik Schramm. Pantheon, 1960. Von Humboldt's adventures in the South American jungles are vivid and unforgettable in this life story of the explorer-naturalist. 11-15

ISABELLA I, QUEEN OF SPAIN (1451–1504)

Noble, Iris. *Spain's Golden Queen Isabella*. Messner, 1969. 12 up

☆ ISHI (d. 1916)

Kroeber, Theodora. *Ishi: Last of His Tribe*, ill. by Ruth Robbins. Parnassus, 1964. 12 up

JACKSON, ANDREW (1767–1845)

Andrist, Ralph K. *Andrew Jackson, Soldier and Statesman*, narrated by Ralph K. Andrist in consultation with Arthur M. Schlesinger. American Heritage, 1963. 12-15

Coit, Margaret L. *Andrew Jackson*, ill. by Milton Johnson. Houghton, 1965. A perceptive biography, not adulatory but candid about the deficiencies that made Jackson so controversial a figure, yet written with sympathy for the unhappy personal life and the political sniping that he suffered. 12-15

De Kay, Ormonde. *Meet Andrew Jackson*, ill. by Isa Barnett. Random, 1967. 7-9

Vance, Marguerite. *The Jacksons of Tennessee*, ill. by Nedda Walker. Dutton, 1953. 11-14

JADWIGA, QUEEN OF POLAND (1370–1399)

Mills, Lois. *So Young a Queen*. Lothrop, 1961. Story of the lovely Jadwiga, fourteenth-century queen of Poland. 12-15

JEFFERSON, THOMAS (1743–1826)

Barrett, Marvin. *Meet Thomas Jefferson*, ill. by Angelo Torres. Random, 1967. 7-9

Fleming, Thomas J. *Thomas Jefferson*. Grosset, 1971. 11-14

Johnston, Johanna. *Thomas Jefferson, His Many Talents*, ill. by Richard Bergere. Dodd, 1961. 11-14

Judson, Clara Ingram. *Thomas Jefferson, Champion of the People*, ill. by Robert Frankenberg. Follett, 1952. 9-11

Lisitzky, Gene. *Thomas Jefferson*, ill. by Harrie Wood. Viking, 1933. A well-balanced picture of the many facets of this complex man. 12-16

Miers, Earl Schenck. *That Jefferson Boy*, ill. by Kurt Werth. World, 1970. 8-10

Moscow, Henry. *Thomas Jefferson and His World*, narrative by Henry Moscow in consultation with Dumas Malone. American Heritage, 1960. 11 up

Wibberley, Leonard. *A Dawn in the Trees: Thomas Jefferson, the Years 1776–1789*. Farrar, 1964.

______. *The Gales of Spring: Thomas Jefferson, the Years 1789–1801*. Farrar, 1965.

______. *Man of Liberty; A Life of Thomas Jefferson*. Farrar, 1968.

______. *Time of the Harvest: Thomas Jefferson, the Years 1801–1826*. Farrar, 1966.

______. *Young Man from the Piedmont: The Youth of Thomas Jefferson*. Farrar, 1963. 12-15

JOAN OF ARC, SAINT (1412–1431)

Churchill, Winston. *Joan of Arc: Her Life as Told by Winston Churchill*, ill. by Lauren Ford. Dodd, 1969. 8 up

Fisher, Aileen. *Jeanne d'Arc*, ill. by Ati Forberg. T. Crowell, 1970. 8-10

Paine, Albert. *The Girl in White Armor*, ill. by Joe Isom. Macmillan, 1967 (first pub. in 1927). 11-14

JOHN (POPE JOHN XXIII; ANGELO RONCALLI) (1881–1963)

Mac Gregor-Hastie, Roy. *Pope John XXIII*, ill. with photos. Criterion, 1962. There is humor, vitality, and reverence in this fine biography of the "Pope of Peace." 11 up

JONES, JOHN PAUL (1747–1792)

Sperry, Armstrong. *John Paul Jones: Fighting Sailor*, ill. by author. Random, 1953. The life of the naval hero who suffered ingratitude and injustice throughout his career. 10-13

☆ JOSEPH, NEZ PERCE CHIEF (1840–1904)

Davis, Russell, and Brent Ashabranner. *Chief Joseph, War Chief of the Nez Perce*. McGraw, 1962. The tragic story of a peace-loving chief forced into war as his people opposed the westward movement. 12-16

JOSEPHINE, CONSORT OF NAPOLEON I (1763–1814)

Vance, Marguerite. *The Empress Josephine: From Martinique to Malmaison*, ill. by Nedda Walker. Dutton, 1956. 12-14

KEATS, JOHN (1795–1821)

Gittings, Robert, and Jo Manton. *The Story of John Keats*, ill. by Susan Einzig. Dutton, 1963. An outstanding and objectively written story of the young English poet who in his short life created lyrics of rare loveliness. 14 up

§ KING, MARTIN LUTHER (1929–1968)

Clayton, Ed. *Martin Luther King: The Peaceful Warrior*, ill. by David Hodges. Prentice, 1964. 9-11

De Kay, James T. *Meet Martin Luther King, Jr.*, ill. with photos and drawings by Ted Burwell. Random, 1969. 7-9

KcKee, Don. *Martin Luther King, Jr.* Putnam, 1969. 11-14

Patterson, Lillie. *Martin Luther King, Jr.: Man of Peace*, ill. by Victor Mays. Garrard, 1969. 8-9

Young, Margaret B. *The Picture Life of Martin Luther King, Jr.*, ill. with photos. Watts, 1968. 7-8

KINGSLEY, MARY HENRIETTA (1862–1900)

Syme, Ronald. *African Traveler*, ill. by Jacqueline Tomes. Morrow, 1962. A British woman exploring West Africa alone was unprecedented in the 1890s but Mary Kingsley did just that. A colorful biography with a blending of heroism and humor. 11-15

LAFAYETTE, MARIE ADRIENNE FRANCOIS (DE NOAILLES), MARQUISE DE (1759–1802)

Wilson, Hazel. *The Little Marquise: Madame Lafayette*, ill. by Paul A. Sagsoorian. Knopf, 1957. Lafayette's aristocratic wife emerges as a figure of unforgettable courage as she shares his imprisonment and fights for his freedom. 12-15

LAFAYETTE, MARIE JOSEPH PAUL YVES ROCH GILBERT DU MOTIER, MARQUIS DE (1757–1834)

Eaton, Jeanette. *Young Lafayette*, ill. by David Hendrickson. Houghton, 1932. 12-16

Gottschalk, Fruma. *The Youngest General: A Story of Lafayette*, ill. by Rafaello Busoni. Knopf, 1949. The author had access to unusual original sources in writing this life of Lafayette. 10-14

Graham, Alberta. *Lafayette: Friend of America*, ill. by Ralph Ray. Abingdon, 1952. 8-10

Wilson, Hazel. *The Story of Lafayette*, ill. by Edy Wilson. Grosset, 1952. 9-11

LAWRENCE, THOMAS EDWARD (1888–1935)

MacLean, Alistair. *Lawrence of Arabia*. Random, 1962. The absorbingly told life story of the great military leader in the Arab-Turkish revolt. 11-14

LEE, ROBERT EDWARD (1807–1870)

Commager, Henry Steele. *America's Robert E. Lee*, ill. by Lynd Ward. Houghton, 1951. Lee is a hero all America should be proud of, and this biography shows why. 11-15

Freeman, Douglas Southall. *Lee of Virginia*. Scribner's, 1958. A difficult, but excellent, biography of the man of honor who was his greatest in defeat. 12 up

Vance, Marguerite. *The Lees of Arlington: The Story of Mary and Robert E. Lee*, ill. by Nedda Walker. Dutton, 1949. The story of the Lees' family life. 11-14

LILIUOKALANI, QUEEN OF THE HAWAIIAN ISLANDS (1838–1917)

Wilson, Hazel. *The Last Queen of Hawaii: Liliuokalani*, ill. by W. T. Mars. Knopf, 1963. 11-14

LINCOLN, ABRAHAM (1809–1865)

Bulla, Clyde. *Lincoln's Birthday*, ill. by Ernest Crichlow. T. Crowell, 1966. 8-9

Daugherty, James. *Abraham Lincoln*, ill. by author. Viking 1943. 12-15

d'Aulaire, Ingri and Edgar Parin. *Abraham Lincoln*, ill. by authors. Doubleday, 1939. 12-14

Fisher, Aileen. *My Cousin Abe*, ill. by Leonard Vosburgh. Nelson, 1962. Dennis Hanks tells the story of his younger relative with the warmth and tenderness inspired by the close family relationship. Although introducing a narrator, the author faithfully follows the details of Lincoln's life. 11-15

Foster, Genevieve. *Abraham Lincoln: An Initial Biography*, ill. by author. Scribner's, 1950. Other Initial Biographies include *Andrew Jackson* (1951), *George Washington* (1949), and *Theodore Roosevelt* (1954). 9-12

Judson, Clara Ingram. *Abraham Lincoln*, ill. by Polly Jackson. Follett, 1961. 7-9

———. *Abraham Lincoln, Friend of the People*, ill. by Robert Frankenberg and with photos. Follett, 1950. 11-15

Sandburg, Carl. *Abe Lincoln Grows Up*, ill. by James Daugherty. Harcourt, 1928. 11-16

LINCOLN, MARY TODD (1818–1882)

Randall, Ruth Painter. *I Mary*, ill. with photos. Little, 1959. A sincere and honest biography of Mary Todd Lincoln which helps to dispel some of the unhappy legends associated with her life. 12-16

LINDBERGH, CHARLES (1902– )

Dalgliesh, Alice. *Ride on the Wind*, ill. by Georges Schreiber. Scribner's, 1956. 7-9

LONDON, JACK (1876–1916)

Franchere, Ruth. *Jack London: The Pursuit of a Dream*. T. Crowell, 1962. The author has skillfully conveyed the poverty, the rough adventurous life, and the taste of glory achieved by London in his brief forty years, without emphasizing the details more suited to an adult biography. 12 up

§ LOVE, NAT (1854?–1921?)

Felton, Harold W. *Nat Love, Negro Cowboy*, ill. by David Hodges. Dodd, 1969. 9-10

LOW, JULIETTE (1860–1927)

Pace, Mildred. *Juliette Low*, ill. by Jane Castle. Scribner's, 1947. A vivid picture of the founder of the Girl Scouts of America. 10-12

§ LUMUMBA, PATRICE (1925–1961)

McKown, Robin. *Lumumba; A Biography*, ill. Doubleday, 1969. Although the sympathetic tone verges on the adulatory in some passages, this is an excellent biography. The complicated history of Congolese independence is made as clear as possible. 12-15

LUTHER, MARTIN (1483–1546)

Fosdick, Harry Emerson. *Martin Luther*, ill. by Steele Savage. Random, 1956. Written by one of the best-known Protestant ministers, this is a thoughtful biography of the great reformer. 12-16

McNeer, May. *Martin Luther*, ill. by Lynd Ward. Abingdon, 1953. The fighting spirit of Martin Luther makes his complex life both difficult and thrilling. Superb illustrations add distinction to this book. 12-14

MC KINLEY, WILLIAM (1843–1901)

Hoyt, Edwin P. *William McKinley*. Reilly, 1967. 13-15

§ MALCOLM X (1925–1965)

Adoff, Arnold. *Malcolm X*, ill. by John Wilson. T.

Crowell, 1970. 8-10
Curtis, Richard. *The Life of Malcolm X.* Macrae, 1971. 11-15

§ MARSHALL, THURGOOD (1908– )
Young, Margaret B. *The Picture Life of Thurgood Marshall.* Watts, 1971. 8-10

§ MARTIN DE PORRES, SAINT (1579–1639)
Bishop, Claire Huchet. *Martin de Porres, Hero,* ill. by Jean Charlot. Houghton, 1954. 12-14

MARY II, QUEEN OF GREAT BRITAIN (1662–1694)
Kyle, Elizabeth. *Princess of Orange.* Holt, 1966. 12-15

MARY STUART, QUEEN OF THE SCOTS (1542–1587)
King, Marian. *Young Mary Stuart, Queen of Scots.* Lippincott, 1954. A moving tale of the young queen which places emphasis on her childhood and the years in France. 11-14
Vance, Marguerite. *Scotland's Queen: The Story of Mary Stuart,* ill. by J. Luis Pellicer. Dutton, 1962. 13 up

MATHER, COTTON (1663–1728)
Wood, James Playsted. *The Admirable Cotton Mather.* Seabury, 1971. 13 up

MAURY, MATTHEW FONTAINE (1806–1873)
Latham, Jean Lee. *Trail Blazer of the Seas,* ill. by Victor Mays. Houghton, 1956. Absorbing story of the scientific U.S. Naval Lieutenant Matthew Fontaine Maury, who studied winds and currents to reduce ships' sailing time. 11-15

MICHELANGELO. See BUONARROTI, MICHELANGELO.

MILLAY, EDNA ST. VINCENT (1892–1950)
Gurko, Miriam. *Restless Spirit: The Life of Edna St. Vincent Millay.* T. Crowell, 1962. 13 up
Shafter, Toby. *Edna St. Vincent Millay: America's Best-Loved Poet.* Messner, 1957. 12 up

● MOTT, LUCRETIA (1793–1880)
Sterling, Dorothy. *Lucretia Mott, Gentle Warrior.* Doubleday, 1964. 11-13

MOZART, JOHANN CHRYSOSTOM WOLFGANG AMADEUS (1756–1791)
Komroff, Manuel. *Mozart,* ill. by Warren Chappell and with photos. Knopf, 1956. Written to commemorate the two-hundredth anniversary of Mozart's birth, this is an outstanding biography. 11-15
Mirsky, Reba Paeff. *Mozart,* ill. by W. T. Mars. Follett, 1960. 9-11
Wheeler, Opal, and Sybil Deucher. *Mozart, the Wonder Boy,* ill. by Mary Greenwalt. Dutton, 1934. 9-10

MUIR, JOHN (1838–1914)
Swift, Hildegarde. *From the Eagle's Wing: A Biography of John Muir,* ill. by Lynd Ward. Morrow, 1962. A fascinating biography for budding naturalists. 12 up

MUSIAL, STANLEY FRANK (1920– )
Robinson, Ray. *Stan Musial: Baseball's Durable "Man."* Putnam, 1963. Comments from Musial's colleagues attest to the popularity of "Stan the Man." 10-12

NANSEN, FRIDTJOF (1861–1930)
Hall, Anna Gertrude. *Nansen,* ill. by Boris Artzybasheff. Viking, 1940. Stirring biography of the famous Arctic explorer and Nobel Peace Prize winner. 12-16

NEWTON, SIR ISAAC (1642–1727)
See Bixby entry under GALILEO.

NIGHTINGALE, FLORENCE (1820–1910)
Nolan, Jeannette Covert. *Florence Nightingale,* ill. by George Avison. Messner, 1946. Florence Nightingale's life story stresses her work rather than her personal life. 11-14

NOGUCHI, HIDEYO (1876–1928)
D'Amelio, Dan. *Taller Than Bandai Mountain: The Story of Hideyo Noguchi,* ill. by Fred Banbery. Viking, 1968. 10-12

● OCHS, ADOLPH S. (1858–1935)
Faber, Doris. *Printer's Devil to Publisher: Adolph S. Ochs of The New York Times.* Messner, 1963. 11-13

O'NEILL, EUGENE GLADSTONE (1888–1953)
Coolidge, Olivia E. *Eugene O'Neill.* Scribner's, 1966. A stark and sophisticated biography of the American dramatist. 14 up

● OPPENHEIMER, J. ROBERT (1904–1967)
Royal, Denis. *The Story of J. Robert Oppenheimer.* St. Martin's, 1969. The emphasis is upon Oppenheimer's academic career, the laboratory at Los Alamos, and the political indictment that affected his scientific career. A mature style of writing. 12 up

PAINE, THOMAS (1737–1809)
Coolidge, Olivia E. *Tom Paine, Revolutionary.* Scribner's, 1969. An infinitely detailed and vivid picture of affairs in France, England, and the colonies during Paine's career, and an objective picture of the man. Sophisticated biographical writing. 12 up
Gurko, Leo. *Tom Paine: Freedom's Apostle,* ill. by Fritz Kredel. T. Crowell, 1957. 12 up

PANDIT, VIJAYA LAKSHMI (NEHRU) (1900– )
Guthrie, Anne. *Madame Ambassador: The Life of Vijaya Lakshmi Pandit,* ill. with photos. Harcourt, 1962. Both an absorbing personal story of India's great stateswoman and a unique picture of India's changing history. 13-16

PANKHURST, EMMELINE (1858–1928)
Noble, Iris. *Emmeline and Her Daughters: The Pankhurst Suffragettes.* Messner, 1971. 11-14

PARACELSUS, PHILIPPUS (1493–1541)
Rosen, Sidney. *Doctor Paracelsus,* ill. by Rafaello Busoni. Little, 1959. 12-16
Susac, Andrew. *Paracelsus; Monarch of Medicine.* Doubleday, 1969. A good biography of the sixteenth-century Swiss physician which gives a vivid picture of the state of medicine and, to some extent, all learning in Europe at that time. Skillful fictionalization. 12-15

§ PARKS, GORDON (1912– )
Turk, Midge. *Gordon Parks,* ill. by Herbert Danska. T. Crowell, 1971. 7-8

● PENN, WILLIAM (1644–1718)
Aliki. *The Story of William Penn,* ill. by author. Prentice, 1964. 8-9
Gray, Elizabeth Janet. *Penn,* ill. by George Gillett Whitney. Viking, 1938. 12-16

PETIGRU, JAMES (1789–1863)
Edwards, Sally. *The Man Who Said No.* Coward,

1970. James Petigru was an established member of South Carolina society, but he was also a Unionist and opposed to the spread of slavery. A good biography with well-integrated historical background and with restrained fictionalization. 12-15

PIKE, ZEBULON (1779–1813)

Baker, Nina Brown. *Pike of Pike's Peak*, ill. by Richard Powers. Harcourt, 1953. Well-paced, entertaining biography of a famous soldier and explorer. 11-14

Wibberley, Leonard. *Zebulon Pike, Soldier and Explorer*. Funk, 1961. 13-15

☆ POCAHONTAS (1595?–1617)

Bulla, Clyde. *Pocahontas and the Strangers*. T. Crowell, 1971. 8-10

d'Aulaire, Ingri and Edgar Parin. *Pocahontas*, ill. by authors. Doubleday, 1949. 7-9

Graham, Shirley. *The Story of Pocahontas*, ill. by Mario Cooper. Grosset, 1953. 9-11

Martin, Patricia Miles. *Pocahontas*, ill. by Portia Takakjian. Putnam, 1964. 7-8

Wahl, Jan. *Pocahontas in London*, ill. by John Alcorn. Delacorte, 1967. 8-9

POLK, JAMES KNOX (1795–1849)

Hoyt, Edwin P. *James Knox Polk*. Reilly, 1965. 12-15

Lomask, Milton. *This Slender Reed, a Life of James K. Polk*. Farrar, 1966. 11-15

Severn, William. *Frontier President: James K. Polk*. Washburn, 1965. 12-15

POTTER, BEATRIX (1866–1943)

Aldis, Dorothy. *Nothing Is Impossible: The Story of Beatrix Potter*, ill. by Richard Cuffari. Atheneum, 1969. 9-11

Lane, Margaret. *The Tale of Beatrix Potter: A Biography*, ill. by Beatrix Potter. Warne, 1946. Delightful story of the Victorian artist whose Peter Rabbit tales have delighted young children. 13-16

POWELL, JOHN WESLEY (1834–1902)

Wibberley, Leonard. *Wes Powell, Conqueror of the Grand Canyon*. Farrar, 1958. One of America's little-known heroes is Wes Powell, who explored the Colorado River and Grand Canyon and foresaw the importance of irrigation for arid western lands. 11-16

RALEIGH, SIR WALTER (1552?–1618)

Baker, Nina Brown. *Sir Walter Raleigh*. Harcourt, 1950. This author can be depended upon to write an exciting biography, somewhat fictionalized but authentic in the main and exceedingly readable. 12-14

REVERE, PAUL (1735–1818)

Forbes, Esther. *America's Paul Revere*, ill. by Lynd Ward. Houghton, 1946. Vigorous prose and superb illustrations do much to illumine the history of the Revolutionary period. 11-15

RICHARDS, ELLEN HENRIETTA (1842–1911)

Douty, Esther M. *America's First Woman Chemist, Ellen Richards*. Messner, 1961. 11-14

RINGLING BROTHERS

Cone, Molly. *The Ringling Brothers*, ill. by James and Ruth McCrea. T. Crowell, 1971. 7-9

§ ROBINSON, JOHN (1919– )

Robinson, Jackie, and Alfred Duckett. *Breakthrough to the Big Leagues*. Harper, 1965. Candid about Robinson's problems as the first black player in the major leagues, and very well written. 11-14

Rudeen, Kenneth. *Jackie Robinson*, ill. by Richard Cuffari. T. Crowell, 1971. 7-9

ROOSEVELT, ELEANOR (1884–1962)

Davidson, Margaret. *The Story of Eleanor Roosevelt*. Four Winds, 1969. 9-11

Eaton, Jeanette. *The Story of Eleanor Roosevelt*, ill. with photos. Morrow, 1956. 12-15

ROOSEVELT, FRANKLIN DELANO (1882–1945)

Peare, Catherine Owens. *The FDR Story*, ill. T. Crowell, 1962. A remarkably perceptive biography of Roosevelt as an individual and as a political figure. 12-15

ROOSEVELT, THEODORE (1858–1919)

Monjo, Ferdinand. *The One Bad Thing About Father*, ill. by Rocco Negri. Harper, 1970. 7-8

§ ROSE, EDWARD (1811–1834)

Felton, Harold W. *Edward Rose, Negro Trail Blazer*, ill. with photos and prints of the period, and maps. Dodd, 1967. 10-14

☆ ROSS, JOHN (1790–1866)

Clark, Electa. *Cherokee Chief: The Life of John Ross*, ill. by John Wagner. Crowell-Collier, 1970. John Ross was a man whose Scottish ancestors had married into the Cherokee Nation and whose integrity earned him the respect of white statesmen as well as the leadership of his tribe. A dramatic and tragic story of the persecution of the Cherokee people. 10-14

§ RUSSWURM, JOHN BROWN (1799–1851)

Sagarin, Mary. *John Brown Russwurm; The Story of* Freedom's Journal, *Freedom's Journey*. Lothrop, 1970. The subject is interesting both as a little-known figure in antebellum black history in the United States and as an important one in the turbulent early days of Liberian history. 12-15

☆ SACAJAWEA (1786–1884)

Farnsworth, Frances Joyce. *Winged Moccasins: The Story of Sacajawea*, ill. by Lorence Bjorklund. Messner, 1954. An interesting and authentic account of the life of Lewis and Clark's Indian guide. 12-15

SAMPSON, DEBORAH. See GANNETT, DEBORAH (SAMPSON).

SCHLIEMANN, HEINRICH (1822–1890)

Braymer, Marjorie. *The Walls of Windy Troy*. Harcourt, 1960. Distinguished biography of Heinrich Schliemann, who achieved his dream of archeological research on the site of ancient Troy. 12-16

SCHUBERT, FRANZ PETER (1797–1828)

Wheeler, Opal, and Sybil Deucher. *Franz Schubert and His Merry Friends*, ill. by Mary Greenwalt. Dutton, 1939. 9-10

SCHUMANN, ROBERT (1810–1856)

SCHUMANN, CLARA (1819–1896)

Kyle, Elizabeth. *Duet: The Story of Clara and Robert Schumann*. Holt, 1968. 11-14

SCHWEITZER, ALBERT (1875–1965)

Manton, Jo. *The Story of Albert Schweitzer*, ill. by Astrid Walford. Abelard, 1955. Beautifully written biography of the famous musician and missionary to Africa. 12-16

☆ SEQUOYAH, CHEROKEE INDIAN (1770?–1843)

Kohn, Bernice. *Talking Leaves: The Story of Se-*

*quoyah*, ill. by Valli. Hawthorn, 1969. 6-8

Marriott, Alice. *Sequoyah: Leader of the Cherokees*, ill. by Bob Riger. Random, 1956. Story of the scholarly Indian who made a syllabary of the Cherokee language so that his people could learn to read and write. 10-14

SHAW, GEORGE BERNARD (1856–1950)

Coolidge, Olivia E. *George Bernard Shaw*, ill. Houghton, 1968. Objective, thoughtful, and astute, this entertaining biography is written in a vigorous style. 12-17

● SINGER, ISAAC BASHEVIS (1904– )

Singer, Isaac Bashevis. *A Day of Pleasure: Stories of a Boy Growing Up in Warsaw*, ill. with photos by Roman Vishniac. Farrar, 1969. National Book Award. 11 up

☆ SITTING BULL, SIOUX CHIEF (1831–1890)

Garst, Shannon. *Sitting Bull, Champion of His People*, ill. by Elton C. Fax. Messner, 1946. 11 up

§ SMALLS, ROBERT (1839–1915)

Meriwether, Louise. *The Freedom Ship of Robert Smalls*, ill. by Lee Jack Morton. Prentice, 1971. Simply told, the story of the Captain of *The Planter*. 8-10

Sterling, Dorothy. *Captain of the Planter: The Story of Robert Smalls*, ill. by Ernest Crichlow. Doubleday, 1958. 12-15

§ SMITH, BESSIE (1894–1937)

Moore, Carman. *Somebody's Angel Child; The Story of Bessie Smith*. T. Crowell, 1970. The dramatic and sad story of the greatest blues singer of them all. 11-14

☆ SQUANTO, PAWTUXET INDIAN (d. 1622)

Bulla, Clyde. *Squanto: Friend of the Pilgrims*, ill. by Peter Burchard. T. Crowell, 1954. 7-9

STEINMETZ, CHARLES (1865–1923)

Lavine, Sigmund. *Steinmetz: Maker of Lightning*, ill. with photos. Dodd, 1955. This biography of the crippled German immigrant is a happy combination of good characterization and scientific information. 13 up

§ STEVENS, THADDEUS (1792–1868)

Meltzer, Milton. *Thaddeus Stevens and the Fight for Negro Rights*. T. Crowell, 1967. 13 up

STEVENSON, ROBERT LOUIS (1850–1894)

Proudfit, Isabel. *The Treasure Hunter, the Story of Robert Louis Stevenson*, ill. by Hardie Gramatky. Messner, 1939. A full-length biography of a favorite children's author. 10-14

Wood, James Playsted. *The Lantern Bearer: A Life of Robert Louis Stevenson*, ill. by Saul Lambert. Pantheon, 1965. 12 up

SUN YAT-SEN (1866–1925)

Spencer, Cornelia. *Sun Yat-sen: Founder of the Chinese Republic*. Day, 1967. 12-15

☆ TALLCHIEF, MARIA (1925– )

Tobias, Tobi. *Maria Tallchief*, ill. by Michael Hampshire. T. Crowell, 1970. 7-9

TERRY, ELLEN ALICIA (1848–1928)

Fecher, Constance. *Bright Star; A Portrait of Ellen Terry*. Farrar, 1970. The author makes her subject move with reality and warmth. Excellent both as a personal portrait and as a large plummy slice of theatrical history. Enticing photographs. 12 up

§ TOUSSAINT L'OUVERTURE, PIERRE DOMINIQUE (1746?–1803)

Syme, Ronald, *Toussaint: The Black Liberator*, ill. by William Stobbs. Morrow, 1971. 10-13

§ TRUTH, SOJOURNER (1790?–1883)

Bernard, Jacqueline. *Journey Toward Freedom; The Story of Sojourner Truth*, ill. with photos and engravings. Norton, 1967. An impressive biography of the indomitable and dedicated woman whose courage and work made her one of the most famous blacks of the nineteenth century. The book is smoothly written and well researched. 15 up

§ TUBMAN, HARRIET (1820–1913)

Lawrence, Jacob. *Harriet and the Promised Land*, ill. by author. Windmill, 1968. In this story of Harriet Tubman, the writing is simple, rhythmic, and effective and the pictures are dramatic and vigorous. There has been disagreement about the paintings as the faces are distorted and sometimes grotesque. 7-9

Petry, Ann. *Harriet Tubman: Conductor on the Underground Railroad*. T. Crowell, 1955. A well-documented, thrilling story. 12-16

Sterling, Dorothy. *Freedom Train: The Story of Harriet Tubman*, ill. by Ernest Crichlow. Doubleday, 1954. 10-12

Swift, Hildegarde. *Railroad to Freedom: A Story of the Civil War*, ill. by James Daugherty. Harcourt, 1932. 12-14

TYLER, JOHN (1790–1862)

Hoyt, Edwin P. *John Tyler*. Abelard, 1970. 12-17

VAN BUREN, MARTIN (1782–1862)

Hoyt, Edwin P. *Martin Van Buren*. Reilly, 1964. 12-15

VESPUCCI, AMERIGO (1451–1512)

Baker, Nina Brown. *Amerigo Vespucci*, ill. by Paul Valentino. Knopf, 1956. 9-12

§ WASHINGTON, BOOKER TALIAFERRO (1859?–1915)

Graham, Shirley. *Booker T. Washington: Educator of Hand, Head and Heart*. Messner, 1955. 10-12

Washington, Booker T. *Up from Slavery*. Houghton, 1917. 12 up

Wise, William. *Booker T. Washington*, ill. by Paul Frame. Putnam, 1968. 7-9

WASHINGTON, GEORGE (1732–1799)

Bulla, Clyde. *Washington's Birthday*, ill. by Don Bolognese. T. Crowell, 1967. 6-8

d'Aulaire, Ingri and Edgar Parin. *George Washington*, ill. by authors. Doubleday, 1936. 7-9

Eaton, Jeanette. *Leader by Destiny*, ill. by Jack Manley Rosé. Harcourt, 1938. 12-15

______. *Washington, the Nation's First Hero*, ill. by Ralph Ray. Morrow, 1951. 7-9

Foster, Genevieve. *George Washington*. Scribner's, 1949. 9-11

Judson, Clara Ingram. *George Washington, Leader of the People*, ill. by Robert Frankenberg. Follett, 1951. 11-15

Lowitz, Sadyebeth and Anson. *General George the Great*. Stein and Day, 1964. 8-10

Wilson, Hazel. *The Years Between: Washington at Home at Mount Vernon, 1783–1789*. Knopf,

1969. 10-12

WASHINGTON, MARTHA (1731–1802)
Vance, Marguerite. *Martha, Daughter of Virginia; The Story of Martha Washington*, ill. by Nedda Walker. Dutton, 1947. 9-11

WAYNE, ANTHONY (1745–1796)
Wilson, Hazel. *The Story of Mad Anthony Wayne*, ill. by Lawrence Smith. Grosset, 1953. 9-11

WAYNE, KYRA PETROVSKAYA
Wayne, Kyra Petrovskaya. *Shurik; A Story of the Siege of Leningrad*, ill. Grosset, 1970. A dramatic, true story of World War II. A nurse in a hospital during the siege of Leningrad adopts Shurik, a homeless orphan. Chilling descriptions of the besieged city and impressive pictures of compassion and courage. 12-15

WELLS, HERBERT GEORGE (1866–1946)
Wood, James Playsted. *I Told You So! A Life of H. G. Wells*. Pantheon, 1969. 13 up

● WEST, BENJAMIN (1738–1820)
Henry, Marguerite, and Wesley Dennis. *Benjamin West and His Cat Grimalkin*, ill. by Wesley Dennis. Bobbs, 1947. An enchanting biography of one of America's first artists. 9-12

§ WHEATLEY, PHILLIS (1753?–1784)
Graham, Shirley. *The Story of Phillis Wheatley*, ill. by Robert Burns. Messner, 1949. 12-14

WHITMAN, NARCISSA (PRENTISS) (1808–1847)
Eaton, Jeanette. *Narcissa Whitman: Pioneer of Oregon*, ill. by Woodi Ishmael. Harcourt, 1941. This inspiring life of a great pioneer woman is based on early letters and memoirs. 12-16

WHITMAN, WALT (1819–1892)
Deutsch, Babette. *Walt Whitman: Builder for America*, ill. by Rafaello Busoni. Messner, 1941. A sensitive study of the man, illustrated with copious selections from his poems. 14-16

WILLARD, FRANCES (1839–1898)
Judson, Clara Ingram. *Pioneer Girl*, ill. by Genevieve Foster. Rand, 1939. 8-9

WILLIAMS, ROGER (1603?–1683)
Eaton, Jeanette. *Lone Journey: The Life of Roger Williams*, ill. by Woodi Ishmael. Harcourt, 1944. Story of the courageous Puritan who left the Massachusetts colony and helped establish Rhode Island. 12-16

WILSON, WOODROW (1856–1924)
Peare, Catherine Owens. *The Woodrow Wilson Story; An Idealist in Politics*. T. Crowell, 1963. 12-15

ZAPATA, EMILIANO (1869?–1919)
Syme, Ronald. *Zapata, Mexican Rebel*, ill. by William Stobbs. Morrow, 1971. 9-11

ZENGER, PETER (1697–1746)
Galt, Tom. *Peter Zenger: Fighter for Freedom*, ill. by Ralph Ray. T. Crowell, 1951. Biography of a famous pre-Revolutionary War printer, who faced trial and prison rather than yield the right of freedom of the press. 12-15

# Chapter 16
# Informational Books

As the name implies, informational books, in contrast to books of fiction, are primarily concerned with facts. The distinction between these two types is somewhat nebulous in the books for younger children. For example, Elsa Beskow's *Pelle's New Suit*, like a book of fiction, tells an interesting story, but, like the informational books, is based on facts—explanation of the various steps that go into the making of a suit. In books for older children, the distinction is usually more marked. Their informational books ordinarily have no obvious story framework, though the authors usually try to present facts interestingly.

The first chapter of this book spoke about man's hungry curiosity which through the centuries has kept him searching for more accurate information in more and more fields. Children today are born into a world which has assembled and systematized that information in numberless books which are usually called by the names of their subjects: geography, astronomy, physics, ornithology, or history. But children's books carry no such ponderous titles. Their informational books are called variously *My Village in Ghana*, *Paddle-to-the-Sea*, *The World You Inherit*, *In Their Own Words*. The books as well as their titles are often designed to attract children to subjects they might otherwise pass by.

## EVALUATING INFORMATIONAL BOOKS

These informational books represent an astounding variety of subject matter and approaches, from the simple concept books planned to give very young children an idea of roundness, for example, to books intended to introduce older children to a whole

### VIEWPOINTS

If his knowledge is to grow through the books a child reads because of his desire to know, it must be the kind of knowledge that grows with his growth. Even a simple, elementary presentation of a subject that has interest for quite young children can awaken curiosity and suggest extensions of knowledge through books beyond the one a child is immediately reading. His interest in the subject may thus become a reading interest developed through childhood into maturity. The satisfactions of such continuous reading interests in the field of knowledge have permanent and rewarding values for children. Their reading of these books is complementary to their pleasure in creative literature, and both are necessary to the mental and imaginative growth of children.—Lillian H. Smith, *The Unreluctant Years*, American Library Association, Chicago, 1953, pp. 180–181.

complex field of knowledge such as physics. The best informational books are written by people who not only know their subjects well but write about them freshly and vividly, with an understanding of the needs and limitations of their audiences. The happy combination of these talents is not always found. The subject matter expert may take background knowledge for granted and so write above the heads of children, or he may write down to them. He may tend toward verbosity, toward polysyllabic language, or sometimes toward the jargon of his special field. On the other hand, a technical writer who communicates well may be hampered by a lack of knowledge in depth. There are a great many commonplace, even downright misleading, books in this genre, and then again there are many splendid books written by authors who are steeped in and fascinated by their subjects and who are able to communicate their knowledge and insights and enthusiasm to young people.

### Accuracy

Accuracy is one of the most important criteria for judging any informational book. There has never been a greater need for accurate information than there is today to help counteract the widely disseminated misinformation to which children are subjected. Adults should encourage them to check so-called facts in reliable sources. This is one way of arming children against credulity and teaching them to weigh arguments, question sources, and search for facts.

If we supply children with factual information which is out of date or superficial, we only add to their confusion. Suppose, for instance, we give children purportedly modern books about the Holland of picturesque costumes and quaint, old-fashioned customs or about the old China of rickshaws and queues or about the South America of primitive Indian villages only. Meanwhile, newspapers, magazines, and television newscasts show them pictures of progressive Holland today, China's program of industrialization, and large South American cities. Discerning children can only conclude that books are less reliable references than other sources.

Of course, authors must simplify scientific information for young readers. For example, a description of our solar system for young students could not present complete information, and so such an account would not be wholly accurate—or, at least, not comprehensively so. Minor facts or details may be omitted, major ones cannot be.

### Organization and Scope

In considering the accuracy and therefore the effectiveness of any informational book, we must decide how successfully the author has simplified his material and limited the scope of his subject for his audience. One reason the Crowell science books for beginning read-

---

VIEWPOINTS

The difference between the good and bad historian is not so much the difference between a wide, regular, well-ordered and a narrow, irregular, and ill-ordered reading of record. It lies much more in the two qualities of proportion and imagination. Two men, for instance, may sit down to write as historians the events of an ancient battle.

. . . But the space of each is limited, and even if each had an unlimited canvas on which to paint, the truth of the result would still depend upon proportion—upon the discovery of the essential movements and the essential moments in the action; and upon imagination, the power of seeing the thing as it was; landscape, the weather, the gestures and the faces of the men; yes, and their thoughts within.—Hilaire Belloc, *One Thing and Another*, Hollis and Carter, London, 1955, pp. 24, 25.

---

ers have been successful is that the authors and editors, in limiting the scope of their material, have been careful to select the important facts about a subject and to present them in logical sequence. Too much information, or information that is ancillary, may confuse and mislead a child even though there are no inaccurate statements in the text.

The presentation of material in logical sequence is particularly important. Only in very short books is a continuous text appropriate; in books of substantial length, the text should be broken up with heads and subheads that clarify the relations of the separate parts. A table of contents can also help make clear the organization of the text and the contents of each chapter. Few books for very young children have an index, although this is becoming more common, but for most informational books for children in the middle grades and up, an index is a necessity.

### Currency

Currency is closely related to accuracy. In many informational books, the date of copyright is especially important. Of course, some books have a timeless quality—Scheele's books on prehistoric life, for example, have been for many years, and are likely to be for many more, some of the best of their type—but even in history or archeology there are new discoveries or new theories. Currency is usually a preeminent factor in choosing the best science books. In many science experiment books, great changes have taken place, and any evaluation of these books would need to consider their currency. Formerly, directions might be given something like this: "Take a teaspoon of this, a teaspoon of that, mix, and . . . will happen." This kind of instruction reflected traditional teaching methods: the teacher demonstrated an experiment, the students tried to duplicate it, and results were expected to be identical. With the discovery method, which emphasizes *why* things happen, new books give children options as they experiment and stress observation of scientific method, keeping records, and drawing inferences from conclusions. Changes in educational practices in any area, then, should be reflected in changes in the literature.

### The Author's Responsibility

Any book that teaches a child how to make something, as with experiment books, should include safety rules and should present lists of materials needed and sources for acquiring them if they are not available in the home. Science experiment books and cookbooks should also make clear when adult supervision or adult participation in a stage of the procedure is needed.

Authors should carefully distinguish between fact and theory or opinion. To signal an opinion or a theory, they should use such phrases as "In my opinion," "It may be that . . . ," "One group of scientists believes . . . ." They should avoid the unsupported generalization and the untenable, all-inclusive generalization, which lets the reader assume that the part he has been reading about is the whole. It just isn't true that if you've seen one, you've seen them all, and to imply this is particularly reprehensible in a book about people. Professional men and women often have a bias about theories in their field, and the dependable author informs the reader that he holds one idea, but that there are others, or that the text covers only some aspects of a subject. Some of these facts can be learned from the author's background; both the limitation of coverage and the adherence to a theory should be clear.

### The Author's Competence

One of the clues to the author's competence is the material he or she considers relevant. John Navarra, for example, includes a chapter

## VIEWPOINTS

I like books of knowledge; not those that want to encroach upon recreation, upon leisure, pretending to be able to teach anything without drudgery. There is no truth in that. There are things which cannot be learned without great pains; we must be resigned to it. I like books of knowledge when they are not just grammar or geometry poorly disguised; when they have tact and moderation; when, instead of pouring out so much material on a child's soul that it is crushed, they plant in it a seed that will develop from the inside. I like them when they do not deceive themselves about the quality of knowledge, and do not claim that knowledge can take the place of everything else. I like them especially when they distill from all the different kinds of knowledge the most difficult and the most necessary – that of the human heart. – Paul Hazard, *Books, Children and Men*, The Horn Book, Inc., 1944, p. 43.

on pollution and politics in *The World You Inherit* presumably because, as an expert in the field, he is aware of the urgency of getting enabling legislation for corrective measures.

Evaluation of the writer's competence is made easier if his credentials are given. The book's accuracy may be further confirmed by a list of readers whose specialties qualify them to vouch for the book's information. A list of sources, a bibliography, or a chronology add to the value of a book and usually attest to the authoritative knowledge or research involved.

### Format

Format should be examined in evaluating an informational book. The child in fifth grade will scorn the book that, because of its size or shape or style of illustration, looks like second-grade fare. The type size and page layout are of more importance in informational books than in other types of books. The reader can be confused by paragraphs irregularly arranged on a page with not enough blank space to make sequence apparent. A photograph or map can lose its value if it is located too far from the discussion to which it pertains. The illustration should always complement and clarify the printed text. Inadequate labels or captions can lessen or obviate the value of maps, pictures, and diagrams. Photographs that are posed or that are decorative rather than informative are an irritant. The best illustrations reflect some quality of the text, as Leonard Everett Fisher's black and white scratchboard drawings reflect the sturdy individuality of the colonial craftsmen in books like *The Tanners*, or as Edwin Tunis' meticulous and detailed drawings enhance the reference use of *Frontier Living*.

### Style

Finally, informational books must be interestingly written. Nonfiction can be abysmally dull. The wrong way to combat dullness is to dress it up. Information can and should be written in a straightforward fashion; young readers need no palliative with books on science or geography or nature study. No "Mother Nature knew it was springtime" is admissible in children's books, nor does a squirrel need to be referred to as "Little Nutsy." Children don't like to be talked down to. They can take information straight, although they can be bored stiff if the writing is too dry or too heavy. A book may be useful – and there are many that are mediocre in style but useful – but a child will not cherish it unless it is also interesting.

The vocabulary should be geared to the reading ability of the child. A controlled vocabulary may be helpful for the beginning reader, but most children enjoy writing that has some unfamiliar words. Older children appreciate the challenge of some new terms that expand their vocabulary and widen their horizons.

## VIEWPOINTS

In the hunt for facts and the ascertaining of truth, the historian must be as conscientious as the scientist. In the presentation he must be an artist, a true one, not one of those who favor vain embellishments. . . .

The historian's means of communication with the public is writing, as color is for painters. An historian who uses so dull a style that he will not be read is as useless as a painter who should use invisible colors. He is, moreover, sure not to do justice to realities, thus swerving from truth, for realities are not dull. Those for whom they are so suffer from a dull mind and a dull heart. In them is the fault, not in the things.—From *The Writing of History* by Jean Jules Jusserand, Wilbur Cortez Abbott, Charles W. Colby, and John Spencer Bassett, Charles Scribner's Sons, New York, 1926, pp. 3–4, 5.

Accuracy, careful organization and presentation, currency, responsibility in dealing with fact and opinion, format, and interesting style are some of the criteria by which informational books can be judged. In the rest of this chapter, these criteria will be further examined as they pertain to particular books. The first section presents in alphabetical order twenty-nine outstanding authors of informational books for children and some of the books they have written. The second section discusses briefly a number of other important authors and significant books organized by subject matter (the biological sciences, the physical sciences, the social sciences, religion and the arts, activities and experiments, and reference books). This discussion gives a glimpse of the variety and the riches available in today's informational books.

### IRVING ADLER

*The Wonders of Physics*

Irving Adler, who has been a teacher of mathematics at the high school and college levels, is the author of more than fifty books on scientific subjects. His work is notable for the skill and lucidity with which he makes complicated material comprehensible. In *The Wonders of Physics* (1966), for example, written for older children, the clarity of his prose is such that the book can be given to a seven-year-old to explain the difference between the Centigrade and Fahrenheit temperature scales.

*The Wonders of Physics* bears out Jerome Bruner's assertion that ". . . the foundations of any subject may be taught to anybody at any age in some form."[1] Adler defines the four states of matter (solid, liquid, gaseous, and plasma) succinctly, then discusses them, using subheadings and drawings to make the material easier to understand. Using pictures of a tire pump pushing air into a bicycle tire, he describes the phenomenon of increasing air pressure and the temperature rise as the air is compressed. In discussing temperature scales, the author carefully identifies each type, along with the scientist after whom it was named, and provides complete descriptions and diagrams. In discussing heat engines, Adler skillfully explains the three laws of thermodynamics. The work is excellently indexed, with more than 720 entries, including some "see also" references. Page numbers in boldface type refer to a page where there is an illustration of the subject. Throughout the text, cross-references are excellent.

*Tools in Your Life* (1956) is an account of man's development of tools from the primitive axe to atomic energy, tracing the sociological effects of the adoption of new tools or of the clinging to old ones. *Magic House of Numbers* (1957) describes number systems built on bases other than ten, and includes many intriguing puzzles. These books are illustrated by Ruth Adler, who was also coauthor and illustrator of more than thirty titles in "The Reason Why" series. These are short, useful books with a descriptive table of con-

1. Jerome S. Bruner, *The Process of Education* (Harvard Univ. Press, 1966), p. 12.

tents but no index. Two books for children in the middle grades are *Evolution* (1965) and *Sets* (1967), and for those even younger, *Sets and Numbers for the Very Young* (1969).

### ISAAC ASIMOV

*Words from History*

Biochemist Isaac Asimov has written his own reference book, *Asimov's Biographical Encyclopedia of Science and Technology*, and his writing includes a wide range of subjects, from authoritative discussions of measuring systems (*Realm of Measure*, 1960) and distinctive science fiction to a story for the preschool child, *The Best New Thing* (1971).

*Words from History* (1968) is a good example of Asimov's work in a field outside his own. Like all of his other books, it is distinguished for a witty, informal style that smoothly carries authoritative information. Using one page of text for each word, he gives its etymology and sets it in historical perspective. The book is delightful for browsing as well as useful for the facts it gives. The following quotation shows how clearly Asimov writes and how much to the point his explanations are:

> *As Roman dominion spread, other roads were built, extending outward from Rome like so many tentacles reaching to the far corners of the Empire. It is from this that the old proverb "All roads lead to Rome" originated.*
>
> *Along the Roman roads, the legions tramped, guarding the frontiers and suppressing revolts (and sometimes marching on Rome itself to snatch at the Imperial crown). Distance was important and was measured off by the tireless pacing of the legionaries in convenient units of a thousand paces. In Latin, a thousand paces is "milia Passuum," and this was gradually shortened to the first word alone, in English* mile. *Our present "mile" is a little longer than the Roman, however, and comes to about 1050 paces or 1760 yards.* (p. 141)

Among his other "Word" books are *Words on the Map* (1962) and *Words of Science; and the History Behind Them* (1959). Each of these books follows the same format as *Words from History*, that is, one word and its explanation on one page. *Words from the Exodus* (1963) and *Words in Genesis* (1962) show how much a part of our everyday speech comes from the Bible.

*Building Blocks of the Universe* (1957) won the Thomas Alva Edison Foundation Award for the best science book published for youth in 1957. An excellent book on chemistry, it also contains little sidelights which make the scientific words come alive for young people. *Realm of Numbers* (1959) is a popularizing of arithmetic for those who don't have a knowledge of algebra, geometry, and calculus. One of the most successful of Asimov's many books about space is *ABC's of Space* (1969), which is illustrated with brilliant photographs and drawings from the space program, with short paragraphs for each item. This may be used with very young children, despite the fact that the terminology is sometimes complex.

### JEANNE BENDICK

*Names, Sets and Numbers*

An author or illustrator of more than 100 books for children, Jeanne Bendick is probably best known for her lively, humorous illustrations. Her easily recognizable style, which she describes as "relaxed representational" is echoed in the brisk and vigorous writing that skillfully clarifies difficult concepts. Her interest in science developed after she had illustrated a number of science books and had done a lot of reading in order to draw her pictures accurately. She found that she had the ability to present a complex subject in simple terms and in a light, often breezy manner.

*Names, Sets and Numbers* (1971) is typical of her direct, crisp approach. Although it is recommended by the publisher for grades four to six, younger children can understand the content. The approach, as a matter of fact, with many pictures, is more that of a picture book, and as such, much more palatable to younger children. The text also is appropriate for this level:

*Names*

*First, we give names to things.*
*People have names, like Mike and Karen.*
*Planets have names, like Earth and Mars.*
*Every plant we know has a name.*
*"Buttercup" is a name. So is "pine."*
*Every animal we know has a name.*
*"Earthworm" is a name. So is "lion."* (p. 8)

Beginning with names of things as a reference point, the author then moves into sets in a very smooth transition. Making small things out of big ones gets across the concept of subsets and classification, another subject to which very young children are being exposed.

Jeanne Bendick has written a number of books, all with the same straightforward tone, in the Watts' "First Book" series. *A First Book of Space Travel* (1969, revised four times) is a comprehensive yet simplified look at the subject, from "What Space Is" to "What Space Science Has Done for Earth." *The First Book of Time* (1963) begins with a question: what do we know about time? It discusses measurement of time, calendars, and clocks, including plant and animal clocks. *A Place to Live* (1970) is a book for the read-aloud audience; it deals with the interdependence of human, plant, and animal life. Two of Bendick's books deal with weather phenomena, *The Wind* (1964) and *Lightning* (1961). The latter begins with an excellent chapter on the beliefs of different civilizations about the causes of lightning, and explains what lightning is and how to protect oneself from it. *The Wind* is organized in similar fashion, the scientific information preceded by a discussion of myths and superstitions the world over. *What Made You You?* (1971) asks

*Did you come like a chicken out of an egg? Like a flower out of a bud? Like a rainbow out of raindrops? Like music out of a horn? No, but just as wonderful. YOU were born!* (pp. 38, 39)

Blithe as it is, the text gives accurate and explicit information about reproduction and heredity.

*Electronics for Young People* (1960) and *How Much and How Many* (1960) are for older children and contain more text than pictures. *Television Works Like This* (1965), covering the technical aspects of the receiving set and of broadcasting, was written in collaboration with Jeanne Bendick's husband, Robert.

## SONIA BLEEKER

*The Ibo of Biafra*

Sonia Bleeker said, in *The Ibo of Biafra* (1969), "A man must dance the dance of the times, is an Ibo proverb. To the Ibo, it means that they are ready to accept change." And change is what the Biafrans have had, and more than their share, since October of 1960, when Nigeria obtained her independence from Britain. Because of unrest and lawlessness within the young republic, there were massacres of defenseless Ibo, and on March 30, 1967, the Ibo declared their independence of the Nigerian government, which led to a bloody civil war.

Sonia Bleeker was an anthropologist whose books are distinguished for their simplicity of style and for the objective assessment of cultural patterns. There is never any insinuation in her writing that a food is exotic or a rite strange; from her viewpoint as a scientist, all customs of all peoples have an equal validity, and this admirable attitude is communicated to her readers. All of her books give both historical background and a description of the tribe's way of life today, but

*Illustration by Edith G. Singer for* The Ibo of Biafra *by Sonia Bleeker. Copyright 1969. Reproduced by permission of William Morrow & Company, Inc.*

the major portion of each is devoted to an examination of cultural patterns. In *The Ibo of Biafra*, for example, earlier chapters of the book deal with the people, their mores, home and marketplace, clothing, and economy. "Growing Up" is a detailed description of the way the child is born, is raised, and matures. Many pages are given over to the courtship and marriage ceremonies. "The Marketplace" discusses the slave trade, which was not abolished until early in the nineteenth century, and actually continued until the beginning of the twentieth century on a small scale. The marketplace is also the local courtroom, and the elders sit as judges to hear cases brought before them.

Sonia Bleeker went to Africa four times to do research for her books, and each is made vivid by the small details that can only come from personal observation. In *The Pygmies: Africans of the Congo Forest* (1968) she describes a ceremony of the Mbuti, one of the four major Pygmy groups. The Molimo is a beautiful and moving rite, a memorial honoring the Pygmy dead, usually a beloved old person, in which the participants give thanks to the forest for its abundance.

In addition to her more recent books on Africa, Mrs. Zim (she was married to author Herbert S. Zim) wrote seventeen books about Indians of the Americas, among which are *The Sea Hunters: Indians of the Northwest Coast* (1951), which describes the history and living patterns of Indians on the Alaskan and Canadian coasts, and *The Maya: Indians of Central America* (1961), which includes some discussion of archeological exploration in the area. In *The Eskimo: Arctic Hunters and Trappers* (1959), a mass of factual material is presented in simple but vivid writing.

## FRANKLYN M. BRANLEY

*The Milky Way: Galaxy Number One*

Franklyn Branley is an astronomer on the staff of the American Museum-Hayden Planetarium, and Director of Educational Services. Both his professional knowledge and his familiarity with presenting facts to the layman are reflected in his many books on astronomy and other scientific subjects. He collaborated with Eleanor K. Vaughan in two interesting books for the very young, *Mickey's Magnet* (1956) and *Timmy and the Tin-Can Telephone* (1959), which present scientific facts in attractive format.

*The Milky Way* (1969) is one of his books for older readers, using scientific terminology and a scholarly approach. It begins with a history of astronomy, describing early telescopes, the beliefs of early scientists and laymen, and the problem of changing men's minds so that they might be persuaded to give up Ptolemaic theory and accept the

Copernican theory on the nature of the universe.

Chapter Four describes a development of the 1940s, exploring by radio astronomy. In the author's words, "when we say we can 'see' or 'view' a region we do not mean in the literal sense. Rather, we mean that we can pick up radio energy and so obtain knowledge of the manner in which the material that produces the radio waves is distributed." Thus it is that with a new device the shape of the Milky Way became more discernible. The last chapter describes the way in which the galaxy may have evolved, and makes conjectures about where it may go from here. The book includes an appendix for finding stellar magnitudes and distances, intended for those who understand logarithms, and a bibliography for further reading. Other books for older readers are *Mars: Planet Number Four* (1966), a revision that includes the findings of Mariner IV, and *The Sun: Star Number One* (1964).

Branley has also written books on these subjects for younger children. *The Sun: Our Nearest Star* (1961) is a simple explanation in picture-book format, and *A Book of Mars for You* (1968) speculates about an unmanned landing. *A Book of Stars for You* (1967) is an excellent introduction to stars, and *The Moon Seems to Change* (1960), handsomely illustrated with woodcuts by Helen Borten, is a clear explanation for the changes in the moon's appearance. All of these books are in the Crowell "Let's-Read-and-Find-Out Science Books" series. He has also written *High Sounds, Low Sounds* (1967), which explains how we hear, and *Floating and Sinking* (1967), which uses an experiment with sand in a bottle to explain the processes.

None of Franklyn Branley's books has been more popular than *The Christmas Sky* (1966), which is based on the Christmas lecture at the Hayden Planetarium. It discusses the Biblical, historical, and astronomical clues to the true date of the birth of Jesus, and deftly combines scientific facts and a reverent approach.

## CHARLES COOMBS

*Skyhooks; The Story of Helicopters*

Charles Coombs in *Skyhooks* (1967) describes the tasks that the helicopter can perform and gives a brief history of man's struggle to discover a way to move vertically into space, including a description and photograph of Leonardo da Vinci's model which he called a helixpteron—from which the modern term *helicopter* evolved. The basic controls of a small helicopter are described, with a labelled photograph as a guide and a step-by-step procedure outlining just how it is flown. Specific uses of helicopters are explored in the next chapters: air taxis which operate out of airports, private use, police patrol and rescue work, helicopters as they are used in industry and in the armed forces. The book has clear black and white photographs, with captions, well placed in relation to the text. Particularly interesting are pictures of the proposed compound helicopter, a machine which folds its wings and becomes a jet airplane, and the SC0142A, a tilt wing variety of experimental machine which has flown with considerable success.

In all he writes, Coombs presents facts clearly and simply, in a smooth and fluid style. He writes about aircraft and inner space flight from experience, and most of his books are about airplanes and space. His major work is *Skyrocketing into the Unknown* (1954), a book about significant jet and rocket-powered aircraft developments which contains not only excellent photographs throughout the text, but a comprehensive representation of the aircraft under discussion in 46 captioned pictures at the center of the text. It is an exciting story of test pilots and their vehicles.

*Lift-off; The Story of Rocket Power* (1963), a basic book about rocket power, including a short history, deals with liquid and solid rocket engines and guidance systems. *Spacetrack; Watchdog of the Skies* (1969) is the little-known story of keeping track of the objects that are launched into space, a fascinating look at the underground quarters of the Space Defense Center and the North American Air Defense Command, including pictures and a diagram of the complex in the heart of the Cheyenne Mountains. It is a comprehensive look at the worldwide system of tracking by radar. *Cleared for Takeoff; Behind the Scenes at an Airport* (1969) has all the allure of any "backstage" book.

### OLIVE EARLE

*Praying Mantis*

The clear, accurate details of Olive Earle's illustrations are one of the most attractive features of her books, most of which deal with one form of animal life or one aspect of it. The books are meticulously detailed, solid enough to be used by the beginning student of natural science or by the nature lover, and brief enough to be read aloud to younger children.

About one half of *Praying Mantis* (1969) is spent on the description and life cycle of the female praying mantis while the other half deals with a firsthand account of a specific Chinese mantis observed in Olive Earle's garden. Organized in a step-by-step fashion rather than by chapters, the book begins with a description of the egg case and the curious way that it is made and describes the wintering of the egg case, the hatching of the baby mantises, the physical characteristics of the insect, its food, the origin of the name, and other details of the life cycle, ending with the cold weather signalling the end of the life span of a mantis. The gentle, poetic tone of the book is sustained in its final paragraph:

> *Perhaps in the hope of flying to some more sheltered spot, the mantis spread her wings slightly. Then it happened. A strong gust hit her and caught her up. She was blown like a falling leaf. Blown up in the air. Blown over the hedge. Blown out of the garden forever.* (p. 48)

Other nature studies written by Olive Earle include *Strange Lizards* (1964), *Camels and Llamas* (1961), and *Birds and Their Beaks* (1965). She has also written two books that are useful for school-age children and adults as well: *State Trees* (1960) and *State Birds and Flowers* (1951). An earlier volume, *Paws, Hoofs and Flippers* (1954), is an imaginative treatment of mammals, classified according to their feet. The illustrations are accurate and add much to the text. This book is useful for middle-graders and could be used at the junior-high level.

*Illustration by Olive Earle from* Praying Mantis *by Olive Earle. Copyright 1969. Reproduced by permission of William Morrow & Company, Inc.*

### LEONARD EVERETT FISHER

*The Tanners*

*The Glassmakers* (1964) was the beginning of a distinguished set of books by Leonard Everett Fisher on "Colonial Americans and Colonial American Craftsmen," a series admired as much for the excellence in its design, illustrations, and format as for its content. Long a subject studied in schools and of interest to young persons, colonial people had not been dealt with in single volumes in quite this fashion, and the books were welcomed, for they filled a great need. They are designed so that a full-page picture on the right faces three quarters of a page of text on the left, with an occasional double-spread picture. The illustrations, drawn with vigor, picture costume details and daily customs. There are many small, accurate drawings of the tools of each trade, and each drawing is carefully labelled and described. The first third of *The Tanners* (1966) is devoted to history, the last two thirds to technique. The author includes a glossary of tanner's terms and an index, but provides no bibliography or acknowledgments of any kind. The text is replete, however, with references which are evidence of research. The tools of the tanner are pictured on page 18, and from then on each page describes a step in the tanning process. Fisher explains how the tanner played an important part in making a free nation of the American colonies. The tanner prepared the skins for the parchmentmaker, and he in turn made vellum, a superior writing surface—on which were written both the Declaration of Independence and the Constitution of the United States.

Among his books on Colonial Americans are *The Schoolmasters* (1967), *The Peddlers* (1968), and *The Architects* (1970). In the series on Colonial American Craftsmen are *The Silversmiths* (1964), *The Cabinetmakers* (1966), and others. For younger children he wrote a book about fire engines entitled *Pumpers, Boilers, Hooks and Ladders* (1961). *Two If by Sea* (1970) is a dramatic and detailed description of the actions of four men during two hours of an eventful evening: April 18, 1775.

*Illustration by Leonard Everett Fisher from* The Architects *by Leonard Everett Fisher. Copyright 1970. Reproduced by permission of Franklin Watts, Inc., Publishers.*

## GENEVIEVE FOSTER

*George Washington's World*

Like some other authors in the children's field, Genevieve Foster wrote her books because no book or teacher ever told her what she wanted to know: who the important figures were or what was happening all over the world at the same time. As a matter of fact, history confused her as a schoolgirl and she says she was more confused than ever by the time she was graduated from college. When she decided to write books for children, the idea was born for this unique look at history, through the events and personalities of people and happenings all over the world. By using primary sources from which she quotes, Foster imparts a sense of nearness to the happenings of long ago.

*George Washington's World* (1941) is divided into six parts beginning when Washington was a boy and ending with his presidency. The book does an admirable job of presenting a horizontal look at history, a slice of life crosswise instead of strung out chronologically. When George Washington was a farmer, for instance, James Watt invented the steam engine, James Cook discovered Australia on the other side of the world, and Pompeii was uncovered. California was settled, Japan was a feudal state closed to the world, Marie Antoinette was married in France; all of these events and more were taking place during the period when Boston had a tea party and Paul Revere took his ride.

This book, like its counterparts in the series, is a large volume with interesting illustrations, full index, and separate indexes of places, nations, and events. Although these books are graded for twelve- to sixteen-year-olds, the style is so lively and understandable that they are excellent sources for teachers and parents to read to their children, for the volumes themselves are rather formidable for elementary children to tackle independently.

*The World of Columbus and Sons* (1965) and *Augustus Caesar's World* (1947), two other books in the series, are richly documented and have the same original approach to history; the former seems more difficult than *George Washington's World*, and is not so fully illustrated. In *Augustus Caesar's World* there is a comprehensive discussion of the Roman gods.

*The Year of the Pilgrims—1620* (1969), for a younger audience, is more simply written and introduces color in a small volume of 62 pages. In this and in *Year of Columbus—1492* (1969), also for younger children, the text is not placed solely at the date given in the title.

## JEAN CRAIGHEAD GEORGE

### *All Upon a Stone*

Many of the books that Jean George has illustrated or written were discussed in Chapter 12. All of her books are distinguished for their minute knowledge of the habits and the habitat of wild creatures, and *All Upon a Stone* (1971) has been singled out not because it is more profound or perceptive than others, but because of the unusual and explicit way in which it presents ecology to young children.

The book is notable for the harmony between the graceful writing and the handsome pictures by Don Bolognese, who painted a three foot by four foot canvas in acrylics first, then used details of the larger work to fill each of the pages of the book. Bolognese chose this technique to reflect the unity of the microcosm of the life on the stone. The whole picture is shown at the end of the book. The opening paragraph draws the analogy:

> *A stone by a stream in the woods is like a tiny country. It has its own forests, valleys, and pools. It has its own creatures that live out their lives, hunting, sleeping, and working all upon a stone.* (p. 1)

As the mole cricket tunnels under the ground and makes his way upon the stone, he meets all of the animal and plant life in this environment, including algae, rotifers, fresh-water jellyfish, and sponges in the water of the rock pool. In two outstanding pictures in the center of the book, the illustrator has painted lacy winged stone flies above a cluster of bluet blossoms along with a starflower, and we see how well the text matches:

> *Silver wings flashed. The mole cricket lifted his knees. The clatter of stone flies was all that he heard. They had hatched in the stream by the stone and were dancing above the bluet grove.* (p. 23)

*The Hole in the Tree* (1957), profusely illustrated by Jean George, can be enjoyed by very young children. It is the story of various occupants: a bark beetle, a carpenter bee, a black-capped chickadee family, and so on to the family of raccoons that is born there. *The Moon of the Bears* (1967) is one of a series of nature books, "The Thirteen Moons." These books have grown out of Jean George's interest in ecology, especially in the study of the relationship between climate and periodic biological events. As part of her research for *The Moon of the Wild Pigs* (1968), she visited the Arizona-Sonora Desert Museum, where she talked with scientists and observed the peccaries in their natural habitat. In *Snow Tracks* (1958), clear drawings by the author tell the story as much as does the simply written text, as a fresh snowfall shows what happens to a child, a weasel, a skunk, a fox, and a white-footed mouse.

## SONIA and TIM GIDAL

*My Village in Ghana*

Sonia and Tim Gidal have often traveled abroad to acquire facts and photographs for their "My Village" books, and the wealth of detail in that series is evidence of their careful scholarship. Limiting their subject to one child, his friends and family, they give a detailed account of the activities which take place in his home, school, and recreation areas during the span of one day, although there may be references to past events.

*My Village in Ghana* (1969) has a full-color photograph of young James Kodjo Badu on its cover and it is through his first-person, present-tense account that we learn about life in Makranso, which is the center of Ghana. Through Kodjo we learn about the customs, schooling, food, folklore, dress, arts and crafts, and economy of the village as well as the interpersonal relations within his extended family. Kodjo's day begins in his Aunt Lucretia's household as he helps with the chores, then joins a group of happy younger children to hear a story about Ananse the spider and why the snake has no legs, told by Nana, the chief. On his way to school Kodjo sees a friend kill a python, an exciting interlude complete with photographs. The children then chop the grass in front of the school. Kodjo explains that it must be cut every few days or they could not play soccer, which incidentally is played with a grapefruit, because a real soccer ball is too expensive. As the day progresses we look into almost every side of village life.

Sonia is the writer in the husband-wife team and Tim, the photographer. This volume has more than eighty black and white photographs of many aspects of life in the village. While some are obviously posed, others are candid. In addition, there is a well-drawn map at the end of the book, as well as a sketch of the village in a two-page spread at the beginning. A glossary of foreign words appears (although they are explained the first time they are used in the text). There is also a one-page history of Ghana.

The "My Village" series has had many imitators, but other authors have not quite achieved the natural quality of the Gidals' books. They have also done *My Village in Germany* (1964), *My Village in Italy* (1962), *My Village in Denmark* (1963), and others, numbering over twenty volumes in the series.

## SHIRLEY GLUBOK

*The Art of Ancient Greece*

Shirley Glubok majored in art and archeology, received her master's degree in early childhood education, and lectures to children's groups at the Metropolitan Museum of Art. She is well prepared, then, to explain and introduce the arts and crafts of ancient cultures, and her books are impressive because of the combination of authoritative knowledge, simple presentation, dignified format, and a recurrent emphasis on the relationships between an art form and the culture in which it was created.

From the handsome endpapers which show the frieze of the Parthenon, through every page of this striking book, *The Art of Ancient Greece* (1963) has clearly reproduced sculpture, architecture, pottery, and reliefs in a survey of Greek art. Presented for the middle grades, it is a guided tour in print of art objects gathered from museums all over the world. The book begins with a paragraph describing Greece, and then discusses ancient Greek vases, their beauty, and their various uses. As the author describes paintings, she tells a little about each. Greek sculpture is discussed, with reproductions of Aphrodite and Apollo and of the Parthenon and its sculpture. Enlarged photographs of the heads are shown so that the children can see the details in the carving. The pages on armor are particularly well designed, with the figures facing each other from opposite pages, both backed by squares of brilliant pink to set off the black and white photographs, with the bronze gleaming as smooth as satin. Glubok has expanded this theme into an entire book, *Knights in Armor* (1969), which is based mostly on the splendid collection of armor in the Metropolitan Museum of Art.

In all of Shirley Glubok's books the page layout and the quality of the reproductions are good; the correlation between the text and the pictures has been careful, and locations in museums are given for all of the objects pictured.

*The Art of Ancient Mexico* (1968) is simply written and includes some materials children would be interested in for their familiarity: a pottery figure which appears to be a child in a swing, a man playing a drum and one blowing on a conch shell, and a series of pieces on an ancient ball game, including a player wearing helmet, knee guards, and ankle guards for protection. *The Art of the Etruscans* (1967) gives a good look at the Etruscan civilization through its art, much of it bronze statues and terra-cotta figures of athletes, gods, and warriors.

While most of the books in the series are about ancient cultures, Glubok has also written *The Art of Colonial America* (1970) and *The Art of the Old West* (1971), both of which have supplementary curricular use. This series is unique in its field. It does not give a comprehensive art history of a culture, but it is unexcelled as an introduction for the beginner.

## ROBERT HOFSINDE (GRAY-WOLF)

*Indian Sign Language*

Robert Hofsinde is not an Indian, but was born in Denmark and received his art training at the Royal Art Academy of Copenhagen. He has lived in America since coming over here as a young man. He saved the life of a Chippewa Indian boy while trapping in the Minnesota forests, and in gratitude, the Chippewas made a blood brother of him and gave him the name "Gray-Wolf."

A glossary of over five hundred universal signs used by North American Indians, *Indian Sign Language* (1956) is profusely illustrated by the author-artist. The book has an organic pattern of development, beginning with "man, woman" and "father, mother." In his acknowledgments, Hofsinde mentions Chief Blow Snake of the Winnebago tribe and the late Chief Crazy Bull of the Sioux, who verified many signs for him. Nowhere, however, is it mentioned whether the book encompasses most of the words in the language, or only a part. The words given are mostly nouns, verbs, adjectives, and adverbs, with few abstract concepts listed. Love, for instance, is not indicated as either a verb or noun, but simply an all-encompassing sign of crossing arms over the chest, right arm close to body, and pressed with the left arm. Many words are combined signs such as *dam*, which is a compound of *river* and *hold*. Occasionally, after the description of the sign is concluded, the author lists other words the same sign stands for. In addition to individual words in the list, the book cites common Indian tribes, the Twelve Moons (the months), totems, and a counting system.

Hofsinde has written a number of books on Indians, such as *Indian Warriors and Their Weapons* (1965), which treats seven tribes, describing their costumes and illustrating their arrows, war clubs, and drums. *Indian Music Makers* (1967) explores musical instruments and reproduces some of the Chippewa music originally recorded by Francis Densmore in the early part of this century. In *Indian Arts* (1971), objects are grouped by the material of which they were made.

Like Sonia Bleeker, Robert Hofsinde restricts his writing to one area of information, making a contribution that is not duplicated by any other writer for children. It is the combination of a sympathetic approach, authoritative knowledge, and an eye for vivid details that gives his books their usefulness and their appeal.

## HOLLING CLANCY HOLLING

*Paddle-to-the-Sea*

In a book as imaginative as its title, Holling C. Holling sets down the travels of a little wooden Indian sitting in a canoe carved of wood. Launched in the water in Nipigon country in Canada, the Indian boy floats down through all of the Great Lakes, and finally reaches the sea. During this odyssey of *Paddle-to-the-Sea* (1941), he becomes frozen into the lake water, caught in a forest fire, and picked up by strangers, but always they heed the carving on the bottom of the canoe: "Please put me back in the water. I am Paddle-to-the-Sea," and he is put back in the water to continue his journey. Fictionalized, this is also a geographical tour de force and a description of the ecology of the land through which Paddle floats. While *Paddle-to-the-Sea* is in truth a demonstration that water from north of Lake Superior makes its way to the Atlantic Ocean, it is much more. It is an imaginative dream of the real-life Indian boy who made the carving, and who later heard that it had gone far across the ocean to France; it is a picture of the wildlife that surrounds Lake Superior; it is all these things, but because it is the sum rather than the parts, it is a unique work of art. *Paddle-to-the-Sea* was a Caldecott Honor Book in 1942.

Each chapter consists of one page of print alternating with full-page illustrations in full color, so that the story unfolds quickly

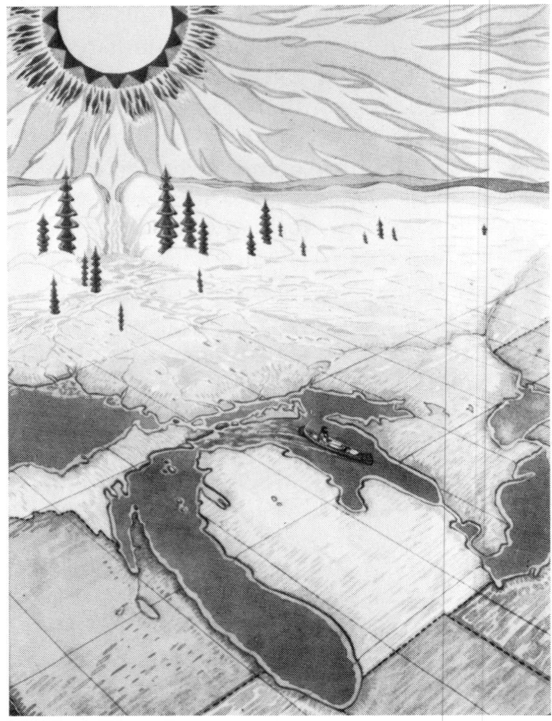

*Illustration from* Paddle-to-the-Sea *by Holling Clancy Holling. Copyright 1941. Reproduced by permission of Houghton Mifflin Company. (Original in color)*

as Paddle makes his way from the north, through the locks at Sault Ste. Marie, and on down to the ocean. The author shapes each chapter or page around a momentous happening, such as the breaking up of the ice on the river, or going over Niagara Falls. His easy, descriptive style, interspersed with lively conversation, makes the book attractive to children. Just as attractive are the pencil drawings which decorate the margins of the text, intricate accurate diagrams of the locks at the Soo, of a sawmill, or a lake freighter. Labelled well, they describe material which is not covered in the text. Coupled with the full-color paintings, these drawings both complement and enlarge the text, and they show as well as the text does the extensive historical research that Holling does for his books.

Although *Minn of the Mississippi* (1963), a Newbery Honor Book, is almost identical in format and approach with *Paddle-to-the-Sea*, it is usually classified as a book about a reptile rather than fiction. Minn is a three-legged turtle who travels down the Mississippi from Lake Itasca, Minnesota, to the Gulf of Mexico, which enables Holling to describe the history, geography, climate, and geology of the river's regions. *Pagoo* (1957) details the life of a hermit crab, and *Tree in the Trail* (1942) is the story of a tree's life over two centuries.

## GERALD W. JOHNSON

*The Presidency*

It was the shock of becoming a grandfather, Gerald Johnson says, that made him decide to write books about the history of the United States and its government. He wanted his grandson Peter to know that "it is in some ways better and in some ways worse to be an American than to be an Englishman, or a Frenchman, or a man of any other nationality"; and he wanted Peter to know exactly why. Such knowledge, Mr. Johnson believes, inevitably leads to an increased understanding of the rest of the world; and to understand other nations is the heaviest responsibility of the rising generation of Americans.

One of a trilogy about the branches of government in our country, *The Presidency* (1962) deals with only three subjects: What the President Does, How the Presidency Has Changed, and The Strong Presidents. In an easy, flowing style with a simple vocabulary, Johnson communicates well, sometimes quoting Presidents to make his story more lively, drawing always on historical events, choosing down-to-earth details such as the way Secret Service men guard the President.

Particularly interesting to some readers will be the intimate details of the President's life. The descriptions of the way materials are excerpted for his survey on a typewritten page and of his daily appointments list may give readers some idea of the mass of detail the President works with each day. Johnson describes the five duties of the President as listed in the Constitution, as well as the restraints put upon him by Congress, and the way some of the restraints have been ignored. In the concluding paragraphs, Johnson describes the leadership qualities which are necessary for a man to be a good President,

*Illustration by Leonard Everett Fisher for* The Presidency *by Gerald W. Johnson. Copyright 1962. Reproduced by permission of William Morrow & Company, Inc.*

then talks about the responsibilities of the voters in a democracy. The book includes, in an appendix, a list of all the Presidents and their terms, and is well indexed.

*The Supreme Court* (1962), while it has the same readable style as *The Presidency*, is set with more lines to the page so that it does not have as easy an appearance. The third book in this trilogy is *The Congress* (1963), a lucid and occasionally humorous look at the remaining branch of the government.

*America Is Born* (1959), *America Grows Up* (1960), and *America Moves Forward* (1960) are outstanding history books. Written for Johnson's grandson, *American Is Born* begins with "A Letter to Peter," a deeply moving statement of what it means to be a part of America. This sense of obligation, this profound moral sense, is what makes Gerald Johnson's books come alive as something more than just dry facts on a page.

## PATRICIA LAUBER

*Who Discovered America?*

In a sharp departure from her earlier works, Patricia Lauber, in *Who Discovered America?* (1970), has written a speculative view of early explorers of America beginning with the people who may have crossed the land bridge between Siberia and Alaska; the Paleo-Indians, who may have inhabited the state of California 17,000 years ago; people who may have come from Southeast Asia to Middle America; the ones who named Vinland; on up through the voyages of Columbus. Lauber has done an excellent job of gathering and synthesizing the current and often controversial material about this important subject.

Two chapters are particularly interesting: "Visitors from Distant Lands" and "Vinland the Good." In the first, the author presents photographs and documentation of inventions, designs, and motifs that are common to Asia as well as Latin America and asks the question, "Borrowed from the old world or invented in the new?"

> *This story is not easy to believe. It seems almost impossible that the fishermen could have drifted 8,000 miles and landed in Ecuador, where they taught the Indians to make pottery. Yet archeologists cannot find another way to explain the sudden appearance of this particular pottery in a region where there are no traces of earlier pottery.*
>
> *About 2,000 years ago, Ecuador seems to have had another visit by voyagers from Asia. The evidence is a collection of pottery objects that were common in Asia but have not been found anywhere else in the New World. They were discovered by archeologists digging near the north coast of Valdivia . . .*
>
> *These pottery objects found together in one part of Ecuador are nearly impossible to explain, unless they were introduced by people from Asia. They appear suddenly in Ecuador. They seem unrelated to New World pottery objects, but they are like objects that were widely used in the Old World. (p. 64)*

In the chapter on Vinland she presents the evidence for the discovery of Vinland as it is outlined in *The Saga of Eric the Red* and *The Greenlander's Saga* and tends to agree with scholars who think that the basic events of these sagas are true. The format of the book is attractive, and the reproductions of photographs, prints, and maps are excellent. The book's nine chapters are well organized and well indexed.

Lauber has written widely in the science and social studies fields. *All About the Planets* (1960), which includes an introductory chapter on the formation of the solar system, a chapter on the moon, and information on the planets, is a competent work. *All About the Ice Age* (1959) is illustrated with drawings, maps, and twelve pages of photographs of glaciers and the scientists exploring them. Three easy-to-read volumes are: *Your Body and How it Works* (1962), *The Story of Num-*

bers (1961), and *The Friendly Dolphins* (1963). The latter is based on current studies of the intelligence of dolphins. A quality that makes Lauber's books stimulating is their sense of lively curiosity, a provocative relish that can be shared by the reader and may send him, titillated, to seek more information.

## ROBERT M. McCLUNG

*Thor: Last of the Sperm Whales*

In a book with overtones of *Moby Dick*, Robert McClung begins with the story of a sperm whale which destroyed the ships of whalers hunting him 150 years ago. *Thor* (1971) goes on to describe a sperm whale of today that bears the same marking as his ghostly forebear, ramming into the stern of a modern-day catcher boat carrying harpooners. In between there is a detailed description of the birth, feeding, growth, mating, and death of the great sperm whale as it travels the oceans, a great monster of the deep, fifty feet in length and "forty tons of bone and muscle, overlaid by an insulating blanket of blubber nearly a foot thick on his breast." While this is a scientific description of the life of the sperm whale, it is also a story of the slaughter of whales in our century, destruction so great that three species, the great blue whales, the finbacks, and the sei whales, are in danger of extinction. McClung graphically describes modern hunting techniques, in their relentless efficiency.

Robert McClung, a major author in his field, has written sympathetically but without sentimentality of all kinds of wildlife. He manages to be thorough, but not dry, and weaves a story without anthropomorphism into his factual approach. Threaded through all of his work is the persistent theme of good conservation practices, and his very early work *Spike: The Story of a Whitetail Deer* (1952) is a fine illustration of this. In it, the reader is exposed to the illegal practice of hunters shining a flashlight at night to attract deer. These early books are particularly attractive to youngsters because they have large type and are easy to understand. The vocabulary is not written down, however. In *Shag, Last of the Plains Buffalo* (1960), the author documents the savage slaughter of the buffalo as the white men drove westward with their guns and railroad tracks. *Honker: The Story of a Wild Goose* (1965) and *Black Jack: Last of the Big Alligators* (1967), which contains an afterword about the alligator being an endangered species of American wildlife, continue the conservation story.

## MILTON MELTZER

*In Their Own Words*

The first of the three-volume survey of black history in America, *In Their Own Words*, contains material not previously known to many readers, drawn from letters, diaries, journals, autobiographies, speeches, resolutions, newspapers, and pamphlets of black people in slavery. It traces life on the plantation and conditions in the North in letters from escaped slaves in the free states, and tells of the day of Emancipation. In these excerpts, one can see the selectivity that Milton Meltzer has employed to show the wide range of activity and writing of slaves and freed slaves. The three books are an excellent source of information on what living conditions have been for black people through this country's history. Volume One is illustrated with black and white paintings, drawings, engravings, and photographs, and includes reproductions of a list of slaves belonging to Thomas Jefferson and of posters announcing the sale of slaves. Each excerpt is short, some only two pages; occasionally a document is quoted in full. Each has an introduction by Meltzer and the source is identified at the close. The volumes cover these three periods: 1619–1865, 1865–1916, and 1916–1966.

Milton Meltzer's books show his interest

in social reform and its effects on the American people. His biographies of Langston Hughes, Samuel Gridley Howe, and Lydia Maria Child, discussed in Chapter 15, are indicative of this concern, as is *Time of Trial, Time of Hope* (1966), written in collaboration with August Meier. The book describes the many problems and few victories of black people in the United States between the First and Second World Wars. The authors write with authority and from a broad viewpoint that includes political, economic, educational, and cultural problems as well as the role of labor.

Meltzer's book on the labor movement in the United States, *Bread and Roses* (1967), gives a vivid history of the struggles of the laboring class up to 1915. Using comments from contemporary sources, Meltzer documents the grim story of child labor, sweat shops, and defeated attempts to organize.

## ANTHONY RAVIELLI

*Wonders of the Human Body*

*Wonders of the Human Body* (1954) has never been surpassed in showing children the intricate marvels of the human form. Written by a man with a passion for communicating by word and illustration, the book has on every page a dramatic and illuminating picture that reveals the inner workings of the body. Anthony Ravielli is fascinated by what holds us together and makes us function, and he makes the subject a fascinating one for his readers. The book describes the skeleton, the muscles, the digestive system, and the brain and nervous system. One double-page spread shows the spine as a long string of spools. Then Ravielli uses two pages for a labelled, anatomically correct drawing of the spine, and the text describes what the spine is and does. In like fashion, another two-page picture shows wire attached to the spools: "These are your ribs." The next page likens the thorax, or rib cage, to a bird-cage. And

*Illustration by Anthony Ravielli from* Wonders of the Human Body *by Anthony Ravielli. Copyright 1954 by Anthony Ravielli. Reprinted by permission of The Viking Press, Inc. (Original with two colors)*

there it is—a black and white bird-cage, complete with bird, slipped down over the realistic drawing of the actual rib cage. His text describes the ribs and their functions, and on that page there are small detailed drawings of cartilage and of two boys, one with chest empty of air, and one with chest expanded. The economy of Ravielli's prose and the grace of his style are evident. He limits his description always to one or two pages, and always the illustrations are coordinated. There is a very complete table of contents.

Anthony Ravielli has written *An Adventure in Geometry* (1957), a book bursting with action drawings which relate forms in nature with geometric forms. *The World Is Round* (1963) deals with the earth as a large spinning sphere, and likens human life on the earth to that of a fly on a giant ball the size of a house. Ravielli gives a history of men's beliefs about the shape of the earth, and concludes with a prophetic statement about men landing on the moon. In *From Fins to Hands: An Adventure in Evolution* (1968), the author-illustrator has produced another handsome book, printed in two colors, on the importance of the development of the hand from prehistoric times to the present day of automation. Ravielli says of hands that "The human brain made man a civilized being, but it was his hands that recorded his progress and made human culture possible."

### KATHARINE SAVAGE

*The Story of World Religions*

A historical as well as descriptive approach, Katharine Savage's *The Story of World Religions* (1967) is a comprehensive, well-written book, useful at both the junior-high and elementary levels, which gives a dispassionate, objective view of religions of the world. The book covers the world's major religions, but it does not include the area south of the Sahara in Africa, or reflect the many changes in the rituals and dress in the Catholic religion, nor does it encompass the unrest in the priesthood of the Roman Catholic Church. It is organized into fourteen chapters, which are roughly chronological, and each treats one religion, sometimes several, of a given area. Well researched, the book has an extensive bibliography, and in her acknowledgments the author cites numerous sources of information as well as sources for the photographs.

Savage's style is dignified but not dry, sympathetic but not sentimental, and her distinction as a writer of informational books is based on comprehensive treatment, reliable research, logical organization of material, and a sense of perspective which sees and emphasizes those aspects of a subject that have real importance. Her other works include *The Story of the United Nations* (1962), in which the first third of the book describes the inception and formation of the U.N., and the last third chronicles crises such as the birth of Israel, the Berlin airlift, and attempts to bring peace to the Congo; and *The Story of Africa: South of the Sahara* (1961), which gives a history of the exploration and exploitation period in Africa and a look at some of the countries: Ghana, Nigeria, Rhodesia, and Kenya, among others. *People and Power* (1959) gives the histories of Russia, Japan, and Germany (each in a separate section) up to the beginning of World War II. Objective and lucid, the book is a good source of information and can give young readers an understanding of some of the forces that led to a world war and that are still in effect in international politics.

### MILLICENT E. SELSAM

*Benny's Animals*

Millicent Selsam, one of the most dependably competent authors of science books, writes for all age levels, but she is undoubtedly best known for her books for young readers. Her style is simple and clear, with no extraneous material and no trace of popularization. She defines good science books as "those that show the methods of science at work, that elucidate basic principles of science and are not a mere assembly of facts, that convey something of the beauty and excitement of science, and that interest young people in thinking up good questions for new young scientists to test by experiment."[2]

*Benny's Animals* (1966) is a particularly good example of the inclusion of methodology and basic principles in a science book for the beginning reader. It is a clear lesson in how animals are classified, with a fictional

2. "Writing About Science for Children," by Millicent E. Selsam, from *A Critical Approach to Children's Literature*, ed. by Sara Innis Fenwick (Univ. of Chicago, 1967), p. 99.

framework that facilitates the explanation. Benny was a child with a passion for neatness and order, who wanted to organize his collection of material from the seashore, and this led to questions about the differences between animals. Finally Benny went to the museum to talk with Professor Wood, who suggested that he put the specimens in two piles according to whether or not they had a backbone; then his next step was to divide the animals with backbones into fish, amphibians, reptiles, birds, and mammals. Benny wanted to take classification a step further, but Professor Wood dissuaded him, saying that it would be a lifelong job. The book ends on just the right note, having explained the basic steps in classification and having made the point that there is a rational way of dividing living things. The format is excellent, with continuous text, large print, and plenty of leading between the lines. Arnold Lobel's illustrations are appropriate in their earth colors, casually realistic when he portrays the boys and the family, and close enough to reality to be recognizable when he draws the animals, often giving them a little personality. *Greg's Microscope* (1963) and *Let's Get Turtles* (1965) are other titles in this "Science I Can Read" series.

*The Carrot and Other Root Vegetables* (1971) and *Peanut* (1969) are for ages seven to nine, illustrated with large handsome photographs, some in color, by Jerome Wexler. A group of books which are illustrated by several different artists are *See Through the Jungle* (1957); *See Through the Sea* (1955), a story of underwater life; and *See Along the Shore* (1961), a colorful volume which deals with tides and animals and plants of the seashore.

For still older children are *Animals as Parents* (1965) and *The Language of Animals* (1962), the latter a fascinating story of communication between animals including sounds, smells, facial expressions, and tail positions. In *Plants That Move* (1962), Selsam tells about the sundew plant, which catches insects, as well as the better-known venus

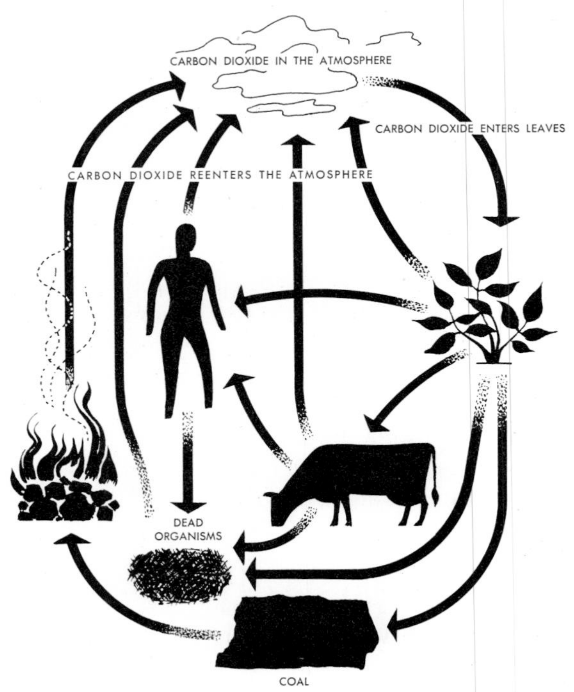


*Illustration by Weimer Pursell from* Biography of an Atom *by J. Bronowski and Millicent E. Selsam. Copyright © 1963 by J. Bronowski; renewed 1965 by J. Bronowski and Millicent E. Selsam. Reprinted by permission of Harper & Row, Publishers.*

flytrap; and in *Plants That Heal* (1959), she writes an intriguing chapter on plant medicines that are in use today. One of Selsam's most interesting books for older readers was written in collaboration with Jacob Bronowski —*Biography of an Atom* (1963), which traces the history of one carbon atom from its birth in a young star, through the millennia, to a conjectural fate today.

## KATHERINE B. SHIPPEN

*Men, Microscopes, and Living Things*

Katherine Shippen's books reflect a wide-ranging interest: science, biography, history, music, industry, and other fields. *Men, Microscopes, and Living Things* (1955) exemplifies her careful research and the vitality and grace of a writing style that give her work authority and elegance. In this survey of the work of great biologists, she uses quotations from their writings to enliven the book. Her own obvious zest echoes a comment from Marcello Malpighi, professor at the medical school at Pisa in the seventeenth century:

> *In performing these researches so many marvels of nature were spread before my eyes that I experienced an internal pleasure that my pen could not describe.—Marcello Malpighi (1628–1694)*

This excitement in discovery is also evident in Shippen's description of Anton van Leeuwenhoek's joy in using the beautiful and precise lenses he had ground. He looked at everything he could find, each object a fresh marvel as he saw the minute details made clear by the microscope. To his amazement, there were "little beasties" swimming about in a drop of water! Most of his neighbors thought him queer, but one who sensed the man's genius wrote to the Royal Society in London, which invited a correspondence. Each chapter deals with some aspect of experimental science, concluding with Thomas Hunt Morgan's work in this century, using the fruit fly in studies of heredity. Anthony Ravielli's spidery, delicate line drawings, quite unlike his other work in children's books, give added appeal to this Newbery Honor Book. It is indexed in full; for example, there are eighteen entries under "Darwin, Charles."

Quotations are used also, as chapter introductions rather than within the text, in *The Great Heritage* (1947), which is timely because of the wide interest in conservation. *The Bright Design* (1949), a book based on talks to young people at the Brooklyn Chilren's Museum, is about scientists and how they studied electricity. *Miracle in Motion: The Story of American Industry* (1955) concisely gives a history of three centuries of industry, from the "Buy American" slogan after the American Revolution to Henry Ford's "Five Dollars a Day." In another book for older readers, Shippen collaborated with Anca Seidlova in writing *The Heritage of Music* (1963), a comprehensive and scholarly history of music from its beginning to Edgar Varèse's electronic music. *This Union Cause* (1958) is a history of organized labor in the United States and *The Pool of Knowledge: How the United Nations Share Their Skills* (rev. ed., 1965) is an informative contribution to young people's understanding of many of the peoples of this world as well as of some of the work of the U.N.

## PAUL and KAY SHOWERS

*Before You Were a Baby*

*Before You Were a Baby* (1968) is an excellently paced book for readers in the second and third grades, and it is clear enough to be read aloud to younger children. There are repetition and rhythm in sentences like "This new cell grew and grew and grew. And at last it became you." Particularly dramatic are the pictures which show, in color, the increasing size of the baby inside the uterus. On these pages the text is almost nonexistent, and the reader's eye is carried forward by the power of the graphic drawings as they progress from the hunchback figure at six weeks to the completely formed baby of eight months. Using all of the correct terms, such as *testes*, *sperm*, and *penis*, the book gives an accurate explanation of conception without being either coy or evasive. The book's tone is captured in its opening and closing paragraphs:

*Once you were a baby. You were very small. A little boy could lift you easily and carry you.*
*Before you were a baby, you were much smaller.*
*No one could even see you.*

then,

*Now the baby is born.*
*This baby,*
*and you,*
*and every baby in the world—*

*came from two tiny cells that nobody could see—*
*an ovum*
*and a sperm.*

The simple style and the use of large print, with a minimum of labelled diagrams, is typical of the Crowell series which includes *Before You Were a Baby*. Showers gives accurate information in the very simplest language, chooses important facts, and tells them in logical sequence, so that the child can read the books himself or the adult can use them as a springboard for discussion.

Showers' other books include *Your Skin and Mine* (1965) and *Look at Your Eyes* (1962). The first gives some of the basic facts about skin: sensation, temperature adjustment, hair follicles, and color differences, explaining the latter so that the message about skin color is casual, while the illustrations show children of various colors in connection with the text rather than as an ethnic spectrum for its own sake. For example, a black child's daily activities are used to show how eyes adjust to light, that eyes are different colors, how the parts of the eye work.

*Use Your Brain* (1971) and *A Drop of Blood* (1967) are other science books by Paul Showers, and he has also written *Indian Festivals* (1969) and *Columbus Day* (1965) in the same direct and pithy style.

## A. HARRIS STONE

### *The Chemistry of a Lemon*

In a disarmingly simple volume of experiments, *The Chemistry of a Lemon* (1966), A. Harris Stone has presented a series of approaches to some aspects of chemical phenomena, which are brief, open-ended, and thought-provoking, and which teach much about scientific method. The child is encouraged to think beyond the pages of the book.

"Cleaning with lemon juice," for example, begins with two questions: "What does lemon juice do to a dirty copper penny?" and "Are there other liquids that will clean pennies?" A discussion of the process of oxidation is followed by a brief explanation of why the lemon juice acts as it does. Then the section ends, as it began, with a series of six questions leading to six experiments. This is far different from most other chemistry books in print, many of which set up experiments with only one conclusion, and guide the child each step of the way.

After twenty-five of these brief experiments, the author leaves the child with still more ideas to motivate him in a section called "A Last Word."

> *If you've experimented right to this page, you are now an experienced chemist. If you have kept notes on your work, you will be able to check each idea that you worked on. You can design and write about your own experiments, too. Look around! Have you overlooked other elements you can combine with a lemon or some part of a lemon to get a new chemical reaction? Keep trying and see what you can discover.* (p. 58)

A glossary of twenty-one terms is furnished, and a paragraph for each explanation. No index is given, none is needed.

The humorous black and white line drawings by Peter Plasencia complement the casual, off-hand style the author establishes throughout. Stone uses short sentences, short paragraphs, and uncomplicated vocabulary, but never writes down to his readers. Thus, while the book might conceivably be used by junior-high students where experiments are regularly in the science curriculum, the appeal is wide enough so that elementary students can use the book, both at home and in the elementary-science programs.

Stone's other books include *Puttering with Paper* (1968) and *Turned On* (1970). Both are coauthored with Bertram Siegel. *Puttering with Paper*, which is based on discoveries of important scientists from Leonardo da Vinci to Sir Robert Hooke, is certainly more than "puttering." Children are likely to be intrigued by the title, however, and if they

*From the book* The Chemistry of a Lemon *by A. Harris Stone, illustrated by Peter P. Plasencia. © 1966 by A. Harris Stone. Published by Prentice-Hall, Inc., Englewood Cliffs, New Jersey. (Original with color)*

heed the advice in the introduction, they will "be willing to experiment without much knowledge about the problem and to experiment in ways not described in this book." Experiments range from testing the tension and absorption rate of paper to making folded paper airplanes. As in other Stone books, the drawings demonstrate procedures in step-by-step fashion.

Stone was one of the first authors to use the process approach that is now a part of the science curriculum; and his writing is so imbued with an enjoyment of investigation that it stimulates the child's need to know.

### ADRIEN STOUTENBURG

*People in Twilight: Vanishing and Changing Cultures*

Adrien Stoutenburg is one of the most versatile of contemporary writers: poetry for children and adults, biography, retellings of tall tales, fiction, and informational books. Perhaps it is her familiarity with other genres that gives her factual writing a smooth narrative flow; at any rate, her books have an impetus that is most satisfying. Her later books have been concerned with extinct and vanishing wild life, and in *People in Twilight* (1971) she turns to the subject of threatened humanity, a moving description of the struggles of small bands of people all over the world to keep their cultures intact. In many cases, these peoples are threatened by the harsh imposition of another culture, in others by a recent exposure to technology because of war, and in some cases—like the Pygmies in the Congo Basin—by fast becoming a tourist attraction. The treatment is brief, but the author has done an excellent job in documenting the crucial aspects of the problem. Certain cultures are described more fully, complete with historical background, as in the case of the Hawaiians. Some of the passages in this chapter are impressive in their recital of the evils brought by other countries and cultures. This chapter begins with Captain Cook's visit to the islanders (in 1778), who welcomed him at first as the God Lono but became hostile to his party when the natives discovered he was not a supernatural being. Cook's unfortunate end and the culture of the islands at that time are described at length: the religion, dress, housing, surfing, and social conduct. The book includes a colorful map of the world with the cultures under discussion color-coded, which is very useful, as is a list of books for further reading.

In *A Vanishing Thunder: Extinct and Threatened American Birds* (1967) Stoutenburg discusses the disappearance of the passenger pigeon, drawing on John J. Audubon's account of the slaughter of these birds, and ending with the death of the last of the species in 1914. Other extinct or threatened birds described are the ivory-billed woodpecker, the great auk, the California condor, the American egret, and the whooping crane. *Animals at Bay: Rare and Rescued American Wildlife* (1968) also describes creatures threatened with extinction due to man's carelessness, but has a more hopeful tone, since such animals as the sea otter are increasing in number under strict protection.

### ALVIN TRESSELT

*The Beaver Pond*

Alvin Tresselt and his illustrator, Roger Duvoisin, have produced in *The Beaver Pond* (1970) a beautiful picture book which vividly describes the chain of ecological events that result from the damming of a stream. We see the beaver and his coworkers gnawing down aspen trees for food and material for their beaver dam. As the dam grows in the small stream, ducklings and fish join the pond family, and green reeds grow along the shore. As winter approaches, the beavers are shown first underwater, in an electric blue-green setting, then above ground as the shore takes on autumn colors. Winter scenes and breaking ice follow as spring approaches; and as the years pass, the stream brings fine silt into the pond, and the beavers finally move on to newer, deeper water. Without the industrious beavers to dam up the pond, the swiftly running water eats away at the remains of the dam and beaver houses, sweeping all of them away; and the stream reverts to its former leisurely pattern. The calm picture of winter quiet that the artist has painted is echoed in this prose:

*The frost bit deeper and deeper into the ground*
*as a sheet of ice spread over the top of the pond.*
*And the frogs slept deep in the mud at the bottom.*
*The winter snows swept down, filling the hollows*
*and covering the secret runways of field mice.*
*The frozen earth slept under the snow.*
*The pond slept under the ice,*
*and the beavers were safe from the wolf,*
*the prowling lynx, and the wolverine,*
*under the icy roof of the pond and the frozen domes*
*of their houses.*

*The Beaver Pond* is both an explanation of ecological balance and a story of an animal's life cycle, and its text demonstrates the reason for Tresselt's durability as a writer for small children. His prose is direct and unornamented, yet it has a poetic quality, and he sees in natural beauty, in wild life, and in the variations of weather those aspects that are exciting or curious to a child.

His earlier books of nature are still standbys on library shelves and favorites with children. *Sun Up* (1949) is a day on a farm, from the time the rooster crows until nightfall. *Rain Drop Splash*, a Caldecott Honor Book for 1946, is the story, in very large print

*Illustration by Roger Duvoisin for* The Beaver Pond *by Alvin Tresselt. Copyright 1970. Reproduced by permission of Lothrop, Lee & Shepard Co. (Original in color)*

and large pictures, of rain and its travels through a pond, a brook, a lake, and a river down to the sea. This book is illustrated by Leonard Weisgard, but most of Tresselt's work is illustrated by Roger Duvoisin, and the two have made an important team over the years. *White Snow Bright Snow* (1947; Caldecott Award) is the delightful story of a big snowstorm and the troubles of all the people who have to brave the elements, compared with the delight of the children in being snowed in. It is interesting that these early books have always stressed ecology and the interdependence of life and its surroundings. *Hide and Seek Fog* (1965), a poetic description of a weather phenomenon, was a Caldecott Honor Book. *It's Time Now!* (1969) portrays in light and easy tone the drama of the changing seasons as they affect activities in the city. It is an evocative book that should help small children associate the cycle of weather and the passage of time.

### EDWIN TUNIS

*Frontier Living*

The immense amount of detail produced in *Frontier Living* (1961) reflects painstaking research; the text contains little conjecture, but only fact upon fact about all aspects of frontier living. Organized generally in an east-to-west pattern, the book, by the author's admission, concentrates mostly east of the Mississippi because, as he says, "Nearly every phase of the far West has been dealt with . . . while the forest frontier, with a few notable exceptions, has been bypassed since James Fenimore Cooper stopped romancing about it." And so the book progresses from sections dealing with the Piedmont, in which Indians, forts, and medicine and witchcraft are described, on through the old Northwest Territory, passing then out to Kansas, Colorado, and California. "The Old Northwest" has much excellent material on day-to-day living, and the section on housekeeping is an example of both the author's style and the meticulousness of his research.

> *Corn bread by no means disappeared, but the family could now eat wheat bread as well, kneaded with home-cultured yeast, put to rise in a covered dough trough, and baked in the stone oven beside the fireplace. This oven was itself a small fireplace with its own flue leading into the main one. A hot fire was maintained in the oven until the masonry around it was deeply heated; then the fire was raked out with a special hoe, and the flue was plugged. The cook slid the loaves from a flat shovel, called a peel, onto some leaves placed on the oven floor to keep the bottom of the bread from burning. She then closed the oven with a wooden door, sealing the cracks with clay, and left the loaves to bake slowly to thick-crusted excellence. (p. 80)*

The black and white line drawings are of uniform excellence and accuracy, whether of a panoramic view of moving half of a canal boat over a mountain, or detailing the intricate works of a small arsenal of early western arms. The author's captions are revealing, too, and often humorous. Of the illustrations of the Bowie knife, he writes: "The mild and quiet Colonel Bowie didn't design this toadsticker; he gave it his name by way of the mayhem he did with it."

*Frontier Living* was a Newbery Honor Book, and *Colonial Living* (1957), with a similar format, won the Thomas Alva Edison Foundation's Children's Book Award for special excellence in portraying America's past. *Wheels: A Pictorial History* (1955) and *Indians* (1959) are so comprehensive and profusely illustrated with authoritatively detailed drawings that they have reference use. *Shaw's Fortune* (1966), the picture story of a plantation, differs from earlier books in being chronological, following the growth of the plantation from a cabin in the wilderness clearing to a self-sufficient community in 1752. *The Young United States—1783 to 1830* (1969) is topically organized, covering both daily life and historical events. Edwin Tunis' wit had been evident in his other

*The Tea Water pump*

*Illustration by Edwin Tunis reproduced from his book* The Young United States—1783–1830 *by permission of The World Publishing Company. Text and Illustrations Copyright © 1969 by Edwin Tunis.*

books, but with the publication of *Chipmunks on the Doorstep* (1971), his first book in the field of natural science, he added a wry humor to the appeals of perceptive observation and beautiful pictures.

## HARVEY WEISS

*Pencil, Pen and Brush;*
*Drawing for Beginners*

A major criterion for an activity book is that the instructions tell the reader exactly how to perform the activity. Harvey Weiss' arts and crafts books are clear in explaining procedures, and they encourage the reader to use his own initiative.

*Pencil, Pen and Brush* (1961) has a sophisticated approach for a how-to-do-it book. Using the work of major artists, from Leonardo da Vinci to Maurice Sendak, as well as photographs for models, Weiss presents his instructions in easy steps, never talking down to his readers. Practical advice is given for each step, and the reader is given suggestions for striking out on his own; the discussion ends on an encouraging note, with questions and suggestions.

An example of the matter-of-fact procedure used throughout the book is this selection from "Tones":

> *A tone is a shade of black or a shade of color. When you use a tone combined with simple line, your drawing will look more solid and more interesting. Here is a way to make a figure drawing using tones. Get a small sponge, or a piece of sponge. (If you can't find a sponge a crumpled-up facial tissue will do.) Pour two or three drops of ink onto a plate and add about two tablespoons of water. Mix the ink and water. Dip your sponge lightly into the mixture then press the sponge down lightly on a piece of scrap paper and quickly lift it straight up again. You'll see that the sponge leaves a large and pleasantly textured tone of gray.*
>
> *Use the sponge to put the main masses of the figure on paper—a few big dabs for the body, some slimmer dabs (with the narrow part of the sponge) for the arms and legs. Then take your pencil, or pen and ink, and draw in the figure with lines. Try using colored ink, instead of black ink, for your tones. Or use water color, which is a transparent paint.* (p. 24)

At the end of the book the artist has included a section "About the illustrations" identifying each artist included in the book by the title of his work, and giving the museum in which the original art is located.

Other books deal with three-dimensional materials: *Clay, Wood and Wire* (1956) and *Ceramics from Clay to Kiln* (1965). Again, the artist uses pieces of sculpture, artifacts, woven fabrics, a Buckminster Fuller geodesic dome, masks, and Egyptian pottery as his models. *Paper, Ink and Roller* (1958) is on print-making for beginners. Although Weiss has reproduced some artists' prints for this book, he uses many examples of his own prints.

Weiss has also written *Sailing Small Boats* (1967) and *Motors and Engines and How They Work* (1969), an accurate and useful book for the child with a mechanical bent and one that requires no previous knowledge.

### HERBERT ZIM

*Dinosaurs*

Among the many books that Herbert Zim has written in various scientific fields, *Dinosaurs* (1954) is a good example of the logical organization, simple and succinct writing, and provision of background information that make his approach admirably suitable for presenting complex information to a reader unfamiliar with the subject. Zim explains the ways in which fossils are formed and the ways in which scientists are able to determine what dinosaurs looked like, and what they ate, by comparing their skeletal structure with those of known creatures. He describes the evolution of dinosaurs, gives details on how the species differed, and provides brief descriptions of some of the better-known kinds. The meticulously drawn black and white illustrations parallel the text and are always adequately captioned. The book concludes with a discussion of the ways in which dinosaurs changed through the long years of the Age of Reptiles and offers possible reasons for their extinction.

Herbert Zim has taught for over thirty years in the fields of science and science education. With his wife, Sonia Bleeker, he wrote *Life and Death* (1970), which stands alone in the field of children's literature; no one else has attempted a work quite like it. The book discusses life expectancy, aging, the clinical definition of death, and the rituals and legal procedures that are followed after death occurs. It concludes with a brief description of death rituals as they are practiced throughout the world.

Zim's lifelong interest in collecting nature specimens is reflected in *Golden Hamsters* (1951) and *Frogs and Toads* (1950), two of a series of small volumes with large print that have proved most attractive to young children. His books on the human body, *Our Senses and How They Work* (1956), *Your Food and You* (1957), and *Your Heart and How It Works* (1959), are for the slightly older child. He has also contributed to the field of informational books as editor and coauthor of a series of Golden Nature Guides, small pocket-sized volumes in full color. They are widely circulated in outlets other than libraries and are probably the one most handy tool for quick identification of trees, fish, sea-shells, fossils, and flowers.

It is manifestly impossible to include, in the discussion and the bibliography that follow, all the good informational books or indeed books on every subject. The chapter and the reading lists are meant to give the reader a broad picture of the kinds of material that are available to provide children with pleasure and to satisfy their need for information.

Whenever books are classified as in the following discussion, problems arise, because some of them simply refuse to fit neatly into preordained slots. For example, the early concept books for very young children could be in a separate group: books that present ideas of big and small, books that simply introduce familiar objects, books that familiarize a child with colors. There are books that bridge the physical and biological sciences, books that are about religious holidays but are also activity books, books that describe musical instruments and also tell the reader how to make simple instruments. Books on pollution, for instance, involve weather, natural resources, and chemical change; they involve living things; and they illustrate the problems created by man's careless destruction of his environment, problems that have sociological repercussions. Since pollution is a tragedy created by mankind, such books have been placed in the social science list.

The books have been arranged in five broad categories: physical sciences, biological sciences, social sciences, religion and the arts, and activities and experiments. The bibliography at the end of the chapter follows the same pattern.

## VIEWPOINTS

To write about science for children an author needs to know science, to know children, and to know how to write. . . .

. . . It is not enough to say, "Here is an exciting thing. See the way a caterpillar spins a cocoon." The role of the writer is to write the book so that a child can feel he is *participating* in an observation. . . .

Good science books should communicate some of the excitement of discovery—and the triumph that goes with the solution of scientific problems. They should make a young person understand why Archimedes could jump out of his bath to rush through the streets of Syracuse shouting "Eureka" when he discovered a new physical principle.—Millicent E. Selsam, "Writing About Science for Children," *A Critical Approach to Children's Literature*, edited by Sara Innis Fenwick, The University of Chicago Press, Chicago and London, 1967, pp. 96, 98–99.

## THE BIOLOGICAL SCIENCES

Partly because of the nationwide concern for more science in the schools, the list of science books grows phenomenally each year as publishers rush more of them to press. The list has also grown in breadth of subject. No longer are books in the biological sciences confined to those about familiar plants and animals—today they cover almost every topic from a hen's egg to cryogenics and space medicine. Children's books have abandoned, for the most part, the pseudo-scientific stories and watered-down information of the past and have adopted instead a seriousness that children and adults alike can appreciate.

Reports from teachers and librarians show that science rates high in both the types of questions children ask and in the types of books they request. The secret of this success lies, of course, in the writing. Properly presented, almost any area of scientific knowledge can be made both fascinating and comprehensible to children.

The criteria for informational books discussed earlier in this chapter (see pp. 586–590) of course are applicable in evaluating science books. Perhaps of most importance is that the author write from the child's point of view.

Writing from the child's point of view, the author begins within the framework of the child's limited world. He must expand that world *step by step* at a pace which the child can follow—if he leaps, he may leave the child behind. Leading, though, is not enough, for the child will choose to stay behind if the journey becomes uninteresting. What, therefore, is necessary to maintain interest?

Naturally clarity and good organization are of primary importance. Yet no matter how carefully and logically an author develops his material, if it sounds like an article for an encyclopedia, the child will often lose interest. Unfortunately many adults look upon science as a cold collection of facts. To them it is devoid of emotion, entirely unrelated to imaginative writing. To the child, however, science is quite different. For him finding out is full of excitement, fascination, joy, and reassurance. What are the books that not only present information clearly and understandably but maintain the reader's interest?

Some books include both the biological and the physical sciences, like Bertha Parker's *Golden Book of Science* (1956), which is designed to introduce the child to a many-faceted field and to encourage him to pursue the facets in detail.

Books like Sarah Riedman's *Naming Living Things* (1963) discuss seriously the classification of plants and animals. There is a wide spread between the sophistication of this book and the simple approach of *Benny's Animals* by Millicent Selsam, described earlier, but in terms of accuracy each fulfills its purpose.

With the current stress on ecological balance, many books explore both the plants and the animals of a living community. *The Living Community* (1966) by Carl Hirsch is an introduction to interrelationships among plants and animals.

In Margaret Waring Buck's *In Yards and Gardens* (1952) the relationships among living things in an easily accessible environment are made as interesting as are those of the more exotic flora and fauna in *Tropical Rain Forests* (1957) by Delia Goetz.

Lucy Kavaler's *The Wonders of Algae* (1961) is an engrossing report on the versatility of one of the simplest of plant forms and of the experiments that have proved its usefulness to man: as a food, as a life-sustaining system for space ships, or as fuel. Other unusual subjects explored by Kavaler are *Mushrooms, Molds, and Miracles* (1965) and *Wonders of Fungi* (1964). The latter discusses the myriad uses of some of the 100,000 known species of fungi that are disease producers or that are used as food or medicine. For younger readers, a good book about the plant kingdom is *Green Is for Growing* (1964) by Winifred and Cecil Lubell. The illustrations are accurate and beautiful; the rhythmic, flowing text describes the characteristics of each group of plants, and it is pervaded with an awareness of the importance of ecological balance.

Both plants and animals are discussed in Glenn Blough's *Soon After September* (1959), the story of what happens in winter to plants, hibernating animals, and migrating birds. *After the Sun Goes Down* (1956) is a story of animals at night, and *Who Lives in This House* (1957) is about animal families. All of these books are illustrated by Jeanne Bendick and are appealing to younger children; the type face is large and clear, and the language is simple, yet Blough does not talk down to his readers.

Probably the greatest number of books about the animal kingdom are accounts of a single animal. Alice Goudey's stories are authoritative and simply written, giving the life cycle, habits, and habitat in such books as *Here Come the Cottontails* (1965), *Here Come the Lions* (1956), and *Here Come the Dolphins* (1961). Another author whose books are dependably accurate and have a direct and dignified style is Dorothy Shuttlesworth, who writes chiefly about insects, although her works include *The Story of Rodents* (1971). *The Story of Flies* (1970) is well organized, its introduction discussing some of the fly's unpleasant characteristics as well as the usefulness of the fruit fly in the study of genetics. The text covers classification, and describes in detail the house fly, tsetse fly, mosquito, and others, a final chapter describing the "flies" that are not true flies, like the dragonflies and fireflies. The evidence here of thorough research is seen also in Shuttlesworth's similar books on ants and on spiders.

Roy Chapman Andrews' *All About Whales* (1954) has the stamp of personal observation, since Andrews worked with these great mammals. *The Whales Go By* (1959) by Fred Phleger is a simple, easy-to-read picture book about whales. Certainly the most beautifully written book on the subject is Victor Scheffer's *Little Calf*, discussed in Chapter 12.

Of all the books about dinosaurs, Roy Chapman Andrews' *All About Dinosaurs*

(1953) adds another dimension to information, for a large part of the book is devoted to a description of his own experiences in hunting reptile fossils, and he conveys with relish the excitement of locating the first dinosaur eggs found by man in our time. The text covers both the varied species of dinosaurs and the mysterious ending of their long reign. He also wrote, for younger children, *In the Days of the Dinosaurs* (1959). Basic information on the subject is given clearly and briefly in two quite similar books, *Dinosaurs* (1955) by Marie Bloch, and *Discovering Dinosaurs* (1960) by Glenn Blough.

Louis Darling's *Sixty Million Years of Horses* (1960) is an interesting story of the evolution of the modern horse from its ancestor, eohippus; and his *Kangaroos and Other Animals with Pockets* (1958) includes an illuminating passage about the newborn baby and the way it finds its way into the pouch of its mother.

Darling's most impressive book is *The Gull's Way* (1965). Here there is excellent correlation between Darling's text and his pictures. On a remote coastal island, he observed closely the behavior of two herring gulls as they courted, mated, brooded their eggs, and departed when their offspring became independent. Darling's style changed,

*From* The Gull's Way *by Louis Darling. Copyright 1965. Reproduced by permission of William Morrow & Company, Inc.*

in this book, from his competent but conventional description of a bird in *Greenhead* (1954), the study of a mallard duck, to a philosophical, almost tender, outlook on wildlife.

*Bird Watchers and Bird Feeders* (1963) by Glenn Blough discusses migration and banding as well as menus. Written for children in the primary grades, the text with its colorful drawings helps the beginner identify species. *The Bird Watcher's Guide* (1961) by Henry Collins is for older readers, a comprehensive book on all aspects of birdwatching.

A good book for identifying sea shells is Elizabeth Clemons' *Shells Are Where You Find Them* (1960), which gives advice on collecting and on a separate page describes each shell listed. Glenn Blough's *Who Lives at the Seashore* (1962) includes clams, shells, jellyfish, starfish, crabs, barnacles, and seaweed. A charming book to use with very young children is Alice Goudey's *Houses from the Sea* (1959). The slow, easy pace and the delicate illustrations by Adrienne Adams make it a good choice for reading aloud; the fact that two children, wandering along the beach, find fifteen kinds of shells means that there is not too much information for small children to assimilate. The book is prefaced by a note on collecting and closes with a brief account of how shells are formed. *Houses from the Sea* was a Caldecott Honor Book.

In addition to books on animal species, there are excellent ones that explore some special aspect of animal life. Dorothy Shuttlesworth, for example, in *Animal Camouflage* (1966), explains countershading, disruptive coloration, and mimicry. Hilda Simon investigates behavior in *Exploring the World of Social Insects* (1962) and an aspect of morphology in *Feathers; Plain and Fancy* (1969). One of her most outstanding books is *Living Lanterns: Luminescence in Animals* (1971), which includes forms of animal life of land, sea, and air. She discusses both the phenomenon of cold light and the research that has been done, particularly in the artificial creation of luciferin.

All kinds of vertebrate life are considered in Margaret Cosgrove's *Bone for Bone* (1968), a study of comparative anatomy by a medical artist. One of the first drawings in the book, for example, shows skeletons of the mouse and the elephant, divergent outwardly but strikingly alike in their skeletal patterns. Also compared are the similar musculature of a human being and a dog, and the embryos of a turtle, a pig, and a human being. Cosgrove discusses, in graceful prose, the relationships between parts of the body, the graduation from simple to complex vertebrates, and the adaptive process by which each animal fits into a way of life.

Cosgrove's *Eggs—and What Happens Inside Them* (1966) is for a slightly younger audience, and deals with eggs that develop in water or on land, and eggs without shells, concluding with a discussion of the parts of the egg that develop into different parts of the body. A book with remarkable photographs is *Window into an Egg: Seeing Life Begin* (1969) by Geraldine Lux Flanagan. Through a glass window sealed into an eggshell, we see an embryo develop into a chick.

The miracle of reproduction is described in books for every age, from Paul and Kay Showers' *Before You Were a Baby*, discussed earlier in this chapter, to Eric Johnson's *Love and Sex in Plain Language* (1967), which discusses sexual intercourse and sex mores with frankness and dignity. In Marie Hall Ets' *The Story of a Baby* (1939), the text begins after conception has taken place and ends with the baby's first smile. For the child of eight to ten, Sidonie Matsner Gruenberg's *The Wonderful Story of How You Were Born* (1970) is a direct and simple text, illustrated with tender and dignified drawings by Symeon Shimin; and for children just a bit older, Sadie Hofstein's *The Human Story* (1967) adds to its information on reproduction such practical concerns as voice changes in boys, acne, and menstrual hygiene.

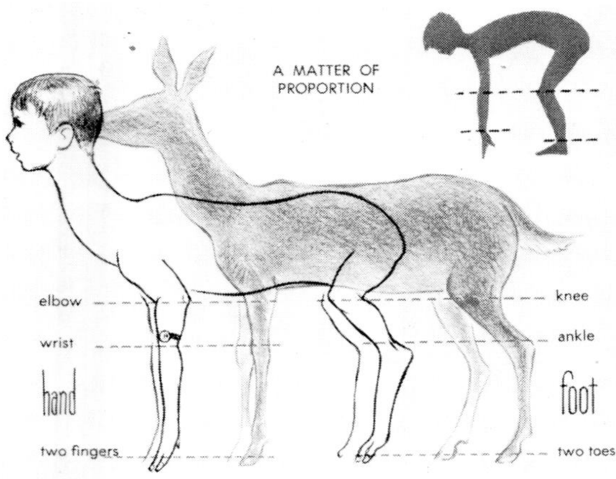


*Illustration by Margaret Cosgrove. Reprinted by permission of Dodd, Mead & Company, Inc. from* Bone for Bone *by Margaret Cosgrove. Copyright © 1970 by Margaret Cosgrove.*

Although the subject of hereditary characteristics is touched on in many books for younger children, the complexity of genetics is fully explored only in books for older readers. Two excellent books that complement each other are Aaron Klein's *Threads of Life* (1970), which surveys the work of scientists whose findings contributed, over the centuries, to the body of knowledge that led to the discovery of DNA; and *The Language of Life* (1966) by George and Muriel Beadle, a comprehensive and authoritative book on genetics that uses only the minimum of necessary scientific terminology.

## THE PHYSICAL SCIENCES

Many of today's children know more about science than do some adults. Parents can sympathize with the mother and father who hadn't the remotest idea of the answer when their fourth-grader asked them whether the ionosphere or the troposphere was nearer the earth. Teachers can report numerous situations similar to the one in which a fifth-grader was able to give his class an impromptu lecture in answer to another child's question on how a rocket works. Where are the children getting this information?

Some of it may come from television programs, but science books for children are certainly one of the most important sources of information. In both the extent of subjects covered and in the vocabulary used, children's science books show that there is a new respect for the reader's intelligence and his interest.

Jeanne Bendick has written two books which aim to encourage children's natural curiosity and enthusiasm for finding out. Her first, entitled *All Around You* (1951), is subtitled "a first look at the world." It encourages the child to observe the many wonders that can be found right at his feet or over his head, and its simple prose conveys the kind of excitement the young child feels upon discovering these things for himself. The second book, *What Could You See?* (1957), begins by inviting the child to imagine what he might see on certain exciting adventures—blazing a trail through an uncharted forest or rushing through space toward the moon. Then in each case the child is led to realize that many of the fascinating things he imagines can be found right in his own backyard.

Alvin Tresselt's picture books about the weather; Isaac Asimov's story about gravity, *The Best New Thing* (1971); books like Illa Podendorf's *Things Are Alike and Different* (1970); and *How Big Is Big? From Stars to Atoms* (1950) by Herman and Nina Schneider all lead the young child to curiosity about the world in which he lives and about why things happen the way they do. When the child begins to ask "how" and "why," then we know that he is ready to explore further in the world of science. It is the primary purpose of all of these books to encourage this desire to know more.

One of the first things a child becomes aware of is the weather. A good first book on the subject is Julian May's *Weather* (1967), which uses technical terminology rather heavily but gives broad coverage. *The First Book of Weather* (1966) by Rose Wyler is for readers in the middle grades and includes simple experiments; and in John Navarra's *Wide World Weather* (1968), older readers can investigate the scientific, social, and governmental aspects of getting and sharing information, and of weather control and weather satellites.

Walter Buehr's *Water: Our Vital Need* (1967) and Fran Harvey's *Why Does It Rain?* (1969) explain the water cycle and the variation in rainfall in different parts of the earth. A good first book about the earth is *Your Changing Earth* (1963) by Hy Ruchlis, which describes the beginnings of the earth and the solar system; the development of land, sea, and air; and the ways in which natural forces change the earth's surface. The same material is covered by Jeanne Bendick in *The Shape of the Earth* (1965), in which the close integration of text and illustrations, and the brisk, authoritative tone of the writing are typical of her style. For older readers, a book that is as enjoyable for its fluency and wit as for the breadth of its treatment is George Gamow's *A Planet Called Earth* (1963), which discusses theories of planetary formation, composition of bodies in the solar system, weather, the living cell, and earth's future. One of the most provocative books about our earth is Alan Anderson's *The Drifting Continents* (1971), which describes the evidence that has led to acceptance of the theory (not new, but long disputed) of continental drift, and the possibilities of new research that may stem from this revolution in geological thinking.

Oceanography is another rapidly expanding frontier; like many other areas of science, it is a subject in which many books bridge the scientific disciplines. Although newer books report some of the more recent knowledge about the sea floor, no book on the subject is more exciting than Rachel Carson's *The Sea Around Us* (1958), which describes the formation of the oceans, tides and currents, marine flora and fauna, and the ocean floor with its volcanic activity. A book that adds immediacy to the information it gives is Peter Briggs' *Science Ship* (1969). Briggs spent three weeks aboard an oceanographic research vessel, *The Discoverer*, and his report gives facts about techniques, equipment, and findings; it also shows how today's scientific investigations demand the skills of scientists from many fields.

Millicent Selsam's *Birth of an Island* (1959) describes, in a text simply written but communicating a sense of wonder, the bare rock that rose from an undersea volcano and became a green and pleasant land. A good first book on volcanoes is Patricia Lauber's *Junior Science Book of Volcanoes* (1965), a simple and accurate explanation of volcanic activity that also describes some of the ways in which it benefits mankind.

Books about the earth and volcanic activity may stimulate a child's interest in the past ages in which the earth as we know it was shaped. *First Days of the World* (1958), by Gerald Ames and Rose Wyler, explains the formation of the solar system, the beginnings of oceans, atmosphere, and living things, and goes on to describe the geological changes through the ages. For older readers, Charlton Ogburn's *The Forging of Our Continent* (1968) is a concise overview of the geology and physiography of North America, with emphasis on the area of the United States.

Men have always been fascinated by the stars, but never before the space age has there been such general interest and such immediate concern with the far reaches of our universe. Two of the best introductions to astronomy for children of ten to twelve are *The New Golden Book of Astronomy* by Rose Wyler and Gerald Ames (1965), which covers the atmosphere, seasons, and phases of the moon, the members of the solar system, gravity and tides, how stellar measurements are made, and man's plans for continuous exploration of space; and Roy Gallant's *Exploring the Universe* (1968), which presents the theories of early astronomers in an easy, informal style. Many of Franklyn Branley's books were discussed earlier in the chapter; no writer in the field of astronomy is more adept at writing simply for young children.

Another clever approach, designed for beginners, can be found in *You, Among the Stars* (1951) by Herman and Nina Schneider. As in other books by these same authors, the emphasis is on orienting the young child. Through the theme of an envelope address, the child moves from his own home outward into space step by step until his familiar street address becomes greatly elaborated.

Finally, there are two books for older children by Irving Adler which are outstanding because of their emphasis on proof. In the words of the author:

> *To see the difference between fact and fancy, we have to follow the thinking of the scientist, and see what proof he has for the things he asks us to believe.*[3]

Both of these books—*The Stars: Steppingstones into Space* (1956) and *The Sun and Its Family* (1958)—offer excellent information about *how* scientists have found out facts about the universe and also *why* they know that these facts are true.

Ask children today what area of science they want to study, and more often than not they will answer "space." In the minds of today's children, studying space often means studying rockets and satellites, not the sun and moon. *Rockets and Satellites* (1970) is one of Franklyn Branley's many books for children in the primary grades, and his *Man in Space to the Moon* (1970), for readers in the middle grades, explains each step in the historic flight of Apollo 11. John Wilford's *We Reach the Moon* (1969) is based on the original adult book and gives the step-by-step development of the NASA program, concluding with some results of the scientific experiments carried out by the astronauts.

To understand the mechanics of the space program, so much of which is based on intricate mathematics, readers must be aware of the mathematical computations on which

3. Irving Adler, *The Stars: Steppingstones into Space* (Day, 1956), p. 14.

scientists rely. Irving Adler explores advanced math in *The New Mathematics* (1958) and fundamental concepts in *The Giant Golden Book of Mathematics* (1960). Lancelot Hogben's *The Wonderful World of Mathematics* (1968) relates the growth of mathematics as a science to the changing needs of mankind. With the modern curriculum, in which children are learning new concepts at earlier stages, there have been many books published that use the process approach or deal with one aspect of mathematical concepts. Rolf Myller's *How Big Is a Foot?* (1962) is a fictionalized picture book, but it lucidly presents the reasons why standards of measurement are needed. An excellent series, the Crowell "Young Math Books," examines one aspect in each volume. Typical of the series is *Long, Short, High, Low, Thin, Wide* (1971) by James Fey, which discusses measurement and encourages the reader to observe and compare; all of these books teach something about scientific methods as well as the immediate subject with which they are concerned. Jeanne Bendick's *Take Shapes, Lines, and Letters* (1962), written in conjunction with Marcia Levin, deals with ideas and relationships rather than with numbers, and the basic principles of computer mathematics are explained in *The New World of Computers* (1965) by Alfred Lewis.

When we come to physics and chemistry we are entering realms of science which have increasingly enabled man to reorder natural existence to suit his particular desires or needs. While we want our children to appreciate fully these achievements of applied science, they must also be helped to recognize its limitations if they are to gain a realistic picture of the world in which they live. In this nuclear age, it is perhaps more apparent than ever before that science can bring great good *or* harm, depending on how man puts it to use.

The science of chemistry can be traced back to early man. Roy A. Gallant's *Exploring Chemistry* (1958), for example, begins with the discovery of fire and thereafter tells the absorbing history of man's efforts to understand and change matter. Ira M. Freeman elaborates upon this story for older children in *All About the Wonders of Chemistry* (1954), describing at greater length such things as molecular structure, the elements, chemical change, and the many ways in which chemistry has contributed to medicine, farming, and industry, for the benefit of modern life. Older children will also enjoy a book entitled *Elements of the Universe* (1958), by Glenn T. Seaborg and Evans G. Valens, which contains dramatic accounts of some of chemistry's greatest discoveries, written by men who have directly participated in the thrill of such achievements. Ira Freeman and A. Rae Patton, in *The Science of Chemistry* (1968), give basic facts about the ways in which atoms and molecules function chemically, and formulas are introduced only in relation to relevant theory. Isaac Asimov, in *Building Blocks of the Universe* (1961), makes clear, in his usual witty and informal style, the chemical elements that are the foundation of all matter.

In the purest sense, chemistry is the study of matter only—its composition, its nature, and the changes it constantly undergoes—while physics is the study of matter and energy and the relationship between them. Even at the elementary-school level, more and more books are appearing that cross boundary lines and reveal the strong interrelationship between these sciences. For example, there are now several books which borrow learnings from chemistry regarding atoms and molecular structure and then go on to apply these learnings to the recent developments in physics regarding atomic energy and its many uses.

An excellent example for younger children is John Lewellen's *The Mighty Atom* (1955), which very simply, with the aid of familiar analogies and Ida Scheib's clever illustrations, moves from a discussion of the atom with its neutrons, protons, and electrons, to molecular structure and the basic elements, and finally to atomic power, the construction and operation of atomic furnaces and engines, and the uses of atomic energy in both war and peace. Margaret Hyde's *Atoms Today and Tomorrow* (4th ed., 1970), written with Bruce Hyde, describes the production and uses of atomic energy, and David Woodbury's *The New World of the Atom* (1965) stresses the uses of atomic energy in medicine, in carbon-14 testing, and in nuclear power plants for space exploration.

Mechanics, an area of great interest to children, paves the way for a study of transportation, and is one of the areas in which children can observe and experiment from the first time they are fascinated by the moving parts in their toys. An interesting book for young children is *The True Book of Toys at Work* (1953), in which John Lewellen describes the mechanical principles involved in such things as whistles, electric trains, and balloons. Hy Ruchlis' *Orbit: A Picture Story of Force and Motion* (1958) successfully explains Newton's law of universal gravitation plus his three laws of motion in terms that can be understood by most children above the fourth grade. Action-packed photographs of such things as "flying" cars, acrobatic stunts, and daredevil sports, plus excellent diagrams by Alice Hirsch, help to illustrate these scientific laws, all of which contribute a great deal toward an adequate understanding of transportation vehicles and particularly of space flight.

Naturally the machines which man has built on the principles of mechanics would have limited use indeed without the harnessing of some type of energy other than man power to run them. One of the most comprehensive books on this subject, excitingly illustrated in color by John Teppich, is Lancelot Hogben's *Wonderful World of Energy* (1957). This book constantly reminds the child that, of all the many sources of energy, the greatest is the one which has mastered the others—man's own will and drive to go forward. We learn how man has gradually harnessed and put to work energy from wind, water, steam, fire, electricity, and now the atom and the sun. This last source of energy, vast and unlimited, still requires a great deal of study. Its history, present status, and future possibilities have been extensively discussed by Franklyn M. Branley in a book entitled *Solar Energy* (1957).

Of all the forms of energy, however, the one with which the child has had the most direct experience is usually electricity. This is not an easy subject for children, and yet it plays such an important role in their everyday lives that we should help them gain at least an appreciation of its great value and some understanding of how it operates. One of the clearest and simplest explanations of this complex subject can be found in *The First Book of Electricity* (1953) by Sam and Beryl Epstein. Since this book is designed for the beginner with no previous knowledge of electricity, new concepts have been fully explained. In addition, there are pages of easy-to-follow instructions for experiments. For older children who already have a basic knowledge of this subject, the greater complexities of electricity are explained in Ira M. Freeman's *All About Electricity* (1957), which introduces a good deal of the history of the development of electrical power and contains whole chapters on various uses of electricity, such as the telephone, radio, motion pictures, and television.

Actually, the science concerned with the communications devices just mentioned is now called electronics. John Lewellen's *Understanding Electronics* (1957) and Jeanne Bendick's *Electronics for Young People* (1960) are lucid and detailed books for children of twelve and older.

Many of the topics we have mentioned are included in *Understanding Science* (1956) by William Crouse. It is a panoramic view in which no subject is treated in depth, but it gives the reader a broad picture of the worlds of pure and applied science. For such background, books like Corinne Jacker's *Window on the Unknown: A History of the Microscope* (1966) and Irving Adler's *The*

*Tools of Science: From Yardstick to Cyclotron* (1958) are invaluable.

## THE SOCIAL SCIENCES

Under the rubric of the social sciences are those subjects that have to do with men in their association with other groups of men: history, political science, anthropology, economics, geography, law, and many others, often—as is true of other sciences—overlapping each other or other disciplines. With so broad a scope, this chapter can only mention some of the good books in areas so extensive yet so finely divided.

Since an understanding of many of these areas is partially dependent on seeing a relationship between past and present, perhaps the best background book for a young child is one that clarifies time concepts. Two such are *The True Book of Time* (1956) by Feenie Ziner and Elizabeth Thompson, which teaches children that there are other ways, in addition to clocks, for measuring time, and Miriam Schlein's *It's About Time* (1955), which helps clarify the puzzling relationships implied in "long time, short time."

Often small children are fascinated by dinosaurs before they understand the earth's time scale, and books about dinosaurs can be used to introduce the beginnings of man's prehistory. Julian May's *The First Men* (1968), for the early grades, may be followed in the middle grades by *The First People in the World* (1958) by Gerald Ames and Rose Wyler. For older readers, Eleanor Clymer's *The Case of the Missing Link* (1968), which describes the search for man's ancestors and the theories held about them, gives a good account of the way scientists carefully evaluate evidence.

Two reliable books about prehistoric man in North America are William Scheele's *The Earliest Americans* (1963), which investigates the puzzle of when men first migrated to this continent, and Anne Terry White's *Prehistoric America* (1951), which describes modern discoveries that have led to a better understanding of prehistoric times. Scheele's *The Mound Builders* (1960) is an imaginative reconstruction of what may have happened when a new burial site was created at Hopewell, Ohio.

To understand how information about prehistory and early civilizations is acquired, children may turn to a book about archeology as a science. Anne Terry White's *All About Archeology* (1959) or Leonard Cottrell's *Digs and Diggers: A Book of World Archeology* (1964) give information about the development of the science, its methodology, and some of the great discoveries of the past. Dora Hamblin's *Pots and Robbers* (1970) tells some true stories about the dramatic aspects of archeology, many incidents involving thefts and forgeries.

There is a wealth of material on ancient civilizations, for many facets of which the art books by Shirley Glubok are good supplementary reading. Victor von Hagen's *Maya, Land of the Turkey and the Deer* (1960) is based on scholarly documents and vividly evokes the people and the period. Hans Baumann's *In the Land of Ur* (1969) is written with a sense of excitement, and Franklyn Branley's *The Mystery of Stonehenge* (1969) explores various theories about why and how the stones were erected. *Classical Greece* (1965) by C. Maurice Bowra, a volume in the "Great Ages of Man" series published by Time-Life, is comprehensive and beautifully illustrated.

Many of the Columbian biographies include conjecture about the first "discoverers" of America, with honors usually divided between Columbus and the Vikings. Ellen Pugh, in *Brave His Soul* (1970), presents convincing evidence for the theory that a Welsh prince exiled himself and came to North America in 1170. A stunning book that uses source material and binds the excerpts smoothly with the compiler's comments is *The New Land* (1967) by Phillip Viereck.

There is a gratifying abundance of books in world history. One book that exemplifies a fine series about major cultures of the world, published by World, is Thomas Chubb's *The Byzantines* (1959). The learning, the technological skills, and the pride of a prosperous civilization are made excitingly real by the vivid writing. Each volume in the series has a chronological chart that correlates other world events. Isaac Asimov makes a long and complicated historical chronicle clear and meaningful in *The Dark Ages* (1968), which covers the period from the year 1000 to the last of the Carolingians and the advent of the medieval knight. Alfred Duggan, who was one of the great historical writers of our time, described *Growing Up in 13th Century England* (1962) with authoritative knowledge and sophisticated wit; by portraying five households at different social levels, he was able to show minute details of daily living as well as social customs, recreation, and education.

Often books that are not written as history can illuminate a period. One such book is *The Bayeux Tapestry* (1966) by Norman Denny and Josephine Filmer-Sankey, which describes the Norman Conquest as it is told in the tapestry; another is Grant Uden's *A Dictionary of Chivalry* (1968), which won the Greenaway Award for Pauline Baynes' exquisite illustrations and was a runner-up for the Carnegie Award, a book as useful as it is handsome.

The editors of *American Heritage* have written *Discoverers of the New World* (1960), one of a series about American history. From the account of the geographers of the fifteenth century, who believed there was only a scattering of islands in the ocean from Spain to China, to the true story of Sir Francis Drake, who docked in Plymouth, England, in 1580 to tell of his world adventure to the delighted Queen Elizabeth I, this book holds the reader's interest.

Other books which give children a factual account of the early history of America, its discovery and settlement, include Alice Dalgliesh's *America Begins* (1958) and Louise Rich's *The First Book of New World Explorers* (1960). And for a record of our country's history from 1492 to the present, we have *The First Book of American History* (1957) by the noted historian Henry Steele Commager.

Enid Meadowcroft's *The Land of the Free* (1961) reflects the careful study, shown in her bibliography, which preceded the writing of the book. It is a brief history, but it weaves together the straws of events that form America's history from 1492 to the end of the Second World War. Reading like fiction, *The Land of the Free* points out America's failures as well as her triumphs and so places our country's character in true perspective.

The American Revolution and the Declaration of Independence are events of special significance for our youngsters. Fortunately, we have a number of good books to offer them about this period of revolution and confederation. *The First Book of the American Revolution* (1956) by Richard B. Morris will help younger readers understand what these events meant then and what they mean today. Both books are effectively illustrated in color. At the junior-high level *The Golden Book of the American Revolution* (1959), adapted by Fred Cook from the *American Heritage Book of the Revolution*, provides an excellent summary of events leading to the war and covers the tactics of battles on land and sea, the development of our armed forces, the contributions of our allies, and the final victory. Prominent men of the newly formed government are well drawn in *The Great Declaration* (1958) by Henry Steele Commager. The author uses excerpts from official documents, letters, and diaries in weaving together the story of the Declaration of Independence. An unusual viewpoint is given by Clorinda Clarke in *The American Revolution 1775–83; A British View* (1967), a book that has a judicious, long-range outlook and a lively style.

For the very young child interested in American pioneers, Mabel Harmer's *The True Book of Pioneers* (1957) is brief but does an admirable job of covering the subject. William O. Steele's *Westward Adventure* (1962) comprises the true stories of six pioneers and is based on material in diaries and journals. Also well-researched, Robert West Howard's *The Wagonmen* (1964) is profusely illustrated with photographs of vehicles from the Smithsonian Institution and other sources.

Charles Flato's *The Golden Book of the Civil War* (1961) is adapted from an American Heritage picture history. Profusely illustrated, it gives a broad and vivid picture of the war years. G. Allen Foster's *Sunday in Centerville* (1971) is as interesting for the discussion of the complex causes of the war, and the preparations for it, as it is for the detailed account of the first Battle of Bull Run.

Daniel J. Boorstin's *The Landmark History of the American People* (2 vols., 1968, 1970) deviates from the usual compilation of facts and dates to discuss the people who influenced patterns of change, and its emphasis is on movements and on regional and national patterns. The approach is stimulating, the style informal, and the analyses acutely perceptive, as might be expected from an eminent historian.

Of the many books on black history, three of the best are Robert Goldston's *The Negro Revolution* (1968), Dorothy Sterling's *Tear Down the Walls!* (1968), and Johanna Johnston's *Together in America* (1965), all comprehensive and as objective as is consistent with a history of slavery and oppression. Unfortunately, no comparable body of material exists for other minority groups in the United States. The American Indian, for example, is represented by very few books, and most of those are concerned with a tribe, an Indian leader, or an event. Ann Nolan Clark's *Circle of Seasons* (1970) is a dignified and reverent description of the rites and observances of the Pueblo year. *Red Hawk's Account of Custer's Last Battle* (1970), by Paul and Dorothy Goble, is historically accurate and is told dramatically from the viewpoint of a boy who realizes, after the battle at Little Big Horn, that the Indian victory was definitive, the Indian's fight against white invasion hopeless. There is, of course, a wealth of material in Sonia Bleeker's books or in a compendium of information like *Indians* (1959) by Edwin Tunis. Probably the two best books available are *The American Indian* (1960) by Oliver La Farge, which has both historical and contemporary material, and May McNeer's *The American Indian Story* (1963), which is more an introduction than a survey, but is distinguished in illustration.

Several books provide information about Canada. Regina Tor, in *Getting to Know Canada*, describes the people of the various provinces, their government, customs, and industries. Lithographs by Lynd Ward help to make May McNeer's *Canadian Story* an exciting account of the history of Canada from the time of the Vikings to the opening of the St. Lawrence Seaway.

Among the books that, in addition to those by Sonia and Tim Gidal, give information about countries in other parts of the world are *The First Book of South America* (1961) by William Carter, which gives an account of the folklore, religions, and history of the continent; John Gunther's books about Africa; the Lippincott series on "Land and People of . . ."; Armstrong Sperry's *All About the Arctic and Antarctic* (1957); and Lois Hobart's *Mexican Mural* (1963). In fact, there are so many that a representative list would be impossible in one chapter on informational books.

Because of the spread of urbanization, the interest in cities is greater today than it has ever been, both from the standpoint of allure and, alas, from the standpoint of the complex problems in urban life. None is more urgent than pollution. In *Dangerous Air* (1967), Lucy Kavaler cites the causes of air pollution throughout the world and discusses what government, industry, and individual citizens must do to eliminate this danger. John Navarra considers the same problem in *The World You Inherit: A Story of Pollution* (1970) and adds, in a cogent chapter, the legislation and litigation that are involved; in *Our Noisy World* (1969), he discusses the problem of noise pollution.

*Illustration from* This Is New York, *written and illustrated by Miroslav Sasek. Copyright 1960. Reproduced by permission of The Macmillan Company, and W. H. Allen and Co., Ltd., London. (Original in color)*

No author has made cities more enticing than Miroslav Sasek. Despite the crime and grime, New York is beautiful in *This Is New York* (1960), with gay, colorful pictures and a lively, humorous text describing the grandeur of a bridge span, the bustle of the garment district, the biggest traffic jams in the world. Of his other books in the series, two of the most attractive are *This Is Edinburgh* (1961) and *This Is Greece* (1966). A sharply different picture emerges in John Holland's *The Way It Is* (1969), a series of photographs, with captions, taken by black and Puerto Rican schoolboys in their home neighborhood.

Alvin Schwartz, in *Old Cities and New Towns* (1968), shows Philadelphia as it is, and as it might be if present plans for its renovation and renewal were followed. In a book for young children, *Let's Look Under the City* (1954), Herman and Nina Schneider show the maze of service facilities but emphasize the interdependency of people in making services universally available.

Children are indefatigably curious about the way other people live and where they live—and why they live there if it's hot (or cold, or rainy, or mountainous . . .). They are curious about differences, open-minded rather than insular. Books can help foster their awareness of the superficiality of differences and the similarity of people everywhere. *Why We Live Where We Live* (1953) by Eva Knox Evans helps them understand the interdependence of people and the geographic limitations upon the choice of homes.

Many of the recent books for children have been written with the objective of making the story of man's past and present a "real experience" rather than a superficial one. A stimulating volume to which older children can be guided is *People and Places* (1959) by Margaret Mead. The book is richly informative, springing out of her expert knowledge of people and countries. She begins her first chapter, "Man's Discovery of Man," by stating that human beings are curious about each other and that even the most primitive peoples in the world today wonder about those unlike themselves, and she concludes with discussions about "Man Asks About Man," in which she talks about similarities and differences among peoples of the world. She also offers suggestions as to what steps must be taken to solve man's problems so that all may live in a more orderly world. All in all, Margaret Mead's book challenges its readers to a deeper understanding not only of themselves but also of other people and places.

## RELIGION AND THE ARTS

Books of religious instruction and prayers are used by devout families in the home, and biographies of religious leaders or stories that present religious diversity can help children understand and respect the beliefs or the non-belief of others. Books on comparative religion, however, belong in any collection to which children turn for information.

Ruth Smith's *The Tree of Life* (1942) is an anthology consisting of selections from the world's great religions, and is an excellent companion volume to Katharine Savage's *The Story of World Religion*, discussed earlier in this chapter. *Religions Around the World* (1967) by Leonard and Carolyn Wolcott is not as detailed as the Savage book, nor is the scope as great, but it discusses people and beliefs that are not included in the other. The *Life* volume, *The World's Great Religions* (1958), a special edition for young readers, limits its coverage to six major religions, with half the volume devoted to Christianity.

The series of books about religious denominations by Kathleen Elgin, of which *The Unitarians* (1971) is an example, describes the history and the beliefs of the denomination, lists some of its famous members of past and present, and gives at length a biography of a leader or prominent member. In *The Vatican* (1970), the managing editor of *Commonweal*, John Deedy, describes the Vatican community's members and its art and history. Roland Gittelsohn, a rabbi, discusses the origins of Jewish tradition and observances in *The Meaning of Judaism* (1970), and describes the differences among the three groups within that faith.

Books that encourage the child's interest in music range from such narrow treatments as Larry Kettelkamp's *Flutes, Whistles and Reeds* (1962), which introduces woodwinds and explains how they produce sounds, to the comprehensive treatment in *The Wonderful World of Music* (1958) by Benjamin Britten and Imogen Holst, a history of music, musicians, and instruments that is mature in concept. Much of the book can be appreciated by the reader with no musical background, but the discussions of theory and harmony may present difficulties for the general reader. A similar book is *The Heritage of Music* (1963) by Katherine Shippen and Anca Seidlova, which describes musical forms and instruments, and is enlivened by anecdotes about musicians.

There is comparatively little material available about the music of other countries. Betty Warner Dietz and Michael Babatunde Olatunji have written an outstanding book about the way music is used in African cultures south of the Sahara in *Musical Instruments of Africa* (1965); and in *Folk Songs of China, Japan, and Korea* (1964) Dietz collaborated with Thomas Choonbai Park. These books have been compiled with scholarly care, and can help children understand other cultures through their music.

Langston Hughes wrote several books about music: *The First Book of Rhythms* (1954), *Famous Negro Music Makers* (1955), and *The First Book of Jazz* (1955). The latter presents a concise history of the development of jazz in the United States and of its spread to other countries. Hughes discusses the diverse elements that contributed to the complex rhythms of jazz: African, French, and Spanish elements in New Orleans; worksongs and blues; spirituals, ragtime, and minstrel music. Although not written as an informational book, Nat Hentoff's *Jazz Country* (1965) conveys the essence of the jazz world. (See Chapter 13 discussion.) Another book that gives a history of a popular type of music is Arnold Shaw's *The Rock Revolution* (1969), which includes discussions of performers and comments of critics. In *Golden Guitars* (1971), Irwin Stambler and Grelun Landon tell the story of Country and Western music.

Books about opera, or libretti of individual operas, and books that describe the composition and arrangement of orchestras are listed in the bibliography, as are some of the many song books published for children. There is also a considerable amount of information about music and musicians in the biographies cited in Chapter 15.

A book that bridges the worlds of music and of the dance is *American Indians Sing* (1967) by Charles Hofmann, in which the information about music, dances, and song-poems includes melodic and dance notation. Perhaps the most comprehensive book on the dance is Arnold Haskell's *The Wonderful World of Dance* (1969). In an impressively authoritative volume, Haskell describes the evolution of the dance and dance forms, with biographical material about famous dancers and choreographers, and with many diagrams of dance notation. There is an especially good section on ritual dances of the Orient; and, throughout the book, dance forms are related to the cultural context in which they evolved. Narrower in scope, *Ballet: A Pictorial History* (1970) by Walter Terry is a good introduction for the reader who is not a balletomane, but it has enough material about outstanding dancers of each historical period to appeal to the lover of ballet.

Olga Maynard's *American Modern Dancers: The Pioneers* (1965) is an excellent survey of the evolution of modern dance through discussions of the work of great dancers, giving authoritative analyses of techniques, theories, trends, influences, and comparative schools. Maynard gives, in *The Ballet Companion* (1957), a detailed guide to four ballets, and a glossary of ballet terms and techniques.

Undoubtedly because dancing is a performing art there is comparatively little about it. When we turn to books about art, however, there is a positive cornucopia of fine books. One of the best general surveys is Janet Moore's *The Many Ways of Seeing* (1968), which discusses the relationship between art and nature, and the relationship between the artist and the world in which he lives. It analyzes the ways an artist perceives in terms of light, color, composition, and line; it also describes media, materials, and techniques, and suggests ways in which the reader can try some of the ideas discussed and learn to see the elements of an art form. A similar book, with examples ranging from ancient treasures to contemporary works, is *Looking at Sculpture* (1968) by Roberta Paine.

Marion Downer's *The Story of Design* (1964) uses a variety of art objects, shown in photographs, to illustrate the appreciation of design the world over, from primitive times to today. In *Looking at Art* (1966) Alice Elizabeth Chase, an art historian, describes the ways in which artists have interpreted their worlds, and the author's explicit and clearly presented views on what art is make the book an excellent choice for the reader who is on unfamiliar terrain.

*The Pantheon Story of Art for Young People* (1964) by Ariane Ruskin is competently written but slights contemporary work; it has, however, an unusually large number of full-page, full-color illustrations. Ruskin's books in the McGraw art series have more depth. Some of the series are by Ariane Ruskin, some by Michael Batterberry, some written jointly by the two. Ruskin's *Art of the High Renaissance* (1970), for example, emphasizes painters and painting, but the comprehensive text covers all art forms. All of the books in this series are profusely and handsomely illustrated.

There are few art books written for adults that cannot be enjoyed by children, if the books are illustrated. The Time-Life Library of Art has magnificently illustrated volumes, each devoted to a single artist. The biographies by Elizabeth Ripley could almost as well be in this chapter as in Chapter 15. Books on color for the preschool and primary child can encourage aesthetic appreciation as well as teach colors, and some of the first concept books, like Tana Hoban's *Shapes and Things* (1970), can stimulate an awareness of form as well as encourage observation. In other words, information about art can come from many sources other than books about art.

Friedrich von Schlegel called architecture "frozen music," and in Mary Louise King's *A History of Western Architecture* (1967), the illustrations show the patterned precision of Greek temples and the soaring lift of Gothic cathedrals that make this phrase so apt. King emphasizes the new developments of each period, and discusses the factors that influence style. A simpler book that gives architectural history more succinctly is *Understanding Architecture* (1971) by George Sullivan, which explains styles and construction techniques from the rudimentary post-and-lintel buildings to today's skyscrapers and the plans for ecologically oriented homes of tomorrow.

Anne Rockwell's *Glass, Stones and Crown: The Abbe Suger and the Building of St. Denis* (1968) is as interesting for its historical background as it is for the story of Suger, the boyhood friend of Louis Capet, whose life as abbot was devoted to rebuilding St. Denis and incorporating those features that became popular throughout Europe: stained glass windows, flying buttresses and piers, and ribbed vaulting.

The construction of a modern building is described in Ely Jacques Kahn's *A Building Goes Up* (1969), in which the erection of an office building is detailed from planning to completion.

## ACTIVITIES AND EXPERIMENTS

One of the most popular kinds of activity books is the puzzle book. Martin Gardner's *Perplexing Puzzles and Tantalizing Teasers* (1969) contains riddles, scrambled words, mazes, and puzzles that require logic for solution. It has enough difficult puzzles to tempt the quick child but not so many as to discourage the one who is slow. More difficult is *Math Menagerie* (1970) by Robert Kadesch, in which the material is grouped under such headings as probability, binary numerals, and soap-film mathematics. Another kind of brain-teaser is *The First Book of Codes and Ciphers* (1956) by Sam and Beryl Epstein, which describes codes used in history, explains how to concoct or decipher messages, and explains the difference between codes and ciphers. *Egyptian Hieroglyphs for Everyone* (1968), by Joseph and Lenore Scott, gives an explanation of how the language developed and makes it easier for the reader to understand hieroglyphic writing.

At the other end of the spectrum are the books that give instruction for physical activities, usually sports. One such is S. H. Freeman's *Basic Baseball Strategy* (1965), which is packed with so much information that it can be used by players older than the middle-grades audience to whom it is addressed, or by coaches for the lucid explanations of such fine arts as base stealing, the squeeze play, and when to use the hit-and-run. In Jim Moore's *Football Techniques Illustrated* (1962), there are discussions of offensive and defensive play, advice on running, kicking, passing, and tackling, and the rules of play. Other how-to-do-it sports books can easily be found listed under the names of the sports in such guides as *Children's Catalog*.

A useful group of activity books are those in the fields of arts and crafts: *Papier-Maché* (1958) by Lillian Johnson gives techniques for making three-dimensional objects; in *Collage* (1968), Mickey Klar Marks gives instructions for seven different kinds of collage; *The Complete Crayon Book* (1969) by Chester Jay Alkema suggests a variety of projects, from simple to complex, and gives an excellent discussion of media and techniques. Among the many books on puppetry, two of the best are Eleanor Boylan's *How to Be a Puppeteer* (1970), which gives directions for making and costuming puppets, manipulating them, making sets and scenery, etc., and *Hand Puppets; How to Make and Use Them* (1969) by Laura Ross, which has clear instructions and gives suggestions for writing a puppet play.

There are general craft books like Susan Purdy's *Festivals for You to Celebrate* (1969), in which the projects are grouped by seasons and suggestions are given for group activities. Camille Sokol's *The Lucky Sew-It-Yourself Book* (1966) is a hand-sewing book with very simple projects for the seven- to nine-year-old. An example of the specialized book is Jan Beaney's *The Young Embroiderer* (1967), with imaginative suggestions that can stimulate original work. Older children can use almost any cookbook, but *Kids Cooking* (1970), by Aileen Paul and Arthur Hawkins, makes cooking easy by listing ingredients and implements on one page, and giving the instructions on the facing page.

Film-making has become tremendously popular, and Robert Ferguson's *How To Make Movies* (1969) gives detailed and practical advice on every aspect of the art. Yvonne Andersen gives both the techniques of preparation and the intricacies of filming in *Make Your Own Animated Movies* (1970).

One of the most sensible books on pets is Dorothy Broderick's *Training a Companion Dog* (1965), which is explicit and detailed and gives advice on equipment. Harriet Howard's *If You Had a Pony* (1965) uses photographs to teach the care and training of a pony and to give some information on riding. In *Look What I Found!* (1971), Marshal Case explains how to capture small wild creatures, with suggestions for duplicating the animal's natural habitat and an emphasis on showing kindness and respect for all life forms.

In addition to the books that describe specific activities and crafts, there is the comprehensive "doing" book, which presents information about a variety of scientific topics through suggested experiments and activities.

The experiment book has a definite value in that it guides the child toward direct participation in the discovery of knowledge, and, since so many experiences must be gained vicariously, first-hand discovery should be encouraged whenever possible. But experiment books also have a more subtle value. We realize today that education must do more than impart knowledge—it must also teach the child how to *use* that knowledge in the solution of problems. Glenn Blough once stated:

> *If pupils are to grow in ability to solve problems they must grow in ability to think of appropriate things to do to discover solutions.*[4]

Teaching the child how to set up sound experiments and how to interpret the results of these experiments is one way of training him to "think of appropriate things to do."

Good experiment books, for obvious reasons, will suggest only those activities which are safe and those which can be performed with readily available and inexpensive materials, and there are such books today for every age level.

*Prove It!* (1963), by Rose Wyler and Gerald Ames, is for the beginning reader and presents simple experiments performed with ordinary objects. Franklyn Branley's *Timmy and the Tin-Can Telephone* is written as a story in which two children learn about the transmission of sound by making a "telephone" out of tin cans, string, and buttons. Harry Milgrom's *Adventures with a Paper Cup* (1968) has an assortment of easy experiments in which a cone-shaped cup is used to demonstrate such phenomena as air resistance and sound amplification. This and similar books by Milgrom, or Nancy Larrick's *See for Yourself* (1952), which has simple experiments with air, water, and heat, can stir or encourage an interest in scientific exploration and discovery in young children.

One of the most varied books of experiments, containing material in many of the sciences, is *700 Science Experiments for Everyone*, compiled by UNESCO in 1956. William Moore's *Your Science Fair Project* (1964) has projects grouped by levels from grades three to eight, and is particularly useful for the average student who is required to participate. Alfred Morgan's *Boys' Book of Science and Construction* (1959) has more advanced experiments, and also includes instructions for making such things as steam turbines, pinhole cameras, and weather vanes.

Elizabeth Cooper's *Science in Your Own Back Yard* (1958) suggests ways of observing, collecting, and experimenting in the field of nature study, in a book that can stimulate the individual reader or be used by a group. There is an emphasis on conservation in Ted Pettit's *A Guide to Nature Projects* (1966).

4. Glenn O. Blough, "Quality Is What Counts!" *Instructor*, September 1958, p. 6.

Each section of the book deals with a single aspect of the subject and gives background information before discussing experiments.

For the child who has a specific interest, there are such books as Harry Sootin's *Experiments with Magnetism* (1968) or his mineralogy book, *The Young Experimenter's Workbook* (1965), written in collaboration with Laura Sootin. Both books require only materials that are available in the home or are inexpensive, and the experiments are practical and clearly explained. Rocco Feravolo's *Easy Physics Projects: Air, Water and Heat* (1966) and A. Harris Stone's books are for children of the same age, but they are quite different in approach. Rather than using the open-ended process approach of the Stone experiment books, Feravolo answers the questions raised; little is left to the student's imagination, but the concepts are lucidly presented and the book can be useful to children hesitant about taking initiative.

## REFERENCE BOOKS

Although encyclopedias and dictionaries, fact books and almanacs, and indexes and bibliographies are the kinds of books usually meant when reference books are referred to, it should be remembered that many other kinds of books have reference use.

Children's rooms in public libraries often have books that reflect the particular interests of their community, such as foreign language source books, reference materials that give information about local industries, or books about indigenous flora and fauna. School library collections may stress books that fit into curricular units. Both will gather as much as they can about local history, and both will include in their collections some books intended for adult reference use.

There are so many dictionaries and encyclopedias that are valuable, that guides to them are reference books in themselves. Most professional journals include reviews of reference books; *Booklist* and *Wilson Library Bulletin* have special sections devoted to them. Carolyn Sue Peterson's *Reference Books for Elementary and Junior High School Libraries* is a useful annotated bibliography that suggests in its introduction methods of evaluation, most of which require examination of the volumes being considered. Another good source is *General Encyclopedias in Print*. Almost every dictionary and encyclopedia has a coterie of devoted users who feel that their favorites are the best. Each differs, and libraries that can afford to buy all the reference books which meet critical standards usually do so.

In assembling a home reference library, parents would do well to examine the different reference books they are considering. If it is possible, a home collection should include one of the major children's encyclopedias; a reliable dictionary like *Webster's Seventh New Collegiate Dictionary*, the *Harcourt Brace Intermediate Dictionary*, or one or more of the four graded Thorndike-Barnhart dictionaries; and an atlas such as the *Rand McNally World Atlas*, *Goode's World Atlas*, or *Aldine University Atlas*. Parents of children with limited vision may want the *Large-Type Hammond-Jennison World Atlas*, which is also a good first atlas for young children because of its clear maps.

Most adults feel that children should have their own dictionaries, but they are not so sure that children need their own encyclopedias. In homes where books must be carefully budgeted, many families feel that an adult encyclopedia is the better investment. When children are young, parents can help them use the books, and the older children can use them themselves. The best adult encyclopedias last for a lifetime; they may become dated in some respects, but the bulk of the material will carry a child through high school, college, and adult life. If a choice must be made, then decidedly the adult set should be purchased because of its greater richness and long-range value. But when a family can afford both, the child should have his own set.

Many informational series books have reference use, from such erudite books as the Time-Life Library of Art and the American

Heritage historical series, to Leonard Everett Fisher's books on colonial craftsmen. But each book in a series must be evaluated on its own merits. As is true in library collections, a home reference collection will include such books when they are appropriate for the family's particular interests. And if a member of the family is a bird watcher or a stamp collector, Roger Tory Peterson's *Field Guide to the Birds* or *Scott's Standard Postage Stamp Catalogue* may seem an absolute necessity.

Family use of religious books is discussed in Part Six, but the library reference collection should include the Bible and other sacred writings and books on comparative religion, whether they are discussions of denominations like Kathleen Elgin's separate treatments or a compendium like Katharine Savage's *The Story of World Religions*. Also useful for information about religion are biographies of religious leaders and such books as Susan Purdy's *Jewish Holidays: Facts, Activities and Crafts*.

Despite the abundance and variety of informational books, they are often given short shrift in discussions of literary quality. To be sure, some are distinguished more for their usefulness than for their style, but many of these books such as *Chipmunks on the Doorstep* by Edwin Tunis are as graceful in their prose as are some of the works of fiction that have won awards. And remember that the first Newbery Medal was given to Hendrik Willem Van Loon for *The Story of Mankind*, a history of man's origin and evolution that is witty and authoritative, the sort of informational book that amuses, informs, and stimulates readers to further inquiry. What more could one ask?

## ADULT REFERENCES[5]

DEASON, HILARY J., comp. *The AAAS Science Booklist.*

HUUS, HELEN. *Children's Books to Enrich the Social Studies for the Elementary Grades.*

IRWIN, LEONARD B., comp. *A Guide to Historical Reading; Non-Fiction.*

LOGASA, HANNAH. *Science for Youth.*

PETERSON, CAROLYN SUE. *Reference Books for Elementary and Junior High School Libraries.*

SUTHERLAND, ZENA. *History in Children's Books: An Annotated Bibliography for Schools and Libraries.*

TITOWSKY, BERNARD. *American History.*

VANCE, LUCILLE, and ESTHER TRACEY. *Illustration Index.*

WENZEL, EVELYN L., and MAY HILL ARBUTHNOT. *Time for Discovery.*

WILTZ, JOHN E. *Books in American History; A Basic List for High Schools.*

## THE BIOLOGICAL SCIENCES

ADLER, IRVING and RUTH. *Evolution*, ill. by Ruth Adler. Day, 1965. 8-10

ANDREWS, ROY CHAPMAN. *All About Dinosaurs*, ill. by Thomas W. Voter. Random, 1953. 9-12

———. *All About Whales*, ill. Random, 1954. 9-11

———. *In the Days of the Dinosaurs*, ill. by Jean Zallinger. Random, 1959. 8-11

ANDRY, ANDREW C., and STEVEN SCHEPP. *How Babies Are Made*, ill. by Blake Hampton. Time-Life, 1968. Includes other forms of life but emphasizes human reproduction. 5-9

ASIMOV, ISAAC. *ABC's of the Ocean*, ill. Walker, 1970. From aquaculture to zooplankton, an introduction to aspects of marine life and oceanography. The alphabetical format is somewhat limiting, but the facts given are interesting and lucidly presented. 8-10

BEADLE, GEORGE and MURIEL. *The Language of Life; An Introduction to the Science of Genetics*. Doubleday, 1966. 14 up

BENDICK, JEANNE. *A Place to Live*, ill. by author. Parents Magazine, 1970. 5-8

———. *What Made You You?* ill. by author. McGraw, 1971. 4-7

BEVANS, MICHAEL H. *The Book of Sea Shells*, ill. by author. Doubleday, 1961. A survey of mollusks in the United States. 10-14

BLOCH, MARIE H. *Dinosaurs*, ill. by George F. Mason. Coward, 1955. 8-10

BLOUGH, GLENN O. *After the Sun Goes Down*, ill. by Jeanne Bendick. McGraw, 1956. 7-9

———. *Bird Watchers and Bird Feeders*, ill. by Jeanne Bendick. McGraw, 1963. 6-8

———. *Discovering Dinosaurs*, ill. by Gustav Schrotter. Whittlesey, 1960. 8-9

———. *Soon After September; The Story of Living Things in Winter*, ill. by Jeanne Bendick. McGraw, 1959. 7-9

———. *Who Lives at the Seashore*, ill. by Jeanne Bendick. McGraw, 1961. 6-9

———. *Who Lives in This House; A Story of Animal Families*, ill. by Jeanne Bendick. McGraw, 1957. 7-9

BUCK, MARGARET WARING. *Pets from the Pond*, ill. by author. Abingdon, 1958. Good fresh-water biology. 9-11

5. Complete bibliographic data are provided in the combined Adult References in the Appendices.

———. *In Yards and Gardens*, ill. by author. Abingdon, 1952. 9-12

CLEMONS, ELIZABETH. *Shells Are Where You Find Them*, ill. by Joe Gault. Knopf, 1960. 8-10

COLLINS, HENRY HILL, JR. *The Bird Watcher's Guide*, ill. with photos; line drawings and cover by Richard Harker. Golden Pr., 1961. 10-13

COSGROVE, MARGARET. *Bone for Bone*, ill. by author. Dodd, 1968. 11-15

———. *Eggs—And What Happens Inside Them*, ill. by author. Dodd, 1966. 8-12

———. *Strange Worlds Under a Microscope*, ill. by author. Dodd, 1962. Includes historical developments and techniques of microscopy. 12-14

DARLING, LOIS and LOUIS. *Sixty Million Years of Horses*, ill. by authors. Morrow, 1960. 9-11

DARLING, LOUIS. *Greenhead*. Morrow, 1954. 10-14

———. *The Gull's Way*, photos and ill. by author. Morrow, 1965. 11-15

———. *Kangaroos and Other Animals with Pockets*, ill. by author. Morrow, 1958. 9-11

EARLE, OLIVE L. *Birds and Their Beaks*, ill. by author. Morrow, 1965. 8-10

———. *Camels and Llamas*, ill. by author. Morrow, 1961. 8-10

———. *Paws, Hoofs, and Flippers*, ill. by author. Morrow, 1954. 10-14

———. *Praying Mantis*, ill. by author. Morrow, 1969. 8-10

———. *State Birds and Flowers*, ill. by author. Morrow, 1951. 9-11

———. *State Trees*, ill. by author. Morrow, 1960. 10 up

———. *Strange Lizards*, ill. by author. Morrow, 1964. 8-10

ETS, MARIE HALL. *The Story of a Baby*, ill. by author. Viking, 1939. 8-10

FLANAGAN, GERALDINE LUX. *Window into an Egg; Seeing Life Begin*, ill. with photos. Scott/Addison, 1969. 9-11

GANS, ROMA. *Birds Eat and Eat and Eat*, ill. by Ed Emberley. T. Crowell, 1963. A book on bird feeding that includes instructions on making a feeder from a milk carton. 6-7

GEORGE, JEAN CRAIGHEAD. *All Upon a Stone*, ill. by Don Bolognese. T. Crowell, 1971. 7-8

———. *Gull Number 737*, ill. by author. T. Crowell, 1964. 12-15

———. *The Hole in the Tree*, ill. by author. Dutton, 1957. 8-10

———. *The Moon of the Bears*, ill. by Mac Shepard. T. Crowell, 1967. One of a series. 9-11

———. *Snow Tracks*, ill. by author. Dutton, 1958. 7-9

———. *Spring Comes to the Ocean*, ill. by John Wilson. T. Crowell, 1965. A tremendously impressive book written with quiet authority, imbued with a sense of wonder and pleasure in the marvelous intricacies of marine creatures. 11 up

GILBERT, BIL. *The Weasels; A Sensible Look at a Family of Predators*, ill. by Betty Fraser. Pantheon, 1970. Mink, ferret, marten, fisher otter, skunk, badger, wolverine, and weasel—and their place in the ecosystem. 12 up

GOETZ, DELIA. *Tropical Rain Forests*, ill. by Louis Darling. Morrow, 1957. 8-11

GOUDEY, ALICE E. *Graywings*, ill. by Marie Nonnast. Scribner's, 1964. The life cycle of a herring gull. 6-10

———. *Here Come the Cottontails*, ill. by Garry MacKenzie. Scribner's, 1965. 7-9

———. *Here Come the Dolphins*, ill. by Garry MacKenzie. Scribner's, 1961. 7-9

———. *Here Come the Lions!* ill. by Garry MacKenzie. Scribner's, 1956. 7-9

———. *Houses from the Sea*, ill. by Adrienne Adams. Scribner's, 1959. 5-7

GRUENBERG, SIDONIE MATSNER. *The Wonderful Story of How You Were Born*, rev. ed., ill. by Symeon Shimin. Doubleday, 1970. 8-10

GUILCHER, J. M., and R. H. NOAILLES. *A Fern Is Born*. Sterling, 1971. Clearly detailed photographs and a concise style make this and other books in the series admirable examples of nature writing. 9-12

HEADY, ELEANOR B., and HAROLD F. HEADY. *High Meadow; The Ecology of a Mountain Meadow*, ill. by Harold F. Heady. Norton/Grosset, 1970. Large print, clear illustrations, good organization, and easy style add value to a book that gives a lucid picture of the intricacies of an ecological situation in seasonal change. 11-14

HELLMAN, HAL. *Biology in the World of the Future*, ill. Evans, 1971. A knowledgeable and witty foray into the frontiers of biological research, well organized and provocative. 12 up

HIRSCH, S. CARL. *The Living Community: A Venture into Ecology*, ill. by William Steinel. Viking, 1966. 12-14

HOFSTEIN, SADIE. *The Human Story; Facts on Birth, Growth, and Reproduction*. Lothrop, 1969. 10-12

HOLLING, HOLLING C. *Pagoo*, ill. by L. W. Holling. Houghton, 1957. 8-10

HUTCHINS, ROSS E. *The Ant Realm*, ill. with photos by author. Dodd, 1967. The author describes, with his usual zest, the fascinating behavior of various species of ants, both group and individual behavior. 10-14

———. *The Travels of Monarch X*, ill. by Jerome P. Connolly. Rand, 1966. The description of a southward migration of a tagged Monarch butterfly from Toronto to Mexico. 8-10

JACKER, CORINNE. *The Biological Revolution; A Background Book on the Making of a New World*. Parents' Magazine, 1971. 13 up

JOHNSON, ERIC W. *Love and Sex in Plain Language*, rev. ed., ill. by Edward C. Smith. Lippincott, 1967. 12-17

KAVALER, LUCY. *Mushrooms, Molds, and Miracles; The Strange Realm of Fungi*. Day, 1965. 12 up

———. *The Wonders of Algae*, ill. with photos and with drawings by Barbara Amlick and Richard Ott. Day, 1961. 11-14

———. *The Wonders of Fungi*, ill. with photos and with drawings by Richard Ott. Day, 1964. 11-14

KLEIN, AARON E. *Threads of Life; Genetics from Aristotle to DNA*, ill. Natural History Pr., 1970. 12 up

LAUBER, PATRICIA. *The Friendly Dolphins*, ill. with photos, with drawings by Jean Simpson, and with diagrams by Charles Gottlieb. Randon, 1963. 9-11

———. *Your Body and How It Works*, ill. by Stephen

Rogers Peck, photos by Florence Burns. Random, 1962. 8-10

LUBELL, WINIFRED and CECIL. *Green Is for Growing*, ill. by Winifred Lubell. Rand, 1964. 8-10

MC CLUNG, ROBERT M. *Black Jack: Last of the Big Alligators*, ill. by Lloyd Sandford. Morrow, 1967. 8-10

______. *Honker*, ill. by Bob Hines. Morrow, 1965. 8-10

______. *Shag, Last of the Plains Buffalo*, ill. by Louis Darling. Morrow, 1960. 8-10

______. *Spike: The Story of a Whitetail Deer*, ill. by author. Morrow, 1952. 8-9

______. *Thor: Last of the Sperm Whales*, ill. by Bob Hines. Morrow, 1971. 8-10

MC COY, J. J. *The Hunt for the Whooping Cranes; A Natural History Detective Story*, ill. by Rey Abruzzi. Lothrop, 1966. A detailed and fascinating account of the search for the nesting grounds of the whooping cranes and efforts to save this endangered species. 13 up

MARI, IELA and ENZO, ills. *The Apple and the Moth* and *The Chicken and the Egg*. Pantheon, 1970. First published in Italy, two charming books for the youngest biologists that tell their stories clearly without text. 3-5

NAPIER, JOHN. *The Origins of Man*, ill. by Maurice Wilson. McGraw, 1969. A fine introductory interpretation of evolution. The author (Director of the Primate Biology Program at the Smithsonian) adds to his professional competence a sense of drama and a simplicity of approach. 9-11

NOURSE, ALAN E. *The Body*, by Alan E. Nourse and the Editors of *Life*. Time-Life, 1964. Illustrated with superb photographs. 13 up

PARKER, BERTHA MORRIS. *The Golden Book of Science*, ill. by Harry McNaught. Golden Pr., 1956. 8-10

PERRY, BILL. *Our Threatened Wildlife; An Ecological Study*, ill. Coward, 1970. An excellent survey of wildlife resources. Discusses extinct and endangered species, conservation agencies, types of refuges, and kinds of research. 12-15

PHLEGER, FRED. *The Whales Go By*, ill. by Paul Galdone. Random, 1959. 6-7

RAVIELLI, ANTHONY. *From Fins to Hands: An Adventure in Evolution*, ill. by author. Viking, 1968. 9-11

______. *Wonders of the Human Body*, ill. by author. Viking, 1954. 10-12

RIEDMAN, SARAH R. *Naming Living Things; The Grouping of Plants and Animals*, ill. by Jerome P. Connolly. Rand, 1963. 10-12

ROUNDS, GLEN. *Rain in the Woods; and Other Small Matters*, ill. by author. World, 1964. The author discusses the small and startling events in nature in a rambling, informal, and lightly humorous style. Handsomely illustrated. 9-12

SCHALLER, GEORGE B., and MILLICENT E. SELSAM. *The Tiger; Its Life in the Wild*, ill. with photos, drawings, and maps. Harper, 1969. The author's firsthand experiences add interest to this account of much that is known about tigers. Myths about these animals are also recounted. 10-12

SCHEELE, WILLIAM E. *Prehistoric Animals*, ill. by author. World, 1954. Describes the first five million years of earth's life forms. Cites locations of fossils in museums. 9 up

SCHEFFER, VICTOR. *Little Calf*, ill. by Leonard Everett Fisher. Scribner's, 1970. 12 up

SCHNEIDER, HERMAN and NINA. *How Your Body Works*, ill. by Barbara Ivins. W. R. Scott, 1949. Does not include all physiology but concentrates on digestive and nervous systems. 9-11

SELSAM, MILLICENT E. *Animals as Parents*, ill. by John Kaufmann. Morrow, 1965. 10-12

______. *Benny's Animals, and How He Put Them in Order*, ill. by Arnold Lobel. Harper, 1966. 6-8

______. *The Carrot and Other Root Vegetables*, photos by Jerome Wexler. Morrow, 1971. 7-9

______. *Egg to Chick*, ill. by Barbara Wolff. Harper, 1970. The instances of oversimplification in the first edition have been eliminated, the new illustrations are an improvement, and some of the longer sentences have been broken down into separate sentences for easier reading. 6-8

______. *Greg's Microscope*, ill. by Arnold Lobel. Harper, 1963. 6-8

______. *The Language of Animals*, ill. by Kathleen Elgin. Morrow, 1962. 10-14

______. *Let's Get Turtles*, ill. by Arnold Lobel. Harper, 1965. 7-8

______. *Peanut*, ill. with photos by Jerome Wexler. Morrow, 1969. 7-9

______. *Plants That Heal*, ill. by Kathleen Elgin. Morrow, 1959. 11-14

______. *Plants That Move*, ill. by Fred F. Scherer. Morrow, 1962. 8-11

______. *See Along the Shore*, ill. by Leonard Weisgard. Harper, 1961. 7-9

______. *See Through the Jungle*, ill. by Winifred Lubell. Harper, 1957. 7-9

______. *See Through the Sea*, ill. by Winifred Lubell. Harper, 1955. 7-9

SHIPPEN, KATHERINE B. *Men, Microscopes and Living Things*, ill. by Anthony Ravielli. Viking, 1955. 13-15

SHOWERS, PAUL. *A Drop of Blood*, ill. by Don Madden. T. Crowell, 1967. 7-8

______. *Look at Your Eyes*, ill. by Paul Galdone. T. Crowell, 1962. 6-7

______. *Use Your Brain*, ill. by Rosalind Fry. T. Crowell, 1971. 5-8

______. *Your Skin and Mine*, ill. by Paul Galdone. T. Crowell, 1965. 6-8

SHOWERS, PAUL and KAY. *Before You Were a Baby*, ill. by Ingrid Fetz. T. Crowell, 1968. 7-8

SHUTTLESWORTH, DOROTHY. *Animal Camouflage*, ill. by Matthew Kalmenoff. Natural History Pr., 1966. 11-14

______. *The Story of Flies*, ill. by Barbara Wolff. Doubleday, 1970. 6-12

______. *The Story of Rodents*, ill. by Lydia Rosier. Doubleday, 1971. 9-12

SIMON, HILDA. *Exploring the World of Social Insects*, ill. by author. Vanguard, 1963. 9-13

______. *Feathers: Plain and Fancy*, ill. by author. Viking, 1969. 11 up

______. *Living Lanterns; Luminescence in Animals*, ill. by author. Viking, 1971. 12 up

STEVENS, CARLA. *The Birth of Sunset's Kittens*, ill.

with photos by Leonard Stevens. W. R. Scott, 1969. No cute posed pictures, no saccharine comment, just the miraculous facts of kittens being born. 5-8

STOUTENBURG, ADRIEN. *Animals at Bay: Rare and Rescued American Wildlife*, ill. by John Schoenherr. Doubleday, 1968. 12-14

______. *A Vanishing Thunder: Extinct and Threatened American Birds*, ill. by John Schoenherr. Natural History Pr., 1967. 10-12

TRESSELT, ALVIN. *The Beaver Pond*, ill. by Roger Duvoisin. Lothrop, 1970. 5-7

TUNIS, EDWIN. *Chipmunks on the Doorstep*, ill. by author. T. Crowell, 1971. 10 up

ZIM, HERBERT S. *Dinosaurs*, ill. by James G. Irving. Morrow, 1954. 9-11

______. *Frogs and Toads*, ill. by Joy Buba. Morrow, 1950. 8-10

______. *Golden Hamsters*, ill. by Herschel Wartik. Morrow, 1951. 8-10

______. *Our Senses and How They Work*, ill. by Herschel Wartik. Morrow, 1956. 9-11

______. *Your Food and You*, ill. by Gustav Schrotter. Morrow, 1957. 9-11

______. *Your Heart and How It Works*, ill. by Gustav Schrotter. Morrow, 1959. 9-11

ZIM, HERBERT S., and SONIA BLEEKER. *Life and Death*, ill. by René Martin. Morrow, 1970. 9-12

## THE PHYSICAL SCIENCES

ADLER, IRVING. *The Giant Golden Book of Mathematics*, ill. by Lowell Hess. Golden Pr., 1960. 10-14

______. *Magic House of Numbers*, ill. by Ruth Adler. Day, 1957. 10-14

______. *The New Mathematics*, ill. by Ruth Adler. Day, 1958. 11-14

______. *The Stars: Steppingstones into Space*, ill. by Ruth Adler. Day, 1956. 12-14

______. *The Sun and Its Family*, ill. by Ruth Adler. Day, 1958. 12-14

______. *Tools in Your Life*, ill. by Ruth Adler. Day, 1956. 10-14

______. *The Tools of Science: From Yardstick to Cyclotron*, ill. by Ruth Adler. Day, 1958. 12-14

______. *The Wonders of Physics; An Introduction to the Physical World*, ill. by Cornelius DeWitt. Golden Pr., 1966. 12 up

ADLER, IRVING and RUTH. *Sets*, ill. by Ruth Adler. Day, 1967. 9-11

______. *Sets and Numbers for the Very Young*, ill. by Peggy Adler. Day, 1969. 6-8

AMES, GERALD, and ROSE WYLER. *First Days of the World*, ill. by Leonard Weisgard. Harper, 1958. 8-10

ANDERSON, ALAN H. *The Drifting Continents*. Putnam, 1971. 12 up

ASIMOV, ISAAC. *ABC's of Space*, ill. Walker, 1969. 8-10

______. *The Best New Thing*, ill. by Symeon Shimin. World, 1971. 5-7

______. *Building Blocks of the Universe*, rev. ed. Abelard, 1961. 14-17

______. *Realm of Measure*, ill. by R. Belmore. Houghton, 1960. 12 up

______. *Realm of Numbers*, diagrams by Robert Belmore. Houghton, 1959. 12 up

______. *Words of Science; and the History Behind Them*, ill. by William Barss. Houghton, 1959. 12-17

BENDICK, JEANNE. *All Around You: A First Look at the World*, ill. by author. Whittlesey, 1951. 6-8

______. *Electronics for Young People*, 4th ed., ill. by author. McGraw, 1960. 11-13

______. *The First Book of Space Travel*, rev. ed., ill. by author. Watts, 1969. 8-10

______. *The First Book of Time*, ill. by author. Watts, 1963. 9-11

______. *How Much and How Many; The Story of Weights and Measures*, ill. by author. McGraw, 1960. 10-12

______. *Lightning*, ill. by author. Rand, 1961. 7-9

______. *Names, Sets and Numbers*, ill. by author. Watts, 1971. 7-10

______. *The Shape of the Earth*, ill. by author. Rand, 1965. 9-11

______. *What Could You See?* ill. by author. Whittlesey, 1957. 6-9

______. *The Wind*, ill. by author. Rand, 1964. 8-10

BENDICK, JEANNE, and MARCIA LEVIN. *Take Shapes, Lines and Letters*, ill. by Jeanne Bendick. McGraw, 1962. 10-12

BENDICK, JEANNE, and ROBERT BENDICK. *Television Works Like This*, 4th ed., ill. by Jeanne Bendick. McGraw, 1965. 10-12

BRANLEY, FRANKLYN M. *A Book of Mars for You*, ill. by Leonard Kessler. T. Crowell, 1968. 6-10

______. *A Book of Stars for You*, ill. by Leonard Kessler. T. Crowell, 1967. 6-10

______. *The Christmas Sky*, ill. by Blair Lent. T. Crowell, 1966. 9-11

______. *Floating and Sinking*, ill. by Robert Galster. T. Crowell, 1967. 6-8

______. *High Sounds, Low Sounds*, ill. by Paul Galdone. T. Crowell, 1967. 6-8

______. *Man in Space to the Moon*, ill. by Louis S. Glanzman. T. Crowell, 1970. 9-11

______. *Mars: Planet Number Four*, rev. ed., ill. by Helmut K. Wimmer. T. Crowell, 1966. 12-15

______. *The Milky Way: Galaxy Number One*, ill. by Helmut K. Wimmer. T. Crowell, 1969. 12 up

______. *The Moon Seems to Change*, ill. by Helen Borten. T. Crowell, 1960. 6-7

______. *Rockets and Satellites*, rev. ed., ill. by Leonard Kessler. T. Crowell, 1970. 6-9

______. *Solar Energy*, ill. by John Teppich. T. Crowell, 1957. 11-14

______. *The Sun: Our Nearest Star*, ill. by Helen Borten. T. Crowell, 1961. 5-8

______. *The Sun: Star Number One*, ill. by Helmut K. Wimmer. T. Crowell, 1964. 11-14

BRANLEY, FRANKLYN M., and ELEANOR K. VAUGHAN. *Mickey's Magnet*, ill. by Crockett Johnson. T. Crowell, 1956. 5-7

BRIGGS, PETER. *Science Ship; A Voyage Aboard the Discoverer*. Simon, 1969. 11-15

BRONOWSKI, JACOB, and MILLICENT E. SELSAM. *Biography of an Atom*, ill. by Weimar Pursell and with photos. Harper, 1965. 10-14

BUEHR, WALTER. *Water: Our Vital Need*, ill. by author. Norton/Grosset, 1967. 9-11

CARSON, RACHEL. *The Sea Around Us*, ad. by Anne

Terry White, ill. with photos, maps, and drawings. Golden Pr., 1958. 11-14

CHAROSH, MANNIS. *Straight Lines, Parallel Lines, Perpendicular Lines*, ill. by Enrico Arno. T. Crowell, 1970. One of a new series of mathematics books for the young, each volume examining basic ideas and demonstrating patterns and relationships. Brisk, straightforward text; large, clear illustrations. 8-9

COOMBS, CHARLES. *Lift-Off: The Story of Rocket Power*, ill. by R. H. Foor. Morrow, 1963. 9-11

______. *Skyrocketing into the Unknown*, ill. with photos. Morrow, 1954. 12-17

CROUSE, WILLIAM H. *Understanding Science*, rev. ed., ill. by Jeanne Bendick and D. Mahanes. McGraw, 1956. 10-14

EPSTEIN, SAM and BERYL. *The First Book of Electricity*, ill. by Robin King. Watts, 1953. 9-12

FEELINGS, MURIEL. *Moja Means One*, ill. by Tom Feelings. Dial, 1971. Soft illustrations add appeal to a counting book that gives numbers 1–10 in Swahili. 5-8

FEY, JAMES T. *Long, Short, High, Low, Thin, Wide*, ill. by Janie Russell. T. Crowell, 1971. 7-9

FREEMAN, IRA M. *All About Electricity*, ill. by Evelyn Urbanowich. Random, 1957. 10-13

______. *All About the Wonders of Chemistry*, ill. by George Wilde. Random, 1954. 10-13

FREEMAN, IRA M., and A. RAE PATTON. *The Science of Chemistry*, ill. by Zenowij Onyshkewych. Random, 1968. 10-12

FREEMAN, MAE (BLACKER). *Finding Out About Shapes*, ill. by Bill Morrison. McGraw, 1969. A good introduction to spatial conceptualization, with simple definitions. 5-8

GALLANT, ROY A. *Exploring Chemistry*, ill. by Lee Ames. Garden City, 1958. 9-13

______. *Exploring the Universe*, ill. by Lowell Hess. Garden City, 1956; rev. ed., 1968. 9-13

GAMOW, GEORGE. *A Planet Called Earth*. Viking, 1963. 13 up

GOUDEY, ALICE E. *The Day We Saw the Sun Come Up*, ill. by Adrienne Adams. Scribner's, 1961. Two children rise before dawn, and mother explains night and day, shadows, and the turning earth. 5-7

HARVEY, FRAN. *Why Does It Rain?* ill. by Lucy and John Hawkinson. Harvey, 1969. 7-9

HOGBEN, LANCELOT. *Beginnings and Blunders; or Before Science Began*. Grosset, 1970. Primitive man moves toward the earliest civilization, from the first tools to the first cities. 11-14

______. *The Wonderful World of Energy*, ill. by Eileen Aplin and others. Garden City, 1957. 11-14

______. *The Wonderful World of Mathematics*, ill. by Andre, Charles Keeping, Kenneth Symonds. Garden City, 1955; rev. ed., 1968. 10-14

HYDE, MARGARET O., and BRUCE G. HYDE. *Atoms Today and Tomorrow*, rev. ed., ill. by Ed Malsberg. McGraw, 1970. 11-13

JACKER, CORINNE. *Window on the Unknown: A History of the Microscope*, ill. by Mary Linn and with photos. Scribner's, 1966. 13 up

LAUBER, PATRICIA. *All About the Ice Age*, ill. Random, 1959. 10-12

______. *All About the Planets*, ill. by Arthur Renshaw. Random, 1960. 9-11

______. *Junior Science Book of Volcanoes*, ill. by Mathew Kalmenoff. Garrard, 1965. 7-9

______. *The Story of Numbers*, ill. by Mircea Vasiliu. Random, 1961. 8-10

LEWELLEN, JOHN. *The Mighty Atom*, ill. by Ida Scheib. Knopf, 1955. 8-10

______. *The True Book of Toys at Work*, ill. by Karl Murray. Childrens Pr., 1953. 6-8

______. *Understanding Electronics*, ill. by Ida Scheib. T. Crowell, 1957. 12-14

LEWIS, ALFRED. *The New World of Computers*, ill. with photos. Dodd, 1965. 9-12

MAY, JULIAN. *Weather*, ill. by Jack White. Follett, 1967. 7-9

______. *Why the Earth Quakes*, ill. by Leonard Everett Fisher. Holiday, 1969. A discussion of geologic theory about the earth's mantle and ocean floor. 9-11

MYLLER, ROLF. *How Big Is a Foot?* Atheneum, 1962. 5-7

NAVARRA, JOHN GABRIEL. *Wide World Weather*. Doubleday, 1968. 11 up

OGBURN, CHARLTON. *The Forging of Our Continent*. American Heritage, 1968. 11-13

PODENDORF, ILLA. *Things Are Alike and Different*, ill. by John Hawkinson. Childrens Pr., 1970. 7-8

RAVIELLI, ANTHONY. *An Adventure in Geometry*, ill. by author. Viking, 1957. 14-17

______. *The World Is Round*, ill. by author. Viking, 1963. 7-10

REED, W. MAXWELL. *The Stars for Sam*, rev. ed., ed. by Paul Brandwein, ill. with photos. Harcourt, 1960. Describes the solar system and the universe and exploration of outer space. Reed's books on the earth and the sea, all durable sources of information, have also been revised. 10-13

REISS, JOHN. *Numbers*, ill. by author. Bradbury, 1971. Beautiful illustrations show numbers 1–20, by tens to 100, and then—1000 raindrops! 2-5

RUCHLIS, HY. *Orbit: A Picture Story of Force and Motion*, ill. by Alice Hirsch. Harper, 1958. 10 up

______. *Your Changing Earth*, ill. by Janet and Alex d'Amato. Harvey, 1963. 7-9

SCHNEIDER, HERMAN and NINA. *How Big Is Big? From Stars to Atoms*, ill. by Symeon Shimin. W. R. Scott, 1950. 8-11

______. *You, Among the Stars*, ill. by Symeon Shimin. W. R. Scott, 1951. 8-10

SEABORG, GLENN T., and EVANS G. VALENS. *Elements of the Universe*, ill. with photos, charts, and diagrams. Dutton, 1958. 12 up

SELSAM, MILLICENT E. *Birth of an Island*, ill. by Winifred Lubell. Harper, 1959. 8-10

SHIPPEN, KATHERINE B. *The Bright Design*, ill. by Charles Daugherty. Viking, 1949. 10-14

SILVERBERG, ROBERT. *Wonders of Ancient Chinese Science*, ill. by Marvin Besunder. Hawthorn, 1969. Following a brief background history of China from 1994 B.C., this most informative book surveys the achievements of Chinese scientists, some familiar but many neglected for centuries. 12 up

TRESSELT, ALVIN R. *Hide and Seek Fog*, ill. by Roger Duvoisin. Lothrop, 1965. 5-8

______. *It's Time Now*, ill. by Roger Duvoisin. Lothrop,

1969. 5-8

______. *Rain Drop Splash*, ill. by Leonard Weisgard. Lothrop, 1946. 4-8

______. *Sun Up*, ill. by Roger Duvoisin. Lothrop, 1949. 5-8

______. *White Snow, Bright Snow*, ill. by Roger Duvoisin. Lothrop, 1947. Caldecott Medal. 5-7

TUNIS, EDWIN. *Wheels: A Pictorial History*, ill. by author. World, 1955. 11 up

WEISS, HARVEY. *Motors and Engines and How They Work*, ill. by author. T. Crowell, 1969. 10-12

WILFORD, JOHN NOBLE. *We Reach the Moon*, based upon the original book published by *The New York Times* and Bantam Books. Norton/Grosset, 1969. 10-12

WOODBURY, DAVID O. *The New World of the Atom*. Dodd, 1965. 9-11

WYLER, ROSE. *The First Book of Weather*, ill. by Bernice Myers. Watts, 1966. 9-11

WYLER, ROSE, and GERALD AMES. *The New Golden Book of Astronomy*, rev. ed., ill. by John Polgreen. Golden Pr., 1965. 10-12

## THE SOCIAL SCIENCES

ABELES, ELVIN. *The Student and the University; A Background Book on the Campus Revolt*. Parents' Magazine, 1969. The "background" of the subtitle is the prime emphasis of the book, which traces European and American developments from feudal times to today. The final sections which discuss the changing university and the contemporary student movement are measured and objective. 13 up

ADOFF, ARNOLD, ed. *Black on Black; Commentaries by Negro Americans*. Macmillan, 1968. A collection of material spanning the thinking of black Americans from Frederick Douglass to Dick Gregory. Their viewpoints may differ but they unite in speaking of the problems of a fragmented society. 13 up

AMERICAN HERITAGE. *Discoverers of the New World*, narrative by Josef Berger in consultation with Lawrence C. Wroth, ill. American Heritage, 1960. 10-14

AMES, GERALD, and ROSE WYLER. *The First People in the World*, ill. by Leonard Weisgard. Harper, 1958. 8-10

ARCHER, JULES. *The Extremists; Gadflies of American Society*. Hawthorn, 1969. Illustrated with old prints and cartoons, a detailed and objective history of extremists in this country. Useful as a source book and eminently readable. 13 up

ASHE, GEOFFREY. *King Arthur in Fact and Legend*. Nelson, 1971. A scholarly, lively investigation of the fictional Arthur and the Arthur of historical and archeological fact. 12 up

ASIMOV, ISAAC. *The Dark Ages*, ill. Houghton, 1968. 12-17

______. *Words from History*, ill. by William Barss. Houghton, 1968. 11 up

______. *Words from the Exodus*, ill. by William Barss. Houghton, 1963. 11 up

______. *Words in Genesis*, ill. by William Barss. Houghton, 1962. 11 up

______. *Words on the Map*, ill. by William Barss. Houghton, 1962. 12 up

BAUMANN, HANS. *In the Land of Ur; The Discovery of Ancient Mesopotamia*, tr. by Stella Humphries, ill. Pantheon, 1969. 13 up

______. *Lion Gate and Labyrinth*, tr. by Stella Humphries, ill. Pantheon, 1967. The archeological discoveries of Troy, Crete, and Mycenae are described along with some of the history, myths, and legends of those civilizations. Includes color plates of archeological sites and finds. 12-15

BAYLOR, BYRD. *Before You Came This Way*, ill. by Tom Bahti. Dutton, 1969. Walking in the quiet of a canyon in the southwest, you wonder if you are the first to pass this way and then you see the wall paintings of the past. A handsome, thought-provoking book. 7-9

BERNHEIM, MARC and EVELYNE. *African Success Story; The Ivory Coast*, ill. Harcourt, 1970. A lucid and authoritative description of the growth and prosperity of the Ivory Coast since it gained independence. 11-14

BIRMINGHAM, JOHN, ed. *Our Time Is Now: Notes from the High School Underground*. Praeger, 1970. Excerpts from high school papers show the intense concern of young people. 13 up

BLEEKER, SONIA. *The Eskimo: Arctic Hunters and Trappers*, ill. by Patricia Boodell. Morrow, 1959. 9-12

______. *The Ibo of Africa*, ill. by Edith G. Singer. Morrow, 1969. 10-12

______. *The Maya, Indians of Central America*, ill. by Kisa N. Sasaki. Morrow, 1961. 9-12

______. *The Pygmies: Africans of the Congo Forest*, ill. by Edith G. Singer. Morrow, 1968. 9-12

______. *The Sea Hunters: Indians of the Northwest Coast*, ill. by Althea Karr. Morrow, 1951. 9-12

______. *The Sioux Indians; Hunters and Warriors of the Plains*, ill. by Kisa N. Sasaki. Morrow, 1962. 9-11

BONTEMPS, ARNA. *Story of the Negro*, 3rd. ed., ill. by Raymond Lufkin. Knopf, 1958. An authoritative and perceptive black history. 11-14

BOORSTIN, DANIEL J. *The Landmark History of the American People*, 2 vols., ill. Random, 1968 and 1970. 10-14

BOWRA, C. MAURICE. *Classical Greece*. Time-Life, 1965. 12 up

BRANLEY, FRANKLYN M. *The Mystery of Stonehenge*, ill. by Victor G. Ambrus. T. Crowell, 1969. 9-11

CARTER, WILLIAM E. *The First Book of South America*. Watts, 1961. 9-12

CHASE, STUART. *Danger—Men Talking! A Background Book on Semantics and Communication*. Parents' Magazine, 1969. The author writes with profound perspective about the tyranny of words, discussing human speech and semantics, techniques of improving communications in human dialogue, and many ancillary topics. 12-17

CHUBB, THOMAS CALDECOT. *The Byzantines*, ill. by Richard M. Powers. World, 1959. One of a fine series of books about major cultures of the world (Arabs, Aztecs, Slavic peoples, etc.). 11 up

CLARK, ANN NOLAN. *Circle of Seasons*, ill. by W. T. Mars. Farrar, 1970. 10-14

CLARKE, CLORINDA. *The American Revolution 1775–*

*83; A British View*, ill. McGraw, 1967. 10-14

CLYMER, ELEANOR. *The Case of the Missing Link*, rev. ed. Basic, 1968. 15 up

COHEN, ROBERT. *The Color of Man*, ill. with photos by Ken Heyman. Random, 1968. A fine book on the physical differences among people, and on the nature and dangers of prejudice. 10-13

COMMAGER, HENRY STEELE. *The First Book of American History*, ill. by Leonard E. Fisher. Watts, 1957. 10-12

———. *The Great Declaration: A Book for Young Americans*, ill. by Donald Bolognese. Bobbs, 1958. 12-14

COOK, FRED, ad. *The Golden Book of the American Revolution*, adapted from *The American Heritage Book of the Revolution*, ill. Golden Pr., 1959. 12-14

COOLIDGE, OLIVIA. *Tales of the Crusades*, ill. adapted from prints by Gustave Doré. Houghton, 1970. Each of the stories that chronicle some facet of the long years of the Crusades is a splendid entity, wonderfully evocative, and vividly written. The book is not a cohesive picture but is impressive both as a literary and a historical work. 13 up

COOMBS, CHARLES. *Cleared for Takeoff: Behind the Scenes at an Airport*. Morrow, 1969. 11-15

———. *Skyhooks: The Story of Helicopters*, ill. with photos. Morrow, 1967. 9-11

———. *Spacetrack: Watchdog of the Skies*, ill. with photos and diagrams. Morrow, 1969. 10-12

COTTRELL, LEONARD. *Digs and Diggers; A Book of World Archaeology*, ill. with photos. World, 1964. 13 up

DALGLIESH, ALICE. *America Begins: The Story of the Finding of the New World*, rev. ed., ill. by Lois Maloy. Scribner's, 1958. 8-11

DENNY, NORMAN, and JOSEPHINE FILMER-SANKEY. *The Bayeux Tapestry; The Story of the Norman Conquest: 1066*, ill. Atheneum, 1966. 11-15

DOBRIN, ARNOLD. *The New Life—La Vida Nueva; The Mexican-Americans Today*. Dodd, 1971. A survey of attitudes, problems, and factors that influence the Chicano, using interviews. 10-12

DUGGAN, ALFRED. *Growing Up in 13th Century England*, ill. by C. Walter Hodges. Pantheon, 1962. 11-14

DURHAM, PHILIP, and EVERETT L. JONES. *The Negro Cowboys*, ill. with photos. Dodd, 1965. A great deal of information about the Negroes who participated in the westward expansion. 13 up

ELLIOT, SARAH. *Our Dirty Air*, ill. with photos. Messner, 1971. Suggests ways that children can help. 8-10

EPSTEIN, BERYL and SAMUEL. *Who Says You Can't?* Coward, 1969. Instances of causes that seemed lost and the determined people who campaigned for those diverse causes are described in a lively and provocative book. 12 up

EVANS, EVA KNOX. *Why We Live Where We Live*, ill. by Ursula Koering. Little, 1953. 9-12

FISHER, LEONARD EVERETT. *The Architects*, ill. by author. Watts, 1971. 10-12

———. *The Cabinetmakers*, ill. by author. Watts, 1966. 10-12

———. *The Glassmakers*, ill. by author. Watts, 1964. 10-12

———. *The Peddlers*, ill. by author. Watts, 1968. 10-12

———. *Pumpers, Boilers, Hooks and Ladders*, ill. by author. Dial, 1961. 5-8

———. *The Schoolmasters*, ill. by author. Watts, 1967. 10-12

———. *The Silversmiths*, ill. by author. Watts, 1964. 10-12

———. *The Tanners*, ill. by author. Watts, 1966. 10-12

———. *Two If by Sea*, ill. by author. Random, 1970. 10-11

FLATO, CHARLES. *The Golden Book of the Civil War*, ad. from *The American Heritage Picture History of the Civil War*. Golden Pr., 1961. 10-12

FOSTER, G. ALLEN. *Sunday in Centerville; The Battle of Bull Run, 1861*, ill. by Harold Berson. White, 1971. 12 up

FOSTER, GENEVIEVE. *Augustus Caesar's World; A Story of Ideas and Events from B.C. 44 to 14 A.D.*, ill. by author. Scribner's, 1947. 12-16

———. *George Washington's World*, ill. by author. Scribner's, 1941. 12-16

———. *The World of Columbus and Sons*, ill. by author. Scribner's, 1965. 12-16

———. *Year of Columbus—1492*, ill. by author. Scribner's, 1969. 8-10

———. *The Year of the Pilgrims—1620*, ill. by author. Scribner's, 1969. 8-10

FRIEDLANDER, JOANNE K., and JEAN NEAL. *Stock Market ABC*, ill. by Tom Dunnington. Follett, 1969. A lucid description in a light tone of the intricacies of the stock market. 12 up

GIDAL, SONIA and TIM. *My Village in Ghana*. Pantheon, 1970. And other titles in the series. 9-12

GOBLE, PAUL, and DOROTHY GOBLE. *Red Hawk's Account of Custer's Last Battle*, ill. by authors. Pantheon, 1970. 10-12

GOLDSTON, ROBERT C. *The Negro Revolution*, ill. Macmillan, 1968. 13 up

GORODETZKY, CHARLES W., and SAMUEL T. CHRISTIAN. *What You Should Know About Drugs*. Harcourt, 1970. The dispassionate tone and straightforward style add to the usefulness of this source of information for the young reader. 10 up

GREENFELD, HOWARD. *The Waters of November*, ill. Follett, 1969. A dramatic, detailed account of the Florentine flood of 1966. Included is a description of the sophisticated techniques of restoration of the art treasures. 13 up

HAMBLIN, DORA JANE. *Pots and Robbers*. Simon, 1970. 12 up

HANFF, HELENE. *The Movers and Shakers; The Young Activists of the Sixties*. Phillips, 1970. Often passionate, always candid, carefully researched, and only occasionally given to generalized statements, this is exciting to read and furthermore is a valuable document about the youth movement of the 60's. 13 up

HARMER, MABEL. *The True Book of Pioneers*, ill. by Loran Wilford. Childrens Pr., 1957. 7-9

HIRSCH, CARL. *The Globe for the Space Age*, ill. by Burt Silverman. Viking, 1963. A book that traces the development of globes and stresses their advantage over maps in studying the sphere on which we live. 11-14

HOBART, LOIS. *Mexican Mural: The Story of Mexico, Past and Present.* Harcourt, 1963. 15 up

HODGES, C. WALTER. *Magna Carta,* ill. by author. Coward, 1966. An excellent survey of the conditions leading to the signing of the Magna Carta. 10-14

______. *The Norman Conquest,* ill. by author. Coward, 1966. A companion volume to the above title. The text is crisply informational; the illustrations unusually beautiful and informative. 10-14

______. *Shakespeare's Theatre,* ill. by author. Coward, 1964. The beautiful pictures are filled with informative detail and the text is written with simplicity and authority. The book is a delight. 11 up

HOFFMAN, EDWIN D. *Pathways to Freedom; Nine Dramatic Episodes in the Evolution of the American Democratic Tradition,* ill. Houghton, 1964. Nine episodes in the history of this country, each episode illustrating some facet of the democratic tradition. Well-written and well-researched. 13 up

HOFSINDE, ROBERT (GRAY-WOLF). *Indian Sign Language,* ill. by author. Morrow, 1956. 9-13

______. *Indian Warriors and Their Weapons,* ill. by author. Morrow, 1965. 8-13

______. *Indians at Home,* ill. by author. Morrow, 1964. A discussion of six major types of Indian homes. One of the best of the author's books on the cultures of North American Indians. 9-12

HOLLAND, JOHN, ed. *The Way It Is,* ill. with photos. Harcourt, 1969. 8-10

HOLLING, HOLLING C. *The Book of Cowboys,* rev. ed., ill. by author and Lucille Holling. Platt, 1968. 12 up

______. *The Book of Indians,* rev. ed., ill. by author and Lucille Holling. Platt, 1962. 12 up

______. *Minn of the Mississippi,* ill. by author. Houghton, 1951. 10-12

______. *Paddle-to-the-Sea,* ill. by author. Houghton, 1941. 9-11

______. *Tree in the Trail,* ill. by author. Houghton, 1942. 9-12

HOWARD, ROBERT WEST. *The Wagonmen.* Putnam, 1964. 11-14

HOYT, EDWIN P. *Whirlybirds: The Story of Helicopters,* ill. by George J. Zaffo. Doubleday, 1961. Attractive color illustrations. 10-13

HUGHES, LANGSTON. *The First Book of Africa,* rev. and rewritten, ill. with photos. Watts, 1964. Explorers, missionaries, the history of ancient Africa, and an evaluation of Africa today are included in this fine introductory book. 10-12

______. *The First Book of Negroes,* ill. by Ursula Koering. Watts, 1952. Not comprehensive, but a competent introduction to black history. 9-11

JANEWAY, ELIZABETH. *The Vikings,* ill. by Henry C. Pitz. Random, 1951. Includes a chapter on Vineland. 9-11

JENNESS, AYLETTE. *Dwellers of the Tundra; Life in an Alaskan Eskimo Village,* ill. with photos by Jonathan Jenness. Crowell-Collier, 1970. In easy, straightforward style the author describes the impact of white culture on an Eskimo village where she and her anthropologist-husband lived for a year. The approach is candid and mature, the material fascinating. 11-15

JOHNSON, GERALD W. *America Grows Up: A History for Peter,* ill. by Leonard E. Fisher. Morrow, 1960. 10-13

______. *America Is Born: A History for Peter,* ill. by Leonard E. Fisher. Morrow, 1959. 10-13

______. *America Moves Forward: A History for Peter,* ill. by Leonard E. Fisher. Morrow, 1960. 10-13

______. *The Congress,* ill. by Leonard E. Fisher. Morrow, 1963. 9-12

______. *The Presidency,* ill. by Leonard E. Fisher. Morrow, 1962. 9-12

______. *The Supreme Court,* ill. by Leonard E. Fisher. Morrow, 1962. 9-12

JOHNSTON, JOHANNA. *Together in America; The Story of Two Races and One Nation,* ill. by Mort Künstler. Dodd, 1965. 11-14

KAVALER, LUCY. *Dangerous Air,* ill. by Carl Smith. Day, 1967. 12 up

KIRK, RUTH. *David, Young Chief of the Quileutes: An American Indian Today,* ill. with photos by author. Harcourt, 1967. The true story of a Pacific coast tribe that has moved gracefully into modern life while keeping its respect for Quileute tradition. 9-11

______. *The Oldest Man in America: An Adventure in Archeology,* ill. with photos by Ruth and Louis Kirk. Harcourt, 1970. The story of a search for records of prehistoric man is made more dramatic by the fact that a new dam threatened the project. 10-14

KURTIS, ARLENE HARRIS. *Puerto Ricans; From Island to Mainland.* Watts, 1965. A simply written survey, with historical background provided. 9-12

LA FARGE, OLIVER. *The American Indian.* Golden Pr., 1960. 10-12

LAUBER, PATRICIA. *Who Discovered America? Settlers and Explorers of the New World Before the Time of Columbus.* Random, 1970. 9-11

LESTER, JULIUS. *To Be a Slave,* ill. by Tom Feelings. Dial, 1968. Excerpts from source material, chronologically arranged, give a moving and explicit picture of slavery. 11-14

LIFTON, BETTY JEAN. *Return to Hiroshima,* ill. with photos by Eikoh Hosoe. Atheneum, 1970. A matter-of-fact, serious, objective assessment of the enduring ramifications of the bombing of Hiroshima. Excellent photos. 10-17

LIPSYTE, ROBERT. *Assignment: Sports.* Harper, 1970. A compilation of articles covering many sports and sports figures. The author, sports columnist for *The New York Times,* writes with authority and a facility for quick and vivid character portrayals. 11-15

LOBSENZ, NORMAN M. *The First Book of Ghana,* ill. with photos. Watts, 1960. A competent historical and cultural overview. 9-11

MC NEER, MAY. *The American Indian Story,* ill. by Lynd Ward. Farrar, 1963. 9-11

MAY, JULIAN. *The First Men,* ill. by Lorence F. Bjorklund. Holiday, 1968. 7-9

MEAD, MARGARET. *Anthropologists and What They Do.* Watts, 1965. The interview technique is used to introduce some of the specialized fields and diversified techniques of anthropology. A lively, varied, and informative career guidance book. 12 up

______. *People and Places,* ill. by W. T. Mars and Jan

Fairservis and with photos. World, 1959. 12-14

MEADOWCROFT, ENID LA MONTE. *The Land of the Free*, ill. by Lee J. Ames. T. Crowell, 1961. 8-10

MELTZER, MILTON. *Bread and Roses: The Struggle of American Labor, 1865–1915*, ill. Knopf, 1967. 12-15

———, ed. *In Their Own Words: A History of the American Negro; Vol. 1, 1619–1865*. T. Crowell, 1964.

———, ed. *In Their Own Words: A History of the American Negro; Vol. 2, 1865–1916*. T. Crowell, 1965.

———, ed. *In Their Own Words: A History of the American Negro; Vol. 3, 1916–1966*. T. Crowell, 1967. 12-15

MELTZER, MILTON, and AUGUST MEIER. *Time of Trial, Time of Hope: The Negro in America, 1919–1941*, ill. by Moneta Barnett. Doubleday, 1966. 11-14

MORGAN, EDMUND S. *So What About History?* Atheneum, 1969. In this stimulating and unorthodox approach to history (this is not a history book), the author stresses the significance of historical interpretation of material objects, from discarded junk to imposing government buildings, as evidence of living patterns. 9-11

MORRIS, RICHARD B. *The First Book of the American Revolution*, ill. by Leonard E. Fisher. Watts, 1956. 9-13

NAVARRA, JOHN. *Our Noisy World: The Problem of Noise Pollution*. Doubleday, 1969. 11-14

———. *The World You Inherit: A Story of Pollution*. Natural History Pr., 1970. 12-14

NICKEL, HELMUT. *Arms and Armor in Africa*, ill. Atheneum, 1971. The Curator of Arms and Armor for the Metropolitan Museum of Art describes both contemporary and ancient weapons and armor and relates this information to facts about the cultures of the peoples discussed. 9-14

NOLEN, BARBARA, ed. *Africa Is People; Firsthand Accounts from Contemporary Africa*, ill. with photos. Dutton, 1967. An interesting anthology, each selection preceded by a brief note on the context of the excerpt and on the author. Varied backgrounds and varied topics. 13 up

OGLE, LUCILLE, and TINA THOBURN. *I Spy; A Picture Book of Objects in a Child's Home Environment*, ill. by Joe Kaufman. American Heritage, 1970. Two labelled pictures on each page afford small children the pleasure of recognizing familiar objects or learning new ones. Useful for extending vocabulary, for classifying objects, and for environmental concepts. 2-5

PARNALL, PETER. *The Mountain*, ill. by author. Doubleday, 1971. Pollution ruins the peace and beauty of a mountainside. 5-7

PERKINS, CAROL MORSE, and MARLIN PERKINS. *"I Saw You from Afar"; A Visit to the Bushmen of the Kalahari Desert*, ill. with photos. Atheneum, 1965. The daily life of the bushmen in photographs and simple text. The treatment is sympathetic and dignified. 9-11

PRICE, CHRISTINE. *Made in Ancient Egypt*, ill. Dutton, 1970. Written in a direct and dignified style, this is a fascinating study of the ancient Egyptians through their tombs, temples, and the many artifacts recovered from burial chambers. A dynastic table and map precede the text, which is profusely illustrated. 11 up

PUGH, ELLEN, with the assistance of DAVID B. PUGH. *Brave His Soul*, ill. Dodd, 1970. 12-15

RICH, LOUISE DICKINSON. *The First Book of New World Explorers*, ill. by Cary Dickinson. Watts, 1960. 9-11

SASEK, MIROSLAV. *This Is Edinburgh*, ill. by author. Macmillan, 1961.

———. *This Is Greece*, ill. by author. Macmillan, 1966.

———. *This Is New York*, ill. by author. Macmillan, 1960. 8-11

SAVAGE, KATHARINE. *People and Power: The Story of Three Nations*. Walck, 1959. 13 up

———. *The Story of Africa; South of the Sahara*, ill. with photos and maps. Walck, 1961. 12 up

———. *The Story of the United Nations*, maps by Richard Natkiel. Walck, 1962, rev. ed., 1970. 13 up

SCHECHTER, BETTY. *The Peaceable Revolution*, ill. with photos. Houghton, 1963. The nonviolent way of solving human problems is traced through the perspective of history: Thoreau, Gandhi, and into today's civil rights movement. 13 up

SCHEELE, WILLIAM E. *The Earliest Americans*, ill. by author. World, 1963. 10-14

———. *The Mound Builders*, ill. by author. World, 1960. 10-14

SCHLEIN, MIRIAM. *It's About Time*, ill. by Leonard Kessler. W. R. Scott, 1955. 6-8

SCHNEIDER, HERMAN and NINA. *Let's Look Under the City*, rev. ed., ill. by Bill Ballantine. Scott/Addison, 1954. 8-10

SCHWARTZ, ALVIN. *The City and Its People: The Story of One City's Government*, ill. with photos by Sy Katzoff. Dutton, 1967. An excellent description of a city of 300,000 people, its administrative structure, problems, and planning. 9-12

———. *The Night Workers*, photos by Ullie Steltzer. Dutton, 1966. Interesting chronological treatment. 7-10

———. *Old Cities and New Towns*, ill. with photos. Dutton, 1968. 11-14

———. *University: The Students, Faculty, and Campus Life at One University*. Viking, 1969. An overview of student activity and the roles of faculty and administration. 12-15

SHIPPEN, KATHERINE B. *The Great Heritage*, ill. by C. B. Falls. Viking, 1947; rev. ed., 1962. 12-16

———. *Miracle in Motion: The Story of America's Industry*. Harper, 1955. 12-17

———. *The Pool of Knowledge: How the United Nations Share Their Skills*, rev. ed., ill. with photos. Harper, 1965. 11 up

———. *This Union Cause: The Growth of Organized Labor in America*, ill. with photos and drawings. Harper, 1958. 14-17

SHOWERS, PAUL. *Columbus Day*, ill. by Ed Emberley. T. Crowell, 1965. 5-8

———. *Indian Festivals*, ill. by Lorence Bjorklund. T. Crowell, 1969. 5-8

SPERRY, ARMSTRONG. *All About the Arctic and Antarctic*, ill. by author. Random, 1957. 9-11

SPIER, PETER. *Of Dikes and Windmills*, ill. by author. Doubleday, 1969. A remarkably interesting book about the long struggle of the Netherlands to claim and hold land from the sea. Written with articulate ease, the book contains a large amount of historical information. 11 up

STEELE, WILLIAM O. *Westward Adventure; The True Stories of Six Pioneers*. Harcourt, 1962. 9-11

STERLING, DOROTHY. *Tear Down the Walls! A History of the American Civil Rights Movement*, ill. Doubleday, 1968. 12 up

STEVENS, LEONARD A. *The Town That Launders Its Water*, ill. with photos. Coward, 1971. A California town has eight man-made lakes for recreation, the water reclaimed from sewage. 11 up

STOUTENBURG, ADRIEN. *People in Twilight: Vanishing and Changing Cultures*, ill. with photos. Doubleday, 1971. 11-14

TREASE, GEOFFREY. *This Is Your Century*, ill. Harcourt, 1966. An impressive twentieth-century history—chiefly of the western world—written in an easy but dignified style, with good organization and reasonable objectivity. 13 up

TRIPP, ELEANOR B. *To America*, ill. Harcourt, 1969. The author, in an unusual approach, has chosen nine highly localized sources of American newcomers, each demonstrating a different reason for coming to a new land. A vivid picture of the diversity of our forebears. 11-14

TUNIS, EDWIN. *Colonial Craftsmen and the Beginnings of American Industry*, ill. by author. World, 1965. Well-organized and superbly illustrated, the text is comprehensive, lucid, and detailed. 11-14

______. *Colonial Living*, ill. by author. World, 1957. 10-12

______. *Frontier Living*, ill. by author. World, 1961. 10 up

______. *Indians*, ill. by author. World, 1959. 11 up

______. *Shaw's Fortune; The Picture Story of a Colonial Plantation*, ill. by author. World, 1966. 9-12

______. *The Young United States—1783–1830*, ill. by author. World, 1969. 10-14

TURNBULL, COLIN M. *Tradition and Change in African Tribal Life*, ill. World, 1966. An anthropologist looks at the institutions of tribal life in an effort to see how they meet the needs of people. 13 up

UDEN, GRANT. *A Dictionary of Chivalry*, ill. by Pauline Baynes. T. Crowell, 1968. 11 up

VIERECK, PHILLIP, comp. *The New Land; Discovery, Exploration, and Early Settlement of Northeastern United States, from Earliest Voyages to 1621, Told in the Words of the Explorers Themselves*, ill. by Ellen Viereck. Day, 1967. 14 up

VON HAGEN, VICTOR W. *Maya, Land of the Turkey and the Deer*, ill. by Alberto Beltrán. World, 1960. 11-14

VAN LOON, HENDRIK WILLEM. *The Story of Mankind*, ill. by author. Liveright, 1921, rev. ed., 1951. Newbery Medal. 12-14

WALTON, RICHARD J. *America and the Cold War*. Seabury, 1969. An important book, this is a detailed and passionate history of the tangled international situation that followed World War II. The author offers neither verdict nor solution and is careful to so state when comments are conjectural. 12 up

______. *Beyond Diplomacy; A Background Book on American Military Intervention*. Parents' Magazine, 1970. A fine history of aspects of American foreign policy, objective in appraising the discrepancies between fact and popular belief. 12-17

WESTMAN, WESLEY C. *The Drug Epidemic; What It Means and How to Combat It*. Dial, 1970. A thoughtful and objective book, written for the mature reader, by a clinical psychologist working in the field of drug abuses. He discusses the medical, psychological, and sociological aspects of the problem. 12 up

WHITE, ANNE TERRY. *All About Archaeology*, ill. by Tom O'Sullivan and with photos. Random, 1959. 10-13

______. *Prehistoric America*, ill. by Aldren Watson. Random, 1951. 9-11

WHITE, THEODORE H. *The Making of the President, 1960*. Atheneum, 1961. A compelling look at what goes on behind the scenes during a campaign. 15 up

WHITNEY, DAVID. *The First Book of Facts and How to Find Them*, ill. by Edward Mackenzie. Watts, 1966. Author discusses the sorts of questions that can be answered by reference books and describes the major types of reference sources. Not comprehensive, but clear; valuable for the discussion of opinions vs. facts and of discrepancies. 9-11

WINN, MARIE. *The Fisherman Who Needed a Knife; A Story About Why People Use Money*, ill. by John E. Johnson. Simon, 1970. A companion book to the following title, this introduces the concept of money as a common medium of exchange. 4-7

______. *The Man Who Made Fine Tops; A Story About Why People Do Different Kinds of Work*, ill. by John E. Johnson. Simon, 1970. A light fictional framework describing the father who made his son a top is used to explain the division of labor. The ideas are perfectly clear and the author wisely stopped when her point was made. 5-7

ZINER, FEENIE, and ELIZABETH THOMPSON. *The True Book of Time*, ill. by Katherine Evans. Childrens Pr., 1956. 6-8

## RELIGION AND THE ARTS[6]

BONI, MARGARET BRADFORD, ed. *The Fireside Book of Favorite American Songs*, arr. for piano by Norman Lloyd, ill. by Aurelius Battaglia. Simon, 1952. From songs of the Pilgrims to ballads of the Nineties. 8 up

BORTEN, HELEN. *A Picture Has a Special Look*. Abelard, 1961. Describes and illustrates some of the media used by artists. 9-11

BRITTEN, BENJAMIN, and IMOGEN HOLST. *The Wonderful World of Music*, rev. ed. Doubleday, 1968. 8-12

BULLA, CLYDE ROBERT. *Stories of Favorite Operas*, ill. by Robert Galster. T. Crowell, 1959. Twenty-three libretti of popular operas. 10-14

CHASE, ALICE ELIZABETH. *Famous Artists of the Past*,

6. See also the Children's Religious Books listing in the bibliography for Part 6.

ill. with reproductions. Platt, 1964. A very good sampling of the works of some two dozen great artists. There is discussion of the artists and some analysis of most of the pictures in the book. 11-15

———. *Looking at Art*, ill. T. Crowell, 1966. 12 up

DEEDY, JOHN. *The Vatican*, ill. with photos. Watts, 1970. 10-12

DE MILLE, AGNES. *The Book of the Dance*, ill. by N. M. Bodecker. Golden Pr., 1963. Social, ritual, and theatrical dance history in full, with many color photographs. 11 up

DIETZ, BETTY WARNER, and MICHAEL BABATUNDE OLATUNJI. *Musical Instruments of Africa*, ill. by Richard M. Powers and with photos. Day, 1965. 11-12

DIETZ, BETTY WARNER, and THOMAS CHOONBAI PARK. *Folk Songs of China, Japan, and Korea*, ill. by Mamoru Funai. Day, 1964. 9 up

DOWNER, MARION. *Discovering Design*. Lothrop, 1947. An analysis of the elements of design in nature. 11 up

———. *The Story of Design*, ill. with photos. Lothrop, 1964. 11 up

———. *Roofs Over America*, ill. with photos. Lothrop, 1967. Two or three paragraphs on each page, accompanied by full-page photographs introduce 32 roofs in this unified treatment of American architecture from the Plymouth Colony to the present. 11-15

ELGIN, KATHLEEN. *The Unitarians*, ill. by author. McKay, 1971. And others in the series. 9-11

FREEDGOOD, LILLIAN. *An Enduring Image; American Painting from 1665*, ill. T. Crowell, 1970. A good survey of American painting, the emphasis on individual artists, with background discussion of trends here and influences from abroad and with a lucid discussion of contemporary art. All illustrations are in black and white. 12 up

GITTELSOHN, ROLAND. *The Meaning of Judaism*. World, 1970. 13 up

GLUBOK, SHIRLEY. *The Art of Ancient Greece*, designed by Oscar Krauss. Atheneum, 1963. And other books in this series. 10-13

———. *The Art of Colonial America*, ill. with photos. Macmillan, 1970. 9-12

———. *The Art of the Old West*, ill. with photos. Macmillan, 1971. 9-12

———. *Knights in Armor*, designed by Gerard Nook. Harper, 1969. Clear descriptions and photos give minor reference use to a handsome book. 9-14

GRIGSON, GEOFFREY. *Shapes and Stories: A Book About Pictures*. Vanguard, 1965. Perceptive comments about a selected group of pictures. 10-12

HASKELL, ARNOLD LIONEL. *The Wonderful World of Dance*. Doubleday, 1969. 11-14

HIRSCH, S. CARL. *Printing from a Stone: The Story of Lithography*, ill. Viking, 1967. A most interesting book that describes the history of lithography. The writing style is straightforward, lucid, and a bit dry. 12 up

HOAG, EDWIN. *American Houses; Colonial, Classic, and Contemporary*, ill. Lippincott, 1964. Writing in a straightforward style, the author relates developments always to influences of heritage, materials and climate, function, or period-fashion. 12-15

HOBAN, TANA. *Look Again!* ill. Macmillan, 1971. A book of photographs that can pique the young child's curiosity. Blank pages with a square cut out of them expose a portion of a picture behind. 2-4

———. *Shapes and Things*, ill. Macmillan, 1970. 2-5

HOFMANN, CHARLES. *American Indians Sing*, ill. by Nicholas Amorosi. Day, 1967. 10-13

HOFSINDE, ROBERT (GRAY-WOLF). *Indian Arts*, ill. by author. Morrow, 1971. 8-11

———. *Indian Music Makers*, ill. by author. Morrow, 1967. 9-12

HUGHES, LANGSTON. *Famous Negro Music Makers*. Dodd, 1955. 11-14

———. *The First Book of Jazz*, ill. by Cliff Roberts, music selected by David Martin. Watts, 1955. 11 up

———. *The First Book of Rhythms*, ill. by Robin King. Watts, 1954. 11-14

JOHNSON, JAMES WELDON, and J. ROSAMOND JOHNSON. *Lift Every Voice and Sing: Words and Music*. Hawthorn, 1970. Simply arranged for piano and guitar chords, a song that has endured as a hymn of black hope since it was written in 1900. 9-11

KAHN, ELY JACQUES. *A Building Goes Up*, ill. by Cal Sacks. Simon, 1969. 10-14

KETTELKAMP, LARRY. *Flutes, Whistles, and Reeds*, ill. by author. Morrow, 1962. 9-11

KING, MARY LOUISE. *A History of Western Architecture*, ill. with photos and diagrams. Walck, 1967. 12-16

LIFE MAGAZINE. *The World's Great Religions*. Special edition for young readers. Time-Life, 1958. 13-15

MANCHEL, FRANK. *When Movies Began to Speak*, ill. with photos and line drawings by James Caraway. Prentice, 1969. A history of the industry from the time of *The Jazz Singer* to the advent of the large screen, the impact of television, and the competition of foreign films. 12-15

———. *When Pictures Began to Move*, ill. by James Caraway. Prentice, 1969. One of the best histories of the motion picture industry for young people, ending with the death of the silent film. Good bibliography. 11-14

MAYNARD, OLGA. *American Modern Dancers: The Pioneers*. Atlantic/Little, 1965. 11 up

———. *The Ballet Companion*. Macrae, 1957. 11-15

MOORE, JANET GAYLORD. *The Many Ways of Seeing; An Introduction to the Pleasures of Art*, ill. World, 1968. 13 up

PAINE, ROBERTA M. *Looking at Sculpture*, ill. Lothrop, 1968. 9 up

PURDY, SUSAN GOLD. *Jewish Holidays; Facts, Activities, and Crafts*, ill. Lippincott, 1969. Each holiday is described and each is followed by directions for some project associated with it. Useful for religious education or for craft groups. 10-12

RADFORD, RUBY L. *Many Paths to God*. Theosophical, 1970. The basic ideas of twelve living religions and many of their parallel teachings. Each chapter has a list of suggested readings. 10-14

REISS, JOHN. *Colors*, ill. by author. Bradbury, 1969. Not only useful for color identification, but for awakening aesthetic appreciation. 2-5

ROCKWELL, ANNE. *Glass, Stones, and Crown: The Abbe Suger and the Building of St. Denis*. Atheneum, 1968. 11-13

ROGERS, W. G. *A Picture Is a Picture: A Look at Modern Painting*. Harcourt, 1964. An informed survey of the development of modern painting, including schools, techniques, and theories. 13 up

______. *What's Up in Architecture; A Look at Modern Building*. Harcourt, 1965. Trends, styles, and architects are discussed in informal, lively writing. 11 up

RUSKIN, ARIANE. *Art of the High Renaissance*, ill. McGraw, 1970. 12 up

______. *Nineteenth Century Art*. McGraw, 1968. 13 up

______. *The Pantheon Story of Art for Young People*, ill. Pantheon, 1964. 11-14

______. *17th and 18th Century Art*, ill. McGraw, 1969. Lucid and informative, a book that serves as an excellent introduction to the art history of two centuries, but is comprehensive and authoritative enough for the knowledgeable reader. 12 up

SAMACHSON, DOROTHY and JOSEPH. *The First Artists*, ill. Doubleday, 1970. A competent survey, with good photographs of cave paintings and engravings, more extensive than the usual treatment of the subject. 10-14

SAVAGE, KATHARINE. *The Story of World Religions*, ill. with photos and maps. Walck, 1967. 13 up

SHAW, ARNOLD. *The Rock Revolution*, ill. Crowell-Collier, 1969. 12 up

SHIPPEN, KATHERINE BINNEY, and ANCA SEIDLOVA. *The Heritage of Music*, ill. by Otto van Eersel. Viking, 1963. 12-16

SMITH, RUTH, ed. *The Tree of Life*, ill. by Boris Artzybasheff. Macmillan, 1942, 1946. 13 up

STAMBLER, IRWIN, and GRELUN LANDON. *Golden Guitars, the Story of Country Music*, ill. with photos. Four Winds, 1971. 12-16

SULLIVAN, GEORGE. *Understanding Architecture*. Warne, 1971. 10-14

TERRY, WALTER. *Ballet: A Pictorial History*, ill. Van Nostrand, 1970. 10-12

WARREN, FRED and LEE. *The Music of Africa; An Introduction*, ill. with photos and line drawings by Penelope Naylor. Prentice, 1970. Includes lists of books and recordings. 11-14

WILDER, ALEC, music by. *Lullabies and Night Songs*, ed. by William Engvick, ill. by Maurice Sendak. Harper, 1965. The choice of songs is very good, the arrangements are simple, the lyrics smooth; the illustrations are delectable. all ages

WOLCOTT, LEONARD and CAROLYN. *Religions Around the World*, ill. by Gordon Laite. Abingdon, 1967. 11 up

## ACTIVITIES AND EXPERIMENTS

ALKEMA, CHESTER JAY. *The Complete Crayon Book*. Sterling, 1969. 10 up

ANDERSEN, YVONNE. *Make Your Own Animated Movies; Yellow Ball Workshop Film Techniques*. Little, 1970. 10-13

ARCHER, ELSIE. *Let's Face It: The Guide to Good Grooming for Girls of Color*, rev. ed. Lippincott, 1968. Hair, complexion, makeup, clothes, speech, manners are all covered in this guide. 11-14

BEANEY, JAN. *The Young Embroiderer*. Warne, 1967. 10-13

BOYLAN, ELEANOR. *How to Be a Puppetter*, ill. by Tomie de Paola. McCall, 1970. Gives directions for making and costuming puppets, manipulating them, making sets and scenery, etc. Plays for a single puppeteer and a group are included. 8-10

BRANLEY, FRANKLYN M., and ELEANOR K. VAUGHAN. *Timmy and the Tin-Can Telephone*, ill. by Paul Galdone. T. Crowell, 1959. 5-7

BRODERICK, DOROTHY. *Training a Companion Dog*, ill. by Harris Petie. Prentice, 1965. 9-12

BUSCH, PHYLLIS. *A Walk in the Snow*, ill. with photos by Mary M. Thacher. Lippincott, 1971. An unusually good correlation of pictures and text make clear the methods of observing and enjoying some of the natural phenomena in snow time. 7-9

CASE, MARSHAL T. *Look What I Found! The Young Conservationist's Guide to the Care and Feeding of Small Wildlife*, ill. with photos by author. Chatham/Viking, 1971. 9-11

COLMAN, HILA. *Making Movies; Student Films to Features*, ill. by George Guzzi. World, 1969. Explicit and very comprehensive, written in a direct style. The advice is pertinent to career guidance. 12-15

COOPER, ELIZABETH K. *Science in Your Own Back Yard*, ill. by author. Harcourt, 1958. 10-13

EPSTEIN, SAM, and BERYL EPSTEIN. *The First Book of Codes and Ciphers*, ill. by Laszlo Roth. Watts, 1956. 9-12

FENTEN, D. X. *Plants for Pots: Projects for Indoor Gardeners*, ill. by Penelope Naylor. Lippincott, 1969. Informal style and precise drawings give information on the propagation, potting, and care and feeding of house plants. 10-14

FERAVALO, ROCCO V. *Easy Physics Projects: Air, Water and Heat*, ill. by Lewis Zacks. Prentice, 1966. 8-10

FERGUSON, ROBERT. *How to Make Movies: A Practical Guide to Group Filming*. Viking, 1969. 13 up

FREEMAN, S. H. *Basic Baseball Strategy*, ill. by Leonard Kessler. Doubleday, 1965. 10-14

GARDNER, MARTIN. *Perplexing Puzzles and Tantalizing Teasers*, ill. by Laszlo Kubinyi. Simon, 1969. 8-11

HAWKINSON, JOHN. *Pastels Are Great*. Whitman, 1968. The author explains the basic skills of the technique with enticing examples and explicit instructions. 8-10

HELFMAN, HARRY. *Making Your Own Movies*. Morrow, 1970. Lucid instructions on preparation, equipment, and filming. 10-14

HOWARD, HARRIET SHRIVER. *If You Had a Pony*, ill. with photos by Susan Rosenthal. Harper, 1965. 9-11

HUDLOW, JEAN. *Eric Plants a Garden*, ill. by author. Whitman, 1971. Clear photographs show a beaming young gardener planning, planting, tending, and harvesting his crop. 7-9

JOHNSON, LILLIAN. *Papier-Maché*. McKay, 1958. 11 up

KADESCH, ROBERT R. *Math Menagerie*, ill. by Mark A. Binn. Harper, 1970. 11-14

KIDDER, HARVEY. *Illustrated Chess for Children*, ill. by author. Doubleday, 1970. A really fine book for the beginning chess player. The clear diagrams are very helpful, as is the proceeding from basic moves to increasingly complicated ones. 10-13

LAFFIN, JOHN. *Codes and Ciphers; Secret Writing Through the Ages*, ill. by C. de la Nougerede. Abelard, 1964. An excellent book on cryptography, written with style and clarity and well organized. Cryptograms and solutions for the reader are appended. 12 up

LARRICK, NANCY. *See for Yourself*, ill. by Frank Jupo. American Book, 1952. 6-8

LOPSHIRE, ROBERT. *A Beginner's Guide to Building and Flying Model Airplanes*. Harper, 1967. Step-by-step instructions for assembling planes, and many small tips to ensure good workmanship. 10-12

———. *It's Magic?* ill. by author. Macmillan, 1969. Simple tricks are described within the framework of a humorous story. 7-9

MARA, THALIA, and LEE WYNDHAM. *First Steps in Ballet: Basic Exercises for Home Practice*, ill. by George Bobrizky. Garden City, 1955. Twelve basic barre exercises meant to be used in conjunction with formal training. 8-14

MARKS, MICKEY KLAR. *Collage*, ill. by Edith Alberts and with photos by David Rosenfeld. Dial, 1968. 8 up

———. *Painting Free: Lines, Colors and Shapes*, ill. by Edith Alberts and with photos by David Rosenfeld. Dial, 1965. Step-by-step instructions for the beginner interested in abstract painting. 11 up

MEILACH, DONA Z. *Creating with Plaster*. Reilly, 1966. A straightforward text with tips on techniques that give a professional touch. 12 up

MILGROM, HARRY. *Adventures with a Paper Cup*, ill. by Leonard Kessler. Dutton, 1968.

———. *Adventures with a Straw*, ill. by Leonard Kessler. Dutton, 1967. 4-7

———. *First Experiments with Gravity*, ill. by Lewis Zacks. Dutton, 1966. A series of home demonstrations, each prefaced by an explanation of the principle involved. 8-10

MOORE, EVA. *The Seabury Cook Book for Boys and Girls*, ill. by Talivaldis Stubis. Seabury, 1971. A very good first cook book containing nine easy recipes. 7-9

MOORE, JIM. *Football Techniques Illustrated*, rev. ed., ill. by Tyler Micoleau. Ronald, 1962. 10-14

MOORE, WILLIAM. *Your Science Fair Project*. Putnam, 1964. 8-13

MORGAN, ALFRED POWELL. *Boys' Book of Science and Construction*, rev. ed., ill. with plates and diagrams. Lothrop, 1959. 11-14

MOTT, CAROLYN, and LEO B. BAISDEN. *The Children's Book on How to Use Books and Libraries*, ill. Scribner's, 1961. Meets a wide variety of elementary grade needs ranging from writing a book review to using reference books and the library catalog.

NEUMANN, BILL. *Model Car Building*, ill. with photos. Putnam, 1971. Full instructions on building, painting, tools, materials, and adhesives. Big, clear photographs of equipment and procedures. 10-14

PAUL, AILEEN, and ARTHUR HAWKINS. *Kids Cooking*. Doubleday, 1970. 8-11

PETERSON, JOHN. *How to Write Codes and Secret Messages*, ill. by Bernice Myers. Four Winds, 1966. Lucid explanations of an alluring subject. 9-11

PETTIT, TED S. *A Guide to Nature Projects*, ill. by Walt Wenzel. Norton/Grosset, 1966. 9-12

PURDY, SUSAN. *Festivals for You to Celebrate: Facts, Activities, and Crafts*. Lippincott, 1969. 9-12

ROSS, LAURA. *Hand Puppets: How to Make and Use Them*, ill. by author. Lothrop, 1969. 9-12

———. *Puppet Shows Using Poems and Stories*, ill. by Frank Ross, Jr. Lothrop, 1970. Each poem, story, or excerpt from a book is provided with production notes. Simple enough for children to use alone, yet good source material for adults. 9-11

ROTH, ARNOLD. *Pick a Peck of Puzzles*, ill. by author. Norton, 1966. Varied selections; riddles, rebuses, tongue-twisters, pictures with hidden clues, etc. 8-10

SCOTT, JOSEPH, and LENORE SCOTT. *Egyptian Hieroglyphs for Everyone: An Introduction to the Writing of Ancient Egypt*. Funk, 1968. 11 up

SOKOL, CAMILLE. *The Lucky Sew-It-Yourself Book*, ill. by Bill Sokol. Four Winds, 1966. 7-9

SOOTIN, HARRY. *Experiments with Magnetism*, ill. by Julio Granda. Norton/Grosset, 1968. 9-12

SOOTIN, HARRY, and LAURA SOOTIN. *The Young Experimenter's Workbook: Treasures of the Earth*, ill. by Frank Aloise. Norton/Grosset, 1965. 8-11

STONE, A. HARRIS. *The Chemistry of a Lemon*, ill. by Peter P. Plasencia. Prentice, 1966. 8-11

STONE, A. HARRIS, and BERTRAM M. SIEGEL. *Puttering with Paper*, ill. by Peter P. Plasencia. Prentice, 1968. 9-12

———. *Turned On: A Look at Electricity*, ill. by Peter P. Plasencia. Prentice, 1970. 10-12

TISON, ANNETTE, and TALUS TAYLOR. *The Adventures of the Three Colors*. World, 1971. Shows color mix by use of transparencies. 5-8

UNESCO. *UNESCO Source Book for Science Teaching: 700 Science Experiments for Everyone*, 2nd ed. UNESCO, 1962. 10-14

UNKELBACH, KURT. *You're a Good Dog, Joe: Knowing and Training Your Puppy*, ill. by Paul Frame. Prentice, 1971. Includes warnings on safety of the puppy and very sensible training procedures. 7-9

WEISS, HARVEY. *Ceramics from Clay to Kiln*. W. R. Scott, 1964. 10-14

———. *Clay, Wood and Wire; A How-To-Do-It Book of Sculpture*. W. R. Scott, 1956. 8-17

———. *Collage and Construction*, ill. W. R. Scott, 1970. A good do-it-yourself book in art, simple enough for the younger reader, dignified enough for the older. Discusses not only the materials (easy-to-get) and techniques, but artistic conception. 9-12

———. *Paper, Ink and Roller; Print-Making for Beginners*. W. R. Scott, 1958. 9 up

———. *Pencil, Pen and Brush; Drawings for Beginners*. W. R. Scott, 1961. 11 up

———. *Sailing Small Boats*, ill. by Peter Barlow. Scott/Addison, 1967. 10 up

WYLER, ROSE, and GERALD AMES. *Prove It!* ill. by Talivaldis Stubis. Harper, 1963. 5-8

YOUNG, RAY. *Bridge for People Who Don't Know One Card from Another*, ill. by Tom Dunnington. Follett, 1964. There's no assumption of previous knowledge, yet the author never talks down. A lucid book for beginners. 11 up

# Part Six
# Bringing Children and Books Together

*The Role of the Adult*
*Techniques for Using Books with Children*
*Notes on Chapters 5–15*
*Religious Books in the Home*

# Bringing Children and Books Together: Introduction

Bringing a child and a book together in a happy way is a rewarding experience for teachers, librarians, and parents. And it needn't be difficult. Among the thousands and thousands of titles there are many splendid ones to meet the interests and needs of every child. There are books to take the child to places he may never see in person, to acquaint him with peoples and periods of the past, to answer his questions and broaden his horizons, to help him empathize with others through experiencing their tragedies and joys, to understand himself better through meeting people with problems like his own, and to give him relaxation, stimulation, and sheer pleasure.

How can these benefits be made available to children? First of all, adults must know books firsthand—not just from critics' annotations giving capsule accounts of content and suggested age levels. Such guides are eminently useful—they can, for example, alert the adult to books he might otherwise miss—but they are guides only. Fortunately, knowing children's books firsthand is a pleasant duty, because many of these books are as appealing to adults as to the children for whom they were written.

Most important, though, adults must know children, must know their general and specific interests and needs. They can learn much from reading some of the fascinating and thoughtful studies of children (see the bibliography), but they can learn most from observing children and talking with them and *listening* to them. They must respect and value children and always expect the best from them.

Parts One through Five have discussed children's needs and interests, ways of judging books, illustrations and illustrators, history and trends (to provide the reader with perspective for viewing books old and new), and all kinds of books from *Mother Goose* to informational books. This section gives suggestions for bringing books and children together through reading aloud, discussions, dramatizations, and so on. These, though, are only suggestions. It is well to remember that each situation is different—communities are different, schools are different, curriculums are different, teachers are different, and students are different. Teachers and librarians must develop the techniques that suit their children best. Although this section discusses ways of bringing children and books together primarily from the point of view of the teacher, many of the techniques may be used by librarians and parents. The ones described here have proved successful in many situations. The bibliography, too, lists books that suggest other successful ways—both traditional and excitingly innovative—of bringing children and books together.

Adults must also see that there is an abundance of books—as varied as the children's needs and interests require. The hundreds of excellent titles available in paperback editions make the acquiring of a respectable collection relatively easy. Children should be introduced, too, to the facilities of their school and community—the school library, the public library, and the bookstores, if any. And above all, their experiences with books should always, always be rewarding, unforced, and joyful.

## The Role of The Adult

### IN THE FAMILY

If literature is to come to mean more than mere diversion to youngsters, the process of introducing them to its emotional and intellectual satisfactions is best begun at home. At the baby's bedtime the mother can begin to say "Hush-a-bye baby" or "Bye, baby bunting." The infant responds to the love in her voice and to the security of her arms rather than to the words themselves.

It is the association of the sound of words with pleasure in the attention of the mother that first kindles an interest in the raw material of literature—words. Later, after the infant has learned to participate in the play of "Pat-a-cake" and "This little pig," the pleasure of the association with a happy setting is joined by the pleasure of achievement. Although in the happy exchange of nursery rhymes the infant's role is only simple hand clapping or the offer of his fingers, he begins to move toward literature—to bring something of himself.

As soon as the baby begins to like pictures, the mother should have a *Mother Goose* to hold on her lap along with the infant. It is good to say the verses over and over as many times as he wants them, but never to force him to listen or to urge the book on him. He will come to it when he is ready. When the child begins to know the verses, the mother can say them with him at any time, with or without the book. It is this happy and mutually enjoyed play that strengthens the bond between children and their parents. Through this bond parents may lead their children toward eventual independence and personal satisfaction in literature.

Unfortunately, during the years from two to five, this developmental process of disposing children toward books is sometimes suspended, perhaps because as the child becomes able to walk about by himself and feed himself, he is no longer as dependent and demanding as he was when an infant. As he begins to explore his little world he does so on his own. Mealtime may not be the mutually delightful time that it once was. As the child discovers the joys of play and staying up, bedtime can become a strain on everyone. Or perhaps another baby comes along and the mother no longer has the time to spend with the firstborn and he turns, sometimes at the mother's harried suggestion, to the cartoons and the latest fad in children's shows on television. There he forms a new bond: undemanding, inexhaustibly diverting, and impersonal. There is, though, something chilling in the sight of preschoolers sitting mutely in front of a television set playing finger games with a teacher who can't see them. This bond, sometimes forged out of necessity, is not necessarily harmful. As children sit spongelike before the screen, they are absorbing more information about the world than children their age had a few decades ago. Children entering school today know a great deal about outer space and far-off places. But this vast store of information, accumulated without direction, is often unsorted and uninterpreted. If it is to be useful as the raw material of ideas and dreams, it ordinarily must be acquired under the loving care of discriminating adults.[1]

Lucky is the family that not only shares its enjoyment of good television programs but reads aloud together, not every night or perhaps not even every week, but on all those occasions when the outstanding book comes along—so well written or beautiful or humorous or all-round compelling that the entranced reader can't bear to have the other members of the family miss it. It doesn't matter whether the content is for the oldest or the youngest, just so it is first-rate reading with depth and significance.

Of course, the prereaders in the family have special privileges beyond the communal reading-aloud sessions. Going to bed is made bearable by the stories that accompany it. It doesn't matter whether they are told by Great-Aunt Mary, read by mother, or made up by father.

The induction of the prereading child into the magical variety of stories and books should continue after he is six. For such a child, who has already known the heady delights of books, that first year of learning to read may come as something of a shock. He generally thinks he will be reading by the end of the first day, and great is his amazement at the slowness of the process. Here parents can help the school by providing the child with book experiences that keep him wanting to read for himself.

Reading aloud in the family is one of the most precious memories a child can have. It means enjoyment shared—the younger children trying hard to understand what makes the older children and the grownups laugh or weep, the adults stopping to explain the joke or the tragedy or to help the young members of the family understand what is at stake. Thus is the family at one, united warmly and happily through shared enjoyment. Families that send their children out of the home knowing good books of many kinds, honest, dependable books, sensibly written and absorbing, written with imagination and beauty, have given their children a lifelong source of strength and enjoyment.

1. See "Television: The Impact and Influence of Another Medium," in Part Seven.

## IN THE CLASSROOM

For the children who come from families where reading is an accepted and satisfying occupation, the teacher merely becomes another member of the brotherhood of literature. Her role is similar to that played by the parents—one who advises, shares, and appreciates. For the children who went from their mother's arms to television, the role of the teacher is more difficult. She must reestablish or, in some cases, establish books as the center of communal enjoyment and must devise ways of using books to make an impact on children and help them identify books as a source of delight and satisfaction.

### Getting to Know the Needs and Interests of Children[2]

The interests of primary children are easily identifiable. They are interested chiefly in themselves, their families, and their pets. The interests of older children are more disparate and less obvious. The attraction of the peer culture is difficult to resist, and although literature can help satisfy their unexpressed needs, children of the middle grades must be persuaded. In general, children have similar needs: to be secure, to love and be loved, to belong, to achieve, to change or play, to know, to experience beauty and order. Individual children will vary in the depth to which they feel one need or another. A teacher with a knowledge of children's literature

2. See Chapter 1, pp. 3–16; Chapter 2, p. 21.

must take the initiative in presenting literature with the potential of fulfilling these needs.

### Making an Impact

The easiest need to satisfy is that for play. Teachers who tell or read humorous stories create a climate of mutual enjoyment. This should be but the first step. The climate of enjoyment modulates easily to a climate of mutual respect in which the teacher can lead children to understand and appreciate the less obvious satisfactions of literature. When reading aloud, with the use of brief asides, the teacher can stimulate reflection on what a character means by what he says, or what motivates him to act as he does. With older children, these provocative thoughts can lead to discussions that can make literature relevant to their own lives, their aspirations, and disappointments. If the teacher is sensitive to children's comments and facial expressions, their misconceptions can be brought to light without threat.

While some children can see beyond the printed word and be moved by what they visualize and feel, many children remain solidly on the page. The teacher must take the initiative, and through the use of sensitive reading aloud, so stir the emotions of children that they experience the power of language to convey a mood. She must come to know her students—their potentials and limitations. Through the selection of literature that is both appropriate and relevant, she can help them see what the literature experience has to offer them. Through the use of dramatization, music, and the visual arts, they may gradually realize how much more satisfying the experience can become when they bring something of themselves to it.

## IN THE LIBRARY

The key person in bringing children and books together may be the librarian. Librarians all over the country, in school libraries and in public libraries, gather young children around them and with their stories cast the magic spell of literature. Teachers who bring their classes for a story hour discover the impact these stories can have by watching the reactions of their children and they also learn a multitude of techniques from the storyteller.

The most important role of the librarian is that of adviser. It is she who knows books and knows the resources of her library. Teachers come to know their children more quickly and may recognize the needs and interests that can be met with literature, but it is the sensitive and understanding librarian who knows what materials may be used to meet those needs and interests. The teacher who works closely with the librarian will find that her classroom activities will be richer with the librarian's help, whether that help consists of providing seven books on dragons, recommending films and film strips, or providing display space for completed projects.

This is not to say that children do not benefit from the librarian's understanding and expertise. It may take children a while to trust someone they see only periodically, but once that trust is established, the librarian, only remotely connected with the possible inhibitions of classroom and home life, becomes the one who can locate the books that will provide answers.

Parents, too, can make valuable use of the librarian. Many parents, interested in encouraging their children to read, buy the books they enjoyed as children. Sometimes they choose stories that never grow old but often they choose books too dated to appeal to today's children. Librarians are in the best possible position to recommend books for purchase. Those parents who have induced a love of literature in their children will find, when their children are old enough to go to the library by themselves, that the librarian is ready and able to encourage children's further growth in the love of literature.

# Techniques for Using Books with Children*

The following section discusses telling and reading stories aloud, reading poetry aloud, choral speaking, discussion, interpreting literature, developing sensitivity to style through written work, dramatization, using music, using visual material, helping children spread their enthusiasms, and a literature program.

## STORYTELLING AND READING ALOUD

Today, more than ever before, youngsters need the security and comfort that the sharing of literature brings. Children love to listen to a good story that is well told or well read. Parents, teachers, and librarians can captivate them with tales of fancy and wonder.

### Values of an Oral Presentation of Literature

**For younger children.** Storytelling and reading aloud are the primary teacher's most powerful charms for luring children to books. By skillful use of the entertainment value of the many stories and poems she reads, she not only persuades children to undertake the trials of learning to read but also introduces them to a wide variety of literature.

Through listening to stories told or read aloud, children develop their powers of aural comprehension. The ability to hear, comprehend, and react intelligently to the spoken word is of great importance. In one nursery school where many picture stories were available, the children, it was discovered, required pictures in order to attend to or understand a story that was told or read. This is a serious limitation in learning a language. Picture clues are valuable aids to reading in the beginning years, but children should also have continuous practice in hearing poetry and stories which are not illustrated. With such balanced experiences, their vocabularies will grow and so will their ability to comprehend the meaning of the spoken word. Moreover, a word that has been heard and understood is more easily recognized when a child encounters it in print.

These are utilitarian reasons for storytelling and reading aloud to young children, but there are other equally important reasons. Unconsciously, children's ears are becoming accustomed to the tune and cadence of English, such English as they may not hear on the streets or perhaps even in their homes. Traditionally, the difficulty encountered by middle-class teachers in lower socioeconomic areas has been communication. The teacher spoke a different kind of English from that spoken in the homes and on the streets. Some students, either because they identified with the teacher or because they recognized that if they were to find a better life than they had they must learn to speak as the teacher spoke, learned two languages: one to communicate with the teacher and one to communicate with their families and friends.

Recently, teachers, more mindful of the need to communicate with their students, have begun, consciously or unconsciously, to speak the language of their students. Although interpersonal communication may have increased, exposure to standard English has decreased. A storytelling and reading-aloud program beginning with very young children and continuing throughout the elementary school would insure the exposure to a wide variety of English patterns in a situation that would not interfere with interpersonal communication.

Also, when the teacher tells or reads sto-

*Some of the material in this section was first published by Raymond Lubway as articles in three Supplementary Educational Monographs, the proceedings of the University of Chicago Reading Conferences: pp. 19–23, *Oral Aspects of Reading* (1955) and pp. 78–81, *Developing Permanent Interest in Reading* (1956), edited by Helen Robinson, and pp. 85–89, *Reading: Seventy-Five Years of Progress* (1966), edited by H. Alan Robinson. University of Chicago Press © 1955, 1956, 1966 by The University of Chicago.

ries to children, they hear and enjoy stories they cannot yet read for themselves. A first-grader whose reading vocabulary is limited and his reading materials something less than enthralling may experience a sense of defeat. Then the well-told or well-read story, dramatic and full of suspense, fills the gap between what he can read and what he would like to read. The story acts as a stimulant to his flagging will by reminding him of delights that await him.

Finally, young children hear and enjoy types of literature they might never read for themselves, but find delightful when they listen to them interpreted by someone who understands and thoroughly enjoys them.

**For older children.** While the practice of reading aloud and telling stories is common in the primary grades, it is not fully exploited by many teachers of the middle and upper grades. The responsibility to "cover material" is a worry of many middle- and upper-grade teachers and understandably so. The curriculum contains a wide range of content subjects, and the press of their demands worries some teachers to the extent that calling the class together for a story seems, if not unwise, at least questionable.

Another explanation is that reading aloud does not perform exactly the same function that it does in the primary grades. Reading aloud to first-graders allows the teacher to display the delights of literature in order to attract them to the task of learning to read. Most of the children in the middle and upper grades, on the other hand, have learned to read with some degree of competence and independence. Many teachers feel the responsibility to refine the reading skills of their students and do so in the reading period with questions and answers. If this is the middle- and upper-grade child's only experience with literature, what then has happened to the promise of delight made to him when he was a first-grader? It would be a skillful teacher, indeed, who could convey the luster of literature through a written assignment. If a child's interests are to be broadened, his enjoyment heightened, and his understanding deepened, there is no substitute for reading aloud or storytelling.

Of course, some of the values of reading aloud to younger children are equally important for older children. By the time some children reach the middle grades, there may be considerable discrepancy between what they *can* read and what they can appreciate and enjoy. This discrepancy, if not reduced, often produces the reluctant reader—that gadfly of the classroom who has cut himself off from books and thereby pricks the conscience of every teacher. While there is no sure way to snare the reluctant reader, reading aloud is an important bait for books. Such children have been known to check out a book that the teacher has just finished reading to the class in order to read it for themselves. Because the story is already known, the reading struggle is eased somewhat.

When children reach the middle grades, many of them have developed a well-rounded interest in reading. Some, on the other hand, have narrow interests: only family stories or fantasy or sports stories or nonfiction. When the teacher reads aloud, these children hear and enjoy types of literature they would never read for themselves.

The teacher who has several anthologies of good poetry and a book of short stories on her desk will never be at a loss when the movie projector fails to arrive on time, or the math lesson ends ten minutes before the period is over. Not only will an emergency have been met but valuable time that could have gone to waste will have been put to good use.

Many teachers of older children have recognized the values in reading a continuous story to their classes—an entire book taking several months to finish. This regularly scheduled storytime is a quiet period when the problems of the day are set aside. A powerful bond is established between teacher and class as, together, they follow the wonderful adventures of Taran in *The High King* or laugh at the hilarious antics of Mr. Toad in *The Wind in the Willows*.

The contributions to the mental health of

a classroom would be justification enough for taking the time to read aloud to children. The bond of mutual enjoyment that is established between teacher and class during storytime pervades their relationship throughout the day. As a teacher reveals her understanding and sympathy with the plights of fictional characters, she also reveals her potential of understanding and sympathy for the plights of the children in her class. As she reveals her delight in a vivid phrase or a fresh bit of imagery, she is also revealing something very personal about herself. It is an act of trust to which children are very responsive. Once that mutual trust is established, the child finds it easier to cope with threatening moments of tension.

A final value for reading aloud to middle schoolers presupposes a bond of mutual trust between teacher and class. Growing up is a puzzling, exhilarating, and sometimes frustrating process. Teachers and parents do what they can to help children interpret behavior that is puzzling, but generally they handle such problems on a one-to-one basis. Many books today deal in fictional terms with this very crucial process of growing up. While it is risky to practice group therapy when one is not trained to do so, teachers who read such stories as *The Loner, Queenie Peavy*, or *A Room Made of Windows* may bring comfort to a child in conflict over his yearning for the rights of adulthood and his treasuring of the privileges of childhood. Discussions that these stories might stimulate may be little more than the ventilation of worry, but talking about worry is a respected therapeutic device.

## Storytelling and Reading Aloud: A Comparison

There is no doubt that of the two techniques, storytelling has the greater impact upon the listener. It is more direct than reading. There is no book between you and your audience, and you can give the story plus your own enjoyment of it unhampered by following the precise words on the page. Your facial expressions, your occasional gestures, and your inflections all respond to the audience just as they do when you regale your family or friends with an account of some exciting experience you have just had. When you can tell the story of "Boots and His Brothers" or "The Fire-Bird, the Horse of Power, and the Princess Vasilissa"[3] with the immediacy and freshness of a personal adventure, you can be sure that you have given your listeners more than just a story; you have given them something of yourself.

Many teachers feel that they don't have the time to prepare stories. Obviously, reading a story does not require as much preparation time as telling one does, although a teacher must certainly be familiar with the story she plans to read. Knowing the story enables her to anticipate what is ahead, to make use of the suspense-heightening pause, to slip in, parenthetically, brief explanations of unusual words. But being poorly prepared to read a story does not necessarily lead to disaster; being poorly prepared to tell one always does.

Another difference between the two techniques concerns the range of choice of material. Although some types of books are better read silently, it would be safe to say that most books can be read aloud to children with impact. Not so with storytelling.

There are some books, like Kipling's *Just So Stories*, that depend for their charm and meaning upon the exact words of the author. Such stories offer not only a good tale but a matchless style that is the author's alone. The telling of these stories would require memorization, which is never storytelling but something much more formal.

Another type of story that should not be told is the so-called picture story. A picture story is one in which the pictures are an integral part of the text, as in Marjorie Flack's *The Story About Ping*, or Louise Fatio's *Happy*

3. See *The Arbuthnot Anthology*, pp. 340 and 393.

*Lion* series. Such picture stories lose a great deal if they are told without the accompanying illustrations.

The choice of material for storytelling is further limited by the age of the audience. As has been said, the informal, intimate approach to literature that storytelling provides has enabled teachers and librarians to entice young children to the delights of literature. The younger the child, the shorter his span of attention. Therefore the stories he is told must be of a length to reach the climax before the fidgeting begins.

While reading aloud is perhaps the more versatile, and skill in its use the easier to acquire, the storyteller has two important advantages.

First, the teacher with a head full of stories to tell never has the need to carry books with her. When the class goes on a field trip, the bus is invariably late. The storyteller can gather the class around her and make the time pass quickly. Many a crisis, which can alarm children unnecessarily or require a restless waiting, has been soothed with a story that dispels distraction or alarm.

Second, the successful storyteller learns how to capture the attention of her audience and hold it. She learns to observe those subtle signs of interest: the staring eyes, the still hands. She learns the signs of flagging interest: the shift in position, the head turning. By interpreting these signs correctly, the storyteller uses the tricks of the trade to revive interest, to retrieve the little boy on the fringe of the story. With the knowledge of her audience, she emphasizes those elements of a story that she knows will be relished.

## HOW TO TELL STORIES

An agreeable voice and clear, pure diction are perhaps the first requisites for the storyteller. Needless to say, there should not be a special voice reserved for storytelling. You have sometimes heard the saccharine voice that talks down to children. You should take stock of your own vocal equipment. Ask others to evaluate your voice honestly. Record it if possible, so that you can listen to it yourself. If your voice is nasal, harsh, or monotonous, try to improve it for everyday use to the point where it is agreeable. Most women can profitably pitch their everyday speaking voices a key or so lower, and both they and the children will be more peaceful as a result. Go to the theater, turn on the radio or television, or play some recordings of gifted readers, and carefully listen to and compare their voices. Try to discover what makes the voices of artists like Katharine Cornell, Helen Hayes, Sir Laurence Olivier, Richard Burton, Maurice Evans, and Dylan Thomas so moving and satisfying. Lessons with an expert in voice placement and production will help you, but by cultivating a listening ear you can do much for yourself.

A good voice is invariably supported by deep and controlled breathing. Breath must come from the diaphragm, not from the upper chest. Read aloud sustained passages from the Psalms or from Shakespeare. Put on Maurice Evans' recording of the lines from *Richard II* or Sir John Gielgud's "Ages of Man," and read the lines with the record. You can then tell when you run out of breath and shouldn't. Breathe deeper, and not only will you be able to sustain those long sonorous passages, but your voice will grow in richness and resonance. Shallow breathing makes thin, tired voices, which are apt to become shrill and sharp. Deep, controlled breathing gives to the voice both support and increased range and color.

Clear articulation of words is as essential as an agreeable voice. Of course, nothing is worse than an artificial, overprecise enunciation, except perhaps an attempt to imitate the speech of another district that is quite foreign to us. If we are New England, Southern, Midwestern, or Western, let's not try for Oxford English or any other accent unnatural to us. Instead, let's eradicate the impurities of our own particular region (every region has them), and try to speak the purest, most vigorous pattern of English that obtains in our section of the country. Storytelling is ruined if it sounds artificial or pretentious, for it is the homiest of all the arts.

In telling stories, you should always maintain the quiet, intimate tone of friendly conversation, but you must also speak so that everyone in your audience can hear you easily. How can you be heard by those farthest from you without shouting at the people sitting nearby? Deep, controlled breathing should build up resonance in your voice, and resonance plays a large part in the carrying quality of the spoken word. But it is not the whole secret. Light, sweet voices are often perfectly audible in the most remote corners of a theater or an auditorium. To be clearly heard at a considerable distance, you must consciously *direct or send your voice* to the most remote people in your audience. If it is possible to see their faces, watch to determine whether they are hearing comfortably. If they are leaning forward, tense or uneasy, they are not hearing. When this happens, women, in particular, tend to pitch their voices higher and shriller. Don't do it. Instead, take a deep breath, keep your voice pitched low and then consciously send your words to the farthest members of the audience.

Storytelling is an art that requires disciplines of many kinds, and one of these is the choice of words. As a storyteller, you cannot go far with a meager vocabulary; moreover, you must develop a sensitivity to words, so that you cannot possibly tell an Irish tale with the same vocabulary and cadence you use for a Norwegian story. Read the story aloud first until you get the feel and flavor of its peculiar vocabulary and word patterns. While exact memorizing is usually the wrong approach to the folk tale, the other extreme is much worse—a slipshod telling, a careless use of words. Such modern colloquialisms as "Boots got real mad," or "the princess looked perfectly lovely," or "'O.K.,' said the lad," can ruin the mood and magic of a tale. Words must be chosen with a sensitive perception of the individual style of each tale. The dreamlike romance of "Sadko" calls for a very different choice of words from the rural dialogue of the old man and his good wife in "Gudbrand on the Hillside." Voice, diction, and vocabulary demand the training of your ear. Listen to yourself—to your voice, your speech, and, above all, to the appropriate words for your story.

A second aspect of the word problem is the effect the peculiar language of the folk tales has upon children. For instance, consider words like "pate," "goody," "lassie," "mare," "foal," "tapers," "minstrels," "spindle." One of the easiest ways to explain these baffling words to young listeners is just to paraphrase them casually as you tell the story: "Just then he met a lassie—a young girl—'Good day, lassie,' said he." And the word is established. There is no reason why children should not hear a much wider range of words than they are going to use, but there is every reason why you should help them understand the words as they hear them, either by paraphrasing or systematical explanation before or after the storytelling.

Your particular style of beauty or plainness is of no consequence to successful storytelling, but certain other elements of appearance are. Whether you sit or stand, you must be relaxed and easy. If you have to stand to tell your stories, then practice them standing until you are at ease and so can enjoy yourself. If you sit with your children grouped comfortably close to you, then practice telling your story sitting down until you are used to telling stories in that position. For most of us, it is safest to practice both ways, so that we can forget ourselves in either position and be ready for any storytelling situation in which we may find ourselves. Forgetting ourselves does not mean that we can afford either to sit or to stand sloppily. Practice in front of a mirror for a little while until you know what a comfortable good posture looks like; then hold it. Either sitting or standing, you should keep your hands free of handkerchiefs or pencils or other impedimenta, free for the occasional gesture most people make in emphasis. Your clothes should be the kind your audience forgets the moment the tale begins. If you wear chains or necklaces, don't fuss with them and don't wear clanking bracelets. In short, avoid any distracting element in your dress that centers attention on you and takes it away from the story.

The important elements of your appearance come from within. These are your genuine, unaffected smile of enjoyment, the twinkle in your eye, the sudden gravity, the warning frown—in short, those slight but unmistakable responses to the changing mood or matter of the tale. The elaborate pantomime and large dramatic gestures of the stage have no place in storytelling. You need only the subtle expressions of the face and eyes, responding even as the voice responds to the import of the story.

### Selecting a Story to Tell

The easiest stories to begin with are the folk tales. They are easy because they were created orally by storytellers and have perfect form for narration. The form is invariable: a clear, brief introduction that launches the conflict or problem; the development or body of the story with a rising action, increasing suspense, and an exciting climax that marks the turning point in the story and the fortunes of the hero; and, finally, a satisfying conclusion that winds up everything—problems, conflicts, and villains all suitably disposed of. From the simplest cumulative "Pancake" type of story, through "Snow White" and "The Bremen Town Musicians," to the more subtle "Clever Manka" for the oldest children, these folk tales tell with ease and will help you fall into the storytelling habit and develop your own unique style.

The next richest source of stories to tell are the myths, but here there is a problem of adapting your story, generally from several sources, until you have a version you thoroughly enjoy. Many of the myths are long and may take two or three story periods to tell, for example, the stories of Perseus and of Theseus. Fortunately these two tales have been well told by Ian Serraillier in *The Gorgon's Head* and *The Way of Danger*. Reading these books will show you why even the simplest myths demand more imagination in the telling and a more choice vocabulary than the folk tales.

The hero cycles or epics, such as the *Odyssey*, *Sigurd*, *Beowulf*, and *Robin Hood*, are the hardest of all stories to tell. They demand long and careful preparation, a study of sources, a comparison of versions, and considerable practice before they are ready for telling. The *Odyssey* and *Robin Hood* are the easiest, *Sigurd* the most difficult. Which do you care about so strongly that you are willing to study and work long and hard on the adaptation and telling? The epics are well worth your time and the children's, because as you tell them over a number of weeks the children are steeped in heroic struggles and noble achievement as they never are in listening to a short story.

Most stories written these days are for reading, not for telling, but here and there you will find little stories that are as perfect for telling as any folk tale. "Paddy's Three Pets" by Mary Phillips is a good example, also *Torten's Christmas Secret* by Maurice Dolbier, "Peter the Goldfish" by Julian Street, and *The Bears on Hemlock Mountain* by Alice Dalgliesh.

If you begin with your favorite folk tales and tell enough of them to get the feel and fun of storytelling in your very bones, then you will be better able to spot a likely candidate for your repertoire, whether it is a tale as old as old or as new as today.

### Learning and Telling a Story

Probably no two people learn and re-create stories in quite the same way, but visualizing characters and scenes often helps. In "The Pancake," you might see a snug kitchen with a mother standing close to the stove, her seven hungry children crowding much too near her to watch that fat sizzling pancake. An old grandfather is sitting over in the corner smoking his pipe. Through the open door—it must be open because the pancake rolled through it—you might see a road winding over the hills and across the country and clear out of sight. You must see the characters, too, some in more detail than others, depending upon how dramatic their words or their roles are in the tale. Visualizing them undoubtedly helps in characterizing them; so if you see the sneering faces of Cinderella's sisters, undoubtedly something of the sneer gets into your interpretation of their words and behavior. Not that you do actually sneer, of course—that is stage business, not storytelling—but still a sneerful suggestion undoubtedly creeps in. And if you are telling a hero tale, something noble and serious comes into your voice, face, and manner.

Obviously, if you are going to tell a story you must know it thoroughly. This involves overlearning to such a degree that you cannot possibly forget the tale, but you can stand aside and play with the interpretation of your story because you have no worries about the mechanics of recall. Some people feel that memorizing is the only solution. Others consider memorizing the wrong approach to the folk tales for two reasons: First, these naïve tales do not have the formal perfection of the literary story; they were always kept fluid and personal by the old tellers. If they are memorized, they are likely to sound stilted and impersonal. Ruth Sawyer, in *The Way of the Storyteller*, pays a tribute to the storytelling of her Irish nurse, who was proud of her art and used it with great dignity. She would close a story with the saying, "Take it, and may the next one who tells it better it." This is exactly what happens.

A second reason why exact memorizing is not recommended is that the forgetting of a single phrase or a connecting sentence will throw the teller completely off, so that she has to stop or start over or pause awkwardly while she racks her brain for the lost words. This of course spoils a story. On the other hand, if the story is thoroughly learned but not memorized it will remain in your memory for years.

Psychologists say that the greatest carryover in learning and the least loss through forgetting are insured by practicing in the same way in which you are going to use your material. Since storytelling is oral, learn your story orally, in the sitting or standing position you expect to employ, and with an imaginary audience around you. Of course you read your tale once or twice silently until you are thoroughly familiar with its sequential action, its mood, its areas of suspense, and its climax. You may then read it aloud once or twice if you wish to hear it, listening especially for its peculiar cadences, its folk flavor. Then begin telling it aloud, with the book at hand to refer to when you forget. It will be heavy going at first, with more rough spots than smooth, but go through the tale as a whole once or twice. Then polish the beginning and the end until both are easy and sure. Dialogue is the most difficult and the most fun. The dialogue sections you must lift out and work at until you make the right connections and they come naturally and spontaneously. Every time you single out a special section for practice, go back and tell the whole story again until it comes to life as a whole.

Perhaps one storyteller's[4] experience will illustrate the difference between memorizing and the process just described. In telling "The Pancake," she had no idea when and to whom the pancake says, "How do you do," or "As well as I may," or "Good day to you," or "The same to you." The pancake and the characters he encounters exchange all these various forms of greetings and responses. These she knew in general and applied as she wished. As a matter of fact, her use of them seemed to follow a definite pattern that was never the modern "Hi-yah," or

4. This is May Hill Arbuthnot's own experience.

the stately "God rest you, stranger" of some other tale. Her version was both the pattern of the "Pancake" and her own personal pattern. It was learned, but not memorized.

The other spots in the story which you lift out for special practice are those which stir the emotions. Listen to yourself. If you are waxing overemotional, tone down; or if you muff the climax, go back and heighten the suspense that leads up to it, bringing out the climax on a fine crescendo. The great virtue of working orally is that you can hear your weak spots and strengthen them. You can hear where the story becomes a little dull or slow, where your dialogue halts or the vocabulary is obscure for the particular group you have in mind. In short, oral practice for oral presentation is the safest, the quickest, and the most effective method of learning, whether you memorize your material or not.

The beginnings and endings of your stories should be polished until they are smooth and sure. The beginning requires special care because it establishes the mood of your tale. You announce your story informally in any of a dozen ways: "Today we are going to hear about our old friends, 'The Three Billy-Goats Gruff.'" "I've a new story for you today, and it's called 'The Fox and His Travels.'" "You have all heard stories about 'Jack the Giant Killer,' but do you know there was one *girl* who got the best of a powerful giant? Our story is about her, and her name is 'Molly Whuppie.'"

Then, having announced your story, pause a moment—not too long, not long enough to let the children start squirming again, just long enough for a deep, quiet breath—and then begin. The beginning of a nonsense tale is very different from the beginning of a romance, as you can hear when you read these lines aloud:

> *Once upon a time there was a man who had a goody who was so cross grained that there was no living with her. ("Goody Gainst the Stream" from* Tales from the Fjeld.*)*

> *Once, in the golden time, when an Irish king sat in every province and plenty covered the land, there lived in Connaught a grand old king with one daughter. She was as tall and slender as the reeds that grow by Lough Erne, and her face was the fairest in seven counties. ("The Princess and the Vagabone," from* The Way of the Storyteller.*)*

> *There was once upon a time a Fisherman who lived with his wife in a pig-stye close by the sea, and every day he went out fishing; and he fished, and he fished. ("The Fisherman and his Wife" from* Grimm's Fairy Tales.*)*

> *As Chicken-Licken went one day to the wood, an acorn fell on her poor bald pate, and she thought the sky had fallen. ("Chicken-Licken," from* Popular Rhymes and Nursery Tales.*)*

Here are the beginnings of a droll, a romance, a comic-tragedy, and a nursery tale. In your telling, you establish the right atmosphere for your whole story with these opening lines; you put your audience in the right mood and build up anticipation.

So with the endings you should leave your audience satisfied, with a sense of completion. Good stories have been spoiled by a weak, inconclusive telling of the end. It must come with conviction, whether it is nonsense, romance, poetic justice, or one of those surprise endings which are fun for everyone. The noisy grunt or inhalation with which you finish off "The Pancake" ought to make the children jump and then laugh. This is primitive slapstick humor but well worth practicing for its gratifying results. Very different are the surprise endings of "Clever Manka" and "Sadko," or the romantic conclusions of "The Princess and the Vagabone" and "East o' the Sun," or the poetic justice of "The Fisherman and His Wife." These satisfying conclusions are characteristic of the folk tales and should be enhanced by the way you tell them.

Storytelling is essentially the art of the fireside, the campfire, the cribside, the classroom, and the library. It should be kept simple and informal, or else it goes over into the realm of the stage, where it does not belong.

Yet the folk tales are dramatic and should be dramatically told in the restrained drama of everyday talk.

Young children are so motor-minded that they can't talk about a train without "choo-chooing" and making the appropriate scuffing, shuttling motions of feet and arms. So in telling stories to them, you unconsciously use more gestures and more pantomime than you would ordinarily. It may not be necessary, but it seems entirely natural to roll the pancake out of the door with a big circular motion of the hand when you say "and rolled out of the door like a wheel," or to suggest the length of the troll's nose with hand to nose and then hand extended full arm's length away as you say, "and a nose as long as a poker." Most nursery-school and kindergarten teachers and most mothers of young children do something of the sort. If such gestures are not overdone, they are natural and legitimate.

## HOW TO READ STORIES ALOUD

Everything that has been said about appearance, dramatic simplicity, voice, and diction for storytelling applies also to reading aloud. It must be remembered that one of the most important purposes of reading to children is to make an impact on them—to make them curious about what is inside a book and to feel glad when they have found out. To do this, you must use the power of your voice, intonation, and personal delight to bring the fictional characters to life, to make their problems and frustrations real, to spread the contagion of their joys and triumphs.

### Reading to Younger Children

When you read to children you must remember that you have a book between yourself and them. You can easily lose the attention of young children in particular if your own attention is confined to the book. Acquaint yourself with the text in advance. Make maximum use of your voice, intonation, and a dramatic pause if you can anticipate a change in mood, the introduction of a new character, the building up of suspense, a smashing climax, or a surprise ending. You must know the book so well that you can look over it directly into the eyes of the children.

Getting the attention of young children is sometimes a challenge. Teachers have devised many ways of announcing that it is time to change activities: the tinkling of a tiny dinner bell, the soft but penetrating sound of chimes. Some techniques have the solemnity of a ritual—the lighting of a story candle is dramatic enough to signify that something very special is about to happen. Usually, though, a simple announcement of "storytime" is enough to settle the most rambunctious of children.

There are some stories that begin with first sentences so startling or intriguing that no introduction is needed. "Rose Birnbaum hurried down the street, clutching an overflowing shopping bag in one arm and four rolls of wallpaper in the other. She was on her way to visit her son Bernard, the detective, and give him some chicken soup" (*Inspector Rose* by Ben Shecter). Obviously, such sentences provide their own introduction. Although you do not have to "sell" a book to children already interested in reading, a dramatic or tantalizing introduction will not be wasted on them. You must think of those children who have resisted the attractions of books and those who are still diffident. An introductory question or comment can often build up an anticipation that will last until the story is well on its way. The first sentence of *Mr. Popper's Penguins*, for example, gives no clue to the hilarious adventures to follow. One teacher introduces it by asking, "Have you ever heard of a pet that lives in a refrigerator?" The children, intrigued by pets anyway, usually respond scornfully, "In a *refrigerator!*" If the children start guessing what kind of pet it will be, the teacher usually lets it go on until someone guesses penguins or until she senses that too much delay will dissipate their initial curiosity.

A librarian who usually tells and reads folk tales sensitizes children to style by asking, "Do all stories begin, 'Once upon a time'? Here is one that doesn't," and goes on to read, "It is the dead of night. The old farm lies fast asleep and everyone inside the house is sleeping too." And so *The Tomten* by Astrid Lindgren is launched.

If the book to be read is a picture story, it is essential that the children be comfortably seated as close to you as possible. This will avoid craning necks and a chorus of "I can't see!" Hold the book with the pictures facing the children so that everyone can see them. This can be done easily with such glorious picture stories as *The Story About Ping*, *Curious George*, *Petunia*, *The Happy Lion*, or *Madeline*, because the text is so simple and direct that an upside-down clue is all you will need. If the text is longer, then hold the book to one side, with the pictures still in view. You can take a long look at the text while the children study the pictures.

Children may love one book because it is funny, another because they can see themselves in the characters. By being clear about the needs that literature can help satisfy, you will find the task of selecting books to read aloud much simpler. By being clear about the chief appeal of a particular book, you will be better able to use your voice and facial expression to heighten that appeal.

**Reading books to amuse.** After a hard work session there is nothing like a funny book to refresh and revitalize a group. Although there is no hard-and-fast rule to help one predict what children will think is funny, stories of mischief are always safe choices.

The mischief of *Curious George* is not only hilarious but innocent. Once children understand what *curious* means and how George's curiosity gets him into trouble, they begin to chuckle with anticipation. When you notice this happening, you can use the "pause" to prolong the delicious suspense. Allowing time for speculation on what is to come is effective if it does not go on too long and if it can be kept within some limits by the text. Aimless speculation is time-consuming and rarely accurate.

Young children may be introduced to grave nonsense with Russell Hoban's *The Sorely Trying Day*. Although they may not understand all of the words, they will recognize with quiet amusement the common phenomenon of passing the blame and telling half the truth. You should be sure that the class understands what "sorely trying" means. Then they will understand Father's irritation with the uproar in the house when he returns from "a sorely trying day."

**Reading books to reassure.** As a child grows and encounters varieties of human behavior, his as well as that of others, he finds much that is curious and sometimes bewildering. There are many books available that deal with situations and feelings very familiar to young children. If a child hears these stories and is assured that the characters in stories behave much the same as he does, he may begin to acquire a faith in literature as a source of explanations of more complicated situations and feelings.

In Russell Hoban's *Bedtime for Frances*, Frances, though a little badger, is definitely human in the ploys she thinks of to put off going to bed and staying there—a familiar situation to children. Her struggle to stay up ends suddenly when the "smack and whack" of a moth's wings against the window pane remind her of a spanking. Then, "All of a sudden she was tired. She lay down and closed her eyes so she could think better." There is no need for you to draw any parallels between Frances' experience and real life; you will see that the children have done it themselves by the knowing, somewhat sheepish smiles on their faces.

Maurice Sendak in his *Where the Wild Things Are* effectively puts chains around another night fear—monsters. Children love this book—perhaps because they empathize with a boy who conquers the monsters with such casual aplomb. You should allow enough time for children to study the details of the exquisitely ugly beasts and keep the book in the classroom for individuals to pore over later.

A storm with lightning and thunder can really disrupt a classroom. The brave children will rush to the windows to watch it and the fearful ones will stay glued to their seats. In this situation Charlotte Zolotow's *The Storm Book* would be a good one to read. It is the story of a storm and of a little boy's wondering questions. The violence of the storm is vividly described, but in sharp contrast are the mother's quiet, gentle, simple explanations.

When you read stories that portray real situations and concerns in fictional form, the reading should be straight and unforced. If there is a message there for children they will receive it. This is especially true when reading stories that treat such delicate themes as size, loss of a pet, and death. Some teachers prefer not to read such stories as Jerrold Beim's *The Smallest Boy in the Class*, because the child who is the smallest is extremely sensitive to the fact; others feel that reading such a book aloud to the entire class may alter the attitudes of those who pick on him. Taro Yashima treats the subject more subtly in *Crow Boy*.

**Reading to stretch thinking and doing.** By reading a few of the beginning-reading books, you may snare the reluctant readers. By reading Crosby Bonsall's *The Case of the Cat's Meow*, you may capture the interest of others with a type of fiction that fascinates everyone—the mystery. You would do well to have copies of other Bonsall books as well. Second-graders might be ready for *Basil and the Pygmy Cats* by Eve Titus.

Another type of literature that children should be exposed to is the fanciful tale. Although you should not saturate very young children with fanciful and folk tales, you should read a few. You might find, as one first-grade teacher did, that their simple plots make it possible for children to notice similarities in different versions. The teacher had read Esphyr Slobodkina's *Caps for Sale*. A peddler of caps fell asleep under a tree. When he awoke, his caps had been stolen by monkeys. In his rage, he shook his finger and his fists and stamped his foot; the monkeys out of reach in the tree merely imitated him. Exasperated, he threw his cap to the ground. And so did the monkeys. Some weeks later, the teacher read Mary Hemingway's *The Old Man and the Monkeys*. The children saw that although this story was set in China, the old man's hats were straw, and he threw a pine cone at the monkeys, the stories were the same. Certainly a mind-stretching experience for seven-year-olds.

### Reading to Older Children

Whether you read to younger or older children, try to arrange the seating so as to approximate the warmth and closeness of a gathering at a campfire, and sit as close to the class as space and comfort permit. You should read the book beforehand so that you are freed from complete dependence on the text and can read to the children more directly. By maintaining eye-contact, you can gauge the effect the story is having on them. If their eyes show they are absorbed, you can put more drama into your voice and drag out the delicious spell. If they are listless and restless, you can put more pep into the reading and possibly summarize long descriptive paragraphs.

The more familiar you are with the book you are reading, the better prepared you are to anticipate what is coming and to make effective use of brief asides to enrich the appreciation of literature by pointing up interesting use of imagery, character development, and style.

**To widen reading interests.** A fifth-grade

teacher, who, as a matter of routine, asked his students to keep a record of their reading, noticed after a few months that the same titles were appearing again and again. When he asked the school librarian's advice, she pointed out that many good books in the library were rarely checked out. "Sometimes I think that it is because they are on the bottom shelf and the children never stoop down." The teacher asked the librarian to select ten of those books and provide him with a brief synopsis of each, so that he could take them to his class and try to "sell" the books.

At the beginning of the next literature period, he placed the books with great ceremony on one of the front desks and then announced: "The school librarian says that there are a great many good books in the library that you people have missed. She thinks that it may be because they were on the bottom shelf and you were too lazy to bend down. She gave me a few and I am going to read the first couple of pages just to show you what you have missed." The teacher read *The Trumpeter of Krakow*, a classic with a style that does not have obvious and immediate appeal. Then he added some titillating bits about a hidden precious stone and asked, "How many would like to read this book?" The hands flew up. He gave it to one child and assured the rest that there would be a sign-up sheet on the bulletin board for anyone else who wanted to read it. Then he went on to the next book and the next and the next. After each synopsis and reading, the book was offered to the class and was received with all the excitement of an auction. Sign-up sheets were duly posted, and after each child read a book he passed it on to the next child on the list. The teacher continued to bring a wide variety of books to his class every two weeks for the rest of the school year and the children's reading records took on a very individual look. The presentation and reading aloud by the teacher had had an impact. At the end of the year, when children were permitted to take out ten books for the summer, the librarian reported that one girl from the class came to ask, "Do you have any more of those 'bottom shelf' books?"

**To develop an appreciation of style.** The practice of reading aloud an entire book during a regularly scheduled storytime offers you the widest range of opportunities for portraying literature not only as entertainment but as a source of new and intriguing satisfactions. With brief asides as you read, you will find that you can stretch your students in many different directions: extending their intellectual interests, sharpening their perceptions of the world, and deepening their understanding of themselves and others. No one book can do all this at once, of course, but with experience and advice from the school librarian, you will find particular books to serve particular purposes.

*Mr. Revere and I* by Robert Lawson is an especially versatile book to read aloud. It has action, humor, and dramatic suspense. But most important of all, it has style. When they hear the title page read aloud and see what it looks like, even fifth-graders know that they are in for no ordinary story. In elegantly old-fashioned script on what looks like a decorative plaque appears:

*Mr. Revere and I*
*Being an Account of certain*
*Episodes in the Career of*
*PAUL REVERE, Esq.*
*as recently revealed by his Horse,*
*SCHEHERAZADE,*
*late Pride of his Royal Majesty's*
*14th Regiment of Foot*
********
*Set down and Embellished with*
*Numerous Drawings by*
*ROBERT LAWSON*

The well-read youngsters giggle at the name of the horse, and their appreciation of the aptness of the name is communicated to the rest of the class when they explain that the other Scheherazade was a storyteller too.

At first, children may not sense Lawson's tongue-in-cheek approach to the representatives of British might. If you want them to notice a skillful use of language, paragraphs such as Scheherazade's description of George III must be read a second time. Once the children are asked to picture the king of the most powerful nation in the world reviewing his troops from a wheelchair with his foot propped up, they begin to sense Sherry's implied disappointment and to appreciate her apology for his appearance. It is worth interrupting the story at this early stage to talk about words and what they mean so that children may begin to tune in to the use of language.

Sherry's blind loyalty and, to employ a word one child used, her "honesty" are revealed in her description of her master.

> *On this memorable occasion my rider, and owner, was Leftenant Sir Cedric Noel Vivian Barnstable, Bart., a Gentleman and Officer in the highest tradition of British Arms. My Leftenant was the perfect picture of the ideal Military Man. Just turned twenty-one, tall and slender (not spindly, as some said), he had the true proud nose of the conqueror, rather like that of a puffin, but less elaborately colored. He was blessed with splendid strong teeth not greatly different from my own. These were quite prominently displayed, because his mouth was usually partly open and his chin was merely a slight ripple in the flesh, a highly prized characteristic of the Barnstable family.*

When first read, the description usually makes a strong impact on the good readers who giggle at the thought of a puffin's nose likened to the "true proud nose of a conqueror." Because they are laughing they usually miss the likeness of Sir Cedric's teeth to Sherry's own. Here again it is worth taking the time to go back over the description to bring out the humor. You should remind the class that this is a description of "The Ideal Military Man." To fully appreciate Sherry's loyalty to her master and her charity, the children must have some picture of what an ideal military man looks like.

The first chapter goes very slowly because of the many explanations of words, connotations, and motives, but the time is well spent. Because of the humor, the children become attentive to the language.

Sherry's slanted viewpoint is revealed when she describes Boston:

> *Rising up from the water on some unimpressive hills, the town of Boston looked pleasant enough, but countrified and flimsy compared to our English cities. While there were a good many presentable brick buildings, the majority were constructed of wood, many of them unpainted. The streets were rambling, muddy and filled with puddles. Most of them seemed mere cowpaths. There appeared to be an unnecessarily large number of church spires.*

This prejudiced and superior view of a budding colonial city might pass right over the children's heads if you don't ask, "Do you think Boston really looked like that?" In one sixth-grade class, a boy responded, "It probably did, but she makes it sound terrible." The teacher asked if a citizen of Boston might describe it differently. The teacher then reread the details of the description given by Sherry and the class provided an alternative. (See Sherry's and "A Bostonian's" descriptions of Boston, at the top of the next page.)

Interestingly enough, despite her arrogance and pride, Sherry remains in the children's eyes an appealing character; perhaps it is her frankness. When she is abandoned by her master and taken over by Nat Sime, owner of a glue factory, genuine sympathy is aroused. They rest more easily when circumstances bring her to the happy household of the Revere family, where, eventually, she becomes a full-fledged and almost equal partner in their mutual love and trust.

Perhaps the best testimonial to *Mr. Revere and I* came from a fifth-grade girl who had already read it before the teacher read it aloud to the class. After the book was finished, the teacher asked, "Was it boring to you?" The girl answered, "Oh, no. When I read it, I didn't notice the language."

| *Sherry* | *A Bostonian* |
|---|---|
| *Rising up from the water on some unimpressive hills* | *The town of Boston rises up from the bay on lovely hills. They are not too high; just right for walking.* |
| *The town of Boston looked pleasant enough, but countrified and flimsy compared to our English cities.* | *It is a pleasant town, with lots of trees. It is not crowded and polluted like the English cities we left.* |
| *While there were a good many presentable brick buildings, the majority were constructed of wood, many of them unpainted. The streets were rambling, muddy and filled with puddles. Most of them seemed mere cowpaths.* | *We have many fine brick buildings but the town is growing so fast that we don't even have the time to paint our wooden buildings or to pave the streets.* |
| *There appeared to be an unnecessarily large number of church spires.* | *We are a God-fearing people and the first buildings we built were our churches. We have built a lot of them.* |

**To explain wonderings.** Children in the middle grades experience many changes in their bodies and in their outlook. The tumult that is adolescence is beginning to stir. What are these new feelings and how will they affect tomorrow? As the middle-grader's awareness of himself and others increases he begins to wonder who he is and where his place in the world is and will be. Many of these questions are raised by characters in books. Sometimes they find answers; sometimes they don't. In either case, for the child who reads these stories or hears them, literature becomes a rich source of reassurance that he is not alone in his bewilderment. The time for the teacher to show literature in this light is before a child's wondering turns to anguish.

There are many books that portray "growing up." A useful one for fifth- and sixth-graders is Madeleine L'Engle's *Meet the Austins*, which has warmth and humor in describing a family's adjustment to a spoiled child who comes to live with them, and perception in their reaction to the death of a beloved uncle.

**To ventilate feelings.** Another kind of book that is useful to read aloud to older children is the one that illustrates real problems of living. One such problem that many middle-graders are keenly aware of is the use and misuse of authority. Those children who have older brothers and sisters are very much aware of the abuse of authority when it is directed toward themselves. On the other hand, they rarely regard their behavior toward younger brothers and sisters as abuse but rather a legitimate exercise of authority. Often a book will stimulate a discussion that will broaden a child's understanding of the privileges and responsibilities of authority and their effect on harmonious group living.

One such book is T. H. White's *Mistress Masham's Repose.*[5] The story concerns a little girl, orphaned by an accident, who, under the tutelage of a callous governess and an unscrupulous vicar, lives unhappily in a dilapidated palace. One day Maria discovers a

5. T. H. White, *Mistress Masham's Repose* (G. P. Putnam, 1946).

colony of Lilliputians, who become the delight of her life. Her size, a handicap in her relations with the governess, becomes a source of power in her relations with the Lilliputians. As she misuses this power, relations between the Lilliputians and herself become strained. It becomes increasingly apparent that their relations are handicapped not only by her size but by her unwillingness to accept and appreciate the Lilliputians' desire to work for themselves and thereby maintain their integrity.

This book was read to a sixth-grade class. As each incident was read, the cause for the growing coolness of the Lilliputians was discussed briefly. The children sensed a build-up to a breakdown in the relationship that had been pleasant and beneficial to both parties. But the fictional situation did not touch the class until they saw in it the very common problem of dominance. The teacher asked them if they ever had had the feeling of being "bossed." They certainly had. Only after their accusations against older brothers and sisters had been exhausted were they able to discuss the distinction between legitimate authority and the usurpation of authority. Their older brothers and sisters with delegated parental authority were not necessarily being bossy in insisting that they go to bed at the prescribed time, but Maria had no authority to require the Lilliputians to play with her whenever she wished.

## READING POETRY ALOUD[6]

In poetry, as in music, some will like certain selections better than others. This should be made clear to children so that they will not feel forced to approve of every poem they hear. Nor would you want them to be glibly disapproving. Children who are being introduced to a new collection of poems will be put at ease if you say, "Do you know that the first time you hear a poem you can't always tell whether or not you like it? Sometimes you have to hear it several times before you know. That is why I always read new poems twice or even three times. Then we can see which poems we remember, or think about, or would like to hear again." This suggests a positive reaction, rather than the negative one which comes all too easily to children and adults as well.

Even with two hearings some poems still remain obscure to children unless the baffling words that block their comprehension are cleared up in advance. Poets have a high regard for words and employ no vocabulary studies to inhibit their use of them. They fling words around with blithe disregard for the audience to whom their poems are addressed. "Aye, marry, two," says *Mother Goose*, and talks nonchalantly in terms of "farthings," "sixpence," "tuffet," "grenadier," "dun," "mare," and dozens of other words that never yet crashed the gate of any respectable vocabulary list for the young. What are we to do with such words and the consequent confusion which they may occasion to young readers?

First, there are the unimportant words which are not essential to the meaning. In all the times that children have heard "Is John Smith within?" not one ever seems to have inquired about "Aye, marry, two." Here, obviously, is just an explosive affirmative to the question, "Can he cast a shoe?" Well, of course he can, my goodness, yes,—*two* of them, all condensed into "Aye, marry, two." There is no use being heavily pedantic about trivia. Any sensible child gets the meaning of that expletive without your going into the ancient and honorable lineage of "marry." On the other hand, most children are bewildered by Elizabeth Coatsworth's "strong-withered horse." If he is to see anything but a "wrinkled" horse, "withered" and "withers" should be explained before the poem is read. Any key word which is obscure should be explained casually in advance.

6. Many suggestions have been made in Chapter 9 for reading poetry aloud and using poetry with children. See pages 285–299.

Sometimes it is better to read a poem first, letting children catch its sound and movement, and then go back to clear up obscurities. Take Winifred Welles' "Dogs and Weather." Decidedly this is a poem to read first and then go back and mull over, dog by dog.

In short, children need not know the meaning of every word—some they can deduce from the context; some are too unimportant to bother about. Key words, however, should be cleared up before reading the poem, while other meanings may be developed casually after reading. Indeed, savoring the full flavor of the unusual words in poetry is part of the pleasure it gives and can result in an astonishing enrichment of vocabulary and a livelier feeling for words.

After you finish reading a poem, *wait for the children's questions or comments.* The worst thing you can do is ask them if they liked the poem. If the class is really with you, they, in their earnestness to please, may chorus docilely, "Yes!" But if they are not, the question will invariably bring forth a strong-lunged, "No!" This reaction can be devastating to any teacher. Instead of embarrassing children with such interrogations, wait for them to speak or to ask a question or to make an honest if hesitant comment that is really their own. If nothing comes, there is a good chance that they have taken your advice and are waiting for a second reading before they make up their minds about it. Thoughtful adults need time after a moving experience, such as listening to a new symphony, for mulling it over—a little baffled, or too much under its spell to be capable of marshaling their reactions and translating them into words. They may know that they feel something, but what it is they are not too sure. It is the same way with children listening to a poem for the first time. For this reason, if the children make no comments and never ask to hear a poem again, it might be slipped in a day or two later and perhaps once again. Then, if there is still no response, no request for it, it should be tucked away. It may be good poetry, but if the children don't respond to it, it is not for them, at least not now.

To introduce children to what John Ciardi calls "the bribe of pleasure that is poetry" (*I Met a Man*), the teacher should be ready with the right poem at the right time. The right time is when the children's feelings have been generated—by the first snowfall of the year, for example; the right poem is the one that puts those feelings into words. The first snowfall always stirs up great excitement and wonder. The whole world suddenly looks different and one does very different things in it: wearing boots, plowing through drifts, making tracks. Lilian Moore in her poem "Snowy Morning" (see p. 286) puts into words the feeling of hushed wonder at the world draped in white overnight.

In quite a different mood, a small third-grader, looking out at an April day of sleet, slush, and grayness, wrote his discouragement:

*Snow is here,*
*Snow is here,*
*But spring is*
*Spost to be here!*

The teacher said, "That's just the way I feel about this weather. I don't know why, but your poem makes me think of another spring poem that is just the opposite of yours." And she said for him the verse of Robert Browning's poem beginning

*Such a starved bank of moss*
*Till, that May-morn,*
*Blue ran the flash across;*
*Violets were born!*

No one can say how much this poem meant to the boy, but he certainly had a strong feeling that he and the teacher had a lot in common—a dismal spring day with better days just around the corner, violets for her maybe and outdoor play for him.

## CHORAL SPEAKING

If you find that your class is responsive to poetry, you may want to introduce them to choral speaking to give an added dimension to their enjoyment. Choral speaking is an art that is old in the history of the race. "A speaking choir," according to Marion Robinson and Rozetta Thurston, "is a balanced group of voices speaking poetry and other rhythmic literature together with a unity and a beauty born of thinking and feeling as one."[7] In an age of emphasis upon "individualized" learning, the discipline required to speak poetry as "one" would seem out of place. And yet group activities which require extraordinary self-discipline are welcomed by middle-school children, even those most outrageously individualistic, provided they feel *with* the teacher and enjoy the material.

The kindergarten and first grade—perhaps the second, too—are merely periods of preparation for choir work. In these early years, saturate the children with poetry; let them say *Mother Goose* and other simple poetry with you, keeping their voices soft and light just as you do in their singing. When you read a poem with a refrain, let the children come in on the chorus and then *mark the time as you do when they sing* to prevent them from dragging. Let the children discover that a poem can be as good a march or walk or skip or run as music. While the group says "Hippity hop to the barber's shop," let one or two children skip it—a high, free skip with arms swinging. They may gallop to "Ride a cock horse" or march to Milne's "Buckingham Palace"[8] or walk laggingly to "A dillar, a dollar" or rock to "Hush-a-bye-baby." In this way they discover varieties of rhythm in poetry and respond appropriately. Even in the kindergarten, you might take such a little conversation piece as "Susan Blue" (p. 283), and let half of the children say the first three lines and the other half the concluding three lines.

Hearing a great variety of poems from nonsense verse to lyrics, developing a sense of rhythm, entering into the saying of these verses individually and in a group, never letting poetry drag or turn into singsong but keeping it light, crisp, and clear in sound and meaning, the children will have as much of a foundation for choral speaking as you should expect at the five- and six-year-old levels. If the results of your efforts are the children's whole hearted enjoyment of poetry and the feeling that it is fun to speak together, then you are happily on your way.

If you are starting this work with older children, begin in much the same casual way. First, there must always be a preliminary saturation with all types of poetry until the children acquire an ear for rhythm and a quick sense of mood. The informal speaking of some of their favorites follows naturally. This is one of the tests of their genuine liking for a poem—they begin to say it with you. With these older children, too, always mark the time (with hand or finger, as you do for singing) when they speak together and hold them to standards of suitable tempo and of light, pleasant voices. Never, even on the lustiest chorus, should the children's voices become harsh or loud. Sweet, light voices are, for children, one mark of good choral speaking. Their vocal cords are immature, and volume can strain and injure these cords with a resultant injury to voice quality. In verse choirs, children naturally tend to become shrill or loud and harsh; so it is important to remember the warning—*keep these young voices light.*

These older children may explore the rhythms of poetry, and they are mature enough to find their own examples of poems that swing, run, walk, hop, gallop, or skip. They may discover, too, the silent beat in poetry that is like the silent beat in a bar of music. Read aloud to them Stevenson's "Windy Nights," asking them to tap on their desks with one fingertip or to mark time in

7. *Poetry Arranged for the Speaking Choir,* p. 13.
8. Most of the poems mentioned in this section are found both in *Time for Poetry* and *The Arbuthnot Anthology.*

any way that is natural and noiseless. They will soon discover the silent beat between certain lines and realize that it must be observed in poetry just as the rest is in music.

*Whenever the moon and the stars are set,*
*Whenever the wind is high,**
*All night long in the dark and wet,*
*A man goes riding by.**

This discovery of the silent beat is important for the correct reading of poetry, and many children are soon able to recognize it independently.

At this point, when the children are used to poetry, when they have discovered how much like music it is in its variety of rhythms, moods, and melodies, and when they like it well enough to explore further, you may tell them something about speaking choirs. Perhaps you will tell them that just as there are choirs for singing together, so there are choirs for speaking together, called verse choirs or choral speaking.

To begin choir work, try contrasted examples of short verses that cannot be spoiled by speaking them in unison. While unison speech in its finished form is extremely difficult and requires the greatest precision and sensitivity, nevertheless, start with it in its simplest form for several reasons: first, because ever since the children could say the words of *Mother Goose* with you they have been speaking in unison; second, because such choral speech loosens their tongues and increases their speech agility without any conscious drill; finally, because there is a contagion and fun about speaking poetry together that delights the children and gets the choir off to an excellent start.

If you have seven-, eight-, or nine-year-old children, you might begin with this rousing march from *Mother Goose:*

*The grand Old Duke of York*
*He had ten thousand men,*
*He marched them up a very high hill*
*And he marched them down again.*
*And when he was up he was up*
*And when he was down he was down*
*And when he was only half way up*
*He was neither up nor down.*

Say it to the children first with the spirited marching rhythm the verse demands, and then let them say it with you, keeping the voices light. After they have it on the tips of their tongues, let half of the children say it and, as the last word is spoken, see if the other half can pick up the first line in perfect rhythm and say the verse through. Later, when the children are used to speaking together, it is fun to begin this march softly as if far away, to grow louder as if the marchers were coming nearer, and then, on a second saying, to carry it far away again and fainter and fainter. A child suggested this variation, and the group thoroughly enjoyed it.

A gallop guaranteed to rouse the most apathetic is Rose Fyleman's "Husky Hi." Say this to the children and let them say it with you. Make the "husky hi" a vigorous staccato from way down in the diaphragm. You probably won't mention diaphragm to the children, but you will suggest that they get the feel of this gallop into their voices and into the words. Then let half the children take imaginary reins in their hands and "cluck" to their horses while the other children say the words. Or two or three children might be Keery and gallop to the verse. Don't use more than three, because the noise of their feet will drown out the speakers or force them to get louder and louder. If the gallopers don't get back to their chairs on the last word, just keep on repeating the last two lines.

For a contrast to these lively rhythms, try this one from *Mother Goose:*

*Blow wind, blow, and go mill, go,*
*That the miller may grind his corn;*
*That the baker may take it,*
*And into bread bake it,*
*And bring us a loaf in the morn.*

Say this to the children first, giving full value

to the long vowel sounds and the sustained tone in the opening lines. Note the interesting contrast between the long, slow beat of the first two lines and the light staccato of the next two. The children can soon say this smoothly, bringing out the contrast that falls so pleasantly on the ear.

If you are beginning this work with children ten, eleven, and twelve years old, you might want to start with Shakespeare's walking song:

*Jog on, jog on, the footpath way,*
*And merrily hent the stile-a:*
*A merry heart goes all the day,*
*Your sad tires in a mile-a.*

Of course, say it to the children first. Doesn't it sound like a detachment of Boy Scouts on a hike? *Stile* may have to be explained—steps over a fence—but even though *hent* is not used today, every child can tell from the context that it means climb over, or get over the stile. Use this song much as you did "The Grand Old Duke of York."

You can use "Jog on" to illustrate an important distinction between a metrical singsonging of verse and the natural rhythmic emphasis that is desirable. If you mark the metrical beat, you will discover that in the last line it falls on *in*—"Your sád tires ín a míle-a." If you read it that way or let the children do it, you get a droning singsong that is tiresome and meaningless. You should speak it as you would naturally, accenting *sad* and prolonging the emphasis on *tires*—"Your *sad tires*—in a mile-a." Over and over again, you will discover that when the children singsong, it is because they strike the metrical beat so hard that they destroy the meaning. Here meaning depends on the contrast between the *merry* heart that goes all day and the *sad* that *tires* in a mile-a.

For a gallop, use "Husky Hi" or the unfamiliar "Master I Have." This you can label "traditional," and so avoid the older children's reproach that *Mother Goose* is "baby stuff":

*Master I have, and I am his man,*
*Gallop a dreary dun;*
*Master I have, and I am his man,*
*And I'll get a wife as fast as I can;*
*With a heighly gaily gamberally,*
*Higgledy, piggledy, niggledy, niggledy,*
*Gallop a dreary dun.*

Say it to the children first, explaining that here is a young man who is delighted to have a job, "a master." He may have to ride a dreary old dun-colored horse, doing errands, but he doesn't care. A master means wages; wages mean a chance to get married. So he pounds along, celebrating his good luck with a song—and a rollicking, hard-riding song it is! Let half the children say it and, as the last word dies away, let the other half pick it up and say it again. Notice if you prolong the *n* sounds in the final words of the lines, you make them sing. This verse is especially good for learning breath control, which you may or may not call to the children's attention. They generally discover they have difficulty when they try to say those last three lines all on one breath. When the children can say "Master I Have" well, you might try Robert Louis Stevenson's "Windy Nights" (p. 344), another good gallop but much harder to say.

For a contrast, try the amusing surprise of Mary Austin's "Grizzly Bear," which tickles children of any age.

These are a few examples of the way you may begin your speaking choirs with either younger or older children. Say a poem first so that they are clear about the words, the mood, the tempo, and the meaning. Then let them say it with you, keeping their voices soft and light. When they know the words, they should speak the poem without your voice to help them, although you will still mark the time.

Probably you should not go much further than this with a speaking choir unless you have studied and acquired some knowledge of the detailed techniques of developing the work.[9]

9. For more detailed techniques, see *Time for Poetry*, pp. 233–246, or *The Arbuthnot Anthology*, pp. 1119–1127.

## DISCUSSION

### Purposes of Discussion

When children read a story silently, it is the story they are attending to. Although some may react unconsciously to the characters, the events, and the climax, they are essentially absorbing, not reflecting. And yet true appreciation of literature and ultimate satisfaction derive from reflection on the significance of what one reads.

If a teacher wishes to bring out the significance of what an author has to say, he must provoke the children's minds with questions. The mere asking of questions makes it clear to children that there is more to a story than simple enjoyment. Often children don't realize as they read that what they like about the story is the idiosyncratic behavior of a character, the chilling mood, or a sympathetic character coping with problems they themselves have encountered. Putting a feeling into words makes it more tangible. Once a child has had that experience and found it intriguing, his mind as well as his emotions will be working the next time he reads a story.

Getting children to articulate is a major goal of elementary education rather than an objective solely of the literature program. It is in the child's interest that he learn to put his thoughts into words, whether they are about history, geography, mathematics, or science. Also, a wise citizenry is composed of people who react, hold opinions, express them clearly, and judge them sensibly. It is important for children to have an arena in which their opinions may be freely expressed and gently judged. The discussion of a story provides just that. It is a time when reaction to the behavior of fictional characters can be stimulated, opinions expressed and judged, and basic values and assumptions about human behavior brought to light.

### Important Questions to Ask

A question of fact will always receive an answer of fact. When a teacher asks, "Who was a llama herder?" she will get what she asked for—a name. When she asks, "Was Jack poor?" the children will answer, "Yes." This is not a discussion. This is not to say that the facts of a story are not important—they are. They are like the playing pieces of a game. They must be all there before the game starts. With younger children and with older children who struggle with reading, it is a good idea to make sure that the children know all the facts of the story. But so often teachers stop there. The discussion really begins when the teacher asks questions of interpretation—questions which require an act of inference. These are the "why" questions. True discussion begins not with "What happened?" but with "Why did it happen?" One kind of question that usually elicits a response deals with the fears, the aspirations, the frailties, the limitations, the desires that motivate behavior. In Kenneth Grahame's *The Wind in the Willows*, for example, the question of why Toad is called Mr. Toad when his friends are called Badger, Ratty, and Mole might lead to a recalling of his vanities, which are many. Through discussion, a child's initial amusement with the romantic Toad may give way to a sympathetic understanding; and, like Toad's friends, he may see Toad as a worthy if extravagant being.

Another kind of question children will respond to deals with their judgments of behavior. In folk tales that tell of the triumphs of the youngest brother, the question might be asked, "Why does he succeed? Is he smarter?" In a story like "Beauty and the Beast," the questions might be asked, "Why does the father allow Beauty to go to the beast? Was he foolish, frightened, or wise?"

A third kind of question that might be used with older children focuses on what the author believes. In discussing Rudyard Kipling's "The Elephant's Child," the question might be asked, "Does the author think curiosity is a good thing and that spanking is bad?" In the folk tale: "Does the author think that Rumpelstiltskin is evil? If so, why does he save the girl's life?"

As children reveal their values, beliefs, and misconceptions, further questions can make them clear not only to themselves but to others. Although you may determine in advance a central problem of a story and frame a question to shed light on it, you should not feel a serious obligation to ask only questions for which there are answers. As adults well know, there are many questions for which there are no answers: questions of living within a changing society, of living with others of differing values. An answer that works today may not work tomorrow. But children must learn how to seek answers. When fictional characters are brought to life in a discussion, children have an opportunity to see how vital problems are encountered. In searching their own experience for explanations of behavior, connections are made between fiction and reality, thereby establishing literature as a source of explanation of their own vital problems.

### The Teacher's Stance

If discussion is to achieve its purposes, it must be carried on in an atmosphere where deviant points of view may be expressed and respected. Children who respond to open-ended questions do so either by parroting the beliefs and values of their parents or by drawing upon their own emerging beliefs. Children of the middle grades have already amassed a store of experiences with interpersonal relations and have made judgments (not always accurate) about what certain kinds of behavior mean. A discussion of motivation forces them to draw on that store of experience. While you may recognize misconceptions arising through inexperience and may be tempted to set children straight right then and there, you shouldn't. If further experience is needed by the children, then you should plan for it at a later time, as one sixth-grade teacher did.

The class had read Constance Hieatt's *Sir Gawain and the Green Knight* and was asked, "Why did Sir Gawain agree to meet the Green Knight when it apparently meant certain death?" One boy expressed the opinion of about half the class when he said, "He was stupid." Clearly, those children had had little experience, in real life or in literature, with the causes for which men give their lives or, indeed, with pure courage. Instead of responding with a lecture, the teacher made plans for a series of readings including biographies such as Iris Noble's *Emmeline and Her Daughters: The Pankhurst Suffragettes* and Milton Meltzer's *Langston Hughes*. After reading and discussing the raw courage of the characters, the teacher recalled Sir Gawain. Although he had no way of knowing how deeply the class as a whole was affected, he was pleased that the boy who started it all agreed that soldiers in wartime often willingly did battle against overwhelming odds. The boy still may have had no conception of why they do it, but reading about people with courage had certainly given him awareness.

As teacher, you must act as an interested, objective inquirer into the meaning and significance of a story. This neutral stance helps you withstand the temptation to be didactic and opinionated. By keeping the discussion relatively impersonal, the intensely personal and subjective contributions of the children will continue to be made. In this way, you are in a position to ask the questions that expose ambiguities and clear up misconceptions. The response, "I don't think I understand you. Are you saying . . .?" sets the stage for clarifying vague statements and disconnected thought. The response, "If that is so, then . . . ," presses the class to think of the implications of a statement and its relevance to the story.

Discussions need not be long-drawn-out affairs to be effective. If children are moved to reflect for even one moment upon an idea suggested by a story, they have come one step closer to regarding books as a source of stimulation, as one fourth-grade teacher discovered. After his class finished the story

"The Princess Who Couldn't Cry,"[10] the teacher asked, playing the devil's advocate, "Why were her parents so upset because she laughed all the time? Don't all parents want children to be happy? What is wrong with them?"

The group looked puzzled and mildly vexed as if they knew that there was something specious about that point of view but couldn't figure out what. Finally, one boy, with some exasperation, gently instructed his teacher, "It is not good to laugh all the time. It is not good to cry all the time. A person has to laugh some of the time and cry some of the time. The king and queen knew *that!*"

That this brief interchange was a discussion could be argued; that it achieved the purposes of discussion is clear. The teacher's provocative question put the group into the position of articulating a sensible philosophy of life that, to their minds, needed no defense.[11]

## INTERPRETING LITERATURE

Through discussion you can be sure that the children understand the elements of a story—(1) the setting: *Where and when does the story take place?* (2) the point of view: *Who tells the story?* (3) the characters: *What are the characters like? How are they revealed?* (4) the plot: *What happens in the story?* (5) the theme: *What is the main idea of the story?* and (6) the style: *How is the story written? How are the ideas expressed?*[12] If a child seems to be confused about any one of these elements, ask him to read aloud the passage or passages that prompted his response, and encourage the class to listen carefully and weigh the evidence. Remember that you are not infallible. You may find that *you* have not read carefully enough. Listen thoughtfully to the children's comments and consider carefully the passages the children cite. Obviously this is not only better for the children but better for you, too—and more fun!

Many of the points made in Chapter 9, "Deepen Children's Understanding of Poems," pages 291–294, apply to fiction as well as to poetry—supplementing children's background of experience if necessary, "reading between the lines," comparing the ideas expressed in a poem with those expressed in a story, and so on.

Most children who reach the middle grades as competent readers come with an adequate grasp of the literal meaning of what they read. That is, they know who the characters are, where the story takes place, what happens and in what order, and how the story ends. Their primary source of satisfaction is *plot*. This means that the primary teachers have done their work well. They have enticed children to books by dangling the entertainment value of stories and now in the middle grades children are seeking that entertainment on their own.

There is, however, more to appreciate in literature than plot. Some children, on their own, rise above the literal meaning of a story and see its broader significance—its theme. They have developed a concept of characterization which, together with a sense of motivation and causation, enables them to relate and therefore give meaning to story events. Some middle-graders are beginning to acquire a feeling for style, imagery, the sound of language, and the author's point of view.

But what of those children who have not learned to see beyond the printed word? To go beyond literal meaning—to see broader significance or underlying meaning—is an act of interpretation. In real life when we are puzzled by the behavior of others we seek an explanation in broader terms. When we ask "why?" we are going beyond what they literally said and did. This act of interpretation is usually involuntary and egocentric. When a

10. "The Princess Who Couldn't Cry," from Kathleen Adams and Frances Atchinson, *A Book of Princess Stories* (Dodd, 1927).

11. For other suggestions for discussing books with children, see "Talking About Books with Children," pp. 17–19; "Discussing Books with Children," *Time for Stories of the Past and Present*, pp. 233–239; "Discussing Books with Children," *The Arbuthnot Anthology*, pp. 1144–1151.

12. See Chapter 2, pp. 23–32.

child identifies with a book character, he may see something in the character's temperament, dreams, or personality that matches his own. This kind of involuntary interpretation cannot be assumed to take place automatically in children when they are asked to speculate on the motives of book characters; they may or may not be personally involved with them. Further, the accuracy of interpretative skill is determined by the breadth and depth of life experience. The interpretations made by young children are particularly revealing of their limited life experience.

The serious teacher can do a great deal to broaden and deepen the life experiences of children by incorporating into their lives the experiences of book characters. By continually asking "why" you can tap the natural inclination to speculate on behavior. Such speculation or interpretation tends to make the characters more real and therefore more worthy of thought, and their problems more vital. Once children have gone beyond what the characters say and do to wonder "why," they have risen far above literal meaning and are ready to grapple with the truly sophisticated questions: What is this story all about and why is the author telling it?

This process of development is described in the following account of the experiences of a sixth-grade teacher of English.

The students in the class were fairly competent readers. They had a sure grasp of plot and an accurate recall of detail. However, when the teacher tried to direct the discussion toward the broader significance of a story, he was greeted with silence, puzzled stares, or irrelevant recitals of detail. The children were prepared to tell him *what* happened, but he wanted them to speculate on *why* it happened. Obviously, they could not speculate about why characters behaved as they did without a concept of characterization. So the teacher changed his strategy.

### Characterization, Motivation, Logic

He asked the class to read "For Sale: Dragon's Breath," an excerpt from *Young Fu of the Upper Yangtze*, by Elizabeth Foreman Lewis. Young Fu, a bright but naïve apprentice, is flattered into buying an overpriced watch. With the debt due and no money to pay for it, he flees to relatives in the mountains. There he finds snow, Dragon's Breath, which he brings back to the city to sell.

The teacher then asked the class to list the characters in the story and describe each one with a word or a phrase. Their responses were accurate enough, if superficial. Young Fu was "foolish and clever." (They were not worried about the apparent contradiction.) Fu Be Be, his mother, was "poor, weepy, and worried." One child even used the word "cruel." These characterizations were interpretations because nowhere in the text did the author so describe Young Fu or his mother. These characterizations were inferred from their actions. The children had unconsciously risen above literal meaning.

The teacher's next question was, "How do you know?" Then he and the class sat down with the text to hunt for support. Sure enough, the class found dialogue and actions to support their descriptions: Fu was foolish for buying the watch and clever in imagining snow as Dragon's Breath and seeing its commercial value. The next question was designed to point up the contradiction between foolish and clever. "How does his feeling of obligation to pay the debt fit your description of him as a fool." This led to a reexamination of the watch-buying incident. One boy, after some reflection, offered the word "uneducated" as a clearer description of Young Fu. A fool would know little of honor but an uneducated person might. The class agreed.

Although Fu Be Be did not emerge as a finely drawn character in this excerpt, the teacher was able to use one incident to show that, although two interpretations were possible, one view of the character was more probable than the other. When Young Fu, pressed for payment of the debt, asked his mother for the money, she wailed and scolded, telling him that his foolishness was his own affair; her poor savings were reserved to buy her coffin. Although this action seemed "cruel," one girl refused to accept this description and asked, "Would a cruel mother work far into the night to feed and clothe her son?" This apparent contradiction in behavior clearly lay outside the personal experience of most of the class. Finally one boy said he had read somewhere that old people in China worried a lot about proper burial. "She was mad at her son for buying that dumb watch. Paying her son's debt wasn't as important to her as being buried properly." He also offered his personal observation that old people had concerns which, if not entirely sensible to children, were common enough.

After some discussion, the characters in this story had become more and more real. The class began to look at what was said and done in the story as clues to personality, fears, and dreams. As their knowledge of the characters, revealed through inference, became more detailed, the class began to see motives for action and logical consequences of action.

### Problems and Solutions

After a reading of "Rikki-Tikki-Tavi," from Rudyard Kipling's *The Jungle Books*, and a recounting of Young Fu's problem and his solution, the teacher proposed the idea that all stories are about problems and their solutions. To test this hypothesis he asked the class to list each character in "Rikki-Tikki-Tavi" and to state his problem. He also asked them to choose what they considered the *main* character. Almost unanimously they agreed that Rikki (the mongoose) was the main character. There was considerable variance in the statement of his problem: some said it was to bring peace to the garden; some said it was to save the family from the cobras, Nag and Nagaina; some said it was to kill the cobras. The class seemed to sense that these three statements were not contradictory, but they could not see how they were related until one girl argued that peace in the garden and the safety of the family would be *effects* of killing the cobras. Therefore, the cobras, she insisted, were the basic problem.

Except for a few, the students said that the problem of the Tailorbird Darzee and his wife was to save their babies and that Chuchundra the Muskrat's problem was fear of going into the middle of the room. These interpretations were revised once the central position of the cobras was established. The class ultimately agreed that the cobras were everyone's problem. With the cobras dead, the baby birds would not be in danger and Chuchundra could go anywhere he liked. Since nowhere in the story does Kipling describe his characters and their situations in these words, the class's conclusions were clearly based on inference. They had already come a long way from their dependence upon literal meaning.

Having risen so far above the concrete detail, they seemed ready for another push. "Why did Rikki want to get rid of this danger when the task involved so much personal risk?" The text offered little tangible help, and the teacher suspected that those children had had little personal experience with heroes and matters of life and death. In the discussion that followed they tasted the anguish and delight of pursuing a philosophic question. The clue that led to an acceptable explanation was the reference that Rikki wanted to be a house mongoose. The question was asked, "What do you think that means?" Kipling didn't say; but the class, now confident of their ability to make educated guesses, reasoned that a house mongoose must be like a watch dog. He would protect the family against cobras, a more common danger in India than burglars, and, in turn, the family would care for him. As a house mongoose he would no longer have to worry about food, shelter, or companionship. Although they didn't say so in so many words, they seemed to feel that Rikki's decision to fight the cobras was a choice of life and security over insecurity or death.

In the discussion of "Rikki-Tikki-Tavi" the practice of supporting assertions became usual—a practice that served to keep interpretations of the text sensible rather than whimsical. The concepts of motivation, problem, and solution gradually became more stable and comfortable as a framework for discussion. In addition, the distinction between immediate and long-range problems not only became useful as a device for viewing a story as a whole but, in the next story, provided a basis for speculation on the author's purpose.

### The Author's Purpose

The next story the class read was Katherine Mansfield's "The Doll's House."[13] In the story, the Burnell sisters, from a well-to-do family in a small town, are given a magnificent doll's house—complete in every detail even to a tiny oil lamp. This treat is shared, two at a time, with all the girls at school—all, that is, save the Kelveys. Although the Kelvey girls, daughters of the woman who does most of the washing of clothes in town, are not "respectable," Kezia, the youngest Burnell, on impulse, lets the Kelveys see the doll's house. For this she is scolded and the Kelveys are angrily chased out of the yard. Though shaken by the experience, the littlest Kelvey softly crows to her sister, "I seen the little lamp."

It is a good story for sixth graders because it so easily stirs up their strong sense of fair play. Confident of the success of his teaching strategy, the teacher again asked the class to list the characters and their problems and to select the main character and her problem and solution.

There was no disagreement on the characters and their problems. In fact, except for one boy who listed the doll house as a character, no member of the class listed a minor character. (That boy, incidentally, with dogged insistence, proposed at intervals that the doll's house was the main character because without it there would have been no story.) There was, however, an outburst of disagreement on the main character. Some said that the main character was Kezia, whose problem was her discomfort about denying the Kelveys a visit to the doll's house; her solution was to allow the Kelveys to see it. Some said that it was the Kelveys, whose problem was to see the house and who finally did see it.

The children asserted positions and defended them by appeals to text, personal experience, and logic. They used as evidence for their arguments not the events themselves but their import. They were obviously looking at the story as a whole and trying to make the pieces fit together.

On the other hand, they were having difficulty in giving weight to parts of the story. The strategy which had worked so well in the previous story had somehow led to arguments. As the children became personally involved with the characters, the factor of personal bias, so much a part of artistic interpretation and criticism, threatened to disrupt the class. In fact, by asking the class to select a *main* character, the teacher had actually invited haranguing! When he realized this, he stepped in to point out that they were all essentially in agreement about who in the story was important and why. The disagreement arose when they tried to make one character more important than another. Clearly, Kezia was a "doer," but her action would have had no meaning if the author hadn't created the strong feeling between the Burnells and the Kelveys. If the Kelveys hadn't been there, would the nasty streak in the town girls have been seen? And, of course, if the doll's house hadn't been given to the Burnell sisters, there wouldn't have been a story at all. (The boy who had first proposed this argument looked smugly satisfied.) Instead of considering the main characters and their individual problems further, the teacher suggested, "Let's look at the problem of the story as a whole."

Just then, a boy raised his hand and said that this story reminded him of the stories of prejudice. The Kelveys were different from the girls in town. It was as though a line were

13. Katherine Mansfield's "The Doll's House," in Avery and others, *Author's Choice* (Crowell, 1971).

drawn between them. Kezia's letting them see the doll's house was like saying they were equal; the line was cut and that made everybody mad.

The boy's metaphor immediately made all the pieces fall into place for the class. The immediate problem of the story was solved when the Kelveys saw the house. The long-range problem of prejudice was not solved in the story, only exposed. Was this the author's purpose? The class thought so.

It takes time for children to acquire a concept of characterization, theme, etc. The serious teacher realizes that no matter how successful, one experience is not enough to establish the habit of questioning, speculating, and interpreting. The experience must be repeated with different stories, different themes, and different characters. The teacher who reads aloud to a class has many opportunities to invite interpretation: "Why do you suppose he said that? Is he really the kind of person who would say that? Then why did he say it?" The more children are maneuvered into interpretative activity, the faster their stockpile of vicarious life experiences will grow. The greater the stockpile, the more accurate their interpretations.

## DEVELOPING SENSITIVITY TO STYLE THROUGH WRITTEN WORK

There is much a middle-grades teacher can do to make children aware of and sensitive to the literary devices of style used by authors.[14] There can be no doubt, however, that their awareness of how an author uses words to create a mood, convey a feeling, or reveal his point is heightened after they have tried to manipulate words themselves. Teachers have used a wide variety of techniques to help children transfer their awareness of stylistic devices to their own writing. Having children experiment with the many words that can be used instead of "said" can be intellectually interesting and have the effect of stimulating them to tune in to other words authors use in stories they read or hear. Without a context, however, or without any other goal in sight, it can be a deadly exercise. Having children write a descriptive paragraph of a place can often spark an idea for a story. A gifted teacher can even make the writing of such paragraphs the springboard for an absorbing discussion of the use of words to create a mood. Some teachers after asking children to read a story told from one character's point of view, have had success in having them write the same story from another character's point of view.[15]

One technique usually arouses interest and impels older children to write. It is to ask them to rewrite a known story, for example, "The Three Billy Goats Gruff" in 100 words. Although many other such short tales might be used just as well, almost every child knows "Billy Goats Gruff," and those who don't, learn it very quickly. Using a well-known tale relieves children of the necessity to be creative in plot; thus relieved, their attention is fully focused on style. By asking them to limit themselves to 100 words, you avoid the perennial question, "How long does the story have to be?" Experienced teachers know that the answer, "As long as the story you have to tell requires," is not much help to most children. Also, by keeping a running count of the words they have written, and every child does it, children know how far they have come and how far they have yet to go.

A way to begin is to assert that the same story may be told in many ways. An author by his selection of words and by his way of reporting what happened can emphasize one side of the story more than another. The way he feels about the characters will affect the

14. See, for example, the account of reading *Mr. Revere and I* aloud, pp. 661–663.

15. A review of Mary Stolz' *A Dog on Barkham Street* and *The Bully of Barkham Street* would be a good preparation for this assignment. See page 18.

way he writes about what they do. Two different authors may see the same series of events in such different ways that when they have written them down we may have two completely different stories, as in the old legend of the four blind men who encountered an elephant—each pictured the elephant according to the part of the elephant he touched.

To make sure that everyone in the class knows the story of "The Billy Goats Gruff," have one child tell the tale. Then give the assignment: "There are only two rules you must follow. The events in your version must be those we have heard today and you must tell the story in one hundred words." Of course, someone always asks, "Does it have to be one hundred words exactly?" While you should hold the children fairly strictly to the two rules, you might bend a little and say, "You may go as high as one hundred ten or as low as ninety." You might also suggest at this point that they write on every other line: "You may find yourself using too many words at the beginning and will have to go back and rephrase something you have written." This possibility never seems likely to children.

When they start writing, few children appear to believe that they will run out of words before they will run out of story. They will usually start with "Once upon a time." Some will continue with a detailed description of the setting of the story. Some will continue with a detailed description of the three goats. There are always those who know that they are "padding" the story without knowing the name for what they are doing and write in nonsensical details.

All the children in that class were very much surprised to learn how easily words flow when they had something to say. Most of them underestimated the number of words needed to tell the story and indeed padded when it wasn't necessary. However, with the rules of the game clearly in mind, they scratched out, counted, rewrote, and recounted. Even those who preferred to skimp in the telling of the story rather than to prune the padded introduction could see the imbalance between a lengthy description of the setting or the detailed description of the personalities of the goats and a fifty-word retelling of the events. Albeit somewhat grudgingly, they rewrote their stories to restore balance.

The next task brought forth anguished cries of "It can't be done!" The teacher asked them to retell the same story in twenty-five words, plus or minus two. This task forced them to scrutinize the story line and distinguish the essentials from the embellishments—as one does when writing an overseas cable. Embellishments are truly seen and appreciated when they are absent.

Not every child was able to do this, but the discussion of those that were produced was fruitful and enlightening. One girl wrote:

> *Three goats wanted to cross a troll's bridge. He threatened first the smallest, then the middle goat. Biggest goat butted the troll into the river.*

A boy offered this twenty-word version:

> *Of three goats to cross a troll's bridge, two tricked the troll. The biggest one butted him into the river.*

In the discussion of the two writing tasks, the class agreed that although it is possible to write the story in one hundred words and even twenty-five, the result wasn't very interesting. What made a story interesting was the dialogue, the description that helped the reader picture what was happening, and the details about the personalities of the characters.

The teacher then asked if a more interesting story could be told in five hundred words. "Sure!" was their response. And they wrote such stories. In every version that was read to the class (only by those children who wished to) could be seen confident excursions into the realm of personality and brave attempts to characterize it through dialogue and action. The listeners were quick to point out characterless characters or dialogue and action that were either consistent or inconsistent with personality.

In all these attempts could be seen the children's sincere efforts to draw upon what they knew of style and apply it to the bare bones of a simple tale. One can imagine, after this struggle to use language purposefully, with what attention they listened to stories, noting not only what was written but how.

## DRAMATIZATION

### Dramatic Play for Young Children

Very young children respond quite naturally to the strong rhythms of the *Mother Goose* rhymes. At first the teacher may have the children clap the rhythm of "Jack Sprat." Even the self-conscious children will forget their inhibitions momentarily so long as they are sitting on the floor and are doing what everyone else is doing. The clapping response can be varied a number of ways: various combinations of clapping and touching the floor or touching their knees. Those children who know "Patty Cake" may suggest working with a partner. With "One, two, buckle my shoe," half the class could clap and chant the rhyme, while the other half could pantomime the activities.

**Using stories in books.** Children can soon go beyond these rhythmic activities to acting out brief rhymes or folk tales that they know or ones that the teacher reads to them. "Little Miss Muffet" and "The Three Billy Goats Gruff" provide simple but varied action. The characters are few, but if you wish to involve more children in the action there can be several Miss Muffets and spiders playing the story simultaneously. With "The Three Billy Goats Gruff" you can help the children invent characterizations and you can even raise the question, "Where does the story really begin?" In this manner, you can introduce some creative thinking into the planning of the play. In Sendak's *Where the Wild Things Are*, all the author tells at the beginning is "The night Max wore his wolf suit and made mischief of one kind and another, his mother called him 'Wild Thing!'" If you ask, "Where should *our* story begin?" the children will probably decide that it should begin with Max's naughtiness. Thus the reading between the lines, so important a part of bringing stories to life, begins.

If you want to stretch children with more complicated stories, there are many cumulative stories in which characters travel and meet others on the way. "Chicken Licken" is a classic of this type. Marjorie Flack's *Ask Mr. Bear* could also be used effectively as well as "The Bremen Town Musicians" and *Finders Keepers* by Will and Nicolas. It would be wise to leave the traditional tale intact and concentrate on characterization and movement. In the more contemporary tales, however, you could ask, "Who else might the character meet and what would happen between them?"

Children's interests in an activity can fade if they stay with it too long. For this reason, formal productions by very young children can be disastrous. If, on the other hand, the story is simple and straightforward and the interest of the children is high, you might suggest that they play their story for another classroom. The painting of masks for *Where the Wild Things Are* might provide a diverting and attractive embellishment.

**Puppets.** Children of all ages love to play with puppets. You might ask some children to work simple hand puppets as you read a story. However, puppets are best used in the primary grades in formal play and in the occasional production of a play by individual children. A primary teacher should have some puppets in the classroom especially for the few extremely shy children. Although they may not be brave enough to participate in a story, they may, hidden by a cardboard stage, find that their tongues become untied and that they can put on a creditable performance.

### Dramatization with Older Children

A class discussion stimulates children to reflect on the personal characteristics of fictional characters and their motivations. But a child in a dramatic situation not only must *understand* the feelings, reactions, and motivations of the character he is playing but must convey them himself—with his voice, his face, and his body. Once the words of dialogue are spoken with understanding, they acquire a meaning far richer than any in the dictionary. Once those words are literally brought to life in a dramatization, a significant gap between the child and literature is bridged.

**Pantomime.** It is well to begin with pantomime. Children of eleven and twelve often are gripped by a perfectionism that inhibits their personal and creative expression. They will say with embarrassed anguish, "I can't" or "I'm not very good." Any forced or mechanical dramatization will certainly result in stilted performances by children fearful of forgetting their lines—an embarrassment for all. On the other hand, in a relaxed atmosphere where the emphasis is on understanding and conveying meaning, children tend to forget themselves. Pantomime is a reassuring technique to children because it relieves them from speaking dialogue. And if the teacher focuses the group's attention on the precision and clarity of movement and ways to improve it, their emotional interests are more objective and less personal.

One teacher who uses dramatics as much to build a class spirit as to show his students a new way to regard literature, introduces pantomime as a change of pace from writing stories. "Here is another way to tell a story—but without words." He then performs one of Marcel Marceau's pantomimes—the balloon seller in the park. Then he asks the class to explain the story step by step. If there is a difference of opinion about the significance of one movement, the teacher repeats it, explaining what he was trying to do, then asks if anyone can suggest a clearer way of doing it. After the discussion, he asks the class to come prepared with a pantomimed story the next day. The subject for the pantomimes should be some common activity that would be familiar to everyone. Many of the pantomimes center about the routine activities of living: getting up in the morning, going shopping. But in every class there are a few inspired tales of frustration. One fifth-grade boy pantomimed a story in which a man tries to make a call in a telephone booth. At first it is occupied. Then he has forgotten the number and must look it up. Halfway through the dialing he has forgotten it again. And so on, until he devises a way to manage the phone, get the phone book close enough to read the number, and insert the coin. No one is home. In disgust, he tries to leave but finds the door jammed. He breaks the glass to escape.

**Creative dramatics.** After a class has been loosened by pantomime, they are ready to try the dramatization of stories. Folk tales are the best because the action is simple and direct and the point is clear. "Nail Soup" is a good one to use for fifth- and sixth-graders, even seventh-graders. It is a tale of a penniless, hungry soldier[16] who comes to a village with nothing but a few nails. With a wide range of excuses, the selfish villagers defend their hardhearted refusals to give him a meal. His offer to show them how to make nail soup appeals to their greed and they eagerly provide him with the few extra ingredients to make it taste better: potatoes, carrots, celery, a bit of meat, etc. The foolish villagers readily agree that nail soup is the finest they have ever tasted.

After you read the story, the first question you might ask is, "Where should we begin *our* version? Should it start with the soldier entering the village? How then will we explain that he is poor and hungry?" Some-

16. In some versions it is a tramp, in some a group of soldiers, etc. Two good retellings are *Stone Soup*, told and pictured by Marcia Brown (Scribner's, 1947), and *Nail Soup*, retold by Harve Zemach (Follett, 1964).

times children will suggest that he just say it or that a previous scene be inserted, perhaps showing how he lost his money. This discussion of causation will begin to give dimension to the soldier and the story. It will also enlarge the cast, a consideration that is always in the minds of children who are planning a dramatization of a story with few characters.

Next comes the discussion of the characters of the villagers. The story will provide some dialogue, but as each villager is discussed, his character should fill out. You can encourage such inventiveness by asking children to think of what the particular villagers would say and how they would say it. Using a line of dialogue, such as, "We have little enough food to feed ourselves!" you might ask how a person who was truly sorry she couldn't feed him might say it, then ask how some of those villagers would say the same line and show that they didn't mean it.

The discussions, if they are to be useful rather than delaying, should stimulate suggestions and demonstrations. The demonstrations should lead to new conceptions of the characters and the story. Individual scenes might be tried out in a number of versions and evaluated. You must keep in mind that although creative dramatics is marvelous for stimulating children to interpret, characterize, act out, and think creatively, these purposes will be achieved only if the children are having fun at the same time.

**Using a script play.** Being in a play, especially if it is well received, can be one of the most vivid experiences a child can have. As a class project, nothing is more successful than the production of a play in engendering teamwork, camaraderie, and a sense of achievement.

For the children, the goal is the actual performance. For the teacher, the values of dramatization are achieved in its preparation. If you have reservations about your successful handling of the freewheeling excitement of creative dramatics you will find working with a script play much easier. The dialogue is there, the characterizations are there, and the story line is clear. And yet you will have the same opportunities to help children understand and portray the feelings and characteristics of fictional characters. A useful source for many teachers is *Plays, the Drama Magazine for Young People*, which is published monthly, October through May.

It is true that children unconsciously regard a script as unchangeable. But if you explain that it is only a springboard, then the class may suggest additions and modifications that will make that play their own. Telling the children this is not enough. One teacher began the process by suggesting that another character might be needed and explained why. The children then realized that some dialogue had to be changed and additional dialogue invented.

**Writing an original script.** Some children in the middle grades are fascinated with the idea of writing their own play. What they produce usually consists of 14 scenes with three lines of dialogue in each. The curtain puller usually has the most active role. Obviously children need guidance. One fourth-grade teacher sees the real value of dramatization as the writing of a simple but well-developed play. With her guidance, she feels that her children acquire a sense of character and plot development. The ideas that are used are always those of the children. She sees her function as that of stimulating such ideas and giving them shape. The themes are usually mischief, mistaken identity, running away to have an adventure. The dialogue, because it is supplied by children, is wonderfully realistic.

One teacher had difficulty finding a play that would suit his class. The boys were rambunctious, the girls painfully shy, and they did not work together very successfully. Yet they expected to put on a play. The teacher chose a variant of the Cinderella story, set in Egypt, thinking that the idea at least would appeal to them. (*The Egyptian Cinder-*

*ella* by Lowell Swortzell was published in the February 1962 issue of *Plays, the Drama Magazine for Young People.*)

With the teacher's guidance, three scenes of the Cinderella tale were outlined. Among the Egyptian modifications was the substitution of a White Spirit Cat for the godmother. Four other cats were added when the problem of how to manage a change of costume on stage came up. One child suggested that if five cats had capes, they could dance around Rhodopis (Cinderella) with their capes spread wide, thus allowing Rhodopis to slip off her rags to reveal her ball dress. The cats could then carry the rag costume off the stage without the audience realizing how the magic was accomplished.

After the plot outline was completed, three children volunteered to write the script, one scene for each. The class was set on authenticity and so they liked the teacher's suggestion that they perform the play as though an Egyptian wall painting had come to life. They adopted the two-dimensional postures that characterize the paintings, and their tunics were decorated with authentic Egyptian designs. The performance was a wholly satisfactory one—to the other fifth-grade classes in the audience and to the young actors themselves. And the experience was rewarding in many other ways. The children learned a great deal about such matters as plot structure and characterization; they happily and vigorously delved into detailed research; and, best of all, they developed a class spirit that amazed even their teacher.

**Puppets.** Puppets are fascinating to manipulate, and few middle-grade youngsters can resist slipping one on and making it perform. The teacher who has a stable of stock characters on hand—an old man and woman, a boy and girl, etc.—will discover that children are marvelously inventive at changing them into any character they need. One teacher had her class make papier-mâché puppets as a project, and the characters were used all year in impromptu dramatizations. A group of versatile puppet characters may be created by a small group of children as an extra project. Once they are available, the puppets can be used for any number of impromptu skits, to perform adaptations of stories.

Puppetry is the ideal medium for the beauty and fantasy of fairy tales. "Hansel and Gretel," "Cinderella," "Sadko," and "Rumpelstiltskin" can be remarkably beautiful when given as puppet shows. Scenery, properties, and puppets are fun to make and to work with. The dreamlike quality and magic of the fairy tales can be more exquisitely suggested with these small creatures than they can be by human beings. And the tiny properties only enhance the magic—Rumpelstiltskin's pile of straw turned to gold, the Czar of the Sea's coral palace, the old witch and her gingerbread cottage, and Cinderella's pumpkin transformed into a splendid coach are especially convincing in the small. These glorified dolls, with personalities, movement, and speech, have interested adults through many centuries and make a delightful hobby for children.

## USING MUSIC

Music induces a sympathetic reaction in the body, and its melody and color stir the emotions. These reactions are involuntary even in young children. Viewed in this way, Sousa's *Stars and Stripes Forever* and "One, two, buckle my shoe" have a great deal in common: they almost push one into a marching step. The well-known theme from the *William Tell* overture and "If wishes were horses then beggars would ride" could, if there were room, propel one into a gallop. Some children, listening to Debussy's *Clouds*, may say that it is happy, and others may say that it is peaceful. The accuracy of their interpretations is not as important as the fact that they have responded in terms of feeling. When the emotions have been stirred, the mind is ready to seek visual images that will give them substance. By using the evocative power of music in connection with poetry and stories, teachers can make children much more receptive to the beauty and mood of language and at the same time offer them outlets for the creative expression of their own feelings.

### To Capture Mood

Kindergarten teachers who play soft music on the piano or on the record player know the soothing effect it has on their children during rest time. Teachers of older children often play soft music during a free reading period. With first- and second-graders music can be brought closer to the foreground by playing a recording as the teacher reads poetry or a story. Kaye Starbird's reverie in her poem "One Leaf" (see p. 376) is one that young children can understand, especially in autumn. Imagine the impact on them if a teacher reads it on a day when the blustery winds strip the trees of their leaves and at the same time plays a recording of Debussy's *Afternoon of a Faun*.

Children need no help in appreciating humorous or fanciful poetry; the words speak for themselves. But mood or feeling is not transmitted by the literal meanings of words. Very young children may not understand all the words of a poem, and certainly nostalgia would not be an emotion that they would have experienced. But with poems that are short and effectively presented with voice and music fitting together, even first-graders will sense that they have experienced something!

With a number of such experiences behind them, in which they sense a feeling perhaps without understanding it, children will become used to the combination of literature and music and can enjoy Aileen Fisher's *In the Middle of the Night*[17] with Debussy's *Clouds* played in the background. The wonder and excitement of a walk in the night with Father—a birthday present—suddenly is not only felt but understood. You would be wise to record the music on tape ahead of time. The musical selection is quite short and although it fits beautifully, it ends too soon. Record the entire selection and merely start over again. In this way there will be no break in the mood that the story and music create.

### To Stir Colorful Images

Program music can be extremely useful in stirring a child to visualize. A fourth-grade teacher played Stravinsky's *The Firebird* for her class. Before she started the record she asserted that the instruments of the orchestra and the melodies they played often make people think of colors. "Put your heads on your desks and close your eyes. As the music plays, if the sounds make you feel colors in your head, say so." After a second or two of the brooding low introductory bars, the teacher heard, "Black!" "Purple." When the shrill swirling fifes and flutes announce the entrance of the Firebird, one little fellow with his eyes squeezed shut, lifted up his head, waved his arms in a swift circular movement and almost shouted, "Red and yellow! Red and yellow!" Although not all children did in fact see or feel colors as they listened, at least a third of them did. Their visions shaped the further listening of the others.

### Using the Native Ballads

If children are to be stirred by music they must have some experience in participating in it. Older children who have not shown any interest in creative movement and whose imaginations have not been aroused by music, may yet see the connection between words and music through exposure to our native ballads. The popularization of the folk song and ballads and the current interest in the guitar may interest such children in learning new songs and singing them in

17. Aileen Fisher, *In the Middle of the Night* (T. Crowell, 1965).

class—either as a refreshing break in the day or in connection with a unit of study.

In the Library of Congress, Washington, D.C., in the Archives of American Folk Song, are some 6000 records, including of course many ballads. Some of these records contain apparently recent and as yet unpublished material. This is the greatest collection of native ballads in existence and one that should be known and used. Albums are available for loan or for sale and might provide a happy way of introducing children to ballad literature. Folk-song albums from the record companies are as varied in quality as they are numerous. In work with children you should avoid the obviously commercial.

The collections made by John and Alan Lomax and by Carl Sandburg are admirably classified for school use,[18] for example: "Pioneer Memories," "Great Lakes and Erie Canal," "Mexican Border Songs," "Railroad and Work Gangs," "Cowboy Songs," "Sailors and Sea Fights," "Lumberjacks, Loggers, and Shanty-Boys." Obviously such ballads will correlate with United States history and with the study of types of work that children find most picturesque and fascinating.

One group studying the Great Lakes and using *Paddle-to-the-Sea* as the literary focus of a geography unit became so interested in lake lore and accumulated such a rich mass of factual material that an assembly was, of course, inevitable. "Red Iron Ore," with its vigorous lilt and dramatic story of shipping on the Great Lakes, was exactly what the children needed to make a lively interlude in their informative program.

Another group studying Westward expansion enjoyed the tall tales for their English work and some of the cowboy ballads for their music period. Since they were reading the hilarious tall tale *Pecos Bill*, for their ballads they chose the contrasting melancholy of "Oh, Bury Me Not on the Lone Prairie." The Lomax section on "Breakdowns and Play Parties" might well be used with the study of the Daniel Boone, Davy Crockett, or Lincoln periods. All three men, the children like to remember, could dance at play-parties the whole night through.

18. Carl Sandburg, ed., *The American Songbag;* John A. Lomax and Alan Lomax, eds., *American Ballads and Folk Songs* and *Cowboy Songs and Other Frontier Ballads.*

### Dramatizing a Recording

One way of getting shy children off their chairs and onto their feet was discovered by a fourth-grade teacher who played for her class a recording of *Cinderella* produced by the Children's Record Guild. The story is narrated with an accompaniment of Prokofiev's music from his ballet of the same name. The children knew the story of course, but the music and the occasional bits of dialogue gave novelty to this rendition.

During the ball scene, the teacher noticed three girls in the back of the room, arms stretched outward, swaying to the waltz music. On impulse she went back to them and whispered, "Here is the ballroom. Pretend you are guests." The girls, sensing a game, got up and waltzed around the back of the room. The rest of the class, who had seen what was happening, readily joined in as she pointed to individuals and cast them. As the narrator went on, the new characters began pantomiming the story. The recording acted as a crutch. One needn't remember exactly what was to come in the story; one needed only to listen.

This experience created a thirst for dramatics in that class. Stories were turned into skits. Their study of the hot dry lands concluded with an original play that illustrated what they had learned and a bit more. It would never have happened if three little girls had been able to resist the compelling rhythm and melody of Prokofiev's *Cinderella*.

### Enhancing the Mood of a Story

Reading a story silently with appropriate mood music playing in the background can be a startling experience for middle-graders. The teacher should prepare the class for the experience by first discussing musical sounds and instruments and the effects they can create. A wide variety of short musical selections should be played and the students asked how they are affected by them. Without forcing any consensus, the teacher should encourage as wide a participation in the discussion as is possible. The purpose of this preparatory work is to provide a conceptual framework in which melody, rhythm, and tone color are connected with descriptive phrases.

In one sixth-grade class, the children read the Norse myth about Thor's stolen hammer. The teacher said that he would play some music in the background and as they read the story they should notice, if they could, how often the music fitted the words. As the overture to Wagner's *Die Meistersinger* played, surprised and pleased smiles appeared. One boy whispered gleefully, "It fits! It fits!"

After all the class had finished reading the story, they agreed that the music didn't always go with the part they were reading, but when it did, it made the story much more exciting.

Another time the class read the opening paragraphs of Joan Aiken's *The Wolves of Willoughby Chase*. Imagine listening to Debussy's *Clouds* and reading:

> *It was dusk—winter dusk. Snow lay white and shining over the pleated hills, and icicles hung from the forest trees. Snow lay piled on the dark road across Willoughby Wold, but from dawn men had been clearing it with brooms and shovels. There were hundreds of them at work, wrapped in sacking because of the bitter cold, and keeping together in groups for fear of the wolves, grown savage and reckless from hunger.*

You would be unwise to use this technique too often. Senses that are sharpened by a dramatic experience can be dulled by overexposure. Besides, the point is not to emphasize the musical arrangement of stories, in the manner of films and television, but to stir children's emotions so as to stimulate the visualization of a story with greater intensity. Once the point is made, it would be hoped that reading would become a more exhilarating experience.

## USING VISUAL MATERIAL

### With Young Children

To the very young, books are pictures. Whether he is in his mother's lap or seated on the floor near his teacher, the small child's eyes are glued to the pictures. It is in the illustrations that he finds all the colorful details of facial expressions, posture, and setting that the words of the story do not provide. The picture stories are a first step in the process of helping children visualize the story; they provide beginning definitions of such words as *ugly, beautiful, sad, happy*. A child may feel sorry for "The Ugly Duckling" when he hears the story, but it is when he sees a picture of the scruffy little thing that he feels the full impact of the dreadful situation in which the little outcast finds himself.

**To stimulate interest.** Although the story should be the main attraction, the illustrations can be shared with children as illustrations. Without spending too much time on them, you might direct the children's attention to the way the artist has interpreted the story and the characters in terms of color and style. Among the hundreds of children's books published each year are just as many styles of illustrations. Children may or may not unconsciously sense the difference between stylized and realistic illustrations. Their impressions can be made more conscious by noticing the dreamy reality of Clare Newberry's cats as opposed to Dr. Seuss' flashy, colorful creatures; the muted line drawings of Lynd Ward as opposed to the boldly stylized woodcuts of Antonio Frasconi. Occasionally you may touch on the concept of the harmony of illustration and text by asking, "Why do you think the artist drew the pictures for *The Biggest Bear* the way he did?" Some children may notice that the drawings are realistic, drawn with tiny lines, and have no color. Even if some second-graders see the relation between the story and the illustrations, you should not belabor the point. It is enough merely to establish the fact that pictures are a part of books worthy of discussion.

Showing children various editions of *Mother Goose* serves two purposes. First, the different pictorial interpretations of the characters in the rhymes provide a freshness while the children are being saturated with the rhymes. Second, the concept of comparison is introduced in a pleasant and undemanding way. As with the characters in the fairy tales and folk tales, what they really look like is anybody's guess. The child who is exposed to a range of visual interpretations becomes more free to visualize the characters in his own way.

Occasionally the technique used by an illustrator can serve to stimulate children to examine the illustrations closely and speculate on how the illustrations were produced. Lionni's *Swimmy* is a good example of a technique within the reach of young children. Once children have recognized that many parts of the illustrations have been produced by a simple printing process, an art project may be born. With trays of tempera paint and a variety of textured materials such as paper doilies, crushed paper, and packing material, the children will be well on their way to producing their own conceptions of Swimmy's undersea world.

**To sensitize children to color.** Films and filmstrips, along with illustrations, can add the richness of color to the visual images that stories provoke. After seeing Coronet Films' series of sound filmstrips on color, young children can be motivated to create their own color story. One teacher reads Mary O'Neill's *Hailstones and Halibut Bones* to her first-graders to extend their concept of color. The extension of color to describe mood can lead almost anywhere, particularly if paints are immediately available. Color can stir emotions just as powerfully as can music.

**To stimulate a reaction—creative or otherwise.** For young children whose writing and reading skill is still primitive, drawing is a way of expressing their own very personal reaction to an experience. While the hearty, outgoing first-grader may eagerly express his opinions voluntarily or impulsively ask questions, the shy child will not. His pleasure, his reactions are locked inside. But with crayons and paper, his feelings can be expressed nonverbally.

A picture in his hand often gives a first-grader the courage to stand before his group and tell about it. At first, perhaps, he may merely hold it up for everyone to see, and the teacher will have to point out its merits, the use of color, the originality of his interpretations. But experience gives confidence. Later, even a painfully shy child will respond to the praise of his work.

In a primary classroom, a sensitive and responsive teacher will create an atmosphere that will allow children to become sensitive and responsive. Creativity engenders creativity. It is a fresh wind that sweeps through and revitalizes everything it touches. A young, creative, enthusiastic student teacher's experience in a second grade, for example, showed her experienced critic teacher a new way to look at children.

The student, unhappy that the children had little exposure to literature and creative writing, appealed to her supervising instructor. Through his intercession, the critic teacher put aside her firm belief that all learning activities should be correlated and permitted the student to experiment with literature for two weeks. The student began by reading stories. The children were enraptured by the stories and by the novelty of the experience. After each story, she asked them to draw a picture of the part they liked best. Each child, if he wished, could show his picture to the class and tell about it. At first there were only a few brave enough, but as the stories continued, more and more children wanted to share their pictorial reactions. The critic teacher said she was amazed at the willingness and ease of these otherwise mute and uninterested children. Before long, some children found themselves unable to settle on one favorite part and drew first two, three, and then a comic strip illustrating the stories they had heard. Their pictures were displayed on the bulletin board, and each morning they were scrutinized by the children.

**Using a flannel board.** The flannel board is a useful device for giving children experience in telling a story. You will need to prepare the colorful flannel characters and have them in readiness. If the flannel board were to be used for the retelling of one story only, it would require more work than the one experience warrants. However, the characters could also be used to stimulate the writing of a story, cooperative in kindergarten or individual in second and third grades. Figures of dragons, kings, and witches might be used in various combinations to add variety to the children's creative products.

**Using various media for artistic expression.** Artistic modesty is uncommon among first-graders. Once they complete a drawing, they are rarely critical of it. By the second and third grade, however, some children become critical of their draftsmanship. This is the time for you to introduce them to media other than drawing that will enable them to express their reactions to literature.

With a supply of cardboard tubes, egg cartons, brightly colored wool, colored tissue paper, and construction paper, you can introduce the children to the visual impact of texture. It may take longer to glue together some balls of crushed newspaper, cardboard boxes, and tubes to make a Wild Thing and then paint it, but children will be absorbed in Sendak's story all the while and have the personal satisfaction of creating their own wild things to carry them through. The Wishing Bird in Lionni's *Tico and the Golden Wings* can be a magnificent thing in a collage of torn bits of colorful tissue paper. Also, children who have wishes of their own can be as specific as they choose with crayon, paints, and cardboard sculpture.

There are many outstanding books that explain art techniques in detail. Some require that you try them out first, if only to learn to anticipate difficulties. Some require a large store of materials. When working with young children you would be wise to avoid ambitious projects that tend to focus attention on the technique itself rather than on its potential for artistic expression.

**Group projects.** The group planning of a bulletin-board display or a mural can be an enormously rewarding experience, provided that it is stimulated by high interest. You can create a theme by reading stories and poems. If one of the stories has made more of an impact than others, it may serve as a stimulus for a mural. A specific story such as Norris Lloyd's *The Desperate Dragons* (Hastings, 1966) may lead to a discussion of dragons—fierce ones, shy ones, comical ones. When the discussion is at its peak, is the time for you to suggest that each child make his own dragon—whether with chalk, paint, or crayon. After each dragon is finished and cut out, it may be tacked to a bulletin board, or fastened to a large sheet of butcher paper. With the entire collection in place, you may pose the question of setting. "Let's think of where our dragons are. What kind of place should it be?" Then the details of trees, rocks, caves, and water are added.

In a primary classroom it doesn't matter if the pattern of activity is from books to theme to artistic expressions, theme to artistic expression to creative writing, creative writing to drawing pictures to discussions of books on similar themes. What matters is that literature can stir the imagination of young children and that with the materials and techniques of the visual arts, a teacher can help children express what they see and feel in a creative way.

## With Older Children

Book illustrations are not as essential to children of the middle grades as they are to primary children. True, when a story is read aloud to a middle-grade class, there are always some children who will ask to see the pictures, and certainly the work of distinguished illustrators such as Robert Lawson and Garth Williams should be shared. Other children may say that they prefer not to see the pictures because they do not want their own visualizations to be disturbed.

**Art techniques can lead to books.** Sometimes art or music or the dance will lead into literature. For instance, in one class, listening to the record of Stravinsky's *Firebird* led to the folk tale and that in turn suggested a dramatization using puppets. So dance-pantomime might well lead to the myths. The following account gives a striking example of an art project enormously expanded and enriched with music, myth, poetry, and stories.

"Birds of a Feather" was the title the children in a sixth grade gave to their pictures of birds, produced by a technique their teacher had seen and liked. The bird was drawn, then individual feathers of different colored construction papers were snipped, bent, and pasted to the body of the bird. The results were astonishingly beautiful. Incidentally, what interested adults was that each of these bird portraits somehow suggested the child who had made it. When the portraits were completed, teacher and children were so proud of the results that they offered the collection to the school librarian for exhibition in the library. The librarian, a creative and gifted person, saw at once the far-reaching possibilities of those handsome birds and accepted them with enthusiasm. Once mounted and hung, they brought color and drama into the room. All classes used this library, both in groups and as individuals, so the librarian began assembling related books.

For the kindergarten-primary groups, picture stories were displayed, and since the pictured birds were both fanciful and realistic, the literature included both. For example, Roger Duvoisin's *Petunia* and Beatrix Potter's *Jemima Puddle-Duck* were lined up side by side with *Fly High, Fly Low* and *Come Again, Pelican* by Don Freeman.

Another exhibit contained the factual books—how to identify birds, how to build birdhouses, feeding stations, and the like. Because these informational books are so handsomely illustrated, this exhibit vied with literature in appeal.

For the middle and upper grades there were such books as Dhan Gopal Mukerji's *Gay Neck*, Meindert DeJong's *Wheel on the School*, and Jean George's *Summer of the Falcon*.

Folk and fanciful tales ranged from Hans Andersen's "The Emperor and the Nightingale" to bird myths, bird folk tales, and *Summer Birds* by Penelope Farmer.

Poetry was plentiful. The librarian listed anthologies containing bird poems, for example, Walter de la Mare's *Tom Tiddler's Ground* and James Reeves' *Blackbird in the Lilacs*. Favorite poems were typed and placed on the bulletin board or attached to the mount of one of the birds. For example, Tennyson's "Eagle" appeared with that fine swooping bird; "The North wind doth blow" with one of the robins, and "What Robin Told" with the other one; and of course, "There Once Was a Puffin" accompanied that fanciful bird.

As each class came to the library to see the birds for the first time, the librarian talked to the children, introducing the pictures and the books. On later days she told bird stories and myths, had them listen to records of actual bird songs, and then included the music gradually. For the youngest children she began with simple folk songs and carols about birds, and for the older children with Stravinsky's *The Firebird*, Rimski-Korsakov's *Le Coq d'Or*, Tchaikovsky's *Swan Lake*, the garden section of Respighi's *Pines of Rome*, and Wagner's "Forest Birds" from *Siegfried*.

Such an outline can barely suggest the richness of this experience. The children read, painted, listened, and were thrilled. They found stories and poems on their own. They brought their parents to see the pictures and the books. And later in the year, when the pictures had been taken down and new books were displayed, the children still harked back to the birds. Such a rich experience with related arts cannot take place without genuinely creative adults to show the way. In this case a deeply interested principal, a creative teacher, and an equally creative librarian worked together to encourage and develop this continuously expanding project.

**Books can lead to art techniques.** In the example above, a teacher's interest in an art technique led to a theme, Birds, and the birds led to appropriate literature. In the same manner, literature may stimulate the interest to learn a new technique. It is easy, for example, to imagine a sixth-grade class seeing the harmony between Joan Aiken's *The Wolves of Willoughby Chase* and the stark, brooding effect of woodcuts. Fifth- and sixth-graders are able to handle the cutting tools for linoleum-block printing. Suppose a classroom teacher, during the reading of this semi-Gothic Victorian chiller, displays some medieval woodcuts and suggests that the class produce their own illustrations. The cutting technique almost dictates starkness of line; the story strongly suggests dark colors.

The harmony between text and illustrations can be an intensely interesting inquiry for middle-grade youngsters. Although they would never be caught with a picture book under their arms lest other children think them childish, a project of studying various techniques of illustration can stimulate them to pore over the scratch-board technique of Leonard Everett Fisher, Blair Lent's cardboard cuts in *John Tabor's Ride*, and the combinations of watercolor, collage, and stamp printing in Leo Lionni's *Swimmy*.

**Writing and illustrating children's books.** In a sixth-grade class there was high interest in writing a book for young children. The students checked out a great many picture books in order to see what appealed to young children. Then each child wrote his own story. To be sure that their original stories did in fact appeal to young children, they asked teachers in the kindergarten and in the first and second grades for permission to read their creations to their classes.

Confident that their stories would appeal, they turned their attention to illustration and layout. In their art period, the children labored over their illustrations. An astonishing range of style, technique, and media was represented. The art teacher then explained the process of bookbinding and helped them produce their finished products.

The project took several weeks to complete, but it was well worth it. The children became absorbed in many facets of literature. They learned what in stories appealed to small children and how to make that appeal come through with words and visual images. The project illustrates another point. Art teachers, whose main concern is how to convey something visually, often are not as experienced as a classroom teacher in knowing what is important to convey. The classroom teacher, on the other hand, who knows the impact that literature can have on children and who wants them to be able to express that impact creatively, is often hampered by her inexperience in the nonverbal arts. By working closely with the art, drama, and music teachers, the classroom teacher can provide the stimulus for expression, the specialists can provide the modes.

**Using slides and films as a stimulus to creative writing.** Slides can be used very effectively to help children capture a mood. In a dark room, a brilliantly colored field of poppies or the gloomy recesses of a cathedral become, as if by magic, the place of a story. Some teachers have used films in this same way. The difficulty is that if the film tells a story, a mental set is induced in children which restricts the play of their own imagination. However, the film may be stopped halfway through, as one teacher did in her fifth-grade class with the exquisite film *The Loon's Necklace*. It relates the Indian legend of how the loon got his necklace of brilliant feathers, and colorful masks are used to tell the story. After she stopped the film the teacher asked the children to retell the part of the legend they heard and saw and then finish it. This superlative film has a haunting mood which was reflected in their writing. After the children read their versions of how the legend ended, the film was shown in its entirety. This activity, because of the drama of its introduction, can interest a class in myths and legends, and in the need that man has felt to explain what he doesn't understand.

## HELPING CHILDREN SPREAD THEIR ENTHUSIASMS FOR BOOKS

The sharing of a very personal delight is a delicate matter. Children in particular are properly cautious about revealing what appeals to them to any but the most receptive audience. If their enthusiasms are to be infectious enough to draw another child to a book he never thought of trying, the atmosphere in the classroom must be friendly and supportive. Further, without being so stated, books must be understood and appreciated by all as worthwhile experiences to be shared.

The teacher must take the initiative in creating this atmosphere by her own interest in stories and books, freely, eagerly, and continually expressed. She should bring books to her class—old ones that have been overlooked and new ones to be tasted. In an atmosphere of mutual regard, literary differences of opinion can be an invigorating stimulus for discussion. At first, the teacher serves as a model of attentive consideration, the exponent of the pleasures of literary delight, the interpreter of the wide applicability of literature, and the propelling force toward its exploration.

### With Young Children

With young children, informality is the keynote. Attractive bulletin boards set up by the teacher will identify one place for sharing in general. After a class has become involved in some of the activities suggested in the previous sections, they will turn readily to the bulletin boards as the place for their pictorial interpretations. In schools where Show and Tell is an important part of the program, children may not think of sharing a book they have enjoyed with their classmates. When a child who has delighted in a book insists upon telling the teacher about it, she may suggest that there might be other children who would like to hear about it. Once one child shares his book with his classmates, there is every chance that others will come to regard a book as something worth sharing. In fact, so often the experiences that young children usually share are those that the others may enjoy only vicariously; a good book is an experience that all may ultimately enjoy.

Toward the end of first grade and certainly in second and third, the children can be encouraged to make dioramas of their favorite stories. There is something fascinating about turning a plain shoe box into a miniature, miraculous world, and children from eight to twelve take to the activity with serious satisfaction. Perhaps the fascination comes from the fact that a child literally creates a world and is master of it; certainly the satisfaction comes from making tangible a pleasant though ephemeral experience.

### With Older Children

**The required book report.** For many years, teachers in the middle grades, in all good faith, have sought to help children crystallize their experience with books by asking them to give a report—either written or oral. Too often, however, the task has led to an excruciating experience which has turned children away from books. Basically, the problem has been that many children do not recognize the experience as one to be crystallized. Although they may have enjoyed a book, they do not see writing about it as a means of expressing that pleasure. Hence, some children may resort to plagiarism; they copy from book jackets or recopy reports that other children have written. The worthiness of the teacher's original intention then becomes lost in the game of wits; the child's efforts to disguise his plagiarism and the teacher's efforts to uncover it.

Teachers must recognize that not all children will be drawn to the solitary rewards of literature. Why should they be? To many children, playing a game of baseball is infinitely superior to reading about one. Once you have identified those children you shouldn't force them to "enjoy" a minimum of four books a year. A tension-free atmosphere will allow for the easy sharing of enthusiasms by the children who do love books—and, who knows, the others may be drawn into vicarious enjoyment in spite of themselves.

**A written record of reading.** If you wish to know what your students are reading, you may prepare a simple reading record form for each student. The child needs only to list the author and title of the books he has read. Some children find great satisfaction in keeping such records; others may have to be reminded. As long as the emphasis is not on the quantity of books read but rather on their quality, appropriateness, and variety, the reading record will become a mirror of the true reading tastes of the class. It helps to identify those children who do not read at all. If low-keyed salesmanship on your part fails to reach those children, you should rely on the rest of the class to infect them with an interest in books.

**Informal chatting about books.** The teacher who brings books to class, reads parts of them aloud, and is ready to distribute them to those children eager to read them has taken the first steps toward the informal sharing of an interest in books. Eager hands, wildly waving to get the first chance at a book, attract the notice of even the most reluctant of readers. They may not join in the game, but if you are alert, you will notice the first time their eyes seem to light up with an interest in a particular book. If you follow through with a private suggestion of another book of the same type, you may be rebuffed at first—reluctant readers are a notoriously stubborn lot—but there is always the chance that one day a child with a blank reading record will accept your offer.

Working in this manner, you are providing a model for the informal sharing of books. By telling the class what you like about a book, and admitting candidly what you don't care for, you are saying that quick judgments are not always accurate nor wise. By reading judicious selections, you are demonstrating a way for each child to make up his own mind about the attractiveness of the style for him.

At this point, one teacher turns the Book Chat period over to the class. There are always children who like to talk about what they've enjoyed—the suggestion that they read an exciting part relieves the monotony of repeated, "This is really a good book!" or "It is really funny!" At first, this oral reporting of pleasure in a book is done by individuals. Children can sign up for Book Chats on a sheet posted on a bulletin board. If you notice that the same children sign up week after week, suggest that, in addition to their names, they also post the name of the book they intend to chat about. Knowing that there are children who may not have the courage or even the interest to stand alone before a group, but would be willing to join someone else, you may suggest, "If you have read and enjoyed a book someone intends to talk about, join him in the chat—you may have liked a part of the book that he doesn't mention." This suggestion usually brings a few new faces, voices, and opinions to the Book Chat period. At times when three or more children talk about a book, excitement is aroused, and at times disagreements. What comes through to the class on such occasions is that books are something worth talking about and getting excited about, and that they possibly warrant further investigation.

**Accessibility of recommendations.** All libraries, school or public, have numerous publications which list recommended books. The teacher, however, should not attempt to draw up a list to be used with her class without consulting the librarian. Nothing could be more frustrating to a child who has become interested in a recommended book than to find that the library doesn't have it. Preferably, the librarian and teacher should sit down together and draw up a list of the books in the library that will serve and stretch the interests of the teacher's class.

If facilities permit, this list of available books, in a wide range of categories, may be distributed to the children and will probably stir the spontaneous recommendations of children who have read them. To give the list more dimension and tangibility, categories can be used as the focus of a bulletin board with book jackets and illustrations. Displays may be set up of books and/or artifacts to dramatize the appeals of sports stories, science fiction, or fanciful tales. After the teacher has shown the way by preparing one such display, there are always some children who, propelled by their own enthusiasm, will volunteer to set up one themselves. While the displays serve primarily as a general direction post, a handy list of books in a category gives a child the name of a specific book where the satisfaction is to be found.

**Children's recommendations.** You should not underestimate the impact on children of another child's recommendation, particularly if that child is a friend. A teacher who had taken her class to the school library noticed two of the most popular boys in class looking through the books on the shelves. A third boy, who was sitting nearby, was aimlessly leafing through a magazine and didn't appear to be interested in checking out a book for himself. As the teacher approached the trio, she heard one of the two say as he pointed to a book, "I read that one; it's really good!" His friend responded, "Yeah, so did I; it's cool!" After the two made their way along the shelves, the third boy got up, took Jean Merrill's *The Pushcart War* off the shelf, and checked it out. The two boys were not aware that they had recommended a book, but they had.

One teacher makes use of the enormous potential of children's recommendations by asking her class, about the middle of the school year, to select one book they have read and enjoyed and fill out a simple 4-by-6 card.

*TITLE* ________________________
*AUTHOR* ________________________
*This book is about* ________________________
________________________
________________________
________________________
________________________
*In my opinion, this book is* ________________________
________________________
________________________
________________________
*Name* ________________ *Grade* ______

This form is simple and relatively undemanding. There is little space for writing anything but the simplest of synopses and opinions. The cards are then placed in a shoe box which is available to any child who is looking for a book someone else has recommended. This device places the recommendations of every child at the disposal of every other child. The children are encouraged to add to the file whenever they wish. Some never do; others review every book they read.

Although the teacher initiated this procedure as a minimal and painless method of reporting, she found the file to be a useful source of recommendations attractive to children. Thereafter, she bound the cards into a booklet at the end of the year. At the beginning of each succeeding year, when she introduced the procedure to her new class she showed them the booklet prepared by the previous class as a record of what *they* liked in literature. She found that the new class was just as interested in those recommendations as they were in those of their own classmates.

**Using games and quizzes.** There are many literary games and quizzes that teachers have introduced to their classes with significant effect. They can be found in professional journals and texts, and many teachers devise their own. Basically, they are guessing games which appeal to the child's fondness for play and pleasure in his achievement. They range from a series of clues to book characters and titles to the more elaborate crossword puzzles, from simple charades to competitive team games. All presuppose a certain amount of experience in literature. For the child who has read a great deal, a literature quiz is not only a challenge but an opportunity to display his knowledge. These youngsters find in literary games not only a showcase but a stimulus to further reading. On the other hand, for the youngster who hasn't found much pleasure in reading, and hasn't read a great deal, these games may have the effect of boring him to the point of resentment. It is rare that such a child, excluded from participation by his own inexperience, will determine to gain that experience. The teacher who has a class that is actively interested in literature and is therefore sure that prepared puzzle activities will be an invigorating challenge should, by all means, try them.

**Dressing up for biographies.** It is interesting to note the appeal that dressing up in costume has for children—even sixth-graders. A sixth-grade English teacher exploits this interest in a unit she teaches on biography. There are children who love biographies and read them all the time. It is more difficult to attract lovers of sports stories or fanciful tales to the lives of great men, especially with an informal approach. With the plan of having children write their own autobiographies toward the end of the year, the teacher introduces them to a biographical style of writing through the assigned reading of several short biographies. In their discussions, the relevance to achievement of various factors is brought out: childhood interests, skills, family environment, obstacles overcome. Then each student is asked to select a famous person he admires, read all the biographical material he can find, and write a short biography. This is where many teachers would stop. This teacher asks that the identity of their choice of person be kept a secret and on the day they are to read their biographies to the class they should come dressed as that person. The costumes every year range from the elaborate knee breeches, waistcoat, and tailcoat of J. S. Bach to the white lab coat and spectacles of George Washington Carver. There is predictable excitement in a classroom with five or six costumed personages, and the prior guesswork as to their identity gives the reading of the biography a luster. In addition, the ingenuity of the costuming gives drama to what otherwise might be an ordinary oral report.[19]

There is no one strategy to spread enthusiasm for books. Each class, being composed of different individuals with differing interests, is unique. In general, however, you may start off in the same way—by being enthusiastic about books yourself, by showing your class a variety of ways of sharing enthusiasm, and by providing every opportunity and en-

19. See also "Writing Autobiographies," pp. 705–706.

couragement for children similarly inclined to join in the adventure. There will be some years when nothing will come of your efforts and those of your group of enthusiasts; there will be others when, thanks to the delight and energy and imagination of some of the children, literature will become the focal point of all activity for everyone.[20]

## A LITERATURE PROGRAM

Suggestions were made in the previous sections for using specific techniques to bring children and books together. The approach suggested thus far has been an informal one. Its success depends upon a rapport between teacher and class that will insure continuing delight in literature and also develop a faith that the thought-stretching activities will indeed lead to richer satisfactions. However, this approach does not guarantee that children will have the opportunity to taste the full range of our literary heritage. Without the aid of a well-thought-out literature program, many children can proceed through elementary school without having any experience with one genre of literature or another—fables and myths, for example. Many responsible educators, administrators, and teachers feel that contact with so important a part of our civilization as literature should not be left to chance, whim, or narrow personal interest; hence the justification for using a literature program.

### What a Literature Program Can Do

One of the chief difficulties faced by a beginning teacher and even by an experienced teacher who feels inadequate in the field of children's literature is selecting books from every genre that are appropriate to the level of maturity of her class. Such teachers often rely upon the school librarian for advice, but they must remember that no matter how knowledgeable and sensitive the librarian is, it is next to impossible for one person to keep in mind the literary experiences of every class in an entire school. If there are gaps in the literary experience of a class, the classroom teacher must discover them. If, for example, she finds out that her class has had little or no experience with myths, then the librarian can suggest appropriate editions and recommend appropriate myths.

Most literature programs suggest a core of basic stories in every genre for every grade level in the elementary school. The categories may be different, but the full range of types of stories will be represented. After all, does it really matter to a child whether Andersen's "The Snow Queen" is a fairy tale or a folk tale? What does matter is that the child has the opportunity to experience the magic of Andersen's writing and the power of his stories.

Armed with copies of *Teaching Literature in Wisconsin*, the Nebraska *A Curriculum for English*, or the *Handbook for Language Arts* from New York City, the teacher has a balanced and sequential list of books which she may use as a check list to assess the literary experience of her class. This is the very lowest practical level of usefulness for such guides.

Another difficulty faced by novices in the teaching of literature is deciding what to do with the books. Some teachers, particularly primary teachers, simply read them informally without stressing the characteristics of the genre. The discussion afterward, if any, is directed by the interests of the children. Teachers of older children may, after examining the children's reading records, fill in gaps by bringing books of ignored categories to the classroom and chatting about them.

Teachers who wish to take more direct action will find in guides, such as *Teaching Literature in Wisconsin*, sample lesson plans. The plans may or may not suit a particular class, but they can be used as models for questions and as guides to what is important

20. See "Book Promotion" in Part Seven for other ways of creating enthusiasm for books.

to discuss in a story. Once a teacher is clear herself about the components of narrative fiction and once she has developed skill in framing questions that will make the components clear to children, she no longer will need to adhere strictly to published lesson plans and will be able to devise her own.

Guides that offer analyses of stories as background information for the teacher are especially helpful. The Nebraska *A Curriculum for English*, for example, prefaces each suggested presentation of a story with a discussion of the stylistic characteristics of the story: its structure, motif, theme, style, and, where pertinent and possible, background information about the author. This information is not intended for communication to children as lectures or ready-made analyses. Rather,

> *These materials are provided on the assumption that a teacher will teach more effectively if she understands something of the literary nature of stories and of their place in the curriculum. The teacher should know all that she can about the meaning and literary method of the work so that, whenever and wherever she can, she may bring to the students those insights that she has and, more importantly, so that she can encourage her students when they show evidence of gaining insights themselves.*[21]

For the second grade, the folk tale, for example, is represented by "The Story of the Three Bears," "Little Red Riding-Hood," and "The Story of the Three Little Pigs." The guide suggests that the plot structure of the three stories is similar in that a child or childlike creature begins in a secure home, wanders off, and encounters a monster or monsters. They differ in that Little Red Riding-Hood is eaten up, one of the three pigs outwits the "monster" and creates a new security, and Goldilocks presumably returns to the security of her home. By the third grade, children have been exposed to four basic structural motifs: (1) journey from home to isolation ("Sleeping Beauty"), (2) journey from home to confrontation with a monster ("The Story of the Three Bears"), (3) rescue from a harsh home and the miraculous creation of a new one ("Cinderella"), (4) the conflict between the wise beast and the foolish beast ("The Rabbit and the Fox").

While the applicability of the foregoing motifs to the particular stories might be argued and others might be devised, still, a teacher who sees commonalities in stories is in a better position to lead children to discovering some themselves. And, as similarities are identified, so are differences. As long as the teacher resists the temptation to force a particular analysis on children, but rather, as the guide suggests, uses the suggestions to bring children through her insights to acquire some on their own, a literature program can serve education in the richest way.

Some curriculum programs treat literature as a separate part of the language arts program; others treat it as an integral part. The Nebraska *Curriculum for English* uses literature as the springboard to a wide variety of language instruction. After the presentation of the stories in a particular genre, suggestions are made for composition activities and language explorations. The latter include, where appropriate, vocabulary, phonology, punctuation, morphology, diction, syntax, and history of the language. Suggestions for poetry and extended activities in art and dramatization are also made.

## Factors Affecting the Use of a Literature Program

A literature program, like a mathematics program, is concerned with materials, concepts, and activities to suit the maturity level of children and arranged sequentially to insure steady growth. The concept of a hero, for example, given merely as a definition is not nearly so meaningful as one that begins with the appreciation of the wit and courage of the

21. *A Curriculum for English*, University of Nebraska Press, 1966, Grade 1, p. xiv.

third little pig, is added to by the outrageous feats of Pecos Bill, and enriched by the sensitive fortitude of Johnny Tremain. A spiral curriculum, such as the Nebraska *Curriculum for English*, is planned so that the work of one year is built on the foundation laid by that of previous years. The best use of a literature program, then, is dependent upon the wholehearted commitment of the entire school and of each teacher.

The Nebraska curriculum guide, for example, stresses over and over again that a growing love of literature is its primary concern. The suggested activities, insofar as they require analyses of stories, should never become so forced and mechanical as to sour that love. There is a temptation to adhere to the array of lesson plans and activities exclusively. The teacher who succumbs to that temptation runs the risk of turning children away from literature. If she becomes more concerned with *talking about literature* than with *communicating the enjoyment of it*, then her efforts are in vain.

A third factor that can affect the use of a literature program is the very richness of its offerings. Curriculum guides, like teacher's manuals for the teaching of reading, whether it be literature or reading, extend radiating arms to all the other areas of the language arts. This situation can be confusing to beginning teachers who wonder where to look for guidance in the teaching of spelling: in the literature guide, the reading guide, or the spelling guide. The solution to this problem is not found through strict and unthinking adherence to printed advice, but from selecting from the many suggested activities those which suit a particular class and its needs. The teacher who uses the suggestions in any curriculum guide as models for her own invention will bring more of herself into the teaching-learning act to the benefit of all.

### How a Literature Program May Be Used

If an entire school has not agreed to use a given literature program and yet some teachers feel that the place and values of literature should have more organized emphasis, they need not despair. A group of middle-school teachers realized that the reading interests of their children had become very narrow and that there were serious gaps in their acquaintance with literature—notably myths. With the approval of their principal, they agreed to follow the treatment of myths in the Nebraska *Curriculum for English* for three years, evaluating their progress at the end of each year. In addition, they agreed to make a serious attempt to use tall tales and fanciful tales in their language arts program but not necessarily in the manner suggested by the guide. They reasoned that, at the very least, their classes would be assured of acquaintance with these three genres and some gaps in knowledge would be filled.

If you find yourself in a school where other subject areas are emphasized more than literature, you can work out a similar plan. Of course, the sequential aspect of a literature program can be an obstacle, but one that can be overcome. You may select a literary genre you feel your children have ignored, and during the year provide them with many rich experiences with the genre. Teachers of older children may have greater difficulty in finding the time in one year to provide the growth planned for five years, but it will be worth the trouble.

## Notes on Chapters 5–15

Pages 650–694 have discussed techniques for using books with children. The following pages relate these techniques to specific kinds of literature presented in Chapters 5–15.

### CHAPTER 5: MOTHER GOOSE (pp. 108–125)

Occasionally, teachers get a little weary of *Mother Goose*. "The same old thing!" they say, and hurry the children to A. A. Milne, or

Myra Cohn Livingston, forgetting that to each crop of children *Mother Goose* is brand-new and endlessly diverting. So if you do find yourself a little tired of "Miss Muffet," try a new edition. Different illustrations will provide a fresh experience, and you will soon discover that you enjoy *Mother Goose* again.

In large cities there are many children with foreign accents. Everywhere, there are children whose speech is slovenly. These verses are the best possible speech exercise. Children can look at the pictures and say the rhymes effortlessly and the improvement in speech agility will be surprising.

These are utilitarian reasons for using the verses. The chief reason is enjoyment. Whole class periods may be devoted to going through a new edition, saying the verses, savoring the pictures, discussing and comparing different collections the children know. A book that is completely worn out, past all further patching and gluing, may be cut up and such pictures as you can retrieve mounted on boards. These may go up on the walls or be used as you would use a book with the children. Sometimes older children "read" these to a younger group. Inexpensive editions should be on the children's own bookshelves for them to pick up in spare time.

Use *Mother Goose* to finish out a class period or to fill in a time of waiting, just saying the verses spontaneously without a book. Let the class dramatize some of the verses, with no set stage procedures. Of course, occasionally they are fun to use for an assembly, with the little children in the simplest costumes or just as usual. One kindergarten had a big wooden book built by the manual training department. The cover opened and through the pages came the children as their favorite story-book characters. *Mother Goose* always supplied a group of these.

There are an infinite number of ways of using these old verses. Our goal is to see that no child goes out of our homes, our kindergartens, or our first grades without knowing by heart dozens of these artless, picturesque, lyrical rhymes that constitute the child's most entertaining introduction to English poetry.

## CHAPTER 5: THE TRADITIONAL BALLADS (pp. 125–134)

The old ballads are not for the primary grades but belong to the children of the middle and upper grades or of junior high school. One glance at these ballads shows the reading difficulties they present for even eleven- and twelve-year-old children. Not only do they employ difficult and obsolete words, but some of the ballads are in dialect, some are in a phonetic idiom that can only be guessed at, and others use familiar words which are so oddly spelled or abbreviated ("ba" for ball) that the average reader doesn't recognize the words when he sees them. Most of these difficulties, however, disappear when the child hears the ballads read aloud.

Children generally like dialect. If, then, you are going to read "Sir Patrick Spens" to the children, you can tell them that it is in Scottish dialect and old, old dialect at that. You might tell them something about the story first, or you might even read the ballad in modern English, either before or after reading the original version. This is the way the first two stanzas read in modern style:

*The king sits in Dumferling town,*
*Drinking the blood red wine:*
*'O where will I get a good sailor,*
*To sail this ship of mine?'*

*Then up and spoke an elderly knight,*
*Sat at the king's right knee:*
*'Sir Patrick Spence is the best sailor*
*That sails upon the sea.'*

In the fourth verse where "a loud laugh laughed he" and then "a tear blinded his eye," a good rhyme is upset but can be restored when you swing back to the "ee" of dialect. This may be a very unorthodox way of dealing with folk ballads, but the barrier of language should not keep these exciting story-poems from children. They like to hear the dialect if they know what it means. Translating it into modern English will make the meaning clear.

A sixth-grade teacher had a group of overage children who were addicted to comic books and the more lurid movies. She started reading some of the old ballads aloud to them. The ones they liked best she read over and over, letting them say the verses along with her. To the children's surprise, they learned a number of the ballads in this way without consciously trying to memorize. When they commented on this, she told them she supposed people had always found ballads easy to learn, and had enjoyed repeating them. That is why they still exist today, after hundreds of years of being learned and passed on from one person to another.

Since the teacher kept the discussion unforced, a few of the ballads drew no comments from the children. If the children never asked for those ballads the teacher let them drop. On the other hand, with every saying of the favorite ballads, questions would come with a rush. "Did that old knight have it in for Sir Patrick Spens when he got the king to send him off to sea in the middle of the winter?" "Did Sir Patrick have to go to sea when he knew there was going to be a storm?" "Why couldn't he just throw the king's letter away and not go?" Such questions provoked considerable discussion and led to some wholesome conclusions about duty and courage. Another group argued at length about the conduct of the wife in "The Raggle, Taggle Gypsies." Why did a fine lady leave her home and her husband, they wondered. Was she just a faithless woman like the wife in "The Daemon Lover"? One of the girls thought not. "Perhaps," she said slowly, "perhaps she was a gypsy girl herself." Others caught the implication immediately and carried it further. "Maybe she thought it would be a fine thing to have a grand house and a rich husband, but when her own people came for her, she just couldn't stand being cooped up any longer; so she went with them." A logical and charitable conclusion!

The Scottish and English ballads may be utilized in several ways. If the children are reading a prose version of Robin Hood, the teacher can read aloud to them the ballad sources of the tales. Or, in a dramatization of Robin Hood, Allen a Dale can sing some of the other old ballads, and the merry men can sing or say still others. The ballads make a fine center for English-class activities. A ballad assembly can be given by a group of children. In a dramatization of medieval life, a wandering minstrel can entertain the company in the great hall by saying or singing the ballads. Some of these he can say alone, but the company can join in with other ballads that have refrains. Many ballads lend themselves to choral speaking and to dramatization, and a few of the farcical ones are excellent for shadow or puppet plays. The heroic ballads, though, are usually better read or spoken by a single individual.

## CHAPTER 6: THE FOLK TALES (pp. 138–174)

Most children reach the peak of interest in fairy tales when they are around seven, eight, and nine years old. There are some stories, of course, that the youngest children ask for again and again: a few beast tales like "The Three Little Pigs" and "The Little Red Hen," and also the accumulative stories. The prereading child should not miss these nursery classics. But for the most part, he is passionately concerned with his own realistic world of trains and cars, stores and houses, real dogs and real goats. Fairies and giants are not for him as yet, although he accepts the troll under the bridge matter-of-factly enough. For him, apparently the troll is just something to wheedle or to fight with.

"Cinderella," "Hänsel and Gretel," "East o' the Sun," and "Mollie Whuppie" are far better for children of eight or nine than for those of five or six. And some folk tales are best for ten- and eleven-year-olds and even older—tales like "Clever Manka," "The Most Obedient Wife," and the American tall tales. Since there are some fairy stories right for every age, it is unnecessary to force the stories on children who are too young for them.

First and foremost, these old tales should be told or read just for fun. The relaxation and entertainment in the promise of "Once upon a time" are a justification for the stories at any age or any hour. When things have been tense or difficult, try a story and relax. Have the kindergarten children just had their first fire drill? Tell them "The Pancake" and make them laugh. Or when a factual study has pressed the older children hard, read them "Urashima Taro and the Princess of the Sea" and they will be refreshed. Keep a book of these tales in the room to pick up at any time just for pleasure. These stories do not have to "correlate" with any study unit; they do not have to teach something. Whether romance or sheer nonsense, nursery tale or allegory, their power of entertainment is their first reason for existence and our first reason for using them.

### Using Folk Tales with National Groups

The folk tales may become a teacher's open sesame to friendship in a neighborhood made up of a somewhat homogeneous national group. One teacher will never forget telling Irish fairy tales at a mothers' and daughters' party where most of the mothers had been born in Ireland. When she began, the girls looked a bit self-conscious, but the mothers' eyes were bright and responsive.

"I heard that story another way," said one mother when the teacher had finished.

"How did yours go?" she asked. The mother outlined the differences clearly, but added, "Mrs. O'Connor's the one for stories. She knows dozens of them."

Between them, they persuaded the reluctant Mrs. O'Connor to tell a story. Proud of her art, she told "Hudden and Dudden and Donald O'Neary" to perfection. They all laughed, and the girls lost their self-consciousness. Over the refreshments, everyone compared notes on the Irish stories she knew and agreed to exchange some of her favorites the next time they met. So began a series of storytelling exchanges ranging from the hilarious "King O'Toole and His Goose" to bits of the Cuchulain epic. Even by the second meeting, they were no longer teacher, pupils, and mothers; they were just friends.

So folk tales may lead straight into the homes of the children and develop a common bond between two generations and between two or more national groups. In a school where different nationalities mingle, a rich and beautiful program can be developed around "Folk Tales of Many Countries," with typical stories told, dramatized, played by puppets and marionettes, and illustrated by the children with paints and clay modeling. The likenesses as well as fascinating differences among all peoples will be dramatically evident.

### Illustrating the Folk Tales

As subjects for modeling or painting, the fairy tales are unsurpassed. One man's guess is as good as another's in illustrating them, because no one can tell anyone else the precise measurements and equipment of a fairy godmother. "Hänsel and Gretel," "Mother Holle," "Cinderella," and dozens of others are beautiful subjects for illustration and send the children's imaginations soaring. Needless to say, no book pictures should be visible when the children are making their own illustrations.

### Dramatizing the Folk Tales

Most of the folk tales have a dramatic quality, and any discussion of children and these old tales eventually leads to the possibilities of dramatization. Pages 677–680, offer suggestions for classroom dramatization.

### Storytelling by Older Children

Upper-grade children had unusual fun with folk tales in one school which was an experiment station for English activities of all kinds. The fifth-grade children had listened to stories told over the radio by one of the best storytellers in the city, and had read other tales as well. They decided to tell some of their favorites to younger children. They formed themselves into the Children's Storytelling Club, learned their stories well, and told them to the primary grades with such zest that the primaries were charmed. The fifth-grade storytellers carried on this activity for a whole semester and not only enjoyed themselves thoroughly but grew in poise, language power, and ability to interest and hold an audience.

## CHAPTER 7: FABLES, MYTHS, AND EPICS

### Using Fables with Children (pp. 184–190)

The highly intellectual quality of fables, proverbs, and parables is quite apparent when they are compared with the folk tales. Just because the fables happen to use characters that sound like those of the folk tales, and because large, colored illustrations usually play up this resemblance, and because they are brief, they have often been given to small children for entertainment. Then we are surprised when the children don't warm up to them. But let's keep our definitions clearly in mind. All three of them—proverbs, parables, and fables—are attempts to make abstract ideas sufficiently striking or objective to be understood and remembered. Every one of them *is* an abstraction—a maxim, an adage, a brief sermon on morality—and, because of this, the least appealing of all story types with children.

**With young children.** In spite of the bright-colored pictures which adorn many an edition of Aesop or La Fontaine, the fables should be used chiefly with the older children. To be sure, a few may be told to young children in anticipation of the whole books later on, but they should be the ones which have the most story appeal or an obvious bit of humor: for instance, "The Lion and the Mouse," "The Town Mouse and the Country Mouse," "The Hare and the Tortoise," and "The Fox and the Crow." Two or three such fables a year, slipped in among warmly appealing folk tales and modern realistic stories, are about as many abstractions as the primary school child enjoys.

**With older children.** On the other hand, children ten, eleven, and twelve years old can read for themselves and enjoy a good collection of the Aesop fables. They like to tell a fable to the class, omitting the moral to see how closely the group can come to supplying it. This, by the way, is no mean intellectual feat but is one item often used in intelligence tests. Try this project: take a maxim or proverb (see those given on page 135) and try to evolve a fable. This is too hard for children to do individually but can be great fun for a whole class. Because the pithy maxims of Aesop and La Fontaine have passed into our language and our thinking, every child should have some experience with them.

With a study of India, introduce the stories of *The Panchatantra* and *Jatakas* as told by Ellen C. Babbitt and Joseph Gaer. Their three books have stories that are worth using at any time, with or without a unit on Indian life. "Greedy and Speedy," "The Lion and the Wily Rabbit," "The Hermit and the Mouse," "The Merchant of Seri," "Grannie's Blackie," and "The Banyan Deer" are all entertaining tales.

After the older children have had some experience with the fables and with several of the fable adaptations like James Daugherty's *Andy and the Lion* and John Ciardi's *John J. Plenty and Fiddler Dan*, they may discover the fablelike qualities of such stories as Wanda Gág's *Nothing at All*, Munro Leaf's *The Story of Ferdinand*, and Anita Brenner's *A Hero by Mistake*. For the moral of this last story they may think of the song from *The King and I*, "Whenever I feel afraid, I whistle a happy tune." A few experiments with double meanings will go a long way with children. Even so, these old moralities, these priceless bits of wisdom we call fables, are an essential part of their literary heritage, too good to miss.

### Using Myths with Children (pp. 190–199)

**As the religion of a people.** Some people believe that myths should be studied as the religion of a people. As a matter of fact, some church schools are using mythology in this way, including the myths in a comparative study of religions for adolescent boys and girls. *The Tree of Life* is a collection of selections from the religious literature of the world. The selections show the emergence, here and there throughout the centuries, of great religious ideals which are universal and command our respect today. Ideas of sin, repentance, expiation, and purification, and ideals of faithful love and self-sacrifice are all to be found in the old symbolic myths. This sort of study probably belongs to late adolescence but is certainly a matter for church schools and families to decide individually.

**With the study of a people.** The elementary schools often use the myths in connection with the study of a people. That is, the children who are studying the Vikings explore the Norse myths in order to understand the motives for and the standards of behavior, the moral code of the Vikings. Or, if they are following the vicissitudes of the Greek hero Odysseus, they study the Greek mythology in order to understand the Olympian battle of the gods—some ranged on the hero's side and some opposed to him. A study of certain forest Indians reveals a far less advanced mythology than that of the Navahos, but no tribe can be understood without the background of its particular ideology of the supernatural. It is, then, not only desirable but essential that any unit about a people shall include a study of its religious ideals.

**As literature.** Reading the myths in connection with the study of a people would seem to take care of these stories. Unfortunately, in many school systems the studies of early people are being replaced by units that are either "here and now," or tied into United States history or civics. Since the high schools generally take for granted that something has been done with myths in the elementary schools, secondary schools may also omit them from the curriculum. The result is that many college freshmen today have no knowledge of mythology.

Certainly, if the high-school curriculum does not include myth, then the elementary schools should—if not as the study of a people, then simply as literature. In the literature periods we need not give children all the involved and confusing ramifications of the gods' genealogies, but we could introduce the major gods to them through stories which illustrate the characteristics and powers of the gods. Older children will be interested in the following Greek gods (Roman names in parentheses):

*Zeus* (Jove or Jupiter), the chief of the Olympian gods
*Hera* (Juno), wife of Zeus, goddess of women and marriage
*Athena* (Minerva), goddess of wisdom
*Aphrodite* (Venus), goddess of love and beauty
*Apollo* (sometimes called Phoebus Apollo), the sun god and the god of health and healing
*Eros* (Cupid), god of love
*Artemis* (Diana), the virgin huntress, who is associated with the moon
*Poseidon* (Neptune), god of the sea
*Hades* or *Pluto* (Dis), god of the underworld
*Dionysus* (Bacchus), god of wine and the harvest
*Hermes* (Mercury), messenger of the gods

*Ares* (Mars), god of war
*Hephaestus* (Vulcan), god of fire and metalworking
*Demeter* (Ceres), goddess of agriculture
*Persephone* (Proserpina), goddess of the underworld, spring

Decide to use consistently either the Greek or Roman names. The Greeks created the gods and the stories about them; the Romans merely adapted them, but the Roman names are more familiar and more generally used. Even the Greek hero Odysseus is better known to most people as Ulysses. To give children both sets of names is generally confusing; so keep to one or the other, perhaps according to the central book you may be using with the children.

The myths are indeed entirely appropriate for the literature period. Many stories about the gods are much like the finest of the fairy tales and are perhaps, in some cases, the sources of certain fairy tales. In "Baucis and Philemon," the gods, Zeus and Hermes, are glorified versions of the folk-tale godmothers or mysterious strangers who grant wishes as the rewards of hospitality or goodness. Older children who know "The Sleeping Beauty" find that the Greek "Demeter and Persephone" is a mature edition of their old friend. Older children find the myths even more beautiful and memorable than their favorite fairy tales. Certainly they have a more intellectual appeal.

### Using Epics with Children (pp. 199–206)

Telling epics or hero cycles generally requires drastic adaptation. Some are easier than others. The *Odyssey* requires, for example, a complete reordering of the episodes. In the original story the actual chronological beginning does not appear until the ninth book, an arrangement which is at first confusing. Fortunately, most children's versions relate the story in chronological form.

The Norse epic *Sigurd the Volsung* is especially difficult to adapt for children and calls for expert handling, but it is magnificent to tell. The *Odyssey* and *Robin Hood* are the easiest and most rewarding epics to tell, but if you have a special fondness for *Sigurd, Cuchulain, Beowulf,* or *King Arthur,* work on your favorite by all means.

Perhaps, in the schools, two epics in the years from ten to fourteen are about as many as the children can comfortably enjoy. Of the rich offering available, the *Odyssey* is of first importance and *Robin Hood* is the most popular. These may be supplemented with such single hero tales as the stories of Moses, Jacob and Esau, and Joseph and his brethren, since those also have entered into our speech, our thinking, and our moral code. Choose, then, from the epics the one or two which you yourself enjoy and which you believe will give the children the greatest enjoyment and enrichment. Then live with these, joyously and intensively, for six to eight weeks.

## CHAPTERS 9, 10, AND 11: POETRY (pp. 277–389)

### Using Poetry with School Subjects

While an unexpected event may be made more significant by saying the right poem at the right time, it is also obvious that there are many predictable uses of poetry for which suitable verses can be collected. We know, for instance, most of the child's nature interests: the change of seasons; the weather; birds, flowers, and insects; the sun, moon, and stars. For all of these interests we may well collect matching poems and have them ready.

So much poetry is devoted to nature subjects that we can find excellent material to correlate with the children's science experiences throughout the year. In social studies it is not so easy. Of course there are many poems about the farm; and a few about boats, trains, airplanes, and buses; but for the fire department, colonial life, and many other "units" there are almost no poems worthy of the name. When good poetry is lacking, do not yield to the temptation to introduce any old doggerel because it is conveniently titled "The Fireman" or "When George Washington Was a Boy." If there is fine poetry available, use it. If not, don't waste time with the second-rate. Instead, introduce the children to all the splendid informational books now available for almost any subject you can think of. Then for their literature period, use poetry that is a complete contrast. For instance, when you are having a particularly factual unit of work—transportation or post office or tropical countries, for example—that might be the very time to treat the children to a satisfying feast of nonsense verse, or to investigate fairy lore and the delicately imaginative poetry that "correlates" with no facts but is precious in its own right. In short, correlate school subjects with poetry when you can legitimately do so with authentic poetry, and when you can't, use poetry for contrast and enjoy the change.

### Using Poetry with Festivals

Celebrate festivals with poetry as well as with music and art. Beginning with the first festival of the school year, Halloween, teachers give the children a background of fairy lore and set them to looking for fairy poems and the favorite jack-o'-lantern verses. They may start with Sandburg's "Theme in Yellow," but they progress to the idea of fairies abroad on Halloween and use Walter de la Mare's "Little Green Orchard," "Tillie," "Some One," and (for the older children) "The Rides-by-Nights," and John Ciardi's or Marie Lawson's poems called "Halloween."

For Thanksgiving, develop the real meaning of the word—literally, "giving thanks"—and introduce the children to that great body of Thanksgiving hymns, the Psalms.

Christmas is actually richer in poetry than in stories. Indeed, the offering is so wide and splendid that there is no excuse for wasting time on the multitude of trivialities that afflict us with rhymes about Santa bringing *toys* for girls and *boys*. From Clement Moore's "'Twas the night before Christmas" (which is a perennial command performance for the youngest children) to the second chapter of St. Luke (which is for children of all ages), the poetry of Christmas is both gay and rich in meaning. Some of the old carols are good to say aloud: "I saw three ships come sailing," or "As Joseph was a-walking," or

*Beggar's Rhyme*

*Christmas is coming, the geese are getting fat,*
*Please to put a penny in the old man's hat;*
*If you haven't got a penny, a ha' penny will do.*
*If you haven't got a ha' penny, God bless you!*

For the older children, Robert Herrick's "Ceremonies for Christmas" makes lusty reading. The youngest should have—along with Martin Luther's "Cradle Hymn"—Eugene Field's "Song." All these and many others are to be found in the best anthologies of children's poetry. And it will be especially worth while to look at *Come Christmas*, the collection of poems of Eleanor Farjeon.

### Making Your Own Collection of Poetry

To be ready with the right poem at the right moment means at least two first-rate anthologies on the teacher's desk or on the home bookshelves, but in addition to these, it is a great satisfaction to have a choice poetry selection of your own making. Cards four by six inches are convenient for this purpose. They are enough to take a poem of several stanzas on one card if you use both sides, and they can be conveniently filed in a shoe box, which the ingenious teacher decorates attractively and keeps on her desk. Poems should be copied accurately and clearly so that you won't stumble over words when you read from your cards. You may file them alphabetically, according to authors, or under subject-matter heads. Many people use both classifications—they file the full text of the poems according to author, and then make a cross-reference index under subjects, copying on these subject cards only the titles and authors. Blake's poem "The Lamb," for instance, would be copied and filed under Blake, but its title might appear on two different cards in the subject-matter index, perhaps once under animals and once under religious poems. Your subject index will include all those areas of interest that you have discovered both in the children and in your curriculum. Each person's index will be different, although animals, the four seasons, play, just-for-fun, going places, and several other topics will occur rather universally.

The children themselves are fascinated with these handmade anthologies. In group after group where they have been used, a child or two has started his own collection, and, whenever the teacher has permitted it, the children have used her file themselves, lovingly and with pride in the teacher's unique possession. Few of us can reach a library and get out six books by six authors on the particular morning when the daffodils have bloomed and we must celebrate with poems on the bulletin board and with poems to be said together. Then you will be thankful for your cards, for the fact that tucked away in your "anthology" you have the very best poems you need, the ones last year's children liked best, and a few new ones to try out.

### Writing Poetry

Sometimes children may become so obsessed with rhyming that anything that rhymes is automatically a good poem to them. When this happens, read them Hilda Conkling's poems and ask them why they think people call these unrhymed verses poems. This proved a poser when tried with a group of children. It took time and listening over and over to some of the verses (see p. 374) before they arrived at these conclusions: (1) She says a lot in a few words. (2) She says things that no one has ever said before. (3) What she says about weather "is my wonder/About the kind of morning/Hidden behind the hills of sky" surprises you. (4) It's like seeing something you never saw before, like the snail's shell being "his umbrella."

The children always came back to the poet's unique, surprising, new way of looking at and saying things. Freed of the burden of rhyme, children can write more naturally. The upper grades can handle rhyme with more ease than the lower grades, but over and over, when they are deeply moved, or sometimes when they need to clarify an idea, the older children, too, will use free verse.

Here, for instance, is a somber reflection of a deep emotion, written by a fifth-grade girl living in a depressed area of a big city. It was a dark, gloomy day with a steady downpour of rain. She stared out of a third floor window in her school, looking down on the wet city streets full of hurrying people. Soberly she walked back to her seat and wrote the following lines:

*When raindrops fall,*  
*It seems as if they were tears of God,*  
*God weeping over the people of the streets.*  
*But the people put umbrellas over their heads.*[22]

Here was a precocious sensitivity expressed in strong, simple words, unrhymed but beautifully cadenced and climactic.

In *Elementary English*, June 1961, Elizabeth Scofield gave a delightful account of what resulted from her reading haiku to the children and letting them try to write in this form. The children made their own rules which permitted considerable leeway: (1) Write the poem in three lines. (2) Tell what

22. Jennie Ross, fifth grade, William Brett School, Cleveland, Ohio.

the subject is. (3) Tell where the subject is. (4) Tell when the action is taking place.

Miss Scofield added, "the most important rule came out in our discussion, although it was not verbalized as such. The poem must be something expressed from one's heart." These rules ignored syllable counts and said nothing about double meanings although such meanings do occur in the poems—for example,

*The deer!*
*Look how gaily he bounds—*
*then goes.*

Did this fourth-grade boy have any consciousness that his verse is a moving expression of the evanescence of life? Probably not, but perhaps from reading and hearing this particular type of verse, he was conscious of overtones of feeling beyond explanation. Who knows?

This subtle form of poetry requires extreme condensation, gives vent to feeling, and, finally, as Miss Scofield suggests, the three lines require clear thinking and free the writer from the burden of many words—"leaving a picture of beauty etched in fine clear lines." One of her boys wrote:

*Petals on the ground—*
*beautiful, so beautiful!*
*birds singing in the starlight.*

Here are sight and sound expressed simply with no extraneous decorations.

Scrutinizing diverse examples of children's use of haiku, we discover certain outstanding qualities. The idea or picture is fresh and unhackneyed and is expressed with the utmost economy. They may not be exact haiku, but in their poems, the youngsters catch a more subtle sense of secondary meanings than is usual with children. If through attempting to write haiku, children learn disciplined economy in the use of words, teachers will probably find the form well worth trying with children.

## CHAPTER 13: REALISTIC FICTION (pp. 420–493)

It is increasingly important for adults to be able to distinguish a good story from synthetic, made-to-specification fiction. To reinforce our judgment, we have enough fine realistic fiction for children, which was created not because a slogan or a curriculum outline seemed to require it but because an author had something to write about, a robust story to tell. The children themselves, given the opportunity, pick out these books unerringly, regardless of Newbery Medals or social-studies' endorsement.

Along with this adult obsession to provide realism in books for children has gone the emphasis on correlation of literature with social studies. Many social-studies units can be greatly enriched by good fiction related to the unit under consideration. But correlation of literature and social studies should not become constant. It is necessary to remember that a good story is a good story regardless of whether or not it correlates with social-studies outlines, and a poor story is a poor story even if it was written with a particular outline in mind. To fail to promote fine literature because it does not happen to fit curriculum units is as short-sighted as to promote commonplace, second-rate fiction because it was written particularly for such a unit. It is far better to turn to the substantial factual books in this field and allow the child to take his fiction along other lines. Certainly it would be just as absurd to expect all the child's reading to correlate with his social studies as it would be to expect adults to forego their favorite novels because such reading did not correlate with their workaday interests.

Perhaps by being aware of the richness of the whole offering in the realistic field and of its wide range and variety, we can develop a feeling for what is substantial and fine and a corresponding sensitivity to what is thin, labored, or trivial. It should not trouble us if right in the middle of his study of the Congo or of medieval times some child wishes to read *Tom Sawyer.* Why shouldn't he? Often a change is a good thing. It is quite conceivable that he is temporarily fed up on jungles or knights and wants to get back to his own boy's world. Let him read *Tom Sawyer,* by all means. He'll return to his geography or his castles and moats with a fresh perspective. So, whether children are at the moment following the rise of the guilds in medieval days or good neighboring with South American countries or being interracially conscious, they should have the best realistic fiction available, let the slogans and the units fall where they will!

## CHAPTER 14: HISTORICAL FICTION (pp. 494–531)

Today, when historical fiction for adults contains much that is sensational and erotic, historical fiction in the juvenile field includes some of our finest books. And though adults flit from one historical novel to another, children read and reread their favorites. Such stories as *Calico Bush, Johnny Tremain, Caddie Woodlawn, The Courage of Sarah Noble, Tree of Freedom, Winter Danger,* and the fine Laura Ingalls Wilder series are good literature and are also continuously popular with young readers.

A sixth-grade teacher, Miss Ophelia Smith of the Cleveland Robert Fulton School, made the Wilder books the center of a valuable unit of work. For their English, the children read the whole series; each child reported in detail on one particular book; and the group evaluated them all at the conclusion of the reports. They noted the geographical setting of each story, the growth and development of the characters, the problems, difficulties, and joys the family shared. They wrote about or discussed such items as the author's powers of characterization, her ability to rouse sympathy and hold interest, her descriptions, humor, and general style. In science they studied the flora and fauna of the tales and also noted every implement or mechanical device employed by Ma, Pa, or their neighbors in subduing the wilderness and making life more comfortable. They looked up the historical aspects of the books, for example, the homestead laws. A visit to the Historical Museum clarified and enriched their ideas of clothing, transportation, household equipment, farm implements, even the games of the times. In music they learned Pa's songs and many others, as well as the dances of the times. Their art work centered on the animals or favorite scenes from the different books, and finally they made a mural summarizing the whole series. The synthesis of all these activities was a spirited assembly program for the whole school, with reports, exhibits, and discussions of the Wilder books. This unit occupied almost two months, but the children's interest never flagged.

## CHAPTER 15: BIOGRAPHY (pp. 534–585)

Biographies for important periods in history and for many notable men and women are available at almost any reading level. Take the period of the American Revolution and such men as Washington and Franklin, for example. There are the picture biographies of the d'Aulaires, the simplified stories of the heroes' boyhoods in the Bobbs-Merrill series, the Initial Biographies of Genevieve Foster, or Enid Meadowcroft's easy-to-read books, and, finally, the mature and detailed records of the men by James Daugherty, Clara Ingram Judson, and Jeanette Eaton. This means that in class discussions even the most retarded readers will have books from which they can obtain facts, anecdotes, and a respectable overall picture of the men and their contributions to the building of our nation. And the superior readers will have detailed records of the men.

### Dramatizing Scenes from Biographies

Both historical fiction and biography are fertile fields for creative expression. Can you think of more thrilling scenes for dramatization than the argument in the tower room between William Penn and Admiral Penn on the question of his Quakerism, or the great court scenes with Penn caged at the back of the room, pleading and winning his own case? (See Elizabeth Janet Gray's *Penn.*) The great scene of surrender with Lee and Grant at Appomattox (see MacKinlay Kantor's *Lee and Grant at Appomattox*) is another thriller, or the scene in the House of Burgesses with Patrick Henry pleading the cause of freedom (see Nardi Campion's *Patrick Henry: Firebrand of the Revolution*) is a natural for dramatization.

One student teacher used *Young Walter Scott* with a sixth-grade class which was reading some of Scott's poems. These poems, together with the biography, led back to the old English ballads which Scott collected. From the biography and the ballads, an exciting assembly program was developed.

There are scenes from Lincoln's boyhood which may be dramatized effectively—the "blab" school, the coming of the new stepmother, Lincoln with his rain-soaked *Life of Washington*, his farewell to his father and stepmother, and that great farewell to his fellow townsmen in Springfield with the speech that forecast the ever-growing greatness of the man. In all such plays and pageants, costume design, stage settings, and scenery would occupy the artists of the school and stimulate profitable art work for everyone.

Three notable books about the Lewis and Clark expedition—James Daugherty's *Of Courage Undaunted*, Julia Davis' *No Other White Men*, and Frances Farnsworth's *Winged Moccasins*—suggest a whole series of scenes for either a play or a pageant: the gathering of the men and the start of the expedition; a scene with one of the Indian tribes—arrival, gift giving, feast, games, and dancing afterwards; winter quarters; the encounter with the bear; Charbonneau and Sacajawea hired as guides. Sacajawea may tell her story of capture. There is the dramatic meeting with the Shoshones when Sacajawea finds her brother, and then the Pacific at last. For the final scene there could be the parting with Sacajawea and her little son as the men return to the East. These and other scenes could be portrayed by children in a wonderful series of paintings or crayon pictures to be brought together in a mural.

### Discussing Biographies

Reading biography opens up some excellent opportunities for airing honest differences of opinion about the acts and policies of some of these men. Why was Jefferson's clause abolishing slavery struck out of the Declaration? Was Franklin conciliatory to the English too long? Who was right in his view of Jackson's Indian policy—Davy Crockett or Sam Houston? If Sam Houston had been nominated for the Presidency on the Democratic ticket, he might have been elected instead of Lincoln. Would Houston's election have prevented the Civil War? What was Lincoln's real stand on slavery at the outset of his Presidency? These are all good subjects for speculation and debate, and the children can find in these biographies different kinds of evidence justifying various and conflicting answers.

### Writing Autobiographies

Robert Lawson's *They Were Strong and Good* may serve as a stimulus for writing. To start youngsters collecting and recording the unique stories about their own families is not only good motivation for writing but a good habit to grow up with. Amateur historians are contributing much lively information to our pictures of the past, and twelve-year-olds are not too young to begin a little local research. Mr. Lawson's sketches are brief, and yet each one is a dramatic unit. Such a pattern is easier for children to comprehend and try than a long biography. Even so, biography reading is almost certain to inspire some child to embark on an autobiography. Some of these family sketches and personal reminiscences illustrated with snapshots or old photographs have given great pleasure to the children and have inspired some amazingly good writing.[23]

### Fiction and Biography

Sometimes fiction will send children to biography. An amusing example of this was in a classroom where the teacher was reading Robert Lawson's *Ben and Me* to her children. They found it hilarious, but one day she stopped her reading and remarked, "It just occurred to me that here we are laughing over this funny story about Benjamin Franklin, but how much do we know about his real life?" Precious little, they soon discovered, and the teacher, too, admitted frankly that she had forgotten a good deal of what she had once known. "So—" said she, "I am not going to finish reading *Ben and Me* until you and I among us can piece together the main events of his whole life." The children rallied enthusiastically. One group took Franklin's childhood and youth, another his life through the Revolution, another his years in France and his death in this country. The local librarian could not imagine what had happened when the whole mob descended upon her demanding everything available about Benjamin Franklin. In a week's time they had their material. Every child reported some facts, and together the children covered the story of Franklin's whole life, supplemented by significant episodes from the teacher, who assured them that she, too, had been working. After that, the reading of *Ben and Me* was resumed, and the children agreed that it seemed funnier now that they knew the real facts. (This project could also be used with Robert Lawson's *Mr. Revere and I*—see pp. 661–663.)

23. See also "Dressing Up for Biographies," p. 691.

### Using the Biographical Anecdote

Another teacher, whose children were sure they "just hated biography," used the anecdote to illumine her history periods. These anecdotes she chose from various juvenile books of biography. In the English period they discussed the anecdote and its power to reveal a man's character or attitude. The children were then to find anecdotes by themselves which would show something important about a man. They went to their school library, chose a biography that looked readable, and went to work. Sometimes the librarian guided their choices or even gave chapter references. The children enjoyed relating their anecdotes and presently were making reports of whole books. These reports led readily into the use of some of the newer biographies in connection with their history.

## Religious Books in the Home

If we are to live realistically and tolerantly in our modern world, adults and children must learn to understand and accept the wide religious diversity in this country. Fortunately, children can become sympathetically familiar with this diversity in many of their books. For examples, examine some of the books discussed briefly in Chapter 1, page 10.

Some decades ago, there was daily Bible reading in many homes, a time set aside for "family prayers." Now, it is said, there is some evidence of a revival of interest in family worship—briefer, more informal, but equally reverent, and with every member of the family taking his turn, even the youngest. Needless to say, each home will choose and interpret according to its own ideology the books it uses for religious education and family worship. The following discussion can only suggest the types of books now available.

## BOOKS OF PRAYERS

There are a number of prayer books for children, and they range from mediocre to excellent. The illustrations for these books often seem to have an overliteralness and oversweetness that reduce their imaginative appeal. Even for very small children "Give us this day our daily bread" need not be limited to the tight literalness of a fat loaf of white bread, and praying children need not be so plumply cute or ethereally sweet as some of the illustrators have made them. As a matter of fact, the illustrations for prayers often seem to be adult reminiscences of childhood, *about* but not *for* children. Several books of prayers, though, can be recommended both for their selections and their pictures.

Tasha Tudor has created some of her loveliest watercolors for her *First Prayers*. The collection includes well-known prayers and some less familiar. The Twenty-third Psalm is there, as are the words of several hymns.

For use with children of all ages is *Bless This Day*, compiled by Elfrida Vipont and illustrated with great beauty and strength by Harold Jones. This is really a book for the whole family. It contains prayers for different age levels, Bible verses, and the words of some of the great devotional hymns that can be read without the music. This book has more range and more depth than any of the others.

Elizabeth Orton Jones' pictures for *Small Rain* are more childlike and illuminating than her pictures for *Prayer for a Child*, a Caldecott winner. *Small Rain* contains a well-selected group of Bible verses. It is illustrated with pictures of children's activities which interpret the verses in terms of the child's understanding without being too tightly literal. A small pajama-clad boy gazing at myriads of stars is the illustration for

*The Heavens declare the glory of God;*
*And the firmament sheweth his handywork.*

One illustration, portraying children of different races and colors playing together, is interpreted by the single line:

*All of you are children of the most High.*

Individual as well as racial differences are unobtrusively and cheerfully suggested.

Elizabeth Orton Jones has also made some exquisite pictures for Eleanor Farjeon's *A Prayer for Little Things*. Pictures of fledglings, drops of rain, colts, and children make this a beautiful book which expands rather than limits the imagination. The same imaginative beauty is found in her interpretation of St. Francis' *Canticle of the Sun*.

Barbara Cooney's *A Little Prayer* is a translation of an old French prayer, illustrated with charming pictures.

## THE BIBLE

The Bible as a book for children offers certain obvious problems which we worry over, perhaps unnecessarily. Our real worry should be over modern children's and young people's ignorance of Bible literature. Today, large numbers of college students are not sure who Moses was or what he did, know Joseph only as a modern novel (if at all), and have encountered Paul chiefly as a popular name for churches.

The Bible is a book to grow on and rediscover at different stages of our lives for different reasons, partly because it contains one of the most civilized codes of morals in existence, couched in memorable words. The Old Testament tales, the Book of Psalms, and the dramatic sequence of the New Testament not only are great literature but have the power to widen our vision and renew our strength. Believe or reject whatever you wish theologically, the Bible will continue to be a source of strength and wisdom, if children know it well enough to turn back to it and search its richness.

In Alvin Tresselt's adaptation of *Stories from the Bible*, the grace of Biblical language has been preserved although the writing is simplified, and the reverent tone is complemented by the handsome lithographs by Lynd Ward. Even simpler, but equally dignified, *Brian Wildsmith's Illustrated Bible Stories* has lovely, colorful pictures. The text, adapted by Philip Turner, a British minister and Carnegie Medal winner, is useful both for independent reading and for reading aloud.

Elvajean Hall has compiled *The Proverbs: A Selection* and *The Psalms: A Selection*, with excellent background material prefacing the selections. A book to add breadth to the study of the Bible is Barbara Johnson Shissler's *The New Testament in Art*, which has reproductions of sculpture and paintings. Another book to use as a companion volume is *A Time for Peace*, verses on the subject of peace, selected from the Bible by Louis Untermeyer.

There have been many Biblical stories published singly. Among the best of these are Clyde Robert Bulla's *Joseph the Dreamer* and *Jonah and the Great Fish*, both told with a dramatic sense and fidelity to the Old Testament. Lorenz Graham's *David He No Fear* and *Every Man Heart Lay Down* are picture-story versions of tales that first appeared in Graham's *How God Fix Jonah;* the stories are told in the style of African-English dialect, tender and poetic.

## RELIGIOUS INSTRUCTION

Mary Alice Jones has done a long series of books of religious instruction for young children, beginning with *Tell Me About God* and *Tell Me About Jesus*. Some parents like these books and use them gratefully. Others feel that the primer-like language completely destroys the majesty of the ideas, and that if the ideas are too difficult for a young child, they should not be introduced until the child is old enough to understand them. A pedestrian text will induce neither wonder nor reverence. Bright, large pictures have made these books exceedingly popular. You must decide for yourself whether or not you wish to use them.

Meindert DeJong's *The Mighty Ones* is a well-written but somewhat controversial book. Each story is introduced with an excerpt from the Bible. Then DeJong takes over and gives his elaboration and interpretation of the story in modern language. The book reads beautifully, but not everyone will agree with his interpretations. Look it over and decide for yourself. The questions of interpretation of the Bible stories themselves and of the use of the fiction that has grown about and around these Bible times and figures will have to rest with the individual.

Florence Mary Fitch in *One God: The Ways We Worship Him* provides children with a feeling for the beauty and likeness in dissimilar religious practices. Appealing photographs and a clear forthright text bring "The Jewish Way," "The Catholic Way," and "The Protestant Way" to children's attention. This clear, sympathetic interpretation of different religious beliefs can do much to give children respect for their neighbor's pattern of worship.

Many of the books discussed in Chapter 16, such as the series of explanations of denominations by Kathleen Elgin, are as appropriate for home collections as they are for libraries. This is true also of the biographies of great religious leaders or of such books as Ann Petry's *Legends of the Saints*, ten stories skillfully told and handsomely illustrated. There are many books that impart religious concepts without dogma, editing or retelling Biblical literature, and illuminated by authentic and memorable illustrations. The spirit of these books emphasizes the points of agreement in all religion. Regardless of what faith or form of orthodoxy or unorthodoxy you may belong to, you should know these religious books. Teachers should acquaint themselves with this literature, and parents not only should examine it but should use it with their children.

## ADULT REFERENCES[24]

ANDERSON, HAROLD, ed. *Creativity and Its Cultivation.*

ARBUTHNOT, MAY HILL. *Children's Reading in the Home.*

ARBUTHNOT, MAY HILL, DOROTHY M. BRODERICK, SHELTON L. ROOT, JR., MARK TAYLOR, and EVELYN L. WENZEL. *The Arbuthnot Anthology of Children's Literature.*

ARNSTEIN, FLORA. *Children Write Poetry: A Creative Approach.*

BAIRD, BIL. *The Art of the Puppet.*

BARROWS, HERBERT, HUBERT HEFFNER, JOHN CIARDI, and WALLACE DOUGLAS. *How Does a Poem Mean?*

BROWN, HELEN A., and HARRY J. HELTMAN, eds. *Choral Readings for Fun and Recreation.*

BROWN, JAMES W. *AV Instruction: Materials and Methods.*

CARLSON, RUTH KEARNEY. *Enrichment Ideas; Sparkling Fireflies.*

CATALDO, JOHN W. *Words and Calligraphy for Children.*

CATTERSON, JANE H., ed. *Children and Literature.*

CHAMBERS, DEWEY W. *Children's Literature in the Curriculum.* See especially Chapter 2, Children's Literature and the Social Studies, Chapter 3, Children's Literature and the Sciences, and Chapter 4, Children's Literature and the Arts.

CIANCIOLO, PATRICIA. *Illustrations in Children's Books.*

CLARK, ANN NOLAN. *Journey to the People.*

CLEARY, FLORENCE. *Blueprints for Better Reading: School Programs for Promoting Skill and Interest in Reading.*

CONRAD, EDNA, and MARY VAN DYKE. *History on the Stage; Children Make Plays from Historical Novels.*

COOK, ELIZABETH. *The Ordinary and the Fabulous; An Introduction to Myths, Legends, and Fairy Tales for Teachers and Storytellers.*

CULLINAN, BERNICE E. *Literature for Children: Its Discipline and Content.* See especially Chapter 5, Literature Study by Elementary School Children.

*A Curriculum for English.*

DENNISON, GEORGE. *The Lives of Children: The Story of the First Street School.*

DEUTSCH, MARTIN, and others. *The Disadvantaged Child.*

DEWITT, MARGUERITE E., and others. *Practical Methods in Choral Speaking.*

DUFF, ANNIS. *"Bequest of Wings"; A Family's Pleasures with Books.*

______. *"Longer Flight"; A Family Grows Up with Books.*

DUNNING, STEPHEN. *Teaching Literature to Adolescents: Poetry.*

______. *Teaching Literature to Adolescents: Short Stories.*

EVERETTS, ELDONNA, ed. *Explorations in Children's Writing.*

FADER, DANIEL N., and ELTON B. MC NEIL. *Hooked on Books: Program and Proof.*

FEATHERSTONE, JOSEPH. *Schools Where Children Learn.*

FELDMAN, EDMUND BURKE. *Becoming Human Through Art: Aesthetic Experience in the School.*

*For Storytellers and Storytelling: Bibliographies, Materials and Resource Aids.*

FOSTER, FLORENCE P., comp. *Literature and the Young Child.*

FREEMAN, LA VERNE, and RUTH SUNDERLIN FREEMAN. *The Child and His Picture Book.*

GILLESPIE, JOHN, and DIANA LEMBO. *Introducing Books; A Guide for the Middle Grades.*

______. *Juniorplots; A Book Talk Manual for Teachers and Librarians.*

GLASSER, WILLIAM. *Schools Without Failure.*

GOODRIDGE, JANET. *Creative Drama and Improvised Movement for Children.*

GULLAN, MARJORIE. *The Speech Choir.*

HENTOFF, NAT. *Our Children Are Dying.*

HERNDON, JAMES. *The Way It Spozed to Be: A Report on the Crisis in Our Schools.*

HOLT, JOHN. *How Children Fail.*

______. *How Children Learn.*

______. *What Do I Do Monday?*

HOPKINS, LEE BENNETT. *Let Them Be Themselves.*

JACOBS, LELAND B., ed. *Using Literature with Young Children.*

JOSEPH, STEPHEN M., ed. *The Me Nobody Knows; Children's Voices from the Ghetto.*

KELLOGG, RHODA, and SCOTT O'DELL. *The Psychology of Children's Art.*

KOCH, KENNETH. *Wishes, Lies, and Dreams; Teaching Children to Write Poetry.*

KOHL, HERBERT R. *The Open Classroom: A Practical Guide to a New Way of Teaching.*

______. *Teaching the Unteachable; The Story of an Experiment in Children's Writing.*

______. *36 Children.*

KOZOL, JONATHAN. *Death at an Early Age; The Destruction of the Hearts and Minds of Negro Children in the Boston Public Schools.*

LARRICK, NANCY. *A Parent's Guide to Children's Reading.*

______. *A Teacher's Guide to Children's Books.*

LINDSTROM, MIRIAM. *Children's Art; A Study of*

24. For additional useful reading suggestions see the bibliographies accompanying the ten articles in Part 7. Helpful ideas on various aspects of "bringing children and books together" can also be found in various issues of such magazines as *Elementary English, Childhood Education, Horn Book Magazine, The Instructor, School Library Journal,* and *Wilson Library Bulletin.* See also Appendix A: Book Selection Aids and Appendix B: Adult References for complete bibliographic data.

*Normal Development in Children's Modes of Visualization.*
LOWNDES, BETTY. *Movement and Creative Drama for Children.*
MEEKER, ALICE M. *Enjoying Literature with Children.*
MILLAR, SUSANNA. *The Psychology of Play.*
*Once upon a Time . . . .*
*Plays, the Drama Magazine for Young People.*
POWER, EFFIE. *Bag O'Tales; A Source Book for Story-Tellers.*
RICHARDSON, ELWYN. *In the Early World.*
ROBINSON, MARION P., and ROZETTA L. THURSTON. *Poetry Arranged for the Speaking Choir.*
SAWYER, RUTH. *The Way of the Storyteller.*
SHEDLOCK, MARIE. *Art of the Story-Teller.*
SIKS, GERALDINE BRAIN. *Creative Dramatics.*
SILBERMAN, CHARLES E. *Crisis in the Classroom; The Remaking of American Education.*
*Six New Plays for Children*, ed. by Christian Moe and Darwin Reid Payne.
*Stories to Tell to Children.*
STRICKLAND, RUTH G. *The Language Arts in the Elementary School.*
*Teaching Literature in Wisconsin.*
*Teaching Reading Through Children's Literature.*
THOMAS, R. MURRAY, and SHERWIN G. SWARTOUT. *Integrated Teaching Materials.*
TOOZE, RUTH. *Storytelling.*
WHITEHEAD, ROBERT. *Children's Literature; Strategies of Teaching.* See particularly Chapter 6, Appreciating Literature Through the Creative Arts, and Chapter 7, Literature Games and Puzzles.
WILSON, ROY R. *Teaching Children Language Arts.* See especially Chapter 2, Providing Experiences in Creative Dramatics, and Chapter 3, Involving Students in Classroom Discussions.
WITUCKE, VIRGINIA. *Poetry in the Elementary School.*
WOLSCH, ROBERT A. *Poetic Composition Through the Grades; A Language Sensitivity Program. Practical Suggestions for Teaching.*

## CHILDREN'S BOOKS: ACTIVITIES

BOIKO, CLAIRE. *Children's Plays for Creative Actors.* Plays, 1967. Thirty-five short plays include material for special occasions. 8-11

BOYLAN, ELEANOR. *How to Be a Puppeteer*, ill. by Tomi de Paola. McCall, 1970. Instructions for making and manipulating puppets, with six plays included. 9-12

CARLSON, BERNICE W. *Act It Out*, ill. by Laszlo Matulay. Abingdon, 1956. Suggestions for creative dramatization, pantomimes, and the use of many kinds of puppets and marionettes. 8-12

———. *The Right Play for You*, ill. by Georgette Boris. Abingdon, 1960. Practical suggestions for producing plays accompany twenty original plays. 9-12

DURRELL, DONALD D., and B. ALICE CROSSLEY. *Teen-Age Plays for Classroom Reading.* Plays, 1971. Twenty selections from *Plays*, a drama magazine for young people, chosen for use by students whose interest is high but whose reading level is in the middle grades. Useful for both groups. 11-14

FOSTER, JOANNA. *Pages, Pictures, and Print; A Book in the Making*, ill. by author. Harcourt, 1958. A clear explanation of each process, from manuscript to bound book. 10-12

HARSHAW, RUTH, and HOPE HARSHAW EVANS. *In What Book?* Macmillan, 1970. The creator of a series of memorable radio programs about children's books asks questions that challenge the reader. Grouped by three broad age levels. 5-13

HARSHAW, RUTH, and DILLA MACBEAN. *What Book Is That?* ill. by Grace Paull. Macmillan, 1948. Games, quizzes, and brief dramatic sketches test the reader's familiarity with children's books. 5-13

KAMERMAN, SYLVIA, ed. *Dramatized Folk Tales of the World.* Plays, 1971. A broad collection of one-act plays, royalty free. 9-12

———, ed. *Little Plays for Little Players.* Plays, 1969. Fifty plays with inexpensive costumes and easy parts. 6-9

MENOTTI, GIAN-CARLO. *Amahl and the Night Visitors*, adapted by Frances Frost, ill. by Roger Duvoisin. McGraw, 1952. A narrative form that keeps the dialogue of the opera libretto. 10-12

MERRIAM, EVE. *A Gaggle of Geese*, ill. by Paul Galdone. Knopf, 1960. A picture book that presents group-words in the animal world. Can be used by teachers in the middle grades to provoke discussion of interesting words. 7-9

OLFSON, LEWY. *Classics Adapted for Acting and Reading.* Plays, 1970. Half-hour dramatizations, with each group (acting and reading) separate. 11-14

PLAGEMANN, BENTZ. *How to Write a Story.* Lothrop, 1971. Discusses form, characters, point of view, dialogue, narration, etc., and stresses the importance of grammar and syntax and the need for rewriting. 11-13

ROSS, LAURA. *Hand Puppets; How to Make and Use Them*, ill. by author. Lothrop, 1969. Includes simple directions for making, costuming, and handling puppets; stage directions; and three plays. 9-12

———. *Puppet Shows Using Poems and Stories.* Lothrop, 1970. Especially useful in the literature program. 9-12

SMITH, MOYNE RICE. *Plays and How to Put Them On*, ill. by Don Bolognese. Walck, 1961. Seven one-act plays with production notes are followed by a useful bibliography of additional sources. 9-11

SWORTZELL, LOWELL, ed. *All the World's a Stage; Modern Plays for Young People.* Delacorte, 1971. Twenty-one plays by eminent writers, with introductions that discuss each playwright and the play. 11-14

THANE, ADELE. *Plays from Famous Stories and Fairy Tales.* Plays, 1967. Twenty-eight one-act plays, many from the classics. 8-10

TICHENOR, TOM. *Tom Tichenor's Puppets*, ill. by author. Abingdon, 1971. Discusses creative dramatics for the story hour as well as making and using puppets, and includes plays for marionettes and for hand puppets. Can be used by children ten and up as well as by teachers and librarians.

WORRELL, ESTELLE. *Be a Puppeteer: The Lively Puppet Book*, ill. by author. McGraw, 1969. A good guide to manipulating puppets and staging puppet plays. 8-11

YATES, ELIZABETH. *Someday You'll Write.* Dutton, 1962. Practical and flexible, a book that encourages the aspirant writer—but not unduly. 11-13

## CHILDREN'S RELIGIOUS BOOKS

BULLA, CLYDE ROBERT. *Jonah and the Great Fish,* ill. by Helga Aichinger. T. Crowell, 1970.

———. *Joseph the Dreamer,* ill. by Gordon Laite. T. Crowell, 1971. 5-7

COONEY, BARBARA. *A Little Prayer,* ill. by author. Hastings, 1967. all ages

*The Creation,* ill. by Jo Spier. Doubleday, 1970. The text from Genesis pleasantly illustrated. 5-8

DeJONG, MEINDERT. *The Mighty Ones: Great Men and Women of Early Bible Days,* ill. by Harvey Schmidt. Harper, 1959. 11 up

FARJEON, ELEANOR. *A Prayer for Little Things,* ill. by Elizabeth Orton Jones. Houghton, 1945. 3-8

FITCH, FLORENCE MARY. *One God—The Ways We Worship Him,* ill. with photos chosen by Beatrice Creighton. Lothrop, 1944. 8-12

FRANCIS OF ASSISI, SAINT. *Song of the Sun,* from *The Canticle of the Sun,* ill. by Elizabeth Orton Jones. Macmillan, 1952. 6-9

GRAHAM, LORENZ. *David He No Fear,* ill. by Ann Grifalconi. T. Crowell, 1971.

———. *Every Man Heart Lay Down,* ill. by Colleen Browning. T. Crowell, 1970. 5-8

HALL, ELVAJEAN. *The Proverbs: A Selection,* ill. by Charles Mozley. Watts, 1970.

———. *The Psalms: A Selection,* ill. by Charles Mozley. Watts, 1968. 10 up

JONES, JESSIE ORTON, comp. *Small Rain,* ill. by Elizabeth Orton Jones. Viking, 1943. 4-8

JONES, MARY ALICE. *Tell Me About God,* ill. by Pelagie Doane. Rand, 1943.

———. *Tell Me About Jesus,* rev. ed., ill. by Dorothy Grider. Rand, 1967. 5-7

KLINK, J. L. *Bible for Children.* Volume I. Old Testament with Songs and Plays, tr. by Patricia Crampton, ill. by Piet Klaase. Westminster, 1968. Translated from the Dutch, these Bible stories are interspersed with comment, songs, plays, and poetry, and effectively illustrated in black and white. Volume II. New Testament. Westminster, 1969. A companion to Volume I. 9-11

PETRY, ANN. *Legends of the Saints,* ill. by Anne Rockwell. T. Crowell, 1970. 8-11

SHISSLER, BARBARA JOHNSON. *The New Testament in Art,* designed by Patricia Koskey. Lerner, 1970. 11-14

TRESSELT, ALVIN, ad. *Stories from the Bible,* ill. by Lynd Ward. Coward, 1971. 9-12

TUDOR, TASHA, ill. *First Prayers,* Cath. and Prot. eds. Walck, 1952. 4-7

TURNER, PHILIP, ad. *Brian Wildsmith's Illustrated Bible Stories,* ill. by Brian Wildsmith. Watts, 1968. 5-12

UNTERMEYER, LOUIS, ed. *A Time for Peace; Verses from the Bible,* ill. by Joan Berg Victor. World, 1969. 9-11

VIPONT, ELFRIDA. *Bless This Day,* ill. by Harold Jones. Harcourt, 1958. all ages

# Part Seven
# Areas and Issues Related to Children and Their Books

*Research in Children's Literature*
*The School Media Center*
*The Censorship Dilemma and Youth's Right to Learn*
*Involving Parents in Education*
*Pressure for Pluralism: The Blacks, the Chicanos, the Native Americans, and Women*
*Popular Literature*
*Series Books*
*Television: The Impact and Influence of Another Medium*
*Internationalism in Children's Literature*
*Book Promotion*

# Areas and Issues Introduction

As the title suggests, Part Seven, "Areas and Issues Related to Children and Their Books," is not strictly about children and books in that even when the discussion is directed at print materials, it is not always concerned with adult-approved reading materials. An assumption that runs through all the topic and issue discussions is that media, in whatever form, do more than provide information: they do have an impact and influence upon behavior and attitude formation, even though it is still impossible to isolate in research the precise nature of such influence.

The areas and issues presented here are crucial ones for students, teachers, librarians, and all adults interested in children's reading and in child development. Since most of the topics have had books written about them and others have been the subjects of major research studies, the discussion can do little more than provide introductions to the topics, supply bibliographies, and suggest questions for further study and research ranging from term papers to doctoral dissertations. The bibliographies reflect as wide a range of opinion as possible. In "The Censorship Dilemma," for example, the bibliography provides access to books and articles that support censorship as well as to those that oppose it and to those that take a middle ground. On the other hand, "Book Promotion" is not by nature a controversial issue.

Obviously, these ten topics represent only a small proportion of possible areas of concern available for research studies. As Lukenbill observes in "Research in Children's Literature," the entire field of children's literature is open for study. Among the numerous topics that are not covered, but might have been, are: (1) the extent and nature of specialized children's book collections; (2) the various book award organizations and the criteria established for the awards; (3) the quantity and quality of newspapers and magazines for children; (4) the quantity and quality of criticism and evaluation of children's books and related media as exemplified by various review media; and (5) the issues raised by the current controversy over the structure and role of the public-school system.

Solid research in a field does more than establish the respectability of the field. It aids the practitioners in identifying what is known as well as what remains to be discovered. It also aids in the development of new research techniques as older established methodologies prove inadequate to the needs of the field under study. In the area of children's literature in relationship to its impact upon children's reading and attitudes, it may be that new techniques will have to be developed before the critical questions can be answered. —*Dorothy M. Broderick, Editor, Part Seven, Areas and Issues Related to Children and Their Books.*

# RESEARCH IN CHILDREN'S LITERATURE

*W. Bernard Lukenbill**

## A General Premise

Social science research seeks to establish normative principles rather than to search for laws. Therefore, accepting the study of children's literature as a part of the social sciences entails developing research studies which are capable of adding to broad and correct generalizations and principles concerning children and their relationships to books, literature, and reading. The researcher might view his work as contributing to an eventual understanding of youth literature and its possible environmental and behavioral influences.

Often assertions are made by teachers, librarians, and parents concerning the positive effects of good books and literature on the behavioral patterns of youth. Yet few of these traditional assumptions have been consistently determined through research evidence. Helen Huus (see bibliography) wrote in 1964 that researchers had not been able to ascertain the effects of various social variables on children and their reading, and subsequently on their behavioral patterns; nor had they formulated research techniques and designs capable of answering some of the basic problems posed in their studies. From such a report, it is evident that children's literature clearly has a mandate to come to terms with itself: to understand its past and its present, to direct its future, and through research to document its claims as a positive influence on the behavioral modes of youth.

In attempting to verify these claims, the researcher must ally himself with research methodologies originated in other disciplines, yet applicable to children's literature study. The investigator will find several methods and techniques available to him; but whichever method he selects, he should always operate on the assumption that his work will add something to the general understanding of children's literature as an influence on children's behavior.

*W. Bernard Lukenbill is a U.S.O.E. Doctoral Fellow, Higher Education Act, Indiana University.

## Research Trends

Today, most research in children's literature is conducted either as masters' theses or as doctoral dissertations. Although some research is conducted by practitioners or college professors acting as independent investigators, most researchers seldom have adequate time or finances required to carry out a well-designed and executed research project. Interestingly enough, psychologists and behavioral scientists have intermediately conducted studies in the area of reading's influence on behavioral changes, but only rarely have these studies involved children's literature. Nevertheless, such studies do exist, and they offer examples of techniques and procedures to be studied and perhaps emulated. Such studies also help in the establishment of generalizations concerning reading as a behavior-influencing factor.

Historically, probably the most popular areas of investigation in children's literature have been reading-interest studies. Generalizations based on these reading-interest studies usually can be accepted, but even here one will find contradictions and changes, depending upon the samples and time periods.

How to teach youth to enjoy reading and literature and how to use children's literature in the instructional curriculum are popular topics of investigation. But these studies often suffer from inadequate statistical and sampling techniques. Another common deficiency of these studies is their evaluation instruments. Two opposing questions can be raised about these instruments: (1) are they sensitive enough to measure the extent of learning taking place in the children involved in the experiment; and (2) do they over-measure the degree of learning taking place? Again, generalizations about the effectiveness of such teaching methods should not be accepted without question.

Specialized historical studies have also been popular as research topics. Literary developments in the colonial period, the Civil War period, the post-Civil War period, etc., have proven popular with investigators. Many studies both here and abroad have also been devoted to the history of foreign children's literature; and a number of translations of works concerned with children's literature in other countries are available, especially works from Germany, Spain, and France. England has also published some notable historical studies. The historical development of juvenile periodicals has also been researched, and these studies have been worthwhile. Nevertheless, much work still remains to be done in this area. More critical interpretative historical studies are certainly needed.

Literary studies in children's literature based on the general historical method of inquiry have produced studies dealing with various genres, including biography, drama, fantasy, historical fiction, humor, and poetry. This method has also lent itself to author studies and literary criticism.

In recent years, many studies have been devoted to the sociological aspects of children's literature. Researchers have been especially interested in analyzing the content of books for children relating to both blacks and American Indians. Some studies have also attempted to determine how exposure to youth literature might affect attitude change toward minority groups. Although most of these studies have shown some sort of attitude change, additional study is required before sound generalizations can be drawn regarding this question. Social values and attitude concepts appearing in youth literature have also been popular areas of investigation.

## Research Methods

Most research methodologies used in social sciences are applicable to research in children's literature. These methods include (1) the historical; (2) the descriptive—including its many techniques (survey, questionnaire, interview, group behavior analysis, content analysis, observational studies, and appraisal techniques); (3) the experimental; (4) the case study; and (5) the genetic or developmental study. The researcher should have some familiarity with all these techniques. Two excellent sources for background reading in research methodologies are Good and Scates' *Methods of Research* (1957) and Selltiz and Jahoda's *Research Methods in Social Relations* (1957). Excellent articles on research also appear in Lindzey and Aronson's *Handbook of Social Psychology* (1968–1969) and Sills' *International Encyclopedia of the Social Sciences* (1968).

Of the methods cited above, the historical and the descriptive methodologies have been most widely used in research in children's literature. Further study requiring the experimental method seems also warranted in order to increase our understanding of the effects of books, reading, and literature on the learning and on the behavioral and attitudinal changes and patterns of children. But it should be remembered that in the experimental method, environmental and social variables are extremely difficult to control.

The case study method has not been widely used in children's literature research, although it is applicable. Prominent library school educators such as Frances Henne and Alice Brooks McGuire have suggested that this method be used more extensively in studying characteristics, interests, and responses of readers. The genetic or developmental study method seems to be seldom used in children's literature study. Its purpose is to study the developmental pattern of an individual or group over an extended period of time; consequently, it is often too involved and expensive for most researchers to undertake, even though it would be beneficial to children's literature.

### Research Procedures and Sources

Before a research idea can be formed into a research design and executed, the researcher must obtain a sound knowledge of the general area to be investigated. This knowledge can be acquired through experience and association, and/or through reading. It is advisable to first formulate a general theory about the area to be studied. This theory should normally include some broad generalizations which have not yet been tested. From this generalized theory, a hypothesis should be formulated. The hypothesis is simply a statement asserting that some element contained in the general theory is true under certain conditions and can be tested through research. Once the hypothesis has been stated, the research design, including appropriate research methodologies and techniques, can be developed.

Students and teachers who are interested in finding research topics need to keep up with professional developments and to read extensively in professional journals and monographs. A review of the bibliography for this article and of the bibliographies for the following nine articles will identify periodicals which present current problems involving children's literature. Actual research studies are often found in these periodicals, offering examples for the researcher. Research journals such as *Review of Educational Research* also occasionally carry research studies devoted to children's literature. One who is interested in conducting research should also be aware of social issues and cognizant that social developments influence children's literature, thus providing fruitful areas for research.

Several bibliographic sources which list research studies in children's literature are included in the following bibliography. These sources should be consulted before any serious research planning is done. The researcher should also read as many actual research studies, including dissertations, as possible. In this way, he will develop an understanding and feel for methodology and research procedures and will learn to identify the strengths and weaknesses of various research techniques.

Primary sources for the study of children's literature are extremely important to the researcher, especially if biographical, literary, or historical studies are contemplated. Although the *National Union Catalog of Manuscript Collections* is available and should be consulted, its holdings now are generally sparse and incomplete in the area of children's literature. Carolyn Field's *Subject Collections in Children's Literature* (1969) is an excellent source for locating both collections of children's books and manuscripts relating to children's literature.

## SUGGESTED RESEARCH NEEDS

The entire area of children's literature is available for research. The following topics seem to be particularly in need of study:

1. The effects of reading on behavior and learning patterns (bibliotherapy, retarded readers, etc.).
2. The sociology of children's literature (both past and present).
3. The publishing industry both in the United States and abroad (including regional presses).
4. The history of children's literature (including regional developments).
5. Personality studies (including authors, editors, reviewers, teachers, creative process in authors).
6. The teaching of children's literature (including college instruction, use of innovation, mediated approaches).
7. The review media (including regional coverage, characteristics of reviewers, etc.).
8. Subliterature (comics, underground presses, rock music).

9. Nonbook literary sources (including relationship of multimedia stimuli and reading).

10. Linguistic features of children's literature (including reading levels, etc.).

11. Art and media format studies (illustrations, paperbacks, typography, etc.).

12. Prognostic studies (prediction of future developments in book or media forms, reader use characteristics, etc.).

## BIBLIOGRAPHY

### Research Reviews

BROWN, GEORGE I. "Literature in the Elementary School." *Review of Educational Research*, v. 34 (April 1964), pp. 187–194. Excellent review of research studies pertaining to reading interests; the elementary school library and its relationship to literature programs; evaluation and analysis of children's literature; individualized reading and literature; and psychological processes and literature. Calls for more significant research work in the areas mentioned.

BURTON, DWIGHT L. "Research in the Teaching of Literature." *Review of Educational Research*, v. 19 (April 1949), pp. 124–134. Cites research studies in the area of teaching techniques, evaluation, social and personal adjustment, and reading interests. National and state surveys are also discussed. Bibliography of research studies included.

CHAMBERS, DEWEY W. "The Didactic Theory," in *Children's Literature in the Curriculum*. Rand, 1971, pp. 137–162. Discusses several major research studies dealing with the ability of literature to influence behavior.

DAVIS, JAMES E. "Recent Trends in Fiction for Adolescents." *English Journal*, v. 56 (May 1967), pp. 720–724. A review of research studies to determine trends in adolescent fiction. Concludes that the adolescent novel is being perpetuated and generally improved.

HUUS, HELEN. "Interpreting Research in Children's Literature," in *Children, Books, and Reading*. International Reading Association Perspectives in Reading, No. 3, 1964, pp. 123–145. Major discussion on research in children's literature. Outlines five areas of popularity: (1) reading preferences; (2) poetry; (3) mass media; (4) reading materials; (5) effects of reading. Lists areas of needed research. Bibliography of studies included.

JAHODA, MARIE. "The Impact of Literature: A Psychological Discussion of Some Assumptions in the Censorship Debate." American Book Publishers Council, March 1, 1954. (Mimeographed.) Summary reprinted in Mary V. Gaver, ed., *Background Readings in Building Library Collections*. 2 vols. Scarecrow, 1969, v. 1, pp. 350–353. Points out some psychological concerns of censorship. States that reading has little to do with causing juvenile delinquency and that the mass media are not as effective as molders of opinion as is generally thought. Indicates reading may, nevertheless, have some causal effect on children's behavior.

KINNEL, ERIC. "Can Children's Books Change Children's Values?" *Educational Leadership*, v. 28 (November 1970), pp. 209–214. Discusses selected studies dealing both with the effects of reading on children and the social content of books that might influence behavior. An excellent selected bibliography included.

LOWRY, HEATH W. "A Review of Five Recent Content Analyses of Related Sociological Factors in Children's Literature." *Elementary English*, v. 46 (October 1969), pp. 736–740. Reviews studies by Chambers, Homze, Lowry, Shepherd, and Walker. Concludes that these studies have contributed to an understanding of social values appearing in children's materials. Suggests areas for additional research.

MECKEL, HENRY C. "Research on Teaching Composition and Literature," in *Handbook of Research on Teaching*. Rand, 1963, pp. 966–1006. Thorough discussion of research in the areas of language and literature as applied to teaching. Discusses specific types of research concerned with literature study and points out three areas for future investigation: (1) the teaching core of appropriate titles; (2) classroom atmosphere and approach; and (3) audiovisual teaching devices. Extensive bibliography.

PILGRIM, GENEVA HANNA, and MARIANA K. MCALLISTER. "Research on Reading Interests," in *Books, Young People, and Reading Guidance*. 2nd ed. Harper, 1968, pp. 53–68. Gives general research findings about reading interests of the adolescent. Short bibliography includes citations of worthwhile studies in reader interests.

RUSSELL, DAVID H. "Some Research on the Impact of Reading." *English Journal*, v. 47 (September 1958), pp. 398–413. Summary of research findings concerning the influence of reading on behavior. Discusses the characteristics of reading materials, ideas contained in reading materials, reader characteristics, and reader behavior. An excellent bibliography is included.

SHAFER, ROBERT E. "The Reading of Literature." *Journal of Reading*, v. 8 (April 1965), pp. 345–349. Brief review of several major studies in reading and literature. Calls for additional research to develop an understanding of the impact of literature on human behavior.

SQUIRE, JAMES R. "English Literature." *Encyclopedia of Educational Research*. 4th ed. Macmillan, 1969, pp. 461–473. Gives an extensive review of research studies relating to the teaching of literature. Both elementary and secondary level approaches are given with emphasis on the secondary school aspect. Comprehensive bibliography included.

TEMP, GEORGE. "Literature in the Secondary School." *Review of Educational Research*, v. 34 (April 1964), pp. 195–202. Surveys of the more important studies conducted in the area and comments on the problems of research in literature. Studies discussed are noted in the bibliography.

## Source Guides

*Dissertation Abstracts* and *Dissertation Abstracts International.* 1952– (monthly). Includes abstracts of dissertations accepted by participating colleges and universities. Comprehensive subject and author indexes have recently been published which add greatly to their usefulness.

FIELD, CAROLYN W., ed. *Subject Collections in Children's Literature.* Bowker, 1969. Describes the holdings of collections useful in children's literature research. Books, manuscripts, and other items included.

HAVILAND, VIRGINIA, et al. *Children's Literature: A Guide to Reference Sources.* Library of Congress, 1966. Extensive guide to various sources of materials relating to children's literature. Subject approach provided.

*Library Literature,* 1933/35– (quarterly). Contains lists of masters' and doctoral theses on children's literature under the heading "Library Schools—Theses."

LITTLE, LAWRENCE, comp. *Researches in Personality, Character and Religious Education; A Bibliography of American Doctoral Dissertations, 1885–1959.* Univ. of Pittsburgh Pr., 1962. Provides a specialized approach to research in children's literature. Annotations are not given for entries.

LUKENBILL, W. BERNARD. "American Doctoral Dissertations in Children's and Adolescents' Literature; A Working Bibliography of Dissertations Recorded in Selected Bibliographical Sources from 1930 through 1970." Univ. of Illinois Graduate Library School. *Occasional Papers.* [In preparation.] Identifies and describes 215 doctoral dissertations accepted by American colleges and universities. Extensive bibliography included.

MC NAMEE, LAWRENCE F. *Dissertations in English and American Literature; Theses Accepted by American, British and German Universities, 1865–1964.* Bowker, 1968.

———. *Dissertations in English and American Literature. Supplement One; Theses Accepted by American, British and German Universities, 1964–1968.* Bowker, 1969. Although limited, these works offer access to some foreign dissertations dealing with children's literature.

*Research Studies in Education; A Subject and Author Index of Doctoral Dissertations, Reports and Field Studies, and a Research Methods Bibliography.* 1941–1951– (annual). Excellent source for both dissertations completed during the preceding year and proposals accepted. Children's literature topics generally appear under the subject heading "Methods of Teaching; Teaching Aids; Libraries."

U.S. Educational Research Information Center. *Research in Education.* 1966– (monthly). Commonly known as ERIC, this is a comprehensive source for all types of material dealing with education, including children's literature. Entries include dissertations, reports, conference proceedings, books, unpublished material, etc.

U.S. Library of Congress. *National Union Catalog of Manuscript Collections.* 1959– (annual). Describes the manuscript holdings of participating libraries in the United States. Subject index approach offers access to a limited amount of material relating to children's literature.

## Representative Published Studies

DARLING, RICHARD L. *The Rise of Children's Book Reviewing in America, 1865–1881.* Bowker, 1968. Traces the growth of children's literature in the post-Civil War period through a study of the contemporary review media.

KARLINS, MARVIN, and HERBERT I. ABELSON. *Persuasion: How Opinions and Attitudes Are Changed.* 2nd ed. Springer Publishing Co., 1970. Gives summaries with discussion of research. Discusses many forms of change instruments, including reading.

KIEFER, MONICA MARY. *American Children Through Their Books, 1700–1835.* Univ. of Pennsylvania Pr., 1948. Study of the adult concept of childhood as pictured in contemporary books written for children.

KUJOTH, JEAN SPEALMAN, comp. *Reading Interests of Children and Young Adults.* Scarecrow, 1970. A collection of actual research studies on reading interests. An excellent source book.

LIND, KATHARINE. "Social Psychology of Children's Reading." *American Journal of Sociology,* v. 41 (January 1936), pp. 454–469. Series of case studies in which 24 adults recall their childhood memories relating to reading. Concludes that reading is a highly important social experience.

LORANG, SISTER MARY CORDE. *Burning Ice; The Moral and Emotional Effects of Reading.* Scribner's, 1968. Study attempts to show through research evidence how books and reading influence moral and emotional behavior of youth.

O'BRIEN, MAE. *Children's Reaction to Radio Adaptations of Juvenile Books.* King's Crown Pr., 1950. Studies the reaction of ten-year-old children to a series of children's books adapted for and broadcast on radio. Found that most of the adaptations were enjoyed by the children and children were stimulated to express interest in reading the original books.

WERTHAM, FREDERIC. *Seduction of the Innocent.* Rinehart, 1954. Popularly written account supporting through research evidence the opinion that comic books have an immense effect on the minds and behavior of children.

## Research Guides

BARZUN, JACQUES, and HENRY F. GRAFF. *The Modern Researcher.* Rev. ed. Harcourt, 1970. Suggests ways to do research. Especially strong in library and document analysis.

GOOD, CARTER V., and DOUGLAS E. SCATES. *Methods of Research; Educational, Psychological, Sociological.* Appleton, 1954. Well-known text designed to introduce standard research methods.

KENT, SHERMAN. *Writing History.* 2nd ed. Appleton, 1967. Classical work which describes the historical research method. Gives details on topic selection, writing styles, and language usage suggestions.

LINDZEY, GARDNER, and ELLIOT ARONSON, eds. *The Handbook of Social Psychology.* 2nd ed. 5 vols. Addison, 1968-1969. Excellent background guide for those interested in research in socio-psychological relationships. Especially worth noting are volume 2, which has excellent articles on interviewing and content analysis techniques, and volume 5, which has the article "Effects of the Mass Media of Communications," by Walter Weiss.

RILEY, MATILDA WHITE, and CLARICE S. STOLL. "Content Analysis." *International Encyclopedia of the Social Sciences*, v. 3, Macmillan, 1968, pp. 371–377. Explanation of the content analysis technique as used in social science research. Includes excellent bibliography.

SELLTIZ, CLAIRE, et al. *Research Methods in Social Relations.* Rev. one-volume ed. Holt, 1957. Outlines basic approaches to the practical application of research. Standard research techniques are explained.

### Literary Theory

ALBRECHT, MILTON C. "The Relationship of Literature and Society." *American Journal of Sociology*, v. 59 (March 1964), pp. 425–436. Theoretical discussion of the interplay of social organization and literature.

WELLEK, RENÉ, and AUSTIN WARREN. "Literature and Psychology," pp. 81–93. Discusses theoretical aspects in the study of psychology of the writer, the creative process, and psychological types and laws within literature. "Literature and Society," pp. 94–109. Discusses literature as a social institution. Cautions researchers not to use literature uncritically as social documents. *Theory of Literature.* 3rd ed. Harcourt, 1956.

## THE SCHOOL MEDIA CENTER

*Sara Innis Fenwick**

While the centralized school library is largely a development of this century, the concept of access to a wide range of instructional materials is as old as formal education. An early quotation from an English publication, *Ashton's Ordinances*, at Shrewsbury, in 1578, stated "buildings should include a librarie and gallerie for said schooles, furnished with all manner of books, mappes, spheres, instruments of astronomye and all other things apperteyninge to learning, which may be either given to the schooles or procured with schoole's funds."

Throughout its history, the school library has reflected the changes in educational philosophy and in the school as an institution. During the past decade the direction of all innovation has been toward individualization of instruction. This emphasis can be seen in new programs directed toward making the "right to read" for all children in the 1970s a reality.

With every new development have come needs for a greater variety of learning resources and for increasing accessibility through organization and interpretation. Individualization of instruction is not accomplished with one textbook per student, or even with a battery of supplementary textbooks. It becomes more likely if there is available, in addition to a range of textbooks at several different levels of difficulty: (1) a variety of published opinion and interpretation of facts or events; (2) biographies of important people associated with the field of study; (3) novels, drama, and poetry for the expression of men's thoughts and feelings—now and in the past; (4) films for the visual and auditory reproduction of action and time change; (5) filmstrips for introducing new topics or picturing difficult-to-explain concepts; (6) sound recordings of speech, songs, and instruments; (7) models to handle and manipulate; (8) museum objects, crafts, art prints, and sculpture to interpret culture and to share creative expression; (9) maps and globes to investigate the relationship of location and space; (10) copies of documents with primary evidence; (11) tape recorders and cameras to make possible students' own reporting contributions; and (12) duplicating

*Sara Innis Fenwick is Professor, Graduate Library School, University of Chicago.

machines and other tools for the creating of teacher- and student-produced materials. Specifically, in the reading field the use of tape recordings combined with projected materials, the typewriter, and the programming of multimedia tools introduces paths to reading that go outside the book.

Such multimedia collections are the basis of media centers in today's schools. *The Standards for School Media Programs*, prepared by the American Asssociation of School Librarians and the Department of Audiovisual Instruction of the National Education Association in 1969, defines the media center as "a learning center in the school where a full range of print and audiovisual media, necessary equipment and services for media specialists, are accessible to students and teachers."[1]

Joined in this definition of the basic collection of learning resources are the other two dimensions of a good learning environment: (1) the services of people who are trained specialists in media and who can provide guidance in their most effective use; and (2) the facilities for organizing and making materials accessible.

Needless to say, not all elementary and secondary schools in the United States have met these standards. Although all state and regional accrediting agencies require some measure of library provision in secondary schools there are a surprising number of schools at this level with no centralized libraries. At the elementary level one fifth of the schools are still lacking centralized libraries. A far higher number have no professionally prepared media specialists. Considerable gains in the acquisition of learning resources in all schools were made possible with federal funds provided through Title II of the 1965 Elementary and Secondary Education Act.

In spite of the fact that virtually all educators have long recognized the importance of a learning environment rich in tools and resources for students and teachers, there have always been differences of professional opinion regarding the most effective way to organize such materials within the school itself. In earlier decades of this century the division was on the issue of a centralized library versus classroom collections. As the library evolved toward an instructional materials center the issue was that of separate centers for print and for audiovisual materials versus a media center. Current discussion centers around the question of the media center as opposed to the individual or tutorial learning center. In good practice, it has generally been demonstrated that the objectives and functions of none of these learning environments are mutually exclusive, and that the best experience might be expected where a combination of the features of all types might be utilized. Nevertheless, these areas of professional disagreement still exist. The new open-space schools "without walls" offer some interesting opportunities for innovative design and organization of media centers that may remove them from the old arguments.

1. American Association of School Librarians, *The Standards for School Media Programs*, American Library Association, 1969, p. xv.

## SUGGESTED RESEARCH NEEDS

The growth of programs for the preparation of media specialists in graduate schools of education and library science holds hopes for some useful research in the various problems recognized by educational media specialists. Among such problems are:

1. What search strategies do students employ in locating information in recorded material, and what methods can help students develop effective strategies?

2. Are there identifiable characteristics for different groups of users among students?

3. What methods help the student become visually literate?

4. Can we develop methods and tools to aid in the evaluation of readers' responses to literature?

5. Is it possible to identify and assess the motivational factors involved in reading experiences?

6. Would longitudinal case studies of the reader and nonreader help identify the characteristics of each?

7. What are the characteristics of the most effective "orchestration" of multimedia?

8. Is it possible to examine and assess individual learning patterns and develop the needed individual programming that allows for such differences?

9. What type of education will assure the preparation of teachers who are knowledgeable about the effectiveness of multimedia in teaching/learning?

10. Do the teaching roles of media specialists as seen by the specialists and the roles as seen by their students differ?

11. Are there fundamental differences in the roles and services of the school media centers and the public library?

## BIBLIOGRAPHY

### Books and Pamphlets

American Association of School Librarians and Department of Audiovisual Instruction. *Standards for School Media Programs.* ALA, 1969. Joint standards which outline the organization, staffing, budgeting, and other aspects of library media centers.

Chicago University Graduate Library School. *New Definitions of School Library Service.* Univ. of Chicago Pr., 1960. Papers presented before the Twenty-fourth Annual Conference of the Graduate Library School; includes papers by educators Francis S. Chase, Robert D. Hess, and Abram VanderMeer, as well as by outstanding librarians.

DAVIES, RUTH ANN. *The School Library: A Force for Educational Excellence.* Bowker, 1969. A useful and comprehensive discussion of the principles and practices that make a media center an educational force in the school.

ERICKSON, CARLTON W. H. *Administering Instructional Media Programs.* Macmillan, 1968. A textbook which emphasizes the organization of centers and materials, and the implementation of various media in educational programs.

GAVER, MARY V. *Effectiveness of Centralized Library Service in Elementary Schools.* Rutgers Univ. Pr., 1963. Research conducted in cooperation with the U.S. Office of Education indicated that there are definite advantages for the schools with school libraries having professional library staffs. Evaluation instruments for collections, skills, and activities were developed.

______. *Patterns of Development in Elementary School Libraries Today: A Five-Year Report on Emerging Media Centers.* Encyclopedia Britannica, 1968. Based on information gathered for applicants to the Britannica school library award, this traces the development of library media centers in elementary schools.

LOWRIE, JEAN E. *Elementary School Libraries,* 2nd ed. Scarecrow, 1970. Presents situations and programs in elementary-school libraries that represent good practice and effective service.

ROE, ERNEST. *Teachers, Librarians, and Children: A Study of Libraries in Education.* Archon Books, 1965. An Australian educator reports on findings of a reading study and asks some important questions about the relevance of libraries to education.

SULLIVAN, PEGGY. *Impact: The School Library and the Instructional Program.* ALA, 1967. *Realization: The Final Report of the Knapp School Libraries Project.* ALA, 1968. In combination, these two volumes trace the progress and report the changing philosophies of the Knapp demonstration schools.

### Articles

"Education of the Media Specialist." *Library Journal,* v. 94 (April 15, 1969), pp. 1719–1737. A symposium on the educational preparation demanded of media specialists by the 1969 standards.

"Educational Trends and Media Programs in School Libraries." *ALA Bulletin,* v. 63 (February 1969), pp. 221–272. A special section devoted to the relationships between school media centers and educational excellence.

GRAHAM, MAE, ed. "Changing Nature of the School Library." *Library Trends,* v. 17 (April 1969). The entire issue is concerned with the development of the school library into the library media center.

### Film

American Association of School Librarians. Knapp School Library Project. *And Something More.* Guggenheim Productions, 1964. 16 mm, sound, color, 28 minutes. Presents the effects of good library service on an elementary school program.

### Periodicals

*Audiovisual Instruction.* Nat. Education Assoc., 1201 16th St. N.W., Washington, D.C. 20036. Valuable source for keeping up with technological progress as well as ideas for use in an instructional program.

Official publication of the Association for Educational Communication and Technology.

*Educational Media International.* 68 Queen St., London EC4N, England. The official publication of the International Council for Educational Media, this periodical gathers scholarly discussions by international authorities, with each issue typically concentrated around a special topic, e.g., multimedia in teacher training.

*Library Journal.* 1180 Avenue of the Americas, New York 10036. Includes in alternate issues *School Library Journal*, which is specifically concerned with the issues, problems, and events in public and school library service to youth, and with print and audiovisual materials for children and young adults.

*Media and Methods.* 134 N. 13th St., Philadelphia 19107. Essential to all media centers, this is devoted to examining various materials. Contains reviews and articles that offer creative ideas for media use.

## THE CENSORSHIP DILEMMA AND YOUTH'S RIGHT TO LEARN

*Diane Chrisman**

One of the most problematic areas facing librarians and teachers in the mid-twentieth century is intellectual freedom. The question permeates society: in the rating of movies, in the banning of books, in the controversies that arise from the purchase by libraries of certain materials and the assignment by teachers of certain books. It is, therefore, incumbent upon the individual working with youth, whether in the schools or in public libraries, to think through the questions that arise and decide where he stands in respect to the many issues involved.

Censorship of reading matter can be traced back to an era long before printing. The *Analects* of Confucius were burned in 213 B.C. in China. Greece and Rome felt the heavy hand of the censor, and when printing began in England, it was assumed that the church and state would control it. In colonial United States, prior to the American Revolution, there were many adamant critics of English censorship, and yet, when the Constitution of the United States was written, the absence of a Bill of Rights almost caused its rejection. It is not accidental that the First Amendment is the one guaranteeing the basic right of free speech. Since that time the Supreme Court has played an important role in the establishment of literary freedom in America.

However, the Court has not been consistently on the side of total freedom or on the side of restrictive measures. It vacillates, according to the makeup of the Court and the societal conditions under which it operates. It has, for example, never made clear whether the phrase "community standards" applies to the nation as a whole or only to the particular community out of which emanates a complaint. The individual who would approach the study of censorship in its legalistic form must be aware that by the time a book on the subject is published, the Court may have made subsequent rulings that alter the interpretation of previous rulings. This is an area where the law changes rapidly.

For example, the people who believe restrictions are necessary for the preservation of society were beginning to feel as if there was no hope that the Supreme Court would help in their fight to combat the prevalence of pornography. Then came the *Sam Ginsberg v. New York* (1968) decision that upheld the right of the state to make illegal the sale of pornographic materials to young people. The case and the resultant discussions have given rise to the phrase "variable obscenity." That is, adults have the right to purchase pornographic material without state restrictions, but the sale of the same material to a person under seventeen years of age constitutes an illegal action for which the bookseller may be prosecuted. It is not yet clear whether this standard can be applied to the lending of material. As now written, the existing state laws limit their concern to the sale of materials.

This point of view was reiterated by the Presidential Commission in *The Report on*

*Diane Chrisman is Coordinator, Work with Children, for the Buffalo and Erie County Public Library, Buffalo, New York.

*Obscenity and Pornography*, in which the majority of Commission members approved the abolition of all restrictions upon the sale of such materials to adults while recommending that the states enact legislation that would protect young people from the materials. A minority of the Commission members objected to this compromise, feeling that state control was essential at all levels.

While the courts have argued the definitions of obscenity and legislatures have attempted to set up controls for questionable material, professional organizations of librarians have investigated the role of the library in regard to intellectual freedom. In 1948 the American Library Association Council adopted the Library Bill of Rights. This document and its amendments (1961 and 1967) along with the Freedom to Read Statement (1953), the School Library Bill of Rights (1955), and How Libraries and Schools Can Resist Censorship (1962) form the backbone of library resistance to censorship. The 1967 amendment to the Library Bill of Rights is especially notable because it states in paragraph five that "the rights of an individual to the use of a library should not be denied or abridged because of his age." Similarly, the National Council of Teachers of English has produced a statement entitled "The Student's Right to Read."

Historically, the public library in its service to youth has encountered less difficulty with censors than the school library has, although the materials that cause the problems are apt to be present in both libraries. Sex education material, nudity in art books, the various "isms," and the theory of evolution are areas of the censor's concern. The public library has always been able to plead that it cannot restrict its materials because the adults who use the library are entitled to find certain items on the shelves. It has taken the stand that parents must be responsible for the reading of their children, but not for the reading of the community as a whole. The liberal public library view is that no one individual should be able to exercise a veto over the reading matter of others.

In the school library, this point of view is more difficult to defend. Books that frankly describe sexual acts and contain taboo words draw heavy fire from citizens who wish to "protect" the young. Not just their young, but all youth. In earlier years, the question involved the inclusion of adult titles in high school libraries, but now that "teen-age" books are treating such subjects as drug addiction, premarital pregnancy, and homosexuality, the question of what is appropriate reading matter concerns librarians and teachers in the junior high schools and elementary schools where such teen-age books are far more popular than in high schools.

While sex materials seem to cause the greatest problem, other areas are equally important, most notably race relations. The turmoil created by the Supreme Court decision of 1954 on school desegregation found expression in many ways besides the open resistance covered by television. For example, books such as *The Rabbit's Wedding* by Garth Williams and *Two Is a Team* by Lorraine and Jerrold Beim were attacked as being "pro-integration."

In recent years, attacks have also been made by such organizations as the NAACP against the inclusion of "racist" materials in libraries. And the 1970 Caldecott Medal book, *Sylvester and the Magic Pebble* by William Steig, has been under attack because it contains an illustration showing pigs as law enforcement officers.

There are many kinds of censors and many kinds of books that cause controversy. Sometimes, in fact, the book under censure is not the real problem at all. It is not unusual for pressure groups to disguise motives involving social and political ideologies. Nor is it unique to find that the roots of the controversy lie in a personality conflict between the censor and the person being attacked. Such complications of motive make it difficult to deal with censorship using the abstract methods discussed by many writers on the subject.

One must not assume that all criticisms of books are unjustified. There is always the possibility that the objector is quite right, and the librarian or teacher should be willing to review his decision about a book without feeling that the defense of intellectual freedom requires him to defend any and all materials. In libraries, as in school assignments, the material may, in fact, be so old as to call for reevaluation. Both teachers and librarians can face attacks with less fear if they have critically reevaluated materials they are offering to the young and have weeded from collections and recommended lists those books that are no longer relevant to modern societal conditions. For librarians, the written book-selection policy and the governing board's adoption of the Library Bill of Rights and the Freedom to Read statement can help prevent controversy and also can aid in the initial selection of material.

By not assigning one single book to an entire class, teachers can do a great deal to forestall attacks. Reading lists should contain materials that have a wide range of reading levels and maturity of content, so that the student may select the book that best suits his needs. If a teacher does assign one book to an entire class, he should be willing to defend its importance against all potential attacks.

Parental objection is a major influence in restricting the purchase or use of reading materials, most particularly in the schools. Many persons feel that the school library, like the school itself, is *in loco parentis* and that the school librarians should not only use sound judgment in book selection, but should also confine purchase to curriculum-related materials. However, many librarians, backed by the School Library Standards, believe that this role is too limited, that school libraries must serve the whole child and that book selection should provide materials for all members of the school, not for just the average students. Most librarians recognize that no one book will be right for every reader, and diversity is the goal of their collection building. These same librarians usually feel that it is the responsibility and prerogative of the parent to restrict and control his own child's reading.

A more subtle form of censorship is self-censorship: the refusal to buy certain materials because they may cause controversy. Unfortunately, studies reveal that this phenomenon is widespread and difficult to counteract. Moreover, self-censorship is usually more restrictive than that which the community would impose. It is interesting to note that many individuals who are staunch supporters of literary freedom for adults are opposed to literary freedom for young people.

## SUGGESTED RESEARCH NEEDS

Librarians and teachers who are deeply concerned about intellectual freedom for children and young people soon discover that there are some censorship problems for which there are no easy answers. The following questions represent just a few of the areas requiring study:

1. Is there an age at which we become less susceptible to the influence of printed materials?

2. Should children and young people be restricted from using adult material in public libraries and, if so, how are the restrictions to be established?

3. Is there a clear line between selection and censorship?

4. How do young people themselves feel about censorship?

5. Is there a relationship between the reading of sexually-oriented materials by adolescents and their behavior patterns?

6. If television programs present such subjects as dope addiction and abortion, should printed materials about the same subjects be available to young people?

7. In a pluralistic free society does one group, even if it is in the majority, have the right to impose its standards and values upon all members of the community?

## BIBLIOGRAPHY

### Bibliographies

GREGORY, RUTH W. "Readings on Book Selection and Intellectual Freedom; a Selected List, 1962–1967." *ALA Bulletin*, v. 62 (January 1968), pp. 64–69. An annotated bibliography of important books and articles that can serve as resources for the librarian.

HARVEY, J. A., comp. *Librarians, Censorship and Intellectual Freedom, An Annual Annotated Comprehensive Bibliography, 1968–1969*. ALA, 1970. Principles, practices, and various activities related to intellectual freedom are included in this list of annotated articles. Especially useful is the section on case histories of libraries and librarians involved in censorship issues.

### Books and Pamphlets

American Civil Liberties Union. *Combatting Undemocratic Pressures on Schools and Libraries; A Guide for Local Communities*. American Civil Liberties Union, 1964. The primary aim of this pamphlet is to prepare citizens to cope with community pressures that infringe on intellectual freedom.

American Library Association. Intellectual Freedom Committee. *Freedom of Inquiry: Supporting the Library Bill of Rights*. (Proceedings of the Conference on Intellectual Freedom, January 23–24, 1965.) ALA, 1965. Important statements about censorship were made during this conference. "Can Reading Affect Delinquency?" by William C. Kvaraceus and "Censorship and the Public Schools" by Lee A. Burress, Jr., are particularly relevant for librarians and teachers working with young people.

BLANSHARD, PAUL. *The Right to Read; The Battle Against Censorship*. Beacon Pr., 1955. A history of censorship, changing standards, and legal interpretations.

BOYER, PAUL S. *Purity in Print: Book Censorship in America*. Scribner's, 1968. Historian Boyer traces the rise of anti-vice societies in the nineteenth century through the heyday of censorship cases in the 1920s to the leveling off in the 1930s. By relating censorship activities to the social and political climate rather than viewing them in isolation, Boyer makes such activities meaningful and shows them to be far more complex than many writers on the subject would lead the reader to believe.

CHANDOS, JOHN, ed. *'To Deprave and Corrupt . . .': Original Studies in the Nature and Definition of 'Obscenity.'* Association Pr., 1962. A British look at the problem of censorship and obscenity that is urbane, scholarly, witty, thought-provoking, and creative.

DANIELS, WALTER MACHRAY, ed. *The Censorship of Books*. (Reference Shelf, v. 26, no. 5.) Wilson, 1959. Basic material on the pros and cons of censorship, including reprints of important documents.

DOWNS, ROBERT B. *The First Freedom*. ALA, 1960. An anthology of notable English and American writings on literary censorship. Especially important is Chapter VIII, "The Librarians Take a Stand."

FISKE, MARJORIE. *Book Selection and Censorship: A Study of School and Public Libraries in California*. Univ. of Calif. Pr., 1959. The effects of self-censorship on book selection in school and public libraries are revealed in this famous study.

GARDINER, HAROLD C., S.J. *Catholic Viewpoint on Censorship*. Hanover House, 1958. The aims and methods of the National Legion of Decency and the National Office for Decent Literature are studied as well as the charges made against them by the American Civil Liberties Union and the American Book Publishers Council.

HANEY, ROBERT W. *Comstockery in America: Patterns of Censorship and Control*. Beacon Pr., 1960. A member of the Unitarian ministry shows the complexities of censorship in a free, pluralistic society and discusses the question of who really does the censoring.

JOHNSON, PAMELA HANSFORD. *On Iniquity*. Scribner's, 1967. Appalled by the "moors murders" in England, the famed novelist has written a book in which she equates the leading murderer's interest in the Marquis de Sade with the violence of his actions.

KRONHAUSEN, EBERHARD, and PHYLLIS KRONHAUSEN. *Pornography and the Law*. Rev. ed. Ballantine, 1964. One of the most important books on the subject, in which the Kronhausens make clear the differences between erotic realism and hard-core pornography. For readers who have never encountered hard-core pornography, the section detailing the plot structure of the more famous titles will be of major importance.

KUH, RICHARD H. *Foolish Figleaves? Pornography in-and-out-of-Court*. Macmillan, 1967. Writing from his experiences as an assistant district attorney, Kuh outlines the problem of defining obscenity and pornography; traces the legal history in this country, and discusses memorable cases, including Lenny Bruce's. His detailed recommendations for legislative action that would bar the sale of pornography to young people are reflected in the New York State law that was upheld by the Supreme Court in the *Sam Ginsberg v. New York* ruling.

MC CLELLAN, GRANT S., ed. *Censorship in the United States*. Wilson, 1967. Reprints of articles and excerpts from books, this compilation is designed to show how our freedoms are currently affected by censorship activities.

MC KEON, RICHARD, ROBERT K. MERTON, and WALTER GELLHORN. *The Freedom to Read; Perspective and Program*. Bowker, 1957. An examination of the philosophical, political, and moral arguments for and against censorship.

MERRITT, LE ROY CHARLES. *Book Selection and Intellectual Freedom*. Wilson, 1970. Following a chapter on book selection in public libraries are directions for writing a book selection policy, sample policies and methods of evaluation. The basic documents concerning intellectual freedom are also included.

MOON, ERIC, ed. *Book Selection and Censorship in the Sixties*. Bowker, 1969. Primarily an anthology of articles written for *Library Journal*, these essays contribute to a full understanding of the development of intellectual freedom during the 1960s.

National Council of Teachers of English. *Meeting Censorship in the School: A Series of Case Studies.* Nat. Council of Teachers of English, 1967. Each report describes the community, school, complaint, the objector, and the reaction to the complaint. Cases include those the censor won as well as those he lost.

New Jersey Committee for the Right to Read. *A Survey of New Jersey Psychiatrists Pertaining to the Proscription by Legislation of Sexually Oriented Publications for Persons under 18 Years.* Final Report. New Jersey Committee for the Right to Read, 1967. The results of a questionnaire concerning the effects on a young person of reading sexually-oriented material are tabulated and summarized.

*The Report of the Commission on Obscenity and Pornography*. Bantam, 1970. The report pleased no one. The President, who commissioned it, refused to accept it; those who see a need for curtailing pornography found it too liberal; those who advocate no restrictions found it too confining. Nevertheless, it is essential reading.

WOFFORD, AZILE. *Book Selection for School Libraries.* Wilson, 1962. A chapter entitled "Censorship and the School Library" describes ways in which censorship becomes evident, lists areas of controversy, and makes suggestions for solving the problem.

## Articles

American Library Association. Intellectual Freedom Committee. "How Libraries and Schools Can Resist Censorship." *ALA Bulletin*, v. 56 (March 1962), pp. 228–229. Principles and procedures basic to the preservation of intellectual freedom in schools and libraries.

ASHEIM, LESTER E. "Not Censorship But Selection." *Wilson Library Bulletin*, v. 28 (September 1953), pp. 63–67. Probably the most quoted article in library literature in which the selector's approach is differentiated from the censor's.

ASHER, THOMAS R. "A Lawyer Looks at Libraries and Censorship." *Library Journal*, v. 95 (October 1, 1970), pp. 3247–3249. A workable balance between the risks of absolute censorship and the objectives of intellectual freedom is suggested by a lawyer who is active in the American Civil Liberties Union.

BACH, HARRY. "A Clear and Present Danger: The Books—or the Censors?" *Library Journal*, v. 90 (September 15, 1965), pp. 3681–3685. The pressures that can be exerted by censors on school libraries are described along with resistance procedures.

BERNINGHAUSEN, DAVID K. "The Librarian's Commitment to the Library Bill of Rights." *Library Trends*, v. 19 (July 1970), pp. 19–38. The Director of a Library School and deeply involved in the ALA Intellectual Freedom Committee, Berninghausen traces the historical development of library dedication to intellectual freedom.

BOND, ELIZABETH M. "Censorship and Your Library." *Illinois Libraries*, v. 48 (May 1966), pp. 358–361. Reprinted from the September 1953 *Minnesota Libraries*, the article discusses the implications of the Library Bill of Rights point by point. This entire issue is devoted to intellectual freedom.

BRIGNOLO, DONALD E. "Censorship Pressure Rising, Missouri Librarians Told." *Library Journal*, v. 94 (June 1, 1969), pp. 2188–2190. A report on a conference entitled "The Censor Always Rings Twice" that considered the problems of censorship in schools, libraries, mass media, and political life.

BURKE, JOHN G. "To Be Professional." *American Libraries*, v. 2 (February 1971), p. 159. An editorial comment that advocates the inclusion of *Sylvester and the Magic Pebble* in children's book collections.

BURRESS, LEE A. "Censorship Is Capricious." *Top of the News*, v. 20 (May 1964), pp. 281–287. The chairman of a college English department explores the hidden motives that can foster a censorship controversy.

CARNOVSKY, LEON. "The Obligations and Responsibilities of the Librarian Concerning Censorship." *Library Quarterly*, v. 20 (January 1950), pp. 21–32. Distinction is made between censorship and selection, and areas of controversy are explored.

"Censorship: Librarians, Administrators and Boards." *Library Journal*, v. 95 (December 15, 1970), p. 4309. Censorship activities throughout the country are reported. They vary from the removal of 40 pages on human sexuality from a high-school textbook to restrictions on underground newspapers.

FARLEY, JOHN J. "The Reading of Young People." *Library Trends*, v. 19 (July 1970), pp. 81–88. The Dean of a School of Library Science explains why the question of intellectual freedom becomes most perplexing when a high-school youngster is involved.

GARD, ROBERT R. "Censorship and Public Understanding." *English Journal*, v. 60 (February 1971), pp. 255–259. The necessity for building public trust and some recommended procedures for the educator to follow.

GAYLIN, WILLARD M. "The Prickly Problems of Pornography." *Yale Law Journal*, v. 77 (1968), pp. 579–597. In the course of reviewing Kuh's *Foolish Figleaves?* psychiatrist Gaylin analyzes the problem of pornography from a mental health viewpoint. He makes the point, among others, that a child reading pornography with the knowledge that it is disapproved of will not likely be harmed, but a child reading pornography without such knowledge may be harmed.

GOTHBERG, HELEN. "YA Censorship: Adult or Adolescent Problem?" *Top of the News*, v. 22 (April 1966), pp. 275–278. A high-school librarian describes her methods of preventing censorship. Important factors are anticipating needs, recognizing the latent censor in the student, and teaching the young person how to handle his reactions to certain types of materials.

GRANNIS, CHANDLER B. "Shifting Winds That Affect Censorship." *Publishers' Weekly*, v. 194 (July 1, 1968), p. 33. The possible effect of pornography on young people has brought a demand for new restraints in communication.

———. "Where Do You Draw the Line?" *Publishers' Weekly*, v. 195 (April 14, 1969), p. 73. Objections are made to the withdrawal of the Xerox reprint of the original *Mother Goose Nursery Rhymes and Fairy Tales*. Grannis claims that this case is evidence of the pressure organized groups exert on publishers.

GREEN, BERNARD. "Obscenity, Censorship, and Juvenile Delinquency." *University of Toronto Law Journal*, v. 14, no. 2 (1962), pp. 229–252. After reviewing what we know and don't know about the relationship between reading and juvenile delinquency, a Canadian lawyer makes suggestions for legal controls that will protect the young but leave adults free.

JOHNSON, PAMELA HANSFORD. "Speaking Out: We Need More Censorship." *Saturday Evening Post*, v. 240 (January 14, 1967), pp. 8–10. A novelist states her case against total license in the arts. Not concerned about sex, she worries about the presentation of cruelty for the purpose of "kicks."

KILLIFER, CONSTANCE. "Double Standards: Intellectual Freedom and the Post-Modern Generation." *Top of the News*, v. 25 (June 1969), pp. 392–399. A high-school librarian sees the need for new standards and believes that the questioning attitude of the "post-modern" generation is a step toward their attainment. The article also appeared in the October 1968 *Bay State Librarian*.

KRISTOL, IRVING. "Pornography, Obscenity and the Case for Censorship." *The New York Times Magazine*, March 28, 1971, pp. 24+. A strongly reasoned statement, stressing the dehumanization effects of pornography. Kristol describes the difference between repressive laws and laws that regulate and concludes that "liberal censorship" is both possible and desirable.

LADOF, NINA SYDNEY. "Censorship—The Tip of the Iceberg." *American Libraries*, v. 2 (March 1971), pp. 309–310. An experienced librarian suggests that there may be more to the problem of censorship than what we see or hear. The harassment of bookstores by police is one form of extralegal pressure.

"Library Ban on Karate Hit by Publisher." *Library Journal*, v. 94 (November 1, 1969), p. 3959. A publisher criticizes the public library for its hesitancy to buy books on karate and offers reasons why these books belong on library shelves.

"Library Still Free in Philly." *Wilson Library Bulletin*, v. 45 (January 1971), p. 450. The decision of the Philadelphia Free Library to retain Jerry Rubin's *Do It!* on open shelves is reported in this news item as well as the reaction of some citizens to the decision.

MESIANO, LINDALEE. "Even When It Offends." *Library Journal*, v. 94 (May 15, 1969), p. 2031. An editorial on the decision of the Xerox Corporation to withdraw its facsimile reprint of an 1895 edition of *Mother Goose Nursery Rhymes and Fairy Tales* because of the charges by the American Jewish Congress that the work is "racist."

NORRIS, HOKE, JAMES SQUIRE, and ROBERT F. HOGAN. "Should We Censor What Adolescents Read?" *PTA Magazine*, v. 59 (March 1965), pp. 10–12. Emphasis is on a positive approach to book selection and on a broad program in literature that parents can understand and support.

OBOLER, ELI M. "Intellectual Freedom, Censorship and Library Associations." *Drexel Library Quarterly*, v. 3 (October 1967), pp. 399–400. A university librarian discusses specific ways in which state library associations can promote intellectual freedom.

RAFFERTY, MAX. "The Other Side: Hardest of All to Come By." *Wilson Library Bulletin*, v. 42 (October 1967), pp. 181–186. The text of an address given by the ex-Superintendent of Public Instruction in California to the Library Trustees' meeting at the annual ALA Convention in San Francisco, 1967. Among Rafferty's points concerning the relationship of schools and libraries to youth is a strong plea for censoring what youth reads.

REISCHE, DIANA. "Censorship and Obscenity: What's Happened to Taste?" *Senior Scholastic*, v. 89 (October 14, 1966), pp. 12–15. Changing tastes and public morals are part of the reason why censorship questions are so difficult. The problems and judicial attempts to clarify and solve them are explained.

SABADOSH, AUDREY. "Teenagers View Censorship." *Top of the News*, v. 22 (April 1966), pp. 278–280. Thought-provoking responses to a questionnaire on reading that was distributed to high-school English students. Thirty six percent indicated a definite belief in censorship.

"School Censors Hit N.Y., Ohio, Maryland and California." *Library Journal*, v. 96 (January 15, 1971), pp. 228–230. Censorship incidents involving books ranging from Cleaver's *Soul on Ice* to Steig's *Sylvester and the Magic Pebble* are reported. Many of the cases bear out the observation of Judith Krug, Director of ALA's Office for Intellectual Freedom, that "during the past two years the obscenity issue has been used as a smokescreen to obscure the political and social issues behind censorship."

SHUMAN, R. BAIRD. "Making the World Safe for What?" *Education Digest*, v. 34 (December 1968), pp. 36–38. (Condensed from *Illinois Schools Journal*, Fall 1968.) As a professor of education, Shuman speaks out against pressure groups that would decree curricular matters and notes the folly of those who think censorship is necessary to protect youth.

SIEBERT, SARA, and LINDA LAPIDES. "Shuddered to Think . . . " *Top of the News*, v. 22 (April 1966), pp. 259–268. Two young adult librarians describe a complaint concerning a book in Baltimore's Enoch Pratt Free Library and explain precisely how the complaint was handled.

STEINER, GEORGE. "Night Words." *Encounter*, v. 25 (October 1965), pp. 14–19. The point is made that mass-produced pornography is not only monotonous, but it does our imagining for us, invades our privacy, and markets our dreams wholesale. A plea for reticence.

WHITE, LUCIEN W. "The Censorship Dilemma." *Illinois Libraries*, v. 49 (September 1967), pp. 612–621. A brief chronology of major landmarks in censorship legislation and suggestions for implementing intellectual freedom at the practicing level.

### Periodicals

American Library Association, Intellectual Freedom Committee. *Newsletter on Intellectual Freedom*. Published bi-monthly. Available from: American Library Association, 50 East Huron Street, Chicago, Illinois 60611. The *Newsletter* is one of the most valuable resources for locating information concerning censorship activities across the nation. It brings together items that are, of necessity, scattered throughout magazines and newspapers.

*American Libraries*. The official journal of the American Library Association carries a regular column "Intellectual Freedom" written by the Director of the Office for Intellectual Freedom in which is reported major concerns affecting libraries and how they are handled.

### Special Aids

American Library Association, Intellectual Freedom Committee, 50 East Huron Steet, Chicago, Illinois 60611. The Office for Intellectual Freedom will provide, upon request, a packet of material, containing, among other items, The Library Bill of Rights and the statement on Freedom to Read.

California Library Association, Intellectual Freedom Committee. *Intellectual Freedom Kit*. Sacramento, 1964. This is an example of the type of kit provided by some professional associations to help the local librarian resist censorship. Basic documents are included as well as bibliographies of pertinent readings and reprints of articles.

National Council of Teachers of English. Champaign, Illinois. The NCTE has endorsed a document entitled "The Student's Right to Read," which is available from that organization, among other documents concerned with the problems of teaching in a free atmosphere.

## INVOLVING PARENTS IN EDUCATION

*Mildred Beatty Smith**

Almost everyone knows a family of dedicated readers in which there is one child who completely rejects books. We also know there are children like the essayist-novelist James Baldwin, who, finding himself overwhelmed by the horrors of the Harlem ghetto, turned to books and libraries for his salvation. There are always exceptions, but they remain just that—exceptions. On the whole, children who read easily and well come from homes that encourage reading.

The lack of home reading is not a matter of class or race; it is not a matter of being an urban, suburban, or rural inhabitant: it is indigenous to American life. The vast majority of adult Americans do not read one book in the course of a year. It is the challenge of the schools and libraries to find ways of involving parents in order to create an atmosphere conducive to learning and one that stimulates intellectual curiosity.

Since reading is a process and not a "subject," one becomes proficient by practice. Thus the goal of parent involvement is to encourage the child to read widely beyond that reading he does in the classroom situation. With wide outside reading, the child can come to discover that reading is a joy in and of itself and not simply something to do connected with school work. For, if he acquires the latter attitude, he ceases to read when he stops attending school, and our complex technological society cannot support a citizenry that does not read. Democracy demands informed citizens if it is to function well.

The idea of involving parents in the educational process is not new—in America, this idea is as old as education itself—but recent trends indicate that we can expect renewed emphasis on this aspect of community-school relationships. While much of the present research and experimentation is directed toward involving parents within the group known as "the culturally deprived," it is reasonable to expect that more will be done in the future with middle-class parents. An

*Mildred Beatty Smith is Director of Elementary Education for the Flint (Michigan) Public Schools.

important side benefit to this involvement is helping parents see the school as "theirs" and not as some remote institution to be respected and/or feared.

Underlying this renewed emphasis is educators' realization that children do not operate in a vacuum. Their behavior patterns and value systems are products of a total environment of which the school is one part. The home, the neighborhood, and the peer group all play roles in influencing a child's behavior. We also know that non-human influences such as television exert some impact upon the child, although it is not clear precisely what the nature of that impact may be (see "Television: The Influence and Impact of Another Medium"). One result of this understanding of multi-influential forces has been to recognize more clearly that many of a child's patterns and values are established before he enters school. Thus, educators are realizing that they must—and can—play some role in the child's preschool life.

In the Flint (Michigan) Community School Program, an activity known as the The Preschool Story Hour is scheduled in elementary-school buildings for mothers and their children between the ages of three and five. These mothers bring their children to the story-hour sessions for one hour one morning each week. During this activity period the mother can check out books suitable for home reading. The mothers are provided with some techniques about how to read aloud effectively to the child. These include suggestions concerning the pace at which material should be read; the value of allowing the child time to look at the illustrations before turning a page; how to sustain a child's interest when the book cannot be finished in one sitting, and the importance of allowing time to discuss the book with the child and answer any questions he may have.

Some follow-up was undertaken to determine what influence, if any, this program had upon the child when entering school. The kindergarten teachers noted better adjustment to the school situation as evidenced by less crying during the first days of school. The teachers noted that these children had mastered a more enriched speaking vocabulary and they exhibited more fluency with oral language. The children also displayed more interest in books by frequently browsing at bookshelves located in the classroom.

While similar results have been found for children attending preschool programs in the public library, there seems little question that there is a positive transference made toward school when the child and parent go there together on a regular basis. Too often the only time parents go into a school is for a parent-teacher conference or to a PTA meeting, neither occasion involving the child himself.

As more educators come to understand that they can play only limited roles in conveying attitudes, interests, habits, and values to children, the schools will be organized to bring the adult members of the community inside the buildings. This will mean that the child comes to see school as one aspect of his total environment, integrated with rather than separated from life.

### Obstacles

There are two distinct types of obstacles to be overcome in trying to involve parents in the educational process. The first may be termed technical. A mother with a four-year-old and a baby is going to need some place to leave the baby if she is going to participate in preschool programs with the four-year-old. It may be that the school will have to provide a room equipped with cribs and playpens and responsible supervisors for the younger children.

To involve working mothers would be the biggest challenge. Not only are they not available during the school day, but they are faced with household chores at the end of a day's work on the job. Physical energy is not inexhaustible and must be taken into consideration. It may, of course, be possible to involve the mother substitute in such programs. It may also be possible, if day-care centers grow in number and quality, for the school system to take the program to the center, although certainly getting the children into the school is a preferable approach. A more radical idea might be espousing the concept of "released time" for working mothers. With more and more mothers working, one of the job fringe benefits might be time off to participate in a weekly preschool program.

The second obstacle is emotional in nature. Many adults have only negative feelings toward schools. Their own experiences were not happy ones and either fear of or resentment toward the school may be their only response. Creating an atmosphere of trust in which such parents can feel comfortable and operate successfully demands genuine sensitivity on the part of the school personnel.

The same holds true for public libraries which must be prepared to be partners with the schools in helping parents become involved in education. Many adults feel strained about visiting a library. They perceive the library as an appropriate place for the well-educated, intellectually-oriented person or the eccentric "bookish" individual. When an adult feels this way he can do little to encourage his child to use the library.

The organization, departmentalization, and neatness of a library can be deterrents. But primarily, the problem stems from imposing standards of behavior upon library patrons. Most other places that parents frequent for services such as those provided by the department store, the laundry facility, the grocery store, and the shoe repair shop are not so formally organized nor do their employees tell people how to behave. Also, librarians have not always managed to convey effectively the idea that the library belongs to the people, not to the librarians. Many adults experience concern over borrowing, and possibly damaging, what they consider another's property. This fear might be lessened if they understood that it was their money that provided the materials in the first place.

Librarians must also learn not to treat people as criminals when a book is lost, damaged, or returned late. Such events do not reflect upon the individual's moral or ethical standards: they are part of life's happenings and should be accepted as such by both librarians and patrons.

## Methods of Involving Parents

The Preschool Story Hour mentioned earlier is one technique for involving parents before the child comes to school. Once the child is in school, parents can serve as teacher's aides, correcting papers and providing individual attention while a child reads aloud. Mothers can, and do, serve as volunteers in the school library.

Besides the traditional Parent Teacher Association meetings, parents can help run book fairs (see Book Promotion). With juvenile paperback books increasingly available in quantity and quality, parents can also run a regular paperback bookstore if the school has any free space at all. The ability to buy inexpensive books is one of the great opportunities children have today, and owning their own books is a satisfying feeling. If school space is not available, parents can encourage the local stores that stock paperback books to add juvenile titles to their collections.

The exact form a particular school's program for involving parents will take will depend upon the nature of the community. If the school is a neighborhood school, within walking distance for all attending, there will be more possibilities than if transportation is needed to bring both parents and children to the school. As mentioned earlier, the number of children in a family, their ages, and the work status of the mother will influence a program's approach.

What is most needed at the moment is research in involving fathers. So far, most of the programs reported by Head Start projects emphasize the mother's role. And while she is vital to the child, excluding the father is not sound practice.

When a program is begun, the professional staff of the school or library may be required to assume the entire responsibility for planning it. But once confidence is established and mutual trust is created between the parents and the institution, the programs should be planned cooperatively. One parent may well be able to influence another to participate when a member of the school staff would meet only resistance. It may be that one of the major tasks of the participating parents will be in recruiting others to become involved.

Parents also often know many facts about a community that are not obvious even to trained personnel. When parents see their ideas accepted and put into action they gain self-pride and confidence. There are so many direct and indirect benefits to having the school and the family work together that it is impossible to believe we will not see numerous creative programs come into being in the near future.

## SUGGESTED RESEARCH NEEDS

1. Are there identifiable economic, cultural, and psychological factors that influence parental attitudes toward schools, libraries, and reading?

2. Is there a relationship between prekindergarten programs and the child's subsequent in-school learning?

3. Can the effective methods by which parents teach children to read at home be systematized for potential use by any interested parent?

4. Does the presence or absence of a home library influence a child's reading pattern?

5. How much influence does a parent's own reading pattern have upon the child's interest in reading?

6. What are the distinctive contributions of schools, school libraries, and public libraries to the child's reading development?

7. How much influence does the peer group exert on a child's interest in reading?

## BIBLIOGRAPHY

### Bibliographies

BOOTH, ROBERT E., et al. *Culturally Disadvantaged; A Bibliography and Keyword-Out-of-Context (KWOC) Index.* Wayne State Pr., 1967. Brings together all materials—books, articles, unpublished research, reports—concerning the disadvantaged. By avoiding the rigid traditional subject headings, access to material is not only easy, but interconnections not usually made in indexes are provided.

*Recent Research in Reading, A Bibliography 1966–1969.* New York: CCM Information, 1970. An ERIC (Educational Resources Information Center) publication. Has author, title and subject indexes. Subject index is key word approach, making access easy.

### Books About Learning

CONTE, JOSEPH M., and GEORGE H. GRIMES. *Media and the Culturally Different Learner.* Nat. Education Assoc., 1969. An excellent little book that covers the major concerns, offers concrete suggestions, and provides a fine bibliography. Especially important is the list of characteristics attributed to children of the poor—both strengths and weaknesses that can affect the learning situation.

*Head Start Programs Operated by Public School Systems, 1966–1967.* Research Report 1968–R 3. National Education Association, 1968. In detailing the many types of programs run under Head Start, the report covers parent involvement and its effects upon the programs.

MAGER, ROBERT E. *Developing Attitudes Toward Learning.* Fearon Pub., 1968. Unlike many books on the taxonomy of education, Mager's is a joy to read. His anecdotes and fables highlight his points with humor. Discusses praise-punishment effects upon learning attitudes.

MERGENTIME, CHARLOTTE. *You and Your Child's Reading.* Harcourt, 1963. A detailed presentation of everything an adult should know about reading. Discusses methods of teaching reading, psychological factors involved in learning, and gives precise instructions on how to help a child with reading problems.

PASSOW, A. HARRY, ed. *Developing Programs for the Educationally Disadvantaged.* Teachers College Pr., Columbia Univ., 1968. A major collection of essays covering such topics as "Maternal Attitudes toward the School and the Role of Pupil: Some

Social Class Comparisons" and "School and Home: Focus on Achievement."

SMITH, MILDRED BEATTY. *Home and School Focus on Reading.* Scott, Foresman, 1971. Combines down-to-earth practical suggestions for involving parents in education with a philosophical basis for the importance of doing so.

UMANS, SHELLEY. *New Trends in Reading Instruction.* Teachers College Pr., Columbia Univ., 1963. In the section "Community Resources," Umans discusses the roles parents can play in a reading program. A bibliography offers additional sources for information on parent involvement.

## Articles

BISHOP, EDITH P. "Experiment in Watts." *Library Journal*, v. 91 (January 15, 1966), pp. 338–339. A brief report on ways in which the Los Angeles Public Library involves adults and children in the Watts area in library programs.

BROOKOVER, WILBUR B. "A Social Psychological Conception of Classroom Learning." *School and Society*, v. 87 (February 28, 1959), pp. 84–87. Brookover's point is that people learn culturally required behavior patterns and it is the job of the schools to expose students to a climate that emphasizes maximum achievement, rather than separating and screening students. People learn through self-concept, through the expectations of others, and within an overall atmosphere that can encourage or discourage learning.

"Education for Socially Disadvantaged Children." *Review of Educational Research*, v. 35 (December 1965). The issue is devoted entirely to disadvantaged children and their education. Each bibliographic essay—5 in number—reviews research findings in a particular area and provides a comprehensive bibliography.

"How to Help Your Child Do Well in School." *U. S. News and World Report*, v. 67 (October 6, 1969), pp. 49–50. A survey of 1,045 mothers, dealing with the parental role in the school achievement of first graders, was carried out by Gallup International for the Institute for Development of Educational Activities. Findings suggest "that the parental role in early years is basic in determining how much a youngster is going to achieve in school, once he enters the first grade." Outlines characteristics of high achievers in terms of parental roles.

KAHL, JOSEPH A. "Educational and Occupational Aspirations of 'Common Man' Boys." *Harvard Educational Review*, v. 23 (Summer 1953), pp. 186–203. Report of a study designed to determine the social influences that help account for the fact that boys of a seemingly similar background in terms of IQ and family status differ considerably in their motivation to attend college. Although many factors were discovered, not all of which could be weighted, the results indicated that boys learned to view the occupational system from their parents' perspective to an extraordinary degree.

MILNER, ESTHER. "A Study of the Relationship Between Reading Readiness in Grade One School Children and Patterns of Parent-Child Interaction." *Child Development*, v. 22 (June 1951), pp. 95–112. While 20 years old, it is doubtful that this study has lost much of its validity. Milner found that high achievers possess several or many story books; are habitually read to by mother and/or father, and are involved in family activities. Lower achievers reversed the characteristics, owning none or few books, mostly funny books or school texts; were not read to, and had little interaction with parents.

SMITH, MILDRED BEATTY, and CARL I. BRAHER. "When School and Home Focus on Achievement." *Educational Leadership*, v. 20 (February 1963), pp. 314–318. A report on the Flint (Michigan) program of involving parents in the educational process. Statistically significant improvement was made by the experimental group.

SWIFT, MARSHALL S. "Training Poverty Mothers in Communication Skills." *The Reading Teacher*, v. 23 (January 1970), pp. 360–367. Undertaken in connection with Philadelphia's "Get Set" program, this experiment was designed to help poverty mothers enhance their own skills and to make them aware of their importance to their children's learning abilities.

WILLE, LOIS. "Moms Are a Must." *American Education*, v. 16 (April 1970), pp. 25–29. Participants in this Chicago program were not preselected, but recruited on a door-to-door basis. School is in session 48 weeks of the year, mothers must sign statements that they will participate, and the children retain the same teacher throughout the program. Results indicate that working with the three-year-olds will have more impact than trying to undo the patterns of the older children.

*Wilson Library Bulletin*, v. 45 (November 1970). The whole issue is devoted to "The Librarian and the Teaching of Reading." Provides an excellent bibliography that covers the important aspects of teaching reading.

## Books About Children's Books

Once parents have been involved in helping their children learn to read and achieve in school they need help in selecting the right books to encourage home reading. The following titles will offer the parents a wide range of possibilities.

ARBUTHNOT, MAY HILL. *Children's Reading in the Home.* Scott, Foresman, 1969. Discussion about why reading is important and how to choose books is combined with detailed descriptions of recommended books of all types for all ages of youthful readers.

DUFF, ANNIS. *"Bequest of Wings," A Family's Pleasures with Books.* Viking, 1944. (Also available as a Viking Compass paperback.) A firsthand account of the role books played in the Duff family. Old, but valuable as an example of how reading together is an enriching experience for all members of the family.

FRANK, JOSETTE. *Your Child's Reading Today.* Rev. ed. Doubleday, 1969. A conservative approach to children's reading and other media. Author is Director for Children's Books and Mass Media of The Child Study Association of America.

LARRICK, NANCY. *A Parent's Guide to Children's Reading.* 3rd ed. Doubleday, 1969. (Also available in paperback from Pocket Books, Inc.) A popular book for involving parents in their children's reading.

## PRESSURE FOR PLURALISM: THE BLACKS, THE CHICANOS, THE NATIVE AMERICANS, AND WOMEN

*Dorothy M. Broderick**

Two very divergent themes have run through American history: (1) the idea that America's doors were open to all, but (2) once having arrived, the immigrants were expected to willingly take their place within "the melting pot." The doors have been closed for some time to all but a select group of potential immigrants, and in recent years the melting-pot psychology has been challenged seriously by a wide variety of groups.

The most active groups demanding change in American attitudes are (1) the blacks, (2) the Chicanos (Mexican-Americans), (3) the Native Americans (Indians), and (4) women. All four groups share the common characteristic known as "high visibility." What this means is that they must be accepted for what they are.

The first three groups also share a common characteristic, although it may not be quite so obvious: they are all Americans because the status was forced upon them. The blacks were brought in chains; the Mexican-Americans became Americans when Mexico lost its territories; and the Indians were physically defeated in war by the United States.

*Dorothy M. Broderick is Associate Professor, School of Library Service, Dalhousie University, Halifax, Nova Scotia, Canada. Mark Weber, high-school librarian at Oak Park and River Forest (Illinois) school system, was research assistant.

Until very recently, despite high visibility in one sense, the four groups also shared a type of invisibility. Women were simply adjuncts to men; while the other three groups were barred from access to the mainstream of American society for a multiplicity of reasons.

It is ironic that as white America has become aware of unpaid debts to the blacks, the Chicanos, and the Indians, and shows signs of being willing to open doors to them, the three groups are turning their backs on that society. In place of the melting pot has come pressure for pluralism. Each group is demanding the right to live its own life in its own style, with control over its own destiny.

While much of this rejection of white middle-class values can be traced to the black power revolution, some of it owes a debt to the millions of white youths who are also rejecting society in one way or another. As white youth has spoken sharply against the school system in underground newspapers, in demonstrations, and on occasion, riots, it becomes clear that they feel participation in the mainstream may not be worth their effort.

All of this is placing great pressure on the school system and creating something akin to chaos in many areas of the country. Educators are beset with problems arising out of the need to rethink the traditional role of public education. When public schools were begun, the need was to take many diverse groups of immigrants and show them how to become Americans. The schools did the job well but at a price that we are only beginning to recognize.

When white male America did concern itself with blacks, Chicanos, Indians, or women in the past it was to impose roles upon them rather than to see them as individuals. The black was taught that he must learn to think white; the Chicanos and Indians were made to feel ashamed of their native languages; and women were thought odd if they wanted to be something other than mothers and housewives.

For schools and libraries the challenge is twofold. In those areas where one of the minority groups predominates, the need is to understand the value system of the group, accept it, and work within its parameters. In order to accomplish this, teachers and librarians must immerse themselves in the history and culture of the group. They cannot be content to read children's books and expect to learn what they need to know. No one who has not read *The Autobiography of Malcolm X*, for example, is in a position to evaluate black materials for children.

A second area of concern is the need to develop programs in pluralistic culture for students in all-white schools. Their need to understand that there are as many ways of life as there are different peoples is vital for reaching some national understanding of our problems and possibilities.

The feminist movement differs from the minority groups in a number of ways. First, it is interesting to observe that the minority group revolts have come from the young while the feminist movement has found its leaders among the middle aged. While we have placed the four groups together in this section, it should be noted that the feminist movement appears to be on a collision course with the other groups, most notably at this time with the blacks. The male black attitude is that it will be time enough for black women to be free *after* the black male is free. The struggle is such that black males do not see the two movements proceeding simultaneously and this will surely create difficulties.

## SUGGESTED RESEARCH NEEDS

Among the innumerable questions up for discussion at this time in history, the following seem particularly vital:

1. How valid is the assumption that only members of the minority group should write materials for that group?
2. Is censorship involved in a request to remove racially objectionable materials from libraries?
3. How much diversity can the nation accept and still be one united nation?
4. Does community control of the schools, particularly in large urban areas, mean that whites are to be excluded from all participation or merely from positions of decision-making?
5. Is there a difference between George Wallace standing in the doorway to exclude a black from Alabama University and black parents keeping white teachers out of the Brownsville District School in New York City?
6. How do adults who have long-acquired patterns of thinking change ideas that they have previously never questioned?

## BIBLIOGRAPHY: MULTI-RACIAL MATERIALS

### Bibliographies

American Library Association. *Minority Groups; Selected Bibliographies and References of Materials for Children and Young Adults.* ALA, 1969. A bibliography of bibliographies of materials on blacks, Mexican-Americans, and Indians.

DIMITROFF, LILLIAN. *An Annotated Bibliography of Audiovisual Materials Related to Understanding and Teaching the Culturally Disadvantaged.* Nat. Education Assoc., 1969. A three-part bibliography: (1) films and filmstrips for understanding of and appreciation for the culture of minority groups; (2) phono-records; and (3) films and filmstrips on teaching techniques. While heavily weighted on blacks, it covers all disadvantaged groups to the extent made possible by the availability of materials.

GRIFFIN, LOUISE. *Multi-Ethnic Books for Young Children; Annotated Bibliography for Parents and Teachers.* ERIC Clearinghouse on Early Childhood Education, 1970. Lists and discusses books now available for children who are not white or middle class. Books are grouped by race, national background, ethnic groups, and life style.

HILLYER, MILDRED. *Bibliography of Spanish and Southwestern Indian Cultures Library Books.* Grants Municipal Schools, Grants, New Mexico, 1969. Annotated bibliography of books that would encourage the Spanish-speaking and Indian children to communicate more effectively in English.

Wisconsin Department of Public Instruction. *Ethnic Minorities: A Bibliography.* Wisconsin Department of Public Instruction, n. d. Contains annotated list of books for children on blacks, Spanish-speaking, American Indians, Chinese, and Japanese.

## Books

Many of the books listed in the section "Involving Parents in Education" will prove useful in this category. The book listed below has particular relevance to this section.

FEDDER, RUTH, and JACQUELINE GABALDON. *No Longer Deprived: Using Minority Cultures and Languages in Education of Disadvantaged Children and Their Teachers*, ed. by Esther Lloyd-Jones. Teachers College Pr., Columbia Univ., 1970. Focus is on Spanish-speaking and Indian children. Despite chatty style, a valuable book.

## Articles

BURHANS, GRACE. "The Cause Is Mankind." *Minnesota Libraries*, v. 21 (December 1965), pp. 234–238. An essay-bibliography of children's books about minority groups with stress upon prejudice and discrimination.

GAST, DAVID K. "Minority Americans in Children's Literature." *Elementary English*, v. 44 (January 1967), pp. 12–23. Using children's books with contemporary settings published between 1945–1962, Gast found considerable improvement in the portraits of the minority groups he studied when compared with earlier images, adult fiction, and textbooks.

HADLOCK, RUTH. "Specially Good for Ethnic Groups." *Instructor*, v. 76 (November 1966), pp. 109–111. A librarian on an Indian reservation discusses children's books useful for reading aloud to minority group children.

WASHINGTON, BENETTA B. "Books to Make Them Proud." *N. E. A. Journal*, v. 55 (May 1966), pp. 20–22. The director of the Women's Centers of the Job Corps contends that children's books must help in developing a positive self-image in children from minority groups.

## Periodical

*Interracial Books for Children.* Council on Interracial Books for Children, Inc., 9 East 40th Street, New York, New York 10016. (quarterly) A publication for those concerned with books by and about minority groups. Contains articles, portraits of minority authors and artists, news items, and bibliographies of recommended titles.

# BIBLIOGRAPHY: BLACK AMERICANS

## Bibliographies

American Jewish Committee. *Negro History and Literature: A Selected Annotated Bibliography.* Anti-Defamation League, n.d. Approximately 175 books dealing with the black experience in America. Covers age 5 through high school.

BAKER, AUGUSTA. *The Black Experience in Children's Books.* The New York Public Library, 1971. Supersedes the older *Books About Negro Life for Children.* An annotated bibliography of books for children through age twelve; designed to increase the black child's pride and aid the white child in understanding another culture.

BRITTON, JEAN E. *Selected Books About the Afro-American for Very Young Children.* Massachusetts State Dept. of Education, 1969. Establishes criteria for evaluating books about blacks and recommends 64 titles.

CLANCY, BARBARA JEAN. *Children's Interracial Fiction: An Unselective Bibliography.* American Federation of Teachers, 1969. Contains 328 titles, divided by age groups.

FINNEY, JAMES E. *The Long Road to Now.* Charles W. Clark, 1969. Entries are coded to indicate age and grade levels. Covers all areas including reference volumes.

HUSSEY, EDITH. *The Negro American: A Reading List.* Nat. Council of Churches, n.d. About 250 selected stories, poems, biographies, and histories about American blacks. Classed by age.

JACKSON, MILES M. *Negro History and Culture; A Bibliography for Young Readers.* Univ. of Pittsburgh Pr., 1968. The foreword stresses how easily susceptible children are to prejudice, making the introduction of sound material on blacks vital in the early years of a child's life.

ROLLINS, CHARLEMAE, ed. *We Build Together.* Rev. ed. Nat. Council of Teachers of English, 1967. Excellent annotated bibliography. Introduction outlines criteria for evaluation and discusses stereotypes found in offensive books.

## Articles

ARMSTRONG, H. T., and R. A. ROBINSON. "Books on Africa for Children." *Top of the News*, v. 21 (June 1965), pp. 334–337. An essay and annotated bibliography on books for children about native African cultures and customs. Divided into fiction and nonfiction.

BAKER, AUGUSTA. "Guidelines for Black Books: An Open Letter to Juvenile Editors." *Publishers' Weekly*, v. 196 (July 14, 1969), pp. 131–133. The Coordinator of the Office of Children's Services in the New York Public Library establishes criteria to be used by juvenile editors in the publishing of chilren's books about blacks.

BANKS, JAMES A. "Developing Racial Tolerance with Literature on the Black Inner City." *Social Education*, v. 34 (May 1970), pp. 549–552. Discusses the use of 16 children's books by or about blacks in the inner city school room to help encourage black pride and self-respect.

BIRTHA, JESSIE M. "Portrayal of the Black in Children's Literature." *Pennsylvania Library Association Bul-*

*letin*, v. 24 (July 1969), pp. 187–197. The Children's Book Selection Specialist at the Free Library of Philadelphia discusses some points for the evaluation of books for children that deal with black people.

BRODERICK, DOROTHY M. "Lessons in Leadership; Caricatures of Black People in Recommended Juvenile Fiction Books." *Library Journal*, v. 96 (February 15, 1971), pp. 699–701. Contends librarians must evaluate books by relating them to contemporary issues. Failure to do this in children's books has led to the degradation of minority groups such as the black in children's literature.

COHEN, SOL. "Minority Stereotypes in Children's Literature: The Bobbsey Twins, 1904–1968." *Educational Forum*, v. 34 (November 1969), pp. 119–134. Analyzes the stereotyped blacks found in the popular children's series.

COLBY, JEAN POINDEXTER. "How to Present the Negro in Children's Books." *Top of the News*, v. 21 (April 1965), pp. 191–195. A juvenile editor discusses the pressures she feels keep her from presenting blacks in anything less than totally favorable portraits.

COLES, ROBERT. "What Can We Learn from the Life of Malcolm X?" *Teachers College Record*, v. 67 (May 1966), pp. 564–567. Psychiatrist Coles feels the life of Malcolm X is an illustration of man's ability to grow in spite of seemingly insurmountable odds. Challenges teachers and librarians to be concerned with the lives of their black students.

GELLER, EVELYN. "Aesthetics, Morality, and the Two Cultures." *Library Journal*, v. 95 (October 15, 1970), p. 3581. A comparison of two works that raise the question of speaking for the black experience: *Sounder* by William Armstrong and *Black Folktales* by Julius Lester. Geller contends that the artist has an obligation through his work to sanctify human freedom.

HASLAN, GERALD. "Black and Unknown Bards: American Slavery and Its Literary Tradition." *Review of General Semantics*, v. 25 (September 1968), pp. 411–419. A thoughtful discussion of the oral history of the American slave: expression of desires for freedom, hopelessness, courage, and resignation.

HOPKINS, LEE BENNETT. "Negro Life in Current American Children's Literature." *Bookbird*, v. 6, no. 1 (1968), pp. 12–16. Subdivided into picture books, juvenile fiction, biography, and books about Africa, the article concludes there is a need for children's books to portray the modern black American.

HUNTER, KRISTIN. "The Soul Brothers; Background of a Juvenile." *Publishers' Weekly*, v. 193 (May 27, 1968), pp. 30–31. A black author of the highly acclaimed *The Soul Brothers and Sister Lou* gives some of her reasons for writing the book; stresses the need to confirm the black child's concept of his or her own self-worth.

JOHNSON, EDWINA. "Black History; The Early Childhood Vacuum." *Library Journal*, v. 94 (May 15, 1969), pp. 2057–2058. An excellent article contending that "simply blackening the characters' faces" is not enough. Children's books should present: (1) *Black History*—the record of what black people have created, nurtured, and produced in the past and (2) *Black Culture*—the totality of black people's modes of living.

JOHNSON, GLORIA. "The Fifth Freedom: Presenting the Negro in Books." *Top of the News*, v. 22 (November 1965), pp. 62–63. A school librarian from Pittsburgh contends that blacks have the right to a fifth freedom—freedom from indignities in American society. Urges the establishment of programs to encourage young people to point out the parts of books that seem exaggerated and unfair.

KAY, HELEN. "Black Out of a Negro Child." *Top of the News*, v. 22 (November 1965), pp. 58–61. A response to the Colby article (see above) questioning Colby's acceptance of slavery as all right when the slave had a "good master." Also discusses how Kay's book *Summer to Share* was changed from a black-white relationship to an all-white book.

KOREY, RUTH ANNE. "Children's Literature for Integrated Classes." *Elementary English*, v. 43 (January 1966), pp. 39–42. Suggests representative books for integrated classes in the following areas: picture books, juvenile fiction, biography, and books about Africa.

LARRICK, NANCY. "The All White World of Children's Books." *Saturday Review*, v. 48 (September 11, 1965), p. 64+. Contends that only four-fifths of one percent of books surveyed over a three-year period (1962–1964) contain contemporary black Americans. Presents a depressing look at the lack of realistic black characters in children's books.

MAC CANN, DONNARAE. "Sambo and Sylvester." *Wilson Library Bulletin*, v. 45 (May 1971), pp. 880–881. The author argues that attempts to draw a parallel between the racism in *Little Black Sambo* and the picture of pigs as policemen in *Sylvester and the Magic Pebble* are wrong. While Sambo is racist, Sylvester is by no stretch of the imagination anti-law enforcement.

MILLENDER, DHARATHULA H. "Through a Glass, Darkly." *Library Journal*, v. 92 (December 15, 1967), pp. 4571–4576. A survey of a wide range of books that have portrayed the black in sterotypical ways since the beginning of the century. Looks at the evolving treatment of blacks in relationship to prevailing social trends.

PELLOWSKI, ANNE. "Beyond the Colonial Bias." *Library Journal*, v. 92 (November 15, 1967), pp. 4228–4231. An essay and bibliography concerning the need for books about Africa that not only explain the culture but empathize with it.

PIEZ, ELIZABETH D. "Read to Explore Africa." *Instructor*, v. 79 (April 1970), p. 48. Discusses children's fiction as an excellent introduction to African culture.

ROLLINS, CHARLEMAE. "Progress in Children's Books About Negroes." *Illinois Libraries*, v. 45 (October 1963), pp. 544–546. Rollins states that "great progress has been made in the depiction of Negroes in children's literature." Derogatory words such as "nigger" and "darky" have disappeared from the books as well as the unintelligible dialect to delineate character.

STERLING, DOROTHY. "Soul of Learning." *English Journal*, v. 57 (February 1968), pp. 166–179. A short history of the emergence of the black man in books for children and young adults. Feels that few books honestly present the black experience.

"Take Five, and Add Soul Boss Reading." *Library Journal*, v. 94 (February 15, 1969), pp. 823–834. To emphasize the need for fairer treatment of blacks in children's books, four black children's authors and one black children's artist traveled the west coast during Negro History Week.

TATE, BINNIE. "In House and Out House." *Library Journal*, v. 95 (October 15, 1970), pp. 3595–3598. Good books can help bridge the cultural and social gaps between blacks and whites that society has imposed. A plea to promote a new humanism.

______. "Integrating Culture." *Library Journal*, v. 94 (May 15, 1969), pp. 2053–2056. After three centuries of distortion of, and indifference to, the black American and his African heritage, Tate feels that children's books must play a major role in exploding the myths and racist caricatures of blacks.

THOMPSON, JUDITH, and GLORIA WOODARD. "Black Perspective in Books for Children." *Wilson Library Bulletin*, v. 44 (December 1969), pp. 416–424. While the day of the direct caricature of black people is gone, a less obvious misrepresentation takes place in children's books. In too many "integrated" books the white child still dominates, thus reinforcing the attitude the books are supposed to be trying to dispel.

VIGUERS, RUTH HILL. "A Pinch of This and a Dash of That." *Horn Book*, v. 42 (February 1966), pp. 18–19. Takes issue with Larrick's "All White World of Children's Books" (see above) on the grounds that children are children and race should not matter.

WERNER, JUDY. "Black Pearls and Ebony." *Library Journal*, v. 93 (May 15, 1968), p. 2091. Argues that while honest character representation of the black is important, some stories or books still injure the black child's self-concept through racist symbolism in which white symbolizes good and black bad.

YLVISAKER, MIRIAM. "Our Guilt." *English Journal*, v. 58 (February 1968), pp. 193–195. The point is made that English teachers must take the initiative in introducing books about black people into the curriculum.

## Periodicals

*Crisis*. Crisis Publishing Company, 1790 Broadway, New York, N.Y. 10019. Bimonthly. Official publication of the NAACP. Contains articles and bibliographies of books by or about black people.

*Journal of Negro Education*. Bureau of Educational Research, Howard Univ., Washington, D.C. 20001. Quarterly. Essentially concerned with black Americans but containing more and more material on other minority groups.

*The Negro American Literature Forum*. Indiana State Univ., Terre Haute, Indiana. Quarterly. Good source of current articles, critical reviews, and commentary on works by and about black Americans.

## Dissertations

BINGHAM, JANE MARIE. "A Content Analysis of the Treatment of Negro Characters in Children's Picture Books, 1930–1968." Michigan State Univ., 1970. A total of 1,067 illustrations in 41 books were coded. Bingham concluded that some changes have occurred such as less exaggeration in the eye and lip formations and in body build; a more realistic setting is provided in the later years, and while there was interaction between blacks and whites, there were notable absences.

BRODERICK, DOROTHY MAY. "The Image of the Black in Popular and Recommended American Juvenile Fiction, 1827–1967." Columbia Univ., 1971. Among Broderick's conclusions was the fact that the authors' emphasis in later years on the "we are all alike" theme served to distort and deny the black experience. Most books in the recommended category seemed written to teach white children about black people with very little to offer the black reader.

CARLSON, JULIE ANN. "A Comparison of the Treatment of the Negro in Children's Literature in the Periods 1929–1938 and 1959–1968." Univ. of Connecticut, 1969. Carlson found that a higher percentage of books in the earlier period contained black characters but there was less stereotyping in the later period.

DONAHUE, ELAYNE MEYER. "A Study of the Preference of Negro and White Kindergarten Children for Picture Book Stories Which Feature Negro and White Story Characters." Univ. of Colorado, 1969. The researcher read selected stories to black and white kindergarten children in which one version was presented as being a book about blacks, the other being a book about whites. She concluded that there was no significant difference in preference.

SMALL, ROBERT COLEMAN. "An Analysis and Evaluation of Widely Read Junior Novels with Major Negro Characters." Univ. of Virginia, 1970. Thirty books were analyzed and most were found acceptable in terms of literary style with six earning an overall superior ranking.

# BIBLIOGRAPHY: CHICANOS

## Bibliographies

BLATT, GLORIA. "The Mexican-American in Children's Literature." *Elementary English*, v. 45 (April 1968), pp. 446–451. Contains a list of children's books that treat the Mexican-American fairly. Blatt concludes that children's books are fairer than other media in their treatment of Chicanos.

*Chicano Bibliography; Selected Materials on Americans of Mexican-American Descent*. Sacramento State College Library, 1969. Unannotated bibliography of materials that deal with broad areas: civil rights, education, housing, etc., as they affect Chicanos.

REVELLE, KEITH. *Chicano! A Selected Bibiliography by and About Mexico and Mexican Americans.* 1969. Order from: Latin American Library, Oakland Public Library, 1457 Fruitvale Avenue, Oakland, California 94601. An annotated list of books, newspapers, and magazines concerned with Chicanos.

### Books

BURMA, JOHN H. *Mexican-Americans in the United States; A Reader.* Schenkman Publishing, 1970. (Distributed by Harper.) Excellent collection of articles, divided by topic. Two major areas covered that are of particular importance for librarians and teachers concern "Education" and "Acculturation and Assimilation."

HELLER, CELIA S. *Mexican-American Youth: Forgotten Youth at the Crossroads.* Random, 1966. Covers all aspects of Mexican-American culture. Section Four, "The School Experience," should concern teachers and librarians.

MANUEL, HERSCHEL T. *Spanish-Speaking Children of the Southwest.* Univ. of Texas Pr., 1965. Scholarly but readable overview of the interlocking problems facing the Mexican-Americans. Specially important for educators is Chapter 11, "The Problem of Language."

ROBINSON, CECIL. *With the Ears of Strangers; the Mexican in American Literature.* Univ. of Arizona Pr., 1963. While not concerned with children's books, this scholarly work can help the reader understand the distortions and biases that are transmitted through books and can provide a model for the analysis of juvenile materials.

### Articles

GEREZ, TONI DE. "Three Times Lonely: The Plight of the Mexican Child in the American Southwest." *Horn Book,* v. 46 (February 1970), pp. 66–73. Contends the lonely existence of the Mexican-American child is a challenge to librarians to select the books and poems of the sort that will appeal to the Spanish-speaking child.

ORTEGO, PHILIP D. "Schools for Mexican-Americans: Between Two Cultures." *Saturday Review,* v. 54 (April 17, 1971), pp. 62+. A superb overview of the problems facing Mexican-Americans in Anglo schools. A strong plea for bilingual education plus recognition of the historical and cultural heritage of the Chicanos.

TREJO, ARNULFO D. "Library Needs for the Spanish-Speaking." *ALA Bulletin,* v. 63 (September 1969), pp. 1077–1081. Outlines the problems of Mexican-Americans in the schools—notably a language barrier and the task of acculturation. Schools and libraries can help by providing materials in Spanish and by recognizing the validity of bilingual culture.

*Wilson Library Bulletin,* v. 44 (March 1970). Except for "Regular Features," the entire issue is devoted to the theme "Libraries and the Spanish-Speaking." The usual fine job one has come to expect from this magazine.

### Periodical

*Aztalan: Chicano Journal of the Social Sciences.* Mexican-American Culture Center, Univ. of Southern California, Los Angeles, California 90024. The journal has already carried articles on the treatment of Mexican-Americans in elementary and secondary school textbooks and can be expected to concern itself with trade books at some point in the future.

## BIBLIOGRAPHY: NATIVE AMERICANS

### Bibliographies

HOYT, ANNE K. *Bibliography of the Cherokees.* South Central Regional Education Laboratory, Little Rock, Arkansas, 1968. Lists books, government documents, and periodical articles about Cherokee life. Also has an extensive section devoted to Cherokee life as depicted in children's books.

NEWMAN, KILLIAN, ed. *A Preliminary Bibliography of Selected Children's Books About Indians.* Assoc. on American Indian Affairs, 1969. A selected list of 63 children's books about Indians reviewed by American Indians.

OLSEN, DIANE. *Indians in Literature, A Selected Annotated Bibliography for Children.* Univ. of Minnesota, 1964. Lists children's books in the following categories: (1) biography and fictionalized biography, (2) lore and legend, (3) stories and novels, and (4) general information.

University of Minnesota; Library Services Institute for Minnesota Indians. *American Indians; An Annotated Bibliography of Selected Library Resources.* Univ. of Minnesota, 1970. Lists resources for elementary and secondary schools. Contains a section devoted to children's fiction and a list of Indian periodicals.

### Books

American Indian Historical Society. *Textbooks and the American Indian,* 1970. Order from The Indian Historian, 1451 Masonic Avenue, San Francisco, California 94117. While concerned with textbooks, the volume has implications for trade books as well. The first chapters are especially important and Chapter III, "The General Criteria," can be applied to any medium.

CAHN, EDGAR S. *Our Brother's Keeper: The Indian in*

*White America.* A New Community Press Book, 1969. (Distributed by World Publishing, Cleveland, Ohio.) A searing indictment of white America's treatment of the country's native inhabitants. The chapter "Education as War" will appall readers who care about children.

ULLOM, JUDITH C., ed. *Folklore of North American Indians; An Annotated Bibliography.* Library of Congress, 1969. Lists historical source material and anthologies of American Indian folktales for adults and children. Divided by geographical areas: Woodland, Eskimo, MacKensie, etc. Children's editions are noted.

### Articles

CHARLES, C. M. "A Science-Mythology Relationship Among Indians." *Journal of Educational Research,* v. 57 (January 1964), pp. 261–264. An interesting study in which Charles determined that a major reason Indian children do not do well in science is because the scientific information comes in conflict with the value-beliefs basic to their culture. The use of Anglo norms will not do; the cultural barrier is too strong.

FISHER, FRANK L. "Influences of Reading and Discussion on the Attitudes of Fifth Graders Toward American Indians." *Journal of Educational Research,* v. 62 (November 1968). Establishes that selected readings on the American Indian could influence a more positive attitude toward the Indian when combined with discussion.

FUCHS, ESTELLE. "American Indian Education: Time to Redeem an Old Promise." *Saturday Review,* v. 53 (January 24, 1970), pp. 54+. A brief but vital overview of Indian education in the United States. The author notes how the white man grouped all Native Americans as "Indians," ignoring tribal differences. The emphasis on destroying Indian culture is examined and a plea is made for recognition of the sound values inherent in Indian life.

WELSH, W. BRUCE. "The American Indian (A Stifled Minority)." *Journal of Negro Education,* v. 38 (Summer 1969), pp. 242–246. A Bureau of Indian Affairs official makes a biting condemnation of past treatment of the Indian but recognizes that to talk of an "Indian Nation" is unrealistic. What is needed is an adequate program of education that recognizes Indian character while preparing Indians for life in the modern world.

### Dissertations

NAPIER, GEORGIA PIERCE. "A Study of the North American Indian Character in Twenty Selected Children's Books." Univ. of Arkansas, 1970. One of Napier's conclusions is that the North American Indian character is seldom portrayed in contemporary settings. The implications of this finding are important for teachers and librarians.

## BIBLIOGRAPHY: WOMEN

### Bibliography

Feminists on Children's Media. *Little Miss Muffet Fights Back; Recommended Non-Sexist Books About Girls for Young Readers.* Available from Feminists on Children's Media, P.O. Box 4315, Grand Central Station, New York, N.Y. 10017. A list of books that are not predominantly sexist in nature, although some are not particularly good books.

### Books

LUNDWALL, SAM J. *Science Fiction: What It's All About.* Ace Books, 1971. Chapter 7 is entitled "Women, Robots and Other Peculiarities." Lundwall's point is that while most science fiction is progressive when it comes to the concepts of freedom and equality, the image of women is one of its dark spots. Even when women write the books the image is bad! With science fiction one of the more popular genres with youth, the analysis is important for anyone concerned with the subject.

MILLETT, KATE. *Sexual Politics.* Doubleday, 1970. Essential background reading. While occasionally belaboring or distorting a point, Millett has, on the whole, done a fine job of tracing sexism throughout the "major disciplines" as well as in literary works.

### Articles

Feminists on Children's Literature. "A Feminist Look at Children's Books." *Library Journal,* v. 96 (January 15, 1971), pp. 235–240. A critical look at the roles assigned women in children's books. Four categories are discussed: (1) sexist books, (2) cop-out books, (3) positive images, and (4) especially for girls.

HEYN, LEAH. "Children's Books." *Women: A Journal of Liberation* (Fall 1969), pp. 22–25. Stresses the point that no one is saying a girl shouldn't grow up to be a wife and mother—only that "sex channeling" should be eliminated so that girls have real choices. Heyn feels that children's books can help counteract the image perpetuated by the mass media and expand a girl's freedom of choice.

STAVN, DIANE GERSONI. "The Skirts in Fiction About Boys: A Maxi Mess." *Library Journal,* v. 96 (January 15, 1971), pp. 282–286. An examination of the image of women in popular books for boys. A few bright spots, but mostly the same old picture.

### Periodicals

The two magazines listed below can be expected to pay attention to the role of women in children's books in the future. They are not, as yet, easily available in libraries but should be as interest in the subject matures.

*Everywoman*. 1043 B West Washington Blvd., Venice, California 90291.

*Women: A Journal of Liberation*. 3028 Greenmount Avenue, Baltimore, Maryland 21218.

### Dissertations

GRUBEL, MURIEL WELLY. "A Comparative Analysis and Evaluation of Sex Roles Exemplified in Certain Juvenile Novels About Family Life." New York Univ., 1968. The study analyzed the sex roles in recommended family stories and found there was no statistically significant difference between the sexes in regard to dominance versus passivity, or love versus hate. The study is available from University Microfilms.

KELLY, ROBERT GORDON. "Mother Was a Lady: Strategy and Order in Selected American Children's Periodicals, 1865-1890." Univ. of Iowa, 1970. The period studied was one of great upheaval in American society. The five periodicals analyzed by Kelly offered a portrait of family life and societal values that the social class responsible for the magazines wished children to absorb.

## POPULAR LITERATURE

*Larry N. Landrum and Michael T. Marsden**

Throughout the history of children's literature there has always existed another reading matter, sometimes more widely enjoyed and almost always more widely available than even the best-selling juvenile classics. While it is seldom discussed as literature, it pervades the world of children in the form of comics, Big Little Books, pop-up books, fan and specialized one-issue celebrity magazines, as well as career novels and the formulaic series novels. The scope of reading matter parallels that of adults on many levels, and, of course, the low level of literacy required for many adult magazines opens them to the interest of juvenile readers.

While some of this literature has great appeal to a specialized audience, much of it is truly popular in the sense of being broadly based. More than any other form, it is selected by the children themselves, chosen from racks in drugstores, supermarkets, and newsstands, and traded with other children. Moreover, parents and teachers usually do not share the reading experience as they may with more socially acceptable literature. This is a world of literature which grew up in the semiprivate imagination of children for well over a century. It is a literature full of paradoxes: it is a reasonably accurate index of the prejudices and parochialism of society while it often affects a stilted style and unimpeachable standards of morals and etiquette; it is often at the same time realistic and fantastic; containing large amounts of mystery, gothic, and conspiratorial elements, the fiction rarely leaves unresolved problems. It creates a world steeped in misinformation, half-truths, and improbable standards of behavior, yet it usually remains faithful to the prevailing cultural ideology. In the last third of the nineteenth century, boys' series novels, for example, generally reflected the success ethic, the concern at the turn of the century for regulating competition, and the technical optimism preceding the First World War. In comics, we have seen Superman, whose only weakness was Kryptonite, replaced by Spiderman, the Fantastic Four, and others of the Marvel Group, who are plagued by critical identity problems. These major genres, the juvenile novels and the comic books, form the two central streams of popular literature.

Many of the factors that combined to produce what is often loosely called a mass society were significant in the production of popular children's literature. The invention of stereotype plates and then high capacity presses made it possible by the middle of the nineteenth century to produce large quantities of relatively inexpensive books. Expansion of the railroad system and more and bet-

*Larry N. Landrum and Michael T. Marsden are Associates of the Center for the Study of Popular Culture, Bowling Green University.

ter roads, together with rapid urbanization and the growth of a broad middle class made possible wide distribution and consumption. A more widespread, though often rudimentary, literacy among the young, coupled with a vivid imagination and a thirst for adventure, resulted in an audience ripe for literary hacks as well as for craftsmen.

At the beginning of the nineteenth century there were a number of minor forms of popular literature available to children. The "story papers" and "yellow-covered romances" in America and the "penny dreadfuls" in England supplemented the serialized novels in newspapers and popular adult magazines. Through the 1840s and 1850s Maturin Ballou published *The Weekly Novelette* series, each of which contained one fifth of a novel and sold for four cents a copy. The House of Beadle and Adams began in 1856 to publish the famous dime novels, printing them in lots of sixty or seventy thousand until around the turn of the century, when they began to succumb to the depression and to competition from pulp magazines. The total sales of Beadle and Adams and their four major competitors ran into the tens of millions. Though the readership for dime novels was initially adults, these novels became more and more a juvenile form.

Popular children's literature has endured numerous critics. Though Dr. Bowdler did not begin expurgating texts until 1818, the practice began about forty years earlier and was common by the 1850s. Critics of popular reading matter have included persons and organizations such as Anthony Comstock, the Watch and Ward Society of Boston, and, more recently, the National Office of Decent Literature (NODL).

Competing with the dime novels on a purely juvenile level and at a much lower level of violence and sensationalism were the Oliver Optic novels of William Taylor Adams. Adams combined the didacticism of the primers and Sunday School readers with the adventure of the dime novels and produced what were to be the general guidelines of the boys' and girls' series novels up to the present. Though the stories usually involved incredible plots, the adventure was subservient to the concern with social and moral platitudes. It was Adams who discovered Horatio Alger, Jr. It might be significant that Adams was a schoolteacher and Alger a failed clergyman, but it was Alger who added the prevailing economic and social ideology to the popular juvenile novel. This ideology became the trademark of Alger: be honest, thrifty, and conscientious, and be alert to the opportunity for great wealth that will some day come your way. Alger fostered the ideals of the Gilded Age perhaps better than any other author of children's books, but by the end of the nineteenth century many of these ideals were highly suspect. Boys no longer believed that reality corresponded to Alger's optimism. Rather than face squarely the fact that free enterprise was giving way to the corporations and that boys would likely grow up to become part of the corporate structure rather than free-wheeling individualists, the matter was dropped.

Gilbert Patten and Edward Stratemeyer, who, respectively, created the Merriwells and Rover Boys, dominated the early twentieth century. Stratemeyer quickly formed a syndicate which capitalized on outline plots, characterization, humor, and adventure. The plots were generally presented to salaried or commissioned writers who then filled in background, characterization, and added fifty jokes. Many of the pseudonyms became household names through the years: Laura Lee Hope, Carolyn Keene, Clarence Young, Arthur Winfield, and Frank V. Webster are still recognized by many of the young and the old alike. The Motor Boys, Rover Boys, and Tom Swift series alone had accumulated sales of over sixteen and a half million copies by 1920.

This period also saw the growth of the pulps, magazines printed on newsprint, which contributed to both adult and juvenile markets and competed with such magazines as *St. Nicholas*. The pulps, dime novels, and adventure series provided a stimulus to the traditional children's literature by providing an alternative to the generally dull and didactic fare that was often written *at* children rather than *for* them. Even today the challenge of series novels exists in a muted, but ever present form. Happy Hollisters and the Nancy Drew mysteries still sell very well through children's book clubs and over the counter.

The other major genre of children's popular literature, the comics, is available in several forms in every corner of society. There is perhaps no more pervasive popular art form in America than comics. In his impressive study of the popular arts, *The Unembarrassed Muse*, Russel Nye writes:

> *No popular art, whatever medium, is so pervasive and persistent in American society as the comics. Studies have continuously shown that they reach about half the total population more or less regularly. The comic strip since its beginnings has produced from eight to twelve million drawings, by far the largest body of materials of any popular art.*

The appearance of the "Yellow Kid" on February 16, 1896, in Joseph Pulitzer's *New York World* marked the beginning of the comic strip, one of the staples of an American's reading diet. The average American, after quickly scanning the headlines, heads straight for the comics page in his daily newspaper. From the Katzenjammer Kids, through Little Nemo, Krazy Kat, Gasoline Alley, Little Orphan Annie, Winnie Winkle, Tillie the Toiler, Barney Google, Blondie, Terry and the Pirates, up to Peanuts, we have a dramatic spectrum of the changing reading tastes of the American public, young and old.

Any one of these comic strips would warrant close study by students, who not only would profit from a cultural analysis of America's favorite reading material, but might enjoy preparing it as well!

A distinction needs to be made between the comic strip, as found commonly in newspapers, and the comic book, which was the logical extension of the failing pulp magazine industry. The comic books were aimed essentially at the same audience as the pulp magazines had been, and they enjoyed unparalleled success.

The 1930s saw the emergence of a new publishing enterprise—all in color for a dime. Heroes like Superman, Batman, G. I. Joe, and The Lone Ranger were seen in brightly, but crudely, colored narratives. Mickey Mouse, Donald Duck, and a host of other Walt Disney creations brought to their faithful readers a whole new world of colorful fantasy. In 1950 a funny looking boy and his friends made their first appearance in America's newspapers, and they soon helped their creator to enjoy an unimagined popularity that resulted in the sale of thirty-six million copies of eighteen different Peanuts books between 1963 and 1969. The move from comic strip to comic book (and to animated cartoons) was easily made for popular characters like Donald Duck and sincere Charlie Brown.

The 1960s saw the rise of the more "mature" comics, led by the Marvel Group. A 1971 survey of college America's favorite reading found Marvel's Spiderman and Fantastic Four heading the list. The success of these more sophisticated, and often risqué, publications gave rise in turn to the "underground comics." While underground comics cannot be bought on most neighborhood newsstands, they enjoy immense popularity, are read by all age groups, and have significant influence on younger people. They are best represented by *Zap*, an anti-establishment and blatantly sexual comic book.

What the 1970s will hold for the comic book industry remains to be seen. But the "funnies" are no longer innocuous pastimes. They are a serious part of our culture and are certainly worthy of study. They contain a wealth of information about our culture and, if presented properly, could lead younger students to a more careful and considered awareness of the world around them.

For the concerned educators, both the

juvenile series novels and the comic books present a serious challenge. More children will read *Mad Magazine* in a year than will read the Newbery Medal books in a generation. To ignore these popular forms of literature is to run the risk of leaving unopened a wide door into the minds of the adolescent of the 1970s. To begin to learn how to use these materials is to work from what the students are most familiar with, and to build from there is to proceed in the proper direction.

## SUGGESTED RESEARCH NEEDS

1. What are the ideals of femininity and masculinity as presented in juvenile series books? Compare and contrast two heroines or two heroes from different series.

2. What kinds of cultural stereotypes run through either a particular girls' series or a particular boys' series? For example, what are the attitudes toward immigrant national groups, racial minorities, and occupational stereotypes?

3. The argument has been raised many times before that comics lead to deviant behavior in adolescents and children. Is there any solid research evidence to support this view?

4. Taking a particular comic strip that is nationally syndicated, analyze it for its cultural stereotypes.

5. Does comic book reading help or hinder the reading ability of children and adolescents?

6. How many adults read comic books? Why do they read comic books and how much else do they read?

7. What impact have the "underground" comics had on young people? Have they, in many ways, replaced older forms of pornography?

8. Why is it that the counter-culture uses the comic strip form very heavily to make its social and sexual comments? What is it about the medium of the comic strip that allows this freedom of expression?

9. How much current social and political knowledge must a reader have to fully enjoy *Mad Magazine*, or any of the other comics that are basically satiric?

## BIBLIOGRAPHY

### Bibliography

WHITE, DAVID MANNING. *The Comic Strip in America: A Bibliography*. Boston Univ. School of Public Relations and Communication, 1961. A good checklist of criticism through about 1959. The 450 items include a short list of theses and dissertations on the subject.

### Books

BECKER, STEPHEN. *Comic Art in America: A Social History of the Funnies, the Political Cartoons, Magazine Humor, Sporting Cartoons, and Animated Cartoons*. Simon, 1959.

BERGER, ARTHUR A. *Li'l Abner: A Study in American Satire*. Twayne Publishers, 1970. A perceptive study of Al Capp and his comic art.

COUPERIE, PIERRE, MAURICE HORN, et al. *A History of the Comic Strip*. Crown Publishers, 1968. Probably the best analytical study of the comics available in print. Written with wit and sympathy as well as insight, this history illustrates the key developments in the genre.

CRAVEN, THOMAS, ed., assisted by Florence and Sydney Weiss. *Cartoon Cavalcade*. Simon, 1943. An early, though valuable, study of the comics.

DILLE, ROBERT C., ed. *The Collected Works of Buck Rogers in the 25th Century*. Chelsea House Publishers, 1969. Color and black-and-white reproductions of much of the famous strip which began in 1928. Ray Bradbury contributes a brief introduction to this invaluable collection.

FEIFFER, JULES. *The Great Comic Book Heroes*. Dial, 1965. A nostalgic but important celebration of the origins of the superheroes. Feiffer is able to contribute greatly to the understanding of youthful fascination with comics.

GOODSTONE, TONY. *The Pulps: Fifty Years of American Pop Culture*. Chelsea House Publishers, 1970. Selections and illustrations, together with brief introductory comments to thematically arranged sections.

GRAY, HAROLD. *Arf! The Life and Hard Times of Little Orphan Annie, 1935–1945*. Arlington House, 1970. Introduction by Al Capp. Black-and-white reproductions of ten years of the famous weekly strip which began in 1924 and has continued until today.

GRUBER, FRANK. *Horatio Alger, Jr.: A Biography and Bibliography.* Printed by Grover Jones Pr., 1961. Contains a useful bibliography and a brief biographical sketch which corrects some of the errors of earlier biographies.

———. *The Pulp Jungle.* Sherbourne Pr., 1967. The autobiography of one of the more prolific of the pulp writers. The book gives something of the flavor of the pulp world of the thirties.

HART, J. D. *The Popular Book: A History of America's Literary Taste.* Oxford, 1950. Useful background book on the popular novel, though little on juvenile fiction as such.

HUDSON, HARRY K. *A Bibliography of Hard-cover Boys' Books.* Clearwater, Florida: Privately Printed, c1965. Lists the series of 45 publishers from the period 1900–1950. A valuable source of information.

LUPOFF, DICK, and DON THOMPSON, eds. *All in Color for a Dime.* Arlington House, 1970. Useful for its illustrations, but lacks new information on the artists in the industry.

MOTT, FRANK LUTHER. *Golden Multitudes: The Story of Best Sellers in the United States.* Macmillan, 1947. Covers the same area as Hart, but with a slightly different perspective.

MURRELL, WILLIAM. *A History of American Graphic Humor, 1865–1938.* Whitney Museum of American Art, 1938. A study of humorous art, especially political and satirical cartoons. Well illustrated in black and white.

NYE, RUSSEL B. *The Unembarrassed Muse: The Popular Arts in America.* Dial, 1970. Essential reading for any student or teacher who wishes to understand America's popular arts. A historical approach, includes sections on most popular art forms, placing them in their social and cultural contexts.

O'CONNOR, GERARD. "The Hardy Boys Revisited: A Study in Prejudice," in Browne, Landrum, and Bottorff, eds. *Challenges in American Culture.* The Popular Pr., 1970. Discusses the prejudicial stereotypes in the first edition and the generally futile attempts at later revision.

PERRY, GEORGE, and ALAN ALDRIDGE. *The Penguin Book of Comics.* Penguin Books, 1967. A standard social history of the comics in England and America. Contains information not found elsewhere, but lacks the technical demonstration of the Couperie history.

ROSENBERG, BERNARD, and DAVID MANNING WHITE, eds. *Mass Culture: The Popular Arts in America.* Glencoe, 1957. Now somewhat dated, this anthology contains useful insights by a variety of writers on the comics and popular literature. The introduction contains a debate between the editors over the value of the popular arts.

SHERIDAN, MARTIN. *Comics and Their Creators; Life Stories of American Cartoonists.* Hale, Cushman, and Flint, 1942. Presents 80 comic strips, arranged by categories. Includes a brief biographical sketch of the artist, as well as an analysis of each strip. Illustrated with examples.

SMITH, HENRY NASH. *Virgin Land.* Harvard Univ. Pr., 1950. Contains a chapter on the contribution of the dime novel to popular myth of the West.

STEDMAN, RAYMOND WILLIAM. *The Serials: Suspense and Drama by Installment.* Univ. of Oklahoma Pr., 1971. A thorough study of the serials as found in comics, movies, radio, and television. Important for its discussion of the comic strips' influence on the evolution of subsequent serial forms.

STEELE, ELIZABETH. "Mrs. Johnston's *Little Colonel*," in Browne, Landrum, and Bottorff, eds. *Challenges in American Culture.* The Popular Pr., 1970. A perceptive essay about the cultural values embodied in a very popular book.

WAUGH, COULTON. *The Comics.* Macmillan, 1947. An illustrated history of cartoons from the 1890s to the 1940s, including both comic strips and comic books.

WERTHAM, FREDERIC. *Seduction of the Innocent.* Rinehart, 1954. The classic condemnation of comics by a practicing psychiatrist. Though very influential during the middle fifties, the book is now seen as impressionistic and opinionated, rather than scientifically accurate.

WHITE, DAVID MANNING, and ROBERT H. ABEL, eds. *The Funnies: An American Idiom.* Macmillan, 1963. A useful collection of essays by those who write the comics as well as those who read them. Essays by Al Capp, Allen Saunders, and Walt Kelley are included.

## Articles

BECKMAN, MARGARET. "Why Not the Bobbsey Twins?" *Library Journal,* v. 89 (November 15, 1964), pp. 4612–4613+. Presents the reasons frequently given for excluding series fiction, such as Nancy Drew and the Hardy Boys, from school and public library collections for children.

BERGER, ARTHUR A. "Comics and Culture." *Journal of Popular Culture,* v. 5 (Summer 1971), pp. 164–178. An informal and informative analysis of the important role the comics play in our culture.

———. "Peanuts: An American Pastoral." *Journal of Popular Culture,* v. 3 (Summer 1969), pp. 1–8. An informal biographical sketch of Charles Schulz and his characters, with useful insights into their popularity and effectiveness.

BRAUN, SAUL. "Shazam! Here Comes Captain Relevant." *The New York Times Magazine* (May 2, 1971), pp. 32+. Discusses the growing social and environmental concern in the comic strips and especially the comic books, and the state of the industry.

CAWELTI, JOHN G. "The Concept of Formula in the Study of Popular Literature." *Journal of Popular Culture,* v. 3 (Winter 1969), pp. 381–390. A major contribution to the analysis of popular literature which should be valuable to the study of children's literature.

FAUST, WOLFGANG MAX (with technical assistance

from R. Baird Shuman). "Comics and How to Read Them." *Journal of Popular Culture*, v. 5 (Summer 1971), pp. 195–202. Discusses the problems of seriously analyzing comics and suggests methods.

"For It Was Indeed He." *Fortune Magazine*, v. 9 (April 1934), pp. 86+. Remains one of the primary sources for information about the Stratemeyer syndicate and its competitors.

LATIMER, D. A. "If Harvey Kurtzman Had Written 'Snow White,' the Dwarfs Would Have Gotten Her." *The Paperback Magazine*, No. 3, pp. 135–151. Brief biographical sketch of one of the most influential cartoonists and editors in the genre. Shows Kurtzman's struggle for expression of his ideas in a milieu of vague standards.

MIRA, EDUARD J. "Notes on a Comparative Analysis of American and Spanish Comic Books." *Journal of Popular Culture*, v. 5 (Summer 1971), pp. 203–220. An interesting comparison of American comic book heroes in Spain.

MULHAUSER, FREDERICK V. "A Juvenile View of the Empire: G. M. Fenn." *Journal of Popular Culture*, v. 2 (Winter 1969), pp. 410–424. A study of the imperialist ideology of a popular British writer of juveniles during the latter third of the nineteenth century.

PEKAR, HARVEY. "Rapping About Cartoonists, Particularly Robert Crumb." *Journal of Popular Culture*, v. 3 (Spring 1970), pp. 677–688. A valuable article for its information about the most influential of underground comic artists.

PRAEGER, ARTHUR. "The Secret of Nancy Drew." *Saturday Review*, v. 52 (January 25, 1969), pp. 18–19+. How Nancy Drew retains popularity after forty years.

RACKIN, DONALD. "Corrective Laughter: Carroll's *Alice* and Popular Children's Literature." *Journal of Popular Culture*, v. 1 (Winter 1967), pp. 243–255. Concerns the development of a popular nondidactic, but socially satirical, children's literature which culminated in Carroll's *Alice*.

SADLER, A. W. "The Love Comics and American Popular Culture." *American Quarterly*, v. 16 (Fall 1964), pp. 486–490. Notes persistence of "Puritan" or Algerine moralism in girls' "romance" magazines, specifically in their "integration of virtue with economic reward."

SAGARIN, EDWARD. "The Deviant in the Comic Strip: The Case of Barney Google." *Journal of Popular Culture*, v. 5 (Summer 1971), pp. 179–194. Presents the case of the deviant side of one of America's best-loved cartoon characters.

SONENSCHEIN, DAVID. "Love and Sex in Romance Magazines." *Journal of Popular Culture*, v. 4 (Fall 1970), pp. 398–409. Points up the themes of pulp romances and suggests the extent of their juvenile readership.

YOUNG, JR., WILLIAM H. "The Serious Funnies: Adventure Comics During the Depression, 1929–1938." *Journal of Popular Culture*, v. 3 (Winter 1969), pp. 404–427. An important study of the way in which the comic strips avoided the important social and economic issues during the depression while supporting threatened family structures.

## SERIES BOOKS

*Kathleen Coleman**

As can be seen by the attached bibliography, not a great quantity has been written about publishers' series books, although periodically the subject does arise. The first article in chronological order is Hollowell's, and she reviews much of what had been written before that time. Yet for all the scarcity of articles, the topic is an important one and offers many possibilities for research projects from term papers to dissertations.

Most writers on the subject are agreed that there are too many series and too many titles within each series. They also recognize that standardized format allows for the production of reasonably inexpensive books and that children do seem to be attracted to series titles. So, we might add, do librarians.

Within each series there are some excellent titles and some very poor ones; the average seems to be plain mediocrity. The major problem that arises in relationship to series books is that children become addicted to them and librarians and reviewers cease to evaluate them as individual titles. For children, the result may well be a stultifying effect upon their mental growth. In short, they become lazy since familiarity with a series reaches the point where the reader encounters few surprises and no obstacles. A library collection heavily weighted with series titles has probably sacrificed adding the superior individual books since all budgets are limited and money spent on one type of material is no longer available for other purchases.

One objection made to series books is that authors are often assigned a topic by the series editor. The assumption underlying this objection is that authors cannot write well upon assignment. This seems unrealistic as well as insulting to the authors.

A more important objection has to do

*Kathleen Coleman is a graduate student at The Library School, University of Wisconsin, Madison.

with "scratching the bottom of the barrel." After a series is initiated and the first titles have proved successful (the first titles are almost always superior in order to establish the reputation of the series), the mad search begins to find topics to keep the series going. This is not entirely bad: having polished off Washington, Jefferson, Lincoln, the great generals, and a few scientists, a biographical series may find gold in the lives of lesser known men who lived equally fascinating lives.

One point seldom made is that series exist at all levels of readability. For very young readers, for example, there are "The True Books" and the "I Want to Be" titles; at the intermediate level there are "The First Books" and "The Real Books," while for older readers, there are "The Landmark Books" and "The Land and People" series.

## SUGGESTED RESEARCH NEEDS

1. What would be the child's overall impression of George Washington if he read all the titles in all the series that treated his life?
2. In a similar vein, does the child's concept of science grow in maturity if he pursues a topic throughout the many series?
3. What do children really like about series titles?
4. Does reading a little about a subject in a series title lead the child to other books on the subject?
5. Despite similar format, do titles within a series actually represent a wide range of reading levels and content maturity?
6. It is often said that series books are created as "curriculum enrichment" tools. How many of the titles in a particular series are geared to the grade level in which the topic is emphasized and answer the kinds of questions teachers are most likely to ask?
7. Are controversial subjects treated in series titles and if so, in what ways?
8. How are minority groups treated in series books? For example, in Putnam's "Let's Go to" titles, are all the places visited (excepting foreign countries) depicted as white middle class?
9. Are series titles covering foreign countries and scientific subjects kept up-to-date?
10. Is there a difference in literary quality between the books an established author writes for a series and those he writes as individual titles?

## BIBLIOGRAPHY

### Magazine Articles

CARUBA, ALAN. "Peter Rabbit Is Alive and Well—Despite His Age." *Publishers' Weekly*, v. 198 (July 13, 1970), pp. 82–84. Addressed to the publisher, this article criticizes many existing series, suggesting that editors research the market, advertise more, and publish less.

CLARKE, MARJORIE. "Why Publish Series Books?" *The Calendar*, v. 30, no. 3 (September-December 1971). An editor explains in the Children's Book Council publication the editorial decisions involved in publishing series titles. Brief but highly informative.

GRANNIS, C. B. "Series Books—Treasures in the Jungle?" *Publishers' Weekly*, v. 193 (February 26, 1968), p. 142. Discusses the advantages and disadvantages of nonfiction book series for children, primarily from the publisher's viewpoint.

HOLLOWELL, LILLIAN. "Series in Children's Books." *Wilson Library Bulletin*, v. 27 (May 1953), pp. 736–738. Discusses disadvantages of the juvenile nonfiction series. In particular, individual books of greater merit may be neglected in favor of series purchases.

LARRICK, NANCY. "Series Defended." *Library Journal*, v. 79 (January 1, 1954), p. 6. Protests outright condemnation of book series by librarians and reviewers.

"The 'Series Books.'" *South Dakota Library Bulletin*, v. 40 (January-March 1954), pp. 3–4. (Taken from *Vermont Library Bulletin*, December 1953.) Points out general strengths and weaknesses in the many nonfiction juvenile series offered to schools and libraries since 1950. While they offer cost advantages, they should not be regarded as a shortcut to collection building.

SILL, HELEN C. "Please, Sir, I Want Some More." *Wilson Library Bulletin*, v. 29 (November, 1954), pp. 236–239. Emphasizes the good points of series publications—they provide much information at relatively low cost. A useful annotated list gives price, age level, indication of content, and an evaluation for representative juvenile series.

"Which Children's Books in Series are Suitable for Library Purchase?" *North Country Libraries*, v. 7, no. 5 (September-October 1964), pp. 8–9. Describes three types of juvenile series—publishers' series, subject series, and author series—and suggests series acquisitions policies for libraries.

Workshop on Problems of Book Selection for Children. "Series, Both Factual and Fictional." *Drexel Library Quarterly*, v. 2 (January 1966), pp. 52–57. Summary of a group discussion. Presents objections to series books, and lists criteria for judging both fiction and nonfiction series titles.

## TELEVISION: THE IMPACT AND INFLUENCE OF ANOTHER MEDIUM

*Caroline Feller**

Today, television is so much a part of our lives and the lives of our children that we tend to forget that it was not common in American homes until 1947. It didn't take long, however, for television signals to cover the nation. So pervasive is the television set that now ninety-six percent of the total United States population have sets in their homes. Put another way, 40,000,000 preschool and grade-school children have access to the medium. The set is not just another piece of furniture.

The average American child of sixteen has spent as much time watching television as he or she has spent in attending formal classes in school. Wilbur Schramm and his associates found in their study *Television in the Lives of Our Children* (1961) that the three-year-old averages about forty-five minutes a day watching television. At the age of five or six, he spends about two hours a day in front of the set. Televiewing time slowly increases until the age of twelve or thirteen, when the average child spends three hours a day watching television. Similar findings have been reported by Paul Witty in his 1949–1965 annual surveys of children's television viewing habits. Witty found a weekly average of seventeen hours of televiewing in grade two and twenty-eight hours in grade six. By grades seven and eight, the figure drops to eighteen and continues to decrease throughout the teen-age years. Apparently this is not a cultural pattern since Himmelweit's 1958 English study, *TV and the Child*, and Maletzke's 1959 German study, *Television in the Life of Youth*, found similar viewing patterns for English and German youth.

The researchers have offered several reasons for this extensive viewing. Television provides both escape from and information about the real world. Himmelweit says that television offers "escape from everyday demands with lightheadedness, glamour and romance, and permits the child to identify himself with different romantic heroes." Schramm finds that one major appeal of television is the passive pleasure of being entertained, but he also points out that the acquisition of incidental information is another factor in televiewing's appeal. Maccoby, in an article entitled "Why Do Children Watch Television?" suggests that the child views different programs to satisfy some of his or her personal needs.

One of the most important questions for a teacher is the relationship between learning and television viewing. There is uncertainty among the researchers as to the amount and quality of knowledge that can be gained from televiewing, but most share the opinion that some learning does occur. They generally accept Charles Winick's view that incidental learning is fairly considerable. Some of the uncertainty on this point arises from the fact that television is only one of many undifferentiated and unmeasured formal and informal education influences in a child's life. Researchers do agree that television is one of the most important of these influences on youth. Schramm sums up his view of the impact of television upon learning this way:

*Any experience that commands so large a part of the child's time, absorbs and involves him so deeply, and leads him to identify as much as it*

*Caroline Feller is Assistant Professor of Librarianship, School of Librarianship, University of Oregon, Eugene.

*does must play some part in shaping the kind of child who comes to school, his interests, the breadth of his world, his status figures, his vocabulary, his ability to learn from pictures and the spoken word, and his capacity for being interested or bored.*

It is important that the parent and the professional working with children have some understanding of this important element in the child's life. The television industry has several facets to be considered.

## Commercial Television

The Federal Communications Commission, FCC, is the federal government agency that regulates broadcast station licensing. It is concerned with the technical aspects of broadcasting such as the broadcast frequency and equipment. The FCC is not directly concerned with individual program content, but it does have an interest in seeing that networks and local stations provide overall balanced programming, reflecting a wide range of opinions. It can, and does, occasionally order a station to provide equal time for opposing views. For example, when cigarette commercials were so much a part of television, it was the FCC that opened the channels to antismoking ads.

Responsibility for the content of individual programs rests primarily with the networks and the local stations, although financial considerations mean that sponsors also play a large part in determining content. Commercial television, which comprises the bulk of American broadcasting, is largely supported by advertisers whose goal is to reach as many buyers as possible. The broad appeal required by national advertising may be one of the reasons for the sometimes pallid program fare, characterized at one point by former FCC chairman Newton Minnow as the "vast wasteland."

This wide appeal may be required by the economics of the industry. In pretelevision days, radio programs were often sponsored by an individual advertiser, but television programs are more likely to use the "magazine format," in which several sponsors join together to support portions of programs on this extremely expensive medium. An average half-hour children's cartoon show, for example, may cost $10,000, and prime time segments are even more costly. While advertisers account for the bulk of commercial television programs, either the networks or local stations may sponsor specials that are called "sustaining programs." In order to keep the viewing public oriented toward commercials, such programs will often contain public service announcements in lieu of the standard commercial that is selling a product.

Most commercial children's programming is of undistinguished quality, but undistinguished quality is not unique to television. Books purchased for children in school and public libraries are selected with more care than are the individual programs which a child may watch. Yet many children's books of below average quality, such as the perennially popular books in the Nancy Drew and Bobbsey Twins series, are selected by children.

Commercial programmers are aware of the need for higher quality for children's programming, and each network has attempted to offer some special programs. Such programs include ABC's *Discovery*, which often had ratings equaling the Saturday morning cartoons. The *CBS Children's Hour* included the plays *J. T.* by Jane Wagner and *Toby* by Art Wallace. NBC offered the award-winning *Children's Theatre* started by George Heinemann, the network's director of public affairs broadcasting. Heinemann was helped in his choice of productions by the National Education Association, the American Library Association, and the Children's Television Workshop. The *Children's Theatre* has produced live action dramas, such as *Stuart Little, The Enormous Egg*, and *Little Women*. In addition to programs aimed specifically at children, some of the adult-oriented programs also have large audiences among young viewers.

### Educational Television

The phrase "educational television" has several meanings. It is most often used to describe the channels set aside for noncommercial television, featuring productions by National Educational Television. NET is a nonprofit organization established to create and produce major educational programs with financial assistance from government and private grants.

Educational television has never sought to appeal to the broad segment commercial television attempts to reach. While this narrower scope allows for more specialized programming, it also tends to isolate the system because people are not accustomed to tuning in to the educational channels. In addition, the programs are less lavishly produced, the broadcast hours are limited, and schedules are sometimes less predominately displayed. However, NET did manage to capture a sizable audience and considerable publicity with *The Forsyte Saga*, imported from England.

Several long-run children's programs have been offered on educational television. *Mister Rogers' Neighborhood* and *The Friendly Giant* are aimed at preschoolers. Both programs feature books. *What's New* features a mixture of travel, history, and science. Undoubtedly, the greatest single event in either commercial or educational children's programming has been *Sesame Street*, a presentation of the Children's Television Workshop under the direction of Joan Ganz Cooney. This hour-long, daily presentation was originally developed in 1969 to provide an educational opportunity for culturally deprived preschool children, paralleling the Head Start program. Within six months of its first season, the Nielsen rating survey indicated that over half of America's twelve million three- to five-year-olds had seen the program. *Sesame Street* attempts to make learning fun. After only two seasons on the air, it became an instant national institution supported by parents, teachers, and community organizations, complete with an intensive publicity campaign and the establishment of home viewing centers. One of the major results of the popular acceptance of *Sesame Street* may be a new awareness by television producers of the success that can result from high quality programming. The program has also helped bring attention to the other programs on the educational channels.

The success of *Sesame Street* led the Children's Television Workshop to develop a similar program for the primary grades, *Electric Company*. Using the same combination of animation, abstract visual aids, and music that has made *Sesame Street* a success, the *Electric Company* focuses on word building, word usage, and letter sounds.

There are other types of educational television such as closed circuit instructional television which are receiving attention in public institutions. More and more school systems are installing their own closed circuit television systems. Some schools even produce their own shows.

Another type of educational television is provided by the video-tape machine that can be utilized in a fashion similar to tape recorders, with tapes being available from regional or national distributors. These machines are becoming economically feasible for all school districts. They can be used to record student performances, analyze a teacher's techniques, and record guest speakers' programs for future use. It is becoming more common for a school district to hire a "television teacher" whose sole responsibility is to produce a series of special instructional programs.

While still too expensive for home use, there is little question that the future will see video-tape machines within the price range of large numbers of people. New VTR (video-tape recording) processes will make available tapes that can be stored and used very much like books, films, and audio-tape recordings. These video-tapes may be either reel-to-reel or cassette. Schools and libraries will undoubtedly be asked to purchase video-tapes, enabling home users to choose from a wide selection of television programs.

### The Researcher

Although television seems to be a major influence in our society, little conclusive research has been done recently to examine the viewer's relationship with television. Major research on children and television has been largely confined to two areas. The first type, such as the Schramm and Himmelweit studies, deals with the general habits of and nature of the viewers. The second type deals with effects of specific kinds of programs on learning and on the reactions of children, particularly to violence. In this connection major experiments and studies have been conducted to determine the effects of television violence on children.

Psychologists differ greatly in the interpretations of experiments attempting to determine a relationship between violence on TV and children's behavior. Two major schools of thought have developed. The "chain-of-ideas" researchers, such as Dr. Ralph Garry of Boston University, claim that a child follows the plot of a play or series and retains the major ideas presented. Thus, for example, the violent incident is put into its larger program context. On the other side are the "perceptual-stimulus" researchers, represented by Dr. Albert Bandura of Stanford University, who claim that it is isolated violent action that may trigger undesirable behavior. Viewing a violent incident may lead to violent acts. Other professionals, such as sociologist Wilbur Schramm, believe that most normal children could not be "triggered" by violence to aggressive behavior.

Basic to the violence question may be the whole question of learning from television. That children do learn from television seems to be evident, but exactly *what* they learn and *how* they learn are areas requiring much greater research efforts.

### The Parent

Many parents are greatly concerned with their children's TV viewing habits. They are aware that their children could use their leisure time to greater advantage than by unselective television viewing. Parents often question whether they should limit viewing time and monitor programs so that their children may receive the maximum benefits from their viewing. The answer is not clear. According to some research, the child with the higher IQ may watch even more television than other children simply because he or she does more of everything (reading, viewing, listening) than the slower child. As in many other areas of behavior, children tend to follow the lead of their parents. If parents are consistent viewers, the child will tend to follow their pattern.

One handicap is the shortage of advance critical commentary available to parents. Television criticism in newspapers is not as highly developed as book reviews, for example, and where it is of high quality, it is dealing with shows already seen. Television critics for children's programming are even more scarce.

Parents may wish to use television experiences as the basis for related activities. Programs featuring animals could be the background for a visit to a zoo, or vice versa. Family-centered programs may be an occasion for family viewing with family discussion after the program. A visit to a local broadcast station may be an enjoyable experience.

Some television related publications may be useful. Certain programs, such as *Sesame Street*, have issued magazines to be used with the program. Some states provide guides to educational television programs.

With advance notice of special programs, background reading and discussion during the telecast may make viewing a more meaningful experience.

### The Teacher

Teachers often wish to help educate the child to profit from television. If the teacher can recommend some of the more outstanding programs, it will not only help develop the student's taste, but it will also indirectly encourage the stations and networks to produce more quality programs. Robert Lewis Shayon, a critic, frequently laments the unconcerned teacher who ignores television, which is such a large part of his students' lives. He urges a better understanding of the power of television and suggests that teachers and parents should work together to make television a contributing force in teaching.

For some purposes, even the less distinguished productions can be used by a teacher. As early as elementary school, children can be taught the basic research process known as content analysis. For example, the examination of male-female roles in current television offerings should be of interest to children. Popular programs are often quite revealing. It might be found, for instance, that the programs they are watching are male dominated, both in actors used and activities presented. Cartoons may tend to show the helpless female being rescued by men who succeed solely by physical prowess. *The Flintstones*, a popular long-run cartoon series, features the typical situation comedy family: a blustering, ineffectual, stereotyped husband and a stereotyped scheming wife. Values that might be observed from a critical viewing of such shows could be part of a discussion on individual self-awareness, role, and sexuality.

Television viewing need not be unrelated to other activities. Books obviously can be tied in with television. A comparison, for example, between *Heidi* and its television adaptation might be a profitable critical experience. Cartoon shows can be a basis for introducing picture books like Pat Hutchins' *Rosie's Walk*, which has a "cartoon-plot," or one of the John S. Goodall books such as *Shrewbettina's Birthday*, which tells its story entirely in pictures. A show featuring puppets on television can introduce a puppet project. Bil Baird's *The Art of the Puppet* can be an inspiring beginning for such a project. News programs obviously call for nonfiction material concerning foreign countries or war news might be used with such biographies as Gerda Klein's *All But My Life*, or a more whimsical, but revealing story such as Seymour Leichman's *The Boy Who Could Sing Pictures*, an anti-war story.

### New Broadcast Modes

Three areas that offer interesting new possibilities are developing. Two are technical in nature, the third is the result of an FCC ruling limiting network programming to three and one-half hours of the four hours of prime time. The effect of this ruling may be to encourage local stations to develop meaningful programs designed to reach the network audience.

Community Antenna Television Systems (CATV) were developed to aid communities where reception was poor—the antenna delivers clear programs from large cities within its range. Recently, the FCC adopted a regulation requiring CATV systems with more than 3500 subscribers to originate programs to a "significant extent." The systems must be more than relay stations: they must have facilities for local production and presentation of programs.

Subscription television utilizes cables to bring people programs they cannot receive on their regular channels. It is a commercial version of closed circuit television. Again, the FCC has taken a firm stand on what subscription television can do in regard to its programming. It cannot present series type programs with interconnected plots or substantially the same cast of characters, and not more than ninety percent of the programming can consist of feature films and sports.

These new regulatory schemes are of recent development, and their potential for children's programming is yet to be fully explored.

## SUGGESTED RESEARCH NEEDS

Much of what we need to know in this area can only be carried out by large research organizations. The following questions do seem within the scope of teachers and librarians. Some of them simply call for the adult to think through the concepts involved so he can better function; others offer possibilities for research within the schools.

1. Does television viewing keep children from reading or merely provide an activity for nonreaders?

2. Are there children who learn more easily from visual presentations than from print?

3. Has the fact that *Sesame Street* presents an integrated cast influenced the attitudes of preschoolers toward blacks? For preschoolers living in all white communities, the question has one implication; for blacks, it has another.

4. How can schools develop programs that will aid young viewers in acquiring a critical approach to media exposure?

5. If Bandura is correct in stating that *some* youth are susceptible to violence on television, is that justification for eliminating it from all programs?

6. Since commercial television does reflect acceptable American attitudes, how does one interject diversity into its programs?

7. While technically the American public owns the television channels, advertisers seem to control them. How can democratic procedures and free enterprise be reconciled under such conflicting circumstances?

## BIBLIOGRAPHY

### Bibliography

The International Association for Mass Communication Research, Amsterdam. *The Effects of Television on Children and Adolescents.* Paris, France: UNESCO, 1964. Annotated bibliography of research studies from around the world. The introductory essay is important as a summary of the issues as well as the problems involved in trying to measure effects.

### Books and Pamphlets

*Action for Children's Television.* (Text prepared by Evelyn Sarson.) Avon Books, 1971. A report of "the first national symposium on the effect of television programming and advertising on children." An impressive array of speakers, much information, and numerous ideas for parents who wish to keep television under control.

Association for Childhood Education International. *Children and TV: Television's Impact on the Child.* Association for Childhood Education International, 1967. A collection of articles that examine all the important aspects of television in relationship to the child's viewing habits.

BELSON, W. A. *The Impact of Television: Methods and Findings in Program Research.* Archon Books, 1967. A scholarly presentation of research techniques used in England to analyze television's influence.

BENTON, CHARLES W., et al. *Television in Urban Education: Its Application to Major Educational Problems in Sixteen Cities.* Praeger, 1969. The many charts, graphs, and statistics may appear overwhelming, but a wealth of fascinating information can be found in the text.

BERKOWITZ, LEONARD. "Violence in the Mass Media." In *Paris-Stanford Studies in Communication.* Institute for Communication Research, 1962. Antisocial conduct may be aroused in only a small segment of the population predisposed toward such behavior, but unhappily this group does cause harm to innocent bystanders.

BLUEM, A. WILLIAM, and ROGER MANVELL. *Television: The Creative Experience.* Hastings, 1967. A collection of articles covering many aspects of television in England and the United States. While strong on discussing educational TV, there is no mention of children's programs.

Carnegie Commission on Educational Television. *Public Television; A Program for Action.* Harper, 1967. The focus of the Commission's concern is the need for programming that is of importance but "not at the moment appropriate or available for support by advertising."

COLE, BARRY G. *Television: A Selection of Readings from TV Guide Magazine.* Free Pr., 1970. A wide variety of topics, including "Children: What Is TV Doing to Them?"

COSTELLO, LAWRENCE F. *Teach with Television: A Guide to Instructional TV*. 2nd ed. Hastings, 1965. Treats both closed circuit and standard broadcasting for elementary, secondary, and university levels. Discusses how, when, and where to use it; enumerates technical devices useful for production.

FESHBACH, SEYMOUR. *Television and Aggression: An Experimental Field Study*. Jossey-Bass, 1971. The latest research on violence and television.

FRANK, JOSETTE. *Children and TV*. Public Affairs Committee, 1962. For parents and other concerned adults, a discussion of such questions as how much time a child should spend before the set, selecting programs, and sex and violence.

GARRY, RALPH, F. B. RAINSBERRY, and CHARLES WINICK, eds. *For the Young Viewer: Television Programming for Children at the Local Level*. McGraw, 1962. Descriptions of a wide variety of children's programs offered on local stations across the country and detailed discussions of how children respond to and absorb experiences at various ages.

HALLORAN, J. D., and P. R. ELLIOTT. *Television for Children and Young People*. International Publications Services, 1971. A study conducted at the Centre for Mass Communications Research, University of Leicester, on English television for children.

HAZARD, PATRICK D., ed. *TV as Art; Some Essays in Criticism*. Nat. Council of Teachers of English, 1966. Covers a number of aspects of television. Includes a detailed analysis by Charles and Mariann Winick of the way *Exploring* treated the Renaissance in relationship to the known needs of children and possibilities for teacher utilization of such programs.

HIMMELWEIT, H. T., A. N. OPPENHEIM, and PAMELA VINCE. *Television and the Child*. Oxford Univ. Pr., 1959. This survey of television viewing habits of English children between the ages of ten and fourteen was conducted by social psychologists from the London School of Economics. The team analyzed diaries and questionnaires given the children. One of the major conclusions of the study was that social status and IQ accounted for most of the differences between children who watched television and those who did not. A major importance of the study is that television viewing was evaluated within the total context of the children's leisure activities.

JOHNSON, NICHOLAS. *How to Talk Back to Your Television Set*. Little, 1970. Considers television's monopolistic tendencies, discusses its educative powers, and suggests how viewers can organize to help reform the medium.

KOENIG, ALLEN E., and RUANE B. HILL. *The Farther Vision: Educational Television Today*. Univ. of Wisconsin Pr., 1967. Explores the problems and challenges of ETV; discusses training teachers, and how to develop a curriculum.

MC LUHAN, MARSHALL, and QUENTIN FIORE. *The Medium Is the Message*. Bantam Books, 1967. A somewhat obscure but often quoted discussion of media and society.

MALETZKE, GERHARD. *Television in the Life of Youth*. Hamburg, Germany: Hans Bredow Institute, 1959. The basic German research study that found television imparts some information, is not good for family life, but does not appear to cause juvenile delinquency or affect social behavior of children in any meaningful way.

MOIR, GUTHRIE, ed. *Teaching and Television: ETV Explained*. Pergamon Pr., 1967. A collection of essays about educational television in Britain for both children and adults. Contains one chapter about American educational technology.

MORRIS, NORMAN S. *Television's Child*. Little, 1971. Very readable book by a television producer-writer who obviously believes in the "equal time" concept since he quotes a wide range of differing opinions from innumerable experts. Of concern to educators should be the charge that most school personnel refused to cooperate in the research study planned, thus limiting the human examples. Good bibliography.

National Association of Broadcasters. *The Television Code of the National Association of Broadcasters*, 12th ed. Nat. Association of Broadcasters, 1967. The television industry's policy statement.

PENNYBACKER, JOHN H., and WALDO W. BRADEN. *Broadcasting and the Public Interest*. Random, 1969. A series of provocative articles by television experts. Each chapter contains a section "Critical Analysis and Projects," that students can react to and explore further.

ROE, YALE. *The Television Dilemma: Search for a Solution*. Hastings, 1962. An analysis of important issues in television, such as government control, educational television, advertising, and standards. The author is a broadcasting executive.

ROPER, BURNS W. *A Ten-Year View of Public Attitudes Toward Television and Other Mass Media, 1959–1968*. Television Information Office, 1969. Reports on what Americans think and feel about television in relationship to news coverage, credibility, commercials, and program-type preferences.

SCHRAMM, WILBUR, et al. *The People Look at Educational Television*. Stanford Univ. Pr., 1963. After a discussion of the problems of the ETV beginnings, the report analyzes nine stations and their programs.

SCHRAMM, WILBUR, JACK LYLE, and EDWIN B. PARKER. *Television in the Lives of Our Children*. Stanford Univ. Pr., 1961. The classic American study on children's television viewing habits. The annotated bibliography is extremely valuable.

SELDES, GILBERT. *The Great Audience*. Viking, 1950. An old but sprightly essay on the oddities of the listening and viewing public.

SIMONSON, SOLOMON S. *Crisis in Television: A Study of the Private Judgment and the Public Interest*. Living Books, 1966. A smorgasbord, touching on many subjects. Opinionated and undocumented statements and a misleading title since the author actually feels that there is little wrong with TV as a social influence.

SKORNIA, HARRY J. *Television and Society: An Inquest*

*and Agenda for Improvement.* McGraw, 1965. A highly critical review of the economics and programming of television. Excellent chapter bibliographies.

STEINER, GARY A. *The People Look at Television: A Study of Audience Attitudes.* Knopf, 1963. A report of a study carried out at the Bureau of Applied Social Research, Columbia University. Remains the most scientific investigation of the subject despite its age.

WITTY, PAUL. *Studies of the Mass Media, 1949–1965.* Television Information Office, 1966. Summarizes the results obtained by Witty in his annual surveys of children's viewing habits and preferences. Appeared originally in the March 1966 issue of *Science Education.*

## Magazine Articles

BANDURA, ALBERT, DOROTHEA ROSS, and SHEILA ROSS. "Imitation of Film-Mediated Aggressive Models." *Journal of Abnormal and Social Psychology,* v. 66 (1963), pp. 3–11. The major implication of this control study is that very young children are likely to imitate aggressive actions whether exposed to them in real life or on film.

CRIST, JUDITH. "Sex and Violence in Movies and TV; How Harmful Are They?" *Good Housekeeping,* v. 169 (August 1969), pp. 59–62+. Emphasis is on nudity in the movies and the self-imposed motion picture code rating system. When Crist does discuss television, it is in relationship to whether children watching the news of riots and war will think these people will also rise from the dead to appear next week on another show. Stresses the fact that sex and violence are what the American public wants or they would not be offered.

CULHANE, JOHN. "Report Card on *Sesame Street.*" *New York Times Magazine* (May 24, 1970), pp. 34–35+. An article written as *Sesame Street* was ending its first year. High grades for teaching the alphabet; could have done more with numbers; still not strong in teaching reasoning. Major problem is that many black Americans see woman's role as providing ego-support for black males, yet *Sesame Street* would like to upgrade the female status.

HOLT, JOHN. "Big Bird, Meet Dick and Jane." *Atlantic,* v. 227 (May 1971), pp. 72–78. Noted education critic discusses why *Sesame Street* should stop trying to prepare children for school and begin to prepare them for what school may never teach them. Emphasis is on human values rather than factual learning.

MACCOBY, ELEANOR E. "Why Do Children Watch Television?" *Public Opinion Quarterly,* v. 18 (1954), pp. 239–244. A research study of 379 mothers of five- and six-year-olds in the Boston area revealed class differences among the motivational factors. Frustration plays a large part in why children watch television.

MORRIS, NORMAN S. "What's Good About Children's TV?" *Atlantic,* v. 224 (August 1969), pp. 67–71. After noting that the Nielsen rating finds preschoolers view television over fifty-four hours per week, Morris goes on to look at the few programs that offer worthwhile viewing. *Mister Rogers' Neighborhood, The Friendly Giant, and Captain Kangaroo* are the focus of his analysis. All help develop an ability to fantasize, an important aspect of young children's growth. Concludes that good children's programs must be entertaining, but also must fulfill emotional and/or intellectual needs.

## Periodicals

*Journal of Broadcasting.* Association for Professional Broadcasting Education, Temple Univ., Philadelphia, Pennsylvania. Quarterly. Devoted to all facets of broadcasting: radio and television, commercial and noncommercial.

*TV Guide.* Triangle Publications, Inc., Radnor, Pennsylvania 19088. Weekly. Reports news in and of the TV scene. Behind the camera stories. Popular and readable. Regional editions publish listings of programs.

*Television Quarterly.* The National Academy of Television Arts and Sciences, 54 W. 40th Street, New York, New York 10018. Programming, engineering, production, news, art direction, scenic design, and many other subjects are covered.

## Sources of Information

Action for Children's Television. 33 Hancock Avenue, Newton Centre, Massachusetts 02159.

National Association for Better Broadcasting. 373 North Western Avenue, Los Angeles, California 90004.

National Association of Broadcasters. 1771 N. Street, N.W., Washington, D.C. 20036.

National Association of Educational Broadcasters. 1346 Connecticut Avenue, N.W., Washington, D.C. 20036.

Television Information Office. 745 Fifth Avenue, New York, New York 10022.

# INTERNATIONALISM IN CHILDREN'S LITERATURE

*Anne Pellowski**

Internationalism in children's literature has at least three important aspects. One has to do with the development of printed and visual materials for children in areas of the

*Anne Pellowski is Director-Librarian, Information Center on Children's Cultures, UNICEF.

world which have until recently had no such materials and the development as well of opportunities for children to experience these materials, as in libraries and cultural centers. A second involves the exchange of children's books from one country to another, either in the originals or in translations. A third, and the one which is perhaps most important for the librarian working with children, is concerned with the way different cultures are depicted and represented in the children's books of any given country.

The international organizations which have been most active and influential in the field of children's books and libraries are the International Bureau of Education (Geneva), the United Nations Educational, Scientific and Cultural Organization (UNESCO, Paris), the United Nations Children's Fund (UNICEF, New York), the International Board on Books for Young People (IBBY, Zurich), and the International Federation of Library Associations (IFLA, The Hague). The World Confederation of Organizations of the Teaching Profession (WCOTP) is currently attempting to organize support for children's materials in school libraries at the international level. In addition to this, there are numerous national organizations, such as the Agency for International Development (AID, Washington) and Franklin Book Programs (New York) of the United States and the International Youth Library (Munich) of the Federal Republic of Germany, which have done very much to promote internationalism and children's books.

However, in spite of all these efforts, it can safely be estimated that more than one half of the world's children have absolutely no exposure to children's literature in printed or audiovisual form; it would be too difficult to estimate what percentage hear some literature through oral means because the oral narration of folkloric and mythic stories is a practice which seems to decrease with the advent of mass communication, but this has never been specifically investigated, especially as it relates to children.

There is still an enormous amount of research to be undertaken before we can come to more firm conclusions about the different methods of exposing children to literature; the relative merits of oral, visual, and print exposure; and the differences in response that depend on cultural and social values of the child reader/listener/viewer, rather than on the intrinsic qualities of the literature itself. Such research is hampered by the fact that ninety percent of current print and audiovisual literature for children is produced in a handful of countries, and represents less than one-tenth of the world's population of children.

The exchange of children's books can thus hardly be called international, except in a limited sense. The number of translations grows each year, but this is limited to translations to and from the Western European languages, with only a few exceptions. Still rarer is the use of children's books in other languages, in other than their country of origin. African and Asian countries use a sizable number of materials from England, the United States, and France, because in many of these countries children are growing up with English or French as their only language. A tiny bit of comparison can be found in the current use of East African Swahili materials now being used in a few American schools.

By far the most common aspect of internationalism, then, is the introduction to other cultures, through children's literature. Now culture is not something that can be separated easily into categories like "adult" and "children's." Anyone preparing to expose children in a meaningful way to another culture must first have some understanding of it himself.

The evaluation and selection of the materials that are to introduce children to another culture is most difficult. Our standard selection lists do not include enough items related to each area, and those which are included tend to stress the past more than the present. Specialized lists are more helpful, but very few have been compiled with stated criteria of selection. One must be prepared to use a wide variety of sources in tracking down sufficient materials.

In establishing the validity of *fictional and folkloric materials*, the following represent some of the questions we must ask:

1. Was the material created by a participant of the culture or by an observer of it?

2. Has it been edited to remove all elements which are morally or socially not accepted in our culture or have some of these intrinsic values of the society concerned been allowed to remain intact, e.g., polygamy, matter-of-fact acceptance of body functions, early marriage or love relationships?

3. If it is historical, is this clearly indicated?

In regard to *illustrations, photographs, or films*, the following questions can be asked:

1. Is there obvious stereotyping, such as *always* depicting Chinese children with pigtails, African children without clothes, Mexican children as barefoot boys with burros, etc.?

2. Are the facial characteristics of any race *always* the same, without regard for the fact that there are infinite varieties within all races?

3. Is the comparative wealth or poverty of a nation or people illustrated with honesty or is it exaggerated?

4. Is there overemphasis of rural or village life with no proportionate attention to urban life?

5. Are the unusually different customs depicted more for their shock value than as illuminations of parts of the total structure of the culture?

For *factual materials* we can ask:

1. What is the copyright date? Does this limit the usability of the work?

2. If the copyright date is recent, do geographical and political facts truly reflect the latest changes?

3. Whose point of view is represented—the insider or the outsider or both?

4. What kind of sources are given?

To answer some of these questions demands a firsthand knowledge, which many of us do not have and which is not acquired merely through the reading of a few books and the viewing of fewer films. One can partly test validity without actually knowing all the answers. A condescending tone or an oversimplified explanation of a complex question can warn of bias, even though one might not be able to pinpoint errors.

The popular adage "Every little bit helps" simply cannot apply when one is concerned about introducing children to other cultures. If the material is derogatory instead of objective, or vivid but totally inaccurate, chances are it will hinder rather than help. It would be better not to attempt an introduction to another people if it cannot be done with sensitivity and care.

Finally, there is the question of technique or method to employ in actually bringing these good materials to the attention of children.

In preschool years and the early grades, the child still has few definitely formed concepts of nationality. He is, however, conscious of racial, religious, social, and cultural differences, especially if these differences are visible. Most research indicates that in these early years children need to see and experience the difference of things, since this helps to build up the self-image.

At this level it is best to use good pictures or photographs showing children from many parts of the world; picture stories can be read aloud. Children at this age are very conscious of names of persons, places, and things, so time should be spent on the origin of names and describing customs.

Picture books in other languages can be shown, especially if one is working with children who know another language. In this way, children often learn to take pride in background rather than secretly feeling ashamed of it because it is so different from that of the peer group.

Older children need materials of much more substance, materials which recognize the concepts of nationality and country, region, and continent, as well as social and cultural values.

## SUGGESTED RESEARCH NEEDS

1. Content analysis studies should be made of popular and recommended books from foreign countries that are translated into English and widely available.

2. Content analysis studies should be made of the books published in the United States that are selected to be translated into other languages.

3. The influence of international demonstration libraries for children should be investigated.

4. The United States is often credited with having developed the best public library service to children in the world. Yet adult reading polls show that adults in the United States read less than adults in any of the western European countries. What factors within a nation's culture can account for this disparity?

5. In relationship to international bibliographic control of materials, is it possible to develop subject headings and classification schemes that are culturally neutral, or at least culturally objective?

## BIBLIOGRAPHY

### Bibliographies

Asia Society. *Asia: A Guide to Books for Children*. New York: Asia Society, 112 East 64th Street, New York, New York 10021. Describes 338 children's books on Asia in general and in specific Asian countries.

KEATING, CHARLOTTE MATTHEWS. *Building Bridges of Understanding*. Tucson, Arizona: Palo Verde Publishing Co., P.O. Box 5783, Tucson, Arizona 85705. An extensively annotated list of 215 children's books dealing with numerous minority groups within the United States.

U.S. Committee for UNICEF. *Africa: An Annotated List of Printed Materials Suitable for Children*. New York: UNICEF, 331 East 38th Street, New York, New York 10016. A selective guide to more than 300 English language items published in nine countries. Arranged by country and general regions of the continent.

______. *Latin America: An Annotated List of Printed Materials Suitable for Children*. New York: UNICEF, 331 East 38th Street, New York, New York 10016. Similar to the African list, this bibliography contains over 500 items, including some in Spanish.

______. *The Near East: An Annotated List of Materials for Children*. New York: UNICEF, 331 East 38th Street, New York, New York 10016. This list contains over 500 items covering the Near East, North Africa, Afghanistan, Iran, Greece, and Turkey. Includes a section of the Bible.

### Books

ANDREAE, GESIENA. *The Dawn of Juvenile Literature in England*. Amsterdam: H. J. Paris, 1925. (Available as a reprint from Singing Tree Press, 1968.) The evolution of the child's book through the centuries and the effect this development had on the whole concept of childhood in the eighteenth century. An excellent book with which to begin a detailed study of English children's literature.

BRAVO VILLASANTE, CARMEN. *Historia y Antología de la Literatura Infantil Iberoamericano. (History and Anthology of Hispanic-American Children's Literature.)* 2 vols. Madrid: Doncel, 1966. This is an invaluable aid to the study of Latin-American children's literature; a monumental work.

GOR'KIĬ, MAKSIM. *O Detskoĭ Literature; Stat'i i Vyskazvaniia. (On Children's Literature.)* Moska Gos. izdvo detskoĭ lit-ry, 1958. (Published by Foreign Languages Publishing House, Moscow.) A collection of essays by Gorki pleading for the best writers to devote their talents to writing for children, for in children and education lay the future hope.

HAWKES, LOUISE R. *Before and After Pinocchio; A Study of Italian Children's Books*. Paris: The Puppet Press, 1933. (Available as a reprint from Singing Tree Press, 1968.) A history and criticism of Italian children's literature from classical Roman civilization to 1930. Books are treated as genuine literature, not a sub-genre.

HÜRLIMANN, BETTINA. *Die Welt im Bilderbuch*. Zurich: Atlantis Verlag, 1966. (Published as *Picture-Book World* by World Publishing, 1969.) After discussing picture books from twenty-four countries, the text is divided into topics for a comparison of how various illustrators treat such subjects as animals, ships, rain, and snow.

______. *Europaische Kinderbucher in Drei Jahrhunderten*. 2d ed. Zurich: Atlantis Verlag, 1963. (Published as *Three Centuries of Children's Books in Europe* by World Publishing, 1968.) A lively, personal history of European highlights of children's literature. A good background book.

International Bureau of Education. *Littérature Enfantine et Collaboration Internationale. (Children's Books and International Goodwill.)* 2nd ed. Geneva: Bureau Internationale d'Education, 1932. Contains information on children's books in 37 countries and because of an admirable objectivity, may be termed the first truly international study.

International Federation of Library Associations. Committee on Library Work with Children. *Library Service to Children*, vols. 1, 2, 3. Lund: Bibliotekstjänst, 1963, 1966, 1970. A series of reports covering different countries of the world in relationship to the state of children's literature and library work with children.

______. *Translation of Children's Books*. Lund: Bibliotekstjänst, 1962. A reprint of three papers read at the 1961 IFLA meeting in Edinburgh, together with a list of books recommended for translation.

LEPMAN, JELLA. *Die Kinderbuchbrücke*. Frankfurt-Main: S. Fischer Verlag, 1964. (Published as *A Bridge of Children's Books* by the ALA, 1969.) A moving, personal account of the author's attempts to build a "bridge of understanding through children's books," in the International Youth Library at Munich and later through the founding of the International Board on Books for Young People.

PELLOWSKI, ANNE. *The World of Children's Literature*. Bowker, 1968. A monumental work, listing over 4400 items concerned with children's books throughout the world.

SAHASRABUDHE, PRABHA. *Writing for Children Today: Why, What and How?* New Delhi: Bal Bhavan and National Children's Museum, 1963. A collection of papers delivered at a seminar held at Bal Bhavan and the National Children's Museum in the spring of 1963. Topics include standards of writing and illustrating, reading interests, and science books.

WEAVER, WARREN. *Alice in Many Tongues*. Univ. of Wisconsin Pr., 1964. A very lucid discussion of the problem of translation, and the checklist of editions and translations (in 47 languages) point out that, in fact, *Alice* is many books by many authors.

WOLGAST, HEINRICH. *Das Elend Unserer Jugendliteratur. (The Misery of Our Children's Literature.)* 7th ed. Worms: Ernst Wunderlich, 1950. This is the most important and influential book on the theory of children's literature written in the German language.

ZWEIGBERGK, EVA VON. *Barnboken i Sverige 1750–1950. (Children's Books in Sweden 1750–1950.)* Stockholm: Rabén & Sjögren, 1965. A clearly written, well-organized, and illustrated history of children's literature in Sweden.

## Magazine Articles

For an abundance of articles see entries in Anne Pellowski's *The World of Children's Literature*. Bowker, 1968.

## Periodicals

*Bookbird*. International Institute for Children's Juvenile and Popular Literature. Fuhrmannsgasse 18a, Vienna, Austria. Quarterly (Irregular). 1957– Covers the international children's book scene; reviews recent materials about children's literature; lists recommended books for translation; and, on occasion, publishes in-depth articles.

*Information Bulletin on Reading Materials*. UNESCO Regional Centre for Reading Materials in South Asia, 26/A, P.E.C.H.H.S., Karachi 29, Pakistan. Quarterly. 1959– Although this publication is concerned with all of the problems of general book writing, publishing, and distribution, a major emphasis is on materials for children and new literates. An invaluable aid to the person interested in a study of the newly developing children's literature in South Asian countries.

# BOOK PROMOTION

*John Donovan**

Two factors enter into the promotion of children's books—imagination and time. With an unlimited supply of both, teachers and librarians can have the most satisfying experiences imaginable encouraging young people and adults, too, to read more children's books. But people's time is limited. And while everyone has imagination, bringing it to bear in the cause of promoting books is not feasible for most. Fortunately, promoting books has been a long-standing concern of many dedicated children's specialists, and they have developed for us some extraordinarily useful patterns that are easily followed by even the most harried librarian and teacher.

Success in promoting children's books is easily measured: has a child been led to books as a result of the promotion activity? Not that he will necessarily respond immediately to the stimulus that a particular promotion offers. Some children will; most will not. But if an activity has been successful it will reach a child at a level that will allow him to respond eventually. He may, as a result of a promotional event, *later* look to books for the information he seeks, the laugh he wants, the friend he does not have.

It should be the objective of everyone

*John Donovan is Executive Director of the Children's Book Council.

who cares about children and books to make it possible for this later response to occur. The child psychologist David Elkind calls this "stimulus gating." He observes that when children are taken to a three-ring circus they may seem to adults to be more fascinated by the hot dogs, pop corn, and crazy hats available than they are by the circus itself. It may take many weeks, he suggests, before the child is able to absorb what he has seen, sort it out in his mind, and then respond to it. The child erects gates in front of experiences, and opens the gates when he is ready.

Storytelling by librarians and teachers is a proven way to promote children's books. Literature has roots in stories told by one person to another. Traditional folk tales endured because these stories were told. The Grimms collected German tales that had been passed on orally, just as Richard Chase in the United States collects mountain stories that are told, not written. Folk artists, such as Pete Seeger, sing variations of the stories. Storytelling, and for the very young, conducting picture-book programs, are effective ways to introduce books to children. You tell the story, and nearby you have a book to point to, and you say, in your own way, "It's all in here." If a teacher or a librarian can't tell stories, or sing them, reading them is an excellent, almost preferred, alternative. A young person can see from an effective, but undramatized, reading that the story is available, in print, right away, and just for him.

Many people have raised objections to motion picture and television productions of children's books. There is a feeling among some that children's books of the classic variety have fared poorly in the hands of commercial movie and television producers. It would be interesting to explore this matter in depth. Among the questions to which we do not know the answers are the following: (1) is it better that a film not be produced if it is not faithful to its source; (2) is it better to produce a film that may lead children to the source, which may in every respect be superior to the movie version; (3) are children adversely affected by a bastardization of a classic that may lose its special quality in a medium other than a book; and (4) are children, in fact, led away from books as a result of audiovisual treatments, rather than to them?

Specifically, how many children found the televised version of *Rabbit Hill* sappy, and therefore avoid the book; how many found the television production of *Stuart Little* condescending and therefore will never find the book; and how many found the movie version of *Island of the Blue Dolphins*, one of the great contemporary books, recreated in such a way as to turn children away rather than toward the book? It is the traditional question everyone in the book field asks when bowdlerization is at issue: is it enough to know the who, what, where, and when of a story to understand the genius behind it?

People promoting children's books say that movies, television shows, and, to a lesser extent, recordings, of a children's book will create an interest in a book where that interest did not exist before. Alert librarians and teachers can certainly capitalize on that interest, while those especially alert can use such occasions to explore the possibilities of developing a critical sense among young readers. Questions can be asked of the individual young person who returns *Charlie and the Chocolate Factory* to the library after he has seen its motion picture version, *Willie Wonka and the Chocolate Factory*. A reading club in a library or an entire school class might attend the movie together, either before or after reading the book, and hold a discussion group on the differences, strengths, and weaknesses of the two media presentations. It can be an exciting challenge to try to induce a critical sense in children, perhaps a particular child or two, rather than to select *for* him, and say, in advance, what is good, what bad. Movies, television, even comic books, can offer this opportunity to adults working with children.

Many people have found that plays based on children's stories are an effective way to introduce books to children. It is one of the great regrets of people familiar with contemporary children's theater in the United States that it is a stepchild of both literature and the theater. With some happy exceptions—the late Charlotte Chorpenning, for example, and the contemporary Aurand Harris—children's theater has tended not to look to current literature for inspiration. It has depended on tedious versions of classic stories or delightful improvisations that owe nothing to literature.

Many teachers and librarians use plays successfully, but seldom in relationship to literature. The widely held view seems to be that plays have other functions that are more important than as introductions to children's literature. However, school play productions can lead the child to books on costumes, crafts books that will aid in producing scenery and artifacts, and to books that fill in the background of the story's time and place setting.

Any year by itself presents fine opportunities to promote children's books and reading. The first notable events during the year, vis-à-vis children's books, are the selections in January of the year's Newbery and Caldecott Medal books, and the Newbery and Caldecott Honor Books, as well. Later in the year, usually in March, the National Book Award in the category of children's books is selected. When awards are announced it is clear that there is a chance to promote books as *news;* it is difficult to do this at other times during the year. Some teachers and librarians have a particularly good time running their own Newbery, Caldecott, and National Book Award contests among young people.

April 2 is Hans Christian Andersen's birthday and has been designated International Children's Book Day. It is also the date on which the winner of the Batchelder Award for the best translated children's book is announced. Some schools and libraries use this occasion for Andersen festivals, or to feature foreign cultures in both fiction and fact.

National Library Week is always in April, and this occasion suggests promotional opportunities to many. American Education Week, in late October, is another good promotional week.

One of the most successful book promotion times is summer. Libraries and schools that have summer sessions which concentrate on remedial reading conduct Summer Reading Clubs. The best clubs do not emphasize reading a lot of books, but stress gaining a sense of personal growth through reading. In large systems, promotional material is prepared locally and is geared to specific local interests. For systems that do not have this service, however, the Children's Book Council has materials each year—a poster, summer reading club membership cards, bookmarks, and achievement certificates. Summer is a time for teachers and librarians to encourage personal ownership of children's books, and to work with local booksellers to be certain that recommended books are available to young purchasers. By the early 1970s an extraordinary number of children's paperbacks became widely available and booksellers heretofore uninterested in children's books became helpful participants in the promotion scene.

Summer and early fall is also a good time to stress children's books by having a library booth at the county or state fairs held throughout most of the nation. People are often surprised and delighted to find the library represented, especially if the booth contains chairs where they can sit and rest while looking at the books.

The major time during the year for the promotion of children's books is Children's Book Week, the third week of November. The first Book Week was in 1919. It has been observed every year since and served as the prototype for Book Weeks throughout the world—in Japan, Iran, the Netherlands, Canada, and many other countries. From the first, an annual Book Week theme has been selected, and artists have been invited to interpret the theme. Book Week has been best known through its annual posters that in their special way illustrate the evolution of children's book illustration in America. (See pp. 46–47.) Book Week's sponsor is the Children's Book Council, which provides a wide variety of materials beyond the Book Week poster to help everyone observe this occasion.

*The Calendar*, also published by the Children's Book Council, will suggest to anyone in the field of children's books great opportunities for the encouragement of reading. Exhibits and displays can be created around almost any holiday of the year, for the great variety of children's books practically assures that books on the topic will exist. A teacher or a librarian, however, would have a lot more fun, and be able to exercise far more imagination and ingenuity, if an unusual occasion during the year—Whale Watching Week, for example—is selected as one for the promoting of reading. It would amaze many people to discover how many children's books exist about nineteenth-century whaling, seafaring adventures, both truth and fiction, and the many forms of life that share the sea with the great mammals. Developing a program on an unusual subject is more likely to intrigue children than would yet another activity relating to the first Thanksgiving.

Book Fairs are a favorite book promotion activity. In large cities, in particular, huge book fairs supported by a local institution or a combination of institutions—a newspaper, booksellers, and civic-minded groups such as the Junior League—will draw effective attention to children's books, particularly new titles. The more usual book fair activity will involve a Parent-Teachers Association or some other group working with a school, and is devised as a fund-raising activity. The American Library Association's Children's Services Division has developed criteria for organizing and running worthwhile book fairs, while the Children's Book Council has prepared a manual to assist interested people in this activity. People promoting the cause of good children's books have found that a well-organized fair will stimulate reading and enjoyment of books, but that an ineffective fair may, by its mere existence, discourage children's interest in books.

One of the more creative ideas developed in recent years involves the concept of the "artist in residence" for public schools. While the concept has a long and honored history among universities and colleges, it is only in recent years that it has been thought of as valuable to the younger members of educational institutions. The obvious reason for its failure to be widespread concerns school finances. The idea of employing an author or artist for a semester or a year may strike many as a needless frill. Yet, where it has been tried, it has proved worth the money.

Schools that have Title I funds should contemplate the experiment. In Philadelphia, Lloyd Alexander, a Newbery Medal winner, spent a year visiting Philadelphia schools talking to children about books and the art of writing. The children were motivated to read more, with better insight, and to produce their own creative works. For the author, it is a valuable insight into the thought processes of children and enables him to be more aware of the needs of youthful readers.

Schools lacking the money to employ a full-time artist can provide a great stimulus to reading by inviting an author or illustrator for a one-day program since most schools do have some money for enrichment activities. In these cases the school should be prepared to pay expenses and offer some type of honorarium.

In one school in New Jersey, the fifth-grade class invited Jean Merrill, author of *The Pushcart War*, as its guest. In art classes the children made replicas of the various pushcarts found within the book as well as other artifacts relevant to the story. They wrote their own stories and devised games to be played with the "pea-pin shooter" used so effectively within the book. Preparation for an author's visit is essential if the occasion is to have impact. Equally important is selecting an author or illustrator whose interests are within the range of the children with whom he will be visiting.

Some people think *all* artists and authors live in New York or California. This is far from the case and many schools in small towns may have an author living quite near at hand. Good librarians keep a file of "local resource people" and should be able to provide teachers with such information. The Children's Book Council can also provide information on the availability of authors.

## SUGGESTED RESEARCH NEEDS

Aside from the questions raised in the text concerning children's reactions to books in relationship to motion pictures and television productions, the following areas are possible research topics:

1. Does expanding a library's program to include film programs and records lead to more, less, or the same amount of book reading?

2. Do programs that involve all age groups—Family Night at the Library or Book Fairs—have more impact than those geared just to children or just to adults?

3. What, if any, is the difference in response to a child's hearing a storytelling record and hearing the same story told by a person present?

4. Besides offering a history of children's illustration, do the Book Week posters reflect changing attitudes toward children?

5. Should promotion techniques vary with the age of the children the activities are directed toward? That is, do different aged children respond to different media?

## BIBLIOGRAPHY

### Bibliographies

American Library Association. Children's Services Division. *For Storytellers and Storytelling.* ALA, 1968. Contains "Bibliographies, Materials, and Resource Aids" to help in the task of storytelling. Also contains information on audiovisual materials.

RUDOLPH, BEULAH COUNTS. "Bulletin Boards and Displays to Publicize Books and Reading." *Elementary English*, v. 44 (January 1967), pp. 37–39. Subtitled a "Bibliography of Books, Pamphlets, and Articles on Techniques, Ideas, and Sources," this list includes standard bibliographic information, including price, and very brief descriptive annotations for most of the items.

### Books and Pamphlets

ELKIND, DAVID. "Experience and Cognitive Growth" in *Open Education: The Legacy of the Progressive Movement.* The Nat. Assoc. for the Education of Young Children, 1970. A presentation by a prominent child psychologist of the factors that influence children's readiness to absorb new experiences in their lives.

FOSTER, JOANNA. *How to Conduct Effective Picture Book Programs.* Westchester (New York) Library System. Distributed by the Children's Book Council. While designed to be used with the film "The Pleasure Is Mutual," the manual can stand on its own. Answers all important questions, suggests programs, and provides criteria for evaluation of programs held.

GROSS, SARA CHOKLA. *Planning a School Book Fair.* Children's Book Council, 1970. In 24 pages, Gross tells the beginner all he needs to know about planning a book fair that will be a success rather than organized chaos.

### Articles

CHILDS, MARY C. "Book Fairs and the CBC." *Library Journal*, v. 91 (May 15, 1966), pp. 2586–2588. Advice on how to run a book fair and ideas to help assure its success. Information on the kind of help available from the Children's Book Council.

———. "The Children's Book Council—A Personal View." *Top of the News*, v. 23 (June 1967), pp. 365–370. A former Executive Secretary of the Children's Book Council describes the varied activities of CBC and the joys as well as the difficulties in coordinating its many programs designed to promote children's reading.

DONOVAN, JOHN. "The Congress of the International Board on Books for Young People, 1968." *Wilson Library Bulletin*, v. 43 (January 1969), pp. 432–437. Promoting children's books and reading is a world-wide activity. Donovan relates the fear of political dissension that lurked beneath the surface of the IBBY meeting, but reports that people who believe in children are able to come together in peace and exchange ideas that transcend their home countries' politics.

FINK, RONN. "Book Week on a Budget." *Library Journal*,

v. 92 (September 15, 1967), pp. 3124–3125. Excellent suggestions for ways to celebrate Book Week and attract adults as well as children.

"Looking Ahead to National Children's Book Week." *Top of the News*, v. 25 (June 1969), pp. 414–421. A brainstorming session with two librarians and a publisher's representative discussing ways to develop effective programs.

NORTON, ELOISE E. "Paperback Cornucopia." *Library Journal*, v. 93 (May 15, 1968), pp. 2088–2090. Report on the many ways paperbacks stimulate reading in the elementary school. Also discusses free or inexpensive materials that aid in curriculum enrichment.

OVERTON, ELIZABETH, and LIZETTE HAND. "Making the Summer Count." *Top of the News*, v. 24 (June 1968), pp. 407–409. If children cannot get to the library because they lack transportation, they can't read. One library solved the problem by providing bus service during the summer months.

STRONER, SANDRA, and FLORENCE E. BURMEISTER. "Summer Happening." *Top of the News*, v. 25 (April 1969), pp. 291–300. Report of "six multi-media happenings" presented by the Skokie (Illinois) Public Library in an attempt to reach non-library-using youth. Creative and imaginative approach.

WEISBLAT, GENEVIEVE, and JOHN WEISBLAT. "The Exciting Adventure of the Children's Caravan." *Top of the News*, v. 23 (January 1967), pp. 158–164. The Children's Caravan is a specially designed bus containing facilities for showing films, playing records, making tapes, and lending paperback books. This is a report of its efforts to promote the joys of reading among migrant workers in southern New Jersey migrant camps.

## Special Aids

*American Education Week*. American Education Assoc., 1201 16th Street, N.W., Washington, D.C. 20036. Annual.

*The Calendar*. Children's Book Council, 175 Fifth Avenue, New York, New York 10010. Three times a year. Free. An invaluable source that lists book-related dates, materials available from publishers and organizations concerned with children's books, news items, articles on people in the book field, and special bibliographies.

*Children's Book Week* and *Summer Reading Programs*. Children's Book Council. Annual. Standard kits are available plus numerous options.

*National Library Week*. National Book Committee, 1 Park Avenue, New York, N. Y. 10016. Annual. Provides posters and other materials directed toward the theme of the particular year.

# APPENDIX A BOOK SELECTION AIDS[1]

*The AAAS Science Booklist*, comp. by Hilary J. Deason, 3rd ed. Selected and Annotated List of Science and Mathematics Books for Secondary School Students, College Undergraduates and Nonspecialists. American Assoc. for the Advancement of Science, 1970.

*About 100 Books; A Gateway to Better Intergroup Understanding*, comp. by Ann G. Wolfe. American Jewish Committee, 1969. A sixth edition, largely comprising books published in 1967, 1968, and 1969, reflecting the trends and unsolved problems in intergroup relations during that period. Arranged by age.

*Adventuring with Books; A Book List for Elementary Schools*, ed. by Elizabeth Guilefoile and the Committee on the Elementary School Book List of the National Council of Teachers of English. Signet, 1966. Annotated listings within 32 subject categories and 60 interest level groupings. May be used by children since it is carefully annotated for child appeal.

*Africa; An Annotated List of Printed Materials Suitable for Children*. ALA, Children's Services Division and the African-American Institute. Information Center on Children's Cultures, United States Committee for UNICEF, 1968. An evaluation of all in-print English language materials on Africa for children, arranged by countries.

*Aids to Choosing Books for Children*, prepared by Ingeborg Boudreau. Children's Book Council, 1969. A selected, annotated bibliography of booklists and review media, designed to aid librarians, teachers, students of children's literature, and parents in book selection. Both general and specialized booklists are included as well as a list of general sources of information.

*American History*, comp. by Bernard Titowsky. McKinley, 1964. Annotated selective listings.

*Appraisal: Children's Science Books*. Harvard Graduate School of Education, Cambridge, Mass. Published three times each year. Around 50 books reviewed in each issue, all rated on a five-point scale by both a librarian and a science specialist.

*Asia: A Guide to Books for Children*. The Asia Society, 1966. Asia is defined as all the countries from Afghanistan eastward to Japan. The guide is arranged by country and approximate grade levels are suggested in the annotated listings.

*A Basic Book Collection for Elementary Grades*. ALA, 1960. Suggested as a minimum collection, this is a helpful annotated guide to books in subject fields as well as to fiction and picture books.

*A Basic Book Collection for High Schools*, 7th ed. ALA, 1963. Includes paperbacks, magazines, and audio-visual aids.

1. See also the bibliographies accompanying the ten articles in Part 7.

*A Basic Book Collection for Junior High Schools*. ALA, 1960. Similar in pattern to the book for elementary grades.

*Behavior Patterns in Children's Books; A Bibliography*, comp. by Clara J. Kircher. Catholic Univ. of America Pr., 1966. The purpose of this book is the development of wholesome principles of conduct and the prevention of delinquency through the therapeutic use of books in which good character traits are embodied. The list is arranged by such categories as making friends, spiritual values, or boy-girl relationships rather than age, and is followed by a list of selected readings and a behavior index.

*Best Books for Children*. Bowker, 1959 to date. An annual catalog of 4000 titles annotated and arranged under preschool to grade 3; grades 4–6; grades 7 up; adult books for younger readers; and special subjects.

*Bibliography of Books for Children*, comp. by Sylvia Sunderlin. Assoc. for Childhood Education International, 1968. Annotated list of books for children from preschool through elementary grades, grouped by subject or form in useful categories. In the revised edition two new categories, Negro Heritage and Negro Fiction have been added.

*The Black Experience and the School Curriculum; Teaching Materials for Grades K–12: An Annotated Bibliography*, comp. by Katherine Baxter. Wellsprings Ecumenical Center, 1968. Annotated lists of books grouped by subject matter and age on black history, social studies, biography, fiction, and poetry, with additional material on teachers' guides and audiovisual aids.

*The Black Experience in Children's Books*, prepared by Augusta Baker, rev. ed. New York Public Library, 1971. An annotated bibliography, classified by age and subject matter about black life in America, in the Islands, in Africa, and in England.

BLUM, ELEANOR. *Reference Books in the Mass Media*. Univ. of Ill. Pr., 1962. An annotated, selective booklist covering book publishing, broadcasting, films, newspapers, magazines, and advertising. The bibliography is intended to provide sources for facts and figures, names, addresses, and other biographical information, and to suggest starting points for research.

*Book Bait; Detailed Notes on Adult Books Popular with Young People*, ed. by Elinor Walker, 2nd ed. ALA, 1969. One hundred carefully selected books that young people enjoy. Each title is followed by a summary of the contents, a paragraph indicating the particular audience to which the book appeals, ideas for book talks, and follow-up titles.

*Books for Beginning Readers*, prepared by Elizabeth Guilefoile, ill. by Norma Phillips. Nat. Council of Teachers of English, 1962. A useful and timely bibliography of over 300 easy-reading books for beginners. The majority have been published within recent years to meet the need for entertainment and information.

*Books for Children 1960–1965*, as selected and reviewed by *The Booklist* and *Subscription Books Bulletin*. ALA, 1966. A compilation of reviews of recommended books, expressly for teachers and librarians. Reviews are grouped by subject matter and genre. The first of an annual compilation.

*Books for Friendship; A List of Books Recommended for Children*, 4th ed. of *Books Are Bridges*. American Friends Service Committee and Anti-Defamation League of B'nai B'rith, 1968. Books of high literary quality selected to help boys and girls widen their friendships and follow the path of peace and brotherhood.

*Books for the Chinese-American Child; A Selected List*, comp. by Cecilia Mei-Chi Chen. Cooperative Children's Book Center, 1969. A carefully selected list of books, included for their honesty and literary quality.

*Books in American History: A Basic List for High Schools*, comp. by John E. Wiltz. Indiana Univ. Pr., 1964. Chronological, annotated bibliography.

*Building Bridges of Understanding*, prepared by Charlotte Matthews Keating. Palo Verde, 1967. An annotated bibliography of books about blacks, Indians, Spanish-speaking ethnic groups, Chinese-Americans, Japanese-Americans, Jews, and other minority groups.

*Building Bridges of Understanding Between Cultures*, prepared by Charlotte Matthews Keating. Palo Verde, 1971. A companion volume to the title above, the annotations arranged by age level within each minority group.

*Bulletin of the Center for Children's Books*. The Univ. of Chicago, Graduate Library School, Univ. of Chicago Pr. Published monthly except August. Ongoing review of new titles for children and young people, annotated according to whether the book is recommended, acceptable, marginal, not recommended, or for special collections or unusual readers only. The reviews are detailed, and grade levels and prices are given.

*Children and Poetry; A Selective Annotated Bibliography*, comp. by Virginia Haviland and William Jay Smith. Library of Congress, 1969. With a preface by Virginia Haviland and an introduction by William Jay Smith, this book presents a choice selection of poetry divided into: Rhymes, Poetry of the Past, 20th Century Poetry, Anthologies, and World Poetry.

*Children's Books*, comp. by Children's Book Section, U.S. Library of Congress. An annual bibliography, selective and annotated.

*Children's Books; Awards and Prizes*, comp. and ed. by Margaret Colbert. Children's Book Council, 1971. A compilation of honors awarded in the children's book field by organizations, schools, publishers, and newspapers. A brief description of each award is followed by a list of all the winners since it was first given.

*Children's Books for $1.50 or Less*. Assoc. for Childhood Education International, 1969. Annotated list primarily of paperbacks and grouped by type: fiction, rhymes, biography, etc.

*Children's Books in Print*. Bowker, annual. An index to 35,000 books in print at time of publication, including such books as have become children's classics based on inclusion in publishers' catalogs. There are separate author, title, illustrator, and publisher indexes. Prices are given for trade and library bindings, and for paperback editions.

*Children's Books to Enrich the Social Studies for the Elementary Grades*, comp. by Helen Huus. Nat. Council for the Social Studies, 1966. Excellent annotated bibliographies, topically arranged, cover world history and geography from ancient times to the present.

*Children's Books Too Good to Miss*, comp. by May Hill Arbuthnot, Margaret Mary Clark, Harriet Geneva Long, and Ruth M. Hadlow, 6th ed. The Press of Case Western Reserve Univ., 1971. A select list of books suggested as the irreducible minimum, which every child should be exposed to, grouped by ages.

*The Children's Bookshelf; A Guide to Books for and About Children*, prepared by the Child Study Assoc. of America. Bantam, 1965. Short articles on books and reading; annotated bibliography for different age groups and books for parents about children and family life.

*Children's Catalog*. Wilson, 1971. Annual supp. A selected, classified catalog of children's books, arranged with nonfiction first, classified by Dewey Decimal Classification, followed by fiction, short stories, and the easy books. Five-year cumulations and yearly supplements.

*Children's Interracial Fiction; An Unselective Bibliography*, comp. by Barbara Jean Glancy. American Federation of Teachers, 1969. Comprehensive annotated bibliography, accompanied by articles dealing with the black perspective and a survey-review of children's literature about black people.

*The Dobler World Directory of Youth Periodicals*, comp. by Lavinia G. Dobler and Muriel Fuller. Schulte, 1966. A revised and expanded listing, a successor to the *Dobler International List of Periodicals for Boys and Girls*.

*Doors to More Mature Reading*, prepared by Elinor Walker, Donald W. Allyn, Alice E. Johnson, and Helen Lutton. ALA, 1964. Detailed notes on adult books for use with young people.

*Elementary English*. Nat. Council of Teachers of English. Besides a regular column reviewing children's books, this journal has articles on children's reading and related subjects.

*The Elementary School Library Collection;* Phases 1-2-3, ed. by Mary V. Gaver. Bro-Dart, 1965. Supp., 1966. Contains discussion of selection policy and classification principles and policy. Books, shown on reproductions of catalog cards, are classified according to Dewey Decimal System of Classification in the first section. Section 2 contains author-title and subject indexes.

ELLIS, ALEC. *How to Find Out About Children's Literature*. Pergamon, 1968. Bibliography of bibliographies as well as other useful listings of organizations and collections, both national and international.

*Fables from Incunabula to Modern Picture Books: A Selective Bibliography*, comp. by Barbara Quinnan. The Library of Congress General Reference and Bibliography Division, Reference Department, 1966.

*Fare for the Reluctant Reader*, comp. by Anita E. Dunn, Mabel E. Jackman, and Bernice C. Bush, rev. ed. State Univ. of N.Y., 1952. Annotated bibliography to help teachers and librarians select books for reluctant readers from grades 7 through 12. Books are grouped by age and subject. There are chapters on developmental and remedial reading.

*Folklore of the American Indians; An Annotated Bibliography*, comp. by Judith C. Ullom, ill. Library of Congress, 1969. Carefully selected items arranged by culture areas.

*For Storytellers and Storytelling: Bibliographies, Materials and Resource Aids*. ALA, 1968. Recommended materials on storytelling, including books, pamphlets, and multi-media aids.

*4000 Books for Secondary School Libraries; A Basic List*, comp. by the Library Committee of the Nat. Assoc. of Independent Schools. Bowker, 1968. Arranged by Dewey Decimal Classification; periodicals and recordings are also listed.

*Gateways to Readable Books*, prepared by Ruth Strang, Ethlyne Phelps, and Dorothy Withrow. Wilson, 1966. Annotated graded list of books in a variety of fields for adolescents who find reading difficult.

GILLESPIE, JOHN, and DIANA LEMBO. *Introducing Books; A Guide for the Middle Grades*. Bowker, 1970. Titles for reading guidance and book talks are grouped according to the developmental goals of childhood, and a subject index groups these same titles under their conventional headings.

———. *Juniorplots; A Book Talk Manual for Teachers and Librarians*. Bowker, 1967. Thematic discussions of specific books grouped under eight categories of basic goals of adolescence.

*Good Books for Children; A Selection of Outstanding Children's Books Published 1950–65*, ed. by Mary K. Eakin, 3rd ed. Univ. of Chicago Pr., 1966. The bibliography consists of graded reviews chosen from the *Bulletin of the Center for Children's Books*.

*Growing Point*, published by Margery Fisher. Belmont, 1962 to date. Nine issues yearly, published in England, reviews books for parents, teachers, and librarians in the English-speaking world.

*Guide to Children's Magazines, Newspapers, Reference Books*, prepared by Roberta A. Bouverat. Assoc. for Childhood Education International, 1968. Revised guide to provide a quick index of available materials.

*A Guide to Historical Reading; Non-Fiction*, comp. by Leonard B. Irwin. McKinley, 1970. Annotated selective listing.

*Historical Fiction*, comp. by Hannah Logasa. McKinley, 1968. Chronologically arranged, with separate sections for Canada, Latin America, and the United States.

*Historical Non-Fiction*, comp. by Hannah Logasa. McKinley, 1960. Annotated listing in the McKinley series.

*History in Children's Books: An Annotated Bibliography for Schools and Libraries*, comp. by Zena Sutherland. McKinley, 1967. The fifth in a series of bibliographies for schools, libraries, and teachers.

*The Horn Book Magazine*. Horn Book. Published six times a year. A magazine about children's books, authors, illustrators, with a section for reviews.

*I Can Read It Myself; Some Books for Independent Reading in the Primary Grades*, prepared by Frieda M. Heller. Ohio State Univ., 1965. Annotated lists divided into three levels of competence.

*Index to Short Biographies: For Elementary and Junior High Grades*, comp. by Helen Stanius. Scarecrow, 1971. Collective biographees are listed first by author, then by biographies.

*An Index to Young Readers' Collective Biographies*, comp. by Judith Silverman. Bowker, 1970. The contents of 471 collective biographies for elementary and junior high school readers. The alphabetical arrangement by biographee includes birth dates, nationality, and profession. Section 2 is a subject listing, with cross references and divided by country. Title and subject heading indexes are appended.

*Junior High School Library Catalog*, ed. by Estelle A. Fidell and Gary L. Bogart, 2nd ed. Wilson, 1970. Annual supp. Part 1, the Classified Catalog, is arranged with nonfiction books first, classified according to Dewey Decimal Classification system. Fiction books follow and short stories are next. Part 2 is an author, title, subject, analytical index. Cumulated every five years, with yearly supplements.

*Latin America; An Annotated List of Materials for Children*, ed. by Anne Pellowski, selected by a committee of librarians, teachers, and Latin-American specialists in cooperation with the Center for Inter-American Relations. Information Center on Children's Cultures, United States Committee for UNICEF, 1969. Materials are arranged by country and age-graded.

*A Layman's Guide to Negro History*, ed. and comp. by Erwin A. Salk. Quadrangle, 1966. Comprehensive compilation of books and teaching aids, conveniently categorized, and listings of important dates and people in black history.

*Let's Read Together*, 3rd ed. Children's Services Division, ALA, and National Congress of Parents and Teachers. ALA, 1969. Books for family enjoyment, by age levels and annotated.

MARTIN, LAURA K. *Magazines for School Libraries; A Brief Survey*. Univ. of Ky., 1967. This is a discussion, rather than a listing, of magazines useful to teachers and librarians, as well as students, covering such areas as selection of materials, general comment, family life, fine arts, etc.

*Negro Literature for High School Students*, prepared by Barbara Dodds. Nat. Council of Teachers of English, 1968. A valuable reference guide offering a historical survey of black writers, an annotated list of works about blacks, annotated lists of novels for boys and girls, and biographies, both historical and modern, as well as suggested classroom uses of black literature. Extensive bibliography.

*Notable Children's Books, 1940–1959*. ALA, 1966. Reappraisals of books on the annotated annual lists of the *ALA Bulletin* after a five-year interval to achieve a list of "Books Worth Their Keep."

*Patterns in Reading*, prepared by Jean Carolyn Roos, 2nd ed. ALA, 1961. A useful selection of books for older children, youth, and young adults. The books are grouped around more than a hundred major reading interests and are well annotated and indexed. A valuable reference.

*Periodicals for School Libraries; A Guide to Magazines, Newspapers, Periodical Indexes*, comp. and ed. by Marian H. Scott. ALA, 1969. A buying guide to periodicals and newspapers for school library purchases. Entries are alphabetical, and each is accompanied by appropriate grade level, name and address of publisher, frequency of publication, and price. Annotations describe the nature and scope of the publication and possible curricular use.

*Reading Ladders for Human Relations*, ed. by Muriel Crosby. American Council on Education, 1963. This enlarged and revised edition contains an introduction and bibliographies on the role of reading in developing children's self-knowledge and social awareness.

*Red, White and Black: (and Brown and Yellow): Minorities in America*, Harold H. Laskey, director. Combined Paperback Exhibit, 1970. Catalog of paperbacks on minority groups, with an order form for purchasing books or previewing films.

*Reference Books for Elementary and Junior High School Libraries*, comp. by Carolyn Sue Peterson. Scarecrow, 1970. A very useful annotated bibliography divided into general reference books (dictionaries, atlases, fact books, etc.) and those for subject areas.

*School Library Journal*. Bowker. A journal for librarians especially, it is published monthly, September through May. Approximately 1500 titles are reviewed, sometimes with dissenting opinions. There are also many articles on library services, books, and reading for children and young people.

*Science Books: A Quarterly Review*. Am. Assoc. for the Advancement of Science. Reviews around 100 science and mathematics books, elementary through college and beyond. Reviews are by specialists in the field.

*Science for Youth*, comp. by Hannah Logasa. McKinley, 1967. Annotated bibliography in the McKinley series.

*Standard Catalog for High School Libraries*. Annual supplements. Wilson. Part 1, the Classified Catalog, is arranged with nonfiction first, classified by Dewey Decimal System; fiction next; and then short stories. Each book is listed under one main entry where full information is given. Part 2 contains an author, title, subject, and analytical index of all the books in the catalog.

*Stories to Tell to Children*. Carnegie Library of Pittsburgh, frequently revised. One of the outstanding bibliographies of folk and fairy literature available for the storyteller.

*Subject Guide to Children's Books in Print*. Bowker, annual. A subject index to children's books in 7000 categories.

*Subject and Title Index to Short Stories for Children*. Subcommittee of the ALA Editorial Committee, 1955. Designed to assist librarians and teachers in locating stories on specific subjects. Approximate grades given.

*Subject Index to Books for Intermediate Grades*, comp. by Mary K. Eakin, 3rd ed. ALA, 1963. An index of 1800 titles with emphasis on trade books.

*Subject Index to Books for Primary Grades*, comp. by Mary K. Eakin and Eleanor Merritt, 3rd ed. ALA, 1967. Approximately 1000 textbooks and trade books for primary grades are indexed under detailed subject headings useful for the classroom teacher and librarian.

*Subject Index to Poetry for Children and Young People*. ALA, 1957. Indicates grade level.

*Translated Children's Books; Offered by Publishers in the U.S.A.* Storybooks International, 1968. Annotated list of books, arranged alphabetically according to language of origin, with an author index and a title index.

*Treasure for the Taking*, prepared by Anne Thaxter Eaton. Viking, 1957. First published in 1946, this revised, annotated bibliography is arranged according to many types of children's books.

*We Build Together; A Reader's Guide to Negro Life and Literature for Elementary and High School Use*, ed. by Charlemae Rollins, 3rd ed. Nat. Council of Teachers of English, 1967. A selected, annotated bibliography of picture books, fiction, history, biography, poetry, folklore, music, science, and sports, with an introduction dealing with the criteria by which the books were selected.

*World Culture*, comp. by Hannah Logasa. McKinley, 1963. Arranged in subject categories.

*The World of Children's Literature*, comp. by Anne Pellowski. Bowker, 1968. An annotated bibliography giving a picture of the development of children's literature in every country where it exists.

WRIGHT, SYLVIA HART. *Magazines Recommended for Use with Children, Grades K–12; A Comparative Survey of Six Basic Lists Compiled by Librarians and Educators*, 2nd ed. Franklin Square-Mayfair Subscription Agency, 1969.

*Your Reading; A Book List for Junior High Schools*, ed. by Charles B. Willard and the Committee on the Junior High School Book List of the Nat. Council of Teachers of English. Signet, 1966. Annotated guide to almost 1300 books.

# APPENDIX B
# ADULT REFERENCES[2]

ABRAHAMS, ROGER, and GEORGE FOSS. *Anglo-American Folksong Style*. Prentice, 1968. Although many songs are included as examples, this is primarily an evaluation of the style, content, and form of folksong, and of the types of ballads and the changes in ballad style.

AFANASIEV, ALEXANDER N. *Russian Fairy Tales*, tr. by Norbert Guterman, ill. by A. Alexeieff. Pantheon, 1945. See the valuable "Folkloristic Commentary" by Roman Jakobson.

ALMY, MILLIE. *Ways of Studying Children*. Bureau of Publications, Teachers College, Columbia University, 1969. Chapter 5 relates to the use of literature in studying children.

ALMY, MILLIE, E. CHITTENDEN, and PAULA MILLER. *Young Children's Thinking; Studies of Some Aspects of Piaget's Theory*. Teachers College Pr., 1966.

ALTICK, RICHARD D. *Lives and Letters: A History of Literary Biography in England and America*. Knopf, 1965. With liberal bibliographical notes for each chapter, the author discusses the achievement and influence of literary biographers from the 17th century to today. A thoroughly researched and comprehensive study.

AMERICAN COUNCIL ON EDUCATION. *Helping Teachers Understand Children*. American Council on Education, 1945. Report of a project designed to deepen understanding of children's growth and development by analyzing and identifying causes that underlie children's behavior.

ANDERSON, HAROLD, ed. *Creativity and Its Cultivation*. Harper, 1959. A compilation of outstanding research papers in the field of creativity. Carl Rogers' paper entitled "Toward a Theory of Creativity" presents his findings on psychological safety, which he considers essential to creative thinking.

ANDERSON, VERNA. *Reading and Young Children*. Macmillan, 1968. A survey of the approaches to the teaching of reading, the problems and the techniques of meeting them, and the use of materials with children.

*The Annotated Mother Goose*, with introduction and notes by William Baring-Gould and Ceil Baring-Gould; the complete text and illustrations in a fully annotated edition, ill. by Caldecott, Crane, Greenaway, Rackham, Parrish, and historical woodcuts. With chapter decorations by E. M. Simon. Potter, 1962. Mother Goose and other rhymes, ditties, and jingles of the nursery run side by side with columns of absorbing historical notes. This impressively large, beautiful book contains over 200 illustrations with a first-line index.

ARBUTHNOT, MAY HILL. *Children's Reading in the Home*, ill. Scott, Foresman, 1969. A description of a good home environment for reading followed by a discussion of books according to age range and type.

ARBUTHNOT, MAY HILL, and DOROTHY M. BRODERICK. *Time for Biography*, ill. by Rainey Bennett. Scott, Foresman, 1969. Collection of biographies for children, with a special section on writing and evaluating, and a bibliography.

———. *Time for Stories of the Past and Present*, ill. by Rainey Bennett. Scott, Foresman, 1968. A collection of realistic stories for children with section introductions, headnotes for individual stories, and a special discussion of realistic literature for children.

ARBUTHNOT, MAY HILL, DOROTHY M. BRODERICK, SHELTON L. ROOT, JR., MARK TAYLOR, and EVELYN L. WENZEL. *The Arbuthnot Anthology of Children's Literature*, 3rd ed., ill. by Rainey Bennett and others. Scott, Foresman, 1971. Single-volume edition of *Time for Poetry, Time for Old Magic, Time for New Magic, Time for Stories, Time for Biography*, and *Time for Discovery*.

ARBUTHNOT, MAY HILL, and SHELTON L. ROOT, JR. *Time for Poetry*, 3rd ed., ill. by Arthur Paul. Scott, Foresman, 1968. A favorite collection of nearly 800 poems, with a special section, "Keeping Poetry and Children Together," which discusses reading poetry to children, using poetry in verse choirs, and working toward a greater appreciation of poetry.

ARBUTHNOT, MAY HILL, and MARK TAYLOR. *Time for New Magic*, ill. by John Averill and others. Scott, Foresman, 1971. A large collection of modern fantasy for children, with headnotes, introductions, bibliography, and a special section which discusses briefly the history of its development and standards for its evaluation.

———. *Time for Old Magic*, ill. by John Averill and others. Scott, Foresman, 1970. A collection of folk tales, fables, myths, and epics, followed by a section on storytelling and reading aloud and a bibliography.

ARNSTEIN, FLORA. *Children Write Poetry: A Creative Approach*, 2nd ed. Stanford Univ. Pr., 1967. A teacher's careful record of her step-by-step procedures in conducting an experiment in creative writing with a group of elementary-school children, with discussions of qualities that mark authentic poetry.

*The Art of Beatrix Potter*, with an appreciation by Anne Carroll Moore. Warne, 1956. In a truly beautiful book, landscapes, still life, experimental drawings,

2. This list provides data and annotations for the Adult References in Chapters 1–16 and Part 6. Consult Appendix A for any reference not found here. For additional useful reading suggestions see the bibliographies accompanying the ten articles in Part 7.

and the tiny pictures for her children's classics are reproduced, giving new insight into the versatility of Beatrix Potter.

ASBJÖRNSEN, PETER C., and JÖRGEN MOE. *Norwegian Folk Tales*, tr. by Pat Shaw Iversen and Carl Norman, ill. by Erik Werenskiold and Theodor Kittelson. Viking, 1961. Thirty-six folk tales in an excellent recent translation which reintroduces the original Asbjörnsen illustrators.

______. *Popular Tales from the Norse*, tr. by Sir George Webbe Dasent. Putnam, 1908. A long and rich introduction by the translator is particularly good on changes from myth to fairy tale.

ASHTON, JOHN. *Chap-Books of the Eighteenth Century*. London: Chatto, 1882. (Facsimile of the original: Singing Tree, 1968) The author reproduces the stories and some of the pages and illustrations from the old chapbooks.

ASIMOV, ISAAC. *Words from the Myths*. Houghton, 1961. From the Greek myths come many word roots used in science and daily language. Mr. Asimov tells the legends briefly and explains origins of current usage.

AUSLANDER, JOSEPH, and FRANK ERNEST HILL. *The Winged Horse; The Story of Poets and Their Poetry*. Doubleday, 1927. Written for older children and young people, this is a thoroughly interesting book for teachers and parents as well. Fine references on ballads and epics.

BAIRD, BIL. *The Art of the Puppet*, ill. Macmillan, 1965. A fascinating and handsomely illustrated book "designed to tell people about puppets and how they differ from each other and how they are alike" by a man with "forty years of practice in a profession that has given me the greatest satisfaction."

BARCHILON, JACQUES, and HENRY PETTIT. *The Authentic Mother Goose Fairy Tales and Nursery Rhymes*. Swallow Pr., 1960. Following a scholarly introduction to the history of Mother Goose and the Perrault fairy tales, there are facsimiles of the complete *Mother Goose's Melody*, and of the 1729 English translation of Perrault's *Tales*.

BARROWS, HERBERT, HUBERT HEFFNER, JOHN CIARDI, and WALLACE DOUGLAS. *How Does a Poem Mean?* Houghton, 1959. A college text for the study of poetry in general with an analysis of specific poems. The examples from traditional ballads, nonsense verse, and fine English poetry make the book a good anthology also.

BARRY, FLORENCE V. *A Century of Children's Books*. Doran, 1923; reissued, Singing Tree, 1969. A readable account of early English books for children, with unusually good evaluations.

BAUGHMAN, ERNEST. *A Type and Motif Index of the Folktales of England and North America*. Indiana Univ. Folklore Series, No. 20, 1966. Gives extensive bibliographic references to the well-known folk-tale types.

BEADLE, MURIEL. *A Child's Mind; How Children Learn During the Critical Years from Birth to Age Five*, ill. Doubleday, 1970. A review, prepared for the lay person, of what has been learned in the past 25 years about the child's mind and development.

BECHTEL, LOUISE SEAMAN. *Books in Search of Children*, ed. and with an introduction by Virginia Haviland. Macmillan, 1969. Speeches and essays by a pioneering editor and critic.

BEHN, HARRY. *Chrysalis; Concerning Children and Poetry*. Harcourt, 1968. A children's poet reminisces and writes about children and poetry.

BERRY, THOMAS ELLIOTT, ed. *The Biographer's Craft*. Odyssey, 1967. A textbook with examples of the work of seventeen biographers from Plutarch to contemporary writers, and with one-page analyses of the biographers' genres and output. Introductory essay and short additional-reading list.

BETT, HENRY. *The Games of Children; Their Origin and History*. Singing Tree, 1968. Intended for both the student of folklore and the general reader, this book explores the primitive, often religious origin of many of the games still played by children.

*The Bewick Collector*. A descriptive catalogue of the works of Thomas and John Bewick. . . . The whole described from the originals by Thomas Hugo, M.A., F.R.S.I., etc. London: Lovell Reeve, Vol. I, 1866. Supp., 1868; reissued, Singing Tree, 1968.

BLACKBURN, HENRY. *Randolph Caldecott: A Personal Memoir of His Early Art Career*, ill. with reproductions and photographs. London: Sampson Low, 1886.

BOLTON, HENRY CARRINGTON. *The Counting-Out Rhymes of Children; Their Antiquity, Origin, and Wide Distribution: A Study in Folk-Lore*. Singing Tree, 1969. Almost 900 rhymes in 18 languages, including Japanese, Hawaiian, Turkish, and the Penobscot dialect, as well as the more common European languages.

BOWEN, CATHERINE DRINKER. *Biography: The Craft and the Calling*. Little, 1968. Dealing with the planning, research, and techniques involved, the book analyzes four major biographies, with side excursions for further examples, and provides a good tool for writers in the field.

BRAND, OSCAR. *The Ballad Mongers; Rise of the Modern Folk Song*. Funk, 1962. An excellent survey of the interest in, and development of, the folk music of America, reviewing the contributors of the past as well as major contemporary figures. Only a few excerpts of lyrics are included; the book is a history of the revolution in folk music.

BREWTON, JOHN E. and SARA W., comps. *Index to Children's Poetry*, Wilson, 1942. First supp., 1954; second supp., 1965. Helpful in finding poem sources. Indexed by author, title, subject, and first line. Thorough analysis of book contents, number of poems in a book, and grade placement.

BRIGGS, KATHARINE M. *A Dictionary of British Folk-Tales in the English Language*. Indiana Univ. Pr., 1970. Part A, Folk Narratives, Vols. 1 and 2. Part B, Folk Legends, Vols. 1 and 2. Contains complete texts and summaries of all British tales in English with extensive comparative notes.

BROWN, HELEN A., and HARRY J. HELTMAN, eds. *Choral Readings for Fun and Recreation*. Westminster, 1956.

BROWN, JAMES W. *AV Instruction: Materials and Methods*. McGraw, 1959. A textbook for teacher training sources in audiovisual instruction, with emphasis on interrelatedness of all teaching aids and the role of the instructor in the presentation of such material.

BRUNER, JEROME S. *Toward a Theory of Instruction.* Belknap Pr. of Harvard Univ., 1966. A collection of essays concerned with the relation between the growth and development of the child and the art of teaching.

BRUNVAND, JAN H. *The Study of American Folklore, an Introduction.* Norton, 1968. The best introductory textbook presently available, with excellent bibliographic references for each chapter.

BULFINCH, THOMAS. *Age of Fable; or, Stories of Gods and Heroes,* introduction by Dudley Fitts, ill. by Joe Mugnaini. Heritage, 1958. This handsome edition of Bulfinch is almost completely devoted to the Greek and Roman myths, though it does include brief materials from the Norse, Celtic, and Hindu lore.

CAMERON, ELEANOR. *The Green and Burning Tree; On the Writing and Enjoyment of Children's Books.* Little, 1969. Critical essays by a writer for children, with a special emphasis on fantasy.

CARLSEN, G. ROBERT. *Books and the Teen-Age Reader; A Guide for Teachers, Librarians, and Parents,* rev. ed. Harper, 1971. A practical book for adults who want to help adolescents read with pleasure for growth and personal fulfillment.

CARLSON, RUTH KEARNEY. *Enrichment Ideas; Sparkling Fireflies.* Brown, 1970. For the elementary school classroom teacher, suggestions for dramatization, art projects, language games, and ways of using literature to enrich the curriculum. The suggestions for activities are accompanied by selected references for children and selected references for adults.

CARROLL, LEWIS (pseud.). *The Annotated Alice; Alice's Adventures in Wonderland & Through the Looking Glass,* ill. by John Tenniel. With introduction and notes by Martin Gardner. Potter, 1960. Significant quotations from Carroll biographies and other sources are placed parallel to the story text. An enriching background source for students.

CATALDO, JOHN W. *Words and Calligraphy for Children.* Van Nostrand, 1969. Reproductions of paintings, drawings, and designs by children in an art workshop intended to give, through free expression, a familiarity with language symbols. Arranged by age groups.

CATTERSON, JANE H., ed. *Children and Literature.* International Reading Assoc., 1969. A selection of papers from the Association's annual convention that should help teachers, both elementary and high school, bring literature into the curriculum and provide positive literary experience.

CHALL, JEANNE. *Learning to Read; The Great Debate.* McGraw, 1967. The findings of a three-year study on teaching beginning reading with a sober discussion of conclusions and recommendations.

CHAMBERS, AIDAN. *The Reluctant Reader.* Pergamon, 1969. A lively account by a Britisher of why young people are reluctant to read creative fiction, with suggestions for authors, teachers, publishers, and librarians. Bibliographies for reluctant readers in appendices.

CHAMBERS, DEWEY W. *Children's Literature in the Curriculum.* Rand, 1971. A "plea" to make children's literature "an integral part of the elementary school's curriculum" and "an important factor in the lives of children." The three sections are "The Role of Literature in the Elementary Curriculum," "How Books Can Affect Children," and "Thoughts on Some Controversial Issues in Children's Literature."

CHAMBERS, ROBERT. *Popular Rhymes of Scotland.* Singing Tree, 1969. First published in 1826, this work has been revised and expanded several times. The 1870 edition is reproduced in this volume.

CHILD, FRANCIS JAMES, ed. *English and Scottish Popular Ballads,* 5 vols. Houghton, 1882–1898. This is our most authoritative source for all English and Scottish traditional ballads. Many variants are given for each ballad, together with copious notes.

*Chosen for Children; an Account of the Books Which Have Been Awarded the Library Association Carnegie Medal, 1936–1965,* rev. ed. London: The Library Assoc, 1967. A discussion of the prize-winning books for children by British authors, with excerpts, illustrations, biographical material, comments by and pictures of the authors.

CHUKOVSKY, KORNEI. *From Two to Five,* tr. and ed. by Miriam Morton. Univ. of Calif. Pr., 1965. A book on the language and comprehension of the very young child written by the dean of Russian children's writers, rich in its insights and observations.

CIANCIOLO, PATRICIA. *Illustrations in Children's Books.* Brown, 1970. The book deals with art and design as areas of study in the elementary school: styles, techniques, appraisal of illustrations and their use in class. Up-to-date references by chapters, and with bibliography and index.

CLARK, ANN NOLAN. *Journey to the People,* with introduction by Annis Duff, ill. Viking, 1969. Essays about a lifelong experience with teaching Indian children: Zuni, Navajo, Pueblo, and other tribes of the Southwest, as well as the Dakota Sioux and the Indians of Guatemala and Peru.

CLEARY, FLORENCE. *Blueprints for Better Reading: School Programs for Promoting Skill and Interest in Reading.* Wilson, 1970. Offers both inspiration and ideas to teachers and librarians.

CLIFFORD, JAMES L. *From Puzzles to Portraits: Problems of a Literary Biographer.* Univ. of N. Car. Pr., 1970. An approach to biography writing that deals in anecdotal style with such problems as testing authenticity, the fictional method, the pursuit of vague footnotes, and the ethics of the biographer's selectivity.

———, ed. *Biography as an Art.* Oxford, 1962. A most useful collection of forty-seven essays of selected literary criticism by biographers, ranging from writers of the 16th to the mid-20th century, with an additional bibliography of about 150 modern books and articles.

COFFIN, TRISTRAM P. *The British Traditional Ballad in North America.* The American Folklore Society, Bibliographic and Special Series II (1950, 1963). Contains bibliographic listings for all the versions of the traditional (Child) ballads collected in North America.

COLBY, JEAN POINDEXTER, *Writing, Illustrating and Editing Children's Books*, ill. Hastings, 1967. A rewritten and enlarged edition of *The Children's Book Field*, this covers all phases of juvenile publishing and provides a wealth of practical data for authors and illustrators.

COLES, ROBERT. *Children of Crisis*. Atlantic, 1964. Based on the author's interviews with black and white people in the South, a long-term study of children, analyzing their drawings as well as their conversation.

COLES, ROBERT, and MARIA PIERS. *Wages of Neglect*. Quadrangle, 1969. An examination of the behavior of young children of the poor, their special hardships, and social and personal anxieties that determine their behavior.

COLLINGWOOD, STUART DODGSON. *The Life and Letters of Lewis Carroll (Rev. C. L. Dodgson)*. Gale Library of Lives and Letters: British Writers Series. Singing Tree, 1967. The biography of Lewis Carroll, written by his nephew shortly after his death, is a primary source book of information about the public and private life of this children's writer.

COLUM, PADRAIC, ed. *A Treasury of Irish Folklore*. Crown, 1954. This book gives insight into Irish history and heroism as well as folklore.

COMENIUS, JOHN AMOS. *The Orbis Pictus of John Amos Comenius*. Singing Tree, 1968. The first children's picture book and the most widely known textbook of the 17th and 18th centuries, reproduced from an 1887 photographic copy of a 1728 London edition, this volume is of interest to educators and historians alike.

COMMIRE, ANNE. *Something About the Author: Facts and Pictures About Contemporary Authors and Illustrators of Books for Young People*. Vol. I. Gale, 1971. The inclusion of biographical information and lists of writings gives this reference use for adults.

CONRAD, EDNA, and MARY VAN DYKE. *History on the Stage; Children Make Plays from Historical Novels*, ill. with photos. Van Nostrand, 1971. Approaches the making of plays as a teaching technique, from choosing and reading a book and improvising to develop a script, to performance. Can be used by children 11 to 14 as well as by teachers and librarians.

COOK, ELIZABETH. *The Ordinary and the Fabulous; An Introduction to Myths, Legends, and Fairy Tales for Teachers and Storytellers*. Cambridge Univ. Pr., 1969. The author undertakes to show that an adult understanding of life is incomplete without an understanding of myths, legends, and fairy tales and that there are many ways of presenting them to children.

CRAVEN, PAUL R. *Biography*. Dickenson Pub. Co., 1968. An introductory textbook, organized under autobiography, journals, obituaries, personality sketches, and extracts from books such as Samuel L. Clemens' *Life on the Mississippi*.

CREIGHTON, HELEN, comp. *Songs and Ballads from Nova Scotia*. Dover, 1966. Includes Scottish and English ballads and folk songs of English and Scottish origin as well as songs native to North America.

CREWS, FREDERICK C. *The Pooh Perplex; A Freshman Casebook*, ill. by E. H. Shepard. Dutton, 1963. Brilliant parodies using Milne's stories and verses to satirize various methods of literary criticism.

CROSBY, MURIEL. *An Adventure in Human Relations*. Follett, 1965. Report of a three-year experimental project in schools in changing neighborhoods, with two main goals: improving the schools through developing appropriate curriculum and in-service teacher training and upgrading family and community life through the development of indigenous leadership.

CROUCH, MARCUS. *Treasure Seekers and Borrowers: Children's Books in Britain, 1900–1960*. London: The Library Assoc., 1962. Excellent brief appraisals of authors and books, chiefly British, published during the first sixty years of the twentieth century.

CULLINAN, BERNICE E. *Literature for Children: Its Discipline and Content*. Brown, 1971. For elementary classroom teachers, this book is intended to build effective courses in literature. Well constructed and researched with numerous references for each chapter.

*A Curriculum for English*. The Nebraska Curriculum Development Center. Univ. of Nebraska Pr., 1966. This excellently worked out curriculum covers the years of kindergarten through high school and also makes suggestions for the first year of college.

DARLING, RICHARD L. *The Rise of Children's Book Reviewing in America, 1865–1881*. Bowker, 1968. A scholarly and thorough examination of the publishing and reviewing of children's books, set in the historical context. Thirty-six periodicals are examined, including the most important literary periodicals of the time.

DARTON, F. J. H. *Children's Books in England: Five Centuries of Social Life*, 2nd ed. Cambridge Univ. Pr., 1958. A scholarly study of children's books, from the fables to Robert Louis Stevenson. Chapter VII is about John Newbery and the first English books for children.

DAUGHERTY, JAMES. *William Blake*, ill. Viking, 1960. An appreciative biography by a contemporary illustrator.

DAVIS, MARY GOULD. *Randolph Caldecott 1846–1886: An Appreciation*. Lippincott, 1946. An evaluation of the great English artist's contribution to children's literature.

DE ANGELI, MARGUERITE. *Butter at the Old Price*. Doubleday, 1971. A grande dame of the children's book world describes, in her autobiography, her long career as an author.

DE AUGULO, JAIME. *Indian Tales*, ill. by author, foreword by Carl Carmer. Hill, 1953. The author lived 40 years among the Pit River Indians and thinks as they think and writes in English as they speak in their language. The time of these stories is the historic dawn, "when men and animals were not so distinguishable as they are today." Chiefly an adult source book.

DENNISON, GEORGE. *The Lives of Children: The Story of the First Street School*. Random, 1969. A fascinating account of a free school with three full-time and one half-time teachers working with twenty-three students, white, black, and Puerto Rican, all from low-income homes and half rejects from the public schools, with severe learning and behavior problems.

DEUTSCH, BABETTE. *Poetry in Our Time.* Holt, 1952. This book brings the author's earlier study of *The Modern Poetry* more nearly up to date. It is a detailed and scholarly analysis of new trends in poetry and the output of individual poets, from Thomas Hardy to Cummings, Stevens, Williams, and their contemporaries.

DEUTSCH, MARTIN, and others. *The Disadvantaged Child.* Basic, 1967. Selected papers on the social environment for learning, and on such factors as race, social class, and language in the education of the disadvantaged child.

DE VRIES, LEONARD. *Little Wide-Awake: An Anthology from Victorian Children's Books and Periodicals in the Collection of Anne and Fernand G. Renier,* ill. World, 1967. Interesting examples of what was read by children during the 60 years of Victoria's reign.

DEWITT, MARGUERITE E., and others. *Practical Methods in Choral Speaking.* Expression, 1936. A compilation of papers by American teachers covering methods from the primary grades through the university, with many practical suggestions.

DOMAN, GLENN. *How to Teach Your Baby to Read; The Gentle Revolution.* Random, 1964. Work with brain-injured children has led to a more complete understanding of how all children learn and the development of a startling new reading program.

DORSON, RICHARD M. *American Folklore.* Univ. of Chicago Pr., 1959. A very readable general survey of prose forms of oral folklore in the United States. Devotes little attention to folksong.

———. *Buying the Wind, Regional Folklore in the United States.* Univ. of Chicago Pr., 1964. A good selection of authentic folklore texts with useful notes and introduction.

———, ed. *Folktales of the World.* Univ. of Chicago Pr. This most impressive series for the student of folklore has been published under the general editorship of Richard Dorson, a professor of history and director of the Folklore Institute at Indiana University. In each volume, his foreword is learned, informative, and beautifully written. The editor for each volume is a distinguished folklorist in his or her own right. The full notes, index of motifs, glossary, bibliography, and general index in each volume add to their usefulness for the scholar. Each book contains from fifty to one hundred tales; several titles are discussed in Chapter 6.

*Folktales of Japan,* ed. by Keigo Seki
*Folktales of Israel,* ed. by Dov Noy
*Folktales of Hungary,* ed. by Linda Dégh
*Folktales of Norway,* ed. by Reidar Th. Christiansen
*Folktales of Scotland,* ed. by Hamish Henderson and John MacInnes
*Folktales of Germany,* ed. by Kurt Ranke
*Folktales of Poland,* ed. by Julian Krzyżanowski
*Folktales of Ireland,* ed. by Sean O'Sullivan
*Folktales of Switzerland,* ed. by Robert Wildhaber
*Folktales of China,* ed. by Wolfram Eberhard
*Folktales of England,* ed. by Katharine M. Briggs and Ruth L. Tongue
*Folktales of India,* ed. by Praphulladatta Goswami
*Folktales of the Philippines,* ed. by E. Arsenio Manuel
*Folktales of France,* ed. by Geneviève Massignon
*Folktales of West Africa,* ed. by Jack Berry
*Folktales of Chile,* ed. by Yolando Pino-Saavedra
*Folktales of Greece,* ed. by Georgios A. Megas
*Folktales of Mexico,* ed. by Americo Paredes

DOUGLAS, NORMAN. *London Street Games.* Singing Tree, 1968. Greatly expanded from an article published in *English Review* in 1913, this running account of English street life in the early part of the century captures the vocabulary and tone of the children Douglas collected from.

DOYLE, BRIAN, comp. and ed. *The Who's Who of Children's Literature,* ill. Schocken Books, 1969. Full and lively biographical sketches of authors and illustrators.

DREW, ELIZABETH, and GEORGE CONNOR. *Discovering Modern Poetry.* Holt, 1961. "There is no single 'meaning' to much poetry. Different interpretations are always possible. . . . Analysis is not destructive, it is creative." These are clues to the authors' approach to the interpretation of modern poetry. Modern authors are examined with an appreciation that should help the most skeptical to a better understanding of modern poetry.

DUFF, ANNIS. *"Bequest of Wings"; A Family's Pleasures with Books.* Viking, 1944. A pleasant account of one family's use of books, pictures, and music.

———. *"Longer Flight"; A Family Grows up with Books.* Viking, 1955. Another pleasant, anecdotal account of a family and its reading, and some apt generalizations about what books mean to children and adolescents.

DUNNING, STEPHEN. *Teaching Literature to Adolescents: Poetry.* Scott, Foresman, 1966. Discusses basic principles for the teaching of poetry to adolescents. Includes discussion of library resources and a series of problems for in-class use.

———. *Teaching Literature to Adolescents: Short Stories.* Scott, Foresman, 1968. Contains eight sample stories and provides specific suggestions for the teacher.

EASTMAN, MARY HUSE. *Index to Fairy Tales, Myths and Legends.* Faxon, 1926. First supp., 1937; second supp., 1952. Useful for locating various sources in which individual tales may be found. There are geographical and racial groupings and lists for storytellers.

EASTMAN, MAX. *The Enjoyment of Poetry.* Scribner's, 1921, 1951. This book is an excellent introduction to the pleasures of poetry. Chapter I, "Poetic People," in which he gives his reasons for listing the child as one of the "poetic people," and Chapter V, "Practical Values of Poetry," should be noted.

ECKENSTEIN, LINA. *Comparative Studies in Nursery Rhymes.* London: Duckworth, 1906; reissued, Singing Tree, 1968. A study of the ancient folk origins of the Mother Goose verses and their European counterparts.

EDEN, HORATIA K. F. *Juliana Horatia Ewing and Her Books.* Gale Library of Lives and Letters: British Writers Series. Singing Tree, 1969. The biography of Juliana Horatia Ewing (1841–1885), her letters, and a bibliography, compiled by the younger sister of this esteemed writer for children.

EDWARDS, MARGARET A. *The Fair Garden and the Swarm of Beasts; The Library and the Young Adult.* Hawthorn, 1969. The writer's own experience in developing a young adult library department, recounted in a lively provocative manner.

EGOFF, SHEILA. *The Republic of Childhood; A Critical Guide to Canadian Children's Literature in English.* Oxford, 1967. Creative writing for children by Canadian authors between the years of 1950 and 1965.

EGOFF, SHEILA, G. T. STUBBS, and L. F. ASHLEY, eds. *Only Connect: Readings on Children's Literature,* ill. Oxford, 1969. A compilation of essays by well-known, competent writers and critics covering literary criticism and history, standards, changing tastes, children's responses, writers and their writing, and illustration.

ELLIS, ALEC. *A History of Children's Reading and Literature.* Pergamon, 1968. History of schools, educational practice, and library development in England.

ELLIS, ANNE W. *The Family Story in the 1960's.* Archon Books & Clive Bingley, 1970. A survey, with comments on trends, on family stories, almost all of British origin, published during the decade. Good commentary and checklist.

ERIKSON, ERIK H. *Childhood and Society,* 2nd ed., rev. and enl. Norton, 1964. The noted psychoanalyst's summary of his studies of childhood, emphasizing the importance of early experiences in the development of adult attitudes and actions.

ERNEST, EDWARD, comp., assisted by PATRICIA TRACY LOWE. *The Kate Greenaway Treasury,* ill. World, 1967. A biography of Kate Greenaway, an evaluation of her art, a fine essay about her work by the late Anne Carroll Moore, and an introduction by Ruth Hill Viguers, make this rich collection the definitive study of a beloved children's book illustrator.

EVERTTS, ELDONNA, ed. *Explorations in Children's Writing.* Nat. Council of Teachers of English, 1970. Papers growing out of a conference on teaching elementary English, in which teachers discuss experiences with children writing.

FADER, DANIEL N., and ELTON B. MC NEIL. *Hooked on Books; Program and Proof.* Putnam, 1968. A detailed description of a program to get bored and apathetic students to read, accompanied by a description of a research project evaluating the program.

FEATHERSTONE, JOSEPH. *Schools Where Children Learn.* Liveright, 1971. These are pieces on schools, learning, and teaching that have appeared in *The New Republic.* Part One is about the Primary School Revolution in Britain; Part Two, about The State of the Profession with varieties of good practice and bad.

FELDMAN, EDMUND BURKE. *Becoming Human Through Art: Aesthetic Experience in the School,* ill. Prentice, 1970. An interdisciplinary approach to visual education, primarily for teachers and teachers of teachers.

FENNER, PHYLLIS. *The Proof of the Pudding.* Day, 1957. An entertaining discussion of many books children enjoy.

______, ed. *Something Shared: Children and Books.* Day, 1959. A spirited compilation from many authors interested in children and books offers genuine entertainment as well as inspiration.

FENWICK, SARA INNIS, ed. *A Critical Approach to Children's Literature.* Univ. of Chicago Pr., 1967. Collected papers from a conference on children's literature, representing a variety of aspects.

FIELD, CAROLYN W., ed., with VIRGINIA HAVILAND and ELIZABETH NESBITT, consultants. *Subject Collections in Children's Literature.* Bowker, 1969. Identifies and publicizes special collections of children's literature, especially for those interested in research.

FIELD, ELINOR WHITNEY, comp. *Horn Book Reflections: On Children's Books and Reading.* Selected from eighteen years of *The Horn Book Magazine*—1949–1966. Horn Book, 1969. Contributors are writers, illustrators, teachers, librarians, and parents.

FIELD, LOUISE F. *The Child and His Book: Some Account of the History and Progress of Children's Literature in England.* Singing Tree, 1968. An important scholarly work tracing the history of English books for children from before the Conquest to the 19th century, this book is also a social history of England.

FISHER, MARGERY. *Intent Upon Reading.* Watts, 1962. A refreshing and critical approach to children's books, both recent and standard selections. Though many of the titles are English publications, a great number are familiar to American readers.

FOLMSBEE, BEULAH. *A Little History of the Horn Book.* Horn Book, 1942. A tiny book, beautifully printed, with a history of hornbooks, in all their variations, both in England and New England.

FORD, PAUL LEICESTER, ed. *The New England Primer.* Dodd, 1897, 1962. The subtitle explains the content: "A history of its origin with a reprint of the unique copy of the earliest known first edition."

FORD, ROBERT. *Children's Rhymes, Children's Games, Children's Songs, Children's Stories: A Book for Bairns and Big Folk.* Singing Tree, 1968. The collection is a pioneer effort of the late 19th century to record the natural literature of the children of Scotland; it includes nursery and counting-out rhymes, rhyme games, songs and ballads, anecdotes, and stories.

FOSTER, FLORENCE P., comp. *Literature and the Young Child.* N. J. Dept. of Education, 1967. Criteria for selecting books for young children, techniques for reading aloud and storytelling, and suggestions for ways of stimulating continuing interest.

FRANK, JOSETTE. *Your Child's Reading Today,* rev. and updated. Doubleday, 1969. Sensible advice from a pioneer in the child study movement concerning a child's reading, given from the standpoint of his social-emotional development. Don't deprecate his tastes, she advises, but capitalize on reading enjoyment.

FRANKENBERG, LLOYD. *Pleasure Dome: On Reading Modern Poetry*. Houghton, 1949, 1968. In his Foreword the author says, "I hope to provide a bridge to modern poetry for readers like myself, brought up on prose."

FRAZER, SIR JAMES GEORGE. *The Golden Bough; A Study in Magic and Religion*, 1 vol. abr. ed. Macmillan, 1922. First published in 1890, this is a monumental study (originally 13 volumes) in comparative folklore, magic, and religion.

FREEMAN, LA VERNE, and RUTH SUNDERLIN FREEMAN. *The Child and His Picture Book*, ill. Century House, 1967. A reissue of a pioneer study, updated with particular attention to methods for using picture books to help underprivileged preschoolers and kindergartners get a head start toward successful school adjustment.

FRIEDMAN, ALBERT B. *The Viking Book of Folk Ballads of the English Speaking World*. Viking, 1956. Contains many ballads, with useful notes.

FRYATT, NORMA R., ed. *A Horn Book Sampler*. Horn Book, 1959. Selected articles on authors, artists, and books that appeared in *The Horn Book Magazine* between 1924 and 1948 provide illuminating background to some of the most significant years in children's book publication.

FRYE, BURTON C., ed. *A St. Nicholas Anthology; The Early Years*, ill. Meredith. 1969. A selection from the years 1870 to 1905 of stories, articles, and poems, as well as illustrations which appeared in this most beloved of all children's magazines.

FULLER, MURIEL, ed. *More Junior Authors*. Wilson, 1963. Companion volume to *The Junior Book of Authors*, 1951, rev. ed. Contains biographical material on current juvenile authors and illustrators not included in that work.

*Funk and Wagnalls Standard Dictionary of Folklore, Mythology and Legend*, ed. by Maria Leach and Jerome Fried, 2 vols. Funk, 1949. Working with a staff of internationally known folklorists and anthropologists, the editors have compiled an invaluable source on national folklores, characters, and symbols in folklore and mythology.

GESELL, ARNOLD, and FRANCES ILG. *Child Development; An Introduction to the Study of Human Growth*. Harper, 1949. This research study considers child growth in its broadest sense—intellectual, emotional, and social—from infancy through adolescence. Lucid style and revealing case histories make this a readable and essential book for parents and teachers.

GILLESPIE, MARGARET C. *Literature for Children: History and Trends*. Brown, 1970. Covering time from the 15th century to the present, the book has chapters on fantasy, poetry, realism (catechisms, religion, manners, primers, etc.), and landmarks of publishing, with selected references and index. For elementary teachers.

GLASSER, WILLIAM. *Schools Without Failure*. Harper, 1969. This book presents suggestions for making "involvement, relevance, and thinking realities in our schools . . . combined into a total program they can provide a foundation upon which to build the schools our children need."

GODDEN, RUMER. *Hans Christian Andersen: A Great Life in Brief*. Knopf, 1955. "Life itself is the most wonderful fairy tale." So wrote Andersen, and no one could have told his fairy tale more poignantly than Rumer Godden, the English novelist.

GOODRIDGE, JANET. *Creative Drama and Improvised Movement for Children*. Plays, 1971. Practical techniques, tested in schools and studios, for teaching creative drama and correlating it with other school subjects, such as English, physical education, music, and art.

GREEN, PERCY B. *A History of Nursery Rhymes*. Singing Tree, 1968. Detailed explanations of children's games, potentially useful to kindergarten and nursery school teachers as well as parents.

GREEN, PETER. *Kenneth Grahame*, ill. with photos. World, 1959. This very welcome biography is authoritatively and perceptively written.

GREEN, ROGER LANCELYN. *Tellers of Tales*, enl. ed. E. Ward, 1953; reissued, Watts, 1965. This is a delightfully written discussion of English authors of children's books from 1839 to the present. Only twenty pages are devoted to modern writers.

GRIMM, JACOB and WILHELM. *Grimm's Fairy Tales*, tr. by Margaret Hunt, rev. by James Stern, ill. by Josef Scharl. Pantheon, 1944. The "Introduction" by Padraic Colum and "Folkloristic Commentary" by Joseph Campbell are important contributions.

GUERBER, HELENE A. *Myths of Greece and Rome*. American Bk., 1893; reissued, British Book Center, 1963. A standard reference, retelling and reinterpreting the myths.

GULLAN, MARJORIE. *The Speech Choir*. Harper, 1937. This is one of the most useful of Miss Gullan's books because it is both an anthology and a methods text. It contains American poetry as well as English ballads, with a detailed description of the presentation and development of each poem. Most of the poems are for upper-grade children and the high schools.

HALES, JOHN W., and FREDERICK J. FURNIVALL, assisted by FRANCIS J. CHILD. *Bishop Percy's Folio Manuscript*. London: Trübner, 1967. Here are the ballads that Bishop Percy found, together with the reproduction of an actual page of the manuscript with Percy's notes scribbled in the margin.

HALLIWELL-PHILLIPPS, JAMES O. *Popular Rhymes and Nursery Tales: A Sequel to The Nursery Rhymes of England*. Singing Tree, 1968. This mid-nineteenth-century book is a collection of material of interest to folklorists as well as teachers and librarians.

HALSEY, ROSALIE V. *Forgotten Books of the American Nursery; A History of the Development of the American Story-Book*. Singing Tree, 1969. A reissue of a book first published at the turn of the century, this volume traces the history of children's books in America from colonial days to the early part of the nineteenth century, with emphasis on the light children's books shed on the social history of the country.

HAVILAND, VIRGINIA. *Children's Literature: A Guide to Reference Sources*, ill. Library of Congress, 1966. The only reference tool of its kind in scope and coverage, this book offers bibliographic guidance to books available today and to the history of children's literature.

HAZARD, PAUL. *Books, Children and Men*, tr. by Marguerite Mitchell, 4th ed. Horn Book, 1960. A member of the French Academy and professor of comparative literature both in France and in the United States has written engagingly of the great children's books of many countries.

HENTOFF, NAT. *Our Children Are Dying*, and JOHN Mc PHEE. *The Headmaster.* Four Winds, 1967. Two accounts of the problems and challenges of educators, one set in a public school in Harlem, the other in a private boys' boarding school.

HERNDON, JAMES. *The Way It Spozed to Be; A Report on the Crisis in Our Schools.* Bantam, 1969. An innovative teacher in a slum school reports on war in the classroom. Penetrating and wryly humorous.

HEWINS, CAROLINE M. *A Mid-Century Child and Her Books.* Singing Tree, 1969. The autobiography of a pioneer children's librarian who was also the author of many books on children's literature, this book provides a detailed picture of what life was like for a book-loving child in New England in the mid-nineteenth century.

HIGGINS, JAMES E. *Beyond Words; Mystical Fancy in Children's Literature.* Teachers College Pr., 1970. The author discusses the importance of mystical fantasy in the development of the child and its significance as a literary form, with special detailed analysis of the work of such great authors as George Macdonald, W. H. Hudson, Saint-Exupéry, Tolkien, and C. S. Lewis.

HILDICK, WALLACE. *Children and Fiction.* World, 1971. A critical study of the artistic and psychological factors involved in writing fiction for and about children, suggesting the application of high standards in examining children's literature both from the literary and the sociological point of view.

HILLYER, ROBERT. *In Pursuit of Poetry.* McGraw, 1960. A distinguished poet and winner of the Pulitzer Prize, Hillyer has written an entrancing introduction to the appreciation of poetry, old and modern, with unforgettable examples from some of the finest English poetry.

HODGART, M. J. C. *The Ballads.* Hutchinson's Universal Library, 1950. Useful general discussion of the traditional ballads, stressing the literary approach.

HOLT, JOHN. *How Children Fail.* Pitman, 1964. An important book, based on records of classroom experience, dealing with the ways children meet or dodge the demands adults make on them, the interaction between fear and failure, the difference between what children are expected to know and what they really know, and finally how the schools fail to meet the real needs of children.

______. *How Children Learn.* Pitman, 1967. This book, written in journal form about the reactions of various children in games, experiments, reading, talking, and being involved in arts and math, throws light on using their minds effectively and on the relationship between encouragement and progress in learning.

______. *What Do I Do Monday?* Dutton, 1970. A school teacher's innovative observations on modern education and theories of the learning process, supported by ideas, exercises, and examples in several subjects.

HOMER. *The Odyssey*, tr. by George H. Palmer, ill. by N. C. Wyeth. Houghton, 1929. This cadenced prose will sing in your memory like poetry. For children who are superior readers, this edition illustrated by Wyeth is a superb source for these tales.

HOPKINS, LEE BENNETT. *Books Are by People*, ill. Citation, 1969. Human interest interviews with 104 writers and illustrators for chidren, to be used with children to make their authors "come alive."

______. *Let Them Be Themselves.* Citation, 1969. Recommendations for enriching the language arts curriculum for all children, but especially the disadvantaged.

HUBER, MIRIAM BLANTON. *Story and Verse for Children*, ill. Macmillan, 1965. With introductory chapters on the selection and history of children's books, followed by an anthology of poetry and prose, this book is intended primarily for teachers, librarians, and parents.

HUCK, CHARLOTTE S., and DORIS YOUNG KUHN. *Children's Literature in the Elementary School*, 2nd ed., ill. Holt, 1968. A reorganized and updated revision of a well-known textbooks.

HUDSON, DEREK. *Arthur Rackham: His Life and Work.* Scribner's, 1960. A handsome oversize book copiously illustrated with plates and sketches of Rackham's work for both children and adults.

HUGHES, TED. *Poetry Is.* Doubleday, 1970. Based on a series of BBC talks, a discussion of poetry intended for young writers, but interesting for poetry readers as well.

HÜRLIMANN, BETTINA. *Picture-Book World*, ed. and tr. by Brian Alderson, ill, World, 1969. Modern picture books for children from 24 countries, with introductory chapters on particular countries and a bio-bibliographical supplement.

______. *Three Centuries of Children's Books in Europe*, ed. and tr. by Brian Alderson, ill. World, 1968. A comparative study as well as a history which includes a survey of contemporary books for children in all of the countries of Europe.

HYMES, JAMES LEE. *Understanding Your Child.* Prentice, 1952. This is a practical and entertaining discussion of child behavior and parent-child conflicts. It is built around these four major considerations: children grow, there is a plan to their growth, they want things out of life, and there is a reason for their behavior.

ILG, FRANCES L., and LOUISE BATES AMES. *Child Behavior.* Harper, 1955. Frances Ilg, M.D., and Louise Ames, Ph.D., give direct advice, based on their research at the Gesell Institute, to parents concerning problems of child behavior.

ISAACS, J. *The Background of Modern Poetry.* Dutton, 1952. Scholarly first aid to adults who find modern poetry hard to take.

JACOBS, JOSEPH. See listings of his collections of English, Celtic, and Indian folk tales in the Chapter 6 bibliography. They contain significant introductions, and the notes in each appendix are treasures of folklore information.

JACOBS, LELAND B., ed. *Using Literature with Young*

*Children*. Teachers College Pr., 1965. A collection of papers on providing good literature for young children, storytelling, reading aloud, poetry, choral speaking, dramatization, and relating literature to other school experiences.

JENKINS, GLADYS GARDNER. *Helping Children Reach Their Potential*. Scott, Foresman, 1961. Describes how teachers have handled the particular emotional needs and problems of their pupils.

JENKINS, GLADYS GARDNER, HELEN S. SHACTER, and WILLIAM W. BAUER. *These Are Your Children*, 3rd ed. Scott, Foresman, 1966. A series of case studies with charts of normal child development and the special needs of children at various ages, enlivened by photographs of children in problem situations or normal activities.

JOHNSON, EDNA, EVELYN SICKELS, and FRANCES CLARKE SAYERS. *Anthology of Children's Literature*, 4th ed. Houghton, 1970. The editors in this latest edition have attempted to hold to the long view, choosing from the present that which gives promise of lasting value and fitting it into the interstices of the proven past.

JORDAN, ALICE M. *From Rollo to Tom Sawyer*. Horn Book, 1948. Here in beautiful format with decorations by Nora Unwin are 12 little essays on some of the most important nineteenth-century writers for children.

JOSEPH, STEPHEN M., ed. *The Me Nobody Knows; Children's Voices from the Ghetto*. Avon, 1969. Moving and revealing writing by children, mostly black and Puerto Rican, in the most impoverished city neighborhoods.

KAMM, ANTONY, and BOSWELL TAYLOR. *Books and the Teacher*. Univ. of London Pr., 1966. A handbook on the choice, requisition, and use of books. References are to British authors and publishers, and organizations listed are also exclusively British.

KARL, JEAN. *From Childhood to Childhood: Children's Books and Their Creators*. Day, 1970. An editor's views on children's books.

KELLOGG, RHODA, and SCOTT O'DELL. *The Psychology of Children's Art*, ill. Random, 1967. Selected examples from a collection of over a million pieces of children's art, accompanied by text explaining the developmental phases common to all children.

KIEFER, MONICA. *American Children Through Their Books, 1700–1835*. Univ of Pa. Pr., 1948. The American child at the beginning of the 18th century was too insignificant for physicians to waste time on, the author tells us. She traces his developing place in the world through an examination of children's books.

KINGMAN, LEE, ed. *Newbery and Caldecott Medal Books: 1956-1965*. Horn Book, 1965. A biographical sketch of each author or illustrator, along with his acceptance paper and related material from *The Horn Book*.

KINGMAN, LEE, JOANNA FOSTER, and RUTH GILES LONTOFT, comps. *Illustrators of Children's Books, 1957–1966*, ill. Horn Book, 1968. This volume, a supplement to *Illustrators of Children's Books, 1744–1945*, and *Illustrators of Children's Books, 1946–1956*, reviews the decade, offers biographies of active illustrators and a bibliography of their works.

KITTREDGE, GEORGE LYMAN, ed. *English and Scottish Popular Ballads: Student's Cambridge Edition*, ed. by Helen Child Sargeant. Houghton, 1904. This is the invaluable one-volume edition of the Child collection. It contains the 305 ballads, a few variants of each, brief notes, and the excellent glossary giving the definitions and pronunciations of the difficult ballad words.

KLEMIN, DIANA. *The Art of Art for Children's Books*, ill. Potter, 1966. Examples and commentary on the work of 64 illustrators of children's books.

———. *The Illustrated Book: Its Art and Craft*, ill. Potter, 1970. A contemporary survey with examples and commentary on the work of 74 artists. A chapter on drawing for reproduction is included, which clarifies the process involved in printing.

KOCH, KENNETH. *Wishes, Lies, and Dreams; Teaching Children to Write Poetry*, ill. with photos. Random, 1971. Working with the children of P.S. 61 in New York City, the author, himself an outstanding poet, has developed ways of getting children to release their ideas and feelings into writing. The book is a collection of their poetry preceded and accompanied by his description of his teaching methods.

KOHL, HERBERT R. *The Open Classroom: A Practical Guide to a New Way of Teaching*. New York Review, 1969. Primarily addressed to public school teachers, this book is a "handbook for teachers who want to work in an open environment. . . . [and] is based upon the experience of teachers: their problems, failures, and frustrations, as well as their successes."

———. *Teaching the Unteachable; The Story of an Experiment in Children's Writing*. New York Review, 1967. An innovative approach to teaching in East Harlem, illustrated by examples of the children's writing.

———. *36 Children*, ill. by Robert George Jackson. New Am. Lib., 1967. The author's experiences in a sixth-grade Harlem classroom demonstrate the progress that children can make when a good teacher meets their needs.

KOZOL, JONATHAN. *Death at an Early Age; The Destruction of the Hearts and Minds of Negro Children in the Boston Public Schools*. Houghton, 1967. Serving as a substitute in a ghetto school, the author found the segregated schools rife with prejudice, with black children condemned by brutality, hostility, neglect, and wholly inadequate provisions for physical needs. A bitter indictment.

KRAPPE, ALEXANDER HAGGERTY. *The Science of Folk-Lore*. Dial, 1930. This book covers various types of folk literature, evaluates theories of origin and content, and analyzes motives. Chapter IX, "The Popular Ballad," discusses the ballad as part of the great stream of folklore, related to the epic, the carol, and the folk tale, migrating even as they have.

KUJOTH, JEAN SPEALMAN. *Reading Interests of Children and Young Adults*. Scarecrow, 1970. A collection of research findings and observations by teachers, authors, and librarians on reading interests and how they are influenced. Divided by age groups.

KUNITZ, STANLEY J., and HOWARD HAYCRAFT, eds. *The Junior Book of Authors*, 2nd ed. Wilson, 1951. Biographical sketches of outstanding authors and illustrators of books for children.

LANE, MARGARET. *The Tale of Beatrix Potter; A Biography*, ill. Warne, 1968. Revised and updated, with new material from the secret code journals of Beatrix Potter.

LANES, SELMA G. *Down the Rabbit Hole; Adventures and Misadventures in the Realm of Children's Literature*, ill. Atheneum, 1971. A series of essays, by a reviewer of children's books, exploring the literary and artistic merits of a particular selection of books. A small bibliography of choice books is appended.

LANG, ANDREW, ed. *Perrault's Popular Tales*. London: Clarendon, 1888. A careful study of Perrault and the tales he edited.

LARRICK, NANCY. *A Parent's Guide to Children's Reading*, rev. and enl. 3rd ed., ill. Pocket Books, 1969. Sponsored by the National Book Committee, this is a comprehensive handbook for parents' use in developing reading interests from infancy on.

______. *A Teacher's Guide to Children's Books*, ill. Merrill, 1960. How to stimulate and develop reading interests in the elementary grades, accompanied by extensive bibliographies for the child and the teacher.

______, ed. *Somebody Turned on a Tap in These Kids*. Delacorte, 1971. A lively collection of articles on the changes of attitudes and expectations of young people toward poetry, with liberal examples of what they like and what they write themselves.

LEACH, MACEDWARD. *Folk Ballads and Songs of the Lower Labrador Coast*. Ottawa: Queen's Printer and Controller of Stationery, 1965.

______, ed. *The Ballad Book*. Harper, 1955. Gives about 250 ballads, many in several variants. The major section is "Ballads of England and Scotland with American and Danish Variants." "American Ballads by Origin or Adoption" contains 45 ballads. The headnotes to each ballad are useful and a general introduction gives a brief survey of ballad scholarship.

LENNON, FLORENCE BECKER. *Victoria Through the Looking-Glass*. Simon, 1945; reissued as *The Life of Lewis Carroll*, Collier Books, 1962, paperback. A fine biography of Lewis Carroll.

LENSKI, LOIS. *Adventure in Understanding; Talks to Parents, Teachers and Librarians by Lois Lenski, 1944–1966*, with decorations by the author. Tallahassee, 1968. The author's ideas concerning books and literature in general, young people, the state of the world, and particularly her own ideas on writing books for children.

LEPMAN, JELLA. *A Bridge of Children's Books*, tr. by Edith McCormick. ALA, 1969. Fascinating autobiographical account of bringing books of all nations to the children of postwar Germany to replace their Nazi-oriented literature.

LEWIS, C. S. *Of Other Worlds: Essays and Stories*, ed. by Walter Hooper. Harcourt, 1966. A posthumous collection which includes essays on fantasy and science fiction, three unpublished short stories, and the first chapters of a novel.

LINDSTROM, MIRIAM. *Children's Art; A Study of Normal Development in Children's Modes of Visualization*, ill. Univ. of Calif. Pr., 1970. Illustrated study of stages of development in expression of visual imagery.

LINES, KATHLEEN, ed. *Walck Monographs*. Walck. Personal anecdotes and a pleasing style make these brief biographies and critical evaluations of internationally known authors invaluable to the teacher or student of children's literature. The series includes:
*Louisa M. Alcott*, Cornelia Meigs
*J. M. Barrie*, Roger Lancelyn Green
*Lucy Boston*, Jasper Rose
*Lewis Carroll*, Roger Lancelyn Green
*Walter de la Mare*, Leonard Clark
*Eleanor Farjeon*, Eileen H. Colwell
*Kenneth Grahame*, Eleanor Graham
*Rudyard Kipling*, Rosemary Sutcliff
*Andrew Lang*, Roger Lancelyn Green
*C. S. Lewis*, Roger Lancelyn Green
*John Masefield*, Margery Fisher
*Mrs. Molesworth*, Roger Lancelyn Green
*Beatrix Potter*, Marcus Crouch
*Howard Pyle*, Elizabeth Nesbitt
*Arthur Ransome*, Hugh Shelley
*Ruth Sawyer*, Virginia Haviland
*Noel Streatfeild*, Barbara Ker Wilson
*Rosemary Sutcliff*, Margaret Meek
*Geoffrey Trease*, Margaret Meek

LOMAX, JOHN A, ed. *Songs of the Cattle Trail and Cow Camp*. Duell, 1950.

LOMAX, JOHN A., and ALAN LOMAX, comps. *American Ballads and Folk Songs*. Macmillan, 1946.

______, eds. *Cowboy Songs and Other Frontier Ballads*, rev. and enl. Macmillan, 1948. The Lomax collections of our native ballads are of major importance as sources, not only because they were the first ones made, but also because they were gathered first-hand and the tunes were recorded on wax cylinders, on the spot, unedited.

LOWNDES, BETTY. *Movement and Creative Drama for Children*. Plays, 1971. A description of the movement and drama work carried on in an infants' school in North London with an emphasis on how both can be used to get children to communicate and to learn with enjoyment.

MC GUFFEY, WILLIAM HOLMES. *Old Favorites from the McGuffey Readers*, ed. by Harvey C. Minnich. Singing Tree, 1969. Selections from all six of the readers are of special interest to students of educational and social history.

MAHONY, BERTHA E., and ELINOR WHITNEY FIELD, eds. *Newbery Medal Books, 1922–1955*. Horn Book, 1955. Elementary schools and libraries have for many years needed information about the Newbery winners. Here in one handsome volume are brief biographies of the authors along with their acceptance speeches. See also supplementary volume by Kingman.

MAHONY, BERTHA E., LOUISE P. LATIMER, and BEULAH FOLMSBEE, comps. *Illustrators of Children's Books, 1744–1945*. Horn Book, 1947. A superb history of illustration in children's books considered as a part of the whole stream of art. Many pictures are reproduced from early books as well as from more recent ones. A major reference. See also supplementary volumes by Viguers and others and by Kingman and others.

MAIER, HENRY W. *Three Theories of Child Development: The Contributions of Erik H. Erikson, Jean Piaget, and Robert R. Sears, and Their Applications*, rev. ed. Harper, 1969. The expanded psychoanalytic theory of Erikson, Piaget's theories on the development of behavior, and those of Robert Sears are explicated and compared, and the last two chapters deal with how they can be used in working with children. A useful bibliography is appended.

MATHEWS, MITFORD M. *Teaching to Read; Historically Considered*. Univ. of Chicago Pr., 1966. Survey of methods of teaching reading and the theories behind them.

MAYERSON, CHARLOTTE LEON, ed. *Two Blocks Apart; Juan Gonzales and Peter Quinn*, ill. with photos by the Still Photography Workshop Harlem Youth Unlimited. Holt, 1965. Biographies, from tapes, of two boys in New York, living in the same neighborhood, going to the same school, sharing the same religion, one white middle class, the other Puerto Rican, members of two cultures separated by social and economic conditions.

MEEKER, ALICE M. *Enjoying Literature with Children*. Odyssey, 1969. A book for parents and teachers, with annotated bibliographies for the preschool years, for the culturally deprived, storytelling, poetry, choral speaking, holidays, and teachers' browsing. Though short, the book is full of practical suggestions for helping children enjoy books.

MEIGS, CORNELIA, ANNE EATON, ELIZABETH NESBITT, and RUTH HILL VIGUERS. *A Critical History of Children's Literature*, rev. ed. Macmillan, 1969. Three librarians and an author of children's books have surveyed the field from ancient to recent times. The evaluations of books, authors, illustrators, and trends make this a valuable reference.

MILLAR, SUSANNA. *The Psychology of Play*. Penguin, 1968. Chapter V, "Phantasy, Feeling, and Make-Believe Play."

MILLER, BERTHA MAHONY, and ELINOR WHITNEY FIELD, eds. *Caldecott Medal Books: 1938–1957*. Horn Book, 1957. Stories of artists who have won awards for the most distinguished picture book of each year, together with their acceptance speeches. An invaluable source for schools and libraries. See also supplementary volume by Kingman.

MONTGOMERIE, NORAH. *To Read and to Tell*, ill. by Margery Gill. Arco Pub. Co., 1964. Fairy stories, folk tales, fables, and legends from many lands.

MOORE, ANNE CARROLL. *A Century of Kate Greenaway*. Warne, 1946. An appreciation of the artist and her distinctive contribution.

———. *My Roads to Childhood*. Doubleday, 1939. A distinguished librarian and critic of children's books comments on outstanding books up to the year 1938.

MUIR, PERCY. *English Children's Books, 1600 to 1900*. Praeger, 1954, 1969. Mr. Muir acknowledges his indebtedness to the books of Darton and the Opies, but his work adds to both. There are excellent indexes and lavish illustrations from the books discussed.

MUNCH, PETER A. *Norse Mythology, Legends of Gods and Heroes*, rev. by Magnus Olsen, tr. by Sigurd B. Hustvedt. American-Scandinavian Foundation, 1926; reissued, Singing Tree, 1968. Authoritative and complete interpretation of sources.

MYRUS, DONALD. *Ballads, Blues, and the Big Beat*. Macmillan, 1966. A survey of the singers and the songs of today, with separate chapters on musical genres.

NICHOLSEN, MARGARET. *People in Books: A Selective Guide to Biographical Literature Arranged by Vocations and Other Fields of Reader Interest*. Wilson, 1969. Appended: an index by century and by country; an index to autobiographical books; and an index of persons about whom a book or part of a collective biography is included in the main section.

*Once upon a Time . . .*, rev. ed. New York Library Assoc., 1964. Help for librarians with preschool hours, picture-book hours, and story hours. Suggested programs and bibliographies are included.

OPIE, IONA and PETER. *Children's Games in Street and Playground*. Oxford, 1969. This record of the games children play draws its authority from more than 10,000 children in England, Scotland, and Wales.

———. *The Lore and Language of Schoolchildren*. Oxford, 1959; Oxford paperbacks, 1967. "The curious lore passing between children about 6–14, which today holds in its spell some 7 million inhabitants of . . ." Great Britain, includes rhymes, riddles, childhood customs, and beliefs. Some can be traced back for generations and others are current. "The present study is based on the contributions of some 5000 children attending 70 schools."

———, comps. *A Family Book of Nursery Rhymes*, ill. by Pauline Baynes. Oxford, 1964. In addition to the rhymes, this contains excellent notes on origins.

———, eds. *The Oxford Dictionary of Nursery Rhymes*. Oxford, 1951. This is the most exhaustive and scholarly study yet made of the origins of the nursery rhymes, their earliest recordings, and variations through the years. Copious illustrations from old plates add to its real interest.

*The Original Mother Goose's Melody, As First Issued by John Newbery, of London, about A.D. 1760*. Reproduced in Facsimile from the Edition as Reprinted by Isaiah Thomas of Worcester, Mass., about A.D. 1785, with Introductory Notes by William H. Whitmore. Singing Tree, 1969. Whitmore's introductory notes discuss the origin, development, and popularity of the Mother Goose rhymes in this reprint.

OVID. *The Metamorphoses*, tr. by Henry T. Riley. McKay, 1899. A literal prose translation of the Latin versions of the Greek myths and hero tales, with copious notes explaining their fable or allegorical significance.

PERRAULT, CHARLES. *Perrault's Complete Fairy Tales*, tr. by A. E. Johnson and others, ill. by W. Heath Robinson. Dodd, 1961. The unabridged fairy tales of Perrault, together with tales by Mme. de Beaumont and Mme. d'Aulnoy.

PIAGET, JEAN, and BARBEL INHELDER. *The Psychology of the Child*, tr. from the French by Helen Weaver. Basic, 1969. A comprehensive summary of Piaget's child psychology, tracing the stages of cognitive development over the entire period of childhood, from infancy to adolescence.

PILGRIM, GENEVA HANNA, and MARIANNA MCALLISTER. *Books, Young People, and Reading Guidance.* Harper, 1968. For use by teachers, librarians, and parents, and also as a college text. Emphasis is chiefly on contemporary books.

PINES, MAYA. *Revolution in Learning: The Years from Birth to Six.* Harper, 1967. A report on the growing number of research projects on increasing intellectual growth in childhood.

PITZ, HENRY C. *Illustrating Children's Books: History, Technique, Production.* Watson-Guptill, 1963. Detailed and authoritative, profusely illustrated, a book that is particularly useful for its lucid explanations of techniques of art reproduction and how the artist prepares his work.

———. *The Practice of American Book Illustration.* Watson-Guptill, 1947.

———, ed. *A Treasury of American Book Illustration.* Watson-Guptill, 1947. A distinguished artist discusses illustration as one of the seven lively arts. With many pictures from modern sources he proves his point. The second volume contains a good chapter on "Pictures for Childhood."

*Plays, the Drama Magazine for Young People.* Plays, Inc. 8 Arlington Street, Boston, Mass. 02116. This useful magazine is published monthly, October through May. Each issue, in addition to providing plays for lower grades, middle grades, and junior and senior high, always has a special feature—a dramatized classic, a radio play, or material for an assembly.

POUND, LOUISE, ed. *American Ballads and Songs.* Scribner's, 1922, 1969. A good collection of United States remnants of old ballads along with our native compositions. No music. Excellent introduction.

———. *Poetic Origins and the Ballad.* Macmillan, 1921; Russell and Russell, 1961. The author furnishes lively evidence against the communal origin of the ballad, besides adding ballad history.

POWER, EFFIE. *Bag O'Tales; A Source Book for Story-Tellers,* ill. by Corydon Bell. Dutton, 1969. Stories for little children, folk tales, myths, and tales of heroes and chivalry, with good lists of source material for the storyteller at the end of each section.

RANK, OTTO. *The Myth of the Birth of the Hero: A Psychological Interpretation of Mythology,* tr. by F. Robbins and Smith Ely Jellife. Brunner/Mazel, 1952. A classic exposition of the connection between the form of myths and the unconscious emotions of the child. Studies the myths of the birth of the hero from Moses to Lohengrin, interpreting each myth in terms of the Oedipus complex.

READ, HERBERT. *This Way, Delight.* Pantheon, 1956. An excellent anthology, mentioned here because of its unusual introduction in which the author defines poetry and gives practical suggestions for writing it.

RIBNER, IRVING, and HARRY MORRIS. *Poetry: A Critical and Historical Introduction.* Scott, Foresman, 1962. Designed to help the beginning poetry reader read with greater understanding and appreciation.

RICHARDSON, ELWYN. *In The Early World.* Pantheon, 1969. Written by a New Zealand teacher, this is an exploration of the stimulation of activity and creativity, particularly with reference to appreciation of nature and particularly expressed in the children's writing. Good book on teaching; good book on children's expression of appreciation of the world around them.

ROBINSON, EVELYN ROSE. *Readings About Children's Literature.* McKay, 1966. Excerpts from books, magazines, journals, and newspapers providing an understanding of the child as a reader, criteria for book selection, and appropriate materials. Contributors are well-known writers, librarians, and teachers of children's literature.

ROBINSON, MARION P., and ROZETTA L. THURSTON. *Poetry Arranged for the Speaking Choir.* Expression, 1936. While this anthology is for adult choirs and advises some of the embellishments Miss Gullan disapproves of, it contains such a choice selection of poetry that it should not be missed. There is a fine section answering questions concerning choir work, and a useful discussion of the speaking choir for religious services.

ROSELLE, DANIEL. *Samuel Griswold Goodrich, Creator of Peter Parley; A Study of His Life and Work,* ill. State Univ. of N.Y., 1968. The Peter Parley books, now largely forgotten, entertained children in the first half of the 19th century with cautionary tales, instructive fables, and reports of strange lands.

ROSENBACH, ABRAHAM S. W. *Early American Children's Books with Bibliographical Descriptions of the Books in His Private Collection,* foreword by A. Edward Newton. Southworth Pr., Portland, Me., 1933; Dover (paperback), 1971. Facsimile pages and illustrations (many in color) of American children's books published between 1732 and 1836. Probably the greatest and most comprehensive book on juvenile Americana.

ST. JOHN, JUDITH. *The Osborne Collection of Early Children's Books 1566–1910; A Catalogue,* introduction by Edgar Osborne. Toronto Public Library, 1958. Descriptive notes on this world-famous collection, illustrated with many facsimiles. Fascinating background material for scholars and students of children's literature.

SANDBURG, CARL, ed. *The American Songbag.* Harcourt, 1927. While this collection borrows from others, Mr. Sandburg's illuminating notes make it a particularly useful and enjoyable volume.

SANDERS, THOMAS E. *The Discovery of Poetry.* Scott, Foresman, 1967. An introduction to the aesthetics of poetry, this book discusses how poetry is written and how it can be read in the same creative way.

SAWYER, RUTH. *My Spain; A Storyteller's Year of Collecting.* Viking, 1967. Pleasant account of a journey through Spain in search of folk tales.

———. *The Way of the Storyteller.* Viking, 1942, 1962. Informally written in Ruth Sawyer's fine style, this is a contribution both to the art of storytelling and to the history of the old tales.

SAYERS, FRANCES CLARKE. *Summoned by Books; Essays and Speeches by Frances Clarke Sayers,* comp. by Marjeanne Jenson Blinn. Viking, 1965. Essays by an outstanding and influential children's librarian.

SCHWAB, GUSTAV. *Gods and Heroes,* tr. by Olga Marx

and Ernst Morwitz, ill. with designs from Greek vases. Pantheon, 1946. This large handsome book is not comprehensive, and the English translation from a German adaptation is not always satisfactory, but it is an excellent source nevertheless.

SCOTT, JOHN ANTHONY. *The Ballad of America: The History of the United States in Song and Story.* Grosset, 1966. Chronologically arranged, with musical notation and with substantial comment on the background for each selection.

SHARP, CECIL J., comp. *English Folk-Songs from the Southern Appalachians,* ed. by Maud Karpeles, rev. and enl., 2 vols. Oxford, 1953. A major contribution by an English collector and musician.

———. *Nursery Songs from the Appalachian Mountains,* 2 vols. London: Novello, 1921–1923. A collection that should be better known in our schools. Many selections for the youngest children.

SHAW, JOHN MAC KAY. *Childhood in Poetry: A Catalogue,* with Biographical and Critical Annotations, of the Books of English and American Poets Comprising the Shaw Childhood in Poetry Collection in the Library of the Florida State University, with Lists of the Poems that Relate to Childhood, 5 vols. Gale, 1967. Although the price ($135) of this work makes it inaccessible to many individuals and small libraries, it is a comprehensive bibliographic guide to English-language children's poetry.

SHEDLOCK, MARIE. *Art of the Story-Teller,* 3rd ed., bibl. by Eulalie Steinmetz. Dover, 1951. Guidance in selection of material, techniques of storytelling, and useful bibliographies are included.

SIKS, GERALDINE BRAIN. *Creative Dramatics.* Harper, 1958. Various suggestions for encouraging children to use their imaginations in dramatization.

SILBERMAN, CHARLES E. *Crisis in the Classroom; The Remaking of American Education.* Random, 1970. Addressed to laymen and professionals alike, its four parts include: The Educating Society, What's Wrong with the Schools, How the Schools Should Be Changed, and The Education of Educators. A fascinating account based on a three-and-a-half-year study commissioned by the Carnegie Corporation of New York.

*Six New Plays for Children,* ed. by Christian Moe and Darwin Reid Payne. Southern Ill. Pr., 1971. This is an interesting collection of new plays for child audiences.

SMITH, DORA V. *Fifty Years of Children's Books,* with an introduction by Muriel Crosby, ill. Nat. Council of Teachers of English, 1963. From Dora Smith's years of experience with children and books, she has selected and discussed significant titles which appeared between 1910 and 1959. Numerous illustrations are reproduced from the original books.

SMITH, IRENE. *A History of the Newbery and Caldecott Medals.* Viking, 1957. Excellent historical background material on two major annual awards for distinguished children's books in the United States.

SMITH, JAMES STEEL. *A Critical Approach to Children's Literature.* McGraw, 1967. A serious, careful analysis of children's books as creative literary works.

SMITH, LILLIAN. *The Unreluctant Years.* ALA, 1953; reissued, Viking, 1967. A Canadian librarian writes discerningly of children's literature from the standpoint of literary quality only.

SMITH, RUTH, ed. *The Tree of Life,* ill. by Boris Artzybasheff. Viking, 1942. A distinguished text for a comparative study of religious ideas. It is a compilation of the "testaments of beauty and faith from many lands." Excerpts from the expressions of religious ideals of the Navaho Indians, the Norse, Hindu, Buddhist, Confucianist, and other religions (including the Hebrew and Christian) make up the content of the book, which is for adolescents or for adults to use with older children.

*Some British Ballads,* ill. by Arthur Rackham. Dodd, 1920. This is a superb edition for home and school.

SPACHE, GEORGE D. *Parents and the Reading Program.* Garrard, 1965. Suggestions for a program to inform parents on what is involved in teaching pupils to read; a question and answer format is used.

STIRLING, MONICA. *The Wild Swan; The Life and Times of Hans Christian Andersen.* Harcourt, 1965. Thoroughly documented, a serious and mature study of Andersen's life and work.

STIRLING, NORA. *Who Wrote the Classics?* 2 vols., ill. Day, 1965, 1968. Short biographies of nineteen English and American writers.

STRICKLAND, RUTH G. *The Language Arts in the Elementary School,* 3rd ed., ill. Heath, 1969. Comprehensive treatment of all aspects of language development with three chapters on reading.

TARG, WILLIAM, ed. *Bibliophile in the Nursery.* World, 1969. Articles by scholars, collectors, and authors have been combined into a delightful whole, highlighting developments in children's literature and the joys of collecting. Lavishly illustrated.

TATLOCK, JESSIE M. *Greek and Roman Mythology.* Appleton, 1917. Although intended for high-school study, this is a useful book for teachers. Miss Tatlock retells the myths, gives excerpts from the "Homeric Hymn" and modern poetry, and presents some fine photographs of Greek sculpture.

*Teaching Literature in Wisconsin.* Wisconsin English Language Arts Curriculum Project. State of Wisconsin Department of Public Instruction, 1965. (Madison) A carefully developed approach to a literature curriculum for kindergarten through grade twelve.

*Teaching Reading Through Children's Literature:* Proceedings of the 1971 First Annual Reading Conference, June 21–22. Curriculum Research and Developmental Center, School of Education, Indiana State University, Terre Haute. Articles include "Role Playing in Children's Literature and Its Effect Upon the Affective Domain of Children's Thinking," "Teaching Reading Through the Use of Films and Children's Literature," and "Reading the Pictures in Children's Books."

THOMAS, KATHERINE ELWES. *The Real Personages of Mother Goose.* Lothrop, 1930. Scholarly research into the historical origins of the Mother Goose rhymes as political diatribes, religious philippics, and popular street songs.

THOMAS, R. MURRAY, and SHERWIN G. SWARTOUT. *Integrated Teaching Materials,* rev. ed. McKay, 1963. Designed to help teachers improve their skills in choosing, creating, and using audiovisual teaching materials, including reading sources, this book also presents specific classroom illustrations—both verbal and photographic—which add to its practicality.

THOMISON, DENNIS. *Readings About Adolescent Literature*. Scarecrow, 1970. A collection of 25 articles from professional journals.

THOMPSON, STITH. *The Folktale*. Dryden, 1946. A standard work in the field discusses the nature and forms of the folk tale, traces their spread, analyzes types, describes the North American Indian folk tale in detail, and examines studies of folk tales.

———, comp. *One Hundred Favorite Folktales*. Indiana Univ. Pr., 1968. Tales chosen by a famous folklorist "as the result of more than a half century of almost daily familiarity with these tales." (p. xi)

TOOZE, RUTH. *Storytelling*. Prentice, 1959. Extensive bibliographies add to the value of this helpful guide for storytellers.

TOWNSEND, JOHN ROWE. *A Sense of Story*. Longmans, 1971. An analysis of the work of 19 writers of children's books, American, British, and Australian, with some notes by the authors on their own writing, and short biographical notes.

———. *Written for Children: An Outline of English Children's Literature*, ill. Lothrop, 1967. A short, selective survey of prose for British children from its beginnings to today.

TREASE, GEOFFREY. *Tales Out of School: A Survey of Children's Fiction*, 2nd ed. Dufour, 1964. A highly personal, entertaining critical survey of juvenile fiction.

TUER, ANDREW W. *Pages and Pictures from Forgotten Children's Books; Brought Together and Introduced to the Reader*, ill. Singing Tree, 1969. The introduction offers a description of the various methods used to illustrate children's books published in England in the 18th and 19th centuries: wood blocks, copper plates, and stone lithographs.

———. *Stories from Old-Fashioned Children's Books, Brought Together and Introduced to the Reader*. Singing Tree, 1968. A collection of old children's stories, by a nineteenth-century publisher.

VANCE, LUCILLE, and ESTHER TRACEY. *Illustration Index*, 2nd ed. Scarecrow, 1966. A topical index to illustrations in periodicals such as *Life*, *National Geographic*, and *American Heritage*, ranging from abacus to Zurich.

VIGUERS, RUTH HILL. *Margin for Surprise; About Books, Children, and Librarians*. Little, 1964. Essays by a dedicated and enthusiastic children's librarian.

VIGUERS, RUTH HILL, MARCIA DALPHIN, and BERTHA MAHONY MILLER, comps. *Illustrators of Children's Books, 1946–1956*. Horn Book, 1958. An outstanding supplement to *Illustrators of Children's Books, 1744–1945*. Includes current art trends, artists' biographies, and a wealth of illustrations from modern children's books.

*Volsunga Saga: The Story of the Volsungs and Niblungs, with Certain Songs from the Elder Edda*, tr. by Eirikr Magnusson and William Morris. London: Walter Scott, n.d. This prose translation of the difficult verse form of the *Elder Edda* is easy to read and is the basis for Morris' beautiful verse version of the saga. (In 1962, Collier Bks. published a paperback version using the Morris translation.)

WALSH, FRANCES, ed. *That Eager Zest; First Discoveries in the Magic World of Books*. Lippincott, 1961. Almost 50 delightful verses and sketches about their own childhood reading experiences by such well-known writers as Carl Sandburg, James Thurber, Sherwood Anderson, and Lewis Mumford.

WARD, MARTHA E., and DOROTHY A. MARQUARDT. *Authors of Books for Young People*, 2nd ed. Scarecrow, 1971. Biographical sketches of authors.

———. *Illustrators of Books for Young People*. Scarecrow, 1970. Biographical information about 370 illustrators of books for children.

WEISS, HARRY B. *A Book About Chapbooks; The People's Literature of Bygone Times*, ill. Singing Tree, 1969. A history of chapbooks, their printers, authors, and salesmen, with reproductions of woodcuts and title pages.

WELSH, CHARLES. *A Bookseller of the Last Century, Being some Account of the Life of John Newbery, and of the Books he published with a Notice of the later Newberys*. London: Griffith, Farran, 1885; reissued, Singing Tree, 1969. A readable history of Newbery, his famous bookshop, and his varied activities.

———, ed. *The Renowned History of Little Goody Two Shoes, Otherwise Called Mrs. Margery Two Shoes*, attributed to Oliver Goldsmith. Heath, 1930.

WENZEL, EVELYN L., and MAY HILL ARBUTHNOT. *Time for Discovery*, ill. Scott, Foresman, 1971. An anthology of selections from 57 informational books with a special section which discusses the history of informational books and criteria for judging them and suggests how adults can use them with children. An annotated bibliography is included.

WHITE, DOROTHY MARY NEAL. *About Books for Children*. Oxford, 1947. Although the author selects predominantly British children's books, she also discusses many American publications.

———. *Books Before Five*, ill. by Joan Smith. Oxford, 1954. A New Zealand children's librarian's study of her two-year-old daughter's progression in the experience of books over three years, ranging over more than 100 books, from Adams' *First Things* to Tolkien's *The Hobbit*.

WHITEHEAD, ROBERT. *Children's Literature; Strategies of Teaching*. Prentice, 1968. Specific practices which help the teacher present an attractive and effective program in literature.

WILLIAMS, SIDNEY H., and FALCONER MADAN. *The Lewis Carroll Handbook*, rev. and enl. by Roger Lancelyn Green. Oxford, 1962. A valuable and comprehensive bibliography of Lewis Carroll's own writings and what others have written about his life and works. Descriptive notes are comprehensive and scholarly.

WILSON, BARBARA KER. *Writing for Children; An English Editor and Author's Point of View*. Watts, 1960. Sound comment on writing fiction, nonfiction, and picture books for children.

WILSON, ROY R. *Teaching Children Language Arts*. Parker Pub. Co., 1970. Wilson says that the purpose of his book is to provide practical, imaginative ideas—specifics to try as well as ideas to stir the reader's thinking about "what needs to be done in the language arts classroom."

WITUCKE, VIRGINIA. *Poetry in the Elementary School.* Brown, 1970. An illuminating treatment of strategies for generating interest in poetry, with generous references and unhackneyed selections of examples, including audiovisual materials.

WOLSCH, ROBERT A. *Poetic Composition Through the Grades; A Language Sensitivity Program. Practical Suggestions for Teaching*, ed. by Alice Miel. Teachers College Pr., 1970. A teacher's handbook for teaching poetry writing in the elementary school.

WYNDHAM, LEE. *Writing for Children and Teen-Agers.* Writer's Digest, 1968. Practical, detailed advice presented in a lively style and covering all phases of writing children's books, marketing them, and seeing them through publication, by a woman who is herself a prolific writer for children.

*Yale French Studies: The Child's Part.* Yale Univ. Pr., 1969. A collection of essays exploring children's literature as a vast subspecies, attention to which can illuminate culture, society, and literature itself.

# APPENDIX C PUBLISHERS AND THEIR ADDRESSES[3]

ABELARD. Abelard-Schuman, Ltd., 257 Park Ave. S., New York, N.Y.10010

ABINGDON. Abingdon Pr., 201 Eighth Ave. S., Nashville, Tenn. 37202

ABRAMS. Harry N. Abrams, Inc., 110 E. 59th St., New York, N.Y. 10022

ADDISON. Addison-Wesley Pub. Co., Inc., Reading, Mass. 01867

ALA. American Library Assoc., Pub. Dept., 50 E. Huron St., Chicago, Ill. 60611

AM. ASSOC. FOR THE ADVANCEMENT OF SCIENCE. 1515 Massachusetts Ave., N.W., Washington, D.C. 20005

AMERICAN BK. American Book Co., 450 W. 33rd St., New York, N.Y. 10001

AM. COUNCIL ON EDUCATION. 1 Dupont Circle, N.W., Washington, D.C. 20036

AMERICAN HERITAGE. American Heritage Pr., 330 W. 42nd St., New York, N.Y. 10036

APPLETON. Appleton-Century-Crofts, 440 Park Ave. S., New York, N.Y. 10016

ARIEL. Ariel Books. See Farrar

ASSOC. FOR CHILDHOOD EDUCATION INTERNATIONAL. 3615 Wisconsin Ave., N.W., Washington, D.C. 20016

ASTOR. Astor-Honor, Inc., 205 E. 42nd St., New York, N.Y. 10017

ATHENEUM. Atheneum Pubs., 122 E. 42nd St., New York, N.Y. 10017

ATHERTON. Atherton Pr., Inc., 70 Fifth Ave., New York, N.Y. 10011

ATLANTIC. Atlantic Monthly Pr., 8 Arlington St., Boston, Mass. 02116

ATLANTIC/LITTLE. Atlantic Monthly Pr. in association with Little, Brown & Co.

BALLANTINE. Ballantine Books, Inc., 101 Fifth Ave., New York, N.Y. 10003

BANTAM. Bantam Books, Inc., 666 Fifth Ave., New York, N.Y. 10019

BARNES, A. S. Forsgate Dr., Cranbury, N.J. 08512

BARNES. Barnes & Noble, Inc., 105 Fifth Ave., New York, N.Y. 10003

BASIC. Basic Books, Inc., 404 Park Ave. S., New York, N.Y. 10016

BEACON. Beacon Pr., 25 Beacon St., Boston, Mass. 02108

BEECHURST. Beechurst Pr. See A. S. Barnes

BEHRMAN. Behrman House, Inc., 1261 Broadway, New York, N.Y. 10001

BOBBS. Bobbs-Merrill Co., Inc., 3 W. 57th St., New York, N.Y. 10019

BOWKER. R. R. Bowker and Co., 1180 Ave. of the Americas, New York, N.Y. 10036

3. For the address of any publisher not listed here consult the latest *Literary Market Place* or Bowker's *Books in Print*.

BRADBURY. Bradbury Pr., Inc., 2 Overhill Rd., Scarsdale, N.Y. 10583

BRO-DART FOUNDATION. 113 Frelinghuysen Ave., Newark, N.J. 07101

BROWN. William C. Brown Company, Pubs., 135 S. Locust St., Dubuque, Ia. 52001

CAMBRIDGE UNIV. PR. 32 E. 57th St., New York, N.Y. 10022

CAXTON. The Caxton Printers, Ltd., Caldwell, Idaho 83605

CHATHAM/VIKING. 15 Wilmot Lane, Riverside, Conn. 06878. Distributed by Viking

CHILDRENS PR. Childrens Press, Inc., 1224 W. Van Buren, Chicago, Ill. 60607

CHILTON. Chilton Book Co., 401 Walnut St., Philadelphia, Pa. 19106

COPP CLARK. The Copp Clark Pub. Co., 517 Wellington St. W., Toronto 135, Ont.

COWARD. Coward, McCann & Geoghegan Inc., 200 Madison Ave., New York, N.Y. 10016

COWLES. Cowles Book Co., Inc., 488 Madison Ave., New York, N.Y. 10022

CRITERION. Criterion Books, Inc., 257 Park Ave. S., New York, N.Y. 10010

CROWELL-COLLIER. Crowell Collier and Macmillan, Inc., 866 Third Ave., New York, N.Y. 10022

T. CROWELL. Thomas Y. Crowell Co., 201 Park Ave. S., New York, N.Y. 10003

CROWN. Crown Pubs., Inc., 419 Park Ave. S., New York, N.Y. 10016

DAY. The John Day Co., Inc., 257 Park Ave. S., New York, N.Y. 10010

DELACORTE. Delacorte Pr. See Dell

DELL. Dell Pub. Co., 750 Third Ave., New York, N.Y. 10017

DEVIN. Devin-Adair Co., 1 Park Ave., Old Greenwich, Conn. 06870

DIAL. The Dial Pr., Inc. See Dell

DODD. Dodd, Mead & Co., 79 Madison Ave., New York, N.Y. 10016

DOUBLEDAY. Doubleday & Co., Inc., 277 Park Ave., New York, N.Y. 10017

DOVER. Dover Pubns., Inc., 180 Varick St., New York, N.Y. 10014

DRYDEN. Dryden Pr. See Holt

DUELL. Duell, Sloan & Pearce. See Meredith

DUFOUR. Dufour Editions, Inc., Chester Springs, Pa. 19425

DUTTON. E. P. Dutton & Co., Inc., 201 Park Ave. S., New York, N.Y. 10003

EERDMANS. William B. Eerdmans Pub. Co., 255 Jefferson Ave., S.E., Grand Rapids, Mich. 49502

ERIKSSON. Paul S. Eriksson, Inc., Pub., 119 W. 57th St.,

New York, N.Y. 10019

EVANS. M. Evans & Co., Inc., 216 E. 49th St., New York, N.Y. 10017

EXPRESSION. Expression Co., P.O. Box 11, Magnolia, Mass. 01930

FARRAR. Farrar, Straus &. Giroux, Inc., 19 Union Sq., W., New York, N.Y. 10003

FAXON. F. W. Faxon Co., Inc., 15 Southwest Park, Westwood, Mass. 02090

FERNHILL. Fernhill House, Ltd., 303 Park Ave. S., New York, N.Y. 10010

FLEET. Fleet Pr., 156 Fifth Ave., New York, N.Y. 10010

FOLLETT. Follett Pub. Co., 1010 W. Washington Blvd., Chicago, Ill. 60606

FOUR WINDS. Four Winds Pr. See Scholastic

FUNK. Funk & Wagnalls, Inc., 53 E. 77th St., New York, N.Y. 10021

GALE. Gale Research Co., Book Tower, Detroit, Mich. 48226

GARDEN CITY. See Doubleday

GARRARD. Garrard Pub. Co., 2 Overhill Rd., Scarsdale, N.Y. 10583

GOLDEN GATE. Golden Gate Junior Books, 8344 Melrose Ave., Los Angeles, Calif. 90069

GOLDEN PR. Golden Pr., Inc. See Western

GROSSET. Grosset & Dunlap, Inc., 51 Madison Ave., New York, N.Y. 10010

HALE. E. M. Hale & Co., Inc., 1201 S. Hastings Way, Eau Claire, Wis. 54701

HARCOURT. Harcourt Brace Jovanovich, Inc., 757 Third Ave., New York, N.Y. 10017

HARPER. Harper & Row, Pubs., 49 E. 33rd St., New York, N.Y. 10016

HARVEY. Harvey House, Inc., 5 S. Buckhout St., Irvington-on-Hudson, N.Y. 10533

HASTINGS. Hastings House Pubs., 10 E. 40th St., New York, N.Y.10016

HAWTHORN. Hawthorn Books, Inc., 70 Fifth Ave., New York, N.Y. 10011

HILL. Hill & Wang, Inc., 72 Fifth Ave., New York, N.Y. 10011

HOLIDAY. Holiday House, Inc., 18 E. 56th St., New York, N.Y. 10022

HOLT. Holt, Rinehart & Winston, Inc., 383 Madison Ave., New York, N.Y. 10017

HORN BOOK. Horn Book, Inc., 585 Boylston St., Boston, Mass. 02116

HOUGHTON. Houghton Mifflin Co., 2 Park St., Boston, Mass. 02107

HUBBARD PR. 2855 Shermer Rd., Northbrook, Ill. 60062

INDIANA UNIV. PR. Tenth and Morton Sts., Bloomington, Ind. 47401

KNOPF. Alfred A. Knopf, Inc., 201 E. 50th St., New York, N.Y. 10022

LERNER. Lerner Pubns. Co., 241 First Ave. N., Minneapolis, Minn. 55401

LIBRARY OF CONGRESS. Supt. of Documents, U.S. Govt. Printing Office, Washington, D.C. 20402

LIPPINCOTT. J. B. Lippincott Co., E. Washington Sq., Philadelphia, Pa. 19105

LITTLE. Little, Brown & Co., 34 Beacon St., Boston, Mass. 02106

LONGMANS. Longmans, Green & Co. See McKay

LOTHROP. Lothrop, Lee & Shepard Co., Inc., 105 Madison Ave., New York, N.Y. 10016

LUCE. Robert B. Luce, Inc., 2000 N. St., N.W., Washington, D.C. 20036

MCCALL. McCall Books, 230 Park Ave., New York, N.Y. 10017

MCGRAW. McGraw-Hill Book Co., 330 W. 42nd St., New York, N.Y. 10036

MCKAY. David McKay Co., Inc., 750 Third Ave., New York, N.Y. 10017

MCKINLEY. 112 S. New Broadway, Brooklawn, N.J. 08030

MACMILLAN. Macmillan Co., 866 Third Ave., New York, N.Y. 10022

MACRAE. Macrae Smith Co., 225 S. 15th St., Philadelphia, Pa. 19102

MEREDITH. Meredith Pr., 250 Park Ave., New York, N.Y. 10017

MERRILL. Charles E. Merrill Pub. Co., 1300 Alum Creek Dr., Columbus, Ohio 43216

MESSNER. Julian Messner, Inc. See Simon & Schuster

METHUEN. Methuen Pubns., 145 Adelaide St. W., Toronto 1, Ont.

MORROW. William Morrow & Co., Inc., 105 Madison Ave., New York, N.Y. 10016

NAT. COUNCIL FOR THE SOCIAL STUDIES. National Education Assoc., 1201 16th St., N.W., Washington, D.C. 20036

NAT. COUNCIL OF TEACHERS OF ENGLISH. 1111 Kenyon Rd., Urbana, Ill. 61820

NATURAL HISTORY PR. Am. Museum of Natural History, Central Park W. at 79th St., New York, N.Y. 10024. Distributed by Doubleday

NELSON. Thomas Nelson, Inc., Copewood & Davis Sts., Camden, N.J. 08103

NEW AM. LIB. New American Library, 1301 Ave. of the Americas, New York, N.Y. 10019

NEW YORK LIBRARY ASSOC. P.O. Box 521, Woodside, N.Y. 11377

NEW YORK PUBLIC LIBRARY. Fifth Ave. and 42nd St., New York, N.Y. 10018

NOBLE. Noble & Noble, Pubs., Inc., 750 Third Ave., New York, N.Y. 10017

NORTON. W. W. Norton & Co., 55 Fifth Ave., New York, N.Y. 10003

NORTON/GROSSET. W. W. Norton in association with Grosset & Dunlap

OBOLENSKY. See Astor-Honor

ODYSSEY. See Bobbs-Merrill

OXFORD. Oxford Univ. Pr., 200 Madison Ave., New York, N.Y. 10016

PANTHEON. Pantheon Books, 201 E. 50th St., New York, N.Y. 10022

PARENTS' MAGAZINE. Parents' Magazine Pr., 52 Vanderbilt Ave., New York, N.Y. 10017

PARNASSUS. Parnassus Pr., 2721 Parker St., Berkeley, Calif. 94704

PERGAMON. Pergamon Pr., Inc., Maxwell House, Fairview Park, Elmsford, N.Y. 10523

PHILLIPS. S. G. Phillips, Inc., 305 W. 86th St., New York, N.Y. 10024

PHOENIX HOUSE. See Univ. of Chicago Pr.

PITMAN. Pitman Pub. Corp., 6 E. 43rd St., New York, N.Y. 10017

PLATT. Platt & Munk, Inc., 1055 Bronx River Ave., Bronx, N.Y. 10472

PLAYS. Plays, Inc., 8 Arlington St., Boston, Mass. 02116
POCKET BOOKS. See Simon & Schuster
POTTER. Clarkson N. Potter, Inc., 419 Park Ave. S., New York, N.Y. 10016
PRAEGER. Praeger Pubs., Inc., 111 Fourth Ave., New York, N.Y. 10003
PRENTICE. Prentice-Hall, Inc., Englewood Cliffs, N.J. 07632
PRESS OF CASE WESTERN RESERVE UNIVERSITY. Quail Bldg., Cleveland, Ohio 44106
PUTNAM. G. P. Putnam's Sons, 200 Madison Ave., New York, N.Y. 10016
QUADRANGLE. Quadrangle Books, Inc., 12 E. Delaware Pl., Chicago, Ill. 60611
RAND. Rand McNally & Co., P.O. Box 7600, Chicago, Ill. 60680
RANDOM. Random House, Inc., 201 E. 50th St., New York, N.Y. 10022
REILLY. Reilly & Lee Books, 114 W. Illinois St., Chicago, Ill. 60610
RITCHIE. The Ward Ritchie Pr., 3044 Riverside Dr., Los Angeles, Calif. 90039
RONALD. The Ronald Press Co., 79 Madison Ave., New York, N.Y. 10016
ROY. Roy Pubs. Inc., 30 E. 74th St., New York, N.Y. 10021
ST. MARTIN'S. St. Martin's Pr., Inc., 175 Fifth Ave., New York, N.Y. 10010
SCARECROW. The Scarecrow Pr., 52 Liberty St., Metuchen, N.J. 08840
SCHOLASTIC. Scholastic Book Services, 50 W. 44th St., New York, N.Y. 10036
W. R. SCOTT. See Addison-Wesley
SCOTT/ADDISON. See Addison-Wesley
SCOTT, FORESMAN. Scott, Foresman and Co., 1900 E. Lake Ave., Glenview, Ill. 60025
SCRIBNER'S. Charles Scribner's Sons, 597 Fifth Ave., New York, N.Y. 10017
SEABURY. Seabury Pr., 815 Second Ave., New York, N.Y. 10017
SIGNET. See New American Library
SIMON. Simon & Schuster, Inc., 630 Fifth Ave., New York, N.Y. 10020
SINGING TREE. See Gale
STANFORD UNIV. PR. Stanford, Calif. 94305
STEIN & DAY. 7 E. 48th St., New York, N.Y. 10017
STERLING. Sterling Pub. Co., 419 Park Ave. S., New York, N.Y. 10016
STOKES. Frederick A. Stokes Co. See Lippincott
TAPLINGER. Taplinger Pub. Co., 200 Park Ave. S., New York, N.Y. 10003
TEACHERS COLLEGE PR. Teachers College, Columbia Univ., 1234 Amsterdam Ave., New York, N.Y. 10027
TIME-LIFE. Time-Life Books, Time-Life Bldg., Rockefeller Center, New York, N.Y. 10020
TOWER. Tower Pubns., Inc., 185 Madison Ave., New York, N.Y. 10016
TROUTMAN. Troutman Pr., Sharon, Conn. 06069
TUNDRA. Tundra Books, 465 St. Francois Xavier, Montreal 125, P.Q.
TUTTLE. Charles E. Tuttle Co., Inc., 28 S. Main St., Rutland, Vt. 05701
UNIV. OF CALIF. PR. 2223 Fulton St., Berkeley, Calif. 94720
UNIV. OF CHICAGO PR. 5801 Ellis Ave., Chicago, Ill. 60637
UNIV. OF PA. PR. 3933 Walnut St., Philadelphia, Pa. 19104
VANGUARD. Vanguard Pr., Inc., 424 Madison Ave., New York, N.Y. 10017
VAN NOSTRAND. Van Nostrand Reinhold Co., 450 W. 33rd St., New York, N.Y. 10001
VIKING. Viking Pr., Inc., 625 Madison Ave., New York, N.Y. 10022
WALCK. Henry Z. Walck, Inc., 19 Union Sq., W., New York, N.Y. 10003
WALKER. Walker & Co., 720 Fifth Ave., New York, N.Y. 10019
WARNE. Frederick Warne & Co., Inc., 101 Fifth Ave., New York, N.Y. 10003
WASHBURN. Ives Washburn, Inc. See McKay
WATTS. Franklin Watts, Inc., 845 Third Ave., New York, N.Y. 10022
WESTMINSTER. The Westminster Pr., Witherspoon Bldg., Philadelphia, Pa. 19107
WESTERN. Western Pub. Co., 1220 Mound Ave., Racine, Wis. 53404
WEYBRIGHT. Weybright and Talley, Inc. See McKay
WHITE. David White Co., 60 E. 55th St., New York, N.Y. 10022
WHITMAN. Albert Whitman & Co., 560 W. Lake St., Chicago, Ill. 60606
WHITTLESEY. Whittlesey House. See McGraw-Hill
WILSON. H. W. Wilson Co., 950 University Ave., Bronx, N.Y. 10452
WINDMILL. Windmill Books, 257 Park Ave. S., New York, N.Y. 10010
WORLD. World Pub. Co., 110 E. 59th St., New York, N.Y. 10022
YOUNG SCOTT. Young Scott Books. See Addison-Wesley

# APPENDIX D
# CHILDREN'S BOOK AWARDS

The awards and prizes given in the children's book field by organizations, schools, publishers, and newspapers, in the United States and other countries, have grown to a sizable number.[4] The Newbery and Caldecott Medals and National Book Award for Children's Literature, all given annually, are the best-known United States awards, and the Hans Christian Andersen Medal, given biennially, the best-known international award. In the case of all but the Andersen Medal, the awards are given for books published during the preceding year.

Following are brief histories of these four awards and listings of the winners and runners-up.

## THE NEWBERY MEDAL

Frederic G. Melcher, American editor of *Publisher's Weekly*, donated and named this award as a tribute to John Newbery (1713–1767), the first English publisher of books for children. Beginning in 1922 and every year since, the Newbery Medal has been given by an awards committee of the Children's Services Division of the American Library Association to the author of the most distinguished contribution to literature for children published in the United States during the preceding year. The author must be a citizen or resident of the United States.

**1922** *The Story of Mankind* by Hendrik Willem van Loon, Liveright

Honor Books: *The Great Quest* by Charles Hawes, Little; *Cedric the Forester* by Bernard Marshall, Appleton; *The Old Tobacco Shop* by William Bowen, Macmillan; *The Golden Fleece and the Heroes Who Lived Before Achilles* by Padraic Colum, Macmillan; *Windy Hill* by Cornelia Meigs, Macmillan

**1923** *The Voyages of Doctor Dolittle* by Hugh Lofting, Lippincott

Honor Books: No record

**1924** *The Dark Frigate* by Charles Hawes, Atlantic/Little

Honor Books: No record

**1925** *Tales from Silver Lands* by Charles Finger, Doubleday

Honor Books: *Nicholas* by Anne Carroll Moore, Putnam; *Dream Coach* by Anne Parrish, Macmillan

**1926** *Shen of the Sea* by Arthur Bowie Chrisman, Dutton

Honor Book: *Voyagers* by Padraic Colum, Macmillan

**1927** *Smoky, the Cowhorse* by Will James, Scribner's

Honor Books: No record

**1928** *Gayneck, The Story of a Pigeon* by Dhan Gopal Mukerji, Dutton

Honor Books: *The Wonder Smith and His Son* by Ella Young, Longmans; *Downright Dencey* by Caroline Snedeker, Doubleday

**1929** *The Trumpeter of Krakow* by Eric P. Kelly, Macmillan

Honor Books: *Pigtail of Ah Lee Ben Loo* by John Bennett, Longmans; *Millions of Cats* by Wanda Gág, Coward; *The Boy Who Was* by Grace Hallock, Dutton; *Clearing Weather* by Cornelia Meigs, Little; *Runaway Papoose* by Grace Moon, Doubleday; *Tod of the Fens* by Elinor Whitney, Macmillan

**1930** *Hitty, Her First Hundred Years* by Rachel Field, Macmillan

Honor Books: *Daughter of the Seine* by Jeanette Eaton, Harper; *Pran of Albania* by Elizabeth Miller, Doubleday; *Jumping-Off Place* by Marian Hurd McNeely, Longmans; *Tangle-Coated Horse and Other Tales* by Ella Young, Longmans; *Vaino* by Julia Davis Adams, Dutton; *Little Blacknose* by Hildegarde Swift, Harcourt

**1931** *The Cat Who Went to Heaven* by Elizabeth Coatsworth, Macmillan

Honor Books: *Floating Island* by Anne Parrish, Harper; *The Dark Star of Itza* by Alida Malkus, Harcourt; *Queer Person* by Ralph Hubbard, Doubleday; *Mountains Are Free* by Julia Davis Adams, Dutton; *Spice and the Devil's Cave* by Agnes Hewes, Knopf; *Meggy Macintosh* by Elizabeth Janet Gray, Doubleday; *Garram the Hunter* by Herbert Best, Doubleday; *Ood-Le-Uk the Wanderer* by Alice Lide and Margaret Johansen, Little

**1932** *Waterless Mountain* by Laura Adams Armer, Longmans

Honor Books: *The Fairy Circus* by Dorothy P. Lathrop, Macmillan; *Calico Bush* by Rachel Field, Macmillan; *Boy of the South Seas* by Eunice Tietjens, Coward; *Out of the Flame* by Eloise Lownsbery, Longmans; *Jane's Island* by Marjorie Allee, Houghton; *Truce of the Wolf and Other Tales of Old Italy* by Mary Gould Davis, Harcourt

**1933** *Young Fu of the Upper Yangtze* by Elizabeth Foreman Lewis, Winston

Honor Books: *Swift Rivers* by Cornelia Meigs, Little; *The Railroad to Freedom* by Hildegarde Swift, Harcourt; *Children of the Soil* by Nora Burglon, Doubleday

**1934** *Invincible Louisa* by Cornelia Meigs, Little

Honor Books: *The Forgotten Daughter* by Caroline Snedeker, Doubleday; *Swords of Steel* by Elsie Singmaster, Houghton; *ABC Bunny* by Wanda Gág, Coward; *Winged Girl of Knossos* by Erik Berry, Appleton; *New Land* by Sarah Schmidt, McBride; *Big Tree of Bunlahy* by Padraic Colum, Macmillan; *Glory of the Seas* by Agnes Hewes, Knopf; *Apprentice of Florence* by Anne Kyle, Houghton

**1935** *Dobry* by Monica Shannon, Viking

Honor Books: *Pageant of Chinese History* by Elizabeth Seeger, Longmans; *Davy Crockett* by Constance Rourke, Harcourt; *Day on Skates* by Hilda Van Stockum, Harper

**1936** *Caddie Woodlawn* by Carol Brink, Macmillan

Honor Books: *Honk, the Moose* by Phil Stong, Dodd; *The Good Master* by Kate Seredy, Viking; *Young Walter*

4. *Children's Books: Awards and Prizes* (comp. and ed. by Margaret Colbert, The Children's Book Council, 1971) is a complete compilation of honors awarded in the children's book field.

*Scott* by Elizabeth Janet Gray, Viking; *All Sail Set* by Armstrong Sperry, Winston

**1937** *Roller Skates* by Ruth Sawyer, Viking

Honor Books: *Phoebe Fairchild: Her Book* by Lois Lenski, Stokes; *Whistler's Van* by Idwal Jones, Viking; *Golden Basket* by Ludwig Bemelmans, Viking; *Winterbound* by Margery Bianco, Viking; *Audubon* by Constance Rourke, Harcourt; *The Codfish Musket* by Agnes Hewes, Doubleday

**1938** *The White Stag* by Kate Seredy, Viking

Honor Books: *Pecos Bill* by James Cloyd Bowman, Little; *Bright Island* by Mabel Robinson, Random; *On the Banks of Plum Creek* by Laura Ingalls Wilder, Harper

**1939** *Thimble Summer* by Elizabeth Enright, Rinehart

Honor Books: *Nino* by Valenti Angelo, Viking; *Mr. Popper's Penguins* by Richard and Florence Atwater, Little; *"Hello the Boat!"* by Phyllis Crawford, Holt; *Leader by Destiny: George Washington, Man and Patriot* by Jeanette Eaton, Harcourt; *Penn* by Elizabeth Janet Gray, Viking

**1940** *Daniel Boone* by James Daugherty, Viking

Honor Books: *The Singing Tree* by Kate Seredy, Viking; *Runner of the Mountain Tops* by Mabel Robinson, Random; *By the Shores of Silver Lake* by Laura Ingalls Wilder, Harper; *Boy with a Pack* by Stephen W. Meader, Harcourt

**1941** *Call It Courage* by Armstrong Sperry, Macmillan

Honor Books: *Blue Willow* by Doris Gates, Viking; *Young Mac of Fort Vancouver* by Mary Jane Carr, Crowell; *The Long Winter* by Laura Ingalls Wilder, Harper; *Nansen* by Anna Gertrude Hall, Viking

**1942** *The Matchlock Gun* by Walter D. Edmonds, Dodd

Honor Books: *Little Town on the Prairie* by Laura Ingalls Wilder, Harper; *George Washington's World* by Genevieve Foster, Scribner's; *Indian Captive: The Story of Mary Jemison* by Lois Lenski, Lippincott; *Down Ryton Water* by Eva Roe Gaggin, Viking

**1943** *Adam of the Road* by Elizabeth Janet Gray, Viking

Honor Books: *The Middle Moffat* by Eleanor Estes, Harcourt; *Have You Seen Tom Thumb?* by Mabel Leigh Hunt, Lippincott

**1944** *Johnny Tremain* by Esther Forbes, Houghton

Honor Books: *These Happy Golden Years* by Laura Ingalls Wilder, Harper; *Fog Magic* by Julia Sauer, Viking; *Rufus M.* by Eleanor Estes, Harcourt; *Mountain Born* by Elizabeth Yates, Coward

**1945** *Rabbit Hill* by Robert Lawson, Viking

Honor Books: *The Hundred Dresses* by Eleanor Estes, Harcourt; *The Silver Pencil* by Alice Dalgliesh, Scribner's; *Abraham Lincoln's World* by Genevieve Foster, Scribner's; *Lone Journey: The Life of Roger Williams* by Jeanette Eaton, Harcourt

**1946** *Strawberry Girl* by Lois Lenski, Lippincott

Honor Books: *Justin Morgan Had a Horse* by Marguerite Henry, Rand; *The Moved-Outers* by Florence Crannell Means, Houghton; *Bhimsa, the Dancing Bear* by Christine Weston, Scribner's; *New Found World* by Katherine Shippen, Viking

**1947** *Miss Hickory* by Carolyn Sherwin Bailey, Viking

Honor Books: *Wonderful Year* by Nancy Barnes, Messner; *Big Tree* by Mary and Conrad Buff, Viking; *The Heavenly Tenants* by William Maxwell, Harper; *The Avion My Uncle Flew* by Cyrus Fisher, Appleton; *The Hidden Treasure of Glaston* by Eleanore Jewett, Viking

**1948** *The Twenty-one Balloons* by William Pène du Bois, Viking

Honor Books: *Pancakes-Paris* by Claire Huchet Bishop, Viking; *Li Lun, Lad of Courage* by Carolyn Treffinger, Abingdon; *The Quaint and Curious Quest of Johnny Longfoot* by Catherine Besterman, Bobbs; *The Cow-Tail Switch, and Other West African Stories* by Harold Courlander, Holt; *Misty of Chincoteague* by Marguerite Henry, Rand

**1949** *King of the Wind* by Marguerite Henry, Rand

Honor Books: *Seabird* by Holling C. Holling, Houghton; *Daughter of the Mountains* by Louise Rankin, Viking; *My Father's Dragon* by Ruth S. Gannett, Random; *Story of the Negro* by Arna Bontemps, Knopf

**1950** *The Door in the Wall* by Marguerite de Angeli, Doubleday

Honor Books: *Tree of Freedom* by Rebecca Caudill, Viking; *The Blue Cat of Castle Town* by Catherine Coblentz, Longmans; *Kildee House* by Rutherford Montgomery, Doubleday; *George Washington* by Genevieve Foster, Scribner's; *Song of the Pines* by Walter and Marion Havighurst, Winston

**1951** *Amos Fortune, Free Man* by Elizabeth Yates, Aladdin

Honor Books: *Better Known as Johnny Appleseed* by Mabel Leigh Hunt, Lippincott; *Gandhi, Fighter Without a Sword* by Jeanette Eaton, Morrow; *Abraham Lincoln, Friend of the People* by Clara Ingram Judson, Follett; *The Story of Appleby Capple* by Anne Parrish, Harper

**1952** *Ginger Pye* by Eleanor Estes, Harcourt

Honor Books: *Americans Before Columbus* by Elizabeth Baity, Viking; *Minn of the Mississippi* by Holling C. Holling, Houghton; *The Defender* by Nicholas Kalashnikoff, Scribner's; *The Light at Tern Rock* by Julia Sauer, Viking; *The Apple and the Arrow* by Mary and Conrad Buff, Houghton

**1953** *Secret of the Andes* by Ann Nolan Clark, Viking

Honor Books: *Charlotte's Web* by E. B. White, Harper; *Moccasin Trail* by Eloise McGraw, Coward; *Red Sails to Capri* by Ann Weil, Viking; *The Bears on Hemlock Mountain* by Alice Dalgliesh, Scribner's; *Birthdays of Freedom*, Vol. 1 by Genevieve Foster, Scribner's

**1954** *. . . and now Miguel* by Joseph Krumgold, T. Crowell

Honor Books: *All Alone* by Claire Huchet Bishop, Viking; *Shadrach* by Meindert DeJong, Harper; *Hurry Home Candy* by Meindert DeJong, Harper; *Theodore Roosevelt, Fighting Patriot* by Clara Ingram Judson, Follett; *Magic Maize* by Mary and Conrad Buff, Houghton

**1955** *The Wheel on the School* by Meindert DeJong, Harper

Honor Books: *Courage of Sarah Noble* by Alice Dalgliesh, Scribner's; *Banner in the Sky* by James Ullman, Lippincott

**1956** *Carry on, Mr. Bowditch* by Jean Lee Latham, Houghton

Honor Books: *The Secret River* by Marjorie Kinnan Rawlings, Scribner's; *The Golden Name Day* by Jennie Lindquist, Harper; *Men, Microscopes, and Living Things* by Katherine Shippen, Viking

**1957** *Miracles on Maple Hill* by Virginia Sorensen, Harcourt

Honor Books: *Old Yeller* by Fred Gipson, Harper; *The House of Sixty Fathers* by Meindert DeJong, Harper; *Mr. Justice Holmes* by Clara Ingram Judson, Follett; *The Corn*

*Grows Ripe* by Dorothy Rhoads, Viking; *Black Fox of Lorne* by Marguerite de Angeli, Doubleday

**1958** *Rifles for Watie* by Harold Keith, T. Crowell

Honor Books: *The Horsecatcher* by Mari Sandoz, Westminster; *Gone-Away Lake* by Elizabeth Enright, Harcourt; *The Great Wheel* by Robert Lawson, Viking; *Tom Paine, Freedom's Apostle* by Leo Gurko, T. Crowell

**1959** *The Witch of Blackbird Pond* by Elizabeth George Speare, Houghton

Honor Books: *The Family Under the Bridge* by Natalie S. Carlson, Harper; *Along Came a Dog* by Meindert DeJong, Harper; *Chucaro: Wild Pony of the Pampa* by Francis Kalnay, Harcourt; *The Perilous Road* by William O. Steele, Harcourt

**1960** *Onion John* by Joseph Krumgold, T. Crowell

Honor Books: *My Side of the Mountain* by Jean George, Dutton; *America Is Born* by Gerald W. Johnson, Morrow; *The Gammage Cup* by Carol Kendall, Harcourt

**1961** *Island of the Blue Dolphins* by Scott O'Dell, Houghton

Honor Books: *America Moves Forward* by Gerald W. Johnson, Morrow; *Old Ramon* by Jack Schaefer, Houghton; *The Cricket in Times Square* by George Selden, Farrar

**1962** *The Bronze Bow* by Elizabeth George Speare, Houghton

Honor Books: *Frontier Living* by Edwin Tunis, World; *The Golden Goblet* by Eloise McGraw, Coward; *Belling the Tiger* by Mary Stolz, Harper

**1963** *A Wrinkle in Time* by Madeleine L'Engle, Farrar

Honor Books: *Thistle and Thyme* by Sorche Nic Leodhas, Holt; *Men of Athens* by Olivia Coolidge, Houghton

**1964** *It's Like This, Cat* by Emily Cheney Neville, Harper

Honor Books: *Rascal* by Sterling North, Dutton; *The Loner* by Ester Wier, McKay

**1965** *Shadow of a Bull* by Maia Wojciechowska, Atheneum

Honor Book: *Across Five Aprils* by Irene Hunt, Follett

**1966** *I, Juan de Pareja* by Elizabeth Borten de Treviño, Farrar

Honor Books: *The Black Cauldron* by Lloyd Alexander, Holt; *The Animal Family* by Randall Jarrell, Pantheon; *The Noonday Friends* by Mary Stolz, Harper

**1967** *Up a Road Slowly* by Irene Hunt, Follett

Honor Books: *The King's Fifth* by Scott O'Dell, Houghton; *Zlateh the Goat and Other Stories* by Isaac Bashevis Singer, Harper; *The Jazz Man* by Mary H. Weik, Atheneum

**1968** *From the Mixed-Up Files of Mrs. Basil E. Frankweiler* by E. L. Konigsburg, Atheneum

Honor Books: *Jennifer, Hecate, Macbeth, William McKinley, and Me, Elizabeth* by E. L. Konigsburg, Atheneum; *The Black Pearl* by Scott O'Dell, Houghton; *The Fearsome Inn* by Isaac Bashevis Singer, Scribner's; *The Egypt Game* by Zilpha Keatley Snyder, Atheneum

**1969** *The High King* by Lloyd Alexander, Holt

Honor Books: *To Be a Slave* by Julius Lester, Dial; *When Shlemiel Went to Warsaw and Other Stories* by Isaac Bashevis Singer, Farrar

**1970** *Sounder* by William H. Armstrong, Harper

Honor Books: *Our Eddie* by Sulamith Ish-Kishor, Pantheon; *The Many Ways of Seeing: An Introduction to the Pleasures of Art* by Janet Gaylord Moore, World; *Journey Outside* by Mary Q. Steele, Viking

**1971** *Summer of the Swans* by Betsy Byars, Viking

Honor Books: *Kneeknock Rise* by Natalie Babbitt, Farrar; *Enchantress from the Stars* by Sylvia Louise Engdahl, Atheneum; *Sing Down the Moon* by Scott O'Dell, Houghton

**1972** *Mrs. Frisby and the Rats of NIMH* by Robert C. O'Brien, Atheneum

Honor Books: *Incident at Hawk's Hill* by Allan W. Eckert, Little; *The Planet of Junior Brown* by Virginia Hamilton, Macmillan; *The Tombs of Atuan* by Ursula K. Le Guin, Atheneum; *Annie and the Old One* by Miska Miles, Atlantic/Little; *The Headless Cupid* by Zilpha Keatley Snyder, Atheneum

## THE CALDECOTT MEDAL

This award is named in honor of Randolph Caldecott (1846–1886), the English illustrator whose pictures still delight children. In 1937, Frederic G. Melcher, the American editor and publisher who had conceived the idea of the Newbery Medal some years earlier, proposed the establishment of a similar award for picture books, and since 1938 the Caldecott Medal has been awarded annually by an awards committee of the American Library Association's Children's Services Division to the illustrator of the most distinguished picture book for children published in the United States during the preceding year. The award is limited to residents or citizens of the United States.

If only one name is given, then the book was written and illustrated by the same person.

**1938** *Animals of the Bible* by Helen Dean Fish, ill. by Dorothy P. Lathrop, Lippincott

Honor Books: *Seven Simeons* by Boris Artzybasheff, Viking; *Four and Twenty Blackbirds* by Helen Dean Fish, ill. by Robert Lawson, Stokes

**1939** *Mei Li* by Thomas Handforth, Doubleday

Honor Books: *The Forest Pool* by Laura Adams Armer, Longmans; *Wee Gillis* by Munro Leaf, ill. by Robert Lawson, Viking; *Snow White and the Seven Dwarfs* by Wanda Gág, Coward; *Barkis* by Clare Newberry, Harper; *Andy and the Lion* by James Daugherty, Viking

**1940** *Abraham Lincoln* by Ingri and Edgar Parin d'Aulaire, Doubleday

Honor Books: *Cock-A-Doodle Doo . . .* by Berta and Elmer Hader, Macmillan; *Madeline* by Ludwig Bemelmans, Viking; *The Ageless Story* ill. by Lauren Ford, Dodd

**1941** *They Were Strong and Good* by Robert Lawson, Viking

Honor Book: *April's Kittens* by Clare Newberry, Harper

**1942** *Make Way for Ducklings* by Robert McCloskey, Viking

Honor Books: *An American ABC* by Maud and Miska Petersham, Macmillan; *In My Mother's House* by Ann Nolan Clark, ill. by Velino Herrera, Viking; *Paddle-to-the-Sea* by Holling C. Holling, Houghton; *Nothing at All* by Wanda Gág, Coward

**1943** *The Little House* by Virginia Lee Burton, Houghton

Honor Books: *Dash and Dart* by Mary and Conrad Buff, Viking; *Marshmallow* by Clare Newberry, Harper

**1944** *Many Moons* by James Thurber, ill. by Louis Slobodkin, Harcourt
Honor Books: *Small Rain: Verses from the Bible* selected by Jessie Orton Jones, ill. by Elizabeth Orton Jones, Viking; *Pierre Pigeon* by Lee Kingman, ill. by Arnold E. Bare, Houghton; *The Mighty Hunter* by Berta and Elmer Hader, Macmillan; *A Child's Good Night Book* by Margaret Wise Brown, ill. by Jean Charlot, W. R. Scott; *Good Luck Horse* by Chih-Yi Chan, ill. by Plao Chan, Whittlesey
**1945** *Prayer for a Child* by Rachel Field, ill. by Elizabeth Orton Jones, Macmillan
Honor Books: *Mother Goose* ill. by Tasha Tudor, Walck; *In the Forest* by Marie Hall Ets, Viking; *Yonie Wondernose* by Marguerite de Angeli, Doubleday; *The Christmas Anna Angel* by Ruth Sawyer, ill. by Kate Seredy, Viking
**1946** *The Rooster Crows . . .* (traditional Mother Goose) ill. by Maud and Miska Petersham, Macmillan
Honor Books: *Little Lost Lamb* by Golden MacDonald, ill. by Leonard Weisgard, Doubleday; *Sing Mother Goose* by Opal Wheeler, ill. by Marjorie Torrey, Dutton; *My Mother Is the Most Beautiful Woman in the World* by Becky Reyher, ill. by Ruth Gannett, Lothrop; *You Can Write Chinese* by Kurt Wiese, Viking
**1947** *The Little Island* by Golden MacDonald, ill. by Leonard Weisgard, Doubleday
Honor Books: *Rain Drop Splash* by Alvin Tresselt, ill. by Leonard Weisgard, Lothrop; *Boats on the River* by Marjorie Flack, ill. by Jay Hyde Barnum, Viking; *Timothy Turtle* by Al Graham, ill. by Tony Palazzo, Welch; *Pedro, the Angel of Olvera Street* by Leo Politi, Scribner's; *Sing in Praise: A Collection of the Best Loved Hymns* by Opal Wheeler, ill. by Marjorie Torrey, Dutton
**1948** *White Snow, Bright Snow* by Alvin Tresselt, ill. by Roger Duvoisin, Lothrop
Honor Books: *Stone Soup* by Marcia Brown, Scribner's; *McElligot's Pool* by Dr. Seuss, Random; *Bambino the Clown* by George Schreiber, Viking; *Roger and the Fox* by Lavinia Davis, ill. by Hildegard Woodward, Doubleday; *Song of Robin Hood* ed. by Anne Malcolmson, ill. by Virginia Lee Burton, Houghton
**1949** *The Big Snow* by Berta and Elmer Hader, Macmillan
Honor Books: *Blueberries for Sal* by Robert McCloskey, Viking; *All Around the Town* by Phyllis McGinley, ill. by Helen Stone, Lippincott; *Juanita* by Leo Politi, Scribner's; *Fish in the Air* by Kurt Wiese, Viking
**1950** *Song of the Swallows* by Leo Politi, Scribner's
Honor Books: *America's Ethan Allen* by Stewart Holbrook, ill. by Lynd Ward, Houghton; *The Wild Birthday Cake* by Lavinia Davis, ill. by Hildegard Woodward, Doubleday; *The Happy Day* by Ruth Krauss, ill. by Marc Simont, Harper; *Bartholomew and the Oobleck* by Dr. Seuss, Random; *Henry Fisherman* by Marcia Brown, Scribner's
**1951** *The Egg Tree* by Katherine Milhous, Scribner's
Honor Books: *Dick Whittington and His Cat* by Marcia Brown, Scribner's; *The Two Reds* by Will, ill. by Nicolas, Harcourt; *If I Ran the Zoo* by Dr. Seuss, Random; *The Most Wonderful Doll in the World* by Phyllis McGinley, ill. by Helen Stone, Lippincott; *T-Bone, the Baby Sitter* by Clare Newberry, Harper
**1952** *Finders Keepers* by Will, ill. by Nicolas, Harcourt
Honor Books: *Mr. T. W. Anthony Woo* by Marie Hall Ets, Viking; *Skipper John's Cook* by Marcia Brown, Scribner's; *All Falling Down* by Gene Zion, ill. by Margaret Bloy Graham, Harper; *Bear Party* by William Pène du Bois, Viking; *Feather Mountain* by Elizabeth Olds, Houghton
**1953** *The Biggest Bear* by Lynd Ward, Houghton
Honor Books: *Puss in Boots* by Charles Perrault, ill. and tr. by Marcia Brown, Scribner's; *One Morning in Maine* by Robert McCloskey, Viking; *Ape in a Cape* by Fritz Eichenberg, Harcourt; *The Storm Book* by Charlotte Zolotow, ill. by Margaret Bloy Graham, Harper; *Five Little Monkeys* by Juliet Kepes, Houghton
**1954** *Madeline's Rescue* by Ludwig Bemelmans, Viking
Honor Books: *Journey Cake, Ho!* by Ruth Sawyer, ill. by Robert McCloskey, Viking; *When Will the World Be Mine?* by Miriam Schlein, ill. by Jean Charlot, W. R. Scott; *The Steadfast Tin Soldier* by Hans Christian Andersen, ill. by Marcia Brown, Scribner's; *A Very Special House* by Ruth Krauss, ill. by Maurice Sendak, Harper; *Green Eyes* by A. Birnbaum, Capitol
**1955** *Cinderella, or the Little Glass Slipper* by Charles Perrault, tr. and ill. by Marcia Brown, Scribner's
Honor Books: *Book of Nursery and Mother Goose Rhymes*, ill. by Marguerite de Angeli, Doubleday; *Wheel on the Chimney* by Margaret Wise Brown, ill. by Tibor Gergely, Lippincott; *The Thanksgiving Story* by Alice Dalgliesh, ill. by Helen Sewell, Scribner's
**1956** *Frog Went A-Courtin'* ed. by John Langstaff, ill. by Feodor Rojankovsky, Harcourt
Honor Books: *Play with Me* by Marie Hall Ets, Viking; *Crow Boy* by Taro Yashima, Viking
**1957** *A Tree Is Nice* by Janice May Udry, ill. by Marc Simont, Harper
Honor Books: *Mr. Penny's Race Horse* by Marie Hall Ets, Viking; *1 Is One* by Tasha Tudor, Walck; *Anatole* by Eve Titus, ill. by Paul Galdone, McGraw; *Gillespie and the Guards* by Benjamin Elkin, ill. by James Daugherty, Viking; *Lion* by William Pène du Bois, Viking
**1958** *Time of Wonder* by Robert McCloskey, Viking
Honor Books: *Fly High, Fly Low* by Don Freeman, Viking; *Anatole and the Cat* by Eve Titus, ill. by Paul Galdone, McGraw
**1959** *Chanticleer and the Fox* adapted from Chaucer and ill. by Barbara Cooney, T. Crowell
Honor Books: *The House That Jack Built* by Antonio Frasconi, Harcourt; *What Do You Say, Dear?* by Sesyle Joslin, ill. by Maurice Sendak, W. R. Scott; *Umbrella* by Taro Yashima, Viking
**1960** *Nine Days to Christmas* by Marie Hall Ets and Aurora Labastida, ill. by Marie Hall Ets, Viking
Honor Books: *Houses from the Sea* by Alice E. Goudey, ill. by Adrienne Adams, Scribner's; *The Moon Jumpers* by Janice May Udry, ill. by Maurice Sendak, Harper
**1961** *Baboushka and the Three Kings* by Ruth Robbins, ill. by Nicolas Sidjakov, Parnassus
Honor Book: *Inch by Inch* by Leo Lionni, Obolensky
**1962** *Once a Mouse . . .* by Marcia Brown, Scribner's
Honor Books: *The Fox Went Out on a Chilly Night* ill. by Peter Spier, Doubleday; *Little Bear's Visit* by Else Holmelund Minarik, ill. by Maurice Sendak, Harper; *The Day We Saw the Sun Come Up* by Alice E. Goudey, ill. by Adrienne Adams, Scribner's

**1963** *The Snowy Day* by Ezra Jack Keats, Viking
Honor Books: *The Sun Is a Golden Earring* by Natalia M. Belting, ill. by Bernarda Bryson, Holt; *Mr. Rabbit and the Lovely Present* by Charlotte Zolotow, ill. by Maurice Sendak, Harper
**1964** *Where the Wild Things Are* by Maurice Sendak, Harper
Honor Books: *Swimmy* by Leo Lionni, Pantheon; *All in the Morning Early* by Sorche Nic Leodhas, ill. by Evaline Ness, Holt; *Mother Goose and Nursery Rhymes* ill. by Philip Reed, Atheneum
**1965** *May I Bring a Friend?* by Beatrice Schenk de Regniers, ill. by Beni Montresor, Atheneum
Honor Books: *Rain Makes Applesauce* by Julian Scheer, ill. by Marvin Bileck, Holiday; *The Wave* by Margaret Hodges, ill. by Blair Lent, Houghton; *A Pocketful of Cricket* by Rebecca Caudill, ill. by Evaline Ness, Holt
**1966** *Always Room for One More* by Sorche Nic Leodhas, ill. by Nonny Hogrogian, Holt
Honor Books: *Hide and Seek Fog* by Alvin Tresselt, ill. by Roger Duvoisin, Lothrop; *Just Me* by Marie Hall Ets, Viking; *Tom Tit Tot* by Evaline Ness, Scribner's
**1967** *Sam, Bangs & Moonshine* by Evaline Ness, Holt
Honor Book: *One Wide River to Cross* by Barbara Emberly, ill. by Ed Emberley, Prentice
**1968** *Drummer Hoff* by Barbara Emberley, ill. by Ed Emberley, Prentice
Honor Books: *Frederick* by Leo Lionni, Pantheon; *Seashore Story* by Taro Yashima, Viking; *The Emperor and the Kite* by Jane Yolen, ill. by Ed Young, World
**1969** *The Fool of the World and the Flying Ship* by Arthur Ransome, ill. by Uri Shulevitz, Farrar
Honor Book: *Why the Sun and the Moon Live in the Sky* by Elphinstone Dayrell, ill. by Blair Lent, Houghton
**1970** *Sylvester and the Magic Pebble* by William Steig, Windmill
Honor Books: *Goggles* by Ezra Jack Keats, Macmillan; *Alexander and the Wind-Up Mouse* by Leo Lionni, Pantheon; *Pop Corn & Ma Goodness* by Edna Mitchell Preston, ill. by Robert Andrew Parker, Viking; *Thy Friend, Obadiah* by Brinton Turkle, Viking; *The Judge* by Harve Zemach, ill. by Margot Zemach, Farrar
**1971** *A Story–A Story* by Gail E. Haley, Atheneum
Honor Books: *The Angry Moon* by William Sleator, ill. by Blair Lent, Atlantic/Little; *Frog and Toad Are Friends* by Arnold Lobel, Harper; *In the Night Kitchen* by Maurice Sendak, Harper
**1972** *One Fine Day* by Nonny Hogrogian, Macmillan
Honor Books: *If All the Seas Were One Sea,* by Janina Domanska, Macmillan; *Moja Means One: Swahili Counting Book* by Muriel Feelings, ill. by Tom Feelings, Dial; *Hildilid's Night* by Cheli Duran Ryan, ill. by Arnold Lobel, Macmillan

## THE HANS CHRISTIAN ANDERSEN AWARD

This award was established in 1956 by the International Board on Books for Young People and is given every two years to one living author who, by his complete work, has made an important international contribution to children's literature. Since 1966 an artist's medal is also given. Each national section of the International Board proposes one author and one illustrator as nominees and the final choice is made by a committee of five, each from a different country.

**1956** Eleanor Farjeon (Great Britain)
**1958** Astrid Lindgren (Sweden)
**1960** Erich Kästner (Germany)
**1962** Meindert DeJong (U.S.A.)
**1964** René Guillot (France)
**1966** Author: Tove Jansson (Finland)
Illustrator: Alois Carigiet (Switzerland)
**1968** Authors: James Krüss (Germany)
Jose Maria Sanchez-Silva (Spain)
Illustrator: Jiri Trnka (Czechoslovakia)
**1970** Author: Gianni Rodari (Italy)
Illustrator: Maurice Sendak (U.S.A.)

## THE NATIONAL BOOK AWARD

In March 1969, the National Book Awards included for the first time in its twenty-year history a prize for Children's Literature. The $1000 prize, contributed by the Children's Book Council and administered by the National Book Committee, is presented annually to a juvenile title that a panel of judges considers the most distinguished written by an American citizen and published in the United States in the preceding year.

**1969** *Journey from Peppermint Street* by Meindert DeJong, Harper
Leading Contenders: *Constance* by Patricia Clapp, Lothrop; *The Endless Steppe* by Esther Hautzig, T. Crowell; *The High King* by Lloyd Alexander, Holt; *Langston Hughes* by Milton Meltzer, T. Crowell
**1970** *A Day of Pleasure: Stories of a Boy Growing up in Warsaw* by Isaac Bashevis Singer, Farrar
Leading Contenders: *Pop Corn & Ma Goodness* by Edna Mitchell Preston, Viking; *Sylvester and the Magic Pebble* by William Steig, Windmill; *Where the Lilies Bloom* by Vera and Bill Cleaver, Lippincott; *The Young United States* by Edwin Tunis, World
**1971** *The Marvelous Misadventures of Sebastian* by Lloyd Alexander, Dutton
Leading Contenders: *Blowfish Live in the Sea* by Paula Fox, Bradbury; *Frog and Toad Are Friends* by Arnold Lobel, Harper; *Grover* by Vera and Bill Cleaver, Lippincott; *Trumpet of the Swan* by E. B. White, Harper

# APPENDIX E PRONUNCIATION GUIDE

Symbols used in the pronunciation are as follows: a as in *hat;* ā as in *age;* ã as in *care;* ä as in *father;* e as in *let;* ē as in *see;* ėr as in *term;* i as in *pin;* ī as in *five;* o as in *hot;* ō as in *go;* ô as in *order, all;* oi as in *oil;* ou as in *house;* th as in *thin;* ŧħ as in *then;* u as in *cup;* u̇ as in *full;* ü as in *rule;* ū as in *use;* zh as in *measure;* ə as in the unaccented syllables of *about, taken, pencil, lemon, circus;* H as in the German *ach;* N as in the French *bon* (not pronounced, but shows that the vowel before it is nasal); œ as in the French *peu* and the German *könig* (pronounced by speaking ā with the lips rounded as for ō); Y as in the French *du* (pronounced by speaking ē with the lips rounded as for ü). All other symbols represent the consonant sounds that they commonly stand for in English spelling.

Aardema är dē mä
Abrashkin a brash′kin
Adoff ā′dof
Afanasiev ä fä nä′syif
Agle ā′gu̇l
Agra ä′grə
Aiken-drum ā kən drum
Alcock, Gudrun al′kok, gü′drun
Aldis ôl′dis
Aliki ä lē′kī
Allingham al′ing əm
Almedingen al′mə ding′ən
Ambrus ôm′bru̇sh
Analdas ə näl′dəs
Ananse ə nan′si
Anckarsvärd äng′kȧs verd
Ankhsenpaaten anH′sen pät′en
Arawn ä ron′
Ardizzone är di zō′ni
Arora ə ro′rə
Arrietty ãr′i e tē
Artzybasheff är tsi ba′shif
Asbjörnsen äs′byėrn sen
Asimov as′im ov
Aucassin ō ka saN′
Averill ā′və ril
Ayars ãrz
Ayme e mā′
Baba Yaga bä′bə yä′gä
Babar bä′bär
Bacmeister bok′mī ster
Bandai ban dī′
Banneker bon′nə kėr
Barbauld bär′bōld
Barchilon, Jacques bär shē yoN′, zhäk
Bartusis bär tü′sis
Basho bä shō
Baudouy, Michel-Aimé bô dü ē′, mē shel-e mā′
Baumann bou′män
Behn bān
Beim bīm
Benary-Isbert, Margot ben ãr′ē is′-bėrt, mär′gō
Benedetti, Mario bā′nā dāt′ tē
Benét be nā′
Benezet ben′ə zet′
Beowulf bā′ə wu̇lf
Berquin, Armand bėr kaN′, ar-mäN′
Bertol bãr′tôl
Beskow bes′kō
Bethune, Mary McLeod bā thūn′, mak loud′
Bevis bē′vis
Bewick bū′ik
Bidpai bid′pī
Binnorie bin′ə rē/bin′ô rē
Bishop, Claire Huchet œ shā′
Blegvad bleg′vad
Blough blou
Bogosian bô gōz′yun
Bolognese bō lō nā′zē
Bontemps, Arna bôN tôN′, är′nə
Brinsmead, Hesba Fay hez′bə
Bryson brī′sən
Bubo bū′bō
Budulinek bu dū′lin ek
Bulla bu̇l′ə
Cabeza de Vaca kä bā′thä dā vä′kä
Caudill kô′dl
Cavanna kə van′ə
Cayuse kī ūs′
Chaga chä′gä
Chakoh chä′kō
Chincoteague ching′kə tēg
Christiansen, Reider kris′tyän sən, rēd ər
Chute, Marchette chüt, mär shet′
Chwast kwäst
Ciardi chär′dē
Cinderlad, Per, Paal, Espen sin′dər läd, pãr, pôl, es′pən
Coblentz kō′blents
Collodi kōl lô′dē
Colman, Hila hī′lä
Coombs kümz
Colum, Padraic kol′um, pô′drig
Comenius kə mē′ni us
Contes de Ma Mère l'Oye kôNt də mä mãr lwä
Cowper kü′pėr
Credle crā′dəl
Cuchulain kü chü′lin
Dahl, Roald däl, rō′äl
Dalgliesh däl glēsh
D'Amelio da mēl′ē yō
D'Armancour där môN kür′
Dasent dā′sənt
d'Aulaire dō lãr′
d'Aulnoy dōl nwä′
De Angeli də an′jel ē
De Beaumont, Madame Leprince də bō môN′, ma dam′ lə praNs′
De Brunhoff, Jean də brün′ôf, zhôN
De Gasztold, Carmen Bernos də gaz′tōl, bėr′nōs
De Genlis, Madame də zhôN lē′, ma dam′
DeJong, Meindert də yung′, min′-dėrt
De la Mare də la mãr′
De Luca dā lü′kä
Demetrius of Phalerum dē mē′-tri us, fu lēr′əm
De Pareja dā pə rā′hä
De Regniers də rān′yā
Derleth dėr′leth
De Trevino dā trə vē′nyō
Deucher dü shā′
Deutsch, Babette doich, bab et′
Ditlabeng dit′lə beng
Dobry dō′brē
Dodge, Mary Mapes māps
Domanska, Janina dô män′skä, yä-nē′nä
Doob düb
Douty dü′tē
Du Bois, William Pène dY bwä, pen
Duvoisin dY vwä zaN′
Eckenstein, Lina ek′en stīn, lē′nä
Edda ed′ə
Eichenberg ī′ken bėrg
Engdahl əng′dôl
Epaminondas i pam i non′dəs
Evers, Alf ev′ėrs, älf
Farjeon fär′jun
Farquharson fär′kwėr sən
Feagles fē′gləs
Fenians fē ni ənz
Fflewddur Flam flü′dœr flam
Figgis fig′is
Fiorello fē ō rel′ō
Fjeld fē′el/fyel
Forberg, Ati ä′tē
Forten fôr′tən
Franchere frän′shãr
Frascino frə shē′nō
Frasconi, Antonio frans kō′nē, än-tō′nyō
Frolov, Vadim frō′lof, vä dim
Fyleman fīl′man
Gaer gãr
Gaetano gä′ā tä nō
Gág gäg
Galdone gal dōn′
Galland, Antoine gə läN′, äN twôn′

Gaudenzia gou den′tsya
Gautama Buddha gô′tə mə bu′də
Gengi gən′jē
Gerda ger tə
Gidal gi dal′
Gilgamesh gil gä′mesh
Giuliano jü lyä′nō
Glubok glü′bok
Gobhai gō bī
Goff gof
Gottschalk, Fruma gät′shəlk, frü′mə
Goudey gou′dē
Gramatky gra mat′kē
Gudbrand gu̇d′bränd
Guillot, René gē yō, ru̇ nā′
Guion gī′ôn
Guiterman git′ėr mən
Gurgi gœr′jē
Gwydion gwi′dē on
Gylfi gYl′fə
Haar, Jaap Ter här, yop tėr
Haas häs
Haber hä′bėr
Hader hā′dėr
Haida hī′du
Hakon hô′kən
Hallard hal′lärd
Hanff hänf
Haugaard hou′gärd
Hautzig hout′zig
Hazard a zär′
Hazeltine hāz′əl tīn′
Heinlein hīn′līn
Hepzibah hep′zi bah
Hesiod hē′si od
Heumann hoi′män
Heyerdahl, Thor hā′ėr däl, tu̇r
Heyward, Du Bose dū bōz′
Hidalgo y Costilla ēd häl′go ē kōs-te′yä
Hieatt hi′at
Hitopadesa hi tō pa dā′sha
Hoban hō′ban
Hofsinde hof′sin də
Hogrogian, Nonny hō grō′gē an, no′nē
Hokusai hō ku̇ sī
Homily hom′i lē
Hosford hôs′fərd
Hyndman hīnd′man
Ignatow ig nä′tō
Ishi ē shē
Ish-Kishor, Sulamith, ish′ki shor′, su lam′ith
Issa is′ə
Jahdu jä′dū
Jancsi yan′sē
Jansson, Tove yän′sən, tō′vä
Janosh yä′nōsh
Jarrell jar′rel
Jataka jä′tä kə
Jean-Claude zhôn klōd
Jeanne-Marie zhan′mä rē′
Josian jō sī′ən
Kaa kä
Kahl käl
Karana kä rä′nä
Kästner, Erich kest′nər, ā′rik
Katia kä′tyə
Kaula kô lu
Kavaler ka′vu̇l ėr
Kävik kä′vik
Kenofer ken′o fėr
Kim Van Kieu kēm vən kyū
Kinder und Hausmärchen kin′dėr-u̇nd hous′mār′Hən
Kjelgaard kel′gärd
Konigsburg kō′nigs bėrg
Krakatoa krak ə tō′ə
Kroeber krō′bər
Krush krush
Krylov kril ôf′
Kumin kew′min
Kuskin kus′kin
La Fontaine, Jean de lä fon ten′, zhôN də
La Gallienne lə gal′yən
Lakshmi lok′shmē
Lalu la lü
Latham lā′thum
Lathrop lā′thrəp
Ledoux lə dY′
Le Hibou et la Poussiquette lē bü′e lä pü si ket′
Lexau lex ô
Liam lē′am
Liddell lid′əl
Liers lirs
Lindgren, Astrid lind grən, äs′trid
Lionni lē ō′nē
Lipkind lip′kind
Lippiza lip′it za
Llyn-Y-Fan Hlin′ə van′
Lobel lō′bel
Lorenzini lô ren tsē′nē
Lueders lwē′dėrs
Lurs lürz
McKuen mak kū′ən
Mafatu ma fa tu
Mahabharata mə hä′bä′rə tə
Mali mä′lē
Manolo män′ō lō
Mara mä rə
Mari, Iela and Enzo mä′rē, ī′la, en zō
Märchen mār′Hən
Mary-Rousselière, Guy mä rē′-rü-se li ā′, gē
Massee ma sē′
Massignon mas ē nyōn′
Matthiesen math′i sən
Maurois, André mô′rwā, än drā′
Mayne mān
Megrimum me′grə məm
Mei Li mā lē
Melendy mə lən′dē
Miers mirz
Miklagard mik′la gärd
Milne miln
Minarik min′ə rik
Mirsky, Reba Paeff mėr′skē, rē′bä paf
Mizamura, Kazue mi′zä mü rä, kä-zü′ā
Moe, Jörgen mō ə, yėr′gən
Momolu mo′ mō lü
Montresor, Beni mōn′trə sôr, bā′nē
Monvel, Boutet de môN vel′, bü-tā′də
Moonta mün′tə
Mordvinoff mord′vin of
Mosel mō zəl′
Moskof mos′kof
Mowgli mou′glē
Munari, Bruno mü nä′rē, brü′nō
Navarra na va′ra
Nefertiti ne fėr tē′ti
Nibelungs/Niblungs nē′bə lu̇ngz/nē′blu̇ngz
Nic Leodhas, Sorche nic ly ō′us, sôr′ä
Nicolette nē kô let′
Noguchi, Hideyo no gü′che, hē-de yo
Nootka nu̇t′kə
Okada, Rokuo ō ka da, rō ku̇ ō
Olatunji, Michael Babatunde ō lä-tu̇n′jē, bä bä tu̇n′dē
Orgel or′gel
Orisha ôr ē′sha
Ormondroyd ôr mond roid
Orphelines ôr fel ēnz′
Padre Porko pä′thre pôrk′ō
Palazzo pa lat′zō
Panchatantra pän chə tän′trə
Pandu pän′dü
Pantaloni pan tə lō′nē
Papashvily pa pash vē lē
Paracelsus par ə sel′səs
Pecos pā kəs
Pegeen pe gēn′
Pelle pel′lē
Perrault pe rō′
Petrides, Heidrun pə trē′dēz, hīd′-drun
Petry pē′tri
Pettit pe tē′
Piatti, Celestino pyät′tē, chā lās-tē′nō
Pibroch of Donnel Dhu pē′broH, don′nel dū
Picard, Barbara Leonie pi′kärd, lā′-ō nē
Pincus pin′kəs
Planudes plə nū′dēz
Plasencia plä sen′thyä
Plouhinec plü′i nek
Podkayne pod kān
Politi pō lē′tē
Prelutsky pre lut′skē
Prishvin, Mikhail prēsh′vin, mē-

hä ēl′
Procyon prō′si on
Prydain pri dān′
Pulga pul′gä
Pwyll and Pryderi pü′il, pru dā′rē
Quarles kwôrlz
Rabe rä bē′
Raman rä′mən
Ramayana rä mä′yə nə
Ranke räng′ke
Rasmussen, Knud räs′mus ən, nud
Ravielli rav ē el′li
Repplier rep′lēr
Rey rā
Ripopet-Barabas rē′pō pā-bä′rä bä
Rocca, Guido rôk′kō, gwē dō
Roethke ret′kē
Rojankovsky rō jan kôf′skē
Rossetti rō set′ē
Rugh rü
Rukeyser rü′kī zėr
Rus, Vladimir rüs, vlad′i mir
Saba sä′bä
Sadko säd′kô
Saemund sā′mund
Saint Exupéry, Antoine de san tāg zoe pā rē, än twän′də
Sasek, Miroslav sä′sek, mī′rō släv
Savigny säv′in yē
Scheele shē′lē
Schoenherr shun′hār
Schweitzer shvī′tsər
Seignobosc, Françoise sāngn′yō bosk, fräN swäz′
Sellew se′lü
Selsam sel′səm
Seredy shãr′ə dē
Serraillier sə räl′yā
Seuss süs
Shawneen shä nēn′
Shecter shek′tėr
Sheftu shef′tü
Shimin, Symeon shi′min, sim′ē-un
Shogomoc shō gō môk
Showalter shō′wäl tėr
Shulevitz, Uri shü′lə vitz, ü′rē
Sidjakov sij′ə kof
Sigurdson si′gûth son
Singer, Isaac Bashevis bə shā′vis
Sita sē′tä
Slobodkin slō bod′kin
Slote slōt
Smolicheck smol′i chek
Snegourka snye gür′kä
Sojo, Toba sō jō, to bä
Sokol sō′kol
Sonneborn son′ne born
Soupault sü pō′
Southall south′ôl
Spier spēr
Stahl stäl
Steegmuller steg mul′ər
Steig stīg
Stolz stōlts
Strachey strā′chi
Streatfeild, Noel stret′feld, nō′əl
Sture-Vasa stur-vä sä
Spyri, Johanna shpē′rē, yō hän′ä
Sturluson, Snorri stür′le sôn, snôr′ā
Suba sü′bə
Sundiata sun′dē ä tä
Syme sīm
Tagore, Rabindranath tä′gōr, rā-bēn′drā nät′
Taliesin tal ē ā′zin
Taran ta′ran
Tatsinda tat sin′dä
Tenniel ten′yel
Terzion ter′zian
Thorne-Thomsen, Gudrun thôrn-tom′sen, gü′drun
Thorvall, Kerstin tur′vāl, char′stin
Tistou tē stü′
Tituba ti′tū bä
Tlingit tling′git
Tolkien tôl′ken
Treece trēs
Tresselt tre′selt
Truro trur′ō
Tunis tū′nis
Turska, Krystyna turs′kä, kris tē′-na
Tutankhaten tüt änH ä′tən
Uchida, Yoshiko ü chē dä, yō shē-kō
Udry ū′dri
Ullman ul′män
Undset, Sigrid un′set, si′gri
Ungerer, Tomi un′gœ rœr
Unnerstad un′nėr stadt
Ushinsky u shin′skē
Van Iterson, Siny vän ē′ter sôn, sē nē
Vasilisa va syē′le sa
Vedge vej
Viehmann vē′män
Viollet vē ō let′
Vivier viv ē ā′
Volsung vol′sung
Vulpes vul′pēz
Watie wā′tē
Wayah wā ä
Weisgard wīs′gärd
Weiss wīs
Whippety Stourie wip′ə tē stür′ē/ stur′ē
Whuppie wup′ē
Wibberley wi′bėr lē
Wier wēr
Wiese vē′zə
Wild, Dortchen vilt, dôrt′shən
Wodehouse wud′hous
Wojciechowska, Maia woi je hov′-ska, mä′ē ä
Wuorio, Eva-Lis wür yō, ā vä-lēs
Yashima, Taro yä′shi ma, tä′rō
Yonge yung
Yonie Wondernose yō nē wun′dər-nōz
Yorubaland yôr u′ba land
Yulya yü lyä
Zamani zä mä nē
Zemach zē′mak
Zhenya zhā′nyə
Zolotow zol′ə tou

# SUBJECT INDEX

# AUTHOR, ILLUSTRATOR, TITLE INDEX[1]



1. The color section appears between pp. 68 and 69. See also Appendices A and B for additional authors not included here.